HANDBOOK
of the
INDIANS OF CALIFORNIA

A. L. Kroeber

HANDBOOK
of the
INDIANS OF CALIFORNIA

Dover Publications, Inc.

New York

Published in Canada by General Publishing Company, Ltd., 30 Lesmill Road, Don Mills, Toronto, Ontario.

Published in the United Kingdom by Constable and Company, Ltd., 10 Orange Street, London WC2H 7EG.

This Dover edition, first published in 1976, is an unabridged republication of the work originally published by the Government Printing Office, Washington, in 1925 as *Bulletin 78* of the Bureau of American Ethnology of the Smithsonian Institution.

International Standard Book Number: 0-486-23368-5
Library of Congress Catalog Card Number: 76-19514

Manufactured in the United States of America
Dover Publications, Inc.
180 Varick Street
New York, N.Y. 10014

LETTER OF TRANSMITTAL.

SMITHSONIAN INSTITUTION,
BUREAU OF AMERICAN ETHNOLOGY,
Washington, D. C., February 18, 1919.

SIR: I have the honor to transmit the accompanying manuscript, entitled "Handbook of the Indians of California," by A. L. Kroeber, and to recommend its publication, subject to your approval, as a bulletin of this bureau.

Very respectfully,

J. WALTER FEWKES,
Chief.

Dr. CHARLES D. WALCOTT,
Secretary of the Smithsonian Institution.

PREFACE.

This book is the outcome of 17 years of acquaintance and occupation with the Indians of California; intermittent, it is true, but with these people remaining throughout the first subject of the writer's study. Although it may seem otherwise, it attempts to be a history.

It is not a history in the usual sense of a record of events. The vast bulk of even the significant happenings in the lives of uncivilized tribes are irrecoverable. For the past century our knowledge is slight; previous to that there is complete obscurity. Nor do the careers of savages afford many incidents of sufficient intrinsic importance to make their chronicling worth while.

The book is a history in that it tries to reconstruct and present the scheme within which these people in ancient and more recent times lived their lives. It is concerned with their civilization—at all events the appearance they presented on discovery, and whenever possible an unraveling, from such indications as analysis and comparison now and then afford, of the changes and growth of their culture. There being no written documents, the element of time enters infinitely less than in works which it is customary to designate historical. In the stead of time, the geographical factor looms large. It is not that this dimension is necessarily more important in savage life than that of chronology; but it is a hundred times more readily operated in, and is on the whole the most available means through which some glimpses of time perspective are attainable.

It is for this reason that after long deliberation I have constituted the bulk of the book a series of tribal descriptions. A broader typical treatment of phases of native culture seems theoretically more desirable, especially in the case of a remote and unimportant people. But such a treatment would have led to an unfortunate dilemma. The local variations are so numerous that their consideration would have smothered the systematic presentation of general points of view. On the other hand, the elimination of this detail would have left the presentation as an abstraction, too largely dependent upon the subjective attitudes of the author, and sterile in the sense of lacking the color and life in which, after all, the characteristics of civilizations are manifest.

I have, therefore, proceeded on the plan of picturing as concretely as I might the customs of each of some 50 little nations, adding discussions and comparisons of broader scope wherever the knowledge in hand made such procedure seem profitable. This brings it about that the more general conclusions appear strewn at random through the course of several hundred pages, and to some this will seem unfortunate. I have attempted to meet the difficulty in two ways — first, by a few chapters which are wholly summary and comparative, and which will be found at the end of the work; second, by a carefully prepared subject index, which not only brings together all the references to each phase of culture but often enumerates its principal aspects or elements.

After some hesitation I have omitted all directly historical treatment in the ordinary sense; that is, accounts of the relations of the natives with the whites and of the events befalling them after such contact was established. It is not that this subject is unimportant or uninteresting, but that I am not in position to treat it adequately. It is also a matter that has comparatively slight relation to the aboriginal civilization. It presupposes, indeed, some understanding of that civilization; but it requires also a thorough knowledge of the local history as well as of the institutions of the superior race. It involves prolonged study and acquaintance with Spanish and mission archives, with Government documents, with early California events and pioneer conditions. In all these things many others are more proficient than I can hope to become; and it has seemed that I might better contribute to the future writing of such a history by concentrating effort in the field to which training and predilection have led me, and endeavoring to render the California Indian, as such, a more familiar object to the future historian of his political and economic relations with ourselves. I have, therefore, considered the effect of contacts only in special cases; as when necessary to form an estimate of an ancient vanished culture through the medium of its modern and modified representative.

In the matter of population, too, the effect of Caucasian contact can not wholly be slighted, since all statistics date from a late period. The disintegration of native numbers and native culture have proceeded hand in hand, but in very different ratios according to locality. The determination of populational strength before the arrival of the whites is, on the other hand, of considerable significance toward the understanding of Indian culture, on account of the close relations which are manifest between type of culture and density of population.

It has also appeared most profitable to attempt as little formal separation as possible of the data acquired by ethnological and archeological investigations. I have indeed added a chapter on prehistory, in the nature of a summary and compilation of miscellanea. In the main, however, a detailed survey of the prehistory of California on the basis of its archeology would be a catalogue of sites known to have been inhabited, a list of excavations performed, and a description of objects found. As yet there is little sequence of development traceable in these ancient remains. The objects discovered in any region are very similar to those used by recent Indians. A strictly archeological treatment leaves the greater part of the culture with which it is concerned entirely untouched, and is likely to have undue recourse to pure speculation in its interpretations. In an area of such unusual stability, ethnological data must accordingly be made use of constantly. This being true, a single treatment seems called for. Data from the recent and surviving Indians being on the whole very much fuller, the only practical procedure has been to incorporate the specifically archeological material in accounts that are prevailingly of an ethnological character.

The physical type of the natives is another topic that has been slighted. In this case the reason is its essential aloofness from the main thread of the work. It is a truism that physical type and culture have only the slightest, if any, relation in human history; and one of the earliest maxims impressed on the student of anthropology, although still one of the most frequently violated, is the fallacy of inferring from one to the other. A compact review and analysis of all that is known on the physical anthropology of the natives of California would be exceedingly useful in itself, but would add little to the serviceability of this book. Moreover, it can be better executed by other hands.

As regards the province of speech, I feel no such hesitation of competence, but here again the subject matter is an essentially distinct one, besides being of a nature which generally impresses as technical. The relation of language to civilization is undoubtedly closer than that of head form or skin color, but it is far from intimate. I have therefore considered speech only in so far as the accumulating knowledge of the languages of California has led to their classification on a genetic or historical basis and thus contributes to the insight of the origin, movements, and relationship of the several nations.

One cultural activity of the profoundest emotional import I have regretfully felt compelled to refrain from considering—music. There is no question that any attempt at a well-rounded description of the culture of a people which omits music from its consideration is imperfect. But in the present case the difficulties were enormous. Primitive music is so thoroughly different from our own as to be practi-

cally unintelligible except on long acquaintance. It has been analyzed only imperfectly and usually is even transcribed but inad-
equately.   There is no work which seriously attacks the music of the
California Indians.   A chapter on this fascinating subject would
therefore have had to be either so superficial as to be worthless or
so long and detailed as to become disproportionate.

A considerable part of the information gathered in this book has
never been printed before.   Some of this is my own.   The remainder
has been unhesitatingly put at my disposal by the present and former
members of the department of anthropology of the University of California: Dr. P. E. Goddard, Dr. E. Sapir, Dr. S. A. Barrett, Mr.
N. C. Nelson, Dr. T. T. Waterman, Mr. E. W. Gifford, Mr. L. L.
Loud, Prof. R. B. Dixon, Dr. J. Alden Mason, and the late Dr. Philip
Mills Jones.   In fact, the present work would have been impossible
without the research which has been conducted for the university
since 1901, as a result of the foundation of the department of anthropology by the late Mrs. Phoebe Apperson Hearst.   In a large sense,
therefore, this book expresses the results of the work of the University
of California far more than the labors of one individual.   It has
merely fallen to my lot to combine and present the knowledge which
has accumulated through the efforts of the group of whom I am one.

Mr. F. W. Hodge, ethnologist in charge of the Bureau of American
Ethnology, and Mr. J. P. Harrington, now also of the Bureau, have
put further data at my disposal.   Personally I wish to express to Mr.
Hodge my genuine sense of obligation for the opportunity to carry
through the undertaking.   Without his encouragement and constant
readiness to cooperate it is likely that a work of the scope of the
present book would not have been undertaken by any one for many
years to come.

I am at the more pains to make these acknowledgments because
this is my only opportunity.   It has appeared necessary to omit
references to the sources and authorities for my statements.   This
is an unusual procedure in a work that pretends to scholarship, but
there were many reasons urging its adoption.   Had authorities been
cited at all, it would have been desirable to cite them at every opportunity.   To the nonprofessional reader such an accumulation of references to sources would have been unserviceable and generally distracting.   The anthropologist or historian has an offhand acquaintance with the bulk of the published literature and its detailed cita-
tion would in most cases aid him but little.   Moreover, the abundant
use made of manuscript data would leave serious vacancies in any
list of references to particular passages.   Intending students are the
only ones, it has seemed, who may now and then be seriously inclined

to deplore the lack of citations to the original sources; but their needs, I am convinced, will on the whole be better served by the bibliography which has been appended. This bibliography makes less pretense to completeness than to being an aid to discrimination. With this feature in mind, I have ventured to add brief appraisals to the titles of many of the works there listed.

If it is remembered that at least nine-tenths of the printed information on the Indians of California, certainly in quantity of facts, perhaps also in number of pages, is contained in three sets of periodical publications—those of the University of California in American Archaeology and Ethnology, the Bulletin of the American Museum of Natural History, and the publications of the Federal Government, particularly those of the Bureau of American Ethnology and the National Museum under the auspices of the Smithsonian Institution—together with a small group of books not exceeding 8 or 10 in number, it becomes apparent that the problem of authorities and bibliography for the subject dealt with in this work is in the main a simple one.

I should not close without expressing my sincere appreciation of my one predecessor in this field, the late Stephen Powers, well known for his classic "Tribes of California," one of the most remarkable reports ever printed by any government. Powers was a journalist by profession and it is true that his ethnology is often of the crudest. Probably the majority of his statements are inaccurate, many are misleading, and a very fair proportion are without any foundation or positively erroneous. He possessed, however, an astoundingly quick and vivid sympathy, a power of observation as keen as it was untrained, and an invariably spirited gift of portrayal that rises at times into the realm of the sheerly fascinating. Anthropologically his great service lies in the fact that with all the looseness of his data and method he was able to a greater degree than anyone before or after him to seize and fix the salient qualities of the mentality of the people he described. The ethnologist may therefore by turns writhe and smile as he fingers Powers's pages, but for the broad outlines of the culture of the California Indian, for its values with all their high lights and shadows, he can still do no better than consult the book. With all its flimsy texture and slovenly edges, it will always remain the best introduction to the subject. It is a gratification to remember that there was once a time when an unendowed periodical published in California felt able to command the support of its public by including among its offerings almost the whole of a work of this merit. The "Tribes of California" was first issued in the Overland Monthly of San Francisco.

POSTSCRIPT.

New information on the Indians of California has of course become available during the five years since this manuscript was written. To incorporate even a summary of this would have meant the alteration as well as the addition of numerous passages—an unfeasible procedure. I have therefore only corrected errors, and here and there added footnotes indicating the range or significance of the recent acquisitions to knowledge, and their sources. These notes will serve to guide the reader to the literature that is gradually filling the gaps in the world's knowledge of the tribes in question. Only the bibliography has been brought as fully as possible up to date.

The chapters on the Yurok, Yuki, Yokuts, and Mohave consist almost wholly of previously unpublished data collected by myself. The chapters on the Karok, Wiyot, Kato, Huchnom, Coast Yuki, Pomo, Yahi, Wintun, Maidu, Costanoans, and Serrano combine similar data in greater or less amount with materials from published sources. The chapter on the Miwok embodies a considerable block of unpublished data put at my disposal by E. W. Gifford. The section of the chapter on Prehistory dealing with cultural stratification in the San Francisco Bay shell mounds is based on unpublished preliminary computations by N. C. Nelson.

Certain parts of the present volume have been utilized, with the approval of the Bureau and with changes of greater or less moment, in other publications. Chapter 53 forms the basis of an article, "Yuman Tribes on the Lower Colorado," in volume 16 of the University of California Publications in American Archaeology and Ethnology; chapters 54–56, of "Elements of Culture in Native California," in volume 13; and chapter 59, "California Culture Provinces," in volume 17 of the same series.

A. L. KROEBER.

BERKELEY, CALIF., *February 1, 1923.*

CONTENTS.

LIST OF TABLES.

ILLUSTRATIONS.

PLATES.

MUSEUM NUMBERS OF OBJECTS ILLUSTRATED.

Unless otherwise mentioned, objects shown in the plates and text figures are in the University of California Museum of Anthropology and their numbers bear the prefix " 1-." If there is no designation of specimens by letters on plate or figure, the numbers refer to specimens as shown in order from left to right, or top to bottom, or both.

PLATES.

2: 1542, 1327.

3: armor, in Daggett collection.

15: 2259, 1952, 1866.

16: 1682, 2181, 1538, 1084.

17: 1647, 1618, 2198, 1563, 1679, 1892.

19, *a–e:* 2841, 1073, 937 (Hupa), 1629, 1195.

20: 2069, 1943, 1236, 1099, 2219, 1239, 1240, 1237.

23, *a–c:* 9415, 9394, 11626.

24, *a–d:* 2541, 2530, 2547, 2534.

29: 10529, 19441, 4102, 401.

30, *a–g:* 2760, 2766, 9169, 10800 and 3960, 10358, 2673, 3902.

33, *a–c:* 2581, 2587, 2603.

35: 9461, 16573, 2307.

38: 10500.

39–40, *a–o:* 10259, 13841, 10057, 10235, 10216, 10055, 10731, 10830, 10780, 10817, 2327, 10944, 10730, 3087, 17336.

41: 12–1752.

42, *a–c:* 1399, 9165, 9579.

43, *a,* 9247, 9240; *b,* 10435, 10434; *c,* 10227; *d,* 2410, 103, 2671, 13977, 2714; *e,* 1779.

44, *a–f:* 20978, 14475, 16555, 4035, 9208, 2679.

45: 10715.

49, *a–f:* 19677, 19742, 14057, 11043, 14477, 4367.

50: 10832, 10910, 3951, 4011, 10390, 10899.

51: 14077, 10823, 10889, 14075, 14074, 14076.

52: American Museum of Natural History 50.1-2150, 50–539 (Chumash attribution probable).

53: 14497, 14503, 14502, 14998, 14999.

54: 14495, 14496.

55: *a,* 14524; *b,* 4344, 13828; *c,* 10972; *d,* 20964; *e,* 20926; *f,* Shoemaker collection, 3, 49.

58: 14565, 9580, 10039, 10040.

59: 14540, 4377, 4357.

62: 11067, 11095.

63: 14570.

66: 4301, 14071, 12971.

67, *a–i:* 1754, 1720, 13866, 153, 1413, 1703, 12401, 11235, 1704.

68: 1713, 13783, 13775, 13774, 4321.

72: 14577, 14595.

73: *a,* 10956; *b,* 11125; *c,* 11057; *d,* 11130, 11111; *e,* 1600, 1509, 1601; *f,* 1663.

75: 11960, 12008, 11963.

76: 9920, 10120, 10351.

80: 10038.

81: 12–1734.

TEXT FIGURES.

THE YUROK: LAND AND CIVILIZATION.

This history begins with an account of the Yurok, a nation resident on the lower Klamath River, near and along the Pacific Ocean, in extreme northern California (Pl. 1), surrounded by peoples speaking diverse languages but following the same remarkable civilization. The complete aspect of this civilization is un-Californian. It is at bottom the southernmost manifestation of that great and distinctive culture the main elements of which are common to all the peoples of the Pacific coast from Oregon to Alaska; is heavily tinctured with locally developed concepts and institutions; and further altered by some absorption of ideas from those tribes to the south and east who constitute the true California of the ethnologist.

This civilization, which will hereafter be designated as that of northwestern California, attains on the whole to a higher level, as it is customary to estimate such averaged values, than any other that flourished in what is now the State of California. But it is better described as an unusually specialized culture, for the things in which it is deficient it lacks totally; and these are numerous and notable.

QUALITY OF CIVILIZATION.

In inventions there was no marked superiority to the remainder of aboriginal California; but most arts were carried to a distinctive pitch. Manufactured articles were better finished. Many objects which the central and southern Californians fashioned only as bare utility demanded were regularly decorated with carvings in the northwest. Often the identical object was made of wood in one region and of antler or stone in the other. A new technical process is scarcely superadded by such a substitution. As regards the mere list of knowledges or faculties, the two cultures remain at par. But the northwestern preference for the more laborious material evidences a different attitude, an appreciation of values which in the ruder central and southern tracts is disregarded. That this difference is deep seated, and that it is manifest at almost every point, is evident when the slab house of the Miwok or Yuki, the canoe or maul of the Modoc, the pipe or acorn stirrer of the Pomo, the netting shuttle and spoon of the Maidu, or the obsidian blade of the Wintun, are set by the side of the corresponding utensils of the Yurok or their northwestern neighbors. It is only among the far-away Chumash that technological activities were granted a similar interest and love; and this localized southern culture has long since perished so completely as to make a comparative evaluation difficult.

The implements that are made only in the northwest—the stool, pillow, box, purse, and the like—are not very numerous. They are at least partly balanced by central and southern devices which the northwesterners lack; and they do not in any instance involve a process or mechanical faculty of which the more typical Californians are wholly ignorant.

Much the same holds of wealth. Money is prized and establishes influence everywhere in California. It certainly counts for more in private and public life among the average Californian people than among the tribes of the plains or the settled and unsettled tribes of the southwestern United States. But whatever its influence in southern or middle California, that influence is multiplied among the Yurok. Blood money, bride purchase, compensation to the year's mourners before a dance can be held, are institutions known to almost every group described in the present work. The northwesterners alone have measured the precise value of every man's life or wife or grief. Every injury, each privilege or wrong or trespass, is calculated and compensated. Without exactly adjusted payment, cessation of a feud is impossible except through utter extirpation of one party, marriage is not marriage but a public disgrace for generations, the ceremony necessary to the preservation of the order of the world is not held. The consequence is that the Yurok concerns his life above all else with property. When he has leisure, he thinks of money; if in need, he calls upon it. He schemes constantly for opportunity to lodge a claim or to evade an obligation. No resource is too mean or devious for him to essay in this pursuit.

If such endeavors are to be realized, there are needed an accurately computable scheme of economic valuation, and an elaborate and precise code of rights. The northwesterner has both. His law is of the utmost refinement. A few simple and basic principles are projected into the most intricate subtleties; and there is no contingency which they do not cover. The central Californian has his law also. But it is neither rigid nor ramified. Margin is left for modification according to personality or circumstance or public opinion. There are phases of life in central California into which neither money nor legality enter.

With all this savoring so strongly of Kwakiutl and Haida custom, the Yurok is wholly Californian in his lack of any visible symbolism to give emotional expression to the economic values which are so fundamental with him. He is without crests or carvings or totems; there are no separately designated social classes, no seats in order of rank, no titles of precedence, no named and fixed privileges of priority. His society follows the aims of the societies of the North Pacific coast with the mechanism of the societies of middle California.

Property and rights pertain to the realm of the individual, and the Yurok recognizes no public claim and the existence of no community. His world is wholly an aggregation of individuals. There being no society as such, there is no social organization. Clans, exogamic groups, chiefs or governors, political units, are unrepresented even by traces in northwestern California. The germinal, nameless political community that can be traced among the Indians of the greater part of the State is absent. Government being wanting, there is no authority, and without authority there can be no chief. The men so called are individuals whose wealth, and their ability to retain and employ it, have clustered about them an aggregation of kinsmen, followers, and semidependents to whom they dispense assistance and protection. If a man usually marries outside the village in which he lives, the reason is that many of his coinhabitants normally happen to be blood relatives, not because custom or law or morality recognize the village as a unit concerned with marriage. The actual outcome among the Yurok may, in the majority of cases, be the same as among nations consciously organized on an exogamic plan. The point of view, the guiding principles both of the individual's action and of the shaping of the civilization, are wholly nonexogamic. Such familiar terms as "tribe," "village community," "chief," "government," "clan," can therefore be used with reference to the Yurok only after extreme care in previous definition—in their current senses they are wholly inapplicable.

Shamanism takes on a peculiar aspect in northwestern California in that the almost universal American Indian idea of an association between the shaman and certain spirits personally attached to him is very weakly and indirectly developed. Shamanistic power resides in control of "pains," small animate objects, nonanimal and

nonhuman in shape, which on the one hand cause illness by entering the bodies of men, and on the other endow the shaman with
power when he brings them to reside within himself, or rather herself, for practically all shamans are women. The witch or poisoner
is usually a man and operates by magic rather than shamanistic
faculty. In the remainder of California the distinction between
the maker and the curer of disease is almost effaced, the shaman being
considered indifferently malevolent or beneficent according to circumstances, but operating by the exercise of the same powers.

Concepts relating to magic are as abundantly developed among the
Yurok and their neighbors as shamanism is narrowed. Imitative
magic is particularly favored and is often of the most crudely direct
kind, such as performing a simple action or saying the desired thing
over and over again. The thousand and one occasions on which magic
of this rather bare volitional type is employed reveal a tensity that
usually seems brought on consciously. This emotional tautness,
which contrasts glaringly with the slack passivity and apathetic slug-
gishness of the average California Indian, is manifest in other
matters. Thus, restraint and self-control in manner and in relations with other men are constantly advocated and practiced by the
Yurok.

Northwestern religion is colored by the cultural factors already
enumerated. The idea of organization being absent, there are no
cult societies or initiations. Symbolism is an almost unknown attitude of mind except in matters of outright magic: therefore masks,
impersonations, altars, and sacred apparatus, as such, are not employed. The tangible paraphernalia of public ceremony are objects
that possess a high property value—wealth that impresses, but nevertheless profane and negotiable wealth. The dances are displays
of this wealth as much as they are song and step. All life being individualized instead of socialized, the ceremonies attach to specified
localities, much as a fishing place and an individual's right to fish
are connected. In the remainder of California, where stronger communal sense exists, the precise location of the spot of the dance becomes of little moment in comparison with the circumstances of the
ceremony.

The esoteric element in northwestern dances and rites of public
import has as its central feature the recitation of a formula. This
is not a prayer to divinities, but a narrative, mostly in dialogue, re-
counting the effect of an act or a series of acts, similar to those about
to be performed, by a member of an ancient, prehuman, half-spirit
race. The recital of this former action and its effect is believed to
produce the identical effect now. The point of view is distinctly
magical. Similar formulas are used for the most personal purposes:
luck in the hunt, curing of sickness, success in love, the accumulation

of wealth. These formulas are private property; those spoken at public ceremonials are no exception: their possessor must be paid, though he operates for the good of all.

Yurok mythology is woven in equally strange colors. Stirring plot is slighted; so are the suspense of narrative, the tension of a dramatic situation—all the directly human elements which, however rude their development, are vividly present in the traditions of most of the Californians and many other divisions of American Indians. A lyric, almost elegiac emotion suffuses the northwestern myths and tales. Affection, homesickness, pity, love of one's natal spot, insatiable longing for wealth, grief of the prehuman people at their departure before the impending arrival of mankind, are sentiments expressed frequently and often with skill. Events and incidents are more baldly depicted, except where the effect of the action recounted is the establishment of an existing practice or institution; and in these cases the myth is often nearly indistinguishable from a magical formula. Tales that will interest a child or please a naïve stranger of another civilization do not appeal to the Yurok, who have developed refinedly special tastes in nearly everything with which they concern themselves.

RADIUS AND FOCUS OF THE CIVILIZATION.

The Yurok shared this civilization in identical form with their neighbors, the Hupa and Karok. The adjacent Tolowa, Wiyot, and Chilula adhere to the same culture in every essential trait, but begin to evince minor departures in the direction of less intensive specialization. A peripheral series of tribes—the Shasta, Konomihu, Chimariko, Whilkut, and Nongatl—show the loss of a number of characteristic northwestern features as well as some elements of culture that are clearly due to the example of exterior peoples. To the south the diminution of the northwestern cultural forces can be traced step by step through the Sinkyone and Lassik until the last diluted remnants are encountered among the Wailaki. The next group, the Kato, belong wholly within the civilization of central California. The progressive change from Hupa to Kato is particularly impressive in view of the fact that all members of the chain are of common Athabascan speech.

To the north a similar transition into another civilization could presumably have once been followed. But the societies of southwestern Oregon have long since perished, and the information about them is only sufficient to show the close similarity of the Takelma and Athabascans of Rogue River to the Yurok, and their civilizational inferiority. Southwestern Oregon was culturally dependent on northwestern California.

Eastward, similarities to the northwestern culture appear for considerable distances—almost across the breadth of the State and into the northernmost Sierra Nevada. These are, however, highland tracts of rather thin populations, to whom the typical culture of central California could not easily penetrate in full form, so that they were left open to random influences from all sides.

Furthermore, it is doubtful whether the institutions of northwestern type among the Yana, Achomawi, and mountain Maidu can be ascribed to specific northwestern influences. Most of the cultural characteristics common to northwestern and northeastern California appear to have been found also in Oregon for some distance north. To ascribe to the Yurok or Karok any definite share in the formation of modern Achomawi civilization would therefore be a one-sided view. The whole of the tract embracing northernmost California and western, or at least southwestern, Oregon is in some respects a larger but ultimate cultural unit. Within this unit, groups of peripheral position like the Achomawi have acquired only the more rudimentary elements and generic institutions, which they have further mingled with elements derived in perhaps larger proportion from central California and in some measure even from plateau or plains sources, not to mention minor institutions of local origin. Centrally situated nations like the Yurok, on the other hand, have kept the original cultural supply in less adulterated form, and in building upon it have exerted an expansive influence on their neighbors and through them on peoples beyond.

Useful as the recognition of culture areas is as a scaffolding or preliminary plan for the student, the conditions in this region corroborate wholly the realization which has been gradually arrived at through investigations of civilization in many other parts of America, namely, that the exact delineation of such ethnographic provinces is almost invariably an artificial and unprofitable endeavor. It is the foci that can be tolerably determined, not the limits; the influences that are of significance, rather than the range of the influences.

Such a focus, in some measure for all northernmost California and southwestern Oregon, and absolutely for northwestern California, is constituted by the Yurok, the Hupa, and the Karok.

Even as between these three little peoples of such close interrelations, some precedence of civilizational intensity, a slight nucleolus within the nucleus, can be detected; and the priority must be accorded to the Yurok.

Geographical and populational considerations would lead to such an anticipation. The Yurok live on the united Klamath, the Hupa and Karok on its two arms, the Trinity and the unaugmented Klamath above the Trinity. The numbers of the Yurok were as great as those of the two other groups combined. Of the tribes of the second order or degree of participation in the civilization, the Tolowa, Wiyot, and Chilula, all three were adjacent to the Yurok, one only to the Hupa, none to the Karok. The canoe can be made, in its perfected type, only of the redwood, a tree that grows, within the habitat of the three focal peoples, only in Yurok territory; and in fact the Hupa and Karok buy their boats from the Yurok. The same tree also furnishes the best material for the lumber of which the houses of the region are built.

Actual cultural evidences are slight but confirmatory. Throughout Califonia it appears that adolescence ceremonies having direct reference to physiological functions are not only relatively but absolutely more elaborated among tribes of a ruder and more basic civilization. Groups that have developed other ceremonial institutions to a considerable pitch actually curtail or dwarf this rite. The Yurok make distinctly less of it than either Karok or Hupa. The great ceremonies so characteristic of the region are, however, most numerous among them. The Hupa perform these rituals in two or three towns, the Karok in four, and the Yurok in seven. The elimination of animals as characters in traditional tales is distinctive of the pure northwestern culture. The Yurok are more extreme in this respect than are the Karok. Both Karok and Hupa agree with the larger nation in placing the birth of their culture hero at the Yurok village of Kenek.

Slender as are these indications, they all point the same way. They justify the conclusion that the innermost core of northwestern civilization is more nearly represented by the Yurok than by any other group. Even in a wider view, the center of dispersal—or concentration—of this civilization might be described as situated at the confluence of the Trinity and Klamath, from which the three tribes stretch out like the arms of a huge **Y**. This spot is Yurok territory. It is occupied by the village of Weitspus, now called Weitchpec, and its suburbs. Either here or at some point in the populous 20 miles of river below must the precise middle of the cultural focus be set, if we are to attempt to draw our perspective to its finest angle.

Of course it can not be contended that the whole of the northwestern civilization, or even all its topmost crests, flowed out from this sole spot. Even an Athenian or a Roman metropolis at its height never formulated, much less originated, all of the culture of which it was the representative; and the California Indians were far from knowing any metropoles. It might well be better, in a search such as has occupied us a moment ago, to think of the finally determined location as a point of civilizational gathering rather than radiation. But where most is accumulated, most must also be given out. The difference in cultural potence between upper and lower Yurok, between Yurok and Karok, must have been slight. For every ten ideas or colorings of ideas that emanated from the exact center at least nine must have filtered into it; and even toward remoter regions, the disproportion can hardly have been excessive. As regards any given single item of culture, it would be nearly impossible to assert with confidence where its specific development had taken place. The thing of moment, after all, is not the awarding of precedence to this or that group of men or little tract of land, but the determination of the civilization in its most exquisite form, with an understanding, so far as may be, of its coming into being. It is this purpose that has been followed, it may seem deviously, through the balancings of the preceding pages; and the end having been attained so far as seems possible in the present state of knowledge, it remains to picture the civilization as accurately as it can be pictured through the medium of the institutions, the thoughts, and the practices of the Yurok.

It may be added, as a circumstance not without a touch of the climactic in the wider vista of native American history, and as an illustration of principles well recognized in ethnology, that three of the great families of the continent are represented at the point of assemblage of this civilization. The Yurok are Algonkins, the Karok Hokans, the Hupa Athabascans.

TOWNS.

The territory of the Yurok, small as is its extent, is very unrepresentative of their actual life, since all of their habitations stood either on the Klamath River or on the shore of the ocean. All land back in the hills away from the houses served only for hunting deer, picking up acorns, beating in seeds, and gathering firewood or sweathouse kindlings, according to its vegetation. The most productive tracts were owned privately. They were occasionally camped on, though never for long periods. All true settlements formed only a long winding lane; and along this waterway Yurok life was lived.

The towns—hamlets is an exacter term according to civilized standards—numbered about 54 and are shown in Figure 1. A few of these, such as Kenekpul, Tsetskwi, Himetl, Keihkem, Nagetl, Tlemekwetl, and some on the coast, may have been inhabited only from time to time, during the lifetime of a single man or a group of relatives. The Klamath villages mostly lie on ancient river terraces, which gradually decrease in height toward the mouth of the widening stream. Wahsekw is 200 feet up, Kenek 100, Kepel 75, Ko'otep 35, Turip 25, Wohkel 20. The coast towns are almost invariably either on a lagoon or at the mouth of a stream. Tsurau alone overlooks a cove well sheltered behind Trinidad Head. Like the more wholly ocean-situated Wiyot and Tolowa, the Yurok did not hesitate to paddle out into open salt water for miles, if there was occasion; but their habits were formed on the river or still water. The canoe

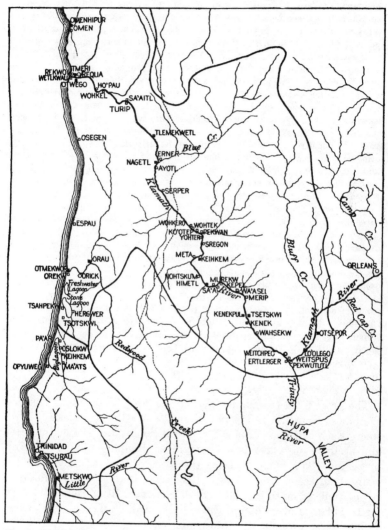

FIG. 1.—Yurok towns and territory. Solid squares indicate sites occupied only during certain periods. Dotted line, redwood timber belt.

was designed for stream use rather than launching through the surf; and the coast itself was designated as downstream and upstream according as it extended north or south. Fishing was done at mouths of running fresh water, or by men standing at the edge of the surf, much more than on the abounding ocean.

The important villages come in groups. The uppermost of these groups is at the mouth of the Trinity: Weitspus, Pekwututl, and Ertlerger. These must have had, a century ago, a combined population of nearly 200. Wahsekw, next below, was isolated and not very large, but wealthy. Those that followed next were of little moment. Kenek, which lies at the best fishing rapids in the Klamath, except possibly the fall near the mouth of the Salmon River in Karok territory, is the town most frequently mentioned in Yurok mythology, and is celebrated even in the traditions of their neighbors, but was always a small settlement in historical times. Kepel, Sa'a, Murekw, and Himetl formed another considerable group of about the populousness of that at Weitspus. Murekw seems to have been the largest of the group, Sa'a its religious center. Several smaller settlements followed at short intervals, among which Sregon enjoyed a reputation for belligerence and wealth. Pekwan Creek brought Pekwan, Ko'otep, Wohtek, and Wohkero. This was perhaps the most populous cluster of Yurok villages. For the next 20 miles the towns were strung apart and mostly quite small: Turip and Sa'aitl, also called Turip-opposite, formed the only larger group. Then, at the mouth, on opposite sides of the tidal lagoon, came Rekwoi and Wetlkwau, with Tsekwetl, Pegwolau, and Keskitsa as quarters or suburbs, and Tmeri and Otwego somewhat doubtful as separate villages. Here also the population must have approximated 200.

On the coast, Tsurau at Trinidad, several miles from its neighbors, was estimated the largest town; Opyuweg on Big Lagoon—also called simply Oketo, "lake"—was next; and Tsahpekw on Stone Lagoon third. Four smaller townlets stood with Opyuweg on Big Lagoon, and Tsahpekw had Hergwer as a minor mate. Of the other coast towns, Orekw at the mouth of Redwood Creek was the leading one, with Espau probably next.

Otsepor was really two settlements: Otsepor, and Aikoo downstream. Ehkwiyer below Tsetskwi, Tekta below Wohkero, Enipeu below Serper, Stowin below Tlemekwetl have been occupied recently, but do not seem to be old sites. Tlemekwetl is also known as Erlikenpets, Hergwer as Plepei, Metskwo as Srepor. Terwer was an important summer camp site on the north bank between Sa'aitl and Wohkel, but appears to have had no permanent houses. O'menhipur included houses on both sides of the mouth of Wilson Creek. Neryitmurm and Pinpa are sometimes spoken of as towns, but may be only parts of Opyuweg.

The great fixed ceremonies were all held at the populous clusters: Weitspus, Kepel-Sa'a, Pekwan, Rekwoi, Wetlkwau, Orekw, Opyuweg. Each of these had a sacred sweat house; and at each of them, and at them only, a White Deerskin or Jumping dance was made or begun. Sa'a alone replaced the dance with a ritually built fish weir at adjacent Kepel. It will be seen that ceremony followed population, as myth did not. Besides Kenek, little Merip, Tlemekwetl, Turip, and Shumig—the uninhabited bluff behind Patricks Point—enter prominently into tradition.

TOWN NAMES.

It is clear from the appended list that in spite of abundant intercourse between the Yurok and Hupa, place names were not adopted into a foreign language, but were made over by these tribes. Sometimes they were translated. Thus the Yurok and Hupa names for Weitspus both refer to confluence, for Nohtskum to a nose of rock, for Serper to a prairie, for Wohkel to pepperwoods. Other places seem to have been descriptively named by the Hupa, without reference to the significance of their Yurok names. Thus they call four villages after the pepperwood, *tunchwin*, the Yurok only one.

YUROK TOWNS.	HUPA NAMES.
Otsepor	Hotinunding.
Pekwututl	Hotuwaihot.
Ertlerger	Tunchwinta'ching.
Weitspus	Tlenalding (Karok: Ansafriki).
Wahsekw	Hotenanding (Karok: Hohira).
Kenek	Choholchweding (Karok: Shwufum).
Merip	Hongha'ding.
Wa'asei	Tunchwingkis-hunding.
Kepel	Ta'tesading (Karok: A'avunai).
Murekw	Tunchwingkut.
Nohtsku'm	Senongading.
Meta	Ninamelding.
Sregon	Kyuwitleding.
Pekwan	Kaikisdeke (Karok: Firipama).
Ko'otep	Hohochitding.
Wohtek	Ninda'sanding.
Serper	Tlokuchitding.
Turip	Ninuwaikyanding.
Sa'aitl	Kitlweding.
Terwer camp	Kauhwkyokis-hunding.
Wohkel	Tunchwingkyoding.
Ho'pau	Chahalding.
Rekwoi	Mukanaduwulading (Karok: Sufip).
Wetlkwau	Tsetlcheding.
Espau	Mingkekyoding.
Orekw	Chewillinding.
Oketo	Chwaltaike.
Tsurau	Muwunnuhwonding.

ORGANIZATION OF TOWNS.

Yurok houses, or their sites, had names descriptive of their position, topography, size, frontage, or ceremonial function. Many of the designations reappear in village after village. The names of abandoned houses were remembered for at least a lifetime, perhaps nearly as long as the pit remained visible. If a family grew and a son or married-in son-in-law erected a new dwelling adjacent to the old, the original name applied to both houses. Sweat houses were usually but not always called by the same name as the house to whose master they belonged, and seem normally to have been built close by.

The habit of naming house sites appears to have been restricted to northwestern California. It is but one instance of many of the intensive localization of life in this region, of its deep rooting in the soil. The origin of the custom is scarcely discernible, but the Yurok made frequent use of it to designate persons without naming them. A person referred to as "the old man of Trail Descends" would be absolutely defined to his village mates, and even in distant villages might be better known by that description than by his personal appellation.

The following are the houses of Weitspus, as shown in Figure 2.

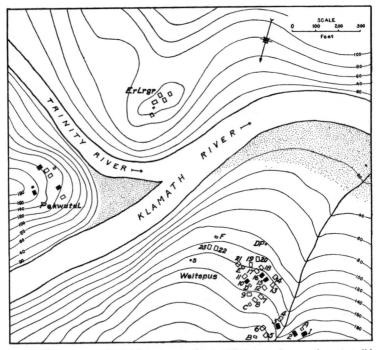

FIG. 2.—Yurok town of Weitspus and associated settlements. Squares, houses; solid squares, standing in 1909; small rectangles, sweat houses. (After Waterman.)

HOUSES.

1. (With 2).
2. Wonitl or Wonoyertl ("up").
3. (With 4).
4. Ra'ak ("in the creek").
5. Sohtsu ("on top").
6. Ketsketl.
7.
8.
9. Oslokw ("trail descends").
10. (With 11).
11. Tsekwetl ("flat").
12.

13. Otsepor ("steep").
14. Kome'r ("last").
15. Ple'l ("large").
16. (With 17).
17. Nikerwerk ("close to dance").
18. Erkigeri ("tie hair" for dance).
19. Wogwu ("in middle").
20. Opyuweg ("dance").
21. Ta'amo ("elderberries").
22. Higwop ("in the water").
23. Petsku ("upstream").

SWEAT HOUSES.

(Named after houses which they adjoin and to which they belong.)

A with 2.	D with 11.
B with 6.	E with 19.
C with 9.	F with 22.

These are the houses of Rekwoi: Oregok ("where rolls down," a game), Ketsketl, Oslokw, Layekw ("trail") or Erkigeri (where they prepared for dancing), Ple'l ("large," in which the Jumping dance was begun), Hokome'r ("end"), Knau, Ma'a, Te'wira, Ma'a-wono ("up-hill from Ma'a"), Sepora ("open place, flat"), Perkweri ("behind the door"), Kekomeroi ("end, last"), Kiwogi ("in middle"), Ernerkw ("narrow"), Kinekau ("on the brink"), Tewolek-repau ("facing the ocean"), Howeyiro'i, Olige'l Ma'a-hito ("this side of Ma'a"), Nekerai. Of these, Ketsketl, Oslokw, Layekw, Knau, Ma'a, Te'wira, Sepora, Kiwogi and Howiyero'i had sweat houses at one time or another; besides which there were sweat houses known as Tetl, Tsa'at'orka'i, and Ki'mo'le'n ("ugly, old"), the last being the sweat house used in the Jumping dance.

Pekwan contained Ereu, Tekor, Ketsketl, Opyuweg ("dance," in which the Jumping dance was made), an unnamed house adjacent to the last and probably belonging to the same family, Etlkero, Wogi, Erkigeri-tserwo (in which the dance was prepared for), Hiwon ("uphill"), Lekusa ("sweat house exit"), Tetl wo'lometl ("the tetl live in it," they being the men who during the Jumping dance frequent the sacred sweat house), Hetlkak, Tso'oleu ("down hill"), Olohkwetoip, Ta'amo ("elderberries"), Hitsao, Ska'awelotl ("buckeye hangs"). The sweat houses were Ereu, Ketsketl, Wogi, Lekusa, Hesier, and Opegoiole, the last used in the Jumping dance. The cemetery filled the center of the village, from Ketsketl to Lekusa, and between Wogi and Erkigeri on the upper side and Etlkero and Hitsao on the other.[1]

POLITICAL AND NATIONAL SENSE.

The national horizon of the Yurok was as confined as that of most northern Californians. Adjacent tribes were visited at ceremonies and to some extent wives were purchased from them. Of those next beyond, there was only the dimmest knowledge; and farther, neither rumor nor legend nor interest. At that distance, there was only the end of the world, or a strange unsighted ocean, and perhaps things that no one wanted to see. The Yurok did not venture into the unknown and felt no desire to. Nor did they welcome strangers. If any came, it must be for a bad purpose; and they were put out of the way at the first opportunity. A man of substance, wealth, or character did not stray or nose about. He remained at home in dignity, or traveled where relatives of old or hereditary friends welcomed him. If ever he went farther, it was with their introduction. An old man of Pekwan, born there of a Tolowa mother from Kohpei, a man of property and many formulas, had traveled in his lifetime as far as Tolowa Eshpeu; Karok Kumawer, not quite as far as sacred

---

[1] Waterman, Yurok Geography, 1920 (see Bibliography), lists the houses of Rekwoi and Pekwan with slight variations from the above, adds town plats, and gives detailed maps of Yurok settlements and habitat generally.

Inam, below Happy Camp; and in Wiyot territory to Eureka. The county seat and its fairs drew him to the latter. Before the white man came he would probably not have passed beyond the mouth of Mad River.

It is essential to bear in mind that since there was no definite community sense within a village, there was no opportunity for a larger or political community to develop out of a group of adjacent villages. One settlement in such a group—a "suburb"—was sometimes involved in a feud while another directly across the river looked on. Of course, wherever kinship existed, it formed a definite bond between towns as within them; but however instrumental blood relationship may sometimes become as a means of political organization, it is not in itself productive of a political sense; and the replacement of the latter by a feeling of kinship or personal relation among people like the Yurok is precisely what makes it necessary to distinguish the two if this peculiar society is to be understood.

It is true that Wahsekw danced against Weitspus, and played against it at shinny, and that under threat of attack from a remote and consolidated alien foe, village might adhere to village in joint war, just as, in lesser feuds, town mates, impelled by bonds of association or imperiled by their common residence, would sometimes unite with the group of individuals with whom the feud originated. But these are occasions such as draw neighbors together the world over, be they individuals, districts, or nations. While they are capable of being utilized in the formation of civic units, they do not in themselves constitute the associated bodies into political societies.

There is one recorded instance of larger community rights. If a whale came ashore anywhere between Atlau, south of Osegen, and Tsotskwi-hipau, south of Dry Lagoon, it belonged to Espau, Orekw, and Tsahpekw jointly, each man taking a cut a half-fathom wide, the rich men a full fathom. This is analogous to a recognition, probably prospective rather than ever actual, that Little River (or perhaps a certain other stream in the vicinity) marked the point beyond which a stranded whale was wholly in Wiyot ownership; to the north thereof the property of the Yurok of Tsurau (including Metskwo); whereas if it drifted to shore across the mouth of the stream, it was shared by the two groups. The Big Lagoon villages probably held corresponding rights for the intervening stretch of coast, and Rekwoi-Wetlkwau the privilege on another stretch of beach to the north. But a whale was an infrequent and uncontrollable event, a half winter's provisions, and yet not so wholly sporadic that definite custom was unable to crystallize about it. There is no instance of a similar law as regards fishing rights on the river, hunting territories, and acorn and seed tracts; all of which were individual or family property and not community rights. Fish dams, intercommunally erected for brief periods at Kepel, at Lo'olego above Weitspus, and on Redwood Creek at Orau at the mouth of Prairie Creek, are perhaps somewhat comparable to the whale claims of the coast.

Yurok speech was uniform along the river. On the coast a difference of dialect became perceptible, according to some accounts, at Espau, a more marked one at Orekw, and a third, most divergent variety, at Tsurau. Actually these differences must have been very slight, since recorded vocabularies and texts show an appreciable difference only for the region of Big Lagoon and Trinidad; and even this dialect was intelligible on the river.

The term "Coast Yurok," in the present account, is used not with reference to this rather slight speech cleavage, but geographically—for the people south of the mouth of the Klamath. These the other Yurok call Nererner. Thus, *ner-nererner*, I speak Coast Yurok; *ne-shagero*, I speak Yurok. Similarly, *ne-kerermerner*, I speak the language of the Karok, the Petsik-la; *ne-we'yohtene*, I speak Wiyot (We'yot); *ne-tolowo*, I speak Tolowa; *ne-mimohsigo*, I speak the Athabascan dialect of the Hupa (Hupo-la) and Chilula (Tsulu-la).

DIRECTIONS.

The Yurok, and with them their neighbors, know no cardinal directions, but think in terms of the flow of water. Thus *pul* is the radical meaning downstream; *pets*, upstream; *hiko*, across the stream; *won*, up hill, that is, away from the stream on one's own side; *wohpe*, across the ocean, and so on. Such terms are also combined with one another. If a Yurok says "east" he regards this as an English word for upstream, or whatever may be the run of the water where he is. The name Yurok itself—which in its origin is anything but an ethnic designation—means "downstream" in the adjacent Karok language. The degree to which native speech is affected by this manner of thought is remarkable. A house has its door not at its "western" but its "downstream" corner. A man is told to pick up a thing that lies "upstream" from him, not on his "left." The basis of this reckoning is so intensely local, like everything Yurok, that it may become ambiguous or contradictory in the usage of our broader outlook. A Yurok coming from O'men to Rekwoi has two "upstreams" before him: south along the coast, and south-southeast, though with many turns, along the Klamath. When he arrives at Weitspus, the Trinity stretches ahead in the same direction in the same system of valley and ridges; but being a tributary, its direction is "up a side stream," and the direction "upstream" along the Klamath suddenly turns north, or a little east of north, for many miles. Beyond their Karok neighbors the Yurok seem to have a sense that the stream comes from the east. At least they point in that direction when they refer to the end of the world at the head of the Klamath.

This plan of orientation is characteristic of all the northwestern tribes, and is followed in some degree in central California. The

Yokuts terms of direction, in the far-away San Joaquin Valley, are at least shifted from the cardinal points in accord with the flow of water, if indeed they do not refer to it. The cognate Maidu words are said to have the same meaning as our own. But it is possible that the Maidu have given a sun-determined meaning to original drainage terms under the ritualizing influence of their Kuksu cult. This may also be what has happened among southern Wintun, Pomo, and Yuki, who constantly use words like "north," while the central Wintun think in terms of waterflow. It has been customary among inquirers to assume that Pomo *yo* means "south" because a group consistently uses it for that direction; which, of course, is no proof. In any event it is likely that exact south, when they knew a south, was determined for most California tribes by the prevailing direction of their streams as much as by the meridian of the sun. The rectangular and parallel disposition of the drainage in the greater part of the State must have contributed to this attitude. Only in southern California, where water runs far apart and intermittently, and the ceremonializing symbolism of the southwestern tribes is a near influence, is it certain that we encounter true terms of solar orientation.

POPULATION.

Yurok population can be more accurately determined than the strength of most other Californian groups, so that a detailed analysis seems worth while.

The most valuable source of information is a census made in 1852 by a trader who spent the most of his life at Klamath. It covers the towns from the mouth of the river to the salmon dam at Kepel. Only 17 are enumerated, but some of the smaller ones may have been counted as suburbs of the more important settlements. Thus Wetlkwau was perhaps reckoned as part of Rekwoi, or perhaps overlooked. The figures are:

	Houses.	Inhabitants.		Houses.	Inhabitants.
Rekwoi	22	116	Yohter	3	13
Ho'pau	6	72	Sregon	7	66
Wohkel	2	15	Meta	6	39
Sa'aitl	2	34	Nohtsku'm	4	15
Turip	14	94	Murekw	14	105
Serper	4	52	Sa'a	3	13
Wohkero	3	51	Kepel	3	10
Wohtek	4	55			
Ko'otep	24	165		141	1,052
Pekwan	20	137			

The total of 1,052 comprises 354 men, 381 women, 160 boys, 157 girls. The 7 per cent deficiency in adult males is about what might be expected as a consequence of feuds.

The house averages per village fluctuate from 3 to 17. This seems excessive; but there is no reason to doubt the grand average of nearly 7½ souls per dwelling. The five largest towns yield 617 persons in 94 houses, or somewhat over 6½.

In the stretch of river covered by the 17 towns of the list, Figure 1 shows 20 standard settlements and 6 others that were inhabited discontinuously or are otherwise doubtful. According as the 141 houses and 1,052 souls are attributed respectively to 17, 20, or 26 settlements, the house average per village is 8⅓, 7, and 5½, the population 62, 53, or 40. The most likely averages for settlements of all sizes and kinds would seem to be:

Persons per house, 7½.
Houses per town, 6.
Persons per town, 45.

Outside of the Kepel-Rekwoi stretch, Figure 1 designates 21 standard and 7 more doubtful towns. These allow of calculations of the whole Yurok population being undertaken:

$$1,052 \ (=26 \times 40) +1,133 \ (=28 \times 40) =2,185.$$
$$1,052 \ (=20 \times 53) +1,105 \ (=21 \times 53) =2,155.$$
$$1,052 \ (=17 \times 62) +1,300 \ (=21 \times 62) =2,352.$$

The conclusion is that the aggregate Yurok population can not have been much below and was certainly not above 2,500.

This figure is precisely the estimate arrived at from acquaintance with the settlements and sites of recent years, their house pits, and discussion with the older Indians of the number of inhabited houses they remember from their youth.

A count of the upper Yurok villages, also made about 1852 by an early resident on the river, is less itemized than the preceding, but yields 544 persons in 68 houses from Wahsekw to Otsepor, and an average house population of eight. The map has only six villages in this reach.

Five hundred and forty-four added to 1,052 makes 1,596. There is a gap of nearly 10 miles, which the first authority estimates to have had 310 inhabitants. This seems a high figure, since there were only five settlements, and two of these not admitted as old or permanent by the modern Yurok. Perhaps Kepel and Wahsekw have been counted twice. A reduction to 200 still leaves the total for the River Yurok at 1,800 in 37 settlements. Seventeen coast villages, exclusive of Rekwoi and Wetlkwau, would have 800 inhabitants at the same ratio. But as the coast towns make the impression of having been somewhat smaller than those on the river, and not more than one or two were distinctly populous, this figure can be reduced to 600 or 700; which, added to the 1,800 on the river, brings us again to barely 2,500. This number seems almost certain to be true within not to exceed 100 or 200 at the time of first American contact.

These data, so far as they relate to house and village population, probably hold with little change for all the specifically northwestern groups; that is, the Karok, Hupa, Tolowa, Yurok, and with some reduction for the Chilula. The populousness per riparian mile fluctuated according to local conditions, as is set forth in connection with the Wiyot; while any computation based on area of land held would be worthless. Prohibitive caution would also have to be exercised in applying any of these figures to other parts of California. Not only the topography and natural resources but customs vary enormously.

The Government expedition sent through the Klamath region in 1851 to negotiate with the Indians did not follow the river below Wahsekw, but 32 Yurok villages were mentioned by the Indians as lying between Bluff Creek and the mouth. This tallies closely with the present map. At the ratio then estimated of 10 persons to the house and 9 houses per village, the population on the river would have been nearly 3,000; but this figure seeming excessive, it was cut in half by the recorder as still liberal. Recent counts of houses and house pits recollected as inhabited, total over 170 for the Rekwoi-Kepel stretch.

	Modern memories.	1852 count.		Modern memories.	1852 count.
Rekwoi-Wetlkwau	23+	22	Sregon	6	7
Ho'peu	9	6	Meta	7	6
Wohkel	2	2	Nohtsku'm	4	4
Sa'aitl	5	2	Murekw-Himetl	21	14
Turip	8+	14	Sa'a-Kepel	14	6
Serper	3	4			
Wohkero-Wohtek	13	7		154+	141
Ko'otep	18	24	Other settlements	19	
Pekwan	17+	20			
Yohter	4	3		173+ [2]	

The Yurok recognize that a village normally contained more named house sites than inhabited houses. Families died out, consolidated, or moved away. The pit of their dwelling remained and its name would also survive for a generation or two. If allowance is made for parts of villages washed out by floods and possibly by mining, or dwellings already abandoned when the American came and totally forgotten 60 years later, the number of house sites on these 30 miles of river may be set at 200 or more in place of 173. In other words, there were two houses to each three recognized house sites among the Yurok in native times.

---

[2] Waterman, Yurok Geography, 1920, p. 206, gives a somewhat different distribution of the number of houses in the towns between Rekwoi and Kepel, but an almost indentical total of 171 plus a few in small settlements. For the Yurok as a whole he tabulates 324 houses in 47 recognized towns, besides which there were 16 minor settlements in which there remained only house pits during native memory or for which recollection failed. The total of 324 multiplied by 7½ yields 2,430 as the Yurok population. Unoccupied houses in the larger towns would probably more than make up for inhabited but uncounted houses in the smaller settlements. On page 209 he lists 107 different names borne by 219 different houses. Of these, 23 names of 111 houses refer to position in the town, 17 names of 24 houses describe the structure, and 6 names of 12 houses have religious reference.

A count of the same 17 villages on the lower Klamath in 1895 revealed a total of 151 houses, or 10 more than in 1852. But instead of 1,052 Indians only 384 were living, and these partly of mixed blood. There were 141 men, 136 women, 55 boys, and 52 girls, or only about 2½ souls per house—a third of the ratio in native times.

The majority of these 151 dwellings were built in American fashion. It was customary, by this time, for a family to have two or three houses, or a native and an American house. The principal change in relative size of villages was between Ko'otep and Wohtek-Wohkero. The former was overwhelmed with mud in the great floods of 1861–62, and most of the inhabitants moved to the latter site. In 1852 Ko'otep had 24 of the 31 houses in the group, in 1895 only 6 out of 37. Turip also suffered from flood and declined from 14 houses to 5 in the interval, while Rekwoi, favored with a trading post like Wohtekw-Wohkero, rose from 22 to 30 in 1895.

On the basis of 382 people in these 17 settlements, the Yurok population in 1895 may be set at 900, or perhaps a little less on account of a more rapid decrease along the coast than on the river.

The Federal census of 1910 reported 668 Yurok. This figure probably includes substantially all full and half bloods, and part of the quarter breeds.

CHAPTER 2.

THE YUROK: LAW AND CUSTOM.

PRINCIPLES OF YUROK LAW.

These are the standards by which the Yurok regulate their conduct toward one another:

1. All rights, claims, possessions, and privileges are individual and personal, and all wrongs are against individuals. There is no offense against the community, no duty owing it, no right or power of any sort inhering in it.

2. There is no punishment, because a political state or social unit that might punish does not exist, and because punishment by an individual would constitute a new offense which might be morally justified but would expose to a new and unweakened liability. An act of revenge therefore causes two liabilities to lie where one lay before.

3. Every possession and privilege, and every injury and offense, can be exactly valued in terms of property.

4. There is no distinction between material and nonmaterial ownership, right, or damage, nor between property rights in persons and in things.

5. Every invasion of privilege or property must be exactly compensated.

6. Intent or ignorance, malice or negligence, are never a factor. The fact and amount of damage are alone considered. The psychological attitude is as if intent were always involved.

7. Directness or indirectness of cause of damage is not considered, except in so far as a direct cause has precedence over an indirect one. If the agent who is directly responsible can not satisfactorily be made amenable, liability automatically attaches to the next agent or instrument in the chain of causality, and so on indefinitely.

8. Settlement of compensation due is arrived at by negotiation of the parties interested or their representatives, and by them alone.

9. When compensation has been agreed upon and accepted for a claim, this claim is irrevocably and totally extinguished. Even the harboring of a sentiment of injury is thereafter improper, and if such sentiment can be indirectly connected with the commission of an injury, it establishes a valid counter-liability. The known cherishing of resentment will even be alleged as prima facie evidence of responsibility in case an injury of undeterminable personal agency is suffered.

10. Sex, age, nationality, or record of previous wrongs or damage inflicted or suffered do not in any measure modify or diminish liability.

11. Property either possesses a value fixed by custom, or can be valued by consideration of payments made for it in previous changes of ownership. Persons possess valuations that differ, and the valuation of the same nonmaterial property or privilege varies, according to the rating of the person owning it. The rating of persons depends partly upon the amount of property which they possess, partly upon the values which have previously passed in transfers or compensations concerning themselves or their ancestors.

One doubtful qualification must be admitted to the principle that the Yurok world of humanity recognizes only individuals: the claims of kinship. These are undoubtedly strong, not only as sentiments but in their influence on legal operations. Yet a group of kinsmen is not a circumscribed group, as a clan or village community or tribe would be. It shades out in all directions, and integrates into innumerable others. It is true that when descent is reckoned unilaterally, a body of kinsmen in the lineage of the proper sex tends to maintain identity for long periods and can easily become treated as a group. It is also conceivable that such patrilinear kin units exist in the consciousness of Yurok society, and have merely passed unnoticed because they bear no formal designations. Yet this seems unlikely. A rich man is always spoken of as the prominent person of a town, not of a body of people. In the case of a full and dignified marriage, the bond between brothers-in-law seems to be active as well as close. Women certainly identify themselves with their husbands' interests as heartily as with those of their parents and brothers on most occasions. These facts indicate that relationship through females is also regarded by the Yurok; and such being the case, it is impossible for a kin group not to have been sufficiently connected with other kin groups to prevent either being marked off as an integral unit. Then, a " half-married " man must have acted in common with the father-in-law in whose house he lived; and his children in turn would be linked, socially and probably legally, to the grandfather with whom they grew up as well as with their paternal grandfather and his descendant. So, too, it is clear that a married woman's kin as well as her husband retained an interest in her. If the latter beat her, her father had a claim against him. Were she killed, the father as well as the husband would therefore be injured; and there can be little doubt that something of this community of interest and claim would descend to her children. Kinship, accordingly, operated in at least some measure bilaterally and consequently diffusively; so that a definite unit of kinsmen acting as a group capable of constituted social action did not exist.

This attitude can also be justified juridically, if we construe every Yurok as having a reciprocal legal and property interest in every one of his kin, proportionate, of course, to the proximity of the relationship. A has an interest in his kinsmen X, Y, and Z similar to his interest in his own person, and they in him. If A is injured, the claim is his. If he is killed, his interest in himself passes to X, Y, Z—first, or most largely, to his sons, next to his brothers; in their default to his brothers' sons—much as his property interests pass, on his natural death, to the same individuals. The only difference is that the claim of blood is reciprocal, possession of goods or privilege absolute or nearly so.

It may be added that this interpretation of Yurok law fits very nicely the practices prevailing in regard to wife purchase. Here the interest in a person is at least largely ceded by her kinsmen for compensation received.

It is men that hold and press claims and receive damages for women and minors, but only as their natural guardians. The rights of a woman are in no sense curtailed by her sex, nor those of a child by its years; but both are in the hands of adult male trustees. Old women whose nearer male kin have died often have considerable property in their possession. The weakness of their status is merely that they are unable to press their just claims by the threat of force, not that their claim is less than that of a man.

It may be asked how the Yurok executed their law without political authority being in existence. The question is legitimate; but a profounder one is why we insist on thinking of law only as a function of the state when the example of the Yurok, and of many other nations, proves that there is no inherent connection between legal and political institutions. The Yurok procedure is simplicity itself. Each side to an issue presses and resists vigorously, exacts all it can, yields when it has to, continues the controversy when continuance promises to be profitable or settlement is clearly suicidal, and usually ends in compromising more or less. Power, resolution, and wealth give great advantages; justice is not always done; but what people can say otherwise of its practices? The Yurok, like all of us, accept the conditions of their world, physical and social; the individual lives along as best he may; and the institutions go on.

MONEY.

The money of the Yurok was dentalium shells. Dentalia occur in California, the species *D. hexagonum* inhabiting the southern coast, and *D. indianorum* perhaps the northern. Both species, however, live in the sand in comparatively deep water, and seem not to have been taken alive by any of the California Indians. The Yurok certainly were not aware of the presence of the mollusk along their ocean shore, and received their supply of the " tusk " shells from the north. They knew of them as coming both along the coast and down the Klamath River. Since the direction of the first of these sources is "downstream" to them, they speak in their traditions of the shells living at the downstream and upstream ends of the world, where strange but enviable peoples live who suck the flesh of the univalves.

Dentalia are known to have been fished by the Indians of Vancouver Island, and were perhaps taken by some tribes farther south; but it is certain that every piece in Yurok possession had traveled many miles, probably hundreds, and passed through a series of mutually unknown nations.

The Yurok grade their shells very exactly according to length, on which alone the value depends. They are kept in strings that reach from the end of an average man's thumb to the point of his shoulder. Successive shells have the butt end in opposite direction so as not to slip into one another. The pieces on one string are as nearly as possible of one size. So far as they vary, they are arranged in order of their length. But shells of sufficiently different size to be designated by distinct names are never strung together, since this would make value reckoning as difficult as if we broke coins into pieces. The length of "strings" was not far from 27½ inches, but of course never exactly the same, since a string contained only an integral number of shells and these, like all organisms, varied. The cord itself measured a yard or more. This allowed the shells to be slid along it and separated for individual measurement without the necessity of unstringing. The sizes and names of the shells are as follows:

Length of shell in inches.	Yurok name of shell.	Hupa name of shell.	Yurok name of string.	Hupa name of string.	Shells to string of 27½ inches.
2½........	Kergerpitl.....	Dingket......	Kohtepis......	Moanatla......	11
2⅝......	Tego'o.........	Kiketukut-hoi	Na'apis........	Moananah.....	12
2¼........	Wega.........	Chwolahit.....	Nahksepitl....	Moanatak.....	13
2—........	Hewiyem.....	Hostanhit	Ta'anepitl.....	Moanadingk...	14
1⅞—......	Merostan......	....	Tsepupitl.....	....	15

The Yurok further distinguish *tsewosteu*, which is a little shorter than *merostan*, though still money. Possibly *tsewosteu* was the name of the 15-to-the-string shells, and *merostan*—sometimes called "young man's money"—denoted a size of which 14½ measured a string. The Yurok further specify the length, both of pieces and of strings, by adding a number of qualifying terms, especially *oweyemek* and *wohpekemek*, which denote various degrees of shortness from standard.

Dentalia which go more than 15 or 15½ shells to the string are necklace beads. These come in three sizes, *terkutem*, *skayuperwern*, and *wetskaku*, the latter being the shortest. The value of all these was infinitely less than that of money, and they were strung in fathoms or half-fathoms, the grade being estimated by eye, not measured. Ten half-fathom strings of *terkutem* were equal to about one 13-string of money; making a rate of an American dollar or less per yard.

The Karok call dentalia *ishpuk*, the broken bead lengths *apmananich*. The largest size of money shells is *pisiwawa*, the next *pisiwawa afishni*, the third *shisharetiropaop*.

All sizes of dentalia have depreciated since first contact with the whites, so that valuations given to-day in terms of American money fluctuate; but the following appear to have been the approximate early ratings, which in recent years have become reduced about one-half:

To string.	Value of shell.	Value of string.
11	$5.00	$50.00
12	2.00	20.00
13	1.00	10.00
14	.50	5.00
15	.25	2.50

From this it is clear that an increase in length of shell sufficient to reduce by one the number of pieces required to fill a standard string about doubled its value.

Dentalia of the largest size were exceedingly scarce. A string of them might now and then be paid for a wife by a man of great prominence; but never two strings. Possession of a pair of such strings was sufficient to make a man well known.

Shells are often but not always incised with fine lines or angles, and frequently slipped into the skin of a minute black and red snake, or wound spirally with strips of this skin. The ends of the cord are usually knotted into a minute tuft of scarlet woodpecker down. All these little devices evince the loving attention with which this money was handled but do not in the least enhance its value.

As might be expected, the value of dentalia was greater in California than among the northern tribes at the source of supply. In Washington or northern Oregon, as among the Yurok, a slave was rated at a string; but the northern string was a fathom long. Among the Nutka, money was still cheaper: it took 5 fathoms of it to buy a slave.

The size of the shells used in the north has, however, not been accurately determined. For the Oregon-Washington region, 40 shells were reckoned to the fathom, which gives an individual length averaging at the lowest limit of what the Yurok accepted as money, or even a little less. In British Columbia it is stated that 25 pieces must stretch a fathom. This would yield an average of considerably over $2\frac{1}{2}$ inches, or more than the very longest shells known to the Yurok. It may be added that the fathom measure was in constant use among the Yurok for almost everything but money.

The actual valuing of dentalia was individual or in groups of fives, the length of men's arms being too variable and the size of shells too irregular to permit of exact appraisals by treating a string as a unit. The shells on a cord were therefore turned over and matched against each other, and then laid against the fingers from crease to crease of the joints. The largest size was gauged from the farther crease of the little finger to the fold in the palm below; according to some accounts, the measure was also taken on the index. Other sizes were matched against the middle finger. A shell from a full 13-piece string was supposed to extend precisely from the base of this finger to the last crease and was called *wetlemek wega*. A 12-to-the-string shell, of course, passed beyond.

Measurement was also by fives, from the end of the thumbnail to a series of lines tattooed across the forearm. These indelible marks were made from fives of known value, and served as a standard not dependent on bodily peculiarities.

The generic Yurok name for dentalium is *tsik*. Since the coming of the whites it has also been known as *otl we-tsik*, "human beings their dentalium," that is, "Indian money," in distinction from American coins. The early settlers corrupted this to "allicocheek," used the term to the Indians, and then came to believe that it was a native designation common to all the diverse languages of the region.

Dentalium is frequently personified by the Yurok. *Pelin-tsiek*, "Great Dentalium," enters frequently into their myths as if he were a man, and in some versions is almost a creator. *Tego'o* is also a character in legend.

All other shells were insignificant beside dentalia in Yurok consideration. Olivellas were strung and used for ornament, but did not rate as currency. Haliotis, which seems to have been imported from the coast to the south of Cape Mendocino, was liberally used on the fringe of Yurok women's dresses, on ear pendants, in the inlay of pipes, and the like. But it also never became money and did not nearly attain the value of good dentalia. Now and then a short length of disk beads from central California penetrated to the Yurok, but as a prized variety rather than an article of recognized value.

A myth, told, it may be noted, by a Coast Yurok of Eshpeu married at Orekw, narrates how the dentalia journeyed by the shore from the north. At the mouth of the Klamath the small shells went south along the coast, but Pelintsiek and Tego'o continued up the river. At Ho'opeu and Serper Tego'o wished to enter, at Turip his larger companion; but in each case the other refused. At Ko'otep and Shreggon they went in. Pekwan they did not enter, but said that it would contain money. Nohtsku'm and Meta they passed by. At Murekw they entered, as at Sa'a and Wa'asei, and left money. At Kenek, Pelintsiek wished to leave money, but apparently did not do so. At Wahsekw and again at Weitspus they went in and left three shells. At Pekwututl also they entered, and there the story ends with Pelintsiek's saying that some money must continue upstream (to the Karok) and up the Trinity to the Hupa. The tale records the Yurok idea as to the situation of wealth; it illustrates their interest in money; and although a somewhat extreme example, is a characteristic representation of their peculiar mythology, with its minimum of plot interest, intense localization, and rationalizing accounting of particular human institutions.

TREASURE.

Of articles other than shells, those that approach nearest to the character of money are woodpecker scalps. These are of two sizes, both of them scarlet and beautifully soft: those from the larger bird are slightly more brilliant. The two kinds of scalp are known as *kokoneu* (Karok: *furah*) and *terker'it*. The former are rated at $1 to $1.50 each, the latter variously at 10, 15, and 25 cents. The native ratio seems to have been 6 to 1. Woodpecker scalps differ from dentalia in that they have value as material, being worked into magnificent dance headdresses, and used as trimming on other regalia. They represent the Yurok idea of the acme of splendor. Dentalium currency is never worn or exhibited in display, and being entirely without intrinsic utility or ornamental possibility, is wholly and purely money.

Deerskins of rare colors and large blades of obsidian and flint possessed high values; in fact, all objects carried in dances represented wealth. But these articles varied so greatly according to color, size, fineness, or workmanship, that their civilized equivalents are jewels rather than money. At the same time, there was a strong tendency, as can be seen from the examples below, to make part of every payment of consequence in a variety of articles. When large sums changed ownership, as in the purchase of a high-class wife or settlement for the death of a rich man, not more than about half the total seems to have been in dentalia. In the same way strings paid over were of graduated sizes, not all of one value. These facts indicate that a proper variety and balance of wealth as well as quantity were considered desirable.

Even a common deerskin represented value when prepared for dance use. Besides the hide, there was the labor of stuffing the head, and woodpecker scalps were needed for eyes, ears, throat, and tongue. An unusually light or dark skin was worth more, and those that the Yurok call "gray" and "black" and "red" are estimated at $50 to $100. A pure albino skin, with transparent hoofs, is rated at $250 to $500. But this is a theoretic valuation given for the sake of comparison. The Yurok state that fine white skins did not change ownership. Their possession was known far and wide and to part with one on any consideration would have been equivalent to a king selling his crown. (Pls. 2, 3.)

Similarly with obsidians. The usual statement that these are worth $1 an inch of length is true for blades of half a foot to a foot. A 20-inch piece, however, would be held at about $50, and the few renowned giants that reach 30 and even 33 inches are, from the native point of view, inestimable. The above applies to black

PLATE 2

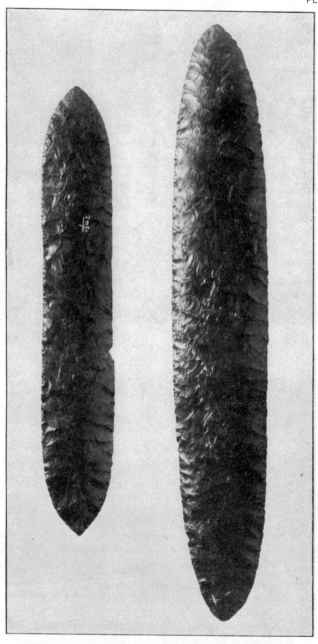

YUROK TREASURES, EXHIBITED IN DANCES:
OBSIDIAN BLADES, THE SMALLER RED, THE
LARGER BLACK AND 13½ INCHES LONG

PLATE 3

HUPA WHITE DEERSKIN DANCE; THE PERFORMERS IN FRONT
OF THE LINE DISPLAYING OBSIDIANS

YUROK MAKING A BOAT

obsidian. The red, which is rarer and does not come in as large pieces, is worth considerably more. Most valuable of all are the blades of white flint, which can not be chipped quite as evenly as the obsidian, but can be worked broader and somewhat thinner. The largest of these run to about a foot and a half long.

VALUATIONS.

The following are some Yurok valuations, apparently on the modern basis of a 12-dentalium string being worth 10 American dollars:

A large boat, that is, a capacious one—the length is uniform—was worth two 12-strings, one full and one short; or 10 large or 60 small woodpecker scalps.

A small boat: One 13-string or 3 large woodpecker heads.

A very small boat carrying two men: Five shells from a 13-string.

The Karok put a boat at two strings of small shells.

A blanket of two deerskins sewn together and painted is said to have been worth a small boat. This seems a high valuation; but the Karok say, 4 to 10 medium or short dentalia or a whole string of small ones, if the skins are ample.

A quiver of otter or fisher fur, with bow and 40 arrows, was the equivalent of a good-sized boat. The Karok reckon an otter skin worth 4 to 7 dentalia.

An entire eagle skin—the birds were shot with the bow at a bait of deer meat on mountain tops—was worth only one shell of smallest size.

A woman's capful of tobacco, one small shell.

A house, 3 strings.

A well-conditioned house of redwood planks, 5 strings.

A fishing place, 1 to 3 strings. Two instances are known of Karok fishing rights having been sold for $5. The value must have been very variable.

A tract bearing acorns, 1 to 5 strings.

The meat from a "small" section—perhaps a half fathom—of a whale, 1 string, presumably of short shells.

A "black," "red," or mottled deer skin, dressed for dance use, 5 strings.

A light gray skin, 6 strings.

A white skin, 10 strings.

Obsidian or flint blades, 2 to 10 strings.

A headband, *sraisplegok*, of 50 large woodpecker scalps, 10 strings. This seems too high a rating in comparison with the others. Small shells must be meant.

Doctors' fees were high: $10 to $20—that is, 1 to 2 strings of good money—are specified as the cost of a treatment.

A slave was rated at only 1 or 2 strings. Evidently the Yurok did not know how to exact full value from the labor of their bondsmen, not because the latter could not be held to work, but because industry was too little organized.

For a wife from a wealthy family 10 strings seem to have been expected, made up, perhaps, of one of 11 shells, one of 12, two of 12 short, and so on, with perhaps a headband of 50 woodpecker scalps, an obsidian, a boat, etc. One Yurok boasted of having paid 14 strings for his wife, plus as much more in other property, including two headbands, the whole representing $300 American at the lower valuation here followed.

For a poorer girl 8 strings and a boat might be given.

The Karok say that a wife was worth 5 to 10 strings. Among both tribes, therefore, a man's life came somewhat higher than what he would pay for a bride of his own rank; which rating, seeing that her relatives did not have to mourn her, is rather favorable to the woman.

For "half-marriage" the price actually paid seems to have been rather less than half.

For the killing of a man of standing the cost was 15 strings, plus, perhaps, a red obsidian, a woodpecker scalp headband, and other property, besides a daughter. The Karok also quote a man's price at 15 strings.

A common man was worth 10 strings, probably of somewhat shorter dentalia, plus, perhaps, 20 large scalps and a good boat.

For a bastard 5 to 6 strings, presumably of small shells, and a few loose woodpecker scalps, are mentioned as usual blood money.

Seduction and pregnancy were rated as calling for 5 strings, or perhaps 20 woodpecker scalps. For a second child the compensation would be less, about 3 strings. The Karok say 2 to 3 strings for seduction, but 4 to 7 if the father took his illegitimate child.

Adultery came at about the same figure.

Uttering the name of a dead man called for the payment of about 2 strings of 13 shells. For a rich man 3 strings of somewhat better money might be demanded.

For breaking a mourning necklace, whether by accident or in play, three or four pieces of money were given.

BLOOD MONEY

The principles of weregild are sufficiently clear from what has been said; an instance or two may be worth adding.

An American at Rekwoi engaged a number of Indians to transport stores from Crescent City. In the surf and rocks at the dangerous entrance to the Klamath a canoe was lost and four natives drowned. Compensation was of course demanded; when it was not forthcoming, the American was ambushed and killed by the brother of one of the dead men. According to one version, the goods were Government property, and the trader responsible only for their transport. The Indians' claims are said to have been forwarded to the Government, but while officials pondered or refused, the Indians, losing hope of a settlement, fell back on the revenge which alone remained to them.

In a Karok myth dealing with the establishment of institutions, it is said in so many words that "if they kill and do not pay, fighting will be perpetual. If a woman is not paid for, there will be bad repute; but if she is bought, everyone will know that so much was given for her, and she will have a good name."

A Yurok myth, which tells of five brothers who made the sky, instituted money and property, and provided for purification from corpse contamination, has them say: "If human beings own money and valuables they will be pleased and think of them. They will not be vindictive; and they will not kill readily, because they will not wish to pay away what they have and prize."

MARRIAGE LAWS.

In marriage the rank of husband and wife and children depended on the amount paid for the woman. People's social status was determined not only by what they possessed, but by what had been given by their fathers for their mothers. Men of wealth made a point of paying large sums for their brides. They thereby enhanced their own standing and insured that of their children. A young man of repute preserved the tradition of his lineage and honored the person and family of his wife in proportion as he paid liberally for her. A poor man was despised not only for his lack of substance, but for the little that he gave for the mother of his children, and for the mean circumstances surrounding his own origin. A bastard was one whose birth had never been properly paid for, and he stood at the bottom of the social scale.

How far the wishes of girls were consulted it is difficult to say, but marriages in which they were unwilling partners are spoken of. We are likely to think in such cases of mercenary fathers intent on profit, when perhaps the main motive in the parents' minds was an honorable alliance and a secure and distinguished career for the daughter.

"Half-marriage" was not rare. The bridegroom paid what he could and worked out a reasonable balance in services to his father-in-law. Of course he lived in the old man's house and was dependent on him for some years, whereas the full-married man took his wife home at once—in fact had her brought to him. It is not certain how often half-marriage was the result of deliberate negotiations, and how frequently a device for decently patching up a love affair.

In a full marriage the groom was represented by two intermediaries, kinsmen, and the price was very exactly specified and carefully considered. A young man rarely possessed sufficient property in his own right, and received the purchase money from his father, or from the latter and his brothers. This was not a formal loan, the blood feeling being very strong among the Yurok. When the bride arrived, at least among the well bred, a considerable amount of property accompanied her. Ten baskets of dentalia, otter skins, and other compact valuables, a canoe or two, and several deerskin blankets, seem to have passed in this way among the wealthy, without any previous bargaining or specification. In this way a rich father voluntarily returned part of the payment made him, the Yurok say. However, on a divorce taking place, these gifts must be returned as fully as the stipulated purchase price.

Sometimes two men traded their sisters to each other for wives; but in such case each nevertheless paid to the other the full amount of money, as if a single purchase were being transacted. In short, the formality of payment was indispensable to a marriage.

On the death of the father of a household, his sons would be entitled to the price received when their sisters were married. In default of sons, the dead man's brothers arranged the marriage of their nieces and received the pay for them. A man sometimes gave to his son part of the money he received at his daughter's wedding, or used the whole of it to buy his son a wife.

Pressing debt sometimes led to betrothal. An infant daughter might be sold to another man for his little boy, the children perhaps remaining in ignorance of their relation. As soon as the girl had passed her adolescence the marriage was consummated.

Sometimes an arrangement was entered into by which a youth received the sister of a sick or crippled man in return for labor or services rendered him.

Divorce was by wish of either party, and entailed only complete repayment. A woman could leave her husband at will, provided her kin were ready to refund; though this was not their usual disposition unless she had been abused. A man, it seems, was not expected to divorce his wife without cause; such as laziness. Probably if a reasonable allegation could not be produced, the woman's relatives would refuse to repay him, in which case the divorce, while still thoroughly open to him, would be an absurd loss.

An implied condition of purchase of a wife was that she bear children. Sterility therefore meant nonfulfillment of contract, and was perhaps the most frequent cause of divorce. If a couple with children separated, the woman could take them with her only on full repayment of her original price. On the other hand, each child left with the husband reduced the repayment, and several canceled it altogether. Theoretically, therefore, the average middle-aged or elderly woman with adult children was free to return to her parents' house, and remained with her husband from choice alone. This privilege is clear, but the Yurok do not seem to formulate it, perhaps because its exercise was not a normal occurrence.

Similarly, it might be inferred that a wife was bought for a natural span of life. If she died young a sister or kinswoman was due the husband. If he passed away first his equity did not lapse but remained in the family, and she was married by his brother. In either event, however, a payment, smaller than the original one, was made to her family. In case of the wife's death this might be interpreted as due to a desire to distribute the loss between the two families involved, since the furnishing of a marriageable and therefore valuable substitute, perhaps repeatedly, wholly gratis, would work hardship on the woman's kin. The payment by the dead man's brother, however, can not well be understood except on the basis that the woman's family retained an interest in her after her marriage. A more likely interpretation of both cases is that the Yurok did not operate on principles so legalistically defined, but held to a generic notion that no union could take place without a payment. The amount given appears to have been nearly half of the original price, although the Indians customarily speak of it as " a little."

It is said that even when a married woman of some age died her kinsmen were required to provide a substitute or repay her original purchase price unless she had borne three or four children. If she had had only one or two children, partial repayment was due.

It may be added that a full year elapsed before the widow's remarriage to her brother-in-law. During this time she kept her hair very short, did not go about much, cried considerably, lived on in her dead husband's house, and kept his property together.

The levirate, as it is called, and the corresponding custom of marrying the sister of the dead or living wife were universal in California, although among many tribes payment for the wife was slight or nominal and among some lacking. The particular legal ideas which the Yurok have connected with these customs can therefore not be regarded as causative of the customs. Historically it is extremely probable that priority must be granted to the levirate, the Yurok merely investing this with the economic considerations that shaped all their life. The foregoing interpretations of Yurok marriage laws must accordingly be construed only as an attempt to make precise a point of view, not as a genetic explanation. Ethnologically, the significance of the group of tribes represented by the Yurok lies largely in the fact that whereas their practices, when compared with those of the bulk of the Indians of California, are obviously closely similar at most points, or at least parallel, they nevertheless possess a distinctive aspect and value throughout.

If a man was jealous and beat his wife without due cause she was likely to return to her parents. Sometimes her father would then dissolve the marriage by returning the purchase price. Her maltreatment did not of itself nullify the marriage transaction. But it did cause a claim for liability, and her relatives seem to have been entitled to keep the woman until her husband had paid them damages for his abuse of her, whereupon he resumed full jurisdiction over her. This provision appeals to us perhaps primarily as one of humanity. Juridically it is of interest as indicating that a woman's kin retained a legal interest in her. Unfortunately we do not know how blood money for a married woman was distributed. It may be suspected that its amount was somewhat greater than her marriage price, the excess going to her relatives.

A curious practice was followed in the Wohtek Deerskin dance following the Kepel fish dam. Before this was finished on the hill at Plohkseu, they danced downstream from Wohkero at Helega'au. Here the old men made men tell what their fathers had paid for their mothers. Those of moderate ancestry were permitted to dance; the rich-born and the illegitimate were both excluded.

A Karok woman born at Ashipak about the time the Americans came had relatives among the Yurok of Rekwoi, the Hupa, and the Shasta. Her grandfather had had wives in or from five different places. For some of these he had paid only partially, the agreement being that the children should remain in the mother's house. It is likely that this is a case of a wealthy man's love affairs legalized after pregnancy set in, rather than of formally proposed marriage; and that the payments made, and the status of the father, were sufficient to remove serious stigma.

Adultery was of course paid for to the husband. From 1 to 5 strings are mentioned as the fine.

Constructive adultery also constituted an injury. Speech or communication between a woman and a former lover made the latter liable. If he met her on the trail he might have to pay a medium-sized string. If he came into a house in which she sat the husband was likely to charge that the visit was intentional, and on pressing his claim might succeed in obtaining double compensation.

Two reasons are given for the payment for seduction. A woman's first bearing is hard and she might die; also, her price to her future husband is spoiled; that is, reduced.

DEBT SLAVERY.

Slavery was a recognized institution but scarcely an important one. The proportion of slave population was small, probably not over one-twentieth, certainly not over a tenth. One Yurok man had three slaves, but he was exceptionally rich, and may not have owned them simultaneously. Slaves entered their condition solely through debt, never through violence. Men were not taken prisoners in war, and women and children were invariably restored when settlement was made; solitary strangers that elsewhere might have been oppressed were suspected and killed by the Yurok. Debt arose from legal rather than economic vicissitudes, Yurok industry and finance being insufficiently developed for a man to fall gradually into arrears from lack of subsistence or excessive borrowing. The usual cause was an act of physical violence or destruction of property; striking a rich man's son, for instance, or speaking the name of a dead person of wealth. Slaves made string and nets, fished, and performed similar work. They were not killed in display of wealth, as farther north on the coast, the Yurok seeing no sense in the destruction of property except when carried away by spite. Slaves, however, were full property. An owner might buy his slave a wife to keep him contented; the children then belonged to the master. The institution seems to have been unknown in California except for the advanced northwestern tribes.

It appears that female relatives paid in blood settlement by poor people became slaves or of kindred status. It is said that if the man to whom such a woman was handed over wished to marry her, or to give her in marriage to a kinsman, he paid a small amount to her family. This indicates that the law accorded him a right to her services, not to her person, and the former was the only right in her which he could transfer on sale.

A bastard, in burning over a hillside, once set fire to certain valuables which a rich man of Sregon had concealed in the vicinity. He was unable to compensate and became the other's slave. Subsequently the Sregonite killed a Tolowa, and transferred the slave as part of the blood money. This was long after the American was in the land; but the slave knew that if he attempted to avail himself of the protection of the white man's law, he would be liable under the native code and probably ambushed and killed by his master. He therefore arranged with him to purchase his liberty, apparently with money earned by services to Americans.

The Yurok state that their slaves did not attempt to run off. A slave might evade a new master; in which case his old proprietor would be appealed to and would threaten him with instant death if he did not return to the service of his new owner. It must be remembered that enslavement of foreigners was not practiced. Among his own or known people, public sentiment would support the master and not the slave. If the latter fled to aliens, his status would at best remain the same, his condition would certainly be worse, and he was likely to be killed at once as an unprotected and unwelcome stranger.

Payment for a murdered slave was, of course, due his master, not his kinsmen. A rich owner would receive a high settlement. It is the old story of values being determined not only intrinsically but according to the value borne by the owner or claimant.

FISHING PRIVILEGES.

If several men jointly owned a fishing place, which seems to have been the case with nearly all the most prolific eddies, they used it in rotation for one or more days according to their share, relieving each other about the middle of the afternoon for 24-hour periods. Thus a famous Karok spot called Ishkeishahachip, formerly on the north side of the river at the foot of the Ashanamkarak fall, but subsequently obliterated or spoiled by the river, belonged for one day to an Ashanamkarak man; for one to a man from Ishipishi, a mile above; for one to the head man of the village opposite Orleans, a dozen miles downstream; and for two days to the rich man of the village at Red Cap Creek, still farther below. A successful fisherman usually gave liberally of his catch to all comers, so that it is no wonder that the Yurok have a fondness for stopping to chat with a fisherman whom they are passing. If a man allowed another to fish at his place, he received the bulk of the catch. If only one salmon was taken, the "tenant" kept merely the tail end.

A fishing place near Wahskw was originally owned by two Weitspus men who were not kinsmen, or at any rate not closely related. One of them dying, his share passed to his son, who sold it to a Wahsekw man for $5 in American money. The new part owner also possessed a place at which he was entitled to put up a platform a short distance below.

It was forbidden to establish a new fishing place or to fish below a recognized one. This provision guaranteed the maintenance of the value of those in existence, and must have very closely restricted the total number to those established by tradition and inheritance.

If one man used another's fishing place, even without explicit permission of the owner, and fell and slipped there and cut his leg or was bruised, he would at once lay claim to the fishing place as damages. People would say to the owner: "It was your place and he was hurt; you should pay him." Perhaps a compromise would be effected on the basis of the plaintiff receiving a half interest in the privilege of the spot.

OWNERSHIP OF LAND.

Up to a mile or more from the river, all land of any value for hunting was privately owned; back of this, there were no claims, nor was there much hunting. It may be that deer were scarce away from the river; but more likely, the private tracts in the aggregate represented accessibility and convenience to the game rather than exhaustive control of its total supply. It may be added that the Yurok country, being well timbered, was poor in small game, deer and elk being the principal objects of the chase. Rich men often held three or four inherited tracts, poor people perhaps a single one, others none. Poachers were shot. A small creek near Weitspus is named Otl-amo, " person caught," because, according to tradition, a poacher was there taken in a deer snare. A wounded animal could be pursued anywhere. It belonged to the hunter, and the owner of the tract in which it fell had no claim upon it.

Certain prairies on the Bald Hills, valuable for seed gathering, belonged to Weitspus and Wahsekw families, who had bought them from the Chilula.

A Weitspus man who had killed a fellow resident of that village fled to the Coast Yurok, bought himself a small stream that flowed into the ocean not far from Osagon Creek, and made his home there. This case is doubly illuminating. It shows the personal heterogeneity of the larger villages, and demonstrates that land was bought and sold for abode and asylum—a rather unusual feature in American Indian society.

The ownership of house sites is discussed elsewhere.

LAW OF FERRIAGE.

Free ferriage must at all times be rendered. At least in theory it is extended also to those who can not reciprocate because of being boatless or in chronic poverty. The underlying assumption of this custom seems to be that ferriage is a primal necessity to which everyone is at times subject and which everyone is also at times in position to relieve. The traveler accordingly has much the status which a guest enjoys as regards food, but his claims are crystallized into a definite privilege. The Yurok and their neighbors extend the right also to Americans resident among them, charging ferriage only to transient voyagers. In the old days even an enemy with whom one did not speak had to be taken as passenger. Such a man on arriving opposite a village shouted. If no one was about but the one who bore him a grudge, the latter nevertheless paddled over. The traveler sat in the boat with his back to the steersman, keeping silence. For a refusal to accord ferriage from three to six short dentalia could be claimed. If a traveler finds a settlement deserted, he takes any boat at the river's edge and puts himself across, without the least care or obligation as to its return.

The carrier being his passenger's agent, the latter becomes liable for any injury to him. A Yurok of Kenek had his house catch fire while ferrying an acquaintance. The latter was due to repay his entire loss: except for the service rendered the owner would have been at hand and might have extinguished the blaze, the Yurok said.

LEGAL STATUS OF THE SHAMAN.

Shaman's fees for the treatment of disease were very high, as the examples previously given indicate. Shamans are said to have frequently urged their female relatives to try to acquire "pains"—shamanistic powers—because wealth was easily got thereby. The rule was for payment to be tendered with the invitation to cure. Usually some negotiation followed. The doctor held out for more; but being legally obliged to go was apt to plead indisposition or illness of her own. The offer was then increased, the pay being actually shown, it appears, and, reaching a satisfactory figure, was accepted, and the shaman went on her visit. Acceptance, however, implied cure, and if this was not attained the entire amount must be returned to the patient or his relatives. This was the old law; but the Karok state that American physicians' example has in recent years caused the practice to spring up of the shaman retaining a small part of her fee as compensation for her time and trouble.

Usually the patient felt improved and the doctor returned claiming a cure. If a relapse followed, she was summoned and came again, receiving a small fee. In strict logic, she should have served for nothing, the patient not having received the complete cure that was tacitly contracted for; but a new effort being involved, there seems to have been some concession to this. The principle is analogous to that which compels a widower to pay a small sum for his second wife, who replaces the first. It is as if the law recognized the equity of partially distributing the loss in cases that are in their nature beyond human agency. This is a mitigating influence that contrasts rather strangely and somewhat pleasingly with the remorseless rigor of the main tenor of Yurok law.

It is a common belief of the Yurok that some shamans would extract one of the pains from a sick person, thus effecting a temporary improvement in his condition, but deliberately leave another within him, in order to be paid for a second treatment. Other shamans sometimes accused them of such malpractice, declaring they could see the remaining pain. It is very characteristic that the Yurok and their northwestern neighbors think in such cases of the shaman's motives as greed, the other California Indians almost invariably as malice.

It is in accord with this diversity of point of view that one scarcely hears among the Yurok of shamans being killed for losing patients, one of the commonest of events elsewhere in California.

On the other hand, the law-spinning inclination of the Yurok is manifest in their absolute rule that a shaman who had declined to visit a patient was liable, in the event of his death, even after treatment by another shaman, for the full fee tendered her, or even a little more. Only a conflicting case, or genuine sickness of the shaman herself, was ground for an attempt on the shaman's part to evade this liability. The argument was that if the fee had been accepted and treatment extended, the sick person might not have died. Hence the liability was complete up to the amount which the patient's family were ready to offer in his behalf. A Karok shaman who had attained some reputation by once appearing to die and then returning to tell of her experiences in the other world, subsequently laid herself open to a claim for not attending a sick person and refused to settle it. The kinsmen of her prospective but deceased patient thereupon waylaid her in the brush and choked her to death. Many a central and south California doctor has met this fate: but his supposed misconduct was intent to kill, as evidenced by failure to cure. The northwesterners took satisfaction because a claim for damages was not met.

It is said that people were bewitched not only by shamans hungering for fees and by avowed foes, but sometimes by mere enviers, who hoped to see a rich man's wealth gradually pass from him to his physicians.

A Karok of Katimin began to suffer with headache, and accused a woman of having bewitched him. Doubtless there was ill feeling between them. He formally voiced his complaint to her brother. The family conferred and offered him three strings as damages. He refused the amount as insufficient, and they, feeling that a sincere effort at reparation had been slighted, announced that they would henceforth be *inivashan*, enemies. Since that time the families have not spoken.

MOURNERS' RIGHTS.

As long as a corpse remained unburied, no one was allowed to pass the village in a boat. If a traveler attempted to go on, the kin of the dead person would lay hold of his canoe. If he succeeded nevertheless, he incurred liability to them. The motive of the prohibition seems to have been that it was a slight to mourners if others transacted ordinary business in their sight or vicinity.

It is, however, specifically stated that this statute did not apply if the dead person had been killed by violence. Similarly those slain were not included among the dead of the year whose kin must be paid before a village could undertake a dance. The reason is clear: if there is a killing, the mourners have been or will be paid, and no further compensation is necessary; while those who grieve for a relative dead from natural causes are enduring an irremediable loss, and their feelings must be assuaged.

If a man died away from home his body might be taken back or buried on the spot. In the latter case the right to interment was purchased. Once payment had been accepted for this privilege, subsequent protest at the inclusion of a stranger's body in a family graveyard subjected the critic to liability for a claim for damages.

Before a major dance could be held, the dead of the year had to be paid for. This was done by contributions of the residents of the village, or by the rich man of the locality. If a village did not hold a dance, the law nevertheless applied, no residents being entitled to visit a ceremony elsewhere until the home mourners were satisfied. This is an extremely characteristic Yurok provision. The dances were held by them to be absolutely necessary to the prosperity and preservation of the world: still, because they afforded entertainment and pleasure to those who assembled, the mourners resented the occasion, and prevented it, until tendered pay for the violation of their grief. In short, a private right is not in the least impaired by coming into conflict with a communal or universal necessity. Since the ceremony is desirable. let those interested in

it extinguish the personal claim, rather than have the holder of
the latter suffer, would be the Yurok point of view. To us, the
legal sanctioning of the obtrusion of a private interest in the face
of a general need seems monstrous. The native probably feels
that the mourners are extremely reasonable in allowing the dance
to be held at all, and that in proportion to the necessity thereof
the community ought to be ready to make sacrifices. This is anarchy; but the Yurok are an anarchic people.

Before the Weitspus dance of 1901, four families were paid $2 each. The
compensation thus amounts to only a very small percentage of the value of a
man's life. The rich man of Pekwututl, across the river, demanded and received $3 because he was rich. Having the money in his possession, he
demanded a second payment of like amount for a relative he had lost at
Hupa. The Weitspus people demurred on the ground that he would be paid
for this death by the Hupa when they held their dance at Takimitlding;
but he stood firm and received what he asked.

If a village did not make or visit a dance for a year the mourners'
claim lapsed totally. There was the same limit to the prohibition
against uttering a dead person's name.

According to a Karok informant the dead of the year were paid
for by the rich men so far as the dead were relatives of those who
contributed dance regalia, whereas even fellow townsmen who were
too poor to help, or had been unwilling, were passed over.

The Yurok declare that the minor "brush dance" was not preceded by payments formerly, but that of late years small compensations have been exacted.
The Hupa, they state, pay more heavily for the privilege of making this dance.
The difference in custom may be due to an earlier abandonment of the great
dances by the reservation Hupa, whereby the brush dance was exalted to a
more significant position. But it seems more in accord with the spirit of Yurok
institutions that the brush dance should also have been permitted only after
compensation; mourners particularly resent hearing singing. The pay is, however, likely to have been small at all times, since the brush dance was instituted by an individual, who was at considerable expense apart from purchasing the privilege.

Compensation for utterances of the name of the dead went, of
course, to the immediate kin—father, brother, or son. A brother
might give part to the widow; but she acted only as custodian of her
dead husband's wealth, and was herself still the property of his family, unless she had borne a number of surviving children. If it was
she that was dead, payment is said to have gone to her husband, not to
her kin. The Yurok state that the amount of compensation depended
solely on the rank of the deceased; age or sex were not factors. After
the name was bestowed on a child of the family, a year having
elapsed, the taboo was of course thereby lifted. This makes it clear
that the conscious motive of the custom is respect for the mourners'
grief for a due season. If two men had the same name, the poorer,

on the death of the richer, would "throw his away," so as to avoid occasion of giving offense. If the wealthy man was the survivor, he would pay his namesake's family, perhaps as much as five strings, satisfy them, and retain his name.

INHERITANCE.

Only a small amount of property was buried with the dead, and none of this of great value. The bulk of the estate went to a man's sons, but the daughters received a share and something was given to all the nearer relatives—at least on the male side—or they would be angry. The kinsman who actually interred the corpse—or rather, the one who assumed defilement on behalf of the others—made a particular claim; no doubt for the restrictions to which his contamination subjected him. Moreover, if there was no one in the family who knew a formula for purification from a corpse, it was necessary for this voluntary scapegoat to hire some one to recite on his behalf; and the fee for this service was high. It is said that poor men were sometimes compelled to give one of their children into slavery in payment for this indispensable release from the excommunicating taboo.

For the building of a house, kinsmen were called upon. They were fed but not paid while they labored; and of course could expect reciprocation. If one of them possessed planks already cut, he furnished them, to be replaced at subsequent convenience. The house was inherited by the son. The brother is said to have received it only if there were neither adult sons nor daughters.

An old and sick Karok woman allowed her half-breed daughter to take possession of her property. Thereupon the sister with whom she lived at Kenek, no doubt in disappointed spite, said to her: "You have nothing. I do not want you," and the decrepit woman went to a more charitable relative at Rekwoi to end her few days.

RICH AND POOR.

The Yurok are well aware of the difference in manners and character between rich and poor in their society. A well-brought-up man asked to step into a house sits with folded arms, they say, and talks little, chiefly in answers. If he is given food, he becomes conversational, to show that he is not famished, and eats very slowly. Should he gobble his meal and arise to go, his host would laugh and say to his children: "That is how I constantly tell you not to behave." If an obscure person commits a breach of etiquette, a well-to-do man passes the error with the remark that he comes from poor people and can not know how to conduct himself. Such a wealthy man exhorts his sons to accost visitors in a quiet and friendly manner and invite them to their house; thus they will have friends. A poor man, on the other hand, instructs his son not in policy but in means to acquire strength. He tells him where to bathe at night; then a being will draw him under the water and speak to him, and he will come away with powerful physique and courage.

Life was evidently so regulated that there was little opportunity for any one to improve his wealth and station in society materially.

The poor, therefore, accepted more or less gracefully the patronage of a man of means, or attempted to win for themselves a position of some kind not dependent on property. A savage temper, and physical prowess to support it, were perhaps the only avenue open in this direction; shamans were women, and priests those who had inherited knowledge of formulas.

The rich man is called *si'atleu*, or simply *pegerk*, "man." Similarly, a wealthy or "real" woman is a *wentsauks* or "woman." A poor person is *wa'asoi*. A slave is called *uka'atl*. A bastard is called either *kamuks*, or *negenits*, "mouse," because of his parasitic habits. *Uwohpewek* means "he is married"; *winohpewek*, "he is half-married."

Even a small village group was known as *pegarhkes*, "manly," if its members were determined, resentful, and wealthy enough to afford to take revenge.

The following Yurok statement is characteristic: "The beautiful skins or headdresses or obsidians displayed at a dance by one rich man excite the interest and envy of visitors of wealth, whereas poor men take notice but are not stirred. Such wealthy spectators return home determined to exhibit an even greater value of property the next year. Their effort, in turn, incites the first man to outdo all his competitors."

The Karok speak of a branching of the trail traversed by the dead. One path is followed by "poor men, who have no providence, and do not help (with regalia, payments, and entertainment) to make the dances." The other is the trail of people of worth.

When an honored guest was taken into the sweat house he was assigned the *tepolatl*, the place of distinction, and the host offered him his own pipe. A common man was told to lie at *legai*, by the door, or *nergernertl*, opposite it. A bastard who entered was ordered out, the Yurok say. It is likely, however, that such unfortunates were more tolerantly treated by their maternal grandfather and uncles.

Food was sometimes sold by the Yurok: but no well-to-do man was guilty of the practice. "May he do it, he is half poor—*tmenemi wa'asoi*" would be the slighting remark passed; much as we might use the term *nouveau riche* or "climber."

PURSUIT OF WEALTH.

The persistence with which the Yurok desire wealth is extraordinary. They are firmly convinced that persistent thinking of money will bring it. Particularly is this believed to be true while one is engaged in any sweat-house occupation. As a man climbs the hill to gather sweat-house wood—always a meritorious practice, in the sense that it tends to bring about fulfillment of wishes—he puts his mind on dentalia.   He makes himself see them along the trail, or hanging from fir trees eating the leaves.   When he sees a tree that is particularly full of these visioned dentalia, he climbs it to cut its branches just below the top.   In the sweat house he looks until he sees more money shells, perhaps peering in at him through the door.   When he goes down to the river he stares into it, and at last may discern a shell as large as a salmon, with gills working like those of a fish.   Young men were recommended to undergo these practices for 10 days at a time, meanwhile fasting and exerting themselves with the utmost vigor, and not allowing their minds to be diverted by communication with other people, particularly women. They would then become rich in old age.

Direct willing, demanding, or asking of this sort are a large element in all the magic of the Yurok, whatever its purpose.   Saying a thing with sufficient intensity and frequency was a means toward bringing it about.   They state that at night, or when he was alone, a man often kept calling, " I want to be rich," or " I wish dentalia," perhaps weeping at the same time.   The appeal seems to have been general, not to particular or named spirits.   Magic is therefore at least as accurate a designation of the practice as prayer.   How far the desires were spoken aloud is somewhat uncertain, the usual native words for " saying " and " thinking " something being the same; but it is very probable that the seeker uttered his words at least to himself.   The practical efficacy of the custom is unquestionable. The man who constantly forced his mind and will into a state of concentration on money would be likely to allow no opportunity for acquisition to slip past him, no matter how indirect or subtle the opening.

According to a Karok myth, the sweat house, its restriction to men, and the practice of gathering firewood for it, were instituted in order that human beings might acquire and own dentalia.

The Yurok hold a strong conviction that dentalium money and the congress of the sexes stand in a relation of inherent antithesis.   This is the reason given for the summer mating season: the shells would leave the house in which conjugal desires were satisfied, and it is too cold and rainy to sleep outdoors in winter.   To preserve his money, in other words to prevent his becoming a spendthrift, a man bathes after contact with his wife, and is careful not to depart from the natural positions.   Strangely enough, the Yurok have a saying that a man who can exercise his virility 10 times in one night will become extraordinarily wealthy; but there are not wanting those who consider this ideal unattainable by modern human beings.

This is a case of typical blending of avarice and magic, as related by the Hupa. The grandchild of the rich man of Medilding had its mouth constantly open. A shaman finally saw and proclaimed the cause. An ancestor of the rich man had asked to kiss a dead friend or relative good-by. He descended into the grave and, bending over the corpse's face, used his lips to draw out from the nose the two dentalia that are inserted through the septum, concealing his booty in his mouth until the grave had been filled. According to report, the rich man admitted that an ancestor of his had actually risked this deed; and the shaman declared that it was the same dentalia that now kept the child's jaws apart.

A man who had borrowed a canoe and wished to buy it might report to the owner that he had broken it; but the possessor was likely to see through the ruse. This is a native instancing of the cupidity which seems to them natural and justifiable.

Gifts were sometimes made by the Yurok, but on a small scale; and while reciprocation of some sort was anticipated, it was generally smaller and could not be enforced. Presents were clearly a rich man's luxury. The host might say to a visitor whose friendship he considered worth strengthening: "You had better return by boat," thereby giving him a canoe. The guest in time would extend his invitation; and the visit would end with his presentation of a string or two of small money, or a quiver full of arrows. As the Yurok say, the first donor had to be satisfied with what he got, because he had given a gift.

MARRIAGE AND THE TOWN.

The Yurok married where and whom they pleased, in the home village or outside, within their nation or abroad. The only bar was to kindred; but the kin of persons connected by marriage were not considered kin. The wife's daughter as well as her sister were regarded suitable partners. The smaller villages were so often composed wholly of the branches of one family that they practiced exogamy of necessity. That such exogamy had not risen to native consciousness as something desirable in itself is shown by numerous endogamous marriages in the larger towns. This point deserves particular consideration because the organization of the Athabascans of the Oregon coast, which seems to have been identical with that of the Yurok, has been misportrayed, simple villages—as ungentile as our country towns—being represented as patrilinear clans, and the mere rule against the marriage of kindred construed as clan exogamy. The subjoined table illustrates the degree of endogamy at one of the larger Yurok towns, Weitspus, and the following examples the distance to which its inhabitants were ready to go for wives when they pleased.

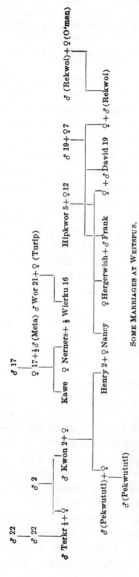

SOME MARRIAGES AT WEITSPUS.

+, married; ½+, half married; 22, etc.: number of house in fig. 2; (Pekwututl), persons from other villages.

House 15 (fig. 2) belonged to the daughter of the former owner. Her half-married husband is of a Karok father from Katimin and a Yurok woman of Ho'opeu. Kewik of Nohtsku'm half-married into Ertlerger, but quarreled with his wife's family, and, moving across the river with her, built himself house 3 in Weitspus, whose site his grandson still owned. The father of the owner of 9 had two wives: The first a Karok from Ashanamkarak, the second a Tolowa. An old man in 10 traded sisters with a Wahsekw man.

THE CRISES OF LIFE.

Births occurred among the Yurok and their neighbors chiefly in spring. This was, of course, not because of any animal-like impulse to rut at a certain season, as has sometimes been imagined, but because of highly specialized ideas of property and magic. The Yurok had made the just psychological observation that men who think much of other matters, especially women, do not often become or remain wealthy. From this they inferred an inherent antipathy between money and things sexual. Since dentalia and valuables were kept in the house, a man never slept there with his wife, as already stated, for fear of becoming poor. The institution of the sweat house rendered this easily possible. In summer, however, when the cold rains were over, the couple made their bed outdoors; with the result that it seems natural to the Yurok that children should be born in spring. A similar condition has been reported from the far-away Miwok region; but the responsible social circumstances, which were certainly different from those of the Yurok, are unknown.

As a girl's property value was greatly impaired if she bore a child before marriage, and she was subject to abuse from her family and disgrace before the community, abortion was frequently attempted. Hot stones were put on the abdomen, and the fœtus thrown into the river. There is little doubt that parents guarded their girls carefully, but the latter give the impression of having been more inclined to prudence than to virtue for its own sake. Probably habits differed largely according to the rank of the family. Poor girls had much less to lose by an indiscretion.

The prospective mother's wish was to bear a small child. Therefore she worked hard and ate sparingly. Difficulty in labor was thought to be caused by undue size of the child brought on by the mother's eating and sleeping too much.

In most of California women sit in childbirth. For the Hupa the same is reported, but the Yurok woman is said to have lain bracing her feet against an assistant. Her wrists were tied with pack straps to parts of the house frame. When the assistant commanded, she raised herself by these thongs. She must shut her mouth, else the child would not leave her body. Many formulas to assist childbirth were known. The most powerful of these, as their own content relates, were thought to become effective as soon as the reciter entered the house with her herb.

If the child during the first five or six days of its life were to take nourishment from its mother, the Yurok believe that its jaws would become affected and it would soon starve. During this period it is fed only a little water in which hazel or pine nuts have been rubbed, and which looks milky. For about the same number of days, or until the child's navel is healed, the father eats apart, touches no meat or fresh salmon, and drinks thin acorn soup instead of pure water. The mother is under the same restrictions for a longer period: 50 days, or 60 for a stillbirth. She spends this time in a separate hut.

The umbilical cord is severed with a piece of quartz clamped inside a split stick, and is carefully preserved in the house for about a year. When the child is about to be weaned the father takes the shred on a ridge, splits a living fir, inserts the little piece of preciousness, and binds the sapling together again. On his return the baby has its first meal other than milk.

If twins of opposite sexes were born, the Yurok smothered one of the pair, usually the girl. They had a dread of such births, which they explain on the ground that if the twins lived they might be incestuous. Boy twins were believed to quarrel all their lives, but were spared. Once triplets were born at Murekw. There was much excitement and much talk of killing them; but a Deerskin dance was made and warded off the sickness which the portent foreboded.

When a girl becomes mature she is called *ukerhtsperek*, and sits silent in her home for 10 days with her back turned to the central fire pit. She moves as little as possible, and scratches her head only with a bone whittled and incised for the occasion. Once each day she goes to bring in firewood; on her way she looks neither to left nor right, and looks up at no one. The longer she fasts, the more food will she have in her life, it is believed. After four days she may eat, but only at a spot where the roar of the river confounds every other sound. Should she hear even a bird sing, she ceases at once. Each evening she bathes, once the first night, twice the second, and so increasingly until on the eighth she pours the water over herself eight times. The ninth night she bathes ten times; and on the tenth day, with declining day, once, squatting by the river, while the small children of the village, one after the other, wash her back. Her mother or another woman then lays 10 sticks on the sand and tells her she will bear so many sons, and places 10 sticks in a row to represent her daughters. The girl's dress during the 10 days is a skirt of shredded maple bark, such as shamans wear during their novitiate.

One in every several hundred Yurok men, on the average, preferred the life and dress of a woman, and was called *wergern*. This frame of mind, which appears to have a congenital or psychological basis well recognized by the psychiatrist, was not combated, but socially recognized by the Indians of California—in fact, probably by all the tribes of the continent north of Mexico. Only among the advanced peoples of that region did the law frown upon transvestites. The Yurok explanation of the phenomenon is that such males were impelled by the desire to become shamans. This is certainly not true, since men shamans were not unknown. It is a fact, however, that all the *wergern* seem to have been shamans and esteemed as such—a fact that illuminates the Yurok institution of shamanism. The *wergern* usually manifested the first symptoms of his proclivities by beginning to weave baskets. Soon he donned women's clothing and pounded acorns.

At death, the corpse is addressed: "*Awok, tsutl* (alas, good-by), look well and take with you the one who killed you with *upunamitl*" (a closure or pressing of internal organs produced magically). The body is then painted with soot, and the septum of the nose pierced for insertion of a dentalium shell. Elderberry sticks measure the length for the grave. This is lined with planks. Boards are removed from one side of the house and the body handed by two mourners inside to two outside. No living soul passes through the opening and the corpse does not leave by the door. The earth on which the person has lain in death is thrown away. At the grave the dead body is washed with water containing herbs or roots and then interred with its head downstream. No one in the town eats during the funeral, small children are taken aside, and all who have looked upon the dead bathe. Those of the mourners who have touched the corpse rub themselves with the grapevine with which the body has been lowered into the grave and hand it from one to the other, thereby passing on the contamination to the last one. This man for five days shuns all intercourse with human kind, does no work, sits in a corner of the house with his back turned, drinks no water, eats only thin acorn gruel, nightly makes a fire on the grave to keep his dead kinsman warm, and finally returns to communion with people by undergoing a washing purification of which the cardinal feature is a long formula.

Cemeteries adjoined towns; often lay in their very heart. Large settlements sometimes had two or three graveyards. Each family plot was small, so that in time numbers of bodies came to be buried in one grave. Old bones were always reinterred. At present each plot is neatly fenced with pickets and posts; but the Yurok say that even in the old days their graves were inclosed with boards. The clothing and some of the personal belongings of the dead were set or hung over the grave; but there was no extensive destruction of property, much less any subsequent offerings to fire, as among most California tribes. People dying away from home were, if possible, transported back for interment; or, a grave was purchased for them where they died.

The dead, called *so'o* or *kesamui*—the words are used alike for "ghost" and "skeleton"—were thought to go below. The entrance was pointed out at a small tree not far above the river just upstream from Sa'aitl, opposite Turip. The Coast Yurok knew a spot in their own territory, and the Karok made the path of the dead go up the ridge southeastward from the mouth of the Salmon. Underground, the dead Yurok came to a river, across which he was ferried by a Charon in a canoe. Occasionally the boat tipped over. Then the corpse revived on earth. Once the crossing had been accomplished, return was impossible. People killed with weapons went to a separate place in the willows; here they forever shouted and danced the war dance. Contentious and thievish men also remained apart: their place was inferior. A rich, peaceable man, on the other hand, who had constantly planned entertainment for dances, came to the sky. Long ago, a young man once followed his beloved, overtook her at the bank of the river, and in his anger broke the ferryman's boat, it is said. He brought back his bride, and for 10 years while the canoe of the lower world was being repaired or rebuilt, no one died on earth.

If a person revived "after having died," a special dance, called *wasurawits*, was considered necessary to bring him back to human intelligence. This seems to have been a modified form of the brush dance, with similar step and positions, held indoors. Only a few feathers were used. All available dresses heavily fringed with haliotis were shaken to drown the voices of the ghosts which the patient had heard and which were rendering him insane. If he was violent, he was lifted on the drying frame within the house and held by two men; when his strength began to return, he was supported and made to dance to speed his recovery.

Should a person already buried make his way out of the grave, the Yurok believed him a monster, from whose insatiable desire for destruction they could only save themselves by killing him once more; but this was only to be accomplished by striking him with a bowstring!

NAMES.

The Yurok avoid addressing each other by name, except sometimes in closest intimacy. It is the height of bad manners to call a person by name, and a Yurok who is so addressed by an American looks shocked. Of course, English names and nicknames do not count. It is not even proper to speak of an absent person by his name before his relatives. All sorts of circumlocution come into use, many of them known to all the Yurok: *Ehkwiyer omewimar*, " Ehkwiyer its old man;" *Meta keryern*, "the proud one of Meta;" *Ra-hiwoi*, "(he has his house) on the side of Ra (a streamlet in Murekw)"; and the like. An old man at Wahsekw was designated by the fact that his house faced upstream. Most of the following names of the women reputed about 15 years ago the ablest shamans among the Yurok, are of this descriptive type.

At Wahsekw (farthest upstream of the towns mentioned) : *Petsi-metl* (pets, " upstream ").

At Sa'a : *Sa'-wayo-metl.*

At Murekw : *Tsmeyowega* and *Mureku-tsewa.*

At Sregon : *Was-metl* and *Pekwisau.*

At Wohtek : *Kewei.*

At Wohkero : *Merit-mela* (Merip, a town, presumably her birthplace).

At Sta'awin : *Kosi-tsewa.*

At Espau : *Kairepu* and *O'men-mela* (O'men, a town).

At Tsurau : *Tsurau-tsewa.*

Most of the true personal names of the Yurok are untranslatable in the present knowledge of the language, but may have meanings : Tsinso, Melotso, Ninowo, Penis, Woilo, Tskerker, O'pe'n, Wilets, Kwegetip ("yearling deer "), Petsuslo ("thrown upstream "). Nicknames like Segep, "coyote," are of course transparent.

As in all California, an absolute taboo is laid on the names of the dead. The violation of this constitutes a mortal offense, voidable only by a considerable payment. We are wont to think of the hardship entailed by such a law on the unwitting and careless; but the Indian, reared since earliest recollection in the shadow of this regulation, makes no mistakes, and when he utters a dead man's name may justly be presumed to do so deliberately. *De mortuis nil*, the Yurok would paraphrase our saying, and live up to it with even greater emotional vehemence. A namesake drops his name at once. Even words that resemble a name are not used. When *Tegis* died, the common word *tsis*, " woodpecker scalps," was not uttered in the hearing of his relatives or by them. Other people, if no tell-tale ill-wishers were about, would be free from such scruple. Whatever may have been the original basis of the custom, it is clear that its force among the Yurok is now more social than religious. They no doubt hold that calling a ghost might bring it, but they hardly entertain such dread about the conversational mention of a dead person.

The name taboo has sometimes been invoked as a contributory explanation of the dialectic diversity of native California. It can not have had much influence. The custom prevails in the Great Basin, throughout whose broad extent no language is spoken but

Shoshonean, and that in only three closely similar forms. Moreover, the Yurok, and with them apparently many other tribes of California, formally end the taboo at the end of a year, by bestowing the dead person's name on a younger relative or child of the same sex. A youth abandons his name to assume that of a dead brother, father's brother, or even mother's brother. This may happen to him several times; but after middle life he changes no more. Children remain unnamed until after they can walk; sometimes they are 6 or 7 years old before a kinsman's name becomes vacant. Some sort of designation for them, of course, comes into use, but this appellation is " picked up " for them and not considered their name. The Yurok state that after a year the family that has lost a relative wishes his name to be out of taboo again.

WAR.

No distinction of principle existed in the native mind between murder and war. It is rather clear that all so-called wars were only feuds that happened to involve large groups of kinsmen, several such groups, or unrelated fellow townsmen of the original participants. Whoever was not drawn into a war was as careful to remain neutral as in a private quarrel. When settlement came it was made on the sole basis known: all damage was compensated. Every man slain or hurt was paid for according to his value, all captive women and children restored, burned houses were paid for, seized property handed back. It seems that actual payments for the aggregate amounts due were made by each side instead of the lesser value being deducted from the greater and the net difference alone paid. This practice was perhaps necessitated by the fact that Yurok money with all its refinement of measurement was not really standardized in the same sense as our own, no two strings, generally speaking, being of exactly the same value. In any event the greater financial drain bore on the winner. There is no group of tribes in California better developed to enjoy tribute than the Yurok and their neighbors, and none to whom the idea was so utterly foreign. The *vae victis* of civilization might well have been replaced among the Yurok, in a monetary sense at least, by the dictum: " Woe to the victors."

When blood money was offered, the exact length of each string was shown by a rod of the precise dimension. This stick was kept by the payee, and subsequently measured against the row of dentalia. To the ends of the rod were lashed little tabs of buckskin, to make possible its being held between the fingers that clasped the string of shells. This device enabled the precise value of each string to be determined during the period when contact between the principals in conflict, or even handling of the property of one by the other, would have been precarious.

The Yurok took no scalps. They did not trouble to decapitate a fallen foe unless it was to make sure of his death. They held no scalp dance or formal victory celebration. They did have a war dance known as the *wertlkerermer*, the songs to which are of a lively if not stirring character. This was essentially a dance of settlement. The participants stood in a row, fully armed, with their faces painted black. A bowshot or less away their opponents performed. Before the actual dance took place, the money or property to be paid over by each side was "cooked." It was laid in baskets, held over the fire, blown upon, and sung over, while the party danced about. No doubt a formula was also recited over the money. The purpose of this practice was to insure that if the recipient of the pay continued to harbor thoughts of revenge against the payers, his wishes would recoil upon himself. After this came the war dance proper, performed by each side standing abreast, very much as in the great dances; and finally the payments by each side were actually handed over, provided the reconciliation had not broken up in a battle meanwhile. It seems that the same or a similar dance was also made as a preparation before war parties started out, but this is not certain.

The chief weapon was the bow. In close fighting, a short stone club, spatula shaped and blunt edged, was used for cracking heads. This was called *okawaya*. Spears were known, it appears, but very little employed. There were no shields, but two types of body armor. One was of thick elk hide, the other a strait-jacket of rods wound together with string. Some men preferred not to be encumbered with so stiff a protection. Women are said sometimes to have rushed into a fight and seized men as if to allay the quarrel, but in reality to hold them for their brothers or husbands to smite.

The greatest war of which the Yurok know took place some years before the Americans came into the country, probably about 1830 or 1840. Some Weitspus men who had married Hupa wives were attacked while visiting there. The cause of the grievance has not been recorded. In the course of the resulting feud the Hupa attacked Weitspus. During the fight a woman was killed who was born of a Weitspus father and Rekwoi mother, and who was herself half married, that is, living at her father's home. Her death angered her relatives at Rekwoi, it is said. At any rate they gathered their forces, to which were added a number of Tolowa. There were 84 altogether, including 6 women to cook for the party. This number shows conclusively that even this war was an affair of families or at most villages. If the Yurok as a whole had mustered against the Hupa they would have been able to assemble nearly ten times as strong. The party traveled toward Hupa by way of Redwood Creek or the hills above it. They journeyed three nights, resting during the day. Early in the morning they waited at Takimitlding. The first Hupa who emerged was killed. Then the fight was on. Many of the Hupa fell, the others fled, and the entire village was burned by the victors, who thereupon seized all the canoes and started homeward down the Trinity River. Two of the men had taken young women whom they intended to marry. But at Weitspus, where the party stopped, probably to eat after the morning's work and no doubt to recount its adventures, some people who pitied the girls enabled them to escape. These connivers may have been individuals with Hupa blood affiliations, perhaps even direct relatives of the two women.

About half a year later the Hupa retaliated. They were helped by their kinsmen up toward the south fork of the Trinity and by the Chilula. Nearly 100 of them are said to have gone. They descended by boat, traveling at night and drawing their canoes up into the brush during the day. Rekwoi was attacked and burned much as Takimitlding had been. Those who were not slain had difficulty living through the winter because their stores of food had been destroyed. The Hupa returned as they had come. This fact again indicates the private nature of the quarrel. Canoes must be laboriously poled and in some spots dragged upstream. Had the Yurok been possessed of any national sentiment in the matter, they could have easily mustered several hundred warriors to overwhelm the Hupa while these were occupied with their difficult navigation. As a matter of fact, the Yurok relate, the villages along the Klamath made no attempt to stop the war party. They concluded that scores being now substantially even, a settlement would soon follow. The Hupa indeed sent to ask for a settlement, and this took place, large amounts being paid on each side.

A feud of some note took place between Sregon and Ko'otep. When the leading man of Sregon lost his brother by sickness, he accused an inhabitant of Wohtek or Wohkero of having poisoned him. The suspect was soon killed from ambush. After this a Sregon man was attacked and killed at Ko'otep, which is only a short distance from Wohtek. This act involved the people of Ko'otep, which was at this time a large village. After a time, settlement was proposed, and the two parties met in an open place below Sregon to conclude the negotiations. Each side was ready to make the customary dance, when some one fired a shot. In the fight that resulted, a Meta ally of the Sregon people was killed. The headman of Sregon now went down river with his friends and lay in wait at an overhanging and bushy bank at Serper, where the current takes boats close in shore. When a canoe of his foes came up, he attacked it and killed four of the inmates. The feud went on for some time. Sregon, never a large village, fought, with only some aid from Meta, against Ko'otep, Wohtek, and Pekwan, but lost only 3 men to 10 of their opponents'. The headman at Sregon was sufficiently wealthy, when settlement came, to pay for all the satisfaction he had earned. He once said with reference to his experience in this and other feuds, that open battles often took place without any-one being killed. Somehow men are hard to hit, he philosophized: arrows have a way of flying past a human being when a hunter is sure to strike a deer at the same distance; as modern military handbooks also tell.

A small feud occurred between Meta and Pekwan. A number of families were camped along the river for fishing, when a man from Wohtek or Wohkero was killed by enemies from Meta. The grievance is not reported. Those who had slain him fled to Osegon, presumably because they had relatives there. The Wohkero kinsmen of the dead man followed them and a fight took place. An Osegon and a Meta man fell in this little battle. Subsequently another Meta man was killed. Afterwards settlement was made.

Many years ago, probably before the arrival of the Americans, Opyuweg, the largest village on Big Lagoon, became involved in a quarrel with the Wiyot, who attacked the town and killed a number of people. Opyuweg subsequently retaliated, but was unable to even the score, the Wiyot being too numerous. Consequently when settlement was made Opyuweg received a large balance. The village fought this feud alone.

Soon after 1860 the Chilula attacked Herwer on Stone Lagoon and killed 10 people. This was at the time the Chilula were in feud with the Americans and Herwer was very likely made to suffer for aid or information given the whites, or thought by the Chilula to have been given. The main grievance of the Chilula, as well as their danger, must have been from the Americans, but satisfaction was more easily taken against the Yurok.

Once there was sickness at Ko'otep. Three Orekw women married at Ko'otep were blamed. An attempt was made to kill them, but one of the Ko'otep men protected them against the others. This angered his fellow townsmen, who, with the aid of friends from Weitspus, succeeded in killing him when he was at Ayotl. One of his kinsmen, probably feeling himself impotent against the actual slayers, revenged himself by killing one of the three women from Orekw, whom he held responsible because it was on their account that his relative had become involved in the quarrel which resulted in his death. This act, of course, meant war between Orekw and Ko'otep. The two parties met several times to negotiate the difficulty before they succeeded. On each occasion some one became excited and fighting commenced over again. Several men were wounded in these skirmishes, but no one was killed. In the final settlement one of the two surviving Orekw women returned to her home, and the other was married by a housemate of the man who had lost his life through championing her cause.

Other wars were waged between Wetlkwau and Ho'opeu; between Rekwoi, aided by Oketo and Tsurau, against the Tolowa of Smith River; and by Weitspus, as an ally of the Karok of Orleans, against the Hupa and Chilula.

CHAPTER 3.

THE YUROK: RELIGION.

GREAT DANCES.

The major ceremonies of the Yuork reveal the following qualities:

1. The motive is to renew or maintain the established world. This purpose includes bountiful wild crops, abundance of salmon, and the prevention of famine, earthquakes, and flood. To a greater or less extent, the expression of these objects takes on the character of a new year's rite. This is particularly plain in the first salmon ceremony at Wetlkwau and the fish dam building at Kepel. Other ceremonies reveal the motive less outspokenly, but all those of the Karok and most of those of the Hupa are distinct world renovation or first fruits rituals; and the equation by all three tribes of the ceremonies of direct with those of indirect new year's type confirms the interpretation. Most of the rites are made in September or October, the remainder about April.

2. The esoteric portion of the ceremony is the recitation of a long formula, narrating, mostly in dialogue, the establishment of the ceremony by spirits of prehuman race and its immediate beneficial effect. This formula is spoken in sections before various rocks or spots that mark the abode of these spirits. The reciter is an old man, usually accompanied by an assistant; any prescribed symbolic acts are performed by them alone. They fast and otherwise refrain from ordinary occupation; inhabit a house sanctified by tradition for this purpose; and spend a number of nights in the associated sweat house, sometimes in the company of several men who also observe restrictions, though they do not directly participate in the acts of magic or recitation. The only offering made is of small quantities of angelica root thrown into the fire, or of tobacco.

3. After the recitation of the formula, or the major portion, a dance begins, and goes on every afternoon, or morning and after-

noon, for 5, 10, or more days.   The regalia are of forms strictly
standardized by custom, but are wholly unsymbolical and in no sense
regarded as sacred.   They comprise the most valuable things in the
world known to the Yurok—all their great treasures, in fact, except
dentalium shells; and the largest obsidian and flint blades, and
whitest deerskins, far outvalue any of their money, while the bands
of woodpecker scalps are each worth more than a string of the
largest shells.   The dances are therefore the one occasion on which
the wealthy can make public display of the property on which their
position in the world, depends; while the entertainment of visitors
from far and near is a burden they are reluctant and yet proud to
bear.   Any man can dance: the lesser regalia are often intrusted to
boys.   The singers are those noted for their ability, and constantly
compose new songs, although the character of the melodies for each
type of dance is so uniform that the novel improvisations prove to be
little but minor variations of one theme, or of a set of similar themes
cast in one rigid style.   Women watch but never dance.   The valuables are not only those of the home town, but of the whole river,
or of long stretches of it.   Men carry their treasures far, and when
they are responsible for a dance, receive reciprocation from those
whose dances they have aided.

4. The dances are of two kinds, known to the Americans as White
Deerskin and Jumping dance.   In some spots only the latter is
made; wherever the Deerskin dance is made, it can be followed also
by a Jumping dance.   In both, the dancers stand in a line abreast
facing the audience of men, women, and children, and some glowing
embers by which sits the formula reciter with angelica incense in
his hand.   The chief singer is in the middle of the line, with an
assistant on each side; the remainder of the rank form a sort of
chorus that adds little but occasional monotone grunts or shouts.
They sway or swing the objects they hold in time to the step or leap
which constitutes the dance.

5. The localization of these ceremonies is extreme.   The formulas
abound in place names.   They are spoken at a series of places in
and about the village which are exactly prescribed.   The sacred
house and sweat house of each ceremony are believed to have stood
since the time when there were no men in the world: the planks, it
is true, are replaced, but the structures occupy the identical spot.
The dance ground itself is always the same; and when a dance moves
from village to village or hillside, it is in invariable sequence.   The
selection of the places that enter into the ceremonies is traditionally
arbitrary.   It is true that the largest villages are the ones in which
dances are held, and that some of the spots of ritual are landmarks;
but there is no appearance of anything symbolic or inherently re-

ligious in their choices.   The places are usually not prominent in myth, and it is evidently the fact that the dance is made at a particular site that has caused the nameless and colorless spirit referred to in the formula to be associated with it, not the reverse.   It is the locality that has ceremonial preeminent sanctity to the Yurok.   Elsewhere in California the Indian thinks first of his spirit or god and his characteristics or history; if a certain spot counts at all, it is because of its connection with the deity.   There is something strangely old world and un-American in the Yurok attitude, a reminiscence of high places and fanes and hallowed groves.

6. The dances are conducted with a distinct attempt at climactic effect.   On the first days they are brief and the property carried is inconsiderable.   Gradually they grow in duration, intensity, and splendor.   The famous treasures begin to appear only toward the last day: the most priceless of all are reserved for the final appearance of that day.   The number of dancers, the vehemence of their motions, the loudness of the songs, the crowd of spectators, increase similarly; even on each day of the series, an accumulation is noticeable.   The performances are always conducted by competing parties.   Each of these represents a village—the home town and from one to five of those in the vicinity.   These match and outdo one another, as the rich man of each village gradually hands over more and more of his own and his followers' and friends' valuables to the dancers to display.

The gradual unfolding of the ceremonies is illustrated by the progress of the Weitspus Jumping dance on its way uphill.   At the first stop, on one occasion, 7 dancers, mostly boys, stood in line, and the songs continued for about 14 leaps. Only two dancers wore woodpecker scalp headbands.   Gradually the dancers became more numerous, the boys disappeared, the songs lengthened, the headbands became 5, then 6, then 9; until, at the summit, 16 men, each with a standard band, danced to songs of nearly 40 leaps.

Such is the character of the great ceremonies.

All ceremonies are likely to have been annual in the old days, but for many years the custom has been to hold them only in alternate years at each locality.   Those on the coast have not been performed in a long time, and of late even the river dances have become very irregular.

Opyuweg is the name the Yurok apply to any form of major dance, and to that only: the "brush" dance is *umeleyek* or *worero*, the war dance *wertlkerermer*, the shaman's dance *remohpo*.   The Jumping dance is sometimes called *wonikulego'* but this is a descriptive term: "they leap up."   The Karok new year's rites at Katimin and Orleans are named *welailek* by the Yurok, the one at Amaikiara *upuntek*, that of the Hupa at Takimitlding *uplopu*.

COSTUME AND STEPS.

The Deerskin dancers wear aprons of civet cat or a deer-hide blanket about the waist, masses of dentalium necklaces, and forehead bands of wolf fur that shade the eyes.   From the head rises a stick on which are fastened two or four black and white eagle or condor feathers, so put together as to look like a single feather of enormous length, its quill covered with woodpecker scalp; or, three slender rods of sinew, scarlet with attached bits of scalp, rise from the stick. The dancers also hold poles on which are white, light gray, black, or mottled deerskins, the heads stuffed, the ears, mouths, throats, and false tongues decorated with woodpecker scalps, the hide of the body and legs hanging loose. A slightly swaying row of these skins looks really splendid. The singer in the center of the line, and his two assistants, add to the costume of the others a light net, reaching from the forehead to the middle of the shoulders and terminating in a fringe of feathers. Their apron is always of civet-cat skins. The step of the entire row is merely a short stamp with one foot. At each end of the line and in front of it is a dancer who carries an obsidian blade instead of a deerskin. Over his wolf-fur forehead band is a strap from which project like hooks half a dozen or more curve-cut canine teeth of sea lions. From the head hangs down a long, close-woven or crocheted net, painted in diamonds or triangles, and feather fringed. A double deerskin blanket passes over one shoulder and covers part of the body; or is replaced by an apron of civet or raccoon skins. Under the left arm is a fur quiver. These two dancers advance and pass each other in front of the row of deerskins several times during each song, crouching, blowing a whistle, and holding their obsidians out conspicuously. In the final drama of the ceremony they may number four instead of two. All the dancers are painted with a few thin lines of soot across the cheeks or down the shoulders and arms; or the jaw is blackened, or the chin striped. The painting is quite variable according to individual, and decorative, not symbolic.

The Jumping dance varies between two steps, which are never changed while a song is in progress. In the first the hand holding a dancing basket is raised, then swung down and the knees bent until the fingers touch the ground, whereupon the dancer hops about half a foot into the air. In the second form of dance one foot is stamped violently as the basket descends. The drop or stamp coincides with the beat of the music; the leap itself is therefore begun at the end of a bar of song.

The principal ornament worn in this dance is a buckskin band, tied over the forehead with the ends flapping. Its central portion is carefully covered with 50 large woodpecker scalps, and bordered with lines of other feathers and a strip of white fur from a deer belly. Before the dance reaches its height, this band is often replaced by a stuffed head ring of skin, to which about five large woodpecker scalps are glued and sewed with sinew. Either headdress is topped by a long white plume on a stick. From the neck hang masses of dentalium beads; about the hips is folded a double deerskin blanket, the fur side inward. In one hand is a cylindrical basket, slit along one side. This has no utilitarian prototype, nor do the Yurok put anything but grass stuffing into it or attach any symbolic association to it. This basket, *ego'or*, suggests in its shape an enlarged native money box; but the Yurok do not see the resemblance. Face and body paint is slight, as in the Deerskin dance.

Not one of the ornaments worn or carried in either of the two ceremonies appears to have the least mythological or ritualistic significance. All the dress is standard, but by meaningless custom alone. Also, not a single one of the numerous ornaments is in use among any of the California tribes except the few adjacent to the Yurok who practice the identical ceremonies. The woodpecker scalp bands alone have some analogues in the lower Sacramento Valley, where belts and headpieces of the type appear in the Kuksu ceremonies. These seem, however, to have been often made on a close network, instead of buckskin, and when intended for headwear to have been broad in the middle and tapering toward the ends. One such specimen of this shape has been found among the Hupa, only a few miles from Weitspus; but its history is unknown, and it may either represent an ancient type or be a traded article. Outside of the partial similarity of these bands, there is no specific resemblance between the northwestern regalia and those of central and southern California. Whether the same uniqueness applies also toward Oregon is not known.

THE DANCES AT WEITSPUS.

The Deerskin dance at Weitspus comes in autumn, and is held on a little terrace facing the village (fig. 2). It lasts 12 to 16 days, according to the number of visitors present, their requests, and the quantity of treasures they bring. There is a short dance late each morning, another before sunset. By the last day the evening dance has grown to occupy most of the afternoon. Wahsekw, Loolego, Pekwututl, and Weitspus equipped the competing parties of dancers in the old days. The concluding dance was formerly made in two large canoes that crossed the river from Pekwututl to Weitspus.

The Jumping dance at Weitspus lasts two days. The formula reciter, followed by a girl assistant or wood gatherer, prays and makes offering, beginning early in the morning at three rocks or bushes in the village, then at five on the way up the mountain Kewet, at a ninth spot near the summit, at a tenth on top, which subsequently serves as a dressing place, and at an eleventh, under a venerated cedar, where a fire is kindled and the dances of the remainder of the afternoon and next day are held. The people follow him up at respectful distance, breakfastless. There is no dancing in the village. At the fourth to eighth halts, small groups of men and boys dance in line to three songs. At the ninth and tenth stops, a larger number of men dance in a circle; under the sacred tree they dance to three songs in a circle and then to three in line. All the way up, the older people occasionally weep as they think of their dead of long ago who used to come with them to these cherished spots; and each man's and woman's wish is to be similarly remembered after he or she is gone. When the tree is finally reached and the dance reaches its height, there is an outburst of wailing: the song and lamentations, the brilliance of the ornaments, and the streaming tears, make an impressive scene. Then everyone, hungry and tired, goes to eat and relax amid merriment.

In the afternoon the village parties begin to dance against each other, and visitors from a distance arrive. Wahsekw has made its own way up the mountain and now endeavors to surpass Weitspus. As it grows dark the dancing ends, and the people camp for the night.

The next day dancing is resumed. The line grows in length, more and more of the gleaming headbands are produced, until in the afternoon the ceremony comes to a magnificent climax of half an hour with hundreds of spectators weeping aloud. Then all pack up and journey well satisfied back to Weitspus.

Here is a case of Indian allegation versus action.

The Deerskin dance at Weitspus is usually stated to continue from 12 to 16 days. In 1901 it commenced on September 3 and ended 18 days later, on September 20, in a great quarrel. Too many old men had saved out their most precious obsidians for the final appearance at the end of the afternoon, no one would withdraw, the altercation soon developed recriminations, old jealousies were awakened, all the men present took sides and participated in the argument, and the end was that everyone wrapped up his regalia and went away. Thus the climax of the dance never came off. The Jumping dance was announced for two days later, and most of the visitors went home to stow away their deerskin ornaments and bring those for the Jumping dance— ostensibly. Actually most of them were much embittered, and there was a general feeling that the Jumping dance would not be held. On September 21 it rained, and the old man who knew the sacred formula for both dances announced that the weather would prevent the dance. The Indian opinion was that he was still angry. He was a poor man, but had become involved in the quarrel.

On September 26 an American visitor attempted to get the dance under way, but the old man refused to take part "because a moon had now gone by since the Deerskin dance begun." Really only 24 days had elapsed. On September 30 he alleged the same reason with more accuracy; if it rained the following day the dance would have to be definitely omitted for the year, because of the interval of a moon. The American persisted, however, and the old formula speaker remaining obdurate, another man who had several times assisted him volunteered to act. He did not know the entire formula, he admitted, but enough of the essential parts to answer. He fixed the payment due him at $4 in American money. This was regarded by the Indians as a reasonable amount, but no one wished to contribute now. Some tentative pledges of small amount were made, however, and by dint of persistent dunning and soliciting, with an addition by himself, the interested outsider after several days succeeded in bringing together the whole of the stipulated sum. As soon as this was handed to the assistant, the native attitude changed to one of interest. The new formula reciter began his preparation. At once his chief decided to officiate in person, and claimed the fee. Part of this having been already spent by the substitute at the trader's store for flour and a shirt, the old man accepted the balance and next morning was at his task. The dancers followed him, and about noon, when the assemblage reached the summit, all differences seemed to have been forgotten and the ceremony developed undisturbed to the end of the next day.

THE KEPEL DAM DANCE.

Perhaps the most famous of all ceremonies among the Yurok is the Deerskin dance associated with the building of a salmon dam at Kepel in early autumn. The dam is made at the upstream edge of that village; the sacred house and sweat house of the ceremony stand in adjoining Sa'a; most of the dancing is in villages downstream.

The ceremony is in charge of the usual formulist, who, with an assistant, restricts himself to a diet of thin acorn gruel and visits many hallowed spots for 10 days. For gathering firewood he has a woman assistant. During the 10 days a band of at least 60 men—a smaller number would be unable to complete the work in time—assemble the posts, stakes, and withes and erect the weir. These materials are obtained in specified ways at designated spots, and, with all the sanctity of the occasion, custom provides many occasions for merrymaking. The weir is built in 10 named sections by as many companies of men. Each group leaves an entrance, behind which is an inclosure: when salmon have run into this, the gate is shut and the fish easily taken out with nets. Comic interludes increase toward the end. On the last day the formulist's assistant, wearing a beard and personating a Karok who has eloped with another man's wife, pretends to be fleeing vengeance and allows his canoe to be capsized in midstream. He swims to Kepel, crouches, and the mass of men, armed with long poles, clash them together over his head and lay them on his back until he is almost covered from sight. This episode is repeated with but little improvised change from year to year, but is received by the multitude with appreciation that grows with familiarity. The end of the dam building is a period of freedom. Jokes, ridicule, and abuse run riot; sentiment forbids offense; and as night comes, lovers' passions are inflamed.

The formula for this ceremony is imperfectly known; but many of the actions, as well as the purpose of the dam, accentuate its tenor as a new year's and world establishing rite.

Before the great weir is finished, a sort of imitation Deerskin dance is held, with long flat cobbles to represent obsidian blades, by the river at Murekw, just downstream. The night of the completion, and the next day, the proper Deerskin dance is danced at Kepel. A few days pass; and then the people gather again about Wohtek-Wohkero, camping in groups, and dancing, for 10, 12, 14, or 16 days, at a spot just downstream from the village, with Wohtek, Ko'otep, Pekwan, Sregon, Murekw, and Kepel-Sa'a competing. After another "ten days," the Jumping dance is made, for a night and a day, at Murekw, or in alternate years on the hill above Merip. Other accounts place the main Deerskin dance at Wohtek, and alternate a brief supplementary Deerskin dance at Halega'u, downstream from Wohkero, with the Murekw and Merip Jumping dances.

Kepel-Sa'a has not been a large community in historic times. Its selection for the dam is no doubt due to a favorable condition of the river bed. The associated dancing is mostly held at larger villages. That at Wohtek-Wohkero may be suspected to have taken place at Ko'otep before the ruination of this town by the floods of 1861–62. Myths tell how the *woge* spirits were about to institute the dam at Turip, and how, when it was moved to Kepel, the Turip people, coming over the hills to take back their rights by force, were turned into redwood trees still visible from Kepel—the farthest of the species upstream. The lie of river and hills at the two places is very similar, and this resemblance to the eye, with the outposts at Kepel of the trees that dominate the view at

Turip, may be the sole foundation of the tale; or a dam at Turip may have been a former actuality.

The dam and dance have not been made for many years, primarily because enough men can no longer be assembled for the construction, but in native opinion because no one can recite the entire formula. A woman married in Meta is reputed to be the only person who knows certain passages, and she will not teach them. She has lost her parents, all her brothers and sisters, and 10 children, it is said. The ceremony would be for the health of the world; and in her own grief, she wishes no one else to be happy among the undiminished array of all his kin. So tell the Yurok; and while they regret her sentiment, they seem to find it natural and scarcely disapprove.

THE JUMPING DANCE AT PEKWAN.

The Pekwan ceremony is a Jumping dance, partly held in a large house. For 10 days the formulist—with a number of elderly companions, women as well as men, the *tetl*—fasts, restrains himself, and spends his time in the sacred house and sweat house. It appears that this group of persons sings much of the time.[1] The last night they remain awake in the sweat house. The next day the people dance by the river, and in the afternoon or evening go up into the sacred house, whose roof and walls have been removed to give a view inside. They dance first before it, then in the interior, which, however, accommodates only about 10 dancers. After this they dance at four spots in or by the village, proceeding in upstream order from one to the other. The competing parties represent Wohtek, Sregon, Murekw, and Pekwan. This continues for two days, after which the old people again sing in the sweat house one night, beating the walls with sticks. This is an early autumn ceremony.

DANCES AT THE MOUTH OF THE RIVER.

Rekwoi had a similar Jumping dance, held partly in a sacred house. The climax was a dance made in two large canoes, which approached across the broad lagoon abreast. The season for the ceremony seems to have been autumn.

Wetlkwau, on the opposite side of the mouth, formerly had a more venerated rite. There was a sacred house and sweat house, and the formulist kept a pipe that was regarded with the greatest fear. Each year, it may be presumed about April, he and his assistant proceeded to the very debouch of the river and speared the first salmon. This was cooked on the beach and the assistant attempted to eat it entire. Should he ever succeed it was thought that he would become extremely wealthy. Some fragments of the formula that are known tell of the coming of the great salmon leader from the miraculous country across the ocean.

---

[1] More on the *tetl* is to be found in Lucy Thompson (see Bibliography).

Wetlkwau also made a Deerskin dance, which, with the shriveling of the village, has long been abandoned. It was evidently an after-math to the salmon rite. In this the competing towns were Turip, Rekwoi, and Wetlkwau. On the last day they danced across the lagoon in boats and finished on the hill above Rekwoi. No one was allowed to witness the boat dance whose father's payment for his mother had not included either a canoe or one of the large Hudson Bay Co. knives, which before 1850 were extremely valuable. Some-times at Wetlkwau the final dance above Rekwoi was omitted and a separate Jumping dance substituted. This is said to have been held 20 miles upstream on the hill back of Pekwan.

DANCES ON THE COAST.

Orekw, at the mouth of Redwood Creek, held a Jumping dance associated with a traditional house.

Another Jumping dance was made at Oketo, or more exactly at the main village of Opyuweg, "they dance," on Big Lagoon, Oketo. This included dancing indoors and in boats on the lagoon. It must have been an important ceremony, since it lasted 10 to 12 days. The formula is reported similar to that spoken at Rekwoi, and different from those of Orekw and Pekwan.

It is rather remarkable that Tsurau at Trinidad, sometimes reck-oned the largest Coast Yurok village, possessed no dance. The Coast Yurok frequented a Jumping dance made by the Wiyot on Mad River, and sometimes went to a ceremony of another type made by the Wiyot of Olog on Humboldt Bay. They declare that these far-ther Wiyot rarely visited them at the Oketo dance, except one famous rich man named Munters, "white," to whom story accredits 10 wives who all drowned at once on Humboldt Bay.

THE BRUSH DANCE.

A minor dance is called the "brush dance" by the Americans. It is ostensibly held to cure an ailing child. As a matter of fact it is often made when the younger men are desirous of a holiday. Whether, however, the initiative comes from an alarmed mother or from those who wish to enjoy themselves, the sick child must be pro-vided. It is kept at the dance all night, and the woman who recites the formula speaks it for the child's benefit. The dance is held in the living house, but the roof and most of the walls of this are taken down for the occasion. On the first night young men dance about the fire for a few hours. They wear no ornaments but hold boughs of foli-age up before them. The following night is an intermission, and on the third or fourth night the dance proper takes place from dark until dawn. The regalia are somewhat variable, especially as regards headdresses, but represent no great value. Arrow-filled quivers and sometimes small obsidian blades mounted on sticks are carried. All ornaments of considerable intrinsic value are reserved for the two great dances. The participants enter the house in competitive parties, each dancing to three songs on every appearance. Two formulas are in use for the dance, or, it would be better to say, two types of ceremonial action in connection with the formula, since the latter is always somewhat different according to the individual reciting it. The *umeleyek* formula is spoken on the first and third nights; the alternative *worero*, which is considered stronger, on the first and fourth, and is followed by the waving of pitch-pine brands over the child.

THE MODERN GHOST DANCE.

The first Ghost dance movement that originated among the northern Paiute reached the Yurok about 1872 via the Shasta, Karok, and Tolowa, but endured only a short time, and vanished with scarcely any effect. It seems that groups like the southern Wintun and Pomo, whose institutions had long been suffering under Spanish and American contact, embodied considerable elements of Ghost dance doctrine into what remained of their religion.

From the Shasta of Scott River the Ghost dance spread to the Happy Camp Karok. Report traveled, and both Tolowa and lower Karok came to see and learned to believe. A woman of Amaikiara seems to have been the first to dream among the latter. Many Yurok were attracted and came to Amaikiara with their dance ornaments. Perhaps they were shocked at the announcement that when the great change came these precious things would vanish. At any rate, most of them grew tired and went home. The Hupa either never came in numbers or failed to be seriously influenced.

The dance actually reached the Yurok from the Tolowa. An old man from Burnt Ranch instituted it at Sta'awin, above Turip, where he came to visit a Yurok nephew. After his return, the nephew began to dream. The dance was then taken down the coast to Big Lagoon, and up the river to Ko'otep, then not yet resettled after the flood of 1862. This was in the summer after the Karok had become converted. The Yurok prophet and his Tolowa uncle announced that the dance must be held also at Weitspus if the dead of that vicinity were to return; but the movement waned before they could effect their purpose. There seem always to have been a number of Yurok who remained unconvinced, and none, except the immediate family of the dreamer, on whose minds the doctrine had more than a passing hold.

The beliefs and practices sound as if taken from a description of the Dakota 20 years later. The world was to end; the dead would return, true converts among the living survive, disbelievers turn to stone. The new world was to be sexless; and in preparation men and women were instructed to bathe together without shame, and husband and wife to ignore each other. All planking was removed from graves to facilitate the resurrection. The prophets visited the dead in dreams and carried messages from them—once even that they would appear the next day. The dancers, men, women, and children, formed concentric circles, revolving in opposite directions.

Local custom, however, colored the doctrine at several points. Dogs were killed. All valuables would turn to rubbish, it was proclaimed, unless exposed in the dance. When there was dancing in the morning, breakfast must be deferred until after it, as in old native ceremonies. Sometimes the dance took place indoors. The officiating prophet remained aloof from the crowd in a house of his own, like the formula reciter of a typical Yurok rite.

SHAMANISM.

A Yurok woman goes through the following stages to become a shaman:

First she dreams of a dead person, usually if not always a shaman, who puts into her body a "pain." The possession of this animate object in her person is what essentially constitutes her a shaman.

Then the *remohpo*, or "doctor dance," is made for her in the sweat house for 10 days, during which she fasts and dances severely under the direction of older shamans. The pain is thereby induced to leave her body, is exhibited, and is then reswallowed by her. The purpose of this dance is to give the novice control of her "pain."

After this, in summer, she goes to a "seat" or little monument on a mountain top, where she spends one night in speaking or dancing. The function of this act is obscure.

After her return she usually goes through the *remohpo* once more.

Then follows the *ukwerhkwer teilogitl*, a dance around a large hot fire, to "cook the pains." The idea perhaps is that the pains are rendered more pliable or amenable to her will. This rite includes a formula. The shaman is now ready to practice her profession.

The Yurok accept as a self-evident fact, which they do not attempt to explain, their conviction that possession of one or more pains enables the carrier to see and extract similar pains from people who have been made sick by their internal presence. The emphasis, in their ideas, is wholly on the "pain." The spirit enters into belief only to bestow the first pain, and seems not to be considered active thereafter. Moreover, the spirit is the spirit of a human being, sometimes of an ancestor, in human form; not of an animal or mountain or lake, rarely of a disembodied divinity. The customary North American concept of the "guardian spirit" is therefore reduced to a minimum among the Yurok. The pain, on the other hand, as a material though animate object operating homeopathically, as it were, and therefore sympathetically, brings Yurok shamanism a step nearer magic than is usual.

This is a native summary of a shaman's inception:

A woman on her way for firewood perhaps begins to think of the dead who formerly lived in her town, notes how grass-grown and dim the path is, clears it of brush, and weeps in recollection. Not long after she dreams. A person says to her: "I pity you as you always cry when you gather wood. You should become a shaman. Eat this!" The woman, not knowing what it is, eats what is offered. She wakes and realizes that what she thought reality was a dream. The base of her sternum hurts; it is a pain growing in her. But perhaps when she is on the path again, she may decide: "Well, I dreamed it so. I will try." Then she tells them in the house of her experience, and her relatives take her into the sweat house and make the *remohpo* for her for 10 days, so she will acquire (her power) readily. The purpose of the dance is to make the pain which she dreamed to have been put into her come out of her body. Perhaps it is displayed on a flat basket. Then she drinks it again. Later, in summer, in the seventh month, a male relative accompanies her to a stone chair (*tsektseya*) on a mountain. There are such on Kewet, the mountain behind Weitspus, and on other ridges. These seats are good for other things also. They can be used to acquire luck in gambling or power of bewitching people; but they can not be used ignorantly. One must know how long to fast, how to offer tobacco, what formula to speak. The seats have been there since the time of the *woge*. The shaman dances by a fire near the chair, and speaks things that are not known to other people. Her kinsman watches that she does herself no harm. In the morning he leads her back. They are already dancing in the sweat house. At last she enters; and then for 10 days the *remohpo* goes on again. Men sing for her; when she is exhausted, one of her relatives dances for her until she recovers. This is the only time a woman enters the sweat house (*sic;* but see below).

According to further accounts, a shaman becomes a shaman by dreaming of a dead shaman, who gives her the initial power. Often a woman seeks to be a shaman. At every opportunity she cries and cries, until finally the desired dream comes to her.

A man who knew the formula and ritual for the "pain cooking" after the second *remohpo* described it as follows:

Two kinsmen of the new shaman bring four limbs of pitch-pine wood and four large slabs of bark from a mountain. A fire is made with these eight pieces of fuel in the house after the roof has been taken off. The novice has been painted, in the sweat house, with black vertical stripes. She now joins the people in the house, who dance in a circle alternately to the right and left about the fire, wearing fir branches in their belts to shield them from the heat. When the ordeal becomes unendurable, they pour over themselves a little water which the ritualist has prepared with herb in it. There is a separate vessel for the novice. Spectators look on from outside. The dancing continues without pause until the fire is wholly consumed. Then some one pretends illness, and the novice seizes and begins to suck him as if to extract his pain. Sometimes, too, a woman falls down during the dance, seized with a pain which will ultimately make her a shaman. Some older practitioner then at once diagnoses her condition. This pain-cooking rite is not indispensable, but novices like to undergo it because it increases their power and enables them to earn more in their profession. The ritualist is in charge because he knows the necessary formula and herbs. He is generally not a shaman himself.

The following is an account given by a shaman of repute of her acquisition of her powers:

I began with a dream. At that time I was already married at Sregon. In the dream I was on Bald Hills. There I met a Chilula man who fed me deer meat which was black with blood. I did not know the man, but he was a short-nosed person. I had this dream in autumn, after we had gathered acorns.

In the morning I was ill. A doctor was called in to treat me and diagnosed my case. Then I went to the sweat house to dance for 10 nights. This whole time I did not eat. Once I danced until I became unconscious. They carried me into the living house. When I revived I climbed up the framework of poles for drying fish, escaped through the smoke hole, ran to another sweat house, and began to dance there.

On the tenth day, while I was dancing, I obtained control of my first " pain." It came out of my mouth looking like a salmon liver, and as I held it in my hands blood dripped from it to the ground. This is what I had seen in my dream on Bald Hills. I then thought that it was merely venison. It was when I ate the venison that the pain entered my body.

On the eleventh day I began to eat again, but only a little.

All that winter I went daily high up on the ridge to gather sweat-house wood and each night I spent in the sweat house. All this time I drank no water. Sometimes I walked along the river, put pebbles into my mouth and spat them out. Then I said to myself: " When I am a doctor I shall suck and the pains will come into my mouth as cool as these stones. I shall be paid for that." When day broke I would face the door of the sweat house and say: " A long dentalium is looking in at me." When I went up to gather wood, I kept saying: " The dentalium has gone before me; I see its tracks." When I had filled my basket with the wood, I said: " That large dentalium, the one I am carrying, is very heavy." When I swept the platform before the sweat house clean with a branch, I said: " I see dentalia. I see dentalia. I am sweeping them to both sides of me." So whatever I did I spoke of money constantly.

My sleeping place in the sweat house was *atserger*. This is the proper place for a doctor. I was not alone in the sweat house. Men were present to watch, for fear I might lose my mind and do myself some harm.

Thus, once while the others slept, I dreamed I saw an *uma'a* coming. One of his legs was straight, the other bent at the knee, and he walked on this knee as if it were his foot, and had only one eye. Then I shouted, dashed out, and ran down along the river. My male relatives pursued me and brought me back unconscious. Then I danced for three nights more. At this time I received my four largest pains. One of these is blue, one yellowish, another red, and the fourth white. Because I received these in dreaming about the *uma'a* they are the ones with which I cure sickness caused by an *uma'a*.

My smaller pains are whitish and less powerful. It is they that came to me in my first period of training. The pains come and go from my body. I do not always carry them in me. To-day they are inside of me.

Again, not long after, I went to the creek which flows in above Nohtsku'm. I said to myself: " When people are sick, I shall cure them if they pay me enough." Then I heard singing in the gully. That same song I now sing in doctoring, but only if I am paid sufficiently. After this I danced again for 10 days.

In my dancing I could see various pains flying above the heads of the people. Then I became beyond control trying to catch them. Some of the pains were very hard to drive away. They kept coming back, hovering over certain men. Such men were likely to be sick soon. Gradually I obtained more control of my pains, until finally I could take them out of myself, lay them in a basket, set this at the opposite end of the sweat house, and then swallow them from where I stood. All this time I drank no water, gathered firewood for the sweat house, slept in this, and constantly spoke to myself of dentalium money. Thus I did for nearly two years. Then I began to be ready to cure. I worked hard and long at my training because I wished to be the best doctor of all. During all this time, if I slept in the house at all, I put angelica root at the four corners of the fireplace and also threw it into the blaze. I would say: "This angelica comes from the middle of the sky. There the dentalia and woodpecker scalps eat its leaves. That is why it is so withered." Then I inhaled the smoke of the burning root. Thus the dentalia would come to the house in which I was. My sweating and refraining from water were not for the entire two years, but only for 10 days at a time again and again. At such periods I would also gash myself and rub in young fern fronds.

In the seventh moon, after nearly two years, I stopped my training. Then the *ukwerhkwer teilogitl* formula was made for me and we danced about the fire. This cooked me, cooked my pains in me, and after this I was done and did not train any more.

When I am summoned to a patient I smoke and say to myself: "I wish you to become well because I like what they are paying me." If the patient dies, I must return the payment. Then I begin to doctor. After I have danced a long time I can see all the pains in the sick person's body. Sometimes there are things like bulbs growing in a man, and they sprout and flower. These I can see but can not extract. Sometimes there are other pains which I can not remove. Then I refer the sick person to another doctor. But the other doctor may say: "Why does she not suck them out herself? Perhaps she wishes you to die." Sometimes a doctor really wishes to kill people. Then she blows her pains out through her pipe, sending them into the person that she hates.

A shaman is called *kegeior;* the pains, *teinom* or *teilogitl; teilek* or *teile'm* is "sick."

DISEASE AND WITCHCRAFT.

The function of shamans is to diagnose in a condition of clairvoyance into which dancing and smoking the pipe has brought them; to manipulate the patient; and to cure by sucking out his pain. They do not ordinarily employ herbs or medicaments, these being reserved as the physical basis of the rituals of which formulas are the central feature. The pipe is the shaman's chief apparatus; she also wears strings of feathers from the two masses of her hair, and a maple-bark skirt. Her song may be learned in her original dream; the words she is said to improvise.

Disease is caused in various ways. The breaking of a taboo or ceremonial regulation often makes illness, but such is perhaps most often treated by another ceremony or a formula.

Shamans themselves make people sick in order to earn fees. They perhaps smoke during the night, then address their pipe, saying: " So and so, I wish you to become ill." When called to treat such a man, they are likely to leave at least one pain in him, that after this has grown they may be summoned with another fee.

Then there are people who have learned or bought a mysterious thing called *uma'a*, with which they destroy those whom they envy or hate. The possessors of such charms seem also to be called *uma'a*. Sometimes this thing is put on the end of a little arrow which is shot, at night from a distance, from a miniature bow at the house of the victim, one of whose inmates soon sickens. At times an *uma'a* can be seen at night, traveling on his nefarious errand. He may be carrying his charm concealed under his arm, but the thing is strong, breaks out, and is visible as sparks or a bluish light that shoots or rises and falls. If this enter a man, he is likely to sleep into his death. Some shamans, however, can suck it out.

Another cause of disease is a sort of poison called *ohpok*, compounded of crushed dog flesh, salamander larva, frog, or rattlesnake. This is put into the victim's food, care being taken that it reaches only him, and that any residue is destroyed. For a whole year he continues in apparent health; but when the same season comes around, he sickens, as the poison grows in him. Strong shamans can see and extract the *ohpok* by the customary means.

Upunamitl is a greatly dreaded swelling or choking of organs, due to an internal growth, but is perhaps to be interpreted as being to the Yurok a physiological process, since it appears itself to be caused by witchcraft, breach of taboo, and perhaps other influences.

The Yurok also fear what they call *sa'atl* or *sa'aitl*, dwarf-like spirits who haunt overgrown spots in creeks, and the like. Sometimes a bark is heard from such a place when no dog is about. Then one stops his ears with his fingers and runs off. Nor is water drunk from such streams. The word *sa'aitl* is probably connected with *so'o*, " ghost " or " skeleton," and *o-sa'ai-wor*, " his shadow."

SPECIAL CLASSES OF SHAMANS.

Three kinds of specialists among shamans, of whom there is frequent mention with most of the other Indians of California, are unrepresented among the Yurok—grizzly-bear shamans, rattlesnake shamans, and weather shamans. The first class, perhaps, have some remote similarity to the *uma'a* wizards. The functions of the second and third are replaced among the northwestern tribes by the recitation of formulas. This is explicitly stated for rattlesnake bites, and was probably true of weather influencing, if the Yurok concerned themselves with this at all. There were shamans who in their initial dream ate a snake, carried it in their bodies, visible to other shamans, and sucked snakes from their patients; but the disease of which they cured was lunacy, not a bite. There was a shaman at Murekw famous for his ability to handle hot stones and eat living rattlesnakes, and after his death one of his kinsmen continued the practice. Such arduous feats, however, are not characteristic of Yurok shamanism, in which juggling is unimportant; and it is significant that both these individuals were men.

A Yurok man who wishes to be brave and fierce—"mean," the Yurok translate their word *tlmei*—goes at night to a lonely mountain pond, swims, and is then swallowed or taken below the surface by a monster. Traditions relate how such men were sometimes " pitied " and helped by the Thunders, and then became wealthy as well as strong. Most men's ambition did not lie in this direction. This belief is rather closer to the notions of the source of shamanistic power obtaining among most North American Indians, but stands well apart from the typical aspects of Yurok shamanism.

TABOOS.

The Yurok are firmly convinced of the definite immortality of the spirits of the game that they kill. Long ago, they say, the salmon declared, " I shall not be taken. I shall travel as far as the river extends. I shall leave my scales on nets and they will turn into salmon, but I myself shall go by and not be killed."

The old deer tell the young to try the house of such a one. Then one of the young deer lies down in that man's snare and dies. He eats its flesh with parched seed meal as flavoring and acorn gruel. The women sit still during the meal. They do not eat the head. None of the flesh is dropped on the floor, so that it may not be stepped on and carried outdoors by the soles; any scraps are scrupulously gathered and put away. After the meal the hands are carefully washed in a basket or wooden basin, then rubbed with fragrant chewed pepperwood leaves. The meat is served on wooden platters, which are washed only with water in baskets, never in a stream. The deer sees everything. After two days it returns. " How do you like that house? " the elders ask. " I do not like it," it says. " He does not wash his hands, and his women shift their feet while they sit at the meal." Or it answers: " He is good. He acts rightly. Smell my hand." They sniff it, like the pepperwood, and frequently go into that man's snares. So the deer never grow less, however much they are killed, the Yurok insist; and the hunter's success is brought not by his own cunning, but by the favor he can win from his game by respectful treatment.

If the hands are washed in flowing water after a meal of venison, it is thought that the deer is drowned. It is believed that deer can not abide the whale; the flesh of the two is not eaten together, and whale meat is called "rotten wood" before a hunter in order not to spoil his luck. It is said that the deer dislike houses that seem dead and empty: "I constantly see smoke there, I will go to that house," they are thought to declare.

Salmon, or fish of any kind, are not eaten at the same time with bear meat, grouse eggs, or acorns blackened by prolonged soaking.

The Yurok avoid strange water, and will not drink from the most familiar stream in certain reaches. River water is never taken. A dog, the deadliest of poisons, might have been drowned, or a girl have thrown in an abortion.

Sometimes, after a killing, the slayer would set up a plank on the ridge above his house, cut the end into the rude semblance of a nose, attach a stick as arm, and fasten to this a bow. Then he addressed the figure: "You killed him. Take the evil that his kinsmen are thinking."

Any things connected with the physiology of sex on the one hand and with deer on the other are thought utterly incompatible by the Yurok. The prospective hunter therefore carefully keeps away from his wife, or counteracts the effect by reciting a formula of special potence. Nor does he approach her after a meal of venison or sea-lion flesh, for fear of bringing illness on their child. Such disease can be averted only by public confession after birth.

A number of taboos were enjoined on boatmen while on the ocean. Under no circumstances would they carry a corpse, a dog, or a bearskin, consume food, or speak of a woman as *wentsauks:* instead they called her *megawitl.* Even on the river, travelers could not eat a meal; but if in haste they might carry fire on a layer of earth, heat stones, and then, disembarking, quickly cook. Near Kenek, Merip, and Kepel, there are large stones at the water's edge, in front of which no corpse may pass, according to the injunction of the ancient *woge* spirits who took up their abodes in these rocks. The one near Merip extended his prohibition to women also, who therefore land above or below the huge block and walk inshore of it.

FORMULAS.

A trait of Yurok formulas is that while those devoted to the same end run along closely patterned lines, no two are alike. One man may even know several formulas serving the same purpose. Thus an old man at Orekw has three formulas for releasing from corpse contamination. One, that of *wertspit*, the insect responsible for death, calls on the spirits of only 3 spots; another names 12 localities; the third, 22, beginning far upstream, proceeding to the mouth of the river, then south along the coast, and ending beyond Orekw.

A Weitspus formula serving the same purpose calls on the spirits in 18 rocks.   They are:

1. Ayomok, far up the river.
2. At the Karok village Inam.
3. At the Karok village Ashanamkarak.   (Pl. 6.)
4. At the Karok village Amaikiara.   (Pl. 7.)
5. At Atskergun-hipurayo, a short distance below.
6. At Wetsets, 2 miles above the Karok village Panamenits.
7. At the Karok village at Camp Creek, Yurok Olege'l.
8. At Otsepor, Bluff Creek, in Yurok territory.
9. Houksorekw, in the river, half a mile above Weitspus.
10. Oreuw, opposite Weitspus at Ertlerger.   (Fig. 2.)

Here the mourner is washed.   The recitation resumes:

11. Otsep, above Kenek.
12. Okegor, at Kenek.   (Pl. 4.)
13. Tsekwa, at Merip.
14. Awiger, below Sa'a.
15. The hill at the mouth of Blue Creek.
16. Sa'aitl, at the entrance to the world of the dead.
17. Below Ho'opeu, perhaps at Omenoku.
18. Oregos, a bold column at Rekwoi, at the very mouth of the river.   (Pl. 5.)

A similar formula belonging to a Rekwoi man names 10 spirits:

1. At the Karok village Kasheguwaiu.
2. At the Karok village Ashanamkarak.
3. At the Karok village Ka'arler at Orleans.
4. At or opposite Weitspus.
5. Okegor at Kenek.
6. Tsekwa at Merip.
7. Merhkwi at Kepel.
8. Awiger below Sa'a.
9. Kemenai at Omenoku.
10. Oregos at Rekwoi.

The spirits in these rocks did not wish human beings to die when "those through whom we die" had their way.   The fifth, sixth, and eighth—corresponding to numbers 12, 13, 14 in the preceding list—objected so strongly that they became the ones who refuse to allow a corpse to pass them on the river. The tenth found a plant which makes the mourners' spoiled body good once more.

With these formulas may be compared one of the same character recorded in both the Hupa and Yurok languages from a Hupa woman of Yurok ancestry.   It is clear from this instance of translation that the exact sound of the words seems of little moment to the Indians, the sense being the effective means of the formula.   This recitation addresses rocks at the following spots on the river bank.

1. Kohtoi, Hupa Haslinding, on the Trinity above Hupa Valley.
2. Below.
3. Petsohiko, Hupa Djishtangading.
4. Ergerits, Hupa Tseyekehohuhw.
5. Oknutl, Hupa Honsading.

PLATE 4

YUROK FISHING FOR SALMON IN KLAMATH RIVER AT KENEK

PLATE 5

MOUTH OF KLAMATH WITH PART OF
YUROK VILLAGE OF REKWOI AND
ROCK OREGOS, ABODE OF SPIRIT THAT
PURIFIES FROM CORPSE CONTAMINA-
TION

YUROK CANOE SHOOTING THE RAPIDS
AT KENEK

PLATE 6

KAROK FISHING WITH PLUNGE NET AT FOOT
OF FALL IN KLAMATH AT ASHANAMKARAK,

ALTAR, AT SAME SETTLEMENT, WHERE FIRE IS
KINDLED ANNUALLY IN AMAIKIARA FIRST-
SALMON RITE

PLATE 7

KAROK FISHING FROM SCAFFOLD OPPOSITE AMAIKIARA

The eddy carries the bag of the net upstream. This is the most common method of taking salmon among the northwestern tribes.

6. Below and opposite.
7. Pekwututl.
8. Merip (compare 6 in the last list).
9. Nohtsku'm.
10. Wetlkwau, at the mouth opposite Rekwoi.
11. Rekwoi-kas, probably the same as Oregos at Rekwoi.

Six of these places are on the Trinity in Hupa territory, 5 among the Yurok on the Klamath. This is the Yurok version. The recorded Hupa original or translation speaks of 10 places, but actually names 12, only 5 of them on the Trinity, the second in the above list being omitted. The 7 in Yurok territory are:

6. Hotuwaihot, Pekwututl.
7. Chwichnaningading.
8. Senongading-tanedjit, Nohtsku'm.
9. Kyuwitleding, Sregon.
10. Kitlweding, Sa'aitl.
11. Tsetlcheding, Wetlkwau.
12. Mukanaduwulading, Rekwoi.

It thus appears that the formulas are not absolutely memorized as to content, even the framework of names and places fluctuating somewhat in the mind of the reciter. The change which a formula can undergo in a few generations of transmission is therefore considerable. It seems that the innumerable formulas known among the Yurok and their neighbors fall into a rather limited number of types, in each of which the idea is identical, but the skeleton as well as the precise wording individually different and unstable. Beyond this, there is a marked fundamental similarity of concepts, and even of stock expressions, extending to practically all formulas irrespective of their purpose. For instance, spirits or plants so powerful that dentalia come to them and remain voluntarily under the most adverse circumstances, such as the presence of human bones, are likely to be mentioned in any kind of a formula.

The Yurok-Hupa recitative just mentioned is an example. It begins thus:

"Hahahahaha—I come to you who sit at Kohtoi. You are said to be the wise one. I am thus as it was left for us of the human world. My body frightens human beings. They make a fireplace while I have none. I make my fire alone. I do not eat what they eat. I do not look about the world. My body frightens them. Therefore, I tell you, let your mind be sorry for me."

"Yes," is the spirit's answer, "I saw him running downstream across the river with string about his head. No, I am not the one. I shall tell you who is the wise one, but in return you must leave for me that which makes human beings happy (tobacco). Hurry on to him who sat down opposite Dyishtangading."

The mourner makes the same appeal and receives a similar answer from each of the other spirits, until he repeats his request to the one at the mouth of the river, adding that he has been in vain at nine (sic) other places, and at each has been told that another is the really wise one. Then the Rekwoi spirit replies:

"I hear you. Do not be afraid. You shall travel again in the human world. You shall eat what people eat. Where they make a fire, you shall have yours.

You shall look about in the world. Your body will be new. I shall lend you this my herb and with it my medicine. You shall hunt and the deer will lie still for you; and it will be the same with dentalia. Now look, here it (my herb) stands outside my house. When it commences to be dark, it is grown high. And to-morrow in the morning it will be eaten down. Deer will have come to feed on it. Look at this, too, which stands erect behind the fire. Dentalia cut it down. At dawn it has grown up again. It has come to my head that it will be so with you (*i. e.*, you have the medicine, food and riches will seek you as if you had never been contaminated). Take my herb with you. I thought that I would lend it. But there will not be many who will know that (formula) by means of which my mind will be made sorry for human beings of the world. Well, take this my herb with you. But leave for me much of that (tobacco) which makes people happy with its body."

There is certainly sufficiency of direct appeal in this to suggest prayer. But it is notable that the spirits' answers are also given; and it is in these recited replies, and in the herb or root with which the formulist has previously provided himself, that the efficacy of the procedure is believed to reside. In fact, the whole, including the minute offerings of tobacco, is a dramatic enactment of a journey believed to have been actually performed by an afflicted ancient in search of relief.

Such, at any rate, is the obvious character of most northwestern formulas, and these differ among one another chiefly in the degree to which they are preponderatingly in the narrative form of a myth or pure dramatic dialogue. A Hupa " brush dance " formula illustrates the tale-like type.

"In the world's middle she and her granddaughter lived. And after a time a person grew in her (granddaughter's) body. 'Hei! Human beings are about to come into being, it seems; their smoke is everywhere,' she said. And the (unborn) child became sick from her. And it came from her. And she thought, 'With what is it that we shall steam this child?'"

Thereupon the old woman sent her granddaughter out to find the necessary medicine. The girl saw wild ginger, dug it, and when the baby was steamed it evinced greater animation. The old woman then found pitch-pine sticks, lit and waved them over the child (as is done in the dance). Then she thought:

"Human beings will soon come into existence. Perhaps their children will become sickly from them. They will think of our bodies. With what is it that we can make them think of us? Yes. One night will pass before (the final night of the dance). There will not be only one herb (in all the ceremony)."

So again she told her granddaughter to look. The girl went east, and at the foot of Mount Shasta saw a basket floating, but it was empty. She followed, lost it, and found it again at Kitokut, then at Kilaigyading, then, still going down the Klamath, successively at Otsepor, above Weitspus, at Weitspus, Kenek, Kepel, Pekwan, north of Rekwoi on the ocean, south of Orekw, and finally, near by, at Freshwater Lagoon, where it came to shore. The basket was still empty, but now she saw a house in which she found an old woman who said she had been thinking of her and her troubles.

"'There in the corner is your basket,' the old woman said, put her hand on it, held it up toward the sky, and (the girl) saw something (yellow pine bark, the desired second medicine) fall into it. She held that (bark) up pointing crosswise and gave it to her and said: ‘Take it and put it in your child's mouth.’ ”

With that attainment ends the formula, which is now used with the vegetables and brands mentioned in curing sickly children.

It is significant of the interrelations of the northwestern tribes that the 12 localities mentioned by name in this Hupa formula are in Shasta, Karok, Yurok, and Coast Yurok territory. On the other hand, the first of eight places designated in an analogous Yurok formula for the brush dance is in Chilula land. The spots are:

Plokseu, on the Bald Hills.
Oreuw, at Ertlerger.
Okegor, at Kenek.
Awiger, near Sa'a.
Oso, a hill opposite the mouth of Blue Creek.
Oka, a mountain downstream from Blue Creek.
Sa'aitl, opposite Turip.
Terwer, at the mouth of the creek of that name.

Several of these spots are prominent in the corpse purification formula and definitely associated with death taboos. It is therefore clear that any religious landmark was likely to be seized upon and worked into a formula, irrespective of what it primarily suggested to the native mind.

MYTHOLOGY.

The Yurok sometimes loosely mention Wohpekumeu, “widower across the ocean,” as the one that made things as they are. But their tales ascribe to him only the institution of a certain limited number of practices. He was born at Kenek, lived there when not traveling in curiosity or under impulse of amatory desires, and was finally carried to the land across the salt water by the Skate woman, to rejoin the other *woge* who had departed from this world before. At Amaikiara in Karok territory he deceived the woman who kept all salmon confined, and liberated the fish for the use of future mankind. From the sky he stole acorns—a benefit attributed also to Megwomets. Until he instituted birth, every woman's life was sacrificed in the production of her first and only child. Everywhere he pursued women, often unsuccessfully; and according as his wooings resulted, he made or marred good fishing places. Eager for feminine conquest, he attempted to deny or evade his son Kapuloyo, and finally, in order to marry the young man's wife, abandoned him on a high tree and blinded his grandson Kewomer. Kapuloyo escaped, gathered to himself all the dentalia in the world, and departed downstream; but near the mouth of the river, Wohpekumeu overtook him and recovered enough money to restock the supply for men.

Almost as great a favorite in tales as this tricky and unreliable benefactor of mankind, is Pulekukwerek, "downstream sharp," so named from the horns on which he sat—a grave, unconquerable character, who smoked tobacco but never ate, passed women by for the sweat house, and by strength and supernatural gifts destroyed monster after monster. His birth, as his name indicates, was far north on the coast at the end of the world. With their own devices he put an end to those who crushed people in pretending to split logs, speared them in playing games, and killed them with overstrong tobacco. He burned blind cannibal women, killed *sa'aitl* monsters with hot stones, and deprived of his power a dangerously jealous man of Merip. He drove women from the sweat house that they still frequented. He stole the boy Night, found the man who could weave the sky, and placed the stars upon it. When the time came, he retired uncompelled to the far-away land of dentalia and everlasting dances. All that the Yurok have of respectful admiration in their mythology they lavish on Pulekukwerek.

At times Pelintsiek, "great dentalium," or some other form of the money shell, appears half divinized in the traditions, and assumes certain of the functions usually ascribed to Wohpekumeu and Pulekukwerek, especially those of a broadly institutory nature. Sometimes the three appear in conjunction with Ki-wesona-megetotl, "Sky holder."

Megwomets, a bearded dwarf, carries acorns on his back and is the distributor of vegetal abundance. He enters into a few myths.

A number of episodes are told of Segep, coyote, but he is less frequently a favorite of invention, even in despicable situations, than among most California tribes, and the only achievement to his credit is the killing of the sun who had caused his children's death. The raccoon alone was able to lift the luminary back to his place: Tlkelikera, the mole, Wohpekumeu's sister, is more rarely mentioned. Wertspit, the locust larva, wished death into the world. Kego'or, the porpoises, lived with most of the foregoing at Kenek until the impending arrival of the human race, when they retired to Sumig, Patrick Point. Thunder and Earthquake were also inhabitants of Kenek, until the latter was beaten at his favorite game of shinny ball by a young man from the mountain Kewet. The house sites of many of these great ones of old are still shown at the little town.

The world is believed to float on water. At the head of the river, in the sky, where the Deerskin dance is danced nightly, are a gigantic white coyote and his yellow mate, the parents of all coyotes on earth.

CALENDAR.

The Yurok monthly calendar commences "at Christmas," that is, with the winter solstice. The first 8 or usually the first 10 moons are numbered, not named. The remainder, up to 12 or 13, are designated by terms that appear to be descriptive.

1. Kohtsewets.
2. Na'aiwets.
3. Nahksewets.
4. Tsona'aiwets.
5. Meroyo.
6. Kohtsawets.
7. Tserwerserk.

8. Knewoleteu.
9. Kerermerk or Pia'ago.
10. Wetlowa or Le'lo'o.
11. Nohso.
12. Hohkemo.
13. Ka'amo.

Informants who reckon 12 moons in the year omit one toward the end, or give *Hohkemo* as a synonym of *Nohso*. The most consistent accounts regularly enumerate 13. *Pia'ago* is said to refer to a red berry gathered then. The meaning of *Le'lo'o* is undetermined, but it is the month of the world renewing ceremonies of the Karok. In *Nohso* the people camp out to gather acorns. *Ka'amo* seems to refer to cold. The older Yurok are aware that some of them allow 13 moons to the year and others only 12. When individual reckonings differ, long arguments result. But when the acorns are ripe for picking, disputes end, for it is then unquestionably *Nohso*. This method of correction by seasonal phenomena is quaint in view of the unquestionable astronomical starting point, and suggests that this was such in theory rather than by close observation. At the same time, the knowledge of the fact that 12 moons do not suffice for a return of the sun indicates a closer reckoning of time than prevailed among central Californian tribes. Of similar order is the Yurok statement that the Pleiades—*teinem*, "the many"—are invisible for one month only. They disappear at the end of the fifth moon, are gone to lie in the water in the sixth, and in the seventh reappear just before daybreak.

CHAPTER 4.

THE YUROK: ARTS.

DRESS.

The dress of northwestern California was essentially that of all the tribes of the State. Young men usually folded a deerskin about the hips. Their elders did not scruple to go naked. A breechclout was not worn. Women put on a buckskin apron, about a foot wide, its length slit into fringes, which were wrapped with a braid of lustrous *Xerophyllum* or strung with pine nuts. From the rear of the waist a much broader apron or skirt was brought around to meet the front piece. This rear apron was again fringed, but contained a considerable area of unslit skin. Women also habitually wore neat, round, snugly fitting caps of basketry (Pl. 73, *f*). These were modeled with a nearly flat top, but degenerated after some months into a peak. In cold weather both sexes threw over the shoulders a blanket or cape, normally of two deer hides sewn together (Fig. 3). A single skin or a garment pieced of small furs might be used instead. This cape was neither fitted to the form nor squared. The Yurok appear to have fancied the somewhat ragged effect of dangling legs and neck. A rectangular blanket woven of strips of rabbit fur, much used through the remainder of California and over large areas eastward, was rare or unknown among the northwestern tribes, perhaps because rabbits are scarce in their country. Capes and men's loin cloths always had the fur left on. Women's aprons were always dressed.

Rich women ornamented their dress heavily. Haliotis and clamshells jangled musically from the ends of the fringes; and occasionally a row of obsidian prisms tinkled with every step. Poor women contented themselves with less. They may sometimes have had recourse to a simple skirt of fringed inner bark of the maple, which was standard wear for adolescent girls and novitiate shamans.

The only footgear of moment was a one-piece front-seamed moccasin without decoration, donned chiefly for travel, by women gathering firewood, or sometimes as part of full dress. It was not worn regularly by either sex. Modern specimens add a heavy sole, but this seems not to have been used in purely native days. Men put on a knee-length buckskin legging and a rude snowshoe—a hoop with a few cross ties of grapevine—when they went up into the hills in winter to hunt.

Men wore their hair at least half long. A confining net of string, customary in many other parts of California, was not known here. In boating, a thong might keep the hair out of the eyes. Before a fight, it was usually piled on top of the head. When the hunter donned a deer hide and stuffed deer's head (pl. 8), a disguise as likely to deceive a puma lurking in a tree as the game, he cushioned his hair over the nape and ran several sharp bone skewers through it. Women gathered their hair in two masses that fell in front of the shoulders and were held together by a thong, or on gala occasions by a strip of mink fur set with small woodpecker scalps.

In mourning, the hair was shortened. A widow cropped hers closely. A necklace of braided *Xerophyllum* was put on by all near mourners.

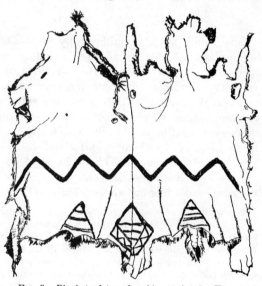

FIG. 3.—Blanket of two deerskins, painted. Hupa.

The Yurok say that this was never removed, being worn until it fell to pieces. It is likely that if it lasted a year, it was taken off when the name taboo of the dead was lifted. Perhaps it usually distintegrated before.

The Yurok did not usually mutilate any part of the body for the attachment of ornaments. Pendants of haliotis were hung around the ears. The nose, contrary to the custom of some adjacent tribes, was bored only after death. A reference to this condition was therefore construed as something like a curse.

Women had the entire chin, from the corners of the mouth downward, tattooed solidly except for two narrow blank lines. A beginning was made with three vertical stripes, which were broadened until they nearly met. Occasionally a row of points diversified the edges of the area. This style is universal in northwestern California.

A little familiarity makes it rather pleasing. Lines and angles and circles always look like something added to the face. The solid mass, conforming to the contours of the chin, favored by the Yurok, soon seems an integral part of the features and serves to emphasize a well-modeled jaw. Certainly it is not long before a younger woman or half-breed who has escaped the tattoo strikes one with a sense of shock, as of something necessary missing. When pressed to explain the custom, the natives, as in all such cases, of course give a reason which is not the cause of the practice, but is interesting as their psychic reaction to the custom. They say that an untattooed woman looks like a man when she grows old. (Fig. 45 *a*.)

HOUSES.

The Yurok house is built wholly of planks split from logs with wedges and more or less adzed. It contains no posts and no beams. The roof planking is supported by three or four plates that rest on heavy planks in the front and rear walls. Two of these plates run near the side walls; the others form ridgepoles. The usual house has two ridges and three roof slopes, the middle one not quite level. A single-ridged house is to the Yurok a sign of the owner's poverty: he builds only 3 fathoms wide; a well-to-do man 4. Actual frontages by measurement are $17\frac{1}{2}$, 19, 20, $21\frac{1}{2}$ feet. The depth is about a yard more. No houses surpassing or falling short of these figures by more than a foot or two were built. (Pls. 9, 10, 11.)

The walls are of planks set endwise in the ground, usually two rows thick. Little care is given the side walls, which are only a few feet high and protected by the overhanging eaves. For the front and rear, splendid solid planks from 1 to 4 feet in width are sometimes used. In the middle of the wall they may rise 10 or more feet. The boards in each wall are held together by two squared poles, one inside and the other out, lashed together with grapevine or hazel withes passing through holes in several of the boards. The plates, which often project several feet, rest in rectangular notches cut into planks of particular strength. The roof boards are as thin and wide as they can be made and from 8 to 10 feet long. They are merely laid on in two overlapping thicknesses. The lower ends are often not squared, and weather and split off irregularly, giving the Yurok house a very untidy look in our eyes. The smoke hole is made by laying aside a board in the middle. In rainy weather this leans over the opening, propped by a stick set at an angle. A refinement is introduced by gouging a gutter along the edges of the two boards bordering the smoke hole, to prevent side flow into the opening. The smoke hole is never used as a door. but it serves as the only window. Measuring about 2 by 7 feet, it admits a little shifting sunshine and a fair illumination to the middle of the house, but this remains cool in midsummer. It darkens early, and the corners are dim and musty at noon. A short log ladder with cut-in notches usually gives ready access from the ground to the roof when the smoke-hole plank is to be shifted or a leak repaired by an adjustment of boards.

The door is a round hole about 2 feet in diameter, cut a few inches above the ground through a plank of exceptional breadth and thickness. This plank

PLATE 8

HUNTER'S HEADDRESS FOR DECOYING DEER. KAROK

PLATE 9

THREE ALIGNED HOUSES WITH STONE PLAT-
FORMS IN FRONT, IN YUROK VILLAGE OF
WAHSEKW

INTERIOR OF YUROK HOUSE AT WEITSPUS;
SALMON HANGING FROM DRYING FRAME

PLATE 10

KAROK HOUSE, SIDE VIEW, SHOWING DOUBLE
PITCH AND RAGGED SHINGLING OF ROOF

INTERIOR OF YUROK SWEAT HOUSE, WITH
EXIT, FIRE PIT, FLOOR BOARDS, AND HEAD
REST

PLATE 11

YUROK TOWN; PLANK-COVERED GRAVES IN FOREGROUND

HUPA MEASURING DENTALIUM MONEY AGAINST TATTOO MARKS ON HIS FOREARM

is always near one end of the front wall. Two stones are planted as convenient grips just inside and often outside the entrance. The door proper is a
plank that slides in a groove—often a piece of gunwale of an old canoe—and
is held upright by two stakes. It can be tied but not locked. The plank in
which the hole is cut is sometimes simply ornamented in geometrical relief.
(Pl. 12.)

Just inside the door a partition extends nearly across the house 3 or 4
feet parallel from the front. The blind alley thus formed serves for the storage
of firewood, and is often littered with carrying baskets and rubbish. This
narrow compartment about takes up the excess of the length of
the house over the breadth.

The square remainder of the interior is on two levels. The
center, for about half the diameter of the whole area, is dug out
from 2 to 5 feet. The surrounding shelf, some 5 or 6 feet
wide, is at the natural level of the ground, or substantially
so. The central depression is the cause of the pits that mark
the sites of ancient houses. It is entered by a notched ladder
(Fig. 4), sometimes as much as 2 feet wide. A second ladder
may stand at the far corner from the door, for convenient
access to the farther sides of the shelf. The corners of the
pit are always cut off, sometimes to such a degree as to make
it more nearly a regular octagon than a square. The sides of
the pit are always carefully lined with thin, even, and smoothed
slabs. These may reach a breadth of 4 feet. In the middle
of the pit is the fireplace, a shallow excavation usually
bordered by five stones. Above it, at less than a person's
height, hangs a huge criss-cross of several tiers of poles in
squares, on which salmon sides or other provisions are suspended. Those on the lower rungs are more easily taken down
than avoided with the head. (Pl. 9.)

The "shelf" area serves for storage. In a prosperous house,
it is largely filled with huge storage baskets, 2 or 3 feet in
diameter, filled with acorns and covered with inverted conical
baskets. The spaces behind and among these are often crowded
with other provisions, baskets, and utensils temporarily out of
commission. Occasionally an elderly relative has her bed on
the shelf, but this is unusual.

FIG. 4.—Yurok
house ladder.

The pit is the area in which women and children sit,
work, cook, eat, and sleep, and men often take a seat on
a cylindrical or mushroom-shaped block or stool. The
hard earth floor is generally kept swept fairly clean, but most Yurok
housewives are untidy, and cooked food, eatables in preparation, un-
finished baskets, materials, implements temporarily laid aside, and a
variety of apparatus litter the cramped space, while from above half-
cured slabs of salmon may drip grease, or gusts of rain drift in.
No matter how old and worn a utensil, it is rarely destroyed or deliberately thrown out; and an accumulation of property in good,
poor, mediocre, and practically worthless condition cumbers most
houses. Orderliness is found in individuals, but is not the rule.

Before the door many houses have a pavement of flat river-worn stones, which provide a pleasant seat in the sun, and on which, when the weather permits, the main or evening meal is generally eaten.

A hut was used by Yurok women in their periodic illnesses. This was a small and rude lean-to of a few planks, near the house or against its side.

SWEAT HOUSES.

The sweat house is smaller than the dwelling and dug out over its entire extent. The frontage is about 12 feet, the breadth 9 to 11, the greatest height 6 or 7. The excavation is at least 4 feet. The longer sides are lined, but have no walls above ground; on the shorter ends, the planks rise 1 or 2 feet above soil level in the middle. From one to the other of these two little peaks runs a ridgepole, further supported, not quite at its middle, by a square post. From the ridge, the roof planks, overlapping along their edges, extend to the ground. These planks are usually much less shaped than those which cover living houses. Evidently lumber is used for them which is too small or too irregular to span the roof spaces of the dwelling. The ridge itself is crowned with a split length of old canoe, which effectually sheds rain from the joint, but adds to the ragged appearance of what little of the structure is visible above ground. (Pls. 13, 14.)

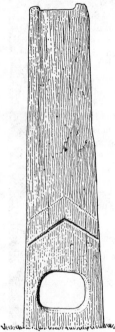

FIG. 5. — End plank of Yurok sweat house, with exit hole.

The interior is neatness itself. The floor is paved either with well-adzed planks which years of contact with human bodies have polished, or with carefully selected and fitted slabs of stone, often of considerable size. There is no furniture about except a few block pillows, cut flat-faced out of redwood with concave top; perhaps a crotched stick or two on which an occupant has hung the net on which he was last working; and sometimes a little heap of firewood at the back. The floor is swept clean. Somewhat toward one end from the middle is the sacred post, toward the other end the fireplace, a cubical hole of a foot and a half, lined with flat stones. (Pl. 10.)

The door is in the middle of one of the long sides, and always faces the river or ocean. It is a roundish, horizontal opening of about a foot and a half, provided with a cover; inside, a ladder with a few notched steps leads down. It, too, is usually worn to dangerous slipperiness

PLATE 12

SACRED HOUSE AND SWEAT HOUSE IN KAROK
TOWN OF KATIMIN, WITH ISHIPISHI ACROSS
THE RIVER

CORNER OF YUROK HOUSE WITH CARVED
DOOR PLANK, AT REKWOI

PLATE 13

CHILULA SWEAT HOUSE

BOAT OF YUROK MANUFACTURE ON TRINITY RIVER AT HUPA

PLATE 14

HUPA WOMAN LIFTING STONE FROM FIRE TO
HEAT BASKETFUL OF WATER TO LEACH MASS
OF ACORN MEAL SPREAD OUT IN SAND PIT

KAROK OLD MEN SUNNING ON STONE PLATFORM
IN FRONT OF SWEAT-HOUSE ENTRANCE

PLATE 15

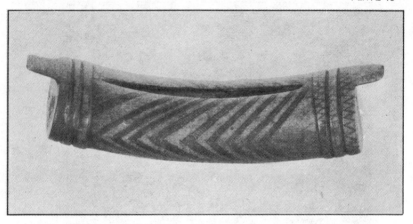

ELK-ANTLER PURSE FOR DENTALIUM MONEY. YUROK

CYLINDRICAL BOX WITH LID IN PLACE. YUROK. THE BOXES
VARY FROM I TO 4 FEET IN LENGTH

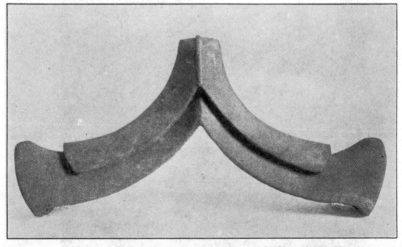

ORNAMENT SET ON PROW OF BOAT. YUROK

for all but bare feet. A second door, used only as exit, is at one of the small ends. This is a minute oval, often not more than 14 by 10 inches, cut through the base of one of the two planks that support the ridgepole (Fig. 5). It is closed by a snugly fitting wooden plug. Many of these exits seem too small for even a medium man to squirm through, yet are habitually used by a little company of varied sizes, as well as their guests. But the bodies are all naked, of course, and supple with perspiration. The exit is some 4 feet below ground level; consequently a pit is dug outside the wall to receive the emerger. The sides of this pit are held by cobbles, in well fashion. After the regular evening and morning sweat, which has a distinctly ceremonial character, the exit is used, because, the Yurok say, those who have completed the purification from corpse contact emerge by the larger door. When a man retires to the sweat house to work, idle, meditate, sleep, or sulk—the latter his usual course when offended—he comes out by the main entrance.

A considerable space in front of this entrance is stone paved, much like the "porch" of the living house, but more invariably so. Here the old men are wont to sun themselves after the "evening" or afternoon sweat, and at other times also.

Firewood for the sweat house is not lightly or randomly gathered. The proper method is to ascend the ridge, often at some distance from the village, climb a tall fir, and cut the branches from near its top. There are many trees in the country of the Yurok and their neighbors which have been trimmed in this way and which when seen against the sky, even at long distances, present the appearance of a gigantic head and outstretched arms surmounting the body. The natives do not seem to be aware of their likeness to the human form. The wood is cut or broken into short lengths, and kindled in the stone pit. Entrance and exit are firmly closed, the former stuffed if necessary, and a small fire soon produces intense heat, besides volumes of smoke. The sweater lies low on the ground and avoids suffocation. When the fire has burned down or out, he opens the exit, wriggles forth, and plunges into the near-by creek, river, or ocean. The smoke gathers in thick velvety soot on the lower side of the roof. The steam sweat bath is totally unknown to the Yurok and to all other California Indians, with the exception of a few groups in the notheastern portion of the State; and there recent influences from the north may have been operative.

All winter long, and often in summer, men and grown boys slept in the sweat house, and passed the evenings in talk and smoking. Seven sleeping places were recognized by name, and each of these was permanently occupied by the same inmate, except when he might yield it to a visitor. The place of honor was in the middle of the end opposite the exit, the two worst by the entrance and in the middle of the opposite side (Fig. 6).

Yurok information as to the number of house and sweat house sites in 36 river and coast villages for which statement appears to be trustworthy, yields 263 houses and 83 sweat houses, a proportion of about 3 to 1. This would make about 23 souls, or 6 to 7 adult males, per sweat house. The omission of slaves and bastards would not materially reduce the number. In other words, most sweat houses appear normally to have had an occupant for very nearly every one of their seven named berths. The actual floor space was great enough to accommodate two men in one place; and this arrangement was presumably followed when necessary.

These figures appear dependable—263 divided by 36 gives over 7 house sites per village. On allowance for inevitable omissions after the lapse of many years, the 7+ would have to be raised to about 9; which, with the previously computed correction of one-third for house sites unoccupied at any given time, makes 6 " live " houses per village—the correct number, according to all available data, and therefore a reasonable check on the sweat-house figures.

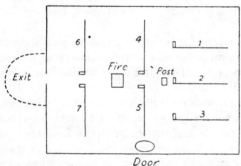

Fig. 6.—Plan of sleeping places in Yurok sweat house. 1, Metlku; 2, tepolatl; 3, hik'es; 4, nergernertl; 5, lega'i; 6, atserger; 7, kwinamet.

BOATS.

The Yurok type of canoe, which was made also by the Tolowa and Wiyot and sold to the Hupa and Karok, is dug out of half a redwood log, and is a clumsy but symmetrical and carefully finished vessel. It is used on the ocean, but is obviously a type devised for a rushing river full of rocks. Its square prow must be awkward in the surf, and is badly designed for cutting through waves or shedding spray. But the round belly of the boat and its gradually curving underside, without stem, allow a single stroke of the steersman's paddle to swing it as on a pivot, and in the rapids many a rock is approached head on and then shot by so close that the hand could reach it. Upstream navigation is tedious. Still reaches can sometimes be paddled through, but over many parts progress is by pushing along the shore or from rock to rock, which requires at least two occupants, while in the hardest places there is no recourse but towing. In every case the stream runs under the bottom of the boat and lifts it, and the square end meets no resistance. (Pl. 13.)

The paddle also is for river use. It is a combination of pushing and sweeping implement, a stout pole 6 to 8 feet long, spreading below to a narrow, heavy blade, and used by standing men. (Pl. 67, *i*.) Only the seated helmsman holds a true canoeing paddle. (Pl. 67, *f*.) In quartering the river the front man always works on the current side, the steersman against him. This affords the latter the chance, by merely reversing his stroke, to turn the prow instantly with the stream, when his vessel is under fullest control. The worst rapids, at Kenek, can be shot at most stages of the river, but goods and passengers are often disembarked, since the passage can rarely be made without shipping considerable water. (Pl. 5.) Other stretches contain dangerous spots for the boatman who is unacquainted or unskillful.

The redwood is the only canoe material, on account of its size, evenness of grain, and softness under tools. It was rarely felled, fallen or drift logs being cut into sections and split. (Pl. 3.) The excavating was largely done by fire, the shaping with a stone-handled adze of mussel shell. The prow and stern rise a foot above the sides in a concave triangle. On them a wealthy man going on a visit sets a projecting cap, something like a huge yoke, which he calls the ears. (Pl. 15.) The upper part of prow and stern, being cross-grained, are the weakest parts, and, unless a boat is split lengthwise on a rock, are usually the first to break out. Such damaged boats are kept for ferrying in comparatively still water. At the top of the prow a sort of handle extends backward, but the Yurok are careful not to grip this in drawing the boat ashore, since half the front is likely to come out with it. This hook is called the boat's nose. The towing rope is fastened to a loop of stout grapevine or hazel, which, passing through holes in the sides, encircles the prow inside and out. This is the necklace. Gunwales extend the whole length, overhanging inward. They turn no wash, and must serve for strength only. At the stern a seat is left, and forward of this two foot braces, called by the same Yurok word as their house ladders. Toward the prow is a rounded knob, known as the heart, and of no apparent use, except that in recent days it is sometimes made to contain a socket in which a little mast is stepped to sail upstream before the afternoon wind for a favorable stretch here and there. Knot holes are plugged with pitch, cracks calked and pitched, or if threatening sometimes held together by lashings. Boats not in frequent use are carefully drawn high and dry under a bush or filled with leafy boughs, that the hot summer sun may not split them.

The Yurok canoes vary considerably in breadth and beam, and the largest must have three times the capacity of the smallest, but the length is standard at 3 fathoms and a hand, about 18 feet. A longer boat would be disadvantageous among the rocks. Measurements of actual beams and inside depths are 51 by 19½, 47 by 19, 45 by 17½, 40 by 13, and 34½ by 10½ inches. The draft is rather shallow, but attains about 6 inches and more in the middle if the boat is loaded.

FOOD.

The Yurok and their neighbors ate very largely of the acorn, the staple food of most Californians; but fish, that is, salmon, constituted a greater proportion of their food than was usual elsewhere. Small game is sufficiently scarce in their territory to make the taking of salmon much more profitable, ordinarily. Deer were abundant and their flesh esteemed, but seem hardly to have formed part of the daily food supply. Bulbs were dug in early summer; seeds were beaten off the open prairies on the ridges. Some varieties of the latter were eaten crushed and parched but uncooked, and were much relished for their flavor. Salt was furnished by a seaweed, *Porphyra perforata*, which was dried in round blackish cakes. The people on the coast secured quantities of the large ocean mussel, whose shells make up a large part of the soil of their villages. The stranding of a whale was always a great occasion, sometimes productive of quarrels. The Yurok prized its flesh above all other food, and carried dried slabs of the meat inland, but never attempted to hunt the animal. Surf fish were the principal species taken along the ocean; there is practically no record of fishermen going out in boats. The myths speak of canoe excursions only for mussels or sea lions. The food supply was unusually ample along both coast and river, and the Yurok ordinarily did not have to condescend to the grasshoppers, angle-worms, and yellow-jacket larvæ whose nourishing qualities other tribes of the State exploited. In time of stress, of course, they fell back on almost anything. The large yellow slug of California, which in the damp northwest grows to enormous size, would then be used. Famines are scarcely alluded to in the myths, but must have occurred, as among every people primarily dependent on one seasonal or migratory animal. The average Californian clearly passed most of his life on a much closer food margin than the Yurok, but the minuteness and variety of his diet seem usually to have saved him from dire extremity.

All reptiles and dogs were considered extremely poisonous by the Yurok.

The old custom was to eat only two meals a day and theory made these sparing. Only a poor fellow without control would glut himself, and such a man would always be thriftless. Most men at least attempted to do their day's labor, or much of it, before breakfast, which came late. Some old men still profess to be unable to work properly after they have eaten. The evening meal came toward sunset.

FISH AND GAME.

Salmon begin running in the Klamath in spring and in autumn. These are the periods of all the great ceremonies, whether or not these

refer directly to the fish. The river carries so much water, however—
more than any California drainage system except the Sacramento-
San Joaquin—that there is scarcely a month in the year when some
variety of salmon can not be taken. It may be added that the stream
is of undiminished volume up to practically the head of the stretch
of Yurok ownership. Fish were taken with dip nets, seines, set
gill nets, and harpoons, but of these devices the first was the most
usual.

The dip net, or lifting net, as it may be called to distinguish it from a
smaller instrument on an oval frame occasionally used by the Karok and other
tribes to scoop boiling riffles and rapids (Pl. 6), was let down from a scaffolding built out over the water, almost invariably at some eddy or backwater.
Here the fisherman sat on a block or little stool, holding the bone button of
the string which closed the entrance to the pyramidal net stretched out in
the current. This net was hung from the bottom of a long A-shaped frame
with a bottom crossbar. The whole was hauled out as soon as a pull on the
cord had inclosed a salmon, which was then struck on the head with a club.
A single night's vigil sometimes produced a hundred salmon, it is stated—a
winter's supply, as the Yurok say. At other times a man will sit for half a
day without a stir. The old men are much inclined to this pursuit, which
would be trying to our restless patience, but gives them opportunity for undisturbed meditation or dreaming or mental idleness along with a sense of profitable occupation. (Pls. 4, 7.)

Lampreys, customarily known as eels, much prized by the Yurok for their
rich greasiness, also ascend the river in great numbers, and sturgeon are not
rare. Both species are taken much like the salmon, though of course with a
different mesh. In the lower river eelpots were also set. Trout in the affluent
creeks are too small to be much considered by a people frequently netting 20-
pound salmon.

Both salmon and lampreys were split for drying—the former with a wooden-
handled knife (Pl. 16) of "whale-colored" flint, as the Yurok called it; the latter
with a bone awl. A steel knife probably involves a different and perhaps a more
precise handling, so that until a few years ago the old women clung to the
aboriginal tools. Most of the fish was somewhat smoked and put away in old
baskets as strips or slabs. The pulverized form convenient for packing, known
also on the Columbia, was probably more prevalent among interior and less-
settled tribes like the Shasta. Surf fish were often only sun dried whole and
kept hung from poles in rows. They make a palatable food in this condition.
Dried salmon is very hard and nearly tasteless, but rather satisfying and, of
course, highly nourishing.

A long net was sometimes set for sturgeon. One that was measured had
a 6-inch mesh, a width of 3 feet, and a length of 85 feet, but in use was doubled
to half the length and double the width.

A measured salmon seine had a scant 3-inch mesh, a width of 3½ feet, and
a length of over 60 feet.

Nets were made of a splendid two-ply cordage rolled without tools
from fibers of the *Iris macrosiphon* leaf. The gathering of the leaves
and extraction of two fine silky fibers from each by means of an
artificial thumb-nail of mussel shell was the work of women. The

string was usually twisted and the nets always knotted by men. The mesh spacer and netting shuttles were of elk antler; net weights were grooved, pierced, or naturally perforated stones. (Fig. 7.)

The salmon harpoon, which could be more frequently used in the aboriginal period than now when mining renders the river opaque, had a slender shaft, sometimes more than 20 feet long. To this were attached two slightly diverging fore-shafts, one a few inches the longer, on which were set the loose barbs of pitched and wrapped bone or horn. The lines were short and fastened to the main shaft, a pay line being unnecessary for prey of the size of a salmon. In fact, an untoggled barbed spear would have sufficed but for the opportunity its resistance offers a heavy fish to tear itself free. This harpoon was made with no essential variation in practically all fish-

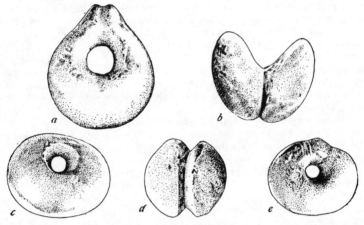

Fig. 7.—Yurok net weights.

able parts of California, and it is the only harpoon known, except for a heavier implement driven by the Yurok and Chumash into sea lions.

Sea-lion hunters took station on rocks, disguised in bear or deer skins. When the animals clambered up, the hunters barked and twisted their bodies, attracting the sea-lions' attention as they approached, then leaped up and harpooned them. The toggle head had two barbs in a row; the line was fastened to the shaft. No attempt was made to hold the bulky prey, but it was followed by boat, the shaft regained, and then at first opportunity the victim was speared again. Sometimes a canoe was dragged out to sea for half a day before the animal was dispatched. For this reason large males were not attacked late in the afternoon.

Deer seem to have been snared more often than shot before the introduction of rifles. They were often driven with dogs.

ACORNS.

Acorns were gathered, dried, stored, cracked, pulverized, sifted, leached, and usually boiled with hot stones in a basket. This gruel, usually known as acorn soup or acorn mush, though it is thicker than the one and more fluid than the other—the Maidu mix it with ten or twelve times the quantity of water—was the chief daily food of more than three-fourths of native California. It is about as tasteless as wheat flour cooked in water would be, nearly as nourishing, but richer in starch, and, when prepared from certain species, perceptibly oily.

In boiling, the hot stones must be stirred to insure cooking the contents equally and to prevent holes being burned through the containing basket. As in the greater part of California, a little paddle is used for this purpose by the Yurok. But they and their neighbors almost invariably carve the handle of this "mush paddle" into geometric ornaments, while among the average Californian tribe the instrument is wholly utilitarian and often short, rough, and unsymmetrical. The Yurok paddle is of madroña, manzanita, oak, or other hard wood, and sometimes nearly 4 feet long and quite unwieldy for a seated woman. (Pl. 17.)

The mealing was done on a hard, smooth slab of rock with a stone pestle usually a foot long. Exceptional specimens reach nearly 2 feet but were too highly treasured to be put into daily service. The better pestles have a raised ring or flange about a third of the way from the butt. (Pl. 16.) This is purely ornamental and makes a distinctive local type, which is evidently well established, since it occurs in ancient examples from the region. Even the commonest work-a-day pestles are dressed rather symmetrically, whereas most of the Californians often contented themselves with a convenient cobble. The acorn fragments and meal were kept from scattering by a flaring hopper of basketry; a soap-root fiber brush swept together what escaped this container. The mortar was not used by the historic Yurok, although specimens are occasionally washed out or mined in their habitat. They are so ignorant of the purpose of the utensil that they conjecture it to have been a cook pot or the like. A similar change of custom as regards the acorn mortar has taken place between prehistoric and recent times in a considerable part of California and constitutes one of the rare instances of a directly traceable cultural change.

The pestle is held near its upper end. As it is raised the wrist is turned until the stone is half horizontal; on the stroke it is twisted back and falls perpendicular. The wrist motion perhaps saves raising the pestle to its full height. The worker lays her legs over the rim of the hopper to hold it down and bring herself close to her labor. (Pl. 60.)

Among acorns, the preference of the Hupa, and presumably of the Yurok, is for those of the tanbark oak, *Quercus densiflora*, but the species *garryana*, *californica*, and *chrysolepis* are used if needed. Acorns were stored, most frequently in the shell, in large baskets set around the sides of the house. Some of these baskets are loose or open work; others have their stitches closely set and are patterned. They are usually covered with an inverted burden basket. Occasionally they are made larger than the door, but are easily moved out if it becomes necessary through the lifting of some planks off the roof.

Acorns were leached of their tannin in three ways. The commonest method was to pour hot water over the meal as it lay spread out in a basin of clean sand. (Pl. 14.) This is the usual Californian method. Cold water apparently also removes the bitterness if given time enough. Thus, acorns buried for a year in swampy mud come out purplish and are ready to be roasted on coals. Again, they were sometimes shelled, set in a basket until moldy, and then dug into clean sand in the river. After some time they turned black, and were then in condition for roasting.

TOBACCO.

All the tobacco smoked by the Yurok was planted by them—a strange custom for a nonagricultural people far from all farming contacts. The custom, which extends also to southwestern Oregon, and in the opposite direction probably to the Maidu, is clearly of local origin. Logs were burned on a hilltop, the seeds sown, and the plants nursed. Those who grew tobacco sold to those who did not. A woman's cap full or not full was the quantity given for a dentalium shell, according as this was of second smallest or shortest length—a high price. Tobacco grows wild also, apparently of the same species as the planted, but is never used by the Yurok, who fear that it might be from a graveyard, or perhaps from seed produced on a graveyard. The plant does seem to show predilection for such soil. Otherwise it sprouts chiefly along sandy bars close to the river; and this seems to have caused the choice of summits for the cultivated product.

The pipe was tubular, as always in California. Its profile was concave, with the bowl flaring somewhat more than the mouth end. The average length was under 6 inches, but shamans' and show pieces occasionally ran to more than a foot. The poorest pipes were of soft wood, from which it is not difficult to push the pith. Every man who thought well of himself had a pipe of manzanita or other hard wood, beautifully polished, probably with the scouring or horsetail rush, *Equisetum*, which was kept in the house for smoothing arrows. The general shaping of the pipe seems to have been by the usual northwestern process of rubbing with sandstone rather than by cutting. The bowl in these better pipes was faced with an inlay of soapstone, which would not burn out in many years. Sometimes pipes had bits of haliotis inlaid next the steatite; others were made wholly of the stone. The pipe was kept in a little case or pouch of deerskin. It could be filled by simply pressing it down into the tobacco at the bottom of the sack. Pouches have been found in California only among the northwestern tribes. Tobacco was stored in small globular baskets made for the purpose. These receptacles are also a localized type. (Pl. 73, *e*.)

A few old Yurok were passionate smokers, but the majority used tobacco moderately. Many seem never to have smoked until they retired to the sweat house for the night. Bedtime is the favorite occasion for smoking throughout California. The native *Nicotianas* are rank, pungent, and heady. They were used undiluted, and the natives frequently speak of them as inducing drowsiness.

BOWS.

The bow was of yew, short, broad, and so thin that only the sinew backing kept it from breaking at the first pull. The grip is somewhat thicker, pinched in, and wrapped with a thong. The string is sinew. Only that side of the tree which faces away from the river was used for bow wood. The sinew backing is often painted with red and blue triangles; the pigment used before blue could be obtained from Americans is unknown. The usual length was 3 to $3\frac{1}{2}$ feet, the breadth $1\frac{1}{2}$ to 2 inches, and the thickness one-half inch, of which a considerable fraction was sinew, whose pull gave the unstrung bow a strong reverse curve. The following are some measurements in inches:

Width of limb	$1\frac{7}{8}$	$1\frac{1}{2}$	$1\frac{11}{16}$	$1\frac{5}{8}$	$1\frac{3}{8}$	$2\frac{1}{4}$
Width of grip	$1\frac{1}{4}$	$1\frac{1}{8}$	$1\frac{3}{16}$	$1\frac{10}{16}$	$1\frac{1}{8}$	$1\frac{3}{8}$
Greatest thickness	$\frac{3}{8}$	$\frac{1}{2}$	$\frac{1}{2}$	$\frac{9}{16}$	$\frac{7}{16}$	$\frac{7}{16}$
Length	$32\frac{1}{2}$	$35\frac{1}{2}$	$36\frac{1}{2}$	39	40	52

The fourth specimen is a shaped but unsmoothed and unsinewed stave. It appears that breadth and thickness vary in inverse ratio, rather independently of length.

Basically, this is the type of bow made throughout California as far as the Yokuts, at least for the nobler purposes of war and the deer hunt. But the extreme flatness is characteristic of the northwestern tribes, who often shave the sides of their bows to a knife-edge. Elsewhere even the most elaborate pieces become somewhat longer, narrower, and thicker. It may be that the material, which among far tribes is rarely yew, has something to do with this difference; or the northwestern extremity of form may be merely a trick of specialization. It is likely to have weakened rather than strengthened the weapon; but the workmanship commands admiration.

The arrow is of *Philadelphus lewisii*, a syringa, foreshafted with a hard wood, and tipped with stone. The length is about 31 inches—from 28 to 32—or so much that the arrow could not be drawn to the head. (Pl. 18.) The marking is in colored rings under the three feathers. The straightener is a little board or flattened stick perforated in the middle. The arrow shaft was bent through the hole. (Pl. 16.)

The usual arrow point was of whitish flint or obsidian. The former material was more abundant, but more difficult to work nicely. The points were small, slender, thin, and neat. Bone points were also known. These were sharpened on sandstone.

The quiver was a skin turned inside out. Otter and fisher fur made the most prized quivers, such as were worthy of gifts or of display in the brush dance.

BASKETRY.

The basketry of the Yurok and their immediate neighbors is the finest ware made in a style that extended with only minute variations south to the Wailaki, east as far as the Achomawi, and north at least to the Athabascan tribes on the Umpqua River, if not beyond. If a number of specimens in the British Museum are representative, the ware of the Kalapuya in the Willamette Valley was similar.

This type of basketry is unusually specialized in the rigid limitation of its processes. Coiling, wicker, checker, and twill work are all unknown. Substantially the only technique is simple twining, with patterns throughout in "facing," that is, overlay. Three-strand twining is customary for starts and strengthening courses, and diagonal twining is known, but neither weave is regularly employed for entire vessels. Wrapped twining and false embroidery are common farther north, and lattice twining and three-strand braiding are used to the south, but are never followed in the local area constituted by northwestern California and southwestern Oregon.

The Yurok employ hazel shoots almost exclusively for their warps. The normal woofs are the split roots of conifers—pine, redwood, or spruce. For special purposes, such as the first courses of a basket or especially fine work, strands split from the roots of willows, grapevines, and other bushes are substituted. The conifer roots are of a gray or buff color, which turns brown with age. Service baskets have their patterns made by facing certain woofs with glistening whitish strands of bear grass or squaw grass (*Xerophyllum tenax*), a material used along the Pacific coast for long distances to the north. Ornamental baskets have the entire surface overlaid with this brilliant facing, except where it is replaced by patterns in glossy black maidenhair fern stems, *Adiantum pedatum*, or fibers of the giant fern, *Woodwardia radicans*, dyed red with chewed alder bark. Occasionally both colors are used on one basket, but this is uncommon except on caps. Rather infrequently yellow patterns are introduced, made by steeping *Xerophyllum* in boiled *Evernia vulpina* lichen, and

PLATE 16

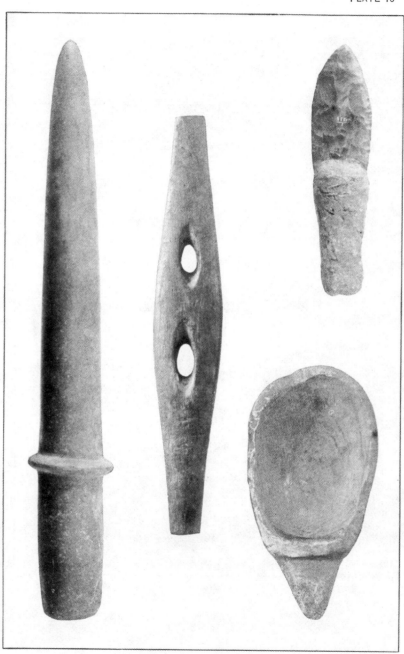

Yurok stone pestle; wooden arrow straightener; "whale colored" flint knife for dressing salmon, the wooden handle lashed with cord and pitched; salmon grease dish of steatite.

PLATE 17

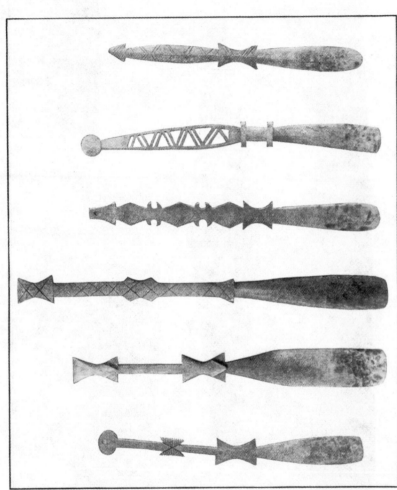

YUROK ACORN GRUEL STIRRERS, THE ENDS CHARRED FROM CONTACT
WITH THE COOKING STONES. LENGTH, 26½ TO 37 INCHES

PLATE 18

KAROK IN WAR COSTUME OF ROD
ARMOR AND HELMET

KAROK DRAWING THE BOW

PLATE 19

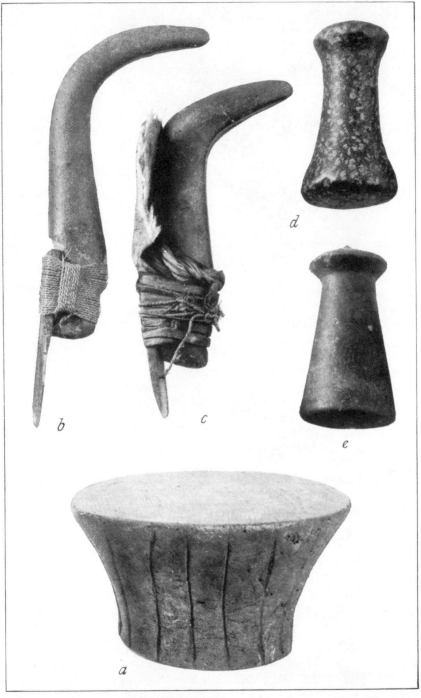

a, Yurok stool of redwood; *b*, *c*, stone-handled adzes, steel replacing the ancient blades of shell; *d*, *e*, mauls to drive horn wedges.

still more rarely porcupine quills are treated in the same manner and inserted. The use of quills seems to have filtered down the river from the Klamath and Modoc. The Yurok keep the overlay constantly toward the outside, so that no color shows on the interior of the basket except where strand edges peep through the interstices. More easterly tribes twist the warp with its facing, so that the pattern is duplicated, though rather roughly, on the inner side. The materials mentioned are varied slightly by some tribes, but, on the whole, are employed without change as far as the type of basketry prevails.

Some 20 forms of vessels are, or were, made in this technique by the Yurok.

The cooking basket, used specially for acorn mush, is a bowl with vertical walls and usually a single band of rather light pattern.

A smaller basket of the same kind is used by individuals to eat from, or sometimes to cook in.

A vessel like the cooking basket, but somewhat higher, and often faced solidly with *Xerophyllum*, serves as a general receptacle around the house. The decoration runs either vertically or in horizontal bands, sometimes diagonally.

Large baskets, up to 3 feet or more in diameter and height, serve for storage. Vertical and diagonal patterns prevail.

Similar baskets are made in coarse or open work, often on multiple warps, naturally without decoration.

Loads are carried in a conical basket, which hangs across the shoulders from a strap passing over the forehead. These baskets are made very neatly in a wide spaced but even openwork. The type is known throughout California as far south as Tehachapi. (Pl. 9.)

Similar baskets for gathering seeds are made somewhat smaller in close stitch, usually faced and patterned.

The seeds are whipped in with a beater, a disk of coarse openwork on a handle.

Similar disks, somewhat more hollowed and lacking handles, are plates for individual portions of fish; and large trays of the same type abound in every house.

A close woven tray, faced and patterned either in bands or in radiating diagonals, is 1½ or 2 feet in diameter, and serves to gather and shake acorn meal.

This meal is sifted by the Yurok from a smaller, stiff, and entirely flat tray, which is tapped with a deer leg bone. The Hupa replace this sifter by one in the form of a very obtuse cone, which does not require tapping.

Similar to the Hupa sifter is a water dipper, used by both tribes. It is usually unornamented.

A very small bowl or tray, decorated inside, serves parched seed meal.

The *rumitsek* is a more or less globular basket in openwork, hung about the house to hold spoons, awls, sinews, and odds and ends. It is sometimes made very prettily with courses of crossed or gathered warp and a pleasingly equal mesh.

The tobacco basket is small, globular or deep, and sometimes provided with a cover of basketry or deerskin. It is overlaid, but commonly patterned simply.

The hopper for the slab on which acorns are pounded is stiffly reinforced, and usually bears an elementary pattern of bars or dots.

The dance basket serves for display only and has been described above.

The woman's cap has already been mentioned. The finest and evenest work is best combined in this article. The disposition of the ornamentation is fundamentally banded, but the principal zone most often contains a series of alternate blocks of triangular pattern. Sometimes the blocks are rhomboids disposed diagonally.

The cradle or baby carrier is a huge sort of slipper of openwork, stood on its toe or hung from the hoop which forms the heel. Some strands shut off the toe: on these the child is set and tied in, its feet hanging free. A more or less dangling round hood may be added to protect the face, but is commoner in specimens made to trade to Americans than in used pieces. This is a form of the "sitting cradle" that prevails in parts of northern California, as contrasted with the "lying cradle" that most Californians use. To the eastward of the Yurok, as among the northern Wintun, a simpler shape is used, which is little more than an ovate tray with a handle at the small end. To the south, the Pomo, a people of great mastery of the textile art, have developed a somewhat different variety of the sitting cradle. (Pl. 35.)

WOODEN IMPLEMENTS.

The only box known to the Yurok was a more or less tapering cylinder of redwood, from 2 to 4 feet long, hollowed out from the top. A lid covered the opening and was lashed on. Occasionally a rectangular specimen is to be seen, but the usual old form is the cylinder. It is difficult to explain this peculiar shape, unless by a transfer of the canoe-making technique. The boxes served to hold obsidians and other dance valuables and were normally transported by canoe; but a square receptacle would have lain on the round bottom of the boat substantially as well as the round form. (Pl. 15.)

Rectangular platters or trays for deer meat, and huge finger bowls carefully used after a repast of the same, were made of wood. The former are often white with hardened fat and black with smoke and dirt.

From redwood or other lumber were also made the only two movable articles of furniture ever reported from aboriginal California: a round block stool, from 3 to 9 inches high and somewhat flaring (pl. 19), of which several stood in every better house, and a pillow for the sweat house (pl. 10). The latter had somewhat the shape and size of a brick stood on edge with the ends a little spread and the top side hollowed. The stool, although in the living house, was used chiefly by men, who among the Yurok rarely follow the general Californian custom of sitting on the ground. Even outdoors they look about for a log or stone, and in default, kneel, squat, lean, or stand. This little habit is a powerful indication of a well-settled mode of life.

In the Southwest it sharply marks off the town-dwelling Pueblos from their nomadic neighbors. In neither region does the custom extend to women.

The standard fire drill was made—both " man " and " woman," as the Yurok call the two parts—of willow root. (Pl. 77.)

UTENSILS OF ELK HORN.

Elk horn was used for the point of the flint flaker, for mesh spacers, and shuttles; sometimes for arrow straighteners, for spoons, and for purses. The spoon is truly such, not a ladle, with a rather flat, cross-grained bowl. The handle always bears some decoration, and often is worked into fairly elaborate zigzags and notches. Sometimes it is cut through longitudinally. One extremely interesting specimen has a thread winding around the handle. Unfortunately there is nothing to prove whether this device is aboriginal or suggested by an American screw. The spoon served for eating acorn gruel, but women contented themselves with a mussel shell or the top of a deer skull. Rich houses kept a store of fine spoons to bring out when they entertained dance guests (pl. 20). Modern spoons are made of wood, but these are likely to be imitations, devised when the supply of antler was no longer obtainable. Most Californians licked their daily gruel from the crooked index and middle fingers, but this does not seem to have been good Yurok manners.

The purse or money box was of the same shape as the large wooden box for dance valuables. It averaged 6 to 7 inches in length. Deerhorn specimens were smaller and less used. Several strings of dentalia could be folded back and forth into an elk-antler purse. The lid was then sprung on under a projection at one end and held in place by a thong wrapping. Now and then a different purse was made from the antler where it forks. This type was triangular. All the horn purses were usually incised with the triangles or zigzags which are the basis of almost all Yurok decoration. (Pl. 15.)

There must have been a needle, since rush mats were made by sewing a cord through the stems; but whether the instrument was of wood, horn, or bone, is not known. The mats were sat and slept on by women in the living house.

RECEPTACLES.

A curious receptacle, known only to the northwestern tribes, was a piece of deer hide, folded hair side out, and with a stick fastened along each edge to spring it closed. The whole somewhat resembled a quiver in outline, but was flat and opened along one edge. It was conveniently carried clamped under the upper arm.

A network sack, with mesh small enough to hold acorns, was much used to carry little objects, from food to money. The shape was trapezoidal, with a deerskin strap. This type was known over most of California, and was chiefly if not wholly man's paraphernalia.

Loose feathers and the like were rolled on a sort of mat of herb stems on which the leaves were allowed to remain and which were twined with string. The object is so shaped as to belly out somewhat when rolled up.

A similar mat case of tules was sometimes made for obsidians.

A small skin of soft fur, spread out flat, often had dentalia rolled up in it. At one end a thong was stitched on, which was tied around the bundle.

TOOLS.

The Yurok were tolerable workmen, but possessed few tools.

Logs and planks were split with wedges of elk horn from a few inches to a foot and a half in length. Some of these were nearly flat, others sharply curved, according to the intended use. The edge was produced by rubbing on stone.

The wedges were driven with pear-shaped mauls, 6 to 8 inches in height, of basalt or mottled metamorphic rock. They are usually quite symmetrical and sometimes beautifully finished. Most California tribes were content with convenient stones. These mauls were one of two kinds of tools on which the Yurok bestowed much care. (Pl. 19.)

The other was the stone handle of the adze. The blade of this is declared to have been of heavy mussel shell. The handle was 6 to 10 inches long, curved up at the end, sometimes with a taper that seems almost too delicate for use. The other end was cut away to receive the butt of the blade, which was lashed on. (Pl. 19.) Most pieces bear two or three ridges or grooves to hold the lashings from slipping. Sometimes the handle end curls but slightly or is blunt and straight; but such pieces have probably been worked over after a break. Steel very early replaced the shell blades, but the stone handles continued in use as long as any members of the generation of discovery remained alive. This implement is restricted to the region in which the Yurok type of culture prevailed, but, like most of the distinctive utensils that withstand time, existed there in prehistoric times.

It is doubtful with what the Yurok did their finer wood carving, as on the acorn mush stirrers. Elk-horn spoons had their designs rubbed into form with sandstone. Purses, of the same material but hollow, must have been gouged with a sharper tool. The method of boring pipes of hard wood and stone is also unascertained.

The old skin-dressing tools were quickly superseded by steel blades. It does not seem that there were well-formed implements for this

PLATE 20

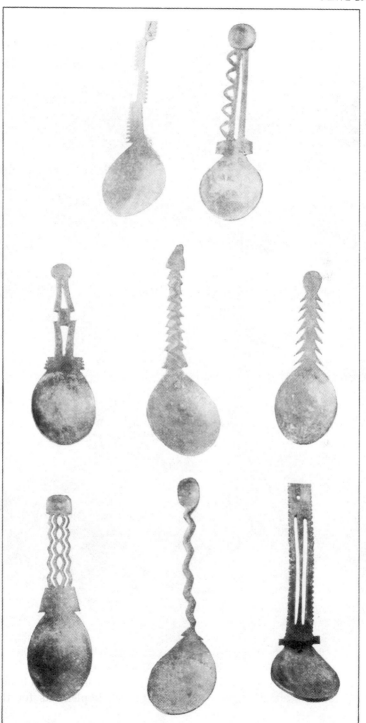

CARVED ELK ANTLER SPOONS FOR ACORN GRUEL. YUROK

PLATE 21

KAROK MAN

purpose, else at least the handles would have been preserved. It is rather likely that a rock was broken to convenient shape, or a bone rubbed down. The Hupa tell somewhat indefinitely of scrapers of stone and deer rib. The only part of the aboriginal technique that has survived is the rubbing of deer brains into the hide. These are preserved in cakes of moss, which are soaked before use. The process softens the skin. True tanning was, of course, unknown.

MUSIC.

Music, like art, is difficult to characterize without a special vocabulary that has grown up around it. Such vocabularies do not exist for most primitive arts because their essential qualities are too foreign from our own. Usually it is only certain incidental features of an alien art that have any meaning in our thinking and feeling. We detach these aspects of expression from their roots and describe them in terms which seem significant but are of real meaning only as they refer to our own schemes. It is only the individual endowed with exceptional sympathy or sensibility that can understand any primitive art without a long acquaintance; and since most people have not the interest to familiarize themselves with the art of their own civilization they are wholly incapable of knowing what a remote foreign one is about. Hence they prefer Indian baskets with bastard European patterns; and though they may find something vaguely pleasing in many primitive works of decoration—if seen sufficiently rarely—the quality which appeals is that of strangeness and the grotesque.

It is the same with music. The first impression of a native song is one of funny noises, grunts, deflected intonations; and the almost invariable report is of plaintiveness, wailing monotony, minor wistfulness—emotions which the hopeful lover, the religious devotee, the community celebrating a victory certainly were not trying to render when they uttered the song. A few examples in our inadequate notation convey but a terribly distorted impression. The music must be heard and heard and heard by those both willing and able to listen to it before it can be understood.

Nevertheless the most casual can discern with ease a distinctiveness in northwestern music. Hear again and again any half dozen songs of the Yurok, the Yana, the Pomo, and the Yokuts. Then listen to a new song from one of the latter three nations. Only a fairly proficient musician would venture its definite attribution to one of the three peoples: their range of stylistic peculiarity is slight. But let the additional song be from the Yurok, and even the novice could usually place it with confidence. It should be added that the

Yurok themselves can not distinguish their own music from that of the Hupa and Karok, and in many cases from that of other near-by tribes.   But the difference of northwestern songs from those of central California in mass is considerable.

A few external traits can be mentioned.   The northwesterner, particularly in the music of his great dances, loves to leap upward an octave or more to a long, powerful note, and then sink back from this by a series of slides, often of a continuous tonal transition. The accompanists at times chant a rhythmic bass pulse without definite melodic relation to the strain.   The levels and climaxes vary enormously in pitch, in rhythm, in intensity of intonation. Central Californian music moves more uniformly in a narrower range of smaller intervals.

These are inadequate hints; but they reveal the rich and unexplored field that lies cultivable for understanding to him with sympathy, patience, and a catholic musical sense.   For centuries hundreds of thousands of human beings in California have been forming a style, a variety of styles, according to nation and occasion, in which they expressed some of their profoundest feelings; and we can not yet make a single exact and intelligible remark about their accomplishments.

MUSICAL INSTRUMENTS.

In instruments the Yurok are remarkable for their paucity.   The sole one was the flute, an open tube of elder wood with three or four equally spaced holes.   It was blown diagonally across one end. If a man could sniff a melody into it with his nose, he was rated a virtuoso.   Many did not even learn to play it with the mouth. The flute was associated with young men's courtship or unexpressed desires; but it was also played by their elders as they sat on sunny afternoons before the sweat house in idle meditation.   The instrument is incapable of accompanying the voice.   A bone whistle used in the Deerskin dance produces only a monotonous blast.

The northwestern tribes of to-day cover a cracker box with horse-hide.   This makes an effective drum to go with the songs that intensify gambling.   But the device is not aboriginal.   The Yurok say that anciently their sole drum was a convenient plank, preferably of seasoned white cedar, thumped with a stick.   If a passer-by wished to join in, he brought his paddle up with him from the boat.

No sort of rattle was used by the Yurok, though several types are known from their nearest neighbors.   The musical bow and the rhythmic rasp of other parts of California were also unrepresented.

This extreme poverty of instruments among a people not deficient in technical devices suggests a strong stylicization of their vocal music.

CONCLUSION.

In addition to the many sorts of baskets and a considerable number of dance paraphernalia, nearly 100 different kinds of implements of Yurok manufacture have been preserved in museums. Adding those which went out of use before they could be collected, it is safe to say that the group made at least 150, and perhaps 200, distinct types of utensils. This is evidence of a fairly rich civilization.

Here ends the description of the Yurok. The next account will be of the Karok, a group so similar to the Yurok in everything but speech that their separate consideration will scarcely be necessary except as their life is conditioned by their geography; and of two smaller peoples, the Wiyot and Chimariko. Next in order are the Californian members of the great Athabascan family, in some ten divisions. The nearest of these, the Tolowa and Hupa, partake wholly of the Yurok type of civilization. From them southward a transition can be followed, from group to group, until with the Wailaki, and especially the ultimate Kato, another culture, that of north-central California, is wholly entered. The Yuki and Pomo and a branch of the Miwok come next in sequence along the coast as far as the Bay of San Francisco. Here the review leaps northward again to the Shasta, neighbors, through the Karok, to the Yurok, and participants in their civilization, although in modified and often diminished state. Beyond the Shasta the central Californian type of culture predominates once more. Some considerable traces of the northwestern civilization are still discernible among the Modoc, the Achomawi, the northerly Wintun, and even certain of the Maidu, but they become fainter and finally fade out.

The relations, intrinsic and distributional, of the northwestern culture to the others in California can thus be set forth with some distinctness. The bonds that link it northward with the cultures of Oregon can not yet be adequately portrayed, intimate as they appear to be. In comparisons in this direction lies the chief avenue to a broader understanding of this peculiar civilization.

CHAPTER 5.

THE KAROK.

NATIONAL RELATIONS.

The Karok (Pl. 21) are the up-river neighbors of the Yurok. The
two peoples are indistinguishable in appearance and customs, except
for certain minutiæ; but they differ totally in speech. In language,
the Yurok are a remote western offshoot of the great Algonquian
family, of which the bulk resided east of the Mississippi and even on
the Atlantic coast; the Karok, one of the northernmost members of
the scattered Hokan group, which reaches south to Tehuantepec. The
nearest kinsmen of the Yurok are the Wiyot, on their south and
west; of the Karok, the Chimariko and Shasta, southward and eastward. In spite of the indicated total separateness of origin, the
two groups are wholly assimilated culturally.

Except for a few transient bands of Hudson Bay Co. voyagers,
the Karok knew nothing of the existence of white men until a
swarm of miners and packers burst in upon them in 1850 and 1851.
The usual friction, thefts, ambushing, and slaughters followed in
spots. The two sacred villages near the mouth of the Salmon, and
no doubt others, were burned by the whites in 1852; and a third, at
Orleans, was made into a county seat. There were, however, no
formal wars; in a few years the small richer placers were worked
out; the tide flowed away, leaving behind only some remnants; and
the Karok returned to what was left of their shattered existence.
Permanent settlers never came into their land in numbers; the Government established no reservation and left them to their own devices; and they yielded their old customs and their numbers much
more slowly than the majority of Californian natives.

The term " Karok," properly *karuk*, means merely " up-stream " in
the language of the Karok. It is an adverb, not a designation of a
group of people. The Karok have no ethnic name for themselves,
contenting themselves, in general Californian custom, by calling
themselves "people," *arara*. They will sometimes speak of them-

selves as Karuk-w-arara in distinction from the Yuruk-w-arara, the
" downstreamers " or " Yurok "; but this denomination seems wholly
relative. In thinking of the Shasta above them on the Klamath, they
would probably name themselves Yuruk-w-arara.

Karok designations for their neighbors are as follows, *-arara* or
-ara denoting " people," and *-hi*, " speech ":

Kakamichwi-arara, the Shasta of Klamath River. This term may refer
to the residents of one village. The speech seems to be called Karakuka or
Karakuha. Shammai is mentioned as a village.

Tishra-w-arara, the Shasta of Scott River.

Mashu-arara, Mashu-hi, the Konomihu and New River Shasta; from Mashu-
ashav, Salmon River. Shamnam is the Konomihu village at the forks, and
Hashuruk one below.

Kasha-arara, Kasha-hara-hi, the Wintun, and probably the Chimariko of
Trinity River; possibly also the tribes on the Sacramento.

Kishake-w-arara, the Hupa on the lower Trinity.

Yuruk-w-arara, Yu-hi, the Yurok.

Sufip-arara, the Yurok of Rekwoi, probably also the Coast Yurok.

Waiyat-hi, the Wiyot.

Yuh-ara-hi, the Tolowa. Yuhanak seems to be a Tolowa village.

SETTLEMENTS.

Knowledge of the Karok settlements is still involved in confusion.
It is clear that there were three principal clusters of towns: at the
mouths of Camp Creek, Salmon River, and Clear Creek. Other
stretches of the river held smaller villages, and in parts even these
appear to have been few.

The farthest Yurok settlement upstream was near the mouth of Bluff Creek,
the lowest downstream of the Karok was Wopum, Yurok Opegoi, Hupa Hai-
wochitding, opposite Red Cap Creek, a considerable village. Between these two
towns a steep peak stands on the south or east bank of the Klamath. This cone
may be regarded as the boundary between the two peoples, although the Indians, always thinking in terms of individuals or collections of individuals
and their personal rights, and rarely in terms of groups as such, almost certainly did not so regard the mountain. Then, until the vicinity of Camp
Creek was reached, followed several minor settlements of which for the most
part only the Yurok names are recorded: Aranimokw, Tu'i, Oler, Segoashkwu.
Above Tu'i was a village called Shavuram or Sahwuram by the Karok, and
Operger by the Yurok. Chiniki and Sanipa were also in this region.

In the Orleans district there were, in order upstream, Chamikininich, Yurok
Oketur, on the south or east bank; Tachanak, Yurok Olege'l, Hupa Dacha-
chitding, on the opposite side at the mouth of Camp Creek; Panamenik, Yurok
Ko'omen, Hupa Nilchwingakading, on the flat at Orleans; and, once more on
the east bank, Katipiara, Yurok Tsano, Hupa Killaikyading. Then followed
Chinits, at Sims Ferry, and Tsofkaram or Tasofkaram at Pearch. The Yurok
mention Wetsitsiko or Witsigo in this region.

About a mile below the mouth of the Salmon the Klamath tumbles down a
low fall, which was a famous fishing station (Pl. 6). Directly at the fall, on the
east side, was Ashanamkarak, Yurok Ikwanek. Opposite, a few hundred
yards below, was the sacred town of Amaikiara, Hupa Djeloding. The Yurok

called this Enek, but distinguished the upstream portion of the settlement as Tumitl. (Pl. 7.) Directly at the mouth of the Salmon, on its lower side, and well known as the spot on which the sacred Jumping dance of Amaikiara concluded, was a little flat, uninhabited in the historic period, called Ashapipmam by the Karok and Kworatem by the Yurok. The latter name seems to be the source of the designation "Quoratean," which an artificial system of priority and synonymy in nomenclature for a time affixed to the Karok nation.

Just above the mouth of the Salmon rises an isolated little peak, cut out between the Klamath and an old channel, which can not fail to impress every imagination: A'uich. Adjoining it, on a bluff that overlooks a shallow rapids in which the river ceaselessly roars among its rocks, lay the most sacred spot of the Karok, the center of their world, *isivsanen ach*, Katimin. Strictly, there was Yutimin, "the lower dam," as well as Katimin, "the upper," and the Yurok distinguished Segwu' and Apyu. Opposite lay Ishipishi, Yurok Kepar, of which Yutuirup was a neighbor or suburb. (Pl. 22.)

Tishrawa, Unharik, Kaus, Inoftak, Iwatak, and Akoteli are villages or parts of villages that can not be exactly located, but which seem to have stood in the vicinity of the mouth of the Salmon.

From this district up villages and information become scanter. A few miles above Katimin was Ashipak, "in the basket," Yurok Hohkutsor; 10 or 12 miles farther, Ahoeptini and Ti. Aftaram, mentioned as rich, may have been in the same vicinity. For 20 or more miles, nothing is known, except Ayis, Yurok Rayoik, and a village called Kumawer by the Yurok. Then, at the mouth of Clear Creek, Inam is reached: a large town, as shown by its boasting a Deerskin dance, and famous even to the Yurok as Okonile'l. Some 8 miles above, at the mouth of Indian Creek, at Happy Camp, was Asisufunuk, the last large Karok village, at which a fish weir was sometimes thrown across the river. The Shasta mention in this region Nupatsu, below Happy Camp, Aukni above it, and Ussini at the mouth of China Creek, beyond which, at Thompson Creek, their own villages commenced. The three words are probably Shasta equivalents of Karok names.[1]

The land of the Karok is substantially defined by this array of villages along the Klamath. There were few permanent settlements on any affluents. All of these were owned by the Karok, and more or less used as hunting and food gathering territories to their heads; so that technically their national boundary followed the watersheds bordering the Klamath. The only exception was in the case of the largest tributary, the Salmon, about whose forks, a dozen miles up, were the Shastan Konomihu. The Karok seem to have had rights along this stream about halfway up to the forks.

Since the American settlement, the Karok have emigrated in some numbers, until now they form the sole Indian population on Salmon River, and are rather numerously mixed among the Shasta.

The dialect of the uppermost Karok was somewhat differentiated, but speech was substantially uniform.

---

[1] Recent unpublished statements obtained from several Karok put their boundary against the Shasta much farther upstream, nearly at Hamburg Bar, and claim Shamai, Seiad Valley, as Karok. If this is correct, the map (pl. 1) must be considerably altered.

Of the wars and feuds of the Karok, little is known, except that the Tolowa sometimes crossed the high southern spur of the Siskiyous to attack villages in the Clear Creek and Salmon River districts, and that the Karok probably reciprocated. Toward the Hupa and Yurok friendly feelings generally prevailed. There no doubt were feuds between individual villages, but there is no record of these ever involving the nations as a whole.

NUMBERS.

The population of the Karok did not exceed 2,000 at the time of discovery, and would unquestionably be put at about 1,500 were it not for the considerable number of survivors. The Federal census of 1910 reckons 775, which makes them one of the largest surviving tribes, and even stocks, in California. This figure seems open to some doubt. Five years before, with a rather high mortality prevailing in the interim, an official investigator, whose statistics everywhere else are more exhaustive than those of the general census, reported only two-thirds as many, distributed as follows:

Panamenik (Orleans) district	178
Katimin (Salmon) district	192
Inam (Clear Creek) district	160
On Salmon River	46
Total	576

To this total would have to be added a number now resident in ancient Shasta territory; but quarter bloods, many of whom now live among the Americans and would be reckoned as whites by the ordinary census enumerator, are included.

The last figures are of particular value because they show the population of the three districts to have been fairly balanced, with some preponderance in the middle one. The circumstances of contact with the whites were much the same in the three regions. Now, an early resident, observant and in unusual relation with the Indians, estimates 425 for the Panamenik district, and for the two above, with part of which he was less intimately acquainted, 1,500. His 425 would rather yield 1,500 for the whole nation.

The official reconnaissance of 1851 reports 250 souls up to Katimin and 600 to 700 for the stock. But these figures are unquestionably too low.

The number of houses noted by the expedition of 1851 is a better index: 37 in and below the Panamenik district, 69 in the region of the mouth of the Salmon, total 106 for very nearly two-thirds of the stock. The maximum number of houses that can be attributed to the Karok is therefore 200; and at the inhabitant ratio of $7\frac{1}{2}$ determined for the Yurok, the population of the stock would be 1,500. This figure seems the most likely; yet, even if it be stretched somewhat, it is clear that the Karok were less numerous than the Yurok, but outnumbered the Hupa.

It may be added that on the basis of 40 to 50 inhabitants per town, as among the Yurok, this population implied something like 30 or 40 Karok villages, which is about the number for which names are recorded.

It is also clear that the populational loss of the Karok in the past 65 years has been relatively mild, possibly not exceeding one-half.

NEW YEAR CEREMONIES.

The Karok brought out more clearly than the Yurok the esoteric first fruits or new year's element that underlies all the great dances of the northwestern tribes. They named the ceremonies "world making." But they reckoned their neighbors' celebrations as equivalent to theirs and visited them regularly. A Karok said that there were 10 of these ceremonies and listed them in geographical order as follows—actually he mentioned only 9:

Inam	Karok.	Takimitlding	Hupa.
Katimin	Karok.	Kepel	Yurok.
Amaikiara	Karok.	Pekwan	Yurok.
Panamenik	Karok.	Rekwoi	Yurok
Weitspus	Yurok.		

Among all three nations the ceremonies were mostly held in early autumn, the remainder in spring, and undoubtedly all have reference either to the beginning of the acorn crop or the run of summer salmon. Among the Karok, that at Amaikiara came about April. Late in August the autumn series commenced at Inam. Some weeks later came Panamenik, and two days subsequently Katimin. The season of these last is close to that of the Takimitlding acorn feast and the Weitspus Deerskin dance; but, so far as evidence goes, conflicts did not take place. A great man could not bring his property to two dances at once; therefore the sequence was, no doubt, nicely adjusted, although the Indians, of course, mention ancient spirit ordainment as the cause. They probably reason that the gods wished the wealth of the rich to be displayed at as many gorgeous dances as possible. The formula speaker at Panamenik, at any rate, began his 10 days' rites in the waning moon, timed so as to conclude with its death. That afternoon and the next day the dancers exhibited their deerskins; and then, as the new moon appeared, visitors and residents alike moved up to Katimin, where the local priest, notified of the start at Panamenik, had so gauged the beginning of his fast that the multitude was present for its ending. Then the Deerskin dance was made for five days. The Inam ceremony having come a month or so earlier, everyone had time to attend, return home from this remote spot, and prepare for the two subsequent ceremonies. At Inam they also danced with white deerskins, but only about a day and a half as at Panamenik. The Amaikiara rite falling in spring, had no competition except for the Salmon ceremony and spring Jumping dance in Hupa, and possibly the similar Yurok ceremony at the far-away mouth of the river. It was followed by the Jumping dance, which the Karok made only at this place.

It seems that the choice of seasons for the ceremonies may also have been determined in part by the climate. September is still normally dry and sunny, and the regalia become little exposed to rain. It is true that the Indians do not cease a dance if it begins to rain; but they do break it off or materially shorten it for a downpour or a storm. Moreover, as visitors can not begin to be accommodated in the houses of the town, and sleep in the open or under the rudest of brush coverings, the rainy season would be very unfavorable for a 2 or 5 or 10 days' dance. It is true that there is still considerable rain at the time of the spring ceremonies; but these are less numerous, and, while of no smaller religious import, are, on the whole, attended by less sumptuous dancing. All the surviving Deerskin dances, among Yurok and Hupa as well as Karok, come in autumn. In central California, where elaborate regalia are again encountered, the Kuksu dances fall during the rainy season; but they are definitely held in the dry and roomy earth house. Southern California is so nearly arid that ceremonies could be held in a roofless inclosure and their time determined other than by the weather.

The esoteric portions of their four great dances were gone through with in full by the Karok priests each year, as is only proper for rites that renew and establish the world. So far as actual records go, however, the Deerskin dances were made only in alternate years, although those of Panamenik and Katimin came in the same year. Biennially the war dance was substituted for them. This calls for no display of wealth and is likely, therefore, to have drawn visitors only from nearer towns, thus lessening the burden of entertainment on the rich men of the home village. Whether the great dances were made biennially or annually before the American intruded is not certain.

RITES AT KATIMIN.

At Katimin the old man in charge of the ceremony sleeps for 10 nights in the sacred sweat house there. This, at least in its present form, is not a true sweat house, but a squarer and higher structure, not slept in at other times. (Pl. 12.) During the days he is in the sacred living house; but each day he visits a different rock or spot in the hills and speaks to it the requisite part of his long formula. It it said that this formula was not treated as private property—that is, not sold or inherited outright—but that the old man would teach it to a younger one who evinced memory, interest, and concentration. This might often be his assistant, it may be assumed, or, if not, then a son or nephew. It does not seem likely that a Karok would allow so important a possession as this knowledge to pass to any other than a kinsman in some degree.

Besides his assistant the priest is accompanied by two virgins, or perhaps girls not yet adolescent, who seem to gather wood for his fire in the living house and to cook the light portions of acorn gruel on which alone he subsists. For the same 10 days he speaks to no person, does not turn his head to look or listen, and is addressed by no one. On each visit to a sacred spot he is followed by a band of young men, who shoot at marks and play along the way. Meanwhile visitors begin to arrive and camp on the sand bar by the river.

The 10 days come to a climax on the last night at the *yuhpit*, a foot-high hillock of clean sand near a large pepper tree at the edge of the bluff on which Katimin stands. (Pl. 22.) The two maidens clean this of any rubbish that may have accumulated and add to it each year one basketful of clean sand from the river. They descend to this, cook acorn gruel at the water's edge, and, carrying it up to the *yuhpit*, give it to the young men who have accompanied the priest on his daily journeyings. In the evening the old man brings out a sacred stool or seat from the sweat house, sets it on the sand pile, and, with his drill, kindles new fire before the assembled people. As he throws something on and the blaze burns up he calls out, and all except he cover their faces until he orders them to cease. Whoever looked would be bitten by a snake during the year. For the remainder of the night he sits or stands on his holy seat, perhaps reciting prayer or formula at times, and the people, or some of them, remain about, " helping him to keep awake " by their jests and laughter.

The combination of the use of sand in the *yuhpit* and of the fact that the Karok name for the world which is established by the rite is *isivsanen*, has led to strange reports that this is a " sift sand " ceremony.

The next day begins the Deerskin dance. The priest is still attended by the two girls, and daily mutters his story while casting angelica root into the fire before the dancers commence. For the last day's dance they line up between the *yuhpit* and the pepperwood. Two parties, representing Aftaram and Katimin, compete in the dance. In old days there may have been more.

RITES AT PANAMENIK AND INAM.

At Orleans the course of the ceremony is similar. Its central feature, the kindling of a fire which may not be looked at, is called *wilela'o* by the Yurok. Whether there is anything corresponding to the *yuhpit* is not known. Elements of this kind are often local among the northwestern tribes. There is some doubt whether the ceremony begins in the Panamenik or Tachanak sweat house. The dance is at Chamikininich, concluding at a spot on the opposite western shore called Tishanishunukich.

Of the Inam ceremony nothing is known except that it is called *irahivi*. It and the two foregoing esoteric rites, as well as public dances, are said to have been instituted by the same *ikhareya* or ancient spirit as he traveled downstream. The formulas are, however, distinct, although no doubt of similar tenor.

RITES AT AMAIKIARA.

The Amaikiara new year ceremony also centers about a fire that mortals may not see; but this is made during the day, and there is a ritualistic eating of the first salmon of the season. The priest or formula reciter is called *fatawenan*, and with his assistant has fasted—that is, subsisted on thin acorn mush—for "many days," probably 10. Early on the morning of the great day the men who have been with him in the Amaikiara sweat house emerge and shout to the people of the town and of Ashanamkarak across the river to leave. Everybody packs up his food and starts uphill. No one may eat until the summit of the ridge is reached. There they feast, play, and shoot at a mark, but never look back, for whoever saw the sacred smoke arising would sicken before long.

A woman assistant is ferried across the river to Ashanamkarak. Going uphill, she cuts down a small madroña tree, splits the whole of it into kindling, and carries the load down to the river's edge at Ashanamkarak, after which she returns to Amaikiara and spends the remainder of the day fasting in the sacred house *wenaram.*

Toward noon the priest and his assistant leave the sweat house, bathe, paint themselves, and cross to Ashanamkarak. Here, in a small cleared space among the tumbled rocks, stands an altar (Pl. 6), a rude cube of stone about a foot high, the only instance known in California of a true altar, unless the southern California ground paintings be so reckoned. This the assistant repairs, then starts a fire near it with the madroña wood. He also cooks and eats a salmon. How and when this is taken, and whether it is caught at the spot, which is noted for its fish eddies, are not certain. The priest himself merely deposits tobacco to the deities, directs by signs, and speaks his formula "inside"—that is, thinks or mumbles it. He utters no word and is in too holy a state to perform any act. Later in the afternoon the pair return to Amaikiara, where they are received in the sweat house by the men who have remained within, to the same song to whose strains they left it. Toward evening these men come out and shout to the people to return.

For 10 days more the *fatawenan* and his assistant remain seated in the *wenaram* and sleep in the sacred sweat house. The people, however, make the Jumping dance at Ashatak, opposite the mouth of the Salmon, and conclude the last day by dancing at Ashapipmam, while those of Katimin come down and dance simultaneously across the mouth at Itiwuntunuta. In the Jumping dance the Karok use eight long poles, *ahuvareiktin*, painted red and black, which afterwards the young men try to take from one another and break. This is a feature not known from the Yurok and Hupa, except for an incident in the customs of the former when they build the dam at Kepel.

GENERAL CHARACTER OF THE RITES.

The ceremonies described are all unquestionably of " new year " type, and have calendrical association with the moon. Yet, to judge by Yurok analogy, the Karok year, or reckoning of the moons, began at the winter solstice, when there were no public rites. The concept of a renewal or reestablishing of the world for another round of the seasons was, however, strong in all four of the ceremonies, each of which was believed to contribute an indispensable part to this end. The new fire element, which is so marked, has not yet been discovered in any part of California other than the northwest; some form of first salmon rite appears to have been in use in nearly all those parts of the State in which the fish abounded.

GIRLS' ADOLESCENCE CEREMONY.

Like the Hupa, but unlike the Yurok, the Karok made a dance for adolescent girls. Contrary to the usual Californian custom, this dance was performed chiefly by men—a distinctly northwestern attitude. The opening was especially reminiscent of the Deerskin dance: men stood in line, the singer in the middle, the girl danced back and forth before them. Then followed a round dance such as is most common in the ceremony elsewhere in California. A ring of men surrounded the maiden, a circle of women stood outside, and both revolved dextrally. One by one the men took the girl from behind and danced with her. Finally the war or defiance dance was made, apparently by the men only, lined up abreast. No one wore regalia of much moment. The girl herself had on a little visor of jay feathers, and carried a rattle of deer hoofs, an implement used in this dance by almost all groups of California. Neither object is employed by the Yurok.

The dance was made at night to keep the girl awake; she herself shook the rattle. For 10 days she ate no flesh and drank no water, might not look at the sun or sky, could not touch water to her face. Each morning she carried to the house 10 loads of wood cut by a female relative. On the last day she emerged early and ran back and forth 10 times, motioning at the morning star as if to catch it, and asking it to give her long life and many dentalia. The entire observance was repeated twice subsequently.

SCOPE OF RELIGION.

Some of the present-day Karok state that they, the Shasta, and more easterly tribes excelled the Hupa in able shamans as well as powerful wizards, but that the Hupa formula for purification from a corpse was longer and more exacting. This belief is probably significant. The formulas are a more specialized development than belief in guardian spirits and poisons. They should therefore be worked out more fully at the center of the area in which they prevail, the generalized practices rather in the marginal and surrounding regions.

The following religious vocabulary may be of interest:

em, supernatural power, such as a shaman possesses.
em-yav, " good shaman."
patunukot, sucking shaman.
maharav, clairvoyance.
anav, a sacred formula.
anava-kiavan, one who knows formulas, either to cure sickness with herbs or for any other purpose.
ara-tamva, "person die," a pain, *i. e.*, disease object.

apuruwan, an "Indian devil," *i. e.*, a person secretly possessing a magical object that produces death; also apparently the object itself.

yumara, ghost, spirit of a dead human being.

ikhareya, ancient spirit, *i. e.*, member of the race of beings that preceded mankind. Yurok *woge*, Hupa *kihunai*.

yash-arara, "real person," a human being; also, a true man, one of wealth and authority, a "chief."

kemish, any monster; also poison; also wickedly fearless.

ipshanmaskarav, poison.

pikship, "shadow," soul.

imya, breath, life.

ikhareya-kupa, ordained by the former spirit race, sacredly established.

pikuah, myths.

ih, to dance; *ih-an.* dancer.

ih-uk, girl's adolescence dance.

hapish, to make the "brush" or curing dance.

wuwuhina, any great dance, either the Jumping or the Deerskin dance; *wuwuhansh*, those who make or provide for such a dance.

ishkaship, "leap up," the Jumping dance.

isivsanen pikiavish, "making the world," the "new year's" ceremonies at Katimin, Amaikiara, etc.

isivsanen pikiavan, "world maker," the old man who recites the formula for this rite.

fata-wen-an, another name for him at Amaikiara.

sharuk-iruhishrihan, "down hill he eats salmon," or *sharuk-amavan*, "down hill he leaves salmon," the assistant in the Amaikiara ceremony.

ahup-pikiavan, "wood maker," the woman assistant who cuts firewood; there are two at Katimin.

imushan, the male assistant at Katimin.

wen-aram, the sacred house at Amaikiara associated with the "new year's" rite.

kimachiram iship, the sacred "sweat house" of the corresponding Katimin ceremony.

isivsanen iktatik, "makes firm the world," a sacred stone kept in this house.

NAMES.

Children were named only after they had attained several years; as the Karok say, so that, "if they died young, they would not be thought of by their names." People will not tell their own names, and are exceedingly reluctant to mention those of their kinsmen and friends, even if the latter are not present to be embarrassed. It is a penalized offense to speak the name of a dead person and the height of bad manners to use that of a living person to his face, unless the closest intimacy exists. Even in reference to living people clumsy circumlocutions spring up, such as Panamenik-wapu, "born at (or belonging to) Orleans," or designations by allusion to the particular house inhabited. This feeling causes even derogatory nicknames, such as Pihnefich, " coyote," to be preferred to the real name. In address, terms such as " old man," " Hupa man," " widower," " married woman," "widow," are very frequent. Most of the personal names seem to us very trivial, when they are not based on some peculiarity of habit; but in the case of girls there appears some inclination to bestow names that are pretty. Perhaps these are secondary pet names, just as the designations by occupation or characteristic are probably not true personal names. A few examples are: Akuni-hashki, " shoots swiftly "; Kemhisem, " roamer " or " traveler "; Anifakich, " walks down hill slowly "; Ma'ikiviripuni, " runs down from up the hill "; Sichakutvaratiha, " wide belt "; Taharatan, " flint flaker " or " bullet molder "; and for girls, I'niwach, " dripping water "; Hatimnin, " butterfly."

CONCLUSION.

Beaver-teeth dice are attributed to the Karok in one or two museum collections. This is an Oregonian form of game, and may have reached the Karok only since the American occupation. It is true that the upper Karok are geographically nearer to tribes like the Klamath and Modoc than to the mussel-gathering Yurok of the coast; but their culture as a whole being so thoroughly northwestern, and showing so little eastward leaning, raises a generic presumption against any eastern practices that are not definitely corroborated.

Data are scarcely available for a fuller sketch of Karok culture. Nor is such an account necessary in the present connection. In at least ninety-five institutions out of every hundred, all that has been said of the Yurok or is on record concerning the Hupa applies identically to the Karok. Here nothing further has been attempted than to depict their relation to their land and to note some of the minor peculiarities of their culture and its departure from the most integral form of northwestern civilization.

PLATE 22

THE KAROK CENTER OF THE WORLD: SACRED TOWN OF KATIMIN ON LEFT BANK OF KLAMATH; ISHIPISHI ON OPPOSITE SIDE ACROSS RAPIDS; AUICH PEAK BELOW, HIDING THE MOUTH OF SALMON RIVER; AND BEYOND, THE RIDGE UP WHICH GO THE SOULS OF THE DEAD

PLATE 23

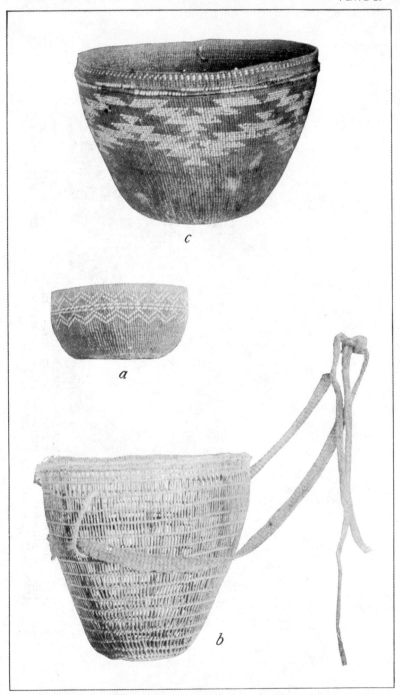

WIYOT BASKETS

For eating (*a*), carrying (*b*), and cooking (*c*).

CHAPTER 6.

THE CHIMARIKO AND WIYOT.

THE CHIMARIKO.

The Chimariko were one of the smallest distinct tribes in one of the smallest countries in America. They are now known to be an offshoot from the large and scattered Hokan stock, but as long as they passed as an independent family they and the Esselen served ethnologists as extreme examples of the degree to which aboriginal speech diversification had been carried in California.

Two related and equally minute nations were neighbors of the Chimariko: the New River Shasta and the Konomihu. The language of these clearly shows them to be offshoots from the Shasta. But Chimariko is so different from both, and from Shasta as well, that it must be reckoned as a branch of equal age and independence as Shasta, which deviated from the original Hokan stem in very ancient times. It seems likely that Chimariko has preserved its words and constructions as near their original form as any Hokan language; better than Shasta, which is much altered, or Pomo, which is worn down.

The entire territory of the Chimariko in historic times was a 20-mile stretch of the canyon of Trinity River from above the mouth of South Fork to French Creek (Fig. 8). Here lay their half dozen hamlets, Tsudamdadji at Burnt Ranch being the largest. In 1849 the whole population of the Chimariko was perhaps 250. In 1906 there remained a toothless old woman and a crazy old man. Except for a few mixed bloods, the tribe is now utterly extinct.

The details of the fighting between the Chimariko and the miners in the sixties of the last century have not been recorded, and perhaps well so; but the struggle must have been bitter and was evidently the chief cause of the rapid diminution of the little tribe.

Since known to the Americans, the Chimariko have been hostile to the Hupa downstream, but friendly with the Wintun upriver from them. Yet their location, with reference to that of the latter people and the other Penutians, makes it possible that at some former time

the Chimariko were crowded down the Trinity River by these same
Wintun.

The Chimariko called themselves Chimariko or Chimaliko, from
chimar, person. The Hupa they called Hichhu; the Wintun, Pachhuai—perhaps from *pachhu*, "willow"; the Konomihu, Hunomichu—
possibly from *hunoi-da*, "north"; the Hyampom Wintun, Maitro-
ktada—from *maitra*, "flat, river bench"; the Wiyot, Aka-traiduwa-

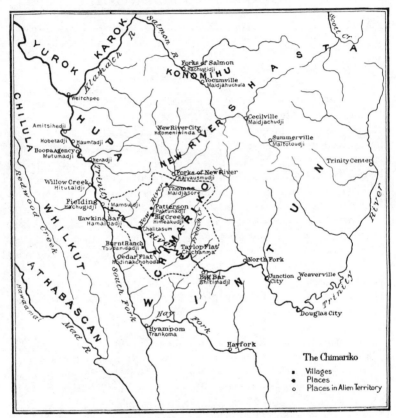

FIG. 8.—Chimariko land, towns, and neighbors.

ktada,—perhaps from *aka*, "water." Djalitasum was New River,
probably so called from a spot at its mouth. They translated into
their own language the names of the Hupa villages, which indicates
that distrust and enmity did not suppress all intercourse or intermarriage. Takimitlding, the "acorn-feast-place," they called Hope-
tadji, from *hopeu*, "acorn soup"; Medilding, "boat-place," was
Mutuma-dji, from *mutuma*, "canoe." The Hupa knew the Chimariko as Tl'omitta-hoi.

The customs of the Chimariko were patterned after those of the Yurok and Hupa in the degree that a poor man's habits may imitate those of his more prosperous neighbor. Their river was too small and rough for canoes, so they waded or swam it. They used Vancouver Island dentalium shells for money, when they could get them; but were scarcely wealthy enough to acquire slaves, and too few to hold or sell fishing places as individual property. Their dress and tattooing were those of the downstream tribes; their basketry was similar, but the specializations and refinements of industry of the Hupa, the soapstone dishes, wooden trunks, curved stone-handled adzes, elaborately carved soup stirrers and spoons, and rod armor, they went without, except as sporadic pieces might reach them in barter.

With all their rudeness they had, however, the outlook on life of the other northwestern tribes—a sort of poor relation's pride. Thus they would not touch the grasshoppers and angleworms which are sufficiently nutritious to commend themselves as food to the unsophisticated Wintun and tribes farther inland, but which the prouder Hupa and Yurok disdained. The only custom in which the Chimariko are known to have followed Wintun instead of Hupa precedent—though there may have been other instances which have not been recorded—was their manner of playing the guessing game, in which they hid a single short stick or bone in one of two bundles of grass, instead of mingling one marked rod among 50 unmarked ones.

The Chimariko house illustrates their imperfect carrying out of the completer civilization of their neighbors. It had walls of vertical slabs, a ridgepole, and a laid roof with no earth covering. These points show it to be descended from the same fundamental type of all wood dwelling which prevails, in gradually simplifying form, from Alaska to the Yurok. But walls and roof were of fir bark instead of split planks. The length was 4 or 5 yards as against 7 on the Klamath River, the central excavation correspondingly shallow. The corners were rounded. A draft hole and food passage broke the wall opposite the door where the Yurok or Hupa would only take out a corpse. And the single ridgepole gave only two pitches to the roof—a construction known also to the lower tribes, but officially designated by them as marking the " poor man's house," the superior width of their normal dwelling requiring two ridge poles and three slants of roof.

Chimariko religion was a similar abridged copy. Sickness, and, on the other hand, the medicine woman's power to cure it, were caused by the presence in the body of " pains," small double-pointed animate objects, which disappeared in the extracting doctor's palm.

The fast and uncleanness after contact with the dead lasted five days, and had to be washed away. Such more elementary beliefs and ritual practices for the individual the Chimariko shared with the other northwestern tribes. But the great national dances of the Yurok, Karok, and Hupa, held at spots hallowed by myth, colored by songs of a distinctive character, dignified by the display of treasures of native wealth, and connected with sacred first-fruit or even world-renewal ceremonies, these more momentous rituals the Chimariko lacked even the pretense of, nor did they often visit their neighbors to see them. They were a little people in its declining old age when civilization found and cut them off.

THE WIYOT.

HABITAT AND AFFILIATIONS.

The Wiyot, a small body of shore-dwelling people, join with the adjacent Yurok to constitute the Algonkins of California. A certain resemblance between the two languages was noted on first acquaintance, and their ultimate affinity suspected. Fuller data revealed a great difference. When a beginning of analysis was finally possible, the structure of the two idioms was seen to be very similar; after which comparison showed a certain number of common stems. They were then united as the single Ritwan stock; but renewed examination established this as but a member and distant outpost on the Pacific of the great Algonquian family of central and eastern North America (Fig. 9).

Wiyot territory fell into three natural divisions: lower Mad River, Humboldt Bay, and lower Eel River. The natives had a name for each district: Batawat, Wiki, and Wiyot. The people of each region were called by names formed from these words by the suffixion of the element -daredalil. Wiyot, while thus properly only the name of a district, was used for the entire stock by most of the neighboring groups: the Yurok say Weyet or Weyot, the Karok Waiyat. The Athabascan Sinkyone, up Eel River, are more correct in restricting the term to the country, and call the inhabitants Dilwishne, which they explain as an onomatopoetic word descriptive of the strange sound of Wiyot speech. As the stock has no name for itself as a body, the designation Wiyot is perhaps as appropriate as can be found. Wishosk, which for a time was in vogue in the books, is a misapplication of the Wiyot denotation of their Athabascan neighbors: Wishashk. Their own language the Wiyot call Sulatelak. The ending of this word is also found in Wishi-lak, Athabascan language.

The Mad River Wiyot associated considerably with the Coast Yurok and were tolerably acquainted with their language. This fact has led to conflicting statements as to the northern boundary of Wiyot holdings. As nearly as can be ascertained, this lay just south of Little River, at whose mouth stood the Yurok town of Metskwo. The upper part of Little River was Chilula hunting ground. On Mad River, Blue Lake, near the forks, was still Wiyot. The main stream from here up was Whilkut, that is, Athabascan. The North Fork was without villages and is in doubt. The Wiyot owned at least the lower portion; and on Map 10 the whole of its drainage has been assigned to

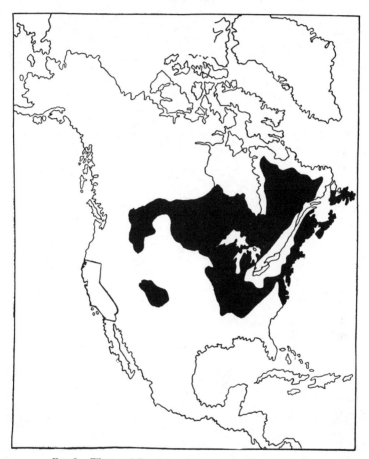

FIG. 9.—Wiyot and Yurok in relation to the Algonkin family.

them. From Mad River south to Eel River Wiyot territory extended to the first range inland. Jacoby, Freshwater, and Salmon Creeks, Elk River, and Boynton Prairie were thus Wiyot; Kneeland Prairie and Lawrence Creek, Whilkut and Nongatl Athabascan. On Eel River the boundary came at Eagle Prairie, near Riodell. Southwest of Eel River, the Bear River mountains separated the Wiyot from another Athabascan division, the Mattole. The spurs of this range reach the sea at Cape Fortunas, between Guthrie Creek and Oil Creek.

The greatest extension of Wiyot territory is only about 35 miles, the greatest breadth barely 15. Their ocean frontage is low and sandy, as compared with the precipitous and rocky coast for long distances on both sides. Three or four miles north of their boundary

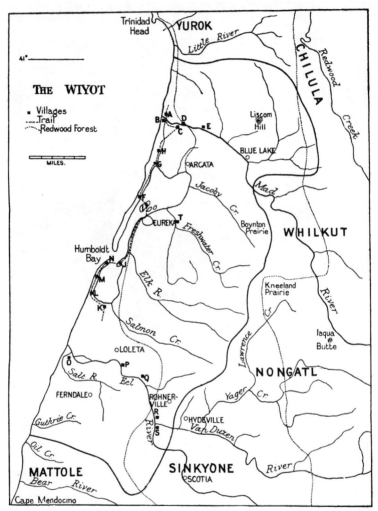

FIG. 10.—Wiyot towns and territory.

is Trinidad Head; 5 or 6 south, Cape Mendocino; both conspicuous headlands. The greater part of Wiyot territory was heavy forest, mainly of redwood. The balance was sand dunes, tidal marsh, or open prairie. Every Wiyot settlement lay on a stream or bay; the majority on tidewater.

SETTLEMENTS.

The Wiyot towns are known only in part. For the plurality the Yurok names are recorded with more certainty than the proper Wiyot designations. On the Eel River section information is particularly scant; most of the entries in Figure 10 may be only place names. Mad River is also likely to have been settled farther up than Osok; and it is not clear whether Kumaidada was a settlement or an uninhabited spot.[1]

WIYOT VILLAGES.

Designation in Fig. 10.	Wiyot name.	Yurok name.
A		Ma'awor.
B	Tabagaukwa (?)	Tegwol.
C	We'tso (?)	Erlerw.
D	Kachewinach (?)	Sepola.
E		Osok.
F	Tabayat; Witki (?)	Teuhpo.
G	Kotsir (?)	Erterker.
H	Tokelomigimitl (?)	Eni'koletl.
I	Dulawat	Olog.
J	Potitlik, Cherokigechk, Pletswak (?).	Oknutl.
K	Yachwanawach	Lumatl.
L	Legetku (?)	Leptlen.
M	Bimire	Pimin.
N	Dakduwaka· Hiluwitl (?)	Ayo.
O	Ho'ket (?)	
P	Wuktlakw (?)	
Q	Dakwagerawakw (?)	
R	Watsayeriditl (?)	
S	Hakitege (?)	
T	Kumaidada	Hikets.

The names of the villages from Salmon Creek to the South Spit (K to N) may be confused.

[1] Loud, Ethnogeography and Archaeology of the Wiyot Territory, 1918 (see bibliography), gives a map with nearly 200 sites, 32 of them the principal settlements in 1850: 10 on Mad River, 14 on Humboldt Bay, 8 on Eel River. A number of these identify with the sites in Figure 10, but in most cases under different names (pp. 258–272, 286–296).

NUMBERS.

The five named towns on Mad River are credited with the following numbers of houses, according to two Yurok sources:

Ma'awor_____ 7   4
Tegwol_____ 3
Erlerw_____ 20
Sepola _____ 15   10
Osok_____ 5   4

This gives averages of 9 and 6 houses per village. The latter figure is that obtaining among the Yurok and probably higher than that for the Chilula, and is more likely to be correct. At this rate, the population of the five settlements would have been a little over 200; and the entire Wiyot population would have amounted to perhaps 800, or not over 1,000. An 1853 estimate set the former figure. The 1910 census yielded over 150; but classed half of them as of mixed blood.

The following estimates are of interest:

	Wiyot.	Yurok.	Karok.	Hupa.	Chilula.
Miles of river navigable to a canoe......	25	50	60	35	(30)
Population.............................	500	1,800	1,500	1,000	600
Per mile...............	20	35	25	30	20
Miles of ocean, bay, or lagoon shore	50	50	....	....	....
Population.............................	500	700	....	....	....
Per mile.............................	10	15	....	....	....

It is clear that streams were more sought as habitations than the coast in this part of California. Furthermore, practically all of the coast settlements, among the Tolowa and Yurok as well as the Wiyot, lay on bays, lagoons, or the mouths of streams rather than on the ocean shore itself.

PLACE NAMES.

These are Wiyot names for foreign places: Datogak, Oil Creek; Chwaregadachitl, Bear River; Tsekiot, Cape Mendocino; Wecharitl, south of the mouth of Mattole River. These are in Mattole territory. Wiyot "Metol" may be the source of this name, or merely taken over from the Americans.

Yurok places: Pletkatlshamalitl, Little River; Dakachawayawik, Trinidad village, Yurok Tsurau; Ktlonechk, Trinidad Head; Chirokwan, Patrick Point; Ri'tsap, a village on Big Lagoon; Tsi'push, St.   Lagoon, Yurok Tsahpekw; Hapsh, Redwood Creek. Yurok Orekw; Chug   echwelage, Redding Rock; Eshkapsh, Gold Bluff, Yurok Espau; Katkadalitl, Requa, Yurok Rekwoi; Ikti'n, the Klamath River; Dalitlrukiwar, Wilson Creek, Yurok, O'men; Takeluwalitl, Weitchpec, Yurok Weitspus, also the Trinity River.

The Karok village of Panamenik at Orleans was Gatsewinas.

In Athabascan territory: Kawa'tlakw, on Redwood Creek, below Bair; Tanataptlagerawakw, at Bair; Dalekwuta'tl, Berry, on the same stream; Wameriwauk, upstream; Talawulitskilik, Bald Hills, between Redwood Creek and the Klamath; Dat-hanetkek, Murphy; Pletalauleli'n, Three Cabins; Pletkukach, Mad River Gap, or near it; Gukech, Kneeland Prairie.

Wiyot names of tribes: All Athabascans, Wishashk; Yurok (the language), Denakwate-lak; Karok, Guradalitl, the speech, Guradalitl-rakwe-lak; Tolowa, Dalawa; Hupa, Haptana; Wintun or Chimariko of the upper Trinity, Deiwin.

It appears from several of the foregoing examples that the Wiyot and Yurok did not always follow the regional practice of translating or making anew each other's village names, but occasionally took them over with merely phonetic alteration.

MATERIAL CULTURE.

In their industries the Wiyot were mates of the Yurok. Their habitat supplied certain distinctive materials and now and then favored a minor degree of specialization. Clams largely took the place of mussels, salt-water fishing was practicable but hunting of little consequence, slightly different basketry woof fibers were available than in the interior, and so on. But the endeavors and methods of the culture are those of Yurok culture; and that on the social as well as the tangible side. Houses, baskets (pl. 23), dentalium money, and a hundred other objects were the same and were used and valued alike, apparently. Together with the lower Yurok and the Tolowa, the Wiyot were the makers of the canoe of northwestern type, whose manufacture can only be carried on where the redwood grows close to the water.

SHAMANISM.

Shamans were chiefly women, and acquired their powers on mountain tops at night. Some people, too, were pitied by powerful lake spirits, and became physically strong and brave. Shamans in practicing wore a headband from which hung two long strings of feathers (Fig. 11, c), and shoved condor feathers into their stomachs. There were those who only diagnosed while dancing and singing and others who also sucked out disease objects and blood. The disease "pains" were minute, wormlike, self-moving, soft, and transparent. They were sometimes sucked through the tobacco pipe (Fig. 11, a), which was a standard unit of the shaman's equipment. The pains were called *silak*. This word recalls the disease-causing apparatus that the Maidu name *sila*.

Dikwa means "spirit" or "supernatural." The word is applied to the Americans and also denotes magical poison. A woman's monthly condition is called *dikwa-laketl*, and the helpers of shamans were *wishi-dikwa*, "inland spirits," from their inhabiting the hills.

ETHICS.

Bodily and social self-restraint in daily life was as much inculcated by the Wiyot as by the Yurok. It was only through this quality that a man could be anything in the world. Only through its exercise could he retain his riches and become wealthier. Self-control marked the rich man and was the evidence as well as the cause of his standing. The poor man was inherently inferior. He did not gravely and naturally hold himself in, because he could not. It was impossible that he should ever kill a white deer or have any other great piece of fortune. The psychic influence of these beliefs

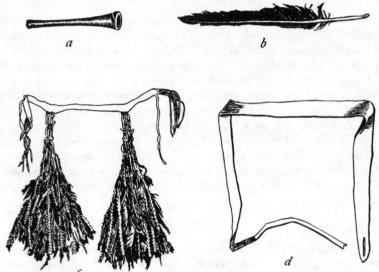

FIG. 11.—Wiyot shaman's outfit.   a, Pipe; b, condor feather; c, headdress; d, elk-skin belt.

must have been profound, so that in large measure they must have justified themselves in experience.

CEREMONIALS.

The Wiyot did not make the White Deerskin dance. They made the Jumping dance only at or near the village of Shepola on Mad River, apparently much as the Yurok made it, and with many visitors from the Coast Yurok.

A dance of somewhat different type, but reckoned as equivalent to the Deerskin dance, was made at Hieratgak, on the North Spit of Humboldt Bay. This was held in a house for five days. A woman stood in the middle of the line of dancers, some of whom wore obsidian blades hanging from the neck, instead of carrying them as among the other northwestern tribes. A Yurok account puts this dance at Olog and has it visited by the more southerly of the Coast Yurok.

The dance on Eel River is entirely unknown.

The adolescence ceremony for girls was well developed. For 5 or 10 days the maiden sat covered in the house fasting. Each night the people danced. At the conclusion she was taken by a number of women into still salt water. They stood waist deep facing the shore in a line and bent forward in unison to the song, sending a miniature breaker up the beach with each sway.

BELIEFS.

Wiyot mythology is of interest because it consists of the usual northwestern ideas to which a strange element has been added which can only have come from central California, through the Athabascan groups to the south. The narrative formulas by which the Hupa and Yurok believed they existed were in full force. Gatswokwire or Rakshuatlaketl is the exact equivalent of the Yurok Wohpekumeu. He wandered over the earth satisfying an unquenchable erotic impulse, but also did good. He obtained for the world the salmon that were jealously hidden away by their owner; he made children to be born without killing their mothers. He instituted dances and many other human practices, the formulas necessary for which go back to his actions. Sometimes his amativeness brought him into trouble, as when the Skate woman lay on the beach to attract him and carried him across the ocean; but he was never permanently vanquished.

With Gudatrigakwitl, "above old man," we encounter a conception of which there is no trace among the Yurok. He existed before the earth, he made it, made the first man Chkekowik or Wat the haliotis, made all human beings, animals, acorns, boats, string, other utensils, the weather, even dances. He used no materials and no tools. He merely thought, or joined and spread apart his hands, and things were. He lives now and will exist as long as the world.

It is possible that this deity has been given increased prominence by the modern generation of Wiyot if the Ghost dance of 1872 reached them, but he is introduced into too many ideas that are ancient and general in northwestern belief to allow his being ascribed in any large measure to that new and passing doctrine. Moreover, the concept of a supreme god and outright creator is found among many Californian tribes: the southern Athabascans, the Yuki, the Wintun, the Maidu.

Another peculiarity of Wiyot mythology is its fondness for animal characters. This is a generic Californian rather than a central Californian trait; but it is a deviation from the specialized northwestern type of myth as revealed in its extreme Yurok or Hupa form.

The story of the origin of death shows northwestern and central motives. Spinagaralu, locust larva, or sand cricket, was responsible. According to one account he disputed with and prevailed over Above old man, who had intended people to be reborn or regenerated 10 times. In another tale, more distinctly central Californian, Spinagaralu refuses to let Frog's dead child come back to life. When his own perishes, he wishes to restore the old order, but Frog is now obdurate.

It is clear that the Wiyot are northwesterners; wholly so in institutions and material accomplishments, but with some first traces of the much wider spread central Californian culture appearing in their religion.

CHAPTER 7.

ATHABASCANS: THE TOLOWA.

THE ATHABASCANS OF CALIFORNIA.

ORIGIN AND MOVEMENTS.

The peculiar conservative genius that pervades all Athabascan tongues rendered the early recognition of those on the Pacific coast easy, in spite of the great distances that separate these tongues from their congeners in the northwestern tundras and forests and in the arid highlands of New Mexico. The origin of the vastly distributed family is, however, as obscure as its coherence is obvious. This is a problem involving an understanding of all ancient North America, and the fragments of the stock in California can contribute only a minute quota to the solution. It is superficially probable, as a glance at a map of the continent will sustain, that the Pacific coast can scarcely have been the first home of the family when it was still united. The Pacific coast Athabascans were therefore immigrants of some remote period; and for those of California, their extreme southerly position makes it probable that they drifted into their present seats from the north.

This movement must not be underestimated as recent; and there must have been many crowdings and rollings about, perhaps even refluxes. On the map, for instance, the Kato look as if they were invaders who had nearly split the Yuki in two and might have made the division complete if the white man had left them alone a few more generations. But such an assumption is pure speculation. It is not beyond the limits of possibility that the Kato have been in their present seats for a very long time, and that in recent centuries it has been the Yuki who gradually confined and nearly surrounded them. Any hypothesis on these points is as yet only a guess.

Two things argue against any rapid conquering march of the Athabascans southward: their assimilation to their linguistically alien neighbors in culture, and in bodily form. The Hupa are as wholly and integrally a part of the hearth of the northwestern civilization as are the Algonkin Yurok or the Hokan Karok. The Lassik show Wintun influences. The Wailaki were similar to the Yuki. And the Kato were substantially one in customs and beliefs with the Coast Yuki. Within the short distance of less than 100 miles, therefore, there were Athabascans of entirely northwestern and of entirely central culture: a situation which could have arisen only among long sessile populations of contracted outlook.

In northwestern California, as in southwestern Oregon, a single physical type is the predominant one among the multitudinous tribes: a tallish stature with round head. These are also the traits of the Athabascans in the northwest and the southwest of the continent.

It is therefore quite possible that the prevalence of this type in the region where California and Oregon adjoin is due to a sustained and abundant infusion of Athabascan blood. But as Athabascans and non-Athabascans are indistinguishable, a considerable period must be allowed for this assimilation of the once separate and presumably different races that now are blended.

In the extreme south the result has been the reverse, but the process the same. The Wailaki have taken on the narrow-headed, stumpy-bodied type of the Yuki—a markedly localized type, by the way.

CLASSIFICATION.

The Athabascan dialects of California fall into four groups: the Tolowa, which is connected with the Oregonian tongues of Chetco and Rogue Rivers; the Hupa group; the small and undiversified Mattole, whose distinctness is not readily explainable either by the topography of their habitat or by a juxtaposition to alien neighbors, and therefore indicates the operation of an unknown historical factor—unless Mattole shall prove to be a subdivision of Hupa; and the Southern or Kineste or Kuneste or Wailaki group, the most widely spread of the four.

For the sake of exactness a fifth group might be added, that of the Rogue River people, to whom a narrow strip along the northern edge of the State, in contact with the Shasta, and another adjacent to the Tolowa, have been assigned on the map. Both these belts are only a few miles wide and high up in the mountains. They may have been visited and hunted in; they were certainly not settled. They represent a little marginal fringe which nominally laps into the present consideration only because the artificial State lines that set a boundary to this study do not coincide exactly with the barriers set by nature.

The Athabascans were a hill people, and most of them inhabited their permanent homes by the side of rivers only during a part of each year. But their territories coincide almost as exactly with stream drainages as if a systematist had planned their ditribution. This relation appears in the following tabulation:

TOLOWA GROUP	Smith River drainage.
HUPA GROUP	Trinity-Redwood-Mad drainage.
Hupa	Lower Trinity River.
Chilula	Lower Redwood Creek.
Whilkut	Mad River (and upper Redwood drainage.)
MATTOLE GROUP (Distinctness doubtful.)	Mattole and Bear River drainages (and a short stretch of Lower Eel River).
SOUTHERN GROUP	All Eel River drainage from the first forks up, except for the headwaters which were Yuki.
Nongatl	Yager, Van Dusen, and Larrabee Creeks (and upper Mad River).
Lassik	Main Eel River in the vicinity of Dobbins Creek.
Wailaki	Main Eel River in the vicinity of the North Fork.
Sinkyone	Lower reaches of the South Fork of Eel River.
Kato	Headwaters of the South Fork of Eel River.

LANDWARD OUTLOOK.

It is a remarkable fact that with all the immense range of the Athabascan family as a whole—probably the greatest, in mere miles, of any stock represented on the continent—they approach the sea in an endless number of places, but actually held its shores over only three or four brief frontages. Two of these lie in California; but even here the strange impulse toward the interior is manifest. The inland range of the California Athabascans has double the length of their coastal distribution. Yurok, Wiyot, and Yukian territories lie between the ocean and an Athabascan hinterland. Not one of the 10 Athabascan groups just enumerated is more than 30 miles from the boom of the surf. Yet only 3 of the 10 hold a foot of beach. It may have been the play of historical accident and nothing more, but it is hard to rid the mind of the thought that in this perverse distribution we may be face to face with something basal that has persisted through the wanderings of thousands of years and the repeated reshapings of whole cultures.

THE TOLOWA.

TERRITORY.

The Tolowa, whose speech constitutes the first and most northerly Athabascan dialect group in California, are the Indians of Del Norte County, in the northwestern corner of the State. The lowest dozen miles of the Klamath River are, it is true, in the same county, according to one of the arbitrary delimitations to which the American is addicted, and there were and are nearly as many Yurok on this stretch of stream as the remainder of the county held Athabascans. But the connections and outlook of these Yurok were up their river or southward along the coast, toward their more numerous kinsmen in what the white man calls Humboldt County. Ethnologically, the Tolowa were the people of Smith River and the adjacent ocean frontage.

Tolowa, like so many California designations of a pseudo-tribal nature, is a name alien to the people to whom it applies. It is of Yurok origin. These people say *ni-tolowo*, "I speak Athabascan of the Tolowa variety," but *no-mimohsigo*, "I speak Athabascan of the Hupa-Chilula-Whilkut variety." As the two groups are separated by the Algonkin Yurok, their distinction by these people is natural, and the considerable differentiation of the two forms of speech is easily intelligible.

SETTLEMENTS.

The names and locations of the Tolowa towns as given by themselves have not been recorded. Some 8 or 10 are known under their Yurok designations, and as many under the names which the Rogue River Athabascans of Oregon applied to them. These two lists, which unfortunately can not be very definitely connected, probably include all the more important villages of the Tolowa without exhausting the total of their settlements.

The Yurok mention Nororpek, on the coast north of Smith River; Hinei, at the mouth of Smith River; Loginotl, up this stream, where it was customary to construct a salmon dam; Tolokwe, near Earl Lake or lagoon, of which Tolokwe-wonekwu, "uphill from Tolokwe," on the Pond ranch, may have been a suburb; Erertl, south of Tolokwe, but on the same body of water; Kna'awi, where the waves dash against a bluff, probably Point St. George; Kohpei, near Crescent City; and an unnamed village on the coast south of this town. There was also Espau, north of Crescent City, and with the same name as a Yurok village at Gold Bluff 40 miles south on the same coast; and Hineihir, "above Hinei," which might mean upstream from it on Smith River or "upstream" along the coast as the Yurok reckon, that is, south. Pekwutsu is a large rock a dozen miles from Crescent City where sea lions were hunted, and not a village. This is likely to be Northwest Seal Rock, where the lighthouse now stands.

The Oregon Athabascans know Huwunkut (compare the Hupa village of the same name) at the mouth of Smith River, and Hosa or Hwasa at one of the forks of the stream. The former is almost certainly Hinei, the latter may be Loginotl. South of Smith River, that is probably on Lake Earl, were Atakut, whence perhaps the American "Yontocketts;" Chestlish; and Echulit or Cheshanme. "Above Crescent City" was Tahinga, perhaps Yurok Kna'awi. Crescent City was Tatin, while to the south, on the coast, lay Mestetl, Tata or Tatla, and Tlusme or Tlitsusme.

The Yurok word Tolowo is apparently connected with the town name Tolok-we. "Henaggi" and "Tataten," sometimes cited as Tolowa subtribes, are only Hinei and "Tata people."[1]

A paternal gentile system that has been alleged for the Tolowa is a misconception derived from imputing to them a social organization that was proper to certain tribes in the central United States, and of which the Tolowa, and their Oregonian neighbors, did not possess a trace. The supposed clans are villages of the kind that form the basis of native society throughout California. In fact, far from being gentile subdivisions of a Tolowa "tribe," the villages were the ultimate and only political units in the Indians' consciousness; and "Tolowa," for which the bearers of the name appear to have had no specific word of their own, was nothing more than a term denoting a certain speech and implying perhaps certain customs—as nonpolitical in significance as "Anglo-Saxon."

LIMITS AND NUMBERS.

On the coast to the north, the Tolowa boundary must have been close to the Oregon line. On the south it is not exactly known. The Yurok had settlements at the mouth of Wilson Creek, 6 miles north of the mouth of the Klamath, and claimed whales that stranded on the shore as much as 3 miles beyond. It is likely that this is where Yurok and Tolowa territorial rights met; but it seems to have been 6 or 8 miles more to the first village of the latter. Inland, Tolowa suzerainty was probably coextensive with the drainage of their principal stream, a high range of the Siskiyous shutting them off from the Karok of the middle Klamath. Most of this interior tract was, however, little used except for hunting, it appears, and the habits of the group were essentially those of a coastal people.

The census of 1910 gave the Tolowa 120 souls, one-third of whom were reckoned as part white. The number at the time of settlement may be guessed at well under 1,000.

---

[1] The Tolowa towns have recently been determined by T. T. Waterman. Nororpek appears to be in Oregon and was not counted as their own by the Tolowa. On the north side of the mouth of Smith River, at Siesta Peak, was Hawinwet (cf. Huwunkut, above), "on the mountain side," Yurok Hinei. On Smith River, at the mouth of Bucket Creek, was Hatsahoto^{n}tne, "receptacle below," probably Yurok Loginotl. Farther upstream, where Bear Creek comes in, lay Melishenten, "close to hill." South from the mouth of Smith River, somewhat inland, at Yontucket, toward Lake Earl, was Yo^{n}takit, "east high," Yurok Tolakwe. In order southward there followed Echulet, Yurok Ertl, on a point projecting northward into Lake Earl; Tagia^{n}te, "pointing seaward," Yurok Kna'awi, at Point St. George; Tati^{n}ti^n, a little beyond; Metetiting, "covered," Yurok Sasoi, at Pebble Beach; Seninghat, "flat rock," Yurok Kohpei, at Crescent City; and Shinyatlchi, "summer fishing," Yurok Neketl with reference to the ending of the beach, at Nickel Creek. Assuming the number to be complete, 10 towns, at the Yurok rate, would make the Tolowa population 450.

FEUDS.

What may be called wars were indulged in between Tolowa towns as readily as between them and alien villages, though it is likely that in the former case each side was likely to be limited to kinsmen, while an expedition for revenge against a Yurok or Karok settlement might unite inhabitants of a number of towns.

In the seventies there was a feud between the Crescent City village and one or more of those on Earl Lake.

Apparently before this was a war between Hinei and Rekwoi, the Tolowa and Yurok villages at the entrance to Smith and Klamath Rivers. Blood relatives of the inhabitants, in other towns, no doubt took part; but it is significant that the other Tolowa villages, though in intermediate position, remained neutral as towns. In one encounter, each party lost three men; in another, five were killed on one side, probably the Yurok one. The occasion of this war was an old woman at Rekwoi, who by her magic stopped the salmon from going up Smith River. Now that the quarrel is long since over, the Yurok appear to take the truth of the Hinei charge for granted—the old lady must have done so, or the Tolowa would not have become angry. Moreover, she had lost relatives in former fighting against Hinei, and though this had been formally ended by money settlements for every one slain or injured, she was believed to cherish continued resentment in secret.

Rekwoi, and the still more northerly Yurok settlement of O'men, were, however, infiltrated with Tolowa blood, and reciprocally there were not a few Tolowa with Yurok wives, mothers, or grandmothers. In the war between Rekwoi and Takimitlding village in Hupa, about 1830 or 1840, the greatest war of which the Yurok have recollection, allies from the lagoon and Smith River, that is, probably, Tolokwe and Hinei, sided with the Yurok against the Athabascan Hupa and Chilula.

The Karok about the mouth of Salmon River also have recollections of a war carried on between them and the Tolowa by surprise attacks across the Siskiyous, but hostile as well as friendly intercourse between these two peoples was infrequent.

CULTURAL POSITION.

From all that is on record in print, as well as from many statements of the Yurok, it is plain that the customs, institutions, and implements of the Tolowa were similar to those of the better known Yurok and Hupa except in minor points. The Tolowa must have served as the principal purveyors to these Indians of the dentalium shells that formed the standard currency of the region and which, in Tolowa hands, must have been near the end of their slow and fluctuating drift from the source of supply in the vicinity of Vancouver Island to their final resting place in northwestern California. The Yurok regard the Tolowa as rich, a distinction they accord to few others of the people known to them.

A Tolowa redwood canoe of the type prevailing in the region, but 42 feet long and 8 feet wide—that is, twice the ordinary size—has been described as made on Smith River and used for traffic on Humboldt Bay. If this account is unexaggerated, the boat must have been made for the transport of American freight by hired Indians. For native purposes, which involved beaching, crossing dangerous bars, shooting around rocks in rapids, and dragging loads upstream, a vessel of this size would have been not only useless but impracticable; besides which it is doubtful if the Tolowa ever visited the Wiyot.

The Tolowa held the Deerskin dance that was made by the wealthier and more populous tribes of the region; and a reference to a "salmon dance" on Smith River is probably to be interpreted as evidence of one of the highly sacred and esoteric "new year" ceremonies that underlie the major dances of the Yurok, Hupa, and Karok. The doctor-making dance is like that of the Yurok; the war dance probably the same; but in the girl's adolescence ceremony and dance, in which a deer-hoof rattle is shaken, the Tolowa possess a ritual that is wanting or obsolescent among the Yurok but which they share with the remoter Karok and Hupa.

The most specific features of the northwestern California culture in its intensive form, such as the Deerskin dance, no doubt reached only to the Tolowa, perhaps in part faded out among them as among the Wiyot to the south; but the general basis of this civilization, its houses, typical canoes, basketry, tools, and social attitudes, extended with but little change beyond them into Oregon, at least along the coast. It is unfortunate that the early and rapid disintegration of the old life of the Oregon Indians makes it impossible to trace, without laborious technical studies, and then only imperfectly, the interesting connections that must have existed between the specialized little civilization that flourished around the junction of the Klamath and the Trinity, and the remarkable culture of the long North Pacific coast, of which at bottom that of northwest California is but the southernmost extension and a modification.

CHAPTER 8.

ATHABASCANS: THE HUPA, CHILULA, AND WHILKUT.

THE HUPA.

TERRITORY, NATIONALITY, AND SETTLEMENTS.

The Hupa, with the Chilula and the Whilkut, formed a close linguistic unit, considerably divergent from the other dialect groups of California Athabascans. They differed from their two nearer bodies of kinsmen largely in consequence of their habitat on a greater stream, in some fashion navigable for canoes even in summer, and flowing in a wider, sunnier valley. Their population was therefore more concentrated, at least over the favorable stretches, and their wealth greater. They were at all points the equals of the Yurok whom they adjoined where their river debouches into the Klamath, and of the Karok whose towns began a few miles above; whereas the Chilula, although reckoned by the Hupa as almost of themselves, remained a less settled and poorer hill people; while the Whilkut, in the eyes of all three of the more cultured nations, were a sort of wild Thracians of the mountains.

Most of the Hupa villages, or at least the larger ones, were in Hupa (or Hoopa) valley, a beautiful stretch of 8 miles, containing a greater extent of level land than can be aggregated for long distances about. Below or north of the valley the Trinity flows through a magnificent rocky canyon to Weitchpec, Yurok Weitspus. In spite of the proximity of a group of populous Yurok settlements at this confluence, the canyon, or nearly all of it, belonged to the Hupa, who now and then seem even to have built individual houses at two or three points along its course. Perhaps these belonged to men whom quarrels or feuds drove from intercourse with their fellows.

The towns in Hupa Valley, in order upstream, and with designation of their situation on the east or the west bank of the Trinity, are as follows:

E. Honsading. Yurok: Oknutl.

W. Dakis-hankut.

E. Kinchuhwikut. Yurok: Merpernertl.

W. Cheindekotding. Unoccupied in 1850. Yurok: Kererwer.

E. Miskut (Meskut). Yurok: Ergerits.

E. Takimitlding (Hostler). Yurok: Oplego. Wiyot: Talalawilu or Talawatewu. Chimariko: Hope-ta-dji. See plat in Figure 12.

E. Tsewenalding (Senalton). Yurok: Olepotl.

W. Totltsasding. Unoccupied in 1850. Yurok: Erlern.

E. Medilding (Matilton). Yurok: Kahtetl. Wiyot: Haluwi-talaleyutl. Chimariko: Mutuma-dji.

W. Howunkut (Kentuck). Yurok: Pia'getl. Wiyot: Tapotse.

E. Djishtangading (Tishtangatang).

E. Haslinding (Horse-Linto). Yurok: Yati.

It is characteristic that while there is more level land on the western than on the eastern side of Hupa Valley, all the principal villages, in fact practically all settlements in occupation when the

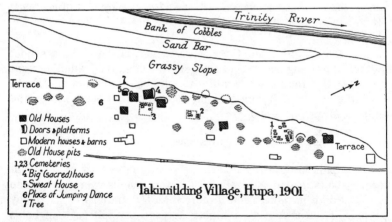

FIG. 12.—Plan of Hupa town of Takimitlding.

Americans arrived except Howunkut, were on the eastern side of the river, with exposure to the warm afternoon sun.

Above Hupa Valley is the small "Sugar Bowl," whose bottom harbored the little village of Haslinding. Some miles farther up begins a string of patches of valley to where Willow Creek comes in. Here there were two permanent settlements, Kachwunding and Mingkutme. Sehachpeya, Waugullewatl, Aheltah, Sokeakeit, and Tashuanta are mentioned in early sources as being in this region: most of these names seem to be Yurok. And still farther, at South

Fork, where the river branches, was the town of Tlelding—whence the "Kelta tribe"—with subsidiary settlements about or above it. The farthest of these was Tl'okame, 5 miles up the South Fork. These southerly Hupa were almost out of touch with the Yurok, and held intercourse with the Wintun and Chimariko. Their outlook on the world must have been quite different, and it is known that their religious practices were distinctive. In implements, mode of life, regulation of society, and speech they were, however, substantially identical with the better known people of Hupa Valley. And the Yurok knew Tlelding, which they called, with reference to its situation at the forks by the same name as their own town of Weitspekw.

The Hupa derive their name from Yurok Hupo, the name of the valley. The people the Yurok knew as Hupo-la, their speech as Omimoas. The Hupa called themselves Natinnoh-hoi, after Natinnoh, the Trinity River. Other tribes designated them as follows: The Wiyot, Haptana; the Karok, Kisha-kewara; the Chimariko, Hichhu; the Shasta, Chaparahihu. The Hupa in turn used these terms: For the Yurok, Kinne, or Yidachin, "from downstream"; the Karok were the Kinnus; the Shasta, the Kiintah; the Chimariko, the Tl'omitta-hoi, the "prairie people"; the Wintun of the south fork of the Trinity, the Yinachin, "from upstream"; the Wiyot of lower Mad River, Taike; the Whilkut, Hoilkut-hoi; the Tolowa language was Yitde-dinning-hunneuhw, "downstream sloping speech."

That something of an ethnic sense existed is shown by a gender in the Hupa language. One category included only adult persons speaking the tongue or readily intelligible Athabascan dialects. Babbling children, dignified aliens, and all other human beings and animals formed a second "sex."

NUMBERS.

The population of the Hupa as far as the South Fork of the Trinity may be estimated at barely 1,000 before the discovery. There do not appear to have been much more than 600 Indians in the valley proper. Even this gives a higher average per village than holds through the region. The first agent in 1866 reported 650. In 1903, a careful estimate yielded 450. The Federal census of 1910 reckons over 600, but probably includes all the children of diverse tribal affiliation brought to the Government school in the valley. In any event, the proportion of survivors is one of the highest in California. This may be ascribed to three causes: the inaccessibility of the region and its comparative poverty in placer gold; the establishment of a reservation which allowed the Hupa uninterrupted occupancy of their ancestral dwellings; and an absence of the lamentable laxity of administration characteristic for many years of the other Indian reservations of California; which fortunate circumstance is probably due in the main to this reservation having been long in charge of military officers.

In 1851 the Yurok listed to the Government officials 99 Hupa houses, distributed as follows:

Honsading	9
Miskut	6
Takimitlding	20
Tsewenalding	10
Medilding	28
5 other villages in and above Hupa valley, not positively identified	23
Tlelding	3
Total	99

The enumeration may not have been complete—it would yield only 750 Hupa; but even a liberal allowance for omission of small settlements would keep the entire group within the 1,000 mark.

The following report of the population in 1870 is of interest:

	Males.	Females.
Honsading	25	30
Miskut	32	49
Takimitlding	51	74
Tsewenalding	14	31
Medilding	75	100
Howunkut	31	39
Djishtangading	14	36
" Sawmill "	16	24
	258	383

Total Hupa	641
Chilula, Nongatl, Wiyot, etc	233
	874

These figures may not be taken with too much reliance. There is nothing that has so great an illusory accuracy as the census of an Indian reservation as it has been customary to make them. In the same year another agent reported only 649 Indians on the reservation—301 males and 348 females. But the figures, like those that precede, give some conception of the relative importance of the villages, with Takimitlding and Medilding, the religious centers of the two halves of the valley, far in the lead. And they indicate that 20 years of contact with the Americans had been heavily disastrous only to the Hupa men. Bullets, not disease, killed in these first years.

But native practices also contributed. About the late sixties a feud arose between Takimitlding and Tsewenalding. A woman of the latter place was assaulted by an American soldier and stabbed him. Not long after, either in resentment or for some other cause, soldiers killed a Takimitlding youth. The Takimitlding people could not or dared not revenge themselves on the military, but holding the woman ultimately responsible for the loss of their man, sought reprisals among her relatives of Tsewenalding. In the "war" that followed the people of the smaller village suffered heavily. The aggregate losses of both sides were about 20. The towns belonged to the same division and stood a scant mile apart on the same side of the river.

Dams were built across the river to catch salmon in alternate summers at Takimitlding and Medilding. There is in this arrangement a wise adjustment between the two largest and most sacred towns and the rights of the upper and lower halves of the valley.

COMMERCE.

The Hupa traded chiefly with the Yurok. From them they received their canoes, which their own lack of redwood prevented them from manufacturing; and dried sea foods, especially surf fish, mussels, and salty seaweed. Most of their dentalia probably reached them through the same channel; although this money, however hoarded, must have fluctuated back and forth from tribe to tribe and village to village for generations. The articles returned are less definitely known, but seem to have consisted of inland foods and perhaps skins. With the Karok the Hupa were in general friendly, but the products of the two groups were too similar to allow of much barter. The Tolowa seem to have been met at Yurok dances. The Chilula were close friends, the Whilkut disliked. There was very little intercourse with the Wiyot, Nongatl, or Wintun, evidently because other tribes intervened.

PLAN OF SOCIETY.

The following account of Hupa society also applies to all the northwestern tribes.

A typical family consisted of the man and his sons, the wife or wives of the man, the unmarried or half-married daughters, the wives of the sons, and the grandchildren. To these may be added unmarried or widowed brothers or sisters of the man and his wife. The women of the first generation are called by the same term of relationship by the third generation whether they are great-aunts or grandmothers. So, too, the old men of the family were all called grandfathers. All the children born in the same house called each other brothers and sisters, whether they were children of the same parents or not.

The ultimate basis of this life is obviously blood kinship, but the immediately controlling factor is the association of common residence; in a word, the house.

Continuing, with omissions:

The next unit above the family was the village. These varied greatly in size. Where a man was born there he died and was buried. On the other hand, the women went to other villages when they married and usually remained there all their lives. The inhabitants of a village were related to each other, for the most part, on the side of the males. They had other relatives scattered through different villages where their daughters and sisters had married.

Each village had a headman who was richest there. Besides riches he had hunting and fishing rights, and certain lands where his women might gather acorns and seeds. The men of the village obeyed him because from him they received food in time of scarcity. If they were involved in trouble they looked to him to settle the dispute with money. As long as they obeyed whatever he had was theirs in time of need. His power descended to his son at his death if his property also so descended.

The villages south of and including Medilding were associated in matters of religion. There was no organization or council. The richest man was the leader in matters of the dances, and in war, if the division were at war as a unit. All to the north of Medilding constituted another division. The headman of the northern division because of his great wealth was the headman for the whole lower Trinity River. He was the leader when the tribe, as a tribe, made war. This power was the result of his wealth and passed with the dissipation of his property. He was the leader because he could, with his wealth, terminate hostilities by settling for all those killed by his warriors. There seem to have been no formalities in the government of the village or tribe. Formal councils were unknown, although the chief often took the advice of his men in a collected body.

There are here male ownership, patrilinear descent, and well-defined laws. There is no trace of exogamous clans, of hereditary power as a part of society, of political machinery. The stage seems all set for these institutions. A slight increment and we can imagine them developing to luxuriance. But the growth would have involved a total change in outlook—the sort of change that comes slowly and which affects at once the subtlest and deepest values of a culture.

DAILY LIFE.

The daily life, not only of the Hupa but of all the northwestern tribes, has been well described in the following passage:

At daybreak the woman arose and went to the river for a complete bath. She then took the burden basket and brought a load of wood for the house fire. She was expected to have finished her bath before the men were astir. They too were early risers. The dawn was looked upon as a maiden. She would say: " I like that man. I wish he will live to be old; he always looks at me." The men always bathed in the river on rising. A light breakfast was eaten by the family in the house and each went to his day's task. The older men preferred to do most of their work before this meal. In the afternoon, the old men, and the religiously inclined young men, took a sweat in the sweat-house, followed by a plunge in the river. After the bath they sat in the shelter of the sweat-house and sunned themselves. As they sat there they engaged in meditation and prayer. In the evening the principal meal was served. The men ate very slowly, looking about and talking after each spoonful of acorn soup. The women sat in silence without caps and with hidden feet, that they might show great respect to the men. A basket of water was passed after the meal that the men might wash their hands. When they were through they retired to the sweat-house, where they spent several hours in converse.

DIVINITIES.

The greatest divinity of the Hupa is Yimantuwingyai, "the one lost (to us) across (the ocean)," also known as Yimankyuwinghoiyan, "old man over across," believed to have come into being at the Yurok village of Kenek. He is a sort of establisher of the order and condition of the world and leader of the *kihunai*, or preceding race; a real creator is as unknown to the Hupa as to the Yurok and Karok. They can not conceive the world as ever different from now except in innumerable details. Yimantuwingyai seems to be a combination of the tricky and erotic Wohpekumeu and the more heroic Pulekukwerek of the Yurok.

A suggestion of the latter god is found in the Hupa Yidetuwingyai, "the one lost downstream." A myth concerning him tells of the time when the sun and earth alone existed. From them were born twins, Yidetuwingyai and the ground on which men live. This sort of cosmogony has not been found among the Yurok or Karok and may be supposed to have reached the Hupa through the influence of more southerly tribes.

Yinukatsisdai, "upstream he lives," is the Yurok Megwomets, a small long-bearded boy who passes unseen with a load of acorns and controls or withholds the supply of vegetable food.

GREAT DANCES.

The Hupa made two ceremonies of the new year or first fruits type, both, of course, with the recitation of a mythological formula as the central esoteric element. One of these was performed at Haslinding by the people of the Medilding division in spring at the commencement of the salmon run. The first salmon of the season was caught and eaten. In autumn, when the acorns first began to fall freely, a ceremony for the new crop was made for the northern division at Takimitlding, "acorn-ceremony place." The reciting formulist took the place of the divinity Yinukatsisdai. The new acorns were eaten by the assembled people. The stones used in cooking the gruel were put in a heap that has attained a volume of 200 cubic feet and must be adjudged to have been at least as many years in accumulating, or more if tradition is true that the river once swept the pile away. A lamprey eel ceremony was also enacted at the northern end of the valley by a Takimitlding man each year. It was a close parallel of the salmon "new year," but much less important.

The Hupa held two Jumping dances and one Deerskin dance; in former times annually, they say; in more recent years biennially. These are all associated with Takimitlding, and at least one if not two are connected with the first acorn ceremony there.

The Deerskin dance, *honsitlchitdilya*, "summer dance," or *hunkachitdilya*, "along the river dance," came about September. The formula was spoken at Takimitlding, it appears, or begun there. The dancers then went upstream in canoes, and on 10 successive afternoons and evenings danced at Howunkut, below Takimitlding, at Miskut, below Kinchuhwikut, upstream again opposite Cheindekotding, then at the foot of the valley, and finally at Nitltukalai, on the slope of the mountain overlooking the valley from the north. On the fourth day, at Miskut, the dance was made in three large canoes abreast, which ten times approached the shore. This spectacular performance, with its peculiar song, recalled to the old people their dead who formerly witnessed the dance with them, and they were wont to weep, deeply affected.

A Jumping dance, *tunkehitdilya*, "autumn dance," was held, also for 10 or more days, half a month or so later, before a board fence or hut erected near the sacred sweat house at Takimitlding. At least on the last day, the Medilding danced against the Takimitlding division, that is, in turn and in a competition as to excellence of song and step and particularly as to sumptuousness and value of the regalia displayed.

Another Jumping dance, *haichitdilya*, "winter dance," seems to have come in spring. It was not associated with any first-fruits ceremony, but seems to have had as its purpose the driving away of sickness. Its season, however, is that of the first salmon rites of Medilding and of the Karok, and it is not unlikely that the dance once rested upon a similar ceremony made at Takimitlding. For 10 nights the dance went on in the "great" or sacred dwelling house which was believed to have stood in that village since the days of the *kihunai*. Then followed 10 days of open-air dancing at Miskut. The apparel and conduct were the same as in the autumn Jumping dance.

GIRL'S ADOLESCENCE DANCE.

The Hupa stand one slight grade lower than the Yurok in the scale of civilization by one test that holds through most of California: the attention bestowed on the recurring physiological functions of women. The influence of their hill neighbors may be responsible. At a girl's adolescence, when she was called *kinatldang*, 10 days' observances were undergone by her which are very similar to those followed by the Yurok. In addition, there was a nightly dance in the dwelling house which the Yurok did not practice, although they knew it among the Hupa, and similar rites were followed among the Karok, Tolowa, and Wiyot. A number of men wearing feather-tipped caps of buckskin from which a flap falls down the back entered several times a night to sing about the blanket-covered girl. They vibrated long rattles which are a modification of the clap stick that is used in dances throughout central California. The end of the Hupa stick is whittled into five or six slender and flexible rods. These rattles were not used by the Yurok. One dancer wore a headdress belonging to the Deerskin dance; another, one from the Jumping dance; both carried small thin boards cut and painted into a rude suggestion of the human figure. In the intervals, seated women sang and tapped the girl with the rattles. After the tenth night, the girl finally threw off her blanket, went outside, and looked into two haliotis shells held to the south and north of her, seeing therein the two celestial worlds.

WIZARDS AND SHAMANS.

It is in keeping with the peculiar form which shamanism assumes in northwestern California that the doctor and the witch are more clearly separated in the native mind than in the remainder of California. Disease was caused by the breaking of some observance of magic, perhaps sometimes was thought to occur spontaneously, or was brought on by people who had become *kitdonghoi*, in Hupa terminology. These were not shamans of avowed training, but men of secret evil proclivities. They did not control animate "pains" or spirits, but operated through material objects possessing magic powers. These objects were also called *kitdonghoi*. A favorite instrument was a bow made of a human rib with cord of wrist sinews. From this, after the proper mythic formula had been recited—the Hupa or Yurok can imagine nothing of real consequence being done successfully without a formula—a mysterious little arrow was shot which caused almost certain death. These devices, or the knowledge of them, were secretly bought by resentful and malicious people from men suspected of possessing the unnatural powers. The *kitdonghoi* might sometimes be seen at night as something rushing about and throwing out sparks. His instrument enabled him to travel at enormous speed, and to turn himself into a wolf or bear in his journeys. This is the only faint suggestion in northwestern California of the bear shaman beliefs that are so prevalent everywhere to the south.

It is evident that the northwesterner distinguishes black magic and curative doctoring rather plainly—much as superstitious Europeans might, in fact. The central and southern Californian, it will be seen hereafter, deals essentially in undifferentiated shamanism, which can be equally beneficent or evil. This contrast is connected with several peculiarities of northwestern culture. The Yurok and Hupa are far more addicted to magic in the narrower sense of the word, especially imitative magic, than the unsophisticated central Californians. The formulas with which they meet all crises rest essentially on this concept; and there are literally hundreds if not thousands of things that are constantly done or not done in everyday life from some motive colored by ideas that are imitatively magical. Though the world is full of deities and spirits, these also are approached by the avenue of magic, by the performance of an action which they like and which compels their aid, rather than by any direct communication as of person with person. As already said of the Yurok, the idea that the shaman owns guardian spirits and operates through communications with them, is feebly developed and expressed only indirectly. Shamans work primarily through "pains"; and these, although alive, are material objects. A true "bear doctor," as the Yuki and Yokuts know him, is therefore an impossibility among the Hupa. Finally, it is no doubt significant in this connection that the professional shaman in the northwest is normally a woman, the *kitdonghoi* or *uma'a* more often a man.

The Hupa distinguished the *tintachinwunawa*, the dancing or singing doctor, who diagnoses by clairvoyance or dream, and the *kitetau* or sucking doctor, who removes the disease object. Often the same shaman performed both operations, but there were dancing doctors who never attempted to extract a "pain." This differentiation of function has been reported from groups in several other parts of northern California. The dancing doctor sometimes used a deer-hoof rattle.

Illness is also treated by *kimauchitlchwe*, people who know formulas that they have been taught by an older relative. In connection with such a recitation an herb is invariably employed, although almost always in such a minute quantity or so indirectly or externally applied that its physiological effect must be insignificant. Pregnancy and childbirth were always so treated, but of actual diseases apparently only a few, of chronic and annoying rather than alarming character.

THE CHILULA.

The Chilula, who constitute one larger ethnic group with the Hupa and Whilkut, are almost indistinguishable from the Hupa in speech, and were allied with them in hostility toward the Teswan or Coast Yurok and in frequent distrust of the Yurok, Wiyot, and Whilkut, and differed from them in customs only in such matters as were the result of habitat in an adjacent and smaller stream valley. Like all the Indians of the region, they lacked a specific designation of themselves as a group. Chilula is American for Yurok Tsulu-la, people of Tsulu, the Bald Hills that stretch between Redwood Creek and the parallel Klamath-Trinity Valley. Locally they have always been known as the Bald Hills Indians.

The Chilula villages lay on or near lower Redwood Creek from near the inland edge of the heavy redwood belt to a few miles above Minor Creek. All but one were on the northeastern side of the stream, on which the hillsides receive more sun and the timber is lighter. A few were as much as a mile or more from the creek, but the majority conformed to the invariable Hupa, Yurok, and Karok practice of standing close to the stream. In summer the Chilula left their permanent homes, near which they fished, and dwelt chiefly on the upper prairielike reaches of the Bald Hills ridge, where seeds as well as bulbs abounded and hunting was convenient. This is a much more distinctively central than northwestern Californian practice. Some of these summer camps were on the Klamath or Yurok side of the range, so that in this rather unusual case the boundary between the two groups was neither a watershed nor a stream. In autumn the Chilula either continued their residence in the Bald Hills or crossed Redwood Creek to gather acorns on the shadier hillsides that slope down to their stream from the west.

Eighteen of their former villages are known. These are placed in Figure 13. The towns there designated as A to R were, in order, Howunakut, Noleding, Tlochime, Kingkyolai, Kingyukyomunga, Yisining'aikut, Tsinsilading, Tondinunding, Yinukanomitseding, Hontetlme, Tlocheke, Hlichuhwinauhwding, Kailuhwtahding, Kailuhwchengetlding, Sikingchwungmitahding, Kinahontahding, Misme, Kahustahding.

Five of the principal Chilula settlements are reported to have been called Cherr'hquuh, Ottepetl, Ohnah, Ohpah, and Roquechoh by the Yurok. From these names Cherhkwer, Otepetl, Ono, Opau, and Roktso can be reconstructed as the approximate original forms.

On the site of six of the identified settlements, 17, 7, 4, 2, 4, and 8 house pits, respectively, have been counted. This ratio would give the Chilula a total of 125 homes, or about 900 souls. As Hupa and Yurok villages, owing to all house sites not being occupied contemporaneously, regularly contain more pits than houses, and the same ratio probably applied to the Chilula, or if anything a heavier one, the figures arrived at must be reduced by about a third. This would make the Chilula population when the white man appeared some 500 to 600, and the average strength of each settlement about 30 persons. This is less for the group than for the neighboring ones, and less, too, for the size of each village; as is only natural for dwellers on a smaller stream.

The trails from Trinidad and Humboldt Bay to the gold districts on the Klamath in the early fifties led across the Bald Hills, and the Chilula had hardly seen white men before they found themselves in hostilities with packers and miners. Volunteer companies of Americans took part, and desultory and intermittent fighting went on for a dozen years. Part of the Chilula were placed at Hupa, others captured and sent to distant Fort Bragg. These attempted to steal home, but were massacred by the Lassik on the way. The Chilula remaining in their old seats and at Hupa avenged their relatives by several successful raids into the territory of their new Indian foes.

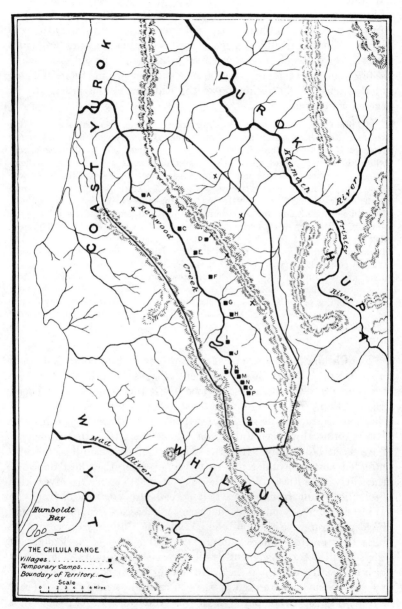

Fig. 13.—Chilula land and towns.   (After Goddard.)

On one of these parties, they still mustered, with their Hupa and Whilkut connections, 70 men. Nongatl Indians closely related to the Lassik also once were confined on Hupa Reservation, which led to further troubles. Other fights took place with certain Yurok villages. Thus the Chilula wasted away. As a tribe they are long since gone. Only two or three households remain in their old seats, while a few families at Hupa have become merged among their kinsmen of this tribe, in the reckoning of the white man, and practically in their own consciousness.

A Chilula who had killed a Hupa, or who was held responsible because his kinsmen were involved in the killing, attended a brush dance at the Yurok town of Kenek after the American was in the land. His foes attacked, and while his hosts apparently scattered to keep out of the way of harm to themselves and possible claims arising from participation, he resisted. He was shot, but evidently only after a little battle, since several bullets were found where he had put them in his piled-up hair ready for quick loading. He had no doubt come to the celebration prepared for a possible attempt on his life. His companions were probably outnumbered and ran off. The next day word was sent from his village that he should be buried at Kenek and payment would be made for the favor. The risk of ambush to the party bearing his corpse home was seemingly considered too great to brave. This was a private or family feud, such as would now and then occur among the Hupa themselves, and was hardly likely to disturb the amicable relations between other members of the two groups. The scale of the affair was probably typical of most of the "wars" of the region, except when most of the embittered Chilula stood desperately together for a season against the American and the native foes instigated by him.

The Chilula built the typical northwestern plank house and small square sweat house in their permanent villages. (Pl. 13.) They were the most southerly Athabascan tribe to use this type of sweat house. In addition, two villages contained large round dance houses of the kind characteristic of the region to the south, but not otherwise known in northwestern California. It is conceivable that these may have been built only after the white man indiscriminately commingled northern and southern tribes, or after the ghost dance of the early seventies. While the Yurok and Tolowa received this revivalistic cult from the east, it spread also northward from the Wintun, Pomo, Yuki, and southern Athabascan groups, and may have penetrated to the Chilula. When the Chilula camped in the hills they erected square but unexcavated houses of bark slabs of the type used for permanent dwellings by the Whilkut. They knew or occasionally attempted the art of sewing headbands of yellow-hammer quills, such as are used by the central Californian tribes. (Fig. 20, d.) Thus, as compared with the Hupa and Yurok, some first approaches to southerly customs are seen among the Chilula.

Their lack of the redwood canoe proves less, as their stream would have been unnavigable except in times of torrential flood. There is a tradition that they once practiced the Deerskin dance, but neither the form of the ceremony nor the spot at which it was held is known. They no doubt participated, as guests and contributors of regalia, in the Hupa dances, as they do now; and possibly also in those of the Yurok at some villages, though many of the Yurok have been their enemies both before and since the arrival of the American.

THE WHILKUT.

The Whilkut are the third division of the Athabascans speaking dialects of the Hupa type. They held Redwood Creek, above the kindred Chilula, to its head; and Mad River, except in its lowest course, up to the vicinity of Iaqua Butte. They also had a settlement or two on Grouse Creek, over the divide to the east in Trinity River drainage. To the south they adjoined Athabascans of a quite different speech group, the Nongatl. On the west and east they were wedged in between the Wiyot and Wintun.

Those of the Whilkut on Redwood Creek almost merged into the Chilula on the same stream, but that there must have been a consciousness of difference is proved by the Hupa regarding the latter as kinsmen and the Whilkut at least as potential foes.

The Whilkut are practically unknown. The general basis of their culture must have been northwestern, but they lacked some of the specific features, and probably replaced them by customs of central Californian type. Their houses were of bark slabs instead of planks, and without a pit, and must therefore have been smaller and poorer than those of the Chilula, Hupa, and Yurok. They also did not dig out the small, rectangular, board-covered sweat houses of these northern neighbors, but, at least since the American is in the land, held indoor ceremonies in round structures, erected for the purpose and presumably dirt-covered. This is the central Californian earth lodge or dance house.

A very few coiled baskets have been found among them. These may have been acquired, or the art learned in the alien contacts enforced on them by the Americans. If coiling was an old technique among the Whilkut, it was followed only sporadically.

As to former population, villages, and the size of the latter, we are also in ignorance. In spite of a considerable extent of territory, the Whilkut can not have been very numerous—perhaps 500. The Government census of 1910 reports about 50 full-blood Whilkut, besides some mixed bloods; but Chilula and members of other tribes may have been included in these figures. The Whilkut suffered heavily in the same struggles with the whites which caused the Chilula to melt away; and similar attempts were made to settle them on the Hupa Reservation, but without permanent success. Their name is of Hupa origin: Hoilkut-hoi.

CHAPTER 9.

ATHABASCANS: SOUTHERN GROUPS.

The Mattole.

The Mattole or Mattoal are one of the rare Athabascan coastal
tribes. Cape Mendocino was in their territory. They held the
Bear River and Mattole River drainages; also a few miles of Eel
River and its Van Dusen Fork immediately above the Wiyot. How
far the sites of their villages were divided between the banks of these
streams and actual ocean frontage is not known, but the climate and
topography of the region indicate inland settlements as predominating. The origin of their name is not clear. The Wiyot call them
Metol or Medol, but this may be a designation taken by the Wiyot
from the white man. Originally the word Mattole may have been
only the name of a village.

In speech the Mattole differ considerably from all nearby Athabascans except possibly the Hupa—sufficiently, it appears, to constitute them one of the primary divisions of that family in California.
They lie somewhat on one side of the main north and south axis of
Athabascan territory in the State; yet there is nothing in their
location or in the nature of their habitat to suggest any very compelling cause for their rather high degree of dialectic specialization.
They may have been influenced by a long contact with the Wiyot. In
certain phonetic traits their speech resembles the Hupa group of
dialects.

Not a single concrete item of ethnology is on record regarding
the Mattole, other than the statement that they burned their dead;
which, if true, carries this funeral mode considerably farther north
in the coast region than all other knowledge would lead one to
anticipate. More likely, some settler has reported the exceptional
funeral of natives shot by his friends.

There may be half a dozen full-blood Mattole scattered in and near their ancient land. The Government census of 1910 gives 10, with two or three times as many mixed bloods; but these figures may refer in part to Athabascans of other divisions, who here and there have drifted into the district. The Mattole had their share of fighting with the whites, the memory of which is even obscurer than the little history of most such pitiful events. Attempts were also made to herd them onto the reservations of Humboldt and Mendocino Counties. But like most of the endeavors of this sort in the early days of American California, these round-ups were almost as inefficient and unpersisted in as they were totally ill judged in plan and heartless in intent, and all they accomplished was the violent dispersal, disintegration, and wasting away of the suffering tribes subjected to the process.

THE NONGATL.

The Nongatl or "Noankakhl" or Saia are the northernmost of five bodies of people into whom the Athabascans of the southern dialect group, whose habitat is in Eel River drainage, appear naturally to divide. The Nongatl territory is that drained by three right-hand affluents of Eel River: Yager Creek, Van Dusen Fork, and Larrabee Creek; also the upper waters of Mad River. They are scarcely to be distinguished from the Lassik, except for their adjacent range and perhaps some consciousness of their own separateness. Saia is not a group name, but a descriptive epithet taken by the Americans from the Hupa: it means " far off." It is probable that the Hupa knew the Nongatl but dimly if at all before the whites forcibly planted some remnants of the latter in Hupa Valley in the sixties, after first having placed them on a reserve in Del Norte County. The survivors now live in their old haunts, but number a mere handful. The census of 1910 enumerated just 6: there can be but few more.

THE LASSIK.

The Lassik are little better known than their close kinsmen the Nongatl, whom they adjoin on the south. They occupied a stretch of Eel River, from a few miles above the mouth of the South Fork not quite to Kekawaka Creek; also Dobbins Creek, an eastern affluent of the main stream, and Soldier Basin at the head of the tortuous North Fork, another eastern affluent. To the east, they extended to the head of Mad River. This stream, and with it the uppermost Van Dusen, may have been Lassik as far as Lassik Peak, rather than to the point shown in Plate 1. Still farther east, over another of the endless parallel ridges, was the uppermost course of the South Fork of the Trinity, which may have been hunting territory of the Lassik or of the Wintun. Claims of the latter are likely to have preponderated, but the tract was probably not settled.

The Lassik appear to have had some intercourse with the Wintun and have in consequence sometimes been erroneously designated as Wintun. Their own name is not known, if indeed they had one. Their current designation is taken from that of a chief, whose name survives also attached to a prominent peak. This man was part Wintun in ancestry. Direct Wintun influence is visible in Lassik mourning ceremonies; they practiced a burning of property at death to which the Wintun and Pomo were addicted, but which was not followed by the tribes to the north. Their basketry is of the northwestern variety, but roughly made (Pl. 24); their houses are mere conical lean-tos of fir bark slabs—a central Californian type. They seem to have had neither the northwestern rectangular sweat house nor the central round dance house. A legitimate inference is that their ceremonies were simple. Eel River and its tributaries ran with salmon in winter, when the Lassik lived close to the streams; but in summer they moved up into the hills, where *Brodiœa* bulbs, seeds, acorns, small game, and deer were within convenient distance.

A few ethnographic facts can be extracted from their recorded traditions. Two forms of war dance are mentioned: that of preparation for revenge, and that of triumph over scalps. It is rather strange to find among one people, even though an intermediate one, these respectively northwestern and central Californian institutions, which usually replace each other. Somewhat analogously, the dentalia of the north and the disk beads of the south are referred to in conjunction. Moccasins are spoken of as if put on only for journeys. Two interesting hunting methods are alluded to: running down elk on foot by ceaselessness rather than speed of pursuit; and driving deer into a corral of logs and brush provided with a gate. It is true that the latter achievement is performed by mythical heroes through the use of magical songs. But the concept of the enclosure for game is likely to have had some foundation in fact.

The Lassik, inhabiting a tract that is still thorough backwoods and in early days was completely beyond the control of organized government, suffered severely at the hands of self-reliant but prejudiced settlers. They also lived far enough south to be within range of the slave traffic in Indian children that seems to have been instituted by the Mexicans of Sonoma County and developed by the more enterprising Americans of Mendocino. There are scarcely as many Lassik living to-day as they once possessed villages, to judge by the house-pit marked sites the survivors can point out.

PLATE 24

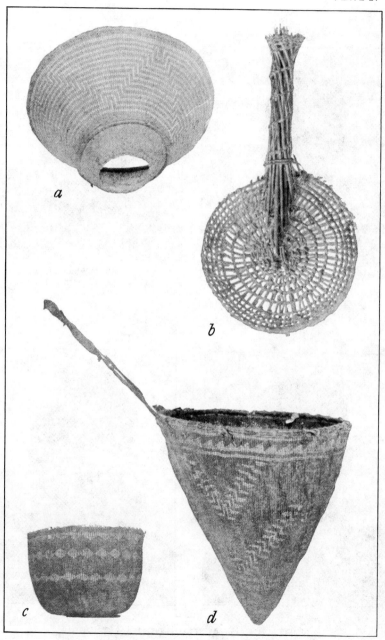

a, Mortar hopper; *b*, seed beater; *c*, for cooking; *d*, for gathering seeds.

LASSIK BASKETRY

PLATE 25

Pomo

Woman, half Northern Wintun, quarter Klamath
Lake, quarter Northern Paiute

Modoc

Huchnom

NORTH CENTRAL CALIFORNIAN TYPES

THE SINKYONE.

LAND AND SETTLEMENTS.

The Sinkyone are those Athabascans of the southern group who live on Sinkyoko, the South Fork of Eel River. They held the whole of this stream and its tributaries except the headwaters, which were Kato range; and in addition they occupied the adjacent coast from above Shelter Cove to a point between Usal and Rockport, where they met the Coast Yuki.

Those of the Sinkyone on lower South Fork have sometimes been known as Lolonko or Flonko; but this word, properly Lo'langko, is the name of Bull Creek or a settlement at its mouth, not of the group of people. The Wailaki are said to call them and the Mattole jointly Tulbush, a term which recalls the Sinkyone appellation for the Wiyot: Dilwish-ne.

The coast Sinkyone are called by those inland Mankya or Bankya, from mancho, ocean. By Americans they have sometimes been named Usal. This word seems to be from Pomo Yoshol, denoting either the Coast Yuki or the Mankya, both of whom are north of the Pomo; but yo is "south" and shol "eastward" in that language.

Sinkyone place names are: Tangating, Shelter Cove; Kileting, Needle Rock; Chelehdang, Bear Harbor; Djokniki, Usal; Sitltsitako, Uantsintyoko, Tantangaiko, Tewitltsintastangko, Kyintigesolko, a series of tributaries of the South Fork between Bull Creek and Salmon Creek; Shahena'ko, Salmon Creek.

Outside of their own territory were Tatyi, Mattole River; Djangko, Bear River; Hatyo, Eel River proper; Setlbaiko, Yager Creek; Kyineko, Van Dusen Fork; Gitel, Bridgeville; Silangko, Larrabee Creek; Djetenang and Koshkatinik, near Blocksburg; Kohtinik, Mad River; Natinik, Trinity River. The stream names, it is likely, are extensions of designations of the places at their mouths.

The narrow horizon of many of the Californian tribes is illustrated by the travels of an old Sinkyone, who was born and lived and died at the mouth of Bull Creek. He recited that in the course of his years he had been downstream to the Wiyot boundary, upstream to one of the South Fork tributaries still in Sinkyone territory, coastward to the Mattole River, and inland to the ridge beyond which lies the Van Dusen Fork. A circle with a 20-mile radius around Dyerville would more than include this little world of his life's experience.

Like most of the surrounding groups, the Sinkyone were quite definite in the habit of occupying their permanent villages in the stream valleys only in the winter half of the year, while in summer they dwelt on the more open mountain sides and hilltops. Thus the Bull Creek people spent the dry season at a variety of places in the hills, living on game and vegetable food. After the first rains, when Eel River and the South Fork began to rise, they came down to them to fish. After these large streams were swollen, the smaller water courses appear to have offered better facilities for taking salmon, and the heart of winter was spent in the home villages on Bull Creek. With this dependence on the food in the hills during a large part of each year, it seems that the limits of the territory of each little local group must have been accurately observed upland, as well as along the streams, and that the fixed boundaries must have given something akin to political cohesion to the people of each unit.

CUSTOMS.

What is known of the customs of the Sinkyone puts them ethnically halfway between the tribes of distinctive northwestern type and those of central Californian character. In short, they shared some cultural traits with the Yurok and Hupa, others with the Yuki and Pomo; while if they possessed any of their own, these were few and rude. They remained backwoodsmen, like their American dispossessors.

The women's tattooing was a superimposing of the horizontal cheek lines favored by the Yuki upon the solid chin ornamentation of the Hupa. (Fig. 45, d.)

Dentalia served as money, but they were the broken, fathom-strung shells which the Yurok class as beads, not the long and accurately measured pieces which alone they treat as standard currency. The price of a man was from 5 to 15 strings—nominally the same as among the Yurok and Hupa—but in their estimation the actual value handed over would have been far too little. The price of a wife was also smaller, and perhaps rather in the nature of a gift to be partly reciprocated than a formal purchase payment. The Hupa both bought and gave at a marriage, but the buying was in conformity with law, the donations a matter of custom. Illegitimate children were paid for by the Sinkyone as by their northern kinsmen, but they took no debt slaves. Feuds and wars were closed only on payment for every life lost.

The regular disposal of the dead was by burial, as on the Klamath, but central influences appear in the habit of cremating those slain in battle, or dying at a distance from home or under circumstances imposing haste. It has already been noted that the statement that the Mattole cremated may rest upon the testimony of whites who noted Indian funerals chiefly after a slaughter.

HOUSES AND BOATS.

The Sinkyone house was of central Californian type. It was unexcavated, and the material was slabs of redwood bark. Wooden planks may also have been used, but there is nothing in the structure of the edifices to require this more laborious material. There were two forms. The *yi-kyiso* or *bang-kyiso* was a conical lean-to. The *yi-taslai* or *min-taslai* was wedge-shaped, of pieces of bark leaned against a pole resting in two upright forks, the front nearly vertical, the combined back and roof gently sloping. The north-western rectangular sweat house was not built. Dances were held in larger conical or circular structures, but these were primarily dance houses, as farther south, and not sweat houses.

The Sinkyone used the northern redwood canoe so far as the streams in their habitat rendered the employment feasible. They declare that the Mattole, whose inland watercourses are small, did not use the canoe, even on the ocean. The southern limit of this cultural element, which, of course, is only a local form of the canoes

FIG. 14.—Sinkyone ring-and-pin game of salmon vertebrae.

of British Columbia and Alaska, can therefore be set definitely at Cape Mendocino on the coast, and near the confluence of Eel River with its South Fork in the interior.

BASKETS.

The basketry is also of pure northern kind: wholly twined; patterns in overlay; and made of hazel shoots and redwood root fibers, with *Xerophyllum* and maidenhair fern and alder-dyed brake for the decoration. The technique is much less finished than among the Yurok, and the ornamentation simpler. Minor distinctions, such as a somewhat greater depth of flat baskets, the occurrence of four vertical dyed stripes on conical burden baskets, and some tendency toward a zigzag pattern arrangement, do not obscure the complete adhesion to the fundamental type, which in fact persists without essential modification to its southern limit among the Wailaki.

OTHER MANUFACTURES.

The elk-horn spoons of the north were used by the Sinkyone, but not the elk-horn money boxes. Their lengths of little dentalia were rolled in mink skins. The smoking pipe was northern, but unskilled workers sometimes contented themselves with an instrument of knobbed shape at the bowl end—a Yuki-Pomo type. The acorn-

grinding pestle also varied to approximate both the Yurok and the
Pomo form. String was of iris fiber, as in the northwest. On the
main rivers, the principal net for salmon was a deep bag flowing
from the base of a triangle of poles held by the fisherman from a
scaffolding over the stream. This is the typical Yurok net. When
the water muddied, a shallower net on longer poles was held nearly
horizontally from shore. This is probably a form with central affinities. Suckers and small fish in the creeks were taken with a net
fastened to a stick whose bent ends were held together by a string,
while a bisecting pole served as handle. This is a distinctively central type, being found as far away as among the Yana and Maidu.

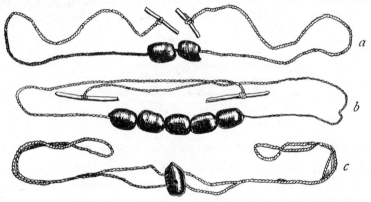

Fig. 15.—Acorn buzzer toys. a, Sinkyone; b, Pomo; c, Miwok.

The games were those of the northwestern tribes: The bundle of
slender sticks with one marked ace, the mussel-shell dice, the cup and
ball of salmon vertebræ. (Figs. 14, 15.)

RITUAL.

Sinkyone ceremonies were few and simple. The specific dance
cults of the Yurok and Hupa and those of the Pomo and Yuki were
both lacking. The only ceremonies were those of the underlying
undifferentiated California culture: The puberty dance for girls;
the doctor dance, in which older shamans helped the novice to fortify
himself in his profession; the war dance for incitement and perhaps
celebration; and the *nadelos*, made at night, outdoors, around a fire,
by men, women, and children, probably with a religious basis, but
largely serving social pleasures. The fighting dance was northern
in form: Armed men stood abreast in a row, with one or two dancing
back and forth before them. The puberty dance was made twice for
five nights for each girl. She was made to dance by a woman who

held her from behind, while the seated singers struck their hands with stick rattles of the form used in this ceremony by the Hupa. The usual restrictions were imposed on the girl: She fasted, kept awake, and kept her hair over her face in order not to blast the world with her disastrously potent glance. A new shaman fasted and danced at nights for a period of some duration in a conical house erected or reserved for the occasion, while more experienced colleagues accompanied him, interpreting his symptoms and advising him in the gradual acquisition of mastery over the difficulties of his involuntary art.

All of these ceremonies can be found in almost identical form among any of the remoter border or hill tribes of northern central California: The Chimariko, the Konomihu, the Shasta, the Yana, the northeastern Maidu, the Achomawi, and probably the Wintun of out-of-the-way headwaters.

Ritual apparatus is as significant as ceremonial practices of the origin of a people's religion. The Sinkyone lacked all the dance paraphernalia characteristic of the northwest. They used the yellow-hammer quill headbands of central California (Fig. 20; Pl. 71); twisted fur strips tied above the eyes; and in these were set dart-like sticks ornamented with feathers or with little banners of yellow-hammer quills (Fig. 21). These are a familiar central California dance object. The split stick and cocoon clappers of the Yuki and Pomo were not Sinkyone, nor the deer-hoof rattle of the Tolowa, Chilula, and Wailaki. They were a people that got along with little, that little the common stock of themselves and their neighbors, and as impartially the neighbors on one side as the other.

SHAMANISM.

The incipient Sinkyone shaman did not seek supernatural power, but began to dream of a dead relative or of the condor or other powerful spirits in the sky; or he would meet with a terrifying experience in a desolate place.

One man, for instance, returned from hunting with bleeding nose and mouth after a delay that had caused his family to fear for his safety. Converging deer trails led him to a house in the rocks, he recounted, with deer hair and dung lying deep. When he faced two condors with red-striped breasts and spread wings, he fell unconscious and lay until night. He sang with reference to this experience until a dance house was erected for him and older colleagues made him into a skillful medicine man. His success was equal at curing sickness, affecting the weather, succeeding in the hunt, winning at play, and foretelling the future. When he was shot to death in the brush, he caused his body and bones to be undiscoverable, and brought on a tremendous flood next winter. His secret died with him, for he always evaded leading anyone to the place of his supernatural encounter.

Another shaman was without avail against illness, but could predict the exact success of a hunting party, foretell rain, and put an end to a storm by singing. When he lay groaning and singing of nights, he saw the waters of the sky flowing past a displaced stick in the row of stakes that held them back and knew that rain was at hand. His luck in hunting was bound up with a transparent disk that had come to him from the sky, and vanished after his death.

Ordinary disease was cured by sucking out of the body the *sinsing* or material "pains"; but against a rattlesnake bite this remedy proved futile. The afflicted person must have ashes thrown in his face and be requested to die, in order to recover.

The malevolent pain objects, the shaman's beginning with a dream of the dead, his graduation in a dance made for him, are features common to a wide array of tribes in northeastern as well as northwestern California. The vision in the lonely place, the suddenly revealed sitters in a cave, the connection of the condor and the sky with deer hunting, and the acquisition of definite spirits—the sun, the eagle, or other animals—are traits pointing to specific Yuki-Wailaki influences.

OTHER RELIGIOUS ITEMS.

Formulas or prayers similar to those of the Hupa were spoken for purification by girls at the close of their puberty ceremonials and by men who had buried a corpse.

The ritualistic number of the Sinkyone was five.

A woman at her periods kept apart, and touched no deer meat, but did not occupy a special hut. There seems also to have been some laxity, in that venison was allowed to remain in the house with her, and her husband did not necessarily refrain from hunting.

Sinkyone mythology knows a creator called Kyoi, "spirit." The name applied also to the un-Indian and therefore nonhuman whites. More specifically, he was known as Nagaicho, "great traveler," as among the Kato. Compare the Yuki Taikomol, "he who goes alone." This creator made the earth and men. Coyote was present at the former act, and assisted in the establishment of the world, but is also responsible for death and much that is wrong in the scheme of things. These are all standard central Californian beliefs.

RECENT CONDITION.

Between dispossession, ill-managed confinement on badly chosen reservations, and occasional fighting, the Sinkyone suffered the same at the hands of the whites as the neighboring groups. They are so scattered to-day that they are not recognized by either the Government census or the Indian Office. Including half-breeds, their number may be estimated at two or three dozen at the most.

THE WAILAKI.

TERRITORY.

Wailaki is a Wintun word meaning "north language," and is applied by some of the Wintun to certain other Wintun divisions as well as to several neighboring groups of aliens. By what group of Wintun it was used for the Athabascan division to whom the designation has become fastened in American nomenclature, and why it was employed when the Wailaki are west and not north of the Wintun in general, has not been recorded. The Wailaki are said to have known themselves as Kenesti, and to have been called Kakwits, "north people," by the Yuki; but the more general Yuki appellation was Ko'il, "Athabascan."

The Wailaki were the uppermost Athabascan tribe on Eel River, which they held to the Big Bend, from where on all its tributaries were Yuki. They owned also several affluents on the western side, Kekawaka Creek on the eastern, and the whole of the North Fork except the head, where the Lassik lapped over.[1]

MODE OF LIFE.

Like the other Athabascans of the region, they were fishermen in the winter, when the streams carried enough water for the salmon to run, and when their permanent houses in the villages along the river banks were more comfortable than the wind-swept mountains and dripping timber. As spring came on, they moved into the hills, digging bulbs, beating the prairies for grass and Compositæ seeds, and garnering acorns as the summer wore into autumn. They were hunters, and, like the Lassik, took deer and elk by running them

---

[1] P. E. Goddard, The Habitat of the Wailaki (see bibliography), lists the "subtribes" of the Wailaki, which evidently correspond to the political units or "village communities" of the Yuki and Pomo discussed below, and were named after inhabited sites. The number of separate settlements per subtribe, as identified by explanation on the ground with natives, varied from 1 or 2 to 8 or 10: 66 settled sites in 13 communities. The communities on main Eel River were: the Sehlgaikyo-kaiya, east side, Big Bend Creek to McDonald Creek, only settlement Sehlgaichodang; Ninkannich-kaiya, opposite; Nehlchikyo-kaiya, east side downstream to mouth of North Fork; Sehlchikyo-kaiya, east side, downstream; Tatisho-kaiya, west side, opposite mouth of North Fork; Bas-kaiya, east, below Sehlchikyo-kaiya; Sla-kaiya, east, below last; Chisko-kaiya, east, below last; Seta-kaiya, west, below Tatisho-kaiya; Kaikiche-kaiya, west, below last; Dahlso-kaiya, Set'ahlchicho-kaiya, K'andang-kaiya, in order downstream, west side; Ihlkodang-kaiya, west side below Chisko-kaiya; Kasnaikot-kaiya, east side, mouth of Kekawaka Creek. Beyond were the Lassik. As compared with these 15 groups on main Eel River, the lower part of North Fork held 3: The Setandong-kiyahang, the Secho-kiyahang, and the Kaiye-kiyahang, in order upstream, with settlements chiefly on the north side. Farther up North Fork (same author, Habitat of the Pitch Indians, MS. in press) were the "Pitch" or "Salt" Wailaki, with four community groups: The T'odannang-kiyahang, on the North Fork below Hull Creek; the T'okyah-kiyahang, upstream on North Fork; the Chokot-kiyahang, on and above Red Mountain Creek; and the Ch'l'ankot-kiyahang, on Jesus Creek. These spoke Yuki as well as their native Wailaki, much as the Yuki adjoining the Sehlgaikyo-kaiya farthest upstream on main Eel River mostly knew Wailaki in addition to Yuki.

down. This, of course, does not mean that they outsped them, but that in a relentless pursuit they wore down the endurance of the game, until, unable to feed and perhaps overcome by pyschic depression, it succumbed. In fishing, too, they did well. Whether because of better opportunities or more skillful use of them, they surpassed the Yuki, and the latter buy, and perhaps formerly bought, nets and harpoons from them.

ENEMIES.

They fought the Yuki, at least along the Eel River, but also married among them and intruded their customs. The Ta'no'm Yuki obsidian dance and initiation is, if not wholly of Wailaki origin, at least largely developed under Wailaki influence. Not long before 1850 the two tribes united and engaged in a bitter quarrel with the Kato. Before this, the Wailaki seem to have been on good terms with the Kato and their friends the Coast Yuki, and thus to have been able occasionally to visit the ocean shore, from which the Yuki were shut off by feuds.

The Yuki have a story of a young Wailaki, whom they call Imichshotsi, who boasted of his ability to dodge the slow Yuki arrows. His people warned him that the Yuki shafts might be short and thick and their own long and slender, but that the foes' arrows came too thickly to dodge with safety, and that they penetrated bitingly. He offered to prove his contention, and the party set out, Imichshotsi demanding to meet the cowardly Yuki whom his people proclaimed to be always ready to meet them in battle. On the slope of Imtomol, where the dividing line between Yuki and Wailaki ran eastward up from Eel River, they met the enemy in three parties, probably the Ta'no'm and their allies. The Yuki shouted in challenge. Imichshotsi took the lead, urging his companions to follow him if they wished to see how arrows could be evaded. As they approached the first band, the Yuki began to shoot, and soon the Wailaki were giving ground around the hill. Then Imichshotsi commenced to feel weak, and took refuge behind a Wailaki, who, incased in a long elk-skin armor, stood a tower of strength. But even here the arrows, though many fell dead from the unpierceable front of the wearer, came too thickly to make a longer holding of his post safe for naked Imichshotsi behind. He prepared to leap away, but as he crouched for the spring that would launch his retreat an arrow entered his hip and came out at the groin. The Yuki ceased shooting, and the Wailaki carried their fallen champion off to his death. His own father went ahead, calling in mockery that Imichshotsi was cutting off Yuki heads; he alone had a powerful bowstring; the Yuki could not shoot, and were all being killed at Imtomol. When the youth breathed his last, the party stopped and mourned over his body, but the old man announced that he would proceed and announce to the people that Imichshotsi was destroying the Yuki. He arrived and shouted this derision to the village but at this very moment his companions were already burning the body of the slain boy.

This naïvely self-complimentary relation, with its incredible account of the father's ironic mockery of his slain flesh and blood, does not pretend to be more than a tale. But it illustrates with vividness the miniature pitched battles, the long-range shooting and incessant dodging of flying arrows, the occasional invulnerable armor, the slight losses, the immediate mourning, the cremation of those slain away from home, and the lack of all idea of organization, that were typical of the fighting of the Wailaki and their neighbors. Struggles of another character against the same foe, half-avowed and half-concealed feuds, with ambushes and village surprises predominating, are related of the Kato.

TEXTILE ART.

Wailaki basketry is of the northern twined variety—technique, materials, patterns, and all. It marks the southern limit of this type in the Coast Range region. Among the Yuki there is no trace of this ware. With it, too, the woman's cap extended to the Wailaki and no farther. As everywhere in this region, the basketry has a wrinkled surface and a lack of fineness. E v e n and delicate texture was not attained, perhaps not attempted. The forms, too, run d e e p, as in northeastern California. It would seem that the characteristic low basket of the Hupa and Yurok was coextensive in its distribution with the best worked ware. Mortar and carrying baskets are

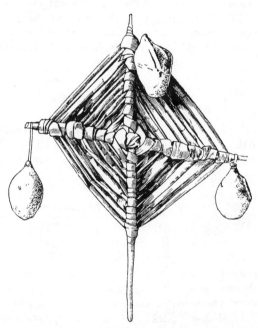

FIG. 16.—Wailaki charm.

strengthened by the Wailaki with one or two stiff hoops, sometimes lashed on with a thong.

While the northwestern basketry has not passed from the Wailaki to the Yuki, the coiled ware of the latter has found some introduction among the former. It is the art that has taken a hold, not a case of objects traded. The Wailaki, however, make but few coiled baskets, and these serve as valuables and gifts rather than practical utensils; and they even seem rather better made than most of their Yuki prototypes. Coiling must be looked upon as sporadic with the Wailaki.

CULTURAL RELATIONS.

Other objects of material culture are little known. On Round Valley Reservation the Wailaki dance in feather ornaments similar to those of the Pomo and Yuki; but this might possibly or partly be an assimilation under American pressure.

Some Wailaki feathered head darts and forks that happen to have been preserved reveal a type that, while central Californian, is perceptibly different from the corresponding Yuki and Pomo ones (Fig. 21); and this distinction is probably significant of others that existed anciently.

Charms of grass or rush wound diagonally around two crossed sticks were used, but their specific purpose is unknown (Fig. 16).

The Yuki state that the Wailaki shamans often dreamed of a spirit coyote, and were able to kill at long distances by means of a magical hulk'oi-tit or " coyote snare." They themselves had no such coyote shamans.

NUMBERS.

The Wailaki population in 1910 was somewhat over 200, mostly on Round Valley Reservation, though only a minority are listed as full bloods. This figure makes them the largest surviving group of Athabascans in California after the Hupa. Their original number may have been a thousand, possibly somewhat more.

The Kato.

THE NATION.

Wedged in on three sides by the Yuki, the Kato or Kaipomo, the southernmost Athabascans on the Pacific coast, held the uppermost courses of the South Fork of Eel River, their only neighbors of their own stock being the Sinkyone to the north and the Wailaki to the northeast. Though they belong to the same speech division as these two groups, their dialect was considerably specialized from that of the Wailaki and only partly intelligible. To the Hupa, of whose existence they had no knowledge whatever in aboriginal days, their idiom is completely unintelligible.

The word Kato is a Pomo place name meaning " lake." Kaipomo means " valley people " in the same language. The Katos' own name for themselves as a group is not known. It is possible that they had none. Their current Pomo designation, the fact that the whites first reached them through the Pomo, and that some individuals among the Kato speak Pomo in addition to their native language, led to their being formerly erroneously classed as Pomo. It is clear, however, that they were considerably influenced by this more advanced group, and, with the Huchnom, served as transmitters of religious cults and other civilizational features from the Pomo to the Yuki and Wailaki.

NUMBERS.

The Kato are said to have had nearly 50 villages. If these had all been inhabited contemporaneously, the population of the group would have been 2,000, which is not only an abnormally high figure for California, but hardly compatible with the rugged nature of their habitat. Part of their country is dense redwood forest and the remainder is well timbered. The permanent settlements must have been generally confined to the three little valleys in which Branscomb, Cahto, and Laytonville now stand. A thousand seems the maximum population that can be assumed; 500 is probably nearer the mark. To-day about 50 persons, mostly full bloods, are reckoned as Katos. Some of these are on Round Valley Reservation, others on land provided them by the government near Laytonville.

MYTHS.

Kato customs are known chiefly through their mythology. Their creation legend refers to two original beings, Thunder and Nagaicho, or " great traveler." The latter is known also to the Sinkyone, and corresponds in function as in the meaning of his name to the Yuki creator Taikomol. Thunder is, however, represented by the Kato as distinctly the more powerful of the pair, and the actual creator of men, many animals, mountains, trees, and springs. The grandeur of the concept of our earth as a vast horned animal that wallows southward through the primeval waters with Nagaicho standing on its head, until it comes to rest lying down in its present position, can not be denied. The making of the sky with its four columns and four cloud gates, the theft of the sun by Coyote, his securing of fire from the spider who alone hoards it, the designation of Coyote as our mother's brother, are told with a similarity to Yuki tales that evinces the close contacts existing between the two peoples.

TRAITS SHARED WITH OTHER GROUPS.

Kato myths and tales refer to two objects which they are not known to have used: the basket hat and the canoe. The woman's cap, so universal in the north, has not been found among any of the tribes grouped together on Round Valley Reservation. It may be suspected that its range at the utmost was that of the northern twined basketry, whose outpost is with the Wailaki. Kato baskets are scarcely distinguishable from those of Yuki manufacture. But it is possible that the Kato now and then traded for objects which they did not make.

The reference to the canoe, *ch'iyashts*, suitable for ocean travel, is harder to understand. The Kato streams are far too small to be navigable, and the Yuki of the coast, to whom they refer as intimate associates, deny having had boats. It is probable that the

Kato knew the canoe only as a possession of the northern Sinkyone. Even the episodes in their legends mentioning it may have been learned from tribes that possessed boats.

The gambling game in which bones are rolled in freshly cut grass, the man's hair net, the many varieties of bulbs cooked in the ground, the large dance house with a roof door, are all traits shared with the Yuki. The employment of an elk-horn wedge and stone maul in the procuring of firewood, and the frequent use of acorns molded or blackened by long immersion in water, are probably common to the northwestern and central groups. Kato women smeared pitch on their foreheads in mourning. This is not northwestern, but has Sacramento Valley and Pomo analogues.

The Yuki *Taikomol-wok* rite—with both its "big-head" dancer and the teaching of children through myths told them by an old man conversant with the ceremony—are said by the Yuki to have come to them from the Kato, and the legends of the latter contain references to the institution, though its name has not been recorded. The Kato in turn probably derived the cult from the northern and these from the eastern Pomo, who in turn were affected by the Wintun, or retained in less elaborate form the elements of an old ritual which was subsequently organized into greater complexity in the Sacramento Valley.

The victory ceremony, danced in line in the dance house with the head of a corpse that had been pulled in two, and the preservation of the "scalp"—probably the entire skin of the head—were substantially like Yuki customs.

Specific references are to cremation and not burial, but it is not certain if this was the universal practice, since all the funerals referred to are those of strangers or people killed in war. The Yuki bury, except—like many other Californian natives—in case of death at a distance, ashes being more transportable than the body; the Pomo burned until the American came.

In speech, an influence of the adjacent Pomo is traceable. The other Athabascans of California all count decimally. The Kato reckon up to twenty by fives. The stems of their numerals are pure Athabascan, the manner of use foreign. They have also the custom of addressing their parents-in-law in plural or dual forms comparable to French *vous* and German *ihr*, in place of the singular, as an expression of respect. This is a Pomo habit, but may have been derived by the Pomo from the Athabascans, since the practice prevails north to the Hupa.

WARS WITH THE YUKI.

A series of hostilities that arose between certain of the Kato and the Yuki shortly before the coming of the Americans has been recorded from a Yuki source. The details are anecdotic; but as the result of the fighting is pictured as mostly in favor of the Kato, the underlying reliability of the account can scarcely be doubted.

Word came to the Lilkaino'm or Lilshikno'm Yuki on Eel River that if they would come to the Kolukomno'm Kato village of Lila^{n}sichma^{n}l or "red-rock-creek," they would receive gifts; that is, that the Kato wanted to trade, making a donation first and then accepting presents in return. When the Yuki arrived an old man and two of his sons were killed and two other young men captured by the Kato. A brother and a son of the old man, named, respectively, Titopi and Pitaki, escaped. The former had indeed been seized, but broke away. As he fled up the canyon he was shot through the hand with an arrow. But he made his escape, and when he arrived on top of the mountain sat down and mourned his brother after the fashion of the Wailaki. The Lilshikno'm and Ta'no'm Yuki were in closer association with the Wailaki than the other Yuki, and this is only one instance of several that they followed the customs which their kinsmen regarded as characteristic of the Wailaki.

The Kato man who was responsible for this attack was called Palmi by the Yuki. One of the three victims had his head cut off by the Kato; that is, they danced over it. The fate of the two captives is not mentioned in the story. To a California Indian this would probably seem naturally equivalent to stating that they were killed. It is characteristiç that the names of the two men who escaped are cited, but those of their slain kinsmen not mentioned.

It appears that the thing attempted was first to get hold of a victim and then dispatch him at close quarters. This practice recurs in the following accounts. Stand-up fighting was not in favor except in a pitched battle, and this was evidently a long-range affair with arrows and infinite dodging.

War was now on, and the Kato, anticipating reprisals, came to Hanchamta^{n}l, a Lilshikno'm or Ta'no'm settlement on Eel River, and succeeded in killing an old Yuki and carrying off his head. This was "too soon," according to the narrator, for the Yuki had not yet made an attack in return for their first loss. But after this they went out.

Near Hayilta^n, in Kolukomno'm territory, the Yuki scouts from Hanchamta^{n}l were run on to by a young Kato known to them as Hutichpalsi. He was seized, bound, his arms stretched out, and his head cut off. There may have been more fighting; but apparently the Hanchamta^{n}l people, having got a head for the one that they had lost, were satisfied and went home. At Tamahan they built a dance house for the occasion and celebrated over the trophy.

The customary intertribal visiting had suddenly ceased under this state of affairs, the native narrator continues; but a Yuki woman, sister of the old man who had been killed at Hanchamta^{n}l, was intent on revenge and pretended a revival of friendship. Supported by a party of Yuki in hiding, she followed her husband to a Kato house. When he had entered, he made as if he were having difficulty passing through the door a large basket of buckeye porridge which his wife had brought up; until one of the two Kato men inside said: "Set down this Yuki blood." At once the husband leaped upon them, his wife rushed in, and between them they overpowered and killed the two inmates. A Kato woman seized up her baby and fled, but the Yuki amazon ran her down at a near-by spring and brained both her and the infant. The main Yuki party probably came up after the affair was over, since the narrative does not mention them again; and if there were Kato in near-by houses, they probably fled at the first alarm, knowing that an attack would not be made without an equipped and outnumbering force in reserve.

The reciprocating Kato offense fell upon the Pomaha^{n}no'm, a group of the Ta'no'm. The Yuki account admits 11 slain, but passes over the painful details.

The Pomaha^{n}no'm, of course, did not sit still. A party went out, but apparently hesitated whether to attack or to treat for settlement. Possibly the offer of peace was a ruse, but it seems that it not infrequently happened that an untoward event would turn a band of willing but suspicious and frightened peace negotiators into aggressors; and, on the other hand, there may generally have been no one who dared treat for a settlement without an armed and ready force standing at his back.

At any rate, the majority of the Yuki went home or turned aside. Two bear doctors, shamans of unusual ferocity, who had the grizzly as their protector and could more or less completely turn themselves into this dangerous and vindictive animal, in native belief, trusted in their power or the fear of their repute and boldly went or remained among the Kato. The latter took one of the two brothers fishing, and after cooking one of the catch offered it to him. The Yuki, however, knew in his heart that the fish had been poisoned by one of the Kato who could exercise magical control, and refused; whereupon a Kato came up to hold him, no doubt preliminary to the others dispatching him. The unarmed bear doctor, however, seized his bone hairpin and, using it as a bear would his teeth, killed the man who had grasped him and several others after him, until the Kato, recognizing his supernatural abilities and invulnerability, desisted. A true bear shaman can not, in fact, be killed with weapons; but they may have been unconvinced that his powers were complete and genuine. About the same time his brother was attacked at the Kato village where he had remained behind, but saved himself by recourse to similar faculties. The Yuki of to-day believe that between them the two medicine men disposed of six of their foes before they returned home, and that so strong and bearlike was the frenzy of the one brother that he chewed and actually devoured part of the arm of the rash man who ventured to be the first to hold him.

However, there was more to this expedition than the story tells, for the Yuki admit that on the same trip the Pomaha^{n}no'm lost an old and a young man. The Kato themselves ran off after the deed. The Yuki must have done the same, for the Kato, returning the next day, found the corpses still on the spot and cut off the heads. They carried these to the coast, presumably to be in a sufficiently remote place to make the dance over the heads safe from an interrupting attack. The choice of this locality indicates that the Coast Yuki were siding with the Kato, or were at least sympathetically neutral. This is not surprising in view of the fact that in times of peace the Kato were constantly visiting the Coast Yuki, while the remoter Yuki rarely if ever ventured to the ocean.

The count stood 17 or 19 killings for the Kato, only 11 for the Yuki, in half a dozen or more encounters, though without a pitched fight, during a period that very likely covered two or three years. Excitement must now have been at a point where larger undertakings might be attempted; and in fact all the Yuki, from the Sukshultatano'm at Fishtown to the Witukomno'm on the slopes of Sanhedrim, talked of combining for one great expedition into Kato territory. Talk and deliberation are, however, the necessary and almost endless preliminary to any joint action of California Indians, however swift and resolute they may be in crises as individuals; and talk it remained. For the whites appeared in the country, upset the native life, and gave Yuki and Kato alike more pressing problems to meet than even their feud.

CHAPTER 10.

THE YUKI: ETHNIC GEOGRAPHY.

The Yukian Family.

The Yuki language and allied dialects have long been recognized as constituting a distinctive group, and even the comparative researches of recent years have failed to reveal much clue of their possible relationship to either Athabascan, Hokan, or Penutian. The general type of the language, it is true, is somewhat similar to that of the Penutian idioms, but specific connections have not been discovered. Yukian, therefore, remains as a small isolated speech family, the only one, in fact, of the many Californian stocks for which original unity with other languages has never been asserted.[1] Its position is somewhat like that of Basque in Europe, so far as can be told to-day; and the people speaking Yukian dialects, or some of their ancestors, must accordingly be regarded as having had a long separate career. (Pl. 28.)

As with the Basques, a peculiar physical type tends to accompany distinctive speech in the case of the Yukian family. The northern tribes of the family possess probably the longest heads in California, and are unusually short of stature. That this physical type is found also among some of the adjacent non-Yukian tribes, and that the southern Yukian divisions depart from it and resemble their broader-headed and taller-bodied neighbors, is easily intelligible as a consequence of gradual intermarriage and the shifting of populations from their former seats; in other words, as a secondary phenomenon. The essential fact remains that Yukian speech and Yukian anatomy are both distinctive and both not definitely connectible with any other group. In this sense, the Yuki may fairly be spoken of as coming nearer, so far as can be judged at present, to being autochthonous Californians than any of the other modern natives of the State.

---

[1] It has been asserted since the above was written: by Paul Radin, in Univ. Calif. Publ. A. A. E., XIV, 489–502, 1919.

The Yuki live in two principal bodies, whose speech, though clearly one in origin, has diverged very considerably. The northern group held the larger territory and was probably more populous. Its seat was between the Athabascans and the Pomo, and between the Wintun and the sea. The southern group, known as the Wappo, was, roughly speaking, south of the Pomo. The Wappo had themselves sent out, or retained, a minute offshoot in Pomo territory. The northern Yukians were almost separated into a coast and larger interior subgroup by the Athabascans and the Pomo, whose territories they themselves separated; but the difference in speech between coast and interior was not very impressive, so that a comparatively recent cessation of contact is indicated. The interior subgroup again subdivides into a smaller, dialectically distinct, southwesterly body known as the Huchnom, much modified in customs by intimate contact with the Pomo; and a main mass that may be designated as the Yuki proper. The latter group subdivides once more into a considerable number of small units which might almost be called tribes, some of which also differed at least dialectically or subdialectically; but as the precise number, dialectic range, and relations of these smaller units are imperfectly known, and the differences between them appear to have been slight, it seems preferable to treat them, except in the discussion of their geography, as a single whole. The four Yukian divisions to be considered separately are thus the Yuki proper, Huchnom, Coast Yuki, and Wappo.

THE YUKI PROPER.

HABITAT.

As seen on the map (Pl. 26), the distribution of the Yuki seems irregular. This is not because their location ran counter to natural topography but because it followed it. Their country lies wholly in the Coast Range mountains, which in this region are not, on the whole, very high, but are much broken. They contain some valleys, but the surface of the land in general is endlessly rugged. The Yuki habitat is, however, not defined, except incidentally, by limiting mountains and ranges, but is given in block by the drainage of such-and-such streams. The native did not think, like a modern civilized man, of his people owning an area circumscribed by a definite line, in which there might happen to be one or many watercourses. This would have been viewing the land through a map, whether drawn or mental; and such an attitude was foreign to his habit. What he did know was that the little town at which he was born and where he expected to die lay on a certain river or branch of a river; and that this stream, or a certain stretch of it, and all the creeks flowing

PLATE 26

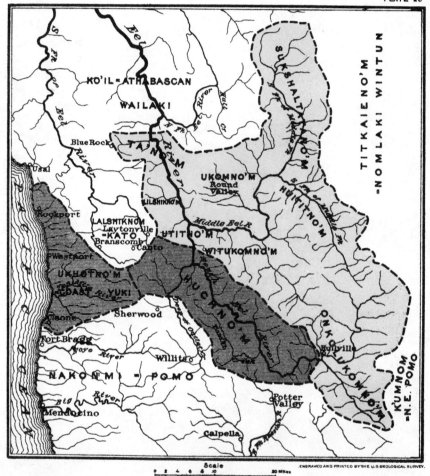

YUKIAN DIVISIONS

into it, and all the land on or between these creeks, belonged to his people; whereas below, or above, or across certain hills, were other streams and tributaries, where other people lived, with whom he might be on visiting terms or intermarried, but who had proprietary rights of their own.

Yuki territory may be described as all the land lying in the drainage of Eel River above the North Fork, except for a stretch on South Eel River where the allied Huchnom were situated. This sounds and is simple enough. It is nature's fault, and not any intricacy of the Yuki mind or subtlety of Yuki institutions, if this extraordinarily compact and unitary fact takes form on our maps in the shape of a meaninglessly curved, indented, and irregular border.

DIVISIONS.

The same basic simplicity of topography applies to the habitat of the larger Yuki divisions. The Ta'no'm were on main Eel River, the farthest down. The Lilshikno'm or Lilshaino'm or Lilnuino'm were upstream from them. Still farther up, where the river forks into the South Eel and the Middle Eel, were the Utitno'm. Each branch can be followed up in the same way. On the South Eel, nearly to its forks, were the Huchnom; from the forks up, the Onkolukomno'm. Along Middle Eel, there were, first, on the south side, especially on the tributaries, the Witukomno'm. Eden Valley was the largest piece of level land in this section. Opposite, where a number of creeks flow into the river from the north and west, mostly through Round Valley—the largest flat tract not only in this area but in the whole Yuki habitat—were the Ukomno'm. Farther up, the Middle Eel also divides. On its South Fork were the Huititno'm, on the North Fork the Sukshaltatano'm.

It would be entirely erroneous, however, to regard these eight or nine groups as being in any way tribes. They were each merely an aggregation of smaller units that happened to live together in a natural area. Among themselves, they probably did not use the designations just mentioned, and thought of themselves as the people of villages A, B, and C, or the people of chiefs X and Y. The broad names were those used by outsiders when they wanted to generalize, just as we, for convenience, speak of the Balkan peoples or the Indo-Chinese, while well aware that Serbia is not Bulgaria and that a Burman does not dream of considering himself of one nationality with an Anamese.

A distinction which has not always been observed must be drawn with scrupulous exactness between the village as a town or physical settlement and the village as a group or community.

The community always might and usually did embrace several settlements. This seems simple enough. What has caused confusion and makes the acquisition of accurate information so difficult, now that the old organization is gone, is the fact that the community was nameless. If designated, it was referred to by the name of the principal village. This place name therefore denotes at one time a cluster of several little towns and on other occasions one of these towns. Even the addition of a term changing the reference from the spot to the inhabitants leaves the situation obscure: "X people" may mean either the residents at the particular settlement X, or those of X, Y, and Z, which together are called X.

The word "tribe" can not be extended to these communities without an entirely erroneous implication, since they possessed, as a rule, no group appellation, no separate dialect, and no distinctive customs. In the sense that the communities were the only political units they were tribes; but as they lacked all the traits of individualized nationality, which it is customary to attach to the meaning of the term "tribe," it is wisest to avoid its use.

THE TRIBE IN CALIFORNIA.

The Yuki type of organization existed among the Pomo and the Maidu, with both of whom the village community and the village settlement can be definitely distinguished in certain areas. It is likely to have been the plan of political society followed by the majority of other Californian Indians, well into the southern part of the State; but, other than among the stocks cited, positive information fails us, except in a few areas where it is clear that a different organization prevailed.

These exceptions are, first, the Yuman peoples on the Colorado River, who were clearly constituted into tribes in the usual sense of the word, and thoroughly similar to the tribes of, for instance, the Plains region in the heart of the continent. This true tribal organization, however, clearly did not extend to the neighboring Chemehuevi, Cahuilla, and Diegueño.

Second, there were the tribes of northwestern California. Here, as described for the Yurok, there were no groups other than the persons, often largely connected in blood, who lived in one spot. Except for their permanent occupation of one site, the Yurok town groups were accordingly in the political status of the primitive horde, as it is theoretically depicted.

The extent of the northwestern type of organization is not clearly known. Besides the Yurok, Hupa, and Karok, the Tolowa, Wiyot, and Chilula participated in it. The Shasta and Chimariko are in doubt. The southern Athabascans, at least the Wailaki and Kato, followed the Yuki plan, and there are indications that the Yukian scheme of organization may have prevailed as far north as the Sinkyone, if not beyond.

The third and last exception is provided by the Yokuts, but it is only a partial one. The Yokuts were divided into tribes, each named and each with a dialect. But, as set forth in the chapter dealing with these people, the Yokuts tribes in size, in relation to territory, and in their own consciousness were rather similar to the Yuki and Pomo community groups, so that their distinctive nature, however significant, was secondary rather than fundamental. Some of the Shoshoneans east of the Yokuts, on both sides of the Sierra Nevada, were organized somewhat like them.

ORGANIZATION OF THE YUKI COMMUNITIES.

The Yuki add the suffix -no'm, " people," to the names of larger regions, districts, villages, or mere landmarks, to denote the inhabitants of these localities or their vicinity. The words containing this increment might be taken for tribal names were it not for the fact that it is always the people that are named after the place, and not the reverse. There is also no restriction of the terms to communities. Ukom-no'm denotes all the inhabitants of the Round Valley region, groups A, B, C, as given below, and as many others as there were. U'witno'm appears to be applicable at will, according to the context, to all the members of group A, of which U'wit was the main town, or to the actual inhabitants of the particular settlement called U'wit.

The ending -no'm is the equivalent of the Pomo increment -pomo or -napo, of the Wappo -noma; perhaps also of the Maidu and Plains Miwok -mni, Sierra Miwok -chi, Costanoan -n. It is often difficult to decide whether the words containing these suffixes denote primarily the village or the inhabitants. Perhaps native usage did not enforce a clear-cut distinction. Wappo -noma, for instance, has been obtained chiefly on names that seem to denote places; yet the element is unquestionably one in origin with Yuki -no'm.

Fortunately there is a restricted area for which specific information has been assembled; and the conditions deducible from these data no doubt applied to all the Yuki. In the northern part of Round Valley and adjacent hills were three such quasi-tribal groups or communities. These constituted only part, and probably a small part, to judge by their area on the map, of the division known as the Ukomno'm. Each comprised several settlements. Each settlement had its headman; but each quasi-tribal group of settlements also recognized a common chief of wider authority.

GROUP OR COMMUNITY A: Northern portion of Round Valley west of the agency. Last head chief, Hunchisutak, who lived at U'wit.

Village or settlement 1: Chochhanuk. Name of chief forgotten. A small settlement.

Village 2: Mameshishmo. Chief: Kumshume. There was a dance house in this town.

Village 3: U'wit. Town chief: Olyosi. The head chief of the group also lived here. This town had a dance house.

Village 4: Hake. Name of chief forgotten. There was a dance house.

Village 5: Son. Olyosi of U'wit acted as town chief for this town as well as his own.

Other villages, probably of minor size and without dance houses, belonged to this group but have been forgotten.

GROUP B: Northern part of Round Valley east of the agency, and northeast over the hills to include Williams Valley. Last head chief, Hultalak at Pomo village.

Village 1: Pomo, in Round Valley.

Village 2: Mo't-huyup, in lower Williams Valley.

Village 3: Kilikot, in Williams Valley, farther upstream.

Village 4: Lelhaksi, in Williams Valley, farther upstream.

Village 5: Nonakak, in Williams Valley, farther upstream.

Village 6: Yukuwaskal, in Williams Valley, farther upstream.

Village 7: Moyi, in Williams Valley, farther upstream.

The names of town chiefs and locations of dance houses have not been learned.

GROUP C: Northeastern corner of Round Valley and eastward to Middle Eel River. Last head chief, Sinchichmopse of Titwa.

Village 1: Titwa or Ona^{n}s, in Round Valley.

Village 2: Sonkash, in Round Valley.

Village 3: Molkus, in Round Valley.

Other villages lay east of the valley, toward the river, but their names and sites are not known.

From the data on group A it appears that the " tribal " chief was more than the headman of the largest village, since his village held a town chief as well as himself; and that the town chief and the dance house have a definite connection. Evidently it was only a recognized headman who put up a dance house, or the man who erected such a structure thereby became the headman of his settlement. It is also evident that the early Spaniards and Americans were not always misunderstanding native conditions in California so completely as sometimes seems to modern ethnologists, in naming villages and "tribes" after their "captains." As the group had no name or single site, its political entity must have been primarily associated with the head chief. His functions are not well known; but it is reasonable to conjecture that he determined war and peace and the time and place of ceremonials, and that invitations for visits, large feasts, and trade meetings with other groups were issued by him. His influence may have extended beyond these matters. On the other hand, it is likely that the relation of each town to its food supply, the decision how long to remain at or away from the winter home, and where to camp or dig or hunt, rested with the town chief.

Many interesting problems must remain unanswered for the Yuki. We do not know how far the head chief's position was hereditary, nor if so, precisely in what manner, nor whether in doubtful or obnoxious cases the consent of towns or town chiefs was required. There is nothing to show whether the head chief got his own food along with his fellows or whether he was supported by contributions and gave his time to being dignified and accumulating wealth by grinding shell beads. And it would be interesting to know his part in the delicate deliberations that must often have preceded the decision to put out of the way a shaman believed to have turned witch and poisoner. Further, we are in ignorance of how substantially the men of each town were a group of kinsmen, presumably in the male line, and whether there was any feeling favoring a man's marrying outside his community, or any unformulated but customary practice of doing so.

OTHER NOTES ON DIVISIONS AND SUBDIVISIONS.

The Ta'no'm, one of the eight geographical groups shown on the map, adjoined the Athabascan Wailaki where a ridge named "Imtomol" comes down to Eel River from the east, at the big bend of the stream, a couple of miles above the mouth of the North Fork. This ridge was the scene of a traditionary fight between the Ta'no'm and Wailaki, which has already been related. Later two groups of Athabascans fought on this same ridge. Probably they were Kato against Wailaki, the latter now aided by the Ta'no'm. This may have been about the time the Americans came. The Ta'no'm were named after Ta', a long open hill slope east of the river. Six of their divisions have been recorded—the Kichilpitno'm, Kasha^{n}sichno'm, Pomaha^{n}no'm, Ma^{n}tno'm, Ha^{n}chhotno'm, and Ulamolno'm. These are likely to have been political units, each with a head chief, corresponding to the Ukomno'm groups A, B, C, described above. Kasha^{n}sich, Pomaha^n, and Hanchhot were places. It is significant that an old Ta'no'm was able to name without effort more than 250 spots in the little territory of his people, in which he had not lived for 50 years. These included summer and winter habitations, hunting places, spots for snaring deer, hot medicinal springs, flint quarries, places where the women leached buckeye mush, or gathered seeds in summer or acorns in autumn, meadows whose grass was burnt to catch the nutritious grasshoppers, spots where the shamans kept their obsidians or where the Wailaki once came to make the obsidian ceremony, and many others. This same informant was married simultaneously to four women—one from Suk'a, one from Nu', two from Ontit.

Other Yuki groups—whether settlements or communities is uncertain in most cases—are the following:

Alniukino'm, in northwest part of Round Valley. K'ilikuno'm, in the northern or lower end of Eden Valley. Witukomno'm is not only the name of the entire group in and around Eden Valley, but of the people of a village near its head. North of the Middle Eel River, between the Ukomno'm and the Witukomno'm, was a group for which no generic name has been obtained, but which included the Suk'ano'm, the Sonla^{n}lno'm, the Chakomno'm, and the Chahelilno'm. Liltamno'm and Nonlachno'm, perhaps synonyms, at Blue Nose, north or northeast of Round Valley. Ukachimno'm, in Poorman's Valley, northeast of Round Valley. Shipima^{n}ino'm and Kichilukomno'm, in Williams Valley— one of these may be the name of the group B above. Ma^{n}lchalno'm at one of the heads of Middle Eel River. Onkolukomno'm, in Gravelly Valley near

Hullville: Nuichukom as the name of this tract seems to be a Yuki translation from the English Gravelly Valley. Hunkalich was a village near Hullville. The Matamno'm were a Yuki group, perhaps of Witukomno'm affiliation, who first learned the Taikomol myth and ceremony from the Kato and spread it to the other Yuki.

GROUP TRAITS.

There are dialectic divergences within the area of the Yuki proper. The speech of the Ta'no'm, Ukomno'm, and Witukomno'm differs. The Utitno'm dialect classed with the Witukomno'm, the Lilshikno'm probably with the Ta'no'm, the group including the Suk'ano'm may have leaned either to Ukomno'm or Witukomno'm, while the affiliations of the three eastern divisions of mountaineers are not known. All the dialects were mutually intelligible, but apparently different enough for any Yuki to recognize the approximate provenience of another.

The Yuki have a saying that the Ta'no'm, Lilshikno'm, and Witukomno'm, in other words, the groups on Main Eel and lower Middle Eel Rivers, were light skinned in comparison with the darker complexioned Ukomno'm of Round Valley.

NOMENCLATURE.

The word "Yuki" is Wintun and means stranger or foe. It is in generic usage by the Wintun, and its application to what we call the Yuki is an American practice. There is no equivalent native name. The Pomo call the Yuki Chumaia; the Wailaki and Kato name them Chiyinch or Ch'inch.

The Yuki, in turn, designate their alien neighbors as follows: The Athabascans in general, and the Wailaki in particular, are the Ko'il or Ko'ol; the Kato, or perhaps a division of the Kato, are the "black stream people" or La^nlshikno'm. The northern Pomo, especially from the vicinity of Sherwood and Willits, are the Nakonmi; the eastern Pomo of Clear Lake, of whom the majority of the Yuki had but vague knowledge before the white man came, the Upochno'm. The Wintun of Stony Creek were the K'umno'm or "salt people"; those of Grindstone Creek the Lilshimteino'm or "shallow black rock people"; those of Thomas Creek—the Nomlaki of the vicinity of Paskenta—the Titkai^neno'm; and those of Cottonwood Creek the Waik'emi. The K'umno'm probably included the northeastern Pomo. Of Yukian divisions, the Huchnom were so called, the Coast Yuki were the Ukhotno'm or "ocean people," and the Wappo were beyond ken or so little dealt with as to carry no distinctive name. The Concow Maidu and Pit River Achomawi that have been introduced on Round Valley Reservation are known to the Yuki there as Inshin and Shawash, respective corruptions of "Indian" and "Siwash."

TRADE.

As regards trade, shells and beads of all sorts came into the country from the south, from the Pomo, but apparently mostly through the Huchnom as intermediaries. Furs were given in return. The Yuki rarely if ever ventured to the coast, perhaps because their kinsmen there stood with the Kato in the prevalent feuds. Ocean foods, dried haliotis, mussel, and seaweed were, however, relished by them, and obtained from the northern Pomo, whose range extended to the sea, and whom they could perhaps meet amicably in Huchnom territory.

WARS.

In general, the Yuki fought all their neighbors, though more or less intermittently, and rarely, perhaps never, as a united body. The eastern groups, in the higher mountains, were at feud with the Wintun on the other side of the range. Ta'no'm and probably Lilshikno'm had a hereditary quarrel with the Wailaki next below them on Eel River; which did not, however, prevent some intermarriage and considerable interchange of customs. About the time of the appearance of the whites, or shortly before, the Wailaki nearest the Ta'no'm seem to have got into a quarrel with other Wailaki or Kato farther north, around Bald Mountain, and to have received Ta'no'm support against these kinsmen. The Lilshikno'm, about the same period, became embroiled with the Kato, with whom they appear to have been on less acute terms before; and before long the Ta'no'm were involved on their side. The Witukomno'm had their own feud with the Kato, and another with the northern Pomo of the vicinity of Sherwood. How the intervening Huchnom stood in this affair is not known. The Onkolukomno'm of the upper South Eel were joined on at least one occasion with the northeastern Pomo of Stony Creek, in the salt district of the region, against the eastern Pomo of the upper part of Clear Lake, to the south of themselves.

Certain of the Yuki wars against their Athabascan neighbors have been described in connection with the Wailaki and Kato; but, as everywhere in California, there were also internecine conflicts.

Apparently in the early days of Round Valley Reservation a woman refused to marry a Chakomno'm Yuki named U'umi and went to live with an U'witno'm, who was at once the father's brother and the stepfather of the narrator. Jealous U'umi prepared a plot. He induced his friends to feign an attack upon himself, but to use arrows without obsidian points. Then he shouted to his brother-in-law and to his U'witno'm rival to help him. They rushed to his aid; but when the U'witno'm's bowstring was void, and U'umi had an arrow aimed at his pretended foes, he swung his bow about and shot the unsuspecting victim at his side through hip and thigh. He fell; and the brother-in-law stepped up and finished him with an arrow above the eye. A clamor arose, and U'umi, with his accomplice, his friends and kin, and the related people of Suk'a, fled southward toward their old homes. The U'witno'm and other Ukomno'm, aided by some Wailaki, pursued. The shooting during the flight must have been at long range, for the avengers related how for all their endeavors they could not get their arrows to penetrate even when they hit. At last the pursuers became discouraged and the fleeing party rallied. The tide turned and Chakomno'm and Suk'ano'm drove the northerners back to the starting point in Round Valley; but also without scoring a kill. There the exhausted combatants quit. The murdered U'witno'm was never paid for by his slayer. Probably the Government officials interfered with the resumption of the feud.

The Round Valley people also fought the Witukomno'm of Eden Valley; but this seems to have been before the appearance of the Americans. It is likely that the murder just related was at bottom a recrudescence of this older enmity, the Chakomno'm and Suk'ano'm standing with the Witukomno'm against the Ukomno'm.

POPULATION.

The original Yuki population is very difficult to estimate. With only 200 to 300 souls to each of the eight or nine geographical divisions, a total of 2,000 is reached. Yet 200 to 300 seems a low average in view of such information as there is of the villages in part of Round Valley alone; whereas, on the other hand, if the total of 2,000 is materially increased, the Yuki as a whole would outnumber important and more advanced tribes like the Yurok and Karok, whose population gives every impress of comparative density. There would also be a tremendous decrease to be accounted for, which is difficult in view of the Yuki not having been drawn upon for the missions, and enjoying the advantage, in comparison with most other tribes, of remaining at least in part in their old homes and inhabiting a region thinly settled by whites—factors which in most of California have operated toward a better preservation of the aboriginal population. Yet the census of 1910 reports only 95 Yuki, three-fourths of them full blood; and this figure tallies closely with an official count. The Indian Office reports are higher, but worthless, since such a factor as tribal or speech difference has been meaningless in the routine administration, and the Round Valley Reservation rolls apparently list Yuki, Wailaki, Wintun, Maidu, Pomo, and Achomawi not according to what they are but on the more convenient plan of assigning each Indian a nationality according to the quarter of the reservation in which his allotted land happens to lie.

Taking everything into consideration, 2,000 is perhaps the most conservative estimate of the original number of Yuki.

CHAPTER 11.

THE YUKI: CULTURE.

CULTURAL POSITION.

The civilization of the Yuki was in some respects anomalous. They were definitely beyond the last influences of the northwestern culture, and yet in many points outside the general stream of customs and thoughts that pervaded the bulk of native California. Toward their wealthier southern and eastern neighbors they stood in the relation of rude and hardy mountaineers. But on the other hand, they possessed some rituals of considerable development, while the rule in California is that the hill tribes lack, in such matters, all that is most elaborate and specialized in the ceremonies of the adjacent lowland people, and content themselves with the simplest and most widespread elements—the earliest elements, to all appearance—of the religion of these neighbors.

Basketry illustrates the peculiar position. The Wailaki are not a northwestern people in any accurate sense as regards their mode of life as a whole. Their basketry, however, is purely northwestern, and indistinguishable from that of the Yurok except in its coarser workmanship and in some subtler details that can be felt but are definable only with difficulty. As far south as the Wailaki, then, a positive northwestern influence penetrates but there stops almost absolutely. The Ta'no'm Yuki interchanged ceremonies with the Wailaki. They may have acquired some of their baskets in trade, now and then. But they did not take over the Wailaki and northwestern art of basketry, or a single one of its features. An absolute line can be drawn here.

The Yuki, in short, and with them the Kato and Coast Yuki, were the northernmost advance guards, in the coast region, of the basketmaking art characteristic of the central Californian culture. But if Wailaki baskets are ill-made Yurok ones, the ware of the Yuki is not merely inferior Maidu-Wintun-Miwok ware, nor even Pomo ware.

A novice can tell it at a glance. It is a basketry with a character of its own.

The Pomo, it is true, had developed a peculiar art, which remained restricted to themselves and the small groups adjacent on their south and east. It is not remarkable that the Yuki in their mountains failed to partake of the specializations of this art, its feather and shell ornamentation, its decorative elaboration of pattern, its variety of techniques and forms. But it might be expected that Yuki baskets were comparable with the substratum of simpler everyday Pomo ware. And yet this is not the case.

Again, it is true that the Pomo art of basket making seems to represent a variation upon an old and well-established widespread central Californian art, which appears with considerable local modifications, but with no basic differences of aim or method, all over the great middle valley of California and the mountains that border it. It might be anticipated that the Yuki ware, failing to keep pace with the advanced Pomo development, represented merely a local survival of this more widely spread underlying art. In a sense, this is undoubtedly the case. Yet it is surprising that so small a fragment as the Yuki were, even if we reckon with them the Kato and Coast Yuki, should have come to acquire so distinct a provincialism in their industry, as great, perhaps, as that of any part of the broad Wintun group and of the widely spread Maidu; and the Maidu basketry shades almost insensibly into that of the Miwok, as again Miwok and Yokuts ware intergrade along their boundary. It is possible that if ever we learn more of the material culture of those of the Wintun immediately adjoining the Yuki, clearer transitions and affiliations will be revealed between them than are evident now. At present we can only separate Yuki basketry quite definitely and without explanation from the general industry upon which it is based.

The other side of the picture comes out in ritual. Two of the three distinctive major ceremonies of the Yuki have come to them from the south. This is quite clear from the character of the ceremonies themselves, and is confirmed by Yuki statements. The most immediate sources were the Kato and Huchnom. Back of them lie the Pomo. And the Pomo rituals themselves are quite clearly a provincial offshoot from the basis of the intricate Kuksu rituals that pervade the middle of the Sacramento-San Joaquin Valley and probably had their source as well as focus among the Wintun. The thing that is difficult to understand is that so much of the influence of this movement reached the Yuki and remained among them, when other hill tribes, whose speech and position and intercourse would indicate that they must have been at least equally subject to the same influence, reveal almost no traces of its effects. The northern

Wintun, for instance, the northeastern Maidu, the Yana, the Atsugewi and Achomawi do not organize themselves into an esoteric society and impersonate gods and spirits in their dances, and even the typical material paraphernalia that accompany these rituals are lacking among them. Not so the marginal and backwoods Yuki. They have, at least in rudiments, the society, the impersonation, and part of the regalia of the lowlanders.

And on top of these surprising connections with the centers of native civilization there is again a local specialization, which links the Yuki with the Athabascan north and divides them further from the Pomo south. The mythological character or creator with whom one of these two rituals of southern origin, the *Taikomolwok*, is associated, is known also to the Kato and even to the northern Sinkyone—under another name, indeed, but a name of the same meaning. And the third of the major ceremonies of the Yuki, the *Kichilwoknam* of the Ta'no'm, has no Pomo or southern equivalents at all, so far as known, but was evolved in association with the Wailaki to the north, if not directly imported from them.

It is in the light of these considerations that the details of Yuki civilization will be presented.

THE ART OF BASKETRY.

The better and decorated Yuki baskets are coiled. This method of manufacture, which is here encountered for the first time in our review, is therefore the one typical of the tribe. The most usual coiling is over a foundation of two rods and several welts. Sometimes a single rod is inclosed by welts, or lies toward the outer side of the basket from them. Poorly made baskets sometimes contain only welts or splints or have rods introduced sporadically. Such baskets usually have their stitches spaced well apart, 3 to 5 to the inch. Splints mostly lie vertically. Pomo coiling dispenses with splints altogether and uses either one or three well-rounded rods. A minority proportion of Yuki baskets are also coiled on a three-rod foundation without splints; but the single-rod foundation is not Yuki.

The materials for the foundation are usually dogwood, or occasionally honeysuckle, hazel, and perhaps also willow; for the sewing, normally *Cercis* redbud, and possibly maple and digger pine. For white portions of the pattern, the inner side of the redbud is used; for red, the outer; for black, the outer bark darkened by long soaking. The *Carex* sedge root favored by the Pomo is employed only occasionally.

The coil of Yuki baskets progresses from right to left, of Pomo ware from left to right, as one looks into the hollow of the vessel.

Baskets of open-bowl form—some almost as flat as plates—are used for parching, smaller ones for sifting meal, both as general receptacles. Hemispherical vessels were cooked in and held food. Some, usually small examples, were almost globular, with the mouth smaller than the body: these served to hold small articles not used for food and were given as presents.

The patterns are remarkably simple. By far the commonest decoration, especially in the flatter baskets, is a series of bands, each one course of sewing in width, encircling the vessel. As each band meets its beginning, the spiral progress of the basket has carried it one course higher, so that the junction would be a step. The Yuki woman meets this decorative awkwardness, in most cases, by leaving a little gap. This break is almost universal in Pomo work, where it is known as the *dau* and is associated with magical ideas, much as among the Zuñi in their pottery. It is not known whether the Yuki hold similar beliefs: at any rate, the gap is often filled in.

A characteristic feature of the ornament are small rectangular patches of varying size irregularly scattered over the white surface.

The hemispherical baskets bear diagonal and vertical patterns more often than the shallow ones, but rarely are elaborate in ornamentation.

The Yuki share the quail plume design with the Pomo, Wintun, and Maidu.

Twined baskets comprise a mortar hopper, of Pomo type but with Wailaki suggestions; a close-woven (cf. Pl. 24, *d*) and an open-work conical carrying basket; a plain twined seed beater resembling that of the Wailaki, though made of split instead of whole sticks (Pl. 29); an open-work sort of plate, with turned-in warp ends; and a similar hemispherical basket for leaching buckeyes. The commonest material for both warp and weft is willow; but hazel, grapevine, and digger pine also occur. The occasional patterns are in *Xerophyllum*.

HOUSEHOLD UTENSILS.

The mortar proper is, as to the north and south, not a hollowed rock, but a stone slab on which the basketry hopper is set. It is so used that it does not indent too deeply in one place. The pestle is the flaring or bulbous ended Pomo implement.

Acorn soup paddles are undecorated, like those of the Pomo, but more roughly made. The pipe is the wooden one with sudden large bowl fancied by the Pomo, but without the long, slender stem often worked by the latter people. (Pl. 30, *f*.) The awl was small and slender, with the joint of the bone ground away to leave no definite handle. (Fig. 67, *f*.)

PLATE 27

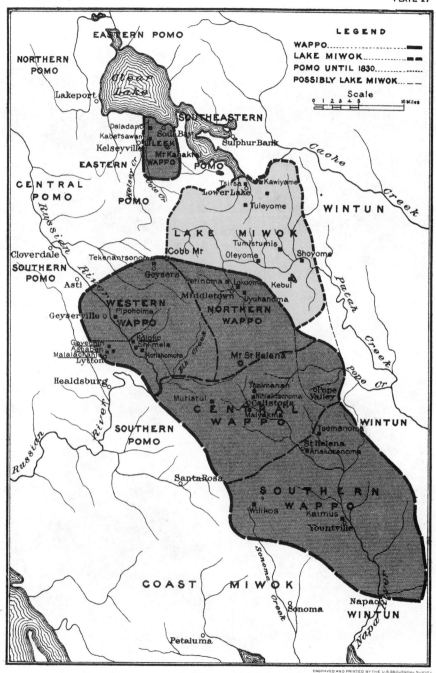

SETTLEMENTS OF THE WAPPO AND LAKE MIWOK

PLATE 28

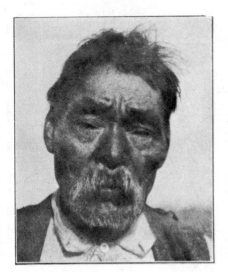

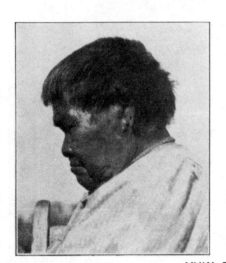

YUKI TYPES

The woman with hair cut in mourning (lower left) is half Huchnom.

PLATE 29

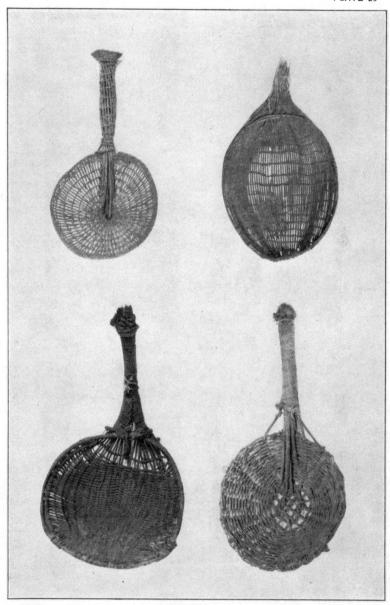

SEED BEATERS

Above, left, Nongatl; right, Chumash.   Below, left, Pomo, wickerwork; right, Yuki

PLATE 30

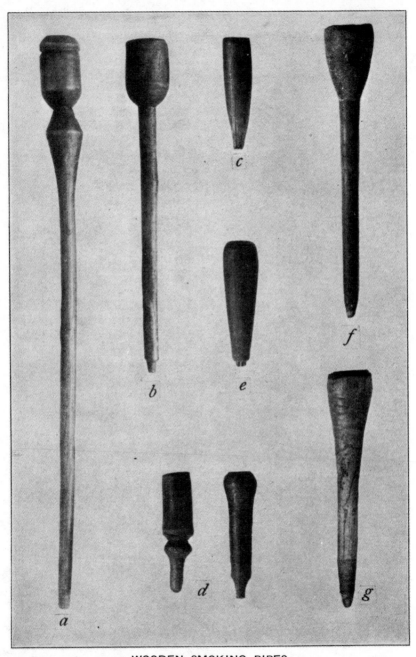

WOODEN SMOKING PIPES

a, b, Pomo; *c, d,* Yokuts; *e,* Miwok; *f,* Yuki; *g,* Wintun

PLATE 31

Salinan

Yana

Hupa girls

CENTRAL AND NORTHERN CALIFORNIAN TYPES

PLATE 32

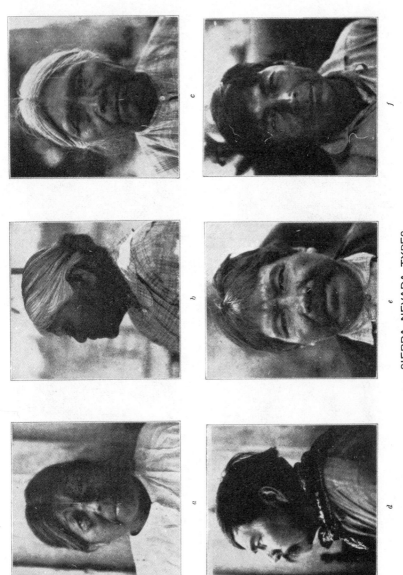

SIERRA NEVADA TYPES

a, *d*, Southern Miwok; *b*, *e*, Chukchansi Yokuts; *c*, Western Mono; *f*, Washo.

PLATE 33

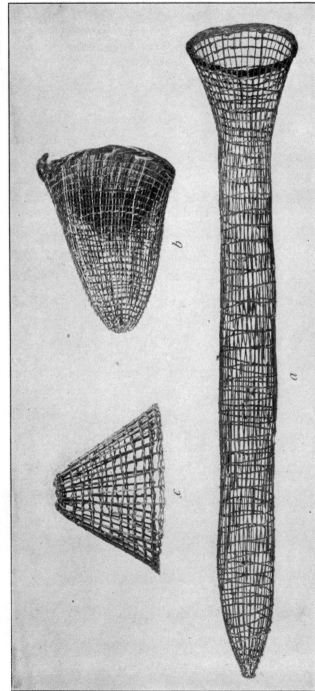

POMO FISH TRAPS

a, Laid in current, which prevents the fish backing out, and the trap is too narrow for them to turn; *b*, funnel pot, for small fish; *c*, open on top, plunged over small fish.

For loads, the Yuki employ both the Wailaki pack strap that passes around the carrying basket and the Pomo carrying net.

DANCE AND GAME OBJECTS.

Religious paraphernalia are of the kind general in central California. They come very close to Pomo forms, but are invariably simpler or less neatly made. The yellow-hammer headband, for instance, has its component quills roughly trimmed and unevenly sewn together (Fig. 20). The forked feather dart, nowadays made on wire instead of wood, is notably less elaborate than the better Pomo pieces (Fig. 21). The cocoon rattle runs to no great cluster and is without interspersed feathers (Fig. 37). The wooden clapper rattle, to judge by available specimens, is unpainted. The Pomo band theirs. The whistle, which may be of bone or reed, single or double, is less accurately cut off, pierced, and tied.

Yuki games are practically undescribed, except for the men's guessing game, which was played as by the Pomo with a pair of bones rolled in grass, and in which the widespread international exclamations *tep* and *wei* were used in designating the bone guessed at.

DRESS.

Little is known of dress, and it appears to have been scant. Women wore the usual fringed skirt or apron made of buckskin, and if necessary drew a deer cape or blanket over their shoulders. Young men wrapped a fur or skin around their hips in place of drawing a breechcloth between the legs. Old men may have gone stark naked. In cold weather a deerskin served as blanket. Rabbit-fur robes are scarcely mentioned. Their advantages are such that they must have been prized; but the timbered country was more productive of deer than of rabbits. The Yuki know the Wintun as being particularly given to taking rabbits by snares.

A basket cap was not worn by the women. This article of dress seems to stop everywhere with the southern limit of exclusively twined basketry, and to reappear again, in coiled form, only some distance to the south, or in diagonal twining in the Great Basin.

A compensation, as it were, for the women's basket caps are the string head nets of the men. Substantially, the two seem mutually exclusive in California; so it is not surprising that the Yuki employed the net, at least when the hair was to hold feathers.

Women's facial tattooing was most prominent on the cheeks and less precisely dictated by an inflexible fashion than in the Northwest, where it was the custom to cover the chin almost solidly but to leave the remainder of the face clear. Cheek tattooing seems to have reached its climax in the region of the Yuki and Wailaki. (Fig. 45.)

FOOD.

The streams in Yuki land are small enough in late summer, but in the rainy season are often torrentially swollen, and their courses are swift and rock-strewn. These were not conditions that encouraged any form of navigation, and the Yuki declare that they made not even rafts or tule balsas. Since many of their women, however, were poor swimmers, even when unencumbered by babies, the men in winter would bank coals of fire in a mass of ashes in a basket and carry this across a river. There they would start a blaze and warm themselves, then return and transport the children and feebler women by setting them in large carrying baskets, which the men pushed across while swimming or fording, as opportunity offered.

Fish nets, spears, and weirs of their own make are no longer used by the Yuki in their reservation life. What they need in this regard they buy from the Wailaki, whom they appear to look up to as superior fishermen. Such complete dependence could not have obtained in native days. But there was probably some tendency in this direction. Certainly the Wailaki on the main river and its immediate tributaries were better situated for fishing than the bulk of the Yuki on the headwaters. The latter, on the other hand, as the heavy winter flows receded and left the large salmon practically shut in pools separated by long and shallow riffles, gave the Yuki a chance to take the fish without nets. Men dived in and came up with a hand in the gills of a salmon, or, it is said, with a running noose slipped around its tail.

Bears were hunted in such wise that one man advanced boldly with nothing but a woman's root-digging stick with which he struck at the animal's pawing legs and stood him off while his companions took careful aim with their arrows.

The salt used by the Yuki came, wholly or mostly, from the K'umno'm, the "salt people," or northeastern Pomo. It may have been gathered there by the nearer divisions, such as the Onkolukomno'm with the consent of the amicable owners of the territory; at any rate, it probably passed through Onkolukomno'm hands. The groups farthest to the northwest were farthest from this source of supply, and in fact the other Yuki say that the Ta'no'm, and with them the Wailaki, having but little salt available, were accustomed to do without and showed little eagerness to obtain it.

The Yuki ate acorn soup by scooping two crooked fingers into the mess and sucking them off. Similar table manners have been reported from other parts of the State, and probably prevailed wherever spoons were not in common use.

HOUSES.

The Yuki house or *han*, and dance or " sweat " house, *iwil-han*, literally " poison-house " or " supernaturally powerful house," were built on one plan, and differed only in size and elaboration. They were circular, conically domed, and earth-covered, with one forking center post. There is no reference to any roof entrance, but the dance house had a small side entrance for fuel. The dance houses and larger houses were probably somewhat excavated, and are said to have had a series of low forked posts around the edge which were connected by the rafters. From these, poles and sticks ran up to the crotch of the center pole. On the poles were put successive layers of bark, grass, pine needles, and earth. The center post was actually somewhat back of the middle, which would give the rear of the roof a steeper pitch unless the house were built on a hillside. There was a short and low entrance tunnel of four forked sticks covered with poles and earth. At the inner and sometimes also at the outer end of this tunnel was a door consisting of a large piece of flat basketry, or a deerskin, around which the corners of the doorway were stuffed with grass.

Smaller houses dispensed with the peripheral uprights and had their poles laid from the central fork directly to the ground. Such a house would be built in a few days by a man working alone or with the assistance of a brother, and would stand without much repair for a year or two.

Still smaller houses were made without a center post, and consisted only of a conical lean-to of poles and bark, with an entrance. These must have been substantially identical with the bark houses of the Sinkyone and Lassik to the north.

It is clear that the distinction between the Yuki house and dance house is not structural, but lies in size, in their names, and in the recognition of the uses to which they are dedicated. This appears to have been the case throughout the northern portion of the central area. The northwestern sweat house differs from the living house in type as well as in service. In south central and southern California there is no true dance house, and the sweat house tends to be built differently from the living house.

The sweat house proper has usually been confused with the dance house on account of the customary designation of the latter as " sweat house " in English. The customs of the other north central Californian tribes suggest that the sweat house proper was earth roofed, but smaller than the dance house and perhaps than the dwelling.

The people lived in their *han* during the winter. They occupied them also in summer when they happened to be at the home village, but, since much of the dry season was spent in the hills, most of the living then was in brush shelters.

Houses stood irregularly in little groups. There would be only one dance house to the village, if that. The geographical accounts given speak of villages with and without dance houses as permanent features, but all the recorded narratives of actual ceremonial events mention such structures as specially erected for each occasion.

MONEY.

The current money was the central Californian clamshell disk bead, and was obtained from the Pomo, most frequently in finished form, but also in the unworked shell for piercing and grinding round by the Yuki themselves. The magnesite cylinders made from a deposit in the territory of the southeastern Pomo and commonly called "gold money" by the modern Indians, also penetrated to the Yuki, who knew them as *ship*, "scars." Most valuable of all were dentalia, *muli*, which came from the northern Pomo of Sherwood and Willits, though where these obtained them, unless at the end of a drift up the South Fork of Eel River through the Sinkyone and Kato, and past the Yuki, is not clear. The involved reflux to the Yuki emphasizes the relative concentration of wealth among the Pomo. These southern dentalia would, however, have been viewed with contempt by the Yurok and Hupa. They were fragments of an inch and less, strung in fathom lengths and more. The northerners would have hung them around their necks as unconcernedly as they were careful to roll up and hide their full-length shells of real money.

The Wintun, at least the Nomlaki of Thomas Creek, had the repute among the Yuki of owning few beads and being uninterested in their acquisition by trade.

COUNTING.

The Yuki system of counting—and it alone among all the Yukian languages—is not decimal or quinary, but octonary. Only the Salinan and Chumash, far to the south, follow an analogous quaternary method. It is remarkable that the Yuki counted on their fingers as regularly as any other people in the State. The explanation is that they did not count the fingers but the spaces between them, in each of which, when the manipulation was possible, two twigs were laid. Naturally enough their "hundred" was 64.

The younger men, who have associated with the Americans, seem not to realize that their fathers thought by eights instead of tens, and are so confused in consequence that they give the most contradictory accounts of even the lowest native numerals. The old generation, on the other hand, is as innocent of our method. One of these survivors, when asked if he knew how many fingers he had, answered without hesitation, *huchamopesul*, ten. Asked how many fingers and toes he had, he replied that he did not know. If the query had been how many spaces there were between his fingers and toes, which would trip up many a civilized person required to answer without calculation or actual count, he would no doubt have known instantly. Two pairs of hands were then spread before him as the accepted equivalent of his own fingers and toes, and he began a laborious count, pushing the digits together into groups of fours. The result he announced was *molmihuipoi*, nineteen. Unaccustomed to handling fingers, he had overlooked a thumb. When the same man was allowed to place pairs of little sticks between his own fingers, as was habitual to him, he reckoned rapidly and correctly.

The Yuki managed their count with only three real numeral words: *paⁿwi*, one; *opi*, two; *molmi*, three. Every other word denoting the numbers up into the hundreds is a description of the process of counting. Thus, a translation of their numerals from four to twenty runs as follows: two-forks, middle-in, even-chilki, even-in, one-flat, beyond-one-hang, beyond-two-body, three-body, two-forks-body, middle-in-body, even-chilki-body, even-in-body, middle-none, one-middle-project, two-middle-project, three-middle-project, two-forks-middle-project. Sixty-four is two-fork-pile-at. There are sometimes several ways of denoting a number. Thus eight is one-flat, or hand-two-only.

As among most Californians, there was no word meaning year. *Pilwan* signified either the summer or the whole year: it is connected with *pilaⁿt*, sun. Or, a man might speak of *paⁿwa ona*, one earth or one world, in the sense of a year having elapsed. But such counts were not carried further than an involuntary memory, unaided by dates or fixed supports, allowed. And of course no one knew his own or anybody's age.

The eastern Pomo called a year *hotsai*, the etymology of which is obscure, but early adopted *ainu*, their pronunciation of Spanish *año*, as a substitute.

THE LEADERS OF SOCIETY.

A rich man was called *wok-huyako'l*, "dance-director," or *atat-iwop*, "person-man," that is, a real man, a man who was a person. A chief was the *ti'o'l*, a war leader *tauⁿ-huyaⁿkiki*. The last two were distinct; how far the rich man and the *ti'o'l* may have merged in native consciousness is not quite clear, though the former seems to correspond to the dance-house owner or town chief, the latter to the head chief of a political group.

The chief is described as being wealthy, friendly to everyone, ready to offer advice, heeded and liked by all, and hospitable. He invited and entertained visitors, and might see that a widower's children were taken care of. He would notify the owner of a dance house and possessor of the necessary paraphernalia when to make, or begin, a dance. He did not lead in battle or fight, but he might tell the war captain when the time for war had come. He might not hold his station all his life, since it was necessary for a chief to retain general liking. Perhaps a chief that permanently lost public approval would be succeeded in influence by a more popular man of prominence without any formal action having been taken; or he may have been deposed. But we know of no such incidents, and they can not have been common.

The "person-man" was probably the informal head of a local settlement, who had a number of able-bodied relatives and a store of shell money, had put up a dance house with their aid, which he was regarded as owning or controlling, and had made and kept a number of dance costumes.

The war leader seems to have been merely a person of bravery above the average, who had displayed his courage and skill in combat and won the confidence of his people. He did not lead the van, in an open fight, but stood aside or behind, advising and encouraging his men. In surprise attacks, on the other hand, it is probable that initiative in action rested directly with him.

BATTLES AND TRIUMPHS.

Fighting was normally concluded by a money settlement. Until a payment were tendered, the losers would be more animated by revenge to continue the conflict than the victors encouraged by their success to persist in the fight. Sometimes, it is said, the side suffering the heavier losses might be willing to quit, in which case the victors would be notified and, with the chief's consent, a payment made to the losers and friendly relations resumed. In such cases persons orphaned in the course of the struggle received the largest share of the compensation. If a son or close relative of a noted war leader fell, the slaying party was likely to make prompt tender of a considerable amount, to forestall the reprisal which would otherwise be certain to be attempted. A bad man, it is said, was not paid for. This statement may be conjectured to refer to unlucky shamans, poisoners, and other objectionable characters disposed of by their own or a friendly neighboring community.

When an enemy was captured or his body secured, he was decapitated and the head taken home. A dance or sweat house was built for the *tau*^{n}-*wok* or war dance. The head was handed to a boy or girl who had lost a father in the feud. The youngster seized the skin with his or her teeth and drew it off. During part of the dance, presumably before this act, the head was thrown on the ground. At other times the head was carried on a stick held by the young men. After this it was given to the young women, who during their dance addressed it as husband, carried it about in their teeth, and chirped "*pi, pi, pi, pi, pi*," as if the head were calling. The dance was continued, it is said, until the head was worn out, after which it was thrown away and covered with stones.

There is no mention of scalping as such nor any suggestion of an idea of permanently retaining a visible trophy. The head was merely the occasion for an expression of satisfaction at the revenge obtained. This attitude is revealed also in the fact that when several foes were slain only one head seems often to have been taken. One gave the opportunity desired and was enough. A Plains Indian on the hunt for scalps or a record of coups would have wondered at this futile moderation as much as a Yuki would have been astonished and perhaps shocked by the Sioux and Cheyenne way of playing the game of war.

That the taking of a head was an event and the war dance much more than a spontaneous celebration is revealed by the circumstance that a full earth-covered dance house was erected for the occasion if the victors did not happen to possess one in their village.

It is characteristic that a man might out of meanness, as the Indians put it in their colloquial English, give the name of the enemy he had slain to his boy or of a female relative of the fallen foe to his daughter. With the intensity of feeling that prevails in California against any allusion to the dead, this was the extreme of vindictive gloating.

MARRIAGE AND SEX.

Marriages were sometimes arranged by the parents. Well-to-do people paid for a wife, whereupon the girl's parents made a return in gifts. Something of the sort probably took place even among the poorest, since there was a name, "dog-child" or "coyote-child," for bastards. This epithet could hardly have existed without a definite recognition of what constituted marriage, and such recognition can hardly be conceived of without being based in part on a payment.

A casual Yuki statement that blood kin sometimes married, to prevent misunderstandings and quarrels, may refer only to one or two exceptional instances; but might also, when followed out, reveal a peculiar and definite system. So, also, the assertion that a widow sometimes married her husband's brother and sometimes another man, is no doubt correct, and there may not have been a rigidly regulatory law; but there must have been quite specific controlling considerations, such as the presence or absence of children, as mentioned by the Huchnom.

In labor, a woman sits, raising herself from the ground on her hands. After birth has taken place, the woman and her husband eat neither salt nor fat for some time; nor does he go to hunt or gamble, in fear of bringing illness on the infant. The child's navel string is carefully kept. If the baby falls sick, the cord is laid in a wet skin or rag which is squeezed out over its body.

The usual type of restrictions for the woman who was after the manner of her kind were in force, but seem not to have been extreme. She ate apart, but was not forced to leave the house for a shelter of her own.

The Yuki appear to impose rather slight restrictions on communication between relatives by marriage, though in reservation life they have learned that the Concow Maidu son-in-law and mother-in-law will not even look at each other. They do not seem to employ the pluralizing circumlocutions to which the Kato and Pomo hold.

The transvestites whose recognition forms so regular a part of Indian custom, were not lacking among the Yuki, who called them *iwop-naiip*, "men-girls." Besides dressing as women they were tattooed and are said to have spoken in more or less feminine voices. Sometimes they married men. There seems to have been no ceremony marking the establishment of their status. Their number, as among other tribes, is difficult to estimate, but may be conjectured to have been in proportion to the normal frequency of well-defined homosexualists of feminine inclination in all populations. An old informant knew of none in his own village of U'wit, and mentioned but two: Ishchosi of Nu' and Chikolno'm of Inkak.

THE DEAD.

Their dead, the Yuki assert, were buried, usually in large baskets. Some of the dead person's belongings were buried with him, but a part was preserved for the survivors. Cremation was practiced also, but was not the standard custom, being reserved for those slain in fighting or dying under exceptional circumstances. Regular burning of the dead is, however, ascribed by the Yuki to their kinsmen the Huchnom, and to the Pomo.

There was also no formal memorial mourning ceremony such as prevailed among the Maidu. In this the Yuki agree with the Pomo, as well as all the groups to the north of them.

NAMES.

Names were bestowed on children about the time they made their first endeavors at speaking. They were given by relatives—the exact kin is not known and may not have been prescribed—accompanied by a gift. The meanings of the names lack what we should consider personal dignity. Some clearly refer to bodily peculiarities; others may allude to trivial incidents. Examples are: Sore-eye, Digging-eye, Striped-acorn, Becoming-summer, Handle-comes-off, Flayed-hide, Bear-walks, Rib-boy, Manzanita-bear, Getting-bloody, Black-to-sit-on, Feet-strung-out, Closing-it-up-with-the-heel. Women's names are Sweet-acorn and Afraid-of-her-shadow.

In regard to the avoidance of the name of the dead the Yuki say that a decent man would not do such a thing as to utter the name. For a breach of the custom the dead person's relatives might lie in ambush or try to poison the violator. It is clear that the idea of the mention carries such an obvious implication of unspeakable offense that it is conceived of as being made only with the most deliberate and hateful intent.

The Yuki have a word equivalent to our "thanks," though of unknown etymology: *yoshimi*. This is used both when a gift is received and as an exclamation to one that sneezes. The first syllable suggests Spanish *Dios*. The Huchnom say *heu*, "yes," or *tatki*, "it is good," to express gratitude; the northern Pomo equivalents are *hau* and *kudi—hudi* in eastern Pomo.

CHAPTER 12.

THE YUKI: RELIGION.

COSMOGONY.

Yuki cosmogony and mythology are thoroughly of the type prevalent through north central California. They revolve around two personages—a creator and an unstable assistant who sometimes mars and again supplements the work of his chief. With the polarity between these figures to build on, the natives manage to develop at once some rude grandeur of conception and a considerable amount of simple philosophy about the dualism inherent in the world, the origin of evil, and similar problems that confront anyone who has lived a life. The mass of the episodes in Yuki mythic narrative is as much part of the common stock of the north central tribes as is the basic motive of the plot; but as among every people there are certain flashes and turns that are national peculiarities and the original product, probably, of individual minds. In their incidents and specific stories the Yuki lean more closely toward the adjacent Athabascans; in their organization of the episodes into a whole, rather to the richer and more studied Pomo and Wintun.

Of the two polar cosmogonic personages the negative one seems to have the older and deeper roots. He has been formulated by all the central tribes and is always identified with the coyote. Even in southern and northwestern California he has not disappeared entirely; and it is well known that he retains many of his aspects throughout the plateau tribes and well up among those of the North Pacific coast.

The concept of his constructive antithesis, the creator, is confined to north central California, and is variable even within that area. To the Yuki he is Taikomol, he who walks alone, to the Kato Nagaicho, the great traveler, to the Wintun Olelbis, he who sits in the above, to the Maidu the ceremonial initiate of the earth or Kodoyanpe, the earth namer. Among the Pomo we do not know the meaning of his name, Madumda. On the fringes of the area thus outlined, he sinks to the level of an animal, such as the silver fox of the Achomawi, or disappears wholly, except for a vague mention or two, as among the Yana and Shasta. In south central California he has an analogue in the eagle, but only a partial one; for to the Yokuts the eagle is not so much the creator as the chief of the assembly of animals who participated in the origin of things. In southern California the creator is replaced, especially among the most advanced tribes, by a parallel but psychologically quite distinct figure, the dying god. In the Northwest, too, Yimantuwingyai and his Yurok and Karok equivalents are only in slight measure representatives of the north central Californian creator: in reality they are a fusion of him with the coyote, placed in a new setting of world inception. The idea of a true creator of the world is thus confined to those of the central California groups that followed the Kuksu cult; is evidently associated with that religion; but may have an even narrower range of distribution.

RITUALS.

Yuki ceremonies are more numerous than might be expected of a tribe the material basis of whose culture was so crude. There were, first of all, among the bulk of the group, two rituals that observed esoteric initiation and practiced divine impersonation: the *Taikomol-woknam* and the *Hulk'ilal-woknam.* These are admitted to have been derived from the Kato and Huchnom, and seem to rest on a Pomo and perhaps ultimate Wintun foundation, though the rituals themselves are no doubt quite different in many respects from those of the tribes that originated their impulse. Among the Yuki of main Eel River in intimate contact with the Wailaki was practiced a Wailaki ceremony, the *Kichil-woknam,* which, though at bottom shamanistic rather than ritualistic, possessed at least some elements of organization and initiation.

The Yuki further possessed all the ceremonies that are conducted without a formal organization, that serve an immediate, specific purpose, and that are the common stock of all the tribes of northern and many of those of south central and southern California: the dance to initiate shamans or *Lamshiwok;* the girls' adolescence dance or *Hamnam-wok*, and the victory celebration dance or *Taun-wok*.

In addition, there was the *Kopa-wok* or feather dance, in which religious and festive social elements were avowedly blended, and for which there are a considerable number of north central Californian parallels; and a somewhat more distinctive dance, the *Lanlhanp-wok*, connected with the acorn crop.

The formal mourning ceremonies of the southern and south central tribes and Maidu were not practiced. Of the specific rituals of the northwest there is not a vestige.

The three ceremonies connected with an organization bear names that end in -*woknam*. *Wok* is "dance," *nam* to "lie"; the compound has about the sense of initiation. The Yuki translate it as "school." The children or young men lay during the prolonged instruction, which, with demonstrations, comprised the bulk of the initiation. No name for the organization or secret society as such has been recorded; but those who have passed through the *Hulk'ilal-woknam* are said to be called *hulk'ilal-woknam-chi* or *lashmil*.

THE TAIKOMOL INITIATION.

The *Taikomol-woknam* refers to the creator *Taikomol*. His impersonator in dances wears the "big head" costume that prevails among the Pomo, Wintun, and Maidu, and the Yuki directly identify their Taikomol with the Kuksu or big head of the northern and eastern Pomo.

The children or youths to be initiated were brought into a dance house in the morning. There they sat with crossed legs, forbidden to move or even to stretch themselves until the middle of the day. Often their parents sat behind to prop them up. They put rope, knives, net bags, snares, furs, and other property in a pile to pay the old man who was to teach their children. The old man then began. He had nothing on or with him but a cocoon rattle and perhaps a feather with which to point and illustrate. He sang a song that referred to the first event in the creation of the world. Then he would tell this episode in prose. Other songs and pieces of narrative followed, interspersed with explanations, applications to life, and a good deal of moralizing. The whole followed the thread of the creation myth. The instructor does not seem to have tried to veil his meaning in cryptic and esoteric utterances; but the numerous repetitions, the constant change from obscure song to story and from narrative to comment, and the self-interruptions, must have produced a sufficiently disjointed effect to make several listenings necessary before a coherent scheme of the myth could be obtained.

Taikomol came from the north. Therefore in this ceremony they put the north first as they point successively north, south, west, east, down, and up. Sometimes they point four times in each of the six directions, then three times, then twice, then once.

There is also a *Taikomol* ceremony distinct from this teaching. This is a doctoring ceremony, and reveals a connection that exists between all society rituals and shamanism among the Yuki. It is called *Taikomola-lit*.

The sick person lies in the middle of the dance house, feet toward the door. Near his head sit five or six singers. Some one goes on the roof of the house and calls *yuhe kokokokok he!* Then the *Taikomol* impersonator, who has dressed himself somewhere out in the brush in a long feather-covered net that conceals his entire face and body, approaches. He stops, retreats, and approaches again. This is counted as four movements. Then, walking backward, he comes close to the house, retreats, approaches again, and comes through the door rump first. This is again counted as four movements. He stands by the side of the recumbent sufferer, who, the Yuki say, believes the feathered figure to be Taikomol himself. This must be taken with a grain of salt, as representing theory rather than practice. Adult males, at least, would certainly have known better. The identity of the impersonator was, however, not revealed. According to one account, there were two Taikomol dancers.

The *Taikomol* now dances to four songs, leaping over the patient, bouncing from the ground, and shuffling along; after which he goes out, and a sucking doctor proceeds to the actual diagnosis, feeling the patient over until he locates the disease object. This act is repeated for four nights. The officiating doctor and the chief singer—the *Taikomol-haᵑp-naᵑho'l*—are paid; the assistant singers and impersonator receive nothing, at least not directly from the patient.

It is said that long ago a man of the Matamno'm, one of the Witukomno'm or other southerly Yuki divisions, bought certain black wing feathers of the condor from the Kato, and information with them. This information was the creation myth as related in the *Taikomol-woknam*. The feathers were worn, but were also like an American book: the knowledge came with them. Because of this event the southern Yuki are said to sing the *Taikomol* songs somewhat differently from the Huchnom and Ta'no'm, to whom, evidently, this importation did not extend. Of course, it is much more likely that a new variety of song, myth, and ritual were superimposed on similar cultural possessions in this introduction, than that a brand new importation of a heretofore entirely unknown *Taikomol* cult took place. The Matamno'm purchaser imparted his knowledge to the grandfather of a man born about 1830, which fact sets the date of the innovation back of 1800.

THE GHOST INITIATION.

The *Hulk'ilal-woknam* is the impersonation of the *hulk'ilal* or ghosts. It is said that this was instituted by Taikomol, but that at first he, or according to another account the bungling coyote, made the ceremony with real ghosts, in consequence of which all the on-looking people died. He then created a fresh set of human beings, and had some of them act as *hulk'ilal* and all went well.

Taikomol also first made a powerful thing like a basket with feathers projecting from it, but this swallowed the people. There-after he had a human being disguise himself in the same way. This is perhaps a parallel myth concerning the " big head " in the *Taiko-mol-woknam*.

Boys and young men were initiated and reinitiated in the *Hulk'ilal-woknam*, but never a girl. No woman was ever admitted into the dance house during any part of the ceremony, nor was she supposed to know anything about it.

The directors of the ceremony meet in the dance house for four days to sing and discuss which children shall be initiated. Apparently, the boys from the settlements or camps for some distance about are gathered up and set in front of the dance house toward evening. As it begins to be dusk, they are picked up and passed through the wood hole in the side of the house, received by another man, and set down. It is pitch dark inside, and the half dozen or so " ghosts " standing about are invisible. When the children are all placed, the singers gathered around the drum start a song, *helina heluli*, the men present put their fingers against their throats, shake them, and shout *yuwuwuwuwu*, the fire is stirred up, and the boys begin to tremble as they see the horrifying *hulk'ilal*.

These impersonators have body, arms, and legs painted in broad horizontal stripes of black and white. They wear false hair of maple bark, and a wreath of black oak, pepperwood, and manzanita leaves to conceal the face. Their faces are distorted. Grass is stuffed in the cheeks. A twig twice the length of the middle finger is split and each half inserted in a nostril. Each is then bent until the other end catches behind the lower lip. This simple device pushes the nostril up and the lip down, and gives the face a monstrous appearance. Of course the voices also sound unnatural.

The director of the ceremony asks the *hulk'ilal*: " Where do you come from? Why are you here and say nothing? " One of them replies: " *E!* We have come to see how you do this. The one above sent us to see how you make it. We came to look at this fire, the drum, and everything else that you have. We shall be here only a little time."

The *hulk'ilal* also pick out men among the spectators to go out for food, specifying what to get from each house. When this is brought in, every one eats. The children in particular are made to eat heartily, as this is their last meal for four days—that is, probably, until the fourth day. They may also not drink. When they have finished, the men shake their throats and shout again.

The fire is kept up and the dance house is hot throughout the ceremony. In addition, the boys are covered with straw or brush.

Then the *hulk'ilal* dance. Their step is a leap up, they swing and twist their hands, and move about randomly. It is apparent that they act as clowns. It is said that the men frequently laugh at them, subduedly but heartily. The *hulk'ilal* point to the sticks in their faces and utter inarticulate sounds. They pull the cheeks down from the eyes. The significance of this is that they bring abundance of acorns, luck in the deer hunt, and plenty of all foods. They hold their privates, or each other's. They direct each other to step in the wrong place, which is their way of indicating where they are to stand. Should one really go where he is told, he has to pay.

The dance centers about the drum. Each *hulk'ilal* leaps on this four times with a tremendous reverberation, crying " *he'ye* " with each jump. The song refrain at this time is *yoho yoho*. The fire is kept especially hot.

The children are kept in the dance house for four days. The *hulk'ilal* are not present continuously but enter at intervals. There is talking in low tones and then the four, six, and eight designated for the next impersonation slip out quietly, so that even the spectators present do not know their identity when they return. They go on a hill to paint and dress. Then they separate in pairs, so as to be able to approach the dance house from different directions.

One of the men inside mounts to the roof and shouts *yuhe kokokokoko*, as in the Taikomol's appearance. They answer *ba, ba, ba*, in long bleats, and as they begin to draw near each other shout *brrrrr!* A singer with cocoon rattle goes out to meet them with a certain song. They approach and enter singly, each going through the same motions as the Taikomol in his ceremony. During this entrance there is also a special song. Then they dance as described, everyone in the house, even the oldest men, standing up and dancing with them; and meanwhile the fire flares up so that all sweat. The men often hold or even carry their sons or grandsons. One or two will take brands and blow sparks on the boys, some of whom instead of shrinking back stretch out their arms and cry *yu'u, yu'u*, to prove that they can meet the ordeal with fortitude. The song for this dance and scene of animation ends with the refrain *hohu hohu hohu!*

It is not clear whether this entry and dance take place once or several times each 24 hours.

The first morning the boys are put in a pit or broad hole which has been dug and lined with grass to the accompaniment of a particular song on the preceding day. This part of the proceedings seems to be connected with sweating the youngsters.

The men have food brought into the house every day, after which some of them go up into the hills to bring wood for the continual fire. On the last day food is brought in also for the boys, but this is kept separate. An old man holding angelica root in his hand goes about to a song *heye hiyohu*, touching each vessel of food or drink with a feather that he licks off, thus imparting health-giving qualities to what the boys will consume.

The ceremony is concluded about noon on the fourth day by throwing the boys out of the dance house through the wood hole by which they entered. Two old men are thrown out first. The boys hold their breaths and keep as still as if they were dead while they are being handled and pitched. Their relatives are outside to catch them or pick them up. In the afternoon the boys seem to reenter to be sweated once more and be rubbed over with ashes.

The initiation, which takes place at intervals of some years, is thought to make the boys strong, swift at running, and enduring on the hunt.

That there is another side to the *hulk'ilal* impersonation beyond that revealed in the initiation of the *woknam*, is evident from the statement that as the *hulk'ilal* approach the dance house they confide or boast to each other that what they are doing will work harm to people of another tribe. A Yuki who went through the ceremony in reservation days partook in it when performed by the northern Pomo there, who made it to poison a Yuki named Mano, on the ground that he knew too much about it.   Perhaps a realization of his knowledge caused motives of having tried to abuse his power by sickening his enemies to be attributed to him, so that the Pomo considered they were acting only in retaliation.   Another statement is to the effect that the northern Pomo on the reservation, known as the Little Lake tribe, are addicted to the *hulk'ilal* ceremonials and visit them when held by the Yuki.   The people of each nation present try to make the others go to sleep.   If they succeed, the man who has slept, or one of his kin, dies soon.

Fat was forbidden during the long duration of the *Hulk'ilal-woknam*, and used sparingly for some time thereafter.

Early in the autumn following a *Hulk'ilal-woknam* there is a ceremony called *Mam*, "mast or crop of black-oak acorns," evidently of the new year's or first fruits type.   The young acorns are gathered and dried and deer are killed, and the older members or people feast, but the novice initiates abstain for their own good.

The graduates of the ghost initiation were looked upon as doctors or the equivalent of doctors, although they had no personal spirits unless they happened to have acquired them outside the course of the ceremony.   Like the *Taikomol* initiates, they sang over the sick, to find out if the illness were caused by the *hulk'ilal* spirits; in which case a sucking shaman, whose power lay in his control of an individual spirit not associated with this ritual, removed the disease object introduced by the ghost.

A BIOGRAPHIC ACCOUNT.

The place of the *hulk'ilal* initiation in the life of the people is more easily deductible from the biographic account given by an old man than from the attempts at generalization made by him and others.

"I am a singing doctor, but not a sucking doctor.   I have made the doctor dance.   I can cure by *Taikomol*.   I have been through the *Taikomol-woknam* and through the Ta'no'm *Kichil-woknam*.   I went through the *Hulk'ilal-woknam* three times.   Doctors take part in this like other men, but those who make it need not be or become doctors.

"When I was a quite small boy, we were at Kolma^{n}l.   From there we went to Suk'a, where a dance house had already been erected for the *Hulk'ilal-woknam*. My maternal grandfather Shampalhotmi of Ushichma^{n}lha^{n}t was at Suk'a.   As we arrived at his house a deer was being brought in.   My grandfather said to me: 'Do not enter on this side but on the other and come to me.'   I was frightened, but went to the left of the fire, around behind it, and back to where he was lying near the door.   We stayed there that night.   Next day it was decided that there was not enough food at Suk'a, and that they would go to Ushichma^{n}lha^{n}t.   Everyone moved there and the same day a dance house was put up. The logs were cut and everybody helped in their erection.

"That night the old men discussed among themselves how they could best catch me next day.

"In the morning they went out to cut the large center post and took me along. They found a good white oak in the canyon and cut its roots. They had no steel axes and worked with a large stone. When they were about to fell the tree itself they ordered me up into it. I was to sit on the crotch with my arms folded. They wanted to test me and see if I was a man and make me into some one who would be a chief. But they made the tree fall as lightly as they could so as not to hurt me. Then they chopped off the top above the fork in which I still sat. Now one of my uncles took off my boy's fawnskin and gave me a man's deerskin to wear. Then they took the log away. I lay flat on it. Thus they brought it into the dance house. They set it up in its hole and still I kept my place. Then my maternal grandfather reached up and took me off, laid me on his lap and cried over me. Then I could not help but cry too.

"When the sun went down, they built a large fire and sweated themselves, but did not trouble me. For four days I was in the dance house with many other boys, all of us eating nothing. My maternal grandfather, and also my paternal grandfather (or grandfather's brother) Lamsch'ala, talked to me about the *hulk'ilal*.

"This was late in the fall, when the river first began to rise (perhaps November). After four days I was allowed to eat and drink again, but all winter they kept me hidden away in the dance house. Whenever I went outdoors my face was covered. All through the winter at intervals they had the *hulk'ilal-lit* (performance or doctoring) for four days at a time. They made it for themselves, not to teach me. But my grandfathers told me to watch them and to see everything that they did. Between times they kept me well covered up. Every evening they sweated. Thus they did until late spring when the grass seeds were ripe (about May or June).

"The second time I went through the *woknam* was at Suk'a. I was a big boy now. This time the ceremonies lasted only four days. After the meal at the end I belonged to the dance house (i. e., I was a full initiate of the organization) and went with the others to bring wood for sweating. Between the first ceremony and this one my grandfathers had taught me fully all the songs and all that I must know.

"The third time I took part I was a grown and married man. Now I took part in the building of the dance house and all the other work. I danced and helped to give orders. I was practicing to be an important man. This was about when the whites were first coming in. There was sickness and the Indians were being killed by the whites, and all things like this stopped being done, all at once as it were. So this time the ceremony was short, only about two days."

GENERAL FEATURES OF THE INITIATIONS.

It is clear from the foregoing account that the " dance house " was at times used for sweating as well as dancing, so that neither the designation here used for it nor the more usual one of " sweat house," nor in fact the English translation of the Yuki word, " poison house," can be taken in a literally descriptive sense. Its use partook of all three functions.

It appears that when a dance house is erected for a particular occasion, as here described, a drum is also specially made, and with considerable ceremony. All the members of the house or organization go out together for this purpose. They make a fire and lay a log on it to burn it out. As they chip off the bark with sharp stones, and perhaps complete the hollowing begun by the fire, they sing a song with the burden *helegadadie hiye*. The convex slab is tested and when it gives a good sound it is addressed: " You shall have much to eat." Then, everyone having painted black, they carry the drum home, singing the same song. Before it is actually put through the dance house entrance, a motion is made, perhaps four times, of thrusting it in. Once inside, it is carried four times to the right and four times to the left of the center post. Again, four starts are made before it is finally set in the resting place over the prepared ditch at the back of the house. All this time the *helegadadie hiye* song is kept up. Finally, much property is piled up by it, to " pay " it.

As practiced in recent years, the *hulk'ilal* dancers are described as belonging to something like a club. Outsiders, if men, may enter as spectators, on payment. There is perhaps an aboriginal basis for this reservation custom.

The *Taikomol-woknam* and *Hulk'ilal-woknam* present many resemblances to the Pomo and Wintun ceremonial organization, and to the more remote but more fully known one of the Maidu. Among these must be mentioned, first of all, the fact of a definite organization or secret society with a membership dependent upon an elaborate initiation, and strictly excluding women. Second is the impersonation of spirits in such a way as to cause women and uninitiated children to believe, theoretically at least, in the actual bodily presence of these gods, and to leave even the members, except for the directing officials, in doubt as to the individual personal identity of the impersonators. The long masking net of feathers and the " big head " of radiating feathered sticks correspond to the Wintun and Maidu *moki* and *yohyo* or *dü*. The latter peoples have separate clowns; the Yuki *hulk'ilal* manifest clownish features. The Pomo call the " big head " *kuksu* or *guksu*, and their *hahluigak* or " ghosts " play like the Yuki " ghosts." The long series of ceremonials from autumn to spring corresponds, although diversified among the Maidu with an endless series of distinctive dances and numerous particular impersonations, and monotonously repetitive with the Yuki. The calling of the spirits from the dance-house roof, their answering cries and peculiar approach, their backward entry, the dancing about and on the drum, the form of this implement, and the general character of the treatment of the initiated boys are so similar as to make any interpretation but that of development under a common influence impossible. The Yuki rituals are much less elaborate than those of the Maidu and Wintun, and somewhat less elaborate than those of the Pomo, but the same ideas and manners pervade them. The comparison is gone into more fully in one of the chapters on the Wintun.

The relation of *Taikomol* and *hulk'ilal* ceremonials to each other is not clear. If Maidu precedent applies, the Yuki had only one society, which performed two or more rituals, the directors and impersonators for each being drawn from those individuals who had been fully initiated into the branch of the ritual in question. The Yuki data give the impression of distinct initiations and organizations; but even if parallel there must have been a relation between them; and there is nothing known that concretely contradicts the assumption that a single general society of Maidu type underlay the two Yuki rituals.

As the accounts of the Yuki ceremonies refer to the days before the coming of the American, they are free from allusions to the modern element that has invaded Pomo and Wintun rituals since the semi-Christian and revivalistic ghost-dance movement of the seventies.

THE OBSIDIAN CEREMONY.

In place of these two ceremonies—*Taikomol* and *Hulk'ilal*—the Ta'no'm and perhaps Lilshikno'm alone of all the Yuki held the *Kichil-woknam* or obsidian initiation. This was practiced by the Wailaki, and the Yuki specifically state that it came to them from the Wailaki. It is also asserted to be an old Ta'no'm ceremony, however. The discrepancy is to be understood thus: The Ta'no'm had long had the ritual, although its ultimate Wailaki origin is probable. About a generation before the coming of the Americans it was decadent among the Ta'no'm. There were no prominent obsidian shamans in the tribe. It was reintroduced by the son of a Wailaki who had married a woman of the Kashaⁿsichno'm division of the Ta'no'm and taken her to his people. About 1835 this half-Yuki made the ceremony among his mother's people, and all the children were initiated; but as he spoke only in Wailaki, it was not very intelligible to the boys. Some years later the same boys were put through a second ceremony held in Yuki.

This double initiation seems to have been characteristic of the ceremony as of the corresponding two ceremonies of the other Yuki. The first initiation took place when the boys were quite small, the second when they were nearly grown or almost men. The ages may be put at about 8 and 15; but as the ceremony was held only at intervals of some years, there must have been considerable variation for individuals.

That girls were also initiated, though once only, marks this ritual off most sharply from the *Taikomol-woknam* and *Hulk'ilal-woknam*, and is indication that it was not a function of a true membership society. All other evidence points the same way, The absence of masked impersonators, for instance, must have given a very distinct tone to the *Kichil-woknam*. Wherever definite esoteric societies are known in California, they impersonate spirits, as in so many other parts of the world. The ceremony was directed by obsidian shamans, and while an attempt was made to have all children participate for their own good, it was also looked upon as a means of determining and perhaps assisting those among them who were or would be endowed with the power of becoming an obsidian doctor. Again, a great part of the initiation took place outdoors, instead of in the dance house. All the basic associations of the *Kichil-woknam* therefore point to shamanism, and it must be looked upon as a development of this activity in the direction of esoteric organization without a full attainment of organization.

Of course shamans and societies, both being religious, can not be wholly dissociated, and in a simple civilization, such as that of all California is at its best, there are certain to be numerous contacts. Even with the Maidu and Wintun such contacts appear to be more numerous than in a highly organized culture such as that of the southwest. The *Taikomol* and *hulk'ilal* practices include doctoring and poisoning; and Yuki informants clearly class these two ceremonies with doctoring by singing, and the *Kichil-woknam* as an expression of the powers of the obsidian doctors and sky doctors, who have a head guardian spirit of their own and, in contrast with the singing shamans, extract disease by sucking. This parallelism is essential to the understanding of the ceremonies; but on the other hand it is also clear that as regards *Taikomol* and *hulk'ilal* we have esoteric societies with some shamanistic functions; in the *Kichil-woknam*, shamanism partly organized into an approach to a society.

This development among the Ta'no'm and Wailaki on the fringe of the area over which the central Californian secret society prevails seems to find a parallel among another border people, the Yokuts on the south. There also there is an initiation and shamans of certain classes act together in public, but formal organization and the recognition of membership, as well as spirit impersonation, are lacking.

The *Kichil-woknam* is in charge of the obsidian-shaman or sky-shaman recognized as ablest. The others assist him. Among themselves they go over the available children and count their number by laying out sticks. This conference seems to be to insure that no children shall be overlooked rather than to select the most worthy and suitable. The children are then gathered without knowing what is in store for them and seated in the place where the singing and most of the treatment will take place. Their parents follow them; in fact everyone gathers there.

Two large baskets of pounded grass seeds and two of water are set down and the children told to eat heartily, as for five days they will receive neither food nor drink and on the sixth day only water.

Then one of the sky shamans takes a long obsidian blade—believed to have fallen from heaven—from a net sack full of such pieces. He goes about among the children rattling this sack and lightly striking them with it. About the same time they begin to keep the children hot, apparently in warmed sand. This outdoor sweating or cooking goes on the whole five or six days of the ceremony except as it is interrupted by special actions. There is an analogue not only in the *Hulk'ilal-woknam* sweating of boys, but in the " roasting of girls " which is so conspicuous a feature of the adolescence ceremonies of the Luiseño and other southern Californians, not to mention the " cooking of the pains " in the Yurok initiating or perfecting dance for adult shamans.

Then they prepare to go to a spirit infested " lake " in the mountains which ordinarily is too dangerous to approach. In reality the lake is only a damp or swampy hollow. Deer have been killed and are eaten by the assembled people, while the children lie about under their hot coverings as if dying. Now one of the shamans proceeds to the lake on a zigzag course, blowing a whistle and approaching the spot cautiously and with stealth. The children and multitude follow along until all are seated in the lake bed. Several of the shamans, one behind the other, sprinkle them with wet pepperwood leaves. Soon water begins to rise in the dry lake. The doctors sing, everyone else dances, and the water splashes about them. After they have come out in single file one of the shamans throws a stone or a stick into the lake to defy those who live there. The shamans poke the boys with a stick to select the one who will wince least and become the bravest man. Now this boy chases the people. They rush about as if attacked, crying out and dragging their children with them. Thus they run away until they are out of sight of the lake.

When they return in the evening they enter the dance house and make the obsidian dance, *Kichil-wok*. The adults dance, and the children—at least the smaller and more exhausted ones—are carried by them. There is a large fire, and the heat is very hard to bear. It is said that even the manliest boys are likely to cry under the ordeal of constant sweating, particularly after they have become thin and weakened from several days' fasting.

This ends the first day.

The second and third days are the same, except that the lake is not visited.

On the fourth day there is a special ceremony, to which, besides the conducting shamans and the children, only those of the people are admitted who have themselves passed through the initiation at some time. To the accompaniment of a particular song, the shamans thrust their sky-obsidians—that is, their long blades—into the children to their stomachs, it is said, and twist them. Those who bleed at the mouth will be obsidian-doctors themselves; the others can not expect this career. Then, to another song, condor feathers are pushed into the patient youngsters so far that only the butt of the quill projects from their mouths. These are also twisted and signs of blood watched for.

This elimination of the future obsidian shamans from the common mass did not, of course, constitute them doctors. In fact, they did not become such until after they were men. But the test foreshadowed their future attainment.

The fifth day seems to be passed like the second and third.

On the sixth day the children are subjected to another ordeal. They are taken out to a shallow hollow, perhaps also a sacred spot, as it is spoken of as being in the mountains. The children are laid down, covered with pine and fir needles, grass, or brush, and logs are laid around the inclosing edge of the little basin. The logs are fired while a shaman runs singing around the circle of fire. Sometimes the flames will spread down into the hollow and the brush on the children will spring into a blaze; but they are never hurt. When the fire has died down, the brush is pulled away and the children taken out, gasping for breath.

On the return, the dance house is visited, and the nightly obsidian dance made around the fire, "to sweat the children." Everyone is present, parents holding their children up by the arms, or carrying them on their backs, which is construed as equivalent to the children dancing. When a child faints in the circle its parents pick it up and cry over it. Sometimes children are so thoroughly exhausted that they have to be taken outdoors. Some boys, however, manage to withstand the stifling heat and continue to dance among the men.

Some time on this sixth day the children receive their first drink of water.

The seventh and last day brings several features, both tests for the children and demonstrations of magic.

The boys are made to run or clamber up a steep hill. In their enfeebled condition, many can progress only a short distance. Some finally arrive at the top. These are the boys who will be courageous and successful in war when they grow up.

Then the children are dragged off to a place in the mountains, one of the shamans leading the way with a song, the words of which are to this effect:

> "This rock did not come here by itself.
> This tree does not stand here of itself.
> There is one who made all this,
> Who shows us everything."

The boys and their parents follow him around every prominent rock and conspicuous tree. When they arrive, the children are seated and strengthened by having the song continued over them.

Seven sticks are counted out for the seven days of the ceremony. Thus the creator did, it is said, and on the seventh day produced water. A shaman now proceeds to do the same. He squats before a sky-obsidian that has been set upright and probes four times in the dry ground with a stick, singing. At the conclusion of his song he draws out the blade and digs the spot where it stood. He digs with his stick perhaps a foot down. Soon the hole fills with water. The shaman says to the multitude: "This is from the creator. I am showing you what he did. I do not do this myself. I was taught by him. If you believe this it will be well with you. People will be good to you. Will you believe what I say?" The shaman is heavily paid for this exhibition.

It is not clear whether the creator referred to is *Taikomol* or some Wailaki equivalent god or the *Milili*, who is the head of the spirits with whom the obsidian and sky shamans are in communication.

This performance could be varied or added to. Thus a Pomahaⁿno'm shaman once announced that he had learned from his spirits that young condors were coming from heaven to be among the people. He set up three obsidian blades at equal distances apart and asked the onlookers to watch for the birds and join in his song when they approached. Soon two condors alighted to the north and south of the obsidians, first turned their heads away and then toward each other, and after sitting a short time flew away. This shaman was also well paid for the act.

It is likely that these demonstrations rest upon sleight of hand, but the filling of the lake on the first day appears to represent a manifestation of the kind which is often ascribed to the power of Hindu devotees and which has sometimes been attributed to the influence of exceptionally concentrated suggestion with an effect akin to that of hypnosis. Of course, the Indian is enormously more suggestible than we when phenomena of this sort are involved.

On the return from the mountains the children are given their first food in the shape of salted clover. Then they are taken to the stream to bathe. As they emerge they are repeatedly pushed back. They return and are painted red and white and down is put in their hair. They follow the shaman in a file, he singing, back to the stream, on reaching the bank of which they dance violently at his command. Coming back to the village once more, he starts his last song, to which they drag brush over the floor of their homes. With this final undoubtedly symbolic act the seven days' ritual ends, and the worn-out boys and girls sit down to their first real meal.

While the demonstrations of magic in this public ceremony recall Yokuts practices, the ordeals undergone by the children savor strongly of the tests of endurance and fortitude to which Luiseño boys are subjected, and stamp the rite as akin on the whole to puberty ceremonies; as an induction to the state of manhood rather than membership in a defined organization.

The *Kichil-woknam* is said to have been made only once on Round Valley Reservation, and can hardly have escaped material modification on that occasion.

The shamans who conduct the *Kichil-woknam* also treat disease. One method employed by them is to construct a kind of little funnel of earth, perhaps 2 feet long. At one end of this the patient reclines; at the other, obsidians are set up. The doctor then blows tobacco smoke through the hole on the sick person.

Kichil denotes both flint and obsidian, but the ceremonial references seem to be prevailingly to the latter material.

GIRLS' ADOLESCENCE CEREMONY.

The girls' puberty rite is the *Hamnam-wok*, the " adolescence dance." The word for adolescence contains the element *nam*, to lie. This idea seems prominent in the Yuki mind in connection with anything like a preparatory or initiatory rite. The girl actually does lie; and her success is in proportion to her quietness. Another feature, also entertained among many other tribes, is that she must not look on the world. The course of the ceremony is much as elsewhere, and the usual taboos against eating meat, or scratching the head with the fingers, prevail. Twice a day the girl is taken out from under the covering basket and made to dance, her face covered, with a woman who holds her arms.

Perhaps the most distinctive trait of this ceremony as practiced by the Yuki is the direct influence which the rite is supposed to have upon food supply. Each night the *la^nl-ha^np* or acorn songs are started and men and women, shuffling in line together, do the *La^nl-ha^np-wok*, the acorn song dance. The house is entirely black, affording opportunity for the abundant licentiousness that is permitted to the participants. Then, it is said that the more the treated girl lies still, the more the sun is pleased, and the more abundant will the natural crops be in the ensuing season.

Finally, at the conclusion of the ceremony, there is a feast, at which a shaman stands and addresses the sun with his hands raised. Soon the *haⁿwaii-no'm* or "food-people," the spirits who cause and control food, begin to come, and the shaman is seen brushing them off his face. Then the people begin to feel them stinging and also brush and scratch themselves. If any skeptic voices his unbelief, the shaman catches one of the little flying fellows in his hand and offers to show it to the doubter. As it is thought that the latter would become blind if he saw the spirit, even for an instant, the demonstration has perhaps never been carried to its conclusion.

ACORN AND FEATHER DANCES.

The acorn song dance just mentioned was also made as a separate ceremony, on four successive nights in winter, in a roofed-over brush inclosure. It may then have been a new year's or new crop rite.

The *kopa-wok* or feather dance was briefer, and largely social in character. In it were worn the dance costumes by which the district is chiefly represented in museums: feather net cape for the back, head net filled with eagle down, forehead band of yellow-hammer quills, and feathered upright forks. The dancing is first in a revolving file, then abreast. The *lil-ha'o'l* or "rock carrier" directs the dancing and beats time with a split stick. He signals the singers to begin by saying *ha'a'a'a'a'a*. As they commence, he calls *hei hei hei*, and as they conclude, *ui ya*. There is a "rock carrier" also in the acorn song dance, although there he limits himself to accompanying the singers, without directing the dancers. A personage with similar functions, and title of exactly the same meaning, reappears among the Pomo.

SHAMANISM.

The Yuki doctor or shaman, *lamshimi*, is a man, rarely a woman. Most frequently he receives the first intimation of his faculties in a dream, but it may also come to him in a waking appearance. His powers rest not upon control of small semianimate disease-bringing objects or "pains" which he normally carries in his body, but upon intercourse with spirits of human shape and speech. There are bear doctors and rattlesnake doctors. In all these respects Yuki shamanism is of central Californian type and contrary to northwestern customs.

Doctors dream of supreme spirits, upon whom their power depends, but they exercise their curative and other functions by the aid of lesser spirits, whom they actually control. Such personally owned spirits are called *mumolno'm*, or *hushkaiemol*, "speaker, instructor." The great spirits are *Milili* and the creator. *Milili* lives in the sky above the visible one, and owns an enormous block of obsidian of which all obsidians in the world are fragments that he has thrown down. He has the shape of an enormous eagle or condor. He controls deer, *mil*, to which his name refers. *Kichil-lamshimi*, obsidian doctors, *mil-lamshimi*, deer doctors, and *mit-lamshimi*, sky doctors, probably corresponding in some measure to the rain makers of the southern half of California, all derive their power from *Milili*. When the creator is a shaman's spirit, he seems to be known under other names than his usual one of *Taikomol*. Rattlesnake shamans have the sun for their spirit, and bear doctors grizzly bears.

The Yuki divide their shamans into those who doctor by singing and those who suck, or perhaps diagnosing and extracting physicians. The two classes correspond more or less with those who derive their power respectively from the creator and *Milili*. Sucking doctors are, however, differentiated into those who extract actual arrowheads from wounds received in battle, and others who suck out invisible obsidian points which the spirits have shot into one in lonely places.

A DOCTOR'S HISTORY.

The attitude of mind underlying Yuki shamanism is perhaps made clearest by an autobiographic account.

"When I was still so young as to have no sign of beard, they were having the doctor dance, *Lamshi-wok*, in summer. They were training two or three new doctors. The older shamans danced with them for five days. Once all the people joined in and danced in a circle with whistles in their mouths. The novices' spirits came to the older doctors and instructed these how to treat the young men, who were not yet able to manage them. The established shamans did this voluntarily. They were paid by the people at large, who were glad to have additional doctors to keep them alive.

"Now it is when new doctors are receiving their training that still younger ones often first learn of their powers; and so it was with me. The first night of the dance I was sleeping outdoors, between my brother, who has the creator as spirit, and another doctor. Then I, too, dreamed of the creator *On-uha^{n}k-namlikiat*. I did not see his face or body; but I was in the sky, and saw many colors, like a mass of flowers. In the morning I was bleeding from mouth and nose and badly frightened. My relatives gathered about me and cried. Finally my brother picked me up and began to sing with me. 'This is what we made the doctor dance for,' he said. Then my relatives rejoiced that I was not to die, and the other people that they were to have an additional doctor, and they gave net sacks, rope, and various property to my brother and the four other doctors who had begun the dance. Now they put me right into the dance with the other novices until it was finished. I was so much younger than usual that the people had not thought my bleeding was due to my becoming a doctor. But as my brother also had dreamed of *On-uha^{n}k-namlikiat*, he knew.

"When I first saw the creator, he sang a song which I was always to sing. Something like a string stretched from him to my head. He sang another song, and told me to use that also.

" Then while I was lying on my back and the other doctors were working over me, after they had received their pay for training me in the dance, I dreamed that I was treating a person bitten by a rattlesnake, by means of a third song. Therefore I can cure snake bites.

" Some time after, on the hunt, a rattlesnake struck three times at one of my companions and bit him once. I ran up and supported him, while he gazed at the sun. I saw at once that he was not seriously hurt, for something like milk appeared to be coming out of his mouth, and the sun spoke and ordered me to cure him. As the others were talking of sending for a certain rattlesnake doctor, I interposed and told them that I had been directed to treat the sufferer. So we made a litter of poles, while one of the party went ahead to give the news and have a place prepared for my doctoring. When we laid the wounded man down he was nearly dead. I painted a flat stone red and white. Then I addressed the sun. Then I sucked the wound twice, and the second time extracted a small but complete rattlesnake, which I spat upon the stone. Immediately the man sat up, folded his arms, and said: ' Good, my father-in-law.' All his property was stacked up before him to pay me. Whenever a man is bitten by a snake he has no belongings left.

"After this, I dreamed again of the creator, who showed me one of the people who live on high peaks, a *mumolno'm* or *huchatat* (mountain person), to be my helper in curing disease. This spirit taught me his song. Other doctors saw in their dreams what was happening to me, and began to fear my power. After that I commenced to doctor sick people.

" I can cure all disease except that caused by spirit obsidians. I did dream of such obsidians once, but did not reply to the spirits who were addressing me, thinking the dream would come to me again and be clearer. Later I was told by the old people that I had made a mistake, that the obsidian spirits never spoke to anyone more than once."

VARIOUS SHAMANISTIC BELIEFS AND PRACTICES.

The *mumolno'm* or personal spirits are small, like boys, with gray hair. Some doctors control several; but one identical spirit sometimes serves two or more doctors. The spirits are called older brothers, and address the doctors as younger brothers. Their communications are sometimes audible to other people, and sound faint and far away, or like whistling.

A doctor who is called by a patient and refuses to come becomes sick himself. The usual custom seems to be for the shaman to order as much property as he thinks proper pay to be hung over the sick person. On cure, this becomes his; but if the patient dies, the property is buried with him.

The following is a case of an appearance outside of a dream. A man on the hunt met two strangers, who had live and wriggling deer tails on the ends of their bows. They talked to him about the hunt and went on. He saw them kill a deer, sit down to smoke, and laugh. Then he fainted. When he revived he was bleeding at all his bodily openings. He arrived home half dead, but the doctor who was called in knew what had happened to him and said there was nothing wrong. Soon the man became very thin. He was fasting and training under the direction of another doctor. After he had made the doctor dance, he became well again and commenced to practice.

When a man finds an obsidian blade, a *mit kichil*, sky obsidian, or *Mililit kichil*, *Milili's* obsidian, he lays his clothes and anything else he may have with him before it and says: "I give this to you." He puts his clothing on again, but is careful not to touch the obsidian, which he raises with a stick, covers with a wrapping, and carries home in his net sack. He says nothing, but before long a doctor comes and says: "Where is what you found?" The discoverer then "gives the obsidian to eat" by providing a public feast. Should he omit this, or the offering of his clothes, he would suddenly find the blade vanished. The Yuki prized such blades for their supernatural potency, and state that they neither manufactured them nor put them to practical use.

Quartz crystals, *wa'i*, were also highly valued and employed in blood letting.

It is in the doctor dance that a young shaman's spirits first come to him outside of dreams. He is frightened, but the older shamans exhort and encourage him. His spirits shoot him with spirit obsidians, to make his heart light and clean. As these same invisible obsidians make ordinary people sick, the idea involved here is akin to the Yurok belief that curative power lies in the shaman's faculty to keep disease-bearing pain objects in her body.

The deer, according to the Yuki, can not be exterminated, as the American game laws fear, for these animals, or their souls, have a permanent home inside a large hollow mountain, and are under the control of *Milili*.

RATTLESNAKE SHAMANS.

When a man walks by a rattlesnake, he is struck or escapes as the sun wishes. If he has nearly stepped on the serpent, he says to it: "Grandmother, I did not see you." If he is bitten, he looks at the sun, which appears to him to dip twice to the horizon and back again. If he sees it milky, he will recover; but if bloody, he knows he will die. When the doctor is summoned, he knows at once the fate of the victim. If it is adverse, he makes no attempt to stay the inevitable, but breaks into mourning. If, however, the sufferer will recover, he begins by threatening or abusing the sun; after which he paints wavy lines, apparently representative of rattlesnakes, on a flat stone, warms the wounded part with hot ashes, lays the stone on for a time, and then begins to suck. The poison operates by reproducing a small but live rattlesnake in the body, which the sucking draws toward the practitioner's mouth and then into it. The patient feels this miniature snake leaving him; and just before it departs from his body it dies; so that the shaman demonstrates only its inert form, of the length of about his hand. On the same principle a rattlesnake shaman sucks out a dead spider in curing the bite of the dreaded *hulmunintata* spider.

Pilaⁿtat lamshimi mihik, " the sun's doctor he is," or *pilaⁿti itin hushkaiemol,* " the sun is my directing spirit," would be said of and by a rattlesnake doctor.

BEAR SHAMANS.

Waⁿshit lamshimi or bear doctors are a special and well-defined class of shamans that prevail among all the tribes from the Yuki south to Tehachapi Pass. They receive their power from bears, transform themselves into bears, are almost invulnerable, or if killed likely to come to life again, and are much dreaded as ferocious avengers or even aggressors. A curious point is that while it is insisted that they have the power of bodily transformation, several accounts speaking of the discomfort of the bear fur growing through the skin and the like, yet the Yuki nevertheless explicitly state that on marauding excursions they were men incased in a hardened bear hide, and that while they pretended to bite their foes with their long teeth, they actually stabbed them with a concealed weapon. The very feats alleged by the Indians as nonmagical are, however, almost as incredible as the supernatural powers ascribed to these shamans; so that it is doubtful whether the asserted practices are not a myth. That there were bear doctors is certain; but that they ever executed the theoretically possible things they are alleged to have done customarily is very questionable.

Bear doctors began by repeated dreaming of bears. Young bear women took them to the woods and lived with them. Sometimes an actual bear was said to carry the man off in the body. An incipient shaman might thus stay away an entire season. Sometimes, it seems, a man deliberately sought the power. He would swim in the pool formed where an uprooted tree had stood. On emerging he would dance toward and back from a tree which sang to him, and growl and scratch the bark of this as bears are believed to do in their dances. Hair would begin to grow over his body, and finally he became a bear.

On his return to human beings the bear novice was taken in hand by older bear shamans, and taught to sing and develop his strength in lonely places in the woods. He hurled logs about as later he was to handle and fling men. He allowed his instructors to roll him down a canyon side in a hollow log. He sat on an oak limb, which they bent down and let spring. Finally he was set on a log and thrown into the air. If he retained his straddling hold, he was a complete bear doctor. During all this period of training the bear doctors associated with actual bears, and ate their food, and at times lived with them. They might be out from spring to autumn.

The powers of the finished bear shaman were several. He cured bear bites. He also gave demonstrations, such as digging in the fire and producing a living snake, or in the hard-baked ground under the fireplace and bringing up a mouse nest. Their most important and spectacular function, however, was to go out, alone or in twos or threes, to kill persons against whom they held a grudge, or people of other localities against whom their own tribe entertained avowed or concealed enmity. Some accounts tell how the bear doctors sang to each other for this purpose until they were transformed into actual bears who set out on their errand of destruction. Other statements relate that they incased themselves in a complete bear skin, the stiffness of which was sufficient to stop arrows. Small baskets were set in the heels of the bear's feet for some unknown use. Another basket had a stone put in it, and was worn so as to rumble like a bear's growl when the shaman shook his head. They carried beads or other valuables with them, so that if they should be killed they would be buried with appropriate belongings. When the foe was attacked he was slapped to blind him, then stabbed with a knife or bone dagger held in the hand close to the mouth to give the appearance of a bite being delivered. The slain were gutted, dismembered, and their flesh scattered about over the brush as might be done by an enraged bear.

This certainly sounds rather unlikely. It may at times have been attempted, but none of the paraphernalia used have ever been seen by students or preserved for museums. The supernatural element was no doubt present for the Indian even in these physically conceivable methods of operation: no one could perform such extraordinary feats of strength and skill without faculties imparted or developed by the bears.

A specific instance of reputed achievements by bear doctors has already been related in the story of the Kato war with the Yuki. Here is another and less sensational incident from an eyewitness:

Several of us were hunting deer, when I heard singing. Peering through the brush, I saw a person lying in a little glade by a spring. I was frightened and ran to my companions. We all went to investigate. Climbing a log, we looked down over it and saw three men lying close together with a bearskin near them. A young man of us said: "Let me shoot and frighten them." An older member of the party objected, but the youth insisted and won assent. He shot and the arrow passed right under the back of the nearest person. The man uttered no sound, and only raised his head to look about and regard the arrow under him. He was just as indifferent as a bear. Then our young man shot a second arrow, which went through his ribs. The shaman jumped and rolled, growling like a bear. The two others leaped up too, but ran off, leaving him lying. Then we went away too. Next morning we returned. Only the bearskin was still there. His two companions had carried the wounded bear doctor away. We left the skin where it was and went home.

It may have been a group of practicing bear shamans who met with this misadventure.

CHAPTER 13.

THE HUCHNOM AND COAST YUKI.

The Huchnom.

LAND AND PEOPLE.

The Huchnom are so called by the Yuki and apparently by themselves. The Pomo know them as Tatu, and the whites usually designate them as Redwoods, a denomination applied also to the remote Athabascan Chilula and Whilkut. Their American name was given to them from their occupancy of a site they call Mulhol in Redwood Valley, near one of the sources of Russian River. They probably visited here in aboriginal times; but the stream was in Pomo ownership, above and below, and the only established Huchnom residence on it was a result of shiftings caused by the coming of the Americans. Huchnom is said to signify "mountain people" and to have been more specifically applied by the Yuki to the northern part of the group of the village of Shfpomul.

The Huchnom territory comprises the valley of South Eel River from Hullville nearly to the mouth, together with its affluent Tomki Creek and the lower course of the stream known as Deep or Outlet Creek. The Pomo had a number of villages on the middle and upper portion of Deep Creek. Whether the Huchnom allowed their share of its drainage to lie idle except for hunting, or whether they also held settlements on its banks which have merely not been recorded, is open to doubt.

The Huchnom territory is typical of California "tribal" distributions. First, it is essentially an area of one drainage. Thus, watersheds and not watercourses mark its boundaries. But, secondly, it is not rigidly confined to these natural limits, spilling slightly over the divides at two points. One village, probably Huchnom, but possibly Yuki, and of uncertain name, was on the headwaters of the South Fork of Eel River—not to be confounded with the South Eel on which the main body of the Huchnom lived. Another, Ukumna, stood on Russian River near the head of its eastern source. These two settlements look like advance posts that have begun to encroach on areas naturally belonging to Athabascans and the Pomo; but they may be rear guards of a Huchnom shrinking from a once wider habitat.

The other main settlements lay on the South Eel, and, in order upstream, were: Shipomul at the mouth of Outlet Creek; Nonhohou; Yek; Mot; Mupan; Mot-kuyuk, at the mouth of Tomki Creek; Ba'awel (this is its Pomo name), only a couple of miles from Ukumna over the divide; Lilko'ol; Komohmemut-kuyuk; Mumemel, just below the forks at Hullville, where Yuki settlements recommenced. On Tomki Creek were Hatupoka and Pukemul farther up.

The Huchnom were friendly with the Pomo. The Ukumnano'm at the head of Potter Valley, for instance, observed no line of demarcation between themselves and the Pomo villages below them. Each people hunted and fished at will over the territory of the other. In the frequent hostilities between the Pomo and Yuki the Huchnom sympathized with the Pomo and no doubt were occasionally involved. Nevertheless they remained the transmitters of many articles of trade, and in the long run of elements of civilization also, to the Yuki.

The original Huchnom population probably did not exceed 500. The census of 1910 recorded seven full bloods and eight halfbreeds. This is probably substantially correct, but the survivors are so mixed in and intermarried with the northern Pomo and the hodgepodge of tribes on Round Valley Reservation that an exact determination would be beyond the efforts of census enumerators.

CULTURAL AFFILIATIONS.

Generic statements made both by the Yuki and Pomo suggest that the Huchnom affiliated in customs with the latter people more than with the Yuki, to whom they are related in speech. This impression is confirmed by reports of their utensils, which seem to be substantially identical with those of the Pomo. It also tallies with their political relations, which were uniformly friendly with the nearer Pomo divisions and with the Kato, but often hostile to the Yuki and Wailaki.

On the other hand, all that is known of the religion of the Huchnom allies them very closely with the Yuki. Like the latter, they practice only two major ceremonies of the Kuksu type; they call these by the same names as the Yuki, and approximate the creation myth of the latter.

Huchnom civilization must therefore be reckoned as on the whole intermediate between those of the Yuki and Pomo, but as tending to adhere to the one or the other type in any single phase. It is a mixture rather than a blend.

RITUAL.

Like the Yuki, the Huchnom practice a *wok* or dance of *Taikomol*, the creator, and of the *hulk'ilal*, the ghosts or spirits of dead human beings. The impersonator of *Taikomol* wears the familiar "bighead" costume, which is the most widespread of all the many accouterments of the Kuksu cult. The *hulk'ilal* are unmasked, but disguised by stripes of black and white paint across face and body. They wear no feathers but tie blossoms into their hair. No women or children, in other words no uninitiated, are admitted into the *hopinim*, or dance house, for either of these ceremonies.

There is also an initiation, or "lying dance," for each of these ceremonies. The *hulk'ilal woknam* comes first. It begins in the autumn, when boys of 12 years or thereabouts are collected and brought into the dance house. Here they spend six or seven months until spring, under restrictions of food and conduct, and listening to the creation myth and its accompanying songs. It appears that a new dance house was put up for such an occasion, which came only infrequently to any one town. When a *woknam* had been announced for the winter among the Huchnom, neighboring Pomo and Kato villages seem to have moved over bodily and brought their children for participation. A year or several later it is likely that a winter might be given up to these rites among one of the other groups, whereupon the Huchnom, or such of them as had boys of the proper age, might bring them. So far as the Kato are concerned, this arrangement is reflected in the fact that the Huchnom know and use Kato songs along with their own. It has already been stated that the Yuki, who were less friendly with the Kato, acknowledge that much of their sacred lore came to them from these people, and it appears below that Coast Yuki and Kato were wont to join in dance celebrations. As regards the Pomo, the situation presents the difficulty that those of them that are best known, the Clear Lake division, practiced a larger number of ceremonies than the tribes heretofore mentioned. It is therefore likely that the most northerly border tribes of the Pomo approximated the Yukians more nearly than the main body of their kinsmen in their ritual system.

After the boys had gone through the *hulk'ilal* they entered the *Taikomol-woknam*, in which they remained throughout the summer. Very nearly a year seems thus to have been spent in this period of induction into the mysteries.

A food taboo which has not been reported from any other people is mentioned by the Huchnom. Their initiated boys ate no small game, such as squirrels, rabbits, quail, or trout. This prohibition is said to have endured throughout life, all meat of this sort being consumed only by women and children. The flesh of the deer, elk, and salmon—in other words, of the larger mammals and fish—was free to men and boys after a special ceremony had been sung over them at the conclusion of their initiation. The reason given for the taboo is that flesh of the small game is incompatible with knowledge of the creation myth. Women were not taught this cosmogony and its accompaniments, and consequently were not injured.

On the other hand, deer meat clashes as violently with anything female, in the opinion of the Huchnom, as in the opinion of nearly all other California tribes. It was not only strictly forbidden to women at the recurring periods of their adult life but was strictly taboo to adolescent girls for about two years. The dance made for them at this time is called the *humnumwok*, and seems to have been performed over them by women at monthly intervals throughout a winter. The girls might not walk about for fear of being paralyzed or otherwise afflicted in body. They were kept away from the sight of men and spent as much time as possible recumbent.

It was women who sang over them, but not in the dance house, which was too intimately associated with the men's mysteries to be profaned in this way. It is clear that we have here a form of the widespread Californian adolescence ceremony for girls, but with an attempt to partially equate or parallel it to the fundamentally different Kuksu type of initiation for boys. A similar phenomenon is encountered several times in California, even among religions of quite diverse type and origin, as among the Luiseño. At the same time it is clear that the idea of initiation in the form of a religious school or "lying dance" has become firmly impressed upon the Yuki and Huchnom alike as one of the fundamental facts of their civilization.

Boys during their period of initiation were allowed to eat only with a spoon of mussel shell or elk horn, and to scratch their heads only with a bone. The latter is a taboo definitely associated with the girls' adolescence rite in the remainder of California, and appears to represent a sporadic Huchnom patterning of the boys' ceremony after that for girls.

The dance house had a smoke hole on top, but as among the Yuki this is said not to have been used as a door, and there is no mention of any ladder for descent. The entrance used was a little tunnel descending from the ground, and was usually at the south end of the dance house.

The owner of the dance house and manager and responsible head of the initiations and dances conducted within it was the chief, *te'ol*, the same individual who led the community in its social and political activities. The Huchnom are clear and emphatic on this point, and the condition they describe agrees rather well with that known from the southern Wintun and with more general statements recorded elsewhere in north central California.

There was, however, at least one official possessing authority to admonish and even strike the chief for ceremonial violations. This was the *wi'hli*, who seems to have exercised a sort of censorship. He is said to have been selected by the chief after a talk in which other men participated. The *wi'hli* ordered the work that was necessary for ceremonies. It is possible that his name is derived from the word meaning "to work."

The *huno'ik* were the watchmen or caretakers of the dance house. While an initiation was in progress one of them was always on duty and awake to report to the chief any violations of the rules by quarrelsome or lazy or recalcitrant boys. The fire tender was known as *yehim k'awesk* or *yehim tateyim*. The director of the steps of the dance, or shouter of orders to the dance performers, was called *lilha'ol*, as by the Yuki.

MYTHOLOGY.

The Huchnom creation, like that of the Yuki, begins with Taikomol alone in the universe. He made the land, built a dance house, made human beings from sticks, and instituted the *hulk'ilal wok*. There was some mistake, however, and things went wrong. The world sank, the primeval water on which it had been floating came up, and the earth disappeared. Taikomol was again alone on the expanse of ocean. He created another world. This had no daylight or sun and was without game, and the people ate one another. This world also did not go right and was burned. Even the water is said to have been consumed. Then Taikomol gave himself his name, and, still singing, said that he was a real man and a chief. Again he made an earth, beginning in the north and extending it eastward. It was new and white and clean, without rivers or mountains. He traversed it southward, and when he looked to the east found it had extended so far that he could no longer see the water on that side. He made rivers and mountains and again built a dance house, but the world was still floating too lightly on its substratum and swayed like a log. Thereupon he set at its northern end a great coyote, elk, and deer to hold it. They, however, also floated about, whereupon he made them lie down and the earth finally came to rest. It quakes now when they stir. Then he laid sticks into his dance house with the wish that they wake up as human beings and hold a feast. He stood at the door of the dance house and listened, and in the morning the people emerged with chatter and bustle. Then he gave them the *hulk'ilal wok*. One of them did something wrong and became sick and died. Taikomol spoke to him: "I shall dig a hole and bury you, but in the morning you will come back." Then in the morning the dead man arose and returned and entered the dance house. Taikomol stood at the door again to listen, and heard them say that he who had returned smelled too strongly. They all became sick. His wish of resurrection was therefore abandoned, but Taikomol enjoined on the people to keep the *hulk'ilal wok* so that they might live well and long. The first man who gave heed to him and carried the ceremony on and taught it to the people was *Lamshim-chala*, "White doctor." When he died, *Shum-hohtme*, "Big ear," was the next teacher, and after him, *Haih-pota*, "Gray net-sack." After that tradition ceases; as the Huchnom say, the succeeding leaders down to the present were only "common men."

This sounds like good myth; but the last part of the story is very likely authentic history. The Yuki mention the same masters and teachers of the Taikomol ceremony as having lived two or three generations before the coming of the white man. It would seem that the Huchnom have projected a set of relatively recent events into the far legendary past; or, perhaps, to put the matter more accurately, that neither Yuki nor Huchnom discriminate clearly between a century or two ago and the time of the creation.

A myth of a contest of the creator and Thunder suggests the rivalry attributed to them by the Kato, but the Huchnom agree with the Yuki in making Taikomol supreme. Thunder challenges him, but fails to carry out his boast of dropping on the ocean and standing on it. He sinks deep into the water, whereas Taikomol succeeds in alighting on it and walking to shore. Thunder is not yet convinced, and suggests a contest of darting down and kicking great stones to pieces. Again he fails, but when the creator follows he drives the rock far out of sight into the ground. Taikomol then sends Thunder north. In spring he is to travel south and play with the hail and return in winter, when the clouds drive north over the ocean.

Taikomol is said to have closed his career by ascending to the sky on a rainbow and to be alive there now. Other details are added, but have apparently been taken over from the ghost dance or directly from Christianity.

THE MODERN GHOST DANCE.

The ghost dance of 1872 came to the Huchnom from the central Pomo of the coast, who in turn had it from the eastern Pomo. From Round Valley and vicinity it was carried north, according to modern survivors, to the Hayfork Wintun and Hupa. The latter statement is probably not to be taken in a literal geographical sense, but it corroborates the inference, already derived from the existence of circular dance houses among the Whilkut, that this distinctly northwestern group derived the type of structure through a northward extension of the ghost dance.

The Huchnom make a good deal of the fact that the ghost dance reached them from the south, whereas their old dances are all believed to have originated in the north. This latter is not a reflection of a historical fact, since it is quite clear that the center of the cults to which they adhere lies to the south and east of them. Their opinion is due to the trend of their mythology, which makes the creator, the world, and everything ancient and venerable begin in the north.

They state that the ghost dance after its spread to the north ceased. This is true so far as concerns its existence as a separate cult connected with the return of the dead and the approaching end of the world. At the same time, traces of ghost-dance influence can be discerned in the cosmogony, ceremonial speeches, and dances of the Huchnom of to-day, so far as they still exist. It is true that the ghost-dance influence seems not to have been as strong among these people as among the Pomo, who were nearer its center of diffusion, but it is perceptible.

CALENDAR.

Their old calendar seems to have become confused in the minds of the few Huchnom survivors. A few of its divisions were numbered, as it were, by the fingers, as in the Modoc reckoning; the majority are descriptive of seasonal events, like the moons of the Maidu. Twenty names of periods are on record, and these do not seem to exhaust the list. There must, therefore, have been synonyms for most of the lunations, or a separate designation for the waxing and waning of each moon. This is the list, the exact sequence being open to some doubt.

> *Mipa'ohot*, "old man finger," thumb (March).
> *Mipa-koye*, "long finger."
> *Mipa'-olsel*.
> *Yoht-umol* (May).
> *Olpalmol*, "tree leaves."
> *Im-pomol*.
> *Yoht-wanmol*.
> *Im-tomol*.
> *Im-pusmol*.
> *Yoht-pomol* (dry).
> *Yoht-usmol*.
> *Olom-tomol*, "mountains burned over."
> *On-tutwin*.

On-woi-mol, "earth smoky" (August or September).
Lehpwanmol or *lehpwene* (beginning of autumn).
Huwol-huntusmol, "acorns ready to drop" (preparations for *woknam*).
Huwol-chukmol, "acorns fall" (new dance house finished).
Muⁿl-naⁿtmol, "ice on streams."
Yem-tamol, "fire ————."
Huⁿw-taⁿkmol, "fish frozen."

This seems to be the type also of the Yuki calendar, which is even less satisfactorily known. *Pal-kush*, "leaves fall (?)" and *uk-hamol*, "waters high"—perhaps they are synonyms—came about the beginning of November; *maⁿl-naⁿtnol*, "streams rise," or *shaⁿwaⁿ lashk'awol*, "winter moon," followed; and *lashk'awol-hot*, "great moon," or *taⁿwish hot lashk'awol*, "principal one," was the time of Christmas and January.

The eastern Pomo system evidently follows a similar plan, since two of its months were *sa'olbi*, "thumb," and *nusutbi*, "index," while others, although not recorded, are said to designate characteristics of the time of year. It is reported that each man who was interested, but especially he who fished or hunted much, kept his own account. Reckonings often differed and there was no standard but nature's by which to settle disputes. When the acorns actually fell, argument as to the acorn moon was decided.[1]

The central Pomo calendar is wholly descriptive. Its beginning is unknown and its order not wholly certain; but approximately its moons corresponded with our months as follows:

Bashelamatau-la, buckeyes ripe (January).
Sachau-da, cold winds.
Kadamchido-da, growth begins.
Chidodapuk, flowers.
Umchachich-da, seeds ripen.
Butich-da, bulbs mature (*bu*, Brodiaca).
Bakaichich-da, manzanita ripens (*kaye*, manzanita).
Luchich-da, acorns appear.
Shachluyiau-da, soaproot dug for fish poison (*sha*, fish).
Kalemkayo, trees felled by fires at butt (*kale*, tree).
Kasi-sa, cold begins.
Stalpkel-da, leaves yellow and fall (December).

CHIEFS.

Chieftainship seems to have rested on the idea that the new incumbent should be a relative of the last chief, with precedence given to his son, but no clearly defined rule of succession. If there were no son, a stepson or sister's son or other relative followed. The same

---

[1] Recent data indicate that the eastern Pomo followed two systems. The less formal was descriptive of movements of fish, the acorn crop, and the like. The other plan was really a count from 1 to 13, with the fingers (from thumb to little finger) replacing the numbers 3 to 7. The first moon seems to have come at the winter solstice.

plan appears to have prevailed among the northern Pomo about Sherwood.

At the same time, the community was consulted, so that conditions were not radically diverse from the customs of the Yuki and Maidu, whose chiefs are stated to have been elective. Thus, the Huchnom report:

> *Mu^{n}ye mose hame*, whom (do) you like?
> *Keu^n iyi k'u^{n}ihke*, him I desire.
> *Kekimko te'ol mehme heu*, his-father chief was yes.
> *Keu^n te'ol tolte iyi k'u^{n}ihke*, him chief's son I desire.
> *Ke miyi tateyimpa*, he you will-care-for.
> *Wi kee kapsheki*, we him install.

And, when the old chief's bow, beads, rope, and other valuables were handed to his successor by the brother of the dead man:

> *Kalu shu'hin ushi nu^{n}wuk*, with-this giving-to-you (?) us watch.
> *Kalu ushi tateyim*, with-this us care-for
> *Me ahtu mehike*, you chief (?) are.
> *Milauhtela ushi ku^{n}imin*, not-be-ashamed us address.

Orating seems to have been one of the principal functions of the chief. He also dispensed food at gatherings, partly from stores collected by him, together with gifts of shell beads, among his people. He built and owned the dance house; and his direction of ceremonies has already been mentioned.

The hereditary principle appears also in the recognition by the Huchnom, as by the Pomo and southern Wintun, of chieftainesses. These were called *mus te'ol*, woman chief, and it was their privilege to harangue women. A chief's wife or daughter might attain to the position, it is said; the former, to judge by Pomo custom, through having a chief for father rather than because of her marriage.

MARRIAGE AND NAMES.

The Huchnom married indifferently in their own town, in another, or among friendly foreigners. A union was usually broached by two mothers; then the fathers conferred also. A youth who hunted or worked actively was looked on with most favor. The four old people being agreed, two brothers or other kinsmen of the groom staked him to shell beads and went with him to the bride's house, where the gift or price was tendered. His companions then returned, and he remained with his wife, but left for his parents' home early in the morning. The youth was extremely bashful toward his mother-in-law at this period and she toward him, and a similar attitude existed between the bride and her husband's father. This feeling was no doubt connected with the young husband's visiting his wife only by night. After he had taken her to his old home for a visit, and especially after the couple had settled in their own house and the fact of the marriage was publicly recognized, the first shame dissipated and the couple and their parents-in-law of opposite sex began to address each other.   The return of the husband to his own people was made the occasion of gifts of food and beads to the pair, which they gave to the wife's parents, besides entertaining their kin. A return visit to the wife's people followed, after which the couple usually founded their own home.   This was always among the group or in the town of the wife.

No cousins or other kin married.   Marriage with the wife's kin was permissible, but there seems to have been a prejudice—rather strange for northern California—against marrying a sister-in-law, except that when a man left small children his brother would take the widow so that his nephews and nieces might be provided for.

Names were bestowed by a relative, who made a present.   The mother's brother was among these, but it seems no more frequently than other older kinsmen.   The Pomo usually named after a grandparent; thus an old woman of Sherwood was named *Shina-toya*, "Striped name," by her father after his mother.   The Huchnom probably followed this plan also.   It is said that no new name was bestowed at initiation, which, although in conflict with the Maidu practice, accords with the greater simplicity of the Kuksu organization among the Yukian tribes.   "Stingy mountain lion" and "Snow old man" are Huchnom names; "Dry black oak" was a Kato chief— *Mam-k'ima*, the Huchnom called him in their tongue.   These appellations are as irrelevant as those prevalent among most of the Californian tribes.

THE COAST YUKI.

GEOGRAPHY.

The Coast Yuki consider their own speech to be more nearly reproduced in the Huchnom dialect than in Yuki proper.   This would mean that they were an offshoot from the Huchnom, or that both were originally a common branch of the Yukian stock.   Their position confirms this.   They are in contact with the Huchnom, but separated from the Yuki by the Kato.

On the other hand, the available vocabularies place the Coast Yuki language as near to Yuki as to Huchnom, so that a critical analysis will be required before a positive determination of their ancient affiliations and history can be made.   All three languages must have been mutually intelligible in some measure, though it is unlikely that a Coast Yuki unacquainted with Huchnom and Yuki could have followed the whole of a conversation in either.   The divergences are in part the result of the formation of words from different stems of similar meaning, and in part the consequence of phonetic changes. The latter seem to be rather consistent. Thus there are regular correspondences of Huchnom *u*, Yuki *a*, Coast *e*, and Huchnom *e*, Yuki *i*, and Coast *i*.

They call themselves Ukoht-ontilka, and are called Ukhot-no'm by the Yuki. Both words mean " ocean people." Their Pomo name, Kamalel-pomo, seems to have the same significance.

The Coast Yuki territory was covered with heavy redwood timber, except for portions of the wind-swept, open coast, which ran to cliffs except at the mouths of the filled streams.

The Coast Yuki settlements have not been recorded. Names of places in their territory, most of which were probably inhabited, are, along the coast from north to south: On-chil-ka or On-chil-em, " land gap," beyond Rockport; Es'im, at Rockport or Hardy Creek; Melhom-i'ikem, " surf fish," Warren Creek; Hisimel-auhkem, " salal-berries having," the next creek; Lil-p'in-kem, " rock lies," De Haven; Shipep or Shipoi, " willows," Westport; K'etim, Chetman gulch; Lilim, Mussel rock; Ok'omet or Shipoi, Kabesillah (*kai* is " willows " in northern Pomo) ⸮ Metkuyak-olselem, the creek north of Ten Mile River; Metkuyaki or Metkuyakem, the mouth of Ten Mile River and also the river, the largest stream in Coast Yuki possession; Mil-hot-em, " deer large," or Lalim, " lake," Cleone.

Here Yukian territory ends and that of the Pomo or Nokonmi begins. Susmel-im, " duck creek," was at the mouth of Pudding Creek; Ol-hepech-kem, " tree foggy," Noyo River; Nehkinmelem, Casper. Inland, Onp'otilkei, " dusty flat," was in Sherwood Valley, and Ukemim, " lake " near Willits.

All Athabascans, Sinkyone, Wailaki, Kato, were Ko'ol. The Kato were specifically designated T'okia. Branscomb or Jackson Valley in their territory was Olohtem-esich-kei, " redwood red; " Cahto was Ukemim, " lake; " and Laytonville or Long Valley, Ukemnini. To the north on the coast, among the Sinkyone, Usal was Nu'chem; the inhabitants of the vicinity, the U'tino'm; Needle Rock or Bear Harbor, Hushki; Shelter Cove, On'pu, " land floats," with reference to the headland as seen from a distance. The people hereabout were the Onpu-ontilka.

The Pomo called K'etim " Se'eshene " and Metkuyaki " Bidato." They recognize another settlement upstream across the river from the latter, one at the mouth of the North Fork, and a third between Onch'ilka and Es'im.

The following was the international status of the tribes in this region at the time of American settlement. The Coast Yuki were friendly with all their neighbors—the northern Pomo of the coast south of themselves and inland on Deep or Outlet Creek; the Huchnom; the Kato; and the Sinkyone about Usal. So amicable were the relations with the Kato that each people constantly and freely crossed the other's boundary.

These various neighbors, however, were often hostile to their neighbors beyond, and this to some extent involved the Coast Yuki in warfare, though at long range and probably with no serious losses. The Usal Athabascans fought their kinsmen of Shelter Cove. The

Kato at times warred against the Yuki and at others against the Wailaki. These two hostile peoples were chiefly embroiled with each other. Shortly before the Americans came, however, they made peace and united against the Kato, who suffered heavily in consequence, according to the Coast Yuki account, although during the portion of the conflict covered by a narrative already related, they inflicted greater injuries on the Yuki than they received. This Coast Yuki friendship for the Kato is the explanation of the statement by the Yuki that they never visited the ocean. The Outlet Creek Pomo fought their kinsmen on upper Russian River, but this did not deter the Potter Valley division of the latter in standing with the Huchnom, who were friendly to the Outlet Creek people, against the Yuki. The northern Pomo on the coast, of Noyo, Fort Bragg, and Albion, were embroiled with those farther south around Gualala River, though whether these were the southwestern Pomo, who held most of the stream, or the nearer central group, who abutted on its mouth, is not clear.

It is evident that relationship of speech and ultimate common origin were of little if any consequence in determining these alignments. It is also clear that travel to any distance, even 50 miles from a man's home, was normally out of the question. Hostile territory had to be traveled before this limit was reached; and beyond were people who, if neutral because unknown, were uneasy in the presence of a stranger.

The Coast Yuki population in 1850 may be set at perhaps 500. In 1910 the census reported 15.

MATERIAL CULTURE.

Manners and thoughts among the Coast Yuki were essentially those of the Kato and Yuki proper, with certain peculiarities in which they utilized opportunities provided by their habitat.

Salmon were speared with the two-pronged harpoon as they went upstream, and caught with a scoop net as they descended. Surf fish, often called smelt, were allowed to run into a net with the receding surf. The net hung from a vertical half hoop, which was probably fastened to the ends of long poles. Eels were caught on a bone gaff at night, the water being randomly raked for them. Deer and elk were sometimes taken in snares. The acorn supply may have been more limited than among most inland tribes, but seeds were obtained in abundance over the hill slopes behind Westport and in the bottoms of Ten Mile River.

The ordinary house was of bark, conical, and probably without a center post, as among the coastal tribes north and south. The dance house had not only a large center post but a peripheral row of forks, from whose connecting beams rafters sloped up to the middle. The pitch of the roof is said to have been steeper than among the Yuki. The side door of the Yuki is not mentioned, but there was a roof entrance. Both exits were closed when the inmates wished to sweat themselves.

The bow was of yew, shaved smooth with flint, and sinew-backed. The width was about two fingers, the middle was not materially narrowed, and the sides were rounded. This is the typical central bow: the northwestern implement being broader, sharp edged, flatter, but distinctly pinched in the middle. The materials, however, are northwestern, as was the habit of overpainting the sinew in red and blue.

In addition, Kato bows were obtained in trade. These were of hazel, somewhat longer, and unpainted.

The pestle was of the bulbous Pomo shape.

Mesh measures were of wood. The central Californian regularly uses this material, the northwestern, elk horn. Slight as this detail is, it is significant. The shape and size of the implement are the same, and rubbing down a slab of antler on sandstone requires no more skill than whittling a stick flat and square at the ends. One product is also exactly as useful as the other. The sole difference of consequence is in the laboriousness of manufacture. That the northwesterner was willing to undergo this is evidence that his standard was another one, and that certain aspects of culture carried distinctive values to him that were of little moment to the central Californian.

Neither the Coast Yuki nor any of their neighbors had canoes, though they knew of them as used by tribes to the north.

Basketry was like that of the Kato and Yuki, it is said, though no examples have been preserved. The Usal Athabascans are said by the Coast Yuki to have made coiled baskets of the same kind. It is likely, however, that as among the Wailaki, and, in another part of the State among the Yana, this ware was only sporadically manufactured by them alongside of the standard forms in twining.

String was made from the fibers of the iris leaf, *ots'ish* or *ts'iwes*, which was split with an artificial thumb-nail of mussel shell. Material and process are wholly Yurok.

The men's guessing game and women's dice were those of the Pomo. The count of the dice was: six marked sides up, two points; six plain, two; three marked and three plain, one point; any other combination, nothing. No form of hoop and dart game appears to have been known. This absence is characteristic of all the coast region to the north end of the State, perhaps even far beyond.

Tobacco was gathered wild in stream valleys, a mountain variety being considered unduly strong. The Yurok planted their tobacco on hilltops, and the wild specimens on the river flats were regarded unsafe to use because liable to pollution. The Coast Yuki pipe is the *woimil-lil*, "tobacco-stone," though invariably made of wood. The discrepancy between the implement and its name recurs among the Pomo.

CUSTOMS.

The Coast Yuki assert that each of the tribes of their neighborhood followed a distinctively recognizable style of women's facial tattoo. The few examples observed or recorded clearly evince variability from individual to individual. A tribal style or significant element, even if not a whole pattern, undoubtedly underlay these arbitrary variations, but is hardly deducible from the scant and scattering data.

Burial was in elk or bear skins, and on the back at full length, it is said, with the head to the north. The stretched position of the corpse is probably due to a remote northwestern influence. The grave was dug with sticks and baskets. There was no anniversary ceremony. Members of a family were buried together, and at their abode. Cremation was resorted to only when it was easier to dispose of the ashes of the deceased than his body. This, the Coast Yuki say, was the habit also of all their neighbors, including the Kato and the northernmost Pomo on the coast. The Pomo in general cremated regularly.

Clamshell disk beads were the standard money, but were little and unsystematically used in many social relations. Thus there was no formal and exact purchase of the wife. The marriage having been agreed upon, groom and father made each other gifts of beads and other property. Consequently the bride did not become the husband's property to take home, nor, if he failed to pay in full, was he under definitely regulated obligation to meet the balance due by service. He might enter the wife's home, take her to his father's, or found a new one. No doubt there was some notion of acquiring title by payment; but at best it was ill defined in comparison with the rigorous precision of the transaction in the northwest.

Just so in war. To a Yurok cessation of the blood feud without full compensation for every life on either side was unthinkable. There was even an exact valuation of each individual according to his social status. If exceptions occurred, they were rare. The Coast Yuki—contrary to the Yuki—state that there was no usual settlement after outright warfare. The sufferers sought revenge or stood their loss—which agrees with the details of the Wappo-Pomo fighting narrated below. But if a member of another community was killed and the murderer or his people were anxious to avoid reprisals, they made a payment to the relatives of the dead man.

The dog of the Coast Yuki was short-haired and sharp-eared. The usual description is given, "like a coyote." It has been the habit to assume from this that the native dog of California was merely a tame coyote or a dog that habitually bred with coyotes. This is surely a hasty and false inference. The Indians state, among this tribe and elsewhere, that their dogs were of all colors, "yellow, red, and black." This argues long domestication and the probability of a disposition very different from that of the wild ancestor. It will require a more exact study than appears yet to have been made before it can be asserted that the Indian dog was even remotely descended from the coyote. For all anyone really knows of the matter, the Indian brought his dog with him when he first settled the continent.

The Coast Yuki and Huchnom did not eat dog flesh. If other northern Californians may be inferred from, they regarded it as the most virulent of poisons. They also did not name their dogs. They did, however, bury them, sometimes even with property.

RELIGION.

Dance ornaments were all like those of the Yuki and Pomo. No doubt they bore their distinctive features, but in the absence of all preserved examples, descriptions are too vague to allow of refinements being discussed with profit. Both kinds of rattles were used, apparently with the same functions as among the Yuki; and the dance house held a foot drum.

The Coast Yuki called the *Hulk'ilal-wok: Yihkim-wok*, which appears to have the same meaning of "ghosts' dance," and it was taught and enacted along similar lines. It is said that women were admitted to the observances when they had become aged. The *Wok-oht*, "great dance," is the Yuki *tau^n-wok* or war dance. The scalp that was put on a stick took in all the skin of the head as far as eyes and ears. The *Shok-hamp*, the Yuki *La^{n}l-ha^{n}p-wok*, is an autumnal acorn dance, made in the dance house by men, women, and children without feather ornaments. In the *Hak'ot-wok*, " south dance," the performers stood in line; in the *Hiltimelk*, or " fire-around," they moved in a circle. Both of these, as well as what was simply called *wok*, dance, correspond to the Yuki " feather dance " in being of no great sacredness. They were made outdoors, and the regalia were showy feather capes, yellow-hammer bands, and feather prongs.

The Yuki creator, " the one who travels alone," is secondary to Thunder among the Kato. With the Coast Yuki, *Taikomol* has disappeared altogether, it would seem, and Thunder, *Ehlaumel*, is the one great deity in the creation.

CHAPTER 14.

THE WAPPO.

ORIGIN.

The Wappo go under an unaboriginal name which is too well established to make its replacement possible. It is an Americanization of Spanish Guapo, "brave," a sobriquet which they earned in Mission times by their stubborn resistance to the military adjuncts of the Franciscan establishments. A similar reputation was enjoyed by the Yuki and Huchnom among the Pomo. It is impossible to imagine an inborn Yukian racial disposition as the basis of this fortitude. So far as their physical type goes, the Wappo and perhaps the Huchnom would seem to have been one in what heredity bestowed upon them with the broad-headed Pomo and other peaceable central Californians, while the Yuki shared their shorter stature and narrower skulls with the Athabascans adjoining them. The superior warlike qualities of all the Yukian divisions must be attributed to somewhat diverse habits formed in adjustment of their culture to a highland and hinterland habitat. They were mountaineers; the Pomo were wealthier lowlanders.

The Wappo proper are separated from the Huchnom by 40 miles of Pomo territory in the valley of the Russian River. Their recent Clear Lake offshoot, the Lile'ek, are nearer still.

Wappo speech, however, is exceedingly different from Yuki and Huchnom. It differs considerably more than Spanish from Italian or German from Norwegian, perhaps almost as widely as German from English. On the basis of such comparisons, a thousand years would be a short lapse to allow for the degree of divergence. On the other hand, the Wappo were a small people and wholly surrounded by half a dozen nationalities of entirely distinct language. Under such conditions of abundant and enforced alien contact a tongue changes with unusual rapidity, not only by the direct importation of loan words but by the absorption of new methods of sound production and perhaps even of structural processes. There is little evidence, it is true, of grammar ever being taken over bodily from another speech, but it is likely that the mere prevalence of bilingualism or trilingualism will disturb the original language to the extent of setting in operation within it impulses that result in new mechanisms of alteration. While the processes are obscure, linguistic geography shows this to have been the fact in all parts of the world, and most precise confirmations are found for California in the aberrant idioms of the outlying fragments of the Pomo, Shasta, Yokuts, and Shoshoneans. The main body of the Yuki, being on the whole far more in contact with each other than with foreigners, would have such impulses checked more frequently, and the constant internal intercourse would hold their local dialects comparatively uniform.

These considerations are sufficiently strong to reduce materially the length of time which their speech divergence at first sight indicates for the period of Yuki and Wappo separation. Half instead of a full or double thousand years seems the more likely figure; and even a somewhat shorter lapse might have sufficed. But is is necessary to be conservative, for while a certain proportion of Yuki and Wappo words are not very different, the majority are totally dissimilar in appearance, and a member of one group would certainly not have caught anything of the drift of a conversation held in the speech of the other.

Within the Wappo area dialectic subdivisions were not very marked. The southern dialect is very scantily known. The central and western dialects were nearly identical. The northern diverged slightly more from these two.

SETTLEMENTS.

The range of the Wappo is peculiar (Pl. 27). Their settlements lay in valleys; but their territory was one of mountains, mostly low, indeed, but much broken. They held the very head of Sonoma Creek; the valley of Napa River down to tidewater; the upper part of Pope Creek; the southern headwaters of Putah Creek, which drains into the Sacramento; the upper courses of Sulphur Creek, particularly its south branch, which runs into Russian River; a short stretch of Russian River itself; and its affluent Elk Creek. The picture of the Wappo which this distribution calls up is not that of militant conquerors who once set out from a northern home to wrest to themselves the fairest of the tracts they might encounter, but an image of a stubborn remnant tenaciously retaining the rough upland core of a once more widely spread domain of mellower lands.

All the known Wappo settlements are entered on the map, but in each district there seems to have been but one larger and continuously inhabited town, the center of a community with some sense of political unity. In the southern area the important towns were Kaimus, at Yountville, and Anakota-noma, near St. Helena, in Napa drainage, and Wilikos, at the head of Sonoma Valley. In the central district there were Mayakma, at Calistoga, and Mutistul to the west.

In the north, in Putah Creek drainage, was Lok-noma, " goose-town," near Middletown. The tract in which this settlement lay was known as " goose-valley " to all the neighboring tribes: as usual in California, they did not employ the Wappo term, but translated it into their own languages. In the western district the principal towns were Tekenan-tso-noma, near Geysers in Sulphur Creek drainage, and Pipoholma, on Russian River near Geyserville

Most of these little towns have had their names perpetuated in the designations of Spanish land grants. The primacy of each in its defined little district was sufficient to lend considerable warrant to the Spanish and early American habit of recognizing in each group a distinct tribe; except, of course, that the native names applied by the whites to these tribes were those of localities and not the designations of tribes as such.

The ending -noma is the same as Yuki -no'm, but appears to mean " town " rather than people. Tso is " earth," and -tsonoma, the probable source of our Sonoma, is a suffix: Tekenan-tso-noma means " village of the place of tekenan."

The map shows a small detached Wappo area north of the main territory, on Cole Creek and the south shore of the main body of Clear Lake. These people are called Lile'ek by their Pomo neighbors, although the word seems to be a Wappo one. They seem to have been a rather recent offshoot from the western Wappo, who visited the Pomo Habenapo for fishing or food, intermarried with them, and were allowed to settle in their territory. Their occupation was recognized; their title may not have been. Later they fought the Habenapo, as recounted below. Their principal village was called Daladano by the Pomo.

No Wappo villages have been placed in Pope Valley, although Indians of to-day assert the region to have belonged to their. forefathers. At least two sources associate the inhabitants of Pope Valley with those of Coyote Valley to the north, which, if true, would make them to have been Lake Miwok and not Wappo.

A WAR.

Alexander Valley, along Russian River above Healdsburg, is one of the very few tracts in the State which are directly known to have changed from the ownership of one Indian group to another. This was some 5 to 10 years before the first Spanish settlements in the region, or about 1830.

At that time the western Wappo had but one village of consequence on Russian River, Pipoholma, whose inhabitants were the Mishewal, the "mishe-warriors," under a chief Michehel. The Pomo called these Wappo A'shochamai or A'shotenchawi, sometimes written Ashochimi. Their land extended to a small creek named Popoech, at which began the territory of a southern Pomo division known to the Wappo as Onnatsilish. The principal villages of these Pomo were Ossokowi, " clover valley," and Chelhelle, " white-oak flat," which the Wappo translated into Shi'mela and Kotishomota. On the same side of Russian River lay Koloko, and across the river to the west were Malalachahli, Ashaben, and Gaiyechin.

One afternoon the Mishewal gathered acorns on their side of the dividing creek, but left them stacked and went home to Pipoholma. During the night the people of Ossokowi made off with the piles; but their proximity threw the first suspicion upon them, and the indignant Mishewal had no trouble in tracing the tracks, at least to their own satisfaction. Michehel, with about 10 of his men, stole at night into Ossokowi and killed two of the inhabitants. During the cremation of these victims in the morning, and the confusion of the funeral wailing, the persistent Mishewal attacked again, this time in full force, slew many of the inhabitants, scattered the rest, and burned the town.

While the victors were cremating the fallen, the survivors sent word from the vicinity of Healdsburg downstream, where they had taken refuge, that they wished to end the feud. A meeting was arranged and gifts exchanged between Michehel and the Onnatsilish chief. As the losses were preponderantly if not wholly on the Onnatsilish side, it is unfortunate that we do not know whether the major payments were also to them, as might be expected. Michehel then told the Onnatsilish that they were free to return in peace to the six villages from which they had fled. But the latter did not feel at ease so near their recent foes—there is no telling now what intermittent feuds and dark suspicions may not have existed between the two groups prior to the recorded outbreak— and they informed the Wappo chief that they would locate elsewhere and that his people were at liberty to occupy the settlements in question. Part of the Mishewal subsequently resettled Ossokowi and Chelhelle, or as they knew them, Shi'mela and Kotishomota. The four other abandoned Onnatsilish village sites were not inhabited by the Mishewal.

That this was not the only fighting between the two nationalities appears from the slurring Wappo name for the Pomo village of Shawako on Dry Creek: Walnutse, "little warriors."

ANOTHER CONFLICT.

For the Lile'ek a war is also reported. Only a mile or two away were the Habenapo division of the eastern Pomo. These people were favored with a certain kind of fish which crowded up their stream, Kelsey Creek, from Clear Lake. Cole Creek, on which the Lile'ek had established themselves by Habenapo sufferance, was avoided by the Kelsey Creek fish, Indian tradition avers. The two streams debouched close together and the Lile'ek proposed commingling their mouths. The Habenapo rejected the little engineering project. Before an issue was reached, winter rains raised both streams bank full. The Lile'ek from Daladano carried their digging sticks to Kelsey Creek and broke through the bank at a low spot. The flooded stream completed the work and tore itself a new channel, or regouged an old filled one, which met Cole Creek just above its mouth; and this is the course to-day.

Later, the Lile'ek are said to have dammed Kelsey Creek above the new junction. The Habenapo tore down the weir and were shot at. Now there was war. The Lile'ek were joined by the southeastern Pomo in their rear, while the Habenapo were supported by their kinsmen, the Kuhlanapo. They fought in a long line along the course of Kelsey Creek. The Wappo line was broken after some hours and driven over the divide into Cole Creek territory. Then the Habenapo ceased. Casualties were few, with only two or three deaths.

POPULATION.

The former number of Wappo must have been over 500 and may have reached 1,000. In 1860, 240 Wappo were reported to have been moved from Russian River above Healdsburg to the Mendocino Reservation since 1856. An estimate giving the Indians of Napa County—Wappo and Wintun combined—3,000 souls in 1843, 400 of them at Kaimus alone, is certainly much too high. The census of 1910, which contains the first data ever made available, reports 73 Wappo, three-fifths of them full bloods, which is considerably more than any ethnologists conversant with the region would have predicted. In 1908 a student familiar with the area had estimated 40 as the number of Wappo, Huchnom, and Coast Yuki, combined, outside of Round Valley. The Lile'ek, always a small group, are extinct except for a few scattered individuals.

CULTURE.

Of the customs of the Wappo there are no specific descriptions. All accounts make them similar to the Pomo in their habits, as in cremating the dead, and the few specimens of their handiwork that have been preserved in collections are practically indistinguishable from Pomo wares.

CHAPTER 15.

THE POMO: GEOGRAPHY AND POLITICS.

ORIGIN.

The Pomo, one of the best-known groups in California, belong in speech and origin to the wide assemblage of Indian natives that have been designated the Hokan family (Fig. 17). They are an isolated member of this group. To the north, 100 miles away, begins the irregular and much diversified north Hokan block, the Chimariko, Karok, Shasta, Achomawi, and so on. Nearly twice as far to the south is another Hokan group, composed of Esselen, Salinan, and Chumash. The Pomo, however, are isolated from all their ancient congeners. The nearest of their relatives, geographically, are the Yana. Less than 50 miles across the Sacramento Valley separate the extreme limits of the northeastern Pomo and the southernmost Yana. More words, too, are superficially common to these two languages than between either of them and their other relatives. Perhaps, however, this is an accident. Structurally, the two tongues differ markedly; a long history must separate them; and it seems possible that instead of the Yana being specially connected, they represent the end of a long development entirely dissociated from that of the Pomo.

HABITAT.

Except for a barely detached offshoot over the main Coast Range in the Sacramento drainage, the Pomo form a wholly continuous and rather compact body. They also harbored no aliens within their exterior boundaries, except for a minute subdivision of the Wappo, the Lile'ek, apparently a single village community, that had moved a short distance from its ancestral hills to the shores of Clear Lake. Roughly, the Pomo are inclosed between members of the Yukian, Wintun, and Miwok stocks and the ocean. In detail and sequence their neighbors are: Coast Yuki, Huchnom, Yuki, Wintun, Lake Miwok, Wappo, Coast Miwok—all, except the Wintun, much smaller bodies than the Pomo.

The heart of the land of the Pomo was the valley of Russian River, whose whole drainage, except for a patch or two, they held. South of the basin of this stream they occupied nothing at all; and to the north, only one affluent of one branch of Eel River, namely, Outlet or Deep Creek, which flows in a coastwise valley almost continuous with that of Russian River, but in the opposite direction. The

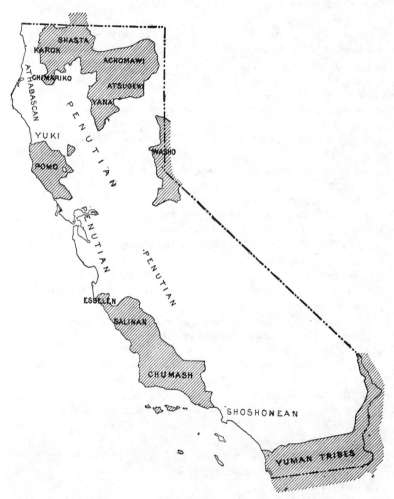

FIG. 17.—Distribution of the Hokan family in California.

sources are together, the mouths nearly 200 miles apart. Except for its headwaters, where the Yuki sat firm, and its very mouth, which the maritime Algonkin Wiyot occupied, Eel River was the stream par excellence of the Athabascans of California as distinctively as the Russian was a Pomo river.

Between Russian River and the cliffy shores of the Pacific runs a heavily forested secondary chain of the Coast Range, or series of chains in places; and the seaward slopes of this are cut into steep transverse canyons—they rarely contain valleys—by a series of rivers from the Noyo in the north to the Gualala in the south. All these were Pomo possession.

Eastward, over another range, the water flows into the Sacramento, but not immediately. The range is double. Between its walls lies a basin, the center filled by one of the few large bodies of fresh water in California—Clear Lake. This sheet more than compensates for an inclination toward an arid climate in the district. Its lower shores are fertile; hills and mountains with their inevitable seepage and flows approach closely; and altogether this was one of the ideal spots for Indian residence in the State. The lake, in whose 30 miles of extent Upper Lake, Clear Lake proper, East Bay or Lake, and Lower Lake are distinguished, ends in Cache Creek, a large and permanent stream which cuts its way in a rugged canyon through the main chain of the Coast Range, to lose itself, after a flow of some length, in the tule marshes bordering the lower Sacramento. In the ultimate reckoning the Clear Lake basin belongs, therefore, to the great interior valley rather than to the coast region. But Cache Creek Canyon is uninhabitable; the mountains to the east are the higher; access from Russian River was far easier; and the occupation of Clear Lake basin by Pomo allied to those on Russian River was accordingly only natural.

In every sense within the interior valley, in outlook as well as in drainage of their soil, were a separate body of Pomo on Stony Creek. They were few and their territory was small, covering only the headwaters of the main course of their stream above its junction with the Little Stony. These northeastern or Sacramento Valley or Salt Pomo—as they may be called from their ownership of a famous deposit of the mineral—were not only cut off from the nearest other Pomo—those of Clear Lake—by a mountain chain of some height, but stood in enmity with them. Their only neighbors to the west were a small and remote branch of the Yuki. With these they maintained a perhaps intermittent friendship, but the northward continuation of the range must have restricted intercourse. On their three other and more open sides, the Salt Pomo were surrounded by Wintun, members of a great stock, through whom nine-tenths of all their contacts with the world must have taken place. It is no wonder, therefore, that they became Wintunized. Their proper dialect specialized farther and farther away, and rapidly at that, from its original form. Many of them, including all the leading men, must have spoken Wintun in addition. They took over Wintun customs and modes of life, and they were so far identified with these more conspicuous people that their own identity was long lost to the American and it was only in recent years that inquiry on the spot revealed their Pomo affiliation.

The Pomo of Lower Lake have also been perceptibly influenced by the near-by Wintun. They have taken over numerals from the language of that people, as well as customs, and an unusual specialization of their dialect must again be attributed to contact with foreign tongues. But they can not be said to have been overshadowed to the verge of submergence by their more populous neighbors.

ENVIRONMENT.

The regions enumerated constitute three principal belts of quite different environment in which the Pomo lived: The coast, Russian River Valley, and the lake district.

The coast region was itself twofold. There was, first, the immediate shore, mostly cliffs or bluffs, with little beach, foggy, and much of the year blown over by heavy, steady winds. There are no harbors and few coves; but the alluvially filled river and creek mouths afforded small level tracts and shelter, and the ocean itself yielded a fair amount of food even to an unnavigating people. Mussels, surf fish, and sea lions replaced the deep-water fish which they were unable to take; and in winter the salmon ran up the rivers and creeks. If the smaller streams held fewer fish, they rendered them easier to take. For a mile or two back from the salt water, up to the timber on or near the crest of the first ridge, the hills were wind swept, but here and there yielded bulbs and seeds; only oaks did not grow near at hand. In this district lived the bulk of the Pomo coast population, moderate in numbers.

From the edge of the forest a belt of dense timber extended inland 5, 10, or 20 miles, with the giant coast redwood, the rival sister of the Sierra Sequoia, prevailing. These gloomy woods, so valuable to our industries, did not attract the Pomo. They did not furnish enough to eat; deer, and acorns in spots, were the only sustenance they provided. In the main, therefore, the redwood belt was only a hinterland, owned but little used by the dwellers on the coast. In a few places open ridges offered sunnier prairies, or a valley was less heavily overgrown. Here permanent settlements sprang up, and little communities had their center; but they remained few, and their affiliations with the shore were at least as close as with the interior.

Russian River flows through a country of hill ridges, which in many places are dignifiable with the appellation of mountains. Like most of California, it is a half-timbered country. Conifers stand on the higher crests, oaks are scattered over the slopes and levels, manzanita and other brush runs up over many of the hills. One can ride anywhere, drive a wagon over most of the country where the grade permits, and yet find few large areas of grass. True meadows are almost lacking; wet, low places run to tule rush instead. Russian River flows through a series of small inclosed valleys, not a continuous plain. Side streams are numerous, often in deep ravines of some length, yet dry in summer; but springs are abundant to any one familiar with the country. It is typical California land: arid to the eye once the winter rains are over, yellow and gray in tone, but fertile; monotonous in the extreme to the stranger, yet endlessly variegated to those familiar with it and its resources.

It is good Indian habitat from the mildness of the climate and the diversity of its products: fishing in winter, plenty of small game the year round, a moderate supply of deer, acorns everywhere, and brush, grass, weeds, and bulb plants in dozens of abundant species yielding their ready quota. Here was situate the kernel and bulk of the nation. More than a third of the Pomo communities were on this river, most of them with their winter quarters almost on its very banks.

On Clear Lake fish and water fowl invited to specialization and permitted of a perhaps even thicker clustering of the population. Yet it is notable that on the upper and main bodies of the sheet the main villages were not so much on the shore itself as near some stream within easy reach of the lake. Evidently these people lived much like their kinsmen of Russian River, with superadded, perhaps seasonal, use of the lake when they congregated in camps on its margin. Only on Lower Lake, whose surrounding hills in the main are arid or excessively mineralized, was there a true lake population. All three of the communities of these southeastern Pomo had their stable seats on islands, whence they navigated to the shore on their balsas of rushes, as occasion advised.

These three areas of environment do not coincide as much as might be anticipated with the lines of speech division among the Pomo; less, too, than among most Californian stock. In some cases, even, the dialects cut clear across the topography, as instanced below. Customs, too, diverged surprisingly little according to habitat. Clothing, houses, boats, and a few other manufactured objects differed somewhat according to districts; but basketry was nearly uniform and religious and social life scarcely affected unless by more or less intimate contact with human neighbors. Pomo civilization was substantially a homogeneous unit, on which natural environment exercised relatively superficial influence.

MAJOR DIVISIONS.

Seven principal dialects of the Pomo language are distinguishable. Perhaps these should rather be called languages, since their differences seem approximately commensurate with those of the Romance tongues, though somewhat other in kind. The natives have no names for these languages. Geographical designations are usually misleading, as most of the idioms are not confined to any natural district. The people of one dialect, the southern, have come to be known by a term of somewhat uncertain origin, Gallinomero or Kainamero, probably based on the Spanish name of a chief, Gallina; but this instance stands alone. The wisest recourse, therefore, is adherence to the directional appellations, "northern," "northeastern," and the like, that came into use with the first linguistic classification of the stock, and whose very unconcreteness averts most of the lurking opportunities for confusion.

The northern Pomo lived on the coast, on Russian River, and on Clear Lake, besides occupying all the Pomo holdings in Eel River drainage. The central division was on the coast and on Russian River; the southern the same. The southwestern dialect was spoken on the Gualala and the coast; but this stream flows parallel and near the shore, and in the wider sense the idiom belongs to a single area. The three other dialects are limited to defined districts: the eastern to main Clear Lake, the southeastern to its lower portion, the northeastern to a nook in the direct Sacramento Valley drainage. Obviously, the distribution of these dialects could not be predicted from a study of the map of the territory.

There are minor divergences of speech in several of these languages, especially the northern and the southern, but they are of so little moment as compared with the primary sevenfold differentiation that they can be passed over. That among the southern Pomo is of interest because the subdialectic line falls at the point where the wedge of Wappo territory has penetrated clear to Russian River, suggesting that occupation of the vicinity by these aliens has existed for some time.

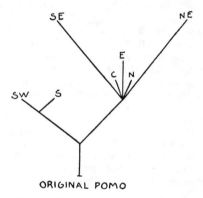

The internal history of the Pomo speech stock as reconstructible by interdialectic comparison is sketched in Figure 18, which gives not only the presumable course of development of the several branches but indicates their respective degrees of affinities by the distances separating the ends of the lines. The northern, eastern, and central languages are fairly close. These represent the

Fig. 18.—Family tree of Pomo dialects.

speech of the great majority of the Pomo. The southern and southwestern idioms form another and less populous unit, which, however, may be equally close to the original, still unified, Pomo languages. The northeastern and southeastern tongues are very evidently extreme but separate local specializations from a common northern-central language before this diverged into these still closely connected dialects.

GROUP NAMES.

The usual designation of a community was by adding *pomo* (or a dialectic equivalent) to the name of the principal site inhabited by the community. Thus, Buldam-pomo, Dapishul-pomo, Sedam-pomo, Pomo-pomo, Shanel-pomo, and so on. It is this element that has given rise to the current name of the stock. It appears also as *poma*. In fact, the latter is perhaps the more usual; but the orthography Pomo is so well established that it would be unwise to disturb it on the ground of a minor accuracy. In the southern dialect, the element is *fo*, and in the eastern, *na-po*, obviously from the same root: in fact *na-po-mo* occurs in the northern dialect, as in Chedil-na-pomo.

The exact meaning of *pomo* is not clear. It is not the word for person or people or house, except that it enters into some such words in the southeastern dialect. It is not known to be used independently; although the eastern Pomo are said to have called themselves Na-po-batin, translated as "many" or "great houses." The meaning conveyed is often rather of inhabitants than of habitations—like Yuki -*no'm*; but the differentiation may well have been less precise in the native language than in our own. Thus, Yuki -*no'm* reappears in Wappo -*noma* in terms that have the semblance of being village names; and in southern Costanoan, *ruk*, house, is found attached to many town names used as if designating the inhabitants thereof. So, too, *pomo* may have meant "town" and denoted either its dwellings or its residents.

The Pomo apply their *pomo, poma, fo, na-po* to groups larger than village communities much as the Yuki do -*no'm*. When there is a valley or naturally defined district that harbors several political units, the neighbors, especially the more distant ones, often lump these, for brevity of designation, under the one title. Thus the Lower Lake Pomo call the people of the Upper Lake district generically Anam-fo, and the Lake Miwok of Coyote Valley Tiam-fo. Other instances are cited in the list of village communities given hereafter.

Now and then, also, there was a name for a single community that appears to have no relation to any of their villages. Usually this occurred where there was a well-defined contrast either of a topographical or a political nature. Thus, on Clear Lake, the Kuhla-na-po or "water lily people" (whence Kulanapan as a synonym of the stock name Pomo) of Kashibadon village; and the Habe-na-po (or Kabinapek), the "stone people" of Bidamiwina.

Six or eight other names of this type are given in the list of village communities below. In general, however, the Pomo seem to have referred by the name of its chief settlement to the distinctive little group that they might have in mind, or, in cases of more generic expression, to have fallen back on such terms as Bokeya, "westerners."

POLITICAL DIVISIONS.

The village community as a political unit comprising ordinarily several settlements, but with one principal village in which lived a chief recognized by all members of the group, had evidently the same form among Pomo and Yuki. Within the tract claimed by the community everyone belonging to it was at liberty to hunt, fish, or gather plant food, it would appear, without limitations of private ownership as among the northwestern tribes. At least, such restrictions have never been reported.[1] The boundaries of the land owned

---

[1] E. W. Gifford, Pomo Lands on Clear Lake (see bibliography), describes family ownership of land among the southeastern Pomo, although the adjacent eastern Pomo of Shigom deny or have forgotten any but ownership by the community. The entire lake frontage of the southeastern division was divided into *ko* or tracts, averaging four or five to the mile, and extending inland several miles. Inheritance seems to have been from the father to his sons, between whom, or whose sons, a tract might be subdivided but would be jointly claimed and defended. Acorns and all vegetal products belonged to the owners of a tract; deer and small game did not; but custom discountenanced hunting on other men's land during the acorn season, as likely to be misconstrued. Fishing in the larger streams and lake was unrestricted within the community, and often even between communities of alien speech. Obsidian and magnesite were also gathered freely in territory of foreign communities.

by the group were, however, definite; and as regards other groups, the rights of property and utilization were clearly established. In case of amity and abundance these rights might be waived. Thus the Pomo of Shanel and Sedam and the Huchnom of Ukuknano'm in Potter Valley used each other's territory freely. The northeastern Pomo were welcome on Little Stony Creek of their Wintun neighbors, just as Coast Yuki and Kato insisted on no boundary. With such laxness between people of utterly alien speech, it is to be presumed that groups of identical language were even more liberally easy-going. But it seems that visitors were always visitors; that the confines of each body were always remembered; and that as soon as suspicion or ill feeling arose the crossing of the boundary was an offense.

As to the relation between the main and the subsidiary villages of a group, it is likely that the adjustment between them varied seasonally, winter bringing the maximum of concentration and summer of dispersal. Often a settlement split: a petty quarrel, a shortening supply of some food in the vicinity, a death, or mere indifferent instability would lead to a living apart without any sense of a division having taken place. Thus settlements of a few houses sprang up, decreased, or were totally abandoned; and then, after the passage of a few years or a generation or two, when the memory of the omen or disaster or feud that had caused their desertion had weakened, might come to be reoccupied. In themselves, the events involved in these little shiftings and recombinings were too trivial to be worth recording in full in even the most painstakingly minute history. But until some instances of such happenings can be concretely followed out as examples typical of the regions in question, our understanding of the motives that ran through and patterned the political and social fabric of the California Indians must remain hazily unsatisfactory.

An instance may make the relation clearer. The principal town of the already mentioned Kuhla-napo was Kashibadon; besides which, they had settlements, at one time or another, at Boomli, Kato-napo-ti, and Hadabutun. The Habe-napo metropolis was centered at Bidami-wina, their lesser settlements, not all contemporaneous, at No-napo-ti, Shabegok, Hmaragimo-wina, Hagasho-bagil, Sedileu, So'-bida-me, Haikalolise, Tsubahaputsum, Hadalam, Lishuikale-howa, Manatol, and Halibem. Further, there was an array of regular camp sites, without permanent houses, in each division.

The number of named and located Pomo settlements reported is 479, which does not exhaust the list of those recollectable by informants, without counting recognized camping places. The number of principal villages or political units was about 75. In the northern, central, eastern and southeastern divisions these are determinable with fair accuracy from the available data; even the boundaries can generally be drawn with reasonable correctness. In the other three groups, matters are much less certain, but some facts stand out. The knowledge on record is summarized in the following list, which adds also any information as to true group names and the like; and is graphically depicted, as accurately as is possible, in Plate 36. All known settlements and sites camped at repeatedly are entered on this map; but only the principal village of each group has its name added.

LIST OF VILLAGE COMMUNITIES.

NORTHERN POMO.

On the coast:

Kadiu, at mouth of Noyo River. The Chedilna-pomo are perhaps the people of this village.

Buldam, at mouth of Big River.

Kalaili, at mouth of Little River.

On Outlet Creek, Eel River drainage:

Mato, northwest of Sherwood.

Kulakai, at lake south of Sherwood. Shibalni-pomo seems to include the people of Mato and Kulakai.

Bakau, at Little Lake, north of Willits.

Tsamomda, west of Willits.

Shotsiu, east of Willits.

Two other main villages, Nabo or Nato and Chauishak, are mentioned in this vicinity in 1851; while the reported name Betum-ki for the valley as a whole is from Bitom-kai or Mtom-kai, which in turn is possibly derived from Mitoma, a site at Willits, plus *kai*, "valley," or from *mato*, "large." Mtom-kai-pomo seems to have had native usage as a generic designation of the Little Lake Valley communities—exactly parallel to Yuki Ukomno'm, for instance.

On upper Russian River drainage:

Shabakana, Bitadanek, and Kobida are three sites successively inhabited by one group whose home was Forsythe Creek.

Dapishu or Kachabida in Redwood Canyon.

Kachake on Mill Creek may have been an independent community.

Masut or Shiyol, on the West Fork of Russian River near the mouth of Seward Creek.

Chomchadila, on the West Fork near Calpella, which town takes its name from the former chief, Kalpela or Halpela.

Shanel or Seel or Botel, at the north end of Potter Valley on the East Fork of Russian River. Shanel proper was east of the river, Seel west, and Amdala adjoined the latter on the north. The relation of these was like that of the wards or suburbs of a city.

Sedam, downstream in the same valley.

Pomo, downstream, still in Potter Valley.

Tsakamo, below, on the same stream, at the mouth of Cold Creek, which belonged to the people of Tsakamo.

Potter Valley as a whole was known as Balo-kai, "wild oat valley," this valuable grain reaching its northern limit at the head of the valley. Djuhulakai, "north valley," is a synonym. Balo-kai-pomo therefore denotes the people of a district in which lived three or four "tribal" communities.

Shachamkau, Chamkawi, or Bomaa, still downstream, in Coyote Valley. Shodakai is a generic name for the entire valley.

Komli, at Ukiah, on the united river.

On upper Navarro River:

Katuli, above the river at Christine.

Tabate, farther upstream, but below Philo.

Lemkolil, on Anderson Creek near Booneville. The people of this district were called Pdateya, "creek-*teya*," in contrast with which those farther upstream, by which the central Pomo on Rancheria Creek are perhaps meant, were known as Danokeya, "rock-*keya*." The two groups appear to have been intimately associated, as is only natural in view of their isolation between the more populous coast and Russian River districts. Together, they have sometimes been known as Komacho-pomo, from a prominent chief Komacho.

Lower Navarro River and the coast near its mouth were claimed by the central Pomo, but appear to have been uninhabited. On the North Fork were three sites occupied by the northern Pomo, Chaida, Chulgo, and Huda. These may have constituted a community and possessed certain rights down the main stream to the ocean.

On Clear Lake drainage:

Shanekai, in a small, elevated valley between the heads of an affluent of South Eel River and a tributary of Middle Creek which drains into the head of Clear Lake.

Tsiyakabeyo, on this same tributary, may have been independent, but is more likely to have constituted only part of Shanekai.

Mayi, on Scott Creek near Tule Lake, not far from the town of Upper Lake. Bochawel, the region from Tule to Blue Lakes, seems to have belonged to Mayi. Haiyau or Kaiyau or Shinal are other names of the valley region in which Mayi was situated. The "Ki-ou tribe" with its chief Bakula was therefore only the Mayi group.

Noboral, on Scott Creek northwest of Lakeport, may have been the principal home of a people called Moal-kai or Boil-kai-pomo. None of the northern Pomo villages in the Clear Lake region were actually on the lake, although these people owned a number of camp sites on the shore, and, conjointly with the eastern Pomo, visited the important fishing site of Kabel or Habel on Rocky Point at the entrance to Upper Lake.

EASTERN OR CLEAR LAKE POMO.

Howalek, on Middle Creek near Upper Lake town. Damot was chief at the time of settlement.

Yobutui, on the opposite side of lower Scott Creek from the northern Pomo village of Mayi. The two towns were rival but friendly metropolises of the region. Djamato was the Yobutui chief.

Danoha, some miles up an eastern affluent of lower Scott Creek. Guki was chief. Connected with this group was Badonnapoti on Bloody Island in Upper Lake off the mouth of Scott Creek. Both sites were permanently inhabited, but the people were a unit. Intermediate in location, and therefore part of the same community, was Behepal or Gabehe, which in the early seventies was the scene of an active ghost dance propaganda initiated by the Wintun of Grand Island on the Sacramento River. Many Indians were killed at Badonnapoti by troops in 1850.

Shigom, on the east side of main Clear Lake.

Kashibadon, at Lakeport on the west side of the lake, was the main town of the Kuhla-napo or "water lily people," who ranged southwestward to Adobe Creek.

Bidamiwina was the more recent, Nonapoti the ancient, and Shabegok a third center of the Habe-napo or "rock people," who lived around Kelseyville between the Kuhla-napo and the Yukian Lile'ek. Kabinapek is another version of Habe-napo, and the near-by Lake Miwok translated the word into Lupu-yama. The Kuhla-napo and Habe-napo chiefs in 1851 were Hulyo and Perieto, as the Indians render their Spanish names.

SOUTHEASTERN OR LOWER LAKE POMO.

Kamdot or Lemakma on Buckingham Island, near the entrance to Lower Lake. The name Kauguma was applied to the people of this village, of Elem, or both. Beubeu seems to have been chief at the time of settlement.

Elem, on Rattlesnake or Sulphur Bank Island in the bay known as East Lake. The group was known as Kamina or Hawina or Kauguma. Notau was chief.

Koi, Hoyi, Shutauyomanok, or Kaubokolai—the Lake Miwok call it Tuli—was also on an island, near the outlet of the lake. The group has been called Mahelchel, which is a Wintun name.

NORTHEASTERN OR SALT POMO.

The village groups are undetermined. Bakamtati at Stony Ford appears to have been the most important town. Cheetido at the salt deposit may have been the seat of a separate community, and Turururaib:da, above the forks of Stony Creek, is sufficiently remote from the others to cause the suspicion that it, too, may have been independent, although its proximity to the crest of the mountains decreases the likelihood of its having been more than an occasional outpost. The entire northeastern Pomo area is not too large to have been the territory of a single political unit.

CENTRAL POMO.

On the coast:

Kodalau, on Brush Creek, some miles from the beach. Camps belonging to this village extended to beyond Greenwood Creek.

Pdahau or Icheche, on lower Garcia River.

Lachupda, on the upper waters of the North Fork of Gualala River.

On Rancheria Creek in Navarro River drainage:

These seem to be the people already referred to as the Danokeya and as part of the Komacho-pomo. Late, near Yorkville, was one of their settlements, but whether the principal one, is not known. Bo-keya, "westerners," is what the Russian River Pomo called these people.

Three or four settlements at the very sources of Rancheria Creek and across the divide on the upper waters of Dry Creek may have constituted a separate community.

On Russian River:

Shokadjal, in Ukiah Valley. Kalanoi was chief about 1835.

Tatem, downstream in the same valley. The two villages together were known as Yokaia, "south (end of the) valley."

Shiego, at the mouth of McNab Creek.

Lema, a mile or two up McNab Creek. The upper Feliz Creek drainage may have belonged to these people.

Shanel, near the mouth of McDowell and Feliz Creeks, in Hopland Valley, which was called Shokowa-ma as a whole. Sokowa as a tribal name is therefore probably a synonym of Shanel.

Kahwalau, at the mouth of Pieta Creek. This is specifically the name of the mouth of the creek, in a wider sense of the adjacent level area, and followed the village to its various sites on the flat, one of which was also called Kabe-chehoda.

Shepda, at the entry of Wise Creek.

Koloko, at the mouth of Squaw Creek.

SOUTHERN POMO OR GALLINOMERO.

This group was partly missionized and then more or less subjected to Mexican influences, so that, although many inhabited sites and their names are known, the old grouping of these can be traced but imperfectly.

On Gualala River drainage:

The topography indicates three units, one comprising Rockpile Creek, another Buckeye Creek and the mouth of the Middle Fork of the Gualala, and the third the upper waters of the Middle Fork. Kubahmoi, Shamli, and Hiwalhmu were villages in the three divisions, but whether the central ones is not known.

On Russian River drainage:

Makahmo, at the mouth of Sulphur Creek, was the principal village of a group most frequently referred to as Musalakon.

Kalme is mentioned as a division, but can not be located.

Upper Dry Creek, with its affluent Warm Springs Creek, probably was the home of one or possibly two units.

Shawako, Walnutse in Wappo, on Dry Creek at the mouth of Piña Creek, is likely to have been the center of another group.

On lower Dry Creek and on Russian River in the vicinity of Healdsburg a great number of villages have been recorded, but their grouping is entirely obscure. They are likely to have been at least two or three units. Wotokkaton was the seat of one of these divisions, as a prominent chief—Santiago or Soto—is mentioned, after whom the village or "tribe" was also called Sotoyome.

On Russian River, from the mouth of Elk Creek halfway up to Geyserville, was a Pomo group, apparently centering at Ossokowi, which came into conflict with the Wappo of Pipoholma, as previously related. After peace was restored it abandoned its territory, which the Wappo then occupied. The Wotokkaton group was involved in this conflict in some measure, and the Shawako people at one time or another were in hostilities with the same Wappo.

South of Russian River, Wilok, which was at the head of Santa Rosa Creek, is mentioned as a "tribe" in Spanish times. Other accounts place the principal village in the district near Santa Rosa city, which would make it to have been the settlement Hukabetawi. Perhaps two communities should be reckoned in place of one.

Batiklechawi, at Sebastapol at the head of the slough known as Laguna de Santa Rosa, was an important town, and therefore presumably the headquarters of a division.

Another group may tentatively be inferred as having occupied the bulk of the shores of the laguna.

SOUTHWESTERN OR GUALALA POMO.

The groups among this people are even more problematical than those of the southern Pomo. Nine have been tentatively delimited on the map—five on the coast itself and four on Gualala River and the interior; but except for some villages of consequence, there is no clue as to the number and territory of the groups other than the uncertain suggestions afforded by topography. It is hardly likely, however, that there were more than nine units, and there may well have been fewer.

Kowishal was at Black Point.

Danaga was at Stewart's Point.

Chiti-bida-kali lay north of Timber Cove.

Meteni is cited by the natives as the old name of the site of Fort Ross. Madshuinui has also been mentioned. The Russians called the group in this vicinity "Chwachamaju," or in their language Severnovskia, "northerners." Erio and Erussi are perhaps native corruptions of Spanish designations.

Chalanchawi and Ashachatiu were villages at the mouth of Russian River, and no doubt connected.

Hibuwi was a place of some note on the Middle Fork of the Gualala.

Potol is a still inhabited site which perhaps was the center of a group on Haupt and Hopper Creeks.

DISTRIBUTION OF THE COMMUNITIES.

It is clear from this list that, assuming the communities to have averaged about the same in population, the members of the Pomo stock were quite unevenly distributed, both as regards the seven dialect groups and the three environmental regions. The fewness of the units on the coast is especially striking. Salt water can have had little attraction for this people. They got more to eat, it would seem, on a lake than along an ocean frontage of the same extent; and 5 or even 3 miles on an inland river, with a creek or two coming in and some miles of hill country on each side, would hold as large a population as 10 miles on the ocean with an even greater extension inland.

It is also noticeable that where two or more communities abutted, their principal towns might be close together. From this center of population the hunting and camping districts then radiated out. Just so among the Yuki: the Ukomno'm villages of U'wit, Pomo, Titwa, and no doubt others, were all close together in Round Valley; the tracts of which they were the "capitals" reached far out over the hills and into smaller remote valleys. Evidently there existed no marked striations of highlanders and lowlanders, or poorly and unfavorably located groups, within these stocks. Each community had its bit of valley and its range of hill or mountain land.

This distribution is connected with the homogeneity of Pomo culture, as compared with that of the stocks of the great interior valley. Among the Maidu and the Yokuts, for instance, there were groups that held their territory entirely in the plains, others wholly in the foothills, and still others in the high mountains. Adjacent groups on different levels invariably evinced some divergence of speech. In the whole Penutian family, valley dialects stand off from hill dialects, either as the primary divisions of speech or as noticeable secondary modifications of other lines of linguistic cleavage. And so, in the Sacramento as well as the San Joaquin region, a civilizational distinction has constantly to be followed: the lowlanders are richer, possess more organization and specialization, and much more complex institutions than the hill people.

It may be that the large-scale topography of the great valley and Sierra Nevada region as compared with the broken character and little patches of level land in the Coast Range region lie at the bottom of this difference between the Penutians on the one hand and the Pomo and Yuki on the other. But whatever the ultimate reason provided by nature, the people of the two areas had adjusted their intercommunal lives in distinct ways.

A majority of the principal villages of the Pomo, in fact of all their settlements, lie on the north or east sides of streams. Not only was the sun grateful, or when too hot easily avoided, so that a southern or western exposure was the pleasanter; but the vegetation is invariably thickest, in all California, on the northern and eastern slopes of hills, where ground and foliage hold moisture better through the long rainless summer. The same inclination has already been noted among the Yurok, the Hupa, and the Chilula. It applies also to the Shasta. In the interior, conditions are scarcely comparable. In the treeless plains of the great valley the sun did not matter: elevation and other factors determined. In the Sierra the streams are usually too deep in canyons and bordered by too little level land to furnish suitable habitation. The villages are therefore on crests, or on the slopes of ridges. Here, too, open places, and that means sunny exposures, were sought; but they did not lie with direct reference to the streams.

WARS.

Besides what has been related under the caption of Yuki, Coast Yuki, and Wappo, little is known of the wars of the Pomo communities, either among themselves or with their neighbors. They were on the whole, there is little doubt, peaceably inclined. There was hostility between the Kuhla-napo and Habe-napo at one time; and the southeastern people of Kamdot must have had their quarrel with one of these divisions, because they supported the Lile'ek against them. The Komli group in the north end of Ukiah Valley fought the Yokaia-pomo, that is, Shokadjal and Tatem communities of the south end, and was worsted. This was a quarrel between people of different dialect.

This feud may be placed between 1830 and 1835, or earlier. According to the Yokaia-pomo, they owned the entire valley, up to the mouth of the East Fork of Russian River, but had allowed a body of northern Pomo to settle at Komli and utilize the northern end of the valley. A dispute arising about hunting or fishing rights, the southerners attacked the hitherto tolerated intruders and drove them to Scott Valley or Clear Lake, from where the local chief, probably of Noboral, finally purchased peace for them.

The northern Pomo assert that one end of the valley had always been theirs, and that the trouble arose not over violations of boundaries but because their famous shaman Sikutsha was accused of having "poisoned" a man in one of the central villages. An attempt was made to obtain revenge by force, but Sikutsha escaped to friends in the Upper Lake region. The Komli people as a whole had not been drawn into a battle, but were ill at ease, and left their village, journeyed up the East Fork to Blue Lakes, and finally settled in Scott Valley.

It is not impossible that both conflicts took place as stated, though at different times.

THE SALT WARS.

The northeastern Pomo owned a far-famed and prized salt deposit that brought them several conflicts. This is a spot near their village of Cheetido, less than an acre in extent, on the surface of which each summer a layer of salt crystallizes out which is derived from brackish seepage from the adjacent hills. Although mixed with earthy matter, the salt itself is more than 99 per cent sodium chloride.

The northeastern Pomo exacted payment; that is, no doubt, expected presents, from those who came to gather salt here; although they seem sometimes to have extended the right gratis to particular friends. There were, however, attempts to steal the salt, either by ancient foes or by those who became enemies through the act, for the local owners bitterly resented any such endeavors.

The Potter Valley people were long in the habit of visiting across the mountains and purchasing salt. A party that attempted to make away with a supply secretly was discovered, attacked, and in part destroyed. In revenge the Potter Valley people killed certain of the northeasterners who happened to be among them, after which they thought it wisest to refrain from attempting to reestablish intercourse and secured such salt as they could get from the ocean. This was before the arrival of Americans.

The Clear Lake Pomo—at least the Kuhla-napo, Habe-napo, and people of Shigom—were also in the habit of journeying to this region. About 1830 a party went over to combine trading with a dance. According to the account of the Clear Lake people, this entire party, with the exception of two men, was treacherously murdered in the dance house. The scalps were stretched over wicker frames hung on poles, ornamented with beads, carried across the mountains to a Yuki village probably in Gravelly Valley, and there danced over. The reason assigned for this transfer is that the Yuki were more accustomed to scalping and could conduct a better dance; but we may imagine that the triumphant celebrators felt more at ease from reprisals far away than in their own homes, much as the Kato took their Yuki scalps to the coast.

For something like 10 years no revenge was taken. Then a Clear Lake party went to the head of Stony Creek and lay in wait by a dam. When fishermen appeared, two of them were killed. Their scalps were danced over on the farther side of Clear Lake. This act being avowedly a reprisal, may prove little as to established custom. It is said that the Pomo rarely scalped or danced over scalps.

POPULATION.

The Pomo are to-day the second most populous group in California—their 1,200 souls, as reported by the census of 1910, being exceeded only by the number of the Mono. At that, the count may not have done them full justice, but it is greater than expected. A few years earlier an observer thoroughly familiar with the whole territory of the group estimated 800, plus a few on Round Valley Reservation. About three-fourths are still full blood.

The ancient population is estimated, for the comparative purposes of the present work, at 8,000, or an average of a little over 1,000 for each of the seven divisions. If this figure seems low for the northern Pomo, it is probably excessive for the southwestern and southeastern divisions, and certainly so for the northeastern one.

At any rate, the total appears liberal rather than close. M'Kee, in 1851, before any but the southern Pomo had been seriously affected by Spanish or American contact, computed far fewer. His counts on Clear Lake, and possibly that on Outlet Creek, are of little value as wholes, because the Indians were frightened and many ran off; but he had unusual opportunities for forming estimates on the spot. He calculates 1,000 Indians about Clear Lake, 1,200 in Sonoma and Russian River Valleys, 450 to 475 in the Outlet Creek region in Eel River drainage, and guesses 500 along the coast from Fort Ross to San Francisco Bay. The latter number was no doubt excessive even for that day. Besides, it comprised chiefly Coast Miwok. The Clear Lake estimate included Wappo and perhaps Lake Miwok. This would bring the number of his Pomo down to about 2,500. On the other hand, the coast villages north of Russian River are omitted and a definite decrease in the south must be allowed for. With these corrections, the aboriginal total might possibly be restored to 5,000 on the basis of M'Kee's information; so that the 8,000 of the present reckoning can scarcely be accused of undue parsimony. It may be added that M'Kee and his aide, Gibbs, gave every indication of having judged sanely as well as utilizing all possible sources of knowledge. Their figures for the Yurok, Hupa, and Shasta are below rather than above the mark, but reasonably close to what appears to be the truth.

M'Kee's figures as to the size of villages are of interest. They are for "rancherias" under the authority of a chief—that is, not for physical towns but for the political units that in the present work are called village communities, and which might comprise one or several settlements. The Kuhla-napo and Habe-napo, two bodies notable among the Indians even to-day, came to 195 and 84. Four other "tribes" in the Clear Lake region aggregated only 232. Twenty-five per cent were estimated to have been absent. Even this addition brings the average per group to barely over 100. On Outlet Creek the villages ran to 75, 77, 89, 80, 59, or about 75 souls each. It may be concluded that the village community in this part of California normally was likely to consist of less rather than more than 100 persons.

Government reports as to the number of Pomo brought to the Mendocino Reservation in 1856 yield about the same figure: From Ukiah Valley, at least two communities, over 200; Rancheria Valley, near Anderson Valley, at least one community and possibly two, 180; mouth of Sulphur Creek, the Makahmo group, 60.

Mato, in Sherwood Valley, had 75 inhabitants in 1853, according to the first American settler.

There are early estimates of 300 to 400 people for Shodakai, Coyote Valley, and the Russian River Shanel, but these seem excessive, even though the latter was an unusually large community.[2]

On these data one other calculation can be attempted. It has been shown that the number of village communities was probably not over 75 among all the Pomo together. At the rate of a scant 100 souls each, the population of the entire stock would come to about 7,000, or well within the assumed figure of 8,000.

NUMBERS AND FOOD SUPPLY.

One derives the impression that the Pomo, and all the stocks in the Coast Range north to the Yurok, were not pressed for food; that a comfortable margin existed between their needs and what nature supplied; and in a measure this is true of all the Californians outside the deserts. First of all, there are almost no references, either in myth or tradition, to famines, which find fairly frequent mention in the tales of much more advanced groups like those of the Plains and the North Pacific coast. Secondly, many bits of specific evidence indicate an easy superfluity. It has already been told how communities in friendly relations welcomed each others' hunters or acorn-gathering women. When they resented poaching, a justified moral grievance is implied, and there is no reference to an infringement of needs. At that, hostility, or at least suspicion, seems usually to have come first, indignation at violation of community hunting rights second. When a witch is believed to have poisoned one's brother, one does not look with equanimity upon the witch's people helping themselves to the produce of the land to which one has undisputed claim; and this seems to have been the usual course of events, not the reverse. Again, when the Pomo of Ossokowi made formal peace with the Wappo of Pipoholma, as already related, they voluntarily withdrew from their land and invited their late conquerors to take it, rather than continue in the vicinity of such doughty warriors. It may have been a whole community that thus rendered itself homeless and went to live with kinsmen of its own stock, or only part of the tract of a community may have been surrendered; in either event, there can have been no serious thought of hunger, else residence in the neighborhood of the reconciled foe would have been risked, or even the conflict continued.

It does not follow that the population of aboriginal California was increasing at the time of discovery. A high mortality may

---

[2] E. W. Gifford, in a census of Shigom on Clear Lake, recently enumerated 235 individuals in 20 houses at the time of earliest recollection of living informants.

have held numbers steady. Nor is it maintained that only a fraction of the resources were utilized: it was rather the bulk; and a material increment to the population would undoubtedly have resulted in hardship, until new methods of utilization of the food supply had been developed. But there was a margin; it was fairly liberal; and the variety of resources probably led to its exhaustion only at intervals, and to acute want still more rarely. The Californian could not go for any considerable period without busying himself with procuring food, in which respect he was handicapped against the Indians that had specialized their food production; but the very diversity and multifariousness of the supply, and of his quest of it, while robbing him of leisure and of concentration, gave him also comparative security against want.

CHAPTER 16.

THE POMO: CIVILIZATION.

DRESS.

Men went naked or wrapped a skin around the hips. Women's clothing was scarcely more elaborate: the one article of regular wear, other than ornaments, was the double skirt. Wherever deer were procurable in sufficient numbers, this was probably of skin; but the commonest form was of shredded inner redwood bark, willow bark, and tule rush respectively on the coast, in Russian River Valley, and on Clear Lake. The Pomo are the first people of all those so far described with whom the fiber skirt seems to have been standard.

Basketry caps were not made or worn. The Pomo carrying net is woven into a broad band in front to ease the strain on the forehead. Sometimes small, thick, highly polished beads were inserted in this band, to roll over the forehead as the load swayed, and prevent a sidewise chafing.

Besides the clumsy soft-soled moccasin usual in California, sandals and leggings of tule and perhaps of netted string were worn by the Pomo. The use of all these was, however, occasional, as circumstances demanded. No Californian, except possibly in the desert tracts, wore any footgear habitually.

Men wore ear tubes of long, incised bird bones, or wooden rods tipped with a bead and small brilliant feathers. The nose was pierced for a pin or shaft of haliotis.

HOUSES.

The types of dwelling used by the Pomo depend upon the climate and vegetation of each district, and their distribution runs across the lines of linguistic cleavage.

On the immediate coast and in the adjacent belt of heavy timber the living house was built of slabs of redwood bark leaned together into a cone 10 to 15 feet in diameter and little more than half as high. True planks were not used, and there was no covering of earth. An incipient approach to the semisubterranean house is found in the fact that there was a center post. This type of dwelling was made also by many of the Athabascans to the north of the Pomo, and by the Maidu and Miwok. The construction prevented any considerable size from being attained, and each dwelling seems to have been occupied by a single household.

The Russian River Pomo erected a framework of poles, bent together at the top, and thatched with bundles of grass. These were attached to horizontal poles on the frame, and each course clamped down by another horizontal stick. The shape of the structure was sometimes circular, perhaps more often rectangular, or like the letter L.

The door seems to have been at the end, perhaps at both. A long narrow slot along the middle of the top served as smoke hole. A house of this sort shed the winter rains, but scarcely lasted into a second season. It was easily built of ample size; and often sheltered several families; although interior compartments may have been used only after the coming of the whites.

The Clear Lake Pomo built a similar dwelling, usually elliptical in plan, with the door in the side, and with thatching of tule replacing the more laborious grass. The long axis measured up to 25 or 30 feet; poor or old people and individual families were content with an humbler abode. The tule used is the circular *bago, Scirpus lacustris*, or the triangular *gushal, Scirpus robustus;* or the cat-tail rush *hal*, probably *Typha*. The inside of the walls was lined with mats sewn or twined from stems of one of the varieties of Scirpus. On the outside, mats are not reported to have been used, although such is the custom of a number of other Californian tribes.

All these were winter houses. In the rainless summer simpler brush shelters sufficed for the more temporary occupation of one spot.

The shade was a brush roof on four or more posts. It was made by the Clear Lake Pomo who were in contact with the Wintun of the hot interior valley; perhaps also by the other Pomo.

The Pomo had a true sweat house, distinct from the assembly or dance house, though the two were identical in plan and differed only in size, use, and name. A diameter of 15 or 20 feet sufficed for this sudatory or "fire lodge," *ho shane* or *holi shane*. The men, besides sweating daily, usually slept in this structure which was peculiarly theirs and spent much of their spare time during winter within it. Evidently the *cha* or *gha*, the living house, was for women, children, property, cooking, and eating; a man's normal place was in one of the two *shane*.

The dance or assembly house, *ke*, *kemane* or *kuya shane*, literally "singing lodge" or "ceremony lodge," was earth-covered and 40 to 60 feet in diameter. A large center post was surrounded by a polygon of eight smaller ones connected by stringers. Across these stringers radiating rafters were laid and fastened with grapevine or withes, and on the rafters four circles of poles. Then followed successive layers of interwoven sticks placed horizontally, another radiating,

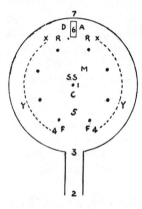

mats of rushes, dried grass, mud, and earth that had been taken from the excavation. One entrance was at the south end, through a long, descending tunnel; another, probably used only in certain ceremonies, was the smoke hole directly over the fire. At the rear the wall was prepared so that it could be readily pushed out to furnish an emergency exit. The posts were often crudely painted. (Fig. 19.)

It is likely that important ceremonies, such as the ghost rite and Kuksu initiation, were made in any one locality only at terms of some years, and were marked by the erection of a new dance house for the occasion. In the intervals, the community visited the performances of its neighbors and took part in them. Whether any fixed and accepted rotation ever grew out of this custom can not be stated. The practice of erecting new dance houses accounts for the number of pits on some village sites; lower Shanel showed five in 1873.

Fig. 19.—Pomo dance house, after Barrett: 1, Center post, surrounded by eight lower posts connected by rafters; 2, 3, outer and inner doors; 4, firewood; 5, fire; 6, drum, with stake for grasping; 7, emergency exit; A, ash ghost performers; C, chief; D, dancer about to drum; F, fire tenders; M, director of dancers; RR, dancers at rest; SS, singers; X–Y, visiting spectators; Y–4, home spectators.

Before a dance house was erected the *dakoi*, or mourners of the year, were placated. The village chief received contributions of shell money for this purpose and added what he thought would make an appropriate total. After delay appropriate to the solemnity, the mourners were asked to assemble and formal presentation of the gift was made to the spokesman of the loudly wailing gathering. Each woman danced with the strings of beads, which were then put aside to be offered to the dead. The chief thereupon announced his intention, and the mourners replied that their sorrow was no reason why the pleasure should not be indulged in by others of erecting a lodge and dancing in it.

The Clear Lake Pomo had taken over from their Wintun neighbors the habit of storing their acorns in large outdoor granaries or caches.

These were substantially of the type made by the Miwok and other Sierra tribes (see Pl. 40), except that the elevated floor was usually rectangular and of somewhat greater area. The Russian River and Coast Pomo kept their acorns in large baskets in the living house, like the northwestern tribes.

BOATS.

On Clear Lake boat-shaped rafts of bundled tule rush were used, accommodating three or four or more persons. These balsas, to use the customary Spanish word, were trimly modeled in the best examples, with rising sharp prow, a stern, and gunwales to prevent the waves from washing over the top. They were in every way boats except that it was the specific gravity of their content and not their displacement that floated them. They could scarcely last more than a season or two, but were much less laborious to build than a canoe.

Russian River is not navigable except in the last few miles of its course, and tule balsas were not used in its drainage except in the Santa Rosa Lagoon.

The coast people used a raft of a few logs when needed to cross stream mouths and to visit mussel and sea-lion rocks offshore. A balsa, of course, is not practicable in the surf, but it is rather remarkable and very indicative that a shore people, deriving much of their sustenance from the ocean and with the best and easiest of all canoe materials—the redwood—at hand in superabundance, should have been entirely boatless. This is not a Pomo peculiarity. All the coast tribes, from near Cape Mendocino to the vicinity of Point Concepcion, faced salt water all their lives without ever riding upon it except now and then on a few rude logs. But the lack of canoes over this long stretch reminds the student how unsafe it is to infer from geography to civilization without as thorough knowledge of one as of the other, and illustrates incisively the abortive condition of the manual arts among most of the California Indians. It is true that this coast is forbidding to the mariner. And yet a heavy dugout canoe would have been entirely usable and a great convenience to a people that made no long voyages nor cruised about, but could have launched their boats in any minute cove or stream mouth and waited for a calm day and quiet surf to make their brief trips to some point or rock a mile or two away. This is proved by the use which the Yurok and Tolowa made of canoes on a wholly similar coast. It is true that the northwestern canoe is evidently a type developed on rivers, but its serviceability on the ocean is manifest; and but for the makeshift character of central California culture, which in most material concerns is content with a bare sufficiency of attainment provided the means remain the lowest and directest possible, it is certain that the art of canoe building would have spread from the Wiyot and Mattole to the Sinkyone and Coast Yuki, and thence to the Pomo. It has already been mentioned that the Kato knew of the canoe. The characteristic thing is that with this knowledge they and their neighbors of the coast were satisfied to do without.

Matters stand differently in two industries—basket making and money manufacture. In these the inclinations of Pomo women and men toward manual dexterity found vigorous expression.

BASKETRY.

Pomo baskets have the name, among Americans, of being the finest made in California; according to many, in the world. Such comparisons are perhaps best avoided. But it is clear that in a variety of ways Pomo basketry has undergone a special development quite unparalleled in California; and so far as concrete evidence establishes the facts, it tends to corroborate the subjective judgment cited.

First of all, there are technical peculiarities. The Pomo are the only people in California to employ lattice twining. Along with some of the Wintun and Maidu, and in special cases the remote and semisouthwestern Yuman tribes, they are the only ones to make use of wickerwork—the technique of ordinary cloth fabric applied to freely handled woody materials. It is true that their wicker ware is restricted to a type of seed-beater (Pl. 29); but still, the occurrence is significant.

Then they coil and twine to about equal extent; and they are the only group to do so. In all northernmost California coiling is never practiced. Everywhere south of this area twining is restricted to coarsely utilitarian objects—burden baskets, seed beaters, parching trays, cradles, traps and fish weirs, and the like. Baskets made for gift or show, those seriously ornamented or worn as caps, and all intended to hold water or to be cooked in, whatever vessels, in short, are made decoratively or for permanent use, are invariably coiled. The Pomo follow both processes. Their boiling receptacles, it is true, are usually twined, their feathered and gift baskets chiefly coiled, and to this point their habits might be interpreted as transitional between those of the twining and coiling tribes—they following the central method but not in its entirety. But that this is an incomplete view of the situation is evident from the fact that the Pomo cooking and storage baskets are exceptionally well twined and intricately ornamented; and especially because of the geographical circumstance, previously commented on, of the Pomo not being in a border area, as regards basket technique. On their north, between them and the twining tribes, are the Yuki, as essentially a coiling group as any. This distribution establishes that the relatively strong tendency of the Pomo toward twining is not due to any immediate influence of the northern tribes; they form instead an island of semitwining, cut off from the pure twining area by a tract where coiling prevails. In fine, the Pomo balance between the two techniques is the result of a specialization on their own part.

Further evidence of the many-sidedness of the Pomo weaver is to be found in the fact that in addition to latticing she employs diagonal twining with fair frequency by the side of plain twining, whereas in the northwest diagonal twining is known, but the simple twine is the one standard technique. Just so, in coiling, other Californians use a foundation either of three rods, or of a bundle of grasses, or a rod and welt combination; but only one of these is customary to a tribe. The Pomo coil over three rods or over one rod with nearly equal frequency. A single rod foundation, by the way, is found nowhere else in California, except in a subsidiary measure among the Washo and Miwok.

The complete independence of Pomo and northwestern twining is apparent as soon as specific comparison is instituted. The one method of ornamentation employed by the northwesterners is overlaying, that is, twining with double woof. This is not known to the Pomo. The shapes, texture, and pattern arrangements are also quite unlike. Even the materials are mostly different. The Yurok use hazel, sometimes replaced by willow, for the warp; conifer roots, *Xerophyllum*, maidenhair fern, and *Woodwardia* fern for the weft. The Pomo warp is willow; pine root, *Carex* sedge root, and redbud (*Cercis*) enter into the woof.

The usual rule in California is that a certain technique, or a certain variety of one technique, is invariable for an object serving a given purpose among one tribe. If a group twines its parching trays it never coils them; if it coils its caps it never twines them; and vice versa. The Pomo break through this natural inclination. Their carrying baskets are twined both simply and diagonally; their trays, their cooking baskets, and their storage receptacles are made at will in plain, diagonal, or lattice twining; the beaters in twining or wicker (Pl. 29). Evidently basket manufacture is no mere utilitarian routine to them, in which they have settled into mechanical habits like other tribes, but an art, the mastery of which is a stimulus and whose possibilities are played with.

Various external devices, intrinsically of no deep moment, but in the present case unquestionably significant as a manifestation of this creative impulse, have helped to make the finest Pomo baskets splendidly showy.

The most important of these devices is the use of feathers. Black, wavy quail plumes may be scattered over the surface of a basket, or fine bits of scarlet from the woodpecker's scalp worked into a soft, brilliant down over the whole of a coiled receptacle; or both be interspersed; or small woven-in beads be included among the feathers. The height of display is reached in the basket whose entire exterior is a mass of feathers, perhaps with patterns in two or three lustrous colors. A gently flaring bowl of this sort, a luminous scarlet intersected by lines of soft, brilliant yellow, with a solid edge of beads and fringe of evenly cut pendants of haliotis, the whole 12, 15, or 18 inches across, radiates a genuine magnificence that appeals equally to the savage and the civilized eye. It is not inappropriately that American fancy has denominated these masterpieces "sun baskets"; although the native has learned the designation from the white man. To him they served as gifts and treasures; and above all they were destroyed in honor of the dead. It is impressive and representative not only of the gently melancholy sentiments of the Pomo but of the feelings of the California Indians as a whole, that these specimens of the highest artistic achievement that their civilization has been able to produce were dedicated to purposes of mourning their kindred.

As against these elaborate jewels, the ring of plumes that the Yokuts sometimes insert at the shoulder of their best baskets is but a feeble attempt; and even this is not made by most other tribes.

Only in one respect do the Pomo exercise a greater restraint than some other basket makers. This is the employment of color. Their twined baskets have patterns in red only; the coiled in either red or black, but never in both together; only feather work is now and then polychrome. The southern Californians, the Chumash, the Yokuts, in the north all the noncoiling tribes, frequently work two or even three colors on the background. It is only the far less elaborate ware of several groups near the Pomo—the Yuki, Wintun, Maidu, Washo, and Miwok—that is characterized by the same modest limitation.

Even in decorative patterns, which are so endlessly variable, the characteristic traits of the Pomo art are traceable. The details can not be gone into without elaborate graphic illustration; but, in general, it is clear that the Pomo feel themselves freer than other groups to follow any type of design arrangement: horizontal or banded, diagonal, crossing, vertical or radiating, or isolated. The frequency is about in the order named. Elsewhere, one or two of these schemes are followed to the practical exclusion of the others.

Pattern names are descriptive, often elaborately so, with reference to size, position, or combination of elements. Their forms breathe no prayers, express no wishes, and serve no ulterior purposes; in short, they are not symbolic. Their general nature, which may be slightly more elaborate than among most other groups, is, however, not distinctive; and the subject as a whole is discussed in the chapter on the Yokuts.

Only at the start of their baskets the Pomo sometimes, for religious reasons, place an initial design or *shayoi;* and if the pattern is an encircling band, they scrupulously leave a break of some sort in its course, that they may not be struck blind. This gap, or suggestion of an interruption, they call *dau, hwa,* or *ham.* It is not observable in the basketry of any other nation in California, with the exception of the Yuki; and whether it has magical import with these people, or is only a by-product of their clumsy handling of the coiled pattern, is not known.

Pomo men perform the coarser labor of openwork twining in most instances. Not only portable traps and weirs (Pl. 33), but cradles, wood-carrying baskets, and the like, issue from their fingers. It is the women, relieved of this dull and heavy practical industry, who were stimulated to attempt the achievement of a true art.

Men and women generally twist the weft in different directions in twining. It would be absurd to think of inherent sex impulses in this connection. It is even doubtful whether a sex consciousness or habit enters into the matter.

The grade of work, the pliancy of the materials handled, may be the determining factor.

The perfection with which the Pomo woman combines fineness and evenness of stitch, especially in her coiled wares, is truly remarkable. So far as texture goes—and this, after all, is the side on which manual skill tells most—the Yokuts, Tübatulabal, Koso, and Chumash work is not inferior; in fact, comparatively coarse-working groups like the Maidu attain splendid evenness and closeness. But the combination of this quality with minuteness of foundation and weft is reserved for the Pomo. Elsewhere, 30 wrappings per linear inch make an unusually fine basket; among the Pomo this is rather common, and 60 stitches, and even more, can be found.

Strictly, the traits here enumerated are not confined wholly to the Pomo. In certain measure, in some instances in their entirety, they apply also to the basketry of half a dozen of the small groups that adjoin the Pomo: the Huchnom, Wappo, Lake and Coast Miwok, and southern Wintun. But these peoples are all fragments of larger stocks; each of them was inconsiderable in size as against the Pomo; and they formed a fringe around that central nation. It may therefore be concluded with fairness that whatever is peculiar in this art is essentially Pomo; and that historically they were the creators, their neighbors the imitators, in this localized achievement.

LOADS.

Whenever the textile art is spoken of in California mention of the carrying basket is soon forthcoming. This article is of universal occurrence. Its invariable shape is conical. Its precise form is more or less peaked; its weave changes from locality to locality; and it is made in closely knit and openwork forms—often side by side among the same people, according to the service intended. But it is always a basket; only in the extreme northeast and southeast do rawhide receptacles appear beside it or stick frames replace it. Some tribes, though the minority, occasionally insert four heavier rods for stiffening. Now and then the head strap is fastened to the structure. But usually the carrier is a basket and nothing more, without wooden reinforcement, and without attachments of any sort; the strap or net is simply slung around it. The constance with which the type of this utensil is adhered to throughout California is remarkable in view of the diversity to which back carriers are subject in other parts of the world and even in North America, and stamp the device as one of the fundamental ones of the region, besides serving as a definite illustration of the hold which basket activities had on Californian civilization to the exclusion and virtual suppression of every other cultural means that might have been a competitor.

The burden basket is supplemented by the carrying net, also slung from the forehead. The Pomo being situated near the northern limit of the distribution of this implement, its form and use can be better discussed in subsequent chapters. But it may be well to note here that the net and the basket together, with the paucity of canoes, and the nonuse of dogs, stamp the entire California region as one of transportation by human carriers. The load is also placed in distinctive fashion—always on the back, never on the head—and regularly hung from the forehead, rarely from the chest.

CRADLES.

The Pomo cradle is a well-marked subtype of the northern Californian sitting cradle, as contrasted with the lying form universal in the central and southern parts of the State, and described in a chapter on the Yokuts. It is made of rather heavy warp sticks laid close and twined together. The bottom, in which the child is set, is round; the sides are straight. The northwestern cradle has a more boat-shaped effect. Its bottom comes to a wedgelike and apparently useless end, the child not being set into this but on a few lashings across the upper part of the end. Throughout, the opening is smaller than the periphery. A strong but obscure stylistic influence is evident. More to the east, among the Shasta and northern Wintun, a third and simpler subtype is in use. This is little but an oval basketry bowl, rather flaring, with a loop handle at one end. There is no great step from this form to the entirely flat base of the lying cradle, and less yet to the soft enfolding case of rushes into which the infant is first laid among many tribes.

Hoods are occasionally used with the sitting cradle, but are never an integral part of the fabric. They are not arches, as in the lying cradle, but a separate little cone of openwork basketry, hung or tied so as to allow a skin or mat to be laid in front of the child's face.

The center of dispersion for the sitting cradle, at least so far as California is concerned, is likely to have been among the northwestern tribes rather than the Pomo. This appears not only from the northwestern subtype being the most elaborate, but from the general distribution of the utensil.

The middle cradle in Plate 35, a Wintun piece, approximates the Pomo type.

MONEY.

The Pomo were the principal purveyors of money to central California. The chief source of supply was Bodega Bay, in Coast Miwok territory, where a large clam abounded; although the northernmost Pomo seem to have got their stock from the Athabascan coast about Shelter Cove. The shells were broken up, ground approximately round on sandstone, bored, strung, and then finished by being rolled on a slab. The value varied according to the diameter of the disks; according to their thickness; and according to the degree of polish. Old strings were prized highly. The handling of a lifetime imparted a gloss unattainable in any other way, and was appreciated as fully by the natives as by any ethnographic collector.

The value of this money varies greatly in different parts of the State. The older Pomo valuation of $2.50 for 400 beads, quoted below, gives less than a cent a bead, or perhaps $1 a yard. The southern Maidu reckoning 40 years ago was a full twenty times as high for large disks, at least four or five times as much for the smallest size. Still farther away, however, among the Miwok, Yokuts, and southern Californians, the value sinks heavily once more. Perhaps the San Joaquin Valley supply was derived from a more abundant source in the south, in which case price would be in direct proportion to distance and rarity. It is clear that the interesting economic relations involved depend for their understanding on a knowledge of where the raw material was obtained, by whom it was worked, and by what routes transported.

According to Yuki statements, dentalium shells reached at least the northern Pomo. They do not, however, seem to enter seriously into Pomo reckoning or their enumerations of wealth; and it is to be presumed that dentalia, at least in whole pieces, did not reach them in sufficient quantities to become standardized into an important currency.

There was, however, another form of money that was prized highly by the Pomo and the stocks as far away as the Sierra Nevada. These are cylindrical beads, from 1 to 3 inches in length, of a variety of magnesite found at White Buttes, near Cache Creek, in the territory of the southeastern Pomo. These were ground down, perforated, baked, and polished. The heating changes the color of the stone from a dull white or streaked gray to a lustrous buff, salmon, or red, often beautifully banded or shaded. These cylinders, which the Indians often call their " gold," as compared to the more numerous " silver " disks of clamshell, were too valuable to be sold by the string and were negotiated for individually or inserted like jewels or as finishing pendants in lengths of the shell beads. The material seems quite similar to the meerschaum of our pipes.

These magnesite cylinders were called *po, pol,* or *fol* by the Pomo; *ship* or " scars " by the Yuki; *chuputa* by the Coast Miwok and *awahuya* by the Lake Miwok; and *turul* or *tulul* by the Wintun; and they were known at least to the northern Miwok of the Sierra. The value also increased with remoteness. A cylinder an inch long and a third in diameter was worth five American dollars to the southern Maidu; the Pomo would scarcely have paid this for any but the largest and finest pieces.

FIRE.

Besides the usual drill, the Pomo had a fire-making device not yet reported from any other tribe. Two lumps of quartz were rubbed or rapidly struck against each other and the shower of sparks caught on tinder.

The pump drill, which the modern Pomo use for bead boring, though not for fire making, was not invented by them, but adopted from the Spaniards.

GOVERNMENT AND DESCENT.

Pomo official authority was vested in a manner that has not been definitely reported elsewhere in California, though it may well have obtained. The chiefs, *cha-yedul*, *cha-kale*, *a-cha-pte*, or *gahalik*— each dialect, in fact, possessed a quite different word—were of two classes: the major, *chayedul bate*, or " great chiefs," and the lesser, *malada chayedul*, or " surrounding chiefs." The former was the head of the community—not only his own town, it appears, but the group of little settlements that constituted a political unit. His office, among the northern and eastern Pomo, was hereditary, whereas a record that appears to relate to the central Pomo states expressly that he was chosen by general consensus of the inhabitants from among the minor chiefs. These minor chiefs represented neither political nor geographical but consanguineous units; and they succeeded a near kinsman. Each body of blood kindred living in one spot had as its head one of these lesser chiefs, and the total of these formed a sort of informal council that cooperated with the head chief. General consent was requisite for any decision in this council, as among so many American Indians. In fact, it is probable that unanimity within the entire community was sought for, and that any matter would continue to be debated as long as a single individual contested the project, and that when a recalcitrant acquiesced it was rather from deference to public sentiment at large than from want of admitted right to maintain his stand.

The inheritance of office among the Pomo is veiled in some contradictions. The information which makes the community chief elective and only the head of a group of kinsmen derive his position by descent, specifically cites the sister's son and not the own son as the inheritor. Even though the remainder of California always reckons in the male line, this attribution of the matrilineate to certain of the Pomo is so definite that it can hardly be conceived as wholly lacking in foundation. Moreover, there is a certain slight corroboration in the fact that the Wappo, and perhaps the southern Pomo, denominate several of their kindred by terms which fit perfectly with matrilinear institutions, but whose origin would be very difficult to understand under a patrilinear status with which they would conflict. Now, it is true that the Wappo at present have no recollection of clear-cut matrilinear practice; but this terminological suggestion of its former prevalence among them does fit in rather nicely with the quoted reference to matrilinear inheritance of Pomo chieftainship. Renewed inquiry has brought some confirmation from the southern Pomo, not wholly conclusive, it is true, because flatly contradicted by most informants from the northern, eastern, and central divisions, but yet sufficient to indicate some local and incipient or vestigial inclinations toward the accordance of priority to the female line in kinship. This matrilineal tendency, manifest so far as known only in the inheritance of chieftaincy in one Pomo group and in a few terms of nomenclature among an adjacent Yukian branch, stands out wholly unique not only in California but on the whole Pacific coast of the United States.

The northern, eastern, and central Pomo, on the contrary, say that the son succeeded the father;[1] that the impulse to have the office remain in the lineage was so strong that in default of a son the succession often devolved upon a daughter, or her husband; and that nephews were chosen only if there were no direct heirs, and that even then precedence was given the brother's son over the sister's son. For instance, in one of the communities near Sherwood, the chief, on aging, wished his son-in-law to succeed him. This could not have been felt by the people to be amiss, since they began to assemble beads and property to contribute for his formal installation. Before this took place, however, he died; and the office passed in time to his son, the grandson of the old incumbent. The young man would have passed the title on to his son if the old life had continued.

These statements seem to refer to community chieftaincies. It is hardly likely that the matter would have been so closely regulated where nothing more was involved than the leadership of a small body of kinsmen living together. Such leadership, however autocratic in special cases, must necessarily have been more or less informal. But hereditary succession to the community chieftainship clashes with the reports of " election " to the office; unless the explanation be invoked that succession was indeed by rule of inheritance or wish of the incumbent, but that the public was formally consulted for approval, participated in the installation, and might cause the withdrawal of an unpopular heir apparent. Such a procedure might well in some instances resemble an election and yet be far from it in fact. That a feeling for inherited social status was fairly strong among the northerly divisions is shown by the circumstance that besides *ga-halik* or chiefs the eastern Pomo recognized *da-halik*, " queens "

---

[1] A recent eastern Pomo informant makes the succession indeterminate, with preference given the son of the late chief's oldest sister. Apparently the incumbent's wishes counted considerably, especially when he retired on account of advancing age.

or women chiefs, and *guma-halik* or chief's children. Whenever possible, marriages were contracted between such *guma-halik*.

The authority of the head chief was slight, in that he exercised but few of the powers of an officer of a civilized government. To compensate, his prominence was assured, and his opportunities for prestige limited only by his personality. He welcomed visitors, entertained them, and had a dignified and distinguished place reserved for him on all public occasions, especially in ceremonies, over which he may be said to have presided, though the actual direction was in the hands of others. His greatest prerogative was publicly lecturing his people—"preaching" the modern Indians appropriately call it. Standing in a conspicuous place, he shouted to them in a peculiar jerky delivery, in detached statements, with endless repetitions, mingling instructions as to some matter in hand with generic advice as to behavior, and particularly dilating on what custom had made obvious since time immemorial or on sentiments that everyone already entertained, such as the intention to enjoy a dance and feast.

In case of war, a chief of sufficient influence could end hostilities by a gift of shell money to the head of the enemy. The recipient usually considered himself morally bound not only to accept the donation but to reciprocate it without diminution, thereby bringing the conflict to an end. It is evident that in wars between entire village communities the head chiefs acted in this way. See, for instance, the Wappo account of their war with the Pomo. But in case of feuds it is expressly cited that the minor chiefs had the power to conclude the enmity in the manner stated whenever they saw fit. Again, however, it is needful not to read too much of our ideas into this statement. The chief who was a member of a group of blood kindred would hardly prefer peace to revenge for his people unless the situation stood so unfavorably that his relatives themselves thought it best to desist; which would mean that after all the decision rested not with him but with all members of the body involved.

It is tempting to connect the Pomo head chief with the Yuki group chief, and the "blood family chief" of the former with the "town chief" of the latter. It has been set forth how the Pomo of one community lived more or less irregularly in smaller bodies, often at a distance of some miles from their principal or permanent town. If the people who thus separated themselves for a season or for a few years were in the main a group united by consanguinity, the head of each of these "families" would also be the head of a settlement or village. Such a conjecture does not seem unreasonable, and if substantially correct, the Yuki "town chief" would also have been in effect a "family chief," and the difference in organization between the two stocks would lie chiefly in our nomenclature, or in an accident of the manner of approach of the matter by students.

In much the same manner the Yokuts, who are tribally organized, seem not to feel themselves materially different from their nontribal neighbors in social scheme, and it is quite possible that there is no intrinsic distinction except in the circumstance that among the Yokuts the community, the body politic, as such, has a name and a slight dialectic separateness, which facts in our eyes superficially endow them with a quite unique sense of national cohesion that they may actually possess in only a slight measure. It is through the just appraisal of subtle differences such as these that the true nature of the socio-political development of the California natives will be illumined as further information flows in.

A similar relation obtains between the "peace chief" and the "war chief," as the Americans have denominated them, among the Yuki, for instance. The former is simply the chief; the latter no chief at all, but the leader in whatever fighting there may be, without any loss of prerogative to the chief, even in the thick of war time.

DEATH.

The dead were burned by the Pomo. Some marginal fragments of the stock may have practiced burial also. There was no subsequent anniversary ceremony comparable to the Maidu burnings or the elaborate rituals that prevail among the south-central and southern tribes. The widow cut or burned off her hair and smeared her forehead with pitch and ashes. Eyewitnesses report that pieces of flesh were sometimes snatched from the corpse during its cremation and devoured. This would seem scarcely credible were it not that the same custom is reported from the Juaneño, of southern California. At that, the distance between the two nationalities is great, and nothing of the kind has been asserted of any intermediate tribe.

Seed or acorn meal was sprinkled to the dead for some time after their burning. As balls of flour were also thrown at certain ceremonial performers, it seems that the Pomo belonged to those tribes that made meal offerings. It is probable that this practice was more or less general in southern California, though the circumstance that it has been mentioned only scatteringly indicates that the act was either infrequent or, as seems more likely, conducted without the impressiveness of which it was capable. The custom is, however, likely to be an ancient one; of southwestern origin or perhaps dating to the remote civilization which underlies those of California and the Southwest, and to have spread from the southern parts of the State about as far as the Pomo. It has never been reported among the tribes on their north.

The decrepitly aged are said to have been sometimes strangled with a stick pressed down at each end. Disposal of the senile infirm has been reported so often from the eastern desert tracts of California that it must have been fairly frequent; but in these regions sustenance was scant and life difficult. Among the affluent Pomo the practice must have been rare.

BIRTH.

Birth observances were of a widespread type. The baby was subjected to prolonged steaming, as by the Shasta. The water in which it was washed was thrown out of the house gently, and by some person other than the father or mother, else rain resulted. The mother used the scratching stick, for fear her nails would leave permanent marks. She was fed, so as to avoid picking up her food; and ate no meat. The father observed a mild couvade, as among so many Californian tribes. He did not lie in, but for four days remained in the house. After this, he began to go out, but not to any distance, and at first carefully kept from mingling with any crowd. He did not hunt for some two or three months.

ADOLESCENCE.

The Pomo, at least those of the eastern group, assert that they held no adolescence dance, the girl merely beginning the monthly observances which she was to follow through her mature life. The feeling of all California Indians in regard to the exceptional supernatural power inherent in girls at this period is so deep-seated that it is scarcely likely that the occasion was allowed to pass without some accentuation of the subsequently recurrent taboos. These were numerous, explicit, and of the usual type. If the woman scratched her head with anything except a special bone or stick, she would shed her hair. If she washed, her face wrinkled; should she work on a basket, she would become blind. If she went to fetch water, she might see a monster in the spring; and eating meat would make her sick. Her husband also refrained from hunting or gambling, and from at least certain religious participations. Evidently her condition was essentially potent for evil and easily transmissible. She occupied a separate hut.

MARRIAGE AND SEX.

Marriage was by exchange of gifts rather than true purchase. The groom presented beads and deerskins to his parents-in-law, and they might reciprocate with baskets, but it is significant that there was no exact fixing of a valuation, no admitted property right in the wife, no going into debt if the payment were insufficient, no restraint of divorce until the exact price had been refunded. With all their developed arithmetical powers, the Pomo did not bargain and exact at marriage like the northwestern tribes. The simple exchange of gifts appears rather as an expression of good will and dignified but affectionate etiquette. It can not be doubted that the Pomo and the Yurok type of marriage have a basis in common and are historically connected. But their institutional and emotional flavor were thoroughly distinct; just as bride purchase meant quite different things to the Kwakiutl and the Dakota.

The eastern Pomo call the first and principal payment for a wife *da-nakil*. This brought the young husband into his bride's home. After a month or two, the couple were escorted by the bride's family to the husband's house, and gifts made by them to its inmates. This was a formal visit with entertainment. Before long, the husband took his wife back to her people, bringing new gifts to them, though less valuable ones than the *da-nakil*. This procedure was repeated several times. The final abode of the couple was, wholly by their preference, either with the husband's or the wife's parents or apart from both. Between settlements at a distance, the reciprocal visits were continued for some time, and the presents were considerable. A man that married at home gave less and dispensed much more quickly with the etiquette of residing occasionally with his father-in-law.

The northern Pomo seem to have followed very similar customs, and expressly state that until the birth of the first child, the abode of husband and wife fluctuated between the houses of their respective parents, but that after this event the couple usually began to inhabit a house of their own. This contrasts with the rather fixed rule of the neighboring Huchnom that the husband settled permanently with his wife's people.

The northern Pomo observed very strictly the custom of a taboo of shame and reticence between husband and mother-in-law. She kept her face covered or turned away from him as long as she lived. A man and his father-in-law were less scrupulous and conversed. Polygamy was practiced without much restriction, even cowives who were not kin living sometimes under one roof.

In the eastern division plural marriages were more frowned upon, and the mother-in-law taboo was much weaker. Bride and groom had their faces washed by each other's mothers. They are somewhat bashful toward them as well as toward their fathers-in-law, but do not avoid their presence. They are polite by speaking to them in the plural, and the old people reciprocate. Relatives-in-law of one's own generation are not accorded this deference, but a man may continue the expression of respect to his parents-in-law even after his wife's death. In place of calling his father-in-law by this term of relationship or simply "thou," he says to him: *mal butsigi hibekal*, "ye old-man them." As this instance shows, some curious logical inconsistencies of grammatical number and person are not shrunk from in adherence to this practice. Even the downright pronoun of the third person is used alone: *Hibek*, "they" or "those," is said for *ma*, "thou," almost exactly as the German employs "*Sie*" for the familiar "*du.*" The native development of this device on substantially the same lines as in modern European languages is an interesting instance of independent origin of cultural devices.

The Pomo do not share the custom followed in some parts of California, as among the Yana and Mono, of observing shame and maintaining silence toward their sisters. Bashfulness toward blood kindred would be ridiculed, they declare, as being treatment proper only toward a bride, and shame would be construed as a symptom of sexual love. This association evidently holds true of their actual attitude. As a man and his wife can hardly be timid toward each other long after marriage, they transfer the emotion to each other's nearest kin.

The status of Pomo women was rather high. Besides the inclinations to matrilineal descent already discussed, there may be cited the native mention of titular women chiefs; the admission of some women to the secret society, with a tradition of at least one community having once had a woman head for the society; the joint " preliminary " initiation of boys and girls; the attribution by the eastern Pomo of ownership of the house to the oldest wife among the several households inhabiting it; and perhaps the fact that men relieved women from the manufacture of coarse burden baskets. The impression is one of definitely greater social equality of the sexes than among the northwestern tribes.

Another trait that must possess a certain cultural significance is the presence of sex gender in the Pomo demonstrative pronoun. It is entirely obscure how this feature could have originated, especially since sex is expressed grammatically by only a very small number of American Indian languages, and no other one in California or pertaining to the Hokan family.

MATHEMATICS.

The Pomo are great counters. Their arithmetical faculties must have been highly developed. They counted their long strings of beads. Methods of measuring such as most California tribes use were probably also in vogue, but must have been less usual, since they have not been described. In early days of contact with Caucasian civilization the unit of exchange was 400 clam-shell beads for $2.50. After the introduction of the pump drill the beads were manufactured more readily, and the value of the same unit quantity fell to $1. A tale relates that the first bear shaman gave 40,000 beads in pretended sympathy for the victim whose death he had caused. The use of these enormous figures is not incredible.

A unit of 100 fours being once established, a reckoning to 100 such units presented no great difficulty to one who was interested. The significant thing is that the Pomo were interested. They evidently liked to deal with numbers, which had come to have a meaning to them and whose mere size did not terrify them. That they were a wealthy people would accordingly go without saying, even if we did not know that they were the principal purveyors of the standard disk currency to north-central California. It can also be inferred that this advance did not proceed without a corresponding development in other fields of the intellect or a reflection in many of their institutions.

There is nothing to show that the Pomo multiplied or divided in our customary sense of these operations. But constant dealing with units and higher units—fours, tens, hundreds, or four hundreds—must have resulted in a frequent familiarity with the result of many combinations of fairly large figures and some facility in dealing with new ones.

The Pomo calendar, with its tendency toward counting, has been discussed in connection with the Huchnom calendar in Chapter 13.

TRADE.

Little is on record as to intercommunal trade relations. The Kuhlanapo and Habenapo of Clear Lake received trade articles as follows: From the north came iris fiber cord for deer snares; arrows; and sinew-backed yew bows, the native backed bow being of mountain mahogany; from the east, magnesite; from the south, clam shells; from the west, mussels, seaweed, haliotis shells, and furs of small seals (" water bear ") or possibly sea otters. For these objects the Clear Lake people gave fish, acorns, skins, and magnesite.

CHAPTER 17.

THE POMO: RELIGION.

SHAMANISM.

Little is known of the manner in which the Pomo medicine man acquired his power, except that it might be derived from one's father or from a shaman whom the novice had assisted and who fell heir to his teachings and paraphernalia. The power was also received directly from the spirits, but this method is less frequently mentioned and appears to have been relatively less developed than among most other tribes. In short, pure shamanism was more or less overshadowed by fetishism and ritualism among the Pomo.

The fetishism is particularly evident in the importance attached to the sacks owned by a certain class of medicine men. These were animal skins containing bull roarers, obsidian, colored pebbles, bones, roots, sticks covered with snake skins, shaped amulets of stone, dried lizards, snakes, coyote feet, or any deformed or unusual object. The type of this outfit is that employed by the Plains Indian shaman. The bag was thought extremely powerful: its shadow would kill a child on which it might fall.

The ritualism appears in the use of these things. The contents of the sack were laid by the fire. The medicine man shook his cocoon rattle and began a song and dance. Handing the rattle to his assistant, who also took up the melody, he danced over the patient. Selecting one of his amulets, that had been sufficiently warmed, he pointed with it to the four directions—or the four " winds," as the Pomo say—and thrust it against the seat of pain, then followed with another and another. This was done for four nights, during which the medicine man fasted and drank no water. The seemingly regular presence of an avowed assistant gives the entire procedure an unusual flavor.

It is probable that the actions performed with each fetish object were more elaborate than here stated. For instance, a bear doctor, before putting on his accouterment, began by dancing up to each part of it four times from each of the four directions. This scheme was multiplicatively enlarged by dancing also with the object, toward the place of its deposit, and holding it in the left instead of the right hand; after which the entire cycle was repeated in reverse order, making all told 170 successive movements, each performed four times. The singing assistant kept the complete tally of 680 with sticks. This, again, is a type of procedure the like of which has not been reported from any other Californian group.[1]

BEAR SHAMANS.

The grizzly bear-shaman's activities are reported on by the Pomo much as by the Yuki and Maidu. Incased in a complete bearskin, his body wrapped with belts of beads serving as armor, and with a horn dagger concealed on him, this nefarious being roamed the hills in search of his human prey, not sparing even people of his own town, if he owed them the least grudge or if their spoliation seemed sufficiently profitable.

But the Pomo accounts of their "bear doctors" are remarkable in making no reference whatever to the animal as the source of the magical power enjoyed. Their bear doctor was not a person who possessed the bear as his guardian spirit, but one who owned the skin suit and necessary outfit, and had learned its use from a human instructor. In short, he was the possessor of a fetish that increased his strength and endurance, and not a shaman at all, if the native information available may be relied on. This fact is of interest because the shamanistic character of the bear doctor is very plain among the Yuki, whose practice of the art closely resembles that of the Pomo, while with tribes like the Yokuts the material paraphernalia appear to be wholly dispensed with and the doctor, through his *tipni* or *mana*, turns his own person into a bear's body. There can thus be no doubt that the basis of the belief throughout California is shamanistic, and that the bear doctor falls into a class with the malignant shaman or evil witch.

Pomo descriptions of the apparatus used are so detailed that they must have some foundation in fact, which is confirmed by at least one model in a museum. At the same time it is impossible for a man to travel considerable distances on all fours with any speed; to fight as well while cumbered with heavy wrappings and a bulky false head over his own, as when stripped for action; or to gain an advantage through being armed only with a dagger. Now and then the repute of the dreaded human bears might have paralyzed a hunter and made him fall a terrified victim; but more often the bear man himself would have succumbed. It can only be concluded that there were bear doctors; that they believed in their powers; that they possessed

---

[1] L. S. Freeland, Pomo Doctors and Poisoners (see bibliography), makes clear the Pomo discrimination of the *k'o'o-gauk*, "poison man" or bewitcher, as against the shaman who cured and was not held responsible for his patient's death. The shamans were of two kinds: *k'o'o-bakiyalhale* "performers for the poisoned"—"singing" or "outfit" doctors in colloquial English—who used the sacks and paraphernalia, and had been taught their knowledge by an older man; and *madu*, the "sucking" or "dream" doctors, who had had a supernatural experience and followed the methods more usual in California and no doubt of greater institutional antiquity. It is interesting that the *madu* were less numerous and less well paid. Sacks belong also to the Guksu society. See below.

actual disguises and found pleasure in donning these and acting the animal in privacy or in the company of their assistants or like-minded associates; but that their feats of slaughter existed chiefly if not wholly in the imagination of themselves and their public; unless indeed, as one hint suggests, the bear doctor was not a shaman at all, but a bear impersonator in more or less public exhibitions of the esoteric ritual society.

CEREMONIAL SYSTEM.

The general religious organization of which the Pomo form part is discussed, for all the tribes involved in it, in chapter 26 on the Wintun. In the present connection there will be mentioned chiefly the principal traits peculiar to the Pomo.

Very little is known of the form which the secret society takes among the Pomo. It may have been somewhat less definitely organized than among the Wintun and Maidu. But any divergences along this line remain for positive determination by study.

The Pomo call a dance, as such, *he* or *ke*, "sing." A ceremony, on the other hand, that is to say, a four days' complex of dances, including separate impersonations, was called *haikil* (or by some dialectic or grammatical equivalent) which means "stick hang." This designation is probably derived from the apparatus employed when invitations were sent out to other villages. Several short sticks, equal in number to the days until the beginning or close of the ceremony, were tied together in a little parallel screen which was hung by a string from the end of a wand. Each day one stick was detached. Sometimes an acorn or fishtail was fastened to the bottom of the little mat. In this case acorns or fish were presented to the visiting chiefs at the conclusion of the ceremony, in value equivalent to the shell money which they had brought with them and given to the resident chief.

The ritualistic features of Pomo dancing, at least so far as the spirit impersonators are concerned, are closely similar to what are known of the corresponding practices of the Yuki, Wintun, and Maidu. The impersonators dressed outdoors at a distance. They were summoned from the roof of the dance house by means of calls -which they answered, each according to his character. Each entered the assembly house, usually progressing backward, and performed his dance separately. The middle of the house, from the door to the drum at the opposite end, was the dancing place, but the focus of the performer's activity was the vicinity of the drum itself. Spectators sat on the right and left of the house behind the side posts. The dance step was mainly an alternate raising of the knees, the foot being stamped with violence. The drum was usually leaped over, sometimes jumped on. Most of the spirit impersonators were led and directed by special officials who were themselves in costume, and in a measure participated in either the dancing or the singing.

The ritualistic circuit among all tribes was antisunwise. The cardinal directions were named in identical order, but the Pomo commenced with the south, the Wintun with the west. The ceremonial number among all tribes is invariably four, except for an occasional amplification to six.

Among the Yuki a simple form of the esoteric system prevails, based primarily, perhaps wholly, on two rituals. The Pomo scheme is ampler, approximating that of the Wintun and Maidu. Its Yuki affinities, however, are revealed by the fact that while the Pomo practice a fair number of ceremonies, these fall into two groups. One of these groups, into which the *Kuksu* or *Guksu* character enters, corresponds to the Yuki Taikomol ceremonies. The other, the *Hahluigak* or ghost ritual, is a close counterpart of the Yuki *hulk'ilal* rites.

These are the eastern Pomo designations. The northerners about Sherwood say *dasan ke* and *chaduwel ke;* and mention the *te ke* as equivalent to the Yuki and Huchnom feather dance, and the *yeu ke* as the one made at a girl's maturity.

Of these two sets of rituals, the one which is perhaps most frequently referred to in reports is the ghost ceremony, which possessed a similar status not only among the Yuki but probably among all the minor groups west of the Wintun among whom the Pomo are central and culturally dominant. Among the Sacramento Valley tribes the ghost ceremony is either unrepresented or reappears in so changed a form that its identity with the Pomo prototype has not been noted.

The kernel of the Pomo system is, however, associated with the *Guksu* rites. This is clear from the fact that the old men in charge of the *Guksu* also direct the ghost ritual, whereas the reverse does not obtain. The head of these old initiates had charge of the feathers and other paraphernalia used in the ghost ceremony, while his companions helped to dress and paint the ghost dancers.

GUKSU CEREMONIES.

Few spirits were impersonated by the Pomo. They were *Guksu*, the principal; *Shalnis*, his associate; and, less frequently, a few animals. *Guksu* was thought to live in a large dance house at the south end of the world; *Shalnis* or *Madumda* at the east; while the corresponding gods at the north, west, above, and below were whirlwind, water, sky or thunder, and earth occupant or spirit.

The last-named four were not represented in ceremonies. *Shalnis* was impersonated by one dancer only, and the *Guksu* by several. *Shalnis* is described as readily moved to anger.

The meaning of the word *Shalnis* is not known. The apparel of the impersonator, however, suggests him as similar to the *Moki* of the Wintun and Maidu. A feather-covered mantle of network fell from the crown of his head so as to conceal entirely his identity. Any visible portions of his body were painted black, and he carried a plain black staff.

The *Guksu*, as with other tribes, wore the "big head" ornament of radiating feather-tipped sticks, though formerly this seems to have been replaced by a smaller tuft of feathers supplemented by a band of yellow-hammer quills. Attached to his head he wore a long nose or horn of feathers painted red. He carried a double bone whistle and a long staff tipped with feathers.

A sort of initiation that formed part of the *Guksu* rituals was called *Gahagaha*, which means "cutting," and which was performed upon children. The cuts were made on the first and last days of a ceremony, by means of a sharp-edged shell drawn across the back of the prostrate child. There was no insistence on the children restraining themselves in their pain, but every precaution was taken to prevent them from looking up during the act. They were also forbidden to look up into oak trees for fear they should blast the crop of acorns. Ideas of this kind are strongly developed in the adolescence ceremonies for girls among most of the tribes of California. It is accordingly not surprising that the Pomo inflicted their hurt on girls as well as boys. As women, however, were not admitted to some sacred rites in the dance house, the ceremonial action must have been thought to have a different effect according to the sex of the children. At that, it is almost certain that the cutting alone did not make a small boy a full member of the organization. From what we know of parallel conditions among the Yuki and Maidu, we may infer that a second initiation was gone through toward early manhood. It is possible, therefore, that the Pomo cutting ceremony for boys was intended only as a preliminary preparation for the future final rite, and that its immediate purpose for boys as well as girls was to insure their speedy growth and vigor, as indeed the Pomo themselves declare.

There are only hints as to the second or more esoteric initiation. Its central feature may have been a stabbing or shooting with spear or arrow. What sort of devices were employed in this exhibition, and how crude or skillful their execution was, can only be conjectured. After a pretended wounding the initiates were healed. In some instances the use of the bow and arrow is reported. In others a spear was thrust at the subject, who stood behind a screen of brush. Still other descriptions refer to spears apparently thrust directly into the naked body. It would seem that demonstrations of this type may have been given as an exhibition of supernatural power rather than as an initiation, since women are mentioned as having been thus operated upon.

The opening of one ceremony was marked by the ritualistic bringing in and erection of a large pole in front of the dance house. While some of the men climbed this pole balls of seed meal were thrown at them. The actions performed in connection with this pole are probably old, but modified by recent "ghost-dance" movement introductions. Among the Wintun, also, outdoor pole rituals are intimately connected with the modern ghost dance. On the other hand, the climbing of a tall post must have some ancient foundation, since it is found as far away as southern California, although there in connection with mourning ceremonies.

At least once on each day of larger ceremonies the *Guksu* impersonators appeared from outside and danced in the assembly house. The intervals between their exhibitions were filled out by the people eating, gambling, or witnessing other dances.

There is a definite association to the Pomo between the *Guksu* and the curing of disease, although the doctor or shaman as such must be sharply distinguished from the *Guksu* impersonator. The patient was approached by the *Guksu* in full costume, danced over, and then prodded or pried with the staff, particularly at the seat of pain. Or, the *Guksu* blew his whistle—which represented his speech—at the affected spot. This rite is practically identical with the *Taikomol* doctoring of the Yuki, but has no known parallels among the Wintun and Maidu.

HAHLUIGAK OR GHOST CEREMONY.

The ancient ghost or *Hahluigak* ceremony must be carefully distinguished from certain recent modifications worked in surviving Pomo and Wintun cults by what is historically known to Americans as the " ghost-dance movement," or, rather, the earlier wave of this, which originated in Nevada about 1870 to 1872 and swept over northern California.

The *Hahluigak* expressly excluded women from participation, and even from witnessing what went on within the dance house. Sometimes four poles were planted around the house to form an exterior barrier that must not be crossed by any but the initiated. The ghost performers frequently conducted themselves in as terrifying a manner as possible, and it scarcely seems open to doubt that in a measure they attempted to instill fear into nonmembers. On the other hand, the assumption that the prime purpose of this ceremony was to keep the women in subjection by threats and terrorization is obviously a crude assumption of the kind that often enters into the naïve thinking of civilized white men not in sympathy with Indian mentality. That the Pomo dancers frightened their women, and deliberately so, is no doubt true, but that a sacred four days' ceremonial should essentially be a device for keeping wives faithful and obedient is surely an interpretation foreign to native psychology.

While it is generally stated that every uninitiated person was scrupulously excluded from the dance house during any performance of the ghosts, the Pomo, like the Coast Yuki, affirm that old women were nevertheless among the spectators. Whether these attended in virtue of their age, or whether there was any formal rite of admittance, is not known.

Among the Yuki only one kind of *hulk'ilal* has been reported. It is characteristic of the general cultural relation of the two stocks that the Pomo impersonators are of two kinds—the *Hahluigak*, or ghosts, and the *No-hahluigak*, or ash ghosts. The latter, who gave demonstrations of their power over fire, appear to have been the higher class. During the dances of the ordinary ghosts, it is true, the ash ghosts served almost in the capacity of attendants to them. It may be more just, however, to understand them as being present in the capacity of watchers to see that the ghost ceremonies were conducted properly. Their own exhibitions were conducted chiefly at night.

On his head the ghost dancer wore a net filled with down, a feather tuft, a band of yellow-hammer quills that followed the crown and hung down behind, and a circlet of pepperwood leaves. No other regalia were worn except a girdle and sometimes a necklace of the same foliage. The entire body was covered with paint. The most common pattern was a horizontal banding, but the style of application, as well as the colors used, were left to the choice of each performer. There was no covering for the face, although the combination of shadowing leaves and crudely smeared paint no doubt effectually disguised identity.

The ash ghosts were more simply dressed. Their ornaments were restricted to a few feathers on the head. A screen of leaves to hide the face is mentioned. The body was completely painted.

The badge of authority of the ash ghosts was a crooked stick, the butt of which was fashioned to represent the head of a crane.

When the ghosts arrived before the dance house the fire tender or headman who called them addressed them thus:

napo putsal giwale	village healthy run to!
mayawale-kale putsal giwale	girls healthy run to!
hahalik putsal giwale	chiefs healthy run to!
dahalik putsal giwale	chieftainesses healthy run to!
kawik putsal giwale	children healthy run to!

In form this invocation closely resembles the Wintun ritual orations.

At times the ghosts carried living rattlesnakes, and on approaching the dance house at night they are reported to have worn on their heads some sort of flaming device. It is not altogether clear whether these statements refer to the ordinary or the ash ghosts.

Even the ordinary ghost dancers would scatter coals of fire about the house when angered, but outright exhibitions, such as eating live coals and plunging the hands into the fire, were reserved to the ash ghosts. They designated coals of fire as their *bu* or edible bulbs, and were called *bu-hiemk* or "bulb watchers."

Both classes of impersonators acted as clowns in some measure. Their speech was reversed, and they followed instructions in an opposite sense. If they were to go to the west of the drum, for instance, it was necessary to direct them to the east. The ash ghosts in particular adhered to some of the practices of the Yuki *hulk'ilal* in rendering their appearance grotesque, stuffing their cheeks, propping their eyelids, and stretching their mouths. Any manifestation of laughter by the spectators caused anger and the exaction of a fine of beads. The fire in the dance house was considered the property of the ash ghosts. Any man who wished to light his pipe or to leave the house while the ash ghosts were performing paid for the privilege with false shell money of tule.

On the other hand, the ash ghosts could claim any visible property to which they took a fancy and pay for it in this same worthless currency.

The ash ghosts also threw boys across the fire as a sort of initiation. This act in itself can hardly have constituted the youths into ash ghosts, but was possibly performed as a preliminary to their becoming such subsequently.

At times a woman of wealth would be told that her dead husband or brother would appear to her. She might be torn between fear and desire; if she yielded to the latter, she was directed to give beads for him to carry back with him. The old men then selected an initiate as like the deceased as possible in figure and concealed him in a hole covered with leaves. His body was painted black and white; his hair and face were completely whitened. As he raised himself from the excavation, the blanching completely disguising his features, the poor woman thought that she recognized her beloved, whitened by the ashes of his funeral pyre, and burst into tears and wailing.

While it is not so stated by the Pomo, it is quite likely, from a Miwok and Wintun parallel, that this deception took place in the gloom of the dance house, and that the excavation was the hollow under the sacred drum. The practice also throws light on the status of women toward the society and the circumstances of their admittance to its rites, as well as suggesting why the fire-playing impersonators were called "ash" ghosts: the Pomo were a cremating people.

COYOTE CEREMONY.

The coyote ritual, *I'wi* or *Gunula* according to dialect, is very little known. It is mentioned as a dance by the Pomo, but several considerations indicate it as a ceremony. Both Wintun and Maidu recognize a coyote ceremony. The Pomo participants were but slightly adorned, except for a complete coat of white paint; which is also the distinguishing mark of certain Miwok clowns who seem to represent coyotes. Finally, the Pomo coyote dancers carried twigs which were held so as to obscure the face as much as possible. This attempt at disguise appears to rank them in native estimation as spirits. Whether, however, there was a separate four-day ceremonial in which these coyote impersonators were the leading performers, or whether they merely entered into other rituals, is not clear. They are said to have been accompanied in their dancing by women.

THUNDER CEREMONY.

The *Kalimatoto*, or thunder ritual, has no known parallel among other stocks. It is possible that it may be a well-known ritual whose identity among the Pomo has been disguised by a distinctive name.

The costume of the thunder dancers was simple, their body and face paint applied chiefly in vertical stripes.

DAMA CEREMONY.

The *Dama* was a ceremony of much consequence and sacredness, but appears to have gone out of use early, and little is known about it. The name may possibly be derived from *dam*, meaning " feather down." In this case a mythological reference is not unlikely, since the Yuki believe the Creator to have made himself out of a down feather. This was a full four days' ceremony with acrobatic displays that suggest those in the creeper and other Maidu dances. The participants crawled on the dance-house ceiling, descended the center pole head first, and displayed other feats of agility on ropes. It is said that one of them, having his power challenged, and a price having been named, once lifted the center post of the house out of its place and laid it on the ground, later putting it back.

Such displays, however, were not entirely limited to the *Dama* among the Pomo, since participants in the ghost dance would sometimes dive headlong through the roof door. They could do this in safety because of a net stretched out to receive them; but to the women and children outside it must have appeared as if the ghost were dashing himself upon the hard floor 15 or 20 feet below.[2]

DANCES.

The various *he*, or dances, were performed by the Pomo either as interludes in the major rituals or separately on occasion. They comprise, besides those listed in the table in chapter 26 on the Wintun, the *Hoho*, *Shokin*, *Tutaka*, and *Yaya*, which are more or less simi-

---

[2] L. S. Freeland, Pomo Ceremonials, MS. records, University of California, gives new data on the eastern Pomo ritual system. These people danced in a thatched house; only the *dama-hai* was made in the earth-covered house customary elsewhere. The secret society was limited to members of certain lineages and such other individuals as they took in, but included some women. Members were known as *matutsi* or spirits and had each a bag similar to the shaman's sack; the head of the society was the *yomta*. There was not more than one *yomta* per political community. Initiation occurred about puberty, by the *yomta*, in a private place; there was nothing corresponding to the formal *woknam* or " school " of the Yuki. The *gaha* or cutting of boys and girls with a bit of shell drawn across their backs was a health-giving rite rather than an initiation into membership. The ritual season, in contrast with the Sacramento Valley custom, was in summer. Ceremonies numbered barely half a dozen, and came without rigorous order, usually, however, beginning with the *budu-bahar* in which a pole was climbed and ending with the Thunder rite, in which the bull roarer was swung. Impersonations, also known as *hai*, were scarcely as numerous as ceremonies, the most important, who appeared in all rituals except the *Hah-luigah*, being the *Guksu*. There was also a bear impersonator, whose description seems to absorb much of the puzzling functions hitherto attributed to the bear shaman. The *Hah-luigah* took in all men, initiation, during a ritual, being on boys before puberty, and women being rigorously excluded. There were no impersonators except the ghosts and ash ghosts. The latter were *matutsi* of the general ritual organization, and direction of ghost rituals was in the hands of the *yomta*.

lar; the *Yo*, or south dance, known also to the Coast Yuki; the *Lehuye*, *Helahela* (possibly connected with the Maidu turtle dance), *Macho*, *Karaya*, *Sawet*, *Taugu*, *Macho*, *Sitaya*, *Badjusha*, and *Momi-momi*. Women as well as men participated in all of these. In fact, the only dance, other than spirit impersonations, restricted to men

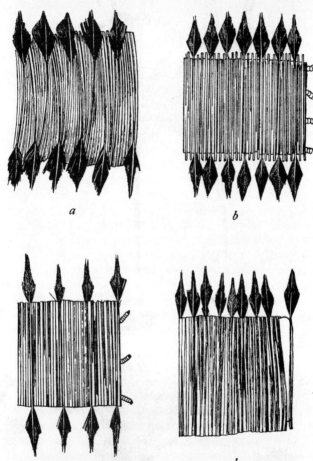

FIG. 20.—Sections of head bands of yellow-hammer quills. *a*, *b*, Pomo; *c*, Yuki; *d*, Chilula. (Compare Pl. 58.)

was the *Hiwe;* except the *Idam*, which is perhaps only a variant name of the dance characterizing the *Dama* ceremony. On the other hand, the only dance made by women only, besides an apparently modern *Mata* or " woman " dance, was the *Lole*.

The standard costume, worn with but little variation in the great majority of these dances, was that of the Yuki *K'op* or *La^nlha^np wok*, and spread, with only minor changes, as far as the Miwok: a feathered net hanging down the

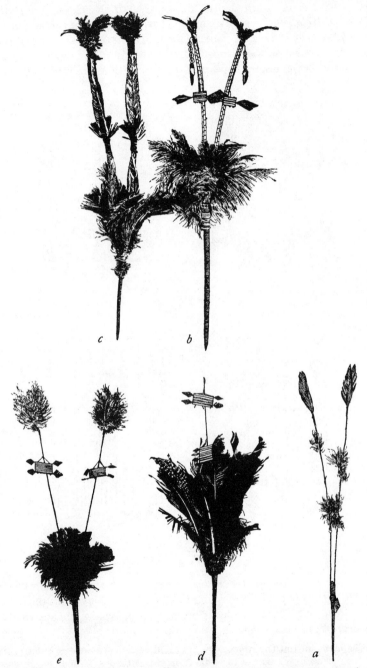

FIG. 21.—Central Californian dance headdresses. *a*, Yuki; *b*, *c*, Pomo; *d*, *e*, Miwok.

back from the armpits; a tuft or bunch of owl or hawk feathers skewered to the hair within the head net; a sewn band of yellow-hammer quills (Fig. 20), worn either across the forehead or along the top of the head and hanging down the back; and a pair of " plumes," each forking into two slender pliant rods, feather wrapped or tipped, and often with little dangling mats of yellow-hammer quills attached (Fig. 21). In a few dances a head net filled with fine down was worn, or down was stuck to the face. A whistle might be blown. A long rattle of cocoons or a bunch of twigs held up to conceal the face was occasionally carried. In general, however, these additions were used in dances of particular character, especially those in which spirits were represented.

Women wore all or part of the men's regalia, but possessed one ornament of their own: a thick forehead band from projections on which little mats of orange quills swayed.

The styles of face and body paint were far more variable than the feather costumes, and most of the dances seem to have been characterized by distinctive patterns.

In the same way, the steps were much the same in nearly all the dances, while it is probable that the songs differed so as to be immediately recognizable to the native.

It is significant that the characteristic dances of the less cultured tribes of northern California, those made on the occasion of a girl's adolescence, the constituting of a shaman, and the preparation or celebration of a fight, are all either wanting or weakly developed among the Pomo.

THE MODERN GHOST DANCE.

The ghost dance that originated in Nevada one or two years before reached the eastern Pomo in 1872, it seems. It was continued for some years, after which its concepts and practices largely merged into what remained of the ancient ceremonial system. For about 40 years past, accordingly, Pomo dances, like those of the Wintun, have been a blend of two quite separate strains.

The ghost dance was under the leadership of dreamers or prophets who communicated in dreams or trances with the spirit world of the dead and with a great creator or superdeity. These propagandists and instigators were called *maru*, whereas ordinary dreaming is *hadum*. Women sometimes became *maru*. There was no order of *maru* and of course no initiation, the idea being very clear that the *maru's* authority and power sprang directly from his achievements, and that these depended on his inherent individual faculties. The *maru* would dream of *waimai*, " our father," the one supreme god, and receive orders from him how to conduct rituals and what to communicate to the people. The world was soon to end, it was universally taught. The believers would live, doubters and apostates turn to stone, at that time. No doubt the whites were included in the latter category, so that the movement was in a sense a revivalistic one. But

it is clear that this renaissance was based on the concept of an antithesis to the whites far more than it was an attempt to rejuvenate
the old native life as such. The movement was a reaction against
smothering by the intrusive American, a convulsive, defensive gasp,
not a new impulse of vitality in the old channels. This is shown by
the fact that the ghost dances, the *maru he*, were distinguished from
the *hintil he*, the " gentile " or ancient native rituals. New ceremonial
patterns were evolved, such as banners; women and children were
admitted; and this last feature was felt to be an innovation in the
direction of American manner, because the new rites were often called
" whisky dances," not because intoxication was favored, but because
whisky was to the Indian the most insistent symbol of his contact
with civilization. There is curiously little reference to the return
of the dead. This element is the one that surely had the deepest
emotional hold on the eastern Indians in the ghost dance of 1890: it
was the prospect of seeing father or husband or brother once more
that stimulated them more than the cosmic cataclysm that impended
or the ensuing return to the old unconfined life. This side must have
been less developed in California in 1872, else the references to the
movement would make more mention of it.

So far as the eastern Pomo know, the ghost dance originated in the
east. This is much more likely to mean the southern Wintun of the
Sacramento Valley than the Paiute of Nevada, of whom they seem
never to have heard. The other Wintun gave the dance to those of
Long Valley, from where it was carried successively to the southeastern Pomo of Sulphur Bank, the eastern Pomo at Kelseyville, thence
to the Pomo of the coast, and to the mixture of tribes in Round
Valley.

In conclusion, it may be added once more that this modern ghost
dance has no connection at all, except in our terminology, with the
old ghost or *Hahluigak* ceremonies. Not only was the character
of the two sets of practices thoroughly distinct, but the Indians are
clear and emphatic on the point.

MYTHOLOGY.

Pomo mythology knows of a high and wise deity Madumda, in the
sky, whose younger brother, the coyote, enterprising, mischievous,
reforming, and tricking, formerly roamed the earth, begot children,
fanned a world fire, created human beings, stole the sun for them,
and transformed the animals into their present condition. Coyote,
accordingly, is the real creator, so far as the Pomo recognize one.
Madumda is so inactive that he scarcely forms a full counterpart of
the Yuki Taikomol, Wintun Olelbis, Maidu Initiate-of-the-Earth;
but he is of their type. It is possible that he and Kuksu, who is also

mentioned in the ordinary tales, entered more prominently into unrecorded esoteric myths connected with the dance organization.

TYPE OF CULTURE.

The Yuki have already been designated as a people whose civilization partook of a largely different color from that of the northwestern groups. With the Pomo, nearly all vestiges of specific northwestern traits are left behind. But they possessed not only a thoroughly central Californian civilization, as shown for instance by their participation in the Kuksu religion: they had worked into its fabric innumerable specializations and refinements of their own: their superb basket industry, their count of beads, certain approaches to a matrilineate, linguistic devices of social significance, and the like. These individualizations were not only developed by them to a point of definiteness, but borrowed, in large measure, by the smaller groups that are clustered about the Pomo; so that the civilization must be reckoned a distinct and rather notable subtype of the wider central culture that extended from Mount Shasta to Tehachapi Pass.

CHAPTER 18.

THE COAST AND LAKE MIWOK.

RELATIONSHIP.

Two branches of the Penutian Miwok that are best considered in anticipation of their congeners lived apart from the bulk of the stock, in the basin of Clear Lake and along the coast north of the Golden Gate: ancient emigrants of enterprise toward the west, or remnants of a once wider distribution of the group. The latter conjecture seems perhaps more plausible. In miles, it is no great distance from the nearest members of the Plains division of the Miwok to these two outposts; and the gap of dialect, particularly from Plains to Lake, while considerable, is nothing exceptional as such things go in California. The Coast speech, on the other hand, is the nearest of all Miwok dialects to Costanoan in its organization; which fact is not surprising in view of the circumstance that there is only a mile of water between the most proximate points held by the two groups.

Within Coast Miwok, the speech of Bodega Bay can be distinguished from the talk of the remainder of the area; and the latter also may have comprised subdialects. But all differentiation is unimportant.

GROUPS OF THE LAKE MIWOK.

The Lake Miwok were squeezed in between Pomo, Wappo, and Wintun. They held the drainage of a couple of small streams flowing into the very lowest mile or two of Clear Lake, and the southern bank of Cache Creek, the lake outlet, for a short distance beyond. Here, in the valley where the American town of Lower Lake now stands, they had several settlements, with Tuleyome as metropolis. But none of these villages was actually on the lake and they do not seem to have navigated it as extensively as the adjacent Pomo. (Pl. 27.)

To the south, over a divide, are the headwaters of Putah Creek, which drains Coyote Valley. Here lived a second group in several villages, of which Oleyome, "coyote place," was perhaps the principal. This region was named after the coyote in all the surrounding languages—thus, Pomo Gunula-hahoi or Kliwin-hoi according to dialect—just as the district of Middletown, on one of the affluents of the upper Putah and in Wappo possession, was "goose land" or "goose valley."

Both these little Lake Miwok groups occupied natural territories and are likely to have constituted political units of the kind described among the Pomo, but there is no definite information.

There may have been a third group of the Lake Miwok in Pope Valley, where there is mention of a "Reho tribe." This region has, however, been assigned also to the Wappo. Plate 27 shows the disputed area.

GROUPS OF THE COAST MIWOK.

The Coast Miwok have also been spoken of as comprising three "tribes": the Olamentko of Bodega Bay, the Lekahtewut between Petaluma and Freestone, and the Hookooeko of Marin County. Likatiut was, however, a village near Petaluma; the name Olamentko may be misapplied from Olema or Olema-loke near the head of Tomales Bay; and Hookooeko may be a similar local designation extended, after contact with the whites and when the population had shriveled, into a quasi-ethnic significance. It is likely that the three names rest on place names that distinguished as many political units; but there must have been more than three of these among the Coast Miwok, and the selection of any of them as denotations of larger linguistic or national bodies seems somewhat fortuitous.

Marin County and its environs are extraordinarily diversified in coast line, nature of the shore, topography, exposure, temperature, and vegetation, and much of the district must have been unusually favorable for native occupation. Settlements clustered mostly about estuaries or their vicinity. Bodega Bay was surrounded by several. Others stretched along the sunny side of Tomales Bay. Point Reyes peninsula seems to have been uninhabited. A reference by the narrator of Drake's voyage to a settlement three-quarters of a mile from the landing may point either to a permanent village or to a summer camp site. Bolinas Bay probably had at least one village. Thence south, to beyond the Golden Gate, cliffs made the shore unsuitable for residence; but, once in San Francisco Bay, Sausalito and the shores of Richardson Bay were inviting. Beyond, San Rafael and the adjacent shore were attractive. In the region of Ignacio and Novato, hills and bay sloughs are still in proximity, and there are records of several settlements as well as abundance of shell deposits. On San Antonio Creek—the eastern one of the two streams so named—were Olompolli and its outposts. Petaluma Creek, from the head of tidewater up, also drew to it a number of little towns, of which Petaluma and Likatiut were perhaps the principal. The ridged and forested interior of the peninsula contained several villages, all on or near running streams; but the preponderating majority were in the bay districts enumerated. It was evidently more convenient to live in the open, close to the supply of mussels, clams, fish, and water fowl, and occasionally visit the hills to hunt, than to live in the shade inland

and travel to the shore. Mollusks perhaps made a more dependable if less prized diet than venison.

Sonoma Valley up to about Glen Ellen has been attributed to the southwestern Wintun as well as the Coast Miwok. The evidence is so directly conflicting that a positive decision is impossible.

Tchokoyem or Chocuyen has been used as a designation for the Coast Miwok in Sonoma Valley or in general. Its origin is unknown. Other "tribal" denomi-

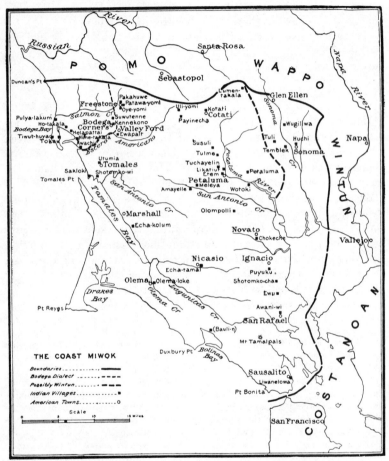

Fig. 22.—Coast Miwok territory and settlements. (After Merriam and Barrett.)

nations, such as Timbalakees, Petalumas or Yolhios, Olompalies, Tamalanos or Tumalehnias, Baulines, and Oleomi, appear to have no other basis than village names. If a generic term of native origin were desirable to introduce for the group as a whole, Micha, "person," or Micha-ko, "people," would be most appropriate.

Similarly, Hotsa-ho might be coined as a designation for the Lake Miwok, if there were need.

The southern Pomo call the Bodega people: Akamtata; the Wappo, those about Petaluma: Onwalisa.

Figure 22 summarizes what is known of the territorial history of the Coast Miwok.

NUMBERS.

The population of the Lake Miwok can safely be estimated to have been not in excess of 500; the Coast branch may have numbered 1,500. There remain a handful of scattered survivors. The missions have played their usual part. The nearer Coast Miwok were first taken to San Francisco. Later, San Rafael and then Sonoma were established in their territory and Pomo, Wintun, and Wappo mingled with themselves. The Lake Miwok fared a little better, being more remote. But they also can muster only a dozen or two to-day.

CIVILIZATION.

Of the recent culture of both groups little has been recorded. They were undoubtedly closely allied to the Pomo in their habits. This is particularly clear of the Lake Miwok, who made feathered baskets and earth-covered dance houses scarcely if at all distinguishable from those of the Pomo. The Coast group, being in contact with the most southerly Wintun and northerly Costanoans and with only one division of the Pomo, and inhabiting a larger and more peculiar territory, may be presumed to have evinced more independence of civilization; but even among them particularities are likely to have consisted chiefly of minor matters. In any event it would be erroneous to infer any resemblance with the interior Miwok from the connection in origin demonstrated by speech. Culturally the Coast and Lake Miwok were tributaries of the Pomo, not of their own Valley and Sierra kinsmen.

DISCOVERY BY DRAKE.

The Coast Miwok are the third body of California Indians to have been discovered by white men and the first with whom English-speaking people came in contact. Thirty-seven years after Cabrillo sailed up the Santa Barbara Channel, in 1579, Francis Drake spent five weeks in a bay on the California coast repairing his little "Golden Hind," and entered into close touch with the natives. San Francisco Bay was for a time believed the scene of this experience, but opinion has now settled in favor of a lagoon inside of Point Reyes, christened Drake's Bay in consequence.

NATIVE CUSTOMS IN 1579.

The principal narrative that has survived of Drake's circumnavigation is surprisingly detailed in its account of the inhabitants of "Nova Albion." The passage is a somewhat prolix mixture of narration and depiction, and, as it has been reprinted several times, need not be recited in full; but some quotation and commentary on the native customs mentioned may be worth while. It can be said that in general the culture described agrees very closely with that existing among the Pomo and their neighbors in the past century.

The dwellings were the typical semisubterranean structures of north central California:

"Their Houses, which are dug round into the Earth, and have from the Surface of the ground, Poles of Wood set up and joined together at the top like a spired Steeple, which being covered with Earth, no Water can enter, and are very warm, the Door being also the Chimney to let out the Smoak, which are made slopous like the Scuttle of a Ship: Their Beds are on the hard Ground strewed with Rushes, with a Fire in the midst round which they lye, and the roof being low round and close, gives a very great Reflection of Heat to their Bodies."

Dress accords equally well: "The Men generally go naked, but the Women combing out Bulrushes, make with them a loose Garment, which ty'd round their middle, hangs down about their Hipps: And hides what Nature would have concealed: They wear likewise about their Shoulders a Deer skin with the Hair thereon." "The Common People, almost naked, whose long Hair tied up in a Bunch behind, was stuck with Plumes of Feathers, but in the forepart only one Feather like an Hord." The "King" had "on his Head a Knit work Cawl" (the net cap of central California), "wrought somewhat like a Crown, and on his Shoulders a Coat of Rabbet Skins reaching to his Waste"—the usual woven blanket of fur. Even the net cap filled with eagle down that the Yuki, Pomo, and other tribes wore until recently seems to be described: "Cawls with Feathers, covered with a Down growing on an herb, exceeding any other Down for Fineness."

Absolutely typical Pomo basketry of the ornate type can be recognized: "Their Baskets are made of Rushes like a deep boat, and so well wrought as to hold Water. They hang pieces of Pearl shells" (haliotis), "and sometimes Links of these Chains" (disk beads) "on the Brims, to signify they were only used in the Worship of their Gods: they are wrought with matted down of red Feathers" (of the woodpecker's scalp).

The money of central California is also unmistakable, although the shell was taken to be bone, and the half mediaeval imagination of the English enacted sumptuary regulations of which the Indians were certainly ignorant. "The Chains seemed of Bone, the Links being in one chain was almost innumerable, and worn by very few, who are stinted in their Number, some to ten, twelve, or twenty, as they exceed in Chains, are therefore accounted more honourable." This is only one of several passages which reveal a curiously naive blending of the most accurate objective description with far-fetched interpretation. All the references to the King, his Guard, the Sceptre or Mace Royal, the Crowns, and the like, are of course fancies; but as soon as the objects themselves are pictured or the King's actions narrated, aboriginal California reappears in its most pungent flavor. Thus: "Their chief Speaker wearied himself, and them with a long Oration, using such violent Gestures, and so strong a Voice, and speaking so fast that he was quite out of Breath. Having done, all the rest bowed their Bodies very low and reverently to the Ground, crying Oh." And again: "Sent two Ambassadors before, to tell the General their Hioh, or King, was coming; one of them in delivering his Message spake low, which the other repeated Verbatim with a loud Voice, wherein they continued about half an Hour." And later: "After Silence, he who carried the Sceptre, prompted by another assign'd by the King, repeated loudly what the other spake low, their Oration lasting half an hour, at the close whereof they uttered a common Amen, in Approbation thereof."

The "Bunch of Feathers, like those of a black Crow, neatly placed on a String and gathered into a round Bundle, exactly cut, equal in length," tallies closely with Pomo and Maidu specimens used in the *Kuksu* ceremonies.

"Their Bows and Arrows (which are their only Weapons, and almost all their Wealth) they use very skilfully, yet without much Execution, they being fitter for Children than Men" (which would be an exact description from the point of view of the powerful English archer) ; "though they are usually so strong, that one of them could easily carry that a Mile together without Pain, which two or three Englishmen there could hardly bear" (not a remarkable feat for a people whose only accustomed transport was on their backs). "They run very swiftly and long, and seldom go any other Pace: if they see a Fish so near Shoar as to reach the Place without swimming, they seldom miss it." Diving for fish in the ocean has not been reported for any Californians, but several tribes are said to have taken salmon by hand in pools of considerable depth.

Only the "canoe," in which one man put out to meet the ship and in which others subsequently appear to have paddled when the English boats "could row no way, but they would follow them," presents a discrepancy. There is no authentic record of true canoes on the whole coast from near Cape Mendocino to the vicinity of San Luis Obispo. Either custom changed after Drake's day or his "canoe" is a loose term for the tule balsa, which was often boat shaped, with raised sides, especially when intended for navigation.

There is no doubt that, like Cabrillo among the Chumash, Drake was received with marked kindliness. Only the extreme veneration accorded him is difficult to understand. The simplest explanation is that the Indians regarded the whites as the returned dead. Such a belief would account for their repeated wailing and self-laceration, as well as the burned "sacrifice" of feathers.

THE PROBLEM OF IDENTIFICATION.

The evidence on the final test—speech—is too scant to be conclusive, but is at least favorable to the interpretation of Drake's friends having been Coast Miwok. The herb "Tobah" which was presented in little baskets is, of course, tobacco, and the "Root called Patah (whereof they make Bread, and eat it either Raw or Baked)" refers to the *Brodiaea* and other lily bulbs consumed in quantities by all Californians. The word, however, stands for "potato," as "Tobah" does for "tobacco." It is to be noted that the narrative does not specify who called the plants thus. Three interjections are mentioned: "Gnah," when the natives wished their visitors to continue singing; "Oh I," uttered when the English read their prayers; and "Oh," at the conclusion of their own speaker's oration. The last two find some reflection in the exclamations *o*, *yo*, or *iyo*, commonly used to-day by the Coast Miwok and Pomo as evidences of public approval. The only real word mentioned in such a way as to indicate that it was native is "Hioh," King. If this was pronounced "hayo" or "haio," with the so-called long sound of English "i," it has a fair parallel in Coast Miwok *hoipa*, "chief," and a closer one in Sierra Miwok *haiapo*.

Documentary evidence has recently led to the theory that Drake's landing occurred some 10 degrees of latitude farther north than has generally been believed. The question thus raised is for historians and geographers to solve. Should their views be favorable to the new opinion, it would follow that an attempt would have to be made to fit Drake's Indian descriptions to the customs prevalent farther north. Whether this could be accomplished with equal success seems very doubtful. The Pomo-like baskets alone present an almost insuperable obstacle. If Drake's occupation of a more northerly portion of the coast is confirmed on other grounds, the interpretation of his voyage that will therefore almost necessarily follow is that he touched at two points, and that the native culture noted by his men in the south was, in the condensed narratives that have been preserved, attributed to the inhabitants of the more northerly harbor. A theory of the prevalence of a perfectly characteristic central Californian culture in the region of Cape Flattery only two centuries before white men came permanently into both districts can not possibly be entertained, in whole or in part.

The ethnologist thus can only conclude that Drake summered on some piece of the coast not many miles north of San Francisco, and probably in the lagoon to which his name now attaches. He is assured that the recent native culture in this stretch existed in substantially the same form more than 300 years ago, and he has tolerable reason to believe that the Indians with whom the great explorer mingled were the direct ancestors of the Coast Miwok.

CHAPTER 19.

THE SHASTAN GROUP.

SHASTAN GROUPS.

RECOGNITION.

The six Shastan languages are, in the light of present knowledge, the northernmost members of the scattered family designated as Hokan. As a group they are also one of the most divergent subdivisions of the family. A tendency to change and specialization has penetrated even within the group, nearly all of whose members are so different from one another that some analysis is required before their kinship is perceptible.

On older ethnological maps only two languages appear in place of the half dozen now recognized: the Sastean and the Palaihnihan. The one is the Shasta, the other the Achomawi, but to the former were attributed territories subsequently discovered to have held three other idioms, while under Palaihnihan Atsugewi had been merged into Achomawi. The reason for the long ignoring of the three languages adjacent to the Shasta is simple: no vocabularies were recorded, the tribes being numerically insignificant, and in one case on the verge of extinction when the white man came to northern California. Now they have dwindled so far—in fact, to all practical purposes perished—that when we are hungry for any bits of information that would help to untangle the obscure history of these remnants of what may once have been greater peoples, we must content ourselves with brief, broken vocabularies and some general statements about their speakers obtained from the neighboring nations.

For the long hiding of the identity of the Atsugewi under that of the Achomawi no such valid reason exists, since the Atsugewi people survive to-day to the number of several hundred. Nor was a similarity of the two tongues the cause of the fault. Kindred, indeed, they are, in the sense and measure that French and Spanish are related; but they are also at least as different. Idioms in which *l* corresponds to n, w to p, p to k, and m to r, are not so similar that they are confounded by those interested in them. In fact, a bare third of the more usual stem words seem to the unaided ear or eye to be common to Achomawi and Atsugewi; and on the pioneer student's basis of overlooking trifles, there would have been almost as much justification for separating Atsugewi from Achomawi and erecting it into a separate family as for keeping Achomawi and Shasta apart, as ethnologists did for half a century. What lay at the bottom of this inconsistence was that the Atsugewi live in a region topographically tributary to the larger Achomawi habitat; that the two tribes were in close association and friendly; and that they followed very similar customs. No one troubled to make a speech record, native statements minimized the difference, and the situation was conveniently simplified, as compared with what a little inquiry would have revealed as being true.

Substantially, the Shastan habitat falls into two nearly equal halves—a western, the old " Sastean," in Klamath drainage, and an eastern, the former "Palaihnihan," in the drainage of the Pit. As the two systems of waters reach the ocean nearly at the Oregon line and at San Francisco, respectively, the outlook and connections of the two areas were obviously far from identical.

THE " SASTEAN " DIVISION.

The overwhelming body of people in the eastern or " Sastean " half were the Shasta proper or Shastika, on the Klamath River and its tributaries above the Karok and below the Klamath-Modoc. They ran over, also, into the Rogue River headwaters in Oregon.

Fairly close to them in speech, in fact clearly a later offshoot of the Shasta themselves and not one of the original divergent branches of the general Shastan trunk, were the Okwanuchu, outside the drainage area of the Klamath and in that of the great central valley of California. They held the heads of the Sacramento and McCloud.

At the source of Salmon River, an affluent of the Klamath, and of New River, tributary of the Trinity, which is also an affluent of the Klamath, was the little nation which in default of a known native name has come to be called the New River Shasta.

The third of these decayed Shastan groups, the most divergent, and the earliest to perish completely, were the Konomihu, on the middle course of Salmon River.

POSSIBLE CONNECTIONS WITH NONSHASTAN GROUPS.

It is not without significance that in the same region was another and distantly allied Hokan, though non-Shastan, tribe that survived only in minute proportions at the time of discovery: the Chimariko. Crowded against each other and into the deep canyons of a jagged country, the coexistence of these three fragments is certainly not without historical significance, which the imagination can sense though an ever-lost knowledge forbids it to penetrate.

In fact, another Hokan division, the Karok, also lived adjacent, so that five groups of the same ultimate origin jostled each other in this rugged region: the perished New River Shasta, Konomihu, and Chimariko, wedged in between the surviving and more broadly spread Karok and Shasta. It is quite possible that when comparison of all the Hokan languages shall have progressed farther, these five idioms may appear to form a single larger group or subfamily, and that even the few bits of knowledge available concerning several of them will suffice to indicate a new arrangement for the group: Konomihu might prove to have its nearest congener in Karok, and New River in Chimariko, rather than both in Shasta, for all that it is possible to judge to-day. Or such a classification might prove the three little peoples the remnant of one Hokan wave or layer that was later almost submerged by another that brought Karok and Shasta into the vicinity; or the Karok may be the representatives of one stream, the four others of a separate one; or still different affiliations and consequent conclusions as to origin and movements may be imagined. It is useless to speculate at the present time when only a small part even of the scanty recorded material on the several languages has found its way into print.

The situation is one of those not infrequently arising in which the philologist, and only he, can come to the ethnologist's or historian's rescue. A dozen randomly preserved facts from the history or civilization of a nation are almost certain to be so disconnected as to allow only of the most general or doubtful inferences; the same number of words, if only they and their meanings are carefully written down, may, if there are more fully known cognate tongues, suffice to determine with reasonable assurance the provenience and the main outlines of the national existence of a lost people. The student of history who permits the difference of material and technique of the sister science philology to lead him into the lax convenience of disregarding it as something alien and useless, withdraws his hand from one of the most productive tools within his reach—on occasion his only serviceable instrument.

Bearing on the jostling of the three perished and two larger but divergent Hokan peoples in this congested section of California, and the probability that time has wrought concentrated even if slow changes in the ethnic conditions of the area, is the fact that it is in this vicinity that four great stocks meet and touch: the Athabascans, as represented by the Hupa and other members of their Pacific coast branch; the Algonkins, in the shape of their most westerly branch, the Yurok and Wiyot; the Penutians, of whom the Wintun are the most northerly, at any rate in California; and the

Hokan family, of whose many far-stretched divisions along the
Pacific coast from Tehuantepec up, our very Shastans are the extreme northern representatives.   Again, a present interpretation in
detail would be pure speculation, tempting though it is to undertake;
but it is clear that this extraordinary agglomeration not only has a
meaning but that it bears a significance which may some day carry
us back into remote periods.

THE " PALAIHNIHAN " DIVISION.

The eastern or "Palaihnihan" branch of the Shastan complex
comprises the before-mentioned Achomawi and Atsugewi, one occupying the larger part of the valley of Pit River, and the other the
remainder.   The Pit joins the Sacramento and McCloud; in fact has
a much longer course and more extensive catchment basin, and
carries more water, so that it must properly be regarded as the real
head of the entire Sacramento River system.   The Okwanuchu on the
McCloud are therefore in the same drainage as the Achomawi-
Atsugewi.   But their speech indicates their primary affinity with the
Shasta; and they must accordingly be regarded as an offshoot from
the latter, which has drifted or been crowded over the watershed.

The New River Shasta.

Of the three minor Shastan tribes the New River people were perhaps rather nearest to the major group in speech, although at that
their tongue as a whole must have been unintelligible to the Shasta
proper.

Their designation is somewhat of a misnomer.   They held only
the upper waters of the torrent known as New River; from the forks
down the stream was Chimariko.   (Fig. 8.)   The larger part of their
habitat was the area of the upper Salmon, both forks of which they
occupied to within half a dozen miles of the junction.   Both these
tracts are inconceivably rugged; except along the tops of the innumerable ridges, it is doubtful if there is a single 5-acre patch of
level land in the whole ownings of the tribe.   The streams carry
water the year around, and in winter rage in volume; but they rush
in twisting beds of rocks.   The entire territory lies high; and the
divide between New and Salmon Rivers is snow-covered the larger
part of the year.   It was a craggy home that these people called their
own.

There must have been deer, salmon, and acorns in tolerable abundance, if little else; but the population was sparse.   In 60 years the
tribe melted away without a survivor, leaving only a fragmentary
vocabulary and conjectures as to their mode of life.   There could not
have been more than two or three hundred souls when the American
came in 1850; and there may not have been so many.

The Hupa seem to have called them Amutahwe. This would make a convenient designation for them if "New River Shasta" were not already in use. Djalitasum is probably not their Chimariko name, but the Chimariko appellation of New River, probably from the settlement at its mouth.

THE KONOMIHU.

The Konomihu are the most divergent of the marginal Shastan tribes. In fact, it is still questionable whether their speech is more properly a highly specialized aberration of Shasta or of an ancient and independent but moribund branch of Hokan from which Karok and Chimariko are descended together with Shasta.

The principal Konomihu village—apparently called Shamnam by the Karok—was between the forks of Salmon River in Siskiyou County, on the right side of the south branch just above the junction. They owned some 7 miles up the south fork, 5 up the north, and 4 down the main river, where the Karok mention Hashuruk. This may mean that the Konomihu maintained settlements at these points, in which case their hunting claims are likely to have extended 2 or 3 miles farther. But their territory was exceedingly restricted at best, and devoid of rich or even tracts. Below them on the Salmon were the Karok; above, the New River Shasta. These two tribes entirely shut them off from the outside world, so far as the map shows; but they maintained relations and intermarried with the Shasta proper. (Pl. 1; Fig. 8.)

Salmon River was mined over in the early fifties, and the industry is still not defunct. This usually meant trouble between Indians and whites, and helps to account for the total disappearance of the Konomihu. But their population must have been very small when the American came, else they would have made more of an impress.

The Salmon River Indian population of to-day is Karok, and mostly mixed blood, much of it heavily diluted. It is all drawn in in the train of the white man.

Konomihu is their own name. The Chimariko call them Hunomichhu, which sounds like a variant of the same word, but might be from Chimariko hunoi-da, "north." The Karok group them and the New River Shasta together as Mashu-arara, "Salmon-river people."

Konomihu customs were like those of the Shasta, not of the Karok. They wore fringed and painted buckskin clothes, including leggins. Their carrying receptacle was of skin, and water vessels were of the same materials. They made few or no baskets; such as they had, they got from the Karok. Their creator was the coyote. These are all specific traits of the Shasta, and mark this little people off sharply from the nearer Karok.

The house was a conical lean-to of bark, slightly excavated. This is a much inferior structure to the Shasta one, which in turn is a sort of imitation of the Karok house. The type of sweat house is unfortunately not known. There was no dance house. The Karok dances were not made by the Konomihu. This might be anticipated, since the whole character of these dances demands wealth, which this poor little group of mountaineers was not likely to possess.

They did get some dentalia along with their baskets from the rich people of the Klamath, though what they could offer in exchange except the furs and deerskin clothing which they traded to the Shasta for disk-bead money would be difficult to conjecture. Elk-horn spoons and steatite dishes of Karok type were used by the Konomihu; where they were manufactured is uncertain.

The dead were buried.

Fish are said to have been taken only or chiefly with spears. The rapid, tumbling streams would afford more frequent opportunity for the use of the harpoon than of nets. Acorns, the statement goes, were crushed in wooden mortars; which if true is quite unexampled for this part of California.

THE OKWANUCHU.

The Okwanuchu held the upper Sacramento from about the vicinity of Salt and Boulder Creeks to the headwaters; also the McCloud River and Squaw Creek from about their junction up; in other words, the heads of the streams draining south from the giant Mount Shasta. The upper waters of the McCloud were probably not permanently settled; whether Okwanuchu or Acho-mawi had the better fortified ancient hunting rights there is not certain; the line on the map makes no pretense as to proved exactness. The entire Okwanuchu habitat is a mountain region, cut and broken, but not as rugged as some areas in the northern coast ranges; and very heavily timbered—as usual in California, with conifers.

The dialect is peculiar. Many words are practically pure Shasta; others are distorted to the very verge of recognizability, or utterly different.

It is not known whether Okwanuchu is their own name or what the Shasta called them. The Achomawi and Atsugewi knew them as Ikusadewi, or Yeti, from Yet, Mount Shasta.

There may have been a few dozen or two or three hundred Okwanuchu two generations ago; not more. There is not one now. There are Indians on the upper Sacramento and McCloud to-day; but they are Wintun, who have come in with the American, and their current name, "Shastas," means nothing more than that they live in Shasta County or near Mount Shasta.

CHAPTER 20.

THE SHASTA.

DESIGNATION.

The origin of the name Shasta, made famous by the great extinct volcano to which it now attaches, is veiled in doubt and obscurity. It seems most likely to have been the appellation of a person, a chief of some consequence, called Sasti.

Besides the now standardized form of their name, the Shasta have been known under the appellation Saste, Shasty, and Shastika. The latter contains the native nominative suffix. The Achomawi and Atsugewi call them Sastidji, which seems to be a native coinage from the name given by the whites. The Achomawi also employ Nomki-dji, which appears to be a similar formation from a Wintun root, and Ekpimi, which may be a native term but denotive of a locality. The nearer Wintun say Waikenmuk, which has reference to their northerly location. The Karok call the Shasta language Tishraw-ara-hi; the group itself they designate as Tishraw-arara, the branches on Salmon River as Mashuh-arara. The Takelma in Oregon know the Shasta as Wulh or " enemies."

HABITAT AND DIVISIONS.

The Shasta held the Klamath River between the Karok and the Lutuamian Klamath and Modoc; to be specific, from a point between Indian and Thompson Creeks to a spot a few miles above the mouth of Fall Creek. They occupied also the areas drained by two considerable southern tributaries of the Klamath, Scott River and Shasta River. Their limits in this direction were formed by the watershed that separates from the Sacramento, Trinity, and Salmon. Eastward, their boundary was also marked by drainage; roughly, it ran north from Mount Shasta to Mount Pitt in Oregon. Finally, Shasta territory comprised a tract on the north side of the Siskiyous, in Oregon, on the affluents of Rogue River known as Stewart River and Little Butte Creek.

This habitat must be described as mountainous. The plateau which forms its base is from 2,000 to 4,000 feet above the sea, with peaks and ridges rising well up into the snow line during much the greater part of the year. The food supply is not particularly favorable. Oaks begin to approach their northern and eastern limit, and are less numerous than down the Klamath and in the Sacramento drainage system. The Klamath is but little smaller than among the Yurok and Karok. In considerable part it is bordered by little strips of valley, whereas among the lower peoples it is so confined in its canyon as to afford few spaces for towns except narrow sites on old river terraces. The result is that the Shasta traveled mostly on foot, the Yurok by boat.

The Shasta territory falls into four natural drainage areas of about equal size. The people within each tract were marked off by certain peculiarities of dialect and custom. There is no precise record of these distinctions, but they do not seem to have been considerable. The Rogue River division was called Kahosadi; that on the Klamath, Kammatwa or Wiruhikwairuk'a. The Scott Valley people were the Iruaitsu; those of Shasta Valley, the Ahotireitsu. The term "Kikatsik" sometimes refers to the Scott and Shasta Valley groups combined, sometimes to the former alone.

The people of each district were thrown by circumstances into closer internal association. Each group looked up to the richest man within its confines as the one most to be respected. There was little that could be called governmental unity within the groups.

The known Kammatwa settlements were, in order up the Klamath, and always on its sunny northern side unless the contrary is specified: Chitatowoki, Ututsu, Asouru, Sumai, Arahi (south side), Harokwi, Kwasuk (south side), Aika, Umtahawa, Itiwukha, Ishui, Awa, Waukaiwa, Opshiruk, Ishumpi, Okwayig, Eras (south side), Asurahawa (south side), Kutsastsus.

Among the Iruaitsu, Orowichaira and Itayah are known.

Ahotireitsu towns were Ihiweah, Kusta, Ikahig, Asta, Ahawaiwig.

The Scott and Shasta Valley divisions, or villages within them, were sometimes in embittered feud.

It has been thought that the position of the Shasta with reference to the minor Shastan fragments bordering them on the south might indicate that their drift had been from the north across the Siskiyous toward a submersion of these more ancient Californian relatives of theirs. But the revelation of their affinity to the great Hokan family negates this theory, since it makes the Shasta proper the most northerly member of the wider group to which they belong, and their Oregonian subdivision on Rogue River the extreme outpost of the family. Whatever minor and more recent fluctuations the Shasta may have been subject to, it therefore seems impossible to avoid the conclusion that in all probability their general movement in the past has been from the south northward. The particular shiftings of all the northern Hokans, the Karok and Chimariko and Yana as well as the six Shastan groups, with reference to the family as a whole, to each other and to alien tribes, give every indication, on the ground of topographic as well as linguistic relations, of having been intricate.

TRADE.

There was considerable trade down the Klamath with the Karok, and possibly through their territory. Dentalia, salt or seaweed, baskets of all kinds, tan-oak acorns, and canoes were the articles that came to the Shasta. In return they gave obsidian, deerskins, and sugar-pine nuts. From the Wintun to the south the Shasta had less that they could get. They did, however, receive acorns, and gave for them the same goods which they traded to the Karok, plus some of the dentalia which they themselves purchased. There was considerable intercourse with their own kinsmen and the Athabascans on Rogue River. Oaks become scarce or cease near the northern line of California, and any surplus of acorn flour that the Shasta possessed found ready takers among these Oregonian people. In return a stream of dentalia—which came, of course, ultimately from the same source on the far northern coast as those which traveled up the Klamath—flowed up Rogue River into Shasta possession. With the Modoc and Klamath Lake peoples on the head waters of the Klamath the Shasta traded comparatively little.

POPULATION.

The numbers of the Shasta were sparse. A Government field census in 1851 yielded 24 towns on the Klamath, 7 on the Scott, and 19 on the Shasta River, or 50 settlements of an estimated average population of 60. This figure is too high, however, since many villages comprised only two or three houses. Even the populous Yurok averaged only 45 souls to a town. If we allow the Shasta 40, their total is 2,000. If this figure is posited for the California Shasta alone, exclusive of those on Rogue River, it is likely to be a full allowance.

For to-day there are no reliable statistics; but the reduction since 1850 has been heavy, even for California. The 1910 census names 255; but as Shasta has become the designation of any Shasta County Indian, or any native of the vicinity of the peak, and the Indians have largely accepted this terminology, the figure has no ethnic meaning. Nearly all of the most northerly Wintun pass as " Shastas."

The number of survivors to whom the true tribal epithet applies is scarcely likely to be in excess of 100, if indeed it reaches that figure.

CULTURE.

Shasta civilization is a pallid, simplified copy of that of the Yurok and Karok, as befits a poorer people of more easily contented aspi-

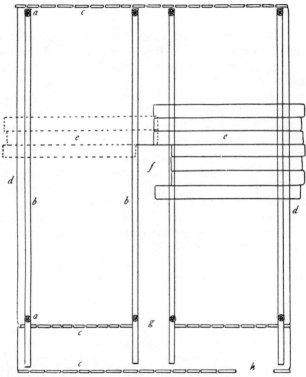

FIG. 23.—Plan of Shasta house. *a*, Posts; *b*, plate logs; *c*, vertical planks of end walls; *d*, low side walls of earth lined with bark; *e*, roof planks; *f*, fireplace and smoke hole; *g*, inner, *h*, outer door; wood room to left of doors. (After Dixon.)

rations. There are some evidences of eastern influences from the Columbia River and Great Basin region, but less than among the Achomawi and far fewer than the Modoc evince. In many features there is an approach to the customs typical of central California: not to the complex institutions of the Sacramento Valley, but to the cultural background of the peripheral hill tribes such as the Yana, the mountain Maidu, the southern Athabascans, and the adjacent Wintun.

In short, the Shasta constituted a fringe of both the northwestern and the central civilizations of California, with more leanings toward the former. They displayed national peculiarities, of course; but these usually take the aspect of modifications rather than elaborations.

HOUSES.

The house is a case in point. It is essentially the Yurok board house with many of its most distinctive traits retained; but altered also in the direction of simplicity of construction. The ridge pole is double, but the roof comes to a single crest, as in the Yurok poor man's house. The ridge poles as well as side plates rest on posts, as in the central Californian dwelling. The Yurok practice of laying them into notches in the end walls argues heavier planking and a

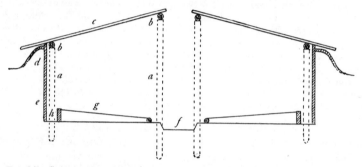

FIG. 24.—Cross section of Shasta house. *a*, Posts; *b*, plate logs; *c*, roof planks; *d*, side walls of earth, lined with, *e*, bark; *f*, fireplace pot; *g*, bed of pine needles; *h*, storage space. (After Dixon.)

more painstaking workmanship in spite of its theoretical structural inferiority. The Shasta dig out the whole interior, adding a small shallow pit for the fireplace. Thus the Yurok distinction between the deep central sitting and sleeping place around the fire and the elevated storage shelf surrounding it is lost. Evidently the Shasta had less to store. Their house also had no real side walls. Earth was piled up to reach the eaves, and this lined interiorly with slabs of cedar bark. Even the poorest Yurok in the degenerate days of the present would think he had sunk below decency if he introduced mere bark into any part of his home. The door was made by omitting the lower half of one of the boards in the end wall and hanging in a mat—a much simpler proceeding than the northwestern one of carving a round hole in a 4-inch plank and providing a wooden slide panel. The four roof rafters appear to have been logs—a central Californian habit. The true northwesterners hewed theirs out into beams set on edge. (Figs. 23, 24.)

The Yurok entrance passage or wood room was retained by the Shasta; but it was essentially a porch outside the house, and its entrance was not closed by any door.

The Shasta lived in their permanent houses only part of the year. The summer camp was a roofless windbreak of brush.

There was a small menstrual lodge.

The sweat house, literally "large house," was the man's sleeping place in winter. It does not seem to have been a dance house like the round "sweat house" of the central Californians, but, on the other hand, was resorted to for gambling, which no Yurok would have done, and for ordinary assemblages.

The plan of this "large house" was part central and part northwestern in character. The size, up to 30 and 40 feet in length, was central; the rectangular shape, northwestern. The roof was of planks covered with pine needles and earth—clearly a compromise between two independent motives, since rough poles will answer as well as boards to support a layer of dirt, while a good plank roof needs no earth finish. A center post, connected with one at each end by the ridge pole and holding up a roof that slopes but slightly, are Yurok and Karok features. The door was close to the middle of one of the ends; it was cut in a circle through a plank and closed by a wooden slide, as in the northwestern living house. A second opening was in the roof, as in the Sacramento Valley. The floor was either of packed earth, as in the latter region, or of split lumber, as lower on the Klamath.

It is clear that this Shasta "large house" is not a survival of an undifferentiated form from which the Yurok and Maidu types of sweat houses have gradually been elaborated. One can not have seen the two latter and know the intimacy of religious associations with each, and be aware of the regularity with which each of their features recurs among tribe after tribe, without being firmly impressed with the conviction that the Shasta structure is a hybrid makeshift, the hesitating product of a people who, historically speaking, did not know their own minds.

Even the function of this edifice was vague. When a Shasta really wanted to sweat he did not enter the "large house" which he had helped his headman to build, but crawled into a sweat lodge of Plains type, a small hemisphere of pine bark and skins thrown over a few bent willows; unfortunately, it is not reported whether he smoked or steamed himself in this. With neither dances nor sweating taking place in the "large house," the most specific uses of this structure, by either central or northwestern standards, were lost.

MANUFACTURED OBJECTS.

Among utensils identical with those of the Karok, or closely similar, the following may be mentioned: Pipes with stone bowls; spoons, though these were often of wood in place of elk horn, and simple in decoration; acorn mush paddles, also with rudimentary carving; acorn meal brushes; cradles, some of which approach the shallower northern Wintun form; probably bows; ring-and-pin games of salmon vertebræ; and the deer-hoof rattle of the Tolowa and Wailaki. The lack of the wooden clapper and cocoon rattle is also shared by the Shasta and Karok. The pestle evinces only occasionally an approach to the ringing of the northwest, and that at the tip in place of two-thirds of the way to the butt; and it is short and inclined to be asymmetrical.

An ingenious device was followed in boring pipes. Sticks of a certain hard kind were stood in a little salmon oil, which was drawn up by the softer core. After one end of this had been picked out with a bone point, a grub from a piece of dry salmon was pushed into the excavation, and confined with a daub of pitch. By spring the prisoner had either died or eaten his way out along the oil-soaked pith to the other end.

The Klamath is fairly favorable for navigation in Shasta territory. Yurok redwood canoes were occasionally bought from the Karok, and now and then rough imitations were made at home out of sugar-pine logs.

The stone mortars which are found in their land are never used by the Shasta, who, like all northern Californians, pound in a basketry hopper set on a slab.

String was either of iris or *Apocynum* fibers.

BASKETRY.

Shasta basketry has disappeared. The reduction and breaking up of the stock may account in some measure for the perishing of this art. It is, however, the native industry which among other tribes is usually retained after all others have vanished. It is therefore difficult to understand why basket making should have gone out of use so completely among the Shasta, except on the suspicion of the correctness of their own statements to the effect that they always depended in considerable measure on trade with the neighboring Karok for their supplies of woven vessels. Even this relation of dependence is an anomaly in California.

Such ware as the Shasta manufactured was entirely of Yurok and Karok type. The materials, technique, patterns, shapes, and uses were the same. Even such pattern names as have been recorded show approximation to those of the Karok.

Besides the usual cone-shaped basket, the Shasta made another carrying receptacle of rawhide on a wooden frame, they say. The seeds struck into this were beaten with an implement whose network was also of skin. Taken in connection with the buckskin clothing, there is here undoubted evidence of an eastern influence upon the Shasta.

Dentalium shells were traded from the Karok and the Rogue River Athabascans of California; they seem to have been measured and rated in the same way, but had a higher purchasing power. Scarlet woodpecker scalps also served as currency; but those of the large bird possessed only twice the value of the smaller crests, whereas among the Yurok the ratio was six to one. The central Californian disk bead of hard clamshell was less prized than dentalia; its measure was a long fathom, drooping to the navel.

CLOTHING.

Clothing was the same as that worn lower down the Klamath, with the addition of some elements that must be ascribed to eastern influences. Women's costume was identical with that of the Karok, except that in some instances the braided front-apron was replaced by a buckskin, and that occasionally a rude unsleeved shirt or gown of deerskin was added to the two-piece skirt.

The men's costume comprised a similar shirt with short sleeves, leggings, and moccasins, all of buckskin. This is the description which the Shasta themselves give of their ancient clothing, but it is doubtful on the one hand how far the account may refer to more recent conditions obtaining since the presence of the whites caused a greater intermixture of diverse tribes and, on the other hand, how far this dress may have been truly Shasta but worn only on special occasions. The buckskin shirt is said to have varied from a true garment to nothing more than a deerskin. The leggings extended from ankle to hip and were worn with the breechclout. The Hupa knew leggings, but wore them only for hunting deer in the snow-covered mountains, and did not extend them beyond the knee. On the other hand, a full-length legging is reported from the Achomawi, a people related in origin to the Shasta, similar to them in degree of culture, and virtually their neighbors on the east. The moccasin was sewed with a single straight seam up the front and carried a heavy sole of elk or bear skin. For winter wear the inner sole was cut out and the foot rested upon the fur side of the bearskin. Sometimes the winter moccasin was made large enough to allow the foot to be wrapped with squirrel skin, wild-cat fur, or moss. This stuffing of the shoe has parallels among the Modoc and Achomawi. At the same time the soled moccasin is not Californian. It is accordingly a question whether its use by the Shasta is to be ascribed to extra-Californian influences from the north or east or is to be set down merely as a modern improvement. In any event it is unlikely that the Shasta habitually wore either the moccasin or the legging. Both articles were probably reserved for travel, especially in winter.

Men allowed their hair to grow long. It either hung loose or was gathered on top of the head by means of a bone pin, according to occasion.

Women wore their hair in two wrapped clubs in front of each shoulder—in Yurok style.

The villages in Shasta Valley used the central Californian head net; the other divisions did not. This may be an incident of the recent introduction of *Kuksu* dance costumes from the Sacramento Valley.

Tattooing was identical with that in vogue down the Klamath. The operator was an old woman who was paid; the instrument, a flake of obsidian. The entire chin was scratched with parallel cuts at one time, and the operation repeated after an interval, if necessary. Tattooing was in some measure a puberty rite. It was performed shortly before the girl's adolescence, and her dreams during the night following the first operation were believed to be presages of her career.

FOOD.

The acorn most esteemed by the Shasta, as apparently by most tribes who could secure it, was that of the tan oak (*Quercus densiflora*). The Shasta obtained this in quantity, however, only by trade with the groups lower down the Klamath. Of native species, preference was given to the black oak (*Quercus californica*), and next to the white (*Quercus garryana*). Black-oak acorns were treated as by the Yurok, with one exception: Leaching is said to have been done on an elevated platform of sticks covered with pine needles, on which was a layer of sand. This looks like a compromise between the usual northern method of leaching directly in the sand and the southern, and sometimes central, device of employing a basket or layer of fir leaves without sand. A step in the acorn preparation process that has often been overlooked is the removal of the membrane covering the kernel. The Shasta rubbed this off by hand, which was probably the procedure elsewhere also. A surplus of black-oak acorn-meal dough was often dried for storage or trade.

The treatment of white-oak acorns was the same, but the mush from them was somewhat slimy and less esteemed. Live-oak acorns (*Quercus chrysolepis*) were buried in the shell in mud until they turned black. The Yurok similarly lay acorns in water for a protracted period. The Shasta ate these darkened kernels cooked whole or roasted them in ashes.

Manzanita berries were crushed for cider, as by the Wintun, Yokuts, and other tribes. Meal made from the dried and pounded berries was sometimes mixed with acorn-flour soup. Sugar-pine nuts were steamed in an earth oven, then dried and stored. After being ground they were either eaten in cakes or mixed with dry powdered salmon.

Salmon was split and lightly smoked for drying. It was kept either in thin slabs or completely pulverized. This salmon dust was stored in large, soft baskets or sacks of tule. No such pliable rush baskets have been reported from the culturally so much better preserved Karok, Yurok, or Hupa. Crushed salmon bones and crushed deer bones were similarly stored, to be made into soup in winter. Venison was hung up and smoked to dry, but bear meat was boiled first.

Salt is said to have been obtained from the Karok: seaweed is likely to have been meant.

Fish dams were built across the Klamath River at the mouths of Shasta River, Scott River, and—by the adjacent Karok—at Indian Creek. The Yurok made only two dams, and the Karok not more than three, it appears. Each of the Shasta dams was the property of one family. To the head of this family belonged all the salmon that were caught in the willow fish traps placed in the openings. Custom prescribed, however, that he should give to everyone who asked for them as many fish as could be carried away. All were also at liberty to spear at the dam.

The Shasta salmon net differs only in details from that in use by the Yurok and Karok. It is a long, flowing bag attached to the base of a triangle of poles the upper end of which is held by the fisherman who sits on the scaffolding projecting over an eddy in the stream. The chief peculiarity of the Shasta net seems to be that its frame is held in place along one side by a grapevine rope tied to the shore, and on the other side by a sliding loop that passes over a stake in the water.

The Shasta believed that the first salmon to reach them each spring was sacred from the medicine and prayer put upon it in the Yurok ceremony at the mouth of the river, and that it must therefore be allowed to pass. Any succeeding fish were caught, but none could be eaten until the first one taken had been completely dried and had been eaten by those assembled for the fishing. It has not been reported whether any further ceremony attended this regulation. The corresponding rituals among the downstream tribes are of great sanctity and their esoteric features are jealously guarded.

Dogs were carefully trained for hunting, and when proficient were kept in sheltered kennels behind the living house. A blowfly song and a grizzly bear song were sung to them, to increase their power of scent and their ability to frighten game. They were employed in driving deer into the water, into corrals with snares in the openings, and apparently through the snow.

The elk being rather too large an animal to be successfully snared, was most frequently run down in winter, the hunter following it on snowshoes and dispatching it with arrows.

If the arrows of several hunters struck the same deer, that one was reckoned as having killed it whose arrow first found the mark, whether mortal or not. Part of the flesh was always given away, but the hide and legs were retained by the slayer, for fear that if they came into other hands his luck might be lost to him through these portions being brought in contact with a woman in tabooed condition. Perhaps the risk was thought to be greater as regards those parts that were not promptly consumed. At that, it is unlikely that a hunter would have allowed any of the meat of his kill to go into a house upon the friendship of whose inmates he could not thoroughly rely.

For a year after he began to hunt a boy never ate any game of his own killing for fear of his luck leaving him permanently. From his very first quarry his entire family refrained. When the year was up the boy was whipped with his own bowstring by his father. This was evidently a minor puberty rite, since whipping with the bowstring formed an essential part of the more elaborate puberty ceremony of the Achomawi. Among the Yurok whipping with a bowstring was thought to be the only means of self-protection against a supposedly dead person who pushed his way out of the grave and who was then as invulnerable as he was destructive.

GAMES.

The Shasta play the guessing game both in its central Californian "grass" and its northwestern "many-stick" forms. It is interesting that men use the former and women the latter. Outwardly the men's game resembles the northwestern type, since it comprises 15 or 20 slender rods. As only two of these, however, one marked and one unmarked, are used at any one time, the use and manipulation of the pieces are like those of the central tribes. The men play for 14 counters, the women for 10. It is reported that these counters are not, as usual in California, in a neutral pile at the start, but that half are in possession of each contestant, as among ourselves. A man stakes his last two counters as a unit on the result of two consecutive guesses, in the second of which he must make choice from among three bundles of grass. If either guess is correct, he keeps both counters and wins his turn to play.

Dice have not been reported.

Double-ball shinny was a woman's game, as in most of California, whereas among the true northwestern tribes it was played by the men.

The hoop and dart game was known to boys, who shot with arrows at a rolling disk of pine bark.

The ring and pin game was played with salmon vertebræ. The number of bones was 12, each representing a month, and play occurred during the wane of the moon, to hasten its death during the long winter.

SOCIAL RANK.

In a sense it can be said that Shasta chieftainship was hereditary in the male line, but the implication of the designation is misleading. The chief was the head of the richest family in the district, and his succession to the "title" was only incidental to his inheritance of the family's wealth. The son is said to have succeeded only if there was no surviving brother. One family was recognized as preeminent in each of the four geographic divisions into which the Shasta are grouped.

The functions of this so-called chief were governmental only in so far as they could be exercised in relation to property. He acted as mediator in quarrels by influencing the adjustment of the payments due for injuries. If the payer was poor or embarrassed, the chief frequently advanced him the necessary compensation or even met the claim against him. The obligations accruing in this way must have had far-reaching effect in enhancing the power of the rich man. In the same way the chief avoided participation in warfare so far as possible, but became prominent as soon as terms of peace came to be discussed—that is, when monetary settlement was undertaken. This has many central Californian analogues.

Slaves were held by the Shasta as by the northwestern tribes, but were probably even less numerous than there. It is said that they were acquired in war. The northwestern slave normally entered his condition through debt.

LAW AND MARRIAGE.

Legal regulations were probably less refined, and the compensation accorded smaller, among the Shasta than among the Yurok, but the basis of equity was identical. Injuries of all sorts, from loss of property and petty theft to murder and killing in avowed warfare, were settled by payments. The blood money payable for every individual was exactly the same as the amount paid for his or her mother by her husband. This is an efficient device which might well have been the custom of the northwestern tribes, though it has not been reported from them. It is, however, possible that the Shasta were readily content with such a simple and fair solution, whereas the mercenary tendency of the Yurok and Hupa may have actuated them to attempt to secure all obtainable compensation in every case. Like the northwestern tribes, the rule of the Shasta was that a fair offer of blood money might not be declined, and that its acceptance absolutely forbade any subsequent revenge.

If vengeance was exacted on one of the blood kin of the murderer before settlement was made, the victim on each side was paid for. If the murderer or a member of his family met with a serious accident soon after the killing, this was attributed to the natural wishes and prayers of the family of the victim, who were thus given credit for having attained their desired vengeance and were as fully liable for the wound or death as if they had physically inflicted it.

Marriage was by payment or specified contract to pay, and people's social status depended upon the amounts paid by their fathers for their mothers. A rich man might buy his son a wife of high standing while he was still a small boy. Although the marriage was not consummated for many years, payment was made immediately. Should the betrothal be broken by the death of the girl or for any other reason, full repayment was of course requisite. Young men of medium wealth were assisted by their relatives in accumulating the property necessary to obtain a wife. If the amount thus gathered remained insufficient, the youth often received his wife on promise to make up the amount later. A poor man lived with his father-in-law and hunted and worked for him until considered to have liquidated his debt. It seems, however, that, as by the Yurok, such a union was not regarded a marriage in the full sense, since in case of outright purchase the husband always took his wife to his own house.

Not long after marriage the bride's relatives visited her in state at her new home, and the visit was then reciprocated by the husband's people. On each occasion the ornaments and clothing worn by the guests were presented to the hosts. This interchange of property seems to have been something in the nature of a matching of liberality, to have been conducted without bargaining or stipulation, and to have had, therefore, no direct relation to the marriage payment.

The levirate followed as a natural consequence upon the monetary basis of marriage. The wife having been paid for, her return to her kin on the death of her husband would have been equivalent to a loss of wealth to his family. For this reason she was married to a brother, or to another relative in case of there being no brothers. In the same way, if the wife should die, particularly without issue, she must be replaced by a sister or other relative. Accepting the native premises, such a substitute wife should, according to our logic, be furnished free; but the Shasta, like the Yurok, paid a small amount for her. It is stated that a widower must remarry within his wife's family unless released by them; but this can hardly have been much else than theory, since there would have been no reason for a man's buying himself a wife out of a new family when he had one available with little cost in the old.

A divorce was a reexchange of the woman and the property paid for her. For infidelity or barrenness the husband could exact divorce or a sister in his wife's place. Without such cause, he was not at liberty to demand the return of the purchase payment, although he was, of course, free to send his wife back to her family without claim, if he were sentimental enough. In no event, however, could a woman remarry whose price had not been refunded. If she went to live with a new husband it was he rather than the woman's kin who was held responsible for payment and likely to be killed if it were not forthcoming.

It would seem that adultery was considered a sort of irremediable offense, since it is said that payment was not even offered, and blood revenge taken as soon as possible. The slayer in such a case, too, paid but a nominal price for his victim. A husband who lived with his father-in-law, in other words was in debt to him for his wife, was entirely without redress in case of adultery committed against him; but possibly some claim rested with the woman's father.

The normal price paid for a woman of average standing is said to have been 15 or 20 full-sized dentalium shells, 10 to 15 strings of disk beads, and 20 to 30 woodpecker scalps, with one or more deerskins added for good measure. This is not more than a half or a third of the amount that the Yurok would consider appropriate, they paying 10 strings of medium-sized dentalia, or about 125 all told, plus other property amounting to half as much or more in value. The lower price establishes the Shasta money as more valuable and themselves as correspondingly poorer.

WAR.

War was chiefly conducted by raiding hostile villages. A preparatory dance would be held for several nights. The members of the prospective party stood in line, carrying bows or knives, and stamping one foot: Position and step are characteristic of all the dances of the northwestern tribes. Women stood at the ends of the line. They are said sometimes to have accompanied the party. That they then actually succeeded in cutting the enemy's bowstrings is more likely to be a tradition than a fact. They may have gone along in order to carry food and to cook. The warriors were elaborately painted with circular spots. They sometimes wore elk skin or rod armor similar to that of the Hupa and Yurok, and a headband or helmet of hide, such as the Hupa and Karok seem also to have known. (Pl. 18.)

BIRTH.

Customs concerned with birth are of the Yurok type. Delivery takes place in the woman's hut. The mother remains in this hut for a month. For the first five days she uses a scratching bone for her head. The father for the same period observes restrictions of the kind followed by the northwestern tribes for purification. There is nothing, however, that gives the impression of any form of the couvade; although the father, from fear of prenatal influences, hunted less and less as the time for birth approached.

Delayed delivery was remedied by songs which are clearly equivalents of the northwestern formulas. These songs are in narrative, or at least refer to myths. They are private property sold for high amounts.

For the first five days infants were steamed over baskets of water kept boiling as constantly as possible. It seems that this practice is connected with the northwestern habit of giving the child food in only nominal quantities for the first five days. The umbilical cord was either burned or carefully wrapped and secreted at a distance from habitations.

Up to the age of about 3 years children had all their hair burned off close to the head. For girls this process was continued over a stripe from the forehead to the nape until they attained adolescence.

ADOLESCENCE.

Both boys and girls had their ears pierced amid simple ceremonial observances shortly before puberty. This custom seems a weakened reflection of the corresponding Achomawi practices.

The observances for *waphi* or adolescent girls are mainly, but not wholly, of northwestern type. The girl's period of fasting and seclusion is 10 days, and each night she participates in a dance made for her. She wears a band or visor of blue-jay feathers like those used by the Karok to shield the eyes. She is forbidden to look upon fire, sun, moon, or human beings. She does not speak except perhaps to whisper to her mother. She may not wash or comb her hair, can scratch her head and eyes only with a bone, and wears moccasins continually—perhaps because the only activity besides dancing permitted her is to gather wood for the dance fire and for every house in the village. She sleeps as little as possible, with her head in a mortar basket. While in her hut she holds and occasionally shakes a deer-hoof rattle, the implement associated with this class of observances throughout the greater part of northern California.

A curious and unexplained symbolic reference to the east pervades the whole of this ceremony. The girl faces east while in her hut. She faces east while dancing. The dancers mostly look in the same direction. On the morning after the tenth night the girl's blue-jay band is very gradually removed from her eyes, being successively lifted and replaced more and more. At high noon it is at last wholly taken off and thrown toward the east. This act marks the real conclusion of the ceremony, although it is followed by the dance of war preparation.

The adolescence dance itself is conducted on a much more sumptuous scale by the Shasta than by most other tribes, evidently because it is one of their few opportunities for indulging in rhythmic ritual. It takes two principal forms, a round dance and one in which the men lock arms and rock sideways while women hold on to their belts from behind. There is also a welcoming dance to parties of visitors. The last night was one of freely tolerated license. To maintain this ceremony for 10 days, and then repeat it in full on two subsequent occasions, meanwhile feeding all visitors from other villages, entailed great expense on the *waphi's* parents.

The Shasta relate one curious belief which they formerly entertained. All dreams of an adolescent girl during her first ceremony were omens and were confessed to her mother. Should she dream of a disaster, such as a conflagration or the death of a member of the village, the impending calamity could be averted only by the family's decking her in her finery and burning her alive. This custom can hardly have had an existence outside of native opinion.

DEATH.

A person dying indoors is taken out through a hole in the roof instead of the door. If possible, interment takes place in the middle of the day. While the corpse is lying outdoors, a fire is kept burning near it, and it is moved about at short intervals. Relatives and friends wail and dance about the body with fir staves in their hands or fir branches attached to their bodies. For a man slain in war, bows, arrows, and knives are substituted for the branches. The body is rolled in skins and laid full length and on its back in the waist or shoulder deep grave with the head to the east. Friends and kindred bring small quantities of currency of which part is destroyed or placed with the body, the remainder returned to them. Sometimes the grave is undercut and the corpse put into the recess at the side and blocked in with stones before the grave is filled, to prevent depredation by bears. This practice was probably rendered necessary by the fact that some of the Shasta cemeteries were at a distance from the village, whereas the true northwestern tribes bury their dead close to the town and often in its middle. The branches worn in the dance were used to line the grave, and the staves to erect a paling around it. If a man died at a distance, he was either cremated or buried in the local graveyard. In the latter event his relatives would subsequently pay the residents for the exhumation of his bones and transportation to his ancestral cemetery.

Near relatives, or possibly only those who had come in contact with the corpse, were considered unclean and fasted and sweated for five days. The Shasta, however, make no mention of any purification formula such as the northwestern Indians deemed absolutely indispensable on the occasion.

The hair that was shortened as a sign of mourning was either burned off or cut and preserved, to be made into belts. A widower kept his hair short until he remarried. A widow, in addition, rubbed charcoal and pitch on her face and head. This disfigurement was maintained for several years, unless she married a relative of her husband at the expiration of a year. Widows, widowers, and parents who had lost a child wore a mourning belt made either of their own hair or of willow bark. The hair belt is also an Achomawi institution. The northwestern tribes use neck strings neatly braided of basket material.

SHAMANISM.

Shasta shamanism and ideas of disease and control of spirits are very similar to those obtaining among the northwestern tribes.

The shaman was almost always a woman. The power usually came by inheritance; but it is necessary to bear in mind that the natives do not seem in the least degree to have thought of the office as hereditary. The inception of the acquisition of supernatural power was invariably by dreams, and in these dreams a former ancestor who had herself been a shaman frequently or regularly appeared to the woman.

Catastrophic dreams also soon asserted themselves, and after a time swarms of yellowjackets were seen. This last type of dream was regarded as a conclusive proof of impending shamanistic power, the insects being interpreted as spirits. During this period of dreaming the woman ate no meat and avoided its sight and smell so far as possible. If she refused to take notice of her dreams or to refrain from meat, it was believed that she would inevitably fall ill, whereupon a practicing shaman being called in, the cause would be announced. A persistent refusal of the dreamer to accept the power thrust upon her by the spirits would result in her death.

About this period, also, it was customary for the prospective shaman to be addressed by a voice and to see a spirit aiming an arrow at her heart while he commanded her to sing. This occurrence might take place while the woman was at work or in the presence of her family. She at once fell down in a senseless seizure in which she remained for some time. During this period the spirit taught her his song, which she repeated faintly while appearing to moan or whine on the ground. In the evening she gradually revived and sang her song loudly, upon which the spirit told her his name and place of abode. She then called out his name, while blood repeatedly oozed from her mouth, after which she rose and danced. She was then carried 10 times around the fire, or swung over it hanging by her knees from a rope, or underwent some other treatment that the spirit had directed.

For three days and nights thereafter she danced. After this the spirit reappeared and warned her that he would shoot her with his "pain"; if she were strong enough to bear the pain in her body she was to be his friend. As the pain entered her she again fell in a catalepsy. After reviving she drew the pain out of her while dancing, and displayed it to those present. She manifested her power over it by making it disappear into her forehead, pressing it into her shoulder or ear and extracting it from the other, and so on. The dancing continued altogether for five nights from the time of the first appearance of the spirit. On the last night or two, other spirits appeared and shot her with their pains, until she might have four or five. The pains were kept in the shaman's body. Her power depended upon the number as well as the size of the pains. All shamans had at least three, which were kept in the two shoulders and in the back of the head, but some carried a larger number.

After the visit the shaman, except for 10 days of fasting, enjoyed a period of rest, until she had accumulated a considerable and apparently specified stock of ritualistic paraphernalia consisting mainly of certain skins, bird tails, feathers, baskets, and paint, usually in groups of ten. One year or several might elapse while these objects were assembled.

The first winter thereafter the novice summoned her friends for a final dance, to which one or two experienced shamans were also invited. This dance was held in the living house, not in the sweat house, as by the northwestern tribes. During the dance her spirits reappeared to her and inspected the paraphernalia which she had prepared. After three days of dancing the novice was a fully qualified shaman.

The guardian spirits were of the shape of men but smaller size. Each one inhabited a definite locality. The "pains," of which each spirit owned one, were small clear objects, pointed at each end. It was their presence in the shaman's person that made her able to discern spirits, converse with them, see pains in other people, and extract them; but it was the residence of a pain in nonshamans that caused sickness, it preying on the body and sucking the blood like a parasite. Disease and the power of curing it thus had the identical cause. It is, therefore, no wonder that the acquisition of shamanistic power was a trying ordeal.

It is notable that the Shasta called the "spirits" and the "pains" by the identical name: *aheki*. The distinctive English translations are justified only by the confusion which the use of the single native term would have caused in the presentation of the foregoing beliefs. It is possible that a similarly undifferentiated nomenclature prevailed among the northwestern tribes. All the accounts which these give of their shamanism are very difficult to understand; the "pains" and "devils" mentioned, even in the Indian idioms, seeming at one moment to be objects and in the next personalized spirits.

Stone pipes, mortars, and in some measure pestles, such as abound as relics of the past in most of California, were greatly feared by the ordinary Shasta and prized by their shamans. They were said to be *aheki*, or to indicate the proximity of the abode of an *aheki*, and to be endowed with the power of gradual locomotion over or under ground.

On the death of a shaman, the pain *aheki* returned from her body to the spirit *aheki* who had sent them into her, to be retained until the same spirits manifested themselves, in all probability, to one of her descendants. There were, however, spirits who had no affiliations with a family, or had abandoned them. Such unattached *aheki* might associate themselves with any shaman. A few of them, in fact, acquired many and influential friends in the spirit world in additon to those which their mothers and grandmothers had possessed. Such powerful shamans would sometimes convey part of their ability even to people who had not dreamed—for a sufficiently large price—by pressing one or more of their private pains into the recipient's forehead, whereupon the novice could see and hear the corresponding spirits. The course of dancing must, however, be performed by such buyers of the spiritual exactly as by natural shamans.

The Shasta shamans seem to have been unusually unreserved about their spirits. They announced the name and place of residence of their spirits not only when they first acquired them, but in approaching a patient. This is evidently part of the professional stock in trade.

To cure, the shaman sucked out a clotted mass, in order to clear the body, though she had already seen the pain inside and weakened and drawn it near the surface by her songs. The final extraction, contrary to the custom of most Californian tribes, was not by sucking. The shaman danced before the patient and suddenly, with a rush, seized the pain and pulled it out with her hand.

If the shaman broke the pain in two, the hostile shaman who for hire or from malevolence had shot it into the sufferer's body died at once. Evidently not all illness was thought to be the result of such witchcraft, and certain pains were believed to proceed from malice of their own or their owning spirit, since in many cases the shaman threw the pain back to its spirit owner, burned it, or swallowed it.

The repeatedly unsuccessful shaman met the usual fate: a justified violent death. The Shasta, however, were peculiar in compelling the doctor who had lost her patient to restore only half the fee. The legal reasoning that justified this compromise is difficult to reconcile with all that is known of the attitude of the Californian Indians toward their doctors.

A shaman who had a rattlesnake spirit cured snake bites. The cover of her pipestem and a headband which she wore were of rattlesnake skin, and around her neck were tail rattles. She painted with dust. After sucking and dancing, she reported the appearance and actions of the rattlesnake spirit, and finally his words, which chiefly related to the gifts he desired for himself and the doctor; after which the patient, or a relative, must entreat the spirit for pity.

The same procedure applied to victims of grizzly bear attacks: the bear spirit was addressed by the patient. The grizzly bear shaman, who simulated the animal while dancing, was a man, not a woman. He extracted the bear's tongue from the wound.

Women who knew songs to prevent snake bites were sent for every winter and went through all the houses of the village after the children were asleep, chanting their exorcism. It is not clear whether these women were rattlesnake shamans or had inherited or bought a self-sufficing formula such as those which answer so many of the needs of the Hupa and Yurok. At any rate, the practice is a faint vestige of the far-away Yokuts public annual rattlesnake-doctors' ceremony.

RITUAL.

The Shasta, strictly speaking, have no community dances, no worship for its own sake or the good of the world. When they dance, it is for a specific purpose, for the use of a particular individual or assemblage of individuals. They dance to prepare themselves for war, to help a girl at the crucial period of her adolescence, to acquire shamanistic power, or to cure a sick man; and there they stop. It is the dozen times iterated story of the relation of the poor highlanders to their more organized neighbors. The contrast is peculiarly striking, because the Shasta on the Klamath were close neighbors to the Karok at one of the most renowned centers of northwestern ritual, Inam at Clear Creek. The Shasta visited and watched here, but seem never to have thought of imitating.

No formal victory or scalp dance has been reported from the Shasta. This negative evidence can probably be accepted, since the lack of such a dance is typical of the northwestern culture. The " war dance " is one of incitement and preparation, or made on the occasion of a formal settlement of peace.

The earlier ghost dance reached the Shasta from the Modoc about 1872 and was passed on by them to the Karok and perhaps the Wintun. Associated with another wave of this movement seems to have been the introduction into Shasta Valley of the " big head " dance of the Sacramento Valley Kuksu system, via the Wintun on the south.

Five or its multiple ten is the only ritualistic number of the Shasta. It is not associated with the cardinal directions.

MYTH.

Shasta mythology consists of tales of magic and adventure, with an interlarding of coyote trickster stories, but without order, sequence, or more than incidental explanations of the present condition of the world.

The individual stories and episodes recounted by the Shasta are in great measure the same as those of the Achomawi and neighboring tribes; but they lack the systematized if crude cosmogony that occurs in the myths of these groups. There is no creator and hardly any version of a creation. Nor is the sharp impress of the idea of an ancient prehuman but parallel race visible as among the Karok and Yurok. The disintegration of Shasta culture in the past two generations may have aided the more rapid decay of the reflective than of the anecdotal parts of their traditions; but the qualities described must have attached to the mythology in considerable degree even before the modern break-up began.

CHAPTER 21.

THE ACHOMAWI AND ATSUGEWI.

The Achomawi.

HABITAT.

The territory of the Achomawi comprised the drainage of Pit River—an eastern affluent of the Sacramento much larger than the so-called main river—from near Montgomery Creek in Shasta County up to Goose Lake on the Oregon line; with the exception of the territory watered by three southern tributaries, Burney, Hat, and Horse or Dixie Valley Creeks, along which the Atsugewi were lodged.

Like the northwestern Californians and the Shasta, the Achomawi were a stream people. Their villages were all on Pit River itself or on the lower courses of its affluents. The back country was visited and owned, but not settled. A solid color on the map accordingly gives a one-sided impression of the relation of many Californian tribes to their habitat.

This is particularly true of the Achomawi, all of whose territory is high and comparatively barren as soon as the streams are left behind, while a large part of it, particularly to the north of Pit River, is pure waste lava.

For this reason the boundaries of Achomawi land are of little significance compared with an understanding of the narrow tracts actually dwelt in.

On the north, toward the Modoc, the Achomawi territorial limits are particularly vague and immaterial. We know merely that they hunted to Mount Shasta and Medicine Lake; but the Modoc may have gone as far or farther south in legitimate pursuits. The essential relation was that the settlements of the one people were on Lower Klamath and Rhett Lakes and Lost River, of the other on Pit River, with a great emptiness between.

The shores of Goose Lake, out of which Pit River flows, have been claimed in their entirety for the Achomawi, the Modoc, and the Northern Paiute. As there appears to be no specific mention of villages of any of the three groups as actually on the shores of the lake, the uncertainty has been compromised on the map by extending the Achomawi to it and giving the bulk of its shores to the Paiute. The mountains west of Goose Lake would seem to have formed the western boundary of the Paiute; but we do not know.

The range between the Achomawi South Fork of Pit River and the Paiute Middle and Lower Lakes can hardly have been other than a recognized limit. Still farther south and west the undrained Madeline plains and Eagle Lake Basin offer difficulty to the cartographer. The latter has been variously assigned to Achomawi, Atsugewi, Maidu, and perhaps Paiute, though no authority appears to have asserted that any of them lived on the lake drainage. The region is more similar in its character to the territory of the two northern groups than to the Maidu range; and of the two northern and allied peoples, the Atsugewi had the nearer habitations in Dixie Valley.

Our knowledge also fails to suffice for the drawing of a real line between the Achomawi and the Atsugewi, except that the former, on Pit River, held the mouths of the three streams along which, farther up, the latter lived. Beaver Creek is between Dixie Valley Creek and Hat Creek, but is specifically assigned to the Achomawi. The reason for this distribution is evidently the fact that Beaver Creek flows parallel and close to Pit River, while the other streams come in from a distance and at right angles.

On their lower Pit River range the Achomawi border on Yana, Wintun, and Okwanuchu. The stated boundary between Achomawi and Okwanuchu cuts across the headwaters of the McCloud, which may be true, but would be bad Indian custom unless the Achomawi had villages on these headwaters. The recorded line perhaps signifies nothing more than that the Okwanuchu had no villages there. At that, it is hardly conceivable that they should not have hunted on these upper courses, and the real question would seem to be whether the Okwanuchu and Achomawi avowedly shared the right of visit to the district, or whether the former owned the tract and the latter poached on it when they felt themselves strong enough.

As to Mount Shasta, there were no Achomawi near it. That they hunted to it, and did so within their rights, is likely. It was customary for great peaks to be regarded by Californian peoples as the starting points of their several boundaries.

DIVISIONS, NAMES, AND POPULATION.

We know no Pit River villages. Some 8 or 10 group names on record are given below. They refer collectively to the people of natural areas, such as valleys or drainage basins. It is needful not to apply habits of interpretation formed from acquaintance with eastern tribes to these names. There is little to show whether or not the villages in any such area felt themselves united politically; in other words, whether it would be justifiable to reckon them as tribes. Even the names appear to be geographic and not national, much as in a larger view we speak of Sudan or South American peoples. It is even doubtful whether the inhabitants of each valley used their name, except as now and then they might on occasion copy the practice of outsiders. To themselves they may have been only the people of this and that particular village. But when they thought of the inhabitants of the next basin, and particularly of those still farther away, they no doubt generally spoke of them under their generic designations.

A similar situation has been described among the Yuki. The apparent difference between these people and the Achomawi, on the one hand, and, say, the Miwok on the other, may be a reflection of a different topography, rather than of another type of political organization. Where the country falls into naturally habitable basins separated by unsettled tracts, group names spring up. Where, as among the Yurok, villages are threaded along a single stretch of river or, as with the Miwok, scattered indiscriminately over a broken but generally uniform country, all parts of which are about equally favorable to permanent location, the larger group names have less occasion to arise. It is only where we encounter definite group consciousness not based on topography but frequently transcending it, and expressed in an individual dialect and a group name, as among the shifting but solidary Yokuts divisions, that we can begin justly to speak of tribes. Everywhere else the only recognizable political unit remains the small cluster of adjacent villages recognizing the authority of the same head man. Whether the Achomawi divisions, such as the Ilmawi and Hantiwi, were such unit communities, corresponding to the Pomo political groups that have been enumerated, or comprised each several communities, there is little present means of deciding.

These are the divisions: Madehsi, lowest on Pit River, along the big bend; Achomawi, on Fall River; Ilmawi, on the south side of the Pit, opposite Fort Crook; Chumawi, in Round Valley; Atuami, in Big Valley; Hantiwi, in lower Hot Springs Valley; Astakiwi, in upper Hot Springs Valley; Hamawi, on the South Fork of Pit River.

Of the several subdivisions, the Astakiwi or Astahkewa are said to have been named after a principal village near Canby, Astake, " hot spring." The Atuami have also been recorded as the Tuhteumi and Hamefkuteli, though there is no ƒ in Achomawi or any adjacent language. All three of the supposed synonyms may in reality refer to the people of three villages rather than to the Big Valley people as a whole. The Madehsi are called Puisu or Pushush, " easterners," by the Wintun whom they adjoin; and the name Yucas or Yuki has also been recorded for them from the same source, though without specific force, since Yuki means merely " foreign " or " foe " in Wintun, and in ethnological usage has come to be restricted to the entirely distinct people in the Coast Range on the other side of the Wintun. A group known as Idjuigilumidji were called Akowigi by the Atsugewi. Itami seems to be a synonym for the Achomawi division.

On the basis of speech conditions elsewhere in California, it may be suspected that the Achomawi language was not identical from lower Pit River to Goose Lake; but nothing is on record concerning dialectic variations.

In native parlance, Achomawi is the name only of that part of the group living in the basin of Fall River. For what ethnologists call the Achomawi, the Atsugewi generic term Pomarii, which denotes all the people speaking the same language—the Hamawi, Atuami, Ilmawi, and others, as well as the Achomawi proper—would therefore have been a more appropriate designation. But Achomawi is so well rooted that a new term would cause confusion. The universal local denomination "Pit Rivers" is appropriate even if it is inelegant and without native flavor.

The Maidu call the Achomawi Kom-maidüm—that is, "snow Maidu," more literally, "snow people." The old book name Palaihnihan is said to be based on Klamath-Modoc Palaikni or P'laikni, "mountaineers," which may perhaps be taken as the specific name of the group in that Oregonian tongue. The Yuki know a few Achomawi transplanted to Round Valley reservation as Shawash, a name that is of interest only in that it evidences the southward extension of the Chinook jargon, or fragments of it, as far as northernmost California. Siwash ("sauvage") is jargon for Indian and not a Yuki or Achomawi word. The two peoples did not know of each other's existence until the Americans threw them together.

The Achomawi population in 1910 was almost 1,000, three-fourths still full blood, according to the Government's reckoning. About a tenth had drifted out of the Pit River Valley into Oregon or remained at Round Valley Reservation. The thinness of the American population over their habitat has unquestionably preserved the Achomawi in a more favorable proportion than tribes in densely settled districts; so that, instead of a tenth or a fiftieth, we may reckon their present numbers as constituting perhaps a third or more of the original population. This may be set roughly at 3,000 for the Achomawi and Atsugewi combined.

WAR AND TRADE.

The Modoc, and with them their close kinsmen the Klamath, fought the Achomawi. Their proximity to northern tribes who formerly kept slaves, and to the great intertribal market at The Dalles, made the taking of slaves from the Achomawi profitable to these Oregonians, and stimulated them, at times, to raid for booty. The Achomawi had the usual Californian point of view: a stranger would usually be killed on principle because he was a stranger, and a neighbor would be attacked when he had given grievance. But war for the fun of the game, or for gain, was foreign to their ideas, so that they would be actuated to retaliate against the Modoc only by revenge; and as they scarcely even made the attempt, it is likely that fear tempered their desire for vengeance. Specific evidence as to Achomawi relations with the Klamath-Modoc is, however, conflicting. An American writer speaks of the Astakiwi and Hantiwi as much harried by the northerners, while the near-by Atuami were nearly exempt. Yet the Atsugewi of Hat Creek remember Modoc or Klamath attacks in which women were carried off. It is not unlikely that local feuds underlay the warfare here as elsewhere in California, and that slave raiding was a superadded and later feature, encouraged by the introduction of the horse. We do not really know.

With the Atsugewi and Wintun to the southwest the Achomawi were friendly. How they stood with the Okwanuchu and Yana on the west and the northern Paiute on the east seems not to have been recorded. In some measure the Achomawi served as transmitters in trade between the Sacramento Valley Wintun and the Modoc and perhaps Paiute farther inland. Shell beads traveled up Pit River, furs down the stream. As in the civilized world, the lowlanders received raw materials and gave manufactures to the back peoples.

FOOD.

Oaks become scarce in Achomawi territory in proportion to the distance from the Sacramento Valley, and the eastern divisions of the nation, while they might now and then secure a temporary supply of acorns by trade, subsisted rather on the plant food used in the Nevada and Oregon portions of the Great Basin than on those characteristic of most of California. Salmon hardly ascended beyond Fall River, so the easterly groups had to go without a regular supply of this food also. The lower Pit River tribes got the fish in abundance, however. It was sun dried, slightly roasted or smoked, and then put away in large bark-covered baskets, either in slabs or as a crumbled powder.

Deer can not have been especially abundant in the dry habitat of the Achomawi, so that their development of a particular method of taking the animal, in addition to those common to all the Californian tribes, is interesting. This device, as simple in plan as it must have been laborious in execution to a people operating only with sticks and baskets, was to dig concealed pits, 2 or 3 yards deep, in the runways. These holes, which were a great nuisance to the settlers until abolished by their edict, were numerous enough to give its name to Pit River; of which "Pitt" is a misspelling. Deer hunting was preceded by rituals; and while the specific taboos prevalent in other parts of northern California and designed to prevent any association of the hunt, the animal, or its flesh with sexual intercourse or menstruation, have not been mentioned for the Achomawi, it is not unlikely that they were also observed. Adolescent girls during their maturity ceremony stuffed their nostrils with fragrant herbs to avoid smelling cooking meat. This precaution may have been intended chiefly as regards venison.

Ducks were snared in nooses stretched across streams. Rabbits were often driven into nets. The large lifting net of the northwest is not referred to by any writer among the Achomawi. The dip net was reserved for trout and suckers in the small streams. Salmon were taken with the harpoon, by seines, or in nets and cratings hung above the water at falls and dams. There may have been some animals whose meat was not eaten, but none have been mentioned except the domestic dog—the most powerful poison known to all the Indians of northern California. Salt was avoided as causing sore eyes, a statement scarcely to be credited except on the assumption that, the supply being scant, over-indulgence was viewed with disfavor.

INDUSTRIES.

Achomawi basketry is of the twined type common to all northernmost California and southern Oregon. At its best it is not quite so well made as the finest Hupa and Yurok ware. The technique is identical and the materials appear to be so. Achomawi baskets are softer and average somewhat higher in proportion to diameter, and their pattern in consequence is less frequently disposed in a single horizontal band. The shapes rather approximate those of Modoc baskets, but the Modoc reliance on tule as a material is not an Achomawi trait. Nearly all baskets in collections are solidly covered with the white overlay of *Xerophyllum*. This may, however, mean that they are trade articles and that the Achomawi of to-day no longer cook in baskets, since the overlay stains when wet for a time, and is used only as a sparing pattern by the Yurok on baskets meant to hold water or to boil in. Or it may be that the difference is old and connected with the scarcity of acorns and comparative nonuse of gruel among the Achomawi.

Other affiliations in material arts to the focus of the northwestern civilization are seen in the sinew-backed bow, only slightly less flat than among the Yurok; in the long body armor of hard elk or bear hide; the waistcoat armor of slender sticks wrapped together; and in the occurrence of the Yurok and Shasta type of guessing-game implement by the side of the Maidu form. Dugout canoes of pine or cedar were made, but lacked the characteristic details as well as the finish of the Yurok redwood boats. They were longer, narrower, scarcely modeled, and little more than punts for poling. They approximated the Modoc canoe, but without the thinness of wall that made the latter a notable achievement in spite of its lack of shape. Sacramento Valley influences showed themselves in the occasional use of the rush raft.

Maidu and other central Californian resemblances are manifest in the undecorated mush paddle, the crude bone spoon, the yellowhammer forehead bands for dancing and shaman's operations, and in the fact of the double ball game being a woman's activity.

DRESS.

Achomawi dress was not only of buckskin but included a sort of coat or shirt, which, however rude, is a quite un-Californian idea.

A deerskin with a hole cut in the middle was slipped over the head after the sides had been sewn together below the armholes, and then belted. Buckskin leggings, with fringes, were not common, but were known. The commonest moccasin was of openwork twined tule stuffed with grass, but in dry weather deerskin moccasins were also favored. We have here the essential articles of the dress fashionable east of the Rocky Mountains. The only Pacific coast resemblance is an apron-like kilt, which substituted for the eastern breechclout. California scarcely knows the latter.

Women's dress was more of a compromise. They wore a short gown or bodice, it is reported, much like that of the men. This would seem to be an abbreviation of the usual woman's dress of the Plains. From the hips down, a wrapping of deerskin formed a sort of separate skirt. Or this might be replaced by a fringed apron of northern Californian type. Leggingless buckskin moccasins and a basketry cap added further Pacific coast features to this hybrid attire.

Both men's and women's garments are spoken of as having been sometimes decorated with porcupine-quill embroidery. It is necessary to understand by this something simpler than the tasteful and showy ornamentation which the Plains women lavished upon nearly all their skin articles; but a specific eastern influence must be admitted nevertheless. The Achomawi received this influence, probably, from the Klamath and Modoc, who in turn were in more or less contact, at least after horses were introduced into the Columbia Valley, with the Sahaptin tribes, whose culture was superficially encrusted with elements from the Plains. The Modoc seem to have used some porcupine embroidery, and not infrequently introduced quills into their basket caps. It is interesting, however, that though this eastern influence penetrated into the northeastern gateway to California which the Achomawi occupied, it did not travel farther, even in fragments.

Tattooing was slight. The women had three lines under the mouth, which are but a slender remnant of the almost solidly blue chin of the northwestern women; and added a few lines on the cheek in Yuki and Wailaki style. Men had the septum of the nose pierced for insertion of a dentalium shell or other ornament. This is also a Yana, Karok, and Tolowa practice.

MONEY.

In trading, the Achomawi are said to have used beads, from which it may be inferred that while they had dentalia as well as the central Californian shell disks, the latter were their principal currency.

DWELLINGS.

The summers were spent in the open, under a shade or behind a windbreak of brush or mats. The ordinary permanent or winter house was of bark, without earth covering, and little else than a sloping roof over a shallow excavation. It has no northwestern affinities except the quadrilateral shape: the bark house of the central tribes was conical. The size, too, was not northwestern: only 8 by 12 feet or less. The most distinctive feature was a deliberate departure from rectangular form, the southern end being wider than the northern by the breadth of the included door. The two door posts matched a single post in the middle of the opposite end. The ridge pole consequently was double also. The narrow triangular space between the ridge poles, or part of it, was left open for a smoke hole.

The so-called "sweat house," which was primarily a dance house, chief's home, or dwelling for several families, was like the ordinary house except so far as its greater size, up to 20 by 30 feet or so, enforced modifications. The most important of these was a center post, without which no Indian of the northern half of California would have thought a ceremonially used house complete. This was set not in the exact middle, but about two-thirds of the way from the broader front end. The roof was supported by two rafters laid transversely from the center post to the sides, and by two others reaching from these two to the door posts (Fig. 25). A second feature which proves this structure to have been essentially a form of the central Californian ceremonial chamber, was the earth roof; the bark of the living house was replaced by a layer of poles and brush. Finally, the smoke hole

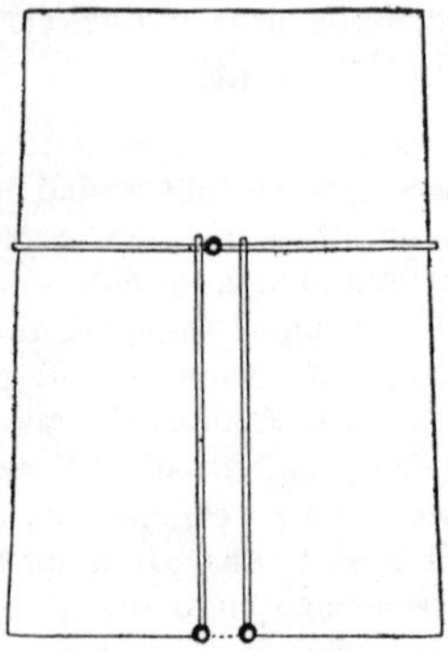

FIG. 25. — Achomawi large house, skeleton plan.

probably replaced the door as the normal entrance, the door being kept as a draft hole. There is some doubt on this point, but as the closely allied Atsugewi favored the entrance and exit by the roof, and since this is a frequent north central Californian practice, it is hardly likely that the Achomawi diverged materially on a point to which so much significance was attached in custom. The ladder is stated to have been made of two poles with crossbars tied on by withes, a surprising fact—although mentioned also for the Maidu— since the ladder of both northwestern and central California is a notched log. The " sweat house " was dug out about a yard. Some villages contained more than one of these large structures.

In the recent period the Achomawi used the small steam-heated sweat house of the Plains. It came to them from the Klamath and Modoc, who in turn perhaps derived it from the Warm Springs and Umatilla groups farther north.

SOCIAL INSTITUTIONS.

Little is known of the formalities of marriage or the rigidity of the purchase side of the arrangements. The bridegroom lived in the bride's home for a short time, hunting and otherwise working for her relatives, then usually took her to his people. This is perhaps the reality of what has been described as a sort of customary honeymoon. The custom indicates that so far as priority of descent was distinguished at all, it was reckoned in the male line. A statement that a chief was usually succeeded by his own eldest son points in the same direction. Betrothal of children was frequent. Food restrictions and seclusion were prescribed for both husband and wife until the end of their babe's umbilical cord fell off. One of each pair of twins was destroyed at birth.

The widow, as all through northernmost California, cropped her hair. She smeared the stubble with pitch, and added more on her face. She also wore a thong with lumps of pitch around her neck, and a carefully made belt of the hair she had cut. All this disfigurement might be left on for two or three years. After her hair had regrown to the upper arm, the widow married her dead husband's brother.

There is some conflict of information as to disposal of the dead, but it seems that they were normally buried, in flexed position, on the side, facing east, and if possible in a large basket. Cremation was used for those who died at a distance, and the ashes buried at home. In either event, the dead person's belongings, increased by offerings of his relatives, went with him, and his house was burned. There was no funeral dance or anniversary mourning ceremony.

RITUAL.

Ceremonies were slight and few: the girl's adolescence ritual that prevails over most of California; a puberty rite for boys connected with the seeking of shamanistic power; and the victory dance, made around the head of a foe with women participating. Even the doctors' initiation dance, so prevalent in northern California, was lacking; and of anything like an esoteric society or impersonations of the gods, there was not a trace. There is mention of a first salmon ceremony, suggestive of the northwestern new year's rituals. Old men fasted in order to increase the run of the fish, while women and children ate out of sight of the river. But no further details are known.

The ceremonial number appears to be five, but the tendency to its use was not strong.

A girl in the physical condition that marks the threshold to womanhood had her ears pierced by her father or other relative. She was then lifted, dropped, and struck with an old basket and ran off, her father praying to the mountains in her behalf. In the evening she returned with a load of wood—symbolic, like the basket, of her career—built a fire before the house, and danced back and forth by it all night, accompanied by some of her relatives. Others might be dancing in the house. The singing was to a rattle of deer hoofs. Deer meat, in fact all meat and fish, were, however, strictly taboo to her, and to prevent herself even from smelling them cooking she stuffed scented herbs into her nostrils. In the morning, having been lifted up and dropped again, she ran off as before, but with the deer-hoof rattle. This was done for five days and nights. After the last night she returned quickly from her run, was sprinkled with fir leaves, and bathed. This ended the ceremony for the time, though it was repeated on the two following occasions.

The boy's puberty rite runs along parallel lines, but adds an element that is akin to the seeking of shamanistic power by eastern tribes. As soon as the ears are pierced, the boy is struck with a bowstring and runs off, to fast and bathe all night in a lake or spring while his father calls to the mountains and to the Deer Woman to watch him. In the morning he returns, lighting fires on the way, eats a little without entering the house, and goes off again. In this way several nights are spent in the solitude of the hills. Besides making fires, he piles up stones and drinks through a reed to keep his teeth from contact with water. In the pond on the first night he may see an animal, which becomes his personal protector, or he may dream of it. But not all boys have this vision which makes them doctors.

SHAMANISM.

A shaman's power rests ultimately upon the protecting animal or spirit sought and acquired at puberty; but a shaman's business, both malevolent and beneficent, at least so far as disease is concerned, is with the " pains "; minute, animate, and motile objects of nonhuman shape. Sickness is caused by pains which have been snapped or shot at people by hostile shamans. The curing doctor frequently swallows the pain after extracting or catching it. All these beliefs as to pains are typical of the northwestern tribes. There were women doctors, as in the northwest, but men on the whole had greater powers.

Pains grow ferocious after causing a death, and the shaman who has sent one out is under particular care to catch and subdue it, lest he fall its next victim. Sometimes a pain will be sent against a village instead of a person. It then buries itself in the ground near the settlement, spreading disease about, until found, extracted, and made harmless, or, like an unexploded grenade, dispatched on a return missive of death. Disease, it appears, is as wholly due to shamanistic power as is cure. The doctor is not a protector against the miscellaneous forces of evil, but himself the dispenser of death as well as life. That killing was frequently resorted to when reprisal by magic failed or was beyond reach follows naturally; and even a doctor who had lost enough of his own friends under his treatment was under so dark a cloud as to run much risk of being murdered. With his death, all his controlled pains died, too.

It is clear that, as among the tribes to the west, the idea of the " pain " was so vividly held and fully worked out by the Achomawi that it had taken upon itself many of the functions elsewhere attributed to the guardian spirit. Thus an extracted pain can be made to tell a shaman who it was that sent it. The Achomawi, it is true, have better preserved the idea of the familiar spirit than the Shasta or the Yurok; but it appears to be preserved in theory rather than in shamanistic practice, which is pervaded throughout by concepts of the animate pain object.

A special feature of Achomawi shamanism is a sort of fetish called *kaku*, a bunch of feathers growing in remote places, rooted in the world, and when secured, dripping constant blood. The doctor uses his *kaku* in treating the sick, consults it as an oracle in locating the bodily hiding place of foreign pains, and obtains from it his own pains that are to travel on errands of destruction. It is possible that the *kaku* is a modification of the cocoon rattle, which through most of California was specifically a shaman's implement of special supernal virtue, and which not infrequently had feathers lightly or abundantly interspersed among its rattles.

MYTHOLOGY.

Achomawi mythology is of central Californian type in its formal organization and recognition of dual and contrasting creators, but lacks something of the spirituality of the Maidu and Wintun systems in having an animal, the Silver Fox, as the planner and maker of the world, in place of a more anthropic and remote deity. The northwestern tone is entirely lacking from Achomawi myths, without a compensating distinctive character of their own.

PLACE OF THE CULTURE.

Achomawi culture may be described as possessing nearly as much of the elementary groundwork of northwestern as of central Californian civilization, but without any of the refinements and advanced specializations of the former and without the flavor of the peculiar social attitudes of the great north Pacific coast culture, and as being infiltrated with eastern, perhaps in part specifically Plains, influences, which seem to have come in more by way of the Columbia River than through the Shoshoneans of the Great Basin.

THE ATSUGEWI.

The Atsugewi, the sixth and last of the Shastan groups, lived on three medium-sized streams draining northward into Pit River: Burney Creek, Hat Creek, and Dixie Valley or Horse Creek. The mouths of these streams, like all the banks of the Pit River itself, were in Achomawi territory. The rather unfavorable stretches between the three creeks; the territory to some distance to the southeast, probably including the region of Eagle Lake; and the higher country south to Lassen Peak and to the watershed between the Pit and Feather Rivers were used by the Atsugewi for hunting and the collecting of vegetable foods. They lay claim to having owned Susan River about as far down as Susanville, and Horse Lake east of Eagle Lake—territories which on Plate 1 have been credited to the Maidu and Northern Paiute, respectively. The neighbors of the Achomawi on the south were the Maidu, on their north the Achomawi, to the east the Northern Paiute, and on the west the Yana. There were Achomawi farther down on Pit River than the entrances of the Atsugewi streams, but the distance in this direction from the Atsugewi to the uppermost Wintun was not great.

Atsugewi or Atsugei is either their own name for themselves or that which the Achomawi apply to them. In the former case it probably referred only to the inhabitants of Hat Creek Valley; in the latter and more probable event— the ending -wi occurs on most Achomawi group designations where Atsugewi has -ĭ'i— the name may have been that of the whole people. But Adwanuhdji has also been cited as the Achomawi designation of the entire Atsugewi mass. The resident whites, at any rate, class them all together as Hat Creeks. The Yana call them Chunoya or Chunoyana.

Among themselves, the Burney Valley people were the Wamari'i, those of Dixie Valley the Apwarukei, while the specific name of those on the larger and middle stream, Hat Creek, is not known. Among the Achomawi, Apamadji denoted the Burney, Amidji or Amitsi the Dixie, and Hadiuwi the Hat Creek division. Pakamali or Bakamali has also been cited as the Achomawi name of this last division.

The population by the census of 1910 was not quite 250, nine-tenths of them still full blood. This purity has been maintained through the fortune of a sparse American settlement.

They were friendly with the Northeastern Maidu of Big Meadows and with most of the Yana, but possessed the repute of bravery.

All that is known of Atsugewi customs and beliefs points to their practical identity with those of the Achomawi. The following are the chief known items of discrepancy or corroboration.

The Atsugewi made the usual central Californian headband of yellow-hammer quills. It was worn by shamans in doctoring. The Achomawi used this ornament less or only sporadically. The former observed some sort of rudimentary mourning dance, in which the dead man's weapons were carried and dust was thrown up by handfuls. This seems, however, to have been a ceremony at the time of funeral, not a commemoration. The shaman's kaku was used as by the Achomawi.

To the Achomawi practice of a widow wearing her severed hair as a belt, the Atsugewi added the reciprocal custom of a man cutting his, though the belt made from it was put on by a female relative and not by himself.

The first deer killed during the camping season was eaten clean up without remnants or waste in order to please the mountain, which would then provide more deer.

Private or family ownership in land or its products is denied by the Atsugewi except for a few claims to particular patches of edible roots or seeds, and to eagles' nests, the right to take from which went from father to son.[1]

The ghost dance of 1870–1872 came to the Atsugewi from the west, from the northern Yana, who derived it from the northern Wintun. The Atsugewi transmitted it eastward to the Fall River Achomawi.

The dead were buried, so far as direct memory of the living extends. There is a tradition that corpses were originally cremated, subsequently put into rock crevices and covered with stones, and only in latter times interred. It is not clear whether this is authentic tradition or mythical speculation, nor whether it refers to the Atsugewi or other groups.

The summer or camping house was of cedar-bark slabs, leaned on a conical support of four poles tied near the top. One recent example, 16 feet in diameter, was occupied by three married couples and three children.

The permanent or winter house was oval, with an entrance passage at one end and a main post nearer the opposite end. From this post three diagonal supports ran down to the rear and sides, while a pair of longer beams, laid parallel or nearly so, sloped gently to the door lintel. Between them, in front of the main post and above the fire, was the trapezoidal smoke hole, which also served as roof door. The skeleton of the house was laid over with bark and had earth put on. Money beads were planted and a prayer spoken before the main post was set. The house owner obtained the chief's approval before construction; several families lived under his roof. A house still standing measures 22 feet in greatest diameter. Chiefs' houses were larger. They were used in winter for joint sweating by the men of the settlement, the women and children taking themselves out each time.

FIG. 26.—Atsugewi cradle. (Compare Pl. 35.)

Sweat houses as such are said to have been made only in the summer settlements or camps. They were small, earth-covered, and heated with steam, not by a fire. The eastern sweat house of blankets over a willow frame was introduced among the Atsugewi within the recollection of middle-aged people.

Deerskin clothing was similar to that described for the Shasta and Achomawi: hip-length leggings and a shirt with open sleeves for men, and for women either a skirt from waist to knee or a sleeveless gown from shoulder to knee. It is, however, specified that this was the costume of the well-to-do, worn in winter. The ordinary woman's skirt was rolled or bundled bast, sewn or twined into a mat; the poor man tied a tule mat about his trunk in cold weather and contented himself with a knee-length tule legging. Tule moccasins were worn mostly by women, three-piece deerskin ones by men; for winter use, the latter had the hair left on the inner side. A sort of glove was made by winding a strip of rabbit fur about palm, wrist, and forearm. These devices reflect the fact that the Achomawi and Atsugewi habitat was one of the coldest inhabited winter tracts in California. (Fig. 26.)

---

[1] This and the following notes are from data obtained by E. Golomshtok in 1922.

CHAPTER 22.

THE MODOC.

TRIBAL AND TERRITORIAL STATUS.

This people is one of a group known as Lutuamian, the fourth and uppermost of the native stocks resident on the Klamath River, which perhaps derives its name from the Kalapuya designation for one of the Lutuamian divisions: Athlameth. Two similar dialects and two tribes are recognized as Lutuamian: The Klamath, wholly in Oregon, and the Modoc, in both Oregon and California. It is not likely that the language will stand as independent and therefore of family rank. Possible connections with several tongues of both States were long ago suggested, and some of these seem almost certain to be verified as soon as a systematic analytic comparison is undertaken.

The holdings of the Klamath comprised Upper Klamath Lake, Klamath Marsh—where they gathered their famous palatable food *wokas*—Williamson River, and Sprague River. The Modoc had Lower Klamath Lake, Tule or Rhett Lake, the smaller Clear Lake, and Lost River. To the west, they owned to Butte Lake and Creek; to the south, to the ill-defined and uninhabited watershed between their territory and Pit River; eastward, probably to the divide between Lost River and Goose Lake. The ownership of the shores of the latter is in dispute, and has sometimes been ascribed to the Modoc. But whatever may have been the case as between the Northern Paiute and the Achomawi, it seems probable that the Modoc did not seriously claim any of Goose Lake. If so, the territory of the two closely linked Lutuamian divisions formed a natural topographic area: The high basin of marsh and lake in which the Klamath originates, with the Shasta below on the river proper, Athabascans and Takelmans across the Cascades on Rogue River, and the Northern Paiute in the interior drainage of the desert, across the lower eastern ranges.

On the map, the Modoc lands have been brought down to Mount Shasta. Perhaps this great isolated peak only served them, as all tribes about, as a gigantic landmark. The matter is one that looms large on the map, but is of little actual significance, the mountain itself, and most of its near environs, having been uninhabited. The hunting rights on its north flank may have belonged to the Okwanuchu rather than to the Modoc.

But few old villages of the Modoc are known. Agawesh was where Willow Creek comes into Lower Klamath Lake; Kumbat on the south shore of Rhett Lake; Pashha on its northwestern side; Wachamshwash a few miles up Lost River; and Nushalt-hagak-ni farther up that stream near Bonanza. These sites are about equally divided between California and Oregon.

The Shasta called the Modoc P'hanai and the Klamath Makaitserk and perhaps Auk-" siwash." The Achomawi knew them respectively as Lutmawi or Lutuami ("lake"), and Alamminaktish (Alaming, Upper Klamath Lake); the Northern Paiute as Saidoka and Sayi.

The designation Skachpali-kni, said to have been applied to the Karok, Yurok, and Hupa by the Klamath-Modoc, seems to be nothing but an Indianization of "Scotts Valley," in which the westernmost Shasta lived.

Klamath and Modoc alike called themselves in the usual way: *maklaks*, "people." They distinguished each other, when necessary, by geographic designations. The Klamath, for instance, were the Eukshikni maklaks, from Eukshi, Klamath Marsh and the district toward Upper Klamath Lake; of which, in turn, the derivation is from *eush*, "lake." The Modoc were the Moatokni maklaks, or people of Moatak, as Tule or Rhett Lake was called from lying toward the *muat* or "south."

The two dialects were easily intelligible, but their speakers inhabited distinct areas and felt themselves two peoples. Conflicts between them may have occurred, and in their foreign wars each was likely to go its own way. The Klamath remained neutral in the Modoc war.

The Modoc, as such, probably possessed more tribal solidarity than the great majority of California Indians, and appear also to have had some measure of the warlike spirit and bravery which has been generally attributed to them. But caution is desirable. Their military reputation rests mainly on the famous Modoc war of 1872–73; and the decisive check which they administered in the course of this conflict to four companies of regular soldiers was not a victory won in the open field. The lava beds south of Rhett Lake in which the Indians were driven to bay form a series of natural trenches that without artillery are practically impregnable except to a vastly superior force and then only at heavy cost. The attack was made by much greater numbers—there were four companies against 70 Modoc men with women assisting to load—but without cannon and under the disadvantage of a fog. The Modoc utilized their opportunity to the full; but the fight was a blunder of the American commander.

Their raiding of the Achomawi of Pit River has also been exploited. That they were the better warriors is indisputable. But if they had conducted annual raids, slaughtering the men and dragging the women and children off to sell at The Dalles, the Achomawi would long since have ceased to exist instead of being found by the

Americans a fairly numerous and resistant tribe in a rather adverse habitat, and being to-day one of the most populous groups in California. It is probable that the Klamath and Modoc were stimulated to their raiding warfare, unusual in the California region, by their northern affiliations, which early provided them with an abundance of horses and offered a lucrative market for captives who otherwise would have been killed. In fact, investigation may reveal that the slave raiding consisted of only two or three incidents, and these perhaps indirectly brought on by the changes of conditions caused by the advent of the whites, whose imagination magnified some temporary events into a custom. The basis of all the clashes may have been a mere vengeance feud such as sooner or later embroiled almost all Californian groups. Thus it is known that while the Modoc fought certain Achomawi groups or villages, they remained friendly with others.

Statistics as to the number of the Modoc in the past 50 years are somewhat vitiated by the inaccuracy that pervades most official figures for reservations on which several tribes are joined. This is perhaps not a grave fault of the Indian Office, whose avowed purpose has been the breaking down of national particularity as part of what it denominates tribal life in distinction from American citizenship; but it is unfortunate for the historian. The available data indicate that the Klamath have long been at least twice as numerous as the Modoc; that there were in 1910 not quite 700 of the one and short of 300 of the other; and that the combined population of the tribes at discovery may have aggregated 2,000. The former number of the Modoc may thus be set at about 600 or 700, of whom perhaps half or less lived in what is now California.

Some dentalia and perhaps all the obsidian from which the immense blades were made seem to have reached the tribes of the lower Klamath from the Modoc, but the transfer was apparently through intervening groups rather than directly. The Karok can have had only the dimmest knowledge of the Modoc, and the Yurok do not appear to have been aware of their existence. The latter people, in fact, place a second ocean at the head of the Klamath. This concept is likely to have rested on a vague report of the Klamath Lakes, but was no doubt mainly fashioned by cosmological speculation. Had the Klamath and Modoc been known, these bodies of water could not have been expanded into an ocean.

SOCIETY AND RELIGION.

Social and religious institutions are practically unknown. Chieftainship is said to have been hereditary and endowed with reasonable authority. For how much wealth counted in men's status is uncertain. There was a five nights' dance for adolescent girls: the *Shuyu-*

halsh. Five is clearly the ritualistic number. A mourning rite in the sweat lodge is mentioned as if it were a purification for the survivors rather than a commemoration for the dead.

The earlier ghost dance religion is said to have prevailed in the Klamath Lakes region shortly before the Modoc war, and may possibly have contributed to its outbreak. The date is correct: about 1870 to 1873. The Modoc and Klamath probably received this pre-Wovoka cult directly from their Northern Paiute neighbors, and in turn seem to have passed it on to the Shasta from whom the Northwestern tribes took it.

There are many data in print concerning Klamath and Modoc shamanism, but they enable no picture and remain a disjected mass of allusions to songs, dreams, sucking, charms, and the like universal stock in trade of the institution. The significant facts which would yield a characteristic picture of the type of shamanism, and make precise its relation to the remainder of the culture, remain undetermined. When these clues shall have been recovered, the existing records will contribute to a very vivid understanding of the subject.

Meanwhile, a few specimens of shaman's songs may be of interest. The native word which has been rendered "disease" in several of these is *nepaks*, "that which comes," and is evidently the disease object or cause, the thing which so many northern California Indians call the "pain" when they speak English.

> What do I remove from my mouth?
> The disease I remove from my mouth.
>
> What do I take out?
> The disease I take out.
>
> What do I suck out?
> The disease I suck out.
>
> What do I blow about?
> The disease I blow about.
>
> As a head only, I roll around.
>
> I stand on the rim of my nest.
>
> I am enveloped in flames.
>
> What am I? what am I?
>
> I, the song, I walk here.
>
> I the dog stray,
> In the north wind I stray.
>
> An arrowpoint I am about to shoot.
>
> A bad song I am.
>
> The earth I sing of.

The mythology of the Modoc has been as comprehensively recorded as their religious and social practices remain little known. It is a colorless body of traditions. The leading figure is Kmukamch, "Ancient old man," a trickster culture hero, who, however, is said to have created men. A number of the episodes recounted of him, particularly in connection with his son Aishish, are incidents told also by the Yurok. Another important pair of characters are the Marten, sometimes identified outright with Kmukamch, and his younger brother Weasel. Silver Fox is a personage of distinction, but fails to rise to the creative rank which he enjoys among the Achomawi. In general, much of the mythologic material of the Modoc is common goods over northeastern and even all northern California, but its trend as a whole is neither central nor northwest Californian, and is rather difficult to define because of a general lack of characteristic features. The account of the origin of the scheme of things is brief, pale, and somewhat heterogeneous. There is nothing in it of the fullness, orderly systematization, or concrete picturesqueness of Maidu and Wintun cosmogony. The typical northwestern qualities are also lacking: the lyrical charging of situations, the defined and poignant concept of the prehuman but humanlike race, the intense significance of the localizations. That Modoc traditions refer to specified spots and presuppose a time of animal activities before men existed are not sharp analogues to the northwest, but generic traits common to all American mythologies in only a varying degree. Clearly, these uplanders had not worked out a mythology of maturely developed traits or positive tendency.

CALENDAR.

The Klamath calendar, or month cycle within the year, is basically of the type that counts instead of describing or naming the moons; that is, related to the system of the Yurok and of many tribes to the north. Strictly, however, it does not enumerate but names the fingers used in counting. It is rather remarkable that the order is from thumb to little finger, the reverse of that used by almost all Indians. The first month approximates our August. The method of occasional correction necessary to fit a 12-moon series into a year of 12 and a fraction luminations is not known. As it is said that the year began with the first new moon after the return from the *wokas* harvest, it is possible that the correction was made according to season: whenever the count got too far ahead of the actual seed gathering, the last "month" of the year, that of the return from camp, may have been allowed to stretch over one and a half or nearly two lunations. In this event a seasonal sense, based on experience, must have replaced the system of reckoning, which indicates how little of a "calendar" the native scheme can have been and how little useful it can have been, even in the rudest way, for

most of the practical purposes of our calendar. The beginning of
the year is not solstitial among this people, and there is no evidence
that the solstices were determined or other than casually considered.

Strictly, we do not know that the Modoc used this Klamath moon
count; but if their scheme differed it was probably only in detail.
These are the Klamath moons:

t–hopo	thumb	ca. August	berries dried.
speluish	index finger	September	dancing.
tat–helam	middle finger	October	leaves fall.
kapchelam	ring finger	November	snow.
kapcha	little finger	December	heavy snow.
t–hopo	thumb	January	lakes frozen.
speluish	index	February	rain, dancing.
tat–helam	middle	March	sucker fishing.
kapchelam	ring	April	ipos gathered.
kapcha	little	May	suckers dried.
t–hopo	thumb	June	wokas harvest.
speluish	index	July	return from harvest.

MATERIAL CULTURE.

The material culture of the Modoc is distinguished by the almost
infinite use made of tule and bulrush. Mats, house coverings, rafts,
nearly all basketry, moccasins and leggings, eye shields, baby cradles,
quivers, and receptacles of all sorts are made of this adaptable material. The utility of the two or three commonest species of rush is
recognized throughout California. There is not a people able to obtain tule but employs it to some degree. But much the greatest
development of industries based on tule is found among the Modoc
and Klamath, among the Pomo of Clear Lake, and among the Yokuts
of Tulare Lake and the adjacent tule-fringed sloughs. Superficially
the life of these three groups must have been marked by a great
similarity. Actually the resemblance was not very deep. The identical material was used for much the same purpose but applied in
quite diverse manners. For example, the Modoc only twined their
tule into baskets, the Yokuts chiefly coiled it, and the Pomo, even of
Clear Lake, preferred to use other materials. It is obvious that the
type of culture prevailing in a region has determined the use made
of the material, and that any attempt to infer from mere employment
of material to cultural type is impossible.

FOOD.

The Modoc inhabited nearly acornless country, and mortar and
pestle are rare among them. They are commonly of small size and
used by old people who can not chew. Meat and fish, fresh or dried,
were more often beaten up in these mortars than seeds. The meat

mortar was known through most of California, although generally as a subsidiary to the larger implement for the standard vegetable foods.

The metate is more important. The principal and larger form is for cracking the shells of *wokas* seeds. It is an even-surfaced slab, generally of lava, irregular in shape, or circular, but not typically rectangular, and, as always in California, without legs or tilt. The muller has a round base and rises sharply into two horns or into a single peak bifurcated at the point (Fig. 27). These horns slope and are held pointing away from the grinder, whose thumbs press against the incline while the fingers grasp the two sides of the implement. The very light stroke is back and forth, the pressure applied on the centrifugal movement. The operator does not kneel but sits behind the metate, with her legs under her, or, rather, to one side. So far as known, this is the invariable posture of the California woman at her metate.

A smaller form is used by the Modoc for other seeds. The muller also has a circular base, but lacks horns and its tip is hemispheri-

FIG. 27. — Klamath-Modoc two-horned muller for round metate.

cal. It is perhaps made for one hand. The motion in this case is rotary. Metates with circular wear are found in other parts of California, but the operation by rotating does not seem to have been described elsewhere. The relation of the two types, of both to the hoppered slab mortar, and the possible history of all three forms, are discussed in the chapters on the Maidu, Chumash, Luiseño, and Cahuilla.

The Klamath and Modoc state that their two-horned muller was sometimes replaced by one with a loop handle. This is a northern form, and may represent a sporadic introduction from that direction.

The preparation of *wokas*, the most characteristic food of the region, was more largely a Klamath than a Modoc habit, the greatest source of supply of the large yellow water lily being Klamath Marsh; but it is likely that the Modoc participated in the industry on a limited scale.

The bulk of the crop is unripe seed pods picked from canoes. These are sun dried, the seeds pounded out with a stone, and winnowed. This is *lowak*. Pods in the center of the drying heap that remain moist are beaten to a pulp, spread out, dried, and winnowed. Their seeds, somewhat further ripened than *lowak*, are a superior food, and called *stontablaks*. Both varieties can be stored indefinitely. They are converted into *shiwulints* by parching, cracking off the shells, winnowing, and boiling into a gruel; or the winnowing is dispensed with, and the shells skimmed from the surface of the cooking mass, called *stilinsh* in this case.

When it is impossible to wait for the pods to dry, they are roasted or steamed to *awal*, or more properly two grades of it, *nokapk* and *chiniakum*, the latter being the less ripe. The *awal* pods are pounded into a gluey mass into which ashes, charcoal, punk wood, or other absorbent is rubbed, to allow of its screening or winnowing. The extracted seeds, which are still comparatively fresh, are now parched, ground lightly to crack their shells, and the latter winnowed from them. The product is *lolensh*, which is either sun dried and stored or roasted into *shnaps*, in which form each kernel expands to triple bulk. The *shnaps* is eaten either dry or in cold water, or ground fine into *shlotish* and water poured on it. These various forms of *nokapk* and *chiniakum* are less esteemed than the preparations from *stontablaks* and *lowak*.

The finest *wokas* is the fully ripe seeds, *spokwas*, which are skimmed with a tule spoon as they float on the water in a mucilaginous enveloping lather. *Spokwas* forms barely 10 per cent of the entire *wokas* harvest. The paste is poured into a hole or shaded basket to rot or ferment, the shell-enclosed seeds, however, not being affected. After several weeks a canoe is filled with the paste and water; on stirring, the seeds sink to the bottom, the water, pod fragments, and refuse are drawn off, and the seeds drained in the sun. Parching, grinding, and winnowing convert them into *lolensh*, from which in turn the other products are derived, as in the case of *lolensh* made from *awal*.

While the supply of *wokas* was enormous—Klamath Marsh alone contained 15 square miles of solid growth of water lily—the food was a high grade and industrially costly one. A woman averaged perhaps 4 to 6 bushels of pods in a day of gathering. These would yield 20 to 30 pounds of seeds in the *lolensh* stage. The separation of the seeds, parching, shell cracking, and winnowing of such a quantity may be assumed to have required at least two additional days. The *lolensh* is often roasted and ground before consumption or even cooking. The *lowak* and *stontablaks* can not have been gotten ready to eat very much quicker. It is a fair estimate, therefore, that a day's labor did not yield above 6 or 7 pounds of edible *wokas*.

It is likely that the two-horned mulling stone, which seems to be restricted to the Modoc and Klamath, is to be traced directly to the *wokas* industry. Its primary use is to crack the seed shells without pulverizing the kernels, necessitating a delicate, even stroke. The horns or nibs, against which the thumbs rest, make the requisite control possible. An ordinary muller, which the whole hand clasps from above, is designed to be borne down on heavily, and lends itself awkwardly to a motion that must be at once light and firm.

The salmon are said not to run into the Klamath Lakes or above, and streams are much smaller and standing bodies of water infinitely more important than in the northwest. Fishing methods consequently have little in common with the practice of the Yurok, Karok, and Shasta. The principal net is a large, sagging, triangular piece on two poles held apart by a crossbar, somewhat like the surf fishing net of the Yurok, but operated from the prow of a fast-moving canoe in lake waters. In streams a small dip net on a circular or semicircular hoop and handle is employed. Long, narrow gill-net seines of very fine string with tule floats were set in the rivers and sometimes in the lakes. The stone sinkers were grooved, not perforated, in which they follow the custom of most of California. The harpoon was of the usual Californian double-pointed form, but without barbs, the socket-ended toggles being set directly on the shafts. With small fish the toggle could be thrust clear through and a barb was unnecessary. For lake bottom fish a pole with a dozen hardwood points somewhat spread by a ring was thrust through the muddy water wherever bubbles rose. The prongs held the fish against the bottom, and it was then retrieved with a barbed lance. Fish hooks were of more use than in most parts of California. The simplest form was a double-pointed bone suspended in the middle and entirely covered with bait, swallowed lengthwise by the fish and turning crosswise in its gullet when pulled. A double-pointed hook on a single shank was also employed: two sharp bones were wrapped and pitched to the end of a stick at an acute angle (Fig. 28).

Ducks were taken in long nets stretched over the water and let down over the birds by watchers holding ropes from the ends. The entangled birds were secured by hunters in canoes.

At night a fire was lit in a canoe and birds enmeshed in a net held out from the prow by two poles.

BODILY CARE.

FIG. 28.—Klamath-Modoc fishhooks.

Modoc heads are considerably shortened by deformation. Bandages around the infant's skull compress the forehead and occiput and increase the altitude of the head. This custom undoubtedly came to the Modoc from the north and east. The Columbia River region is a focus of head-flattening customs, and they extend up the Pacific coast for some distance beyond. No interior Californian tribe deforms the skull. Individuals with shortened occiput can be found as the result of cradle-board nurture; but there is no conscious custom of deliberate treatment.

Modoc dress seems also to have been of northern and eastern type: deerskin shirt and leggings. Most of the pieces preserved appear to be new and intended for ceremonial wear, but to represent the prevalent type of aboriginal dress. This conclusion is borne out by the fact that tribes to the south and west of the Modoc, comparatively good Californians like the Shasta and Achomawi, knew the fitted costume of buckskin; as well as by the fact that the fringed petticoat apron of California is not mentioned for the Modoc, whose women seem to have put on full gowns.

The accessories of dress were of tule and of local type. Such are the twined shoe of tule strands lined with grass, a form known also to the Achomawi. With this went a small mat of tule tied on as a knee-high legging. A cape or blanket of shredded tule or sagebrush bark was worn by women, presumably only when needed outdoors. A crownless cap of tule for men recalls the eye shades of rawhide sometimes donned by the Plains Indians.

The tule moccasin is for winter wear, in the house or snow or marsh. The summer moccasin, evidently designed for protection in travel and not for warmth, is of deerskin. It is interesting as of eastern rather than Californian type: a U-shaped tongue, although a short one, is inserted at the instep, where the Californian moccasin has merely a seam running all the way up the front; and the ankle portion is a separate flap normally worn turned down.

The snowshoe is a simple hoop with a few lines of fur or hide lashed across—the universal rude Californian type (Fig. 68). A smaller shoe of the same form is worn in marsh wading.

The hairbrush is a porcupine tail, as among the Achomawi and mountain Maidu.

The Modoc-Klamath cradle is of the sitting type that obtains from the Pomo north. The special base added by the northwestern tribes is wanting. A central Californian touch is given by the hood, which is a mat or fan-like piece loosely attached to a large hoop. Modern specimens are roughly made; old pieces have not been preserved. The first cradle, used only for the first few weeks, is of soft tules. Its precise form is not known, but presumably it was little more than a sort of wrapping.

The board cradle is also employed. This is a type widely spread to the north, in the Plateau, and in the Plains. It may be ancient among the Modoc, or a modern introduction from the Northern Paiute settled on the reservation by the Government.

HOUSES AND SWEAT HOUSES.

The dead were cremated. All adjacent Californians buried.

The Modoc winter house was the earth-covered lodge, dug out 3 or 4 feet and entered through the roof by a ladder. This ladder is described as consisting of a pole with toe holds cut through it. Posts supported the roof beams. Over these were laid poles, then brush of some sort and mats, and a heavy coating of earth. The houses are said to have reached a diameter of 50 feet, with a height of nearly 20 from the roof entrance to the floor.

This is the semisubterranean house which extends with little modification from the center of California to British Columbia and beyond. As used among the Modoc, it has northern rather than

Californian affiliation. First, it is distinctly and only a winter residence. The Californians, such as the Maidu, did not draw so sharp a seasonal distinction.

Secondly, the earth lodge has distinct ceremonial associations in California, particularly as its southern limit of distribution is approached. It was the place in which indoor dances were held, and it, or a small structure of the same type, was used for sweating. Its current English name is " sweat house." Among the southerly Maidu and Wintun and among the Miwok it could appropriately be called " dance house." While used as a dwelling, its larger examples were intimately associated with the Kuksu religion, and the type of structure ceases as soon as the line is reached at which this religion stops.

South central California appears to have no earth-covered houses, but they occur again in southern California. Here, however, they would seem to be of another type. They are low; the entrance is on the ground instead of from the roof; and they are not used ceremonially, rituals being held outdoors or in specially constructed inclosures without roofs. This southern earth-covered house varies between two forms. The simpler is a conical lean-to of logs or poles with earth heaped over them. This is essentially identical with the Navaho hogan. The more elaborate form, and apparently the standard one of southern California, had posts and beams. This approached rather closely to the central California type in its construction.

During the greater part of the year the Modoc lived in brush houses. These sometimes reached a length of 25 feet, but frequently were only half that size. The width was about half the length. The corners were rounded. There was a level ridge and the walls sloped rather steeply. The frame was of willow poles supporting the ridgepole and tied to it. The roof or sides were of three layers of matting of tule. The outer layer of mats was not twined but sewn through, so as to shed the water better. Little time was spent even in this house when the weather was warm, a shade or sun shelter being the customary lounging and working place.

The modern sweat house of the Modoc and Klamath is distinctly un-Californian, and of northern and eastern type. It is a very small structure, is usually more or less temporary, and above all the heat in it is produced by steam instead of a direct fire. Light poles are stuck into the ground and bent over to form a dome-shaped frame just large and high enough to accommodate a few persons seated on the ground. Over this frame are thrown mats. Stones heated in a fire outside are put into a small pit near the back of the sweat house, the entrance is closed, and water is poured on the rocks. This description, with buffalo skins substituted for tule mats, would apply exactly to the Plains sweat house. Nothing of the kind is known from any part of California except among the Shasta and Achomawi, who seem to have taken the type over from the Modoc and Klamath. The Californian builds a structure that will receive a considerable company, covers it with earth, and then starts a wood fire within. He would probably be as much disturbed by the unaccustomed steam that the northerners and easterners breathe as the latter would be distressed at having to inhale the dense smoke which the Californian has learned to tolerate while enjoying its welcome warmth.

There were earth-covered sweat houses among the Klamath and Modoc, but knowledge of them is unsatisfactory. According to one account these were limited in number, maintained only at certain localities, and entered only for purification after a death. The implication is that the structures may have been of some size, but another statement makes them no larger than the mat-covered kind. In any event, both types were steam heated and called by the name *spuklish*.

There is also some mention of a third kind of *spuklish*, a communal dance house or *kshiulgish*, literally, " for dancing "—" a spacious structure erected on the style of earth lodges." This may or may not have been something more than a house of dwelling type used for ritual assemblage.

These three types can hardly have coexisted. It is possible that the old Lutuamian sweat house was Californian and earth covered, heated by fire; and that the smaller temporary structure in which steam was produced came in from the Columbia River with the horse, or even later.

Finally, there was a menstrual lodge, on which, however, information is also lacking.

BOATS.

The Modoc and Klamath used the canoe and the rush balsa. The canoe was dug out of a fir log, and whether 12, 20, or 30 feet long, remained of nearly uniform beam of about 2 feet. The northwestern canoe was of standardized length, but varied greatly in breadth. The Modoc boat was hollowed out to a remarkably thin and light shell. It was high enough for a little of the inclosing curvature of the upper half of the log to form the gunwales, which were finished to a simple edge. There was no stem—no canoe with sharp prow is known from California, except perhaps the Chumash area. Both prow and stern sloped gently upward, the prow being cut away more. The boat was loaded chiefly aft, so that the prow rose clear, which of course made for easier driving in still water. A single paddler sat at the stern; a second would occupy the middle. The cedar paddles are broad and thin bladed, and 4 to 5 feet in length. In *wokas* gathering, or hunting in shallow water, the paddle was discarded for a pole, whose split end was wedged apart with a block or bone. The fork found resistance in the soft mud or caught a lily root.

The Modoc type of canoe seems to have been used, although sparingly, by the Achomawi, Atsugewi, and northeastern Maidu. It differs from the northwestern redwood canoe in several respects, although basically of one form with it. It is longer, narrower, thinner walled, without strengthening gunwale, neither prow nor stern is appreciably elevated, ornaments are never added, no foot rests or seat are carved, there is less flare from the middle of the bottom upward to the ends, the propelling implement is either a true paddle or a true pole, not a hybrid intermediate. The finish is smooth, but often follows the irregularities of the grain of the wood, and the thin shell soon warps, whereas the thick but light walls and even texture of the redwood of the northwestern boat permit of a tooled evenness, and no lack of finish is tolerated. Both vessels are obvious inland water types, but the Yurok canoe would be needlessly heavy and deep drafted in the quiet lakes and marshes of the Modoc plateau, whereas the long narrow boat of the Modoc would be quite unmanageable in the rapids of the lower Klamath area, would split from end to end on striking the first rock, and would soon have its bottom worn through on the gravelly bottoms where the streams riffle wide. The modifications are of interest because they are in use on the drainage of the same not very long river. But apart from adaptation to physical requirements, there is no doubt that the Yurok canoe represents the more elaborate and better wrought type—as is always the case when any northwestern implement is set against one from elsewhere in California.

The employment of the tule raft by the side of the canoe is obscure. It is said to have been used by war parties; perhaps because its dependability made up for inferior motility. It certainly could not well be overturned, broken, or sunk. It may also be conjectured that it was serviceable in duck hunting among the tules, where an inconspicuous and stealthy approach was important, and speed of travel of no consequence. The length was 10 to 15 feet; the component bundles of tule, of which several were lashed together, might each be of a diameter up to 2 feet. Such a mass must have been very unwieldy; but the innumerable air cells of the rush stems, which float lighter than cork, were able to sustain a tremendous burden, until waterlogged by continued use. The propulsion is said to have been by paddling with the hand, the occupants lying along the edge. This statement may refer to the practice of companies intent on an attack, when temporary rafts were hastily constructed and paddles had not been brought along.

The use of the rush raft in war indicates internecine feuds between Modoc villages, or at least between the Modoc and the Klamath; alien groups being accessible only at the end of land journeys of some distance. This point is of interest as indicating that the tribal solidarity of the Modoc was not so much greater than that of other Californian Indians as the usual references in literature indicate.

BASKETS.

Modoc basketry on first being seen suggests very strongly that of the northwestern tribes except for being softer. Actually the two arts, while connected, constitute two distinct variants of the basic type of basket industry that prevails over northernmost California and western Oregon.

The materials of the northwest, to which most of the northeastern tribes also adhere, are replaced among the Modoc almost entirely by a single one, tule rush. The warp in finer baskets is the surface fiber of the circular tule, *Scirpus lacustris*, twisted either on itself or more usually into a 2-ply string. The weft of the undecorated portions of baskets appears to be the same material. Ornamented baskets have a white surface—that is, weft. This is the skin of the leaves of the cat-tail rush, *Typha*. This is sometimes treated to assume a yellow color, or dyed black in mud. Patterns are usually in this black, or in a color that varies from red to brown and is obtained by using tule roots. Coarse baskets are made outright of tule. Vessels intended to be specially decorated have the center of the pattern overlaid in lustrous porcupine quills dyed bright yellow with *Evernia vulpina* moss. *Xerophyllum* is used chiefly on caps and seems sometimes to be overlay. The weft proper, however, is tule, and is reduced to fine strands. *Phragmites* reed is also used for white. Maidenhair fern, black, is rare.

On the whole, accordingly, Modoc basketry is set apart in its use of tule material and its prevailing adherence to plain twining.

Textile ware in woody materials is confined to openwork trays, carrying baskets, fish traps, and the like. The most common material is willow stems; split juniper roots are also employed. The carrying basket is bluntly conical, with braided edge and of Yurok type. The trays are roughly triangular or scoop-shaped, often with a handle at one end, and coarsely made. The form is not northwestern, but approaches a type found throughout the Sierra Nevada.

There is no trace of coiled basketry.

Colors being in the wefts themselves, the patterns show on the inside of Modoc baskets much as on the outside except for some raggedness of the weft ends. In northwestern baskets the overlay is carried throughout on one side, so that the interior of a basket is free from decoration, except as slender glimpses of design may show through interstices of the twining. Northeastern baskets—that is, those of the Achomawi, Yana, and Northern Wintun—resemble Modoc ware in duplicating the pattern on the inner face of the vessels; but the process is the same as that followed in the northwest, except that each faced weft strand is given a half twist with each twining.

Modoc caps average larger than those of the northwestern tribes and sometimes are of a size making it difficult to see how they could fit a head unless a mass of hair were tucked in. The northwestern caps are as trim as possible.

The seed beater has been reported but not described.

VARIOUS.

The bow was of the usual northern California type, broad, flat, rather short, sinew backed, and with recurved ends. The material is not known. Modern hunting bows are clumsier and unbacked. The arrow was often of reed, but light wood was also used, and was foreshafted and obsidian tipped. Water birds were shot with an unbarbed arrow bearing a small ring near the wooden point, this addition causing the missile to skip along the surface instead of burying itself in the water. The arrow straightener was a perforated board, the polisher a longitudinally grooved stone, as in all northern California. The transversely grooved arrow straightener of steatite, which elsewhere in California accompanies the cane arrow, has not been reported from the Modoc or any northern tribe. The quiver was of tule mat.

The Modoc, like many Californians, occasionally used a war spear, but it does not appear to have been a common weapon. It was a rather short stick with an obsidian head, and, although designated a javelin, seems to have been used in close encounters rather than for throwing.

Armor was a body covering of doubled elk skins.

The lumber-working wedge and maul were those of the Yurok, with two reductions. Mountain mahogany was often substituted for elk horn in the wedge; and the maul, while of stone, lacked the concavity of handle and expanding top of the northwestern implement. The Modoc must have had some form of adze for canoe making, but it is wholly unknown.

The fire drill was of willow in cedar, the canoe paddle handle usually serving as hearth. The drill point was of willow root, bound to the drill handle. The method of joining the two pieces is not clear. A socket or mortise is not mentioned, and a mere lashing of the willow along the end of the handle would cause the latter to rotate about a center outside of its own diameter and tend to interfere seriously with steady manipulation. Torches of tightly bound bark of sagebrush are mentioned. Similar devices may have been in use on occasion in most of California but appear not to have been reported.

Neither the iris of the northwestern tribes nor the *Apocynum* of the other tribes of California seems to have served the Modoc for string. Milkweed was occasionally employed, but the standard material was nettle bark. This reappears again among the Luiseño in the extreme south of the State. It is likely to have been known to intervening groups but appears to have been little used by them.

Of games, the ring and pin toy is of tule; and for guessing, the four-stick variety largely or wholly replaces the many-stick form of northern California and the hand bones or grass game of central California. There are two thick and two thin sticks, placeable in six orders under a basket tray. The arrangement rather than a given stick is guessed at. The trays, although twined of soft tule, resemble in size and showiness the coiled trays which Yokuts and southern Californian women use to cast dice on. This similarity may be a case of what is known as cultural convergence; but it is also likely to be the result of secondary variations in an ancient association of the basket plaque and gaming.

FIG. 29.—Klamath-Modoc pipe bowls.

The four-stick game is confined in California to the northeastern corner of the State.

The Modoc and Klamath pipe makes an un-Californian impression. It is a stone bowl smoked with a wooden stem; and it is L-form, not tubular. Some specimens are nearly straight, but even these show a slight upward bend toward the opening. Most common is an obtuse-angled bowl, but right-angled ones occur (Fig. 29). A special variety is a stone disk, with two holes bored to meet at right angles, one for the stem, the other for the tobacco. This form appears to have gained in vogue of late years, but inasmuch as it is quite unlike anything European, and is not known from neighboring tribes, it must be reckoned a native product. California pipes are normally of one material, whether that be stone, wood, cane, or clay; and if composite, they are structurally of one piece. Thus the wood and stone pipe of the Northwest is a wooden implement with a steatite lining to its bowl, the Chumash shell and bone pipe is of stone with a small piece of bird bone inserted for convenience of sucking. True two-piece or stemmed pipes are eastern.

CULTURAL POSITION.

It is evident that the inclusion of the Modoc in this volume is of somewhat dubious ethnological justification. If their civilization is essentially Californian, the same is true of the Klamath, and aboriginal California would have to be extended to take in an area of which at least three-fourths lies in what is now Oregon. The situation is complicated by the elements of northern and eastern origin in Lutuami culture and the fact that no one seems to be in a position to judge whether these are mostly ancient or came to the Klamath and the Modoc only after the horse became common in the middle Columbia Valley. That this factor was of some consequence during the nineteenth century is shown by the occasional finding of parfleche envelope bags of typical Plains Indian form in use among the Klamath. The mat sweat house and perhaps its heating by steam, and possibly any number of other features, may have been introduced along with the horse. It is therefore well conceivable that in 1770 the Lutuamians did not present the eastern affinities which mark them now, but were scarcely distinguishable from the true Californians except in so far as they had worked out proper specializations of culture in their rather unusual and comparatively shut-in habitat. The route of these northeastern influences would have been down the Columbia, up the Deschutes, and over the divide into the drainage of Klamath Marsh; and it is altogether likely that what the Shasta and Achomawi have of these foreign institutions and devices came to them via the Modoc.

Yet this view can not be pressed until further researches have been made. The world possesses depictions of the physical manufactures and of the mythology of the Lutuami, but beyond tantalizing hints scarcely anything else. We have no conception of the basic constitution of their society, and are profoundly ignorant of the true organization of their religious ideas. No one has yet taken the pains to inquire of the people themselves what part of their usages they attribute to recent importation from the Columbia. They may always have had considerable affiliations in that direction.

Apart from this northeastern strain their civilization is likely to have been chiefly Californian, and probably north central rather than northwest Californian. With the Great Basin Paiute on their east they certainly had little in common. Somewhat west of their north, across the Cascade mountains, were the Kalapuya of the Willamette, whose little-known culture was apparently too indistinctive for them to have exerted serious influence on the Lutuami. In fact, Kalapuya culture is likely to have been a blind alley local simplification of the civilization of the Chinookan lower Columbia, which it adjoined. Due west of the Lutuami were the Athabascans and Takelmans and Shasta of southwestern Oregon, whose culture, by all indications, was a reflex of that of the Yurok. Unless, therefore, the Lutuami are to be accredited with a largely peculiar civilization, which neither their numbers nor anything fundamental that is known about them warrant, they must be regarded as essentially Californian with an overlay developed in their isolation, and another, or an admixture, from the middle Columbia. Whether the Californian basis of their culture is mainly of the northwestern type that flourished best on the lower courses of the stream of which the Lutuami inhabited the headwaters, or of the central variety which centers on the Sacramento, is difficult to decide positively. The latter view is probably the sounder. Certainly the flavor of their civilization is markedly different from that of the Yurok, although the two nations possess in common a number of individual traits. The decision is difficult because northeastern California, which most directly adjoins the Klamath and Modoc land, is in the main central Californian but suffused with northwestern elements.

Cultural features of the Lutuami, typical of the middle and upper Columbia River region, and ultimately of the Plains east of the Rocky Mountains, include the sweat house (size, construction, steaming); the employment of the semisubterranean dwelling; dress; perhaps the type of skin moccasin; head deformation; the board cradle; the nontubular pipe; the eye shield; and possibly a superior sense of tribal solidarity.

Northern Californian traits are the bow, arrow straightener, and arrow polisher; the seed beater; the rude snowshoe; the tule balsa; the short spear; the grooved sinker; the mat-covered summer dwelling; the type (not the utilization) of the semisubterranean house. The last five of these are north central Californian only, and not northwestern. Specific northwestern resemblances are found in the wooden canoe, the wedge maul, the sitting type of basket cradle, and the trickster culture hero in myth; but in each of these instances there is a perceptible loss of much of the characteristic quality or refinement that the trait possesses in the northwest.

Local traits of culture connected directly with the physical environment and its products are the tule basis of basketry; the tule moccasin, legging, cape, quiver, and the like; the spreading fish spear; the unbarbed toggle of the harpoon; the extensive employment of fishhooks; the split pole for canoe propulsion; the ring-pointed arrow; and nettle string. Peculiarities not directly referable to environment include the two-horned muller and the discoidal pipe bowl, both quite distinctive forms; the four-stick guessing game; and perhaps the perforated ladder.

CHAPTER 23.

THE YANA AND YAHI.

The Yana.

ORIGIN.

The Yana are a people of fairly extensive territory but rather restricted numbers, concerning whom little general information has been extant, but to whom mystery of some kind has usually been made to attach. They were reputed of a marked physical type; their speech was not only distinctive but abnormally peculiar; in military prowess and cunning they far outshone all their neighbors; they had perhaps come from the far east. As usual, there is a thin sediment of fact to these fancies.

As regards physical type, no measurements are available. Report makes the Yana shorter than their neighbors, and an allusion in one of their myths appears to attribute the same conviction to themselves. But they certainly are not racially anomalous to any notable degree. The few scattered survivors would pass as normal among any group of north central California.

Their warlike reputation may be due partly to the resistance offered to the whites by one or two of their bands. But whether the cause of this was actually a superior energy and courage or an unusual exasperation aided by a rough, still thinly populated, and easily defensible habitat is more doubtful. That they were feared by certain of their neighbors, such as the Maidu, argues them a hungering body of mountaineers rather than a superior stock. The hill dweller has less to lose by fighting than the wealthy lowlander. He is also less exposed, and in time of need has better and more numerous refuges available. All through California the plains peoples were the more peaceably inclined, although the stronger in numbers: the difference is one of situation reflected in culture, not of inborn quality.

The speech of the Yana disposes definitely of all theories of their remote origin. They are members of the great Hokan family. As such, their ultimate source may have been southerly; but no more and no less than that of the Achomawi, the Shasta, the Karok, the Pomo, and others. Their language, so far as its sounds and words are concerned, is perhaps somewhat nearer to the Pomo on the other side of the Sacramento Valley than to the adjacent Achomawi and Atsugewi. It has, however, certainly been long differentiated, since it has entirely lost the prefixes that are found in all other Hokan idioms, and has become a suffixing tongue. It may be added that on the chart (see Pl. 1, inset; and Fig. 17) Yana territory looks like the end of a reflex curling movement of the interior Hokans—Shasta, Achomawi, and Yana—from the northern end of a coastwise distribution that begins in Mexico and ends with the Pomo, Chimariko, and Karok. It is, however, possible that the Yana were once neighbors of the Pomo and became pushed apart from them as the great block of Penutians drifted up or down the Sacramento Valley. Yana tradition is silent on these questions. Like all Californians north of Tehachapi, they believe themselves to have been created in their historic seats.

MEN'S AND WOMEN'S SPEECH.

Yana speech shows one extreme peculiarity, which, as an essentially civilizational phenomenon expressed through linguistic medium, must be mentioned: The talk of men and women differed. Men spoke the women's forms when conversing with them; women always spoke female. The differences are not very great, but sufficient to disconcert one not thoroughly familar with the tongue. Usually a suffix is clipped by women from the full male form. Thus *yana*, "person," becomes *ya* in the mouth or in the hearing of a woman; *auna*, "fire," and *hana*, "water," become *auh* and *hah*. Similarly a mortar, personified and addressed, would be called *keman-'na* if considered male, *keman-yi* if thought of as a woman. Somewhat analogous, though essentially a distinct phenomenon, is the employment of diverse roots to denote an action respectively as it is performed by men or women: *ni*, "a male goes," *ha*, "a female goes." The spring of these remarkable phenomena is unknown.

TERRITORY.

The Yana were surrounded by the Achomawi and Atsugewi, the Maidu, and the Wintun. Their holdings stretched from Pit River, on which they are said to have fronted for a distance, to Rock Creek on the south; that is, more probably, to the ridge on one or the other side of Rock Creek. In general, they ranged from the edge of the upper Sacramento Valley along the eastern tributaries of the Sacramento itself to their headwaters in the watershed beyond which the drainage flows north and south instead of westward. The summit of this divide, and the greatest landmark of the Yana country, was the ancient volcanic peak of Mount Lassen, recently active once more: Yana Wahganupa, literally "little Mount Shasta" (Wahgalu). Here the territory of two of the four Yana divisions met that of the Atsugewi and of the mountain Maidu. The whole of the Sacramento Valley in Yana latitude, east as well as west of the river, was

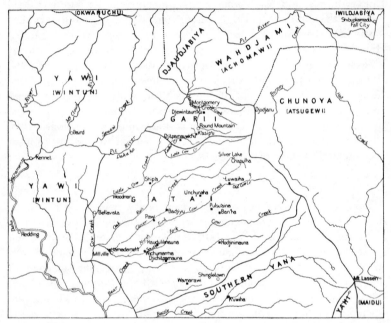

Fig. 30.—Yana territory, northern part. Settlements are shown by squares; alien groups in dotted lines. Unbracketed names are Yana designations.

Wintun. Yana land began with the foothills. In their lowest courses through these hills the streams often flow in narrow canyons; toward their source the beds are deep and rugged. Most of the Yana settlements were therefore in a middle belt. Those that are most accurately known and located are shown in Figure 30. In general, Yana country was a broken and endlessly ridged and furrowed land, timbered in part, mostly covered with brush, rocky, and hard of soil.

DIVISIONS.

The Yana comprised four dialectic divisions, but the speech of the most divergent was largely intelligible. The northern dialect was called Gari'i, the central one Gata'i. The southern dialect is extinct: it may have been included in Gata'i. Beyond it was another, to which the name " Yahi " may be given, that being the term replacing Yana in the mouths of its speakers. This division is also extinct. Its recent history being a different one from that of the three other divisions, it will be treated separately. It should be admitted that the designations here applied to the four Yana groups are awkward, the " southern " one not being the most southerly. The cause is the late recognition of the Yahi division after the names of the three others had become established in print. A renaming to northeastern, northern, central, and southern would be appropriate, but would inevitably cause future confusions.

The northern group held by far the smallest territory ; the drainage of Montgomery Creek into Pit River, and that of Cedar Creek, an affluent of Little Cow Creek. The northern Yana were wedged in between Wintun, Achomawi, and Atsugewi.

The Central Yana held the entire Cow Creek drainage: Cow Creek itself, Little Cow, Oak Run, Clover Creek, and North and South Forks of the Cow. To these must be added Bear Creek. The extreme northwestern corner of the territory shown in Figure 30 between Bellavista, Woodman, and the mouth of Squaw Creek, may have been Wintun instead of Gata'i Yana.

The southern Yana lived on Battle Creek. They also held Payne and Antelope Creeks and one or two smaller streams.

The Yahi held the course of Mill and Deer Creeks.

DESIGNATIONS AND NUMBERS.

The Yana to-day are generally known to the adjacent Indians and resident whites as Noze or Nozhi, a term of unknown origin although a Wintun source is likely. The Maidu said Kombo, although whether by this word the Yahi and southern Yana alone were meant, or all divisions of the stock, is not certain.

Sukoni-ya was a nonethnic term applied by the Yana to distant easterners: the more remote Achomawi and northeastern Maidu; perhaps also the Northern Paiute.

An average of 300 to 500 souls for each division, or 1,500 for the stock, seems a liberal computation of the pre-American numbers. To-day the two northern groups alone survive and between them can muster less than 40 full and mixed bloods, and these much scattered. The Yana as a whole suffered heavily at the hands of the whites in the first 20 years of contact, both by fighting and in massacres, and have never been even partially sheltered by reservations. None of the adjacent stocks and few of the neighboring ones, except possibly the Shasta and the Okwanuchu, have shrunk in the same ratio.

Near the central Yana village of Wichuman'na, some miles east of Millville, was a saline swamp. The dark-colored mud was taken up and dried for use as salt. Achomawi, Atsugewi, and Wintun all resorted to this place—a fact that indicates more or less chronic friendliness. This locality originated the Achomawi name for the Yana, Ti'saichi, " Salt people."

CHARACTER OF CUSTOMS.

However commendably hardy the Yana may have been, it is clear that they did not rank high among the natives of the State. They were perhaps on a level with the near-by Atsugewi and Achomawi. The little coruscations that enliven the culture of the Wintun and Maidu, for instance, are entirely lacking. Mythology, symbolism, ritual, social customs, the uses of wealth, are all of the plainest, most straightforward, and simplest character. Although bordering on both the great valley stocks, none of the Yana had any participation in the Kuksu religion that found its focus there. It is not even possible to ascribe to them any partial reflection of the valley civilization: their culture consisted of the primitive basic elements which other groups shared with them but overlaid with more special developments.

The winter house was the earth-covered one of the Modoc, Pomo, Wintun, and Maidu. They called it *igunna* and *mat'adjuwa* or *watguruwa*. Although generally referred to as a " sweat house," Yana myths make clear that it was a dwelling.

Their thatched summer homes the Yana called *wawi* or *wowi*, which seems to be the generic word for house.

The Yana were situated in the region where two basketry arts meet; the northern of overlaid twining with *Xerophyllum tenax*, which they called *maha;* and the central one of coiling and twining, but without the overlay technique. The two northern divisions followed the former method chiefly if not exclusively. Their ware is scarcely distinguishable from that of the northern Wintun and the Achomawi. The Yahi coiled much like the Maidu; of what precise type their twining was, is not clear. For the southern Yana all data are lacking, but their situation suggests that the line between the two arts ran up the slope of the Sierra Nevada along their northern or southern boundary. It is possible that one or more of the Yana divisions showed an unblended mixture of the two styles, such as is found among the northeastern Maidu, although west of the Sacramento the cleavage of the arts is sharp.

Dentalia, *bahninu,* as well as clam-shell disks, *mats'ewi*, were prized as money. Again we are at the distributional border, and which form prevailed is not clear.

Brother and sister addressed each other in the plural, the singular being considered improper among them, as is the case between parents-in-law and children-in-law among several other stocks. This practice must be interpreted as an approach to a taboo on communication. Some parent-in-law taboos seem to have been observed by the Yana. In a tale, Coyote addresses his mother-in-law freely; but his erotic character in Indian tradition, and his actions in this story, do not allow any certain inference as to the actual custom.

A term for bastard, *wahtaurisi*, "sits at the foot of the ladder," indicates that some observance was given to social station. This position, the nearest the entrance in the earth-covered lodge, belonged to people of no moment.

The two northern divisions buried the dead. During heavy snows people were sometimes interred inside the earth lodge, to be exhumed and reburied later. The Yahi cremated.

The native dog of the Yahi was sharp-nosed, erect-eared, short-haired, of the shape and size of a coyote, but gentle and definitely domesticated since it bred in a variety of colors. It was used in hunting bear and deer, and was more or less fed on meat; but, like most American dogs, died from eating salmon. Its flesh was thought deadly poison to human beings, and was much favored by wizards for evil purposes.

Yana myths are often picturesquely told, but explain little and lack real interest in cosmogony or the origin of human institutions. Attention is concentrated on the incidents of the plot as such. Rabbit, Gray squirrel, and Lizard have been suggested as being to the Yana a creative trinity, somewhat parallel to Earth-Initiate, Father of the Secret Society, and Turtle of the Maidu, with Coyote as antithesis in each instance; but the difference in the spirit of the myths is enormous. The trivial doings of the Yana animals are devoid of all the planning and semigrandiose outlook of the acts of the Maidu gods.

The ghost dance of the early seventies is said to have reached the northern Yana from the Chico Maidu, that is, from the south.

THE YAHI.

HISTORY.

The Yahi, the southernmost division of the Yana, once resident on Mill and Deer Creeks, two eastern affluents of the Sacramento, are of a peculiar interest because of their rediscovery in recent years after they had been believed extinct for 40 years.

For some reason that is still obscure, this little group, that can hardly have numbered much more than 200 or 300, became particularly embroiled with the whites and embittered against them in the period of greatest Indian unrest in northern California—the time, approximately, of the Civil War, a full dozen years after the first contact of the races. The Yahi country lay near American farms and towns, but in the early sixties did not contain permanent settlers; indeed has very few to-day. It is a region of endless long ridges and cliff-walled canyons, of no great elevation but very rough, and covered with scrub rather than timber. The canyons contain patches in which the brush is almost impenetrable, and the faces of the hills are full of caves. There are a hundred hiding places; but there are no minerals, no marketable lumber, no rich bottom lands to draw the American. Cattle, indeed, have long ranged the region, but they drift up and down the more open ridges. Everything, therefore, united to provide the Yahi with a retreat from which they could conveniently raid. Only definite and concerted action could rout them out.

FIG. 31.—Yahi deer decoy, stuffed. (Compare Pl. 8.)

Of course, this action inevitably came. After numerous skirmishes with small parties of Americans, and at least one disastrous fight or slaughter, practically the whole remnant of the group was surrounded and exterminated in an early morning surprise attack by a self-organized body of settlers. This seems to have happened about 1865. If there were known to be survivors, they were so few and so terrified that they were obviously harmless; and no further attention was paid to them. General opinion reckoned the tribe as extinct. After a time, at intervals of years, a cattleman or hunter would report meeting a wild and naked Indian who fled like a deer. Now and then deserted cabins in the hills were rifled. A few of the local mountaineers were convinced that a handful of Indians still remained at large, but the farmers in the valley and the townspeople were inclined to scoff at their stories. In all but the immediate region the Mill Creek Indians had long been forgotten. The last printed reference to them is that of Stephen Powers, who knew them by their Maidu name of Kombo, and related how the last seen of them, in 1872 or earlier, was when two men, two women, and a child were encountered by a couple of hunters, but soon escaped into the brush. There can be little doubt that these were the only survivors.

REDISCOVERY.

At length, in 1908, a party of surveyors half way up the side of Deer Creek Canyon, a mile or two from the nearest cabin and not more than 15 miles from a trunk railroad, ran their line almost into a hidden camp in which skulked four middle-aged and elderly Indians, who fled. There was no doubt that they were untamed and living the aboriginal existence. Arrows, implements (fig. 31), baskets, the stored food, the huts, were purely native; such American objects and materials as there were, were all stolen. It was clear that for 43 years this household, remnant of what was once a nation, had maintained itself in this or similarly sheltered spots, smothering their camp smoke, crawling under the brush to leave no trail, obliterating their very footsteps, and running like animals at the approach of a human being. It was an extraordinary story: the ingenuity of the Indians was almost as marvelous as the secret of their long concealment.

THE LAST SURVIVOR.

The discovery broke up the existence into which the little band had settled. They had lost most of their tools; they feared to remain in the vicinity; their food supply became irregular. A year or two later the huts were found still standing, but abandoned. One after another the handful died. In 1911 a single survivor, a man with hair singed short in mourning for his relatives, remained. Solitary, weaponless, pressed by hunger, desperate and yet fearful of every white face, he wandered away from his accustomed haunts, until, in August, he was found half hiding, half approaching a house, near Oroville, 40 miles south. He was clapped into jail, but treated kindly; and, as the last wild Indian in the United States, his case aroused wide interest. There was no question of the genuineness of his aboriginal condition. He was practically naked; in obvious terror; and knew no English and but a few words of Spanish learned from his own people and considered by him part of his native tongue. He practiced all the ancient crafts, and proved an expert flint flaker and bow maker.

After a few days he was brought to San Francisco, where he remained, under the protection of the University of California, until his death in 1916. He was then about 50 or 55 years of age, and passed under the name of Ishi, an anglicization of his word for man. He refused to return to his old home or to settle on any Indian reservation, and in clothing and personal and daily habits speedily assimilated civilized ways. He learned English very slowly and brokenly, but was volubly communicative in his own tongue on all topics except the fate of his kinsmen, where deeply ingrained sentiment imposed silence. He was industrious, kindly, obliging, invariably even tempered, ready of smile, and thoroughly endeared himself to all with whom he came in contact. With his death the Yahi passed away.

A NATIVE MAP.

A map drawn by Ishi and reproduced as Figure 32 is of interest because it proves the California Indians to have been not totally devoid of faculty in this direction. They usually refuse point-

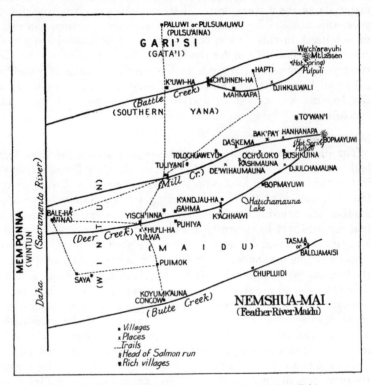

Fig. 32.—Map sketched and explained by Ishi, the last Yahi.

blank to make even an attempt of this kind, alleging utter inability, and it is only in the extreme south of the State that some rudiments of a sense of tracing topography appear. The Mohave readily draw streams and mountains in the sand, and the only native map ever published from California is a sketch of this type. The Diegueño ground paintings also evince some elements of cartographic endeavor, although in ritualized form. Considering the negative attitude of the northern California mind in this direction, Ishi's map is more accurate than might be expected.

YAHI GEOGRAPHICAL KNOWLEDGE.

The sketch is of further interest because Ishi appears never to have visited a considerable part of the area depicted by him, the features shown being known to him only by tradition dating back to the period before 1860.

It must be noted that Ishi applied the term "Gari'si" not to the northern Yana proper, whom he did not recognize as a separate group, but to the central Yana (the Gata'i), and to the southern Yana of Battle Creek. Actually, so far as can be judged, the southern Yana dialect is more similar to Yahi than to central Yana. Tuliyani on Mill Creek, and Yisch'inna on Deer Creek, may be names of chiefs that once lived at these villages, rather than true place names. Ishi employed the term Ga'me'si in connection with the region of these settlements. It is perhaps a designation of his dialect contrasting with Gari'si for the three Yana dialects to the north. Tasma or Baldjamaisi, also Yulwa, are possibly in upper Feather River drainage, in the vicinity of Big Meadows, rather than on Butte Creek. The stream shown is, however, not intended for Feather River, of which Ishi knew by report that it had four large branches and which he had seen before his capture at Oroville, but of the ancient inhabitants of which he knew only that they were distant and unfriendly. Battle Creek he called Chuhnen-ha more frequently than by its usual northern name of K'uwi-ha.

The Memponna on the map may be named after a chief, although he mentioned Pashahi as such. At Baleha, Saik'olohna and a woman Malki were former chiefs; he also knew the group as Malkinena. At Saya, Kinnuichi was chief. North of it, where Singer Creek and Bush Creek emerge from the hills, were Munmun'i and Djaki-ha; north of these, K'aiuwi at Stevens Hollow and Bolohuwi on Mountain Branch. These seem to have been Wintun rather than Yana, but their attribution varied. The Wintun and Yahi appear to have been on friendly terms, the former coming up Deer Creek at least as far as Ya'muluk'u, near the mouth of Sulphur Creek, well in the Yahi country, to camp and hunt. Other places in or near the valley, and presumably Wintun, were Ha'wan'na, south of Deer Creek; and to the north, Eltami, on Dry Creek; Gahseha; Mukaudanchiwa; Shunhun'imaldji; Chiwa'imaldji where the Indians of Paswi lived; Dahauyap'ahdi, on Dye Creek, north of Mill Creek; and the Dachapaumi-yahi. Mimlosi is a term used in reference to the vicinity of Red Bluff, and evidently contains the Wintun stem for water, *mem*. Chupiskoto, Holok'opasna, and Dashtilaumauna are unlocated Wintun places.

Most of the Maidu groups were less known to Ishi, hostility prevailing between them and the Yahi. The Puimok, whose speech Ishi called Homoadidi—the name Puimok is Wintun—once killed two men and a child at Milshna at Six-Bit Ford on Dry Creek, between Deer and Mill Creeks. Evidently warfare between the two groups was on more even terms than the exaggerated American accounts indicate. The Daidepa-yahi seem to have been a Maidu division in the Big Meadows region, with a woman chief Yella.

The Atsugewi of Hat Creek were called Chunoya and were friendly. Three chiefs were remembered: Pumegi, Badetopi, and Kanigi, besides a woman Wamaiki. They are said to have called the Yahi and perhaps all the Yana Dip-mawi.

Ishi knew a fair number of Atsugewi, Maidu, and Wintun words, about in the proportion of this order. Since he had never met a soul of any of the three stocks, this is a fact of interest, evidencing that the California Indians in their native condition took some interest in each other and spent more or less time in the home circle telling one another about strangers and their ways.

The term " Noza " (Nozi) Ishi seems to have applied to the southern Yana, and Wailaka (Wintun: "north language") to the central Yana. Antelope Creek he called Halhala, and Tuscan Buttes Uht'anuwi.

Other group names recorded from Ishi, but only after contact with a central Yana, and therefore not certain as a native possession, are Sasti (Shasta) ; Marak (Modoc) ; Paiuti ; Sun'sona (Shoshone) ; Basiwi, perhaps Washo ; and Shukoni, in the distant east.

CHAPTER 24.

THE PENUTIAN FAMILY.

INCLUSION.

The Penutian family has recently been established by a union of five stocks—Wintun, Maidu, Miwok, Costanoan, and Yokuts. Two of these, Miwok and Costanoan, indeed had long been suspected to have affinity, and certain resemblances had also become apparent between Wintun and Maidu and Maidu and Yokuts. A systematic comparison revealed a unitary basis underlying all the languages. Miwok and Costanoan form a subgroup in which some form of the vocable *uti* is employed in the sense of "two." In the three other languages this numeral is *pene*, *ponoi*, *panotl*. They may therefore be designated as the "pen" subgroup. From the combination of these two words comes the appellation of the whole family: Pen-uti-an. It is always unfortunate when names must be arbitrarily coined, but native terminology offers no assistance, there is no suitable geographical term available, and an artificial designation of some sort was inevitable.

ORGANIZATION.

The territorial disposition of the two subgroups is quite different. (Fig. 33.) The "Pen" languages are stretched in a long north and south belt; the "Uti" dialects follow a broken horseshoe curve. The former occupy practically all of the great valley proper, with tracts of adjoining upland. The latter are dialects of the mountains, hills, and coast.

The Miwok and Costanoan dialects are most similar where they are in contact on San Francisco Bay. From this region the one set becomes more and more specialized as the horseshoe is followed inland, the other as its alternative arm pursues its southward coastwise way. The Miwok idioms of the Sierra, therefore, and the most southerly of the Costanoan tongues, are the most different, though they are not far apart in geographical distance. They were and remain the best-known languages of the subgroup; and it seems chiefly to have been ignorance of the transitions that prevented an earlier recognition of their common source. Much the same can be said of the "Pen" tongues. They, too, were recorded and studied mainly at their peripheries: Northern Wintun, northeastern Maidu, southern Yokuts. As the records of the more centrally located dialects of the same three languages are examined, it is found that many of the peculiarities of the outlying idioms disappear. There is thus ground for the anticipation that if exact knowledge of the most southerly Wintun and Maidu and northernmost Yokuts dialects is ever recovered, they will prove to furnish strong links that now can only be suspected between the three allied members.

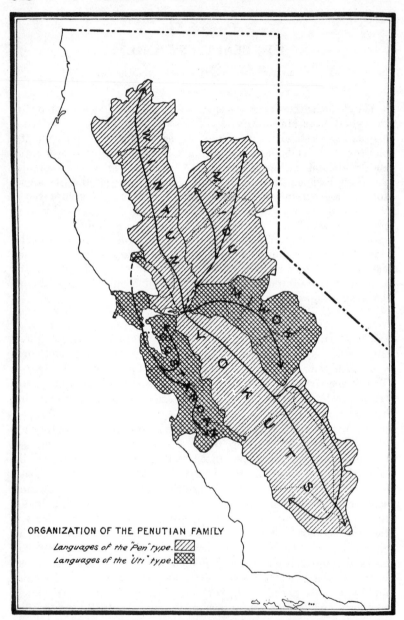

Fig. 33.—Penutian languages of "Pen" and "Uti" types. Arrows indicate degree and direction of dialectic variation.

The hearth of the "Pen," as well as of the "Uti" group, and consequently of the entire Penutian family, is therefore the spot at which all five of the principal languages abut, namely, the region where the conjoined Sacramento and San Joaquin debouch into the head of San Francisco Bay. Here or near this point is the philologist's center of gravity, and in this vicinity, too, the ethnologist must look for the greatest interchange of customs. The historian, however, need be on his guard against assuming this overflowed region of sloughs and tule swamps as the original home of the Penutian family. Natural conditions would render such a conjecture extremely unlikely to be true. This central point is one where rising differentiations were most efficaciously prevented by international contact or covered over by new assimilations. The speech and perhaps the customs of this half-drowned region, where the two great rivers of the State meet tidewater, are likely to be more similar to Penutian speech and customs of a thousand years ago than the tongues and habits of any other Penutian area, and that is all. The first seat of the family while it was yet undivided is entirely unknown.

TOPOGRAPHICAL RELATIONS.

The Penutian family occupied nearly half of California. It also held the core of the State—not only in a spatial sense but physiographically. This heart and kernel is what the geographer knows as the Great Valley of California and the resident as the Sacramento and San Joaquin Valleys, together with the flanking and inclosing mountains—an unbroken plain 400 miles long and a stretch from crest to crest of nearly 500. On one side is the Sierra Nevada, the highest range of mountains and in many aspects the most impressive in our country. On the other side the lower but sharp Coast Range stretches parallel. In the south both chains swing toward each other and meet in the semicircular Tehachapi Range, so that the wall remains continuous. In the north the Sierra breaks down, the Coast Range becomes higher and more irregular; the great volcanic peak of Mount Shasta is roughly where the two systems may be said to meet. Every drop of water that falls within this inclosure flows into the ocean through the channel of the Golden Gate, above which San Francisco sits clustered to-day. There are few regions of the same size that nature has endowed with greater diversity of surface, altitude, humidity, soil, and vegetation than this one. But there are also few that have been so distinctly stamped by her as a compact and indissoluble unit. This unit was the Penutian empire.

Figure 34 reveals with what fidelity they adhered to its limits. In the southeast, Shoshoneans and Chumash occupied a border of highlands inside the oval; in the northeast, Hokan tribes—Achomawi, Atsugewi, and Yana—held the elevated lava plateau through which Pit River has cut its way. But to compensate the Wintun have drifted over their barrier to the northwest and hold most of the drainage of the Trinity; and in the center Miwok and Costanoan long ago spread out from the Golden Gate, where they first came face to face with the roll of the Pacific, over 150 miles of coast. One

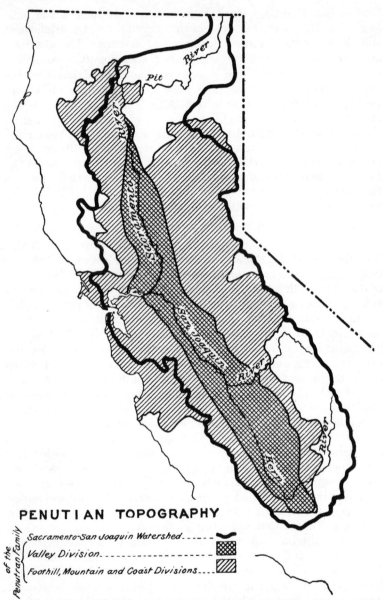

PENUTIAN TOPOGRAPHY

Sacramento-San Joaquin Watershed......
Valley Division....................
Foothill, Mountain and Coast Divisions....

of the Penutian Family

FIG. 34.—Penutian valley and upland dialects in relation to the drainage system of the interior valley of California.

can see them on the map crowding the Hokan tribes away from this outlet, leaving the Pomo a remnant on one side and their kinsmen, the Esselen, a fragment on the other.

CHAPTER 25.

THE WINTUN: GEOGRAPHY AND CULTURE.

The Wintun, the first of the five groups of Penutian affinity to be encountered in this survey, were, both as regards numbers and territory, the largest nationality in the northern half of California, and, next to the Shoshoneans and Yokuts, in all the State. They were also one of the most important in the development and diffusion of customs. It is thus regrettable that they are less known than nearly all their neighbors. The account that it is possible to present here is little more than a series of miscellaneous items, introduced to shed some light on the status of the Wintun in comparison with the neighboring peoples. A more systematic description has been attempted only of the ritualistic aspects of their religion, which has been selected, as being central and probably primary in its region, to serve as a point of departure for a comparative examination of the whole central California cultus.

TERRITORY.

The territory of the Wintun is long from north to south and narrow from west to east. It consists, substantially, of the west side of the Sacramento Valley, from the river up to the crest of the Coast Range. In some parts, however, the Wintun had not fully reached or retained this natural boundary; in others, they had transcended it.

From the mouth of Feather River, or more likely from a short distance above it, up to the mouth of the Pit, the Wintun lapped over on the east side of the Sacramento in a fringe that averaged perhaps 5 miles wide. The exact limits of this belt are difficult to draw on any map that does not show contours in detail. In the south, where the valley is broad, the Wintun appear to have held the tule marsh that fringes the Sacramento. With dry land began Maidu territory. The marsh was permanently habitable at a few knolls or mounds, especially at the river bank; and it furnished a splendid seasonal hunting ground for ducks and geese. In the north, where the valley narrows, the Wintun seem to have owned its entire level floor, the authority of the Yana commencing with the rather abrupt foothills. In the intermediate region, about Chico, the exact eastern limit of Wintun occupation can only be surmised.

It has been customary to assign the whole east side of the valley to the Yana and Maidu. A civilized person inevitably thinks in this way: A narrow overlap across the river which makes the central topographical feature of the map seems arbitrary. We put our counties on one or the other side of the stream: Butte balances against Glenn, Sutter with Colusa, Sacramento with Yolo. But the Indian knew the land with the soles of his feet; he thought of it in terms of its actual surface, of its varying plant and animal population, not as a surveyed chart on which certain great structural traits stand out. The valley offered him one mode of progress, food, occupation, and materials to work with, the hills another; and the same difference existed between the long, reedy marsh and the solid plains. Thus it was almost inevitable that different nations should come to occupy each tract. It will be seen below that where diverse peoples did not suffice, a single nationality generally split into groups marked off from each other by distinctions of customs as well as dialect. On the other hand, the great river as a convenient political boundary meant little to the native because he had developed scarcely the rudiments of our political sense.

From the mouth of the Pit north, the Wintun, here turned hillsmen because there is no valley left, had penetrated farther east from the Sacramento. They held the whole right side of the lower Pit, including the lower courses of its affluents, the McCloud and Squaw Creek, up to the commencement of the big bend of the Pit, about where Montgomery Creek comes in; thus uniting with the Yana on the south side to shut off from the mouth of this lengthy stream the Achomawi who are so identified with its drainage as to be usually known as the Pit River Indians.

The uppermost 20 or 25 miles of the Sacramento, where it flows a tumbling course through a picturesque wooded canyon, were not occupied by the Wintun but by the Shastan Okwanuchu. The boundary between the two stocks was in the vicinity of one of the several Salt Creeks of the vicinity; probably the northern one.

West and southwest of this alien tract on the headwaters, the Wintun occupied a large, rugged tract outside the Sacramento drainage: the whole upper waters of the system of the Trinity, the greatest affluent of the Klamath. These holdings comprised all the territory watered by the main Trinity above Big Bar, with its numerous tributaries and forks; nearly the whole of the South Fork; and all the Hay Fork. In fact, the Trinity may almost be denominated a Wintun stream, the only other natives within its sphere being the Chimariko, Hupa, and New River Shasta, owning restricted areas on its lower reaches.

There are some statements to the effect that the Wintun had drifted across still another chain of the Coast Range, and lived on the very head of Mad River, scarcely 30 miles from salt water as the crow flies. This is entirely possible; but other reports assign the region to the Lassik or some related Athabascan group; and Mad River being in the main an Athabascan stream, the latter statements have been given preference in the delineation of the map.

Toward the south, in the region of the headwaters of the Eel, the main Coast Range served as boundary between the Yuki and the Wintun; but from here south, the heads of all the western tributaries of the Sacramento were in the possession of a variety of non-Wintun groups.

First, upper Stony Creek, above Little Stony Creek but not including this, was northeastern Pomo, these people being wholly surrounded by the Wintun except where the Yuki backed them behind the mountains.

Next, the beautiful Clear Lake basin, the source of Cache Creek, was also in possession of the Pomo, who lived here in two groups, perhaps representing distinct drifts of occupation.

Farther south, in part in the same basin, but mainly on upper Putah Creek, were the Coast Miwok, a little isolated group with all its nearest relatives to the south and southeast.

Then, and last, came the Wappo branch of the Yuki: in the hills on the headwaters of Putah Creek and the Sacramento affluents to the south, and on Napa River.

We are now close to San Francisco Bay, whose upper divisions, Suisun and San Pablo Bays, are only the drowned lower reaches of the united Sacramento and San Joaquin Rivers. The flow, so to speak, here is west, instead of south; so that the western or Wintun side becomes the northern shore. This the Wintun held all along Suisun Bay and along part of San Pablo Bay; the Suisun "Valley," and the Napa Valley to the end of tidewater, being theirs. On the map this is the farthest territory downstream accredited to them, and the divide between Napa and Sonoma Valleys has been set as their limit. There is, however, much doubt about Sonoma Valley, whose native inhabitants are extinct. The Wappo held its very head; but its bulk, according to some accounts, was Wintun; according to others, Coast Miwok. If the former are correct, the Wintun extended almost to Petaluma Creek, or to within a scant score of miles of the ultimate goal of the Sacramento, the sheer defile of the Golden Gate into the broad Pacific.

DIVISIONS AND DIALECTS.

Wintun speech is very imperfectly known, and its ramifications have been determined only in the rough. Three great areas of distinct dialect are clear, which may be described approximately as consisting of a central block in Glenn and Tehama Counties, and a northern and a southern in the modern counties respectively on those sides. Beyond this basic classification, information quickly fails us; but it is clear, both from fragmentary evidence as well as from the size of the tracts involved, that these, like the corresponding Maidu divisions, are areas of groups of dialects, not of single, uniform idioms. In other words, the basis of customary classification is different for the Wintun and Maidu on the one hand, and stocks such as the Athabascan, Yuki, Pomo, and Miwok on the other; and there is no reason to doubt that when the two former tongues are recorded with the same nice discrimination of petty differences that has been directed to the other languages, the same conditions of local diversification will become evident, and the abnormal extension of the Wintun and Maidu " dialects " will be seen to be more apparent than actual. It is probable that the true status of speech among both Wintun and Maidu will ultimately be found to approach somewhat that existing among the remotely allied Yokuts, where the number of slightly different dialects is great, but these fall readily into half a dozen obviously distinct groups.

The northern form of Wintun speech prevailed down the Sacramento to Cottonwood Creek and over the whole Pit and Trinity areas. From all the evidence available, the language was remarkably uniform for a tract of this vastness, as it may justly be described under California conditions. But the very size of the territory precludes absolute identity of tongue. The Wintun of the McCloud and of the South Fork of the Trinity certainly never came in contact, possibly did not know of each other's existence. They must have been separated at least for centuries; and it is therefore impossible that every word and grammatical form in their languages should have been the same.

Cottonwood Creek is the boundary usually mentioned toward the central Wintun, and in default of any more precise knowledge has been so entered on the map. But the true line very likely followed the minor watershed on one or the other flank of the stream.

For the central Wintun one subdivision is known: that of the valley dwellers and the hillmen. But their dialects were not very different, and there may have existed equal or greater divergences between northern and southern settlements within the group. On the great map of the State, which alone shows the whole Wintun territory (Pl. 1), no attempt has therefore been made to indicate any internal demarcation.

Among the southern Wintun the cleavage between plains and hills continues, in fact is accentuated; and this block has therefore been represented not as a unit, like the others, but as consisting of a southeastern and a southwestern half. This gives, then, four instead of three primary Wintun languages and groups of people.

Both the southern dialect groups were subdivided; but the areas of these minor dialects are known in only two or three instances, which are recorded on Plate 37. The impression must be guarded against that these dialect areas were the only ones; from Knights Landing downstream usable data are almost nil, the Indians having disappeared.

The habitable sites in the Sacramento marshes were favorable places in winter, on account of the immense number of water birds which they drew, besides being in proximity to the salmon fishing in the main river. In summer the swampy plains were hot, malarial, and infested with swarming insects, while the hills were correspondingly attractive and productive. There was consequently much seasonal shifting of habitation. This can hardly have extended all the way from river to mountains: friendly people of diverse dialect may have visited each other freely, but if each had lived on the other's territory for half the year, they would have been a single nationality. The dialectic diversity between hills and valley, therefore, is evidence of the restriction of the regular movements of the separate communities to limited areas. The valley people evidently had their permanent villages on the river itself—that is, in the marsh belt—but appear to have left this during the dry half of the year to live on the adjacent plains, mostly by the side of tributaries. The upland people built their winter homes where the streams issue into the open valley, or in favorable spots higher on these creeks, and in summer moved away from the main water courses into the hills or mountains.

A distinction has often been made between a Wintun group proper in the north and a Patwin group in the south. This distinc-

PLATE 34

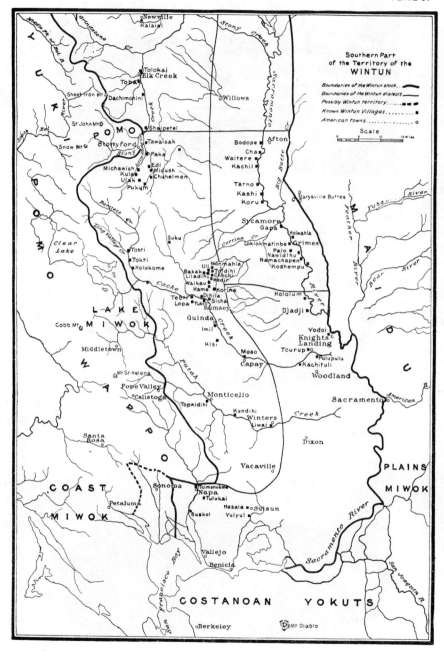

PLATE 35

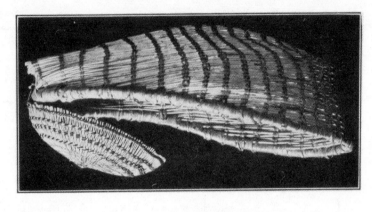

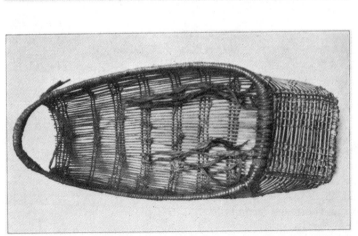

CRADLES, "SITTING" TYPE

Left to right, Yurok, Wintun (Pomo type), Northern Wintun

tion is based on the employment of these terms, in the dialects of the two regions, to denote " person " or " people." There is no doubt that in the north *win-tun*, or perhaps more correctly *win-tu*, is in use where the southerners say *pat-win*. The " Wintun " of this nomenclature seem to correspond rather closely with what are here called the northern and central divisions, the " Patwin " with the southeastern and southwestern. The terminology, being native, is likely to express a line of cultural cleavage of some consequence. It would therefore be desirable to follow, were it not for the confusion that might ensue from the use of " Wintun " to designate sometimes the entire stock and sometimes the northern half alone.

DESIGNATIONS.

The Wintun stock has sometimes been called Copehan in technical literature. This name is supposed to be derived from that of a village. Kope is grapevine in southern Wintun; but no settlement of this designation can be recalled by surviving Indians.

The Shasta knew the Trinity Wintun—the only ones they were in direct contact with—as Hatukwiwa or Hatukeyu; the Chimariko called them Pachhuai or Pachawe. The Yuki named the Nomlaki Titkaieno'm, but seem to have lacked any generic designation for the stock. How the Maidu, Yana, Achomawi, Athabascans, Pomo, and Costanoans called their Wintun neighbors is not known.

SETTLEMENTS.

The names and locations of some 60 sites inhabited by the Wintun are known, mostly in the northern part of the southwestern and southeastern areas. These are shown in Plate 34. Their grouping into political communities such as have been established for most of the Pomo territory can unfortunately not even be attempted.

Tawaisak, on Little Stony Creek, is a Pomo, not a native name.

Kotina, north of Cache Creek, is also not aboriginal. It appears to be the modern Indian adaptation of Cortina, the name of a chief, later used for his group, and then applied to a valley and a stream, or rather three streams. Whether this chief was simply labeled " Curtain " by the Spaniards, or whether his native name suggested this familiar word to them, is not known.

Many of the village names appear with the ending *-hlabe;* but this appears to be a suffix or added word, not a part of the name of the place.

The inequality in distribution of sites on Plate 34 reflects the incompleteness of knowledge, not any notable unevenness of occupancy.

A number of Wintun group names have been reported, but these nearly all refer to directions and boil down to merely relative designations like those used by the Miwok, the same people being northerners and southerners to their several neighbors. Where the directional terms fail to appear, elements like *ol*, " up " or " above," enter into these shifting designations.

Among the names are: Waikenmok, Waikosel, Wailaki (applied to themselves as well as to the Athabascan division on whom the name has crystallized in American usage). From *wai*, " north."

Nomlaki, Nomkehl, Nummok. From *nom*, " west."

Normok, Norelmok, Norbos, Noyuki, Nuimok. From *nor, no*, " south."

Puimok. From *pu*, " east."

Of similar type: Olposel, Chenposel, Wilaksel, Daupum-wintun.

Other cited names are those of places outright: Napa, Liwai-to, Yodetabi (for Yodoi-hlabe). Probably of this class are Suisu-n, Karki-n, Tole-n, and Ulula-to or Ula-to, which appear to have been important villages in extreme southern Wintun territory, in the vicinity of the modern similarly named places; and a few others in the same region: Malaka, Sone-to, Ansak-to, Aklu-to, Churup-to, and Puta-to. Puta or Putah Creek has generally been derived from Spanish *puta;* but the ending *-to* (compare Napa-to) is native. Either the Wintun of a place on Putah Creek accepted the Spanish epithet or the Spaniards put their own interpretation on a native place name.

Places in the north were Waidal-pom, at Ydalpom; Tsarau, at Stillwater; Paspuisono, at Redding; Hin-pom, probably at the mouth of Slate Creek; Tayamnorel, at Trinity Center; Tientien, at or below Douglas City; Haien-pom, at Hyampom. Wini-mem, " middle river," and Pui-mem, " east river," do not denote tribes as sometimes stated, but the McCloud and Pit Rivers.

In Central Wintun territory Paskenta is probably named from a native settlement. The word means " under the bank."

A few terms seem to be group names formed on localities; as Topaidi-sel, from Topai-dihi; and Lol-sel, the " tobacco people " of Long Valley east of Clear Lake. Designations of this sort are parallel to the Pomo group names ending in *pomo* or *napo*.

WARS.

The Cortina Valley people fought the northeastern Pomo, with whom the neighboring Wintun of Little Stony Creek were probably allied. They were also in feud with certain of the Sacramento River people. The hill Nomlaki of Thomas and Elder Creeks also warred with the plains people below them. The latter in turn were unfriendly with the valley people of Stony Creek and southward, if their name for this group, No-yuki or " southern enemies," may be depended on. Another feud prevailed between the Lol-sel of Long Valley and the Chenpo-sel of middle Cache Creek.

Scalps (in the south more probably whole heads) were taken in war, hung on poles, and celebrated over with a dance, but no details of the procedure are known. The Trinity Wintun, like all the northwestern tribes, took no scalps, and may therefore have made the war dance of preparation in place of that of victory. They are said to have fought with slings. This seems to be a mountaineer's accomplishment whenever it occurs in California.

NUMBERS.

If the Pomo aggregated 8,000 and the Maidu 9,000, the former Wintun population may be set around 12,000. To-day, however, the Wintun have shrunk to a less figure than either of these neighbor-

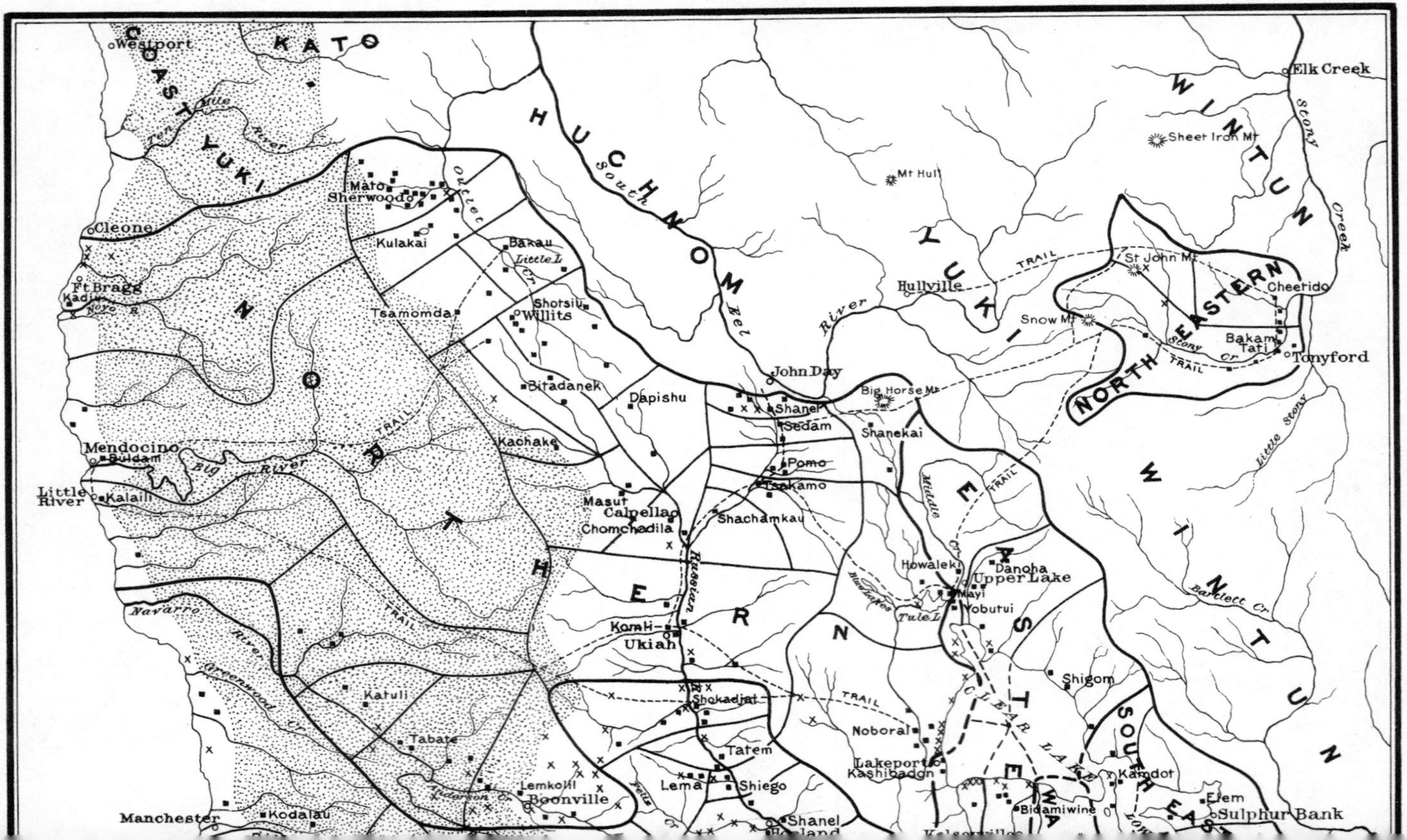

COAST YUKI
KATO
HUCHNOM
YUKI
WINTUN
NORTH EASTERN
NORTHERN
EASTERN
SOUTH EASTERN
Westport
Ten Mile River
Cleone
Ft Bragg
Kadiu
Noyo R
Mendocino
Buldam
Big River
Little River
Kalaili
Navarro River
Greenwood Cr
Manchester
Kodalau
Mato
Sherwood
Kulakai
Outlet
Bakau
Little L Cr
Tsamomda
Shotsiu
Willits
Bitadanek
Dapishu
Kachake
TRAIL
Masut
Calpella
Chomchadila
Katuli
Tabate
Lemkolil
Boonville
Anderson Cr
South Eel
Eel River
John Day
Shanel
Sedam
Pomo
Tsakamo
Shachamkau
Russian
Komli
Ukiah
Shokadjal
Tatem
Lema
Shiego
Feliz Cr
Big Horse Mt
Shanekai
Middle Cr
Howaleki
Danoha
Upper Lake
Mayi
Yobutui
Blue Lakes
Tule L
Shigom
Noboral
Lakeport
Kashibadon
Clear Lake
Kamdot
Bidamiwine
Elem
Sulphur Bank
Mt Hull
Hullville
Sheet Iron Mt
Elk Creek
Stony Creek
St John Mt
Cheetido
Snow Mt
Stony Cr
Bakam
Tati
Tonyford
Little Stony
Bartlett Cr

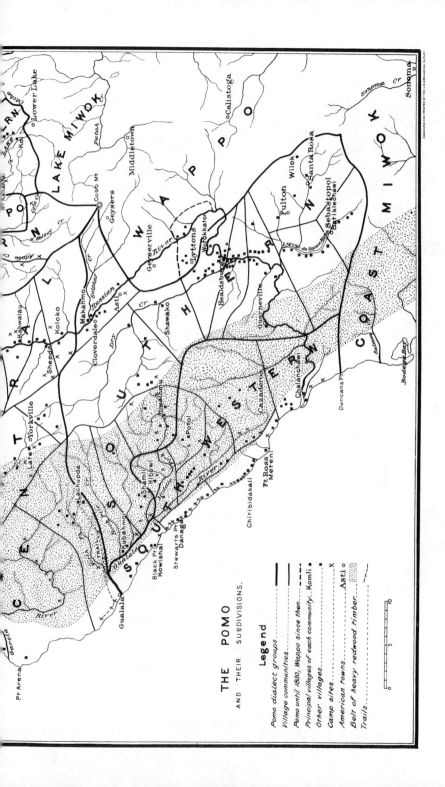

THE POMO
AND THEIR SUBDIVISIONS.

Legend

Pomo dialect groups ....
Village communities ....
Pomo until 1830, Wappo since then ...
Principal villages of each community ... Komli ■
Other villages .... ■
Camp sites .... ×
American towns .... Astio ○
Belt of heavy redwood timber ...
Trails ....

ing stocks. The census, which reports only 710, more than half of mixed blood, does not do them full justice, because many of the Wintun of Shasta County have no doubt been returned as "Shasta," ethnic designations being replaced in local American usage by names based on localities. Thus the Shasta become the "Yreka tribe," or "Scotts Valley Indians," while the northern Wintun are turned into "Shastas," "Trinity Indians," and "Hayforks." At best, however, the survivors of this once great nationality may come to a thousand or so.

The Franciscans drew converts from identifiable places in Wintun territory at least as far north as Puta Creek, and direct Spanish contact and influence extended to about the latitude of Clear Lake, say Cortina Creek or beyond.

CULTURE.

The unusual length of Wintun territory brings it about that this group is exposed to most diverse contacts of social environment. Divisions that live only a short day's walk away from the Hupa obviously will not observe the same customs as those which adjoin on the Pomo; and the Wintun bordering on the Achomawi and those in touch with the Yokuts can have had few specific habits in common. It is probable that the northern, the central, and the southern Wintun differed more from one another than the Pomo did from the Yuki. There is therefore little theoretical justification for a discussion of the culture of the stock as a whole; and such a summary method is followed here only because the available information is so scant that its segregation into three or more bodies would render each of these without shape or coherence.

In certain respects, however, the continuity of basic speech may have operated in favor of a more considerable uniformity of civilization than would be expected. Thus, northern Wintun mythology certainly inclines to the "creator" type that elsewhere is associated with the occurrence of the Kuksu religion which they did not follow.

The uppermost Wintun on Cache Creek and those in near-by Long Valley were cut off by the long canyon below them and the secondary range on their east from the bulk of their kinsmen, and stood in correspondingly closer intercourse with the Miwok and Pomo of Clear Lake, whom they influenced in several traceable particulars, and by whom they in turn were no doubt affected.

ARTS AND CUSTOMS.

Face tattooing for women, which seems to reach its acme in the Yuki vicinity, was practically lacking among the southern Wintun of the Sacramento. Ornamentation of the breast or stomach was more common. In the north the northwestern style of three lines or bands down the chin was in vogue.

The southern house was of the dance-house type, earth covered and dome shaped, at least in the valley. In the hills the conical bark house, and perhaps thatched structures, were in use. The Trinity Wintun used the bark dwelling. The custom of those in the upper Sacramento region is unknown.[1]

Among foods may be mentioned pounded and sifted manzanita berries, cooked; a cider made from the same; and young clover herbage, eaten raw. The inner bark of trees was sometimes resorted to in the hungry time of early spring. All these foods had a much wider distribution than Wintun territory.

Wintun basketry possesses little that is distinctive. In the north it is of the overlaid twined type characteristic of the border region of Oregon and California. On the McCloud the shapes and pattern arrangement are more nearly of Achomawi than of Yurok-Hupa type, as might be expected; along the South and Hay Forks of the Trinity, no doubt the reverse.

The southern limit of all-twined basketry among the Wintun is not known, but can not have been far from the boundary between the northern and central divisions.

In the central group, and among the northerly members of the southern one, baskets were, in a generic way, of Pomo type, but without most of the distinctive traits of the ware of that people. Among the Wintun bordering on the Pomo, as well as those of the extreme south, western influences were stronger. Feathered baskets have been reported from Yodoi on the Sacramento.

The Pomo type of baby carrier prevailed through southern Wintun territory: it is found without material modification on the Sacramento River. The central type is not known, but is likely to have been similar. In the northern group, a crude, shallow form of the sitting cradle was used, flatter even than the Shasta one; but carriers rather similar to the Pomo ones also occur. (Pl. 35.)

---

[1] Southeastern and central Wintun buildings in the Sacramento Valley were earth covered, elliptical rather than round, and uniform in construction, but of four sizes and functions: the dance house, *hlut,* about 50 feet in length; the sudatory, *chapakewe,* larger than the dwelling, and slept in by unmarried men and sometimes by their elders; the living house, *kewe,* 20 to 30 feet long; and the menstrual house, *kula,* up to 20 feet in diameter. There was but one dance, sweat, and menstrual house in a settlement, the first two in proximity at either the upstream or downstream end of the village, the latter at the opposite end. All buildings normally faced east—riverward—but the dance house also had a rear exit. Roof entrance and ladder are not mentioned. The dwelling was shared by several households, each with recognized floor space. There were no partitions, but there were raised bed scaffolds, and a common mortar hollowed in a log lying transversely at the rear, corresponding in position to the drum in the dance house. Summer camping was under rectangular brush roofs, without walls. See McKern, Patwin Houses, in bibliography.

The tule raft was used on San Francisco Bay and no doubt in the marshes all along the Sacramento.

Fishing in the northern streams is often from a scaffold out over the water; but this is simpler than among the Yurok and Shasta, and for spearing rather than netting.

The salmon harpoon runs to three times a man's length; and forks at the end, with detachable points, as in all the northern half of California.

The villagers on the Sacramento used decoys to attract ducks, then scared them into nets. The decoys are said to have been carved and colored, but this was scarcely the way the California Indians exercised their fingers, even in pursuit of a practical object. Models made of bound rush stems, possibly with ducks' heads set on them, are more likely.

Money came from the west, that is, the Pomo. Of late years the shells have been traded, and even the river Patwin know how to round and bore them. In the old days, it is said, only finished beads came in. Beads were counted, not measured. The reckoning was by units of 80 in the south. The thinnest disks were rated 80 to an American dollar, good beads 80 to 4 dollars, exceptionally thick ones 5 to a dollar. This is a quadruplicating count: 320, 80, 20 to 4 dollars. As the latter amount is the fee for each ceremonial initiation or degree, it perhaps represents a native unit of valuation, or at any rate evinces a southern Wintun inclination to reckon by fours.

The northern Wintun must have had and prized dentalia.

All the Wintun used their terms of solar direction freely on the most trivial occasion. "North of you" or "west of the door," would be spoken where we should say "behind" or "to the left." The tribes of northwestern California follow the same usage, except that they think in terms of water: "Downstream," "toward the stream," and the like, with the absolute direction changing to accord with the drainage of each locality.

THE DEAD.

In general, the Wintun buried the dead. This is established for the northern division; for the Nomlaki of the central group; and at least for the northern members of the southern Wintun, of valley and hills alike. The groups near upper San Francisco Bay, and some of those in immediate contact with the Pomo, may have cremated.

The precise customs in the extreme rite are not known; but the Nomlaki and the people about Colusa hunched the body, wrapped it with strings of money, bundled it in a skin—a bear skin if possible— and then wound it around and around with ropes. The grave, which was dug with sticks, was undercut toward the west. The body was dropped in, not lowered, then pushed with rods into the little cave.

The earth was slowly stamped down to the accompaniment of wailing songs. Property was buried with the dead in large quantities, and, in some regions, burned near the grave. Altogether the public ritual of burial and mourning was showy and slowly elaborate, and thus in some ways approximated a substitute for the anniversary burning of the Maidu and southern tribes, which the Wintun knew but did not practice. This statement holds without qualification for the southwestern and southeastern divisions. The central group, and those in the north about Redding, are said to have postponed the burning of property for a month or two after the funeral, a practice probably to be interpreted as an approach to the Maidu custom of annually holding a communal burning of valuables in commemoration of the dead of the year.

The native motive for the destruction of property was pure sentiment rather than a desire to equip the dead. People who did not sacrifice all the belongings of a relative were looked upon as having more regard for falling heir to his valuables than for him and his memory. This seems to be a powerfully rooted idea among all the California Indians. So far as magico-religious concepts enter into the burial or burning of property, they appear to run along the line of not retaining any object that might bring about the return of the dead person, rather than a desire to provide for his spiritual existence, although the Maidu are reported as specifying the latter purpose.

Somewhat similar are the motives that crop out in the universal taboo of the name of the dead. Fear of calling the ghost no doubt existed, at least here and there; but primarily the name was not spoken because its utterance would shock the family. For this reason a nameless reference, if direct enough to be unmisunderstandable, was almost as much to be avoided. No one who has even seen the effect produced on a group of Indians by the well-meant ignorance of a white man who inquires after a relative who in the meantime has died, or by any allusion to the parents of old people, can doubt that their sensibilities are roughly and deeply wounded. It is as when among ourselves the dead are spoken of slightingly or with condemnation; the only difference being that the Indian, feeling far more keenly or morbidly than we, regards any reference at all as an outright slight. Hence the unforgivable nature of the offense if there is the least suspicion of its having been intentional; and among natives, who know native custom and its strength, the breach can not well be other than deliberate. On the other hand, the names of the dead are freely spoken by those not related to them, at least to white men, if only the Indian has confidence that the information will not be allowed to go farther, and is sure that no other native can overhear him; which confidence would not be in him if he seriously feared that utterance of the name would call the ghost. Knowing that un-civilized nations believe in souls and follow magical practices, we are often inclined to rush to the conclusion that all their actions are influenced by these preconceptions, and to divest these people of some of the profoundest and most common human emotions.

Burial was in little graveyards not more than 100 yards from the houses of the living, and often in the village, perhaps in front of the dance house. The reason assigned for this proximity is pre-vention of grave robbery. Ordinary people would not touch any-thing that had been in contact with a corpse; but certain shamans were reputed so powerful that they had nothing to fear, and were likely to be tempted by the valuables underground.

Widows applied pitch to their close-cropped hair and their faces during the entire period of mourning.

SHAMANISM.

The southeastern Wintun, like the Pomo, recognize the transfer of shamanistic ability. Among the hill people, they say, each doctor acquires his own power; but among themselves, a man sometimes receives, not only knowledge or amulets, but the actual shaman's faculty, from a brother or relative.

In the north, shamans are "finished" in a dance held in the sweat house at night. Older doctors suck the novices' bodies clean; then call the *yapaitu* or spirits, who enter the neophytes and render them temporarily unconscious or maniac.

The disease-causing "pains," as the Yurok or Shasta or Maidu call them in speaking English, are named *dokos* by these Wintun, which word means flint or obsidian arrow point. The Yuki hold very similar beliefs. The *dokos* are evidently spirit missiles, and can be extracted, through sucking, only by a shaman who has a spirit stronger than the one which dispatched the death-dealing object. It is specifically stated that the *dokos* are sent into human bodies by benevolent but offended spirits; or by inherently malignant ones; or by such as are controlled by an evil-minded shaman. The sun, stars, clouds, salmon, coyote, dog, wolf, and sucker are all shaman's spirits; the first three benignant, the last three particularly powerful to bring death.

The were-bear shamans exercised their powers chiefly to destroy those whom they disliked. When in the form of the animal, they had the faculty of drawing their victims to them. Grizzly bears were not eaten.

Charm stones were hunting amulets, as among all other California Indians who recognize them. An American, finding one in a slough— they are almost always found in or near water—gave it to a Colusa

Wintun.   An older Indian carried it away on the ground that it was too dangerous an object to have about, and then, in order to retain undisturbed possession for himself, pretended to have lost it.   The old fellow was a constant fisherman and goose hunter, and the stone was known to be of value in attracting game.   This incident, in addition to the instances already on record, should dispose of the tenacious but utterly unfounded interpretation of these artifacts as sinkers. They were undoubtedly often suspended; but a charm can be hung as well as a net weight.   There is no evidence that any recent California Indian ever made one of these objects; but since they looked upon them as magical, it is quite possible that their prehistoric shapers manufactured them for magical use also.

TRADITIONS.

Wintun mythology is represented in the available records by a series of tales of very unusual form, apparently obtained in the region of Redding or above.   The chief deity and creator is *Olelbis*, "he who is above," or in literal idiom "up-in-sit."   He makes streams, game, clouds, mountains, acorns, and shells, or sanctions their production, and reobtains water after its abduction.   Daylight, fire, and flint are all secured from their chary possessors by theft, which is obviously a favorite mythic motive.   A world fire is recounted.   The existing human race supplants the first people, who are endowed with animal or natural attributes.   Coyote causes death and is its first victim; but the antithesis between him and the creator is vague.   Much in the world is brought about through the power of beings who are direct personifications: Water women, Flint, Fire-drill child, Old man white oak acorn, Wind, the Cloud dogs.   There are many episodes in all this to suggest the mythology of the Sacramento Valley Maidu; but again, much of the essential spirit of the systematized traditions of that people is lacking.

The Southern Wintun equivalent of *Olelbis* is not known, except that the hawk *Katit* is said to have been opposed by Coyote, and when he had yielded to him in the matter of death for mankind to have laid the *Equisetum* rush *sohi* in the path of Coyote's son at the burning of property for the dead.   The rush turned into a rattlesnake, which bit the young man as he ran; and when Coyote wished to reverse his law, *Katit* refused.   A world fire is told of; but this idea is Pomo and Yuki as well as northern Wintun.   The attribution of the origin of the earth to the turtle, which dived through the primeval sea, is a bond of affinity with the Maidu, with whom many more may be expected.

DANCES.

An adolescence ceremony for girls has been definitely reported only from the northern Wintun, and even there details are lacking. In general, this rite seems to wane in proportion to the development of the Kuksu cultus which is discussed in the following chapter.

The war dance and shaman's dance have already been commented on.[2]

---

[2] W. C. McKern, Functional Families of the Patwin (see bibliography), distinguishes (1) the household; (2) the *sere* or paternal family, a lineage of kin reckoned in the male line only; (3) the family social group, consisting of a headman and those who acknowledged his authority, viz, his wife, descendants, brothers and their wives and descendants, and young men recently married into the group and not yet returned to their natal one; but excluding older female members living in their husbands' homes and young male members still living in their wives' homes. Names, ceremonial objects, and household utensils were hereditary in the *sere;* strictly personal property was buried or burned at the owner's death.

The chief usually succeeded his father, sometimes a brother or uncle, but always a relative within the *sere;* an unqualified son might be passed over in favor of a more distant relative on his father's death, by agreement of the older men of the community; once in office, he could not be deposed. He consulted formally with the headmen of the family social groups (who evidently corresponded to the lesser chiefs or "captains" of the Pomo and the "town chiefs" of the Yuki) but made his own decisions and was not disobeyed; the dissatisfied left the community. His house stood in the middle and he wore only holiday attire. He is said to have assigned "picking grounds" annually to each family according to its needs, divided all larger game among the family headmen, directed communal hunts, and fixed the first day of fishing. He authorized the holding of the *Hesi* ceremony and gave a ritual name to each initiate. Councils were held, with sweating, in his house; gambling on ceremonial occasions took place in it; he was buried in it and it was then burned.

Each *sere* possessed an esoteric ritual, plus individually inherited charms, which qualified one or more of its members for certain religious, official, or trade functions. Thus the *hlapeta* family fished with the *hlapi* seine; the *chapentu* built salmon dams; the *chakotu* netted ducks; the *kapitu* flaked arrow points; others netted geese, made salt, made feathered or oval baskets or woodpecker crest headbands and belts. Nonmembers of these families were not prohibited from following the same occupations, but specialization and success went with the family medicine. Official and religious families, on the other hand, were monopolistic and provided the *chapatu* or *Hesi* fire tender; *koltu* or song leaders; *holwatu* or *Sika* drummers; *yaitu* or ritual shaman and instructor; *K'aima, Sika, Loli, Toto,* and *Kuchu* dancers; and the *maliomta* or shamans, who were taught by older relatives to influence the spirits. The chief, the war leader, the *chimatu* or *Hesi* manager, the *moki* or *Hesi* head, attained their positions through merit and not because of family charm or ritual. The strict rigor of patrilinear inheritance in these functional families was frequently modified by adoption of unrelated individuals of special aptitude or qualification.

Something of this type of organization would seem to have existed also among the Pomo, since it explains many of their statements; and in some degree among the Maidu and perhaps other groups; and it is evident that further studies along the line of this one will have to be made before the precise relation of the Kuksu organization and rituals, as described in the next chapter, to native society becomes clear.

CHAPTER 26.

THE WINTUN: KUKSU CULT.

The Central California Kuksu Cult.

Among the Wintun, or more specifically in the Patwin half of the Wintun stock, appears to be found the hotbed of the central Californian cult system based on a secret society and characterized by the Kuksu or "big-head" dances. It happens that the Wintun practices in connection with this organization are rather less known than those of their neighbors the Pomo and the Maidu; but as all indications point to their having exercised the most prominent influence in the shaping of this system, it is advisable to consider its general features here.

It must be clearly understood that "Wintun" in connection with Kuksu cult means Patwin only. Few if any non-Patwin Wintun followed this religion until after the white man came.

DISTINCTIVE TRAITS.

The presence of a male secret society must be taken as the first test character of the central Californian religious cult. This means that there is a set of esoteric rites participated in only by those who, usually as boys, have been initiated and instructed.

Hand in hand with secret societies in many parts of the world goes the use of masks and disguises, both traits springing from the same impulse toward concealment. True masks have not been reported anywhere in California; but it is clear that wherever the secret society prevails at least some of its members have their identity concealed during dances. This is accomplished either by crude and heavy coats of paint, or by face curtains of feathers, down, grass, or shredded rushes. As almost everywhere else, these disguised dancers of central California represent spirits or deities, in fact are believed to be such by the uninitiated children and younger women. The lack of an actual mask, in the form of a false face, is probably the result of the much weaker technical inclinations of the Californians than of other nations given to secret associations.

A certain type of place of assembly is a nearly constant feature of this cult: the large earth-covered house, approximately circular, with its domed roof resting on posts and beam logs. Structures of this general type are widespread: the Plains earth lodge—of which the Sun-dance lodge is only the unroofed and unwalled skeleton—the winter house of the interior Salish, of the Modoc on the California border, are all similar in fundamental plan. But these are dwellings. In central California the structure is a ceremonial chamber.

It is true that the living houses of some of the tribes that possessed the Kuksu society were often made like their dance houses, except that they were smaller. It is also true that several of the groups adjoining them on the north, such as the Wailaki, Yana, northeastern Maidu, and Achomawi, built the same kind of structure without devoting it to the uses of a society. But in general, the geographical correspondence of the two traits is close. The Wiyot, Chimariko, and Shasta, who are all but a short distance north beyond the confines of the secret society area, did without the earth lodge. To the south, again, the earth lodge has not been reported from the Yokuts, who had no secret society. They did construct sweat houses covered with soil; in fact, such structures prevail south practically to the limits of the State; but these were comparatively small buildings, devoted to sweating and sleeping, and not employed for dances, initiations, or assemblies. Again, an earth-covered house appears in much of southern California; but this is the living house, and ceremonials are held outdoors.

In the main, then, the spread of the earth house as a ritualistic chamber coincides with that of the Kuksu cult, except toward the north. So far as the correspondence fails in details, the variance can be corrected by consideration of an accessory, the foot drum. This is a large, hollowed slab, 6, 8, or 10 feet long, placed with its convex side up, above a shallow excavation in the rear of the dance house, and stamped on by the dancers. So far as available information goes, this drum is used only by secret society tribes.

The earth-roofed ceremonial chamber is frequently called a sweat house. It is this, at times, though smaller structures, used only for sweating, stood by its side. In uncomfortable weather it probably served as a lounging place for men. It seems sometimes to have been inhabited, sometimes, like the Yurok sweat house, to have been used as sleeping quarters by men only. It differs radically from the sweat houses of northwestern, south central, and southern California, first, in being much larger, and second in being the principal site in which dances and public rituals were held. In the other regions dances were performed in the open, or under booths or shades; an occasional exhibition or practice in the sweat house by disease-curing shamans is no real exception. Neither "sweat house" nor "dance house" is therefore accurately descriptive for the structure of the Wintun area; but the latter term is far more distinctive.

It can hardly be doubted that there is a connection between the dance house and the fact that so far as knowledge goes the secret society rites were prevailingly if not exclusively held in winter. Whether this custom drove the central Californians to build a structure that would afford them shelter from the rains, or whether the splendid roof of the earth lodge and its subterranean warmth drew the ceremonies indoors and therefore into the wintry season, is of course not to be decided offhand. But the latter seems more probable; both because religion may in general be assumed to be more likely to accommodate its details to industrial and material considerations than the reverse; and especially because the dance house, built smaller, served also as the permanent dwelling of the tribes in question. It would seem, then, that because groups like the Wintun and their neighbors lived in suitable houses, they came to conduct their ceremonies indoors and in the period of rains. This fixation in place and time, in turn, could hardly have any other effect than an elaboration of ritual. The same dance performed in the same spot for half a year would have palled even on the decoratively repetitive mood of a California Indian. Much of the systematization of the Kuksu dances and their bewildering ramifications, so unique in California and so reminiscent of Hopi and Kwakiutl, can therefore have its origin laid, with a fair degree of likelihood, to the fact that the people of the environs of the Sacramento Valley lived in good-sized, permanent, and waterproof houses.

At any rate, a causal correlation between buildings and ritual season is clear, because elsewhere, to the north as well as the south, where dances were held outdoors, or under flimsy sun shelters, all evidence points to the dry summer months being the usual time for ceremonies. This applies both to the northwestern tribes and to the Yokuts. The Modoc had the earth house and danced in it in winter, or outdoors in summer. For the southern end of the State, the custom is not so clear; but in this warm arid region every season is reasonably pleasant in the open.

RELATION TO OTHER CULTS.

The secret society, the pseudo-masks, and the semisubterranean dance house with its foot drum are, then, the regular recognition marks of the Kuksu cult that centers among the Patwin.[1]

Not one of these features recurs in the developed ceremonial system of the northwestern tribes. In fact, almost every aspect of ritual is diverse there: dances are occasions for the manifestation of wealth, and the participant enters them to display on his person the valuable splendors owned by his friends or kin, with no more notion of representing a spirit than when we go to church.

The southeastern or desert or Yuman religious system is also organized on a totally distinct plan. The dance is quite incidental, almost immaterial, often rudimentary. Hence the place where it is held, and the regalia worn, are of very little consequence. The center of interest is in the song, which comes in great monotonous cycles, whose words relate mythic events " dreamed " or spiritually experienced by the singer. He tells of the god or repeats his chant and speech, instead of enacting him: the ritual is essentially narrative, as that of the Patwin is dramatic. Again the whole ceremonial technique is fundamentally another one.

The fourth and last of the organized cults of California, that which appears to have originated in the coast or island region of southern California and to have spread north as far as the Yokuts of the San Joaquin Valley—the jimsonweed or toloache religion—has one point of similarity, as it has also geographical contact, with the secret society system: in both, an initiation is a fundamental feature. A group of initiates is in itself a kind of society; and in this sense, the southern religion can be said to be characterized by the presence of an esoteric society. However, the toloache cult stresses the initiation, while the northern appears to have more feeling for the organization as such, for its activities irrespective of the introduction of novices. Thus, the jimsonweed ceremonies are everywhere clearly puberty rites in some measure; among some groups elements taken from them are extended to girls as well as boys; and their avowed intent, as well as obvious purpose, is to render each neophyte hardy, strong, lucky, wealthy, and successful. It is the novice's career in life, rather than membership in an organization, that is thought of. The same qualities attach to the activities of the societies. These, in the south, are directed predominantly to either initiations or mournings, while in the Sacramento Valley prolonged

---

[1] Recent data suggest that among the tribes in the San Joaquin as opposed to the Sacramento half of the Kuksu territory—in other words, the Miwok, Yokuts, Costanoans, and Salinans—the secret society was either unimportant or lacking.

and involved ceremonies like the *Hesi* are practiced which either
are an end in themselves or have as their purpose the benefit of the
world at large, and are in no direct relation to the making of new
members or the commemoration of the old. A difference in emphasis
or meaning is thus quite clear between the half-society of the toloache
using Yokuts, Gabrielino, and Luiseño, and the typical Pomo,
Patwin, or Maidu society.

At other points the gap is complete. The narcotic and dangerous
drug introduces an entirely new element into the southern cult.
There is no approach to masks or disguise—in itself a suggestive indication that the true esoteric society feeling is weak or lacking.
The southern dancer acts as the god acted or taught; he does not
pretend to be a god. A slight and uniform costume suffices where the
northern imagination revels in a dozen or more kinds of attire—one
for each deity.

The associated mythology is quite different in sentiment as well as
in substance. In its most developed form finally, the Chungichnish
worship of southern California, the southern cult possesses features,
such as the ground painting and a type of symbolism, that are
wholly unrepresented in the Sacramento Valley.

DISTRIBUTION.

The one recognizable point of approach between the Kuksu and the
jimsonweed cults may account for the fact that they seem to overlap
territorially. As nearly as can be determined, the Salinan group
and the northern Yokuts followed both systems. But inferences may
be drawn from this circumstance only with extreme caution. Both
groups are extinct for all practical purposes. The survivors are
very few, and of their culture only memories of the grandfathers'
times remain: With the Salinans, evidence for Kuksu practices is
slight and for toloache of the slightest; especially as regards the
latter there is no positive means of deciding whether the recorded
mention refers to natives or to Yokuts foreigners imported to the
Salinan missions. About the northernmost Yokuts, even less is on
record. We barely know that they danced Kuksu, and the attribution to them of jimsonweed drinking rests wholly on statements of
their Miwok neighbors. On the whole, therefore, there is likely to
have been less commingling or co-existence of the two systems than
the map appears to indicate.

Between the Kuksu and the northwestern rituals, on the other hand,
there is an absolute geographical gap. Over a belt of 50 miles or
more of rugged country nothing pertaining to either cult was followed, the rude natives contenting themselves with shamanistic practices, adolescence ceremonies for girls, and war dances.

The distribution of the secret society cult is shown in Plate 74, but requires some amplification.

Actual records of the rituals among the Wintun are chiefly confined to the northerly members of the southeastern and southwestern divisions of the stock. The southerly villages, down to San Francisco Bay, unquestionably adhered to the cult. For the central Wintun, information is doubtful. The Colusa Patwin declare that the characteristic Kuksu forms, such as the Hesi ceremony and Moki impersonator, were not known beyond uppermost Stony Creek, in the region adjoining the northeastern Pomo. This is the end of southwestern Wintun territory. Beyond, on Grindstone and the middle course of Stony Creek, and about Paskenta, only " common " dances were made, the southerners declare, until the ghost dance of about 1872 coming in—the *boli* dancing, as they call it in distinction from the ceremonies relating to the *saltu* spirits—it became connected with some of the old rituals, and carried them north into these regions of the central Wintun.

These central Wintun are situated between the Yuki on one side and the northwestern Maidu on the other. Both these groups followed Kuksu cults in ancient times. The central Wintun are therefore rather likely to have practiced some form of the same religion even before 1870, in spite of the statements of their southern kinsmen. It may be presumed that those of the hills, who have chiefly survived, adhered to a form of the rituals which did not include the most special manifestations of the religion, such as the Hesi and the Moki, and perhaps did not even make use of the name Kuksu; in short, that they were much in the status of the Yuki. The central Wintun of the valley, particularly those on the Sacramento, may have been one with the up-landers; but their contact with the Chico Maidu, as well as with the southeastern Wintun downstream from them, make the conjecture more likely that they shared in some measure in the more numerous ceremonies of Hesi-Moki type. But there is no direct evidence to this effect.

Beyond them, among the northern Wintun, the Kuksu cults almost certainly did not prevail. Neither the mythology of these people, which is rather adequately known, nor any of the more scattering notices as to their customs, contain the least reference to any known phase of the religion. The ghost dance, however, carried the " big-head " impersonation and other Kuksu elements to them also, no doubt in a bastardized form.

From the northern Wintun, one branch of the Shasta, the group resident in Shasta Valley, learned the " big-head " dance since 1870. The Shasta are so overwhelmingly northwestern in their mode of life and point of view that these elements of the central religion would have been wholly in conflict with their civilization before American influences disintegrated it.

All of the Yana are ignorant of the characteristic old costumes, and fail to recognize names like Kuksu.

Of other northern tribes, the Wiyot, Chimariko, Shasta of Scott Valley, Achomawi, and presumably Atsugewi knew nothing of the system.

Among the Maidu, the valley villages of the northwestern division made substantially the same dances as did the Patwin. In fact the fullest information extant upon the complexities of the cult is derived from these people. The northwestern foothill Maidu possessed the same society but less elaborate ritual and a less systematic organization. For the southern Maidu or Nishinam direct data again fail us, but the position of these people, together with their close cultural relations to the northwestern Maidu on the one hand and the Miwok on the other, make their inclusion in the cult a certainty. They had probably developed it in intensity proportional to their proximity to the valley. For the northeastern Maidu, a race of highlanders, a doubtful negative must be recorded. They held indoor dances, among them a goose dance, in which an abundance of feathers was worn, and which are said to have been recently introduced from the northwestern Maidu. But there is no reference to disguises or to impersonations of spirits; the dances are said to have been made randomly and not in sequence; the "big head" costume was unknown; characters like *Kuksu*, so important in the northwestern creation myth, are unmentioned in northeastern tradition; and above all, the secret society organization is not known to have existed. If, then, the northeastern Maidu came under the cult at all, it was but very slightly and may again have been only since the arrival of the white man.

On the Washo there are no data. In spite of their living across the Sierra Nevada, it is not wholly precluded that they had borrowed something from the Kuksu cult; they knew of the earth lodge.

For the Pomo, there are direct accounts for nearly all of the divisions; and circumstantial evidence, such as the presence of dance houses with drums, for the others.

The Yuki ceremonies, which appear to have been only two, have been described in detail. It must be recalled that the two most northwesterly divisions of the Yuki proper, the Ta'no'm and Lilshikno'm, did not perform the impersonations of the other Yuki, and replaced their society by an "obsidian" initiation, of shamanistic inclinations, derived from the Wailaki. The Yuki *Hulk'ilal* and *Taikomol* dances were learned from the Huchnom, and the former ceremony reappears among the Coast Yuki under another name. Thus both these tribal groups must be included also. For the Wappo, nothing is known, but their location renders their participation in the cult certain.

One Athabascan division, the Kato, the southernmost members of the family, practiced the esoteric rites of the society, in fact, helped to convey them to the Yuki, it is said.

The Wailaki followed the just-mentioned "obsidian" cult. This possesses an initiation, but is essentially shamanistic and without impersonations. A Kuksu cult is therefore lacking; but a Kuksu stimulus may be suspected.

The Miwok on the coast and on Clear Lake were so identified with the Pomo in all their customs that they must be reckoned with them in this matter also. As regards the interior Miwok groups on the slope of the Sierra Nevada, definite data are available for the central division, and the character of these leaves little doubt that similar rites prevailed among the other three divisions. What is known of Miwok ceremonies gives them a somewhat different color from those of all the tribes so far enumerated. There is more mention of dances and less of a society organization. But Plate 74 reveals that those of the Yuki, Pomo, Wintun, and Maidu divisions about whom there happens to be information form a compact and continuous group, from which the central Sierra Miwok are removed by some distance; so that a considerable diversity of the latter would have to be expected.

On the large Costanoan and Salinan groups there is only the scantiest information, which in effect reduces to the fact that at both missions San Jose and San Antonio the *Kuksu* dance and one or two other dances with characteristic Kuksu names were performed. This would be sufficient, were it not for the fact that San Joaquin Valley natives were brought to both missions. This circumstance would seriously jeopardize all conclusions, except for one saving grace. The interior Indians settled at the Salinan missions were largely if not wholly central Yokuts tribes such as the Tachi and Telamni, whose survivors in their old homes are totally ignorant both of Kuksu and of any esoteric society, while they do follow the southern jimsonweed cult. The *Kuksui, Hiwei,* and *Lolei* dances at San Antonio are therefore more probably indigenous or long acculturated among the Salinans. With the system established there, the likelihood is increased that it prevailed also among the Costanoans, who lived between the Salinans and the Patwin. The particular *Kuksui* danced near mission San Jose until a generation ago may well have been an importation by Plains Miwok; some native form of the cult would nevertheless be likely to have existed among the Costanoans.

As for the Esselen, it is the same story as in everything else: ignorance. But they can hardly but have belonged other than with the Costanoans and Salinans.

The Yokuts, or the bulk of them, including practically all the survivors, are a toloache-drinking people. It is only the northern valley tribes, and perhaps only the northernmost block of these, that come in question for the Kuksu cult. There is so little known of these natives that there is really nothing to go on in the present inquiry, other than Miwok statements that many of their ceremonies of Kuksu type came to them from these Yokuts of the adjacent valley. Furthermore, the position of these people, between the Miwok on one side and the Costanoans on the other, and actually though barely in touch with the Patwin, makes it difficult to believe that they could have escaped taking up more or less of the ritual.

The secret society or Kuksu cult thus was followed by all or most of the members of eight stocks: the Yuki, Pomo, Wintun, Maidu, Miwok, Costanoan, Esselen, and Salinan, and by fragments of two others: Athabascan and Yokuts. On a wider view, the cult thus appears to be essentially as well as originally a Penutian systematization.

THE ESOTERIC SOCIETY.

Of the society itself our understanding is slight. There seem to have been two grades, although the second may have been entered after a less formal initiation. The first took place when boys were of a tender age, the second when or after they reached puberty, perhaps in early manhood. This has been previously noted for the Yuki; other groups have distinctive names for the two grades, as Pomo *muli* and *matutsi* (or *matutsi* as member versus *yomta* as head of the society), Patwin *yompu* and *yaitu*, Maidu *yombasi* and *yeponi*.

These two age steps were perhaps characteristic of the organization everywhere. There are some indications of further subdividing. Among the Patwin, some men are said to pass through 12 successive "degrees," each preceded by instruction and payment, and leading to knowledge of a new *saltu* or impersonation. There was a seat for each of these *yaitu* stages along the southeastern wall of the dance house, while the *yompu* novices sat on the southwest.

The northwestern Maidu of the foothills called the head of the society in each village *huku*. The valley people in the same group use the term *yeponi*. This term seems to be sometimes used specifically of the individual of highest authority; at other times, to be the designation of any fully initiated adult. The near-by Yahi, who did not have the society, regarded *yeponi* as the Maidu equivalent of their word for "chief" or important person in the ordinary sense, *mudjaupa*. So, too, the Colusa Patwin translate *yeponi* as *sektu*, "chief," and identify the Maidu *yombasi* or preliminary initiate with their *useltu* or night-prowling witch.

An initiate who has never risen to the highest rank is called *beipe* by the Maidu. The word is also used to designate the individual who assists the head *yeponi*. The same conflicting vagueness appears here, to our minds. Whether this is due merely to native etymological undifferentiation, or whether in reality there was only one person, or perhaps a few individuals, who carried the full secrets of the order in each locality, is a tantalizing problem.

The valley Maidu use three other terms that indicate some measure of systematized organization. The *ba'api* is an expelled or degraded initiate. The *kuksu* is the instructor of the *yombasi* or boy novices. The *hinaki* teaches the impersonators of the *Yompui* spirit. The southeastern Wintun do not seem to know the terms *ba'api* and *hinaki*, declare that any full initiate taught the boys, and add that if a member proved refractory he was magically poisoned by his fellows.

There is another side from which the organization can be approached, though here, too, the available information does not carry us far. The Maidu and the Patwin universally accord the highest rank among their spirit impersonations to the *Moki*. They state that for a man to make the *Moki* implies his having enacted all other characters and being acquainted with everything concerning them. Now this, if there are degrees and ranks within the society, looks like an instance of it. And yet the Moki performer attains his post not by any tested proficiency or service to the society, but by having acted as assistant to the individual who was the last incumbent, and having been designated by him as successor.

That is, so far as can be seen, an avowed principle of private arrangements here cuts into the society plan. The same holds true of the Maidu *peheipe* or clown, who retained his position for life or until age induced him to transfer the office to a successor of his own selection. Similarly among the Patwin, the singers, who appear to have been repositories of particular knowledge but who did not impersonate spirits in the dances, and thus almost formed a caste within the society, inherited their office in the male line. It is thus clear that a plan of recognized personal privilege, almost feudal in type, and rather at variance in spirit with the principle of a society of comrades, coexisted within the system.

The Patwin add that there are certain impersonations, such as the *Moki*, *Sili*, *Kot-ho*, *Temeyu*, and *Sika*, which many men receive instruction for but are afraid to enact. Possibly, they think, the teacher was offended at not receiving more pay and in resentment gave erroneous instructions, which, if carried out, would bring death to the performer. They placed full confidence, in such dangerously sacred matters, only in a near kinsman; so that the enactment of these spirits usually descended from father to son. The *T'uya, Dado, Dihli, Wit'ili,* and *Kuksu* impersonations carried much less risk, and were freely assumed by all initiates.

Still another point of view antagonistic to the fundamental scheme of a universal religious society is obvious as having intruded among the northwestern foothill Maidu. The *huku* or head of the society in each locality was a person charged with enormous responsibilities and privileges, but he was selected, not by any esoteric or ritualistic procedure on the part of the society, or any designated element within it, but by the leading shaman. That there is no misunderstanding of the reports on this point, and that it was the shaman as shaman and not as a member of the organization that made the selection, is clear from the fact that he based his choice upon consultation with the spirits—apparently his own private spirits and not the deities presiding over the organization. This status was reenforced by the circumstance that the new head of the society was expected to be a shaman himself, and that if he were not, he would be made such by having an animal or disease-bearing object introduced into his body by some acknowledged shaman.

It may be added that in the Chungichnish religion of southern California it is also often difficult to distinguish between the initiated as such and the shamans; and that the name of the former, *puplem,* appears to be only a reduplicated or collective plural of the word for shaman, *pul.* Evidently, the failure to differentiate completely is in this case in the native mind, and something of the sort appears to have been true also of the foothill Maidu and other northern tribes. For instance, the *huku* had as badge of office a cape, to which were attached objects of a fetishistic character. This cape was made for him by the principal shaman, and buried or burned with him at death. It was fatal even for other members of the society to touch it. When enemies in another village were to be destroyed, magic ceremonies were performed with the cape by its possessor. It is true that the society was less organized among the foothill people than among the valley Patwin and Maidu. But the interweaving with shamanism in the hills is so close that it can scarcely be doubted that in some measure the same processes must have been at work everywhere. Thus, at least some of the Miwok dances pertaining to the cult were made to cure or prevent disease; as has already been noted of the Yuki and Pomo.

Again to return to the *huku* or society head of the foothill Maidu, we have attributed to him functions not only of the shaman but of the governmental chief. He found the best sites for acorn gathering and announced them to the public; if the trees belonged to another village, he negotiated the payment for the crop. Besides inflicting sickness on foes, he warded it off from his own people. He made rain when it was needed, insured abundance of seeds, and a favorable run of salmon. He lit the fires at the anniversary mourning burnings. He knew and taught myths and more recent lore. Enmities were at once reported to him, that he might protect the people. He must understand all smoke signals. He advised about fighting, prepared arrow poison, and accompanied or led all war parties. In fact, his reported duties and prerogatives were so numerous that he must have been priest, shaman, and political and military chief all in one, and it is difficult to see where any room could have been left for the true chief except in matters relating to money and wealth, which it is significant are not referred to in connection with the *huku*.[2]

Now, when the dividing line between the priest and the shaman becomes obliterated in any primitive society, the matter may seem of no great moment to some students, in spite of the ideal difference between the two statuses, because after all both personages are religious functionaries. But when the priest is also the political head, especially as regards all foreign relations of the community, a commingling of what is normally distinct can not but be acknowledged; and this commingling means that social elements possessing no integral relation to the scheme of an esoteric and impersonating religious society have entered and profoundly affected that society.

All these indications together reveal at once the complexity of the connections and functions of the secret society, and its ill-defined vagueness as an organization. Elaborateness is present, indeed evidently in greater degree than we yet have specific knowledge of; but it is not a formally exact elaboration. Here lies perhaps the deepest difference of spirit between the organization of religion in its highest form in California and those expressions which it assumes among the Pueblos, the North Pacific coast Indians, and even those of the Plains.

For this reason the impression must be guarded against of looking upon the society of each village as a branch or chapter or lodge of the society as a whole. This is our modern way of organizing things. There is nothing whatever to show that the California Indian arranged affairs in such a way, and a great deal to indicate that he did not. The society existed only in separate communities. Each communal society no doubt recognized the others as parallel and equal.

---

[2] The difficulties about the *huku* are partly cleared up by the assumption that the foothill Maidu society organization was similar to that of the Pomo as disclosed by recent data: a limited membership drawn chiefly from one lineage in each community, and a marked centering of its authorities in the one person of its *yomta* or head.

In this sense there was a general society; but its existence remained a purely conceptual one. The society custom was widespread and recognized as international. The only societies were those of the town units. They were not branches, because there was no parent stem. Our method, in any such situation, religious or otherwise, is to constitute a central and superior body. Since the day of the Roman empire and the Christian church we hardly think of a social activity except as it is coherently organized into a definite unit definitely subdivided.

But it must be recognized that such a tendency is not an inherent and inescapable one of all civilization. If we are able to think socially only in terms of an organized machine, the California native was just as unable to think in these terms. When we recall with how slender a machinery and how rudimentary an organization the whole business of Greek civilization was carried out, it becomes easily intelligible that the American Indian, and especially the aboriginal Californian, could dispense with almost all endeavors in this direction which to us seem vital.

It is therefore not surprising that no name has been reported for the society. There probably is none. The dance house or ceremonial chamber is *k'um* in Maidu, *hlut* in Patwin, *shane* in Pomo, *iwil-han* in Yuki, *lamma* in Coast and *hangi* in Interior Miwok. No doubt these words are often used in the sense of the society rather than the physical structure itself. So, also, there is everywhere a name for the members as a class: *yeponi* in Maidu, *yaitu* in Wintun, *matutsi* in Pomo, *lashmil* in Yuki; and these terms, in the plural, again imply the organization.

In just the same way there is in southern California a name for the instituting and protective deity, *Chungichnish*, for the initiated, *puplem*, and for the place of ritual, *yoba* or *wamkish*; and there the vocabulary ends. It may even be recalled that among ourselves, who can not dispense with names of organizations as such, terms denotive of membership, like Masons, Foresters, Odd Fellows, and Elks, underlie our designations of the orders themselves. The Indian merely seems to have lacked any abstract word corresponding to our "society" or "order."

THE INFLUENCE OF THE MODERN GHOST DANCE.

The vagueness of purpose and technique which allowed the seeping in of such extraneous features as shamanism appears also in the introduction of "ghost dance" elements in the modern society rituals among the Pomo, southern and central Wintun, and in some measure the valley Maidu. These infiltrations are a consequence of the ghost-dance movement initiated in Nevada in the beginning of the seventies by the father of Wovoka—the Northern Paiute messiah of two decades later. The earlier prophecies came at a time when

the great mass of tribes in the central United States was not yet
ready for them—the last of the buffalo were still roaming the plains,
and the old free life had not yet disintegrated. The consequence was
that this earlier dream religion, instead of sweeping like a blast over
half the country, spent itself in Nevada and northern California, and
drew almost no attention from Americans. It ran, for a brief time,
and in typical ghost-dance form, with dreams of the dead and expectation of their impending return and the end of the world,
through northern tribes like the Achomawi, Shasta, Karok, and
Yurok; and may possibly have had some effect in fomenting the
Modoc war of 1873. Its course in the Sacramento Valley region
is not well known; but it attached itself to the soil and became en-
demic, modifying the old society ritual. The Patwin distinguish between their old worship and the modern *boli* or *bole* or "spirit"
religion—*boli* signifies ghosts or spirits of the human dead, as contrasted with *saltu*, the ancient spirits or divinities. This distinction
does not imply a separate organization and ceremonial existence. In
fact, the *boli* rites have perpetuated themselves, where they survived
at all, only as part of the secret society rites. But the older men
are aware of the difference between the form of religion practiced
in their youth and that prevalent now. Similarly among the Pomo:
recent ceremonies are in charge not so much of the head *kuksu* official,
as of a *maru*, a messianic priest or dreamer or "fortune teller," who
communicates with the spirits of the dead. Among the Pomo the
old society rituals perhaps went to pieces rather more completely than
in the Sacramento Valley; at least, the new cult obtained a firmer
foothold, and seems to have supplanted the ancient rites more.

CEREMONY, DANCE, AND IMPERSONATION.

A distinction of considerable importance between what may be
called the ceremony and the dance, or a ritual and a rite, appears in
native terminology. The Wintun call a ceremony *huya* ("gathering," "assembly"), a dance *tono*, a song *muhi;* the Pomo, according
to dialect, call a ceremony, which they describe as a four days' affair,
hai-kil (*hai-kil-ga*, *hai-kil-ba*) or *hai-chil*, "stick-hanging," and
the individual dances performed in the ceremonies, *he* or *ke*, "singings." [3] It may be added that the native words which we translate
by "sing" and "dance" are used with far less distinction of meaning, or with a different distinction, in some Californian languages,
than we make between them.

In the idioms other than Wintun and Pomo, the same discrimination between ceremony and dance may be expected, though it has
not been reported. As compared to *wok*, "dance," the Yuki say

---

[3] Another account calls both a ceremony and an impersonation *hai*, but distinguishes
a dance without impersonation as *he*.

wok-nam, "dance-lying," for "initiation." *Lit* they translate as "doctoring" or performing on the sick by means of spirit impersonations. This word may really denote "rite" or "ceremony"; especially since the *lit* is said to continue four nights.

Among the Maidu the distinction has not been recorded. This omission is perhaps the reason for the appearance, in the records concerning them, of an unusual elaboration of their dance cycle, and for the conflicting nature of their testimony as to its details.

On the other hand, Maidu accounts make it clear that there is a difference, of which the native is conscious, however difficult he may find it to express in general terms, between the dance or ceremony on the one hand, and the acts of spirit impersonation that enter into the ceremony on the other. Thus the Maidu separate the *loyeng-kamini* or "pay dances," in which payments are made because spirits appear in them, from the *weng-kamini*, which they translate as "common" or "profane" dances, in which there are no disguises.

This provides three elements for consideration: the ceremony, the dance, and the impersonation. Thus, with the Pomo, the *Kuksu* impersonator performs the *Kuksu* dance as part of various ceremonies. It is plain that relations such as these afford broad opportunities for confusion in presentation and apperception of facts known to us only by hearsay; and they have no doubt helped to obscure understanding of the ritual system. It is probably only accident, in other words imperfection of the record, that has led some students to distinguish the *Kakini*, or spirits impersonated by the Maidu, from their *kamini*, but to use the latter term indiscriminately for individual dance performances and for ceremonies that are complexes of dances and other activities; while among the Pomo and Patwin, other students separate the dance and the ceremony, but leave vague the relation of the spirit impersonation to each. The discrimination of these three factors, and of any others that there may prove to be, will have to be pretty accurately accomplished before we can hope to conceive the organic plan of the secret society cult with justice.

So far as the fragmentary knowledge allows, however, the principal ceremonies, dances, and impersonations have been brought together for comparison in the appended tabulations; the ceremonies (including perhaps some of the more important dances), as contrasted with the nonspirit or subsidiary dances, in Table 1, the impersonations or dance characters in Table 2. These lists embody all ritual performances that can be accepted as common to two or more stocks, either through similarity of name, identification by the Indians, or the possession of the same features. In addition, there is a long array of dances that are peculiar to the Pomo, Patwin, Maidu, or Miwok, or whose interrelations remain obscure; such are mentioned in the sections devoted to each of these stocks.

TABLE 1.—PRINCIPAL DANCES OR CEREMONIES ASSOCIATED WITH THE SECRET
SOCIETY SYSTEM OF THE CENTRAL TRIBES.

CEREMONIES OR MAJOR DANCES.

Meaning.	Yuki.	Pomo.	Patwin.	Valley Maidu.	Central Miwok.	Costanoan.	Salinan.
(¹)	Taikomol	Guksu ²	Kuksu ²	(³)	Kuksuyu	Kuksui ⁴	Kuksui.
			Hesi	Hesi			
Duck ⁵			Waima ⁶	Waima			
				Aki			
Grizzly Bear			Silai	Pano	Uzumati		"Bear."
Deer				Sümi			
Coyote		I'wi,Gunula.	Sedeu	Oleli			
Goose			K'aima	K'aima			
Ghost	Hulk'ilal	Hah-luigak			Sulesko ⁷		
Thunder ⁸		Kalimatoto					
Feather Down		Dama					

MINOR DANCES.

Meaning.	Yuki.	Pomo.	Patwin.	Valley Maidu.	Central Miwok.	Costanoan.	Salinan.
(⁹)		Hiwe			Hiwei ¹⁰	•Hiwei ¹⁰	Hiwei.
(¹¹)		Lole	Lole	Loli	Lole		Lolei.
			Keni	Kenu ¹²			
		Toto	Toto	Toto	Totoyu		
(¹³)			Salalu	Salalu			
Grasshopper ¹³				Ene	Salute		
Creeper ¹⁴				Tsamyempi	Akantoto		
Turtle		Hela-hela?	Anosma	Yelimi			
Condor			Moloko	Moloko	Moloku		
(¹⁵)		Gilak	Gilak		Kilaki		

¹ A deity or mythic character among Yuki, Pomo, Patwin, and Maidu; and perhaps among the other groups also. See the table of dance impersonations.

² Described by the Maidu as being a " *Yombasi* making," or initiation of boys among the Patwin, rather than a dance. The Patwin call *Kuksu* a *saltu* or spirit, but deny any *Kuksu* ceremony. The same seems to be true of the Pomo.

³ The first man and instructor of the first people; head of the secret society and instructor of novices among the valley Maidu. Among the majority of tribes the *Kuksu* ceremony heads the list in sacredness. Among the Maidu and Patwin the *Hesi* is accorded this place. The Maidu and Patwin lacked a separate *Kuksu* ceremony. Among the other tribes the "big-head" headdress is used by the *Kuksu* impersonators; with the Wintun and Maidu the wearers of this headdress have other names.

⁴ Reported from mission San Jose, whether among native Costanoans or introduced Miwok is not clear.

⁵ Said by the Maidu to mean "duck" (*wai*), though whether in their own or the Wintun language is not certain. The *Hat-ma* ceremony is the same as the Waima. Probably one is a Wintun and the other a Maidu name of the same dance. Possibly "crane"—northern Wintun *kat*, northwestern Maidu *waksi*— should be substituted for "duck." Compare the crane-head staffs used by the Pomo "ash-ghosts."

⁶ Also given as *Wai-saltu*.

⁷ Means the same as the Yuki and Pomo terms; a specific identification of the ceremonies is not established. See notes 11 and 12 in the following table.

⁸ Thunder is important in Maidu mythology, but no thunder ceremony has been reported from any group but the Pomo. The Kato associate Thunder with Nagaicho—their equivalent of Yuki Taikomol— in the creation and the Coast Yuki replace Taikomol by Thunder.

⁹ The *Hiwei* is specifically a man's dance among all the tribes from whom it is reported and is more or less contrasted with the women's *Lole*.

¹⁰ The central Miwok state this to be a recent dance among themselves, introduced by a Costanoan or northern Yokuts individual.

¹¹ Among Pomo, Maidu, and Salinans the *Lole* is a woman's dance; for the Patwin data are lacking; with the Miwok men are said to participate. See note 9.

¹² Performed by women and children only; the Patwin fashion is not known.

¹³ *Ene* means grasshopper, *salute* grasshopper or katydid. *Salute* suggests *salalu*, which in turn is close to Patwin *saltu*, "spirit."

¹⁴ Probably the nuthatch, at any rate a bird. Some of the features of this dance reappear in the Pomo *Dama* ceremony.

¹⁵ *Kilaki* denotes a small hawk in Miwok; it is not known what the meaning of Pomo and Patwin *gilak* is.

TABLE 2.—PRINCIPAL SPIRIT IMPERSONATIONS IN THE CEREMONIAL SYSTEM OF THE CENTRAL TRIBES.

Meaning.	Yuki.	Pomo.	Patwin.	Maidu.	Miwok.
....	....	Shalnis ¹........	Moki..........	Moki ²........ .	Mochilo.³
Cloud.................			....	Yati...........	
....			Sili............	Sili............	
"Big head" ⁴..........	Taikomol ⁵....	Kuksu ⁶..........	T'uya ⁷.......	Yohyo ⁸.......	Kuksuyu.⁹
"Woman" ¹⁰...........			Dado.........	Dü............	Osa-be.
Ghost ¹¹.............	Hulk'ilal......	Hahluigak......			Sules-be. ¹²
Ash-ghost ¹³.........		No-hahluigak...	Temeyu.......		Temayasu.
Grizzly bear...........			Silai ¹⁴........	Pano..........	Uzum-be. ¹⁵
Deer.................				Sümi.........	
Coyote...............			Sedeu ¹⁶.......	Oleli..........	

¹ The eastern one of six deities of the cardinal directions.

² Wüt'a was obtained as equivalent and is perhaps the native Maidu synonym. It is said to mean "insane."

³ Mentioned as a personage appearing in the Kuksuyu and Mochilasi dances. The impersonator is called Mochil-be. It is probable, but not certain, that the Mochilo corresponds to the Moki.

⁴ This is the current English designation used by Indians and whites. It appears that none of the native terms means "big head." The characters in question are those wearing the typical headdress of a huge ball formed by innumerable feathered sticks.

⁵ "He who goes alone," the creator. The Yuki identify him with the "big head" of the Pomo, but at east in some of his appearances he wears a long feathered net mantle like the Wintun Moki.

⁶ The southern one of six deities of the cardinal directions.

⁷ The Patwin know and some of them impersonate a Kuksu spirit, but if so only in minor ceremonies. The Hesi dancer, who wears the big-head costume, is called T'uya or Tonpa.

⁸ A spirit whose sight causes death.

⁹ A personage in what seems to be the most sacred Miwok dance, which is also named Kuksuyu. The impersonator is called Kukus-be.

¹⁰ The current English designation. Osa is "woman" in Miwok, Maidu Dü and Patwin Dado are untranslated. They very possibly are from eastern Pomo da, northern and central dialects mata, "woman." The Patwin state that the impersonated spirit is female.

¹¹ That is, the spirit of a dead human being. There is no connection with the modern ghost dance.

¹² Sule, a ghost; sulesko, a kind of spirit. There is a Sulesko dance, said to have been introduced recently to cure sickness caused by ghosts, and a Sule yuse "ghost hair," or Sule sikanui "ghost scalp," a dance of revenge with a scalp. Sulesbe is the leader in the Sulesko dance.

¹³ So literally. They play with coals of fire. The Miwok Temayasu does the same; otherwise nothing is known to connect him with the Pomo No-hahluigak. The Patwin Temeyu, who wears a long feather cloak and dances in the Toto and Hesi, is not known to be similar except in name.

¹⁴ Impersonator and ceremony; at some places in Patwin territory, Sika.

¹⁵ The impersonator in the Uzumati or "grizzly bear" dance.

¹⁶ Impersonator and ceremony.

THE DANCE SERIES.

As to the sequence of the cycle of ceremonies, there is information from the Patwin and the Maidu.

The southwestern Patwin begin with the Hesi about October and end with a repetition of the same ceremony in May, with several other dances, such as the Toto, Keni, Lole, Coyote, Grizzly Bear, and Wai-saltu celebrated on a lesser scale during the winter. The particular dances introduced into any one ceremony are not prescribed. The Coyote dance, for instance, must come in the Coyote ceremony, but the Grizzly Bear, the Lole, or dances such as the Gilak that have no ceremony named after them, may also be inserted in the Coyote ceremony. Since the modern decadence, the initial Hesi has been dropped in some localities and commencement is made with the Toto.

The southeastern Patwin of Colusa began with the *Hesi*, followed with the *Sika* or Bear ceremony—which has long since gone out of use and been replaced by the *Toto*—and then made the *K'aima* and *Yuke*. The remainder of the series is not known, but it concluded with a second *Hesi* in spring. When a dance house is built, it is dedicated with the *Hesi*, and the entire cycle must then be gone through. At Grand Island, downstream from Colusa, the *Waima* takes the place of the *Sika*. Although it has no reference to the bear, the two ceremonies are considered similar and called *hlanpipel*, or brothers.

According to the Maidu of Chico also, the *Hesi* is the most sacred ritual; and they, too, make it twice, in October and in May, as the beginning and end of their cycle. The first *Hesi* is closely followed by several profane dances, the *Luyi* and *Loli* and *Toto*, which may almost be reckoned as part of it. Then comes the *Waima*, and, corresponding to it, shortly before the spring *Hesi*, the *Aki*. These two ceremonies are next in importance to the *Hesi*, and are visited by most of the spirits that enter the *Hesi*. Between them come two other spirit dances, the Grizzly Bear and the Deer, and between these again two dances that are somewhat uncertainly reckoned as spirit dances, the Coyote and Goose ceremonies. It is evident that a system is observed here: dances are paired and other balanced pairs of successively less import are inserted between them, the whole sequence—*Hesi, Waima, Bear, Coyote, Goose, Deer, Aki, Hesi*—thus forming a first descending and then ascending scale of sacredness.

The order ascribed to the remaining ceremonies, which are without spirit characters and therefore better described as dances, varies greatly according to informants among the Maidu, and was therefore evidently not rigorously fixed, although there was probably some plan. Thus the *Salalu* appears to have belonged early in the cycle, the Creeper dance near the middle, the Condor and *Yok'ola* toward the close. There is also some associating of the dances, partly corresponding to the balanced pairing of the spirit ceremonies: *Kükit* and Grasshopper, Coyote and *Oya*, *Yok'ola* and *Aloli*, seem to have been made in juxtaposition. In the main, however, all these dances might be performed at any time, or with much latitude of selection of period, between the major ceremonies.

It is possible that the Patwin and Maidu cycles would agree better if contemporary studies of them had been possible. The dances of the former people were continued until recently, but in altered form; the Maidu performances went out much earlier, and their recollection, though less clear, is accordingly purer.

At any rate, incompletely though we can trace it, and fluctuating as it may have been in its less conspicuous features, a definite arrangement pervaded the order of ceremonies made by both tribes between autumn and spring. The same plan will perhaps appear among other stocks, though as yet there is no evidence in this direction, other than that the Yuki initiations and accompanying ceremonies were protracted throughout the winter. But too close a correspondence must not be expected, since each district made and left unexecuted dances which its neighbors respectively omitted or practiced, as shown by the differences between the southeastern and southwestern Patwin.

THE KERNEL OF THE CULT.

One geographic diversity is clear within the system as outlined in Tables 1 and 2: the Pomo and Yuki form a subunit as against the Patwin and Maidu. Among the former the *Kuksu*, or "big head," and the ghost ceremonies are easily the most conspicuous. From the marginal Yuki, in fact, no others are known; and among the Pomo these two easily transcended all the remainder in importance, as is evident from the fact that the others are scarcely known. In the Sacramento Valley, on the other hand, the ghost ceremony appears to be almost unrepresented. *Kuksu*, too, is not a ceremony here but an impersonator or an official. The leading ceremony is called *Hesi*, a name not known elsewhere. The typical costume of the Pomo *Kuksu*, the "big head" itself, reappears in the *Hesi*, but under other names, and as the disguise of a personage of subsidiary rank. In its place the mantle-draped *Moki* has the primacy, accompanied by other spirit characters, the *Yati* and *Sili*, that have not been reported from other tribes.

The Miwok of whom we have information, and apparently the Costanoan and Salinan stocks, seem to have participated rather in the Pomo than in the Patwin form of the ritual. Their *Kuksuyu* is a dancer and a ceremony; they do not use the term *Hesi;* there is some indication that they practiced a ghost ceremony; and the status of the *Hiwei* and *Lole* among the minor dances suggests the Pomo rather than the Patwin-Maidu type. On the other side, as Sacramento Valley resemblances, can be listed only the presence of the minor Condor, Creeper, and Grasshopper dances; of the "Woman" spirit; and of the *Mochilo* as a possible though doubtful equivalent of the Moki.

The inference is that the valley Patwin and Maidu, although centrally located with reference to the distribution of the whole dance system, possessed it in an aberrant form, and that the border tribes, which customarily evince cultural traits in their most pared-down condition, are in this case the more representative. This can mean only one thing. The Maidu and Patwin once shared the generalized or Pomo-Yuki-Miwok form of the cult, perhaps even originated it. Either because of this earlier start, however, or because of a more rapid progression, they developed the generalized form of the system to its limits and then passed beyond it to their own peculiar *Hesi-Moki* form, leaving the outer tribes, such as the Pomo and Miwok, adhering to the older rites, and the extreme marginal Yuki perhaps attaining only to the rudiments even of these. There is thus a ritual superimposed upon a ritual in this cult, a *Hesi* system laid upon an older *Kuksu* system. This crown attained in the *Hesi* belongs only to the

Patwin and Maidu, and it almost certainly is a Patwin product; that the generic *Kuksu* basis also had its origin among the Patwin, at least largely, is therefore a reasonable possibility.

There may have been some secondary specialization also among the Miwok. The great number of their dances points in this direction. But more must be known of the systematic relations of their ceremonies and of their spirit enactments before this clue can be followed with profit.[4]

MYTHOLOGICAL RELATIONS.

The relations of the secret society cult to mythology, among all the tribes, promise to be exceedingly interesting once they are known. A few hints in this direction are embodied in the notes to Table 2. The modern southwestern Patwin place their ceremonies under the guidance of a spiritual *Katit*, a species of hawk, and possibly the equivalent of the northern Wintun *Olelbis;* but *Katit* may be the same word as *K'ütit*, the name of a Maidu dance. The most sacred spirits in Patwin and Maidu ceremonies, the *Moki*, *Yati*, and *Sili*, have not been reported in any narrative myths. They appear to be spirits that are believed still to roam the world and to be sometimes encountered, though only with risk. The Pomo *Kuksu* and *Shalnis* are rather deities, and the Yuki *Taikomol* is the creator himself. The Maidu *Kuksu*, on the other hand, is only the first man. It thus seems that the tribes that follow the cult in its simpler forms connect the ritual rather directly and crudely with the creation, while the more advanced ceremonialists weave it more lightly and subtly into their traditions.

It is, however, evident that there is a connection between the specific creator mythology of north central California and the Kuksu cult, the former being generally found in its purest and most extreme form only among tribes that possess the secret society. In fact, the distribution of the society is perhaps the broader, taking in the Costanoans and Salinans who seem to have known no spiritual or anthropomorphic creator; and with them, perhaps, must be included the Miwok; although for the northern Wintun the reverse condition held.

MINOR EQUIVALATIONS.

The intertribal integrity of the cult may be further illustrated by a few references to one of its most obscure phases, the nomenclature and functions of the various officials of the society and ceremonies.

---

[4] If they lacked the society, their historical status in the cult would be more dependent and marginal, and their type of ritual more primitive, than those of the Pomo.

The eastern Pomo call the general manager of a dance, who directs the movements of the participants, *Habedima*, " stone-hand-hold," that is " stone-carrier," or *Habe-gauk*, " stone person." Among the Yuki a similar personage, at least in minor dances, is known as *Lil-ha'-o'l*, " stone-carrier." Some informants assert that the *Habedima* belongs not to Kuksu, but to the modern *Maru* dances.

The central Pomo name of the same personage or of the singers is *Helima*. The central Miwok have *Helika* and *Helikna* dances. Perhaps this is only a coincidence.

The Maidu name of the *Habedima* is *Meta*. He is said to " coach " the dancers. The Maidu *Mesi* or Patwin *Chelihtu* leads or conducts the dancers into the house and about it. The Pomo *Metsi* or *Medze* was the fire tender or housekeeper, responsible for the care of the dance house during a ceremony. With the Maidu, the clown seems to have been fire tender.

The *Mesi* is frequently referred to by the Maidu, who also use *Huyeyi* as equivalent, which may be connected with Patwin *huya*, " ceremony." Compare central Pomo *kuya-shane*, " ceremonial earth-house," or *ke-shane*, " dance earth-house," as opposed to *ho-shane*, " fire earth-house," the name of the sweat house. Again, the northern Pomo word corresponding to *Hahluigak*, the eastern Pomo designation of the ghost impersonators, is *Kuya*. As northern and central Pomo replace eastern Pomo " *h* " by " *k* " and the latter language is in geographical contact with the Patwin, a connection seems more likely in this case than a coincidence.

The Maidu called the leading singer, who also prayed and harangued, *Yukbe*.

The clown or licensed parodist of the dancers and priests, the *Yohos* of the eastern Patwin, the *Peheipe* of the Maidu — the word is from *pe*, " eat," and gluttony is one of his principal affectations—is a specific and important personage in the Sacramento Valley, but without direct equivalent among the Yuki and Pomo. Certain of his functions are exercised by the ghost impersonators of the latter two tribes; but these represent spirits first, and ridiculous characters only incidentally. On the other hand, the practice of welcoming a distinct comic personage into ceremonies has penetrated farther south than the ritual system as such. The central and southern Yokuts—who know nothing of *Kuksu*, *Hesi*, *Moki*, ghost impersonations, " big head," or foot drum—call their clown *hiauta* or *hiletits*.

MOTIVES OF THE CULT.

The purpose of the Kuksu ceremonial organization is probably not altogether clear to the natives themselves. They appear so thoroughly to accept it as established and unalterable that in the old days any cessation from it would have seemed equivalent to a general catastrophe, perhaps directly productive of a disintegration of the physical world. The purpose of the initiation is generally stated to be to make the boys healthy, long-lived, hardy, swift, strong, and enduring. Again, the general effect, and that primarily a material one, is uppermost in the Indians' consciousness.

In much the same way the specific cycle of dances was thought to bring rains, nourish the earth, and produce a bountiful natural crop; perhaps also to ward off epidemics, floods, earthquakes, and other disasters. The Patwin state that the making of their spring ceremonies results in an abundance of bulbs and greens, and that when the *Hesi* has been properly held in October the fall harvest of acorns will be favorable.

Game was no doubt believed to be affected much as plants. The number of animal dances in the complete cycle suggests that these dances may have been made with such a purpose. That such a concept was lacking from the native mind it would be extreme to deny. But on the other hand there is little to show that the Indians inserted the deer ceremony into their series specifically in order to increase the number of deer. It is clear that such ideas are but little developed in the central Californian mind. The paucity of definitely appropriate symbolism points strongly to this conclusion. One has only to recall the degree to which corn is directly referred to in the ritual of the southwestern agricultural tribes, to realize that the California Indians' thoughts do not run readily in such directions. Questions put to the native are likely to bring deceptive replies: of course the deer dance produces deer; any dance helps to produce everything desirable. Before any conclusion can be drawn as to the notable presence of the factor of exactly applied imitative magic in the animal dances of the Patwin, Maidu, or Miwok, objective evidence to this effect must be available. As yet, such evidence is most sparsely represented.

Moreover, any interpretation of the ceremonies on the basis of a considerable magical symbolism must explain the presence of dances referring to animals that have no appreciable food value, such as the coyote, grizzly bear, condor, nuthatch, and turtle, as well as the absence of ceremonies relating to animals like the rabbit and salmon, which are economically important. Above all this, however, is the fact that the most widespread, spectacular, and sacred of all the rituals, the *Kuksu-Hesi* and the ghost ceremony, have no reference in name, and little if any in symbolic content, to any particular animals and plants. In fine, the dances are spirit dances. Their reference is to spirits or deities, whose control of the food supply is but an incident of their wider powers.

THE PATWIN FORM OF THE KUKSU CULT.

The sequence of ceremonies and the full series of impersonations are much less known for the Patwin than the Maidu, so that the following notes find a fuller significance in reference to the subsequent chapter upon the latter people.

The complete cycle of ceremonies varied not only between stocks but from dialect group to group, and even between villages. A

Patwin town sometimes sold one of its dances to another, the payment going to the chief.

The valley Patwin of Colusa held the *Hesi*, but not the next two most important ceremonies of the Maidu at Chico, the *Waima* and *Aki*. The other Maidu dances which these Patwin admit as being also their own are the *K'aima, Toto, Lole, Keni* (borrowed from them by the Chico Maidu), *Salalu, Moloko,* and *Silai* or Grizzly Bear, which last, however, they called *Sika,* and made in the place of the *Waima*. The *Wai, Waima,* or *Wai-saltu* was a Grand Island ceremony, and the *Gilak* was made there and at Knights Landing. The *Yuke* was an unidentified Colusa dance or ceremony.

At Cortina Valley, in the foothills, the known dances are *Hesi, Toto, Lole, Keni,* Coyote (*Sedeu*), Grizzly Bear (*Silai*), Duck (*Wai-saltu* or *Waima*), *Salalu,* and *Gilak*.

The Grand Island *Waima* is said to have been more like the Colusa *Sika* than like the Chico Maidu *Waima*. The *yaitu* or initiate who is the chief performer lies in the dance house without moving for two nights and two days, except that nightly he pays a visit to his sacred paraphernalia. On the second afternoon a sweating dance is held to four songs. When these are concluded the recumbent performer at last sits up. By this time the dancers are in a frenzy and bleeding at their mouths. Shouting *ho, ho, ho,* they plunge through a little side door in the north wall of the dance house and rush northward. Men standing on the roof answer with the same call, to guide the delirious dancers back, while the singers, who have mounted to the same station, chant a long song which begins by naming all the places within the dance chamber, then the parts of the exit, and proceeds northward, enumerating each slough and spot to the end of the world. The last words are *wanaiyelti yeduro mitalmu mato tawaihla pute tawaihla,* "at-rear-end (the north of the world) on-back you-lie your bed feathers bed"—as the chief performer has been doing. The dancers are followed on their northward course by their relatives, who finally calm them and induce them to return. A man who was not headed off would keep running and never come back, it is declared, and some are said to have been lost in this way. Once a dancer was found two days after with his head in a swamp, and another one drowned. Both were carried back to the dance house, sung over, and restored to life. Even the runners who return on their feet fall insensible at the door and must be treated before they regain their strength and faculties. The same evening the dancers, now enacting deer, are hunted with nets amid great excitement.

This performance seems to be the enactment of a myth. The *Hesi* cycle is said to have originated among the animals at Onolaitotl, the Marysville Buttes. The deer people here sang four songs while they sweated, then rushed to plunge into the water. Their foes used this opportunity to ambuscade and exterminate them, for which reason there are no deer on these peaks.

While there are 12 steps of *yaitu* membership at Colusa, only 10 impersonated *saltu* have been recorded, and it is unlikely that each "degree" corresponds with a spirit enactment, especially since the Patwin, like the Maidu, seem to have no clear idea of ranking the impersonations beyond the two or three most sacred.

The *Moki*, who wears a full-length cloak of crane or heron (*wakwak* or *doritu*) feathers, is the highest. Besides appearing as this spirit, the performer directs the *Hesi*.

The *Sili* comes next in sacredness, and like the Maidu *Sili* wears a fish net around his body. About his head are ropes of black feathers.

The *Yati* is known to the Colusa Patwin from Maidu ceremonies, but was not enacted by them.

The *Kot-ho* is wholly plastered with mud.

The *Sika* appears in the Grizzly Bear ceremony of the same name. There are other performers, called *Napa*, in this dance, who carry staves named *shai*, which are cut at designated places. There they sometimes find bears, who attack them. If a man is killed by the bears he is left unburied until the ceremony has been concluded. This was the practice for any death that occurred during a ceremony. These *Napa* dance but are said not to represent spirits.

The *Temeyu* comes in the *Toto*, a fact that elevates this rite from the rating of a minor dance to that of a fairly important ceremony among the Patwin, as is also indicated by its replacing one of the two annual *Hesi* in recent times. The *Toto* is directed by the *Kuksu*. The *Temeyu* wears a cloak like that of the *Moki*, but made of raven feathers and hung with little tablets of yellow-hammer quills.

The foregoing are the dangerous impersonations. Of the safer ones, those which any initiate undertakes without hesitation, the *T"uya* or *Tonpa* or "big-head" is easily the first or "heaviest," and with it is associated the female *Dado*. A young man first assisted the *T"uya*, then appeared with him as the *Dado*, then was ready to assume the *T"uya* costume. Boys, it is said, were "caught" for the *Hesi*, kept in the dance house until its conclusion, and made to carry regalia and serve the men; but this was not considered an initiation and no payment was rendered for such knowledge as the youngsters might pick up. It was not until they were adult that they really were instructed and became *yaitu*.

The *Dihli* wears long feathered sticks like those that make up the enormous headdress of the *T"uya*, but arranged in a horizontal plane. The one arrangement resembles a magnified pincushion, the other a hat brim.

The *Wit'ili* had grass hung over his face and on his body, and wore two flowing yellow-hammer bands from the back of his head.

The *Kuksu* occupies a special rank. He directs the *Toto* dance, is reckoned a *saltu*, but does not enter the most sacred ceremonies; he serves as messenger and punishes people that misbehave. Anyone that he has punished is thereby qualified to enact the *Kuksu* himself. Among the central Wintun of Grindstone Creek, who did not possess the *Hesi* until after 1870 but with whom the *Kuksu* character is likely to have been ancient, it is said that the man who enacted this spirit received his power by going into the hills and calling upon the *Kuksu* himself. The spirit appeared, cut him into small pieces, and those who followed and were versed in the procedure restored him to life.

Except for the *Kuksu*, none of the most important impersonations of the Pomo are enacted by the Colusa Wintun—the *Shalnis*, Ghosts, and Ash Ghosts.

The *Chimmatu*, or clown, is an important personage, but is not reckoned a spirit, probably because his identity is unconcealed. He is a carrier of news.

The southeastern dance house faces east, with a rear door at which women look in (Fig. 35). In old days they were forbidden to view the *Hesi* and during less sacred ceremonies were allowed in only on the first and last nights. Since the *boli* dances came into vogue the restrictions against their presence have been moderated. The floor, *wole*, is carefully allotted. The left or northern edge is occupied by the uninitiated, or at least by nonparticipants. The south side is subdivided. By the drum, *holwa*, and rear door sit the *yompu* novices. In the middle of the south side is the place of the chief, the owner of the dance house. This position, therefore, is the *sektu wole*, the "chief's floor." By him sits the particular initiate who has charge of the ceremony that is in progress. Between the novices' and the chief's station is the *yai-wole*, consisting of three separately named places for dancers. The *yaitu wole*, or full initiates' place, is by the front door. Between the chief and the full initiates are a number of places or seats, each named after its "degree," in ascending order to the right.

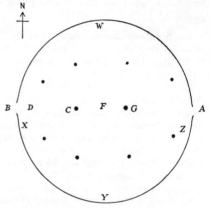

FIG. 35.—Patwin dance house. *A*, Dancers' entrance, replacing ancient roof entrance; *B*, rear door; *C*, chief post; *D*, drum; *F*, fire; *G*, second main post; *W*, uninitiated spectators; *X*, wole or floor of yompu, novices; *Y*, of sektu, chief; *Z*, of yaitu, initiates. (Compare Figs. 19, 39.)   (After Barrett.)

During the *Hesi* the rule is that each of these seats must be occupied by at least one member of the proper rank, otherwise the spirit impersonators become angry and *djurpiri*, that is, throw things about. A boy thus begins his ceremonial life at the rear of the house, moves gradually to the right, and concludes his career at the front entrance. When he begins, his father makes a payment which entitles him to this succession, so that as he advances to a higher seat he may eat there without danger.

The southern Wintun are reported to have possessed one characteristic feature of the Pomo ghost ceremony: the introduction of women into the dance house in order to meet the spirits of their dead relatives or husbands and make gifts to them. Unfortunately there is no hint as to the place in the system at which this enactment was introduced; and the Colusa people deny the practice.

THE PATWIN HESI.

The *Hesi* of the western Patwin begins in the evening and lasts for four days. The modern "ghost dance" rites that have been added to it seem to center about a pole erected in front of the dance house. This pole is wound with cloth of different colors, and carries a species of banner. The Patwin say that these recent elements in their worship relate to the *boli*, who seem to be the spirits of dead human beings, whereas the *saltu* who are impersonated in the older ritual are spirits of more or less divine character. It may be added that flags and wound poles were used elsewhere in the ghost dance of 1872.

The head and general manager of the *Hesi* among the modern hill Patwin is an old man who at times dances in the long enveloping feather cloak of the *Moki*. The identification of the official with the *Moki* impersonator may be an ancient practice.

The *T'uya* or "big-head" dancers are arrayed in the brush at some distance from the dance house, and calls are interchanged between them and the director on the roof. They approach the entrance in a ritual manner, and dance into the house backward. Besides the characteristic headdress, the dancers wear a skirt of feathers or rushes and carry a split-stick rattle in each hand. Each set of dancers is accompanied by one or more *chelitu*, who may be called leaders. The *chelitu* signals the beginning and end of the songs, and directs the steps and motions of the dancers. Part of the time he also dances with or opposite to the "big-head." His costume comprises a head net filled with white down, a tall crown of magpie feathers called *laya* by the Maidu, and the inevitable headband of yellow-hammer quills. In one hand he carries a bow, in the other a quiver filled with arrows. It is evident that the modern *chelitu* is a combination of official and dancer; he does not seem to impersonate any spirit.

Each "big-head" dances a quarter of an hour or more, stopping for brief intervals during which the leading singers, who are armed with cocoon rattles and carry the air, continue, while the chorus, whose main function is to shout *he he he* to the shaking of split-stick rattles, cease temporarily. One "big-head" succeeds the other until the entire set has danced, whereupon they retire to undress at a distance. In a full set of dancers, the "big-heads" are accompanied by one or more "women."

The first dance of the ceremony is made by the people of the home village. By the following day the residents of other towns have arrived, each in a body, and made a formal approach in file to the dance house, headed by their own "big-head" dancers in costume. As things went in the old days of Indian prosperity, there were often enough large villages represented to make the dancing almost continuous after all had assembled.

It is probable that spirits other than the "big-head" and the "woman" appeared either with these or between the big-head dances, since such was the Maidu custom.

Early each morning a fire was built in the dance house, and a song started to which the participants in the ceremony danced, as close to the fire as possible, until they reached a profuse sweat, whereupon they rushed out and into the near-by stream. Except for the dancing and the larger number of participants, this act did not differ from the ordinary daily sweating.

Visitors to the *Hesi* did not live in the village but camped outside. After they had filed into the dance house they were assigned seats in a particular section of it.

The clown wore no special dress. He imitated the *Moki*, or director, in voice and manner of speech, and ridiculed him as well as the dancers and singers. There was one in each village, besides a minor personage who played a similar part in dances of less sacredness. Both positions were for life, and the holders were always addressed by their title in place of their names.

The *Hesi* songs normally consist of a phrase of a half dozen words repeated four times or a multiple thereof. Such a " stanza " may itself be repeated indefinitely or may be varied by the substitution of new words for two or three of those first sung. Part of the language, but usually only a part, is archaic or of esoteric significance, so that the song does not make complete meaning except to the initiated.

Somewhat similar to the songs are speeches made by the *Moki* or person in authority. These are delivered in a very high voice and jerky phrases. Here again an ordinary person can understand perhaps half the words, but others being beyond his comprehension, and some of even the intelligible ones being used in a metaphorical sense, the exact meaning can not be clear to the populace, although the setting of the speech must help to indicate its drift. While the form of these orations is strongly ritualized, the subject matter is prescribed only in the most general way, and they are largely composed on the spur of the moment. The following will serve as examples:

piruboti	Be thus!
piruboti	Be thus! thus!
layakaroboti	Be good!
layakaroboti layakaro	Be good! good!
pima weyuro	That be glad of!
pima lamuro	That rejoice in!
e t'ewe lamuro	This speech rejoice in!
e lamuro	This rejoice in!
e chalal lamuro	These roses rejoice in!
wile chalal lamuro miletihla	Healthy roses rejoice in on you!
ouraboti	Approve! (say yes).
ouraboti	Approve!
outa pele were	Approve we come!
outa pele were	Approve we come!
eura pele piuto	Thus we shall do!
outo	Shall approve!
weyuto	Shall be glad!
we tache uto	Father will be glad!
we apacha uto	Mother's brother will be glad!
we labacho uto	Older brother will be glad!

eura pele huyahla_____ Thus we when gather!
eura pele huyahla_____ Thus we when gather!
pihla pele lamuto_____ Thus we shall rejoice!
peleno t'ewe_____ Our speech!
peleno t'ewe_____ Our speech!
pira weyuro_____ Thus be glad!
weyusha chu weyusha_____ Was glad I, was glad!
chu lamusha_____ I rejoiced!
lamuro opuro_____ Rejoice say it!
lamuro weyuro_____ Rejoice glad!
pima ouro_____ That approve!
pima lamuro_____ That rejoice in!

Another:

wuuu wuuu_____ Wuuu, wuuu!
wile sektu_____ Healthy chief!
wile sektu_____ Healthy chief!
wiledachu_____ Healthy!
nanu wiledachu_____ My healthy!
nanu wilechu_____ My healthy!
wiledachu helairachu_____ Healthy sway! (or shake).
lilainma wile lelorochu_____ Children healthy made!
loibama wile lelorochu_____ Girls healthy made!
seribama wile lelorochu_____ Youths healthy made!
pidachu nanu wiledachu_____ That my healthy!
chalal wiledachu_____ Roses healthy!
bole wiledachu_____. Ghosts healthy!
pidachu pulakiboti boai_____ That come-out with!

The constant -chu may mean "I;" the -da, like the -ro in the preceding sermon, seems to be a grammatical form used chiefly as a formal expletive. It is
clear that these series of ejaculations are not addresses in the sense of our
speeches, but ritual frames of somewhat variable content. The type of oration
is probably old; the content has been made over to accord with mannerisms of
the modern ghost-dance propaganda. Thus, the constant chalal, "rose," in the
sense of "beautiful," is said by the Indians to be a boli word. Wile, "healthy,"
seems to belong to the older saltu stratum, since the older people were wont to
utter: he'some wileda when a person sneezed (compare Yuki yoshimi). Both
in the old and in the modern speeches there are many cryptic words. Thus,
hamak, dried and pulverized salmon, was called "water meal," mem gori; for
hlut, dance house, kul'a was said; for depi, emerge, pulaki; for djoki, salt,
paharakma, with reference to its cracking or crunching sound when chewed.

CHAPTER 27.

THE MAIDU: LAND AND SOCIETY.

TERRITORY.

The Maidu, long classified as an entirely independent stock, are the second branch of the Penutian family encountered in a southerly progress through California.

Their territory may be described as consisting of the drainage of the Feather and American Rivers: or differently stated, the region from the Sacramento River east to the crest of the Sierra Nevada. The precise boundaries of the group are, however, involved in some uncertainty at almost every point.

From Mount Lassen east the line of demarcation toward the Atsugewi followed the watershed between Feather and Pit Rivers. Beyond, it becomes uncertain. Eagle Lake, Susan Creek or River, Honey Lake, and Long Valley Creek—an interior system behind the end of the Sierras—drain a tract the ownership of which is doubtful. Susan Creek and the Susanville region have usually been ascribed to the Maidu, but there are Atsugewi claims. Eagle Lake has been variously attributed to the Atsugewi, the Achomawi, and the Northern Paiute. Atsugewi ownership seems the most likely. Honey Lake was not far from where Maidu, Paiute, and Washo met. It seems not to have had permanent villages, and may have been visited by all three of the tribes in question. On the map the problem has been compromised by extending all their territories to its shores. Long Valley Creek was most likely Washo. Any Maidu claims to this stretch are likely to have been counterbalanced by rights or visits of the Washo to Sierra Valley on the Maidu side of the Sierras. Long Valley was probably habitable throughout the year, at least in places: Sierra Valley could be occupied only in summer. Its winter snows are unusually deep.

South of Sierra Valley the crest of the Sierras takes a westward turn before resuming its south-southeasterly course. In this offset lies Lake Tahoe, a favorite summer home of the Washo. The map makes the upland boundary of the Maidu pass within a few miles of the lake. It is, however, doubtful whether the Maidu followed the various branches of the American River up to their extreme sources. Farther south the Washo are known to have exercised hunting rights across the summits of the Sierra, almost halfway to the plains. It is not unlikely that they similarly crossed the crest in the Maidu region. Since this range is unfit for permanent habitation above an altitude of 4,000 to 5,000 feet, but since its crest runs from 8,000 to 12,000 feet, a belt of considerable width is involved in this uncertainty of ownership. On the other hand, the lack of permanent villages makes the question seem more important on the map than it was in native life.

The southern boundary of the Maidu toward the Miwok has been drawn along the Middle Fork of the Cosumnes. The north, middle, and south branches have all been mentioned in this connection. The actual boundary is more likely to have been the divide between some two of the forks. After the Cosumnes begins to swing south through the plains to unite with the Mokelumne, the interstock boundary left it and cut in a westerly direction across to the Sacramento. Here there is particular conflict of authority: but it would seem that the line in the plains was not far south of the lower American River.

The western limit of Maidu territory has generally been said to be the Sacramento. But actually this main artery served as a line of demarcation only as far up as the mouth of the Feather or a little beyond. From there on the Wintun held the marsh and slough belt on both sides of the stream. Butte Creek is the principal one of a series of south-flowing parallel streams which the Maidu occupied in this region west of the Feather River drainage.

Toward the Yana their boundary was reached either immediately north or south of Rock Creek, and farther up it followed the watershed between Feather River drainage on one side and Deer Creek and Mill Creek on the other, back to Mount Lassen.

DIVISIONS.

A comparison of vocabularies shows very quickly that Maidu speech falls into three languages: a southern one, spoken over a full half of the entire Maidu area, and two northern tongues which pass under the appellations of northwestern and northeastern. The southern Maidu, or many of them, call themselves Nishinam or Nisinan, whereas the two northern divisions use the term " Maidu "—more exactly Maidü, or in the nominative or absolute case of the word, Maidüm. This word means " person." The etymology of Nishinam may be " our people."

The northeastern Maidu inhabit a distinct topographic area: the upper reaches of the ramified drainage of the North and Middle Forks of the Feather River. The long, high wall of the Sierra here breaks up into a less regular formation. Among the masses and spurs of mountains lie flat-bottomed valleys, apparently old glacial lakes. It is these valleys, a dozen or more in number, plus perhaps the valley of Susan River, that provided homes for this division.

The northeastern language is not known to have been split into dialects, and if any existed they are likely to have been of little moment.

The northwestern Maidu were below the high Sierra, part of them in the foothills where the south, middle, north, and west branches of Feather River converge, and on upper Butte and Chico Creeks; and part in the open Sacremento Valley along the lower courses of the same streams. The topography is quite different in the plains and in the piedmont country. Habits of life were consequently somewhat diverse also; and hand in hand with this distinction of customs went one of speech. There are many indications of still further dialectic complication; but as all of them are imperfectly known, the area covered by the northwestern Maidu language has been left on the map without indication of subdivision.

The southern Maidu held the whole of the American drainage plus the Bear and Yuba Rivers, which technically are affluents of the Feather, although entering it in its lowest course. In this vast tract there are almost certain to have been divergences of idiom between the extreme north and south, as well as between those divisions living actually on the Sacramento and those at the upper limit of habitation in the mountains. The available vocabularies indicate that these presumptive differences must have been actual; but again the data on which it is possible to build are too unsystematic to allow of either classification or mapping. The Nisinan are therefore also represented as if they constituted the sort of uniform block which we know they were not.

In any event, however, the speech differences within each of the three Maidu languages were not more than dialectic, or at least not of a character wholly to prevent intelligibility. The primary northeastern, northwestern, and southern idioms, on the other hand, are diverse enough to warrant their designation as separate although cognate languages. Each has a fair proportion of basic words that are peculiar to it. Each also is about equally different from the two others, although northeastern is somewhat the most distinctive.

It may be added that the appurtenance of the dialect of Honcut Creek, between the lower Yuba and Feather Rivers, is uncertain. It has been included in the northwestern language in Plate 1. Actually the dialect seems to have been transitional between the northwestern and southern.

SETTLEMENTS.

Plate 37 shows these fundamental divisions of the Maidu as well as such of their more important local settlements as are known. Information as to the latter is rather irregular. In some regions minor villages have been included, in other tracts even the major towns have not been recorded. At several points the names appear to refer to the particular hamlets, often in the vicinity of some American town, in which the modern Indians have gradually concentrated as their numbers diminished, rather than to the villages that were important in aboriginal times. The securing of information of this character is difficult on account of the disturbance of native life for nearly 70 years, as well as because of the prevailing ignorance of the Indians regarding all tracts more than a few dozen miles from their place of birth.

The settlements recorded on Plate 37 are:

Northeastern Maidu: 1, Oidoing-koyo; 2, Nakang-koyo; 3, Hopnom-koyo; 4, Ko-tasi; 5, Tasi-koyo; 6, Yota-moto; 7, Silong-koyo.

Northwestern Maidu: 8, Paki; 9, Yaukü; 19, Bahyu; 11, Tadoiko; 12, Michopdo; 13, Eskini; 14, Yunu; 15, Nim-sewi; 16, Otaki; 17, Tsulum-sewi; 18, Konkau; 19, Taikus; 20, Toto-ma; 21, Tsam-bahenom; 22, Hokomo; 23, Benkümküimi; 24, Kalkalya; 25, Hoholto; 26, Kulayapto; 27, Tsuka; 28, Tsaktomo; 29, Yuma; 30, Ololopa; 31, Bayu; 32, Botoko; 33, Taichida; 34, Bauka.   (Nos. 35–38 should perhaps be included in this division.)

Southern Maidu: 35, Helto; 36, Toto; 37, Honkut; 38, Tomcha; 39, Yupu; 40, Mimal; 41, Sisum; 42, Okpa; 43, Hoko; 44, Yikulme; 45, Ola; 46, Taisida; 47, Pan-pakan; 48, Yamakü; 49, Wokodot; 50, Tsekankan; 51, Usto-ma; 52, Kushna; 53, Kulkumish; 54, Hembem; 55, Molma; 56, Pitsokut; 57, Pushuni; 58, Seku-mni; 59, Yodok; 60, Yalisu-mni; 61, Yükülü; 62, Chapa; 63, Siwim-pakan; 64, Kolo-ma; 65, Tumeli; 66, Indak; 67, Ekele-pakan; 68, Chikimisi; 69, Oncho-ma; 70, Opok; 71, Bamo; 72, Wapumni.

Spots which are mentioned as inhabited sites but not included in the map are the following: Natoma, Kohes, Kiski, Wili, Hoktem, Tankum, Tsamak, Wesnak. On Bear River below the foothills, in ascending order, are said to have been Homiting, Woliyu, Lelikian, Talak, Intanto, Mulamchapa, Lidlipa, Solakiyu, Kaluplo, Pakanchi, Shokumimlepi, Bushamul, Shutamul, Chuemdu, Opelto, Pulakatu, Kapaka, Yokolimdu, and Tonimbutuk.

A number of endings occur repeatedly on village names. Such are *-koyo,* "valley" or "land"; *-sewi,* "stream"; *-umni* or *-amni,* familiar also on Miwok and Yokuts names; *-oma* or *-omo,* perhaps meaning "people of"; *-ko; -to, -do,* or *-da; -kan* or *-pakan;* and perhaps *-si.* The ending of Nishi-nam or Nisi-nan recurs in Tosim-nan, "north people," a term which the Maidu of the Cosumnes drainage apply to themselves with reference to the adjacent Miwok.

DESIGNATIONS.

Few names for the Maidu are known. Pujunan has had some circulation in books, but is arbitrary as a designation for the stock, being based on the name of a single village, Pushuni. The Atsugewi call the Maidu Tikisuii. The Achomawi are said to call them Pakamali, but this term has also been recorded as the Achomawi name for the Atsugewi. The northern Paiute, it is stated, call the Maidu Wawa. The Washo designation is not known. The Miwok say Tamulüko, which means merely "northerners." The Yana terms are given as Wawaltpa'a and Pachamisi, but these are likely to refer to specific localities. The latter term suggests Baldjamaisi, the Yahi name of a Maidu village or district. The Yahi knew a number of Maidu localities, but lacked a generic term for the people. The Spaniards seem not to have designated them as an ethnic group, and Americans are wont to content themselves with the inclusive "Digger."

POPULATION.

There is no adequate means of estimating the number of Maidu. The figure assumed in this work, 9,000, seems very liberal. It is derived only from comparison with groups like the Pomo and Yokuts for which a measure of computation can be attempted; with consideration of the size, surface, and climate of their respective territories. The actual numbers may well have been several thousand more or less. The ethnologist who has studied them most put them at 4,000. To-day, if the last Federal census may be trusted, they have become the least shrunken of the five Penutian stocks, with about 1,100 full-blood and mixed-blood survivors.

USE OF LAND.

Land as such was not really owned. That is to say, its use was free and common to all members of the community. As to how far fishing and hunting rights in specific localities belonged to individuals or families is not clear. Concrete evidence is lacking and generic statements conflict. It does appear that fish holes were sometimes owned and that fences for deer drives could be erected in particular places only by certain families. The individual hunter, however, it is said, could search for deer and pursue them without restriction of any sort in the entire territory of the community or political group of which he was a member.

Twenty miles is said to have been an unusual distance for a hill or mountain Maidu to travel. In the valley journeys may have been longer. No northern Californian would go far from his home. Beyond a dozen or two villages there lay a narrow belt known only by hearsay or through occasional meetings with other visitors. Everything farther was utterly unknown. It is probable that the westernmost Maidu had only the vaguest cognizance, if any, of the most easterly Pomo; and the intervening Wintun occupied a comparatively narrow and open strip of land. Even within a man's ken, half the villages were likely to be hostile or under suspicion.

Village sites varied according to topography. In the valley they stood beside affluents of the Sacramento.

In the foothills the Feather, Yuba, American, and smaller streams flow through deep, narrow canyons. Permanent settlements were therefore generally on the ridges that separate the parallel streams, either on the crests or on knolls or terraces part way up. Minor features of topography seem to have determined the particular choices. The same was the practice of the Miwok, whose habitat is in the central part of the same slope of the Sierra. As one looks at the map of these two stocks, the villages seem placed quite randomly. The reason is that the basic structure of the land—a vast gentle slope furrowed into innumerable deep gashes by the westward or southwestward drainage—could not be utilized by the Indian, as it was in most other parts of California, in which the location of settlements can be predicted from a good map with some accuracy. For the foothill Maidu and Miwok a spring, a clearing, a level, a southwestern exposure, or any other of a number of essentially local and varying features was the deciding consideration.

The surface of the country is as broken in the Coast Range as in the Sierra, and if anything more irregular; but its scale is smaller and more intimate. The plan of the Sierra is so grand as to be scarcely observable on the ground except as an idea; its effect is one of endlessness and monotony. All the Coast Range people lived on their streams; in the extreme north, the year round; in the Athabascan and Yuki region, throughout the winter; from the Pomo south to the Chumash, perhaps less regularly according to season and with frequent departures, especially in summer, but still with an invariable return to the same home by the flowing water. Much the same habits prevailed among the Wintun and Yokuts of the great valley. Something of this mode of life must have been followed by the Maidu also. But the only reference is to movements in the mountains proper; and in the foothill slopes the conformation of the Sierra may have interfered.

In the northern high Sierras the mountains are practically uninhabitable. The flat-bottomed glacial valleys charm the eye with the soft vivid green of their carpet. But they are snow blanketed half the year, and likely to be spongy meadow or outright marsh most of the remainder. The northeastern Maidu therefore built along the edges overlooking the valley, with the pine timbered highland on one side of them and the open level on the other. A farming or cattle-breeding population might have selected sites in the flat stretches. For a people living directly upon nature, the Maidu choice of locations was by far the most practical.

Like most of the Californians who inhabited timbered tracts, the Maidu frequently burned over the country, often annually. It appears that forest fires have been far more destructive since American occupancy, owing to the accumulated underbrush igniting the large trees. Of course the Indian was not attempting to protect the stand of large timber: he merely preferred an open country. This is shown by the fact that he also burned over unforested tracts. Travel was better, view farther, ambuscades more difficult, certain kinds of hunting more remunerative, and a crop of grasses and herbs was of more food value than most brush.

POLITICAL ORGANIZATION.

The political organization of the Maidu was on the same basis as that of the Yuki and Pomo: a group owning a certain territory in common, knowing themselves as a group, acting largely as a unit, but actually residing in several settlements. In the northeastern division, where the land is mountainous with a few definite valleys interspersed, the houses of each group were in one of these valleys, or in a few cases, such as the larger expanse of Big Meadows, in a part of a valley. In the hills and Sacramento plains, the topographical segregation of the groups was less obvious, but is likely to have been basically similar.

For instance, American Valley, in which the little city of Quincy now stands, harbored one such nameless group. The valley as a whole was called Silo-ng-koyo, that is "Silo valley" or "Silo land." The same name was applied also to one of a half dozen settlements in the valley, that which stood where the high school has since been erected. This, although not the most populous village, had the largest "sweat house" or ceremonial chamber, which probably means that the man who had the most authority within

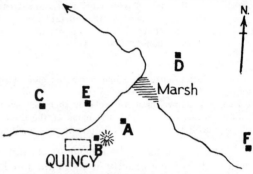

Fig. 36.—Maidu settlements in American Valley.

the group and was its spokesman lived here. This settlement was, however, called Nukuti as well as Silo-ng-koyo. Nukuti is evidently the specific name of the site: Silo-ng-koyo, it would seem, could have been applied to the settlement itself only as a representative of the valley. From our point of view, we should rather expect Silo to be the site, and the valley to have been named from it.

The settlements, as lettered in Figure 36, were as follows:

	Houses.	"Sweat houses."
A. Omhübe	6–7	1
B. Silo-ng-koyo or Nukuti	2–3	1
C. Opüle	4–5	1
D. Satkini	0	1
E. Piteli	4–5	0
F. Bumi	2–3	0
Total	18–23	4

On the basis of 5 souls per house, this would yield a population of about 125 for the "tribe." This basis may be too low. But 10 people in each dwelling is the maximum assumption possible—the Yurok averaged $7\frac{1}{2}$ in substantial houses of wood—so that the group probably did not exceed 200. The mountain Maidu have generally been described as living in the brush-covered *hübo*, which was a small structure. The informant who furnished the foregoing list called the "sweat houses" *k'umü* (northwestern dialect *k'um*), and the "houses" *k'umü-ng-hübo*. The former were entered only through the roof; the latter had a door on the ground. The "sweat houses" must have been inhabited, else Satkini would hardly have consisted of one of these standing alone.

It may be added that Nukuti to-day shows a single pit, 3 or 4 feet deep and about 12 by 18 feet across, lying at the foot of a large rock with a westerly outlook. This pit evidently represents the "sweat house." No other pits remain: from which it would appear that the "houses" were not seriously excavated and therefore presumably slight and rather small edifices. The sweat house, too, does not nearly attain the size of the more capacious earth-covered assembly chambers described in the hills and plains.

Similarly, Indian Valley or Tasi-koyo about Taylorsville had three settlements:

	Houses.	"Sweat houses."
A. Yodawi (with the largest sweat house), 1½ miles from Taylorsville, across the stream__	10–11	1
B. Ong-koyo-diknom, 3 miles distant_____	4–5	1
C. Küshdu (now called Tela-ng-k'umü, "Taylor sweat house"), at Taylorsville_____	6	1
	20–22	3

This tribelet must have had much the same strength as that in American Valley.

In Big Meadows, or more probably their eastern part, Naka-m-koyo was the leading settlement and also the name of the district. The site itself was at the famous Big Spring. Wishotpiming was a village belonging to this group.

There is nothing in the scheme of organization suggested by these data that does not exactly fit the Yuki and Pomo plan: but the unit groups, each comprising several settlements and yet forming a recognized community, are wholly without parallel among the Yurok and Hupa.

It may be added that the northeastern "villages" shown on Plate 37 seem quite generally to be the eponymous settlements representative of such groups, while for the northwestern and southern divisions the entries appear sometimes to comprise the separate settlements of a group and sometimes to be confined to the leading one.

The area claimed by each village community was very definitely known and sometimes marked. It has even been said that the boundaries were more or less regularly patroled to guard against poaching. Even game that had been wounded outside but died within the territory of a community belonged to the latter people and not to the hunter. This rule, however, is said not to have been observed by the high mountain people.

It is stated that four communities in eastern Butte County between Oroville and Mooretown once met to agree on the precise limits of their lands and on certain devices by which these should be marked. One took a crescent, another three vertical lines, and so on. These symbols were then scratched into natural rocks that served as corner stones. This arrangement is almost certainly colored by an imitation of land surveying and cattle branding; but, apart from the marking of lines and the use of symbols, it may rest on a genuinely native practice.

There is no trace of any system of social or political classification other than the village communities, nor of any fictitious or exogamic kinship groups.

THE CHIEF.

The quality of chieftainship varied according to region. The southern Maidu, particularly those in contact with the Miwok, made more of the institution. Their chief was hereditary, received part of all larger game, and sometimes had young men hunt for him outright. He lived in the village dance house, or his dwelling served as assembly chamber for the group. In the north, this close connection between the dance house and the chief perhaps did not obtain as rigorously. The chief is also said to have been chosen here for his wealth and popularity, irrespective of descent. It is further stated that he did not receive more than an average share of food. He could be deposed whenever he became unsatisfactory to the majority. These statements may apply rather to the simple mountain Maidu than to the people of the valley, whose wealth in property and ritualistic organization make it difficult to believe that their chief men should have been so inconspicuous.[1]

Such scanty evidences of descent as succession in office and inheritance of property rights afford invariably point to the Maidu counting in the male line.

TRADE.

The valley Maidu traded considerably with the Wintun. They received beads—that is, money—above all else. What they chiefly gave is not known. The beads were counted by tens, not measured, although handled on strings. From the valley and hills the beads flowed into the high Sierra, together with salmon, some salt, and nuts of the digger pine which grows only at moderate levels. The return was that of a hunting people: bows and arrows and deerskins, sugar-pine nuts, and perhaps some other local food products. A similar trade prevailed between the mountaineers and the Achomawi to their north, and indicates that the general status of northeastern Maidu culture was less advanced than that of the Achomawi, rude as was the life of the latter; or at least, that the mountain Maidu were the poorer. Obsidian for arrow points and a green pigment for bow decoration reached the Maidu from the north, probably also from the Achomawi. With the Paiute and Washo to the east the northeastern Maidu had little communication. The southern Maidu of the uplands may have been in somewhat closer touch with these neighbors. Wild tobacco from the border district of Honey Lake appears to have been traded in all directions.

---

[1] The data on the southern Wintun agree with the statements on the southern Maidu, and further enhance the probability of northwestern Maidu chieftainship being hereditary and influential, especially in the valley.

WAR.

The principal fighting weapon was the bow. Stabbing spears with obsidian heads and simple sticklike clubs were used occasionally. Shields were unknown, but both types of Pacific coast armor were worn now and then. The elk-hide coat was perhaps more characteristic of the valley; the waistcoat of rods, of the mountains. The wood for the latter was mountain mahogany. It is said to have had a high collar, behind which the warrior could shield his head. The rod armor is probably to be viewed as one of the many influences which the Achomawi have exerted on the northeastern Maidu. It is a type that extends from the northwestern tribes across the State to the Achomawi.

Attacks against the enemy were almost always made at daybreak. In open fighting great reliance was placed on dodging arrows and a constant dancing was kept up to disconcert the foe's aim. So far as possible the side of the body was presented to him as being narrower than the front. It is probable that in such battles the two lines were separated by nearly arrow range. At 50 yards an arrow from a powerful bow would be distinctly difficult to dodge.

Men were taken prisoners only to be killed. They were tied to a pole in the dance house and mutilated and burned to death. Several of the devices mentioned show some ingenuity of cruelty, but the torture gives the impression of a spontaneous expression of hatred rather than of any refined system of prolonging anguish. Foes of distinction seem to have been shot to death in a dance around them. If only the dead body or even the head of a foe could be secured, it was brought home and treated as if it were a living prisoner. Scalps were taken and danced about by men and women, but there are no details on record as to the cut of the scalp or the nature of the celebration. This scalp dance appears to have been a mountain rather than a valley practice.

The usual northern Californian system of paying for the slain prevailed. It seems to have been fairly well worked out in the valley, where it is said that war parties, or a group of negotiators dressed as if for war, would meet in a conference to discuss the exact terms of settlement. In the mountains blood money was more irregular, and it is said that it did not always prevent the subsequent taking of revenge. If this statement can be accepted there could have been little incentive to settle for a killing. Possibly the reference is to people who were too poor to pay adequately, and these may have comprised a considerable part of the population.

Feuds are likely to have been almost as common between Maidu villages as between them and foreigners. There is no evidence that any considerable group of Maidu towns ever united in a common movement against aliens. At the same time there were foreign groups toward whom distrust or enmity was chronic. Thus the northern valley people had more or less constant difficulty with the Yana, the northeastern Maidu with the Yana, the Achomawi, and the Washo. Hostilities between the Maidu and Wintun of the valley were intermittent and probably affairs of individual villages. As nations, the two groups seem to have been rather friendly, and at any rate to have communicated considerably. The mountain people apparently got on better with the Northern Paiute than with most of their other neighbors. The friends and foes of the southern Maidu are not known.

MARRIAGE.

Maidu marriage customs exemplify very accurately the variations of levels of culture that coincide with habitat in different altitudes in California.

In the Sacramento Valley the suitor remained at home and sent a representative with shell money. The price was displayed, discussed by the girl's family, and if considered insufficient, returned. The father might also accept the offering, give it to a brother, and then demand an equal amount for himself. It is said that the girl's consent was usually secured, or that at any rate she was likely to be advised of the offer before it was made; but this is not wholly in accord with the custom of other tribes among whom marriage by purchase prevailed.

In the hills, little or no money passed. The young man indirectly declared his suit by repeatedly visiting the girl's home and pointedly engaging in conversation on indifferent topics with her father. Having given due notice in this way, he went hunting or fishing, regularly bringing his catch to the girl's home, without, however, uttering a formal declaration. Acceptance of the gifts encouraged him to continue. After he had sufficiently shown his capacity and good will, he visited once more. A separate bed was now prepared for him and the bride, apparently without any words having yet been spoken on the matter, and the couple were considered married.

The mountain people dispensed even with this indirect and unspecified prepayment. The suitor merely visited in the evening and remained. If the girl did not want him, she sat up all night, if necessary. Otherwise he joined her. She was probably influenced considerably by the attitude of the family, and it is likely that a half understanding, or at least an indication of intention, previously existed among the young people. The only thing that resembled payment was that the young man remained with his bride's parents for some months, hunting and working for them. Even after he took her back to his own parents, or to a separate house in his home village, he occasionally visited and provided food for them during several years. An excellent hunter might even have a girl sent to him as wife; in which case it would be bad form for him to refuse her.

Among all the Maidu, kinship alone is said to have been a bar to marriage, and there existed no artificial incest groupings. The man was free to wed in his own or another village. Since his home settlement, however, consisted largely of kinsmen, he more commonly went elsewhere for his wife. In normal cases the permanent home of a couple was in the man's village, but a first residence with the bride's parents was the rule everywhere. This was clearly to render service as whole or partial purchase payment, and not a reminiscence of any principle of exogamy. Even in the valley it seems to have been added to the formal price as something that custom demanded without bargaining.

As to polygamy, the Maidu rule was the usual one in California. Chiefs, rich men, and old men kept as many wives as they could; the majority contented themselves with one. The levirate was in force among all the Maidu. In the mountains a man had a first claim on his wife's sisters. If he failed to exercise his right, it passed to his brother.

Among the hill and mountain people, where no real payments had been made, divorce was merely a matter of the wish of either party. In the valley a man could return his wife and claim his purchase price if she were unfaithful or otherwise definitely objectionable.

SOCIAL PRACTICES.

The taboo between mother-in-law and son-in-law seems to have prevailed among all the Maidu. It is specifically mentioned that among the valley people the two would neither converse nor look at each other, and that if she met the young man, the old woman would cover her head.

The valley women delivered in their special huts, those of the hills in a secluded spot outdoors, and those of the inclement mountains inside the living house. For a stillborn child, the subsequent observances were made more rigorous, much as by the northwestern tribes.

The mountain Maidu tied the child's umbilical cord to its cradle. This is perhaps a Plateau Shoshonean practice: at any rate it prevails in the Plains area.

The hill people feared and destroyed twins. Sometimes the mother was killed with the children.

Before as well as after the birth of a child the husband and wife alike were under restrictions. These constituted what may be called a semicouvade, such as prevailed over the greater part of California. Meat and fish were forbidden, and both parents abstained as completely as possible from all labor, especially hunting. In the northern valley the period lasted 10 days after childbirth, and husband and wife jointly occupied the woman's hut. In the foothills, the period of restriction was determined practically rather than ritualistically, enduring until the woman was able to walk about easily. She remained in her hut, the husband at home. In the mountains, both parents fasted and kept quiet until the remnant of the umbilical cord fell from the child.

NAMES.

Maidu names generally had a meaning, but this was often trivial, sometimes obscene, and usually of obscure reference. The name of a dead relative was generally bestowed upon the child by the time it was 2 years old. Often an additional nickname came into vogue. At the time of their initiation, the boys received a new name, which was that of a dead member of the society, probably bestowed when a man reached the higher grade of *yeponi*. The mountain people having no Kuksu society, of course did not follow this practice. It is not known whether they had any corresponding device for replacing the child name by an adult one. In the hills women are said to have received new names, or at least new designations in the family, during adolescence, after the birth of the first child, and as old age began to be reached. Among all the Maidu there seems to have been an inclination to terminate the taboo which lay on the names of the dead, by bestowing these names upon a near member of the family at the first opportunity after a year or so had elapsed.

The following are names of hill Maidu, given on entry into the Kuksu cult: Vomiting-baskets, Licking-deer, Licking-head, Tiedwing, Mother's Stomach, Void-in-river, Stuck-in-the-ear, Pine-nut-eater. These can hardly be symbolic of the religion in themselves. They are evidently typical California names of traditional origin and little significance; the cult enters chiefly as machinery for their bestowal.

THE DEAD.

As to disposal of the dead, evidence is somewhat variable. Burial seems to have been the rule, the hill people showing the most frequent inclination toward cremation. In the valley, burning is said to have been resorted to only for persons who died away from home, ashes being more easily transported than a corpse. The mountain division always buried. The southern practice was cremation.

Among all divisions interment was in a flexed position, the body being roped in a skin, that of a bear if possible. Personal property was broken and buried with the corpse, or burned. The house was usually burned down. This was particularly likely to be done for people of note. The cemeteries lay at the edge of the villages, the reason assigned being fear of grave robbery.

Men shortened their hair for the death of a few of the nearest relatives, women for a larger number. A widow cut or burned her hair off close and covered it with pitch, which was never deliberately removed. In the mountains, widows wore a buckskin thong with beads of pitch until the mourning anniversary. The hill people, for the death of a husband or wife, put on a mourning necklace which served as a sort of badge of participation in the next five years' anniversaries. The hair cut in mourning is said by the Maidu to have been secreted, not worked into belts or ornaments, as among certain tribes both of northern and southern California. This statement is confirmed by the absence of any articles of human hair in museum collections from the Maidu region.

CHAPTER 28.

THE MAIDU: ARTS AND IMPLEMENTS.

DRESS.

Maidu clothing was similarly scant in the summer heat of the valley and the snowy winter of the mountains. A deer or puma skin with the hair side next the body, a rabbit-skin blanket, or a pair of skins sewn together, was worn as a loose mantle at need; but there was no true garment. The mountaineers are said to have donned grass-stuffed moccasins for travel in the snow. Such use may have kept the feet warm, but would quickly ruin the footgear. The calf was protected by a deerskin legging, the hair side inward, tied above the knee and wound to the leg with a thong. Both moccasin and legging were presumably for journeys or the hunt rather than for daily wear. The moccasin was of the usual California variety: unsoled, single piece, seamed up the front, and coming well above the ankle.

The snowshoe varies locally in California, but only in detail. It consists of one or two withes or thongs traversing a small oval hoop longitudinally, and two to four crosswise. There is no netting, no tailpiece, and no provision for heel play. The device fulfilled only the most minimal requirement; but it could be made in half an hour by an unskilled operator, and is typical of Californian culture. (Fig. 68.)

The netted cap completed the costume of Maidu men. It was indispensable in ceremony, through allowing headpieces to be skewered into the contained hair; and was convenient in many occupations, although we are uncertain whether it was worn habitually.

Women's clothing was constituted essentially of two shredded bark aprons, preferably of maple, the front one smaller and tucked between the legs when the wearer sat down. Grass may also have been used, and old women occasionally went naked. The mountain women inclined to buckskin fringes, essentially of the type that prevails through all of northernmost California, but, it is said, with less profuse ornamentation of pine nuts. Outdoors in winter, women added moccasins and a skin robe.

There is some doubt whether the Maidu women wore caps. There is not a specimen in any museum. The southern and valley Maidu may be presumed not to have used this article. The northeasterners declare that they had them, and that they were flat-topped baskets like those of the Achomawi, Modoc, and Yana. Perhaps the fashion was imitated from one of these neighboring peoples; or the caps may have formed a more or less regular object of intertribal trade, as between Wailaki and Kato. In any event they are not worn to-day.

Several methods of hair dress are described. It is not clear whether these represent regional customs or individual variation. In the south the bunched hair was tied with string at the back of the head. As this is also a Yana device, it must have been known to the northwestern Maidu, and may have been practiced by them. The northern mountaineers wore their hair loose; the valley people are said to have inclined more to the head net for a forehead band. Women's hair, which was often cut half length, hung loose, or was held by a band passing under the chin. This was a strange habit, and, if correct, indicates that caps were not worn.

Hair was perhaps most frequently trimmed with a glowing coal, but a flint edge bearing on a stick is also mentioned. Combs of porcupine tails, pine cones, and pine needles were in use. Only hair on the face was pulled out; at that the northeasterners are said occasionally to have left the upper lip covered.

The Maidu are on the fringe of tattooing tribes. In the northern valley women bore three to seven vertical lines on the chin, plus a diagonal line from each mouth corner toward the outer end of the eye. The process was one of fine close cuts with an obsidian splinter, as among the Shasta, with wild nutmeg charcoal rubbed in. Toward the east and south the more painful pricking-in method was followed, the cheek decoration becomes lost, the chin lines are fewer, until finally tattooing becomes sporadic and individual in character. For men there existed no universal fashion: the commonest mark was a narrow stripe upward from the root of the nose. As elsewhere in California, lines and dots were not uncommon on breast, arms, and hands of men and women; but no standardized pattern seems to have been evolved by any group, except for the female face. (Fig. 45, *e*, *f*.)

There is said to have been no ritual of any moment when a girl was tattooed. The operation must generally have come near her puberty, but seems not to have been very definitely associated with the adolescence ceremony.

Ornaments were worn in the ear chiefly by women, in the nose only by men. Girls had their lobes pierced in the adolescence dance, but less was made of the act than by the Achomawi. Where the Kuksu society existed, the perforation of the septum occurred more ceremoniously in the initiation of boys. Ear ornaments were pieces of haliotis on thongs; or more characteristically, incised bird bones or polished sticks, with or without feather tufts or shell pendants. The horizontal nose ornament was a feather, a pair of feathers, or a feathered stick.

Glass beadwork has obtained as slight a foothold among the Maidu as with most California groups. Its occurrences can be traced to contact with Northern Paiute and Washo, who in turn appear to owe their inclination to indirect or ultimate influences from the Plains. The western Mono reveal their eastward affiliations in a greater fondness for bead weaving than, for instance, the neighboring Miwok and Yokuts display. The Colorado River tribes have devised some distinctive and well-chosen uses for beads; but these seem to be of local origin. In general, glass beads are woven in California, not embroidered on skins.

HOUSES.

The Maidu possess two names for houses: *k'um* and *hübo*. The *k'um* or *k'umi* or *k'umü* is the large earth-covered structure, the *hübo* a lean-to of bark or brush. But the relative use of the two types is not wholly clear. The *k'um* was the dance chamber; also a sweat house; also a dwelling. The same edifice was not always used for all these purposes; but it is characteristic that the ceremonial, the sweating, and the living house were built alike and called the same. Other than in function, they seem to have differed only in sizes, and these were variable. Villages of consequence had a dance house. Small settlements may have danced in their most available dwelling. An important rite would only be held in a big town, in all likelihood.

The *hübo* was only a dwelling. How far its relation to the *k'um* was determined respectively by the owner's wealth, by the season, or by region, must remain in abeyance; but the last seems the most important factor. The valley people inhabited large and small *k'um* almost altogether. In the foothills and higher Sierra, the much less weatherproof *hübo* was the usual family domicile. Exponents of the direct influence of climate are wont to overlook such cases of the best shelter where it is least needed. There is indeed an unquestionable correlation with environment; but it is subtle. The mountaineers are poor and unskilled; the valley dwellers leisurely, painstaking, and well provided. So it happens that the very ones exposed to inclemence are the least in position and the least accustomed to take efficient action for their protection.

As to season, as soon as the rains were over the hill people abandoned their winter houses, whether these were *k'um* or *hübo*, and lived under open brush roofs, or in the most flimsy shelters of leafage. The mountaineers did the same, so far as their briefer and cooler

summer allowed.   The valley people are said to have remained with
their *k'um* throughout the year, merely moving out under an adjacent
porch or brush shade in the period of heat.   Such a habit, however,
would contradict the normal central Californian practice of more or
less movement in summer.

The large inhabited *k'um* are stated to have contained several
families, each with its assigned portion of floor space.   Whether
these were all kin, or how far the related families were reckoned
as separate families by the Maidu, are interesting but unanswered
questions.

The *k'um* was round, 20 to 40 feet in diameter, and dug out with sticks and
baskets to a depth of a yard.   The sides of this shallow pit were lined with
poles, split logs, or bark.   Two, occasionally three, oak posts were set up in
the middle, in line with the door and fireplace.   The one behind the latter
was the ritual center of the structure, and was called great or spirit post.
It may be conjectured that for a dwelling these uprights sufficed; but a dance
house had four more on each side, between the middle and the walls—10 in
all.   The center posts rose from 10 to 20 feet, according to the size of the
edifice, the side uprights little more than half as much.   The roof was carried
by eight logs, which sloped from the ground over the side pillars and rested
with their higher ends on two larger logs which extended from the main posts
respectively to the entrance and to the rear.   Then came cross poles, more or
less following the circumference of the house; then bark, sticks, pine needles,
and the like; and finally earth to a depth of a foot.   The smoke hole was in the
middle of the roof and served as the principal door.   The descent was by a
notched log.   A two-pole ladder with tied crosspieces is mentioned by some of
the Maidu; but the idea has an unaboriginal flavor, and its report needs corroboration.   The door in the front served for draft, bringing in wood, and
occasional exit or entrance, especially by women or children.   It was built
out into a little tunnel, which must slope up to reach the ground.   The orientation is unknown, except for the valley, where the door faced south or southwest.

This type of earth lodge prevailed among the entire stock with the exception of the most extreme southern Maidu, who, in common with their Miwok
neighbors, replaced the row of two center posts by a square of pillars, interconnected at the top, from which the roof beams radiated; and among the
northeasterners, who set three principal uprights, one behind the fire and
two abreast it.   This gives a pair of longitudinal girders, instead of one,
from the "spirit post" forward; and these run directly into the door-tunnel
frame.   This concept—that of a ridgepole forking into the door—is repeated
by the northeastern Maidu in their *hübo*, and reappears among the Achomawi.
On the other hand, the valley Maidu form of *k'um* is very similar to that of
the Wintun and Pomo in its structural plan.

The *hübo*, in some dialects *uyi*, was a conical hut, 10 to 15 feet across, supported by several poles leaned and tied together over a shallow excavation.
Bark, sticks, slabs from dead trees, pine needles, and leaves in any combination kept out the weather more or less successfully.   Thatching is not mentioned; perhaps the "leaves" imply it.   The disturbed earth was banked up
the sides as far as it would reach, some 2 or 3 feet.   Occasionally a more
pretentious house had a center post.   The northeasterners built a doorway
by setting up two low stakes with a stick across.   From this frame light
beams sloped to the intersection of two or three poles leaned together from

the edges of the hollowed ground. The remainder of the house rested on this primary framework.

At least the northerly Maidu had their women build huts for themselves for solitary habitation during their periodic illnesses; as to the southerly divisions, information fails. These structures were small and poorly made *hübo*.

A little apse or niche was often built at the back of their houses by the mountain Maidu for the storage of food. The Yuki refer to a similar arrangement, which may have had a wide distribution in California.

A bed is reported for the earth lodge: A platform of willow poles, covered with pine rushes or other soft material, along each side of the house, and high enough, at times, to allow of storage underneath. A log along the inner edge served both as part of the framework and as pillow. The inmates consequently slept with their heads toward the fire. Skins, and presumably tule mats, according to locality, formed the bedding; and deerskins, or preferably woven blankets of fur or feathers, the covering. The earth house, however, was so warm when fired and closed that naked sleep was often comfortable. In the smaller houses and brush huts a mere layer on the ground replaced the platform. It will be seen that the Maidu had not attained to the use of individual beds. The Patwin and Chumash are other Californian peoples for whom there is record of beds that consisted of more than mats or skins spread on the floor.

SUSTENANCE.

The list of animals disdained as food was small. Foremost was the dog, regarded as virulently poisonous by most northern Californians; then the wolf and coyote; and, among the southern Maidu, the grizzly bear. The buzzard is the only bird mentioned; and this concludes the number, except for reptiles and amphibians, all of which were scrupulously avoided.

Invertebrates were freely eaten; worms, the larvæ of yellow jackets and probably of other insects, grasshoppers, crickets, locusts, and fresh-water mussels were relished.

Of fish, the salmon came first, in the region of the larger streams, and next the lamprey eel, whose extraordinary fatness appealed to the Indian's palate much as it did to the Roman's. In the higher mountains trout were nearly the only fish available.

Deer vertebræ were crushed in mortars, and the meal caked and set before the fire. Salmon backbones were also pounded, but eaten raw. Both these practices are likely to have had a wide Californian distribution.

Deer were often hunted by companies of men. They were driven over cliffs, or past hunters hidden near the runways. The mountaineers headed the animals against a grapevine fence with egresses, at which the deer were shot, or with angles in which they were cornered and clubbed. It is probable that the barrier restrained the game by the fact of its artificiality rather than by actual strength or closeness. Drives of this type were undertaken with prayers and magical observances, and strict taboos were in force for the families of the hunters.

Individual hunters stalked with the deer-head mask, or ran the game down, either on foot or with snowshoes. Elk were most frequently taken by the latter method. The animal, unable to feed or ruminate, becomes so weak in a couple of days that the hunter can overtake it.

Bear hunts were opened ceremonially. The common species had its cave entered before the end of hibernation, and was then killed by magic plus a well-directed arrow or two. If the proper form were gone through, the natives believed that the animal responded by quietly arising and exposing its heart. Hunting grizzlies with the bow was dangerous, on account of the vitality and frequent ferocity of the wounded animal. The plan was for a number of men, carefully posted behind stones or trees, successively to engage the brute in pursuit while others shot, until it succumbed to the number of arrows.

Rabbits were taken in long nets, as by the Washo and Northern Paiute. The little animals were driven at full speed and enmeshed their heads or entire bodies and were promptly clubbed.

Birds were killed in greatest numbers by nooses and nets. Quail will often follow even a low fence rather than fly over it, particularly along their runways. A fine noose and bait at occasional gates usually trapped a bird. For waterfowl a series of nooses, each held open by a leaf of grass, were stretched over the surface of a stream. Ducks, geese, pigeons, and crows were also netted. The latter were scared up at night and caught in a fan-shaped net held up from a willow bush. Pigeons often flew regularly through gaps in ridges where they were an easy prey. Geese were attracted under a row of nets by a live decoy, and then enmeshed by the pull of a string reaching to the hunter. Ducks sometimes caught themselves under similar nets hung over a bank where they touched releasing strings in the dark. Salmon could be harpooned in riffles and at weir openings. In deep water they were taken with nets held from scaffolds, much as by the Yurok and Shasta. Fishhooks were of little consequence; they consisted of pieces of bone tied and pitched to form an angle.

The acorn cache or granary of the type described for the Miwok was used by the Maidu of the valley as well as the foothills. The northeasterners do not seem to have followed this practice: in addition to the built-in compartment, they wove large baskets like those of the Achomawi and the northeastern tribes.

Of acorns, those from *Quercus kelloggii*, *chrysolepis*, and *wizlizeni* were preferred.

Neither the acorn soup paddle, whose distribution reaches from the Tolowa to the Northern Miwok, nor the looped stick of the Southern Miwok and Yokuts, has been reported among the Maidu.[1] Certainly in most cases they stirred their acorn mush with a mere stick, and picked up the cooking stones with a pair of sticks. The mush was scooped up with the index and middle fingers, and these sucked off— the commonest method in California. Worked spoons were scarcely known, but river mussel shells were occasionally employed.

MORTAR AND METATE.

In the coast region the metate is not known from San Francisco Bay or to the north. In the interior, in the same latitude, the Maidu used the implement. It was nothing but a slab, said to have been set at a slight tilt. The metates of the more southerly Sierra tribes are generally considerably hollowed in all directions, as if the muller were rotated rather than handled with the back-and-forth motion of the typical Pueblo grain metate. With this accords the shape of the muller itself, which is rounded or irregular, whereas the Pueblo "mano" is a rectangular block. The Klamath-Modoc metate is small; the muller has a peculiarly two-horned handle, but its bearing surface is circular. The basic type thus is that of the Sierra; incidentally, a similar implement must have been employed by the Achomawi, to judge by their location. All through the interior region the metate is used for dry seeds. The acorn is probably too oily to be pulverized by rubbing. Nevada has metates of the interior Californian kind. The Mohave, who are agricultural, use a metate which is wholly of the Pueblo variety, except that, lacking stone houses, they do not mortar it into a mealing bin. The nonagricultural tribes of the south have metates whose hollows, to judge by all available specimens, are basin-shaped; that is, they resemble the Sierra utensil in having the surface rubbed circularly. A number of brick-shaped rub stones in museum collections, however, indicate that the Pueblo metate, which wears into a segment of a cylinder under the back-and-forth motion of the hard stone, must also have been known in southern California beyond the Mohave and Yuma; though whether before the advent of the missions and their Mexican followers remains to be determined.

---

[1] In fact, the paddle has been denied; but there is one in the University of California Museum.

The metate has been described by some authorities as part of the maize complex, that is, associated with the cultural influence which, spreading from southern Mexico, carried agriculture into the middle portions of the continent. This is likely to be partly true. Grain is better ground than pounded into flour, apparently. But if this is the origin of the implement, its use has outstripped the cultivation of the plant which was the center of the complex. The southern Plateau and the greater part of California, if not more northerly regions, have then borrowed the grinding concept without taking over the basic agricultural industry which gave rise to it. The alternative interpretation is that the California-Great Basin metate originated independently, in response to a need for the utilization of small dry seeds of grasses, sages, and Compositæ. This is not an unreasonable conjecture; but if true, it raises the question whether the utensil may not also have been devised in Mexico before agriculture was followed, and to have been subsequently associated with that practice. In either event, the association of the metate with maize culture is considerably weakened.

Another problem arises in the relation of mortar and metate. The most obvious form for a mortar is a hole of some depth in a log or block of stone. Both these types are in use in southern California. They continue in central California, although the bowlder mortar begins to be generally replaced by a hole in bedrock. In the northern part of the State, however, the globular mortar was not employed by the recent Indians, except in small forms for special purposes, and is replaced by the flat slab with basketry hopper. The distribution of this type is not exactly definable. It extends farther south on the coast than inland. But the area in which the use of the slab with hopper is exclusive, and therefore most characteristic, is clearly the north coast region, in which the metate is not known. It is a reasonable conclusion that the two phenomena are connected: that one is the equivalent of the other. The metate is almost certainly the more fundamental and ancient. It is a simpler form and it is far more widespread. That pounding should first have been performed on a flat slab is conceivable, but only conceivable. Further, the entire slab and hopper region is archeologically underlain with numerous mortars. Against this fact there can only be set a southward extension of the hopper. But a basketry hopper on a deep globular mortar such as is occasionally found in southern California is essentially a superfluity. It can increase utility but little, and must often add considerably to inconvenience of use. As a matter of fact this anomalous combination seems never to have acquired a firm hold on custom in the southern region in which it is found. In the Chumash area the slab and hopper existed beside the deep mortar, as revealed by excavations. But the globular form is much the more prevalent here; and it is to be doubted whether the use of the hopper is very ancient, since the asphalt joints, which alone survive as evidence, would perhaps not be likely to be preserved buried in contact with a smooth slab for many centuries.

It seems, then, that the ordinary mortar, most commonly hollowed out of a block or bowlder, but made also in bedrock or wood according to local opportunity or exigencies, once prevailed over all California. Then came the metate, perhaps from the southwest area via southern California, or through the Great Basin, or by both routes. In southern and middle California it became established by the side of the mortar, one implement being utilized for seeds, the other for acorns. The metate, as the shell mounds prove, did not come into use on San Francisco Bay, nor did it penetrate to the northern coast. In this latter region, however, as well as in some marginal areas of its own distribution, such as among the most northerly Maidu, the metate appears to have influenced industrial habits sufficiently to cause the adoption of a slab as mortar, which of course necessitated the use of a hopper. The hopper then in reflux may possibly have spread southward to the edge of the agricultural area; but this last conjecture must be carried very tentatively, because the southern Californian hopper is so different in technique and use from that of the north that it might have been devised independently.

The natural supposition that the hopper is the intrinsic result of a high development of the basket industry, an adept people finding it easier to weave a basket than laboriously to peck out a stone, is therefore to all appearance erroneous. Imitation of a utensil of different purpose, or at least a suggestion derived from such a foreign object, seems to have been at the root of the development of the pounding slab which involved the hopper as a by-product. The art of basketry was only called upon to provide the by-product. The originating stimulus came from a stone form, not from any exuberance of basketry activity. This at least is indicated for northern California. The coiled hopper of the south may be a labor-saving device.

Of course, all the evidence for the foregoing chain of reasoning is indirect. Proof or disproof must come from fuller knowledge, perhaps through excavations. If the metate is found in the most ancient deposits through the same regions in which it now occurs, the foregoing hypothesis of its spread from the south will be applicable only to a very remote period, or entirely invalidated. It is conceivable that just as the implement is lacking from the earliest as well as the latest levels of the San Francisco Bay shell mounds, it may have been used in southern California and in the Sierra Nevada thousands of years ago as to-day, in which case the problem concerning it would take new shape. The instance does reveal incisively how little historical use we can yet make out of the data of California archeology, outside of the San Francisco Bay district, in consequence of nearly all explorations having been devoid of stratigraphic determinations or a correlating point of view.

The hopper is said to have been more frequently dispensed with than used by Maidu women. It is very probable that custom was an affair of geography in this matter. The southern Maidu almost certainly followed the Miwok practice of doing without. Bedrock holes are found in their territory, but the basketry hopper has not been reported. Available specimens are wholly from the northeastern division, which has contact with the twined weaving Yana and Achomawi. In fact, the Maidu hopper is made in the characteristic *Xerophyllum* technique of northernmost California, and may therefore be set down, like the patterned burden basket, as a direct imitation of their northern neighbors by the more northerly Maidu.

The globular mortar possessed much of the magical esteem among the Maidu which it enjoyed with the Shasta, except that it was not regarded as self-moving and a spirit. It was called a spirit basket or pain basket; used by doctors as a receptacle for charms; was far too powerful to be tolerated in the house; was sought after but feared: of course was not employed for grinding; and was always found, never made. According to some accounts, mortars were once people; by others, they were attributed to the Creator or his antithesis Coyote. All looked upon them as potential and hallowed; and the meal with which secret society initiates were sprinkled was taken from a mortar, much as the Luiseño drank their toloache from one.

TEXTILES.

The most characteristic Maidu baskets are coiled. The materials are peeled willow and peeled or unpeeled redbud (*Cercis*), the foundation always three-rod, the edge finished by mere wrapping. Normally there are only two colors, a brownish red on a white or neutral background which turns soft buff with age. Rather rarely a black, produced by burying pine root fibers in charcoal and mud, was substituted for the redbud. Patterns are comparatively simple, and show more feeling for the appearance of the basket as a whole than for intricacy of detail. They are most frequently disposed in diagonals, either parallel or zigzag. Horizontal or circumferential patterns are distinctly less common than in the Pomo-Yuki-Wintun region, and vertical or radiating ones are rare. As among the Miwok, the direction of the coil is always clockwise, as seen from the hollow of the basket, except in flat baskets, which invariably run in the opposite direction. This difference seems to be due to the insertion of the awl and sewing splint from the inside or top in flat specimens, from the outside in all others. The Pomo women, by the same standard, appear to work all their baskets from the outside; the Yuki, most of whose vessels are fairly shallow, from the inside. The Maidu use no feathers or pendants in their basketry, and know no oval forms or constricted necks. Their ware is self-sufficient and artistically as pleasing as any in California, but in elaborateness falls short of that of the Yokuts, and especially that of the Pomo.

Twining was used for carrying, storage, and tray baskets, all more or less openwork; for a short-handled seed beater; and for fish traps. Its regular form was two-strand, but it is likely that three-strand twining was known and occasionally employed for starts or strengthening.

The northeastern Maidu, and they alone, have taken over the overlay twining of northernmost California in all its features, including the typical materials: hazel shoots, pine roots, *Xerophyllum*, and maidenhair fern. These were employed chiefly for close-woven and patterned carrying baskets, which are scarcely distinguishable from those of the Yurok and Achomawi. Mortar hoppers and perhaps caps were made in the same technique. In fact, the art has obviously been introduced bodily from the Achomawi or Atsugewi, and exists among the northern mountain Maidu as a current separate from the remainder of their basket making and without appreciable influence on it. It is an instance of a cultural "complex" having been adoped entire and juxtaposed beside an existing one.

In the foothills and perhaps in the valley districts of the northwestern Maidu, seed beaters were often or prevailingly made in wicker ware—one of the rarest techniques in California. This form is closely paralleled by a Pomo one, and may therefore be ascribed also to the intervening Wintun. Except that the unusual degree to which the Pomo had developed all aspects of basketry gives them a probability of precedence, there is nothing to show which one of the three peoples originated this aberrant local type.

The universal Californian tule mat was twined with string by the Maidu. The rushes employed were *Scirpus lacustris* and *Typha latifolia*. The mats served as seats, beds, camp roofing, and doors.

String was a two-strand twist of the bark of *Asclepias* or *Apocynum*. Heavy cord was made by successively joining such twine in pairs, not by uniting three or more strands at a time.

In the sloughs and stiller reaches of the streams in the valley seines could be employed. In the swift waters of the mountains the typical central California dip net was used: a conical sack attached to an arc of stick bisected by the handle, which passed across the opening of the net. The shuttle was a pair of slender sticks lashed in the middle. One or several fingers served to measure the width of the mesh.

The net cap, which confined the men's hair, was begun on a loop hung from an erect stick. A slender rod was slid through the last row of loops. Several stitches were followed, but most or all of these techniques were carried out with a single string knitted or looped on itself.

The woven rabbit-skin blanket, most highly prized for bed covering, but also worn on occasion, is common to California, the Great Basin, and the Southwest. The skins were cut into strips a half inch or more wide, which were left uncured. As these dried, they curled or twisted on themselves, leaving the soft hair side everywhere exposed. The strips were then knotted into a long furry line. This was wound back and forth between two stakes to form a vertical plane of horizontal warps. Into this the continuous double weft, two lines of the same material, was twined alternately up and down, and knitted to the outermost warp on each turn. The completed blanket was thick, soft, and warm, while the hide strips gave it great durability.

In the Sacramento Valley water birds are more numerous than rabbits, and the blankets were usually of feathers. The manufacture was identical except that the more fragile bird skin was first twisted with a string.

It is possible that similar blankets were made of close-woven cord, with feathers knotted in. The valley Maidu and Wintun appear to have used the technique, which has long since gone out of use, but are only known to have employed it for red woodpecker belts and ceremonial apparel. All their more modern pieces of this kind have the feathers glued to a deerskin, like the Yurok headbands.

The carrying net of the Pomo and of the south was not used by the Maidu, but, besides the pack strap of skin, they possessed one of string which was woven and braided into a band where it passed over the forehead, but composed of half a dozen cords through the remainder of its length. The addition of cross strings would convert this "tump line" into a carrying net of Pomo type. The flatness of the band portion confirms the conclusion reached elsewhere that among the majority of the Maidu the women wore no caps.

BOATS.

The valley Maidu navigated on tule balsas, log rafts, or flat, square-ended dugout canoes. The use of all three types by one people is remarkable. It is perhaps to be ascribed to the fact that the employment of boats was only sporadic, in the crossing of streams or hunting of birds. In the foothills, streams are too rapid to be navigable.

In the high valleys of the northern Sierra a canoe was occasionally serviceable. It was made of a fallen pine or cedar burned to suitable length, and hollowed with ignited pitch, which was checked with handfuls of damp earth. This dugout was rough and blunt ended. It was either poled or paddled.

BOWS.

The Maidu bow in its best form was made in the mountains of sinew-backed yew and traded to the valley. It is practically identical with the bow of the Yurok, except for not attaining quite the same degree of breadth and thinness. The sinew was applied in small parallel shreds, each chewed entirely soft and dipped into a glue of salmon skin. The characteristic decoration was bands of triangles painted in a green mineral pigment imported from the north and used also by the northern Wintun.

The best arrows had a foreshaft set into the main shaft of syringa, *Philadelphus Lewisii*, or rose bush, *Rosa pisocarpa*. If the foreshaft was omitted, a "vestigial" wrapping of sinew marked the point where it might have been inserted. Straightening was done with the teeth. The perforated wooden straightener may have been known, but has not been reported. Grooved sandstones served for smoothing. The release is the "primary" one: thumb and index finger. The left hand held the bow nearly horizontally, the index finger crooking over the arrow.

The quiver was the entire skin of a suitable animal, turned fur side in, with a strap from fore to hind legs passing over the wearer's left arm. This appears to be the usual type of quiver in California. In fighting, rapidity of delivery was of course all important. The quiver then was merely a reservoir, and the arrows for immediate use were clamped under the arm.

Arrow poison was sometimes made by teasing a rattlesnake into biting a deer liver. The septic effect of such a preparation is likely to have been much greater than the toxic.

TOOLS.

A skin-dressing tool is rarely mentioned in California and is seldom represented in museum collections. It is possible that a stone broken for the occasion often sufficed. The Maidu hafted a small chipped blade to the end, or both ends, of a wrapped stick; the tool was moved centripetally. The mountaineers frequently substituted a deer ulna rubbed to an edge at one end.

There is some reference to a roughly chipped ax, but its existence is doubtful in view of the Maidu being known to follow the common California custom of working lumber with horn wedges and fire.

It is possible that small trees were occasionally hacked down with a hand-held flint or piece of trap. Larger trees were utilized only after they had fallen, and were burned into lengths.

In the northeastern Maidu territory some ground and grooved ax heads have been found, but the natives disclaim their manufacture. The lucky finder of one might use it for its original purpose or as a weapon. These axes appear to represent an ancient sporadic infiltration from the east, and it is significant that they have not penetrated beyond the border Maidu.

For knives and arrowheads the Maidu used obsidian obtained in trade, apparently from the north, and local flint and basaltlike stones. The latter material answered for a tolerable knife; a good arrow point was possible only in obsidian or flint. A flint mine in a cave at Table Mountain near Oroville was sacred. Offerings—beads or dried meat are specified—were thrown in; only as much material was carried away at each visit as could be detached at one blow; and the operator crawled out backward.

Large blades of obsidian, single or double pointed, were probably not knives, as the local antiquarian usually assumes, but shamans' paraphernalia. All the evidence from central California points to this use: the Maidu add that such pieces were worn hung from the neck.

The Maidu fire drill is that of all California: a flattish hearth with cups near the edge and guide notches for the carbonized wood powder running out from the pits; the drill about a foot and a half in length, and rather less than half an inch in diameter. The buckeye, *Aesculus californica*, furnished the favorite material, and dried grass the tinder, both as among the Yana. There seems to have been no idea that the apparatus would operate better if drill and hearth were of different woods.

PIPES.

The Maidu pipe was normally of wood—apparently a short tube tapering somewhat to the mouth end—the generic Sierra type, as contrasted with the longer stemmed and bulbous bowled form of the Pomo and their neighbors. The stone pipe was similar, though rarer, and mostly used in religion—by shamans or the ceremonial clown. Sometimes a prehistoric specimen was discovered; if made by the Maidu themselves, the stone pipe was gouged through with an end of antler pounded by a stone. It is said that this drill was not rotated, but the use of sand in the bore seems to refute this assertion. Perhaps the statements as to the untwirled tool refer only to work in steatite, which cuts readily.

Tobacco was taken from the roofs of the earth-covered houses: it may have been planted there. The species used by the mountain Maidu was *Nicotiana attenuata*.

MUSICAL INSTRUMENTS.

The flute is a straight tube of elder wood with four holes. It was blown for pleasure and in courtship. It is a curious fact that the only wind instrument capable of producing a tune appears among none of the American Indians to have been used ceremonially.

The musical bow is a device definitely reported from the Maidu and Yokuts, but probably shared by these groups with a number of others. Among the Maidu it was sometimes an original hunting bow that was tapped or plucked for amusement, one end being held in the mouth. At other times the bow was made for the purpose, and was considered a shaman's means of conversation with spirits.

The Maidu used all three central Californian forms of the rattle. The shaman's instrument was of Attacus cocoons containing gravel (Fig. 37). The split-stick rattle went with dances, especially of the Kuksu organization. It was either quivered or beaten against the palm of the hand. The deer-hoof rattle was particularly associated with the girl's adolescence ceremony, as is the case in the greater part of California, and was most prevalent with the northeastern Maidu among whom this ritual looms conspicuously.

GAMES.

Maidu games present several peculiarities. No form of the ring and pin game has ever been found, nor are dice known to the northern Maidu. The pole and hoop game is also unmentioned and, if it existed at all, must have had a scant development. Ball games differed according to sex. Women used a stick to toss a double-ended "ball." This consisted of two billets of wood or a pair of acorns on a string, a braided rope of hide, or a long bundle of bark. The game proceeded either like shinny, or took the form of a race between two lines of women, each line trying to pass the ball to the goal faster than the row of opponents. The men's ball game followed the latter plan, but the ball was of skin stuffed with deer hair and was kicked with the foot along a posted line of players. This method of play is a cross between the two usual Californian types of the game: shinny and the football race. Contests were between villages, and in the valley took place principally at the conclusion of the mourning ceremony in autumn.

The guessing game employed the pair of marked and unmarked bones usual in all of central California. Perhaps its chief peculiarity was that each side started, in civilized fashion, with one-half of the

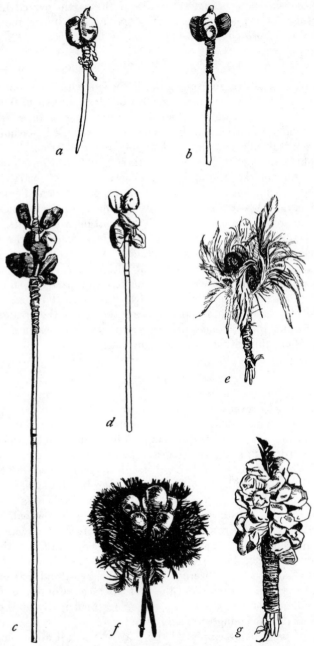

FIG. 37.—Central Californian cocoon rattles. *a*, Yokuts; *b*, Maidu; *c*, *e*, *g*, Pomo; *d*, Yuki; *f*, Miwok.

counters, whereas the usual California custom is to begin with a neutral pile. In the valley the game was for 8 counters, in the hills and mountains for either 10 or 16. The marked bone was called *sulu,* the plain one *hindukü;* but in guessing, the exclamations *tep* and *we* were used to refer to them. In general, the unmarked bone is guessed for, but there existed a great variety of cries and gestures indicative of the choice made. A pair of players shuffle the bones and thus offer four possible combinations. A doubly wrong guess loses two counters, a wholly correct one wins the play. If the guess is half correct, one counter is paid and the divined player surrenders his bones. The next guess, on his partner's shuffling, determines whether the two of them resume or whether they lose the play to their opponents.

MONEY.

The common currency was the Pomo disk bead, transmitted by the Wintun, and perhaps coming from the south also. The beads from the west were often traded unsmoothed, so that the Maidu performed much of their own money polishing, but the clamshells came to them broken and strung, not as wholly raw material. Baked magnesite cylinder beads also came from the west, but completely finished and very precious. Haliotis was another valuable obtained from the Wintun, but went into ear ornaments and necklace pendants, scarcely serving as currency. Dentalia, of unrecorded source, reached the Maidu occasionally. They are said to have been valued highly, but appear to have been too rare to be used as standard money. Their chief use is likely to have been in the northeastern mountains.

The southern Maidu called the standard currency *howok,* olivella *kolkol,* haliotis *ülo.* The following are valuations of nearly 50 years ago.

Howok, 1,160 pieces, stringing to 30 feet, average thickness per bead a little less than a third of an inch, valued at $230, or 5 to a dollar. The largest beads, nearly an inch in diameter, 4 to a dollar. A string of 177 beads of smallest diameter, valued at $7, or 20 beads to the dollar. *Kolkol,* rated at a dollar a yard. A 1-inch magnesite cylinder from the Pomo, valued at $5. These native appraisals are very much higher than any reported from the Pomo or southern Californians; which fact seems to be due to Maidu remoteness from both sources of supply. The southern Wintun valuation of beads as given in Chapter 26 is also lower: about a fourth.

CHAPTER 29.

THE MAIDU: RELIGION AND KNOWLEDGE.

SHAMANISM.

The Maidu shaman operated on "pains" or disease objects, but his power rested less on control of these than on his possession of guardian spirits. The "pain" is called *omeya* in the valley and *itu* in the mountains. The spirits are named *kakini* (*kukini*, *gak'ini*), which is the same word as is applied to the ancient spirits or mythical divinities who are impersonated in the Kuksu ceremonials. The *kakini* acquired by the shaman may be animals, but more frequently are mountains, rocks, lakes, or waterfalls; that is to say, the spirits inhabiting such geographical features and known by the names of these. Among the northern Maidu the novice undergoes a period of instruction at the hands of older shamans; who, without being organized into a body, appear to be actuated by a spirit of professional helpfulness. It should be stated, however, that the first communication with spirits is believed to be excessively and often seriously distressing. The novice becomes very ill, and the older shamans' activity may, in the native view, be as much a treatment of sickness as assistance extended to a prospective colleague.

VALLEY SHAMANS.

The valley Maidu of the Chico region describe the practice of their shamans in very much the same way as do the Yuki; from which fact it can be concluded that the central Wintun served as a connecting link. A man who is out alone, perhaps a hunter in the brush, suddenly has a vision and falls unconscious. During his trance a spirit instructs him. On awakening the future shaman bleeds, and on returning home he fasts. Sometimes the seizure occurs as a person is diving for fish or mussels, and he has to be drawn ashore. The spirit now keeps reappearing in dreams and the man falls ill. He is thoroughly secretive about his experience. In fact, it is not until old age that a shaman begins to tell much about his spirits. The older men, however, recognize his symptoms and treat him, singing by his side all night and toward morning dancing with him or holding him up if he is too weak. The novice seems usually to be very feeble at this period and to bleed frequently at the mouth. The period of treatment is not known, but seems to endure for some time. The older doctors gradually test the young man by throwing into him, or inserting into his nose, magical objects called *sila*. If the candidate bleeds or can not extract the *sila* he will not be a successful shaman.

The "pain" which is sucked out is described as usually feathered. It is powerful enough to cause the shaman to fall in a faint as soon as he gets it into his mouth. It is shown to the patient and then buried.

The valley Maidu also appear to have had a form of nonshamanistic doctoring resembling the Kuksu treatment of the sick by the Yuki and Pomo. This was resorted to for repeated bad dreams. The patient was sung and danced over in the dance house. The chief, it is said, did the dancing, standing by the main post. It is likely that this "chief" was one of the headmen of the Kuksu organization. The account does not mention whether feather regalia were worn or definite spirits impersonated; but the cocoon rattle was used. Very high payment was demanded for this treatment.

HILL SHAMANS.

The hill Maidu make less mention of animals as guardians. Their shamans communicate with spirits as such. It would seem that these are sometimes the ghosts of kinsmen, since there is a distinct tendency for shamanism to be hereditary in this division, and there is precedent in northwestern California and among the Shasta for the idea that a future doctor has his first communication with the spiritual world through his ancestors. Another reminiscence of the customs prevalent to the north is the fact that female doctors are recognized by the hill Maidu, although their ability is usually less than that of men. There is a period of preparation by means of dancing and singing in the dance house, apparently under the supervision of older shamans. At this time the novice gradually comes to be on terms of greater friendship with his spirits, and many other visitors from the supernatural world are believed to attend. Those who are present hear them either uttering the cries of animals or speaking.

The hill Maidu distinguish between doctors proper, that is, shamans who suck, called *yomi*, and others who merely dream and are known as *netdi*. Of course sucking shamans also have dream power. They may therefore be regarded as a class which has attained to higher faculties than the dreamers. This distinction between the clairvoyant and the curing shaman seems to exist among all of the Maidu, as in fact through most of northern California.

The dreaming shamans hold assemblies in the dance house during the winter months. Formal invitations are sent out by means of knotted strings, and a feast is offered for a day or two before. At night the fire is smothered with ashes until the house is perfectly dark. After the dream doctor has sung for a while and beaten the main post with his cocoon rattle, the spirits begin to arrive. The doctor asks them questions and answers them by ventriloquism. The clown of the Kuksu organization is present and mimics the proceedings. In spite of the awe inspired by what is going on, laughter at the clown's apings is in place. A part of such meetings is the singing of certain songs to which the bottoms of large baskets are rhythmically beaten.

The pains sucked out are very various, according to hill Maidu belief: bits of wood, stone, or manufactured objects, bones or teeth, insects and worms of various kinds, and the like. They are exhibited—if animals, always still alive—and then buried.

The shamans' pipe is also considerably used. Smoke is blown on the patient while orders are given to what resides in him to depart. This treatment seems to be particularly favored for headache. It is not known whether the doctor ever attempts to suck through his pipe.

The hill Maidu doctors held public competitions, very much like those of the Yokuts, and somewhat similar to the contests in which the Yuki *hulk'ilal* members engage. They gather in the dance house from long distances. Each doctor, having previously fasted and prepared, dances for himself. The clown is the leader of the dance. Any touching of a competitor, either with the body or with a held object, is debarred. Power is exerted by a supernatural shooting or transmission. The hands are held against the breast and then thrown forcibly forward as if warding off or sending out mysterious influences. After a time the weaker contestants begin to be taken with seizures and pains, some bleeding from the nose, some rolling on the floor. Others follow, and such as have recovered from the first shock busy themselves sucking out the cause of the later victims' succumbing. As the number of competitors decreases and the survivors are those of the intensest power, the excitement and the imaginative faculties of the audience as well as participants increase. Flames and light are seen about the few who are still contending, and they, to demonstrate their strength, cause lizards or mice to appear and disappear. Finally the contest narrows to a pair, and when one of these yields the lone survivor is victor of the occasion. It is said that women have been known to win, although as a rule their milder powers cause them to be among the first to be taken ill.

It is evident that the minds of the contestants must be strangely affected. Whatever legerdemain they may consciously avail themselves of, there is no question that they believe in the power of their rivals. A man might pretend to supernatural powers which he was aware he did not possess, but would scarcely deceive consciously for the purpose of exhibiting his inferiority.

The ceremony concluded, all go out and bathe carefully, then return to purify themselves still further by smoking. The clown, who appears to be no contestant, but who has stood in the thick of the battle, is specially treated to free him from any remaining influences.

This description applies to the northwestern hill Maidu. The southern Maidu held similar competitions; the northern Miwok did not. Shamans' contests, however, reappear among the Yokuts, and, perhaps in simpler form, among the southern Wintun.

MOUNTAIN SHAMANS.

Among the northern Maidu of the mountains the hereditary principle appears still more strongly. It is said that all the children of a shaman invariably follow in his footsteps, death resulting if they refuse to accept his spirits. This is, however, native theory and not practice; for inasmuch as this Maidu division also recognizes shamans whose parents have not been doctors—in fact declare that any man who wishes can acquire spirits—it follows that if the theory were lived up to, the entire population would long since have become shamans. Women doctors are of some importance, particularly in the Big Meadows region where contact with the Achomawi and Atsugewi has been intimate.

A hereditary shaman acquires his parent's spirits only after the latter's death. In this way the identical spirits remain in a line of descent for generations. Dreaming of them makes the novice ill, and with his sickness his dreams increase, the spirits thronging about him and worrying him with their talk and songs. The spirits at first are violent and angry, and it is only gradually, through the efforts of older doctors who are called in, that their aggressiveness and hatred begin to disappear and they become friendly with their new owner, or rather associate. He makes them presents of beads and of feathered wands. The process usually requires a whole winter, the novice, who seems not only genuinely ill but thoroughly frightened, being treated and danced with by the older doctors in proportion as his spirits are numerous and powerful. Often the attendant shamans have to call on their own spirits to hold those of the newcomer that are trying to do him harm. During the dance the novice sings the songs that his spirits have already revealed to him, striking the main post of the house with his rattle. Sometimes the spirits reach down from the smoke hole and carry the rattle up on the roof, where it can be heard pounding.

If the spirits are those of animals, these animals are never eaten or killed by the shaman. More usually, however, they are inhabitants

of topographical features in the vicinity; and in their treatment of
the novice the older shamans begin by calling upon all the rocks and
lakes which are known to harbor spirits.

After the night dancing has gone on for some time, the novice's
ears are pierced. After this he resorts to haunted mountains or
ponds to spend the night. If possible he bathes, losing consciousness
in the water. He awakens on the shore, then walks and sings for
hours about a fire. When he finally sleeps, he once more hears the
spirits thronged about him. In the morning, after another swim,
he hears the spirits talking in other places, and then for two or three
days follows them about the country, lured on by their voices and
totally refraining from food.

There is a discrepancy here. The above is the procedure said to
be followed by hereditary shamans after they have had their first
dreams at home and have begun to be trained. Their purpose is
said to be the acquisition of spirits additional to those which their
father had. Men who are not doctors by heredity, on the other hand,
are stated to seek the lonely places deliberately, obtaining the good
will of the spirits there by gifts, and then to return home to dream
further, or at least to undergo the course of training which has been
described.

The shaman's paraphernalia are not destroyed at his death among the northeastern Maidu, but are carefully preserved for his children. Should they be
too young at the time, their mother or some other relative maintains the knowledge of their hiding place. These paraphernalia include certain objects called
yompa (hill dialect *yomepa*) which apparently are made by the shaman out of
feathers and other objects. Similar devices are employed by the Achomawi.
These charms are used to kill. Singing a certain song, the doctor points the
yompa at his victim, who is thereupon entered by a part of the object. The
sila or killing objects of the valley Maidu are also known here. These are
thrown into people.

The pains which the mountain Maidu believe to cause death are minute,
animate, and more or less movable. Many are sharp, others have the shape of
insects or tiny reptiles. If they are sucked out by a benevolent doctor, they name
the shaman who sent them and then die. The extractor causes them to disappear by rubbing between his hands or buries them. If on the other hand the
pain can not be extracted, it flies back, after death has ensued, to the doctor who
sent it, returning to a place appointed by him. He has instructed one or more
of his spirits to attend this place. They hold the returned pain, and after the
wizard has addressed it soothingly and asked it not to harm him, he suddenly
seizes it, nestles it into feathers, and hides it away. It is not clear whether it
is believed that evil shamans find these pains or whether they frequent the
mountains in order to manufacture them. At any rate, pains as well as spirits
address their controlling shaman as father.

It is clear that two currents of thought have influenced the shamanism of the mountain Maidu. The concepts of female shamans; of
dreaming of ancestors; of the inheritance of spirits; of acquiring

them in lonely outdoor places, particularly lakes; and of the independent power of motion of the pains, are characteristic of the tribes of northeastern and northwestern California. The other traits of the shamanism of the mountain people possess a distinctively Maidu or central Californian aspect.

SPECIAL CLASSES OF SHAMANS.

Rain doctors or weather shamans are mentioned among the Maidu, but little is known of them. This was a profession more important in southern and central California than in the north, and the Maidu appear to be near the limit of its diffusion.

The valley Maidu had rattlesnake doctors whose particular gift was the treatment of snake bites, and who conducted public performances, possibly somewhat along the lines of the great rattlesnake ceremony of the Yokuts. For the southern Maidu a *Kauda* dance or rite is reported, held in spring to prevent snake bites during the year. Certain men were paid for their services in this connection, but the account leaves it obscure whether they were shamans or Kuksu directors.

The grizzly bear shamans clawed out their victim's eyes and then dispatched him. If encountered in their enterprise, they might offer a heavy reward for the preservation of their secret. This would indicate that they attacked those whom they bore a personal grudge, much as a witch might try to poison an enemy. The general basis of this belief is clearly the world-wide werewolf idea; its peculiarly north central Californian flavor lies in the fact, already mentioned in another connection, that, magically endowed as the bear shaman must be, he does not turn himself into the animal, but disguises himself as one by physical apparatus. This is also the Miwok conception. The Maidu and Pomo say that their bear doctors wore long strings of beads as armor within the animal skin: the Yuki explain the beads as intended for burial in case of a fatal mishap. The Maidu mention oak galls as being carried to produce a sound similar to that made by the mass of the bear's entrails as he shuffles along. The Pomo speak of baskets half filled with water for the same purpose. The very detail of all the accounts renders them almost incredible; and complete bear doctors' suits modeled for museums do not dispel doubts because they may only prove the belief in bear shamans, rather than the reality of the practices. Perhaps it is possible to compromise on the interpretation that there were men controlled by an emotion that made them find satisfaction in reproducing the animal as closely as possible in their persons, and hoping or imagining a power over their foes. But that they actually exercised their murderous inclinations while in the disguise passes comprehension.

Another interpretation is that the bear shamans as here described have been fused in native imagination with grizzly bear impersonators in the Kuksu cult, or that white reporters have failed to distinguish them.

GIRLS' ADOLESCENCE CEREMONY.

The Maidu nicely illustrate the universal Californian law that the elaborateness of adolescence rites for girls stands in inverse ratio to the general development of culture.

The northern valley people called the ceremony *dong-kato* or *yüpü-kato;* and apart from the restrictions which the girl herself underwent, the ritual consisted only of singing for about five nights. There was no dance. The nightly songs, in which men as well as women participated, began in the living house with what was called the grasshopper song and concluded in the morning with a song from the top of the roof with the words: " The dawn begins to show on manzanita hill." The girl remained covered the whole time and, except while the singing was in progress, secluded herself in a separate hut. At the conclusion of the period of singing a feast was given, and custom exacted that the parents must give away anything they were asked for.

In the hills a dance called *wulu* accompanies the singing. The girl was painted with five vertical lines on each cheek, one of which was erased each morning. With a companion, both having their heads covered, she was stood in a ring of pine needles which was set on fire and the girls told to escape from it. After this she was washed by women in a sand pit like that used for leaching acorns. The *wulu* dance commenced after dark. Men looked on and women took part. They stood in a circle holding hands. They wore no ornaments. In the center of the ring were several old women, who swung their arms— in which they held a skin, a string of beads, or something similar—alternately up to the right and left, while the circle of younger women and girls, revolving either way, swung their clasped hands in and out to the same rhythm. After a number of hours the dance might cease, but old women continued singing.

In the mountains, both men and women danced, and the ceremony lasted 10 days and was repeated in full a month later. People were summoned from a distance by smoke signals lighted in the hills by the girl and her mother. She carried a deer-hoof rattle during the entire 10 days. Each morning and evening she brought in firewood, and at intervals trained herself for the future, as it were, by carrying and depositing logs and heavy pieces of wood. The first four and last four nights of the ten were spent in dancing: the middle two constituted an interval of rest, marked only on the following morning by the piercing of the girl's ears by her mother with an awl of cedar wood. The dancing was outdoors, men and women holding hands about the fire. At other times they formed a line looking eastward over the sitting singers and the fire. In either case the girl danced with them, yielding her rattle to one of the singers. At dawn the songs were concluded, the rattle was thrown to the girl, she caught it and ran off at top speed. General license was not only tolerated but almost obligatory during each night of the dance.

On the morning following the tenth night came the *wulu*, which was danced as in the hills and by women only, the girl, however, joining with the dancers in this region. The women now used clap-stick rattles. Toward noon the dance ceased, the girl with a number of companions bathed, and then ran them a race back to the house. The remainder of the day was spent in games and feasting.

The customs of the southern Maidu are not known.

Much the same restrictions were imposed on the girl among all divisions. They were of the type customary in California. She ate as little as possible, was permitted neither meat nor fish, might not scratch herself except with sticks or bones provided for the purpose, and so far as possible was kept covered up so that she might not look about.

THE MOURNING ANNIVERSARY.

The Maidu are the first tribe of those considered to this point who practiced a great annual mourning ceremony in honor of the dead. This rite was made among all the tribes of the Sierra Nevada and throughout southern California. It was not practiced by the Achomawi, the Yana, or any of the Wintun divisions. The Maidu therefore represent its northernmost extension. There is little doubt that the origin of the ceremony, in many respects the most outstanding religious practice of the tribes in at least half of California, lay considerably to the south of the Maidu, most likely in southern California. Its general distribution is much the same as that of the toloache cult, but slightly more extensive. It is possible that the two worships had a connected source; but it is only in southern California that they are brought into relation, although even there it is but slight. It is conceivable that the only factor that prevented the spread of the toloache religion to the northernmost groups which made the mourning ceremony, the Miwok and Maidu, was the absence of the toloache plant from their territory. This conjecture could be accepted as practically certain if it were known that the toloache cult was more ancient than the Kuksu religion. If, however, the latter worship existed first in central California, its presence might well have been sufficient to keep out the rival toloache ritual; whereas the mourning anniversary might have been accepted as a nonconflicting addition.

In any event there appears to be no connection or association of any kind between the mourning anniversary and the Kuksu religion among the Maidu.

The mourning anniversary is best known from the hill Maidu, who call it *üstu*. In English it is usually known as " burning " or " cry." It was held in early autumn, about September or October, often on the cemetery site or near it. Since the confusion of the burning offered favorable opportunities for successful attack by foes, a clear rising ground was usually chosen, in which, moreover, the soil was soft enough for interments.

On this burning ground was erected an open inclosure up to 50 or 100 hundred feet in diameter and consisting of a brush fence a yard or two high, following the line of a circle of earth that had been heaped up a few inches. There was always an entrance to the west, and often one to the east also. This simple structure is certainly derived from a southern source. It is the only ceremonial edifice of the southern California Indians. North of Tehachapi it is made chiefly or only for the mourning anniversary, but apparently is invariable for that rite. This circumstance alone would be sufficient to differentiate the mourning very fundamentally from the Kuksu religion, which is so intimately associated with the large semisubterranean dance house.

Each community, whether consisting of one or several settlements, appears to have had only one *üstu* ground, which was used by successive generations. It was in charge of a director, the relation of whose status to that of the chief and the shamans is not wholly clear.

This director issued mourning necklaces on receipt of payment from a member of the family of each dead person. The family then participated in several of the annual rites and at the fifth one redeemed its payment by return of the string, which was then burned by the director. The necklace consisted of a string on which beads were arranged in a certain recurring order of ones, twos, or threes, a certain pattern being traditionally fixed for each community or burning ground. Should a death occur within the five years, the same necklace was worn for a new period of five years. Poor people who could make no payment are said sometimes to have received property instead of giving it; but they made repayment upon the return of the necklace. It will be seen that no one made any profit in either form of the transaction.

According to other statements, the mourners themselves issued necklaces or strings to their friends as invitations. The guest paid, and attended all *üstu* in which his host participated until the latter redeemed and burned the string. Somehow this version seems more consonant with the spirit of the California Indian.

Actual notification was sent to other villages by means of strings with knots, of which one was untied each day. The home community, of course, entertained everyone.

The course of the rite was as follows:

On the first evening the actual mourners visit the burning ground about sunset, cry for a time, and sprinkle meal on the graves.

On the next day the inclosure is repaired and put in order and poles 15, 20, or more feet long are prepared for the offerings that are to be burned. A vast accumulation of valuables of all sorts has long been made for this occasion. A widow, for instance, especially on her first burning, is likely to have spent her whole time since her husband's death in the manufacture of baskets that are to be consumed. Each family prepares its own poles, which in the evening are planted to the north and south of the fire, in sets of about half a dozen. So far as possible each pole is strung from top to near the ground with objects of one kind. Larger articles and quantities of food are piled at the base of the poles. The fire is then lighted by an old man. A period of bargaining often follows, objects that are to be consumed being exchanged or even sold. When this confusion has quieted down, the director delivers an oration of the customary Californian kind, carefully instructing the people in what they perfectly well know how to do. Thereupon wailing, crying, and singing begin, to continue throughout the night. Exclamations of pity for the dead are constantly uttered and bits of food or other small objects are from time to time thrown on the fire. Each group of mourners seems to think of its own dead and to sing its own songs independently of the others. It is the occasion that is joint, and there is nothing in the nature of communal acts.

About the first signs of dawn the poles are lifted down and the objects stripped from them and thrown into the fire. The old people sway and wail with redoubled vigor, and intense excitement is shown by all. Often the offerings smother the fire, which must be given respite to flare up anew. The mourners beat their heads and blow out hard. As it begins to be light, and the last of the goods are being burned, the climax of grief is reached, and old women have to be restrained from throwing themselves into the fire.

The alleged purpose of the ceremony is to supply the dead. The amount of property destroyed must have been immense by aboriginal standards. As late as 1901, 150 poles of baskets, American clothing, and the like, were consumed at a single Maidu burning.

When the fire has finally died down the participants are almost prostrated with fatigue and reaction. After a short rest the director orates again, instructing the people to eat, gamble, and make merry, which they proceed to do for a day or more. Such an aftermath of celebration is a regular part of the ceremony everywhere in California.

While the rite has here been called an anniversary, it will be seen that it is more accurately an annual ceremony among the hill Maidu. Custom varies locally through California between the two forms. On the whole the precise anniversary is the type that prevails where the ceremony is made rather for distinguished individuals than for all of the dead of the year; which is as might be expected.

On occasion the Maidu ceremony is made more elaborate by the introduction of images of the dead. These, of course, are constructed chiefly for persons of note. They are made of stuffed wild-cat skins richly decorated with valuable dance regalia and made up to resemble as nearly as possible the human figure. They are set up on stakes near one of the entrances to the inclosure and during the night are occasionally " fed." Toward the end of the burning the figures are walked toward the fire, as if they were alive, and thrown into the flames. The images are known as *kakini büsdi*, "the spirit is within," and are regarded as actually containing the ghost of the dead person. The Maidu state that an insult offered one of these figures was deadly, and that even an accidental offense against one was heavily atoned for. It is not impossible that a senti-ment prevailed which looked upon injury or revilement of the image as a specially favorable opportunity for the expression of deep-seated hatred; such emotions are characteristic of the California Indians.

In the northern valley the ceremony ran along similar lines as in the hills, but from what little is known of it—its practice having been discontinued for many years—it was considerably different in details. It is said, for instance, that for a man the mourning necklace was made by his brother and given to his widow or a near female relative. At the anniversary he received the string back and paid the wearer, who did not burn or destroy the money thus received. This looks almost like a payment for the wearing of the necklace, and not at all like an invitation or badge of participation. It is also said that the valley Maidu held a circular dance without definite regalia in the dance house on the night following the burning, and before the gambling and merry-making.

The northeastern burning was simpler than that of the foothills. Here the ceremony was made, at irregular intervals, for two successive years, beginning about a year after the death of a person of prominence, to whom it directly referred. The same inclosure was used as in the hill region and the general procedure was similar, except that the number of offering poles is likely to have been much less among the poorer people. Images are also said not to have been used. On the whole it appears that the rite did not exercise the minds of the mountain people very much.

For the southern Maidu information is, as usual, scant, which is doubly to be regretted, since the practice of the valley and the mountains in the region are almost certain to have differed considerably. The ceremony is said to have been comparatively simple, but in view of its holding an important position among the Miwok and Yokuts to the south, this statement must be taken as implying a difference of ritual from the northern Maidu rather than a notably minor significance. It does appear, however, that the southern Maidu agreed with the northern mountain Maidu in making the ceremony irregularly for their notables rather than annually for every one. They used images. The American name for the rite in this section, as among the Miwok, is " cry."

THE KUKSU CULT.

The Maidu form of the Kuksu religion is the best known of any. Its general features having been already presented in the comparative discussion of the cult in a foregoing chapter on the Wintun, it remains only to indicate the tribal individualization.

KUKSU SPIRITS.

The deities enacted by the northwestern Maidu of the valley are listed in Table 3. This enumeration is either exhaustive or nearly so, and appears to apply, with some changes, especially in the names of the spirits, to the valley Patwin as well as the Maidu.

TABLE 3.—MAIDU SPIRIT IMPERSONATIONS.

Character.	Ceremonies.	Apparel.	Notes.
Moki............	*Hesi*, Duck, *Aki*	Complete feather cloak..	Highest in rank.
Yati.............	.....do...........	*Kawe* headdress; bow...	Second highest. No songs for. Cry: *wuhui*.
Sohe............	.....do...........	*Kawe* headdress.........	Not led by *mesi*. Cry: *sohe*.
Hahe...........	.....do...........	.....do...............	No *mesi*. Cry: *haho*.
Wuhui..........	.....do...........	.....do...............	No *mesi*. Cry: *wuhui*.
Tokoiluli.......	.....do...........	.....do...............	Cry: *wuhui*.
Yüyinang-wetu..	.....do...........	.....do...............	
Yohyo..........	.....do	Big-head headdress.....	The *kuksu* of other tribes.
Dü..............	.....do...........	Woodpecker-scalp headdress band.	Represents woman.
Sili............	*Hesi*.............	*Laya* feather mask; net.	Third in rank. Runs race.
Yompui.........	.....do...........	Grass mask; net........	
Koto...........	.....do...........	Net cap; plastering of mud.	
Oleli...........	*Hesi*, Coyote......	*Sikli* feather cape; coyote head.	
K'opa..........	*Hesi*, Goose.......	*Sikli* feather cape......	
Pano-nkakini....	Grizzly bear.....	Bear skin; *ora* headdress.	Cry: *wuk-wuk*.
Sümi-nkakini...	Deer.............	Deer mask.............	

The *Moki* is also called *Wüta*, which seems to be a Maidu equivalent of the more familiar Patwin term.

There appear sometimes to have been two *Moki* in charge of a ceremony. This character differed from all other spirit impersonations in that it was not learned separately and that one did not pay for initiation but was selected for the honor and paid for refusal.

The *Yati* or cloud spirit stands for a long time looking between his legs in the *Hesi* or *Aki*. He is approached with the payments due him by the *Sili*, who is covered, from the crown of his head down, by a plain net. The *Sili*, who is a spirit that is fond of chasing people, then pursues the *Yati* or the two race away from the dance house and back to it. The loser is thought to be in danger of his life. The *Sili*, when angered, throws coals of fire about him like the Pomo ash ghost.

The typical ornament of the *Dü* was an approximately diamond-shaped headband solidly covered with the glistening scarlet scalps of woodpeckers and fringed with raven feathers. This object, *woh-dü* in Maidu and *tarat* in Patwin, is the Sacramento Valley equivalent of the woodpecker scalp bands of the Yurok Jumping dance.

The deer impersonators represented spirits called *Wishdum-sümi*, "lift up the deer."

None of the spirits are mentioned by name in their presence, but are referred to merely as *saltu* or *kakini*.

THE KUKSU DANCE CYCLE.

Table 4 shows the dances of the northwestern valley Maidu, arranged downward in time sequence from October to May, and with the horizontal position indicative of their respective sacredness. The rituals in the first three ranks are all "pay dances" performed by spirits. Those in the two following columns are "common dances," but those in the fourth, somewhat contradictorily, are said to have contained one spirit impersonation each. The essentially supplementary dances of the last rank are little known. The *Loli*, *Luyi*, and *Kenu* follow closely on the *Hesi*. The *Loli* would seem to presuppose the *Hiwe*, its male counterpart elsewhere, but this has not been reported from the Maidu. The *Toto* is Maidu, but its position is undetermined. It seems that these semiprofane dances were likely to be held at almost any time between or even within major ceremonies. Some of them seem to have been acts or exhibitions that might be hitched on to a major ceremony or given in its intermissions.

A like irregularity evidently characterized even the more elaborate common dances, those in fifth position in Table 4, since every informant cites these in a different order. As regards the spirit dances, however, all authorities agree, so that it is obvious that these constituted the unalterable framework of the yearly sequence, into which the common dances were fitted, with some idea of a proper place for each, indeed, but yet rather loosely according to the exigencies of the occasion.

The classification of the dances in this table is substantiated by the number of spirits that might be represented in each, as deducible from the preceding table: *Hesi*, in the first rank, 14; Duck and *Aki*, in the second, 9 each; Grizzly bear and deer, third rank, 1 each; coyote and goose, fourth, 1 each; all others, none.

TABLE 4.—SEQUENCE OF MAIDU DANCES AND CEREMONIES.

Hesi.
               Loli, Luyi, Kenu.
    Waima, duck.
            Salalu.
      Pano, grizzly bear.
        Oleli, coyote.
          Ota.
          Tsamyempi, creeper.
          Woiti.
          Yelimi (or Anosma, turtle).
        K'aima, goose?
          Aloli.
          Yok'ola.
          Weyo.
          Moloko, condor.
    Sümi, deer.
          K'ükit, sitting.
          Ene, grasshopper.
          Ts'amba.
  Aki.
Hesi.

THE SEVERAL KUKSU DANCES.

The *Hesi* was performed substantially as it has been outlined for the Patwin. The two groups seem to have attended each other's ceremonies rather frequently.

The *Loli* was for women only, a line or circle of whom held a long rope of swan or goose down.

The *Luyi* was not instituted at the beginning of the world by the Creator, the Maidu say, but by a man who followed his dead wife to the ghosts' dance house. This story as well as the facts that the usual feather ornaments were not worn, and that the performers, men and women, danced standing in a circle, suggest that the ritual may be a production of the modern " ghost dance " movement, or made over by it.

The duck dance, *Waima-ng-kasi* or *Hatma-ng-kasi*, is or can be visited by a variety of spirits, but possesses none peculiar to it. It comprises a dance made by men not representing spirits who shout *hat, hat, hat,* in imitation of ducks. A statement that the *Waima-ng-kasi* can at will be repeated later in the winter perhaps refers to this particular performance, rather than to the ceremony as a whole.

The *Salalu-ng-kasi* is little known. Its place was early in the series.

In the *Pano-ng-kasi* or *Pano-ng-kamini*, the grizzly bear dance, the *Pano-ng-kakini* or bear spirit impersonators imitated the actions as well as the appearance of the animal. This, with the parallel deer impersonation, is the only spirit that does not enter the *Hesi*. Each enactor had as assistant an initiate into the general society, who was his pupil and successor, and paid for the special instruction received. This tallies with Patwin and Pomo statements indicating that the right or ability to enact this impersonation is not part of membership in the society as such, but individually acquired or inherited; and may help to an understanding of the obscure status of bear shamans.

In the coyote dance the impersonator of this animal, or rather spirit, also mimicked it. Women danced in a part of this ceremony.

The *Oya* is little known, but is in some way asociated with the coyote ceremony. It is mentioned as having been influenced by the *boli,* or ghost dance movement.

The *Tsamyempi* is named after the nuthatch or a similar small bird that circles or "creeps" about tree trunks. After the house is darkened, a performer slides spirally down the sacred main or rear house post, clasping this with his legs while his body hangs down. He and his mates wear curtains of down strings over the face. This disguise suggests an impersonation, but the Maidu refuse to recognize the *Tsamyempi* actor as a spirit. While rated as "common," the dance is, however, clearly one of consequence, as other interludes, in which two men in raven feathers play hide and seek, reveal. Among the Pomo the essential features of the *Tsamyempi* appear in a full four days' ceremony, the *Dama.* The Miwok equivalent is the Akantoto, the Patwin unknown.

No details are available on the *Woiti.*

The turtle dance, called by its Patwin name *Anosma* (or *Akcholma*) more frequently than by its native equivalent *Yelimi,* comprises a two-man performance mimetic of the fox, but how its tortoise symbolism is expressed remains obscure.

A portion of this ritual is named *Hela-ng-kasi* or gambling dance, from the performers holding shredded tule and circling their arms like players. This name points to a connection with the Pomo *Hela-hela,* meaning unknown.

The *K'aima-ng-kasi* is named after a large water bird, probably the goose or crane. It balances the coyote dance. The *K'opa* who appears is reckoned as a spirit. A relation to the Yuki *Kop–wok—kop, kopa,* is "feathers" in that tongue—can not be pressed beyond the bounds of conjecture.

The *Aloli* and *Yok'ola* are associated or come in succession. Perhaps they are only parts of one ritual. In the former there is a curious act performed by two men and two women, who in turn sway a cradle containing a make-believe baby while swinging a pair of feather ropes suspended from the ceiling. In the latter a fringe, similar to that of the *Tsamyempi* but longer, is worn, and some informants connect the two dances.

The *Weyo* is disputed as a true dance. The name may possibly refer to the skunk.

The *Moloko* or condor dance is very little known. The bird is the object of much regard by all the California Indians.

With the *Sümi* or deer dance, about March, the ascending order of major ceremonies is well on its concluding way. The impersonators wear deer heads, but appear to represent spirits associated with the deer and not the animals themselves. Other dancers spot their bodies black and white to resemble fawns.

The *K'ükit* or "sitting," the *Ene* or "grasshopper," and the *Tsamba* dances are undescribed. The first two are associated.

With the *Aki,* in April or when the leaves come out, the last of the great ceremonies, barring the repetition of the *Hesi,* is reached. This ritual can hardly but have had equivalents among other groups, but its name defies translation in Maidu and does not recur elsewhere. In the *Aki* occurs a sort of trapeze exhibition, in which a personage called *Lali,* wearing the woodpecker scalp headdress of the *Dü* spirit, swings by his feet from a roof beam. To this there is a parallel in the Pomo *Dama.*

The cycle thus outlined is that followed by the northwestern Maidu of the valley. The series of the foothill people is less known, prob-- ably because there was much less of it. The northeastern people of the mountains are said to have borrowed some of the dances, or elements of them, from the lowlanders; but as they possessed no secret society, so far as is known, these importations, whether old or recent, must have remained unorganized fragments in their hands.

On the southern Maidu, information fails us, but those of the valley about Sacramento may be conjectured to have adhered fairly closely to the practices of the northwesterners of the vicinity of Chico, with some approximation to Miwok rituals; while the upland villages perhaps again followed them to the extent of an abbreviation.

It should be added that the Maidu, like the Patwin, make use of a number of ritualistic circumlocutions or sacred words in Kuksu songs and orations.

FIRST SALMON OBSERVANCE.

Like many of the northern Californians, the Maidu, at least in the northwestern foothills, had a first salmon observance. It was hardly elaborate enough to be named a ceremony. A shaman caught the first fish of the season, cooked it on the spot, and gave morsels to all in the village. This threw fishing open for the year. There may have been more of the rite than has been recorded, but it must have been a simple affair in comparison with the momentous ceremonies of the Yurok and Karok. It would be interesting to know whether the "shaman" acted in virtue of his actual shamanism—that is, supernatural power over the spirits individually acquired by himself—or because he also happened to have been taught the requisite prayer and rite.

CALENDAR.

The Maidu calendar recognizes 12 lunations with more or less descriptive epithets. It opens in spring, appears to contain no clear reference to the solstices, and to possess no fixed points. There is no mention of a device for correction, and it may be presumed that the Maidu dispensed with any, leaving a lunation unnamed whenever their moons ran too far ahead of the year as determined by seasonal events.

TABLE 5.—NORTHERN MAIDU CALENDAR.

Month.	Valley reckoning.	Foothill reckoning.	Mountain reckoning.
March	Shawi, Sha-kono; flowers.	Kono	Bom-tetno ("t r a i l sit along").
April	Laila; grass	Win-uti ("b l a c k oaks tassel").	Kono.
May	Kon-moko; seeds, fish, geese; *Hesi*.	Tem-diyoko; fawns.	Külokbepine ("old women ——?").
June	Neng-kaukat ("big summer").	Nem-diyoko ("big month"?).	
July	Tumi; smoky	Kaui-tson ("ground burn").	
August	Tem-simi; acorns ripen.	Eslakum ("m i d - dle").	
September	Kum-menim She-meni; acorns gath-ered.	Mat-meni ("acorn-bread").	Se-meni ("seed").
October	Shahwodo; acorns cached; *Hesi*.	Bapaboka	Tem-tsampauto ("s m a l l t r e e freeze").
November	Yapakto; winter di-vided.	Bo-lye ("trail ——?").	Tetem-tsampauta ("l a r g e t r e e freeze").
December	Omhincholi; ice lasts all day.	Sap	Kanaipino ("under burn").
January	Yeponi ("ceremonial initiate") or Bom-pene ("two trails").	Into	Bom-hintsuli ("trail squint").
February	Kaka-kano; pattering showers.	O m i - h i n t s u l i ("squint rock").	Bo-ekmen ("trail breaks open").

It seems that the mountain people actually counted only nine moons, leaving those of summer nameless. It is clear that the reckoning in valley, hills, and mountains has diverged, names originally descriptive having become crystallized rather arbitrarily as regards season. This appears from the fact that month names containing the same element appear in the three regions not only at diverse times of the year but in variable order. Thus:

	Valley.	Hills.	Mountains.
Kono, kon–	May	March	April.
Nem-, neng-, "large"	June	June	
Tem-, "small?"	August	May	October.
Se-meni, "seed"	September		September.
-hintsuli, "squint"	December	February	January.
Bo-, bom-, "trail"	January	November	January, February, March.

The valley people divide their calendar into halves, from *Shawi* to *Temṡini* and from *Kummenim* to *Kakakano*. Whether these divisions refer merely to summer and winter, or whether they represent an attempt to note the equinoxes, is not clear. The two periods are not the dance season and quiet season of the Kuksu cult.

On the whole, a more distinctly unastronomical calendar than that of the Maidu can hardly be imagined.

Four seasons were recognized by the Maidu, counted as commencing with the first appearance of the phenomena referred to. Two lists from the northwestern foothills corroborate each other, and run in the spirit of the month calendar.

> Spring: *Yo-meni*, flowers.
> Summer: *Kaukati*, earth, dust, or *ihilaki*, dry.
> Autumn: *Se-meni*, seeds, or *mat-meni*, acorn bread.
> Winter: *Ko-meni*, snow.

In line with this series is a set of four seasonal festivals or *weda* mentioned by the hill Maidu: the *Hoktom*, an open-air affair in spring; the *Ilakum* in the dry season, about July; the *Üshtu* or *Üshtimo* around September (this is the "burning" or mourning anniversary); and the *Yakai* near Christmas.

The mountain Maidu know the Milky Way as "morning star's path"; the Pleiades as *dotodoto;* Ursa Major is "looking around"; Job's Coffin is *hemuimu*, perhaps from the word for roasting. The rainbow is associated obscenely with the coyote, as by the Yurok.

THE SOUL.

What we call the soul, the Maidu named heart. "His heart is gone away" means that a person is dead. In a swoon or in a dream a person's heart leaves his body. Sickness, however, is due not to the departure or attempted departure of the soul, but to the presence in the body of a "pain" or disease object.

The northern valley people believe that a dead person's heart lingers near the body for several days. It then journeys to every spot which the living person had visited, retracing each of his steps and reenacting every deed performed in life. This accomplished, the spirit seeks a mysterious cavern in the Marysville Buttes, the great spirit mountain of the Maidu, where for the first time it eats spirit food and is washed. Its experiences here are a repetition of those of the first man of mythology. From the Marysville Buttes the spirit ascends to the sky land, flower land, or spirit land, as it is variously called.

The hill residents tell of the same journey traveled by their dead. But these reach the abounding sky land—"valley above" is an equivalent rendering—by going east along the path of the sun, instead of to the Marysville Buttes. The Milky Way is also pointed out as the road of the spirits. Its fork is the parting of the ways for those going to the good or the bad land in the sky according to their life on earth; but it is far from certain that this idea of reward is aboriginal. We may be confronted here by a ghost dance idea.

The mountain people also make their dead wont to linger for a time, particularly those attached to their family. But they describe them as careful not to look on their relatives, for, as among all the Maidu, the glance of a ghost, or sight of it, is fatal. The retraveling of the earthly course is not mentioned by the mountain Maidu. Like the hill people, they believe that their ghosts go eastward and live with the Creator. Once a ghost's face has been washed on its way, it is a spirit forever. Those few who are merely in a trance and are to return to life are not washed at the entrance to spirit land.

THE WORLD.

The earth was believed to be round and surrounded by water. In fact it floated on this sea, held by five ropes that had been stretched by the Creator. A shaking of these ropes made earthquakes. This concept of the tying of the world reappears hundreds of miles to the south among the Luiseño. The ropes of which the mountain Maidu tell reach in our cardinal directions and to the northwest, which by them is also reckoned a direction.

This insistence on five as the ritualistic number is another instance of the influence which the tribes of extreme northern California have exerted on the northeastern Maidu through the medium of the Achomawi. In the hills four is the number of ceremonial import more frequently than five, and in the valley four or a multiple thereof distinctly prevails. It may be added that four exercises this function wherever the Kuksu organization exists.

It is also clear throughout California that four and six tend strongly to be associated with directions, but that five has no such implication. When, therefore, the northeastern Maidu reckon five horizontal cardinal directions, it is plain that an attempt has been made by them to reconcile the quintuple concept of their northern neighbors with the directional number ideas of their southern and western kinsmen.

A new moon was regarded as respectively favorable or unfavorable, with reference to weather, health, and crops, according as its horns pointed up or horizontally. This type of belief is so widespread among American Indians that it can scarcely be interpreted as a concept borrowed from the whites. We may be dealing with an item of folklore which long ago underwent a world-wide diffusion, or possibly with one of those rare and suspected things, a direct and spontaneous projection of the human psyche into culture.

LOCAL CURRENTS IN MAIDU CULTURE.

The traits in which the Maidu of the high northern Sierra—that is, of Plumas country—stand apart from the remaining Maidu and resemble the tribes of northeastern and through them those of northwestern California, may be recapitulated thus: basketry in overlay twining, including several distinctive vessels, such as the cap, the mortar basket, the large storage basket and the close-woven carrier; rod armor in waistcoat form; the porcupine tail comb; the fringed and wrapped deerskin apron; the deerskin legging for men; the use of five as a ritualistic number; the absence of Kuksu cults; and several elements in shamanistic belief, such as the dreaming of ancestors, bathing in lakes, a considerable importance of women, the motility of pain objects.

The valley Maidu resemble the Yurok and Hupa in those customs into which money enters, such as wife purchase and settlement for the slain, and in the failure to elaborate an adolescence ceremony. The content of the two cultures shows very few specific similarities. The resemblances thus spring from likeness of level or degree of civilization, rather than from direct importation as with the northeastern Maidu.

CHAPTER 30.

THE MIWOK.

GEOGRAPHY.

The Miwok comprised three territorially discrete groups: the Coast
Miwok, the Lake Miwok, and the Interior Miwok. The first two
have already been described. The Interior Miwok constituted by
far the largest portion of the stock. With the Maidu on their right
hand, the Yokuts on the left, Washo and Mono behind them, they
lived on the long westward slope of the great Sierra, looking out
over the lower San Joaquin Valley. A few, the Plains Miwok, were
in the valley itself, where this is intersected by the winding arms
of the deltas of the San Joaquin and the Sacramento. The bulk of
the group were a true foothill people, without claims to the floor of
the valley, and moving into the higher Sierra only for summer residence or hunting.

A primary cleavage of speech separates the Plains from the Sierra
Miwok, exactly as among the Yokuts. The Plains speech is a little
the nearest that of the Coast and Lake divisions in its forms as well
as in location. The dwellers in the foothills followed three principal
dialects, which in default of native names have come to be known
as northern, central, and southern. The latter stands somewhat
apart; the two former are similar to each other and evince some
approach to the Plains dialect. There are some subdialects within
several or all of these four idioms; but they are rather insignificant
and may be disregarded.

The Sierra territory of the Miwok extended from the Cosumnes
River on the north to the Fresno on the south. Roughly, the northern division held the drainage of the Mokelumne and Calaveras;
the central, that of the Stanislaus and Tuolumne; the southern, that
of the Merced and adjacent smaller streams. But there was some
transgressing of these natural limits, as appears from Plate 37.

The exact boundaries of the Miwok are still a matter of controversy at many
points, especially as between the Plains division and the adjacent Yokuts,
Wintun, and Maidu of the delta, all of whom are practically extinct.

Thus the entire tongue of land between the lower Cosumnes and Sacramento, as well as Grand, Andrews, Tyler, Staten, and Brannan Islands between the easternmost and westernmost channels of the Sacramento, have sometimes been assigned to the Maidu. Sherman Island and a tract to the southeast seem to have been Miwok, but there is some conflict of evidence as to the location of the line separating the Plains Miwok and the most northerly Yokuts in this vicinity.

The region from Michigan Bar to Plymouth has been variously claimed as Maidu, Plains Miwok, and northern Miwok. The whole northern boundary of the Miwok, in fact, is obscure, the North, Middle, and South Forks of the Cosumnes, as well as various compromises between these, being cited by different authorities. The Middle Fork has been followed in Plates 1 and 37.

On the eastern front discrepancies are even wider, but simmer down substantially to technical differences. The Miwok lived permanently as far up into the Sierra as the heavy winter snows permitted; in summer they moved higher; and no other people held residence between them and the crest. The Washo had admitted hunting and therefore camping rights almost down to Big Trees in Calaveras County. They may have enjoyed similar but unrecorded claims elsewhere; and the same may possibly be true of the Mono. Very likely there were tracts that were jointly visited on friendly terms by the Miwok and their trans-Sierra neighbors. The "boundary" may therefore well have been shifting as amity or hostility prevailed. In this connection it may be noted that in the region of the headwaters of the middle and south Stanislaus the Miwok and Mono were on bad terms in recent times, while along the Merced they were more at ease with each other.

On the south it is reasonably certain that Fresno River itself separated the Miwok from the Yokuts, except for a small tract below Fresno Flats where the Miwok held the southern bank of a northward bend of the stream. The exact location of the village of Hapasau is in doubt. The name is Yokuts; the location may have been on the Miwok side of the river.

As for the West, it has sometimes been assumed that the Miwok ranged as rightful owners over the whole eastern and more fertile side of the lower San Joaquin Valley, but the evidence is nearly positive that this tract was Yokuts, and that the precise commencement of the first foothills marked the boundary between the two stocks. This is the line that has been followed in Plate 37.

Like Wintun, Maidu, and Yokuts, "Miwok" is not originally a distinctive tribal or group name, but the native word for people, plural of *miwü*, "person." The northernmost Miwok respond to the designation Koni, which is their Maidu name; and those of the extreme south are often known as Pohonichi, which appellation seems to be of Yokuts origin; whether connected with Pohono Falls in Yosemite is less certain.

Chauchila appears to be the name of both a Yokuts tribe on the plains and of a Miwok village in the canyon of Chowchilla River, whose designation has been applied also to a larger Miwok group or division. It is scarcely probable that the same name was in use by both stocks in aboriginal times. The American is likely to have been responsible for its spread. Before the conflict can be solved we shall have to be in a position to distinguish between ancient native usage and more modern terminology adopted by the Indians in their relations with the whites.

Moquelumnan is an artificially derived synonym of Miwok that has attained some book usage. An earlier term of similar nature that is now happily obsolete is Mutsun, based on the name of a Costanoan village taken as a designation of the conjoined Costanoan and Miwok groups.

Among themselves the Miwok are content to refer to one another by village, or employ an endless succession of " northerners " and similar directional names that never crystallize into specific designations. The same people that are northerners to their neighbors on one side are southerners to those on the other, and so on ad infinitum, even beyond the boundaries of the stock, as far as knowledge extends. A group of people as a unit possessing an existence and therefore a name of its own is a concept that has not dawned on the Miwok. Humanity must appear to them like a uniform sheet spread over an endless earth, differentiable only with reference to one's own location in the whole. A national sense is weak enough among most of the California Indians; but there are usually a few generic names for outside groups of foreigners. If the Miwok have such, they have not become known; except Koyuwe-k, " salt people," for the Mono. Mono-k seems to be a recent term. Even the Washo are only " easterners " or " uplanders." Lisnayu-k denotes either the Yokuts or the Costanoans of the vicinity of Pacheco Pass.

Their four standard terms are Tamuleko, Tamulek, or Tumitok, northerners; Chumetoko, Chumetok. or Chumteya. southerners; Hisotoko. Hisatok, or Hittoya, easterners; Olowitoko, Olowitok, Olokok, or Olwiya, westerners; or other close dialectic variants.

Among the Plains Miwok names in -mni are frequent which suggest the tribal appellations of the Yokuts: Mokelumni, Mokosumni, Ochehamni, Lelamni, Hulpumni, Umuchamni or Omochumne, Sakayakümni. As with the Maidu, the words probably denote a political community named after its principal or permanent settlement.

The same appears to hold of names ending in -chi.

Something over a hundred Miwok villages are shown on Plate 37. The total number of those whose names have been recorded is considerably larger; but some are in doubtful or conflicting records, others are vaguely located, and in general the condition of knowledge concerning the settlements of the group—even those included in the map—is far from satisfactory. We are in total ignorance, for instance, to what extent near villages were truly independent or only outlying settlements that recognized their political and social unity with a central larger town.

The villages that can be both named and approximately located are, as shown on Plate 37:

Plains Miwok: 1, Hulpu-mni; 2, *Yumhul; 3, *Yomit; 4, *Lulimal; 5, *Sukididi; 6, *Mayeman; 7, *Chuyumkatat; 8, Umucha; 9, Supu; 10, Tukui; 11,

Mokos-umni; 12, Ocheh-ak; 13, Mokel(-umni); 14, Lel-amni; 15, Sakayak-ümni. (Starred names are in the southern Maidu language.)

Northern Miwok: 16, Yule; 17, Omo; 18, Noma; 19, Chakane-sü; 20, Yuloni; 21, Seweu-su; 22, Upüsüni (Fig. 40); 23, Tukupe-sü; 24, Pola-sü; 25, Tumuti; 26, Sopochi; 27, Ketina; 28, Mona-sü; 29, Apautawilü; 30, Heina; 31, Künüsü; 32, Penken-sü; 33, Kaitimü; 34, Hechenü; 35, Huta-sü.

Central Miwok: 36, Sasamu; 37, Shulaputi; 38, Katuka; 39, Humata; 40, Akutanuka; 41, Kosoimuno-nu; 42, Newichu; 43, Yungakatok; 44, Alakani; 45, Tuyiwü-nu; 46, Kewe-no; 47, Tulana-chi; 48, Oloikoto; 49, Wüyü; 50, Tipotoya; 51, Loyowisa; 52, Kawinucha; 53, Takema; 54, Tulsuna; 55, Hangwite; 56, Wokachet; 57, Sutamasina; 58, Singawü-nu; 59, Akankau-nchi (*cf.* 67); 60, Akawila; 61, Kapanina; 62, Chakachi-no; 63, Suchumumu; 64, Waka-che; 65, Kotoplana; 66, Pokto-no; 67, Akankau-nchi (*cf.* 59); 68, Ḳuluti; 69, Pota; 70, Wolanga-su; 71, Tel'ula; 72, Tunuk-chi; 73, Kesa; 74, Hochhochmeti; 75, Siksike-no; 76, Sopka-su; 77, Pasi-nu; 78, Pangasema-nu; 79, Sukanola; 80, Sukwela; 81, Telese-no; 82, Hunga; 83, Olawiye; 84, Kulamu; 85, Hechhechi; 86, Pigliku (Miwok pronunciation of "Big Creek"); 87, Sala.

Southern Miwok: 88, Sayangasi; 89, Alaula-chi; 90, Kuyuka-chi; 91, Angisawepa; 92, Hikena; 93, Owelinhatihü; 94, Wilito; 95, Kakahula-chi; 96, Awal; 97, Yawoka-chi; 98, Kitiwina; 99, Siso-chi; 100, Sope-nchi; 101, Sotpok; 102, Awani; 103, Palachan; 104, Kasumati; 105, Nochu-chi; 106, Nowach; 107, Olwia; 108, Wasema; 109, Wehilto.

In 1817 Father Duran, voyaging from the Golden Gate up San Francisco Bay, through the delta, and some hundred miles up the Sacramento, encountered or reported Chupcanes, Ompines, Quenemsias or Quenemisas, Chucumnes, Ilamnes, Chuppumne, Ochejamnes, Guaypems, Passasimas, Nototemnes, Tauquimnes, Yatchicomnes, Muquelemnes, and Julpunes. The first of these groups were Costanoan; the next probably Maidu or perhaps in part Wintun; from the Ochejamnes on, the list refers to Plains Miwok and the northernmost Yokuts. It seems, therefore, that all five of the great Penutian divisions were represented among the natives of whom this little expedition makes mention.

Nine thousand seems a liberal estimate for the number of interior Miwok in ancient times. This allows more than 2,000 to each of the four divisions. But all specific data are wanting. The 1910 census counted 670, only one-half of them full blood. The Miwok have thus failed to preserve as large a fraction of their numbers as the Maidu, but have done better than the Yokuts. The Plains division came pretty thoroughly under mission control and shows very few survivors. The three foothill groups escaped this well-meant but nearly fatal influence.

CULTURE.

The civilization of the Miwok is imperfectly known, and is the more difficult to reconstruct in that the culture of all their immediate neighbors, except in some degree that of the Yokuts, is also unrecorded in detail.

Even in a larger sense, comparison with the stocks to the east and west is mostly invalidated by the profound difference of habitat. As between the adjacent Sierra dwellers on the north and south, the

Maidu and the Yokuts, Miwok affiliations incline somewhat more to the former; but perhaps this fact is at bottom to be ascribed to environmental adaptations, the Maidu being in the main Sierra dwellers like the Miwok, whereas the Yokuts, although in part situated in the foothills, were so much more extensively a plains people that their civilization as a whole has no doubt been intensively colored by this circumstance.

The strongest link with the Maidu is the presence of the Kuksu cult of the Sacramento Valley, with its long variety of rituals, impersonation of spirits, distinctive costumes, and the accompaniment of the large semisubterranean dance house. The complement is the absence among the Miwok of the Yokuts jimsonweed cult.

Another important link in the same direction is the apparent lack of the more definite tribal organization of the Yokuts.

So far as Miwok mythology is known, on the other hand, it is rather of Yokuts type. This fact is surprising, since an anthropomorphic creator tends to appear in the beliefs of the tribes addicted to the Kuksu religion. It is true the Costanoan and Salinan stocks, who

Fig. 38.—Yokuts loop stirrer and Miwok paddle. (Compare Pls. 17, 44.)

participate in the Kuksu cult and live in the same transverse belt of California as the Miwok, seem also to lean in their mythology toward the Yokuts more than to the Sacramento Valley tribes. A less specialized type of cosmogony is therefore indicated for the southern Kuksu-dancing groups.[1]

The organization of society on the plan of two totemically contrasted halves, which was first discovered in California among the Miwok, extends south from them to the Yokuts and western Mono. It has not been reported from the north.

In material arts the balance again inclines northward. Coiled baskets, for instance, are made on a foundation of rods, as by the Maidu, whereas the Yokuts use grass. The Yokuts cap and constricted-neck vessel are also wanting. So is Yokuts pottery. Games, on the other hand, are rather of Yokuts type, so far as can be judged. Perhaps this is due to an association with the social organization. (Fig. 41.)

In some minor points the Miwok follow varying practices according to the habits of their neighbors. Thus the southernmost Miwok

---

[1] If, as seems probable, the southerly Kuksu tribes (the Miwok, Costanoans, Esselen, and northernmost Yokuts) had no real society in connection with their Kuksu ceremonies, the distinctness of their mythology appears less surprising.

PLATE 37

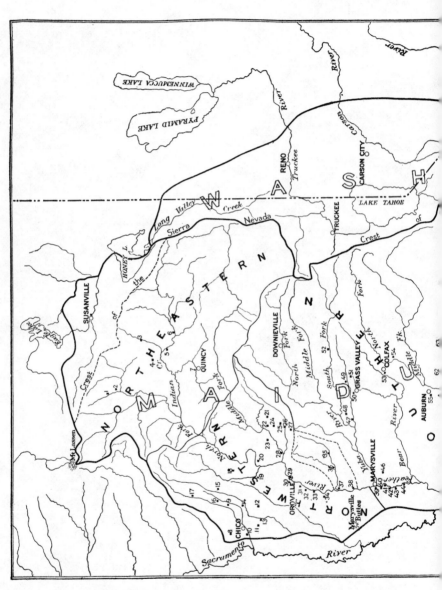

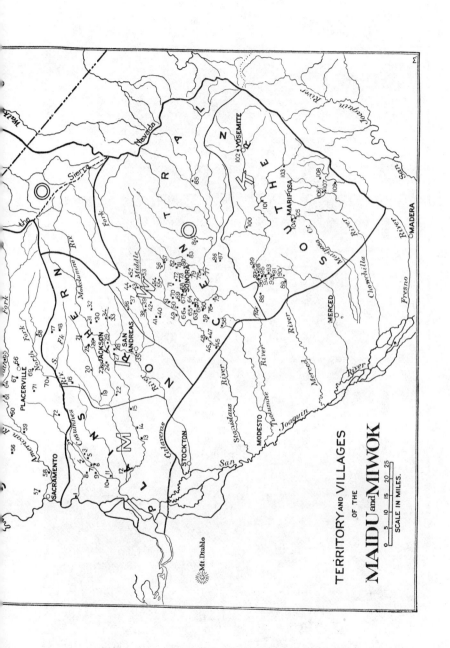

TERRITORY AND VILLAGES
OF THE
MAIDU AND MIWOK
SCALE IN MILES.

PLATE 38

MIWOK ACORN GRANARY

PLATE 39

CRADLES

a, d, e, Southern Miwok; b, Mohave; c, f, Northern Miwok

PLATE 40

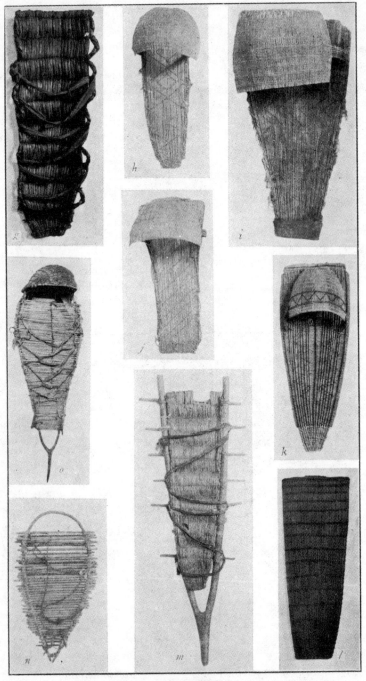

CRADLES

g, m, Valley Yokuts; *h, i, j,* Kings River Yokuts; *k,* Eastern Mono; *l,* Western Mono; *n,* Northwestern Maidu of foothills; *o,* Northwestern Maidu

often employ the grass foundation of the Yokuts and approximate the shape of their "bottle neck" baskets. South of the Tuolumne, too, the Yokuts looped-stick mush stirrer and the Yokuts type of basketry cradle are used. North of the Stanislaus the mush stirrer is a small, plain paddle (Fig. 38), as among the Achomawi and Pomo; and the cradle takes on the peculiar form of being built on two rods whose upper ends are bent forward as a hood support. (Pls. 39, 40.) Also, it is chiefly north of the Stanislaus that one-rod basket foundations are found alongside of the more usual three-rod coil. Here influence of contact with the adjacent Washo is likely.

MATERIAL ARTS.

The distribution of house types in the Miwok region is still far from clear. The semisubterranean dance house or *hangi* was known to the whole group. It rested on a square of four center posts, or on two rows of posts, whereas the Yuki, Pomo, Wintun, and Maidu employed a single large post, or two set in line with the door. The diameter was as great as farther north, up to 20 yards; the door regularly faced eastward; the general construction presented few noteworthy peculiarities. (Fig. 39.)

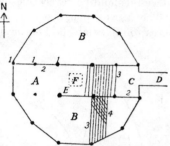

FIG. 39. — Miwok dance or assembly house. Diameter, 25 feet. Construction: 1, tole, posts, forked or notched on top. 2, chawik, main rafters, extending east and west. 3, lolapa, crossbeams on rafters. 4, shuchapa, brush on beams, radiating from center. On this brush was a layer of grass, and then of earth. Parts of house: *A*, wole; *BB*, oni; *C*, hawana; *D*, door or tunnel—always toward east; *E*, smoke hole, 3 feet square; perhaps the entrance in ancient times; *F*, fireplace. (Cf. Figures 19, 35.)

The sweat house was much smaller than the dance house, but built on the same plan.

The Miwok living house, *kocha* or *uchu*, appears to have been often of the earth-covered type, although smaller and ruder than the dance house. It is not certain how far south the range of this extended. It may have been rare in the higher foothills, and was probably not lived in more than half the year. A lean-to of bark was used in the mountains in summer; it may have been the permanent house of some sections.

The cache or granary used by the Miwok for the storage of acorns is an outdoor affair, a yard or so in diameter, a foot or two above the ground, and thatched over, beyond reach of a standing person, after it was filled. Plate 38 shows the type. The natural branches of a tree sometimes were used in place of posts. There was no true basket construction in the cache; the sides were sticks and brush lined with grass, the whole stuck together and tied where necessary.

No door was necessary: the twigs were readily pushed aside almost anywhere, and with a little start acorns rolled out in a stream. Even the squirrels had little difficulty in helping themselves at will.

An outdoor cache coincides rather closely with the distribution of coiled basketry. None of the tribes that twine make use of any granary. This is no accident. A large storage basket is readily twined. Where there is a feeling that the proper way to make a basket intended to be preserved is by coiling, the laboriousness of this technique would incline toward the manufacture by other processes of vessels holding several bushels.

The Miwok pound acorns with pestles in holes in granite exposures; on flat slabs laid on or sunk into the ground without basketry hopper; and grind them by crushing and rubbing on similar slabs. The conical and cylindrical mortars found in their habitat are prehistoric. Occasionally a small one is in use; but if so, it is employed by some toothless crone to crack bones, or to beat an occasional gift of a gopher or squirrel into a soft, edible pulp. Such a mortar may contain a pit or two for cracking acorns, and perhaps a groove in which bone awls have been whetted for a lifetime. In default of anything more practical the owner's husband may now and then grind his tobacco in the same utensils. Ancient stone implements that have been put to secondary uses are rather common in California, and can still be seen in service now and then. That an object is already in use is if anything an added reason why it should be employed for another purpose. A neat people would feel differently; but a glance into almost any California Indian home suffices to reveal that these people are actuated by but little sense of order as compared with the Plains or Pueblo Indians.

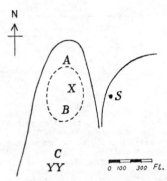

FIG. 40.—The Miwok village of Upüsüni. Lines are hill contours. Dotted line (X), old village site. YY, modern houses. A, pit of oldest dance house, diameter 50 feet. B, dance-house pit, diameter 65 feet. C, standing dance house (plan shown in Fig. 39), diameter 25 feet. S, spring Upüsüni, whence the name of the village.

Clamshell disk currency was less precious than in the north, though that may have been one of the directions from which it reached the Miwok. Its value in American terms is said to have averaged $5 a yard, only a fraction of the figure at which the southern Maidu rated it. Whole strung olivella shells went at $1 a yard among both groups. The cylinders made from magnesite by the southeastern Pomo reached the hill Miwok, but were scarce and valuable. Possibly clamshell money traveled to them from the Chumash via the Yokuts as well as from the Pomo; whence its abundance and comparative depreciation.

THE KUKSU RELIGION.

The Miwok follow the Kuksu ritual organization. It happens that we possess considerable knowledge of their individual dances and none at all of the society underlying these;[2] but the names and character of several of the ceremonies, their large number, the type of feather dress worn, the stamping of the foot drum, and the holding of the performances in the earth-covered assembly chamber, all make the adhesion of the Miwok to the Sacramento Valley scheme of rites clear, even though the precise form which the system takes among them remains undetermined.

The distinction between ceremony and dance and between ceremony and impersonation, as it has been described among the Wintun, evidently recurs among the Miwok. Thus there is the *Kuksuyu*, an exceptionally sacred performance, seemingly occupying the same primary position that the *Hesi* holds among the Patwin and Maidu, and the *Guksu* impersonator among the Pomo. In this *Kuksuyu* appear at least three personages: *Kuksuyu* himself; *Osa-be*, or " woman "; and *Mochilo*, who is perhaps the Miwok representative of the Sacramento Valley *Moki*, and whose impersonator is known as *mochil-be*. In addition, there is the *Mochilasi* dance, held without the drum, in which the *Mochilo* appears impersonated by a *sotokbe*,

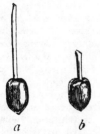

a   *b*

Fig. 41.—Acorn tops. *a*, Pomo ; *b*, Miwok.

and accompanied by the *Osa-be*. At some point in the *Mochilasi*, as in most Miwok dances, women participate; but they do not appear in the *Kuksuyu*.

Besides the Miwok rituals mentioned in Table 1 in the chapter on the Wintun, they practice the following dances:

The *Lileusi* and *Uchupelu* are of a type with the Patwin *Akantoto* or creeper dance, the Maidu *Tsamyempi*, and the Pomo *Dama*, in that in all of them there are acrobatic demonstrations. In the *Akantoto* the performer descends the center post of the dance house head first, clasping it with his legs. The *Uchupelu* is similar, but less spectacular. In the *Lileusi*, in which the drum is not used, the dancer is believed to fly about the darkened house. The songs tell of one, no doubt the impersonated spirit, who thus came to the Miwok country from Mount Diablo, the name of which reflects the native belief in its habitation by spirits.

---

[2] It seems quite doubtful whether there was a society ; there is certainly no trace of a communal one.

The *Kalea* is a frequent and perhaps an important dance, which has survived until more recently than the majority. In it are worn a back cape of feathers similar to the Maidu *sikli* and the corresponding garments of the Patwin, Pomo, and Yuki; a large tuft; and two smaller ones, skewered into the net-gathered hair.

The *Tamula* may be the "north" dance: *tamal-in* is the ordinary word designating this direction.

In the *Temayasu*, a personage of the same name, who is followed by seven *seyapbe*, showers coals on the spectators, who may not laugh, evidently for fear of provoking his anger. The *Temayasu* thus evinces something of the nature of the Pomo "ash ghosts." The Patwin *Temeyu* bears a similar name.

A ritual called *Sule tumum laksü*, "ghost from drum emerging," also has close Pomo parallels. The performer, painted with horizontal black and white stripes, emerges from a tunnel under the drum and then dances upon it. It is likely that he is taken for a real ghost by the uninitiated.

To the *Sulesko*, said to be named after a kind of spirit in some way associated with the *sule* or ghost of dead people, is ascribed a recent origin. It was performed to cure people made ill by such spirits. Four dancers wear something like face coverings of skin. This is a nearer approach to what are ordinarily considered masks than anything yet reported from California; but on the other hand, there is less reference by the Miwok to veiling of the face by feathers or grass in other dances than among the Maidu and Patwin. The Miwok *Kuksuyu*, indeed, has his features hidden by feathers; but the only other personage known to be disguised, other than perhaps by crude paint, occurs in the *Helekasi*, in which a piece of buckskin, with eyeholes cut in it, is worn around the head.

The clowns, or *Wo'ochi*, who shout *woo*, appear in a number of ceremonies in an interlude named after them. They are painted white and evidently represent coyotes. The gluttonous, greedy, tricky, but also insensate nature which the California Indian attributes to this animal is the character which is portrayed in the actions also of the Maidu clown; but no avowed symbolic reference to the contemned canine has been reported from the latter people.

The *Uzumati* or grizzly bear ceremony came to the central Miwok from the west or northwest, they say; that is, probably, the northernmost Yokuts such as the Chulamni of Stockton, or the Plains Miwok. The performer, who was a dance impersonator and not a bear doctor or shaman, carried curved pieces of obsidian attached to his fingers in place of the bear's claws. He imitated the animal in his dancing. This description accounts for the hitherto unexplained "Stockton curves," as antiquarians have come to call the semilunar flaked objects of obsidian found in ancient burials in the San Joaquin delta.

Other dances or ceremonies were the *Mamasu*, *Tula*, *Henepasi*, *Yahuha*, *Alina*, *Hekeke* or "quail," *Wehena*, and *Olochina*. There is also a *Helika*, which may or may not be the same as the *Helekasi* in which masks are worn, and a less sacred *Helikna*.

A leading dancer called *hoyuche*, assisted by several *echuto*, appears in the *Salute*, *Helika*, *Alina*, and other dances. Whether the term indicates his leadership, a particular costume, or a spirit that he impersonates, is not known. A village chief is called *echuto hayapo* in distinction from the *toko hayapo* or head chief of a district.

Besides the *Helikna*, the *Aletü*, *Ahana*, *Ulula*, and *Helkibüksu* are mentioned as at least semiprofane. The drum is not used; the *sobobbe* or shouters who accompany the dancers in the major ceremonies are absent; and some, at least, of these dances are held outdoors, away from the gloom of the assembly chamber. Women take part in all these dances, whose general character is probably analogous to that of the Maidu *Loli* and *Toto*. In or after the *Aletü* two black-painted clowns, called *Humchilwe*, may appear.

It is said that women were allowed to witness all dances, even the most sacred of those held in the assembly chamber. This would indicate a status of the secret society in the community rather different from that which obtains among the tribes in the latitude of the Sacramento Valley. Miwok women seem to have participated in probably the majority of dances.

Nothing has been learned of the order or classificatory relations of the various major and minor dances so far enumerated. Yet it may be suspected that, like the Maidu ceremonies, they came in some sort of an orderly sequence at specified seasons of the year rather than randomly.

OTHER CEREMONIES AND BELIEFS.

Sule yuse, " ghost hair," or *Sule sikanui*, " ghost scalp "— a single word to denote " ghost," " dead person," and " skeleton " seems to be customary in a number of the Californian languages—was the name of the dance of triumphant revenge held over a scalp. It was made in the dance house, as by the Yuki, and the drum was stamped.

The *Pota* was a ceremony in which several rude dummies of tules were put up on poles. It appears likely that songs of malevolence and perhaps other expressions of hatred were directed toward the figures. The images represented foes of the village: murderers, successful war leaders in past affrays, or shamans believed to have caused sickness and death. Care was taken to invite the towns to which these individuals belonged; but as no identification was given the image, and no names mentioned at the time, this method of revenge could contribute little but moral satisfaction to the preformers. The guests might suspect that it was their townsman who was meant, but as no insult was tendered, none could be resented; until later, when care would be taken that the visitors learned that it was their kinsman whom they had helped to revile. The whole procedure is characteristically Californian. By impulse, the native is thoroughly peaceable. A plan of spoliation or oppression rarely enters his mind. But suspicion is ever gnawing within him. Punctilious as he is not to commit a deliberate offense, he constantly conceives that others have wished him ill and worked the contemplated injury. And so he spends his life in half-concealed bad will, in nonintercourse, in plotting with more or less open magic, or occasionally in an open feud. He has always been wronged by some one, and is always planning a merited but dark punishment. Though they are rarely uttered expressly, he mutters his feelings about; with the consequence that those whom he hates soon have equal or greater cause for hating in return. There must be a subtle pleasure in publicly dishonoring and threatening a foe, who may suspect but can not know that he is meant. But the satisfaction thus obtainable is an equally extraordinary one, and obviously peculiar of a people more given to keeping grievances alive by cherishing them than to ending them by an open appeal to the nobler violence that springs from indignation.

The *Kalea* seems to be made in connection with this *Pota* ceremony.

The *Aiyetme*, named from *aiye'a*, the signs of a girl's maturity, is an adolescence ceremony, as is also clear from the fact that the dancers are called *kichaume*, from *kichau*, " blood." There are four of these, men, painted with red streaks down the face, but they wear no feathers or costume. At present the dance is a short performance on and about the drum in the assembly house, and evidently a part of larger ceremonies that have other purposes. Originally, however, it was made for the girl, and probably over her as she lay for four days in a trench dug in the floor of her home.

The Miwok are said to have held that there was no after life; but this is a white man's superstition about them. One of their favorite traditions, which they share with the Yokuts, relates the visit of an aboriginal Orpheus to the western or northern country of the dead in pursuit of his wife.

SOCIAL PRACTICES.

Cremation of the dead was the usual but probably not universal practice of the Miwok.

Widows singed their hair off and pitched the face. In the southern districts the pitch was put on over smaller areas. The levirate was observed, but perhaps not invariably.

The annual mourning ceremony included dancing as well as wailing, culminated in a burning of property, and ended with a ritualistic washing of the mourners by people of the opposite totemic moiety. Rude lay figures were made and burned for people of rank.

Chieftainship was a well-defined and hereditary affair, as is shown by the passage of the title to women, in the male line. In the central division there were head chiefs, *toko hayapo*, whose authority was recognized over considerable districts; *echuto hayapo*, chiefs of villages; and *euchi* or *liwape* (*liwa*, " speak "), who were either the heads of subsidiary villages or speakers and messengers for the more important chiefs. A born chieftainess, and the wife of a chief, were both called *mayenu*. The husband of a born chieftainess was usually her speaker; the latter had authority after her husband's death until the majority of her son.

It is evident that concepts of rank were fairly developed, and it is regrettable that more is not known of this interesting subject.

TOTEMIC MOIETIES.

With the Miwok we encounter for the first time a social scheme that recurs among several of the groups to the south: a division of the people into balanced halves, or moieties, as they are called, which are totemic, and adhesion to which is hereditary. The descent is from the father, and among the Miwok the moieties were at least theoretically exogamic.

The totemic aspects of these moieties are refined to an extreme tenuousness, but are undeniable. Nature is divided into a water and a land or dry half, which are thought to correspond to the *Kikua* and *Tunuka* moieties among the people. *Kikua* is from *kiku*, water, but the etymology of *Tunuka* is not clear. Synonyms, though apparently only of a joking implication, are *Lotasuna* and *Kosituna*, " frog people " and " blue jay people "; or the contrast is between frog and deer, or coyote and blue jay. All these terms apply to the central and southern Miwok. The northern division uses a word formed from *walli*, "land," in place of *Tunuka;* and the animal equivalents are not clear. There is also some doubt as to the form which the scheme takes among the northerners, some accounts denying its existence, or that the individual's adherence was determined by descent. It is apparent that the northern Miwok are institutionally as well as geographically on the border of the moiety system.

There are no subdivisions of any sort within the moieties. Associated with each, however, is a long list of animals, plants, and objects; in fact, the native concept is that everything in the world belongs to one or the other side. Each member of a moiety stands in relation to one of the objects characteristic of his moiety—a relation that must be considered totemic—in one way only: through his name. This name, given him in infancy by a grandfather or other relative, and retained through life, refers to one of the totem animals or objects characteristic of his moiety.

Nor is this all: in the great majority of cases the totem is not mentioned in the name, which is formed from some verbal or adjectival stem, and describes an action or condition that might apply equally well to other totems. Thus, on the verb *hausu-s* are based the names *Hausu* and *Hauchu*, which connote, respectively, the yawning of an awakening bear and the gaping of a salmon drawn out of the water. There is nothing in either name that indicates the animals in question—which even belong to opposite moieties.

The old men who bestowed them no doubt announced the totemic reference of the names; the bearers, and their family, kin, and more intimate associates, knew the implication; but a Miwok from another district would have been uncertain whether a bear, a salmon, or one of a dozen other animals was meant. Just so, *Akulu* means "looking up"—at the sun. *Hopoto* is understood to refer to frog eggs hatching in the water; but its literal meaning is only "round." *Sewati* connotes bear claws, but denotes "curved" and nothing more. *Etumu* is "to bask." An individual so called happens to be named after the bear; but there is nothing to prevent the identical name referring to the lizard, if it were borne by some other man.

It is true that the Miwok seem to pay some attention to these implications of their names, since they are aware of the totemic reference of the names of practically all their acquaintance, as well as of kinsmen for some generations past. At the same time it is certain that whatever totemic significance the majority of the names have is not actually expressed but is extrinsically attached to them.

In fact, the totemic quality of the names is very probably a secondary and comparatively late reading in on the part of the Miwok, since names of exactly the same character, so far as structure and range of denotation go, are prevalent over the greater part of California without a trace of totemism attached to them. Even the adjacent totemic Yokuts, whose names, when intelligible, are similar to the Miwok ones, do not interpret them totemically.

It might be thought that the names are remnants of an older clan system; that what is now the land moiety was formerly an aggregation of bear, panther, dog, raven, and other clans; that for some reason the clans became merged in the two larger groups; that as their separate existence, as social units, became lost, it was preserved for some time longer in the names that originally belonged to the clans. But there is no evidence that such is the case. If a man and his sons and their sons all bore appellations referring to the bear— as among the Mohave all the women in a certain male line of descent are called *Hipa*, which connotes "coyote"—we might justifiedly speak of the Miwok condition as a disguised clan system. But the supposition does not hold. In the majority of cases the child is not named after the same animal as its father; and in a line of male descent extending over several generations the proportion of instances in which the same totemic reference is maintained throughout becomes very small.

By far the most commonly referred to animal in names of people in the land moiety is the bear. On the water side there is no such pronounced predominance, but the deer comes first. This fact is certainly of significance with reference to the bear and deer "totems" reported among the Salinan group across the Coast Range.

A number of animals or objects are referred to in names belonging to both moieties; such are the coyote, falcon, acorn, buckeye, seeds, and bow and arrow. This is an unexplained effacement of the otherwise sharp distinction between the moieties.

Moreover, some of the most important animals, such as the eagle, puma, and rattlesnake, are very rarely or not at all referred to in names, to judge by the available translations rendered by the natives, whereas objects of far less natural importance, such as nose shells, ear plugs, and ceremonial objects, are more common. A truer idea of the totemic classification of the world is therefore obtainable from general statements made by the Miwok. From these the following partial alignment results:

Land side.	Water side.	Land side.	Water side.
Bear.	Deer.	Katydid.	Bee.
Puma.	Antelope.		Caterpillar.
Wildcat.			Cocoon.
Dog.	Coyote.		Butterfly.
Fox.			Snail.
Raccoon.	Beaver.		Haliotis, and other
Tree squirrel.	Otter.		shells and bead
Badger.			money.
Jack rabbit.		Sugar pine.	Jimson weed.
Eagle.		Black oak.	White oak.
Condor.	Buzzard.	Pine nuts.	Vetch.
Raven.		Manzanita.	Oak gall.
Magpie.		Tobacco.	Wild "cabbage."
Hawk.	Falcon (probably).	Tule.	
Chicken hawk.		Salmonberry.	
Great owl.	Burrowing owl.	(And other	(And other
Blue jay.	Meadow lark.	plants.)	plants.)
Woodpecker.	Killdeer.		
Yellow-hammer.	Hummingbird.	Sky.	Cloud.
Goldfinch.	Kingbird.	Sun, sunshine, sunrise.	Rain.
Creeper.	Bluebird.		Fog.
	Dove.	Stars.	Water, lake.
	Quail.	Night.	Ice.
	Goose.	Fire.	Mud.
	Swan.	Earth.	Lightning.
	Crane.	Salt.	Rock.
	Jacksnipe.		Sand.
	Kingfisher, and no doubt other water birds.	Bow, arrows, quiver (probably).	Nose ornament of shell.
Lizard.	Frog.	Drum.	
	Salamander.	Ear plug.	Feather apron.
	Water snake.	Feather headdress.	Football.
	Turtle.		Gambling bones.
	Salmon, and various other fishes.		
Yellow jacket.	Ant.		

It is apparent that every water animal, and all phenomena associated with water, are on the appropriate side; but that the remainder of the world is divided quite arbitrarily, or perhaps according to some principle that is obscure to our minds.

The briefer list of totems which the Yokuts enumerate follows the same lines with but few exceptions: beaver and antelope, and hawks and owls, are transposed to the opposite moieties by these southerners.

The Miwok do not regard the totem animals as ancestors, except in an indirect and vague sort of way, to stress which would result in misconception of their attitude. According to their beliefs, as of those of all Indians, the bear, the coyote, and all the animals were once quasi human. The California belief is that they occupied the earth before there were true human beings. They are therefore predecessors of mankind. From that to ancestors is not a far leap; and it has perhaps been made now and then more or less randomly. But there is no definite theory or understanding to this effect. Least of all does a man with an eagle or deer name believe that he can trace his particular lineal descent back to the eagle or deer.

Nor is there any connection in the native mind between a man's totem and the animal guardian spirit that may reveal itself to him. A bear-named man may acquire the bear for his protector; but he is just as likely to be patronized by any other animal; and if he does secure a bear spirit, the fact seems a meaningless coincidence to him and his fellows. The interpretation of Miwok totemism as a development out of the widespread guardian spirit concept, in other words out of shamanism, would therefore be without warrant. Among other nations this interpretation may here and there have some support. In fact, the two sets of phenomena have enough in common to make it highly probable that the native mind would on occasion connect them secondarily and assimilate them further. And it is an obviously tenable idea that they may spring from a common root. But to derive an essentially social and classifying institution from a religious, inherently individual, and therefore variable one, is, as a proposition of generic applicability, one of those explanations with which ethnological science is choked, but which would be more in need of being explained, if they were true, than the phenomena which they purport to elucidate.

The rule of moiety exogamy is definitely formulated by the Miwok, but has not been very rigidly enforced for several generations. It is therefore doubtful whether the sentiment in favor of exogamy was ever more than a marked predilection. The natives say that marriage within the moiety evoked protest but no attempt at actual interference. At present one marriage out of four is endogamic in

place of exogamic among the central Miwok. A numerical disproportion, which gives the land moiety an average excess of nearly
20 per cent over its rival, may help to account for these lapses,
though marriages within the smaller water moiety also occur.

According to the limited statistical data available, the water
moiety actually predominates in some of the higher villages, while
nearer the plains it is much inferior in strength. As the Yokuts
equivalent of the water moiety is called "upstream" and its antithesis "downstream," it is possible that the greater strength of the
former in the Miwok highlands is more than an accident of distribution.

The moieties compete with each other in games, and they assist
each other at funerals, mourning anniversaries, adolescence observances, and the like. They do not appear to enter at all into the
Kuksu religion.

Thus they possess social and semiceremonial functions besides
those concerned with marriage and descent, but no strong ritualistic
ones.

Many Miwok terms of relationship are applied by any given
individual only to persons of one or the other moiety. But for
many terms such a limitation is inevitable the moment there is any
social grouping on hereditary lines accompanied by exogamy. The
father, mother, son, daughter, brother, sister, and other relatives
must each be exclusively of one's own moiety or of the opposite one.
When it comes to relatives like our "uncle," such a term, because
it comprises the mother's brother as well as the father's brother,
would in Miwok refer to persons of both moieties. As a matter
of fact, like almost all Indians, they possess no word that means
what our "uncle" does; but they have a considerable number of
kinship terms—more than a fourth of the total—that designate, potentially at least, individuals of both moieties; or, after deduction
of the above-mentioned terms denoting the closest relatives, nearly
one-half. The system of relationship accordingly reflects the social
grouping much less than might be anticipated—not nearly so well
as among most Australians, for instance. From this the inference
may be drawn that the moiety organization is either comparatively
recent among the Miwok or that it has failed to impress their other
institutions and their life as a whole very deeply.

MARRIAGE OF RELATIVES.

There is another point which the terms of relationship clear up.
The preferential marriage among the Miwok, the one considered
most natural and correct, was with certain relatives of the opposite
moiety. Now, it was long ago reported that the Miwok married

their cousins, which is a practice horribly repugnant to the vast majority of American Indians. Investigation has confirmed and restricted the statement. The Miwok man did often marry his first cousin; but only his mother's brother's daughter; that is, one of the two kinds of cross cousins, as they are called. Even these marriages were considered too close in some districts and were frowned upon; a first cousin once removed, or second cousin, or some such distant relative was the proper mate.

It proves that all the female blood relatives that a man might marry come under the designation *anisü*, and all the kin that a woman could mate with are included in what she calls her *angsi*. Now *angsi* is also the word for "son" or "nephew" and *anisü* for mother's younger sister or stepmother. It is inconceivable, from what we know of the Indian temper, that the Miwok ever married their aunts; and they indignantly deny such an imputation: it is only the cousin or second cousin called *anisü*, and not the aunt *anisü*, that one espouses.

Further, it is remarkable that not one of the 30 or more words by which the Miwok designate their various blood kindred or relatives by marriage is of such denotation that it in any way reflects or implies cross-cousin marriage as customary.

If to these circumstances is added the fact that a man may never espouse one of his two kinds of cross cousins—his father's sister's daughters—it is clear that the Miwok cross-cousin marriage is an isolated and anomalous institution; and the presumption is forced that it is neither basic nor original in their society.

The foundation of the practice can in fact be traced. It is the almost universal California Indian custom of marrying people who are already connected with one by marriage. To most civilized people such a custom seems quite shocking. But that is only because we introduce a false sentiment, or sentimentality, based in part on confusion of thought, in part on an oversensitiveness, and in part on a fanatical avoidance of everything that even seems to savor of polygamy, whether or not it is connected with that practice. All nations abhor the marriage of near blood kin, but the vast majority distinguish clearly between kindred in fact, such as a sister, and kindred in name, such as a sister-in-law; which of course is the only logical procedure if blood is to mean anything at all. We do not make this distinction with nearly the same force and clearness of perception that most other peoples do. English is one of the few languages in the world that has no independent words for affinities by marriage; "brother-in-law" is based on "brother"; and we show the weakness of vocabulary, and therefore of our thinking in these matters, by not possessing even a single, convenient, generic term for the clumsy "affinities" or "relatives by marriage." Other European nations approach the Anglo-Saxon condition. In short, for better or for worse, we have lost the keenness of a sense that not only primitive people but the civilized ancients possessed. The idea of blood means but little to us. We are given to imagining that we have developed home and family ties far stronger and deeper than any other people; and we do not know half so well as a savage or a Mohammedan what "family" means.

We think of association, when we believe we think of consanguinity. The very word " kin," except as employed in ethnological literature, is nearly dead : it survives only in poetry and in the occasional mouths of the illiterate. There are people to whom the mere mention of marriage with a former brother's wife or dead wife's sister is abhorrent because the word " sister-in-law " reminds them of " sister."

From this particular overrefinement the overwhelming mass of nations are exempt. They often have their own equivalent scruples, such as balking at marrying a " clan-sister." But in the present point they think consistently, and it is we who are exceptionally irrational. Not only in aboriginal America but all over the world people espouse what we miscall " relatives by marriage." Thus, all through California a man is entitled to marry his brother's widow ; and among most tribes it is expected of him. So, too, if his wife dies he weds her sister or some other kin of hers. If he marries the sister while the wife is still living the objection can be only on the ground of the rule of monogamy being violated. If, finally, he adds to his mates his wife's daughter by some other man, he is still adhering rigidly to his premises. We are revolted by a false impression of incestuousness as well as by the polygamy, when actually we might base a valid objection only on the ground of sexual delicacy. This particular delicacy the Indian of many tribes lacks ; but he replaces it by another, in the total lack of which we are utter barbarians and brutes : he will not look his wife's mother in the eye or give himself any opportunity to do so. He will marry his stepdaughter ; but he will refuse ever to address a word to his mother-in-law.

That, then, is the condition of marriage that underlies the practices of the Miwok as of the other Californian tribes. There is only one point at which their possession of the dual organization specializes it. If a Miwok can marry a woman, he can marry her sister, because she is of the same eligible moiety ; and for the same reason he can marry the woman that his brother was wed to. Both these practices are indeed followed. He can not, however, properly marry his wife's daughter, as a Costanoan or Yurok is free to do, because the daughter is of the moiety of her father, which is also that of her stepfather. If no sister is available some other relative of the wife must therefore be substituted for her daughter as successor or cowife the moment the moiety system is operative. The nearest of these kin, of the same moiety as herself, is her brother's daughter ; if the husband is Land, his wife is Water, her brother must be Water, and his daughter Water also, and therefore eligible. Now, the Miwok actually marry their wives' brothers' daughters, and they proclaim such marriages as fitting and frequent.

One more step and we have cross-cousin marriage. Once this type of marriage is fairly frequent the husband is likely to be conceded some right to his wife's niece, just as most nonmoiety tribes in California admit that he possesses at least some preferential priority to his wife's sister. Such a claim once established, no matter how irregularly exercised, would descend to the man's son, who is of the man's own moiety. The father would only have to die before his wife's niece was old enough to be wed ; or he might reach an age in which he would voluntarily transfer his claim to his son, particularly if he had bound it by a payment. But the son in marrying his father's wife's brother's daughter would be marrying his mother's brother's daughter ; that is, exactly the type of cross cousin whom among the Miwok he can and does marry.

It seems rather likely that this is exactly the manner in which the curiously one-sided cousin marriage of the Miwok has come about : it is merely a secondary outgrowth of the more basic marriage to the wife's niece, and this in turn a specialized form of the general practice of wedding a close relative of the wife. This deduction is confirmed by the fact that while there are no terms of relationship that reflect cross-cousin marriage as such, there are a dozen that suggest and agree with marriage to the wife's niece.

Here, too, we have an explanation of the extraordinary fact that the cousins who marry call each other "stepmother" and "son." If the father marries the girl, she becomes a second mother or stepmother to her cousin and he a sort of son to her. She therefore is his potential stepmother until the father vacates his right; when she becomes, or can become, the son's wife instead of his stepmother.

This so exceptional marriage of a relative—quite abnormal from the generic American point of view—thus seems to rest upon the almost universal basis of marriage to an affinity by marriage, modified in detail but not in principle by the exogamic moiety scheme of the Miwok, and given its culmination by the simple transfer of a privilege from father to son. The real specialization of the Miwok lies in this last transfer. Natural as it may seem, it may have caused them a hard wrench; for after all, in spite of its plausibility, it transcended the fundamental principle that kin do not cohabit. What is legitimate for the father is not necessarily legitimate for the son, for after all one is not and the other is related by ties of blood to the woman in question. The problem presented by Miwok cousin marriage is therefore reduced rather than solved: we still do not know what caused the son's right to prevail over the aversion to kin wedlock. If the Miwok were a people with a marked interest in property, as shown by numerous and refined regulations concerning ownership such as the Yurok have worked out, the case would be simple: but their institutions are not of this cast. It is even doubtful whether purchase entered very seriously into their marriages. Nothing to this effect has ever been reported of them; and their neighbors on all sides did indeed give something for their wives, but quite clearly never thought of turning marriage into a wholehearted commercial transaction like the northwestern tribes. Another explanation must therefore be sought: and the only circumstance that appears is the moiety system itself. This, with its accentuation of one-sided in place of undifferentiated descent, may well have accentuated the idea of descent itself, and therefore of inheritance, and thus brought about the necessary reenforcement of the son's claim. A dual organization lends itself particularly to such a development.

Under a multiple clan system a man's nearer kin are overwhelmingly of only two social groups out of several or many, so that normally he would have few or no blood relatives, and those more or less remote, in whatever of the other groups he married into. With a dual organization, however, he must necessarily average as many actual kinsmen in the group into which he is bound to marry as in his own. Under clan organization, therefore, a distinction between kin groups and marriage groups tends to be kept alive; in any moiety scheme it is liable to effacement, at least in mental attitude. As long as a man must marry into a group in which he has many immediate relatives, the feeling that he may marry a relative can not be very remote; and now and then it is likely to crop out and be accepted. Such seems to be the case in Australia, where the dual scheme is very deeply impressed on society and where kin marriage is almost normal. In fact the Australian feeling seems to be as much that one should marry persons standing in a certain relationship to oneself as that one should not marry certain others; just as the Australian classes are now properly recognized as not being really exogamic; one is compelled to marry *into* a particular group, whereas under the clan system one is compelled to marry *out* of it. That the Miwok are dualistically organized, therefore, makes it the more likely that it is this very social scheme of theirs that gave the impetus to the final step that resulted in cross-cousin marriage.

If this argument is valid it reacts to strengthen the probability, already mentioned, that the Miwok moiety scheme is original and not a reduced survival of a former clan system.

No communication is held between a Miwok man and his brothers on the one hand and his mother-in-law and her sisters on the other; nor between a woman and her sisters, and her father-in-law and his brothers. A man also does not address his mother's brother's wife—his potential mother-in-law in that she is the mother of his eligible cross cousin.

It is said that when speech is urgent between such shame-faced relatives, and no go-between or third party to be addressed is present, they will communicate with each other in the plural number—" as though more than one person were there." The feeling, perhaps, is that the individuality of the addressed is obscured by the plurality. The same custom is followed by the Pomo and Kato.

CHAPTER 31.

THE COSTANOANS.

TERRITORY.

The designation Costanoan is from Spanish Costaños, "coast people." Its awkwardness is in some measure atoned for by its consistency of usage in literature. The name would be difficult to replace by one coined from native sources, since the words denoting "men" or "people" vary from dialect to dialect within the group. But the appellation Costanoan is in one respect felicitous: The other main divisions of the Penutian family held the great interior valley of California as their habitat, while with the exception of a small branch of the Miwok, the Costanoan tribes occupied the whole of the shore districts to which the Penutians laid claim.

The San Joaquin River belonged to the Yokuts, the Sacramento to the Maidu and Wintun. At the point where these two streams debouch into San Francisco Bay Costanoan territory begins. The winding north shores of the bay were Wintun and Coast Miwok; but the entire southern border, including the long arm known as San Francisco Bay proper, was Costanoan to the Golden Gate. From here south their range followed the coast to beyond Monterey: to Point Sur, to be exact.

The Costanoan limits inland are not precisely known. They have sometimes been asserted, or loosely assumed, to have been formed by the San Joaquin River, but it is far more probable that the boundary was constituted by the interior chain of the coast ranges, the Mount Diablo Range of the maps.

The included territory falls into two natural divisions. The northern half drains into San Francisco Bay, or by short streams into the adjacent ocean. The southern half includes the catchment area of the Pajaro River and the lower courses of the Salinas and Carmel, all of which flow into Monterey Bay or the ocean just below. The main line of dialectic cleavage within the Costanoan group appears to coincide with the irregular line separating these northern and southern areas.

DIVISIONS.

Seven Franciscan missions were founded in Costanoan territory, and it was not many years before all members of the stock had been brought into association with these establishments. Here Indians not only of distinct villages, but of separate dialects, were brought together, and found themselves mingled with utterly alien converts from the north, the south, and the interior. As along the entire coast of the State, there was no political cohesion worth mentioning between the little towns. Native appellations of wider applicability were therefore lacking; and the result was that the dialects that can be distinguished are known chiefly by the names of the missions at which each was the principal or original one. Where native terms have obtained a vogue in literature, they appear to be only village designations used in an extended sense. Of this kind are Mutsun, for the dialect of San Juan Bautista; Rumsen or Runsien for that of Monterey; and Tamien for Santa Clara.

The records that have been preserved show one principal dialect for each mission. Only at the establishments of Santa Clara and San Jose the speech differed so slightly that the two idioms must be united in a single dialect group. On the other hand, in the extreme north, toward San Pablo and Suisun Bays, there appears to have prevailed a distinctive tongue—which may be named the Saklan after one of the principal villages—that failed to have a mission established within its limits. This makes the number of dialect groups seven, the same as the number of missions.

It is almost certain that minor divergences of idiom occurred in some of these areas. This is specifically mentioned at Monterey and at San Juan Bautista. Nothing is known, however, beyond this bare fact. Our information upon Costanoan speech is restricted to some records, often pitiful at that, of the idiom prevailing at such and such points that happened to be selected by the missionaries for their foundations. We can only start from these points as centers, and conjecture the limits of each dialect group by following the watersheds on the map.

The transition from the northern dialects to the southern seems to have been by way of the speech of Santa Cruz approaching that of San Juan Bautista. The extreme southern and northern idioms, those of Soledad and of Saklan, are the least known, and appear to have been the most specialized. The latter may be suspected of having shown particular affinities to Wintun, Miwok, or Yokuts.

POPULATION.

The Costanoan group is extinct so far as all practical purposes are concerned. A few scattered individuals survive, whose parents were attached to the missions of San Jose, San Juan Bautista, and San Carlos; but they are of mixed tribal ancestry and live almost lost among other Indians or obscure Mexicans. At best some knowledge of the ancestral speech remains among them. The old habits of life have long since been abandoned. The larger part of a century has passed since the missions were abolished, and nearly a century and a half since they commenced to be founded. These periods have sufficed to efface even traditional recollections of the forefathers' habits, except for occasional fragments of knowledge.

The aboriginal population is also difficult to judge. Perhaps an average of 1,000 heads per dialect group, or 7,000 for the stock as a whole, is not far from the mark. The numerous mission statistics are of little service in this connection. The priests were saving souls and not writing history, and no doubt had trouble enough to establish the exact numbers of their flocks without going accurately into ethnic distinctions. Indians from the lower San Joaquin Valley were brought to most of the Costanoan missions. San Carlos received the bulk of the Esselen as well as the local Costanoans. Mission Dolores, at San Francisco, must have contained an extraordinary jumble. Besides natives from the east side of the bay, as well as the peninsula, there were Coast Miwok from the north; perhaps southern Pomo and Wappo; and to these were added from time to time groups of Wintun, Maidu, Miwok, and Yokuts. Here and there a "tribal" or village name, of the many that occur in the mission records, can be identified as belonging to one or the other of these stocks, but the others remain mere names. As the local or nearer Indians died out under the shock of contact with civilization, those from a greater distance were brought in in increasing numbers. The proportional strength of the various stocks at any one establishment was therefore constantly changing and their respective absolute numbers at any given period remain quite conjectural.

SETTLEMENTS.

A long series of village names has been preserved through the notations of the missionaries. Something like 100 such are known to have furnished converts to San Francisco alone. Most of these names are Costanoan in sound. Distinctive elements of the language can frequently be recognized in them, but in most instances there is no record of the location of these villages, or of their interrelations

as permanent towns and suburbs or summer camps. Such villages
as can in any way be identified have been entered in Figure 42;
though a considerable proportion of these can be but vaguely located.

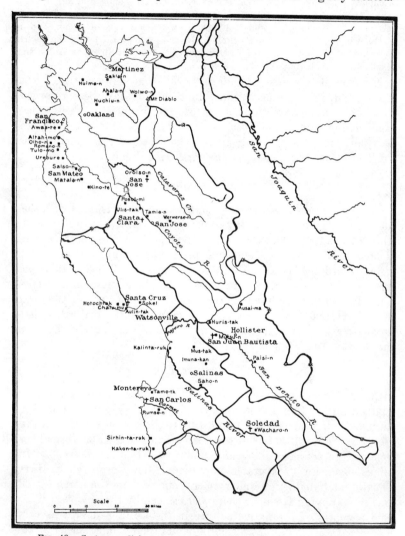

Fig. 42.—Costanoan dialect areas and approximate sites of some settlements.

The ending -n that occurs in so many Costanoan village names perhaps means
"people of." So does -mak, -kam, or -kma, which is the plural suffix for
persons. On the other hand, -tak, -tka, -ta, -te, -to, is the locative case: "place
of." The meaning of -mo, -me is similar. Ruk, "house," is used as an ending
in the plural sense of "town." Kalin-ta-ruk, is "ocean-at-houses," Kakon-ta-
ruk, "chickenhawk-place-houses."

The termination -*n* occurs in numerous names of places or tribes that were outside Costanoan territory but probably first known to the Spaniards through Costanoan guides or interpreters. Such are Essele-n, also Esle-n and Ense-n; compare Esla-n-aga-n, and, in the same territory, Ekhe-aga-n. Wintun divisions are: Suisu-n, Karki-n, Tole-n, Pulpe-n. Coast Miwok—Bauli-n. Yokuts—Choloo-n or Cholovo-n. Plains Miwok or perhaps Maidu—Hulpu-n, Olpe-n. Unknown, perhaps Costanoan—Umpi-n, Lama-n, Piteme-n. Often the -*n* has been added to a term from a foreign language thus: Hulpu-n or Hulpu-mni, Choloo-n or Chula-mni.

Of the little wars—or village feuds—that agitated the Costanoan groups from time to time, the following have been recorded: The Salso-n against the natives of San Francisco; the Sakla-n against the same, or against the Oakland tribe transplanted to the mission; the Ausai-ma against the Mutsu-n; the Wacharo-n or others of the Soledad region against the northern Salinans.

SHELL MOUNDS.

The entire Costanoan frontage on ocean and bay is lined with shell deposits. San Francisco Bay in particular is richer in such remains than any other part of the State, except perhaps the Santa Barbara Islands. Many of these, and probably the upper layers of nearly all, must accordingly be ascribed to the Costanoans. Whether their possession of the district goes back as far as the earliest period represented by the lower levels of the largest shell mounds, a time estimated at 3,000 or more years ago, is entirely problematical. There is nothing to show that the Costanoan tribes were or were not then in their more recent seats.

CULTURAL STATUS.

A number of early voyagers visited the Costanoan missions, especially those at San Francisco and Monterey. Their accounts contain much of value, but are tantalizing to the ethnologist in that they describe the modified life at the missions rather than aboriginal customs. The universal testimony, however, is that the Costanoan Indians made an unfavorable impression. They were dark, dirty, squalid, and apathetic; and travelers coming from the north as well as those arriving from the south were struck by the obvious paucity and rudeness of the native culture in the Costanoan area as compared with other regions. Choris paints their temperament in two phrases: " I have never seen one laugh. I have never seen one look one in the face." The mission atmosphere at San Francisco may have accentuated these traits; but they are typical for much of central California.

CLOTHING.

The men were accustomed to go naked when the weather permitted. The women wore the usual two short skirts, one before and one behind, made either of deerskin, tule, or bark fiber. The rabbit-skin blanket served both as mantle and as bedding. A common custom of the men was to coat themselves thickly with mud in the morning until the sun shone warm. Whether the women wore basketry hats is very uncertain. Face tattooing was customary for women. It ran to lines or rows of dots as among all the central Californians. (Fig. 45, *b*, *c*.)

FOOD.

Mussels, whose shells constitute so large a proportion of the mounds of San Francisco Bay and the coast, are specifically mentioned as an important food of the Costanoans. Sea lions were hunted, though the precise manner is not known. The tule raft must have been an unsatisfactory conveyance, and in most weathers a dangerous one, for reaching the surf-surrounded rocks on which the animals sun themselves. When a whale came ashore food was plentiful, but as there was no way of hunting these monsters the supply which they furnished must have been most irregular and undependable. Salmon begin to be numerous in the streams that enter the ocean in Costanoan territory, or at least were so in former times, though never reaching the numbers which they attained in more northern rivers. South of the Costanoans the salmon ceases as an important food. The taking of this fish, with which that of lampreys was associated, must, however, have been restricted to the winter months of high water. Seaweed replaced salt.

The plant foods were the usual ones. On the immediate coast, where acorns were few or lacking, seeds seemed to have replaced them. Acorn meal was leached both in the southern way through an openwork basket and in the northern style by means of a hollow in the sand in which the flour was spread. The usual California practice was followed of burning the country over in order to clear out the underbrush for facilitating acorn gathering and to foster the growth of seed-bearing annuals. A rabbit stick is mentioned as used in rabbit drives. This suggests a southern Californian influence; but the sticks are specified as straight. Every hunter held one in each hand.

BASKETRY.

Costanoan basketry has perished. One or two older specimens that have been preserved are of little historic value, because shaped according to European ideas. Other pieces, not quite so old, that are attributed to Indians at Costanoan missions, are Yokuts or Miwok in style, and were probably made by members of these stocks that had been taken to the religious establishments. A very few other specimens remain, but the ethnic provenience of even these is clouded. It is not even known whether Costanoan basketry stood in specific affinities with that of the Pomo, or showed any of the distinct traits of Yokuts work; nor in fact how far it was similar to the simpler ware of the Miwok. Baskets ornamented with feathers, shell pendants, and beads are mentioned; but unfortunately we can not be sure that these were truly of Costanoan origin, nor, if so, how prevalent a type they were.

The carrying net for loads and baskets was used by the Costanoans. It may be suspected that this was of the southern or Shoshonean rather than the northern or Pomo type.

HOUSES AND BOATS.

The house in which the Indians lived at the missions appears to have been mainly a native construction on a more or less European plan. The aboriginal house was primarily a structure of poles covered with brush or tule matting. There is no reference to the earth-covered lodges of the interior valley, but it can hardly be imagined that they were entirely unknown. There is some evidence of the existence of a high conical house of thatch. Slender poles and withes held the thatch together from the outside against the interior framework. A few individuals who survived until recently near Monterey recollect a house of redwood planks. Slabs of bark of this tree are much more likely to have been the aboriginal form, since there is no authentic report of any true wooden house south of northernmost California. The sweat house was an institution in daily use, but no details of its size or construction have been preserved.

The tule raft was the only boat known to the Costanoans; and on this they crossed San Francisco Bay, which is normally a sheet of far from calm surface and of strong currents. The balsa was propelled by double-bladed paddles, such as recur in the Santa Barbara Island region, but there in connection with well-made canoes of planks.

SOCIAL INSTITUTIONS.

Chieftainship is stated to have passed by descent, which may be taken as meaning a succession from father to son. The influence of the chief is said to have been limited, but several accounts mention that he took a leading part in war. This, if true, would be rather exceptional for California. Prisoners were not taken, or, if so, dispatched as soon as possible. The slain foe was mutilated or dismembered. His scalp was carried about in triumph. It seems that the "scalp" was of the usual Californian kind: the head, or its entire skin. Some parts of the enemy were eaten, it is said, by the parents of the slayer. Songs of insult or vengeance were common, both as an aftermath and as a new cause of fighting. Here again there are southern Californian reminiscences; as well as Miwok ones.

Marriage was loose and divorce ready. Shell money was tendered for the bride, but the transaction must have been commercially informal or separations could not have taken place as readily as is stated. The fact that the mother retained the children is evidence in the same direction. Among the south Costanoans it is said monogamy was the rule except for chieftains; much as among the Salinans, Chumash, and Juaneño. In the north different practices prevailed, a man espousing his wife's sisters, daughters, or other relatives. A bit of etiquette reported also from the Wintun was for a bride to resist the approach of her husband with her nails. He was expected to appear with his face scratched: if he did not, the young woman seems to have been thought immodest.

Customs of birth and adolescence are undescribed, except that a woman after childbirth lay for a number of days with her child on fresh foliage that covered a pit lined with baked stones. In this custom again there is a suggestion of southern California, although in that region the practice applied primarily to adolescent girls.

Tobacco was smoked. The eating of it with lime is not mentioned.

DEATH.

Accounts of the native method of disposing of the dead are somewhat in conflict, but cremation appears to have been the rule. From San Francisco it is reported that poor people, or those with few or lazy relatives, were buried, but that if the kin or friends would gather wood, the corpse was burned. This is likely to have been the custom throughout the Costanoan area. The funeral took place soon after death. There is no mention in any of the sources of anniversary mourning ceremonies. This omission proves little, but, on the other hand, it is not inconceivable that the Costanoans followed the customs of the Pomo and other tribes of the coast north of San Francisco Bay, among none of whom such rites prevailed. The property of the dead was thoroughly destroyed, the reason alleged being that the deceased would then be no longer remembered. All that we know of other Californian Indians indicates this as a genuine motive; but the coexistence of other reasons is not necessarily excluded.

The universal custom of avoidance of the name of the dead was rigorously adhered to. Even a reference to the deceased was the pro-

foundest affront to his kin. At the height of a quarrel such phrases as
"Your father is dead" were likely to be bandied about.

The dead were believed to go to an island across the ocean, as by
the Yokuts and Miwok. That they were now and then thought to
return from this abode is probable, but that there was a belief in
literal reincarnation is a statement which must be accepted with
caution.

GAMES.

The guessing game was played for 24 counters at Monterey. In
place of one marked and one unmarked bone, each player held a single
bit of bone or shell in one hand and left the other empty. The
manipulating was done under a mat. Two men sat on a side. Their
opponents did not take up the implements until the bones of both
their opponents had been guessed.

Shinny was the simple southern type of game, played by a dozen
or so men on a side, with a wooden báll struck out of a hole in the
middle of the field. Women played the same or a similar game.

The football race of southern California and the Southwest was
also known. A contest is spoken of in which a pair of contestants
ran from San Luis Obispo to San Juan Bautista, a distance of
over 100 miles, in two days, without touching the wooden ball other
than with the feet. In aboriginal times races of this distance could
not have taken place; and in general it is likely that this game was
of less importance until fostered by the settled condition and constant intercourse of the mission period.

RITUAL.

The proximity of the northern Costanoan area to Wintun territory
renders it highly probable that many elements of the Sacramento
Valley ceremonial system, if not the main part of the scheme itself,
must have penetrated some distance south of San Francisco Bay.
In this event it is likely that the specific feather costumes, dances,
and songs were accompanied in their gradual migration by the foot
drum and the earth-covered dance house. There is, however, no
direct evidence of the existence of this cult among the Costanoan
Indians. A few survivors in north Costanoan territory know of
the *Kuksui* dance with the *Lole* and *Hiweyi* as accompaniments; but
as these individuals live with descendants of missionized Plains
Miwok and northern Yokuts, who of late years greatly outnumber
them, it is not altogether certain that the dances are native to the
locality. The *Kuksui* or *Kuksuyu* dancer is said to have had his
face uncovered, and to have carried his whistle projecting horizontally from his mouth. If it were thoroughly certain that the occurrence of this dance personage among the Salinan Indians to the south

of the Costanoans was not due to involuntary importation by the missionaries incident to their transfer of interior tribes to the coast, the existence of the ceremony in this remoter region would render its ancient prevalence throughout Costanoan territory almost certain.

There is no mention of the use of Jimson weed at the Costanoan missions, and it is likely that the cult had not penetrated the area. In fact, the plant seems to grow in only a few spots in Costanoan territory.

Several of the older authors make specific mention of prayers and offerings to the sun, from which may be inferred the existence of a more definite form of sun worship than is usual in California, though all details are lacking. At Mission San Jose a dance was made at the winter solstice. Whether this is to be associated with the supposed sun cult or was part of the Kuksu system, whose dances are winter rites, must be left to conjecture.

Offerings of meal, presumably both of acorns and of seeds, are repeatedly referred to and must have formed a characteristic part of Costanoan ritual. This is a practice that seems most pronounced among the northern Shoshoneans of southern California, and probably reached the Costanoans by way of the Chumash and Salinans. The Yokuts most frequently offer eagle down or tobacco. The latter was employed by the Costanoan peoples, but apparently less extensively.

Besides meal, arrows and little feathered rods were used as offerings. The latter provide an interesting suggestion of the faraway southwestern prayer sticks or prayer plumes; nearer parallels are among the Maidu and Chumash.

Sacred objects, besides the sun, were large redwood trees; and Pajaro River is said to derive its name from a stuffed bird which the natives were found worshipping.

There is some evidence, especially in the fragmentary myths that have been preserved, that the Costanoan ceremonial number was five. The position of the stock among groups that thought in fours or sixes renders it regrettable that this indication of distinctiveness can not be positively substantiated.

Costanoan songs are unusually pleasing to civilized people; but this may be because more than a century of association with Spaniards has conformed their intervals and perhaps their rhythm to the wont of our ears.

A dance song runs:

> Dancing on the brink of the world.

Another, first sung by the wood rat:

> I dream of you,
> I dream of you jumping,
> Rabbit, jack rabbit, and quail.

A blind man's charm, which, played on the flute, drew on a girl who became his wife:

> There goes meat.

Another charm, to bring a man home, was first sung for Fog, who was thus notified that his wife was being maltreated:

> Now he beats your wife,
> Pelican is beating her.

When the hunter wishes to charm the deer into not scenting his approach, he sings:

> Its nose is stopped with (fragrant) *estafiarte*.

A love song, composed in or since mission times, but on aboriginal lines, runs:

> Come! Come!
> I mean you
> With the brown hat.

The character of the words recalls the type of those customary in Yokuts songs.

SHAMANISM.

Costanoan shamanism has passed away with scarcely a trace. We know that the doctor sang, danced, and sucked material objects out of the body of the sick, and that sometimes he was believed to exercise control of the weather and of the natural crops. His relation to his spirits, the precise manner in which disease was caused, the actions attending his entrance into the profession, the probable belief in bear shamans, are all matters on which the evidence is lost.

MYTHOLOGY.

Costanoan myths carry numerous suggestions of Yokuts cosmogony. They commence with the world covered by water, above which rises a single mountain top. In the vicinity of Monterey this is designated as Pico Blanco; farther north, Mount Diablo. The latter mountain, by the way, was so named by the Spaniards with reference to the Indian belief in its habitation by spirits, much like the Marysville Buttes of the Maidu and Doctor Rock peak of the Yurok and Tolowa.

On this lonely spot are the coyote, the eagle, and the humming bird, the eagle being chief of the three; or, according to other accounts, the coyote stands alone until he is joined by the eagle, who arises from a feather floating on the water—like the Yuki Creator. After the ocean recedes the land is explored and human beings made by the coyote at the direction of the eagle. The coyote in particular marries the first woman. He and the humming bird come into conflict, but his smaller antagonist eludes and surpasses the coyote.

The latter is tricky, gluttonous, and desirous of women. At times he loses his wife or otherwise comes to grief. Occasionally he is successful. In still other narratives he appears as the bringer of culture. He institutes tribes and languages, shows people how to secure food, and gives them houses and utensils.

It is impossible to say from what little survives of these traditions whether the Costanoan tribes carried out to any considerable degree the animal characterization that pervades the myths of the Yokuts, just as it is conceivable that the associated San Joaquin Valley system of totemic moieties may have extended to the Costanoans, though we do not know such to have been the case. On the other hand, it is clear that they did not share to any marked degree in the typical Sacramento Valley mythology with its long systematized myths of the origin of the world, its attempts at philosophy, and its formulation of a wise and majestic creator.

THE YOKUTS: GEOGRAPHY.

TRIBAL ORGANIZATION.

The Yokuts are unique among the California natives in one respect. They are divided into true tribes. Each has a name, a dialect, and a territory. The first of these traits, the group name, is wanting in other Californians, who normally are able to designate themselves only by the appellation of the place they inhabit. The second feature, dialectic separateness, of course is an old story for California, but elsewhere in the State each idiom is usually common to a considerable number of tribelets or "village communities." Only in the third trait, their political independence and their ownership of a tract of land, are the ordinary Californian village communities and the Yokuts tribes similar.

Forty of these tribes are sufficiently known to be locatable. In the northern part of the Yokuts areas the map is, however, blank except for a few names of groups of uncertain situation and doubtful affinities. The total number of tribes may therefore have reached 50. Such an array of dialects is unparalleled, and gives to the Yokuts alone nearly one-third of all the different forms of speech talked in the State. The differences of language from tribe to tribe were often rather limited; but they are marked enough to be readily perceptible to the interested Caucasian observer. Since the total length of the Yokuts area does not much exceed 250 miles and the breadth nowhere attains to 100, the individual geographical range of these little languages was exceedingly narrow. Their territory averaged perhaps 300 square miles—say a half day's foot journey in each direction from the center.

Some of the tribes occupied a single spot with sufficient permanence to become identified with it: thus the Wowol on Atwells Island in Tulare Lake, the Gawia and Yokod on opposite sides of Kaweah River where this leaves the hills, the Choinimni at the junction of

Mill Creek and Kings River. Such groups, save for their distinc
tive speech, would be indistinguishable from the village communities of their neighbors if the purely local designations of the latter
were replaced by appellations for the people themselves. Still
fainter is the line of demarcation when the Choinimni, for instance,
are called, as occasionally happens, Tishechuchi after their town
Tishechu; but such terms are rare among the Yokuts.

For other tribes a principal and several subsidiary abodes are
specified; thus the Paleuyami are identified with Altau and sometimes called Altinin, but lived also at Bekiu, Shikidapau, Holmiu,
and other places. The Hometwoli lived at three principal sites, and
the Chukchansi, Tachi, Yauelmani, and others dwelt from time to
time, and perhaps simultaneously, at a number of places scattered
over a considerable tract. These instances confirm the Yokuts divisions as true tribes.

Fully half the Yokuts tribal names end either in -amni, found
also as -imni, -mina, -mani; or in -chi. The former suffix recurs added
to place names among the Plains Miwok to designate the inhabitants
of such and such spots, and among the Maidu as an ending of village
names; the latter among the southern Miwok with the significance
"people of." But the subtraction of either of these endings from the
names of Yokuts tribes usually leaves only meaningless syllables;
and in general the people themselves are well content to employ their
little national designations without inquiring what they may denote.
The few etymologies which they have ventured in response to inquiries are obviously naive and unhistorical.

HABITAT.

The home of the Yokuts was the San Joaquin Valley, the entire
floor of which they held, from the mouth of the river to the foot of
Tehachapi Pass. In addition, they occupied the adjacent lower
slopes or foothills of the Sierra Nevada, up to an altitude of a few
thousand feet, from Fresno River south, but nowhere to the north
of that stream. The San Joaquin River proper flows down only the
lower half of the length of the valley. Above it, Kings and then
Kern River also break westward from the high mountains and
the latter turns north into the treeless plains. Kern River drained
into Tulare Lake, formerly a large, shallow basin of water surrounded
by an even more extensive tract of swamp of tules, as two or three
species of rush are locally known. The swamps are now reclaimed
and much of the lake is normally dry and its area under cultivation.
For most of the year, formerly, the evaporation over this immense
sheet sufficed to equal the intake from Kern River and other streams;
in time of flood the lake might drain north through Fish Slough
into Kings River. This latter stream itself, though of considerable

volume, was nearly lost in a lengthy area of swamp, whence its waters seem normally to have flowed backward into Tulare Lake. It seems that Kings River and Tulare Lake drained into the San Joaquin at no remote time, since the lake is fresh. The San Joaquin, from the point where it reached the central axis of the valley and perhaps once took in the excess discharge of Kings and Kern Rivers, was also bordered pretty continuously by tule swamps, though of less width than to the south. Hence the Spanish name " Los Tulares " for the low-lying portion of the valley and " Rio de los Tulares " for the stream, though by the latter term they understood the main line of the entire drainage system rather than its lower, more northerly portion alone, to which we, with greater precision but more arbitrary logic, restrict the name San Joaquin. Hence also the appellation Tulareños, under which they consistently and appropriately knew the Yokuts. (Pl. 47.)

The eastern side of the level valley is traversed by streams from the Sierra Nevada. A dozen or so of these merit the name " river." The west side of the valley, however, on the lee of the rather low and barren Mount Diablo Coast Range, is arid; and not even one permanent stream of any size whatsoever reaches the central river system from this left hand. The overwhelming bulk of the American population is on the east side. The dispersion of the Yokuts was, if anything, even more unilateral. In the whole upper valley, in which the distribution of the Yokuts groups is pretty accurately known, there were only two tribes, the Tulamni and Tachi, in the large tract west of Tulare Lake and Kings River; and even of these two the Tachi preferred to cross to the east side when summer and autumn dried the overflowed lands and rendered their winter habitat a virtual desert.

Along the west of the San Joaquin we have less certain knowledge. This territory seems to have belonged to the Yokuts, though in default of precise information it has sometimes been attributed to the Costanoan people or to the Miwok. This very doubt indicates an unimportant occupation; and while the area was almost certainly visited by the Yokuts, and probably claimed by one or more of their northerly tribes, the number of residents must also have been very few.

The flow of Sierra rivers of approximately equal length is ever less toward the south, so that Yokuts streams are smaller than those in Miwok territory and much smaller than those occupied by the Maidu. The run-off in millions of acre-feet is approximately as follows. Yokuts: Kern, $\frac{3}{4}$; Kaweah, $\frac{1}{2}$; Kings, 2; San Joaquin, 2. Miwok: Merced, $1\frac{1}{4}$; Tuolumne, 2; Stanislaus, $1\frac{1}{2}$; Mokelumne, 1. Maidu: American, $3\frac{2}{3}$; Yuba, $3\frac{1}{4}$; Feather, at Oroville, 6; the Sacramento at Red Bluff, above the Feather, $10\frac{1}{2}$, most of it from the Pit. Even a short affluent of the Pit, Fall River, the habitat of one Achomawi division, carries about a million acre-feet, or more than the lengthy Kern or Kaweah.

CLASSIFICATION.

The classification of the Yokuts tribes must be made, like that of other Indians, and those of California in particular, on the basis of language. In spite of the number of the tribes, this it not difficult; for the dialects fall clearly into two great divisions, which coincide with the two topographic regions held by the stock: the valley proper and the foothills of the southern Sierra Nevada. Only in the extreme south were there three tribes speaking idioms of the foothill type but dwelling in the plains between Tulare Lake and the Tehachapi region. These three dialects, closely similar to one another, are easily the most divergent of all Yokuts forms of speech, and thus argue an unusual and peculiar history for the little remote group of people whose idiom was derived from that of the mountains while their habitat was in the valley.

The valley dialects are the most uniform, in fact remarkably similar to one another. A Yokuts from Stockton must have been able to understand considerable of the talk of one from Bakersfield—a condition utterly unparalleled for any like distance elsewhere in California; for although the Northern Paiute and Mono afford a technical exception, they are mostly east of the Sierra Nevada and hence in the Great Basin outside the natural limits of California. The Yokuts Valley dialects seem to be classifiable into two groups, a northern along the San Joaquin and a southern from Kings River south; but the former is very little known, and it is possible that fuller information regarding it might shift the line of demarcation.

The foothill dialects, though hardly more numerous and spoken over a very much smaller area, are far more diversified. This might be anticipated from the topography of their territory. Their variety may, however, also be due to the historical fortunes of the foothill tribes. The farther south one progresses along the lower Sierra, the more deviations does one encounter from the type of Yokuts speech which is numerically preponderant and therefore justly to be considered the normal and presumably original form. Now the Yokuts as a whole constitute the southernmost branch of the great Penutian family, which, so to speak, radiates in five directions from the region of the entrance of the Sacramento and San Joaquin into the head of San Francisco Bay; in other words from the lowest and central point of the Great Valley of California. That the foothill dialects of Yokuts become more and more specialized the farther they are situated from this center of influence and possibly of origin is certainly significant; though whether it is significant of successive migrations from the north, of longer contact with Shoshonean and Chumash aliens, or merely of ever reduced intercourse with kinsmen, must as yet be left to conjecture.

The northern group of tribes in the foothill division are those living on the San Joaquin where this stream still pursues a southwesterly course before turning into the main line of the valley. Their dialects are very similar to those of the adjacent northern valley tribes; so much so that they could almost be reckoned as of one group with them were it not that the more and more insistent divergence of all subsequent foothill dialects draws these northernmost idioms into the distinctive hill class. This comparative indeterminateness between the speech of the northern hills and plains is paralleled in the topography. Along the San Joaquin and to the north, the perfectly flat valley shades imperceptibly into the gentlest undulations, which swell and magnify into long low hillocks, until the foothills proper are gradually reached.

From Kings River south the transition from plain to foothills is abrupt, a single step often being literally sufficient to carry one from one area into the other. This means that the physiography is sharply distinct, and that the native modes of life, with their direct adaptation to the soil, can not be identical. It is therefore not surprising that the Kings River group of foothill dialects is well marked off from the adjacent southern valley group.

The Tule-Kaweah group comprises the idioms on these two streams, with which the foothill portion of Deer Creek must be included.

The Poso Creek group of dialects covers not only this stream but White River to the north and a section of Kern River to the south.

With the Buena Vista group, finally, the greatest departure from average Yokuts speech is attained, but, as already mentioned, the foothill habitat of the remainder of the division was abandoned, at least in historic times.

Here follow the names of the Yokuts tribes, their habitats, and their principal known villages. The sequence is from foothills to valley and from south to north, the reverse of that just pursued, in order to allow of procedure from the better to the less known.

TRIBES OF THE BUENA VISTA GROUP OF THE FOOTHILL DIVISION.

The Tulamni (plural Tulalmina) were the tribe in possession of Buena Vista Lake, at some point on whose western or northwestern shore where the hills come close to the water was their main settlement Tulamniu, "Tulamni-place." From there they ranged westward to Wogitiu in the vicinity of McKittrick. (Pl. 47.)

On Kern Lake were the Hometwoli or Humetwadi. This name means "southerners" and is a variant of the common term Homtinin applied by any Yokuts to those of their neighbors who live to the south. The true tribal designation of the Hometwoli has been forgotten. They inhabited at least three principal sites: Halau near the entrance of Kern River into the channel connecting Kern and Buena Vista Lakes; Loasau, somewhere on the north side of Kern Lake; and Pohalin Tinliu (meaning "ground squirrels' hole") in Yauelmani, or Sihetal Daal in the Hometwoli dialect itself, on the south shore.

The Tuhohi, Tohohai, or Tuhohayi (the t is almost like English tr) are extinct. They are said to have spoken a dialect similar to Tulamni and Hometwoli, and to have lived among the channels and tule-lined sloughs of lower Kern River where these became lost in Tulare Lake. They may have ranged as far as Goose Lake. Their principal habitation is spoken of as Tahayu, "Tuhohi-place."

A little mystery may be dispelled here. Stephen Powers found among the Yauelmani one old man, the survivor of a tribe that had once lived on Kern

Lake, and whose numerals, and therefore speech, he recognized as distinctively non-Yokuts. Inquiry proves that the survivor had been at one of the missions, had there learned more or less Salinan, and that some of its vocables suggested to him Yokuts words of entirely different meaning. He used to regale his friends with accounts of his travels; and his rattling off the Salinan count as a meaningless 'string of Yokuts words became a well-known entertainment; much as we might amuse a child with a tale of a strange people called the Spanish who counted "You-know, toes, tray, quarrel." Here are the Salinan originals and his puns:

kitol, kishile_____kile.
kakichu _____choyochi.
lapai_____uyatsi.
kicha _____chuichau (a place name).
olchat, ulchao_____lopchin-tinliu (at the fish hole).
painel, payat_____pokoichin-tinliu.
te, tepa_____tuhtu.
sanel_____pusin-tinliu (at the dog's hole).
tetatsoi_____hosche.
tsoe_____chiwa.

TRIBES OF THE POSO CREEK GROUP OF THE FOOTHILL DIVISION.

The Paleuyami, Padeuyami, Peleuyi, or, as they were called by their Shoshonean neighbors, Paluyam, had their headquarters in the hills beside Poso Creek, especially at Altau ("salt-grass place"), which lay just south of this stream about as far up in the hills as K'ono-ilkin or Kern Falls, to which place, and adjacent sites on Kern River, they, as well as the Yauelmani of the valley, appear to have come. They had also Bekiu and Shikidapau (*shikid*, "arrow") in Poso Flat, and Holmiu in Linn's Valley.

The Kumachisi, Komechesi, Kometsiosi, or Kumachesi (plural Kumachwadi) centered about Hoschiu on White River. They were sometimes known as the Small Paleuyami, the Altinin of Altau being the Great Paleuyami. Some informants identify them with the obscure Shoshonean tribe called the Giamina, whose habitat is said to have been in or near the Paleuyami territory. The majority of the Kumachisi probably knew more than one language; as to whether their native dialect was of the Paleuyami type, or of the valley division, or indeed not Yokuts at all but Shoshonean, there is no certain evidence.

TRIBES OF THE TULE-KAWEAH GROUP OF THE FOOTHILL DIVISION.

The Yaudanchi or Yaulanchi (plural Yauedchani or Yawilchini), also called Nutaa (plural Nuchawayi), "easterners, uplanders"—whence Garcés's generic designation of the Yokuts as Noche—held Tule River in the foothills, especially the North and Middle Forks. One of their principal winter quarters was Shawahtau, above Springville. Near by was Ukunui ("drink"); and house pits at Uchiyingetau ("markings") at the painted rocks, and at Tungoshud ("gate") near the agency, on Tule River Reservation, hark back to either Yaudanchi or Bokninuwad occupancy. In spring and early summer they gathered seeds in the vicinity of Lindsay; in late summer or fall they met with other tribes in Koyeti territory about Porterville for fishing and elk hunting. In dry and hungry seasons the southern end of Tulare Lake would be frequented in search of tule roots. All the Yokuts tribes from the Kaweah River south, except perhaps the Wowol and Chunut of Tulare Lake, and at least most of the adjacent Shoshoneans, were friendly and appear to have ranged over one another's territory amicably and almost at will. The northern Yokuts were more divided by distrusts and hostilities; definite intertribal boundaries are known in several cases; and southern tradition speaks of invading war parties from the north.

The Bokninuwad or Bokninwal (plural Bokenwadi), Garcés's Pagninoas, are in native opinion so named because they had a habit of not returning to their owners lost articles that they encountered (bok, "find"). They appear to have been a smaller tribe than the neighboring and similar Yaudanchi. Deer Creek, in the foothills, was their habitat. Here they lived at K'eyau, near the valley, and perhaps at Hoin Tinliu ("deer's hole"), farther up, not far from Deer Creek Hot Springs, though the Shoshonean Bankalachi seem also to have frequented the region of the latter. The southern forks of Tule River, including the present reservation, were in customary Bokninuwad range.

The Wükchamni, Wikchamni, or Wikchomni (plural Wükachmina or Wikatsmina), whose name was a byword for "gluttons," and who may be the Buesanet of Garcés, wintered on Kaweah River near Lemon Cove and Iron Bridge and frequented the adjacent hills in summer.

The Yokod or Yokol (plural Yuwekadi) had their principal village a dozen miles below the Wükchamni, on a flat near Kaweah railroad station, on the south side of Kaweah River, north of Exeter. Their summer range met that of the Yaudanchi about Lindsay.

The Gawia or Kawia (plural Gaweyayi or Kaweyayi), from whom Kaweah River takes its name, lived at a hill on the north side of the stream, opposite the Yokod. Their recognized northward range included Chidepuish, Calvin Hill, on Big Dry or Rattlesnake Creek. They seem to be the people whom Garcés calls Coguifa.

TRIBES OF THE KINGS RIVER GROUP OF THE FOOTHILL DIVISION.

In this coterie the Choinimni survive to-day in the greatest, although much reduced, numbers. They were perhaps also the most populous before the white man came. Their village was the before-mentioned Tishechu, said to mean "at the gate," a place of some importance on the south side of Kings River at the mouth of Mill Creek.

The Choinimni were the Yokuts farthest up Kings River proper, Mono territory beginning some miles beyond Tishechu. Next up Mill Creek were the Michahai (plural Michahaisha or Michayisa), at Hehshinau, on the north side of the stream, on a flat at the foot of the pine-covered ridge.

Up a small affluent of Mill Creek from the south, in Squaw Valley, some 6 miles from Hehshinau, were the Chukaimina (plural Chokoyemi). These lived at Dochiu and Mashtinau, at the north and east sides of the circular valley.

Up Mill Creek, at Kicheyu near Dunlap, and at another site known as Chit'-atichi ("clover"), were the Entimbich or Indimbich (plural Enatbicha or Inadbicha). These, neighbors of the Shoshonean Wobonuch, have sometimes also been classed as Monos; but a vocabulary of their dialect establishes them as Yokuts.

Below the Choinimni on Kings River, but on the opposite side, were the Toihicha (plural Toyehachi). They lived at Tanaiu ("Jimson weed place"), at Hughes Creek, and at Bochiptau.

Still farther down Kings River, but this time on the south side, were the Aiticha, Aitecha, Aititsa, Aigicha, or Ai'kicha (plural Aiyetatsi or Aiyekachi). Their village was K'ipayu, somewhat nearer to Centerville than to Tishechu.

Kocheyali is mentioned by some of the Yokuts as another name for the Aiticha. This is not, however, their unanimous verdict. Two designations for a single tribe are also without parallel, apart from duplicate appellations based on names of places or terms of direction. There may therefore have been a distinct Kocheyali tribe in this vicinity.

With the Gashowu (plural Gashwusha) Big Dry Creek, losing itself in the plain near Fresno, and Little Dry Creek, draining into the San Joaquin, are reached. The Gashowu dialect also differs somewhat from the idioms of the Kings River group and approaches correspondingly to those of the northern foothill or San Joaquin group; but its general affinities are still with the former. The Chukchansi, for instance, complain of difficulty in understanding Gashowu, which fact, since their own idiom is very similar to Dumna, which in turn was spoken only a few miles from the Gashowu of Little Dry Creek, is significant. The Gashowu ranged to Fresno to gather seeds in spring or summer. Old maps show two Indian rancherias. One of these can be identified with Pohoniu, below Letcher on Big Dry Creek. On Little Dry Creek were Yokau in Auberry Valley, near Opnoniu, and Ochopou, the latter attributed also to the Kechayi.

TRIBES OF THE NORTHERN GROUP OF THE FOOTHILL DIVISION.

The Toltichi (plural Toletachi), the "stream people," were the Yokuts tribe farthest up the San Joaquin and neighbors of the Mono. They are extinct. The recorded fragments of their speech show many distortions, not only from northern foothill but from all forms of Yokuts. It is doubtful whether these divergencies are due to faulty recollection or are real modications caused by prolonged contact of a small and remote mountain group with people of alien language, as in the case of the Paleuyami. It is even conceivable that the Toltichi were Monos, who mispronounced the Yokuts which many of them had partly learned. Tsopotipau, at the electric power site on the large bend of the river below the entrance of the North Fork, was Toltichi.

The Kechayi (plural Keche'wali or Kichainawi) had the south bank of the San Joaquin for some miles above Millerton. A settlement of theirs upstream from this abandoned town and fort was Kochoyu, which seems to mean nothing more than "Kechayi place." Farther up they lived at Kowichkowicho. Below the Kechayi were the Wakichi, a tribe of the valley division.

The Dumna (plural Dumanisha) were on the north side of the San Joaquin, about opposite the Kechayi. Their range took in the country opposite Millerton; Table Mountain; the mouth of Fine Gold Creek; and Bellevue, which they called Dinishneu.

The Dalinchi (plural Da'elnashi) were a little off the San Joaquin. Fine Gold Creek was their territory. Here they inhabited Moloneu; also O'Neals. Dalinau, "Dalinchi place," was over the divide in the Coarse Gold Creek drainage.

The Chukchansi, Shukshansi, or Shukshanchi (plural Chukadnisha) held Coarse Gold Creek, an affluent of Fresno River, and the head of Cottonwood Creek. They are the northernmost of all the foothill tribes, and their border, Fresno River, where they adjoined the Miwok, was the farthest limit of all the hill Yokuts. They appear to have moved and scattered considerably, and, being on friendly terms with their Miwok neighbors, to have had no hesitation in entering their territory. This is probably the reason why the modern Chukchansi list among their settlements certain places across the Fresno River, such as Aplau and Yiwisniu, whereas actually it was the Miwok who seem to have owned a small tract on the south side of the stream. Hapasau, near Fresno Flats, was, however, Chukchansi. Also well up on Fresno River was Chukchanau or Suksanau, "Chukchansi place." On Coarse Gold Creek they inhabited Tsuloniu, near the headwaters; Kowoniu or Kohoniu, on Picayune Creek; Kataniu, the present Picayune rancheria, where the majority of the survivors dwell; and, on Cottonwood Creek, they lived at Ch'eyau, "bone place," near Bates.

It is possible that place names like Kochoy-u, Dalin-au, Chukchan-au are original and that the tribal names Kechayi, Dalinchi, and Chukchanchi are derived from them. However, none of these place names yield to etymology, whereas many that are not related to tribal names do have meanings.

TRIBES OF THE SOUTHERN GROUP OF THE VALLEY DIVISION.

The Yauelmani, Ya'welmani, Yowelmani, Yowenmani, Yowedmani, which forms appear to be the plural of Yaulamni or Yaudimni, perhaps number more survivors to-day than any other Yokuts tribe. Their ancient range was extensive. They held Tinliu ("at the hole") on Paso Creek below the Tejon ranch house—perhaps the most southerly of all Yokuts settlements. This must have been a favorite abode, since it gave them the appellation Tinlinin, which, together with "Tejoneños," is still used as a synonym of Yauelmani. With this spot went ownership of the lower courses of Tejon and other near-by streams. Thirty or more miles to the north they held Woilo ("planting place," "sowing place"—the name was given after mission influences began to reach them), on the site of the town of Bakersfield. Up Kern River they lived at times at K'ono-ilkin ("water's fall") and at Shoko ("wind place," in a gorge), above which began the territory of the Tübatulabal, whom they knew as Pitanisha. These spots were also frequented by the Paleuyami across the divide on near-by Poso Creek, and it is not certain which tribe laid claim of ownership to them. A short distance above Bakersfield in the first foothills was Tsineuhiu ("at the shades" or "ramada place"), not permanently inhabited, but a favorite day resting place between night journeys in the summer; while below the city, on one of the channels of the river draining toward Kern Lake, was Kuyo. The Yauelmani are also mentioned as at Altau with the Paleuyami, at Hoschiu on White River with the Kumachisi, and at Chididiknawasi in the Deer Creek country—all places above the valley. It is therefore not surprising that there are old Indians, born, before the coming of the Americans, of a Yauelmani parent married to a Yaudanchi or Wowol partner. Unions with the Shoshonean Kitanemuk to the south and Bankalachi to the north also occurred.

The Koyeti or Kuyeti (plural Koyetati or Kuyetwadi), now extinct, seem to have been a smaller tribe of almost identical speech with the Yauelmani. They held the swampy sloughs of Tule River from Chokowisho, Porterville, down; this tract being known as Kiawitnau.

The Choinok (plural Choyenaki), the Choinoc of Garcés and Cabot, another small group, were the southernmost of three tribes in the flaring, slough-intersected delta of the Kaweah. They lived south of Tulare City and below Farmersville, probably on Deep and Outside Channels, in which region their town of Ch'iuta may be looked for.

The Wo'lasi or Wo'ladji (plural Wowulasi, Wowelasi, Wowlasi) were north of the Choinok, at and below Farmersville, perhaps on Cameron Channel. This small tribe must not be confused with the more prominent Wowol (plural Wowowoli) of Tulare Lake.

The Telamni, Telomni, Tedamni (plural Tielami, Tielamni, Tiedami, Tiedamni, or Teyelamni), the "Telam or Torim" of Garcés and Telame of the missions, were northwest of the Wo'lasi, at Visalia and Goshen. Among their settlements was Waitatshulul, some 7 miles north of Tulare City. Here for the first time we hear of fixed tribal boundaries. The Telamni, Wo'lasi, and Choinok did not pass over Cross Creek, the northernmost slough fed from the Kaweah, without encountering the hostility of the Nutunutu.

The valley tribes on Kings River appear to have been at least as large as those on the Kaweah, but they have died out almost as completely. At Centerville, also known as King River, at Sanger, and toward Reedley, were the Wechihit, Wechahet, or Wetehit (plural Wichehati). At Musahau, in the low bottoms, between the middle and east channels opposite Sanger, one or two survive near an ancient village site. Wewayo, on Wahtoke Creek, seems to have been a no-man's-land so far as tribal ownership went, but was at any rate visited by the Wechihit. A Wahtoke "tribe," formerly mentioned in this vicinity, was given that designation, which means "pine nut," by the Americans from the name of the chief of the band.

The Nutunutu or Nutuntu (plural Nutantisha) were south of lower Kings River, in a country formerly a mass of sloughs and swamps. Armona, Hanford, and Kingston were their territory; a little south of the latter was their village Chiau. Hibek'ia, where they also lived, can not be exactly located. Their name is puzzling. It probably goes back to the root *not*, upstream (compare the Nuta'a, or uplanders, the mountain Mono or hill Yokuts in general); yet the Nutunutu were certainly a downstream people, if there were any, to all their neighbors except possibly the Tachi.

The Wimilchi (plural Wimelachi) were separated by Kings River from the Nutunutu—and apparently without friendship—much as these kept Cross Creek as a barrier against the Telamni. The Wimilchi in turn observed Fish Slough, connecting Kings River and Tulare Lake, as a boundary against the Tachi. They had Lillis and Laton, and Cold and Murphy Sloughs; and in general seem to have occupied the whole of the Laguna de Tache land grant, though this was named after their better known western neighbors. Ugona was a Wimilchi town.

Tulare Lake and its shores are stated by all the Yokuts to have belonged to three tribes and three only, all of them large and warlike, though not always friendly to one another. These were, in order from south to north, the Wowol, Chunut, and Tachi.

The Wowol, Wowod, Wowal, or Wo'wal (plural Wowowoli, Wowowadi, Wowowali, or Wu'wo'wali) are the Bubol, Hubol, and perhaps Tuohuala of the Spaniards. They are not to be confounded with the Wo'lasi (plural Wowulasi) of Kaweah River. They are said, in a characteristically picturesque but probably unreliable native explanation, to have derived their name from standing ("*wowul*") in rows and lousing each other. Of more intrinsic interest is the fact that they lived on an island off the east shore of the lake, from which they had to cross on their tule rafts to the timbered or brushy stream outlets on the mainland to obtain firewood. This island is said to have been due west of the present Delano, which identifies it with Atwells Island, where old maps show an Indian rancheria on the lake shore. This settlement was called Sukuwutnu, Shukwatnau, or Shugudnu; the name Dulau has also been given it.

The settlement or settlements Miketsiu and Chuntau of the Chunut (plural Chunotachi or Chunotati) can be less exactly located, but the tribal range was the Tulare Lake shore in the Kaweah Delta region. Spanish sources refer to them as Sumtache and Tunctache. These people seem to have penetrated freely up the sloughs. Cross Creek was their northern boundary, as of the Telamni, against the Tachi and Nutunutu, a fact that argues close association between them and their upstream neighbors of the Kaweah.

'The Tachi, Tadji, or Dachi (plural Tachechayi, Tadjedjayi, Dachechayi, Tatsetsai, or Tatetayi), the northernmost of the three Tulare Lake tribes, appear to have been one of the largest of all Yokuts divisions, and still survive to the number of some dozens. The Spaniards frequently referred to the Tache, and a Laguna de Tache land grant survives on our maps. Their country was the tract from northern Tulare Lake and its inlet or outlet, Fish Slough, west to the Mount Diablo chain of the Coast Range, where they bordered the Salinan Indians. Here they wintered at Udjiu, downstream from Coalinga, and at Walna, where the western hills approach the lake. Golon (Huron) was theirs. In summer they crossed to the east of the outlet and gathered seeds in the neighborhood of Lemoore. Chi, west of Heinlen, and Waiu, Mussel Slough, on which stands their present rancheria of Santa Rosa, were in this tract. The various delimitations cited by older Indians as having formerly existed make it seem that the Tachi and Nutunutu were friendly to each other, but suspicious and probably hostile at times toward the Wimilchi on the one side and the Chunut, Temlani, Wo'lasi, and Choinok on the other.

The Apiachi are an obscure and extinct tribelet, living with the lower Kings River tribes, but somehow associated with the Tachi, from whom some of the older Indians now refuse to separate them. They lived north of Kings River and east of its outlet slough, at Wohui, beyond Telweyit or Summit Lake, in the direction of Elkhorn.

TRIBES OF THE NORTHERN GROUP OF THE VALLEY DIVISION.

The Pitkachi, perhaps more accurately Pitkati (plural Pitakati or Pidekati) are said to have received their appellation from an evil-smelling salt or alkali of the same name, which they used to gather or prepare. This in turn is named after feces, *pidik*. They held the south side of the San Joaquin, living at Kohuou, near Herndon or Sycamore; at Weshiu, on a slough; and at Gewachiu, still farther downstream.

The Wakichi or Wa'kichi, plural Wakeyachi, were on the same side of the river but farther up, not quite opposite the Dumna, and just below the Kechayi. Holowichniu, near Millerton, was in their territory. This location would suggest that the Wakichi were part of the northern foothill group, but a few preserved phrases of their dialect indicate that it belonged to the valley division.

The Hoyima, Hoyim'a, or Hoyimha (plural Hoyeyami) were also on the San Joaquin where it still flows west, but opposite the Pitkachi; in other words, on the north side. They may have ranged as far as Fresno River. They had settlements at K'eliutanau, on a creek entering the San Joaquin from the north, and at Moyoliu above the mouth of Little Dry Creek. They were not without fighting proclivities, and at times engaged the Chauchila of the plains and the Chukchansi of the hills.

The Heuchi, Heuche, or Heutsi (plural Hewachinawi) had a large settlement at Ch'ekayu, on Fresno River 4 miles below Madera. They were certainly on the north side of this stream and may have had both its lower banks.

The Chauchila or Chauchili, more correctly Chaushila or Chaushilha (plural Chaweshali), sometimes also called Toholo, "lowlanders, westerners," by the hill tribes, were in the plains along the several channels of Chowchilla River, in whose name their appellation is perpetuated. They lived at Shehamniu on this stream, apparently at the eastern edge of the plains, some miles below

Buchanan. Halau, "cane," near Berenda, which may have been in their range or that of the Heuchi, recalls a town of the same name on far distant Kern Lake. The Chauchila may have been a populous tribe; they were certainly a warlike one, for their name is a byword for bravery to the southernmost end of Yokuts territory among tribes ignorant of the nearer Heuchi and Hoyima. It is frequently translated as "murderous," "cruel," or "aggressive"; but the nearest roots known are not very similar: Yaudanchi *tawidj*, *taudj*, to die or kill, and *taw* (*t* alomst like *ch*), to overcome. Two mythical traditions told by the Yauelmani begin at Kamupau in Chumash territory beyond San Emigdio at the extreme head of the San Joaquin Valley, and progress, one to the ocean on the south, the other north to the Chauchila. Such a range of geographical knowledge, however vague, is quite unparalleled in California, except among the inquisitive and far-traveled Mohave, who, by the way, were also known to the Yokuts through visiting parties from across the desert and by reputation as a fighting people, and who quite correctly termed the Yokuts Kwalinyokosmachi, "tule sleepers."

The Chauchila are the first Yokuts tribe to have no upland neighbors of their own stock, the southern Miwok now being the easterners. They are also the last tribe, until Stockton is reached, concerning whom anything definite is known. In the plains along the Merced, Tuolumne, Stanislaus, and Calaveras Rivers, on the east bank of the lower San Joaquin, and perhaps on its west side also, were Yokuts. There are some names extant; but whether of tribes or towns, or where these were located, is doubtful. Some fragments of language, transmitted from several independent sources, show that there existed a variety of northern valley speech distinguished by a frequent change of *m* and *n* to *b* and *d;* but again there is no certainty where these dialects were spoken. There are known in this region the Nupchinche or Noptinte, not located; the Tawalimni, presumably on Tuolumne River, which appears to be named from them; the Lakisamni, perhaps to be connected with Takin (for Lakiu?) rancheria at Dents or Knights Ferry on the Stanislaus; the Siakumne; and Hannesuk, which sounds like a Miwok place name, but is given as a tribe and placed in territory that was probably Yokuts. Some names can be identified as generically denoting any inhabitants in certain directions, such as Nutu-tamne and Kosmitas or Xosmitamne, Yokuts for "upstream people" and "northern people," respectively; and Tammukamne, Miwok for "northern-ers." Others, like Yachik, Yachikamne, or Yachimesi, refer only to village sites or the inhabitants of particular places, instead of being tribal names. And still others, like Coconoon, an anciently mentioned group on Merced River, whom a vocabulary proves to have been Yokuts, are utterly hopeless, unless one is ready to take such random shots as to identify this term with Gogoni, a spot said to have marked the extreme northern or upland range of the Chauchila. The early travelers often encountered these northernmost Yokuts far from their homes or at the missions, and rarely cared or were able to record their exact habitat. At the present time, when an old Indian can be found who remembers a few words of the Yokuts speech of his father or grandfather, he has usually forgotten the name of the tribe, or, if he remembers this, is in ignorance or in patent error of its former location. A similar dark-ness reigns concerning the Wintun, Maidu, Miwok, and Costanoan groups once on or near San Francisco Bay. In short, regrettable as the fact is, we can scarcely hope ever to have wholly accurate or full information concerning these tribes.

Conditions are a little better for knowledge of the last and probably most northerly Yokuts tribe, the Chulamni, who apparently are the group that fre-

quents the older sources under the designations of Tcholovone and Cholo-
vomne. Fortune preserved until recently a few individuals of this tribe, who
retained a reasonable command of their forefathers' speech. This, on comparison with the Chauchila dialect, has proved to be typical Yokuts of the northern
valley group, making the appurtenance of the intervening tribes to the same
group substantially certain. The Chulamni inhabited Yachik and Wana near
Stockton. the latter just below the landing. Their territory extended at least

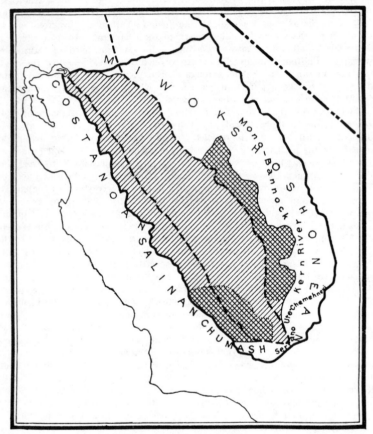

Fig. 43.—Yokuts topography, distribution, and neighbors. The heavy line marks
the San Joaquin-Tulare drainage; the broken line, the level San Joaquin Valley.
Territory of Yokuts of valley division in hatching; of foothill division in cross-
hatching.

some miles down the San Joaquin and up the Calaveras; probably also across
the former stream, possibly as far west as Mount Diablo.

SPEECH AND TOPOGRAPHY.

The very remarkable relation of the Yokuts habitat and of their
speech divisions to topography is shown in Figure 43. It is clear that
they are essentially a valley people. Not only do they hold the whole

of the San Joaquin Valley floor but their extension into the hills is of the slightest. The higher Sierra Nevada everywhere, and the lower slopes in the north, are in the possession of alien nations.

Equally significant is the almost perfect correspondence between topography and speech. The valley dialects are absolutely confined to the plains, except for a small part of the range of the Yauelmani in the extreme south. The foothill group of dialects is restricted with equal exactness to the hills, except where the three southwestern tribes, finding the lee side of the Coast Range too barren for their subsistence, appear to have come down into the adjacent tule swamps. The correlation between speech and soil surface is so rigid that causes of such potency must be inferred to have been operative as could scarcely have prevailed to this extent among the Yokuts without being of some influence elsewhere. Indeed it seems, as already pointed out, that lines of dialectic cleavage followed the edge of the plains in the Sacramento Valley, among Miwok, Maidu, and Wintun. On the other hand, it is dangerous to reason from the mass conditions of the great valley, flanked by the massive, unbroken wall of the Sierra, to circumstances obtaining in regions of more irregular topography. Several Pomo dialects, for instance, extend practically unchanged over belts of coast, timber, valley, mountain, and inland waters.

It is also clear from Figure 43 how much more diversified the foothill tribes were than those of the valley. Holding barely a fifth of the area of the stock, they comprised about one-half of the tribes, and five out of seven of its dialect groups. The diversity of surface in the hill country is only partially responsible. Of more moment, probably, is the fact that the foothill tribes, happening to constitute a fringe, were thrown into more intimate contact with their alien neighbors dwelling higher on the same slope of the Sierra Nevada, and thus had stimulated in them those unconscious influences toward change of language that only association with the foreigner seems to bring.

It is difficult to look at this map, with its enormous solid nucleus of valley, and defend oneself from the impression that this is the original home of the Yokuts group, and that the border foothill tribes represent an upland spilling over. This would be contrary to the view sometimes entertained that the Yokuts once occupied the entire basin to its summit, and were in process of being gradually driven to the center by Shoshonean pressure. From the Yokuts side the appearance is rather of an expansion of this stock and a pushing back of Shoshoneans who previously might have held all of the mountains and perhaps the southern end of the valley.

As a matter of fact, it is impossible to decide. Either alternative looks plausible as the evidence is approached from one aspect or the other. What is most likely is that a condition nearly of equilibrium between the two stocks has been maintained for a long time. The four or five Shoshonean divisions of quite diversified speech did not all crowd westward over the watershed in any short period; nor did the specialized Yokuts foothill dialects, no matter how much effect we allow to topography and foreign association, spring up in two or three centuries.

DESIGNATIONS OF THE STOCK.

The name " Yokuts " is taken from a native word for person or people, appearing as *yokoch* and in similar forms in a number of the dialects of the stock. The Spanish Tulareños, " people of the rush marshes," coincides very closely with modern Yokuts in its ethnic application. Mariposan is a book name, happily moribund, since it is equally arbitrary and erroneous. The Indians of Mariposa County are Miwok, not Yokuts. Foreign Indian names are few. The Costanoans at San Juan Bautista called the Yokuts Yawisun; the Chumash of Ventura, Chminimolich, " northerners "; the Mohave, Kwalinyo-kosmachi, " tule sleep."

YOKUTS AND OTHER CALIFORNIA POPULATION.

The problem of the size of Yokuts' population is crucial for the question of what the number of California Indians may have been, but unfortunately it seems impossible of entirely accurate solution.

The prime factor of uncertainty is the size of the tribe. Two hundred and fifty souls seems an overconservative estimate. There may have been tribes that surpassed 500. On the other hand, this latter figure appears to be excessive as an average. It is difficult to say why, in the absence of any evidence bearing directly on the point; but the nature of the country, the descriptions of travelers, and the Indians' statements as to their great-grandfathers' customs, somehow leave the impression that the Yokuts tribe did not so very much exceed the usual California village community in populational strength. But again, the consistent adherence to the principle that each tribe possessed its peculiar dialect warns against setting the figure very low. Three to four hundred persons is perhaps the soundest estimate that can be made, and with 50 or nearly 50 tribes, this would yield from 15,000 to 20,000 souls for the entire group.

Mission records are of little aid, for although there were Yokuts at nearly all of the church establishments from San Luis Obispo to San Francisco, and a number of tribal names can be recognized, statistics are for the total at one mission at one time. San Antonio may have harbored more Yokuts than Salinan neophytes when secularization came, but the proportions of the two national elements are obscure. It also seems impossible to ascertain how exhaustively the Franciscans drew upon the tribes that they tapped, or how long certain of these were under mission influence. There were Tachi brought across the mountains, but whether the whole tribe was moved or only a fraction, whether it remained a generation or only a few years, no one seems able to say. It is only known that the valley tribes from about the Fresno River northward were removed and missionized almost completely, and that their early virtual extinction was due to the effects of this process.

Nor do figures for the twentieth century population of the stock yield any approach to fixed conclusions for the eighteenth. The Federal census of 1910, the first that attempted to concern itself with such matters, reports only 533 Yokuts. The most widely spread stock in California, after the Shoshonean, to-day ranks twelfth in numbers. Not only Miwok, Maidu, and Wintun, but small localized groups like the Yurok, Karok, and Washo surpass the Yokuts. However much the estimate of original population be scaled down, it is evident that factors of most unfortunate potency have been at work. One such, and of proved fatality, is the concentration of mission life; but it is insufficient, for the southern and eastern Yokuts escaped it. It was apparently their open valley habitat, or at best hill abode, that crushed the Yokuts, through making them more readily and unmitigatedly accessible to the white man. In the mountains, civilization advanced slowly, or receded after the first rush of miners. The Indian shrank back, but had numberless corners left to himself. In the plains, the farmer followed hard on the pioneer, the soil was broken, fences began to stretch, and before long railroads ran their course and cities flourished. There was no way for the native to escape the full brunt of civilization; and it melted him away. In the Sacramento Valley the Plains Maidu and Wintun have vanished, compared with their fellows in the hills. Against 600 Sierra Miwok there are not two dozen of the plains division. More distinctively a lowland people than any of these, the Yokuts as a whole have been more reduced. All they have preserved better is the purity of their blood. The infrequency of half-breeds among them is noticeable; and the census that makes one-half or more of the Wintun, Maidu, and Miwok population mixed blood, credits at least three-fourths of the Yokuts with purity of strain.

If any doubt remains as to the strength of the factor of proximity to centers of Caucasian population, in rapidly diminishing Indian numbers, the Mono clinch the argument. Eastern neighbors of the Yokuts in the higher Sierra and the desert beyond it, they numbered at most a quarter or a third, perhaps not a fifth as many. To-day they are the largest group in California, and total nearly three souls for every living Yokuts.

The survivors, then, tell us nothing of the strength of their ancestors, because the wastage has been too excessive. The fragments are too small for an estimate of the original block. The remnant may be 2 per cent or 5. It does not help to answer the question.

This uncertainty weakens one of the potentially strongest lines of evidence that might bear on the problem of the ancient population of California. The Yokuts held a full tenth, possibly an eighth, of the area of the State. If we knew their numbers, a simple multiplication, corrected by an allowance for productivity of the soil under native exploitation, would yield a total that would be of value for controlling estimates derived by other methods. Groups of narrower range or numbers do not justify the application of such procedure; conditions are too unrepresentative. The Yurok, for instance, owned barely one-half of 1 per cent of the area of California, the Cheme-huevi perhaps 5 per cent: ratios that, with what is known of their numbers, would give in the one case well over half a million and in the other much less than 50,000 for the State.

However, the almost lost opportunity may be essayed. Say 18,000 Yokuts in a ninth of California: 162,000 Indians once in the State. Or, taking the highest possible figures, 25,000 in a tenth, gives 250,000 as a maximum limit.

Then comes the correction. There undoubtedly were areas more densely populated than the average of the Yokuts habitat: the Santa Barbara Islands, stretches of the shore fronting them, certain valleys in the coast region, the district of the lower Klamath. There were probably as many Pomo on Clear Lake as Yokuts on much larger Tulare Lake. But these areas of concentration were small. It was apparently precisely the fact of their confinement that brought about the density. The additions to be made to the total on account of distinctly heavier population are therefore not very great in the aggregate.

The deductions to be made for a sinking of the Yokuts ratio in less favorable regions are more considerable. A full third of the State is thorough desert, substantially desert, high mountains, bare lava flow, or dense timber. In all these environments the population was of the slenderest. Generally such regions were not even inhabited except in oasislike spots; and that the maps in the present and other volumes show continuous territories rather than these significant oases is not because the entire areas have been thought to be inhabited, but because ignorance of precise conditions of habitation has rendered other delineation impracticable for most of the State. Everything east of the Sierra, its entire upper portion, a solid three-fourths of southern California, most of the northeastern angle of the State, and a number of tracts in the coast ranges, belong to these thinly populated regions, which loom broadly enough to bring down by at least a fourth any total computed from the rate prevailing in more favored regions.

Let us balance this reduction by the smaller additions and say that not a fourth but a fifth must be taken from the multiplicative total. That diminishes by 32,000 our apparently soundest estimate of 162,000 and gives for the native population of the State 130,000, or about eight times the present number of full bloods and mixed bloods combined. At any rate, there is a high degree of probability that the actual figure fell between 100,000 and 150,000. The maximum limit under the same process falls from 250,000 to 200,000, or less than almost all published estimates.

We have one check on the estimate of 300 to 400 souls per Yokuts tribe that underlies this total. In 1806 Moraga marched up half the length of the San Joaquin Valley and returned with the names of more than 20 groups and estimates of their numbers. Most of these must have been Yokuts, and about half of them can be identified.

YOKUTS.		YOKUTS OR OTHER.	
Nupchenche (Noptinte)	250		
		Chineguis	250
		Yunate	250
		Chamuasi	250
		Latelate	200
		Lachuo	200
Pizcache (Pitkachi)	200		
Aycuyche (Aiticha)	60		
		Ecsaa	100
		Ehiaja	100
		Xayuase	100
		Capatau	10
		Hual	400
Tunctache (Chunotachi)	250		
Notonto (Nutunutu)	300		
Do	100		
Telame (Telamni)	600		
Do	200		
Uholasi (Wowulasi)	100		
Eagueya (Gawia)	300		
Cohochs (Yokol?)	100		
Choynogue (Choinok)	300		
		Cutucha (Colteche)	400
Tahualamne (Yauelmani?)	200		
Coyehete (Koyeti)	400		
	3,360		**2,260**
		Total	5,620

Five thousand six hundred and twenty people in 23 groups yield an average of less than 250; or, if we divide the 3,360 known to have been Yokuts by 12, the result is 280 per tribe. The earliest observer's estimate is a fifth less than the figure of 300 to 400—say, 350—assumed above. There is thus every reason to believe that the total computed for California does not err on the side of parsimony.

CHAPTER 33.

THE YOKUTS: SOCIAL INSTITUTIONS.

CULTURE.

The extinction of the northern valley tribes prevents their being included in the following account of Yokuts life, which is accordingly confined to those members of the family who live south of the Miwok, or approximately those shown in Plate 47. When such and such customs are ascribed to "the northern Yokuts," the tribes of the upper San Joaquin region are therefore referred to, notably the Chukchansi, who survive in the greatest numbers. Under "southern Yokuts" all the tribes from Kaweah River south may generally be understood, although most of the information relates to the Yaudanchi and Yauelmani. For the "central" tribes of the lake region and the sloughs of lower Kings River the Tachi may be taken as typical. It is regrettable that so little knowledge survives concerning the Yokuts of the lower San Joaquin, as their practices must have been different from those of their southerly kinsmen at many points. Living almost in contact with the Wintun and Maidu, and between the Miwok and Costanoans, it is practically certain that they shared the Kuksu and other ceremonies of the ritual system which is common to these groups and centered in the first-named stock. The Yokuts south of the San Joaquin performed ceremonies of entirely different type. This lack of similarity is probably typical of many other distinctions which can only be suspected.

MARRIAGE.

Marriage was a comparatively informal affair all the way from the Chukchansi to the Yauelmani, though payment was always made for the bride, sometimes by as high as a hundred *chok* measures of beads. A father might send his son to a prospective son-in-law of his choice, with instructions to address him as his brother-in-law. Or a man might suggest to a friend that they be *maksi*—parents of a married couple. The bridegroom would then appear, but if the girl remonstrated vigorously, would probably soon depart of his own accord. If a marriage took place, the husband lived with his wife's people. This is rather remarkable in view of the fact that most and probably all the Yokuts reckoned descent paternally with reference to exogamy and totemism. As usual in loosely organized society, polygamy was not considered objectionable, but was not the common fortune of men and women, probably because there was no noteworthy excess of females. A man with several wives seems normally to have been married in as many villages, dividing his time between his various households. Kindred of any known degree of relationship, except perhaps one class of cousins, were ineligible to marriage; and, what is more interesting, accidental namesakes as well. The Yokuts state that people of the same tribe and town could marry, and this is confirmed by the parentage of old living Indians; but the vast majority of such specific records reveal marriages between people not of the same tribe. This habit is the more peculiar because the dialects of the tribes always differed somewhat; at the same time, the practice must have been a factor of some influence in preventing the rapid drifting apart of the idioms. Naturally, many of the Yokuts were bilingual; and persons knowing three or four dialects, or even distinct languages, are not rare.

Children-in-law and parents-in-law exhibit mutual shame. They avoid speaking, though inmates of the same house; walk apart; and do not even approach each other unless it is absolutely necessary.

MOIETIES AND TOTEMS.

In addition to the politically exogamic tendency, there was a strict rule requiring a man to marry outside his own inherited social division. These divisions were two, and certain animals were symbolically associated with each and transmitted from father to child and son's child. In other words, the totemic moiety system of the Miwok extends also to the Yokuts. It has been found among hill and valley tribes from the Chukchansi to the Wowol. Only the Yaudanchi and Yauelmani, and with them no doubt some of their immediate neighbors, did not possess the organization. For the extinct valley tribes north of the Fresno River there are no data, but their associations with their own kinsmen to the south, as well as with the upland Miwok, render it extremely probable that the same scheme prevailed among most if not all of them. In fact, the existence of a similar organization among the Mono on the east and probably among the Salinan Indians to the west, together with the reappearance of exogamous moieties in southern California, place the Yokuts more centrally than the Miwok as regards the known distribution of this social trait. It is therefore remarkable that their southern tribes know nothing of the scheme.

This seems the more probable from the forms of the system. The Miwok divide all nature into two halves. Every individual's name has some expressed or connoted reference to one of the infinitely numerous animals or objects of the world's moiety that corresponds to his own social moiety. With the Yokuts only a limited number of animals are associated with each division. One of these is held as hereditary totem by every paternally descended family. The names of the people in such a line of descent have no connection with the totem animal, but every individual in the family regards his inherited animal as his "dog"—the one word which the Indian possesses for the idea of "domestic animal" or "pet captive." The Yokuts totemism is thus more direct and emphatic than that of the Miwok, and to this degree may priority in its formulation be attributed to them.

The Yokuts lines of male descent with the same totem obviously resemble clans. They fall short, however, of being clans in that they are not involved in marriage or exogamy, the moiety being the sole regulating factor in these matters, and in that they bear no group names.

This plan of social duality runs at right angles across the many lines of tribal cleavage. The halves are the same, or are equated, everywhere; and a man marrying outside of his tribe confines himself to the opposite moiety exactly as if he chose his spouse at home.

The names of the moieties are the same in all the Yokuts tribes among which they have been recorded: *Tohelyuwish* and *Nutuwish*. *Tohil* signifies "downstream," which varies locally from south to west and northwest; *not*, the opposite direction; *-u-wish* is a reflexive ending forming abstract nouns and names of practices and institutions.

The border Yokuts identify their moieties with the Miwok ones, and in case of intermarriage between the two peoples there is never a question about the proper correspondence of the divisions. The names, too, are similar, but, strangely, rather opposite. The Yokuts "upstream" is the Miwok "water" half, and "downstream" is the equivalent of "land."

The wide-range cleavage implied by this terminology, with its essential polarity, confirms the impression which is given by other features of the Miwok-Yokuts system, that it inherently has a dual ground plan, with the animal totems as an auxiliary development, and that it is not an organization of decayed clans secondarily grouped into moieties.

The representative animal of the *Tohelyuwish* division is the eagle. Of birds, there further belong the raven and crow, blue jay, road runner, and killdeer. Of quadrupeds, the bear is most prominent. Fox, wild cat, jack rabbit, beaver, and antelope are of the same group.

Coyote is the most conspicuous animal on the *Nutuwish* side. Associated with him are the *limik* or falcon, the buzzard, several species of hawks and owls, the quail, and the skunk.

In Yokuts legendary traditions tales of contests and competitions for superiority abound, which may in many cases reflect this totemic duality. Of this sort are struggles between the falcon and raven, coyote and eagle, condor and eagle, and between the deer of the upstream hills and the antelope of the downstream plains. In all these cases, except where the falcon is involved, the downstream animal triumphs. Only in a war of the uplanders against the lake people is coyote successful. In certain other tales the personages are not in opposition, but are all or nearly all of one division. Thus one tale tells of the deeds of coyote, falcon, and white owl; another of coyote, hawk, condor, and owl; a third of eagle, crow, road runner, and fox, with the lone coyote as a disturbing coadjutor; and so on.

It is even possible that the totemic affiliation of certain animals that are as yet unplaced in the social organization of the modern Yokuts can be reasonably predicted from the mythology. This applies not only to the deer and condor, but to the dog, the wood rat, the humming bird, the mountain quail, the woodpecker, and the spider on the *Nutuwish* side; while it seems almost as if in the legends of the southern Yokuts—although the institution itself is lacking—the falcon had been transferred from this to the *Tohelyu-wish* division.

A Yokuts does not ask a stranger whether he is *Nutuwish* or *Tohelyuwish*, nor what his moiety may be, but: "What is your dog?"

As bear doctors speak of the grizzly bear as their "dog," a connection between the moiety animals and the guardian spirits of shamans might be imagined. The Yokuts, however, specifically distinguish between their inherited totemic animals, which they sometimes keep in captivity but which confer no distinctive powers on their persons, and the animals, spirits, or monsters that the impending shaman dreams of or encounters in a trance.

The balance of opposition between animals of the two moieties that runs through the legends has institutional parallels among the Yokuts themselves. Thus, formal games were between moieties. Each moiety had a distinctive style of body paint. In mourning rites the divisions acted reciprocally. From the Chukchansi to the Tachi, and perhaps farther, there was an eagle ceremony. The bird was killed by the coyote division, redeemed and received with manifestations of grief by the moiety of which it was representative.

This rite suggests the eagle-killing mourning ceremony of the Luiseño, among whose neighbors moieties recur. Among the Yokuts the eagle rite may not have stood alone. Other animals, of the *Nutuwish* as well as *Tohelyuwish* division, were killed, redeemed, and bewailed, it seems. So far as can be judged, this intrusion of the moieties into religious activities is greater among the Yokuts than with the Miwok.

As descent was reckoned from the father only, the children of brother and sister were of opposite moieties. Among the Miwok this at least contributed to the permissibility of the marriage of such children—cross cousins they are often called. The similar social organization and kinship nomenclature of the Yokuts suggests that they, too, may have married their cross cousins.

CHIEFS AND OFFICIALS.

The chief, as so often among the Pacific coast natives, was the rich man. A myth tells how Coyote, to avenge his attempted destruction ordered by Eagle, the chief, causes a six months' night to the distress of every one. Eagle sends him three sacks of beads to bring back the sun. Coyote sends back six sacks, restores daylight, and thus wins not only fame for magical power but prestige at outdoing the chief in liberality. Chiefs were also expected to know more, especially regarding religion, than common men. The son succeeded the father. As women occasionally became chiefs, it is evident that inheritance was an important factor, and that chieftainship was a regulated and established institution.

There were chiefs who headed tribes and were influential for several days' journey about. This is only natural under the superior solidarity of Yokuts organization. In addition, it is likely that there were lesser chiefs or headmen for the separate settlements in each tribe. Reports of confederacies of villages and bands formed by powerful chiefs probably rest on misinterpretation of the primacy of the tribal group over the village. The tribes had their chiefs born into them: they were not created by the chiefs. A chief of personality and judgment, especially if supported by wealth, would undoubtedly command attention and respect among his neighbors. But there is nothing to show that in the most favorable case he ever headed a formal league of tribes.

While chieftainship has been spoken of as if it were of the usual single-headed type, it was acually dual in tribes like the Tachi. There was a chief for each exogamic moiety. Whether this polarity applied to the tribal or the settlement heads is not clear. The authority of the pair was reckoned substantially equal; at least, they were expected to exercise it in cooperation. But the *Tohelyuwish* chief was accorded a certain precedence. It is possible that the head of every tribe was always of this division, and that the polarity of authority was more of a formal or ceremonial nature, a half-conscious reflection of the social bifurcation. At any rate, all historical and biographic accounts mention only one chief for each group.

Another position that was hereditary was that of the *winatum*, the messenger or herald. In a typical village the chief was supposed to have his house in the middle, a *winatum* at each end. When one of these heralds was sent to announce a festival he was paid by the invited guests. A chief in need of shell money for any purpose might send his *winatum* to chiefs elsewhere. These would gather their tribes, who would contribute what they thought proper to the occasion.

Two other offices were, if not hereditary, at least held for life. One of these was the clown, Yaudanchi *hiauta*, Yauelmani *hiletits*, Tachi *hohotich*, whose business it was to mock sacred ceremonies, speak contradictorily, be indecent, and act nonsensically. The *tongochim* or *tunosim* were the transvestite sexual perverts recognized by all North American tribes. Among the Yokuts they possessed one unusual privilege and obligation: they alone handled corpses and prepared the dead for burial or cremation, but were entitled to keep for themselves any part of the property placed with the body. Both at the immediate and the annual mourning ceremonies they conducted the singing and led in the dancing. It is clear, once the character of these persons' peculiarity is understood, that they were not delegated to their status, but entered it, from childhood on, by choice or in response to an irresistible call of their natures.

WAR.

Very little is known of Yokuts warfare. The tribes seem generally to have acted as units when conflicts arose. This should have given them some advantage of solidarity and numbers over most of their neighbors; but there is nothing to show that they were specially feared. - Conflicts between tribes were apparently about as frequent as with aliens; and with many of their neighbors they were on friendly and even intimate terms. The Yokuts were evidently on the whole a peaceable people.

It has been said that they did not scalp. As an absolute statement, this is surely incorrect, for a myth tells how the prairie falcon after a battle hung the hair of his slain foes on trees, where it can be seen to-day as moss. But this is certainly a strange use to which to put trophies, and one arguing a lack of the usual Indian sense of such matters. There also appears to be no record of any Yokuts scalp celebration or victory dance. It can accordingly be concluded that scalping customs were of relatively little moment in Yokuts life.

MONEY.

Ordinary money consisted of strings of shell disks, of the wampum type, *keha*. During the past hundred years the Yokuts derived at least part of their supply of this currency through visits to the ocean. It is uncertain whether such trips were made in purely aboriginal times. The unit of measurement in the north was the *chok*, one and a half times the circumference of the hand. In the south the *chok* was somewhat shorter, and was reckoned as half the *hista*, two times the circumference of the hand.

Long perforated cylinders, perhaps made from the columellæ of univalves or from clams of unusual size, were called *humna* or *humana*, and were exceedingly valuable. They came from the south, probably from the Chumash.

GREETINGS.

There was little or no handshaking before the white man introduced the custom. Kissing was another undeveloped greeting. Mothers kissed their children, and lovers each other in seclusion; but no one else. The usual greeting is *hileu ma tanin*, "where are you going?" An old form, now less used, is, in foothill dialect, *ma-wit hide*, "you, hello"; more literally, "you, where?"

Like some other Californians, the Yokuts call the years "worlds." *P'a'an tanzhi*, "world went," denotes the lapse of a year.

BIRTH.

A woman about to give birth sat on the ground grasping a stake set up before her. At the moment of parturition she was raised by an assistant who grasped her from behind. The umbilical cord was tied with one of the mother's hairs, and severed with a knife of cane or elder wood, according to locality. The Chukchansi buried the cord; the Tachi preserved it by having the child wear it over its abdomen.

Husband and wife were under equal restrictions after the birth of a child. They ate no meat or hard food, and did not cook, hunt, work, or touch tools. The Yokuts attached the greatest importance to these observances, some of which were continued until the remnant of the cord dropped from the child's navel. and others for several months.

The monthly condition of women—which was thought to be connected with the dark period of the moon—was viewed with less scrupulous abhorrence by the Yokuts than among many tribes.

There was no separate menstrual hut, nor any dance nor public ceremony at a girl's adolescence. For six days a woman took no meat,
fish, or cold water. Some tribes allowed her to cook, work, and stay
by the sick; others forbade her to prepare food or to leave the house.
The additional observances at puberty were unusually slight, the
most regular being the prohibition against the head being scratched
with anything but a stick—a peculiarly deep-seated bit of taboo,
encountered among Pacific coast tribes as far as Alaska.

NAMES.

The name of the dead could under no circumstances be spoken.
For this reason a new appellation was assumed on the death of any
namesake. Among the southerly tribes the inconvenience caused by
this practice was guarded against by the custom of each child receiving two names, one to be used as a reserve in emergency, as it
were. If nevertheless both namesakes died, the person deprived of
his designations was spoken of and addressed as *k'amun hoyowosh*,
" No-name." Many names are meaningless; some denote animals or
objects, such as " Buzzard," " Otter," " Pine nut "; a few are names
of tribes, as Pitkachi, Yaudach; many are verbs: " Tap," " See,"
" Make-fire," " Dead," to which may be added the curious one of
" Seven." Almost all names were those of ancestors or older relatives.

DEATH AND MOURNING OBSERVANCES.

The Yaudanchi and Yauelmani buried their dead unless they died
at a distance, when they were cremated and the ashes interred in the
graveyard of their home town. The underlying idea seems to have
been to deposit the remains where the person had lived. All California Indians have strong sentiments on this point; old people will
express satisfaction at the prospect of being buried adjacent to the
house in which they were born. The Tachi, like some Costanoan
groups, burned every one of any account, believing that burial gave
wizards an opportunity to steal the hair of the deceased and thus
evoke their ghosts; but they also buried the ashes. A group of
ancient bodies discovered in the Buena Vista hills, in Tulamni territory, included some skeletons painstakingly wrapped in strings or
tules (Pl. 41), and others incompletely cremated before burial.
Perhaps they perished in an attacked and burning house. The Chukchansi left the body one night; then four men carried it on a litter
to the funeral pyre.

The favorite of Yokuts ritual impositions, the abstention from
meat, applied also to mourners for a period of a month. The alleged
reasons are that one would be eating the flesh of his child, or kill his
second wife. The Yaudanchi absolved the mourner only after he
had paid a friend for the privilege; the friend, if the same occasion

came to him, would buy himself free with a larger amount. Among all the Yokuts, parents and spouses were subject to this fast, and sons, daughters, and grandparents exempt; some tribes extended the practice also to brothers, sisters, or near relatives by marriage. Burning the hair short in mourning is a practice which the Yokuts share with all Californian and many other American peoples. As is also usual, men sacrificed less of this adornment than women. The central Californian custom which required a wife to pitch her face and not remove same for a year or until the next annual mourning ceremony, has been reported only from the Chukchansi. The Yaudanchi mourners merely refrained from washing or scraping their face during the briefer period in which they ate no meat.

The body of the dead was not only bewailed but sung over and danced for by the bereaved and the professional mourners or *tongochim*. After each song the latter clapped their hands and the relatives, still standing up, resumed their crying.

The Tachi held a more elaborate ceremony, known as *tonochmin hatim*, "Tonochims' dance," on the occasion of the first gathering after a death. In this the performers wear long false hair, made to project over the forehead like a beak. They represent long-billed birds called *yakeyaknan*, perhaps loons. They have the privilege of taking for themselves any property, which must be redeemed by the owners after the dance. They draw a mark on the ground; whoever crosses this is captured by them and thought to be unable to leave his imaginary inclosure. Even should he escape his watchers, it is believed some mysterious force would compel him to return against his will. Such a person must have his liberty redeemed by payment, else he is kept in confinement until the conclusion of the ceremony. This ritual would appear to have been a local custom.

Toward the end of summer an annual public mourning ceremony was held, called *lakinan*, *lakinanit*, or *tawadjnawash*. This undoubtedly had the greatest hold on the minds of the Yokuts of any of their rituals. It continued for several nights on lines similar to the crying, dancing, and singing over the unburied dead, the *tongochim* taking the same part. The last night ended in a spectacular climax with a destruction of property in honor of the departed, plus special features that varied from tribe to tribe.

Among the Yaudanchi, the mourners, who have been indoors or under a shade while the *tongochim* have been dancing, notify the latter, through the official herald, of their coming. They then approach carrying frames or figures dressed to represent the dead. Standing inside the circle of singing *tongochim*, they sway the images as if to thrust them into the fire that burns in the middle. At the end of each song the *tongochim* clap and the mourners burst into wails. After daybreak the figures are finally burned, and beads, baskets.

and other property are tossed to the *tongochim*, who though already liberally paid, are entitled to keep all that they secure in the scramble. Other valuables are burned with the images.

The use of effigies is of interest because duplicated among many remote groups, but appears not to be participated in by such Yokuts tribes as the Chukchansi or Tachi. Among the latter, after dancing until morning, property is given to visitors through the medium of a sham fight in which they despoil the owners. After this the chief mourner, who has arranged the ceremony and provided food for the guests, wanders through the village crying.

Among the Chukchansi the ritual of the final night takes on many features of the corresponding practices of the neighboring Miwok, whose *yalaka* ceremony they identify with their own *lakinan*. There are two fires, one for the men, the other for the women. The chief is posted at the latter, whence he delivers loud orations, in a peculiar abrupt enunciation. Such "preaching," as the Indians now term it, is indulged in on ceremonial occasions also by the Pomo, the Patwin, the Maidu, the Mohave, the Luiseño, and no doubt most other tribes in the State. Around each fire dancing goes on in a contraclockwise circle, the men holding poles from which hang valuables, the women baskets, and the singers standing outside the circles. Once during the night, and again toward morning, the men and women change to each others' fires. Finally the displayed property is burned in the men's fire. This act is called *tulo* or *yuyahin*, and marks the end of the ceremony. After this the visitors are paid by the residents of the town for purifying them by washing them with water in which a scented plant, *mechini*, has been steeped.

A joyous aftermath during the ensuing day marks the definite cessation of mourning. This is the *ka'm* or *wotii*, meaning simply dance. The step of this, indeed, is the same as that practiced by the *tongochim* during the preceding funerary ritual, and in fact over the unburied dead. It consists of an alternate high lifting of each leg at intervals of a second or less and stamping it down with violence, the performers meanwhile standing still or traveling in a circle. On this occasion of pleasurable reaction the dancers are for the first time painted—the men black, the women red, among the Yaudanchi—and they wear, so far as they possess them, the most elaborate and distinctive of Yokuts regalia: high crowns of crow and long magpie feathers, and skirts of strings of eagle down. Among the Chukchansi the men line up in a row, the women behind them, both facing north. Man after man then pays a woman for taking her from her place, and the couple dance before the double row.

CHAPTER 34.

THE YOKUTS: CULTS.

THE JIMSON WEED INITIATION.

Next to the great mourning ceremony of the Yokuts is to be ranked
a boy's initiation, which centered around the narcotic, and therefore
supernatural, effects of a drug pervading the roots of the Jimson
weed, *Datura meteloides*, commonly known in California by its
Mexican name, toloache.[1] The Yokuts called the plant *tanai* and
the rite *tanyuwish*, which might be translated as "Jimson weeding."

The initiation was into manhood and tribal status, rather than to
membership in any organization. It was therefore in a sense a boy's
puberty ceremony, which was given a distinctive character by intoxication. The same type of ritual prevailed among all the Shoshoneans, and perhaps the Chumash, of southern California. Its
occurrence among the Yokuts is only one of several instances of
customs shared by them with the groups to the south.

To the west there are reports that the Salinan villages followed the
cult, although it is unfortunately not wholly certain that they possessed the custom before the missionaries introduced Yokuts among
them. To the north the Miwok did not drink Jimson weed: in fact,
it probably grows little in their habitat. The northernmost Yokuts
hill tribes, such as the Chukchansi, practiced the rite feebly, if at all,
and the Chauchila are said to have refrained from it altogether. On
the other hand, the Miwok declare that their Yokuts neighbors of
the plains of Stanislaus River had a Jimson weed ceremony. The
cult may have gone farther north than this, to the extreme tribes of
the lowest San Joaquin, since the plant occurs as far north as Stock-

---

[1] W. E. Safford, Daturas of the Old World and New, Smithsonian Report for 1920,
537–567, 1922, gives the following Daturas: *D. meteloides*, Mexico, Utah, California,
used by the Zuñi, Walapai, Luiseño, Yokuts; Aztec name, *coatlxoxuhqui,* "green snake
weed," *ololiuhqui,* its seed. *D. discolor,* closely allied to *D. meteloides,* Mexico and
southwestern U. S.; *toloache;* more common at Yuma than *D. meteloides* (and therefore
probably the species employed by the Yuma and Mohave). *D. innoxia,* Mexico; Aztec
name, *nacazcul* and *toloatzin.* *D. stramonium,* Jamestown weed, Mexico and eastern
U. S.; Aztec name *tlapatl.*

ton in the hot plains. Among Maidu and Wintun there is a complete lack of reference to the plant, its use or any similar ritual. The Yokuts thus were the only Penutians, and virtually the only central Californians, to adhere to the custom. It is hard to believe that they acquired it otherwise than from the south, and that it can be anything but a form of the religion which had its presumable origin among the Gabrielino, among whom its manifestations are most elaborate.

Indians find it difficult to fix the age of the participants, but these are always described as boys, except among the Dumna and San Joaquin tribes, where young men and middle-aged men are specifically mentioned. The estimate of 12 to 15 years, or before sexual intercourse, made by one ancient southern Yokuts is therefore likely to be correct. It is of interest that this man himself never took the drug until in manhood he broke his arm. He then drank the decoction 12 times on alternate nights, remaining throughout in a stupor. The advantage of such a period of quiet during the setting of a bone must have been great. Evidently, however, the intoxication as a pure rite was not considered so overwhelmingly essential as to be enforced on every individual. On the other hand, another old southern Yokuts took the plant ritually three times, his father speaking the requisite prayer before the drinking. On the first occasion the boy was stupefied for six days; the second time three days; the third time he did not "sleep" at all, but walked about as if drunk.

The drug is not only a narcotic but produces visions. This is unquestionably the cause of the tremendous supernatural power ascribed to it, and of its selection as the foundation of an important public ritual. The vision producing effect must also have been enhanced by the preceding period of fasting. Expectation, based on current folkways, would lead the novices to see even inanimate objects as persons, as is said to have happened.

There was no formal structure erected for the ceremony. The root extract was drunk outdoors. During the period of fasting the participants were withdrawn from the public, usually remaining in a separate house or booth. They ate, in conformity with usual Yokuts ceremonial practice, no meat or solid food, and drank no pure or cold water, subsisting on thin acorn soup. The duration of the fast seems to have varied; six days may have been a common period, six being the number most frequently employed by these people in ritual connection. During this time the old man in charge of the ceremony directed the boys' actions, spoke to them of the origin of the world, and preached to them regarding their own future. He himself was expected to sleep little, but to go out at night, deposit eagle down on the ground, and pray.

The Jimson weed roots were crushed and soaked for some days. When the time for drinking came, the old man took the basket of liquid and said:

> Drink this water for Tüüsiut;
> Drink this water for that Pamasiut;
> Drink this water for that Yuhahait.

Twice he moved the basket toward the novice; the third time he held it toward the novice's mouth. When all the boys had drunk, they were taken away from the village, to places where they would be undisturbed, by older men who watched over them. The boys seem to have slept off their intoxication outdoors; as an open-air affair, the ceremony was made during the dry season, apparently in spring.

The participants underwent the rite for their own good. The Jimson weed would give them health, long life, ability to dodge arrows in battle, and general prosperity.

If a boy vomited his dose of drug, it was taken as a sign that he would die, and his relatives paid the old master of ceremonies for praying to avert this threatening fate.

Such was the ritual among the southern Yokuts. The Dumna, among whom the participants were men, practiced it somewhat differently. The roots were shaved instead of pounded. The master of ceremonies is mentioned not as having prayed, but as singing, before giving the liquid. The drinking took place in the sweat house and was followed, before the intoxication took effect, by a brief dance of the participants. Men would experience or obtain what they saw in their visions; the sight of beads would make the dreamer wealthy.

THE RATTLESNAKE CEREMONY.

Other public ceremonials of the Yokuts were in the hands of medicine men. They were not performed by participants following an anciently established ritual learned from preceding generations, nor by initiates into an esoteric cult or priesthood, but by shamans who, in their own persons, held communication with the source of the supernatural. The ceremonies were in essence a demonstration of the *tipni*, the magic power, possessed by these men—sometimes for the public good, at others merely as exhibitions.

The most spectacular of these shaman's performances was a rattlesnake ceremony, somewhat suggesting the famous snake dance of the Arizona Hopi. The Yokuts called this institution, according to dialect, *Daidangich*, *Datela*, or *Datlawash*, namely, " stepping on."

Early in spring, before the snakes had come out, the *tüüdum* or men to whom a rattlesnake had spoken in their dreams, executed the rite in order that none of the people might be bitten during the ensuing year. Proceeding in a procession to a rattlesnake den, they stamped and whistled before it, the head shaman directly facing the hole, the others on the sides to cut off the return of such snakes as might falter at the impending ordeal.

Soon, it is said, the snakes would emerge, usually preceded, it was believed, by a large lizard, and, drawn on by the leading shaman, they crawled straight to his feet, where they buried themselves in a winnowing basket filled with eagle down. Each medicine man in turn pointed out the snake he considered his, distracted its attention by swinging his *wacham* or hand-feathers, seized it, and carried it off in a sack. The worst snake of the lot was left for the head "doctor."

In the evening the tribe gathered under the inevitable shade. While the singers chanted particular melodies to the accompaniment of cocoon rattles the snake shamans walked about whistling, each with his death-bearing sack. They wore down-filled head nets and were painted in alternate horizontal stripes of white and red drawn across the body and limbs. From time to time they placed their bags on the heads of spectators, declaring that thus they determined who was subject to snake bite during the year.

On the following day these prospective victims of the serpents are cured in anticipation in order to prevent their being bitten. Although their infection is entirely imaginary and future, it is treated by the snake shamans by their usual medical means of sucking. The doctors even profess to extract from the not yet existing wound the actual poison—usually a rat's tail or tooth or a small snake—which has already been injected into the body by the future piercing of the skin by the rattlesnake's fangs. This is certainly magic with a vengeance; and it is difficult to imagine a logic of causality more in conflict with our own.

This precaution for the health of the community having been taken, the snake shamans display their powers to the multitude. They play with the snakes, throw them about, tease them to anger, allow them to bite themselves, and even hold them out hanging by their fangs from the thumb or hand.

The *kuyohoch* or "shaman killers"—in California the doctor is also potentially a nefarious wizard—then appear. Pretending to be trying to shoot the rattlesnake shamans, they make these beg for their lives and pay ransom for being spared.

The last act of the ceremony, the "stepping" itself, is also costly to the shamans, who, far from exploiting the community through their powers, as we might anticipate, are forced to accumulate much property in order to pass through the rite. The rattlesnakes are now in a small hole outdoors. The people come with sticks from which hang crude imitations of shell money; the chiefs' prerogative is to bear poles of such length that they can be made only by splicing. Everyone professes a strong wish to prod the snakes in the pit. The shamans feel equal alarm for the safety of their darlings, and purchase the lives of them by paying each man the equivalent in real money of the length of bark or rag on his stick.

Finally the entire community files past the hole, each man, woman, or child placing the right foot into or over it. This insures that for a year every approached snake will rattle in warning instead of striking blindly; and with this act the ceremony ends.

A rattlesnake ceremony song:

> The king snake said to the rattlesnake:
> Do not touch me!
> You can do nothing with me.
> Lying with your belly full,
> Rattlesnake of the rock pile,
> Do not touch me!
> There is nothing you can do,
> You rattlesnake with your belly full,
> Lying where the ground-squirrel holes are thick.
> Do not touch me!
> What can you do to me?
> Rattlesnake in the tree clump,
> Stretched in the shade,
> You can do nothing;
> Do not touch me!
> Rattlesnake of the plains,
> You whose white eye
> The sun shines on,
> Do not touch me!

The implied idea probably is that the repetition of the words used by the king snake when he successfully defied and evaded his venomous opponent will bring about a recurrence of his safety for the human being who in his turn encounters a rattlesnake.

Such was the Yaudanchi practice, which the Yauelmani, Tachi, and Kashowu approximated. Only the Chukchansi are again un-Yokuts-like and dispense with the ceremony.

OTHER CEREMONIES.

The *Heshwash*, or "hiding" ceremony, is a public intertribal contest of medicine men, who test their superiority in bewitching one another. The shamans dress as for a dance. In the evening they seat themselves in two parties under a shade, while special *heshwash* songs are sung to cocoon rattling and the expectant multitude watches. The performers try to inject their disease objects or "poison " into their opponents, and strike at each other with winnowing baskets. Often, when struck, they are able to extract the magic missile, but sometimes fail, whereupon the victors shout " *Wuwuwu-wuwu!* " and receive pay for withdrawing their paralyzing power. On the first evening the performance is brief, a sort of warming up. The next night the shamans go at each other in earnest, and contend until morning. Although no public benefit whatever results, this rite appears to be rated more highly than the rattlesnake ceremony, on the ground that a greater number of medicine men participate. Shamans of special powers as opposed to bewitching and curative abilities do not enter the *heshwash:* rain, bear, and snake " doctors " stay out.

This contest of supernatural abilities has northern parallels; as among the Yuki in their *hulk'ilal* ceremonies. But the setting, meaning, and organization of the performances are different. In the one case there is a secret society of initiated impersonators; in the other an assembly of shamans with personally acquired powers. A nearer parallel is found among the Maidu shamans' competitions.

The *Ohowish* or " wishing " ceremony is also a pure demonstration of supernatural power. Sleight of hand is the central feature, as suggestion is in the *heshwash.* Several shamans gather in a specially made house or booth, behind a screen of tules, and perform to songs appropriate to the occasion. The skins of beavers and otters hang about the walls. These animals are the personal spirits of the *oho-wich* medicine men, the " wishers " or " willers," whose power seems connected with water, as among their achievements mentioned is that of making fish in a vessel of water. Such displays appear to be the kernel of the ceremony, which ends toward morning by the performing shamans " fighting " one another magically.

The medicine bags here referred to savor of Plains Indian ideas more than of native Californian practices; although there is Pomo parallel.

The *Heshwash* and *Ohowish* extend from the southernmost tribes at least to the Tachi and Gashown; the habits of the Chukchansi are not known.

The *Ha'ishat* is a nonshamanistic dance, whose relation to other ceremonies, or purpose other than pleasure, has not become clear. A place and time, perhaps 12 days ahead, are appointed. The invitees then busy themselves securing quantities of food, laden with which they start out, and make camp for the night a mile or more away from the designated spot. In the morning the entire tribe, men, women, and children, every one carrying his pack of provisions, dance in a long single file, to the usual Yokuts " piston-rod step," all the way in to the meeting place. This must have been a most picturesque spectacle when several tribes gathered at once; but it has the appearance of being only a prelude.

The eternal yellow-hammer forehead bands of the California Indians are not lacking among the Yokuts; but the characteristic dance costume of these tribes comprised the *chohun*, a skirt of strings of eagle down, and the *djuh*, a tall headdress of tail plumes of magpies, encircled at the base by crow feathers (Fig. 44). The eagle-down skirt extends across the Sierra to the Shoshonean tribes as far east as Death Valley (Pl. 42). It has not been reported from any part of interior California other than the Yokuts, and in southern Cali-

fornia its place is taken by a skirt of large eagle feathers. In this garment we have thus to recognize either a local development or an influence from the Great Basin. The magpie and crow headdress is found, with some slight variation, among the Maidu and Patwin; and it may accordingly be assumed for the intervening Miwok also, though not yet reported from them. With the Maidu, this ornament is part of the apparel of god impersonators, such as the *Sili* and Bear spirit; among the Yokuts, who do not indulge in such esoteric representations, it is worn in the mourning dance, in the comple-

FIG. 44.—Yokuts dance headdress of magpie and crow feathers.

mentary dance of rejoicing, and by shamans. It is a familiar fact that the same article or element of civilization is frequently utilized for widely different purposes, and in quite diverse connections or meanings, by distinct nations.

The *djuh* was held in place by a stick jammed through its base and the hair as bunched under a tightly drawn head net—the usual central Californian device for fastening large feather ornaments to the head. The *chohun* was made from the down of a large water bird, called *goldat* by the valley tribes, when they experienced difficulty in securing a sufficient supply of eagles. Sticks tipped with the showy crest feathers of the mountain quail were passed through the pierced ear lobes.

Two other ornaments were much used by the Yokuts: the *wacham* and the *notanat*. The former was a loose bunch of feathers carried in the hand and swinging with every motion; the latter, a belt, also worn as leg band, of strings of twisted hair cut off by mourners. This

PLATE 41

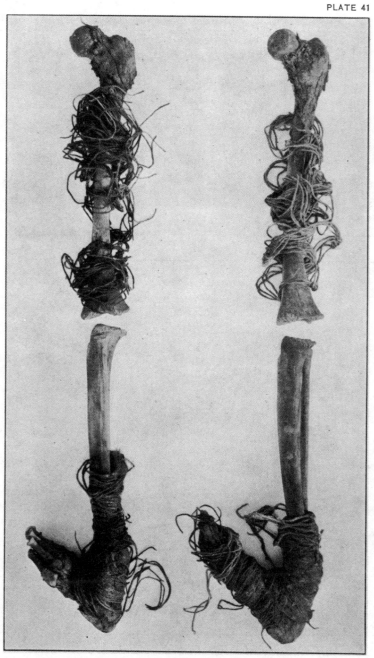

CORD-WRAPPED LEG REMAINS, BUENA VISTA LAKE

PLATE 42

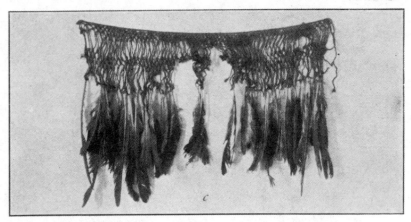

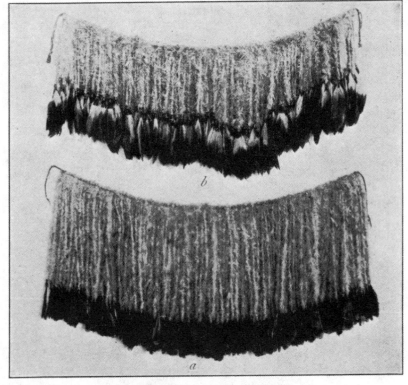

FEATHER DANCE SKIRTS

a, Koso; *b*, Yokuts; *c*, Luiseño

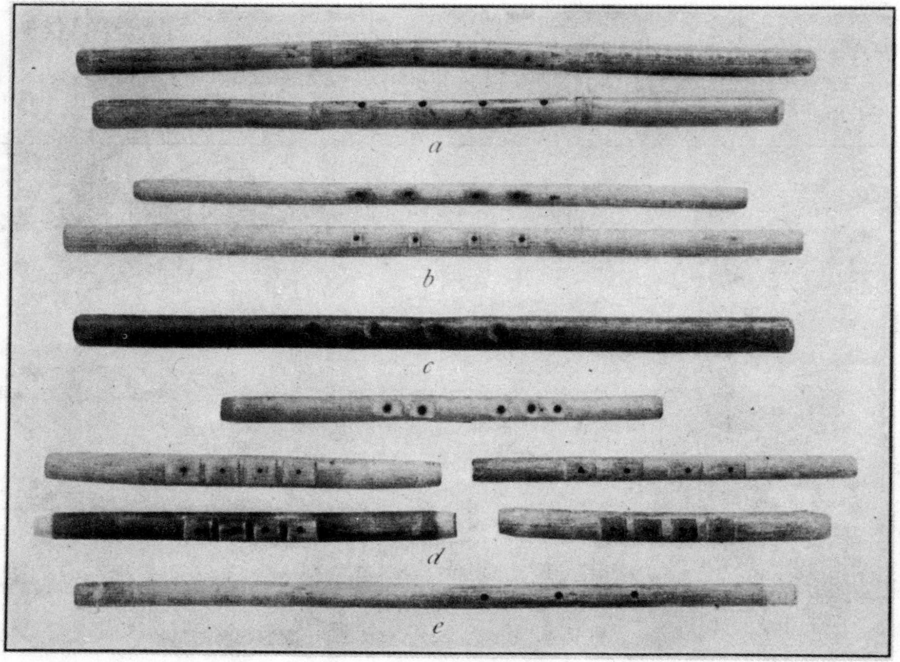

PLATE 43

FLUTES

a, Yuma; *b*, Yokuts; *c*, Miwok; *d*, Pomo; *e*, Karok

PLATE 44

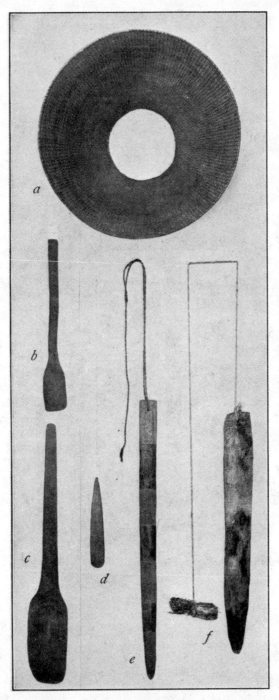

a, Kitanemuk mortar hopper. Acorn gruel stirrers: *b,* Diegueño;
c, Northern Wintun. Bull-roarers: *d,* Yokuts; *e,* Luiseño;
f, Pomo

hair belt recurs as far to the north as the Shastan tribes. Its distribution is likely to have been continuous over a wide area, but there are reports of its use from only a few points.

The dance rattle was the same cleft stick as prevails over all of central California; likewise, the cocoon implement was associated with the shaman. The deer-hoof rattle of parts of northern California and the turtle shell and gourd instruments of the south were unknown. The flute was the usual tube, blown from the end over its edge; the holes were commonly four, grouped in pairs, but without definite rule as to relations of distance. (Pl. 43, *b*.) It was thought to have been invented by the falcon. Drums were not employed by the Yokuts: the foot drum of the Sacramento drainage appears to be part of the dance house. The bull roarer was called *himhimna, huhuudech*, or *hmhm'udech*. It was a toy; but whether it had other purpose and potency is not known. (Pl. 44.)

PRAYERS.

Short prayers in fixed form are spoken on a variety of occasions and are evidently a definite element of Yokuts culture.

When there is an eclipse, this is said:

> Leave me a little of the sun!
> Do not devour it altogether from me!
> Leave me a little!

If one wishes to drink of a strange body of water, he says:

> Let us live long in this world!
> This is our water!

The dead are addressed thus by the Tachi:

> You are going to another land.
> You will like that land.
> You shall not stay here.

There is here an expression of the world-wide sentiment that the career of the departed in this world is finished, that the break is final, and that any attempt at return can only be disastrous to the living and is not desired.

As the language knows no exhortative of the second person, nor any form corresponding to our precative "may," these speeches are either in the unvarnished command of the imperative or direct statements in the indicative mode.

One of the most usual Yokuts offerings is tobacco; another, at least among the hill tribes and those of the south, is eagle down.

The ritualistic number of the Yokuts is most often 6, sometimes 12, not infrequently 7; 3 occurs occasionally, but it is not certain whether with any sense of significance. The universal 4 of the north central tribes, and the 5 and 10 of the northwestern Indians appear to be meaningless to the Yokuts.

MYTHOLOGY.

Yokuts mythology lacks the organization and leaning toward spirituality that characterize native beliefs in the region of the Sacramento Valley. Traditions are not built into a system, and speculation as to the mystery of the world and life is not even naïvely profound. The creators are all animals, with the Eagle at their head as wise and dignified chief. The Coyote is his presuming assistant, often ridiculous, at times inefficient; on other occasions, when not in direct competition with his chief, possessed of strange powers. He brings disaster into the world only rarely; death is the result of the Meadowlark's folly, or the desire of the insect Kokwiteit; but Coyote assents. He aids in securing fire, in stealing the sun for the future world, and advises the Eagle to send the Duck to dive for the earth from the primeval stump which alone projects from the universal first water. A favorite figure is *Limik*, the swiftly swooping Falcon, silent, determined, wise, a warrior, whose only food is tobacco, and whose supernatural abilities are great; but a victim in gambling. His coadjutor is his friend the Raven. The Condor is a plotter, a cannibal and robber, but he is overcome by the Falcon, and by the Eagle when he threatens the latter's supremacy. The Owl is a powerful shaman, the Antelope the swift runner who wins from Deer and helps to steal fire. The Hummingbird is Coyote's son, who excels his makeshift father.

This animal pantheon, varied and distinctive as it is, seems strange as set against the more abstract deities of the Maidu, the Wintun, and the Yuki; or had this aspect as long as it was believed that the Miwok alone observed totemism. Now that it is known that this set of beliefs extends to most of the Yokuts also, their traditions, uncoordinated as they remain on the surface, are perhaps more than mere fanciful beast fables, and may fit into a scheme more or less allied to the totemic classification and its connected dualistic plan of chieftainship, marriage, and ritual.

The southern Californian concepts of the god that dies—Wiyot, Matavilya, Tuchaipa—of the first Sky father and Earth mother; and of the birth and wanderings of mankind; together with many associated episodic incidents, are all lacking among the Yokuts—totally, it would appear. It is clear that mythically a sharp cleavage separates the San Joaquin Valley from the southern end of the State, and that the southwestern influences which have so profoundly permeated the tribes of the latter region, both in traditions and ritual, have not transcended the barrier of the Tehachapi.

The Yokuts Jimson weed puberty rite has already been referred to as of southern origin. The most specific development of this religion, however, a later cult developed by the Gabrielino and spread out from them, failed to reach the Yokuts. This is clear both from their nonuse of sand paintings and their ignorance of the great deity Chungichnish or any equivalent.

On the other hand, the Yauelmani, and perhaps other southern Yokuts tribes, appear to have borrowed from the nearer Shoshoneans or southern Californians, probably the Kitanemuk, the concept of a group of gods, apparently anthropomorphic, and associated with ritual rather than myth. Three of these, who have no exact Shoshonean counterpart, have already been mentioned in the Jimson weed rite; but the full number is seven, of whom four correspond in name to the first four among six Serrano deities. As referred to in an intoned prayer, recited not so much for the achievement of any specific wish as for the general fulfillment of good fortune, these deities are the following:

> Do you see me!
> See me, Tüüshiut!
> See me, Pamashiut!
> See me, Yuhahait!
> See me, Echepat!
> See me, Pitsuriut!
> See me, Tsukit!
> See me, Ukat!
> Do you all help me!
> My words are tied in one
> With the great mountains,
> With the great rocks,
> With the great trees,
> In one with my body
> And my heart.
> Do you all help me
> With supernatural power,
> And you, day,
> And you, night!
> All of you see me
> One with this world!

A certain vastness of conception and profoundness of feeling, rising above any petty concrete desire, can not be denied this petition, crude though the undeveloped vocabulary of its speech leaves its wording.

SHAMANISM.

The Yokuts shaman is called *antu* or *angtu*—with a reference to poisoning—by the southern tribes; *tuponot* by the Tachi; *teish*, "maker," by the Chukchansi. The latter word reappears in the south as *tesh* and with the Tachi as *teshich gonom* as the designation of the "rain doctors" or weather shamans. *Hopodno*, sometimes used as if a synonym, seems to have been the name of an individual of unusual repute in these matters who lived at or near Tejon about two generations ago. Perhaps his appellation too was at bottom a generic one.

The *ohowich*, the " willing " or " seeking " doctor, has already been mentioned. The bear doctor is called simply " grizzly bear," *noho'o* or *ngoho'o*, according to dialect.

MANA.

Supernatural power, beings, or things are called by all the Yokuts *tipni* or *chipni:* a word from which Tachi *tuponot* is probably derived by one of the vowel mutations characteristic of the language. The word *tipni* itself is likely to be connected with *tipin*, " above," in a spatial sense, or "top, high, sky, up." It is the obvious equivalent of *mana, orenda, wakanda,* and *manitou.* In some usages the term clearly refers to beings, monsters, or spirits. In other connections it is said that a man, say a shaman, is *tipni* or possibly that he has *tipni.* In the above prayer to the seven gods, the word seems to mean " with supernatural power "; but a translation by " supernatural ones " is also possible. Altogether, it is clear that *tipni* is used indifferently as a noun and as an adjective; and that it is employed, according to circumstance, to denote spirits, supernatural or monstrous beings of any sort, men who possess spiritual or magical power, and, if indications are not deceiving the essence or power or quality itself.

This diversity of usage seems to be as characteristic of the more familiar synonyms in other languages as of Yokuts *tipni;* and it follows, therefore, that the question of whether these words denote rather an essence or a definite personalized spirit in the literal sense is not a problem to be settled by psychological interpretation, but one for which the tools and knowledge of the philologist are indispensable, and that the latter's answer is likely to be that the terms are used with both meanings and adjectively as well as substantively; with reference on one occasion to quality, on others, to personality. There must have been a time when our own word "spirit " was capable of denoting in one sentence the breath itself, the physical flow of air from the lungs, and in the next an immaterial thing resembling the entire body of a man but possessed of faculties that do not belong to the body. Just so, to-day and among ourselves, " spirit " at times indubitably denotes such an anthropomorphic but intangible personality, and nothing else; at others, an abstract and impersonal essence or quality or force. It would be rash to maintain that its real meaning in our minds and in our civilization was only one of these two aspects and that when used in the other sense it was so used as a conscious metaphor or from deliberate desire to present as personal something known to be impersonal, or as general something known to be specifically limited. It is just as strained, or more so, to force this alternative on the less developed and simpler terminology of uncivilized people.

The choice that has been made between the understanding of *mana, orenda,* or *manitou* as denotive of an essence, or of a particularized ghostlike personality, has done violence to a distinctive quality of the concepts residing in these words, namely, their undifferentiated poise between our two extreme formulations. A native who has learned the significance of our phrases " essence," " pervading quality," " intangible diffused power," will of his own accord give these definitions for his own concept; but at other times he will as blithely render it by " spirit " in the sense of something limited, personal, and spatial.

With the Chukchansi, *beniti* means clairvoyant, and among the Yauelmani *suhua* denotes the faculty of magical creation out of nothing by means of blowing.

A ghost is *hichwaiu* or *hitwaia* to the Yokuts. The soul is called *ilit* by the Tachi. The word for heart, *honhon* or *honghong*, is not used in this sense.

There is bare possibility that shamanism, the individual relation of persons to what is *tipni,* is distantly related to the totemic observances and beliefs of the Yokuts, but specific evidences of direct connections are rare. One of the few is the coincidence that both the " pet " or captive or totemic animal, and the doctor's guardian spirit from whom his *tipni* power emanates, are called *puus* or *cheshesh,* " dog "; *cheshesh nim ngohoo,* " my dog is the grizzly bear," a Yaudanchi bear shaman says. But again, poverty of vocabulary can not be relied upon to prove a common growth of institutions.

SOURCE OF THE SHAMAN'S POWER.

The northern California idea of shamanistic power is bound up with the notion of control over small, animate, disease-bearing objects, these material " pains " having many of the faculties of spirits. This special form of the nearly universal concept that sickness is produced by an injected substance is not even in rudiment a part of the San Joaquin Valley culture. The Yokuts shaman owns a spirit. This may be a monster, or an animal that turns into a man, or possibly a permanently disembodied spirit. It is certainly most often one of the two former. It may be met in actuality, or dreamed of, or both. But it is a being, with an independent existence, and with a defined relation between it and the medicine man; not a little noxious thing, a sort of animated fetish or amulet, that he swallows and keeps inside his body.

Shamanistic power among the Yokuts comes both unsought and to men desirous of acquiring it. It is most commonly derived from animals or monsters inhabiting the water, or from their appearances in dreams after their haunts have been frequented; but visits by dead relatives, which are so frequent a stimulus among the northern California tribes, are also mentioned as a source of the conferment. The bear doctor, of course, has bears as his spirit; the rattlesnake shaman, the sun, as with the Yuki. The rain doctor alone has his power associated more directly with an amulet than with any spirit.

The prospective Tachi doctor bathes nightly for a winter in pools, springs, or water holes, until the inhabiting being meets and instructs him, or comes to him in his sleep. In one such hole lives a six-mouthed rattlesnake; in another, a white water snake; in a third, a hawk which can occasionally be seen flying into or out of its home below the surface. A Yaudanchi, with two boy companions, caught a *wetapkul*, a long, large-eyed fish, which makes doctors by swallowing them. At once a great whirlwind circled, the trees broke, the water rose, and the three persons fled for their lives. That night in his sleep the monster came to the young man and gave him this song:

> Whose is this fish to shoot?
> Your hand feathers are panting!

The hand feathers are the *wacham* dance ornament used by doctors; they seem to symbolize the moving gills of the water monster.

Another southern Yokuts at dusk met two strangers, who took him with them into the stream, through two doors, one formed of a snake, one of a turtle. He had become unconscious. Inside their house the otters, for such they had become, resumed human shape. They offered *tipni* power to their guest, with the threat that he could not live if he refused. He took the gift, but asked for instructions concerning it. " You shall cure the sick, not kill human beings," was the naïve order he received with his song. When the man awoke he was on land once more, and dry as if he had never left the earth. This is his song:

> The other says: Run in the brush;
> Run in the brush, I hear continually.

Two instances of the genesis of bear doctors:

A Yaudanchi hunter was taken by a grizzly into its hidden house inside the rock, where it drew off its skin and became human. Others joined the circle, and a dance began. Suddenly a dog barked and the dance stopped. The man remained with his hosts several days.

A Tachi bathed at night. At last a bear appeared in his dreams and instructed him. After many years, not before middle life, he reached the power of becoming a bear at will. He swam in a pool, emerged as the animal, and went on his errand. To resume human shape a plunge into the same pool was necessary.

The long period of training before full power is attained seems characteristic for Yokuts bear shamans, as for Yuki.

A bear doctor's song:

> Again he comes,
> Again the grizzly bear comes to me.

A shaman named Mayemai dreamed that his father sang to him:

> Listen to me,
> Mayemai!
> There in the east
> I shall emerge
> Twirling
> My hand feathers.

An eagle dance song, originally dreamed:

> The earth quakes.
> See my eagle
> Emerging at the open place!

Coyote songs, dreamed, and perhaps also of moiety totemic reference:

> Whirling in front of you,
> It is mourned for,
> The rope of our world
>
> I am coyote,
> We are coyotes.
> The earth told them,
> The earth said:
> You shall not continually scratch me.

Coyote said:
> What am I?
> I am coyote.
> I am of the water.
> What am I?
> I am coyote.

The frankness of these songs in allusions to the supernatural experience and mention of the guardian, and that in words which are far less altered to fit the rhythm than is customary in California, is remarkable.

The doctor's initiation dance of northern California has not been referred to among the Yokuts and seems not to have been practiced.

DISEASE AND CURE.

Three principal methods of curing disease are followed, besides the administration of herbs and parts of animals. Sucking the disease object, a pebble or bit of something, is universal. This is linked with bloodletting and singing. The Tachi class themselves with the northern tribes as addicted to the former, the southerners as specialists in the latter. A good southern doctor can even kill by his song or restore the dead to life, provided he is summoned in time. Bloodletting was often joined with sucking. The skin was cut, and first blood and then the disease object drawn out. Among the Chukchansi, who have women practitioners as well as men, the inferior shamans sucked only blood. Cuts between the eyes were commonly made for headache, sleepwalking, and other chronic but light ailments. Most of the Chukchansi even to-day carry several such scars.

The use of irritants was not unknown. For stomach ache ants were applied to the abdomen; if the pain did not yield, the insects were wrapped in eagle down and swallowed.

His pipe was one of the resources of a doctor; he could cause sickness by blowing tobacco smoke, and perhaps cure by the same method.

The shaman's rattle was the usual California one, but was a little thing with but one or two cocoons. (Fig. 37, a.) Occasionally a larger number of cocoons were tied up in a mass of feathers. (Fig. 37, f.) A favorite habit was for the doctor to sing softly to himself before lying down to sleep.

The repeatedly unsuccessful medicine man stood in danger of his own life, and it appears that violence was the end of members of the profession as often as among most California tribes. Even to-day American law has not entirely extirpated this system of reprisal. In the early reservation days at Tejon a Yauelmani shaman bewitched a Yaudanchi so that he awoke crazed and soon died. When the Yaudanchi slew the poisoner the Yauelmani were incensed at the summary fate of their compatriot. But one of their chiefs restrained them and they laid down their bows, which seems to have been the end of the matter except for talk.

BEAR SHAMANS.

The bear doctor did not cure disease, though there is a recorded instance of one who eased his daughter's childbirth by giving her bear's hair to drink. On the other hand, the Chukchansi accused bear doctors of making their private enemies ill by shooting little stones into them. Only the Tachi attributed particular curative powers to the song and dancing of the bear doctor. In fact the function of this class of shamans, other than as exhibitors of their powers, is not clear. They were difficult to keep killed; but they seem not to have been dreaded marauders or ferocious fighters as among the Pomo and Yuki. In the hunt, a shaman of this class might enter the retreat of a skulking bear to rout him out.

The Chukchansi know of a female shaman who on being killed and buried emerged from the ground in the shape of a bear and walked off unmolested. The Tachi ascribe to their bear doctors, and of course especially to those of their neighbors, the faculty of surviving repeated killings in their bear shape: the medicine man merely returns to his home the next night as if nothing had happened. A famous shaman of this kind was at San Luis Obispo in mission times, they declare. Once he was trapped or roped, in his animal form, and had the misadventure of being dragged in to fight a bull. This tale seems to include the Chumash among the tribes that believed in bear doctors.

While the valley Tachi bear doctor might dance over a patient, the Choinimni and Yaudanchi had a public dance of such personages, held outdoors. The exhibition is described as harmless in effect, and the dancers were paid, but the purpose of the demonstration, except as a demonstration, is obscure. Obviously the ceremony falls into the same class as the *Ohowish*, *Heshwash*, and rattlesnake stepping rites already mentioned. The two or three participants were painted entirely black, and were naked save for a headband of eagle down and a claw necklace, or skin around the loins, that had been taken from the animal they controlled. The dance was clearly mimetic. The feet were held together, the body leaned forward, the hands hung down. The step was a short stiff leap with a heavy land. Gradually the doctors jumped to their song, growled, spread their fingers like claws, and leaped forward as if to seize a foe.

RATTLESNAKE SHAMANS.

The Chukchansi, among whom the public stepping ceremony was lacking or slenderly developed, nevertheless had shamans who cured rattlesnake bites. The poison was sucked out with a bone whistle, pointed, however, at the sun, and not at the bitten part. The poison was then displayed as a salivalike string—no doubt from the shaman's own mouth—and put away in a basket to be kept by him. The connection of rattlesnake and sun has already been alluded to as regards the shaman's spirit. The Yaudanchi rattlesnake doctor extracted gopher teeth by direct sucking: as the snake feeds on gophers, it retains their teeth to inject as poison.

Rattlesnake doctors are said to have received only moderate fees, as contrasted with the bankrupting payment to the Yuki shaman; and rattlesnakes are declared to have been killed, though reluctance to do this is so great among most other California Indians that it may be supposed that even among the Yokuts a common man would not lightly perform the act.

WEATHER SHAMANS.

The weather doctor chiefly brought on rain, perhaps when it was needed, more often, it appears, like Samuel before the people, to prove his power. Again the national inclination toward public recognition of shamanistic displays is manifest. The famous Hopodno at Tejon, who was half Yauelmani and half Shoshonean Kawaiisu, staked the rain in a game, and when he lost promptly delivered it to the winners.

The Chukchansi mention only blowing and the dipping of fingers into water as means of making rain; but the Tachi and southern tribes describe cylindrical stones, 6 to 8 inches long, pointed at one end, as the necessary apparatus. Moistened or dipped a little into water, the amulet produced a shower; but if the doctor was angered, he plunged the whole stone in and a violent storm followed. These objects, which suggest the well-known "charm stones" of the California archaeologist, but were probably a distinct though similar type, were inherited from father to son; and the Tachi go so far as to say that the theft of his amulet would deprive the owner of his power. Spirits are nowhere mentioned directly in connection with the rain-making faculty.

CHAPTER 35.

THE YOKUTS: THE CONCRETE BASIS OF LIFE.

DRESS AND BODILY HABITS.

Clothing sufficed only for the very limits of decency, as we see them. Men wrapped a deerskin, *sep*, around the loins, or went naked. Old men in particular were wont to go without even this covering. Boys and little girls also were nude; but from the time of puberty on women wore a two-piece fringed skirt of the usual Californian type, the hind part larger. With the Yaudanchi, both portions were made of willow bark, as among the Mohave. The Chukchansi made the back piece of buckskin, the front of pounded masses of a long grass called *chulochul*. The well-known rabbit-fur blanket protected against cold and rain on occasion, and was excellent to sleep in. Moccasins of deer and elk skin were worn only as there was special need. Rude sandals of bear fur have been reported as worn in winter.

Women's hair was worn long, but for men the custom was more variable. Both sexes were wont to gather it under a string when at work. In mourning, men burned their hair off to the neck, women, for a near relative, close to the head. A glowing stick was used, and the Chukchansi controlled the singeing with a natural comb of *tumu*, which has close-set parallel branches.

Women, but not men, had their nose septum pierced for ornaments of bone.

Tattooing was more practiced in the north than in the south, and more extensively by women than by men. It ran in lines, zigzags, and rows of dots, chiefly down the chin and across from the corners of the mouth; the Mono style of marking the upper cheeks was not followed. The general type of women's face pattern tolerated infinite individual variety, as in the Yuki region; the Yurok and their neighbors clung strictly to a tribal style. Chukchansi women might be tattooed across breast, abdomen, arms, and legs also. The method followed was to rub charcoal dust into cuts made with flint or obsidian. Chukchansi face patterns are shown in Figures 45 *h–l*, 46 *m–o*.

Men frequently squatted rather than sat. For longer periods they sat on their heels, with toes turned together and hands on knees. The cross-legged position, the most common of all the world over, was not used, except perhaps on special occasions like gambling. Women stretched one leg out and folded the other back; or, at rest,

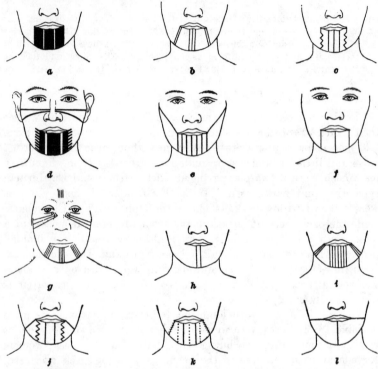

Fig. 45.—Women's tattoo. *a*, Yurok and northwestern tribes; *b*, *c*, San Francisco, probably Costanoan; *d*, Sinkyone; *e*, northwestern valley Maidu; *f*, northeastern and southern Maidu; *g*, Yuki; *h–l*, Chukchansi Yokuts. Compare the Wailaki, Yuki, Huchnom, and northern Pomo tattoos shown in Powers, Tribes of California, pages 116, 130, 140, 142, 144, 158.

drew the knees up and joined the hands in front of them. The Plains Indian woman's attitude, with both legs to one side, was not adopted. The habits of all the California Indians in these interesting matters are little known, but it is clear that custom and not inherited nature is the chief determinant. As at so many other points, nature seems at once to have furnished us a structure that permits a surprising variety of sustained positions, and to have deprived us of instincts favoring one rather than the other; so that culture has a clear opportunity to evolve the most diverse habits.

HOUSES.

The Yokuts built at least five kinds of dwellings.

1. Most distinctive was the mat-covered, gabled, communal *kawi* of the Tulamni, Hometwoli, Wowol, Chunut, and perhaps Tachi. The roof pitch was steep. Probably each family constructed its own portion, with door to front and back, closed at night with tule mats. Each household had its own space and fireplace, but there were no partitions, and one could look through from end to end.

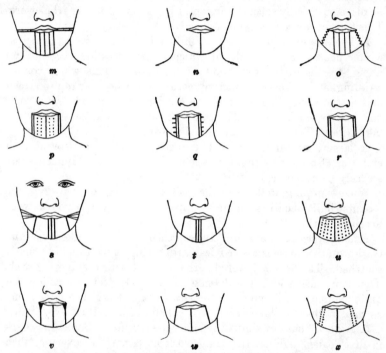

FIG. 46.—Women's and men's tattoo. Women: *m–o*, Chukchansi Yokuts; *p–u*, Mohave. Men: *v–x*, Mohave.

These houses sometimes ran to a size where they accommodated a little more than 10 families. A shade porch extended along the front. The tule stalks were sewn together with an eyed bone needle and string of tule fiber.

2. The Yauelmani and their neighbors of the southern plains off the lake approached this long structure in aligning their wedge-shaped tule houses or *dumlus*, but kept each contiguous family domicile separate.

3. The middle plains tribes, such as the Wechihit and Tachi, to-day build small tule houses of another type, elliptical or oblong

with rounded but vertical ends. There may be a ridgepole on two posts, with perhaps five poles planted along each side and bent over to the ridgepole. In this case the door is on one side of the front post. Or the ridgepole may be dispensed with and the poles bent all the way over or lashed together. The total length is only a dozen feet or so. The covering is of loose tule mats, each stalk wrapped to the next by a hitch in a single strand of string. Floor mats and bedding are sewn through. The Wechihit use a covering of tall *mohya* stems, reaching from the ground to the ridge, and held in place outside by several horizontal poles lashed to the framework. This type of house was called *te* or *chi*.

4. The Yaudanchi, though a hill tribe, built their principal winter houses or *te* of tule, of which a species called *shuyo* grows along streams to the very limit of the plains. This was a conical dwelling, and its most distinctive feature was a hoop at top to attach and at the same time separate the leaning poles of the framework, and leave a smoke hole. The tule mat covering was sewn as by the lake tribes. The houses were placed in rows.

A larger, ridged house, with two fireplaces and a door at each end, was also built by the Yaudanchi. In this a valley influence can scarcely be questioned.

When camping well up in the hills in summer, or traveling, the Yokuts built small structures, apparently conical, covered with brush or bark.

Among the northern hill tribes, such as the Chukchansi and Gashowu, the house is also conical with a ring at the top, but usually thatched. The floor is lowered perhaps a foot with the digging stick. The door faces south, the diameter is 12 to 15 feet, the height not quite as much. Allowing for the lack of tule, this is the same house as that of the Yaudanchi, but it is called *ho*, literally " live," " sit."

5. A bark house of similar type is called *samish*. Sometimes bark is first leaned against the framework as a partial covering, then brush thatch added, and the whole held fast by bands of pliable poles or withes tied around.

It is interesting that there is no reference anywhere to tule thatching. The thickness of this rush may make its sewing or binding into mats more practicable than bundling it into thatch. The Serrano and other southern Californians also built tule mat houses, but the Pomo employed tule thatch.

The *ch'iniu* or shade, a flat roof on posts, was used by all the Yokuts. It must have been almost indispensable in the intensely hot summers of the plains.

The sweat house, *mosh* or *mos*, is a true sudatory, oblong, dug down several feet, with a ridge log resting on two posts at the ends, and dirt covered. It was small, not over 15 feet in length, and in no sense a dance house or assembly chamber. Women never entered it. It was the regular sleeping place of the older men during the winter when they were at the home village. The door faced the creek, or south, and was sometimes sheltered by parallel windbreaks. Often on retiring, the inmates sang and sweated, perhaps in competition along the two sides, the fire being added to to make the opposite row cry out first that they had enough. Then came a plunge into the stream, and a return to dry and sleep. In the morning they ran shouting to the water again.

There is no house for dances and rituals. The rattlesnake "stepping," the mourning ceremony, and perhaps other rites were held in large roofless inclosures of brush, a sort of fence. This is the southern California form of ceremonial structure. North of the Yokuts it reaches to the Maidu as an adjunct of the mourning ceremony.

THE FOOD PROBLEM IN CALIFORNIA.

The California Indians are perhaps the most omnivorous group of tribes on the continent. The corn, salmon, buffalo, reindeer, or seal which formed the predominant staple in other regions, did indeed have a parallel in the acorn of California; but the parallel is striking rather than intrinsic.

To begin with, the oak is absent from many tracts. It does not grow in the higher mountains, in the desert, on most of the immediate coast; and it is at best rare in districts like the baked plains inhabited by the southern Yokuts valley tribes, a fact that may help to explain the permanent association and commingling of the majority of these tribes with their foothill neighbors. It is true that at worst it is rarely a far journey to an abundant growth of bearing acorns anywhere in California; but the availability of such supplies was greatly diminished by the habits of intense adherence to their limited soil followed by the great majority of divisions.

Then, where the acorn abounded, the practices both of collecting and of treating it led directly to the utilization also of other sources of nourishment. The farmer may and does hunt, or fish, or gather wild growths; but these activities, being of a different order, are a distraction from his regular pursuits, and an adjustment is necessary. Either the pursuit of wild foods becomes a subsidiary activity, indulged in intermittently as leisure affords, and from the motive of variety rather than need, or a sexual or seasonal division becomes established, which makes the same people in part, or for part of the year, farmers and in part hunters. An inclination of this sort is not wanting in many districts of California. The dry and hot summer makes an outdoor life in the hills, near the heads of the vanishing streams, a convenience and a pleasure which coincide almost exactly with the opportunity to hunt and to gather the various natural crops as they become available from month to month. The wet winter renders house life in the permanent settlement in a valley or on a river correspondingly attractive, and combines residence there with the easiest chance to fish the now enlarged streams on an extensive scale, or to pursue the swarms of arrived water fowl.

But this division was not momentous. The distances ranged over were minute. Fishing was not excluded among the hills. Deer, rabbits, and gophers could be hunted in the mild winter as well as in summer. And while acorns and other plant foods might be garnered each only over a brief season, it was an essential part of their use that much of their preparation as well as consumption should be spread through the cycle of the calendar.

Further, the food resources of California were bountiful in their variety rather than in their overwhelming abundance along special lines. If one supply failed, there were a hundred others to fall back upon. If a drought withered the corn shoots, if the buffalo unaccountably shifted, or the salmon failed to run, the very existence of peoples in other regions was shaken to its foundations. But the manifold distribution of available foods in California and the working out of corresponding means of reclaiming them prevented a failure of the acorn crop from producing similar effects. It might produce short rations and racking hunger, but scarcely starvation. It may be that it is chiefly our astounding ignorance of all the more intimate and basal phases of their lives that makes it seem as if downright mortal famine had been less often the portion of the Californian tribes than of those in most other regions of the continent. Yet, with all allowance for this potential factor of ignorance in our understanding, it does appear that such catastrophes were less deep and less regularly recurring. Both formulated and experiential tradition are nearly silent on actual famines, or refer to them with rationalizing abstraction. The only definite cases that have come to cognizance, other than for a few truly desert hordes whose slender subsistence permanently hung by a thread, are among the Mohave, an agricultural community in an oasis, and among the Indians of the lower Klamath, whose habits, in their primal dependence on the salmon, approximated those of the tribes of the coasts north of California.

The gathering of the acorn is like that of the pine nut; its leaching has led to the recognition of the serviceability of the buckeye once its poison is dissolved out; the grinding has stimulated the use of small hard seeds, which become edible only in pulverized form. The securing of plant foods in general is not separated by

PLATE 45

MIWOK MORTAR HOLES IN BEDROCK AND BOWLDER
PESTLES

VALLEY YOKUTS MORTAR OF OAK

PLATE 46

DESERT CAHUILLA THATCHED HOUSE

SOUTHERN FOOTHILL YOKUTS PLATFORM
AND BOOTH FOR SNARING PIGEONS

any gap of distinctive process from that of obtaining grasshoppers, caterpillars, maggots, snails, mollusks, crawfish, or turtles, which can be got in masses or are practically immobile: a woman's digging stick will procure worms as readily as bulbs. Again, it is only a step to the taking of minnows in brooks, of gophers, or lizards, or small birds: the simplest of snares, a long stick, a thrown stone even, suffice with patience, and a boy can help out his grandmother. The fish pot is not very different from the acorn receptacle, and weirs, traps, stiff nets, and other devices for capturing fish are made in the same technique of basketry as the beaters, carriers, and winnowers for seeds. Even hunting was but occasionally the open, outright affair we are likely to think. Ducks were snared and netted, rabbits driven into nets, even deer caught in nooses and with similar devices. There is nothing in all this like the difference between riding down buffalo and gathering wild rice, like the break from whale hunting to berry picking, from farming to stalking deer.

The California Indian, then, secured his variety of foods by techniques that were closely interrelated, or, where diverse, connected by innumerable transitions. Few of the processes involved high skill or long experience for their successful application; none entailed serious danger, material exposure, or even strenuous effort. A little modification, and each process was capable of successful employment on some other class of food objects. Thus the activities called upon were distinguished by patience, simplicity, and crude adaptability rather than by intense endeavor and accurate specialization; and their outcome tended to manifold distribution and approximate balance in place of high yields or concentration along particular but detached lines.

The human food production of aboriginal California will accordingly not be well understood until a really thorough study has been made of all the activities of this kind among at least one people. The substances and the means are both so numerous that a recapitulation of such data as are available is always only a random, scattering selection.

Observers have mentioned what appealed to their sense of novelty or ingenuity, what they happened to see at a given moment, or what their native informants were interested in. But we rarely know whether such and such a device is peculiar to a locality or widespread, and if the former, why; whether it was a sporadic means or one that was seriously depended on; and what analogous ones it replaced. Statements that this tribe used a salmon harpoon, another a scoop net, a third a seine, a fourth poison, and that another built weirs, give us in their totality some approximation to a picture of the set of activities that underlie fishing in California as a whole: but for each individual group the statement is of little significance, for it is likely that those who used the nets used the spear and poison also, but under distinctive conditions; and when they did not, the question is whether the lack of one device is due to a more productive specialization of another, or to natural circumstances which made the employment of this or that method from the common stock of knowledge impracticable for certain localities.

There is, however, one point where neither experience nor environment is a factor, and in which pure custom reigns supreme: the animals chosen for the list of those not eaten. Myth, magic, totemism, or other beliefs may be at the bottom; but every tribe has such an index, which is totally unconnected with its abilities, cultural or physical, to take food.

Among the Yokuts, one animal stands out as edible that everywhere in northern California is absolute taboo and deadly poison: the dog. The Yurok give as their formal reason for not drinking river water that a large stream might contain human foetuses or a dead dog. The Yokuts did not shrink from eating dogs.

Coyote flesh was generally avoided, whether from religious reverence or magical fear is not clear. Grizzly bear meat was also viewed askance. The bear might have devoured human flesh, which would be near to making its eater a cannibal. Besides, in all probability, there was a lurking suspicion that a grizzly might not be a real one, but a transformed bear doctor. The disposition of the animal showed itself in the muscular fibers bristling erect when the flesh was cut, the Yokuts say. Brown bears had fewer plays of the imagination directed upon them, but even their meat was sometimes avoided. Birds of prey and carrion from the eagle down to the crow were not eaten. Their flesh, of course, is far from palatable; but it is these very birds that are central in Yokuts totemism, and the rigid abstinence may have this religious motivation. All reptiles were unclean to the southern Yokuts, as to the Tübatulabal; but the northern tribes exercised a peculiar discrimination. The gopher snake, water snakes, and frogs were rejected, but lizards, turtles, and, what is strangest of all, the rattlesnake, were fit food to the Chukchansi. There is a likely alien influence in this, for the neighboring Miwok probably, and the Salinans to the west certainly, ate snakes, lizards, and even frogs. On the other hand, the southern Yokuts relished the skunk, which when smoked to death in its hole was without offensive odor; while to the Miwok and Salinans it was abomination.

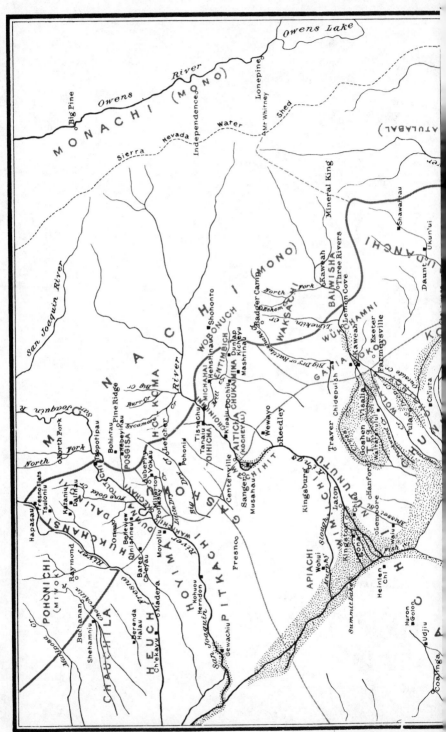

PLATE 47

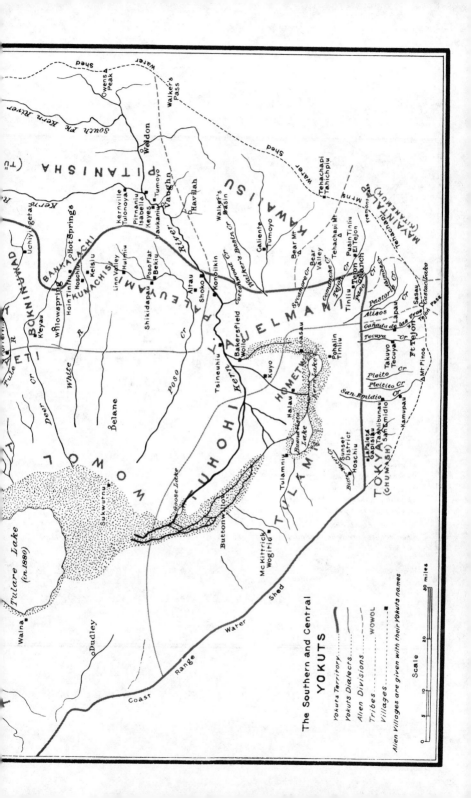

The Southern and Central
YOKUTS

Yokuts Territory ....
Yokuts Dialects ....
Alien Divisions ....
Tribes .... WOWOL
Villages ....■

Alien Villages are given with their Yokuts names

Scale
0   5   10   20   30 miles

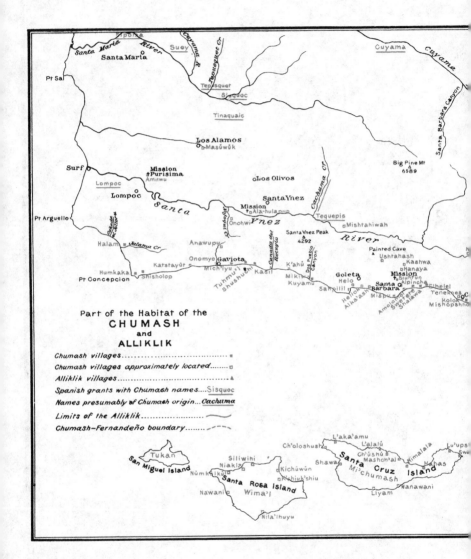

Part of the Habitat of the
CHUMASH
and
ALLIKLIK

Chumash villages............................... ▪
Chumash villages approximately located........ □
Alliklik villages................................. ▲
Spanish grants with Chumash names.....Sisquoc
Names presumably of Chumash origin...Cachuma
Limits of the Alliklik.......................... ‿‿
Chumash–Fernandeño boundary........ ‒ ‒ ‒

PLATE 48

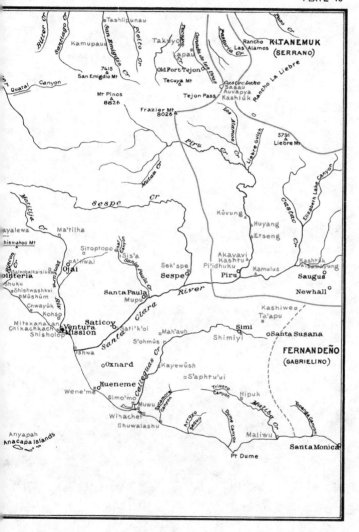

YOKUTS PLANT FOODS AND THEIR PREPARATION.

The buckeye process, which was probably similar to usages elsewhere in the State, was the following: The nuts were broken with a stone and soaked in water for a day. Next, the kernels were crushed to powder with the pestle. The last step was the extraction of the poison, which was done in the acorn-leaching place by the creek. Each time the flour dried a stick was laid aside; the pourings were so timed that the tenth stick was taken as the sun was nearly setting. The woman then cooked the flourlike acorn mush, and it was usually consumed on the spot.

The digger pine nut was not only eaten whole and raw but often treated like small seeds, being winnowed in a scoop-shaped basket, pounded into flour, and cooked.

Acorn granaries were of Miwok and Maidu type. There is no record of their occurrence south of the Yokuts.

Small shallow cook pots of soft stone, perhaps steatite, though described as reddish, were used by the Chukchansi and no doubt irregularly by other tribes who had access to a suitable supply of material. They were dug out with quartz. *Kuyati* and *kulosun* grubs, and angleworms, were perhaps stewed in these vessels, or more likely fried in their own fat at the edge of the fire.

The paddle for stirring boiling acorn mush is not a Yokuts implement, the central Miwok being the most southerly group among whom it makes its regular appearance until southern California is reached. The Yokuts substitute a stick looped on itself, a less efficient stirrer but more serviceable for removing the cooking stones, and far more readily made. (Fig. 38.)

THE MORTAR.

The mortar was a pit in an outcrop of granite, used until the depth of the hole became inconvenient. A convenient exposure of bedrock near a village often contains dozens of holes in all stages of wear within a few yards. (Pl. 45.) Poles leaned together with brush thrown on made an arbor under which a group of women would work for hours, gossiping or singing. Their pestles were often left on the spot; they are rude, irregular, with little taper, and somewhat oval in cross section, even with one or two sides flat or concave; in fact, little more than longish river bowlders, somewhat shaped, partly by pecking with the edge of a flat cobble, and in part by continued usage.

On the alluvial plains portable mortars were necessary. The most common form of these among the Tachi was one of white oak. The flat-bottomed wooden block was little more than a foot high, half as much again in diameter. Except for a narrow rim, the whole upper surface was excavated a few inches, chiefly by fire; but the actual pounding was done in a smaller doubly sunk pit in the center. The pestle was the same as on bedrock. Even the hill Chukchansi knew the wooden mortar, which they called *kowish;* and the Choinimni used it. It is a type that has rarely been observed north of Tehachapi outside the San Joaquin Valley: there are attributions to the Konomihu and the Patwin. (Pl. 45.)

Loose mortars of stone were found and used on occasion by all the tribes, but the universal testimony is that they were not made. In fact, the Chukchansi declare their inability to do so, and attribute all stone mortar holes, in situ as well as portable, to the coyote, who employed an agency of manufacture that decency debars from mention.

It is reported that the Yokuts sometimes fastened a hopper of basketry to the edge of a stone mortar; but this practice is established only for the southern California tribes, and needs confirmation. There is no Yokuts mortar basket, and the few available specimens of the combination suggest that an American may have cut the bottom out of a cooking basket and asphalted it to the stone.

Small stone mortars were probably used for special purposes quite different from those usually assumed. A toothless woman, for instance, was likely to keep such a one for pounding up the whole gophers or ground squirrels that younger relatives might from time to time toss her. Others may have been used for tobacco or medicines.

THE TAKING OF GAME AND FISH.

One hears less of deer snaring among the Yokuts than in the north; but they knew the device. Only, instead of setting the loop in a runway so as to encircle the neck, they laid it in a small concealed pit and fastened the end to a log.

Deer stalking with a deer's head as a decoy was shared with all the tribes of the north and central parts of the State. The Yokuts add that they painted their arms and breasts white like a deer's underside, and aided their traveling on all fours by holding a stick in each hand. When an animal was approached from the leeward, these sticks were rubbed together to produce the sound of a buck scraping his antlers.

Elk were too large to be snared, and in the open plains impossible to approach within bow range. They were chiefly secured in long-distance surrounds and drives called *taduwush.*

Antelope were similarly hunted, the valley groups uniting for intertribal drives, in circles that must often have been many miles in diameter at the start. When the ring had narrowed down so that a shout could be heard across it, two warriors famous for dodging stepped forward from each tribe, and each shot one flint-tipped deer arrow from fully bent bow at his companion. Then these men, and they only, shot the crazed antelopes as they circled about within the human inclosure, or sometimes ran until they dropped from fear and exhaustion. Certain of the antelopes with peculiar horns were believed to sing as they ran, with ground owls sitting on their heads. These individuals were spared. The mimic warfare no doubt had magic intent; but the delegation of the shooting to select men served to keep the circle intact, which would certainly have broken under the excitement of every man aiming his arrow at his own quarry.

A safe though far from certain way of hunting bears was to shoot them on moonlight nights from a sort of nest constructed in a tree in their acorn feeding grounds.

When the geese traveled, inflammable brush was piled up, and when the birds were heard approaching on dark, still nights these were suddenly lit. The birds swooped down to the flare, and in their bewilderment were easily killed.

Pigeons were snared in the earliest morning from a comfortable brush booth with a grass window looking out on a leveled platform on which a live decoy was staked and bait scattered. The running noose was on a stick that was slowly shoved through the curtain until a bird stepped within. The victim was smothered with the knee, and the flock soon returned to feed. (Pl. 46.) The decoy was carried in a spindle-shaped cage.

The Yaudanchi capture of eagles was modeled on the principle of their pigeon taking. The hunter lay in a concealed hut of brush. He did not look at his quarry until it was caught, fearing that it flee his glance. Outside were placed a stuffed animal skin as bait and a live hawk as decoy. The trap was a noose fastened to a bent-over pole sprung from a trigger. Before the eagle was killed by being trod on, it was addressed : "Do not think I shall harm you. You will have a new body. Now turn your head to the north and lie flat!" Only men who knew this prayer and the necessary observances undertook to kill eagles.

Of the many ways of capturing fish, a few more unusual ways may be mentioned. Completely darkened booths were built, in which a man lay to spear the fish passing beneath. This device suggests the pigeon snaring and eagle taking arbor. Small fish could sometimes be taken with the scoop-shaped openwork baskets of the women. Poisons were two: ground buckeye nuts with earth stamped into them and crushed *nademe* leaves. Soon after these preparations were thrown into a small stream the fish began to float on the surface. The *t'unoi* net was fastened to a circular frame on a pole, held vertically, and raised. The more usual Californian net of this type is on a half hoop, and is used rather for scooping or horizontal lifting.

Salt may have been obtained at springs, but the reported cases are from the Pitkachi, whose "salt" stank; from the Chukchansi, who went to the plains to scrape a sort of alkali off the ground; and from the Yaudanchi, who, with other southern tribes, gathered a salty grass known as *alit* and beat it on stones to extract the juice; which was particularly favored with green clover.

THE BOW.

Common bows for small game were little more than a shaped stick; good bows were carefully smoothed of large mountain cedar wood and sinew backed. The commonest type, primarily for the hunt, was nearly as long as a man, of about two fingers' width and the thickness of one. The ends were recurved, probably through a curling back of the thickened sinew. Bows made specifically for fighting were shorter, broader, and flatter, and pinched in the middle. Except for being unpainted and probably not quite so extreme in form, this type appears to have been the same as the northern California one.

Mention of the right and left end of the bow makes it seem to have been held horizontally, or at least diagonally, as by most California tribes.

The arrow, *shikid* generically, had three forms among the Yaudanchi, known as *t'uyosh, djibaku,* and *wuk'ud.* The war arrow had no foreshaft, but a rather long wooden point, notched. It measured from the finger tip nearly to the opposite shoulder or a trifle more than the possible pull of the bow. The Mohave also fought with arrows lacking flint tips. The ordinary hunting arrow had a long sharpened foreshaft, but no real head. The deer arrow had foreshaft and flint head, but the foreshaft was socketed without glue or tie, so that the main shaft would disengage after hitting.

The prevailing arrow straightener among the Yokuts is the southern California form: a well-shaped rectangular block of soft stone, often rounded or ridged on top, and invariably with a polished transverse groove. (Pl. 49, c.) This implement is undoubtedly associated with the employment of cane for arrows: the Yokuts are known to have used this plant, though not exclusively. The joints were warmed in the groove and bent by hand or on the ridge after the stone had been heated; the groove was also used for smoothing. The holed straightener of wood or horn for wooden shafts, as employed all over northern California, has not been reported from the Yokuts.

PLATE 49

ARROW STRAIGHTENERS

a, b, Mono; *c,* Yokuts; *d,* Cahuilla; *e,* Diegueño; *f,* Mohave (pottery)

PLATE 50

a

c

b

d

e

YOKUTS BASKETRY

a, Yokuts shouldered baskets with fringe of mountain quail plumes; *b*, tray for suspension; *c*, soft basket of tules; *d*, seed beater or tray; *e*, diagonally twined winnower or tray

PLATE 51

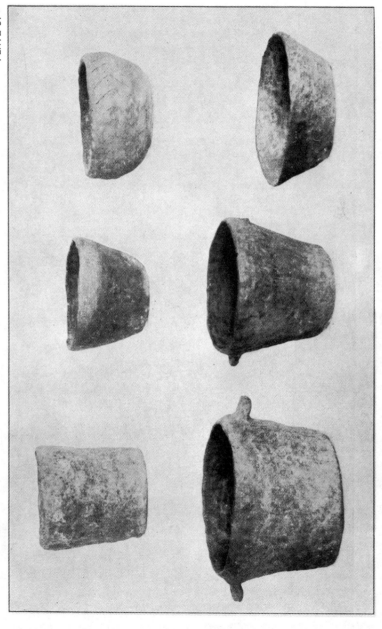

YOKUTS POTTERY

The sling was used only by boys, but the hill tribes report the Mono to have employed it in war. In the high Sierra it might often be more effective than an arrow.

BOATS.

Boats of bundled tule must have been in use among nearly all the valley tribes. On the tumbling streams in the hills these heavy rafts would have been utterly unmanageable. The northernmost Yokuts, below the Miwok of the hills, must have employed these craft constantly in their broad, sluggish streams and multitudinous still sloughs. They remained longest in service on Tulare Lake. Reconstructed models reveal only a cigar-shaped aggregation of bundles of rush, but the best specimens of old days may have approximated real boats in having raised edges. It can scarcely be presumed that the tule stalks could be bundled or beaten together so tight as to exclude the water; rather their lightness raised the whole mass so high that even the bottom of the hollow was above the water line, the gunwales serving only the convenience of preventing wave wash from entering and load or killed game from slipping overboard. Some of these lake boats carried three or four men in comfort, and could bear a small fire on an earth hearth. In maneuvering among the tules the entire vessel and occupants were often covered over with tules, forming a movable blind for the pursuit of waterfowl.

TEXTILES.

Yokuts baskets are distinguished by one special type, a coiled jar-like vessel with flat shoulder and constricted though sometimes reflaring neck. The pattern is one or more bands in red and black, either diamonds or hexagons or alternate trapezoids. The shoulder was often ornamented with a horizontally projecting fringe of quail crests (Pl. 50), for which red worsted is a modern substitute. These "Tulare bottlenecks," as they have come to be known in the curiosity and antique trade, as well as the quail plume decoration, are not found among the Miwok on one side of the Yokuts nor among the true southern Californians on the other. The two-color pattern is also rare if not lacking among the tribes to the north and south, except among the Chumash. The western Mono, Tübatulabal, Koso, Kawaiisu, and Kitanemuk worked according to Yokuts type, but as they form a fringe of Shoshoneans they have probably derived the art from their lowland neighbors. Kawaiisu technique is, however, as fine as Yokuts. The Chumash also did beautiful work, but the shapes which they gave to their incurved baskets are perhaps less specialized. At least they lack the sharp shoulder and distinct neck which the Yokuts fancied; but their baskets are very small-mouthed.

Chemehuevi forms are rounder, while the farthest traceable affinity is the small spherical basket of the Luiseño and Cahuilla. It is therefore possible to set the focus of the constricted neck forms among the southern Yokuts or the Chumash. As between these two groups, general grade of culture favors the Chumash, while the Yokuts are more central in the distribution of the type. The northern Yokuts, on and near the San Joaquin, do a much poorer grade of work than their southerly kinsmen, as do the Mono. But the Tübatulabal approximate the Tulare-drainage Yokuts in fineness of execution.

The woman's basket cap was probably Yokuts. At least the southern Yokuts seem to have shared it with their southern and eastern Shoshonean neighbors. This hat was, however, worn only with a load on the back, not habitually. It is curious that the range of the southern California cap coincides with that of the carrying net; of the northern form, with the technique of exclusive twining.

The pattern scheme of Yokuts baskets varies from the prevailing horizontal banding of southern California to the diagonal, vertical, and broken effects of Miwok basketry—largely according to locality. Materials and technique are also intermediate. The sewing is close, as in the north; in the Shoshonean area to the south, wider spaced. The foundation is a bundle of *Epicampes* grass, as in southern California; the wrapping, however, is not *Juncus*, as there, but more woody materials: root fibers of sedge (*Carex* or *Cladium?*) for the ground color, *Pteridium* fern root for black, bark of *Cercis* or redbud for red.

Very flat trays were made in coiling. The banded decoration of these brings them nearer Cahuilla and Luiseño ware than Maidu, where radiating designs prevail in flat work. Miwok coiled trays have gone out of use, if they were ever made. Yokuts women employed the finest of their trays for dice throwing; but of course the type was also put to more lowly and daily service.

Twined baskets were more poorly made, but filled a greater variety of needs and perhaps outnumbered coiled pieces in the normal household. The carrying basket was loose enough in texture to be describable as openwork. The interstices were filled with a mucilaginous smear. The commonest of all receptacles is an oval or ovate tray, with a rounding bottom. The term "winnower" describes only one of its manifold uses. The seed beater was but such a tray, one end of which was continued to a handle. Another form of tray was rounded triangular, nearly flat, and wholly or partly in diagonal twining. This has almost certainly been borrowed by the Yokuts from the Shoshoneans on their east. The Tulare Lake tribes must once have possessed a considerable array of special ware in

tule, both coiled and twined; but as it made no decorative endeavor
it has passed away with the disintegration of the culture of these
tribes almost without preservation. (Pl. 50.)

The Yaudanchi affirm that they knew the pitched water bottle of
the desert and southern California; but no specimens have survived.

Large baskets were used by the men to ferry women and children
across rivers, as by the Yuki. The Mohave employed pots for the
same purpose.

Basket patterns had more or less aptly descriptive names, but these
were ordinarily without symbolic or religious reference. Some of
the names were adjec-
tival, like " zigzag " and
" crooked "; others de-
noted parts of animals,
whole small animals, or
familiar objects. The significance might be in the
pattern as a whole or in
the design element. (Fig.
47.) The number of names
was not over a few dozen.

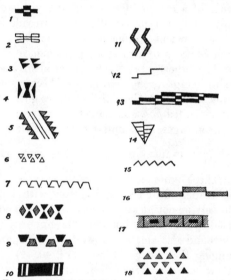

The pattern designa-
tions of the Yokuts, like
most of the patterns, are
g e n e r a l l y confined to
themselves or their imme-
diate neighbors; but their
range, character, and limitation of meaning are
typical for all the Cali-
fornia Indians, whatever
their varieties of tech-
niques, materials, and
forms of basketry. Where

FIG. 47.—Yokuts basket designs. Yaudanchi: 1, 2,
flies; 3, 4, deer foot; 5, arrow points; 6, 7,
crooked; 8, 9, rattlesnake markings; 10, king
snake markings; 11, water snake; 12, *chok*, wood-
gathering crook; 13, tied in the middle. Chukchansi: 14, arrow point; 15, crooked; 16, milli-
pede; 17, king snake markings; 18, rattlesnake
markings.

the matter has been most fully inquired into, as among the Pomo, it is
found that design names are often combined, or modified by standardized epithets, which allow of the accurate description of even a
complex pattern. It is not unlikely that the Yokuts may prove to
have followed a similar system.

The carrying net, *chutia*, into which either a conical basket or a
less shapely load could be set, reappears with the Yokuts. It
seems to have been of southern California type, light and with detachable supporting band or rope. Pack straps of braided string
were also slung around the load and forehead.

The commonest string material was milkweed, *Asclepias,* called *shah* or *chaka.* The stems were collected in early winter, the bark or covering peeled off, and shredded by rubbing between the hands. The thin epidermis was then removed by drawing the mass of fibers over a stick. The fibers were not separately disentangled, but loosely rolled together as they adhered. Two of these rolls were then twisted tight, on themselves as well as on each other, by rolling on the thigh with the spit-into hand, the other hand holding and feeding the loose ends. The exact process of adding further material is not known; it consisted probably of rubbing together the ends of a mass of fibers, perhaps with some twist. String was two-ply. This is a practically universal rule for California. Except for a few ancient fragments, every piece of three-ply rope or twine in the State is of American provenience or obviously modern.

The other great string material of the bulk of the Californians, wild hemp, *Apocynum,* has not been reported from the Yokuts; but this is likely to be only an oversight. The inner bark of a large shrub called *hoh* was made by the Yokuts into rough rope for withes, pigeon cages, and similar bound articles.

CRADLES OF THE YOKUTS AND OTHER CALIFORNIANS.

The Yokuts cradle shows three types. The first is a flat rectangle or trapezoid of twined basketry with a curved hood. The hood is loosely or not at all attached to the top edge of the base, and is carried by a basketry hoop or side supports. (Pl. 40, *h, i, j.*) This type is found also among the western Mono, and, with some modification, among the eastern Mono. (Pl. 40, *k.*) The latter run the rods of their base across instead of lengthwise, and set a smaller and rounder hood on more snugly. The Miwok (Pl. 39, *a, c, d, e*) and western Mono (Pl. 40, *l*) sometimes use the base of the Yokuts, without the hood. The Washo cradle is substantially that of the Yokuts.

The second type is built up on half a dozen sticks lashed across a large wooden fork. A layer of string-twined tules is put over the sticks. (Pl. 40, *m.*)

The third form is a mat of twined tules, with loops at the edges to pull the lashings through. (Pl. 40, *g.*)

The hooded basketry cradle seems to predominate in the north, the forked stick type in the south, and the soft frameless tule form on Tulare Lake; but this distribution is not altogether certain, and it is possible that the age of the child, or the season of the year, may have been of influence.

The Maidu cradle is often made on a forked framework, and in summer carries a basketry hood. It differs, however, in carrying numerous light transverse rods, in having the ends of the fork united by a stick loop, and in often lacking the point of the fork. (Pl. 40, *n, o.*) None of the Yokuts cradles, clearly, is made for hanging, except perhaps by a strap. The Maidu cradle may be described as a combination of the Yokuts first and second types; among the latter people no such combination or transitional type has been found.

The southern California cradle, so far as known, has a ladderlike foundation of a few short sticks on two long ones. The two long rods are, however, joined at the top instead of at the bottom: that is, there is a loop at the top instead of a fork below. The hood is also a separate hoop of wickerwork. (Pl. 39, *b.*)

The cradle of northeastern California, northwestern California, and the Pomo region is, in spite of much local variation, uniformly of a different order. It is of basketry, not of sticks; it is hollow instead of flat; and a rounded bottom is an integral part of the structure, while the hood is clearly a subsidiary feature. This northern cradle is built essentially for sitting (Pl. 35); that of central and southern California only for lying.

The stiff cradles of central and southern California may be schematized as in Figure 48, *a–e* being types with a wooden frame,

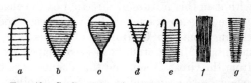

Fig. 48.—Cradle types of central and southern California. *a,* Diegueño, Mohave; *b, c,* Maidu; *d,* Yokuts, Kitanemuk; *e,* northern Miwok; *f,* Yokuts, Miwok, western Mono; *g,* eastern Mono. (Cf. Pls. 39, 40.)

f–g basketry forms. It will be seen that there is a complete transition from *a* to *d*: *b* differs superficially from *c* only in lacking the point of the latter. Structurally, however, the gap in the series comes between these two, *b* being only *a* with the ends of the frame rod joined, whereas *c* is *d,* namely, a natural fork at the bottom, with an added hoop. That form and consequent use may be of more importance than structural plan, so far as connections go, appears from the fact that *b* and *c* are the winter and summer types of the same people, the Maidu.

Even the stick and the basketry types shade into each other: *b* and *c,* whose transverse rods are close and slender, need only the substitution of a few courses of twining for their underlying hoop or fork frame to become *g.*

In Miwok basketry pieces of type *f,* like Plate 39, *e,* the strengthening hoop seems secondary, but may be a vestige of a former wooden foundation.

The hood is primarily associated with the basketry cradle, but again there are exceptions on both sides that make transitions. *B* and *d* are always hoodless, so far as known, and the hood of *a* is structurally separate. C, however, is hooded; on the other hand, f is found without a hood as well as with it.

Finally, the soft tule-mat cradle of the Tachi (Pl. 40, g) is the same in plan as Mono stiff basketry specimens like Plate 40, l, differing only in its pliability.

An aberrant type is e, so far reported only from the northerly Miwok. The frame is wooden, but distinctive in not being in a single plane. The two rods curl up from the base. This enables them to serve at once as hooks for hanging and as a hood frame. (Pl. 39, f.)

The historical interrelations of the several types can only become known through ampler material than is now available, both from within California and without. It is only possible to say that in spite of transitions the basketry and the wooden-frame types seem fundamental.

The former has its rods running longitudinally and is intra-Californian, or rather cis-Sierra, the northern sitting cradle linking with it in this feature of direction of the elements.

The wooden-frame cradle with cross rods is trans-Sierra, including southern California. On this interpretation the hill and mountain Maidu cradle has been shaped by Shoshonean influences from the Great Basin, and the Yokuts have been infiltrated to some extent by the same influences. On the other hand, the Shoshoneans within the Sierra Nevada, such as the western Mono, and presumably the Tübatulabal, follow the Californian method of construction at least as frequently as do the neighboring native stocks.

An interesting minor feature of Yokuts cradles is the expression of sex in the decoration. The Chukchansi put a band of parallel diagonal lines on a boy's hood, a zigzag on a girl's. A number of the Yokuts cradles from other localities show the same designs; several have the twining of the frame analogously disposed (Pl. 40, h, i, j). Diamonds may be the equivalent of the zigzag, in which case a genital connotation is possible. Eastern and western Mono hoods show patterns of the same kind (Pl. 40, k); the Washo denote sex in their hood ornamentation; the Miwok may therefore be guessed to follow the principle also; and the Mohave use distinct patterns for boys and girls in the braided bands with which the child is lashed to the frame, besides putting feathers only on a boy's hood. The device is therefore of some geographical extent, and may represent an eastern influence into California. It is of special appeal because of the rarity of symbolic expression in California outside of ritual; and even in ritual the symbolism is scant compared with the habits of the Southwest, the Plains, and the East.

While the same patterns probably occur over a large area with the same symbolism, the sex denotation itself is expressed in other ways also. Thus the Nutunutu boy's cradle is said to have the hood fastened only at the sides, the girl's at the top and the base also.

POTTERY.

The Yokuts practice one curious and hitherto undescribed art: that of pottery making. The precise distribution of this industry remains to be ascertained. The southern hill tribes made pots; the adjacent valley tribes appear to have; on the lake tribes there is no information; the Chukchansi and probably other northern tribes did not follow the art. Of adjacent Shoshoneans, the Tübatulabal made pots; some of the western Mono probably did. Outside of these groups there is no record whatever of the industry. It is not connected geographically with the pottery-making area of southern California, which does not come north of the San Bernardino Range, so far as known; and the territorial gap is paralleled by a thorough diversity of the ware.

The distinctive feature of this pottery is its excessive crudeness. It appears to have been made by a rough fitting together of pieces of clay, or a pressing out of a lump: there is no evidence of the coiling and smoothing method. It is doubtful whether the clay contains tempering. Glue, blood, or a sticky substance may have been introduced as binding material. The color is from light to dark gray. There is no slip, wash, or pattern, except now and then a rude incision obviously modeled on a basket pattern. The shapes are indefinitely varied, without approach to standardized forms. A row of the vessels looks as if produced by children or experimenters. (Pl. 51.)

Even the uses are not known. Most of the pots show evidences of employment in the fire. But their purposes must have been special, since the ordinary cooking of the Yokuts is as regularly performed in baskets as among other groups. Small vessels may have been intended for services that we can only suspect. Thus the Yaudanchi affirm that they formerly kept tobacco in hollowed clay balls.

Archaeology gives no information as to the age of the industry. There has been little collecting in the Yokuts area and no systematic exploration. The prehistoric clay cooking balls or sling shots of the stoneless Stockton plains, where the Yokuts Chulamni lived in the historic period, suggest a connection; but no vessels of the same material have ever been found with these. The Clear Lake Pomo sometimes make a minute receptacle by pressing a hole in a lump of clay; but they do not bake these little articles. Evidently there were some anticipations toward pottery making latent in parts of California; and the Yokuts carried these tentative steps a little further. But the inference of a stimulus, however indirect, coming through their immediate Shoshonean neighbors from the pottery-making Shoshoneans of the south or east can hardly be avoided; and therewith the interpretation of an ultimate southwestern origin of the art.

PIPES AND TOBACCO.

The pipe is small among the Yokuts. (Pl. 30, *c*, *d*.) A wooden pipe is found among the Chukchansi and Gashowu; the Yaudanchi and southern tribes normally used a bit of cane, which was carried in the pierced lobe of the ear. The northern Yokuts implement suggests the southern Californian stone pipe in size and shape, and the Mohave equivalent of clay. Outwardly it is similar to the abbreviated Miwok pipe, but the latter has a very short reed or stem inserted as a mouthpiece. Occasionally a pipe with enlarged bowl, of Pomo shape but very much smaller, is to be found among the northerly Yokuts. All the Yokuts declare that they did not use stone pipes; and the random finds of prehistoric material in their habitat include very few, if any, such implements.

The reason for the abortiveness of the Yokuts pipe is to be found in the fact that a common practice of all the tribes was to eat tobacco instead of smoking it. This custom is affirmed by the Chukchansi, Gashowu, Tachi, Wükchamni, Yaudanchi, and Yauelmani, and was therefore evidently universal. Garcés, in 1776, found a Serrano Shoshonean tribe bordering on the Yokuts, either the Kitanemuk or the Alliklik, following the same practice, to the serious discomfort of his unaccustomed Mohave companions. One method was to mix the leaves with fresh-water mussel shells that had been burned to lime. This procedure is of interest because it recurs in the northernmost part of the Pacific coast. A probably less usual plan was to drink a decoction of tobacco in water. In either event vomiting followed except for the long-hardened. The after effects of the emetic may have been pleasant. At any rate they were considered beneficial, and in some cases at least they were thought to impart supernatural efficiency. The Chukchansi speak of being able to detect wizards after eating tobacco.

GAMES.

Among the Yokuts the guessing or hand game becomes less important than among the tribes of northern California. Its place in the prime estimation of men is taken, as in parts of southern California, by the hoop and pole and the shinny game, though which of these two enjoyed preeminence it is hard to say—perhaps shinny.

This game, *katauwish*, was named from the shinny stick, *kated*. The ball was called *odot*. It was not shinny in our sense, played with one pall, but rather a form of the ball or stick race of the Southwest, each party propelling its knob of white oak with sticks instead of feet. The course, however, was short, within a definite field, the *katadwishchu;* and among the Chukchansi the ball had to be holed to win.

Chukchansi women played the same game with straighter sticks, and threw a hoop in place of striking the ball.

Another variant, though for men, was lacrosse, *ch'ityuish,* named after the racket, *ch'itei.* The " net " was nothing but a loop that half fitted the ball. This game was secondary to the *katduwish.*

In hoop and pole the throwing stick was called *payas,* the rolling buckskin-wound ring *tokoin,* and the carefully smoothed ground, often by the side of the sweat house, *i'n.* The game itself, *hochuwish,* was substantially that of the Mohave; it extended as far north as the Chukchansi.

In the *aikuich* the pole was thrown at a sliding billet, *t'ieh.* The same name is now applied to the Spanish "nine men's morris": the men are *aiek.*

A third form was the *haduwush,* in which darts were thrown at a mark hidden by a fence of brush.

There is no record of any Yokuts cup and ball game.

The guessing game was called *wehlawash* by the Chukchansi, *a'liwash* by the Yauelmani, *hi'uniwich* by the Yaudanchi. The former, like the northern Californians, used wooden pieces, or in a good set, bones; the latter, bits of cane slipped, as in southern California, over an endless string to prevent the deceit of interchange after the guess. The marked piece was called " man " and guessed for; the plain one was the " woman." The Yaudanchi shot out one finger if he meant the hand at which he pointed, but two to indicate the ignored side as containing the " man." When there were two pairs of players confronting each other, a single finger signified a guess at the hand indicated and at the partner's opposite hand; two fingers, the same hand of both players. These complications look like arbitrary elaborations; but like most such Californian devices, they spring from an intensive development of the spirit of the game. A gesture begun with one finger can be finished with two if the instant suffices for recognition of a trace of satisfaction in the opponent's countenance as he realizes an impending false guess. These attempts to provoke betrayal imply instantaneous shiftings of features and fingers and lightninglike decisions and reactions; and it is impossible to have seen a Californian Indian warmed to his work in this game when played for stakes—provided its aim and method are understood—and any longer justly to designate him mentally sluggish and emotionally apathetic, as is the wont. It is a game in which not sticks and luck but the tensest of wills, the keenest perceptions, and the supplest of muscular responses are matched; and only rarely are the faculties of a Caucasian left sufficiently undulled in adult age to compete other than disastrously against the Indian practiced in his specialty. Seen in this light, the contortions, gesticulations, noises, and excitement of the native are not the mere uncontrolledness of an overgrown child, but the outward reflexes of a powerfully surcharged intensity, and devices that at once stimulate the contestant's energy still further and aid him in dazzling and confusing his opponent. There is possibly no game in the world that, played sitting, has, with equal intrinsic simplicity, such competitive capacities.

The Yaudanchi shuffled under a blanket instead of behind the back or in bunches of hay. Among the Chukchansi only women used the blanket.

Chomwosh is the guessing or matching of hidden fingers. It is too little described to allow of a decision between the possibilities of native and Mediterranean origin.

Dice was the woman's game. There were two forms. *Huchuwish* was played with 8 *huech*, half shells of nut filled with pitch or asphalt and bits of sea shell, thrown from both hands on a basketry tray, *t'aiwan*. The far-away Chemehuevi play this much like the southern Yokuts, though with 6 instead of 8 pieces; it appears to be a game of Shoshonean origin. The Chukchansi keep the name, but use 6 split acorn kernels. Beyond them, the course of the game becomes uncertain. For the Miwok nothing is known, and the Maidu seem to lack all dice. The Yaudanchi played for 12 counters, and the scoring ran: 5 of 8 flat surfaces up, 2 counters; 2 up, 1; any other number, none. The Chukchansi won by taking 10 counters, and considered only the possible combinations of falls, irrespective of side. Six to none counted 4 points; 4 to 2 or 3 to 3, 1; 5 to 1, nothing. Such variations seem to occur in all Californian games, even between adjacent areas.

The second dice game, *tachnuwish*, was played with 6 (or 8) split sticks, *dalak*, of elderwood in the north, of cane in the south, burned with a pattern on the convex side and thrown on end on a skin.

There was a generic word, *goyuwinich*, for gambler. *Gwiunauzhid mak*, "let us gamble," the Yaudanchi would say.

AESTHETICS.

Apart from basket patterns, there was no trace of activity of graphic or plastic art in Yokuts life. The images in the mourning ceremony were symbols of the rudest kind. Anything like the tracing of a picture or shaping of a figure was foreign to the native mind. Even conventionalized symbols were lacking, for conventionalization is a standardization of some artistic impulse, and this impulse never manifested itself. The stiff figures of men and animals that occasionally appear on baskets are invariably due to American influence, among the Yokuts as well as among all other Californian groups. One can not have become imbued with a feeling for the decorative value of California basketry without resenting these childish introductions as fatal to the inherent aesthetic qualities of the work. Our tastes have been infinitely more cultivated than those of the native Californian; but in the few directions, or one direction, in which he had made an incipient progress in ornamentation, his habits had poise and restraint.

The ungraphic, unplastic, and unsymbolic character of native Californian civilization is complete to a degree that is almost inconceivable. It is only rarely that an Indian can be induced to draw in the sand the most schematic sketch of the rivers or mountains of his habitat. In southern California there are indeed some faint stirrings in the sand paintings, but only under a strong ritualistic motive; and the poverty and rudeness of these, compared with their Navaho and Pueblo prototypes, reveal the aridity of the artistic soil which this southwestern religio-aesthetic influence encountered in its invasion of California.

In all the remainder of the State even this trace is wanting. For once the deep cleavage between the northwest and the central south is effaced. The Yurok and Hupa culture may be a North Pacific coast civilization in nine-tenths of its essential impulses and goals; in representative art it is as Californian as that of the Maidu or Yokuts.

How far some beginnings of literary form have evolved in Yokuts traditions, in comparison with those of their neighbors, it would be difficult to state. The languages, the emotions, and the pleasures of the natives are everywhere known with too little intimacy for a judgment to be of value. Myths have been recorded primarily with reference to their episodic content, their religious associations, or their systematic coherence. Such as are available from the Yokuts evince a lower literary pitch, a less intensity of presentation, than those of northern and southern California at their best. But we do not know how far they are artistically representative; and what has already been said about the animal pantheon of these people suffices to reveal that the real merits of their folklore lie implicit in a background or setting of which the skeletonized translations that are available give to us but rudimentary hints.

Much the same must be said of music, only in a still stronger degree. Some differences of external form, or involved system, are apparent between the songs of various parts of California. But as long as no exact analysis has been rendered, and especially as long as no one has approached this music with any desire to enter into its essential spirit, comparisons between the aesthetic value of the inclinations and achievements of this and that tribe are empty.

Southern Yokuts men sometimes played the musical bow after settling themselves in bed; the Chukchansi in mourning the dead. These may be but two expressions of one employment. Modern forms of the instrument have a peg key for adjusting the tension, or are made on cornstalks. In old days a true shooting bow, or a separate instrument made on the model of a bow, was used. *Mawu*, or *mawuwi*, was its name. One end was held in the mouth, while the lone string was tapped, not plucked, with the nail of the index finger; the melody, audible to himself only, was produced by changes in the size of the resonance chamber formed by the player's oral cavity.

THE TYPE OF YOKUTS CIVILIZATION.

The affiliations of Yokuts civilization are nearly equal in all directions. To the north, their system of totemic moieties connects them with the Miwok while certain detailed elements of their culture, such as the Y-frame cradle and the magpie headdress, link them definitely with the Maidu. To the east their twined basketry has close relations as far as the remoter edge of the Great Basin. Toward the Shoshonean and Yuman south there are innumerable threads: the Jimson weed ritual, the arrow straightener, the carrying net, to mention only a few. Toward the west the decay of Salinan and Chumash culture makes exact comparison difficult, but what little is known of the former people evidences a strong Yokuts impress, while with the nearer Chumash relations of trade were close and must have brought many approaches of custom in their train. It is difficult to say where the most numerous and most basic links stretch.

Equally impressive, however, are the features distinctive of the civilization of the Yokuts, or rather of the group composed of themselves and their smaller and less known Shoshonean neighbors on the immediate east and south. These specialties include the true tribal organization, the duality of chieftainship, the regulated functions of transvestites, the coordinated animal pantheon, the eagle-down skirt, the constricted coiled basket, a distinctive pottery, and the communal house, to mention only a few points.

It thus seems that the Yokuts were a nation of considerable individuality. It appears throughout California that the dwellers in the larger valleys, though they were the first to crumble at the touch of the Caucasian, elaborated a more complex culture than the hill tribes; and the Yokuts were a lowland people in a greater measure than any other stock in California.

But it is also evident that wherever the soil of history is really penetrated in California a rich variety of growths is found. If a little mountain group like the Yuki, placed between more highly civilized nations, has been able to evolve feature after feature of cultural distinctness, there is every reason to believe that the same would prove to be true of nearly all the California tribes, if only we really knew them; and a large, compact, and prosperous block of people like the Yokuts would be exceptional only in having carried the development of their originality somewhat farther than the majority.

It so happens that in the long stretch of land between the Maidu and the Luiseño no tribe has yet been exhaustively studied with any array of information. It is therefore inevitable that the present account of the Yokuts, the first rendered in any detail, scattered as that is, should reveal many novelties. But there is nothing to encourage the belief that if the Miwok, the Tübatulabal, the Serrano, or the Salinans had happened to be chosen, there would have been any notably less quantity of interesting peculiarities revealed; not to mention that for the Pomo and Chumash, little known as they are, we have every indication of a civilizational richness greater, if anything, than that evinced by the Yokuts.

In other words, the exact understanding of the Indian history of California still lies before us. Some foundations may have been laid for it in the present work. The outlines were sketched for all time 40 years ago by the masterly hand of Stephen Powers. But the real structure will be a gift of the future; and its materials can only be assembled by investigations far more intensive, as well as continuous, than those yet undertaken.

THE ESSELEN AND SALINANS.

THE ESSELEN.

With this people, we are back in the Hokan family, with which, except for a long Shoshonean excursion, the remainder of this survey will be occupied.

Long reckoned as an independent stock, the Esselen were one of the least populous groups in California, exceedingly restricted in territory, the first to become entirely extinct, and in consequence are now as good as unknown, so far as specific information goes—a name rather than a people of whom anything can be said. There are preserved a few hundred words and phrases of their speech; some confused designations of places, and a few voyagers' comments, so generic in tone as to allow no inferences as to the distinctiveness of the group.

The only clue to their ultimate history is, as usual, afforded by language. On two sides the Esselen had the Penutian Costanoans as neighbors, on the third the Hokan Salinans; they faced the ocean on the fourth. Salinan speech, however, leans toward Chumash, its southern sister; and the obvious affinities of Esselen are toward Yuman, far to the south, and to Pomo, Yana, and other north Hokan languages, before which a broad belt of alien Penutian tongues intervenes. In short, Esselen is free from the peculiarities of Chumash and Salinan, and is a generalized Hokan language. It can not well, therefore, have originated in the same branch of the family as Salinan, and probably represents a separate wave or movement. Further than this, nothing can be said until the internal organization of the Hokan family shall have been better determined.

There is only one conjecture that may be alluded to. The smallness of the group is in marked contrast to the degree of its linguistic distinctness. It is therefore likely to be a remnant of a people that once ranged over a much larger territory. Now the Penutians of California were very plainly the people of the great interior valley. It is chiefly from the vicinity of San Francisco to Monterey that they impinged on the ocean. They have therefore presumably spread out along this stretch of coast, in which their Costanoan division was located in historic times and where it may be supposed to have taken shape as a group. This stretch is adjacent to the soil which the Esselen still held when they were discovered; and it seems reasonable to believe, accordingly, that the Esselen once owned at least part of this region to their north. This ancient extension might have connected them with the northern Hokans, particularly if the Pomo or some allied group formerly lived farther south.

The heart of Esselen territory at the time of discovery was the drainage of Carmel River, exclusive, however, of its lower reaches, where Costanoans were situated and the mission was established. The Esselen also held Sur River and the rocky coast for 25 miles from a little short of Point Sur to Point Lopez. At the great peak of Santa Lucia they met the Salinans. Nearly all of this territory is rolling or rugged, part of it sierra. The Esselen, like most small groups in California, were therefore distinct mountaineers. A thousand souls would be a very liberal estimate for their population. Five hundred seems nearer the mark.

Esselen, Eslen, Escelen, Ecselen, or Ensen, also Ecclemach, is used by all authorities of the Spanish period as a tribal name and commonly provided with the plural ending *-es*. It seems, however, to be the name of a village, after which, following Caucasian custom, the group was denominated. This is borne out by a reference to Eslanagan and Ecgeagan (also recorded as Ekheya) as on opposite sides of the Carmel River. The final *-n* itself is hardly likely to be of native Esselen origin. The word "Eslanagan" looks like a stem *Esla*, plus possibly the common Esselen noun suffix *-nah* or *-neh*, to which in turn the Costanoans added their *-n*. The Eslen or Ensen and Rumsien or Runsen seem to have been habitually distinguished as the two predominant groups at mission Carmelo, much in the sense in which we might distinguish Esselen and Costanoan. The names were easy and rhymed; and travelers came away and reported the two "tribes," sometimes as extending 20 leagues from Monterey. Data were scarce; and for nearly a century almost every book on California refers to the famous "Ensenes and Runsenes," as if they were great ethnic groups instead of villages. Huelel—that is, Welel— is mentioned once as the "language of the Esselenes" attached to mission Soledad.

The settlements cited in various authorities are: Ensen, at Buena Esperanza; Ekheya, in the mountains; Echilat, 12 miles southeast of mission Carmelo; Ichenta, at San Jose (this is certainly a Costanoan name, whoever inhabited the spot; compare the locative ending *-ta*); Xaseum, in the sierra; Pachhepes, near the last; and the following "clans or septs": Coyyo, Yampas, Fyules (*f* is an Esselen sound), Nennequi, Jappayon, Gilimis, Yanostas. These are all in the original orthography, which in most cases is Spanish.

Several terms in the preserved vocabularies may be of ethnographic interest. Thus, *pawi* or *lottos*, arrow (two kinds may have been used); *iwano*, house;

tsila, *ku'uh*, *ishpasha'a*, *shaka*, various kinds of baskets; *ehepas*, rabbit-skin blanket; *shikili*, asphalt(?); *ka'a*, tobacco; *makhalana*, salt; *lelima* a "favorite dance," possibly the *Loli* of the Kuksu system; *tumas-hachohpa*, night spirit; *kuchun*, arroyo; *aspasianah*, dry creek. The last two may be names of places rather than generic terms.

THE SALINAN INDIANS.

The Salinan Indians are one of those bodies of natives whom four generations of contact with civilization have practically extinguished. Some 40 remain, but among these the children do not speak the language, and even the oldest retain only fragmentary memories of the national customs of their great-grandfathers. Missionaries and explorers happen to have left only the scantiest notices of the group; and thus it is that posterity can form but a vague impression of their distinctive traits. Even a name for the tribe or for their language has not been recorded or remembered; so that they have come to be called from the Spanish and modern designation of the river which drains most of their territory.

TERRITORY.

The Salinan language extended from the headwaters of the Salinas, or perhaps only from the vicinity of the Santa Margarita divide, north to Santa Lucia Peak and an unknown point in the valley somewhere south of Soledad; and from the sea presumably to the main crest of the Coast Range. Much of this territory is rugged; nearly all of it is either rough or half barren. Along the steep harborless coast one dialect or division of the language, the extinct "Playano" or "beach" idiom, was spoken; in the mountains and valley the second or "principal." This in turn was divided into a northern and a southern subdialect, of both of which records have been made, and which are usually named after the missions of San Antonio and San Miguel.

The Salinan language is wholly unconnected with the neighboring Yokuts and Costanoan. It has remote affinity with Esselen, and a greater resemblance to Chumash. These three tongues constitute the central Californian representatives of the Hokan family.

NUMBERS.

Cabrillo in 1542 saw no natives on the Salinan coast, and Vizcaino 60 years later only a few on tule rafts. The true discoverers of the group were the members of the Portolá expedition of 1769. In the mountains between the future sites of San Luis Obispo and Monterey they saw, going and coming, 10 different towns whose population they estimated to range between 30 and 400 souls, with an aggregate of 1,200. As Chumash, Esselen, or Costancan villages were included, these figures shed little light on the numbers of the Salinan stock; but they are of interest in giving an average of over 100 people per town.

The records of the missions furnish an approximate Salinan census. San Antonio was founded in 1771, and reached a maximum population of 1,124—or 1,296—neophytes in 1805. San Miguel, established in 1797, had 1,076 converts at the end of 17 years. The sum, about 2,300 souls, includes some Yokuts—Tachi, Telamni, and perhaps other tribes—from the San Joaquin Valley; so that even if allowance is made for conjectural unreduced Salinan villages as late as 1814, the total aboriginal population of the family can not possibly be placed above 3,000; and 2,000 seems a safer estimate. The record of baptisms—not quite 7,000 at both missions up to 1834, during a period which on the average took in nearly three generations—would confirm the smaller rather than the larger figure.

SETTLEMENTS.

Of the 20 or so Salinan villages known other than as mere names, some can be placed on a map only with a question (Fig. 49). Ehmal, Lema, Ma'tihl'she, and Tsilakaka are entirely undetermined except for having been on the coast. Trolole has been located at points so widely separated as Santa Margarita and Cholame. Cholame, the most important town of the San Miguel division, is stated by some to have been situated at that mission, by others on Cholame Creek. As the Cholame land grant lies along this creek, and the Spaniards and Mexicans were rather precise in their application of native names, the latter vicinity seems more likely. But Estrella Creek, as the lower course of Cholame Creek is now designated on maps, flows into the Salinas near the mission; and as it is the general custom of the California Indians to name streams after the sites at their mouths, the name may in this way have been, correctly enough, carried upstream by the Spaniards. Conjecture, however, is all that is possible on such disputed points. The majority of Salinan towns of ascertained location lie on San Antonio and Nacimiento Rivers. In part this unevenness may be the fault of the preservation of knowledge; but it seems also to reflect the preponderating distribution. Even in the barren hills of the Cholame drainage there are known as many villages as in the long valley of the Salinas proper.

TYPE OF CIVILIZATION.

The Salinan Indians were completely omnivorous. Every obtainable variety of fish, reptiles, birds, and mammals, with the single exception of the skunk, and possibly the dog and coyote, was eaten. An incomplete list of their vegetable dietary contains six kinds of acorns, three of grasses, three of clover, six at least of berries, and two of pine nuts; besides wild oats, buckeye, sunflower, chia and sages, grapes, prickly pears, yucca, and Brodiaea bulbs. This wealth of plant foods is typical of aboriginal California.

Salinan industries and customs were largely influenced by those of the Yokuts, with whom they traded, visited, and communicated freely, whereas the Costanoans on the north were generally their bitter enemies, and the main body of the Chumash to the south were too far removed, and of too different an outlook, to hold much relation with them. Baskets were essentially Yokuts in material and technique. Women's hats and mortar hoppers of coiled basketry are

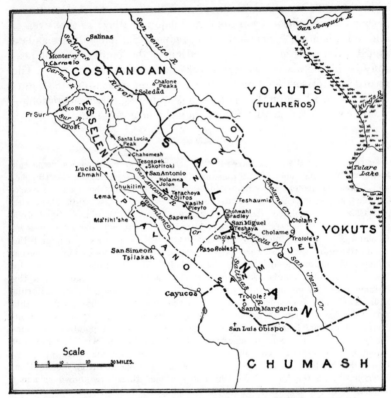

Fig. 49.—Salinan and Esselen territory and probable Salinan settlements.

reported. The former may have been introduced by the missionized Yokuts; the latter is a southern California type that seems out of place in Salinan territory. Roughly interlaced receptacles of willow for the storage of acorns also recall those of southern California. Grooved arrow straighteners, reed smoking pipes, the eating of tobacco mixed with lime, and the practice of cremation indicate Yokuts affiliations. The initiation of boys into manhood with a toloache drinking rite, whereas the advent of adolescence in girls was disposed of with less circumstance, also suggest Yokuts contact.

On the contrary, the few names of Salinan dances that are still remembered point to an origin of these ceremonies from the Patwin-Pomo-Maidu-Miwok cycle in the north. These dances are: the Kuksui, made by a feather-covered performer; the Hiwei, by men; and the Lolei, by women. But their introduction may possibly have been due to commingling of nationalities at the Salinan missions.

Beliefs, again, were substantially those of the Tachi and other valley Yokuts. Certain medicine men were thought capable of bringing rain with amulets; others of turning themselves into grizzly bears. Souls inhabited a western island of the dead. Earth was brought up from primeval water, given shape as this world, and mankind fashioned from it, by a trio of animal creators, the eagle, coyote, and kingfisher.

Only two distinctive peculiarities are known of the rude civilization of the Salinan Indians. One is the use of the musical rasp, a notched stick rhythmically rubbed with another. The second is the remarkable report from mission sources that at San Miguel they lent each other shell money at 100 per cent interest per day! The rasp is a simple implement, easily invented even by a rude tribe, or perhaps learned by it from others who have allowed it to degenerate into a toy, or to go out of use altogether. Usury, however, is contrary to all the known customs of the California Indians, and the rate of increase seems incredible, especially as a temporary or emergency use for money is hard to conceive under aboriginal conditions. Still, a report as definite as this can hardly be without some foundation.

CHAPTER 37.

THE CHUMASH.

HISTORY AND TERRITORY.

Except for a brief and unsettled experience of Alarcon with the aggressive tribes of the lower Colorado a year or two before, the Chumash are the first Californian group discovered by Caucasians. Cabrillo in 1542–43 sailed back and forth among the islands, coasted the shore, had abundant and most friendly contact with the natives, lived on San Miguel, and died there.

Subsequent explorers and voyagers have left a number of casual observations on the Chumash, but none of the missionaries settled among them showed inclination to develop into a painstaking historian like Boscana; and when California was long enough American for ethnologists to survey it, the old life of the Chumash was a dimming memory. The result is that there exist more impressions than information. There is no group in the State that once held the importance of the Chumash concerning which we know so little.

The Spaniards were disposed to regard the Chumash as superior to the other tribes of California with whom they had acquaintance, and on the whole they seem to have been correct in this opinion. We know so little of the religion of the group that it is impossible to decide whether they attained to the comparative height of semi-abstruse symbolism that the Gabrielino and Luiseño displayed. In their industries, in the arts that accompany ease of life, possibly in the organization of society, they rather surpassed these Shoshoneans. The consequence is that Chumash culture presents the appearance of a higher development on the material, technological, and economic side than on the religious, but we can not be altogether certain that such a formulation would be reliable.

The Chumash are predominantly a coast people, and were more nearly maritime in their habits than any other Californian group. They held the three northern large islands of the Santa Barbara archipelago—Anacapa does not appear to have been inhabited permanently. They clustered thickly along the calm shore from Malibu Canyon westward to Point Concepcion, and from there extended northward along the more boisterous and chillier coast as far as Estero Bay. Inland, in general, they reached to the range that divides the direct ocean drainage from that of the great valley; except that in the west their frontier was the watershed between the Salinas and the Santa Maria and short coast streams; and in the east, some small fragments had spilled into part of the most southerly drainage of the San Joaquin-Kern system. The Carrizo plains are doubtful as between Chumash and Salinans, and may not have contained any permanent villages.

Marine life along the Chumash shores is exceptionally rich, the climate far famed, and every condition favored the unusual concentration of population among a people living directly upon nature. The land, however, is dry; the watercourses, though long, are small and rarely run permanently, and each successive mountain chain increases the aridity. Only some narrow stretches among the uplands of the western end of the Tehachapi range are more favorable. There was thus every occasion for the inlander to drift to the edge of the ocean, if he could, but small inducement for the coast people to go to the interior, except for occasional visits. The population in the districts away from the sea must have been comparatively light.

From Point Concepcion north the coast is exposed to westerly winds, fogs, and heavy surfs, and the inhabitants were noted by the Spaniards as less numerous and poorer than on the Channel of Santa Barbara.

Five missions—San Buenaventura, Santa Barbara, Santa Ynez, La Purisima Concepcion, and San Luis Obispo—were established among the Chumash. These being recruited almost wholly from the members of the stock, would argue a population of about 8,000 or 10,000; and this figure seems reasonable on the basis of the character of the land and sea. The Chumash accepted the Spaniards with unusual kindliness. But the subjection which the residence of the superior people entailed broke their spirit and produced a deep inward depression, which manifested itself in the alarming spread of the practice of abortion, and as late as 1824 fanned itself into a feeble and timid flame of insurrection at three of the missions. By the time of secularization, the population was heavily on the wane. The disorganized decade and a half that followed melted it even more rapidly, and when the American came there were scattered peons on ranchos, but no more Chumash nation. To-day there remain scarcely a dozen old men and women who still speak the language of their grandfathers, although the number of individuals admitting pure or partial Chumash blood is somewhat greater.

There was a dialect for each mission; at least one other on the islands; another in the mountain region where the Tehachapis meet the coast ranges; and possibly others. As to the limits of these, there is no information whatever. Some attempt has been made to estimate their boundaries on Plate 1. But it must be frankly confessed that the lines there drawn represent little but conjectures based on topography.

A rough classification of the known dialects is possible. That of San Luis Obispo, the most northwesterly, thrust into an angle between the Salinans and the sea, is the most divergent. Next in degree of specialization seems to be that of the islands. Santa Ynez and Santa Barbara are rather close, Ventura somewhat more different. San Emigdio appears to lean on Ventura.

When it comes to villages, information is abundant as regards names, but often less precise as to location and almost wholly wanting as to relations. Several hundred Chumash place names are on record, the majority referring to inhabited sites. Nearly 100 of these can be located with some approximation to accuracy on a map of the scale of Plate 48; and these undoubtedly include most of the important towns near the ocean. The interior is less satisfactorily represented.

The following may be added to the data contained in Plate 48:

The native name of San Luis Obispo was Tishlini. Pismo and Huasna appear to derive their designations from Chumash originals. Upop is mentioned as near Point Concepcion, Awawilashmu near the Cañada del Refugio, Alwatalam and Elhiman in the Goleta marsh; Shtekolo at the Cienega and Kulalama and Tenenam and Tokin near the mission at Santa Barbara; Skonon and Mismatuk in Arroyo Burro in the same neighborhood; Kinapuich', Mishtapalwa, Kachyoyukuch, Antap, and Honmoyanshu near Ventura; Mahalal at San Cayetano. Ho'ya or Huya has been recorded for San Miguel Island, Santa Catalina Island (which is Gabrielino), and a village on Santa Cruz. Another name for Santa Catalina is Himinakots, with which Cabrillo's Taquimine, "Spaniards," may possibly be connected.

Kamupau, Tashlipunau, Takuyo, and Lapau are Yokuts forms, but some of them may rest on Chumash originals. Takuyo, reflected in the modern name of Mount Tecuya, may be a locative of Tokya, the generic name which the Yokuts apply to the Chumash.

CABRILLO'S DISCOVERIES.

The report of Cabrillo's voyage mentions by name a considerable number of coast and island Chumash villages. As this list antedates by more than two centuries any similar record for other California Indians, its examination is of interest.

Beginning with Xucu, the Pueblo de las Canaos, sometimes placed at Santa Barbara or Ventura but more likely to have been at Rincon, the Cabrillo narrator names Xucu, Bis, Sopono, Alloc, Xabaagua, Xotococ, Potoltuc, Nacbuc, Quelqueme, Misinagua, Misesopano, Elquis, Coloc, Mugu, Xagua, Anacbuc, Partotac, Susuquey, Quanmu, Gua (or Quannegua), Asimu, Aguin, Casalic, Tucumu, Incpupu. The context implies that these extended westward not quite to Dos Pueblos. Subsequently Cabrillo speaks of the greater part of this coast, namely, the stretch from Las Canoas to Cicakut or Pueblo de Sardinas, identified with Goleta, as the province of Xucu, appearing to contrast it with the province of Xexu which reaches from Xexu or Xexo on the lee side of Point Concepcion to Dos Pueblos. From Sardinas to Point Concepcion he then names Ciucut (the "Capital," where an old woman reigned as "señora"), Anacot (or Anacoac), Maquinanoa, Paltatre, Anacoat, Olesino, Caacat (or Caacac), Paltocac, Tocane, Opia, Opistopia, Nocos, Yutum, Quiman, Micoma, Garomisopona.

It is clear from the misspelled repetitions in these lists, as well as their correspondences, that they cannot represent any consistent geographical order. Sopono, Misesopano, and Garomisopona; Potoltuc, Paltatre, Partotac, and Paltocac; Anacot, Anacoat, and probably Nacbuc and Anacbuc; Opia and Opistopia; Cicakut, Ciucut, and perhaps Caacat, are all duplicate references.

The identifications with villages mentioned in more recent sources point to the same conclusion. The more probable of these are:

Xucu: Shuku, at Rincon (not Ventura).
Alloc: Heliok, near Goleta.
Xabaagua: Shalawa, near Santa Barbara (b for l?).
Quelqueme: Wene'me, at Hueneme (q for g?).
Elquis: Elhelel (?), near Santa Barbara.
Coloc: Kolok, at Carpinteria.
Mugu: Muwu, on Mugu lagoon.
Xagua: Shawa on Santa Cruz island, or for Xabaagua (?).
Susuquey: Shushuchi, between Refugio and Gaviota.
Quanmu: Kuyamu (?), at Dos Pueblos.
Casalic: Kasil (?), at Refugio.
Tucumu: Tuhmu'l, near Shushuchi.
Incpupu: Humkaka, on Point Concepcion.
Ciucut: Siuhtun or "Siuktu" in Santa Barbara.
Tocane: Perhaps a misreading of Tucumu, but Tukan, the name of San Miguel Island, may be intended.
Xexo: Shisholop, inside Point Concepcion.

It may be added that Paltocac is placed by a later authority near Goleta, presumably on native information.

The islands present more difficulty, since the expedition may have confounded or rediscovered them. Two of the three Cabrillo names for the islands can not be identified: Liquimuymu, San Miguel, and

Nicalque, Santa Rosa. The third is involved in doubt: Limu or Limun, Santa Cruz.

Liquimuymu is said to have had two towns: Zaco or Caco, which may be for Tukan (the island may well have been named after the principal settlement); and Nimollolo, which suggests Nimalala on Santa Cruz. Liquimuymu itself suggests the Santa Cruz village of L'aka'amu, or, as it has also been written in Spanish orthography, Lucuyumu.

On Nicalque three villages are named: Nichochi or Nicochi; Coycoy; and Caloco or Estocoloco ("este Coloco, this Coloco"?). None of these can be identified. Coloco may be another Kolok distinct from that at Carpinteria: compare Shisholop at both Point Concepcion and Ventura. Nicalque itself might possibly stand for either Nümkülkül or Niakla on Santa Rosa.

Limu is said to contain eight towns, and ten are then enumerated, whose names seem unusually corrupted: Miquesesquelua, Poele, Pisqueno, Pualnacatup, Patiquiu and Patiquilid (sic), Ninumu, Muoc, Pilidquay (sic), and Lilibeque. If these words are Chumash, the initial syllables in P– suggest a native article or demonstrative which has been erroneously included. Not one name of this list can be connected with any known Chumash settlement.

A previous mention of "San Lucas" has been interpreted as referring to Santa Rosa, but several of its six villages can be safely identified as on Santa Cruz: Maxul is Mashch'al; Xugua (compare the mainland list), Shawa; and Nimitopal, Nimalala. The others are Niquipos, Nitel, and Macamo. If we are willing to allow a considerable play to misprints, Nitel might be Swahül (Ni– for Su–), and Macamo, L'aka'amu (M for L). Hahas, one of the principal towns in later times, is not mentioned by Cabrillo. Even if some of these identifications with Santa Cruz settlements seem doubtful, it is significant that not one of the San Lucas villages bears any resemblance of name to the villages of Santa Rosa.

It follows, therefore, that "San Lucas," as the designation of a single island, is Santa Cruz, and not Santa Rosa. Limu or "San Salvador," for which an entirely different list of villages is given, accordingly would be not Santa Cruz but Santa Catalina, as indeed at least one authority has already asserted. There is the more warrant for this attribution, since the name Santa Catalina in the mouths of all Shoshoneans is Pimu, of which Limu is an easy misreading. Hence, too, the eight or ten unidentifiable village names on "Limu": they would not agree with any known designations of Chumash villages because Santa Catalina is Gabrielino, that is, Shoshonean. It is true that the words do not ring Shoshonean. They are almost certainly not Gabrielino, which has "r" where more southerly cognate dialects have "*l.*" Various conjectures can be advanced on this point. Perhaps the simplest is that Chumash names were obtained for Shoshonean settlements.

It may be added that these reinterpretations are much more consonant with a reasonable course for Cabrillo's little vessels. The route formerly accepted is: San Pedro Harbor (San Miguel), then westward to Santa Cruz (San Salvador), back easterly to Santa Monica (Bahia de los Fumos or Fuegos), then west once more to Mugu, and then to Ventura (Xucu); with Catalina, which is in plain sight of San Pedro, unmentioned until later. The following chart is suggested instead: San Diego or Newport Bay (San Miguel); Santa Catalina; either San Pedro or Santa Monica (Los Fumos); Mugu; and Rincon (Las Canaos, native name Xucu). This gives a continuous course.

On the other hand, Limu reappears in later sources, and almost certainly as Santa Cruz. Father Tapis in 1805 wrote of two islands, whose position seemingly best fits that of Santa Cruz and Santa Rosa, as being called, respectively, Limú and Huima. The latter is clearly Wima'l, that is, Santa Rosa. It was said to contain seven settlements, which is the number located on it in Plate 48. Limú must therefore be Santa Cruz. Its 10 rancherias nearly reach the number on the map. The three principal, with populations of 124. 145, and 122 adults, respectively, were Cajatsá—that is, Hahas; Ashuagel; and Liam, the Liyam of the map.

This evidence seems almost inescapable; but its acceptance gives Cabrillo a confused route; makes his San Salvador (Limú) and San Lucas (Maxul, etc.) the same island; furnishes two entirely different lists of villages said by him to be on this island, one of them identifiable and the other wholly unidentifiable by more recent Chumash data; and makes the voyager silent on the inhabitants of Santa Catalina. These difficulties lend a certain seduction to the temptation somehow to regard Cabrillo's Limú as having been Pimu-Catalina; enough, perhaps, to justify the maintenance of some suspicions until further elucidation is forthcoming.

With "San Lucas" and possibly "San Salvador" shifted one island east from the accepted interpretation, it may be that the "Isla de la Posesion" or "Juan Rodriguez," where Cabrillo wintered and lies buried, was Santa Rosa instead of San Miguel. Since nothing certain can be made of the native names that seem to refer to either island, this problem is one for the geographer rather than the ethnologist.

Two things are clear that are of general interest to the historian of the natives of California. First, many place names have endured for centuries in California. And, second, on allowance for the accumulation of errors in successive recording by mariners, copying, and printing of meaningless terms, there is no evidence that the Chumash language has materially altered in more than 350 years.

The Chumash knew the Salinans as At'ap-alkulul; the Yokuts or San Joaquin drainage Indians in general as Chminimolich or "northerners"; the Alliklik, their Shoshonean neighbors on the upper Santa Clara River, by that name; the Fernandeño, Gabrielino, and perhaps the groups beyond as At'ap-lili'ish. Most of these names in their full plural form carry a prefix I-.

All accounts unite in making the Chumash an unwarlike people, although intervillage feuds were common and the fighter who killed was accorded public esteem. A little war between Santa Barbara and Rincon, probably in Mission times, seems to be the chief one of which knowledge has been perpetuated.

SOCIAL INSTITUTIONS.

Notices of the status of the chief, *wot* or *wocha*, are brief and as conflicting as is customary when no intensive study has been made. One statement is to the effect that chiefs had no authority and were not obeyed. This is no doubt true if "authority" is taken in the strict legal sense which the word can possess among more advanced peoples. But, on the contrary, everything goes to show that the Chumash chief enjoyed influence and honor to a rather unusual degree. Cabrillo's reference to his "princess" indicates that rank was carefully regulated. In an anarchic society, leadership would have been in the hands of a man of natural capacity; a woman can attain to accorded preeminence only through definitely crystallized custom. It is also repeatedly stated that the chief received food and shell money from the people—no doubt for a return of some kind. It is specifically said that he was head among the rich men. Ordinarily, he alone had more than one wife. The chief summoned to ceremonies—the general Californian practice; and no doubt entertained the visitors. Refusal to attend was a cause of war. As the same is reported from the Juaneño, the fact can not be doubted. But it is likely that some motive other than resentment at slighted prestige was operative. Declination of an invitation may have been a formal imputation of witchcraft, or a notice that hostile magic had been practiced in revenge.

The Chumash, alone among their neighbors, buried the dead. The Salinans cremated; so did the Shoshoneans eastward; the Yokuts both buried and burned. Only the inhabitants of the three Shoshonean islands followed the Chumash practice. The custom must have been very ancient, since skeletons are as abundant in most of the Chumash area as they are rare in adjoining territory; and there is no clear record of calcined human bones.

The body was roped in flexed position. The prehistoric burials frequently show the same position, and sometimes contain fragments of heavy cord. One man alone carried the corpse and made the grave. This practice indicates belief in defilement. Those who assisted at a funeral were given shell money. The widow observed food restrictions for a year and wore the husband's hair on her head. The cemeteries seem to have been inside the villages, and were marked off with rows of stones or planks. For prominent men, masts bearing the possessions of the dead were erected, or tall boards bearing rude pictures. The mourners, it appears, danced around the cemetery, or perhaps about the family plot within it.

DWELLINGS.

According to all accounts, the Chumash house was large—up to 50 feet or more in diameter—and harbored a community of inmates; as many as 50 individuals by one report, 40 by another, three or four families according to a third. The structure was hemispherical, made by planting willows or other poles in a circle and bending and tying them together at the top. Other sticks extended across these, and to them was fastened a layer of tule mats, or sometimes, perhaps, thatch. There was no earth covering except for a few feet from the ground, the frame being too light to support a burden of soil.

The ordinary sweat house seems to have been small, but nothing is known of its construction. There was, however, also a large type of sweat house or ceremonial chamber, apparently dirt roofed, with steps leading up to the top, where the entrance was by ladder. This is clearly the Sacramento Valley dance house, whose appearance among the Chumash is rather remarkable in view of the fact that otherwise it was not built south of the Miwok, several hundred miles away. Such discontinuous croppings out are not rare in California; witness the distribution of totemic exogamy, of caps, and the acorn soup paddle. They indicate a greater group individuality than has generally been assumed or than appears on first acquaintance. It is extremely probable that of such now separated cultural elements many once extended over a large unbroken tract, from certain middle portions of which they were subsequently eliminated by the increasing activity of other factors of social life.

The Chumash are one of the California nations that knew true beds and made what might be called rooms inside their houses.

The beds were platforms raised from the ground, on which rush mats were spread. A rolled-up mat served as pillow. Other mats were hung about the bed, both for privacy and for warmth, it appears. The islanders, on the other hand, slept crowded and on the ground, according to Cabrillo.

CANOES.

The canoe, *tomol* or *tomolo*, was one of the glories of the Chumash. Their northern neighbors were entirely without; only toward Cape Mendocino were canoes again to be encountered; and these were of a quite different type. The Shoshoneans of the islands, of course, had boats; and in some measure the Chumash-Gabrielino form of canoe was employed southward at least as far as San Diego. But the Luiseño and Diegueño did not voyage habitually; and for local use, the rush balsa seems to have been commoner. The Chumash, however, were mariners; they took to their boats not only when necessity demanded, but daily, so far as weather permitted.

The canoe as generally described was made of separate planks lashed together and calked with the asphalt that abounds on the beach. Fragments from ancient sites tally exactly with the accounts. Whether the dugout form of boat was also made is not altogether certain, but seems not unlikely. The planked vessel has less strength; but the sea is generally remarkably calm in the Santa Barbara Channel, and landings would normally be made in sheltered coves. This type of boat is, of course, also lighter and swifter. It has sometimes been thought that the Chumash had recourse to planks because of lack of timber suitable for hollowing, especially on the islands. This explanation seems to be only indirectly true. Santa Cruz still bears tolerable pines, Santa Rosa was not wholly without trees, and on the mainland there were, of course, forests. But the rainfall is light in Chumash land, and trees of any size grow only on the mountains, in the most favorable cases several miles from the shore. There are no streams large enough to float a heavy log, and the carriage of one would have been extremely laborious at best, perhaps quite impracticable. A long board, however, was easily carried down a trail by a pair of men. The abundance of asphalt remedied any deficiencies of carpentering, so far as tightness to water went. Once the type was worked out and established, it might be given preference over the dugout even in the rarer cases where the latter was practicable.

The larger canoes must have had some sort of skeleton, or at least thwarts; but there are no clear reports as to such constructional elements. Neither do we know if the bow was pointed, as the speed attained would indicate, or blunt, as in the river boat of north-western California. One account mentions that the ends were high. Prehistoric stone models are sharp and raised at both ends, with a vertical drop in the gunwale aft of the stem and forward of the stern.

The canoes are described as holding from 2 or 3 to 12 people; one account even says 20. Another mentions 8 paddlers and 6 passengers. The length is said to have run to 8 or 10 varas, say 25 feet, with a 4-foot beam; but this size must have been exceptional. It is certain that double-bladed paddles were used; their employment has already been noted on San Francisco Bay and recurs among the Diegueño. This implement seems elsewhere in North America to be known only to the Eskimo. The ordinary one-bladed paddle may also have been in use by the Chumash.

The planking was split with wedges, which would be needed also for cemetery boards and probably for wooden dishes. The Chumash replaced the usual Californian antler wedge with one of whale rib. The adze is not known. Its blade must have been of shell, as with the Yurok, since flint chips too jaggedly to be of service for planing, and grained stone can not be rubbed down to a fine enough edge and retain strength. The handle may be conjectured to have been of wood, since no remains of stone or bone have been found that would answer the purpose.

WOODEN IMPLEMENTS.

Another device that is unique among the Chumash, at least so far as California is concerned, is the spear thrower. Our knowledge of this rests exclusively upon a single specimen brought to England by Vancouver. The record that it was obtained at Santa Barbara is not entirely free from suspicion, but seems authentic. It might be conjectured that the Chumash learned the implement from the Aleutians who were brought to some of the islands by Russian sea otter hunters during the latter part of the Mission period; but there is nothing in the specimen to suggest an Alaskan prototype, and Vancouver seems to have preceded the Russians. The shape is remarkable: a very short and rather thick board, nearly as broad as long, and appearing extraordinarily awkward for its purpose. It is, however, indubitably a spear thrower, with groove and point for the butt of the spear. While the circumstances surrounding this solitary example are such as to necessitate some reserve in the acceptance of the implement as native in Chumash culture, it seems sufficiently supported to be added to other instances as an illustration of the technical advancement which this people had reached.

A companion piece in the British Museum is a harpoon quite different from any other known Californian one. It has a rather heavy shaft of wood painted red. Into this is set a slenderer foreshaft, a device never reported from California except in arrows. The head is of bone, with a barb and a chert point. The line is attached to the head in typical Californian manner: lashed on with cord, over which gum or asphalt has been smeared. The weapon is meant for sea otters or seals, not for fish. It is to be hoped that these two remarkable pieces may soon have the remnants of doubt that still cling to them dissipated by a searching scrutiny. A determination of their wood promises to be particularly convincing.

Also unique is a sinew-backed bow in the British Museum; and of special interest because southern California generally used self-bows. This specimen is narrower and thicker than the Yurok bows obtained by Vancouver at Trinidad on the same voyage; and its wood is more yellowish than the northern yew. The attribution to Santa Barbara is therefore probably correct. The grip is thong wound, the cord of three-ply sinew.

Otherwise, the Chumash bow is unknown. The arrow is said sometimes to have been of cane. This report is confirmed by the presence in graves of the grooved arrow straightener of steatite that is the invariable concomitant of the cane arrow in the southern half of California. It is less common, however, than might be anticipated among a people who worked soapstone so freely as the Chumash. The inference results that the cane arrow was less typical than one with a wooden shaft.

Several early sources speak of neatly made dishes and bowls of wood, beautifully inlaid with haliotis; but not a single representative specimen has survived. The type appears to have been confined to the Chumash; though inlaying on a smaller scale was practiced by the southern Californians on their ceremonial batons, and the Yurok and their neighbors occasionally set bits of haliotis into a pipe.

BASKETRY.

Chumash basketry is substantially that of the Shoshoneans of southern California, which is described in detail in the chapter on the Cahuilla, plus some leanings toward the Yokuts and certain minor peculiarities. Perhaps the most important of these is the substitution of three rushes (*Juncus*) for a bundle of grass stems (*Epicampes rigens*) as the foundation of coiled ware. The grass is used both by the Southern Yokuts and the Shoshoneans. The Chumash employed it, but rarely. One or more of their rushes were apt to be split with each stitch: the awl was as likely to pass through as between the soft and hollow stems. Sumac (*Rhus trilobata*) was also coiled about the *Juncus* foundation. The prevailing surface, however, at least in decorative baskets, was of the rush. Typical

PLATE 52

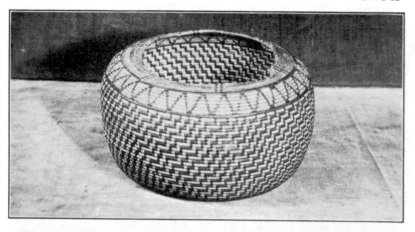

CHUMASH BASKETRY

PLATE 53

a, Ancient Chumash coiled cap; *b*, *c*, *d*, *e*, asphalted water baskets found in a cave. *b*, Plain twining; *c*, same with reinforcement in three-strand twining; *d*, same with more reinforcement; *e*, diagonal twining

PLATE 54

ANCIENT CHUMASH BURDEN AND STORAGE BASKETS, COILED
FOUND IN A CAVE

MOHAVE FRAME FOR WEAVING GLASS BEAD CAPE

PLATE 55

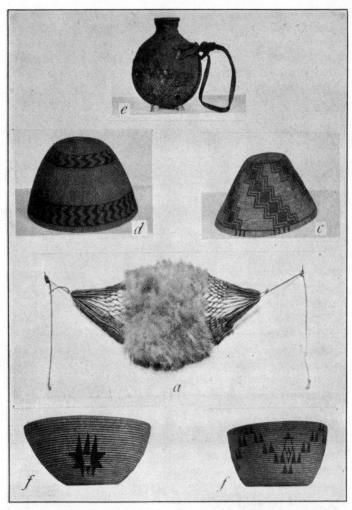

a, Head net for dancing, Northwestern Valley Maidu. Baskets: *b,* Mohave; *c,* Kitanemuk; *d,* Eastern Mono; *e,* Kawaiisu; *f,* Washo

coloration of such vessels was threefold: a buff background, often inclining to red or mottled, with black patterns outlined in yellow or white, all of these shades except the black appearing to have been obtained from the undyed rush itself. This three-color effect is Yokuts rather than southern Californian. (Pl. 52.)

There is also northern resemblance in the shape of baskets intended for gifts or offerings. The shape of these stands midway between the Yokuts bottleneck and the southern California globular basket. They are low, with mouth rather small in the perfectly flat top. Sometimes there is a small rim or neck, but this never rises to any distance. One or two preserved specimens are fitted with a lid, but there is no evidence that this is an aboriginal feature. The direction of the coil in these shouldered baskets is antisunwise, as they are viewed from above, and contrary to the direction in vessels of other shapes. Exactly the same holds for the Yokuts and Shoshonean small-mouthed baskets, which, in all three regions, were evidently held or pierced in reverse position during manufacture.

The best Chumash work is somewhat finer and smoother than that of the Shoshoneans of southern California. In part, the difference may be attributed to the preservation chiefly of exceptional show pieces, which contrast with the average effect of the much more numerous modern utilitarian Cahuilla and Luiseño specimens. But there was no doubt also an actual distinction, in which the southern Yokuts were aligned with the Chumash as against the Shoshoneans. This is what one should expect from the general types of civilization of the peoples. The Chumash at all points show themselves finished and loving artisans of exceptional mechanical skill. The Shoshoneans of the south were coarse handicraftmen, but mystic speculators and religious originators.

An ancient Chumash cap which fortune has preserved in a cave is also southern Yokuts rather than Luiseño in appearance. (Pl. 53.)

Coiled storage baskets, wider at the bottom than at the mouth, were made by the Chumash. (Pl. 54.) These may have been known also to the other tribes of the south, but, if so, they have gone out of use.

Openwork rush baskets, both deep and plate form, were practically identical with those of the Luiseño.

A basketry water bottle must have been of some importance, since a number of prehistoric specimens have come to light. (Pl. 53.) They are usually in simple twining reinforced here and there by courses of three-strand or diagonal twining, flat bottomed, and lined with asphalt, which was applied with hot pebbles. The water bottle of the Plateau Shoshoneans and of the desert tribes of Arizona, which penetrated eastern and southern California at least as far as the Tehachapi range, was in diagonal twining, pitched outside, and

usually pointed or rounded below. It is intended for hanging and
for travel; the Chumash form, to be set about the house. The material of the latter seems most commonly to have been *Juncus*, which
the asphalt stiffened for enduring wear.

The woven fur blanket, which in its characteristic California form
is made, as in the Southwest and Plateau, of strips of rabbit skin, was
partly replaced among the Chumash by one of feathers. Narrow
pieces of bird skin were twisted with a cord to give them strength;
into these were woven shorter strands of plain strings. This is a
form of blanket that appears to have been known through a considerable part of California.

This type of feather blanket is described by the Maidu, and is only a variant
of the rabbit-fur robe. Two specimens preserved in museums, one from the
Chumash and the other from an unspecified group in California, have a different
structure. The former has a long continuous warp of two cords wrapped with
strips of quill, to which feather web adheres. A double woof of unfeathered
cords is twined in. The second piece also has a double warp, but the two
strands are twisted on each other and a bit of feather inserted at each turn.
The woof is inserted in close rows. This makes at least three techniques followed in the manufacture of these blankets.

INDUSTRY IN STONE.

The Chumash did not make the pottery of their southeastern neighbors, and did not acquire it in trade, although stray pieces may now
and then have drifted among them. References to their " pots " or
" ollas " are to steatite vessels, both open dishes and nearly globular
bowls, often large—up to 2 feet in diameter—and usually thin
walled. Some are shell inlaid and have not been subjected to setting
in the fire, but the service of ceremony or show which they rendered
is unknown. When a pot broke, its pieces were used as fry pans; at
least, many such have been found, fired and usually perforated in
one corner, to allow of being moved with a stick.

The Chumash used the metate; the bowlder mortar; the mortar
finished outside; and the pounding slab with basketry hopper. The
latter is attested by numerous circles of asphalt on ancient stones—
sometimes on mortar edges, too. Whether the relation of the several
types was one of use or period, or both, is not known, since no attention appears to have been given to stratigraphy in any of the
numerous excavations of Chumash sites. The deposits are sometimes
of considerable thickness, and once they are examined with reference
to their time sequences, light may be shed on the obscure history of
mortar and metate, which is discussed in connection with the Maidu
and other tribes.

One consideration may be added here. There are indications
that the true or squared metate is a utensil which spread north-

ward from southern Mexico, probably in more or less close association with agriculture. This is the implement with flat or cylindrically concave surface, over which an elongated stone was worked back and forth. In contrast with this is the grinding stone more prevalent in California: an irregular slab on which a roundish or short stone was rubbed with a rotary motion. This is a ruder device, effective enough for the occasional grinding of seeds, and sufficiently simple, both in its manufacture and manipulation, to form part of a very rudimentary culture. It would not answer the daily needs of a population practicing maize agriculture systematically. The question for California is whether the grinding slab may go back to an early period with the metate superadded later, or whether the former is to be regarded as the contemporary equivalent among a lowly civilized people of the more specialized metate. Almost every specimen shows at a glance how its surface has been worn; but no consistent distinction of the two types appears to have been attempted.

Small and large show mortars are not rare in Chumash graves. They are of fine sandstone, flat bottomed, the walls of uniform thickness, and polished outside as well as in. The rim is nicely squared, sometimes even concave, or asphalted and inset with shell beads. Such pieces would necessarily be far too valuable for ordinary use, and would certainly break promptly under wear. That they were made for the toloache ritual is possible, but unproved. They do confirm, however, the early remark that " the constancy, attention to trifles, and labor which they [the Channel Indians] employ in finishing these pieces, are well worthy of admiration; " a fitting characterization, also, of most other products of Chumash industrial art.

Large stone rings or perforated disks have been found in great numbers in Chumash territory. These were slipped over the women's digging sticks to give the stroke momentum. Elsewhere in California such weighting of the stick has not been reported, and since stones with sufficiently large perforations are rare, it seems that the Chumash were nearly unique in not contenting themselves with the simple sharpened shaft. Most of the stones are well rounded and some are beautifully polished in hard, compact material. They were evidently highly prized and illustrate once more the fondness of the Chumash for perfection in manual matters.

There has been some inclination to interpret these objects as warclub heads, net sinkers, and the like, but as native statements on the subject are perfectly clear and decisive, mere conjectures are baseless. It does not matter that now and then a carefully polished piece shows wear as if someone had hammered with it. A hasty woman may occasionally have laid hold of the first implement that came to hand, or young or thoughtless members of the family may have aroused her resentment by putting a carefully preserved treasure to rough and ruinous use in her absence. We do not conclude from coffee stains on a chair that the owner regarded it indiscriminately as a seat and a table, nor from its violently fractured condition that it was intended as a weapon of offense. The remains of primitive people must be judged in the same spirit.

The pipe, as recovered by excavations, is a stone tube, slightly convex in profile, and thinning considerably from bowl to mouth end. A short bone mouthpiece remains in many specimens and is likely to have been set in regularly. The length varies, but 5 inches would be not far from the average. Steatite is perhaps the commonest material, but by no means the only one; a rough-breaking brick-red stone occurs rather frequently. Now and then the pipe is bent near the middle at an angle of from 15° to 60°. This form allowed comparatively easy perforation of pieces more than a foot long, since boring could be carried on in four sections—at each end and in both directions from the elbow. the two latter holes being subsequently plugged.

Analogy with the practices of other California Indians makes it almost certain that the stone pipes of the Chumash were employed by shamans. Their comparative abundance suggests that they were also put to profaner use. But, on the other hand, it is scarcely probable that a man would smoke only when he had a stone implement. Pipes of wood or cane are likely to have been used but to have perished.

SHELLS AND MONEY.

The commonest fishhook among the Chumash and their neighbors to the southeast was of haliotis, nearly circular, and unbarbed. The point is turned so far in as to make it difficult to see how it could have bit; but hooks of similar shape are used in Polynesia and Japan for fish that swallow slowly. As tension is put on the line, the point penetrates the jaw and slides through to the attachment of the line.

Chumash money appears to have been the clam-shell disk bead currency that was the ordinary medium of all those parts of California that did not employ dentalia. In fact, it is likely that the Chumash furnished the bulk of the supply for the southern half of the State, as the Pomo did farther north. The usual south and central Californian method of measuring the strung beads on the circumference of the hand was in vogue. The available data on this system have been brought together in Table 6.

TABLE 6.—CALIFORNIA SHELL BEAD MONEY MEASURES.

	Salinan Antoniano.	Salinan Migueleño.	Central Yokuts.	Southern Yokuts.	Chumash.	Gabrielino.	Luiseño.
Tip of middle finger to crease of palm	wosemah (½)[1]	tewi (½)					
Half of circumference palm and fingers	"1–its–name" (1)	"1–its–name" (1)					
Circumference palm and fingers	mawiya (2)	"2–its–name" (2)		chok	skomuya[2] (½)[3]		
One and a half times around			chok[3]			ponko (1)[3]	[½ ponko.]
Twice around		"4–its–name" (4)		hista[4]	stü[4] (1)[3]		
Circumference elbow and finger tips		hamawi[5]		(6)			ponko.
Four times around palms and fingers		"8–its–name" (8)					
Six times around						sakayo (4)	

[1] The figures in parentheses give the equivalent in Spanish *reales* or American "bits."
Compare *iskom*, two, *skumu*, four.
[2] Plus the length of the middle finger.
[3] Probably the same word.
[4] Reckoned as nearly equal to the "4–its–name."
[5] The measure from the tip of the middle finger "to" the elbow is mentioned as worth 2 *reales*.

The following conclusions may be drawn from this table:

(1) There was no unit of identical length of strung disks that obtained among all tribes that measured on the hand. One, one and a half, or two circumferences, with or without the length of the middle finger of the hand superadded, and the circuit of the forearm, were the basis of valuation among different groups.

(2) The Migueleño system has been renamed, and possibly altered, to fit the Spanish currency of reales and pesos.

(3) The native system was everywhere one of duplicating or quadruplicating units.

(4) The equivalations to silver money must be accepted with caution, because they may date from various periods, when native currency perhaps had reached different stages of depreciation. But it is rather clear that the Chumash, who probably furnished most of the supply, held their bead money in the lowest estimation. It was worth a third more among the Gabrielino and four times as much among the Salinans. With the southern Maidu, who are probably the farthest group to whom money from the Santa Barbara Channel penetrated, the system of measuring on the hand seems to have been no longer in use; but the values were extremely high. A yard would rate from $5 to $25 in American money; whereas the Chumash *stü* and Gabrielino *ponko*, of nearly the same length, were rated at only 12½ cents.

Chumash graves, as a rule, yield but little of this thick clam money. Small curved beads of olivella are far more abundant, and sometimes occur in great bulk. It may be that the Chumash buried these inferior strings with the dead and saved their genuine money to burn at a subsequent mourning commemoration.

Long tubular beads, sometimes of the columella of large univalves, others of the hinge of a large rock clam, are also found. These were prized like jewels from the Yokuts to the Diegueño—much as the magnesite cylinders in the north. Again the Chumash seem to have been the principal manufacturers.

STATUS OF CHUMASH CULTURE.

Practically every implement here mentioned as Chumash was known also to the inhabitants of the Shoshonean islands, and most of them to the mainlanders of the coast for some distance south, especially the Gabrielino. The archipelago must be considered a unit as regards material culture, irrespective of speech and origin of the natives. Santa Catalina remains, at any rate, show all the characteristics of Chumash civilization, perhaps even in their most perfect form. The Chumash coast, however, appears to have been much more closely linked with the Chumash islands, at least technologically, than the Shoshonean mainland with the Shoshonean islands; so that the prevailing impression of the culture as a distinctively Chumash one is substantially correct.

The steatite of the Chumash, so far as known, came from Santa Catalina, although ledges of this stone are reported in the Santa Ynez Mountains and near Arroyo Grande. But it can not be doubted that the island was the source of much of the supply. With it came certain curiously shaped objects—shovel-form, hooked, and the like, even carvings of finned whales, all very variable in size, and clearly serving no utility. They are less frequent in Chumash graves than on Santa Catalina, as might be expected. Since this island is the source of the Chungichnish religion, the most developed form of any cult based on the taking of the toloache plant, it might be suspected that this worship and the soapstone figures, whose import is obviously ritualistic, had traveled to the Chumash together. This may be; but there is no evidence in the scant extant knowledge that any of the specific phases of the Chungichnish religion, such as the sand painting, prevailed among the Chumash. They did use the Jimson weed; but for all that is known to the contrary, the associated cult may have been a generalized one such as flourished among the Yokuts.

It must be plainly stated, in fact, that our ignorance is almost complete on Chumash religion, on the side of ceremony as well as belief and tradition. The plummet-shaped charm stones were regarded magically and made much of. This fact points to central rather than southern California affinities in religion. Seeds, or perhaps meal ground from them, were used in offerings; but this is a custom of wide prevalence in California. Sticks hung with feathers were set up in their " adoratories." Such isolated scraps of information allow of no broader conclusions. Even the habits of the shaman are undescribed. The god *Achup* or *Chupu*, whose " worship " a missionary report of 1810 mentions as being uprooted among the Purisima natives, may or may not have had connection with the toloache cult. We can believe that the great mourning anniversary of the larger half of California was practiced; but we do not really know.

The curious ceremonial baton known to the Luiseño as *paviut* was certainly used by the Chumash, since prettily inlaid pieces, though lacking the inserted crystals, have been found. Again it would be hasty to draw the inference that the outright Chungichnish cult had reached the Chumash. Concrete religious elements often have a wider distribution, especially among primitive peoples, than organized religions, which, like all flowers, are temporary and superficial. It is difficult, to be sure, to picture the Chungichnish religion originating on Santa Catalina and spreading east and south to tribes of much inferior arts while leaving the nearer and more advanced Chumash on Santa Cruz and of Ventura untouched by its influence. An interpretation that avoids this mental obstacle is the conjecture that the Chumash and Gabrielino jointly worked out a well-developed religion based on toloache, of which we happen to know only the Gabrielino or Chungichnish phase because its spread was very recent and its influence affected tribes that have survived.

On the other hand, it is possible that the Chumash were really inferior to the speculating Shoshoneans in power of abstract formulation. Such differences in national spirit exist in California, as witness the Shoshonean Luiseño and Yuman Diegueño. The technological abilities of the Chumash do not by any means prove an equal superiority in other directions. And yet their excellence in material matters is so distinct that it is difficult for the ethnologist to picture them as mere secondary copyists in other respects.

CHAPTER 38.

THE WASHO.

AFFILIATIONS.

The Washo have been unduly neglected by students of the Indian. What little is on record concerning them makes it difficult to place them.

Their speech, which is rather easy to an English tongue and pleasant to the ear, is distinctive and very diverse from that of the Shoshonean Mono and Northern Paiute with whom they are in contact and association. Such investigation as has been made—and it has not gone very deep—points to the Washo language as being Hokan and therefore no longer to be regarded as an independent stock. Still the affiliation with other Hokan languages can not be close. The position of the Washo makes this comparative distinctness remarkable. For a detached and quasi-independent little group the Washo are on the wrong side of the Sierra. Diversity is the true Californian habit. The moment the Plateau is entered single dialects stretch for monotonous hundreds of miles, and the basic Shoshonean tongue continues without interruption across the Great Basin and even over the Rockies. Now the Washo are a Basin tribe. Their settlements were all on streams that flow eastward to be lost in the interior desert. Even as the artificial lines of statehood run they are as much a Nevadan as a Californian people. Their anomaly as a separate fragment is therefore in their location.

It is tempting to conjecture, accordingly, and especially on the basis of their probable Hokan kinship, that they are an ancient Californian tribe, which has gradually drifted, or been pressed, over the Sierra. But there are no concrete grounds other than speech to support such an assumption.

HABITAT.

The Washo territory is the upper and more fertile drainage of the Truckee and Carson Rivers—streams born in California mountains to perish in Nevada sinks. How far down they ranged on these two rivers has not been ascertained with accuracy. It seems to have been but a little below Reno and Carson City. Long Valley Creek, which drains northwestward into Honey Lake, a Californian stream, was also in their possession. West of the crest of the Sierra they had no settlements, but the Miwok acknowledged their hunting rights on the upper Stanislaus nearly as far down as the Calaveras Big Trees. They may have enjoyed similar privileges elsewhere. Where there are no winter villages, information is often conflicting: boundaries may have been in dispute, or amicably crossed. If the Washo hunted on the North Stanislaus they may have come down the Middle Fork also, or frequented the Calaveras, Cosumnes, or American. Sierra Valley has been assigned both to them and the northeastern Maidu. The deep snows prevented more than temporary occupation. Honey Lake, too, may have been more largely Washo than the map (Pl. 46) shows, or entirely forbidden to them.

Lake Tahoe is central to Washo territory, and was and is still resorted to in summer, but its shores are scarcely habitable in the season of snow.

The Washo call themselves Washiu or Wasiu. The names applied to them by their neighbors are unknown, except for northern Maidu Tsaisuma or Tsaisü. Northern Miwok Hisatok or Histoko means merely " easterners."

The Washo were at times in conflict with the adjacent Northern Paiute, whom they call Paleu, and by whom they are said to have been defeated about 1860.

NUMBERS.

There are the usual statements, some made as much as 50 years ago, about enormous decrease and degeneration or impending extinction; but actually the Washo seem to have suffered less diminution as a consequence of the invasion of our civilization than the vast majority of California Indians. Estimates of their population were: In 1859, 900; 1866, 500; 1892, 400; 1910, 300. The Federal census in this last year enumerated over 800, about one-third in California and two-thirds in Nevada, some three-fourths or more being full blood. As the Washo are distinctly separated from the " Paiutes " and the "California Diggers" in the local American consciousness, it is not likely that this figure involves any erroneous inclusions of consequence. Their lack of any reservation, and the semiadjustment of their life to civilized conditions, leading to a scattering habitation on the fringes of white settlements, have evidently caused a persistent underestimation of their numbers.

Their original strength may have been double what it is to-day: 1,500 or under seems a likely figure in view of the nature of their country, their solidarity, and their unity of speech.

CULTURE.

The customs of the Washo will undoubtedly prove interesting once they are known. Their habitat on the flank of the Sierra Nevada must have made them in the main Californians. But being over the crest of the range, they must have had something of an eastern outlook, and their associations with the Northern Paiute, who maintained direct affiliations with the tribes in the Rocky Mountains, and were apparently subject to at least some indirect influences from the Plains. can hardly but have given the civilization of the Washo some un-Californian color.

BASKETRY.

Their basketry, which is deservedly noted for excellent finish and refinement of decorative treatment, is of the central Californian order, with coiling predominating in fine ware (Pl. 55, *f*), whereas the adjacent Shoshoneans, like most of those of the Great Basin, incline to plain and diagonal twining. The nearest analogues are in Miwok work. Both single and triple rod foundations are employed. The shapes are simple; the designs are characterized by a lack of bulk that is typical also of Miwok patterns, as well as by a delicacy and slenderness of motive to which the Miwok do not attain. The direction of the coil is from left to right, as among the Miwok and Maidu; the edge has the herringbone finish of diagonally crossed sewing, where most California tribes, except sometimes the Miwok, simply wrap the last coil.

A twined and pitched water jar is no doubt due to Shoshonean influence. The conical carrying basket is either of plain-twined widespaced openwork of peeled stems, as in northwestern California, or unpeeled like the wood-carrying basket of the Pomo, or diagonally twined in openwork, or closely with a pattern. The nearer Californian tribes use chiefly a narrow mesh filled in by smearing over. Oval and triangular trays, elliptical seed beaters, and the like were of the types common to all the Sierra tribes and the nearer Shoshoneans; with the weave in plain or diagonal twining. The latter technique is in use also for cooking baskets. Three-strand twining is employed for starts and reenforcements.

The almost universal basket material is willow, with fern root (*Pteridium aquilininum*) for the black of patterns, and redbud (*Cercis occidentalis*) for red. The latter material was also used for warp and coiling foundation. It is said to have been imported from west of the Sierras.

Cradles are of the hooded basketry type described among the Yokuts. A band of diagonal bars or crosses—diagonals in two directions—is put on a boy's cradle, of rhombuses on a girl's. Occasionally the cradle and hood are covered with buckskin, as in the eastern Great Basin.

DRESS AND IMPLEMENTS.

Sinew-sewed deerskin clothes for women are mentioned, but may possibly have had the same recent and eastern source as the small sweat lodge. Their description as consisting of a separate waist and skirt sounds rather unaboriginal.

Rabbits were taken in nets of a 3-inch mesh, 1½ or 2 feet wide, and as much as 300 feet in length. These were hung loosely on stakes or bushes. Sometimes two were set at an angle. When the animals were driven, they became entangled in the sagging net, and had their temples crushed by hunters that sprang out from concealment. All hunts organized on a large scale were under the direction of the chief of the rabbit hunt, *peleu-lewe-tiyeli*, whose position was hereditary.

The bow was sinew backed and had recurved ends. The arrow was foreshafted, the quiver of deerskin had the hair side turned in. This indicates the usual north and central Californian type of weapon.

Piñon nuts, *tagum*, usually ground and boiled, were a commoner food of the Washo than acorns, *malil*, although these could also be gathered in some tracts and were obtained by trade from the west. The mortar was a hole in a bowlder, used without basketry hopper; the pestle usually an unshaped cobble. The metate was called *demge*. The mush-stirring paddle was called *k'a'as;* the looped stick which was used for the same purpose Yokuts-fashion, *beleyu*.

BUILDINGS.

The house was of poles joined in an oval dome, thatched with mats of tule, much as among the adjacent Northern Paiute. In the mountains leaves or bark were used for covering. The winter house was a cone of slabs of bark, about 8 feet high in the middle and 12 feet in length, with a projecting entrance. It must have been very similar to the Maidu *hübo*.

The Plains Indian type of sweat lodge, a pole frame temporarily covered with skins or mats, just large enough to sit in, and heated by steam, was used instead of the earth-covered Californian sweat house, it is said. This form is likely to be a recent one, introduced with the horse, or possibly a reflex of a ghost-dance movement.

The dance or assembly house with roof of earth was known to the Washo, who call it *dayalimi;* but whether they built and used it, or had merely seen it in the west, is not clear.

RELIGION AND SOCIETY.

The adolescence dance for girls was practiced, perhaps in a Shoshonean guise, since neither the valley Maidu, the hill Miwok, nor the Yokuts make this dance in developed form.

Some form of mourning anniversary was held—" cry " is its English name in vogue—but all details are lacking.

The chief, *teubeyu*, succeeded in the male line. At marriage an exchange of gifts is said to have been optional. As among the Northern Paiute, there evidently was no bride purchase, even in form. The dead were cremated.

It is clear that some real information on the Washo is highly desirable.

CHAPTER 39.

THE SHOSHONEAN STOCK.

RELATION OF THE STOCK TO THE CALIFORNIAN AREA.

The Shoshonean stock is easily the largest in California, in present-day numbers as well as in territory. It occupied a third of the area of the State. It stretched in a solid belt from the northeastern corner nearly to the southwestern. True, the Washo break the continuity at one point within the State limits. But this is a gap only in a nominal sense, for the Shoshoneans of the north and those of the south of California are connected by a broad band of territory that sweeps over nearly the whole of Nevada.

In one sense, however, the Shoshoneans are an un-Californian people. Except for a highland strip in the south (see Figs. 34, 52), they have nowhere crossed the Sierra Nevada, and therefore failed to penetrate the great valley and mountain area which is the heart and bulk of California. More than half of their territory that we are here concerned with is in that essentially Shoshonean region, the Great Basin. The lines that legislation has seen fit to impose on the States include this tract in California, but nature had planned differently and her line of division between the fertile lands that face the ocean and the deserts that front nothing at all ran nearer the shore. It is this natural line that the Shoshoneans have observed in their history. And in this sense the bulk of them are un-Californian, although within California.

In the south, it is true, they have arrived at the ocean, and there some of the most populous divisions had their seats. But southern California is in many ways a physiographic and climatic area distinct from the bulk of the State. At Point Concepcion on the coast, and at Tehachapi Pass inland, the vegetation, the marine life, the temperature, and the humidity change. The alteration of the land is visible from a train window. The south is in some parts the most fertile as it is the balmiest portion of the State. But the tract to which those traits apply is restricted. It is confined to the immediate drainage into the ocean, and its limits are nowhere more than

50 or 60 miles from the surf. Even of this fortunate belt the Shoshoneans held only part: Hokan, Chumash, and Diegueño clung to more than half.

In any event, the coastal territories of the Shoshoneans were small in contrast with their inland desert range, even within the limits of political California, and, when their whole habitat is considered, insignificant. From north to south the Shoshonean diffusion in the State was 600 miles: their ocean frontage, a scant 100 miles. Of at least 20 known divisions established on the basis of dialect, only 5 bordered on the sea, and only 3 of these in any notable degree.

THE LARGER UTO-AZTEKAN FAMILY.

Reference has been to " Shoshoneans "; but actually this group is only part of a larger one, from which habit rather than conviction has to date withheld the universal recognition which is its due: the Uto-Aztekan family. This mass of allied tribes, which extended from Panama to Idaho and Montana (Fig. 50), is one of the great fundamental families of aboriginal America, of importance in the origins of civilization, politically predominant at the time of discovery, and numerically the strongest on the continent today. The association of our Shoshoneans of east and south California with this aggregate at the centers of native culture opens a far perspective. The lowly desert tribes and simple-minded folk of the southern coast are seen in a new light as kinsmen, however remote, of the famous Aztecs; and an unexpected glimpse of a vista of history opens up before the concrete fact that the sites of the cities of Los Angeles and Mexico were in the hands of peoples whose affinity is certain.

Of course, any recent connections are out of the question. It was the ancestors of the Mexican Nahua and the California Shoshoneans some thousands of years ago who were associated, not their modern representatives; and, as to the former association, no one knows where it occurred. No tribe that could by any legitimate stretch be called Aztec was ever in California, nor for that matter within the present confines of the United States. That the speech of India and that of Germany go back to a common root is a circumstance of the utmost historic import. But no sane mind would infer from the existence of an Indo-Germanic family that Germans were Hindus or Hindus Germans. It is only reasonable that we should accord the Indian a similar discrimination.

The Shoshonean group, however, forms a solid block within the Uto-Aztekan group. It is a well-marked subdivision, with a long and justly recognized unity of its own, though of a lower order. The

speech affiliations of the Shoshoneans of California are all with the
other Shoshoneans, and not with the Pima, Yaqui, Tarahumare, Cora,
and other Mexican groups of the Uto-Aztekan family.   Hence it can
only aid proper understanding to treat the California tribes as Shoshoneans rather than as Uto-Aztekans.   Their relations to Mexico,
however ultimately important, are through the Shoshonean group as
a whole.

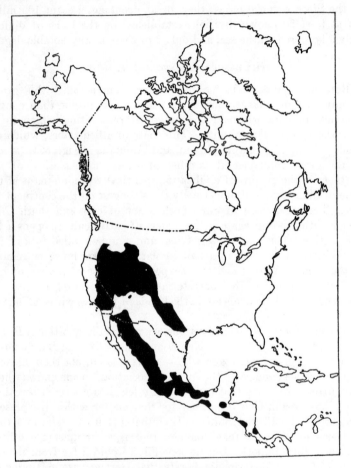

Fɪɢ. 50.—Uto-Aztecan family.

SHOSHONEAN BRANCHES AND DIVISIONS.

The Shoshonean group of languages is divided into four branches:
the most extensive in the Great Basin or Plateau; the next in southern
California; a third between these two on upper Kern River; and the
fourth in the Pueblo area in Arizona.   These are all about equally

distinct from one another, except that the speech of the Hopi, the Pueblo tribe, who are territorially as well as culturally isolated from the others, is somewhat the most diverse. Two of the three other branches are subdivisible; and the organization of the whole body appears in the following scheme:

Groups in California.	Division.	Branch.
Northern Paiute		
Eastern Mono	Mono-Bannock	
Western Mono		
Koso (Panamint)	Shoshoni-Comanche	I. Plateau.
Chemehuevi	Ute-Chemehuevi	
Kawaiisu		
Tübatulabal		II. Kern River.
Kitanemuk		
Alliklik	Serrano	
Serrano		
Vanyume		
Fernandeño		
Gabrielino	Gabrielino	
San Nicoleño		III. Southern California.
Juaneño		
Luiseño		
Cupeño	Luiseño-Cahuilla	
Pass Cahuilla		
Mountain Cahuilla		
Desert Cahuilla		
	Hopi	IV. Pueblo.

The more intimate geography of these groups can be surveyed in Figure 51. The relative position and extent of the branches and divisions appear in Figure 52. The Shoshonean holdings in California will be seen to be but a small fraction of the entire territory of the stock. Yet seven of the eight divisions, or every one except Hopi, is represented within the borders of the State. The inclination to diversity of idiom which has followed us throughout our progress over California greets us once more.

As Figure 52 is regarded, the Shoshonean subdivisions appear as if raying in a semicircular fan from a point in south-central California, on or near Kern River. It is highly improbable that they have actually spread out thus. We must rather look upon the focus as the region where the condensation has been greatest, the tract where newcomers gradually agglomerated, not the hive from which the whole body swarmed.

SHOSHONEAN MOVEMENTS IN CALIFORNIA.

The languages of the southern California branch are sufficiently specialized to make it necessary to assume a considerable period for their development. This specialization could hardly have taken place without either isolation or alien contacts in a marginal loca-

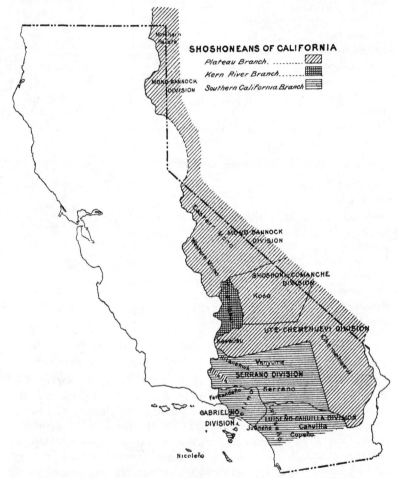

FIG. 51.—Shoshonean branches, divisions, and dialect groups in California.

tion, such as the branch is subject to now. Then, the ramifications of this branch imply a residence of some duration: there are three fully differentiated languages and a dozen dialects in southern California. How long it would take these to spring up it is impossible to say; but 1,000 years of location on the spot does not seem an excessive figure, and perhaps it would be conservative to allow 1,500 years since the Shoshoneans first began to reach the coast. The languages of the Yuman and Chumash peoples, whom the Shoshoneans have apparently split apart in their ancient shoreward drift, are so extremely different from each other now that this period is certainly the minimum that can be assumed for their separation.

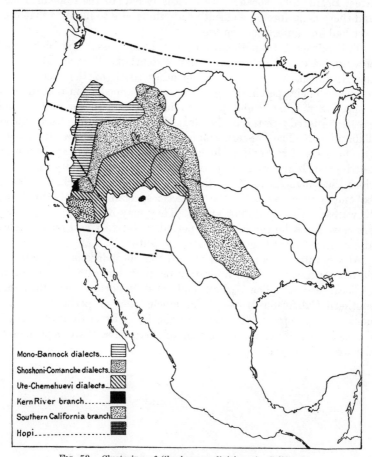

Mono-Bannock dialects....
Shoshoni-Comanche dialects.
Ute-Chemehuevi dialects.
Kern River branch.......
Southern California branch
Hopi.

Fig. 52.—Clustering of Shoshonean divisions in California.

The little Kern River branch, being equally distinctive, would seem to demand a nearly equal antiquity in the vicinity of its present seats. This would involve a drift separate from the last, but a substantially simultaneous one. It is possible that the Kern River group, being a much smaller one, and therefore much more susceptible to foreign influences, reached its high degree of specialization in a somewhat shorter time.

The languages of the Plateau branch in California represent a much more recent stratum. Those east of the Sierra are scarcely distinguishable from their congeners throughout the Great Basin. It is entirely conceivable that these tongues have been spoken in their present locations from time immemorial. Their territory is in the Great Basin; their speakers were actually part of the Plateau tribes; and there is no foreign element or anything else to indicate that they ever had any antecessors on the spot.

Two offshoots from them, however, have crossed the Sierra and entered the true Californian valley system: the Western Mono and the Kawaiisu, one north and the other south of the Kern River branch. Their speech, though somewhat changed from that of their respective neighbors and presumable ancestors to the east, is not greatly altered; certainly far less than that of the Kern River Tübatulabal. The Western Mono and Kawaiisu, then, are late comers. On the basis of reckoning which allows the Kern River and southern Californian branches 1,000 years in their present vicinity and 1,500 since their detachment from the main Shoshonean stock, 500 would be ample to account for the dialectic specialization of Mono and Kawaiisu. But we do not know. They may have been where they are now for a longer or a less period. Native tradition is silent; and civilized records go back barely a century.

At any rate, we can be positive that the Shoshoneans of California do not represent a single migration or drift, but rather a succession of local waves. The earliest and most important was that into southern California proper. Not much later, or perhaps synchronous but separate, was the entry of the Kern River division. Much the most recent was the movement of distinctive Plateau peoples to the west of the watershed.

CHAPTER 40.

THE PAIUTE, MONO, AND KOSO.

THE NORTHERN PAIUTE.

NOMENCLATURE.

The northeasternmost corner of California is held by a Sho-shonean people who popularly are known by the blanket term "Paiute." People of the same speech and very similar customs occupy the adjacent parts of Nevada, in fact the whole northwestern third of that State; the majority of the eastern half of Oregon; roughly the southern half of Idaho; and they extend southward along the eastern border of California, except for the local interruption of the Washo, for 300 or 400 miles. In Nevada and Oregon they are called Paiutes; in central California sometimes by this term and sometimes Mono; in Idaho they are the Bannock. The form of speech over this vast stretch is, however, virtually identical: minor dialects may be numerous, but intelligibility prevails throughout. Mono-Bannock is perhaps the generic designation least open to confusion. Paviotso is the term of the Shoshoni proper for the Nevada members of the group, but, like Mono and Monachi, is too limited in its application to serve for the entire Mono-Bannock body without producing opportunity for error.

The unqualified term "Paiute" is unfortunate because it refers to two quite different peoples, both indeed Shoshonean, and Plateau Shoshonean at that, but of quite distinct divisions. The other Paiute are in southern Utah, southern Nevada, and southern California. Their affiliations are with the Ute and Chemehuevi, and their speech is divergent enough from that of their northern namesakes to be at first contact mainly unintelligible, at least as connected discourse.

As a matter of fact, the Mono-Bannock and Ute-Chemehuevi divisions seem nowhere to be even in contact, Shoshoni-Comanche

581

tribes intervening from California to Colorado. The distinction
between Southern Paiutes and Northern Paiutes will therefore be
rigidly adhered to hereafter whenever the term is used at all. For
the former term, Chemehuevi is a customary and convenient synonym in southern California. For the latter, "Mono" occupies a
similar position in central California. Only the Northern Paiute
in northern California have no alternative epithet. Paviotso originated in eastern Nevada, and is locally unknown in California.
The northwestern Maidu call the Northern Paiute near them Monozi
or Mona, which are evidently forms of Monachi and Mono. This
very fact of its being a related name for a related people would
make Monozi a desirable designation were it not that Mono has
become so definitely identified with the central Californian Shoshoneans of the same division that its extension, even in slightly altered
form, to a people several hundred miles distant would be certain
to cause confusion. For our northeasterly Californians, then, the
unwieldy designation "Northern Paiute" seems to remain as the
only safe one.

The only other native ethnic name known for the Northern Paiute
is Toloma, applied by the northeastern Maidu.

THE GREAT BASIN CULTURE.

These people should be described in connection with those of
Nevada and Oregon, of whom they constitute a minute peripheral
fraction. They can, in fact, not be described here because nothing
of any significance is known of them, and little of moment of their
main body to the east. Their country was un-Californian. What
has been said before of Great Basin tribes that belong to California
unnaturally and only through the courtesy of arbitrary political
lines is particularly applicable here. The land is one of sagebrush
and cedar, as what appears to be really a juniper is currently called.
The acorn of California has vanished. The true pine nut takes its
place only in a measure. The soil is desert, the mountains rocky,
with timber in spots. Lakes are numerous, but they are evaporation
pools, swampy sinks, or salt basins. Streams run only in the mountains, and flow nowhere. The outlook is wide of necessity, the
population scant, travel and movement almost enforced. The Californian self-chaining to a short compass, with a dim gloom everywhere beyond, is impossible. But, to compensate, subsistence is
slender and a constant makeshift. There may be leisure indeed,
but it is an intermittent idleness, not the occupied and productive
luxury of well-fed time. The imagination has little occasion for
flight; or when the opportunity arises, there is but scant stimulus

in the concrete basis of life. Customs, therefore, remain rude. They are too flexible to bear any ramifying elaboration. Ritual, symbolism, and art attain little intensity, and monotonous simplicity takes the place of a rich growth. Where an activity specializes, it develops in isolation, and fails to merge or expand into a broad scheme: eagle hunting, shamans' singing, mourning customs fix the attention, not an assemblage of the gods or a coordinated series of rites.

The very poverty of Nevadan native civilization endows it with an interest. Its numberless little but crudely effective devices to struggle along under this burden, its occasional short plunges here or there, contain a wealth of significance. But we can only glimpse this cultural story from bits of stray knowledge. Its import and tenor can scarcely be mistaken; but the episodes that make the real tale have never been assembled.

We must leave the Northern Paiute of our northeasterly angle of California to some future historian of the bordering States. That they had much in common with their Maidu and Achomawi neighbors in the detail of their existence can not be doubted. But it is equally certain that in other respects they were true Basin people, members of a substantially homogeneous mass that extended eastward to the crest of the Rockies, and that in some measure, whether to a considerable or a subsidiary extent, was infiltrated with thoughts and practices whose hearth was in the Plains beyond. Several traces of this remote influence have already been detected among the Achomawi.

THE TWO GHOST-DANCE WAVES.

It was a Northern Paiute, though one of Nevada, Jack Wilson or Wovoka, who in 1889 in his obscurity gave birth to the great ghost-dance movement; and before him his father, or another relative, about 1870, originated a similar wave, whose weaker antecedent stimulus carried it less far and scarcely impressed the American public. In both cases the fringe of Northern Paiute whom we hold under consideration were involved with the main body of their kinsmen to the southeast, and passed the doctrine westward, the first time to the Modoc, the second to the Achomawi. The later and greater agitation stopped there: the California Indian inside the Sierra had long since given up all hope and wish of the old life and adapted himself as best he might to the new civilization that engulfed him. But in the early seventies less than 25 years had passed since the pre-American days of undisturbed and undiluted native existence. The middle-aged Indian of northern California had spent his early years under its conditions; the idea of its renewal seemed not impossible; and its appeal to his imagination was stirring. From Klamath Lake the tidings were carried to the Shasta; from them they spread to Karok,

Yurok, and Athabascan tribes.   The doctrine, taking new forms, but keeping something of its kernel, worked its uneasy way about and somewhere was carried across and up the Sacramento Valley, until, among the Pomo and southern Wintun, it merged with the old religion, crystallized, and remains to-day a recognizable element in ceremonial.

TRIBAL DATA.

The band of Northern Paiute of Surprise Valley and on Upper, Middle, and Lower Alkali Lakes, south of Fort Bidwell, were the Kaivanungavidukw.   To the north, around Warner Lake in Oregon, but ranging southward toward or to Fort Bidwell, were the Tuziyammo, also known as Ochoho's band.   The Honey Lake group were the Waratika or Wadatika, the "*wada*-seed eaters." East of these, over the State line, the Smoke Creek region seems to have belonged to the Kuyui-dika or "sucker-eaters," the Pyramid Lake people or Winnemucca's band.   (Pl. 37.)

The California limits of the Northern Paiute are not quite certain.   The doubts that exist have been aired in the foregoing discussions of Achomawi, Atsugewi, and Maidu.   The present population appears to be in the vicinity of 300.   It probably never exceeded double this figure.

THE MONO.

DESIGNATIONS.

After the alien Washo have been passed in a southward journey along the eastern base of the Sierra Nevada, Mono-Bannock people are again encountered.   They can now be named Monos with little fear of misunderstanding.

The word Mono means " monkey " in Spanish, but this signification, some guesses notwithstanding, can be eliminated from consideration of the origin of the term.   So can a Yokuts folk etymology, which derives it from *monai, monoyi,* " flies," on the ground that the Mono scaled the cliffs of their high mountains as the insect walks up the wall of a house.   Monachi is the Yokuts term for the people, corresponding to Miwok Mono-k, and to Maidu Monozi for the Northern Paiute.   It is a meaningless name.   The subtraction of the tribal suffix *chi* leaves a stem of which a Spaniard could hardly have made anything but Mono.   Whether the Yokuts originated the word, or whether it comes from some Shoshonean or other source, is not known.   The Mono call themselves only Nümü, which means no more than " persons."

Besides Monachi, the Yokuts call the western Mono Nuta'a (plural Nuchawayi), which, however, is only a directional term meaning "uplanders," and therefore generally easterners.   That it is not a true ethnic term is clear from the fact that Garcés, in 1776, used the same name, in the form Noche, for the southern foothill Yokuts themselves.   Malda is a specific southern Yokuts term for the Kern River Shoshoneans, and perhaps for all members of the family.

The eastern Mono of Owens Valley are called by themselves or their kinsmen Pitanakwat, which probably means "pine-nut-eaters," after a system of tribal or band nomenclature that prevails over much of Nevada and the surrounding Shoshonean regions. The Kern River Tübatulabal call the eastern Mono, Yiwinanghal; the western Mono, Winanghatal.

EASTERN AND WESTERN MONO.

The bulk of Mono territory and population is still in the Great Basin; but a branch is established in the high Sierra, at least in its marginal, permanently habitable portion, from which they look down on the foothill and valley Yokuts. The upper San Joaquin, Kings, and Kaweah comprise this domain, in which all the pine forest, and some stretches below it, are Mono. The dialect east and west of the huge crest is not identical, but appears to be remarkably similar considering that the two parts of the people have only their backs in contact—if contact it be with one of the earth's greatest walls between—and that their outlooks are opposite. The western, cis-Sierra, truly Californian Mono can hardly, therefore, have come into their present seats very long ago, as the historian reckons; and they are certainly newer than their neighbors, the Tübatulabal of Kern River, or the southern Californians of the same family. Both the western and the eastern halves answer to the name Mono, and the Yokuts call them both Monachi.

WESTERN MONO DIVISIONS.

The western Mono have several distinctive names applied to them by the Yokuts. It is not clear whether the Mono themselves employ these, or equivalents; nor whether, as the names might indicate, the Mono have borrowed the tribal organization of the Yokuts, or the latter merely attribute their own political unity to each Mono group to which its habitat gives a topographic unity.

On the North Fork of the San Joaquin, close to the Chukchansi, Dalinchi, and half-mythical Toltichi, as well as the uppermost of the southern Miwok on Fresno River, was a Mono band that survives in some strength to-day, but for which no "tribal" name is known.

South of the San Joaquin, on Big Sandy Creek, and toward if not on the heads of Little and Big Dry Creeks, were the Posgisa or Poshgisha. Their Yokuts neighbors were the Gashowu.

On a series of confluent streams—of which Big, Burr, and Sycamore Creeks are the most important—entering Kings River above Mill Creek, were the Holkoma. Towincheba has been given as a synonym and Kokoheba as the name of a coordinate neighboring tribe, but both appear to be designations of Holkoma villages.

At the head of Mill Creek, a southern affluent of Kings River, and in the pine ridges to the north, were the Wobonuch. Their Yokuts associates were the Michahai, Chukaimina, and Entimbich. In regard to the latter there is some confusion whether they are Yokuts or Mono.

On Limekiln and Eshom Creeks and the North Fork of Kaweah River were the Waksachi, whose Yokuts contacts were primarily with the Wükchamni.

On the Kaweah itself, especially on its south side, the Balwisha had their home. They, too, associated with the Wükchamni lower down on their own stream, but also with the Yaudanchi on the headwaters of Tule River, the next stream south.

This makes six named western Mono divisions, one each, roughly speaking, on each side of the three great streams that flow through their territory. Their more precise location appears on the Yokuts map (Pl. 47).

EASTERN MONO TERRITORY.

The eastern Mono inhabit a long, arid depression that lies along the base of the Sierra. Numerous small streams descend, even on this almost rainless side, from the snowy summits; and through most of the valley there flows one fair-sized longitudinal stream, the Owens River—the Jordan of California—and, like it, lost in a salt sea. The exact southward limits of the Mono have not been recorded, it appears. The line between them and the Koso, the next group beyond, has been drawn between Independence and Owens Lake; but it is possible that the shores of this sheet should have been assigned rather to the Mono.

Eastward and northward the Mono extend indefinitely across the diagonal line that gives the State of Nevada its characteristic contour. There appears to be no consequential change of dialect and no great modification of custom. On Owens River and around Mono Lake the people are sometimes called Mono and sometimes Paiute; in western Nevada they are only Paiutes; as the center of that State is approached, the Shoshoni name Paviotso begins to be applicable. To the Paiute of Pyramid Lake they are all, together with the bands far in Oregon, one people.

To the northwest, toward the Washo, the Mono boundary is formed by the watershed between Carson and Walker Rivers.

NUMBERS.

The Mono are to-day the most numerous body of Indians in California. The eastern Mono alone exceed, according to census returns, every group except the Maidu and Pomo; and at that both the latter are composite bodies, each including distinct languages, and are likely to have been more completely enumerated. The returns show 1,388 Mono in California. But as Mono and Inyo Counties, which are wholly eastern Mono except for a few Koso, are credited with nearly 1,200 Indians; and as the western Mono are about half as numerous as their eastern kinsmen, it is impossible to avoid the conclusion that the total for the combined group is above rather than below 1,500. Part of them have probably been classed under other names, such as Paiute, or reported without tribal designation.

This relatively high standing is, however, of recent date. A century ago the Mono were feeble in numbers compared with many other groups. The very inhospitability of their habitat, which then caused their population to be sparse, has prevented any considerable influx of Americans and has spared them much of the consequent incisive diminution that a full and sudden dose of our civilization always brings the Indian. They may retain in 1916 a full one-half of their numbers in 1816; the proportion among tribes situated as they are is in the vicinity of this fraction. A conservative estimate of their original number is 3,000 to 4,000; 5,000 or 6,000 a very liberal figure.

Much the same result is reached by comparison. If 50 Yokuts tribes totaled 15,000 to 20,000, the 6 western Mono divisions higher in the mountains may have aggregated 2,000 at best; and allowing double for the eastern division, we are still within the range of our estimate.

It is a subject for thought that a body of people that once stood to their neighbors as three or four to one should now be outranked by them one to three, merely because the former were a few miles more accessible to Caucasian contact.

CULTURE.

Mono civilization is little known, either as to customs or preserved implements. It is not even certain that they formed a group other than in speech and origin. There may have been a deep cultural cleft between the two halves, the western people being essentially Yokuts in practices and ideas, the eastern little else than Nevada Paviotso. Or they may really have been one people, whose western division had their civilization overlaid with a partial veneer of Yokuts customs. Information is practically lacking, for ethnologists have put little on record concerning either half of the group.

TOTEMIC GROUPING.

The western Mono, at least those on the San Joaquin and very likely those on other streams also, possessed one important central California institution that had not penetrated to their eastern brothers nor to any trans-Sierra people: the totemic moieties. But these moieties exhibit one feature that is neither Miwok nor Yokuts: they are not exogamous. Marriage is within or without the moiety. Descent is in the male line, and a group of animals is associated as "pets" or "dogs" with each moiety. These animals, at least the birds among them, were sometimes reared in captivity. When adult they were either despoiled of their feathers or released unharmed. The personal name is of Yokuts rather than Miwok type: it is inherited, and generally meaningless, not of totemic connotation. Chieftainship was dual as among the Yokuts, but the chief of the moiety represented by the eagle had precedence.

Besides being nonexogamous, the Mono moieties are peculiar in being definitely subdivided. The entire scheme is:

Moiety I, corresponding to Miwok "land" and Yokuts "downstream;" Yayanchi.

Subdivisions: Dakats, Kunugechi.

Totem animals: Eagle, crow, chicken hawk.

The name Dakats suggests Kawaiisu *adagatsi*, "crow," and Yayanchi the *yayu* hawk, identified with the opposite moiety.

Moiety II, corresponding to Miwok "water" and Yokuts "upstream:" Pakwihu.

Subdivisions: Tübahinagatu, Puza'ots or Pazo'odz.

Totem animals: Buzzard, coyote, *yayu* hawk, bald eagle.

Pakwihu is probably from *pakwi*, "fish"; Tübahinagatu perhaps from *tüba*, which seems to mean "pine nut" in certain Shoshonean dialects—compare "Tüba-tulabal"; Puza'ots recalls *oza'ots*, "magpie"—a bird of the opposite moiety among the Miwok—but the etymology seems more than venturesome. In fact, *oza'ots* may be nothing but a modified loan ward, the Yokuts *ochoch*.

The animal associations are the same as among the Miwok and Yokuts. The *yayu* may prove to be the Yokuts *limik*, the falcon, and as for the "bald eagle" on the buzzard or coyote side, this may be the "fish hawk" whom the Tachi put in the same division. But the Mono totemism is perhaps looser than that of their neighbors; it is said that a person may change his moiety.

OTHER NOTES.

The relationship terms of the San Joaquin Mono are, like those of the eastern Mono, of Great Basin type. Cross cousins are "brothers" or "sisters," not "parents" or "children" as among the Miwok and central Yokuts. This circumstance, coupled with the absence of exogamic regulations, makes it very probable that none of the Mono practiced cross-cousin marriage, a peculiar custom established among the Miwok.

The western Mono observed rather strictly the taboo between mother-in-law and son-in-law. If speech was necessary, these persons addressed each other in the plural, as if to dull the edge of personal communication by circumlocution. This device has already been noted among more northerly tribes. Some restraint or shame, though of a milder degree, was observed also toward the father-in-law; and—as among the Yana—between brother and sister. The eastern Mono knew nothing of these customs.

The rough Yokuts type of pottery seems to have been made by the western Mono but its precise range among them is unknown. Their basketry agreed with that of the Yokuts in forms, technique, and materials. A diagonally twined cap from the eastern Mono is shown in Plate 55, *d*.

The southern Yokuts report that the Mono cremated their dead; but it is not clear to what subdivision this statement refers. The eastern Mono about Bishop buried.

The mourning anniversary of south and central California was probably made by the western Mono. The eastern Mono burned considerable property over the graves of dead chiefs and possibly of other people, too; and saved their remaining belongings in order to destroy them a year later. This is an echo of the standard mourning anniversary.

The ritual number of the eastern Mono was four.

THE KOSO OR PANAMINT.

CONNECTIONS.

With the Koso (also called Kosho, Panamint, Shikaviyam, Sikaium, Shikaich, Kaich, Kwüts, Sosoni, and Shoshone) a new division of the Plateau Shoshoneans is entered—the Shoshoni-Comanche. This group, which keeps apart the Mono-Bannock and the Ute-Chemehuevi (Fig. 52), stretches in a tenuous band—of which the Koso form one end at the base of the Sierra Nevada—through the most desert part of California, across central and northeastern Nevada, thence across the region of the Utah-Idaho boundary into Wyoming, over the Continental Divide of the Rockies to the headwaters of the Platte; and, as if this were insufficient, one part, and the most famous, of the division, the Comanche, had pushed southeastward through Colorado far into Texas.

HABITAT AND POPULATION.

The territory of the westernmost member of this group, our Koso, who form as it were the head of a serpent that curves across the map for 1,500 miles, is one of the largest of any Californian people. It was also perhaps the most thinly populated, and one of the least defined. If there were boundaries, they are not known. To the west the crest of the Sierra has been assumed as the limit of the Koso toward the Tübatulabal. On the north were the eastern Mono of Owens River. Owens Lake, it seems, should go with the stream that it receives; and perhaps Koso territory only began east or south of the sheet; but the available data make the inhabitants of its shores

" Shoshones " and not " Paiutes." On the south the Kawaiisu and Chemehuevi ranged over a similarly barren habitat, and there is so little exact knowledge of ethnic relations that the map has had to be made almost at random. The boundaries in this desert were certainly not straight lines, but for the present there is no recourse but to draw them.

The fact is that this region was habitable only in spots, in oases, if we can so call a spring or a short trickle down a rocky canyon. Between these minute patches in or at the foot of mountains were wide stretches of stony ranges, equally barren valleys, and alkaline flats. All through California it is the inhabited sites that are significant in the life of the Indians, rather than the territories; and boundaries are of least consequence of all. In the unchanging desert this condition applies with tenfold force; but ignorance prevents a distributional description that would be adequate.

It is only known that at least four successive ranges, with the intervening valleys, were the portion of this people—the Coso, Argus, Panamint, and Funeral Mountains, with Coso, Panamint, and Death Valleys. Thirty years ago they actually lived at four spots in this area—on Cottonwood Creek, in the northwestern arm of Death Valley; south of Bennett Mills on the eastern side of the Panamint Mountains, in another canyon leading into Death Valley; near Hot Springs, at the mouth of Hall Creek into Panamint Valley; and northwest from these locations, on the west side of Saline Valley, near Hunter Creek at the foot of the Inyo Mountains.

It is not clear whether the terms " Coso " and " Panamint " were first used geographically or ethnically. The latter is the most common American designation of the group, and would be preferable to Koso except that, in the form Vanyume, it has also been applied to a Serrano group.

Koso population was of the meagerest. It is exceedingly doubtful whether the country would have supported as many as 500 souls; and there may have been fewer. In 1883 an estimate was 150; in 1891, less than 100; a recent one, between 100 and 150. The Koso are not sufficiently differentiated from adjoining groups in the popular American mind to make ordinary census figures worth much.

MANUFACTURES.

The Koso must have lived a very different life from the San Joaquin Valley tribes; but they share many implements with the Yokuts, through intercourse of both with the Tübatulabal; and it can not be doubted that ideas and practices were also carried back and forth.

The ceremonial skirt of strings of eagle down is one such evidence. Whether this traveled from west to east or the reverse, it is almost

PLATE 56

MOHAVE HOUSE INTERIOR, LOOKING IN FROM
DOOR

KOSO SWEAT HOUSE

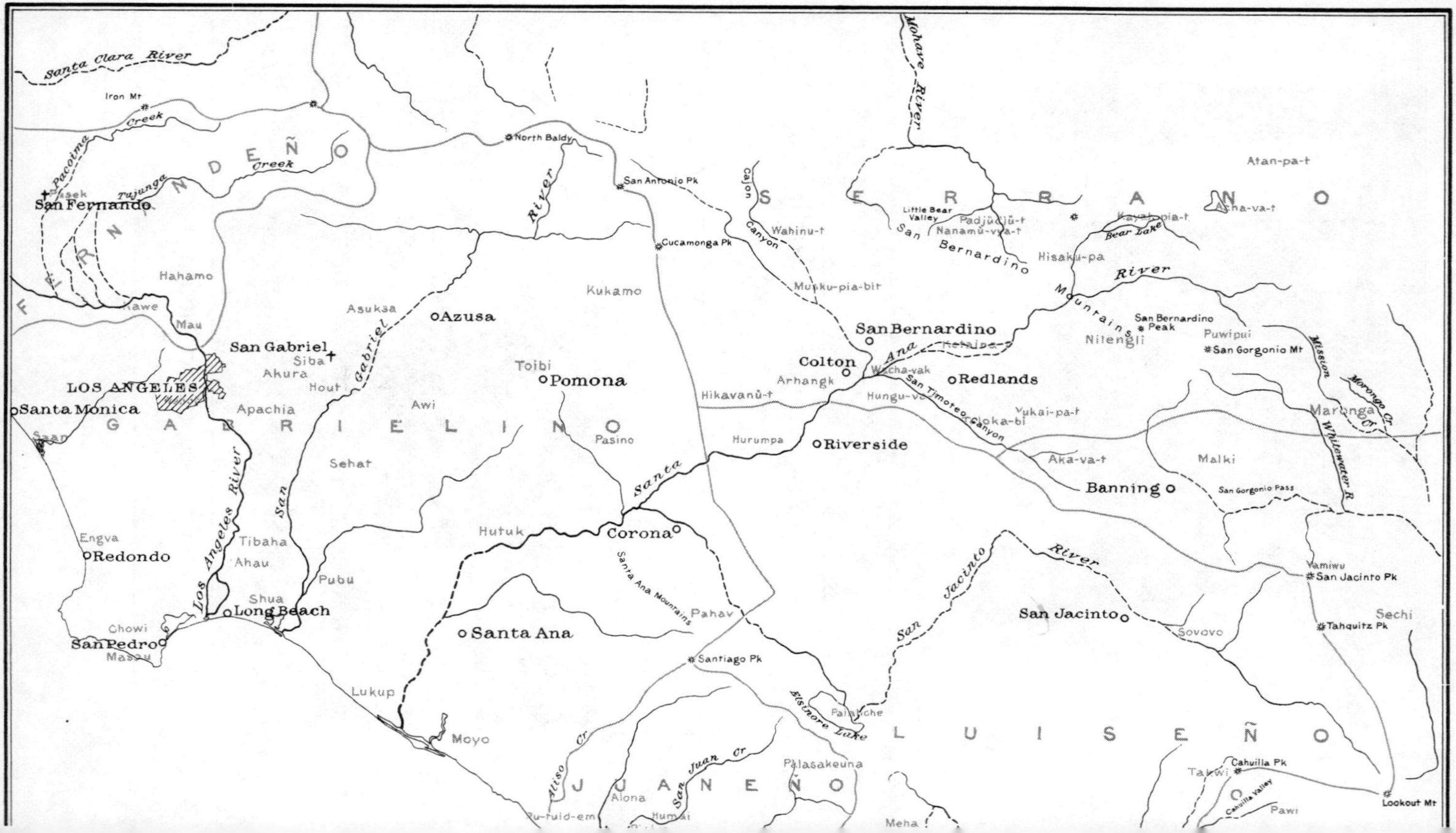
Santa Clara River
Iron Mt
Creek
Pacoima
Tujunga
Creek
San Fernando
F E R N A N D E Ñ O
Hahamo
Mau
North Baldy
River
San Antonio Pk
Cucamonga Pk
Cajon
Canyon
Wahinu-t
Musku-pia-bit
S E R R A N O
Mohave River
Little Bear Valley
Padjüdjü-t
Nanamü-vya-t
San Bernardino Mountains
Hisaku-pa
Bear Lake
Aha-va-t
Atan-pa-t
River
San Bernardino Peak
Nitengli
Puwipui
San Gorgonio Mt
Mission
Morongo Cr
Maringa
Whitewater R
Malki
San Gorgonio Pass
Banning
Aka-va-t
Vukai-pa-t
San Timoteo Canyon
Redlands
San Bernardino
Colton
Arhangk
Hikavanü-t
Hungu-va
Wacha-vak
Ana
Santa
Riverside
Hurumpa
Kukamo
Toibi
Pomona
Pasino
Azusa
Asuksa
Gabriel
San
San Gabriel
Siba
Akura
Hout
Awi
LOS ANGELES
Santa Monica
Apachia
G A B R I E L I N O
Sehat
Los Angeles River
Tibaha
Ahau
Pubu
Shua
Long Beach
Engva
Redondo
Chowi
San Pedro
Hutuk
Corona
Santa Ana Mountains
Pahav
Santa Ana
Santiago Pk
Lukup
Moyo
Aliso Cr
J U A N E Ñ O
Alona
San Juan Cr
Palasakeuna
Elsinore Lake
Palapche
Meha
San Jacinto River
San Jacinto
L U I S E Ñ O
Sovovo
Yamiwu
San Jacinto Pk
Tahquitz Pk
Sechi
Takwi
Cahuilla Pk
Cahuilla Valley
Pawi
Lookout Mt

NATIVE SITES IN PART OF SOUTHERN CALIFORNIA

PACIFIC OCEAN

Las Coyotes Canon
Chawimai
Tule Pk.
*Beauty Mt
Hulwawona
Saipeta
Hot Springs Mt
Kupa
Wilya
San Ysidro Mt
Takwi
Met-hwai

C A H U I L L A

Awa'
Palomar Mt
Takwish-po-shapila
Ngorivo
Weyu
San Felipe Cr
San Felice Cr
Setmunumin
Mitj-ekwokak

S E Ñ O R E Ñ O

Agua Tibia Mtn
Pala
Paumo
Taghanashba
Kapa
Ta'i
Yami
Kuka
Huyulkum
Kolo
Pashkwo
Mesa Grande
Oakumai
Pasha
Atikwana
Sinyau-kehwir
Kosmit
*North. Pk
Lawim
*Middle Pk
Cuyamaca Pk
Ekwianak
Kwatl

Temecula
Temeku
Maiamai
Pala
Anuva
Woshha
Aiapi
Shakishmai
Pamo
Anyaha
Witiltak

Pechanga Cr
Saumai
Panakat
Ahmakatkatl
Pauwai

San Jacinto River
Ushmai
Wiaxio
Hekwish
Keish
San Luis Rey
Palamai
Shikapa
Hakuti
Sinyau-pichkara
Hapai

D I E G U E Ñ O

Elcajon Mt
Amotaretuwe
Sekwen
Hamacha
San Miguel Mt
Otai
*Otay Mt

San Juan
Piwiya
Anachmai
Parih
Arroyo San Onofre
Hechmai
Katukto
Kwalam
Agua Hedionda Cr
Kulaumai
San Dieguito River

Ex Mission
San Diego
Sinyewacha
Kosoi
Nipawai

SAN DIEGO
Coronado
Sweetwater
Pa-shuy
San Diego River
San Diego Bay
Totakamalam
Pt Loma

Otecate

Cocoamuuny Creek
Otay River
Hamul

O C E A N

PLATE 58

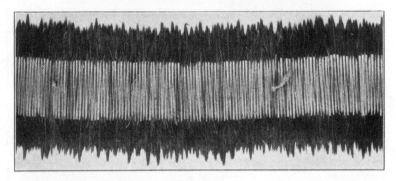

PARTS OF QUILL HEADBANDS

From above, down: Koso, Luiseño, Miwok, Miwok

certain to have transported with it some religious associations. (Pl. 42.)

Flat feather bands are of the type of the yellow-hammer ornaments so characteristic of the whole cis-Sierra region, but their detailed form, as revealed in total length, inaccuracy of stringing, and proportion of feather to quill, allies them more particularly to the corresponding article of the Luiseño and other southern Californians. (Pl. 58.)

Baskets, again, are of Yokuts rather than southern affinities. The plate or shallow bowl, it is true, is coiled; but there is a conical carrying basket, and it is twined. The pitched water basket is indispensable to a potless desert people. The carrying cap was worn by women. It was coiled. The foundation for coiled ware is a bundle of *Epicampes* grass stems containing a single woody rod; the sewing is strands of willow, and black patterns are made with the horns of *Martynia* pods, or *Scirpus* bulrush roots soaked in ashes. For red, tree yucca root is used. Twined vessels are of strands of willow or sumac on shoots of the same. The patterns are also in *Martynia*, or if red, of tree yucca root.

The carrying net is of southern California type (Fig. 53), but without the convenient loops of the Cahuilla form (Fig. 59).

Earth-covered sweat houses were used regularly, at least by some men. They were large enough to stand up in. The soil was heaped over a layer of " arrowweed," *Pluchea sericea*. (Pl. 56.)

The bow is of juniper, short, and sinew-backed. The string is sinew, or *Apocynum*, wild hemp, the usual cordage material. The arrow is of willow, or of *Phragmites* cane; the latter has a long point of greasewood.

FIG. 53. — Carrying net. Koso (Panamint) of Death Valley. (Cf. Fig. 59.)

The cane arrow is heated in the groove of a stone straightener of Yokuts-Cahuilla type, then seized in the teeth and the ends bent.

SUBSISTENCE.

The most important food in the oakless country was the Nevada pine nut, from *Pinus monophylla*. Seeds were gathered by beating as by the more favored Californian tribes. *Oryzopsis*, the desert sand grass, perhaps furnished the most abundant supply. Seeds of evening primroses, of *Ephedra*, and of the devil's pincushion cactus, were also available. Most of these were ground and then parched with coals in a shallow basket. The mesquite bean, *Prosopis*, was pounded in wooden mortars; the stalks of the common reed, *Phragmites*, were treated similarly and cakes of the flour toasted.

The "mescal" of the Southwest and southernmost California hardly penetrates the Koso country, but the tree yucca bud affords a substitute, which has the advantage of being edible after roasting on an open fire, whereas the agave butt or stalk requires prolonged steam cooking in an earth-covered pit.

Prickly pear joints, however, are treated by the Koso in this manner, and can then be kept indefinitely, or are sun dried and boiled when wanted. The thorns are first rubbed off.

The leaves and shoots of several varieties of crucifers are eaten.

In the fertile parts of California clover and other greens are mostly eaten raw, but the desert vegetation requires repeated boiling, washing, and squeezing to remove the bitter and perhaps deleterious salts.

Animal food is only occasionally obtainable. Rabbits, jack rabbits, rats, and lizards, with some birds, furnish the bulk. Mountain sheep take the place of deer as the chief big game. On the shores of Owens Lake countless grubs of a fly were scooped out of the shallow water and dried for food.

CHAPTER 41.

THE CHEMEHUEVI.

AFFILIATIONS.

With the Chemehuevi we encounter the third and last of the Shoshonean Plateau divisions, composed of this people, the Kawaiisu, the Southern or true Paiute, and the Ute, all speaking dialects of remarkable uniformity, considering the extent of territory covered by them.

In fact, the Chemehuevi are nothing but Southern Paiutes, and all their bands have at one time or another been designated as Paiutes, Payuchis, and the like.

Conversely, the term Chemehuevi has been applied to several more eastern bands, in Nevada and Arizona, on whom custom has now settled the name Paiute. The Mohave and other Yuman tribes follow this nomenclature consistently: Chemehuevi is their generic term for Paiute. Thus that remarkable pioneer Garcés, who in 1776 entered Shoshonean territory from the Mohave and with Mohave guides, speaks not only of the Chemegué and Chemeguaba—our Chemehuevi—but of the Chemegué Cuajála and Chemegué Sevinta, that is, the Paranüh Paiute of Muddy River in Nevada and the Shivwits Paiute of Shivwits Plateau in Arizona, the Kohoalcha and Sivvinta of the Mohave. In fact, the name Chemehuevi, whose etymology is uncertain, would seem to be of Mohave or at least Yuman origin.

At the same time, the appellation is a convenient one to distinguish the Southern Paiute of California from their brethren of Nevada, Arizona, and Utah; and it will be used here in this geographical rather than in any essential ethnic sense.

HABITAT.

The Chemehuevi are one of the very few Californian groups that have partly altered their location in the historic period, and that without pressure from the white man. Their shifts emanated in disturbances of the still more mobile and more compact Yuman tribes on whom they border.

Their old territory lay off the lower Colorado River westward. It commenced in the Kingston Range, south of Death Valley, where they met the Koso, and stretched southward through the Providence Mountains and other stony and sandy wastes, to about the boundary of Riverside and Imperial Counties. Roughly, this is the eastern half of the Mohave Desert. Somewhere along the middle of the southern half of this desert an ill-defined line must have run between the Chemehuevi and the Serrano divisions farther west. The oasis of Twenty-nine Palms was Serrano. So was the Mohave Desert to beyond Daggett, and probably to its sink. Somewhat nearer this sink, however, than to the Providence Mountains, Garcés found a Chemehuevi rancheria. North of the Serrano range, and south of that of the Koso, lies a stretch that if anything is more arid still than the neighboring ones—northwestern San Bernardino County. This seems to have formed a westward arm of Chemehuevi territory—if not permanently inhabited, at least visited and owned. True, there is no specific record of any of their bands being in this area, now or formerly. But it has not been claimed for either the Serrano or Koso; and to the west, where the region begins to rise toward the southern Sierra Nevada, it meets the land of the Kawaiisu, whose speech shows them to be a Chemehuevi offshoot. In the absence of knowledge the inherent probability would favor continuity of the territories of the two allied groups; and the Mohave speak of them as in contact. Intrinsically, it is of little import who exercised sovereignty in this tract: to all purposes it was empty. But it is extensive enough to loom large on the map, and in more favored regions three or four stocks like Esselen, Wiyot, Yurok, and Chimariko could be put into an equal area.

In 1776 there were no Chemehuevi on the Colorado River below Eldorado Canyon. The entire California frontage on this stream was in Yuman possession. Subsequently, however, the Mohave and Yuma drove the remnants of the Halchidhoma and Kohuana eastward; and the Chemehuevi, who were intimate with the victors, began to settle on the stream. According to the Mohave, they themselves brought the Chemehuevi to Cottonwood Island, where the two nations lived side by side, to Chemehuevi Valley, and to other points. At all events, when the Americans came, three-quarters of a century after the Spanish priest, they found the Chemehuevi on Cottonwood Island as well as in the valley that bears their name, and on both the Arizona and California sides, apparently.

About 1867 war broke out between the old friends. The Chemehuevi acquitted themselves well, according to the Mohave; but they must have been heavily outnumbered. At any rate, they fled from Mohave proximity to remoter spots in the desert. After a time they returned, and to-day there are even some individuals among the Mohave. A small group, however, remained at their asylum at Twenty-nine Palms, far to the southwest; and in recent years some members of this band have drifted still farther, across the San Bernardino range, to Cabezon in Cahuilla territory.

POPULATION.

The Chemehuevi area is the largest in California occupied by a people of uniform dialect; but it is also easily one of the most worthless, and was certainly among the two or three most thinly populated. A thousand inhabitants is a most liberal estimate.

The last Federal census reports 350 Chemehuevi in all, 260 of them in California. The decrease since aboriginal times has not been heavy in regions so empty and remote as this. A reduction by one-half or two-thirds is all that can be allowed; which would make the primitive population something between 500 and 800.

NAMES AND DIVISIONS.

The Chemehuevi and Southern Paiute name for themselves is only Nüwü, "people," corresponding to Mono and Northern Paiute Nümü. The Chemehuevi proper are sometimes called by their kins-men: Tantawats or Tantüwach, "southerners," an appropriate enough term; and they accept the designation; but it has local, not tribal reference. The various Serrano groups call them Yuakayam. The Yuma are said to name them Mat-hatevach, "northerners," and the Pima: Ahalakat, "small bows." Tribes or local divisions that may fairly be included among the Chemehuevi are the following:

Mokwats, at the Kingston Mountains.

Yagats, at Amargosa.

Hokwaits, in Ivanpah Valley.

Tümpisagavatsits or Timpashauwagotsits, in the Providence Mountains.

Kauyaichits.

Moviats, on Cottonwood Island in the Colorado River.

Shivawach or Shivawats in the Chemehuevi Valley; it is not certain whether this is the name of a band or of a locality.

There must have been others farther west and south.

The Chemehuevi name their neighbors as follows: The Koso-Panamint, Kwiits or Panumits; the Serrano proper, Maringits; the Vanyume Serrano, Pitanta; the Kitanemuk Serrano, Nawiyat; the Kawaiisu, Hiniima or Hinienima; the Cahuilla, Kwitanemum; the Hopi, Mukwi or Mokwits. Yuman tribes are: the Mohave. Aiat; the Walapai, Huvarepats; the Havasupai, Pashaverats; for the Yuma there seems to be only the Mohave term "Kwichyana." The Yokuts were called Saiempive.

Place names are: Nüvant, Charleston Peak in Nevada, the most famous place in the mythology of both the Chemehuevi and the western bands of the Southern Paiute; Muvi, Eldorado Canyon (compare Moviats); Wianekat, Cottonwood Island; Pa'ash, Piute Springs, the Mohave Ahakuvilya, where there are petroglyphs; Toyagaba, near by; and Aipava, farther west on the trail to Mohave River.

WAR AND PEACE.

The international relations of the Chemehuevi were determined in general, and probably for a long time, by a series of interconnected amities and enmities that threw the tribes of southern California, southern Nevada, and western Arizona into two great alignments that ran counter to their origins as well as their mode of life. On one side were the Chemehuevi, Southern Paiute, Mohave, Yuma, Kamia, Yavapai, and Apache. These were generally friendly to the less enterprising and passive northern Serrano of the desert, and, so far as they knew them, to the Yokuts, the Tübatulabal, the Chumash, and perhaps the Gabrielino. On the other side were the Hopi; the Pima and most of the Papago; of Yuman tribes, the Havasupai, Walapai, Maricopa, Halchidhoma, Kohuana, Halyikwamai, Cocopa, Diegueño, and the Cuñeil or northernmost Baja Californians; of southern California Shoshoneans, the Serrano proper, the Cahuilla, and possibly the Luiseño. There was nothing like a confederation or even formal alliance among the tribes of either party. Rather, each had its enemies of long standing, and therefore joined hands with their foes, until an irregular but far-stretching and interlocking line-up worked itself out. Often tribes here grouped as on the same side had their temporary conflicts, or even a traditional hatred. But, on the whole, they divided as here indicated, as Garcés pictured the situation in the eighteenth century, as later reports of narrower outlook confirm, and as the recollections of the modern Mohave corroborate. Small, scattered, or timid tribes, like the Chemehuevi, the Hopi, the Havasupai, and the various Serrano divisions, were less involved in open war and more inclined to abiding suspicions and occasional conflicts, than aggressive, enterprising, or tenacious nations of numbers or solidarity such as the Apache, Pima, and Mohave; but their outward relations were largely predetermined by the general scheme.

This mere list of tribal friends and foes, especially when conceptualized on the map, lifts one with a bound out of the peasant-like, localized, and murkily dim world knowledge of the true Californians into a freer atmosphere of wide and bold horizons.

CULTURE.

The groundwork of Chemehuevi culture was the Shoshonean one of the Great Basin, of the participants in which they were a member

PLATE 59

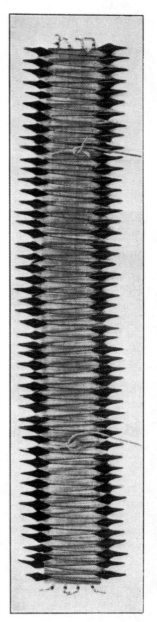

PATWIN YELLOW-HAMMER QUILL HEADBAND; MOHAVE FISH SCOOP; CHEMEHUEVI BASKET

PLATE 60

HUPA WOMAN POUNDING ACORNS,
HER LEGS HOLDING THE BASKET
MORTAR

DESERT CAHUILLA GRANARY

INTERIOR OF SERRANO OR PASS CAHUILLA
SWEAT HOUSE

physiographically as well as in speech and origin. This interior plateau civilization was largely composed of elements ultimately common to itself and the central Californian civilization. But specific Californian influences reached the Chemehuevi only to a limited extent. The civilization of the Pueblos also did not affect them directly. Their life was, however, strongly colored by contact with the quasi-Southwestern Yumans—in its material aspects more by the unsettled tribes, such as the Walapai; in religion especially by the Mohave.

ARTS.

Like the Southern Paiute, the Chemehuevi now and then farmed small patches where they could. In the main, they lived on what their bare habitat provided—game, rabbits, rats, lizards, perhaps other reptiles, seeds, mescal, and the like.

Also in imitation of the Mohave, they now and then, especially since settled along the river, ventured to bake a few pots. But such attempts were sporadic, and the Chemehuevi must in justice be classed as a tribe that made baskets and not pottery.

Their basketry suggests, in its coiling, the San Joaquin Valley and the ware of the Shoshoneans adjacent to this valley, as much as southern California. This is in part due to their presumably enforced use of woody willow or other fibers for the sewing, in place of the reedy *Juncus* of the Cahuilla and Luiseño; in part to their manufacture of vessels with constricted neck—not well definedly flat-shouldered as among the Yokuts, but of an approximating and rounded shape that is clearly due to the same influence. Their twined basketry is also foreign in spirit to that of southern California. Caps, triangular trays, and close-woven carrying baskets in diagonal twining, with an inclination to paint designs on instead of working them in, are pure Plateau types. (Pls. 59, 73, *a*.) The water basket was undoubtedly also used, but seems not to have been preserved.

The bow is distinctly shorter than the Mohave self-bow, with recurved ends. The back is painted, the middle wrapped, and the old game and fighting weapon was evidently sinew-backed, although no specimens seem to have survived. The arrow is at least sometimes of cane, foreshafted, and flint tipped with a small point. It differs entirely from the jointless *Pluchea* arrow of the Mohave, that lacks both foreshaft and stone head.

Women's dice were of gum-filled and shell-inlaid nut shells (Fig. 54), similar to those of the southern Yokuts.

Garcés found the Chemehuevi, at some springs in the desert west of Chemehuevi Valley, wearing "Apache" moccasins, skin shirts, perhaps of antelope or mountain sheep, and feathered caps. This is the dress of the nomadic Southwestern or Plateau Shoshonean tribes, and unconnected with that of the southern or central Californians or the Mohave, although the Serrano tell of having worn a similar costume.

The Mohave, however, declare the Chemehuevi men to have worn their hair in the peculiar style characteristic of themselves and the Yuma.

Houses need have been little else than shelters against the sun and wind. The sweat house has not been reported. Open-air storage baskets are also not mentioned; most of the Chemehuevi habitat would furnish more safe and dry rock crevices than food to keep in them.

BELIEFS.

The Chemehuevi origin myth is free from southern Californian or Southwestern suggestions. It does recall the central Californian

account of the creation, but evidently only in so far as it rests upon a Plateau set of conceptions, and these in turn approximate those current in California. There is little that is common with the mythology of the Yokuts, the nearest of the central Californians.

Fig. 54.—Chemehuevi dice of filled shells.

The heroes are Coyote and his elder brother Puma—the Chemehuevi equivalent of the Wolf of the northern Plateau—who build a house on Charleston Peak while the world is still covered with water. When the earth has become dry through the instrumentality of an old woman in the west, Hawichyepam Maapuch, Coyote, failing to find men, marries a louse, from whose eggs spring many tribes. The Chemehuevi themselves, however, the Mohave, and other southerners come from Coyote's own voidings. They are taught to eat game by being given parts of a person, a human example of animal food. Puma is killed by eastern enemies, who, unwinding a powerful object that he has made, bring on the first and an unbroken night. Coyote mourns, but wishes daylight to burn his brother's belongings. He restores it when he shoots the yellow-hammer. After the completion of the funerary rites—the instituting ones for the world—Coyote recovers his brother's scalp from the foes who are dancing before it and escapes their pursuit.

Mohave traces are visible: the great sacred mountain, the building of an abode, the actionless but all-powerful old woman, the death of the older brother, the mourning for him. But they are elements which tinge rather than shape the story.

RITUAL.

Chemehuevi rituals have been influenced by the Mohave. They may have been equally affected by the religion of other peoples of the region, but these are too little known to estimate. The cremation of the property of the dead, and, no doubt, of added belongings, as a definite rite—especially notable because the body itself was buried and not cremated—extends, it is true, over a wide area. But the fact that the Kaibab Paiute, in the far-away tract where westernmost Arizona and Utah conjoin, possess a long series of mourning songs in the Mohave language, establishes probability that the nearer and intimate Chemehuevi also derived their funeral music, and with it no doubt a large part of the associated practices, from the same source.

Incidentally, the religious dominance of the Mohave over a vast region is clear. The Diegueño myths tell of the sacred Mohave Mountain Avikwame; some of their song cycles are Mohave in words as well as melody and name; and tribes so advanced, self-centered, and remote as the Zuñi perform dances that they attribute to the Mohave and whose songs are possibly derived from a Mohave stimulus.

The Chemehuevi sing four cycles—Salt, Deer, Mountain Sheep, and Shamans' or Doctoring—all of which, in effect, are sung by the Mohave also, though to these people they constitute only a small fraction of a much larger number of different kinds of singings. It seems that each of these song cycles refers to a story, which may or may not be related in the intermissions; and that this narrative is believed to have been dreamed—that is, actually experienced in a spirit condition—but that the presentation of the dream takes an essentially mythological form. Whether, as with the Mohave, dancing or other rudimentary ritual may accompany the singing—though only as a subsidiary feature, the songs remaining the kernel and essence of the complex—is not known as regards the Chemehuevi.

It is possible that these Chemehuevi-Mohave resemblances lie as much in an equivalation made by the Indians as in any similarity of the ceremonies themselves. When the Zuñi perform what they call the Mohave dance it is actually a purely Zuñi ritual in every particular, whatever its origin; but both tribes would nevertheless be likely to assert their corresponding rituals to be the same. It may be that analogous though slighter differences exist between Chemehuevi and Mohave ceremonies, which the native consciousness obliterates, and which therefore will become revealed only when the rites are concretely known in some detail. But this theoretical possibility is unlikely to amount to more than a partial qualification, so far as Chemehuevi similarities to the Mohave are concerned; for all the specific bits of knowledge that are available point to specific Mohave resemblances.

Thus, the Chemehuevi " dream " and tell and sing of the mountain Nüvant as the Mohave do of Avikwame. They see there Coyote and Puma and Yunakat, the personification of food. The shamans acquire their songs and powers from these or other mythological beings at Nüvant. A man " dreams," for instance, of the time when the earth was still wet from the primeval flood and without mountains, when the cane sprang up and Older Brother Puma instructed him in detail how to make each part of bow and arrow. This experience is the source of the " dreamer's " faculty to flake arrowheads. The assumptions, the implied concepts, the whole setting as well as many of the particulars in this instance, are characteristically Mohave.

CHAPTER 42.

THE KAWAIISU AND TÜBATULABAL.

The Kawaiisu.

NEIGHBORS.

An offshoot of no great antiquity, apparently, from the Chemehuevi, the Kawaiisu have become differentiated from the parent body as a result of a new setting. They lived in the Tehachapi Mountains, and therefore half across the watershed that separates the great valley of California from the undrained Great Basin. Behind them remained the westernmost of the Chemehuevi; and nominally the two bodies were in contiguity. Actually, however, the Chemehuevi tract in question was perhaps the least frequented of all the barren lands of that people; and the Kawaiisu had more to gain by clinging to the timbered and watered slopes of their mountains than by wandering among the rare vegetation and dry soda lakes of the desert. Intercourse between the two groups was therefore probably not specially active.

On the other side of the crest, however, the Kawaiisu were pressed close against a variety of neighbors. In the plains below them were the Yauelmani, and beyond them other Yokuts tribes. Relations with these seem to have been friendly, and intermarriages took place.

On both sides were Shoshoneans, but of quite distinct history and speech; to the north the Tübatulabal of Kern River, to the south the Serrano Kitanemuk; and a journey of less than a day led into Chumash territory.

It was inevitable, accordingly, that the Kawaiisu should be essentially Californian in culture, and that their speech should diverge from its original form. In all fundamentals it is pure Ute-Chemehuevi, but superficially, especially in its pronunciation, it is considerably changed. With such close and numerous alien associations as the Kawaiisu were subject to, this degree of alteration might be attained in a very few centuries, possibly in a few generations.

TERRITORY AND DESIGNATIONS.

Tehachapi Pass, a famous Agua Caliente or hot spring in the vicinity, Walker Basin, and probably some southern affluents of Kern River were in Kawaiisu possession. They owned also the eastward drier slope of the same mountains, and perhaps some of the desert beyond; but the limits of their extension in this direction are conjectural.

Tehachapi has its designation from a local name, which has been taken over by the Yokuts as Tahichpi-u. The hot springs were called Hihinkiava by the Kitanemuk; Tumoyo or Shatnau ilak by the Yokuts. Walker Basin, or probably the principal village in it, was Yutp or Yitpe. At or near Havilah were Wiwayuk and Anütap, Kitanemuk and Tübatulabal names of possibly the same locality; it may have belonged to the latter people or to the Kawaiisu, and certainly was near their boundary.

The origin of the name Kawaiisu is not known. The Yokuts call them thus, or by dialectic variants. The Tübatulabal say Kawishm. The Mohave designation, Kuvahya, may be from the same stem; Garcés, the discoverer of the Kawaiisu, writes it Cobaji, and says that the Yokuts call them Colteche. The Chemehuevi designate them Hiniima or Hinienima. The Kitanemuk and Vanyume Serrano call them Agutushyam, Agudutsyam, or Akutusyam. Their own name for themselves is merely Nuwu or Nuwuwu, "people"; it has also been written Newooah. Locally, Americans usually speak of them as the Tehachapi or Caliente Indians.

There were Kawaiisu or Chemehuevi at Victorville on the upper Mohave River some years ago who asserted that this was part of their ancient territory, and that they ranged from there west along the base of the Sierra Madre. Most of them were born in the vicinity of Tehachapi, but they comprised individuals from Sheep and Deadman Creeks, halfway, on the north side of the mountains, between the two railroad lines that cross the Mohave Desert. If these claims prove correct, a considerable part of the desert region that has been attributed to the Serrano must be assigned to the Kawaiisu instead.

The same little group asserted that the southern end of the Panamint Mountains—that is, the general range of which the Panamint Mountains of our maps are part—belonged to their own people, only the northern segments of the chain being "Shoshone" or Koso. They may, however, include with "their own people" the Chemehuevi.

There is in these statements a possible explanation of a puzzling vacillation in the use of the name Panamint. The people of what we call the Panamint Mountains are those here named the Koso, of Shoshoni-Comanche affiliations. The Mohave, and with them the explorer Garcés, apply the name, in the form Vanyume or Beñeme, to the Mohave Desert Serrano, who are Shoshoneans of quite a different branch. Garcés clearly recognizes them as speaking a southern Californian idiom. The Mohave, however, are not consistent, and sometimes place the Vanyume at Tehachapi or Tejon. If the Kawaiisu of Tehachapi, or a division of them, extended on the one hand to the upper Mohave River and on the other to the southern spurs of the Panamints, the application of the name Vanyume-Panamint to people as far separated as these two outlying localities begins to show some reason. This desert region is little known to the ethnologist and would prove a fascinating field for him, and this instance of apparent confusion as to the whole basis of ethnic conditions illustrates how urgently knowledge is needed.

For modern times the census, and for the older period even estimates, fail us in regard to the Kawaiisu. There seem to be nearly 150 of them; and the aboriginal population may have been 500.

SOCIETY.

The Kawaiisu lack the organization of society on a basis of totemic moieties which is so characteristic of the Miwok and most of the Yokuts. As the eastern Mono and even the Kern River people agree with them in doing without this dual plan, it is clear that the system is essentially a Californian one and, far from being in any sense a trait of life in the Great Basin, has scarcely succeeded in reaching the crest of the Sierra. Even traces of the moiety scheme are wanting with the Kawaiisu. Eagles and other birds are indeed kept in captivity; but they are without a personal or taboo relation to the owner, are not inherited, and in fact are released after having been plucked twice.

The mother-in-law taboo is another Yokuts institution that the Kawaiisu lack, no doubt under Plateau or southern California influence. Children are usually named after relatives. Kinship designations are full of reciprocal terms; an old woman will call her daughter's boy by the same word that he applies to her, plus a diminutive suffix. This is a habit widely spread among the Plateau Shoshoneans. Another device of much greater restriction geographically is the custom of altering a term of kinship or affinity when the connecting relative has died, as we might speak of an ex-son-in-law. The Tübatulabal and Yokuts share this practice with the Kawaiisu.

Chieftainship is said to be much less a matter of descent than among the Yokuts and to depend almost wholly and directly on the possession of wealth. If the son succeeded the father it was because he too had accumulated property rather than because of his parentage. As all a man's belongings were destroyed at his funeral the prospects of a chief's son being elevated to his father's place did not so greatly tower above those of other members of the community. In fact the Kawaiisu say outright that any rich man became a chief.

RELIGIOUS PRACTICES.

The inevitable mourning ceremony was practiced, but we know too little of it to relate it specifically to the type of rite prevalent among this or that group of people. As the use of crude representations of the dead occurs among nations to the north as well as to the south of Kawaiisu, the practice might be looked for among them, but it has not been reported. Property seems to have been de-

stroyed at the funeral itself rather than at the subsequent commemoration. This fact, if corroborated, indicates Chemehuevi and
Mohave influences rather than central Californian ones in this set
of customs.

On the other hand, a washing of the participants at the end of
the ceremony points northward; but the connection is weakened by
the fact that the Kawaiisu washed themselves, the Yokuts and
Miwok each other according to moiety affiliations. The commemorative rites are said to have been performed for several nights, a year
or two after a death. The impression given is that the ceremony
was made for one particular person of distinction by one of his close
relatives, who bore the cost of entertainment of visitors. This
suggests the Mohave practice of holding a commemorative rite only
for people of prominence. On the other hand, the difference from
the more communal form of anniversary generally reported from
central California is not so great as might appear. Thus among
the Yokuts, while everyone participated and mourned his dead of
the year, the initiative and direction of the affair, as well as the bulk
of the entertaining, rested upon one person, who undertook to make
the ceremony in honor of one of his relatives of rank or importance.
There is no mention of every mourner appearing with images of his
kin; and it is likely that this representation was confined to the one
deceased individual, or at most to the few persons for whom the chief
entrepreneur undertook the performance. Custom may well have
varied from tribe to tribe, in this point of the degree of association
of the commemorative ceremony respectively with individuals or the
community; but at bottom the divergences may have been differences
of emphasis more than absolute distinctions.

As Jimson weed is employed for religious purposes both by the
Yokuts and the southern Californians, the Kawaiisu might be expected to use it also; and they do. It is associated with puberty rites;
but, contrary to both Yokuts and Luiseño practice, seems to be
administered as regularly to girls as to boys. There are suggestions
of an approximation to shamanistic experiences, and of the initiate
standing in a definite relation to his vision for his adult life. One
girl, for instance, saw and was frightened by the grizzly bear while
under the influence of the drug. He did not address her; but thence-
forth she was forbidden bear meat.

As to Kawaiisu shamanism, nothing is on record, except that they
had powerful rain doctors. Thus, one member of the profession,
while lying on a summer's day with a wound in his neck—perhaps
received from an avenging relative of some one recently dead—
made a light rain to ease his pain and reduce the inflammation.

INDUSTRIES.

The manufactures and industries of the Kawaiisu are scarcely known. There is as yet no report that they made pottery of the San Joaquin Valley type. Their basketry is of Yokuts-Tübatulabal-Koso type rather than southern Californian, and excellently made. Their water bottle is in diagonal twining, round bottomed, and pitched. (Pl. 55, *e*.)

THE TÜBATULABAL.

ORIGIN AND MOVEMENTS.

With the Kawaiisu, the survey of the Plateau Shoshoneans in California is completed. We come now to an entirely distinct branch of the family—that of Kern River. There is only one people included in this divergent stem, the Tübatulabal. Looking downstream, they face the utterly alien Yokuts. On their left are the Kawaiisu, on their right the Mono, at their back the Koso. They are thus nearly surrounded by members of all three divisions of the great Plateau branch.

From what little knowledge is available, the speech of the Tübatulabal is, however, not more similar to the Plateau idioms than to the Shoshonean idioms of southern California. A long separate history is thus indicated for them; and it is hard to imagine a more favorable location for such continued aloofness than the one they now occupy—a clean-cut valley in a high mountain region; within the true California of nature and yet at its edge; outside the wide Shoshonean plateau but at the same time bordering upon it. Even the element of contact with totally strange peoples is given—a factor that would at once stimulate, accelerate, and tend to perpetuate novelties of speech formation, and thus lead to the condition of this little people ranking coordinate with much greater divisions, in the classification of the family to which they jointly appertain.

The situation of the Tübatulabal thus partly accounts for their distinctiveness, and renders it unnecessary to assume any extreme length of time for their separateness. On the other hand, their language is so thoroughly specialized as compared with that of their neighbors, the western Mono and the Kawaiisu, whose location with reference to topography and contact with aliens is similar, that it is clear that the Tübatulabal have lived where they are now, or in the immediate vicinity, for a period several times as long as these two groups of their kinsmen.

The Tübatulabal are the people upon whom in particular has been fostered the slander, or the undeserved reputation, of issuing in warlike mood from their highland fastness and raiding the sluggish, peaceable Yokuts of the plains, dispossessing these, indeed, until the southernmost Yokuts were almost separated from the main body to the north. The story even goes on to picture how they would have seized the entire Tulare Basin had they not become enervated by malaria—somewhat as Greek and Latin civilization perished before the same disease, according to a more recent and famous fancy. Even the fact that the Tübatulabal were all found living in the mountains when the white man came is explained: the same scourge drove them back to the salubrious hills whence they had emerged, and they utilized their conquests only for an annual or occasional visit.

As a matter of fact, the visits took place; but they were the visits of guests. The southern Yokuts tribes, both of the plains and of the foothills, were generally quite thoroughly friendly, and joined one another in their respective territories to such an extent, according to the season of the year, that it is almost impossible to assign an exact habitat to any of them. The Tübatulabal, in spite of their separateness of origin and speech, were also in the main on amicable terms with these Yokuts tribes; and so came to join them in their little migrations. Just as they came down to Bakersfield, to Kern Lake, and to White River, probably even to Tejon and San Emigdio, the Yokuts, as occasion warranted, ascended the Kern for miles to fish, and to its forks, the center of the Tübatulabal home, to visit.

The entire little pseudo-history rests neither upon evidence nor even native tradition, but is solely an imagination developed from a knowledge of the facts that the Tübatulabal are Shoshonean and that eastern tribes are often more aggressive than those of the Pacific coast area.

Of course the amity between Yokuts and Tübatulabal suffered intermissions. But the Yokuts tribes fell out among each other also, now and then; and the relations do not seem to have been different in more than moderate measure.

GEOGRAPHY.

The land of the Tübatulabal was the region drained by Kern River, down as far as a point about halfway between the forks and Bakersfield. The exact spot has not been determined; it was not far from the Paleuyami Yokuts settlements Shoko and Altau, and a few miles above what the Yokuts call K'ono-ilkin, "water's fall," a cascade, or perhaps a stretch of rapids that does not appear on our maps but which served as a landmark to the natives.

The modern Tübatulabal settlements, and apparently the majority of the old villages, were in the vicinity of the forks of Kern, both above and below the junction, and apparently more largely on the smaller South Kern. On the map the entire area tributary to both branches has been assigned to the Tübatulabal; but the upper reaches, which are little else than two great canyons among vast mountains, were assuredly uninhabited, and it is not even certain that the Tübatulabal laid exclusive claim to their hunting rights.

Substantially, this Kern River country is a rugged depression between the southern end of the main Sierra Nevada proper and a secondary parallel range. From this lower range to the west, Tule River, and Deer, White, and Poso Creeks flow westward, through Yokuts lands, directly into Tulare Lake. Kern River, however, is confined to a true southerly course until after it has worked its way around the end of the secondary range, when it sweeps westward, and finally almost northward, until lost in the tule swamps and lakes south of Tulare Lake. At least such was the condition until a generation ago: now the lake is nearly gone, and, except in times of flood, the volume of Kern River is dissipated in endless ditches and over irrigated stretches. The natural course of the stream is thus a great semicircle, open to the north: its upper half Tübatulabal, its lower Yokuts. Only at one point did the Tübatulabal leave their river. In the region of upper Deer Creek a small band seems to have had a home among the Yokuts. This group is referred to below as the Bankalachi.

Only a few names of places in Tübatulabal country can be located, and it is not known how many of these were villages. On the South Fork, Cheibü-pan was at Roberts, Tüsh-pan at Weldon. Yahaua-pan was at the forks; Piliwini-pan near Whiskey Flat or Kernville; Wokinapüi-pan farther up the main fork. Mount Whitney, "where all rivers begin," was called Otoavit. Owens Lake, on one side of the mountains, was Patsiwat, Bakersfield, on the other, Palun-tanakama-pan.

The Yokuts called the village at the forks Pitnani-u; others, at Kernville, Tulonoya, at Keyes, Haukani-u; and at a hot spring above Vaughn, Tumoyo. The Tübatulabal territory is shown in most detail in the Yokuts map. (Pl. 47.)

The name Tübatulabal is Shoshonean and means "pine-nut eaters," but its dialectic source is not established. The Tübatulabal admit the designation, but also call themselves, or their speech, Pahkanapül. The Yokuts sometimes translate Tübatulabal into Wateknasi, from watak, "pine-nut"; but more frequently employ Pitanisha, from Pitnaniu, the central village. They also say Malda, but this term denotes any Shoshonean. Paligawonop and "Polok-wynah" are unidentified names for the Tübatulabal.

They, in turn, name their neighbors as follows: Winanghatal, the western Mono of Kaweah River; Yiwinanghal, the eastern Mono or perhaps the Mono in general; Witanghatal, the Kitanemuk Serrano. These three names present the appearance of being directional terms. The Kawishm are the Kawaiisu, the Toloim the Bankalachi, the Amahaba the far-away Mohave. The Yokuts tribes in the valley along lower Kern River are the Molilabal; for the Yokuts in the foothills, somewhat distorted forms of their proper names are employed, as Witskamin, Paluyam, and Yokol, with perhaps an extension of these terms to wider groups. Thus the "Yokol" of the Tübatulabal seem to have included also the Gawia, Yaudanchi, and perhaps other tribes.

The Tübatulabal of to-day may aggregate 150. Perhaps the number is nearer 100. On the ancient population there are no data. A thousand seems as reasonable a guess as any other: at least it appears ample.

ARTS.

The Tübatulabal are one of the seemingly endless number of California tribes whose customs have never been described in any detail. Intercourse and intermarriage between them and the Yokuts were so frequent that they must have been strongly influenced by this much larger nation.

Their basketry is scarcely distinguishable from that of the southern Yokuts; it appears to average a little better in fineness. Tree yucca root replaced *Cercis* bark for red patterns. They made pottery of the same type as the Yokuts. Like these people, they ate tobacco mixed with lime. Their houses, or at least one form of dwellings, were covered with tule mats.

It is not certain that they had any form of sweat house: what may be remains of such have been reported. Balsas of bundled tules, with a keel, a slender prow, and a square stern, were made.

The dead were buried.

SOCIETY.

In their social life they stood more apart. The exogamous moieties of the Yokuts were not represented among them. There are possible traces of the totemic manifestations that accompany this dual organization. Young eagles were caught and reared. They were not killed, but were ultimately liberated. The plucking of their feathers seems to have been only a minor end of their captivity. Other birds, such as condors, crows, hawks, and geese, and even young coyotes, were kept as pets; in some cases inherited by the son from the father. In mythology the eagle is the chief, the coyote his antithesis; one has as associates a variety of birds, the other lizards, vermin, and trivial or noxious beasts.

In some matters Yokuts practices have failed to obtain a foothold, or a secure one, among the Kern River people. The parent-in-law taboos are not observed, or only by those individuals intimately associated with the Yokuts by intermarriage. This factor, incidentally, has introduced a number of Yokuts personal names among the Tübatulabal, who care very little whether an individual's appellation has any meaning as long as it is the name of an ancestor. The designation of kindred is almost identical with that of the Kawaiisu, and apparently of the Chemehuevi: the terms used are often quite different, but their significance is the same. The two groups thus think alike as regards relationship. A particular trait shared with the Yokuts is the custom of altering the kinship term when the connecting relative has died; but this has already been seen to be a Kawaiisu device, and the custom may well have had a Shoshonean origin and been borrowed by the Yokuts.

Chieftainship, on the other hand, resembles the Yokuts rather than the Kawaiisu institution. The prime requisite is to be the son of a *tiwimal* or chief; the approval of the community and the possession of wealth are also factors. The father selects the son who is to receive the dignity; if there is no male heir, a daughter succeeds. The feeling as regards descent must be strong, since the husband of a chieftainess is accorded no official authority, and the title passes to her son.

RELIGION.

Information fails as to whether the Tübatulabal practiced the southern Yokuts form of Jimson-weed ritual. They did have what the Yokuts seem to have lacked: a definite adolescence ceremony for girls. It is the old story: among the hill men this simple and personal observance stands out conspicuously, while in the more elaborate civilization of the lowlanders it is dwarfed or crowded aside.

The fact that the Tübatulabal are said in this ceremony to put their girls into a pit and cover them suggests an influence from southern California.

The mourning ceremony is called *Anangat*, is made primarily for a single person of prominence about two years after his death, and as among Maidu, Yokuts, and Luiseño, represents him by an image. Such a figure is made of bundled tules, and its sex denoted by bead necklaces and feathers, or an apron. The figure is burned at daybreak of the last night of the rites, together with baskets and other valuables.

So far we have substantially the same features as mark the ceremony among the other tribes mentioned. A trait that may be distinctive of the Tübatulabal is the fact that the mourner puts the observances in charge of visitors from other localities. This may be the substitute of an undivided people for the reciprocal division of function among a dually organized one; or the basic idea of the participation of nonmourners may be older and have been seized upon and fortified by those groups that were subsequently cleft into social moieties.

An invited chief had charge of the burning at the climax. His people gathered wood, tended the fire, burned the image, washed the faces of the mourners afterwards, and performed other services, for all of which they were paid.

THE BANKALACHI.

This small group was an offshoot from the Tübatulabal, that had crossed the divide from Kern River and settled among the Yokuts foothill tribes in the region where Deer Creek, White River, and Poso Creek head. Their speech was only slightly different from that of the Tübatulabal; but their associations were primarily with the Yokuts, and they probably followed the customs of the latter. Bankalachi (plural Bangeklachi) was their Yokuts name: the Tübatulabal called them Toloim. The majority of the little tribe are likely to have been bilingual; at any rate they were extensively intermarried with the Yaudanchi, Bokninuwad, Kumachisi, Paleuyami, and other Yokuts. Some of their blood flows in various of the Yokuts of to-day and something of their speech is not yet forgotten, but as a tribe they are extinct.

THE GIAMINA.

The Yokuts occasionally mention a supposed Shoshonean tribe, called Giamina by them, in the vicinity of the Bankalachi, probably on Poso Creek. It is extinct. A few words have been secured from the Yokuts. These are indubitably Shoshonean, but not of any known dialect nor wholly of affiliation with any one dialect group. It is impossible to decide whether this brief vocabulary is only the result of a distorted recollection by an individual Yokuts of a smattering acquaintance with Shoshonean; or a sort of jargon Shoshonean that prevailed among the Kumachisi or some other Yokuts tribe; or the vanishing trace of a distinctive Shoshonean language and group. The last alternative is by no means precluded; but it may never be proved or disproved. The existence of the name Giamina signifies little, for it may be a synonym. But it is an old appellation. Father Cabot in 1818 encountered the "Quiuamine" in the vicinity of the Yokuts Wowol (Bubal), Choinok, and Yauelmani ("Yulumne").

CHAPTER 43.

SERRANO DIVISIONS.

The Serrano Group.

The fourth and fifth Shoshonean tribes inside the Sierra, the Kitanemuk and the Alliklik, are in the same region of the head of the San Joaquin-Kern drainage as the preceding groups. With the Kitanemuk, however, an entirely new division of Shoshoneans is entered: the southern California branch of the stock.

The Kitanemuk and probably the Alliklik (the latter are extinct) belonged to a northern section of the southern Californians to which the generic appellation "Serrano" has been applied. This is an unfortunate name. Not only is there this Serrano group and the Serrano tribe proper within it, but the name means nothing but "mountaineers"—"those of the Sierras," to be exact. In fact, the Kitanemuk do not know themselves as Serranos, but extend the epithet to their neighbors the Kawaiisu, quite correctly in an etymological sense, since these people happen to live higher in the mountains than they. But an ethnological designation is necessary, however arbitrary. It is in the fertile portion of southern California that the term "Serrano" has acquired a definite ethnic meaning as the name of the people in the San Bernardino Mountains. Their dialect is close to that of the Vanyume and Kitanemuk; Alliklik speech was probably similar; and so "Serrano" is here used also in the wider sense as the name of the division.

The Kitanemuk.

RANGE.

The Kitanemuk lived on upper Tejon and Paso Creeks, whose lower courses are lost in the Yokuts plains before reaching Kern River. They held also the streams on the rear side of the Tehachapi Mountains in the same vicinity and the small creeks draining the northern slope of the Liebre and Sawmill Range, with Antelope Valley and the westernmost end of the Mohave Desert. The extent of their territorial claims in this waste is not certain. The population perhaps resided more largely in the smaller San Joaquin part of the Kitanemuk area; the bulk of their territory was over the mountains in southern California.

A synonym of Kitanemuk is Kikitanum or Kikitamkar. All these words are perhaps from the stem *ki–*, "house." The Yokuts know the Kitanemuk as Mayaintalap, "large bows"; the Tübatulabal call them Witanghatal; the Chemehuevi, Nawiyat; the Mohave, Kuvahaivima—Garcés's "Cuabajai"— not to be confounded with Kuvahye, the Mohave designation of the Kawaiisu. The Americans are content to call them Tejon Indians, which would be satisfactory but for the fact that the former Tejon Reservation contained a little Babel of tribes. Most of the neighbors of the Kitanemuk to-day frequently refer to them as the Haminat. This is not a true designation but a nickname, a characteristic phrase of the language, meaning "what is it?"

It is necessary to distinguish between Tejon Creek, Tejon Rancho, and the old Tejon Reservation, all of which were in Kitanemuk territory, and Tejon Pass and the former Fort Tejon, which lie some distance to the west on the Cañada de las Uvas in Chumash habitat.

A few Serrano place names have been reported. Their present principal village, where Tejon Creek breaks out of the hills, is Nakwalki-ve, Yokuts Pusin-tinliu; Tejon ranch house on Paso Creek is Wuwopraha-ve, Yokuts Laikiu; below it lies Honewimats, Yokuts Tsuitsau; on Comanche Creek is Chivutpa-ve, Yokuts Sanchiu; Tehachapi Peak or a mountain near by is Mavin, perhaps Chapanau in Yokuts.

The Mohave or "Amahaba" of the Colorado River were known as "muy bravos" and were welcome guests among the Kitanemuk, penetrating even to the Yokuts, Alliklik, and perhaps Chumash. They came to visit and to trade. It is characteristic that the local tribes never attempted to reciprocate. Their range was not as confined as that of the northern Californians, but they still had no stomach for long journeys to remote places inhabited by strange people. The Mohave refer to the Tehachapi-Tejon region in their myths; it is not known and not likely that the Kitanemuk traveled as far as the sacred mountains of the Mohave even in imagination.

A curious and unexplained belief prevails among all the tribes in the Kitanemuk neighborhood, as well as among the Mohave, namely, that there is in this vicinity a tribe that in speech, and perhaps in customs too, is almost identical with the Mohave. Sometimes the Kitanemuk are specified, sometimes the Alliklik, or again ideas are vague. The Mohave themselves speak of the Kwiahta Hamakhava or "like Mohaves" as somewhere in this region; they may have meant the Alliklik. There is no known fragment of evidence in favor of this belief; but it must rest on a foundation of some sort, however distorted. Perhaps it is the presence of an Amahavit group among the Serrano, as mentioned below.

CUSTOMS.

Garcés in 1776 found the Kitanemuk living in a communal tule house, which differed from that of the lake Yokuts in being square. His brief description is best interpreted as referring to a series of individual family rooms surrounding a court that had entrances on two sides only, at each of which a sentinel—compare the Yokuts *winatum*—was posted at night. Each family had its door and fireplace. The framework of the structure was of poles; the rushes were attached in mats. The modern Yokuts deny that the Kitanemuk or any hill tribes built community houses, but Garcés's testimony is specific.

He mentions also the eating of tobacco. The leaves were brayed with a white stone (lime) and water in a small mortar, and the end of the pestle licked off. Even some of the natives swallowed the mess with difficulty. The avowed purpose of the practice was the relief of fatigue before sleep.

Seeds, possibly crushed to meal, were scattered in the fire and over sacred objects. The Pueblo sprinkling of corn meal is inevitably suggested.

The priest also tells of vessels, apparently of wood, with inlays of haliotis, "like the shellwork on the handles of the knives and all other manufactures that it is said there are on the Canal" of Santa Barbara—that is, among the Chumash. They trade much with the Canal, he adds, and suspects, though erroneously, that they may be the same nation. He had not himself been with the Chumash.

The Kitanemuk seem to have been at war at the time with the Alliklik, for Garcés mentions their killing a chief on the Santa Clara, and the Alliklik did not conduct him into Kitanemuk territory. Toward the Yokuts, also, there seems to have been no friendliness; he could not get a Quabajáy guide to the "Noches" because these were "bad"—except a Noche married among them.

The Yokuts of to-day declare that the Kitanemuk interred corpses. They danced differently from the Yokuts, and lacked the rattlesnake rite and the *Heshwash* doctor ceremony. They did have a memorial burning of property for the dead, when "clothing was stuffed" to represent them; and they practiced an initiation ritual with Jimson weed, which drug, or its drinking, they called *pa-manit*. The southern California deities to whom the Yokuts pray seem to have had their origin among the Serrano proper or, more likely, the Gabrielino; the Kitanemuk would in that case have been the transmitters.

Basketry (Pl. 55, *c*) seems to have been of the San Joaquin drainage type rather than southern Californian.

THE ALLIKLIK.

Bordering the Chumash, on the upper Santa Clara River, there lived a Shoshonean tribe that was probably of Serrano affinities, although the two or three words preserved of their speech allow of no very certain determination. They can not have been numerous. Taken to San Fernando or San Buenaventura missions, they dwindled rapidly, and the few survivors seem to have been so thrown in and intermarried with people of other speech that their own language became extinct in a couple of generations. In fact, there is nothing known about them except that they held the river up from a point between Sespe and Piru, most of Piru Creek, Castac Creek, and probably Pastoria Creek across the mountains in San Joaquin Valley drainage and adjacent to the Yokuts. The location of a few of the spots where they lived is shown on the Chumash map. (Pl. 48.) Alliklik, more properly I'alliklik in the plural, is the Ventureño Chumash name.

THE VANYUME.

The Vanyume are the Serrano of Mohave River. Dialectically they stand nearer to the Kitanemuk than to the Serrano of the San Bernardino Mountains; but all three idioms appear to be largely interintelligible.

Except perhaps for a few individuals merged among other groups, the Vanyume are extinct, and the limits of their territory remain vaguely known. Garcés makes their habitat begin some few Spanish leagues east of the sink of Mohave River, perhaps a third of the way from it to the Providence Mountains; and Chemehuevi accounts agree. From there up to Daggett or Barstow was undoubted Vanyume land. Beyond, there is conflict. The well-traveled Mohave describe the Vanyume as extending to the head of the river. An ancient survivor not long since attributed the upper course of the stream to the brother tribe, the Serrano proper. Garcés, the first white man in this region, who rode from the sink of the river to its source, does not clear the problem, since he designates the Vanyume, the Serrano, and evidently the Alliklik by a single epithet: Beñeme. The point is of no vital importance because of the likeness of the groups involved. Political affiliations may have conflicted with linguistic ones. The Mohave and Chemehuevi were at times friendly to the Vanyume, but hostile to the Serrano of the San Bernardino Range; there could well have been a division of the Serrano proper settled on upper Mohave River and allied with the Vanyume. The whole relation of Serrano proper and Vanyume is far from clear.

It must also be remembered that there are some Kawaiisu claims to a possession of Mohave River about where it emerges from the mountains.

Vanyume is the Mohave name, whence Garcés's "Beñeme." The Chemehuevi seem to call them Pitanta, The group has also been designated by the term Mühineyam, but this appears to be not so much an ethnic designation as the name of one of the local groups into which the Serrano proper were divided: Mohiyanim. The word Vanyume seems to go back to the radical of our "Panamint," which in turn is a synonym for the Shoshoni-Comanche group called Koso in this work.

The Vanyume population must have been very small. Garcés mentions a village of 25 souls and a vacant settlement on the river between Camp Cady and Daggett. Then there was nothing until a short distance below Victorville he encountered a town of 40 people and a league beyond another where the chief resided. These may have been Vanyume or Serrano proper. In the mountains, but still on their north slope, the rancherias were larger: 70, 25, and 80. These were probably Serrano proper.

The river carries water some distance from the mountains, and seepage beyond; but in much of its course it is only a thin line of occasional cottonwoods through an absolute desert. The people must have been poor in the extreme. At the lowest village Garcés found some bean and screw mesquite trees and grapevines; but the inhabitants had nothing but tule roots to eat. They were naked, and a cold rain prevented their going hunting; but they possessed blankets of rabbit and otter fur. Their snares were of wild hemp. At one of the upper villages there were small game and acorn porridge; and where the chief lived, welcome was extended by sprinkling acorn flour and small shells or beads. The latter were strung in natural fathom lengths.

A punitive expedition against the Mohave in 1819 traversed Vanyume territory and names the following places and their distance in leagues from Cucamonga: Cajon de Amuscopiabit, 9; Guapiabit, 18; Topipabit, 38; Cacaumeat, 41; Sisuguina, 45; Angayaba, 60. The first three names are in a Serrano dialect; the fourth seems to be; the fifth is doubtful; the sixth Chemehuevi. Their locations fall within the territories assigned respectively to the Vanyume and the Chemehuevi on the map.

THE SERRANO.

HABITAT.

The Serrano proper, or "mountaineers" of the Spaniards, are the last of the four bodies of people that have here been united, on account of their similarity of dialect, into a "Serrano division" of the Shoshonean stock.

Their territory was, first the long San Bernardino Range culminating in the peak of that name, and in Mount San Gorgonio, more than 11,000 feet high. Next, they held a tract of unknown extent northward. In the east this was pure desert, with an occasional water hole and two or three flowing springs. In the west it was a region of timbered valleys between rugged mountains. Such was the district of Bear Lake and Creek. In the third place they occupied the San Gabriel Mountains or Sierra Madre west to Mount San Antonio. This range is almost a continuation of the San Bernardino Range. In addition, they probably owned a stretch of fertile lowland south of the Sierra Madre, from about Cucamonga east to above Mentone and halfway up San Timoteo Canyon. This tract took in the San Bernardino Valley and probably just failed of reaching Riverside; but it has also been assigned to the Gabrielino, which would be a more natural division of topography, since it would leave the Serrano pure mountaineers.

There is another territory that may have been Serrano: the northern slope of the Sierra Madre for some 20 miles west of Mount San Antonio, the region of Sheep, Deadman, and Big and Little Rock Creeks. But this is uncertain. The Kawaiisu may have ranged here, in which case this Chemehuevi offshoot no doubt owned the whole western Mohave Desert also, and cut off the two western Serrano divisions, the Alliklik and Kitanemuk, from contact with the two eastern, the Vanyume and present true Serrano. In support of this view is a reference to the "Palonies—a subtribe of the Chemehuevi" as the northern neighbors of the Gabrielino.[1]

The best parts of the Serrano land are shown in the southern California map, Plate 57, which includes place names. Many of the latter no doubt originally denoted villages; but it is usually impossible to determine. The Indians of this region, Serrano, Gabrielino, and Luiseño, have long had relations to the old ranchos or land grants, by which chiefly the country was known and designated until the American began to dot it with towns. The Indians kept in use, and often still retain, native names for these grants. Some were the designations of the principal village on the grant, others of the particular spot on which the ranch headquarters were erected, still others of camp sites, or hills, or various natural features. The villages, however, are long since gone, or converted into reservations, and the Indians, with all their native terminology, think in terms of Spanish grants or American towns. Over much of southern California—the "Mission Indian" district—the opportunity to prepare an exact aboriginal village map passed away 50 years ago. The numerous little reservations of to-day do in the rough conserve the ancient ethnic and local distribution; but not under the old circumstances.

NAMES AND NUMBERS.

The most frequent name for the Serrano among their neighbors to-day is some derivative of Mara or Morongo. Thus, Luiseño: Marayam; Chemehuevi: Maringits; they call themselves Maringayam. These terms are derived from the name of one of the Serrano bands or groups discussed below, the Maringayam or "Morongo," formerly at Maringa, Big Morongo Creek, whence the designation of Morongo Reservation near Banning, on which Serrano are settled among Cahuilla. A similar word, Mara, is the native name of the oasis at Twenty-nine Palms.

---

[1] Recent inquiries by Mrs. Ruth Benedict, as yet unpublished, put Serrano groups in the canyons on the northern face of Mount San Jacinto, in territory assigned in Plates 1 and 57 to the Pass Cahuilla.

Tahtam has been given as the name of the Serrano for themselves: it means merely "people." Kauangachem is of unknown significance; Kaiviatam is only a translation into Indian of Spanish "Serrano."

The Mohave know the Serrano as Hanyuveche, the "Jenigueche" of Garcés.

The population must have been rather sparse; 1,500 seems an ample allowance in spite of the extent of the Serrano range. A part of the group may have kept out of the exterminating influence of the missions; yet few seem to survive. The census of 1910 reports something over 100.

SOCIAL SCHEME.

With the Serrano, the exogamous and totemic moieties of the Miwok and Yokuts reappear. Associated with them is a new feature, a series of bands or local subdivisions.

One moiety is called *Tukum*, "wild cats," after *tukut*, its chief totem. It has as other totems *tukuchu*, the puma or mountain lion, older brother of wild cat, and *kachawa*, the crow, his kinsman.

The other moiety is known as *Wahilyam*, "coyotes," and has as associate totems coyote's older brother *wanats*, the wolf or jaguar, and his kinsman *widukut*, the buzzard.

The word for "totem" is *nükrüg*, "my great-grandparent," or *nüngaka*. The creator established the institution. Moieties joke each other; members of the first are reputed lazy and dull, of the second swift and perhaps unreliable.

The bands offer more difficulty. Some are not assigned to either moiety in the available information. All of them are mentioned as localized within certain districts. Their recorded appellations are mostly either place names or words appearing to mean "people of such and such a place." For some districts a single band is mentioned, for other regions pairs of intermarrying bands.

In general, it would appear that the Serrano bands are not so much clans, as has been conjectured, as they are the equivalents of the "village communities" or political groups of northern and central California—what might be called tribes were they larger in numbers, set off by dialect, or possessed of names other than derivatives from one of the sites inhabited. Each of these Serrano groups or bands owned a creek and adjacent tract; its "village" or most permanent settlement usually lay where the stream emerges from the foothills. Each group was also normally or rigidly exogamous: and there was at least a strong tendency, if not a rule, for particular groups to intermarry. Each group or band was either Wild Cat or Coyote; but it appears that group and not moiety affiliation determined exogamy, since some of the regularly intermarrying bands are assigned to the same moiety.

The known groups, in west-east sequence along the southern edge of the San Bernardino Range, were the Wa'acham of San Bernardino, Redlands, and Yucaipa; the Tüpamukiyam (?) at Tümünamtu between El Casco and Beaumont; the Pavükuyam at Akavat near Beaumont; the Tamukuvayam of Pihatüpayam (*sic:* the name seems that of a group) at Banning Water Canyon; perhaps a group at Nahyu, Hathaway Canyon; one at Marki (Malki), the present reservation near Banning; the Wakühiktam at Wakühi on Cabezon Creek; the Palukiktam in Lyons Canyon; the Wanüpüpayam at the mouth of Whitewater Canyon; three groups, the Maringayam, Mühiatnim (Mohiyanim), and Atü'aviatam, more or less associated at Yamisevul on Mission Creek, Türka on Little Morongo Creek, Maringa on Big Morongo Creek, Mukunpat on the same stream to the north, and at Kupacham, the Pipes, across the mountains. Of these, the second, eleventh, and twelfth were Wild Cat, the fifth and sixth not known, the remainder Coyote.[2]

Other groups were the Tüchahüktam (Coyote moiety) of Tüchahü at Snow Canyon or One Horse Spring at the foot of Mount San Jacinto, on the south side of San Gorgonio Pass; the Coyote moiety people of Mara, Twenty-nine Palms, northeast of Big Morongo Creek; the Yuhaviatam or Kuchaviatam of Yuhaviat ("pine place") in or near Bear Valley, moiety unknown; the Pauwiatum, Coyote; the people of Kupacha, Wild Cat; the people of Kayuwat, Wild Cat (?)—these three in or north of the San Bernardino Mountains. The Mawiatum are described as east of Kayuwat on Mohave River and the people of Amahavit as east of these. Both of these would be Vanyume rather than Serrano proper, by the classification here followed; and Amaha-vit suggests Hamakhava, Mohave, and reminds of the rather close relations between this people and some of the Vanyume. Some Serrano also list the Agutushyam of the Tehachapi Mountains, that is, the Kawaiisu, as if they were one of their own bands. This is in line with certain Kawaiisu claims, already mentioned, to ownership of part of Mohave River and the northern foot of the Sierra Madre.

Each group possessed a hereditary chief called *kika*. This word is from a Shoshonean stem meaning " house " or " live." Associated with each *kika* was a hereditary *paha'* or assistant chief with ceremonial functions. The Luiseño have the same official and call him by the same name. Ceremonies were held in special houses built of tules, not in an open inclosure as among the other southern Californians.

The moieties, at least as represented by the Maringayam and Mühiatnim, partly divided and partly reciprocated religious functions. Each tended the dead of the other before cremation. The Mühiatnim *paha'* named the children of both clans after their dead ancestors. The Maringayam *kika* ordered ceremonies, and his people built the tule house and acted as messengers. The Mühiatnim cooked and served food to the Maringayam at ceremonies.

Acorns were fairly abundant in the western part of Serrano territory, but the eastern bands got their supply from the western ones, or substituted other foods. Storage was in outdoor basketlike caches raised on poles. Houses were covered with mats of tules, which are said to grow along all the streams, even those that lose themselves in the desert. The modern ceremonial house at Banning, apparently kept up for a fragment of an annual mourning, is tule covered. A sweat house that stood there until recently—it may have been built

---

[2] The list is incomplete and may be supplemented and corrected by the unpublished Benedict data already referred to.

by a Pass Cahuilla, but was probably Serrano—was small, earth-covered, and had a center post (Pl. 60). Pottery was made by the Serrano, but rarely if ever decorated. No specimens have been pre-served.

COSMOGONY.

The Serrano origin begins with Pakrokitat, from whose left shoulder was born his younger brother Kukitat. Pakrokitat created men. Kukitat wanted them to have eyes in the back and webbed feet, and quarreled constantly. It was he that caused death. Pakro-kitat finally left him this earth, retiring to a world of his own, to which the hearts of the dead go after first visiting the three beautiful Panamam on the island Payait. This island and its goddesses were also made by Pakrokitat. Before the separation of the brothers, the human race, led by a white eagle, had come from its origin in the north to Mount San Gorgonio. After Pakrokitat's departure, men, under the influence of Kukitat, began to divide into nations, speak differently, and war on one another. They finally became tired of Kukitat and decided to kill him. The frog accomplished this end by hiding in the ocean and swallowing the god's excretions. Kukitat, feeling death approach, gave instructions for his cremation; but the suspected coyote, although sent away on a pretended errand, re-turned in time to squeeze through badger's legs in the circle of the mourners and make away with Kukitat's heart. This happened at Hatauva (compare Luiseño Tova, where Wiyot died) in Bear Valley. People continued to fight, until only one man survived of the Marin-gayam. His Kayuwat wife bore a posthumous boy, who was reared with his mother's people, but returned to his ancestral country, mar-ried two Mühiatnim sisters, and became the progenitor of the Maringayam or Serrano of today.

CHAPTER 44.

THE GABRIELINO.

THE FERNANDEÑO.

This group of people, more properly San Fernandeños, are named from San Fernando, one of the two Franciscan missions in Los Angeles County. At San Gabriel, the other establishment, were the San Gabrielinos, more often known merely as Gabrielinos, popularly Gravielinos. In a larger sense, both people have been designated as the Gabrielino. Their idioms were distinguishable, but not notably so; and if fuller knowledge were extant it might be necessary to recognize half a dozen dialects instead of the two which the presence of the missions has given the appearance of being standard. The delimitation of Fernandeño and Gabrielino on the map is mainly conjectural, and there is no known point in which the two groups differed in customs. It will be best, therefore, to treat them as a unit under the caption of the more prominent division.

THE GABRIELINO.

TERRITORY.

The wider Gabrielino group occupied Los Angeles County south of the Sierra Madre, half of Orange County, and the islands of Santa Catalina and San Clemente. The evidence is scant and somewhat conflicting as regards the latter; a divergent dialect, or even a Luiseño one, may have been spoken there. The local culture on San Clemente, however, was clearly connected with that of Santa Catalina, perhaps dependent upon it; and Catalina was pure Gabrielino in speech.

On the west, the Gabrielino limits—here more exactly Fernandeño—against the Chumash were at the minor watershed through which the Santa Susanna tunnel has been bored; at the coast, between Malibu and Topanga Creeks. Eastward, toward the Serrano and Luiseño, the line probably passed from Mount San Antonio to the vicinity of Cucamonga, Mount Arlington, and Monument and Santiago Peaks; in other words, through western San Bernardino and Riverside Counties—although San Bernardino Valley has also been ascribed to the Gabrielino. Southward, Alisos Creek is cited as the boundary between Gabrielino and Juaneño.

Most of the ascertained place names of the Gabrielino are shown in Plate 57, whose limitations as regards the inclusion of true village sites have already been mentioned. Other places are these: Pimu or Pipimar, Santa Catalina Island; Kinki or Kinkipar, San Clemente Island; Aleupki-nga, Santa Anita; Pimoka-nga, Rancho de los Ybarras; Nakau-nga, Carpenter's; Chokish-nga, Jaboneria; Akura-nga, La Presa; Sona-nga, White's; Sisitkano-nga, Pear Orchard; Isantka-nga, Mision Vieja. Sua-nga near Long Beach is mentioned as the largest village.

Synonyms or dialectic variants of the Gabrielino names shown in Plate 57 are: Tuvasak for Siba; Iya for Wenot; Pashina for Pasino; Ongovi, Ungüvi for Engva; Chauvi and Unau for Chowi; Shua for Sua.

A language of "Kokomcar" and one of "Corbonamga" are mentioned as spoken by the neophytes at San Gabriel besides the "Sibanga"—Siba, the site of San Gabriel—and "Guiguitamcar" or Kikitanum, that is, Kitanemuk.

The Ventureño Chumash knew the Gabrielino, and perhaps all the Shoshoneans beyond, as Ataplili'ish (plural I'ataplili'ish).

GENERAL STATUS.

The Gabrielino held the great bulk of the most fertile lowland portion of southern California. They occupied also a stretch of pleasant and sheltered coast and the most favored one of the Santa Barbara Islands. They seem to have been the most advanced group south of Tehachapi, except perhaps the Chumash. They certainly were the wealthiest and most thoughtful of all the Shoshoneans of the State, and dominated these civilizationally wherever contacts occurred. Their influence spread even to alien peoples. They have melted away so completely that we know more of the fine facts of the culture of ruder tribes; but everything points to these very efflorescences having had their origin with the Gabrielino.

The Jimson weed or toloache ritual is a case in point. The religious use of this drug extends far eastward, and its ultimate source may prove to be Pueblo, like that of the sand painting that is associated with it in the region from the Gabrielino south. The definite cult. however, in which the plant is employed, the mythology with which it is brought into relation, the ritual actions and songs that constitute its body, were worked out primarily if not wholly by the Gabrielino. All southern accounts mention Santa Catalina and San

Clemente Islands as the seat of the source of this cult. Whether it was brought from there to the mainland Gabrielino, or whether these had long shared the ritual with their oceanic kinsmen, is not certain. At any rate, the ritual was carried to the Juaneño; from them to the Luiseño; and they in turn imparted it to the Cupeño and the northern or western Diegueño.

The last of this flow took place in historic time. It reached the interior Luiseño and the Diegueño from about 1790 to 1850. The very missions of the pious Franciscans stimulated the spread. They brought San Clemente Indians to San Luis Rey, and highland Luiseño to mingle with the coast Luiseño and islanders there. The Luiseño and Diegueño to-day sing nearly all their toloache songs in the Gabrielino language without concern at not understanding the words issuing from their mouths.

MYTHOLOGY.

Among the Juaneño and Luiseño the Jimson-weed cult is intimately associated with beliefs in a deity called Chingichnich or Chungichnish. This name has not been reported from the Gabrielino, but Kwawar occurs as a synonym of Chingichnich among the Juaneño and as the "creator" with the Gabrielino. Further, certain of the animals of the Luiseño worship, such as the raven and rattlesnake, reappear with religious significance among the Gabrielino. There can thus be little doubt that these people also acknowledged the divinity. The problem which we can not answer is whether they knew him under another name, or whether Chungichnish is itself a Gabrielino term which happens not to be mentioned in the scant sources of information upon this tribe. Pura, the Luiseño say, is what the Gabrielino called the deity; but the word looks suspiciously like the Luiseño term for shaman: *pula*.

On the other side, to the north, there are some traces of a pantheon of six or seven deities, in part female, more or less associated with the Jimson-weed cult, though whether primarily or not is uncertain. Among the southern Yokuts these divinities present the appearance of being of foreign origin, and this determination is corroborated by their entrance into wider phases of life with the Gabrielino: the names are not only those of gods, but titles of chieftainship. The information on this interesting little system of mythology is sadly fragmentary, but pieces together sufficiently to suggest some idea of the nature of the scheme. It is presented in the following table:

YOKUTS. In fixed order of Jimson-weed prayers.	YOKUTS. In fixed order of other prayers.	FERNANDEÑO. "Gods" in order of mention.	GABRIELINO.	SERRANO.
Tüüshiut....	Tüüshiut....			
Pamashiut..	Pamashiut....			
Yohahait....	Yohahait....			
	Echepat.....	5. Iuichepet..		
	Pitsuriut......	4. Pichurut...		
	Tsukit	3. Chukit....	Chukit (in myth, sister of 4 brothers).	Six stones at Nanamüyiat, Little Bear Valley, were "gods."
	Ukat (their sister).	1. Ukat..		
		2. Tamur....	Tomar (title of oldest son of chief).	
		6. Manisar (wife of 5).	Manisar (title of oldest daughter of chief).	

FORMULA: 7 Yokuts (-t, prayers)−3 Yokuts (-t, Jimson weed)+2 Gabrielino (-r, chiefs)=6 Fernandeño (-t, -r, gods)=6 Serrano (?).

The Fernandeño list is from San Fernando in mission times, and might therefore go back to a Kitanemuk Serrano source. The Kitanemuk at any rate would have carried the religion to the Yokuts, who would not be praying to native gods under names that contain the sound r, which is lacking from their own language. How far the Chumash, Alliklik, Kawaiisu, and Vanyume shared in this complex is entirely undetermined.

It is observable that there is a distinction of function between the gods whose names end in -t and those whose names end in -r, and that this distinction coincides with tribal distribution.

South of the Gabrielino, this mythic-ritual-social six god system has not been reported. Whether it and the Chungichnish complex excluded each other or stood in relation remains to be ascertained by future investigations. But there is an approximation to the Gabrielino plan among the Juaneño, who possessed animal names as titles for their chiefs and chieftainesses; thus "coyote" and "ladybug." It is also possible that the Juaneño female mythological character Ikaiut is to be connected with Ukat.

The meanings of the deities' name are obscure. Manisar is very likely from mani-t, Jimson weed. Pitsuriut or Pichurut suggests Juaneño piuts or piuch, the breath of life. The names Tüüshiut and Yohahait, which have been reported only from the Yokuts, are translated by these people with some hesitation as "maker" and "crusher;" but these may be only folk etymologies of foreign terms, like their rendering of Ukat as "looker, seer." It is not impossible that Tüüshiut is connected with the tosaut or tushaut stone so important in Chumash ritual and Juaneño myth.

The creative mythology of the Gabrielino has been preserved only in the veriest scraps. The reputed creator of the world—he may or may not have been such to the Indians—was called Kwawar ("Qua-o-ar") by his sacred name, and "Y-yo-ha-riv-gnina" otherwise. Neither epithet yields to analysis. He fixed the earth on seven giants whose stirrings cause earthquakes. The first man was Tobohar, his mate Pabavit. Tobohar is from a widespread Shoshonean stem for "earth;" among the Gabrielino themselves *tobanga* means "the world." Perhaps Tobohar and Pabavit should be interchanged. Everywhere else in southern California the earth is the first mother.

Porpoises were believed to watch the world, circling around it to see that it was safe and in good order. The crow was thought to advise of the approach of strangers. This sounds much like beliefs associated with the Chungichnish cult. Still more significant in this direction is the report that a surpassingly wise "chief," before dying, told the people that he would become an eagle so that they might have his feathers for dances; and that consequently ceremonies were made to the eagle. This is surely the dying god of whom all the southern Californians know; perhaps even the very Wiyot of the Juaneño and Luiseño; and the ceremony must be their eagle killing mourning rite.

The origin of mankind was attributed, as by all the Shoshoneans of southern California, to the north, whence a great divinity, who still exists, led the people to their present seats. Perhaps this "capitan general" was the just-mentioned eagle, perhaps Wiyot or his equivalent.

Chukit, the virgin sister of four unnamed brothers, probably all members of the six-god pantheon, was married by the lightning flash, and gave birth to a wonderful boy who spoke when his navel string was cut.

Coyote raced with water, and ended exhausted and ashamed. Whether he entered also into less trivial traditions is not recorded.

The Pleiades are "seven" sisters—six seems a more likely native version—married to as many brothers, who, however, cheated them of the game they killed, until the women rose to the sky. The youngest alone had been good to his wife; he was allowed to follow them, and is now in the constellation Taurus.

A woman of Muhu-vit, married at Hahamo, lazy, gluttonous, and stingy, is said to have been fed with game stuffed with toads and vermin, and given urine to drink by her husband's people. Sick and with her hair fallen out, she returned to her parents, destroying her child on the way. Secretly she was nourished back to health by the old people, until her brother, finding hairs in his bathing pool, discovered her unrecognized presence, and threw her out. Ashamed, she started for the seashore, and drowned herself from a cliff.

Her father threw his gaming hoop in four directions; when it reached the sea, it rolled in, and he knew his daughter's fate. First he revenged himself on his own son, whom, in the form of the *Kuwot* bird, he carried off and destroyed. Then, taking the shape of an eagle, he allowed himself to be caught by the people of Hahamo; but when they touched him, pestilence spread from him, and killed every one except an old woman and two children.

An inconsequential appendix follows. The two children grow up and marry: then the woman maltreats the old grandmother, but is killed by her. The husband mourns his wife and follows her spirit to the land of the dead, where his experiences are like those of the Yokuts Orpheus. Like him, also, he brings his partner back, but loses her once more and irrevocably at the last moment.

The ethical inconsistency of this story is marked to our feelings. The heroine certainly is blameworthy, but those who rid themselves of her, even more so. Hardly is sympathy aroused for her when she dispels it by dashing out her child's brains. Then she becomes beautiful once more, and elicits interest through the disgraceful treatment accorded her by her brother. But this hardly seems sufficient cause for suicide. Her brother, too, committed the offense unwittingly; and his fatal punishment by his father comes to us as a shock. That the old chief should cruelly revenge himself by his magical powers on the foreigners who had first attempted his daughter's destruction seems natural enough; but the focus of interest is suddenly shifted from his means of vengeance to the successful escape from it of the old woman and her grandchildren. Then these, brother and sister as they are, marry. Now it is the old lady who is abused; but suddenly it is her granddaughter who is persecuted and finally slain; after which follows the episode in which the loving and grieving husband is the central character.

Nothing can be imagined farther from a plot according to the thoughts of a civilized people than this one; it appears to revel in acmes of purposeless contradictions. And yet, this trait is undoubtedly the accompaniment of an effect that, however obscure to us, was sought for; since it reappears in traditions, following an entirely different thread, told by the Luiseño and Diegueño, and is marked in the long tales of the Mohave. This deliberate or artistic incoherence, both as regards personages and plot, is thus a definite quality of the mythology of the southern Californian tribes. It has some partial resemblances in the Southwest, but scarcely any in central or northern California except in the loosely composite coyote tales. In central California we have the well-defined hero and villain of the normal folk tale of the world over; and however much the oppressed endure, there is never any doubt as to who is good and who wicked, and that before the end is reached the wicked will be properly punished. That in the southern California traditions this simple and almost universal scheme is departed from, is of course not due to absence of aesthetic feeling, but rather an evidence of subtle refinement of emotion, of decorative overelaboration of some literary quality, to such a degree that the ordinary rules of satisfaction in balance and moral proportion become inconsequential. The traits that shock us ethically and artistically were the very ones, we may be sure, that gave the keenest satisfaction to the craftsmen that told these tales and the accustomed public that delighted to listen to them.

Most likely, as among the Mohave, stories like this one are little else than a web that carries a rich embroidery of songs, which yield their own emotional stimulus, and at the same time endow the plot, when sensed through their medium, with a brilliant and profound luminousness that makes immaterial the presence or absence of everything else.

RITUAL.

Almost nothing specific is on record concerning the Gabrielino Jimson-weed cult, except that it is reported that the plant, called *manit*, was drunk mixed with salt water, in order to give strength, impenetrability to arrows, immunity from bear and snake bites, and fortune in the hunt. These very practical aims in no way indicate that the drinking was not also part of the sacred and esoteric ritual that we know to have been associated with it.

Among the Fernandeño a four-sided and roped-off ground painting was made, in the middle of which a man stood, holding twelve radiating strings, the ends of which were in the hands of as many assistants. When he shook the cords, the earth quaked, and whatever person he had in mind became sick. The setting of this rite is obscure. It suggests the Chumash use of charm stones more than any Luiseño ceremonial act; but the sand painting is Luiseño and not, so far as known, Chumash.

The mourning commemoration was held in the *yoba* enclosure. For eight days songs and perhaps dances were rehearsed outside. The ceremony itself endured another eight days.

On the first, the enclosure was erected or consecrated.

From the second to the seventh day men and boys danced inside the enclosure and women sat in a circle and sang. The dancers' faces, necks, arms, and thoraxes were painted; which makes it seem that their feather costume was the feather crown and skirt of the Luiseño and Juaneño. The songs related to the deceased, or perhaps to the god who first died; some were sung " to the destruction of his enemies." Each song or verse ended with a sort of growl. A pole with a feather streamer was erected at each of the four cardinal points.

On the eighth day the old women made ready more food than usual; about noon it was distributed. A deep hole was then dug and a fire kindled in it, whereupon the articles reserved at the time of death were committed to the flames. Baskets, shell money, and seeds were thrown to the spectators or out-of-town visitors. During the burning, one of the old men, reciting mystical words, kept stirring up the fire to insure the total destruction of the property. The hole was then filled with earth and well trodden down.

The end of this ceremony allies it with the Luiseño *yunish mata-kish*, made for a dead initiate. The rehearsing, the participation of boys, and the type of costume, all point to the existence of the kind of initiatory organization which the Juaneño and Luiseño possessed and in fact believed that they derived from the Gabrielino. The four poles suggest the one erected in the Luiseño *notush* mourning, to which, again, they attribute a Gabrielino origin. The cursing songs of hate are also southern. All that fails of mention is the image of the dead; and with the Kitanemuk on one side and the Luiseño on the other employing this, it is practically certain that the Gabrielino knew it.

It must be said once more that the frequent mention of the Juaneño and Luiseño in connections like the present one must not lead to an inference that the Gabrielino were in any sense dependent upon them. The influence was positively the other way. It merely happens that for the Juaneño a fuller account of the religion, and among the Luiseño the ceremonies themselves, have been preserved; so that the knowledge of the borrowed rites of the southerners must be drawn upon for an understanding of the recorded fragments of the older and probably more elaborate Gabrielino cult. Thus, something is known of the Luiseño *notush* and its *kutumit* pole; for the Gabrielino there is no record other than that at San Fernando a similar pole was called *kotumut*.

Several round stones, perforated, hafted on the ends of rather slender sticks, and feather decorated, have been discovered in a cave in Gabrielino territory. Such stones, which abound most among the Chumash, are ordinarily digging stick weights; but in this case the character of the handles precludes any employment as a tool. An unknown ritualistic use is therefore indicated.

That the Gabrielino word for "tobacco," *shuki*, is not from the usual southern Californian stem *piva*, but borrowed from Yokuts *shogon*, *sohon*, which has penetrated also into the Mono, Koso, and Tübatulabal dialects, suggests that the plant was perhaps more widely used, at least in religious connections, by the Yokuts, and that the neighboring Shoshoneans came under their influence in this matter.

The number most endowed with significance to the Gabrielino seems to have been four, or its double, eight. Six, seven, and ten are also referred to in connections that make probable a certain degree of sacredness or suggestive value; but five, which predominates among the Juaneño, has not been reported here.

SHAMANISM.

The removal of disease was by sucking blood and perhaps the disease object. Smoking, manipulation, and singing preceded. The words of the songs appear to have been descriptive of the practices applied, as among the Mohave. It may be conjectured that the doctor sang not so much of what he was doing as of what had been done to a god in the far past, or what he in a dream had seen a deity or animal perform.

Diseases were also treated by a variety of remedies. Jimsonweed was drunk for paralysis, debility, and stagnation. Whipping with nettles was resorted to in the same cases, as also for side pains. Eating red ants or letting the insects bite the skin, a favorite Yokuts remedy, were remedies for body pains. For local inflammations, blood was drawn. Tobacco, with or without an admixture of shell lime, was eaten for fever, strangury, wounds, stomach aches, and whenever vomiting was desired. Whether the old men habitually ate tobacco and lime, as was customary among the Kitanemuk and Yokuts, is not clear. Against rheumatism, blisters were burned with nettle or wild hemp furze and at once opened. Anise was for purging; *kayat*, "chuchupate," for headache; *ihaiish*, *Echinocystis*, for inflammations, eye disease, suppressed periods, wounds, and urinary troubles; when boiled it was taken to produce sweating.

Medicine men were called *ahubsuvoirot*.

The bear doctor was a Gabrielino institution, although more than the naked fact is not known.

BUILDINGS.

The house was of tule mats on a framework of poles: size and shape have not been recorded. On the islands and in the hills thatch of other materials may sometimes have been used. Earth-covered dwellings have not been mentioned. The sweat house had a roof of soil; but it was small, and a true sudatory, heated by fire and smoke, of course, as in all California, and not by steam. The sweat house of the Serrano or Pass Cahuilla (Pl. 60) probably serves as a representative.

The place of assembly for any occasion not savoring too formally of ritual was presumably any large dwelling, such as the chief's, or the open brush shade. Religious gatherings took place in the open air ceremonial enclosure, the Juaneño *wankech*, Luiseño *wamkish*, Diegueño *himak*. The Gabrielino seem to have called it *yoba* ("yobare," "yobagnar") and to have built it circularly of willows inserted wicker fashion among stakes. It was consecrated for each ceremony. A similar structure, without sanctity, was used for rehearsals and the instruction of children. Each village had one *yoba*.

BASKETRY AND POTTERY.

Few if any baskets authentically assignable to the Gabrielino have been preserved. The type of the tribal ware was that common to all southern California and usually known as "Mission basketry"; it is described in the chapter on the Cahuilla. The pitched water bottle is specifically mentioned.

Pottery had come into use by the end of the mission period. But it is stated positively that clay was not worked in aboriginal days. Archeology confirms: no pottery has been found in ancient remains in the Gabrielino habitat.

STEATITE.

In the soapstone ledges of Santa Catalina the Gabrielino possessed the best available supply of this serviceable material in California; or at any rate the source most extensively utilized. The discoverers found them using stone vessels for cooking; and the condition of the island quarries, with half-finished pieces and tools still on the surface, is evidence that the industry was only interrupted after the importation of our civilization. From Santa Catalina the pots, and perhaps the raw material, were carried to the villages at Redondo and San Pedro and gradually distributed to the inland towns. The eastern Chumash may have got them from the people of Santa Monica and Topanga and from the Fernandeño. But the presence of steatite articles in fair abundance on Santa Cruz and the other northern channel islands suggests also a direct maritime dispersion to these Chumash, and from them to their kinsmen of the Santa Barbara coast. Inland the vessels penetrated at least sporadically as far as the Yokuts of Tulare Lake, if scant archeological records may be trusted. It is not sure that this entire area was served from Santa Catalina. But much of the supply evidently came from the island.

It is interesting that the steatite and the pottery areas of southern California substantially exclude each other. Gabrielino and Chumash were flooded with the one material, and did not touch clay. Juaneño, Luiseño, Cahuilla, Diegueño, Serrano, Mohave, and Yuma made pots; and it is only now and then that small or ornamental pieces of steatite were to be found among them.

When the soapstone pots broke, their pieces were bored at one corner to allow of the insertion of a stick to handle them by, and utilized as baking slabs or frying pans. Hundreds of such salvaged fragments have been found in old village sites. The occasional fine vessels of stone were not cook pots, but religious receptacles— possibly to drink toloache from. They are shell inlaid and untouched by fire. The shape, too, is that of an open bowl, not a jar. They have sometimes been taken for mortars, on account of their general form; but it is obvious that one blow with a pestle would have destroyed irreparably most of these delicately walled, polished, symmetrical, and ornamented objects of sandstone or waxlike steatite.

Most abundantly on Santa Catalina, but also on the coast immediately opposite, on the Chumash islands, and even on the Santa Barbara shore, a profusion of soapstone artifacts have been found. Besides recognizable ornaments and beads, there are several types whose evident lack of any utilitarian purpose has caused them to be generally classed as made with ceremonial intent. Besides peculiar objects of the shape of hooks, spades, and scoops, there are carvings of whales, which are of particular interest as one of the very few instances, in all aboriginal California, of anything like a representation. They are as simple as the stone is easy to work, but suggest a dorsally finned cetacean with considerable fidelity and no shadow of doubt. They may be plastic figures of the porpoises that guarded the Gabrielino world. The hooks and other shapes range from a fraction of an ounce to several pounds in weight, and pass through a transition of shapes which retain indeed a certain decorative or symbolic likeness that makes their unity of class certain, but are so variant in structural features as to dispel any possibility of each type having possessed a common utilitarian purpose. They served a religious purpose, then; and as their source corresponded with that ascribed by evidence and tradition alike to the Chungichnish cult—the balmy island of Santa Catalina—the conclusion is very hard to avoid that the worship and the art forms must have been associated. From this conviction we can argue, with somewhat less confidence, but yet with probability, that something of the same specific Chungichnish ritual and mythology traveled with the figures from Santa Catalina to the Chumash islanders and mainlanders. That the Chumash drank Jimson weed we know; the present reasoning establishes some likelihood that their cult of it was not a particular one.

TRADE AND MONEY.

For the islanders' journeys, canoes of the kind described by the discoverers, and known also from fragments in Chumash graves, were employed. The canoe may at times have been dug out from a log, but owing to the scarcity of suitable timber, especially on the islands, was usually built up out of planks, lashed and asphalted together. For lagoon navigation the rush balsa may also have been used.

Between the coast and interior trade was considerable. The shore people gave shell beads, dried fish, sea-otter furs, and soapstone vessels. They received deerskins, seeds, and perhaps acorns.

The standard currency was the disk bead, of clamshell, from one-half to three-quarters of an inch in diameter, and the thicker the better. The unit of measurement was the *ponko*. This reached from the base to the tip of the middle finger, thence around the outside of the hand past the wrist back to the point of the middle finger, and then once more not quite to the wrist. The length, about 30 inches, is half of the scant fathom reach of a man of small stature. The various local manners of this type of money measuring have been brought together in Table 6 in the chapter on the Chumash.

The next highest unit was four *ponko*, called a *sayako*. Two *sayako* were reckoned, in mission times, a Mexican *peso* or dollar; which made the *ponko* a *real*. This equivalation to the Spanish standard obtained also among the Chumash and Salinans, but the reckoning of values by doubling and quadrupling is probably native.

It is curious that the heavy clamshell beads are rare in ancient Gabrielino and Chumash graves, thin convex disks of *Olivella* being the common prehistoric type. These have also been found among the modern Luiseño and Cahuilla. The *Olivella* shell was known throughout central and northern California, but little esteemed; it ranked as beads rather than money. In the south it was more frequently ground into disks; but at that, it must have been secondary to the heavy clam bead, whose broad edge is susceptible of a much higher polish.

Both types are represented among the Southwestern tribes. The modern Zuñi bead is prevailingly of *Olivella*. The Pueblo, however, never distinguished as sharply between a mere necklace and currency as the Californian; he thought in terms of property rather than of standardized money.

FOOD.

When the Gabrielino first met the Spaniards they politely accepted every gift, but every scrap of food was held in such abhorrence as to be buried secretly. It was not that the natives feared deliberate poisoning, but they were evidently imbued with a strong conviction similar to that of the Mohave, who believed that every nation had its own peculiar food and that for one to partake of the characteristic nourishment of the other or to mingle with its women, or in fact associate in any prolonged contact, was bound in the very nature of things to bring sickness.

The native foods rejected are not known. They can not have been many, as dogs, coyotes, all birds whatsoever, and even rattlesnakes are mentioned as having been eaten. Whether the omission of the bear from the list of edible animals is significant or not must remain doubtful.

The Gabrielino are the first people of all those passed in review to use movable stone mortars to any great extent for the ordinary purpose of grinding acorns and plant foods, at least in historic time. The soil of northern California is studded with pot-shaped mortars, but the natives misunderstand their purpose or regard them as magical objects, and pound on slabs or in holes worn into natural surfaces of rock. In the central part of the State the portable mortar begins to appear, and the basket hopper, the accompaniment of the pounded slab, commences to go out of use, but the bedrock mortar hole remains the standard, at least for acorns. From the Gabrielino on, however, south to the Diegueño, east to the Mohave, and west, perhaps, to the Chumash, the stone mortar is not merely a buried relic from a remote prehistoric age but a utensil of everyday modern use. Some of these southern tribes cement a basket to the rim of the stone; the Chumash asphalt it also to slabs; but the mortar can often be used just as successfully, and sometimes perhaps more conveniently, without this extension. Perhaps this is why the hopper has not been reported from the Gabrielino. That they knew the device is nearly certain from their location between groups that employed it.

VARIOUS IMPLEMENTS.

The Gabrielino war club ranged from a straight heavy stick to a shorter form with a definitely marked cylindrical end—the southwestern type.

A curved flat stick, called *makana*, for throwing at rabbits and birds, is another southwestern type that pervades all southern California and seems to have come to the limit of its distribution among the Gabrielino. (Fig. 55.)

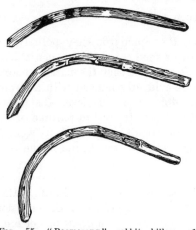

Rattles in the Spanish period were made of gourd or rawhide. These are almost certainly recent modifications of the old turtle-shell rattle still employed by the Luiseño and Diegueño and, as a knee attachment, used from time immemorial by the Pueblo Indians. The modern Mohave rattle is a gourd; but it is not sure that this is native; in any event, the Mohave were an agricultural people, while the Gabrielino and other southern Californians were not.

FIG. 55.—"Boomerang" rabbit killers of southern California. From above downward, Cupeño, Luiseño, Mohave.

A wooden clapper rattle has been reported from the Gabrielino. This is the most southerly occurrence recorded for this universal north and central Californian implement. At that, the Gabrielino rattle is not a half-split stick, as elsewhere, but two boards bound and cemented together at one end.

Meat was cut with a splint of cane and not with a stone knife. Practicability or habit rather than any religious reason appears to have been the motive.

For arrow poison, gall was boiled down.

SOCIAL PRACTICES.

As in the whole of southern California, social institutions constitute the least known side of Gabrielino culture. Marriage was by purchase, but more was made of the wedding rite than of the payment; chiefs and prominent men often had several wives. All this is typical Juaneño procedure. The wife seems to have lived in the husband's village. It is said that he was at liberty to punish her at will for infidelity, even by death; but that the usual solution was to leave her to the seducer and appropriate the latter's spouse, with which practice no interference was tolerated. Deliberate incest was punished by shooting to death. There was a chief in each village. If any exercised wider influence, the fact has not been reported. To judge by Juaneño analogues, as well as the above-mentioned titles for the chieftain's children, the position conveyed much deference and respect. Each chief was known by the name of his town plus the suffix -*pik* or -*vik*. The rank was hereditary, apparently in the male line. It is said that the chief took no action against sorcerers, other than to leave punishment to the magical machinations of the medicine men of his own town. As an absolute negative, this statement may be doubted. It is likely to have been true under the outward restraints of mission life.

Captives taken in battle were tortured and killed.

The hair was at times plastered with clay for 24 hours, to impart gloss and keep it from splitting. The Mohave mix in a vegetable dye for this purpose; plain mud is applied by them to kill vermin.

The dead were burned by both Fernandeño and Gabrielino proper until the padres introduced interment. On Santa Catalina many skeletons have been found, but few if any evidences of cremation. Burial must therefore have been the prevalent manner on this island through most of its history. The mainland, on the other hand, is remarkably free of ancient human bones, except at immediate coast points opposite Santa Catalina, such as Topanga, Santa Monica, Redondo, and San Pedro. It seems, therefore, that an ancient difference of custom separated the islanders from the bulk of the Gabrielino on this point.

THE SAN NICOLEÑO.

San Nicolas, the farthest seaward of the Santa Barbara Islands, foggy and wind blown, harbored a tribe of which the last survivor died more than 60 years ago. Four badly spelled words are all that has been preserved of their speech. These suffice to prove it Shoshonean: they do not establish its dialectic relation. A divergent idiom may well have developed in the isolation of this sand-swept and

rocky island.   It is stated that when the last survivor was brought
to Santa Barbara her speech was thoroughly unintelligible not only
to the Chumash of the vicinity but to the " Pepimaros " of Santa
Catalina (Pimu, Pipimar, the name of the island), of whom some
were sent for from Los Angeles.

The last handful of the natives, who are said to have suffered
previously in quarrels with Aleuts imported by Russian fur hunters,
and whose numbers had probably been diminished by drafts to the
missions, were taken to the mainland in 1835, soon after secularization.   A woman who at the last moment missed her child was left
behind.   Eighteen years later, when California was American, she
was discovered.   Her romantic case aroused the greatest interest, and
she was given the best of treatment in her new home at Santa Barbara; but she died in a few months.   More attention was bestowed
on her humble belongings than on the panoply of many a tribe; and
while the objects themselves seem all to have been scattered and
lost—the last traceable piece perished in the San Francisco fire of
1906—the descriptions, together with random but rather full recov-
eries from ancient village sites, enable a partial insight into the life
of this remote little group, the most westerly of all Uto-Aztekans.

Wood was scarce and small on the island.   There was enough brush
for huts, but most dwellings were reared on a frame of whale ribs and
jaws, either covered with sea-lion hides or wattled with brush or
rushes.   Bone implements were very numerous, and the use of several varieties is far from clear.   The island may have afforded sufficient timber for plank canoes, or dugouts may have been burned from
drift logs.   Steatite was imported from Santa Catalina, but is represented by small ornaments or charms rather than heavy bowls.
Whales must have been very abundant and frequently stranded;
there is nothing to indicate that they were hunted.   Sea otters were
to be had in comparative profusion, and, to judge from the habits of
other tribes, their furs formed the most prized dress and the chief
export in a trade on which the San Nicoleño must have depended for
many necessities.   Seals, water birds, fish, and mollusks were no
doubt the principal food; but roots were dug industriously.   Baskets
are spoken of as of the type ordinary in southern California.   They
were often asphalted, hot pebbles being employed to melt and spread
the lumps.   Water baskets were in plain twining, as among the
Chumash; but the neck was long, much as in our wine bottles.   The
lone woman wore a sort of gown of squares of bird skin sewn together; but this does not seem wholly aboriginal.   The usual dress
may be conjectured to have been the scant costume of all California,
with capes or blankets of woven strips of bird skin added at need.

The cylinder-headed wooden war club was in use. The dead were buried, as by all the islanders, not cremated as on the Shoshonean mainland. Of religion we only know that there were weather invocations and hunting charms; whether the toloache cult or the image form of mourning anniversary had reached the island must remain in abeyance; and as to society, there is total ignorance.

Ghalas-at has been given as the name of the island. This is perhaps the native or the Chumash pronunciation of Gabrielino Haras-nga.

CHAPTER 45.

THE JUANEÑO.

EXTENSION.

The Juaneño Indians are so named after the mission of San Juan Capistrano in their territory. They were wedged in between the Gabrielino and the Luiseño; but their speech was a dialect of the latter language, not a transition between the two. Their land extended from the sea to the crest of the southern continuation of the Sierra Santa Ana. Southward, toward the Luiseño, the boundary ran between San Onofre and Las Pulgas; on the north, toward the Gabrielino, it is said to have followed Alisos Creek. The known settlements of the group are shown in Plate 57.

For Ahachmai, Akagchemem and Kwanisa-vit have also been given as dialectic variant or name of an associated site; for Pu-tuid-em, Niwiti.

The population may have been a thousand; the present survivors may be three or four.

Father Geronimo Boscana's "Chinigchinich," easily the most intensive and best written account of the customs and religion of any group of California Indians in the mission days, relates to San Juan Capistrano; and the pages that follow are almost wholly based on his careful statements. It has been generally assumed that this work referred to the Juaneño; but analysis of its native terms and designations of place leave a doubtful impression. A large part, possibly the bulk, of the information conveyed by the assiduous and sympathetic priest is certainly of Gabrielino origin. What is questionable is whether the lore was taken over by the Juaneño from the Gabrielino of their own accord and in premission times, as part of the Chungichnish cult or as the effect of still earlier streams of Gabrielino culture; or whether the father reported data from local Juaneños and imported Gabrielinos side by side without thinking it worth while for his purposes to specify the tribal differences. On the one hand, we know that the Gabrielino influence existed, for it prevails among the more distant Luiseño. On the other hand, the mission was but a very few miles from the Juaneño boundary, and southern Gabrielino converts must have become attached to the establishment in considerable numbers. The problem can not be answered with exactness; the only recourse is to present the information as a whole and preserve the mental caution called for by the circumstances.

MYTHOLOGY.

The Juaneño story of the creation has been preserved in two versions, one from the inhabitants of the interior, the other from the coast. The former is more similar to the Luiseño account.

According to this version, the first things in the universe were the sky and the earth, brother and sister. From their union were born, first, earth and sand, next, stone and flint, then trees, next herbs, after that animals, and finally Wiyot (Ouiot). From Wiyot were born men, or rather a first race of beings that preceded mankind. As they multiplied in number, the Earth, Wiyot's mother, grew southward, and the people followed. They used soil as food.

Wiyot was plotted against and poisoned. His mother prepared a remedy, but this was spilled and lost through the curiosity of the Coyote. After a sickness of some duration, Wiyot died, predicting his return. After some discussion his cremation was decided upon, but the people feared Coyote, and attempted to conduct the funeral in his absence. He appeared, however, and professing his affection for Wiyot, leaped upon the pyre, tore off a piece of flesh from the body, and swallowed it. Coyote had been the *eyake* or assistant chief to Wiyot.

After this, a new being appeared, who revealed himself as Chingichnich ("Chinigchinich"), with his habitation in the sky, or rather throughout the world. Chingichnich converted the first people into animals and plants, or into spirits having power over animals and plants, and caused them to scatter over the earth. In their place he made a new race, the present human species, out of earth, and taught them their laws and institutions, including the building of the *wankech* (*vanquech*) or ceremonial inclosure.

The coast Juaneño attributed the creation of the world, the sea, and animals and plants to "Night," Tukma or Tokuma ("Nocuma"). He fastened the earth by means of the smooth, black, hard rock called *tosaut*. The ocean at first was small and overcrowded with beings until a large fish brought the *tosaut*, the center of which was filled with gall. This being emptied into the water, it became salt and welled up until the ocean attained its present size. Tukma then created the first human being called Ehoni.

To two of Ehoni's descendants, Sirout ("handful of tobacco") and his wife Ikaiut ("above,")Wiyot was born as son, at Pubu-na, to the northwest of San Juan Capistrano, in Gabrielino territory. Wiyot ruled the people, but according to this story also was plotted against, and poisoned by means of the *tosaut* stone. He sickened, died, and was burned.

In this version also a new divinity appears after Wiyot's death, but under the name of Atahen, "man," who gave to certain of the people and their descendants the power to make rain, cause seeds to grow, and bring about the productivity of game animals.

Still later there was born at "Pubuna"—Pubu-nga, Los Alamitos, in Gabrielino territory—to Taku and Ausar, Wiamot ("Ouiamot"), who is said to have been Chingichnich. He announced that he had come from the stars, gave to the people the feather costume for dancing, instructed them in its use, thus constituting the order of *puplem* or initiated, and gave orders for the ceremonial inclosure to be built.

Wiamot or Chingichnich is also said to have become sick and to have announced that after his death he should ascend to the stars to watch the people; to punish by bears, rattlesnakes, famine, and sickness those who disobeyed his commandments; and to reward the faithful.

There is evidently some confusion in this story. Atahen, the second of the great leaders, is perhaps merely a synonym of either Wiyot, the first, or Chingichnich, the third. The appearance of Chingichnich under the name Wiamot, so similar to Wiyot, is also peculiar. Three other names of Chingichnich are given. He was called Tobet, which is the name of the ceremonial costume worn by those initiated into his cult; Saor, which denotes the uninitiated; and Kwawar, his appellation among the stars. The last name was in use among the Gabrielino also. The close association of myth and ritual at these points is evident. The use of the name of the dance costume for the deity himself, or vice versa, is a fusion parallel to that which has taken place in regard to the Kuksu in the religion of the Sacramento Valley.

The prominence of the *tosaut* stone in the creation myth of the coast Juaneño is partly cleared up by the fact that this word occurs among the entirely alien Chumash as the name of the charm stones used by medicine men, and probably in public ritual also. It follows that the intervening Gabrielino must have had similar sacred stones and given them the identical appellation. In fact it is not unlikely that the practice as well as the name, which is of undetermined etymology, are of Gabrielino origin. It is probably more than a coincidence that all indications of the *tosaut* cult come from coast points.

Tradition further told of a flood which submerged the whole earth except one mountain peak. This event is placed in the time of Chingichnich's appearance, subsequent to the death of Wiyot, and has parallels in Mohave belief. In general, the concept of primeval water is central Californian. In northwestern and in southern California the world is believed to have existed first, and the subsequent flood to have been temporary. Of all the southerners, only the Yuman tribes tend to begin their cosmology with the waters.

Another legend has been preserved which, although trivial and limited in its range, is of interest as evidencing the presence among these people of a migration tradition of the type characteristic of parts of southern California, but entirely without analogues in the central and northern portions of the State. It begins at Sehat, at Los Nietos, a Gabrielino village some 30 or more miles northwest of San Juan Capistrano. Here lived the Chief Oyaison, with his wife Sirorum. After the death of the latter, Oyaison escorted one of his three children, his daughter Korone, together with a portion of his people, southward to Niwiti, not far from San Juan Capistrano. Here, after the return of her father, Korone established a settlement which was named Pu-tuid-em after an enlargement of her abdomen or navel. She was enormously fat, and never married. The newcomers spread out into neighboring settlements and changed their speech from the original Gabrielino tongue which they had brought with them. Korone's body finally swelled up to such a degree, during her sleep, that it turned into a mound or small hill which remains to-day. The inhabitants of Pu-tuid-em then moved to Ahachmai or Akagchemem, a mile or two distant, at the spot where the mission was subsequently founded. They spent their first night in their new home huddled and piled together like a heap of insects, or other animated things, to which fact the name of this new and final settlement refers.

This is almost certainly a true Juaneño story, as shown by its location; but it is noteworthy that it begins in the land of the Gabrielino.

The general cast and tone of this tradition is similar to a number of Mohave legends, although the particular incidents differ throughout; and it obviously recalls the tribal and clan migration legends of the Pueblos, just as southwestern suggestions crop out in Juaneño cosmogony.

CULTS.

Juaneño ceremonies are primarily of two classes: initiatory or puberty rites, and mourning rituals. They were held in a sacred enclosure, and there appears to have been but one standard religious costume.

THE CEREMONIAL STRUCTURE.

The *wankech* or ceremonial chamber was an inclosure of brush, open to the sky, apparently with a subdivision or smaller inclosure. Near or in the latter place was placed the skin of a coyote, filled with feathers, horns, claws, and beaks, including particularly parts of the condor, and a number of arrows. This image or figure has no known parallels in California. It is said to have been the god Chingichnich. At any rate, it constituted an altar, in front of which was made a rude drawing or sand painting. Great respect was shown this sacred place. Conversation did not rise above a whisper, and the uninitiated were not even permitted to enter the outer inclosure.

It is specifically said that the altar in the *wankech* was an inviolable sanctuary, at which murderers, deposed chiefs, and all in fear of punishment found safe refuge. The practice is likely to have been actual, but the formulation of the idea of a recognized sanctuary seems un-Indian; there is nothing like it among any California tribe. It can hardly be doubted that the sanctity of the spot was great enough to prevent a killing or struggle. No matter what the provocation, punishment might be deferred until a more suitable occasion.

RITUAL DRESS.

The *tobet* or ceremonial costume comprised the *palet* ("*paelt*") skirt of eagle or condor feathers, reaching from the waist to the knees. On the head was fastened, by means of a cord of human hair, the *emech*, described as a pad or wig. Into this feathers were stuck, or an upright bunch of feathers called *eneat* was attached to it. The body was painted red and black, or sometimes white.

INITIATION CEREMONIES.

The Gabrielino Jimson-weed ceremonies were practiced by the Juaneño, who in turn helped to convey them to the Luiseño. As among the Luiseño, these were clearly initiation rites, and under the inspiration of the god Chingichnich. Young children were given the drug. From the fact that this is described as *pivat*, which is the native name for tobacco, it seems possible that a mixture of narcotic or stimulating plants was employed. In the visions caused by the drug the children expected to see an animal. In this they were instructed to place entire confidence, and it would defend them from all future dangers in war or otherwise. The animals mentioned are the coyote, the bear, the crow or raven, and the rattlesnake—all except the first specifically associated with Chingichnich among the Luiseño.

The suggestion of a personal guardian spirit in these beliefs must not be overestimated into their interpretation as a part of shamanism, since the protective animals were acquired not through involuntary dreams or individual seeking, but during a state of intoxication produced in a communal ritual.

The term *touch*, still translated by the Juaneño as "diablo," is mentioned by Father Boscana in connection with the Jimson-weed vision, but the context does not leave it entirely clear whether *touch* signified a form or apparition of Chingichnich, or was the generic name of the protecting animal. The Luiseño *towish* means "ghost."

There was another initiatory rite which is said to have been undergone by chieftains' sons and others of high rank who did not partake of the Jimson weed. But it is possible that the account may really refer to a subsequent and higher stage of the initiation, or perhaps to a second initiation leading to a higher degree. This is confirmed by the fact that this ceremony is mentioned as having been undergone by young men. These were painted black and red and wore feathers—a description given also of the initiated wearers of the *tobet*—were led in procession to the *wankech*, and placed at the side of the Chingichnich image or altar. Before them, then, the older initiates made a sand painting—of an animal, it is said—by which the novices fasted and refrained from drink for a period of about three days.

As among the Luiseño, trials of endurance followed the general drinking of the Jimson weed. The novices were blistered with fire, whipped with nettles, and laid on ant hills. These ordeals hardened them, and any who might fail to undergo them were looked upon as unfortunate, feeble, and easily conquered in war.

About the same period of life the boys or young men were prohibited certain foods, both meat and seeds. Some of these restrictions were maintained during manhood.

When boys were initiated—not into manhood, but into the use of the *tobet* dance costume—they were one after another arrayed in this, and danced with a turtle-shell rattle in their right hands. If a boy became totally exhausted from the duration of the ceremony he was carried upon the shoulder of one of the older men, who danced for him. At the conclusion a female relative danced naked. It is not certain whether all young men underwent this initiation, or only those who were of higher social status, or attained a specially advanced religious rank. The nude dancing by women is mentioned as having taken place on other occasions.

GIRLS' RITE.

Girls at their adolescence underwent a ceremony much like that practiced by the Luiseño, except that no mention is made of a ground painting. The girl was laid on branches of " estafiate " (*paksil*) placed in a pit lined with stones that had been heated. The hole is said to have resembled a grave in shape, a circumstance that is paralleled in the Luiseño puberty rite for boys and appears to be symbolic. Here the girl lay for several days fasting, while old women with their faces painted sang, and young women at intervals danced about her.

Girls were tattooed as part of their adolescent training shortly before puberty, from the eyes or mouth down to the breast, and on the arms. Agave charcoal was rubbed into bleeding punctures made with a cactus spine.

MOURNING CEREMONIES.

The dead were cremated, usually within a few hours after their decease. The pyre was lit by certain persons who derived their office by descent, and were paid for the service like the Yokuts *tongochim*. It is said that all but these personages withdrew from the actual cremation, which was followed by several days of wailing and singing. The words of the songs are stated to have related the cause, location, progress, and completion of the disease that had resulted fatally. It is not probable that the illness of the departed was thus described. Such reference to anything savoring of the person of the dead would certainly have been extremely repugnant to all other Californian tribes. The Luiseño on the same occasion sing similar songs about the sickness and approaching death of Wiyot; the Mohave have parallel practices; and it may therefore be concluded that the burden of the Juaneño mourning also referred to the fate of their dying god.

As in all parts of California and nearly all regions of America, the hair was cut in sign of mourning, the length removed being proportional to the proximity of kinship or degree of affection.

The hearts of those of the initiated whose flesh was eaten by the *takwe* were thought to go to the sky and become stars. The hearts or souls of all other persons went to an underground region called *tolmer* (Luiseño *tolmal*), where they spent their existence at ease in constant dancing and feasting.

The usual commemorative mourning ceremony was made for chiefs and prominent persons, although Father Boscana has left no specific account of it, and we do not therefore know whether, as seems probable, it included the burning of an image of the dead. It was, however, an exact anniversary, the precise condition of the moon at the time of death being observed, and the rite held when the moon attained the same size in the month of the same name in the following year.

Father Boscana describes a ceremony similar to the eagle-killing rite of the Luiseño and Diegueño. Although he does not mention it as a funerary observance, it can hardly have been anything else. The bird employed he names *panes*, which has not been identified, but from its description appears to have been the condor. It was carried in procession to the *wankech*, placed upon a sort of altar, and danced to by the initiated, while young women raced or ran about. Later the bird was killed without the loss of any blood. The skin was drawn off and preserved for making *palet* skirts, while the body was interred within the *wankech*, while old women made offerings to it, wept, and addressed it, after which dancing was resumed. This ceremony was definitely associated with Chingichnich. The very identical reincarnated *panes* was believed to be killed not only each year but in every village.

The fire dance was another act which has southern analogues, and is likely to have been introduced sometimes into mourning ceremonies. The dancers leaped into a large fire, which they trod until every spark was extinguished.

On the death of one of the fully initiated a personage called either *ano*, " coyote," or *takwe*, " eater," cut off from the back or shoulder of the deceased a piece of flesh and devoured or appeared to consume it in the presence of the crowd. This character was much feared and was heavily paid for his act by contributions from the populace. The natives specifically connect the ceremony with their myth of the eating of part of Wiyot's body by the coyote.

Nothing like this astounding rite is known from any other region of California nor from any part of the Pacific coast, until the Hamatsa practices of British Columbia are reached, except for a mention that Pomo mourners now and then snatched and ate pieces of the dead.

SHAMANISM.

The source of power of the medicine man and his method of acquiring it are not known with exactness, either for the Juaneño or for the other Shoshoneans of southern California. Besides sucking, blowing was resorted to. The word for shaman is *pul*, which appears to be the unreduplicated singular of *puplem*, " the initiated." There would thus seem to have been a certain lack of differentiation between the shaman proper and the man who had been fully instructed in sacred tribal lore.

ORDINANCES AND BELIEFS.

The regulation that a hunter must not partake of his own game or fish was adhered to tenaciously. Infraction brought failure of luck and perhaps sickness. Often two men went out together, in order to exchange with each other what they caught. It would appear that this rule applied chiefly or only to young men. At any rate, there must have been limitations to its enforcement, since it is stated that sickness resulted only when the game was consumed secretly.

At the appearance of the new moon, old men danced, while the boys and youths raced. The words of the songs used on this occasion referred to the death and resurrection of the moon and were symbolic, although whether of a return to life of human beings in general, or only Wiyot, is not certain.

At eclipses every one shouted and made all possible noise to frighten away the monster thought to be devouring the sun or moon. It is probable that this custom was common to all the Indians in California.

Takwich or meteors were much feared. Young women fell upon the ground and covered their heads, fearing to become ugly or ill if looked upon by the spirit. Takwich or Takwish is prominent in

the mythology of the Luiseño and Cahuilla and the name is presumably connected with *takwe*, the designation of the ceremonial
eater of human flesh. The latter functionary has not been reported
from the Luiseño or Cahuilla, but the traditions of these people consistently depict Takwish as a cannibal spirit.

Of immaterial essences, the *piuch* ("*piuts*") or breath was distinguished from the shun ("*pu-suni*") or heart. The former corresponded somewhat to our idea of life, the latter rather to the soul.

The ritualistic number of the Juaneño is not clear. Among the
Luiseño, Gabrielino, and Diegueño there is also some variability
and hesitance of formulation. Five seems to have been used with
significance at least as often as any other number by the Juaneño.

The Gabrielino origin of a large share of Juaneño ritual and
myth is clear, not only from the fact that both creation and migration traditions commence in Gabrielino territory, but especially
from the names of religious import.

A considerable number of Juaneño ceremonial designations contain the sound
"*r*," and very few contain "*l*." Now "*l*" is the Juaneño and Luiseño sound
that corresponds to Gabrielino "*r*," especially at the end of words. "*R*" does
occur in these two dialects, but is scarce and obviously a development from
some other sound, since it appears only in the middle of native words. At least
the majority of Juaneño terms containing "*r*" must therefore be from a Gabrielino source. Such are: *Saor, Kwawar, Sirout, Ausar, tolmer, Sirorum, Korone.*
The only question that arises in this connection is the one already raised
whether the larger part of the information extant concerning the Juaneño in the
work of Father Boscana may not really relate to the southern Gabrielino
themselves rather than to the Juaneño. Even if this possibility be answered
affirmatively it indicates the cultural leadership of the Gabrielino; since
although San Juan Capistrano lay not far distant from Gabrielino territory, it
was nevertheless in Juaneño land, and for an observer to have slighted the
natives in behalf of imported foreigners detached from their soil and with their
institutions correspondingly weakened, conveys in itself a strong suggestion
of the greater development of the latter.

CALENDAR.

The Juaneño calendar seems to have been unusually definite for
California, and it is exceedingly regrettable that the account of it
which has been preserved is not altogether clear. Ten months are
named, and these are said to have been all that there were. The year
was definitely divided by the solstices. The month or moon in which
the solstice fell was somewhat longer than the others, after which there
followed four regular lunations. If the number of these subsequent
moons was really four and not five, then each of the solstitial months
must have averaged somewhat over two moons in duration. Nothing
like this attempt to combine a lunar and solar count has yet been
reported from any other people in California. A similar plan is,

however, the basis of the Pueblo calendar. We have here, therefore, one more of the many instances of the influence of the tribes of the Southwest upon those of southern California, and it can not be doubted that many others would be discovered if our knowledge were deeper. It is significant that these parallels to the southwest are most abundant in religion; but it is equally striking that they are detached ceremonial elements which ususally crop out in southern California in a quite different setting and organization.

The names of the " months," whose form suggests that they are in part of Gabrielino and in part of Juaneño or Luiseño origin, are the following:

A'apkomil (winter solstice).	Sintekar (summer solstice).
Peret.	Kukwat.
Yarmar.	Lalavaich.
Alasowil.	Awitskomel.
Tokoboaich.	A'awit.

SOCIAL RANKS.

Chieftainship was hereditary in the male line. In default of sons, the title remained in abeyance until a daughter gave birth to a son, a collateral relative meanwhile exercising the power of office. Neither the daughter nor her husband, it is expressly said, acted as chief. The chief was known as *Nu* and his lieutenant or assistant as *Eyake*. The wife of the former bore the title of *Korone*, and of the latter that of *Tepi*. *Eyake* occurs as the mythical name of the coyote; *Korone* as that of a traditional chieftainess who led a migration to San Juan Capistrano. Further, both *Korone* and *Tepi* are names of insects. Similar distinctive names, also appearing in mythology, are found connected with chieftainship among the Gabrielino. There it is the chief's son and daughter that are said to have borne the titles. Whether there was a real difference of detail between Gabrielino and Juaneño custom, or whether the discrepancy is one of report, is not certain.

In any event these names evidence a considerable development of the idea of rank, and according to all accounts chieftainship was invested with much prestige. This is confirmed by the fact that there was a specific ceremony for the installation of a new chief, who appeared in the *wankech* in the *tobet* costume, wearing also a feathered rod or slat bound to his forehead by a cord of human hair.

The authority of the chief is likely to have been less than his dignity, and his power less than his authority. He is said to have decided on war, to have led on the march, and to have made peace. He also announced through a crier or speaker the date of dances, though the fixing of the time of these was in the hands either of the older medicine men or those of high rank among the religiously initiated. The chief received irregular, voluntary contributions of food from the people. When a communal hunt or food-gathering trip was undertaken, it was under his direction, and the larger part of what was secured was turned over to him. In return, he fed the needy and entertained visitors. There seems even to have been some notion of his being responsible for the satisfaction of his village in time of scarcity, through his ability to fall back upon such accumulated stores. Most chiefs also had two or more wives, who seem to have been thought necessary for the acquisition, or at any rate the proper preparation, of the food he was expected to dispense. On ordinary occasions it is specifically stated that the chief was obliged to hunt for his own sustenance.

That the chief's ranking was considerable appears further from the fact that he was treated with the utmost deference, especially by the young; that it is stated, though probably with some exaggeration, that death was sometimes inflicted upon those of his younger people who had been disrespectful to him; and from the circumstance that war might be made upon another village because its chief had not returned adequate presents to the head of the home town. This last cause for fighting has been reported also from the Chumash, and may therefore be regarded as authentic, although actual occasions perhaps occurred only sporadically.

MARRIAGE AND BIRTH.

The bestowing of gifts upon the bride's family was customary. The amount of property, however, was small, and it was tendered when the marriage was first proposed rather than when it was consummated. It is evident that the idea of purchase as such was feeble, but that custom required the gift as a token.

It appears that the accepted suitor spent a certain period in his bride's house before marriage took place, hunting and working for his prospective parents-in-law. It would be rash to assume, from the vague reports that have been preserved, that this practice involved a trial of continence such as the Seri followed; but it is not impossible that this may have been the case. The wedding was a public affair, held under a shade in front of the bridegroom's house, with a prolonged feast and singing. The essential part of the marriage rite lay in the girl's being conducted to her husband, disrobed, and seated on the ground beside him. Small children and even infants were sometimes betrothed by their parents.

Children were named soon after birth, usually by a grandfather or grandmother, who bestowed upon it their own name, or that of another relative of the same sex.

The couvade was practiced for a period of half a month or more after birth. The father fasted from fish, meat, and tobacco, refused to gamble, work, or hunt, and did not leave the house if it was possible.

As nearly everywhere in California, considerable occasion was made of the removal of the remnants of the umbilical cord from the child. This was taken off by old women, in the presence of a gathering of relatives, and buried in a hole either within or outside of the house, after which dancing took place.

Habitual transvestites were called *kwit* by the Juaneño of the coast, *uluki* by the mountaineers. That they were deliberately "selected" in infancy, as stated, seems inconceivable; but it is extremely probable that under the lack of repression customary in Indian society against the involved inclination, the feminine tendencies sometimes revealed themselves in early youth and were readily recognized and encouraged to manifest themselves as natural. Such "women" were prized as robust workers, and often publicly married.

WAR.

The Juaneño "never waged war for conquest, but for revenge; and in many cases for some affront given to their ancestors, which had remained unavenged." Theft, a slight to a chief, the seizure of a woman, and perhaps also the conviction that witchcraft had been practiced, were causes. An assemblage of the initiated was held, over which the chief presided. Other villages were frequently asked to join in an attack. The women ground meal furnished by the chief, and accompanied the expedition, both as provision carriers and to gather up spent arrows. On the march the captain led the way, or delegated this position to another. No quarter was given, and any wounded who could be seized were at once decapitated. Women and children were kept as slaves and taken home without redemption.

As soon as possible the captured heads were scalped. The skin was dressed and preserved as a trophy on certain public occasions. These scalps were hung from a pole near the *wankech*. Strenuous efforts were made by the relatives of the slain to recover the scalps, heavy payment being resorted to if force failed.

CHAPTER 46.

THE LUISEÑO: ELEMENTS OF CIVILIZATION.

TERRITORY AND NUMBERS.

The Luiseño, named after the Mission San Luis Rey de Francia, occupied a somewhat irregular territory, considerably longer from north to south in the interior than on the coast and wholly west of the divide that extends south from Mount San Jacinto. To the northwest and north they had Juaneño, Gabrielino, and Serrano as neighbors; to the east the Cahuilla, and to the south the alien Diegueño of Yuman family. They were a hill rather than a mountain people, and scarcely anywhere reached the summit of the watershed.

The Luiseño lack a native tribal name. Designations like Payamkuchum, "westerners," were applied to the coast people by those of the interior, and perhaps by themselves in distinction from the more easterly Cahuilla and Cupeño. The Diegueño know them as Kohwai; the Colorado River tribes seem to include them with the Cahuilla; if the Cahuilla, Serrano, and Gabrielino have a designation for them it has not been recorded.

Names like Kechi and Kech-am or Hecham, sometimes cited, either mean merely "house, village," or are native designations for the vicinity of the mission.

Plate 57 shows some of the best identified places in Luiseño land. Most of these seem to have been villages, but with the concentration and subsequent dispersal of the population the old continuity of habitation was broken, and to-day most of the names refer to districts, principally the various Spanish land grants.

Place names additional to those listed on Plate 57 are: Topamai (Tapomai); Heish, Gheesh (Keish); Opila (Kwalam); Akipa, Hunalapa, Tutukwimai (near Kahpa); Washka (Woshha); Pa'auw, Wikyo (near Ta'i); Kome (Panakare); camp sites on Palomar Mountain: Wavam, Shoau, Shautushma, Malava, Wiya', Chakuli, Ashachakwo, Pahamuk, Pavla, Tokamai, Mokwonmai.

San Clemente Island, Kinki, may have been Luiseño or Gabrielino. Statements conflict. Culturally, it was certainly dependent on Santa Catalina, of which it formed, in native opinion, a sort of annex.

There are slight dialectic differences within the Luiseño range, especially between the extreme north and south, but on the whole the speech is remarkably uniform for so considerable a tract.

The ancient population is difficult to estimate: 3,000 seems rather a low figure, 4,000 a liberally allowed maximum. In 1856 the Indian Office reported over 2,500; in 1870, 1,300; in 1885, 1,150; but tribal discrimination is likely to have been inaccurate. To-day there are less than 500, according to the Federal census—an infinitely larger proportion of survivors than among the Gabrielino, but a distinctly smaller ratio than the Diegueño have succeeded in maintaining.

ETHNOBOTANY.

The following are the plants known to have been used for food by the Luiseño. It will be seen that seeds are the most numerous. Next in importance come plants whose foliage or shoots are eaten raw or boiled. In the third place are fruits and berries. Roots are of less consequence than other parts.

Seeds: *Artemisia dracunuloides, Layia glandulosa, Malacothrix californica, Helianthus annuus, Bigelovia parishii; Cucurbita foetidissima; Salvia carduacea, S. columbariae, Ramona stachyoides, R. polystachya; Opuntia* (several sp.); *Gilia staminea; Trifolium ciliolatum, T. tridentatum; Prunus ilicifolia; Lepidium nitidum; Calandrina caulescens; Chenopodium californicum; Avena fatua, Bromus maximus.* The seeds eaten by the California Indians are often spoken of as from grasses; but it appears that Compositæ and Labiatæ are drawn upon more than Gramineæ. Some varieties were employed as flavoring rather than foods.

With the seeds must be reckoned acorns, for which a grinding process is also required, though leaching replaces parching. In order of esteem, the acorns from these species are taken: *Quercus californica; agrifolia* (oily); *chrysolepis* (hard to grind); and *engelmanni, wizlizeni*, and *dumosa*, used only when the others fail. The Luiseño are still essentially an acorn people; the Cahuilla are not.

Stems and leaves, or parts of them, are sometimes cooked, sometimes eaten raw: *Carduus* sp., *Sonchus asper; Solanum douglasii; Ramona polystachya; Phacelia ramosissima; Philibertia heterophylla; Viola pedunculata; Sidalcea malvaeflora; Psoralea orbicularis, Lotus strigosus, Lupinus* sp., *Trifolium ciliolatum, T. gracilentum, T. microcephalum, T. tridentatum, T. obtusiflorum; Lepidium nitidum; Eschscholtzia californica; Portulaca oleracea, Calandrina caulescens, Montia perfoliata; Chenopodium album; Scirpus* sp.; *Yucca whipplei*, the source of baked "mescal," may also be included. Clovers are perhaps the most important in this group.

Pulpy fruits are small and not especially abundant in Luiseño habitat. Those eaten include *Sambuscus glauca; Opuntia* sp.; *Arctostaphylos parryi; Vitis girdiana; Rhus trilobata; Rubus parviflorus, R. vitifolius, Prunus demissa, P. ilicifolia, Heteromeles arbutifolia; Mesembryanthemum aequilaterale; Yucca mohavensis* (flowers boiled, pods roasted), *Y. whipplei* (flowers). Rosaceæ are the most numerous.

Of edible roots, the country affords *Orobanche tuberosa, Bloomeria aurea, Brodiaea capitata, Chlorogalum parviflorum,* and probably others, but the variety is not great.

All the California Indians used a considerable number of vegetal medicaments. Among the Luiseño, whose knowledge may be assumed typical, more than 20 species are known to have been employed. All these medicines appear to have been household remedies, whose use was not specifically associated with shamanistic practices.

Ambrosia artemisiaefolia, a species of *Adenostegia,* and one of *Malvastrum* were emetics. Wounds, ulcers, and sores were washed with an infusion of the leaves of *Baccharis douglasii,* the roots of *Psoralea macrostachya,* galls from *Quercus dumosa,* or *Woodwardia radicans* root decoction. *Echinocystis macrocarpa, Mirabilis californica,* and *Sisyrinchium bellum* roots served as purgatives. The flowers of *Sambucus glauca* were thought to cure women's diseases. The sap of *Solanum douglasii* berries was put on inflamed eyes. *Erythraea venusta* yielded a tea drunk in fever. *Croton californica* was reputed to produce abortion, and *Euphorbia polycarpa* to be of aid after a rattlesnake bite. *Ribes indecorum* or *malvaceum* was employed against toothache. Other medicinal plants, whose specific virtues have not been reported, are *Artemisia dracunuloides* and *heterophylla, Bigelovia parishii, Monardella lanceolata, Micromeria douglasii, Eriodictyon parryi* and *tomentosum* or *crassifolium, Deweya arguta, Cneoridium dumosum, Houttuynia californica, Rumex* sp., and *Pellæa ornithopus.*

A combined pharmaceutical and botanical study would be required to reveal what plants of therapeutic value grew in the territory but were not employed by the Luiseño. Such a determination, particularly if prosecuted to the point of an understanding of the motives which led to their neglect, would be extremely interesting.

Although knowledge is far from complete, a review of the plants used in technology may not be wasted.

Houses were thatched with *Pluchea borealis* or *Croton californicum;* near the coast, with tule, probably a species of *Scirpus.* These may be considered the typical materials; but it is scarcely open to doubt that others were also employed.

Bows were of willow, elder, ash, mountain ash, and an undetermined mountain shrub. Willow was perhaps the least esteemed but commonest for light hunting bows. Neither juniper nor cedar are mentioned. The bowstring was either of sinew or of any of the fiber cords.

The characteristic arrow was of cane, *Elymus condensatus,* with a foreshaft of greasewood, *Adenostoma fasciculatum.* This is the south central and southern Californian arrow with which the grooved straightener of soapstone is used, although different species may have replaced the above elsewhere. Inferior or smaller Luiseño arrows had the mainshaft of *Heterotheca grandifolia* or *Artemisia heterophylla.* These were straightened with the same implement. A totally distinct type of arrow, especially characteristic of the Yuman tribes of the Colorado River, was made by the Luiseño of *Pluchea borealis.* This was not foreshafted and presumably without stone point.

For string, the outer fibers of the two plants most commonly used in California, *Asclepias eriocarpa* (perhaps other species also) and *Apocynum cannabinum*, milkweed and Indian hemp, were of prime importance. The stinging nettle, *Urtica holosericea*, was also used, but less prized. *Yucca mohavensis* fiber was less employed by the Luiseño than that of *Agave deserti* by the Cahuilla, whose environment rendered them largely dependent on it.

The main or back petticoat of the women was made of the soft inner bark of either cottonwood or willow, as among the Mohave. The smaller front piece may sometimes have been constructed of the same material, but its standard form was a sheet of cords of the usual string materials.

Coiled baskets were made, as by all the Shoshoneans of southern California, on a foundation of *Epicampes rigens* grass stems, wrapped either with splints of sumac, *Rhus trilobata*, or with the stems of a species of rush, Juncus. The same rush was made into mats for wrapping ceremonial paraphernalia, while mats for household use were presumably of tule, where this could be obtained, although none such have been preserved. Twined baskets were apparently of another species of rush, *Juncus mertensianus*. These served for gathering food; as "sieves" or leachers; and, it is said, for cooking acorn meal. The latter type, which is entirely unknown except from description, must have been closely woven; the two former were openwork. (Pl. 73, *b*.) The seed beater was of sumac stems. The complete restriction of the entire art of basketry to three or four materials is significant; the attitude involved, characteristic of the California Indian generally. The Luiseño lacked the favorite hazel and redbud of the northern and central groups; but there was nothing to prevent them from employing conifer roots and willow shoots and splints.

The brush auxiliary to meal grinding was made, as in nearly all of California, of the bulb fibers of soap weed, *Chlorogalum pomeridianum*, but there is no mention of the plant for lather. Instead, the root of *Chenopodium californicum* and the ripe fruit of *Cucurbita foetidissima* served as soap.

Several woods appear to have been employed for drilling fire, but *Baccharis douglasii* was usual. Both hearth and drill were of the same material. Although such a practice is contrary to current theories among ourselves, which demand variant hardness in the two parts, it seems to have been frequent in California. The Yana and Maidu availed themselves of buckeye in this way.

The only known vegetal dye of importance was a yellow obtained by boiling the roots of *Psoralea macrostachya*. There may have been others. Blackberry juice was sometimes used to stain wooden objects. A red for rock paintings and perhaps other purposes consisted of scum from iron springs mixed with pine turpentine and oil from ground *Echinocystis macrocarpa* seeds. This mixture, which resisted weather admirably, suggests imitation of civilized technique, but the Luiseño declare that they never mixed their pigments with fat. The black of basket patterns was mineral; splints were boiled with mud and iron scum.

The juice of the berries of the black nightshade, *Solanum douglasii*, is said to have been used for tattooing. All other records for California refer to charcoal.

Gum came from pines, or more frequently from an exudation caused by a scale on the chamisal or greasewood, *Adenostoma fasciculatum*. Where it could be obtained, asphalt was probably used more than either.

The only plants known to have been employed ceremonially are tobacco, an undetermined species of *Nicotiana;* and the Jimson weed or toloache, *Datura meteloides*, mentioned in connection with so many Californian tribes.

ANIMAL FOOD.

The animals not eaten by the Luiseño included the dog, coyote, bear, tree squirrel, pigeon, dove, mud hen, eagle, buzzard, raven, lizards, frogs, and turtles. It is probably significant that snakes are not mentioned. Deer were shot, with or without decoy, or snared. A noose was laid in a runway, fastened to a bent sapling. Rabbits furnished a more regular supply of food. They were shot, knocked over with the curved stick called *wakut*, driven into long nets, or snared. Wood rats, ground squirrels, and mice were not disdained. They were sometimes taken in a deadfall of two stones held apart by a short stick stood on an acorn. Quails were shot, attracted at night by blazing cholla cactus and knocked down, or run down by boys in cold, rainy weather. Ducks were killed with the *wakut* or arrows: nets are not mentioned, and would not have been of service in the Luiseño country except on the lagoons at the entrance of streams into the sea.

Small game was broiled on coals; sometimes, too, venison and rabbits. The two latter were also cooked in an earth oven, whatever was not immediately eaten being crushed in a mortar—bones included in the case of rabbits—dried, and stored. The pounding of flesh is a habit common to most of the California Indians. Venison was sometimes boiled, though not often.

When grasshoppers were abundant in the wingless stage they were driven with branches into a pit, into which fire was then thrown.

The coast people fished from canoes or balsas with dip nets, seines, and lines of yucca fiber. The hook was of bone or cut from the central portions of haliotis shell where the grain twists. A harpoon was also used, no doubt of the customary type. Mollusks, of course, were important.

The mountain people had only a few trout and minnows, which they took by poisoning or with dip nets.

IMPLEMENTS.

The bow and arrow were of the usual southern Californian types: the one long, narrow, and unbacked, the other often of cane and generally foreshafted. Bow strings were of *Apocynum* or other cord materials, which in this case were sometimes three and four ply. Sinew bowstrings were regularly three ply, as among the Cahuilla and Mohave. The arrow hold is specifically described as the Mediterranean one; the primary release was employed only for unforeshafted or small arrows. The Mediterranean release has heretofore not been reported from North America except among the Eskimo.

Pottery and basketry need no description, being substantially identical with that of the Cahuilla.

The pipe, *hukapish*, was chiefly smoked lying down, presumably at bedtime. This is the favorite occasion for smoking among most California Indians. The pipe is described as most commonly of pottery, but shamans used ancient stone pipes in their practices.

Chisels, perhaps more accurately described as wedges, were of deer antler, driven by a stone. The present is the most southerly occurrence reported for this tool, which is the universal Californian substitute for the ax.

The Luiseño use the bedrock mortar of the northern tribes, and add a movable one. *Topal* and *arusut* are native names. The portable mortar was usually excavated in a large bowlder, that might weigh 200 pounds or more, and was evidently not intended to be carried away every time residence was shifted. A coiled basket hopper set on the stone is described as intended for new and shallow mortars, being discarded as the hollow deepens. If this is correct, the southern California mortar basket is a device to save labor in stone working. The northern California form, whose twining indicates an independent origin, is an outright substitute for the mortar, never being set on anything but a flat slab.

The toloache mortar, *tamyush*, was more symmetrical, often finely polished, and sometimes ornamented with exterior grooves. It was not used for profane purposes. Its pestle, too, was neatly shaped, instead of being merely a convenient bowlder. Paint mortars, also having religious association, were equally well finished, and were called " little tamyush," *tamya-mal*.

Some of the Luiseño profess that the metate is a Spanish importation, but their statements, which employ the name *ngohilish*, probably refer to the well-made three-legged article, introduced by the Mexicans and used by the Indians at the missions. This interpretation is confirmed by the designation of the muller, *po-ma*, " its hand," Spanish " mano." The crude grinding slab is undoubtedly native among all the tribes of southern California. The Luiseño name it *malal*, which is the same word as " metate," Aztec *metlatl*. It has been indicated above, in the chapter on the Maidu, that there is some evidence for believing the concept of the metate to have been introduced into California from Mexico. If this had happened after the Luiseño were in their present seats, they would not be designating the article by a word formed from an ancient common Uto-Aztekan stem. Nor, on the other hand, would they know the name if they had come as a metateless people into California after the metate was established there. It seems, therefore, that they always had the implement and brought it with them; in fact, it may possibly have been the Shoshonean drift of which the Luiseño were part that introduced the metate to California; but our uncertain chronologies of national migrations and archeology forbid such a hypothesis being taken very seriously.

Besides the balsa, the coast Luiseño knew the canoe, which they called *pauhit*, "yellow pine." The same name was given to boxes hollowed out of wood as receptacles for ceremonial feathers—another of the many cultural reminiscences of the Southwest. Incidentally, the name suggests that the canoe was a dugout, not a plank-built boat as among the Gabrielino and Chumash. It is said that canoe voyages were sometimes made to San Clemente Island.

DRESS.

Clothing was of the common type—nothing for men, a back and front apron for women, with yucca fiber sandals and caps on occasion. The cap was worn chiefly with loads. The Luiseño women of to-day do not habitually wear it; and it seems that this is the old fashion. A twined cap of *Juncus* is described besides the stiff coiled one that is still to be seen. The Diegueño knew both kinds also. As everywhere, there were two names among the Luiseño for the two pieces of skirt: *shehevish*, the larger, made of inner bark, and *pishkwut*, the front piece, of twine, and partly netted. Both sexes in cold weather wore long capes or robes of woven rabbit fur, deerskins, or sea-otter furs. The latter were highly prized.

HOUSES.

The permanent houses of the Luiseño were earth covered and built over an excavation some 2 feet deep. As in the case of the Cahuilla, accounts vary between descriptions of a conical roof resting on a few logs leaned together, and of a less peaked top supported by one or two planted posts. The inference is that both constructions were employed, the latter especially for large dwellings. For less permanent residences, the ground might not be dug out, and the dirt covering was presumably also omitted. The earth was kept from dropping through the framework of the roof by a layer of cedar bark in the mountains, of stems in the lower belt, and of tule or sedges on the coast. There was a smoke hole in the middle of the roof, but entrance was by a door, which sometimes had a short tunnel built before it. Cooking was done outdoors when possible, on the central hearth when necessary. People slept with their feet toward this.

Except for its smaller size and lack of a roof entrance, this dwelling resembles the earth house of the Wintun, Maidu, and Miwok. No direct relationship may, however, be inferred until the steps of the connection have been ascertained. The intervening Yokuts and Gabrielino had no earth-covered lodges. The immediate linkage of the Luiseño is through the Cahuilla and Diegueño with the Mohave and Yuma structure; but the latter, which has several center posts and definite though low walls instead of an excavation, is a more advanced type. On the other hand, the conical form of the Luiseño earth lodge seems to have been rather similar to the Navaho *hogan.*

The sweat house was similar to the dwelling, except that it was smaller, elliptical, and had the door in one of the long sides. It rested on two forked posts connected by a ridge log. Men sweated in the evening, perhaps in the morning also, but did not regularly sleep in the sweat house. Perhaps it was too small an edifice to serve as a club. The heat was produced, as almost everywhere in California, directly by a wood fire.

The *wamkish* or "temple" or religious edifice was a mere round fence or *hotahish* of brush. The opening was usually to the north, although some accounts mention the east. On both sides were narrower openings for the dancers. The more esoteric actions were carried on toward the rear, if possible. Spectators looked in at the main entrance or saw what they could through and over the fence. No particular sanctity appears to have extended to the structure when not in use. Performers prepared and dressed in another but smaller circle, which stood some distance off on the side toward which the opening faced.

This unroofed ceremonial inclosure is found as far north as the Yokuts, and, for the mourning anniversary, even among the Maidu. It seems also to be distributed through the Shoshonean Plateau, and may have an ultimate connection with the Sun dance lodge of the Plains, although this, in turn, resembles the Missouri Valley earth lodge minus walls and covering, and may therefore be compared, in type if not in origin, with the Sacramento Valley ceremonial chamber and house. In California, however, the inclosure is, as its distribution shows, definitely associated with the mourning anniversary and the toloache religion. Both these religious cycles are quite undeveloped among the Colorado River tribes, especially the Mohave, and the inclosure is not known to them. It is therefore doubtful how closely the Navaho ceremonial inclosure may be historically connected with that of the southern Californians.

With the Mohave and Yuma, as with the Yokuts, the shade roof appears as a place for singing or religious exhibition, though apparently more as a convenience than with any attached idea of a definitely ritualistic structure. The shade was much used by the Luiseño and their neighbors in daily life, but not in ceremonial connections.

RELIGIOUS SCHEME.

On the side of its plan, the religious life of the Luiseño comprises two classes of ceremonies: initiations and mourning rites. These seem to be of distinct origin, but have come to be interrelated at several points. This interrelation appears to be due to their association with a relatively late form of the Jimson-weed cult, the form built around the deity Chungichnish or Changichnish, and carried to the Luiseño through the Juaneño, among whom it has already been mentioned, from its Gabrielino source, ascribed by tradition to Santa Catalina Island. Among the Luiseño this version of the Jimson-weed religion has touched the girls' adolescence rites, whose basis seems to be independent of it; and has colored the mourning observances, and even allowed these to react in some measure on itself. The god of this religion seems to be forced rather lamely into the cosmogony of the Gabrielino and Juaneño: what is said of him lacks the true mythological ring, the color of incident; the statements are abstract or rationalizing. Among the Luiseño he enters hardly if at all into narrative. The Diegueño, finally, though they have taken over most of the Luiseño practices, do not seem to know the god: at least his name has never been recorded among them, nor any synonym.

But with the Luiseño, Chungichnish is still the god who ordained the sacred practices, except the mourning ceremonies, which were instituted on the death of the more mythological divinity Wiyot; and he is also a living god, who watches and punishes. He is distinctly a Jehovah; and if it were not for the wholly native flavor of the ideas connected with the cult, and the absence of European symbols, it might be possible to think of missionary influence. At that, Christianity may well be the indirect stimulus at the root of the Chungichnish movement, since its spread into Luiseño territory went on at least in part, and may have occurred entirely, during the mission period.

This idea of a present and tremendously powerful god, dictating not only ritual but the conduct of daily life—a truly universal deity and not merely one of a class of spirits or animals—is certainly a remarkable phenomenon to have appeared natively among any American group north of Mexico.

It is clear that the Chungichnish cults are totally diverse from the elaborate rituals of the north that have been described as the *Kuksu* ceremonials, in spite of the fact that the central feature of both sets of practices is the initiation into a kind of esoteric society. The Sacramento Valley religion is conceptual only in spots; its cults as such, not any single idea permeated with some quality of grandeur, are its fundamental and subsuming element.

This conclusion of separate developments is borne out by the distribution of the two religions. They are separated by a tract of the magnitude of a third the length of California, in which indeed toloache is used in religion but Chungichnish and the symbols peculiar to him are unknown.

But before the initiation rites and then the mourning observances are described it is necessary to examine certain definite religious devices or forms, which have, it is true, become embodied in the Chungichnish cult, but seem to be neither an intrinsic nor an original part of it.

SONGS.

Luiseño ritual is complicated by the coexistence of two currents of expression. Until the relation of these is more exactly determined, the organization of the tribal religion will remain obscure at many points. On the one hand, there are ceremonies; on the other, songs. The more important ceremonies have each a set of its own songs. But there are series or kinds of songs that do not pertain specifically to any ceremony. These, as well as songs from other ceremonies, are freely introduced into almost any rite.

Thus, in the *Tauchanish*, there are sung in order the following: *Pi'mukvul*, *Temenganesh*, *Cham-towi*, *Kamalum*, *Kish*, *Anut*, *Nokwanish*, *Totawish*, *Monival*, *Nyachish*. In the *Wekenish*, the *Ashish* or *Wekenish* songs proper are followed by the *Cham-towi* set.

Songs forming part of a ceremony.

Totawish, name given the dancer in the *Morahash*.
Anut, "ant," from the initiatory ant ordeal.
Ashwut, "eagle," from the eagle killing.
Ashish, "first menses," from the *Wekenish* or adolescence ceremony.
Tauchanish, the memorial mourning rite with figures.
Shungamish, sung as the figures burn in the mourning ceremony.

Songs not belonging to specific ceremonies.

Pi'mukvul, "death."
Cham-towi, "our spirit," or *Kwinamish*, "root, origin."
Kamalum, "sons," referring to the first people.
Temenganesh, "season" (*teme-t* is "sun").
Nokwanish, sung for men dancing. First sung by the rabbit.
Tapa'sash, sung for men dancing.
Kish, "house."
Monival, "travel, tracks."
Nyachish, containing maledictions of foes.
Chatish, shamans' songs.
Numkish, shamans' songs to cause the growth of food.
Tuknish, the same in puropse, but distinct.

The "death" songs all refer to the death of Wiyot, and many are put in his mouth. Wiyot counsels the people before his departure, or enumerates the months in which he may die. Others allude to Wiyot's death through the frog, or the digging of the pit for his funeral pyre.

" Our spirit " songs contain passages such as these:

"North, east, south, west, the hair lives." Hair is symbolic for spirit; and there is allusion to hair ropes at the four ends of the sand painting representing the world.

" North, the hair, the *wanawut*, lives tied, fastened. My origin lives there." Presumably the other directions are also mentioned. The *wanawut* is the sacred rope in the initiation rite.

" I thought ('hearted') at the *hayish*-racing at the moon, I thought with surprise at the moon." Death is connoted.

Another song refers to sky's heart as well as the *wanawut* and sand painting.

From songs of " Season ":

"All named *wanawut*."

" Hid the season in the water," an act of frog and earthworm.

" The ant has his speech,
" The butterfly has his *wamkish* inclosure,
" The chipmunk has his hollow log for acorn storage."

" I am doing something." The month Nemoyil, when the animals grow fat, is mentioned or connoted.

" North the *uchanut* bears young,
" North the elk bears young,
" East the mountain sheep bears young,
" East the horned toad bears young,
" South the *awawut* bears young,
" South the *tamyasowut* bears young,
" West (the ocean) tosses.
" In the middle here the deer sheds its hair,
" The sky sheds its hair (changes color)." The reference is to the month Pahopil.

" At Malmus rose the son Sun."

" See ye that San Gorgonio mountain." Cahuilla Valley, Kupa, Volcan, Pine Mountain, and Malava on Palomar Mountain are also mentioned.

Part of a " Travel " song:

" Then I do not know the tracks,
" Then I err in the tracks."

A number of places are mentioned, apparently beginning with the spot near San Gorgonio Mountain at which the ancient people could not pass through a defile and their language became different, and proceeding southward to Temecula.

An *Ashish* song beginning with the words: " I am adolescent " seems to name a similar series of mountains: San Gorgonio, San Jacinto, Kupa, Volcan, Cuyamaca, Cahuilla Valley, Pine Mountain, Palomar.

The closing song of the same series begins near Bonsall, proceeds to Santa Margarita, and ends at Elsinore, where Swift and Kingbird were the first girls to be adolescent.

Another *Ashish* song refers to Deer's desire and failure to escape from death, which he found waiting at the north, east, south, and west. The same idea, but with Eagle as character, inspires a recitative in the Wiyot myth. Eagle goes from Temecula to mount San Gorgonio, Cuyamaca, Palomar, and returns to Temecula to die: the directional circuit agrees.

An "Ant" song:

"They did not wish to give their kill that they had." Puma, Jaguar (?), and Thunder Cloud seem to be referred to; Deer is their game.

A Toloache drinking song:

"*Tamyush* walked twisting." *Tamyush* is the sacred mortar from which the Jimson weed is drunk.

From shamans' *Chatish* songs:

"From my feet, from my hands, was drawn, was drawn."
"Something thundered from their feet, from their hands." This and the last refer to curative power.
"To me it comes, *Towut* comes, *Yawut* comes." *Towut* and *Yawut* are names for a fine dust or mist. This is evidently a weather shaman's song.
"Shot, shot, *towauya.*" This word is from the stem of *towish*, spirit. The reference is to killing by means of the shaman's stick.

It appears that nearly all the songs except those of a specific shamanistic character consist of mythological allusions. They may be said to float in a web of tradition. Those that are not mythological are directly descriptive of the ritual to which they pertain.

Further, the songs of different series are similar not only in character but in detailed content. The rising of constellations is mentioned in *Tauchanish*, Death, and Season songs. Long enumerations of places are frequent, whatever the connection; and these frequently begin or end at the same spot, such as Mount San Gorgonio or Temecula. *Ashish* and Ant songs both refer to Deer; Death and Season songs enumerate or allude to months. The indiscriminate prevalence of a certain ritualistic phraseology is thus obvious; and this must be admitted as being patterned in a fashion that can only be called highly decorative, in the sense that it is symbolic, abbreviated, and only conventionally representative.

This strong uniformity explains the frequent transfer of Luiseño songs from one ceremony to another.

All these traits recur in undiminished or exaggerated vigor in Mohave, Yuma, and Diegueño songs. As to their northward and westward distribution, enough is indicated by the statement that a large proportion of the songs sung by the Luiseño are in the Gabrielino language. Yokuts songs, on the other hand, as the examples quoted establish, lack all the peculiar traits of those of the south: they are more concretely picturesque, but are unmythological, ungeographical, and nearly lacking in astronomy and symbolism.

Precisely to what extent the Luiseño and Gabrielino songs of each kind constitute a series strung on a single plot can not yet be said. But is is clear that they approach closely to the song cycles of the Mohave and Yuma. On the coast, song and ceremony are two parallel developments, interconnected at innumerable points, yet essentially pursuing separate courses. In the Colorado Valley ritual has been nearly effaced, or has come to consist essentially of singing, with the choice of series dependent on the singer rather than the occasion. This allows the Mohave songs to be dreamed by the individual, in native theory, in place of being acquired by avowed tradition. The Mohave songs seem also to have reached a greater extremity of dependence on myth and wealth of geographic allusion; but, as might be anticipated from the greater poverty of ritual accompanying them, they are less permeated by metaphoric symbolism.

DANCES.

Much as songs of various kinds were introduced into the most diverse rituals, so the Luiseño had two or three standard dances which they performed on several occasions as part of their initiation as well as the mourning rites. It seems, therefore, that the dances, like the songs and in a measure the sand painting, were fixed elements upon which the ceremonies as larger wholes were built up.

The paucity of dances and abundance of song types among the Luiseño marks an approach to the method of religion of the Mohave and Yuma.

The commonest Luiseño dance to-day is the *Tatahuila*, which is always made by a single performer. *Tatahuila* is uniformly regarded by the Indians as a Spanish word. The Luiseño word is *Morahash*, which means "whirling for;" the dancer is called *totawish*, which may perhaps be regarded as a dialectic form of *tobet* (Spanish for *tow-et*), the name the Juaneño are said to have given the costume. The Diegueño say *Tapakwirp*. Besides the headdress, the principal apparel is a skirt of eagle feathers, which swing effectively in the very characteristic motion of the dance, a continued and very rapid whirling. The body was painted; probably as by the Diegueño, with horizontal white bands.

The fire dance, of which the native name is not known, served as a climax and was part of the magical stock in trade of the toloache initiates. A large fire was danced out, the performers approaching the edges, stamping the embers, falling back, rushing up once more, and sitting down to kick the blazing coals inward. The feet were bare and there seems to have been no treatment or mechanical preparation, but a certain amount of earth was pushed on the flames with the feet and when possible unobtrusively thrown on with the hands. As each dancer's attack lasted only a few seconds at a time, while he was in rapid motion, and the number of performers was great, it is probable that most of the blaze was extinguished by actual stamping. There is nothing astounding or cryptic about this exhibition, but it unquestionably was spectacular, and is described as impressive even to white people. No public fire dance is known anywhere to the north in California, and eastward it seems not to be encountered again until the Pueblos are reached.

Like the fire dance, the *Morahash* appears to have been in the hands of the toloache initiates, but both were certainly made as part of mourning rites.

The Diegueño add to these two dances a third, the *Hortloi*, which can probably be identified with the Luiseño *Tanish*, since the latter is described as the dance of the initiates or *pumal-um* in mass, which accords with the performance of the *Hortloi;* also because the songs of the latter are in the Gabrielino language. This Diegueño exhibition is the one that Americans have come to know as the "war dance," but it appears to have no reference whatever to war. The step is a forward jump with both feet, followed by a stride. To successive songs the dancers circle contraclockwise, stamp standing, and jump backward in line.

GROUND PAINTINGS.

With the Luiseño we encounter for the first time detailed references to a ritualistic device of the greatest interest, which is known to have been used also by the Juaneño, Gabrielino, and Fernandeño: the ground or sand painting. The Diegueño sand painting has also been recorded, and the Cupeño apparently used it. The Cahuilla and Chumash are in doubt. It is therefore rather clearly a development of the Shoshoneans of the coast region. It is connected with the Chungichnish form of the Jimson-weed cult, and about coterminous with it.

This sand painting of southern California is unquestionably connected with that of the Pueblos and Navahos. There can also be little doubt that it originated in the much more complex ceremonialism of these southwestern nations. But it is not a recent importation; and the history of its diffusion can only be appreciated properly with reference to the fact that not even a trace of the custom exists among the intervening tribes of the Colorado

River, nor apparently among the Pima. Like the Chungichnish religion with which it is associated, it is clear that the Californian sand painting rests upon old cultural materials common to the Southwest and southern California and probably evolved chiefly in the former region, but that its actual essential form is a purely local growth. This is not only indicated by its geographical distribution but confirmed by its subject matter, symbolism, and style, which reveal scarcely anything specifically southwestern.

The painting was made in the *wamkish* or ceremonial enclosure, the " temple " of older authors. The Luiseño brought it into the Jimson-weed initiation for boys; the *Yunish Matakish* or death rite for initi-ates; and the girls' adolescence ceremony. With the Diegueño the latter ceremony belongs to an old native stratum and has not been colored by Chungichnish influences as among the Luiseño. They therefore do not use the painting in this connection.

The Luiseño call the sand painting *torohaish* or *tarohaish*, or in ritualistic speech, following their usage of doubling terms. *eskanish tarohaish*.

Figure 56 shows all known restorations of Luiseño and Diegueño ground paintings. In spite of the variability, which may have been nearly as great in practice as in these reproductions, a distinct tribal style as well as a fundamental uniformity are apparent. This fact renders it highly probable that the lost paintings of the Juaneño and Gabrielino were similar in tenor but also distinctive in manner.

The elements in the Luiseño and Diegueño ground paintings shown in Figure 56 are as follows: 1, Milky way. 2, Night (or sky). 3, Root (of ex-istence), *kwinamish*. 4, Our spirit or soul. 5, World. 6, Hands (arms) of the world. 7, Blood. 8, Rattlesnake. 9, Spider. 10, Raven. 11, Bear. 12, Puma. 13, Wolf.[1] 14, *Apmikat.* 15, " Breaker." 16, Stick, wood. 17, Coyote. 18–21, Black, gopher, garter, red racer snake. 22, Sun. 23–24, New and full moon. 25, Pleiades. 26, Orion. 27, Altair. 28–29, " Cross " and " Shooting " constellations. 30, Sea. 31, Mountains. 32, Hill of *hulwul* plant. 33, Boil, abscess. 34, Coronado Island. 35, Mountain of creation. 36, San Bernardino (Gorgonio?) Mountain. 37, Santa Catalina Island. 38, Four avenging animals. 39, Ceremonial baskets. 40, Toloache mortar and pestle. (The last two may be the actual objects rather than representations.) P, Pit in center. S, Spitting hole.

In all cases, it is clear that the essential subject of the depiction is the world. The Luiseño, however, are chiefly concerned with re-vealing its subtler manifestations—the mysterious encircling Milky Way, the all-encompassing night or sky—or its still more spiritual phases as expressed in a symbolism of human personality: the arms, the blood, our root or origin, the spirit. Within this frame are in-dicated—depicted would be an exaggerated word—the punishers sent by the invisible Chungichnish: the raven, rattlesnake, spider, bear, wolf,[1] mountain lion, and the cryptic *Apmikat* and " breaker."

---

[1] Or jaguar (?).

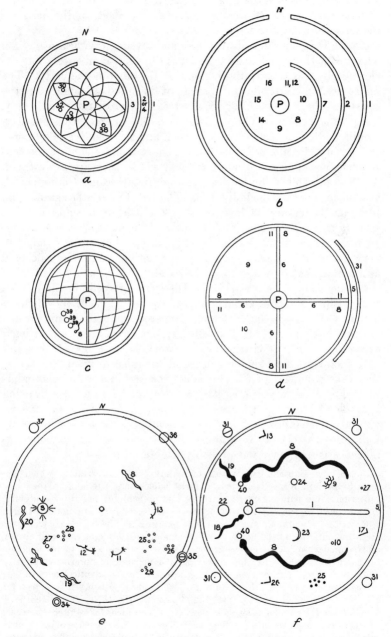

FIG. 56.—Southern California ground paintings (altars).   *a–d*, Luiseño; *e–f*, Diegueño.

In the very center is the hole symbolical of death and of the burial of human ashes: called *tolmar* or *tolmal*, the abode of the dead; or the navel—of the universe.

To the Diegueño this abstruseness and mystic craving are foreign. They paint the world indeed; but it is the visible universe. The enclosing circle is merely the horizon or the edge of the earth. The figures within it are a downright map of the mundane surface and the celestial sphere. The Milky Way stretches across the middle as it bisects the heavens. On one side are the summer constellations Aquila and Cygnus, on the other Orion and the Pleiades of winter—each group identifiable by its form. The sun and moon are too conspicuously visible overhead to be omitted: so they are represented. To the Luiseño the luminaries mean nothing, because Chungichnish symbolism does not include them. The navel of death, again, is an idea, not a feature of land or sky—the Diegueño omits it. His mountains, too, are not vague harborers of the messengers and avengers of a cult, but actual named peaks; and the four in figure *e* stand in very nearly the relative geographical position, with Diegueño land as a center, that they occupy in the painting.

Having mapped his world, the Diegueño proceeds to fill it with living beings. These are not mere heaps of pigment to which an old man can point while naming dangerous animals in his sermon on the punishment of disobedience, but actual representations: excessively crude, it is true, even abbreviated to a few strokes, but still pictures. The spider can be distinguished from the snake, the snake from the wolf. This is not the case in any Luiseño painting. For good measure, as it were, perhaps because their drawing is easily effective, the Diegueño add to the dread rattlesnake (whose eyes are of haliotis and whose diamond-back pattern is carefully indicated) sketches of several harmless species, whose symbolic significance is unknown and probably slighter.

Among the Luiseño, two styles of painting are discernible, which appear to pertain respectively to the girls' adolescence rite and to the boys' initiation. The painting for the girls (*a* and probably *b*) has three concentric circles, open to the north; within, the several avengers are indicated in a more or less circular arrangement. The painting for the boys (*c*, *d*) perhaps lacks the gateway to the north, has only one or possibly two enclosing circles, and is quartered. The representations of the avengers seem to predominate in the western half. At the same time the network of interior lines in *a* and *c* is not very different, and may be intended for an identical pattern.

The diameter of the ground painting is described as being 2 to 3 feet for the girls' painting (*a*), and 4 (*c*), 12, 15, or 18 feet (*d*, *e*, *f*) for the boys. The materials include ashes and powdered soapstone for white; charcoal; reddish iron rust or scum; yellow may also have been used; and variously colored " sands " and " earths " are mentioned more vaguely. The harmless snakes in the Diegueño paintings were of " seeds."

PLATE 61

DIEGUEÑO "TATAHUILA" PERFORMER, IN THE
STANDARD DANCE COSTUME OF SOUTHERN
CALIFORNIA

POMO WOMAN PARCHING CATERPILLARS

PLATE 62

CAHUILLA SANDAL OF YUCCA FIBER

CAHUILLA PAINTED POTTERY JAR

There is some mention of cords of human hair leading from the Luiseño painting to sticks or canes planted in four little mounds on each of the cardinal sides: these tied the world and probably the human spirit also. It is not certain whether these objects were actual or only painted: the former seems more likely, since ropes that were pulled are mentioned of the Fernandeño ground painting.

CEREMONIAL OBJECTS.

The *pa'lut* was perhaps the most showy of Luiseño religious regalia. This was a net tied around the waist, from the lowest loops of which hung eagle or condor feathers. It was worn in the *morahash* dance, as part of what the Juaneño would call the *tobet* costume, and its free swishing added to the effect of the rapidly turning dancer. (Pls. 42, *c*; 61.)

Headdresses are simple, but the native recognition of types is not altogether clear. The commonest form was a bunch of owl or spotted hawk feathers, more or less slashed, and mounted on a stick. These appear to be called *cheyat*. They were worn in pairs, one at each side of the head, held by a band. The *hainit*, Juaneño *eneat*, apparently was a band or upright row of feathers encircling the head. The *apuma* is mentioned as an erect eagle feather headdress. Not one of these pieces was notably brilliant, large, or elaborate.

The *yukish* was an ancient headdress of human hair, held in place by a cord of the same material. Its form is not clear. It may have corresponded to the Juaneño *emech*. Hair was very sacred to the southern Californians, and the Luiseño used it with evident reference to the idea of human personality and employed the name *yula* as a constant metaphor for " spirit."

The yellow-hammer forehead band typical of central California is not found in most of the southern part of the State. The Luiseño, however, made *tuminut*, long bandoliers of dark feathers, less trimmed than in the central Californian ornament, but, like them, laid in opposite directions and sewn through. (Pl. 58.) Similar pieces have been found among the Koso and in an ancient cave cache in Gabrielino territory. The occasions on which they were worn are not known.

The *paviut* was a hand wand a foot and a half long, associated with the Chungichnish cult. It consisted of a board more or less pointed below, somewhat flaring at the upper end, where it was inlaid with haliotis, and tipped with a crystal or large flint.

The *elat* was also a board, a foot long, painted red, with snake rattles or the like attached, held upright by the feathered *cheyat* band against the forehead of the *pula* when he doctored, made rain, or juggled. The employment of this standardized piece of costume by the shaman is one of many links that closely ally him with the initiate or *pumal*.

Wooden "swords," that is, really, flexible wands, were swallowed either by the *pula* or the *pumal*, probably the former. This is a southwestern trick of which little is heard in central and northern California.

The rattle was a turtle shell on a stick, the openings wound with cord. Wild cherry pits made the sound. The deer-hoof rattle associated in northern California with the girls' adolescence ceremony was known to the Luiseño, but used only, it seems, in hunters' rites. Neither the clap stick nor the cocoon rattle of central California was employed.

The whistle of *huikish*, *Elymus* cane, stopped with asphalt, was blown by the men who sang and danced about the boys undergoing the ant ordeal. It was called *pahal*.

The bull-roarer, *momlahpish*, is a crude board, whirled as a summons to religious assembly and as a starting and stopping signal. Its size—from 1 foot to nearly 2—stamps it as an implement for outdoor use. (Pl. 44.)

Two traits characterize the religious regalia of the southern Californians as typified by the Luiseño.

First, they are simple and comparatively somber. Although of feathers, they lack the bright colors and showy forms that characterize the area of the Kuksu religion and of the northwestern open-air dances. There is not a trace of anything like a mask or a disguise of the performer. These qualities are a reflex of the toloache religion, which at least in its Luiseño form knew a god too lofty and pervading to be impersonated, but no nearer spirits other than animals. Hence while the initiates constituted a body that must unquestionably be considered as a sort of organization, they did without the masking which is so frequent an accompaniment of the esoteric society in aboriginal America. The comparative simplicity of dance costume is already observable among the Yokuts, the most northerly of the toloache-using tribes.

Second, the powerful psychic effect of the Jimson weed caused the cult based upon it to take on a specifically inward character. There are innumerable references to the human spirit, to the relation of life and death. What we should call the soul is constantly being symbolized or alluded to. The Maidu and Wintun have very little to say about the soul of man, but more about the spirits or minor gods that populate the world or helped to shape it. Thus their ritual is comparatively dramatic, representative, spectacular, its costuming diversified, picturesque, impressive; but both are symbolic in only minimum degree. The southerners thought of life as such, not of events. Their concepts must of needs be ritualized; yet as their abstractions were better expressible in the sand painting, in the *wanawut* representation of the grave, or in the burying of the dead *pumal's* badge than in any apparel of feathers and sticks, the costume, like their dance movements and cries, became wholly unrepresentative. It was worn because ancient tradition so ordained, not because it illustrated. Its form, therefore, crystallized largely along lines of simple convenience, and it came to matter little whether the regalia were diverse or the same for all occasions, as long as their conformity to custom indicated the sanctity of the occasion. The history of dance costume in southern California can accordingly not be traced from anything intrinsic to religious thought or feeling.

In general, then, ceremonial paraphernalia and dance actions stand apart from religious beliefs in southern California. Songs and ground paintings directly reflect concepts and myths, but run a course largely independent of ritualistic actions. Hence all four sets of elements are made use of in the scheme or organization of religion almost as if they were foreign matter.

ESOTERIC NAMES.

The Luiseño consistently employ a distinctive device in their ritualistic designations. A double name, consisting of a pair of juxtaposed synonyms or approximate synonyms, is given to many ideas. So strong is this inclination that where two words are not available, as for animals, two of these are coupled as if they were one: compare "bear mountain-lion" in the little sermon quoted in the section headed Morality. The cosmogonies outlined also offer abundant illustrations. *Yunish matakish, eskanish tarohaish, wanal wanawut, antish tivihayish, kimal chehenish* are other examples; also the star names *piwish ahuta* and *ngoiwut chawochmush;* and *sivut paviut,* the crystal-tipped stick. There are indications of a similar habit among the Juaneño, as in the various names of *Chingichnich: Wiamot, Kwawar, Saor, Tobet,* and in the two terms *ano* and *takwe* applied to the ceremonial cannibal. Among the Luiseño even place names are usually coupled in myth or song: *Pawi Chawimai,* Cahuilla Valley, *Kupa Kawimal,* "Kupa little hill," *Ehva Temeku,* Temecula; two spots in the same vicinity appear to be treated as one.

CHAPTER 47.

THE LUISEÑO: ORGANIZATION OF CIVILIZATION.

THE TOLOACHE INITIATION.

The toloache ritual is the heart of the Chungichnish religion. In the main, it consists of a series of acts initiating boys, but there is also a feature that is rather uncommon in American Indian esoteric associations, a mourning observance for dead members. As is frequent, however, among primitive people, there is no formal ritual for adherents as such. The normal function of the society is to perpetuate itself rather than accomplish some clearly realized end.

The initial and most significant proceeding in the initiation, as the natives seem to see it, is the taking of the *Datura* drug. This act is called *pa'nish mani*, or *mani pa'ash*, or simply *mani*. As *pa–* means "to drink," *mani* appears to denote Jimson weed, which in fact is the meaning of the stem throughout the Shoshonean dialects of southern California. The Luiseño, it is true, call the plant itself *naktomush*. It is therefore probable either that *mani* has become with them a synonym of exclusively religious denotation or that *mani* means the principle or decoction.

The drinking takes place at night. All uninitiated boys are gathered and brought together. Small boys are sometimes carried in asleep. Any man who may have escaped initiation in his youth, or alien resident, is given the drug with the youngsters. A fire is lighted in the *wamkish*, and the people begin to gather there. The various *tamyush* or toloache mortars are dug from their hiding places, repainted, and set in the *wamkish*. Only the mortar actually to be used, together with a *tukmal* or flat basket, are brought to the small or preparatory enclosure which stands near the *wamkish*. It is in this smaller place, unlit and without audience of the uninitiated, that the toloache is drunk, and there the boys are taken. One of the *paha'*, ceremonial chiefs or managers, pounds the dried roots in the reserved mortar, to a sacred song or recitative, after which the potion is prepared with hot water. The usual way seems to have been to sift the powder from the basket back into the mortar and add the water, which was allowed to stand for a while. In other cases the hot water was poured over the basket, or the powder boiled in a pottery jar. The drinking itself, however, was from the mortar in which the plant was crushed, the boys kneeling before it. The manager held the forehead of each in turn, to pull it back when he had drunk enough. The drug was powerful, and the Luiseño tell of cases of fatal result.

Meanwhile one of the managers has gone three times to the large inclosure to notify the people there that *mani* is coming. Each boy, after the drinking, is taken in charge by a man who appears to direct and steady him. The procession to the *wamkish* seems to be performed crawling on hands and knees, by the men at least, each of whom utters the cry of an animal. Possibly this act takes place on later days of the ceremony. The mortar and baskets are believed to march along. There may have been a simple legerdemain to produce this effect. The party divides in two, each half making a three-quarter turn about the enclosure and entering by one of the side gates. They then march or stand the boys around the fire, apparently dancing the *tanish*. The youths soon begin to sway and reel and have to be supported under the armpits. Before long they fall and become entirely unconscious, and are then carried to the smaller enclosure, where they lie in complete stupefaction, watched only by a few men. The other adult members remain in the *wamkish*, dancing the *tanish* until morning. They seem to stand in a semicircle back of the fire, with a line of seated men singers facing them across it, and women, also singing, behind the men. Still farther back, outside the main entrance, stand the spectators.

The duration of complete narcosis is not quite certain. The Diegueño appear to reckon it one night, and speak of quantities of warm water being given the boys in the morning to remove the remaining effect of the drug. A Luiseño account speaks of two or three nights, and of a stupefaction of four being excessive. It is probable that the period was variable: there was no definite measure to the bulk of root used nor was accurate control possible of the quantity of liquid drunk by each novice; besides which, the boys were of different ages and their constitutional resistance to the drug must have varied individually. It may be added that the ceremony was not performed annually or at a fixed season, but every few years, as the old men might decide that there was a sufficient crop of fresh boys. Nor did anyone drink toloache twice.

The so-called intoxication is in any event the cardinal feature of the entire initiation, and therefore the heart of the cult. There is no doubt that its sacredness and supernatural basis lie to the native mind in the physiological effect of the drug. It produces visions or dreams as well as stupor; and what the boys see in their sleep becomes of lifelong intimate sanctity to them. This vision is usually an animal, and at least at times they learn from it a song which they keep as their own. It seems also that they will not kill any individual of the species. It is clear that the concept of the vision corresponds exactly with what among certain primitive tribes has been unfortunately denominated the "personal totem." It is certain that a special and individual relation of a supernatural kind is believed to exist forever after between the dreamer and the dream. The similarity to shamanism is also obvious; but it would be as misleading to name the Luiseño institution outright "shamanistic" or "totemic."

The duration of the ceremony is not clear, and may not have been fixed. A Luiseño account speaks of men from other villages dancing with the boys for four or five nights after the first one, painting and instructing them, and teaching them their songs. A Diegueño version is to the same effect, adding that each boy thus acquired a kind of proprietorship over certain alien songs in addition to those given him by his kinsmen; but this account makes the visitors come in only after six nights of dancing with the home people.

At any rate, a fast is observed by all the boys for about six days, complete at first, and relaxed later to a limited amount of acorn mush, but no meat or salt under any circumstances; and they dance— apparently the *tanish*—nightly and sleep during the day.

The first period is followed by a more temperate one of perhaps a month, and a third and still milder one of another month, during which the night dancing continues, but for briefer hours, and the novices are allowed all the acorn or sage-meal gruel they wish.

Even after this time has elapsed, the boys are forbidden meat for several months, and are then encouraged to refrain from it, or at least to eat it sparingly, for as much longer as possible. This commencement with the main act of the ceremony and gradual dying away of the ritualistic observances without definite end, instead of a climax, recurs also in the girl's initiation, and seems characteristic of Luiseño procedure.

Various other things are taught or half revealed to the boys, probably during the first intensive period of initiation. These include the fire dance, with its appearance of magic; the putting of feather headdresses into the flames and taking them out whole; the shooting of men; the cutting off of one's tongue; and the like. These tricks are at any rate performed; and while it is not likely that they are deliberately and wholly exposed to the youths at this time, they are no doubt carried out for them to know something about.

That some sort of progress in knowledge is made by the boys is likely from a Diegueño account of the boys instead of the men crawling to the *wamkish* on the second, third, and fourth days of the initiation.

A month or so after the toloache drinking, the boys dispose of the belts which they have heretofore worn on account of their hunger, and run a foot race back to the *wamkish*. At the end of the second month they are presented each with a feather headdress and a painted dance stick, which, though lacking the sacred crystal, is a sort of imitation of the *paviut*. After this the ground painting is made and then comes the final rite of the *wanawut*. A different account speaks of this being performed three days after the drinking, but all other informants agree that the *wanawut* act takes place after the period of fasting.

The ground painting is made in the *wamkish*, and has been described before. As its meaning is explained, the boys are given an elaborate lecture, passages from which are quoted below in the section on Morality. At the last, a lump of sage meal and salt is put in each boy's mouth, after having been touched against several parts of his body as in the girls' rite, and is spat by him into the central hole of the painting. This is then erased by pushing the pigments into the hole, so that no uninitiated may see the figure.

THE WANAWUT.

Either the same day or the next, toward the end of the afternoon, the *wanawut* rite takes place. Ceremonially this object is called *wanal wanawut* or *yula wanawut*, *wanal* being a seine or long net, *yula* hair or spirit. The *wanawut* is a long mesh of milkweed or nettle twine, the size of a man, and having head, legs, arms, and perhaps a tail. Its name is undoubtedly a derivative from *wanal;* its association with *yula* is probably only symbolic of spirituality, but may mean that the object was sometimes made of hair. In the net are three flat stones, or according to another statement, four are set upon it. The entire figure is laid in a trench, the feet apparently to the north: the Diegueño say east.

Each boy in turn now enters the trench, supported by the old man who has acted as his sponsor, and at a signal leaps from stone to stone. Should he slip, it is an indication that he will die soon. Very small boys are partially assisted by the old men. When all have jumped, they help the old men push the earth into the trench, burying the figure.

The symbolism of this strange rite clearly refers to life and death. The trench represents the grave: the Luiseño cremated their corpses over a pit which was filled when the embers and bones had sunk in.

The figure is human. It is specifically said to denote the Milky Way—otherwise a symbol of the spirit or soul. There seems also to be present the idea that the spirit of the dead is to be tied, perhaps to the sky, at any rate away from earth; and the cordage of the object is probably significant in this regard. It is obvious that there existed a rich though perhaps but half-expressed symbolism in connection with the *wanawut*, of which only fragments are known to us.

When the *wanawut* is finally buried, the *tanish* is commenced for the last time and danced through the night, ending toward daybreak with the fire dance. There are some references to burning the *wamkish* about this time, or part of it for the whole. It may be conjectured that it is the brush enclosure that furnishes the fuel for the final fire dance. At any rate, this destruction of the sacred enclosure marks the termination of the collective acts of the initiation.

THE ANT ORDEAL.

The *Antish* (literally " anting," from *anut*, " red ant "), also called *Tivihayish*, was an ordeal for boys or young men, probably made within the toloache initiation, but perhaps held as a separate supplement. In the latter event, many features of the initiation were repeated, such as fasting, the foot race, and the ground painting. The rite itself was carried out with secrecy toward the public.

The boys were laid on ant hills, or put into a hole containing ants. More of the insects were shaken over them from baskets in which they had been gathered. The sting or bite of the large ant smarts intensely, and the ordeal was a severe one, and rather doubtfully ameliorated when at the conclusion the ants were whipped from the body with nettles.

There are special *anut* or *antish* songs, whose use, however, following Luiseño custom, is not restricted to this ceremony.

Ant bites were used medicinally as far away as the Yokuts, but an ant ceremony has not been reported from farther north than the Juaneño and probably did not extend beyond the Gabrielino at most. The animal is, however, very distinctive of southwestern ceremonialism. Many of the Pueblos have ant fraternities, and among probably all of them there exist esoteric rituals for curing sickness brought on by ants. These particular concepts are of course not Luiseño; but there can be little doubt that the southern California ordeal has at least received its impetus from the same source that caused the growth of the Pueblo ant ceremonies.

THE YUNISH MATAKISH.

The Yunish Matakish appears to be held as part of the mourning anniversary, but is a specific Chungichnish rite, of which the central feature is the burial, in the central hole of the ground painting,

of the feather headdress and other cermonial paraphernalia which
the dead man has had since initiation. The ritual seems to come
on the last afternoon of the mourning, just preceding the night in
which the images are burned. The painting is made in the *wamkish*, the sacred toloache mortars and baskets are set out, and the
general aspect of events is similar to those which marked the entrance of the member into the religious life of his people years
before.

His late companions have gathered at the small enclosure, and
amid wailing by the spectators approach one by one toward the
wamkish, imitating the deceased as well as they can. Finally, among
the Diegueño, the whole membership crawls into the *wamkish*, each
man painted with the footprint of the animal that he saw in his own
toloache vision, and uttering its cry. It is very probable that the
practice of the Luiseño is the same.

After the men are seated about the ground painting they grunt and
blow, the feathers are placed in the central pit, and then the company
buries them by pushing the painting into the hole.

The " grunting " is an element of all Luiseño ceremonies. It is a
ritualistic sound, sometimes described as a groan or growl, ending
in a marked expulsion of the breath, and accompanied by an exclamation *mwau* or *wiau*. It seems always to occur in threes and to have
symbolic reference to the spirit or soul.

THE GIRLS' CEREMONY.

The *Wekenish* or girls' ceremony has as its central feature an
act practiced by all the Shoshoneans of southern California: the
" roasting."

The ceremony, according to established Luiseño practice, was called
and financed by the home village, but its direction was in the hands
of the ceremonial head of another village or " clan." Several girls
of one " clan " were usually treated at once, only one, however, being
at the actual physiological period indicated by the word *ash*. As it
is said that they did not undergo the rite a second time, the number
of performances of the ceremony in each locality can have been only
a fraction as numerous as the arrivals at womanhood. Perhaps the
wealthiest or most prominent men had the ritual made as their daughters reached the requisite period, while other parents availed themselves of the opportunity thus offered their younger girls to participate.
Among small and poor hill tribes, having few public rituals to occupy
them, the coming to age of each young woman may have furnished a
welcome occasion for a general gathering. To relatively populous
groups like those of southern California, with wider range of acquaintance and alliance and frequent festivals produced on a large

scale, an equal attention accorded to every female member of the tribe would be likely to be monotonous, if not burdensome. Two alternatives are open: to maintain the ceremony as an important one but reduce its frequency by grouping the girls, or to minimize the significance of the rite, leaving it an affair for kinsmen and fellow residents rather than the larger community. The southern Californians followed the former plan; the Yurok and Hupa, and the Mohave, the latter.

The first step in the ceremony was to make the girls swallow balls of tobacco as an ordeal. Only those who did not vomit were considered virtuous. As the Indians say, this was a hard test.

The girls were then placed on their backs in a pit that had previously been lined with stones, heated, and then carpeted with tussock grass and sedge. Two warmed flat stones were put on the abdomen of each maiden. The girls lay as still as possible for three days. At night men and in the day women danced around the pit. Each girl had her head covered with an openwork basket to keep the flies off, the Luiseño say—perhaps to prevent undue and prejudicial movement. Northern Californians give as the reason for a similar veiling the balefulness of the young woman's glance at this time. Such ideas are, however, in the background if they enter the southern Californian's mind at all. It is an interesting case of an identical act having almost contrary import according to cultural attitude.

Scratching with the finger nails would be very bad. In former days the girls were therefore furnished with scratchers of haliotis.

The girls did not wholly fast, but refrained from meat, fish, and salt. Once every 24 hours they left the pit, which was then reheated.

When finally taken out the girls had their faces painted by the wife of the officiating chief. Bracelets and anklets of human hair and necklaces of *Echinocystis macrocarpa* were put upon them. They were now free to go about, but the food restrictions endured another month or several, and might be voluntarily prolonged for a year or two. Cold water was especially to be avoided.

At the end of the first month the sand painting is made, and its explanation is combined with a sermon by the ceremonial chief on the subject of good conduct in life and its rewards, as quoted below. Each girl then has her head, shoulders, arms, breast, and knees touched with a ball of sage meal and salt, whereupon this is put in her mouth. Leaning on hands and knees she spits this mess into the central hole of the painting. The painting itself is then shoved into the hole by the men seated about it, exactly as in the *yunish matakish* for dead initiates, and as the *wanawut* trench is filled in the boys' initiation.

The girls, accompanied by friends, thereupon run a race—another ceremonial device of which the Luiseño are fond. The chief's wife then again paints them. With the same paint she makes a large geometrical pattern upon a rock, or according to another account, the girls themselves do so. Their hair ornaments are deposited on the rock.

This face and rock painting is performed monthly three or four times. The last occasion marks the final act of the ceremony.

At some time in the period of the observances the girls are tattooed.

MOURNING CEREMONIES.

The impress of death is heavy on the mind of the California Indian. He thinks of it, speaks of it, tries to die where he has lived, saves property for years for his funeral, weeps unrestrainedly when the recollection of his dear ones makes him think of his own end. He wails for days for his kin, cuts his hair, and shudders at their mention, but lavishes his wealth in their memory. It is no wonder that he institutes public observances for them. In the north, indeed, these are scarcely developed; but from the Maidu south, the mourning anniversary has followed the course of our description with growing intensity. The Luiseño practiced at least half a dozen mourning ceremonies after the cremation of the body.

The relation of these is not altogether clear. The *Tuvish* appears to be first in order and simplest. This hinges about a ritualistic washing of the clothes of the deceased, as part of a night of singing, declaiming, and dancing in the ceremonial inclosure. Kin and fellow residents participate; the rite is for an individual. It is held soon after death, and its purpose is to banish the spirit from its familiar haunts.

The *Chuchamish* came next and ran a similar course. Here the clothing was burned and the dead instructed to depart to the sky.

The *Tauchanish* is the great public observance for the dead of the year, or several years, marked, as among many other tribes, by the exhibition and burning of images of the dead, rude figures of rushes, but often hung with valuable clothing and beads. The signal to start and stop the songs to which the images are carried is given with a bull-roarer. The rite is instituted and provided for by the chief, but conducted by the ceremonial leaders of invited clans or villages. The guests receive presents, and are privileged to despoil the images. This observance is not part of the Chungichnish cult, and is probably far older: in fact according to the Diegueño it was the first ceremony in the world; but, like almost everything in Luiseño religion, it has been affected by the Chungichnish worship.

The *Notush* was a local correlative of the *Tauchanish*, perhaps introduced from the Gabrielino to the northern Luiseño. It does not seem to have become established among the southern Luiseño in the mountains, but was brought to mission San Luis Rey probably in the time of the padres. It is described as a more elaborate and costly rite than the *Tauchanish*. The use of images is not mentioned. The characteristic feature was a tall painted pole representing the spirit of the dead person and called *kutumit*, Fernandeño *kotumut*, in Luiseño esoteric language *kimal chehenish*, that is, "little-house appearances." Each portion of the pole denoted a part of the body, but there seems to have been no attempt at actual representation. The top was painted white and bore a raven skin, called *levalwush*, " wide; " below this were baskets and other valuables, which apparently became the property of those who succeeded in climbing to them. Contests were a distinctive feature of the *Notush*, as the following " origin " tradition of the ritual reveals.

The first *Notush* ceremony was held between Pala and Temecula. Sea fog erected the great pole, and the uplanders of the east gathered to contend with the westerners of the coast. Squirrel alone climbed to the top, cut the string, and won the baskets for his mountain companions. *Mechish*, who crawls in the sea, carried off the great sack in which was all the gathered food, but this victory was in turn balanced by wide-mouthed Nighthawk, who was the only one able to devour the mass. Then the owl and a fish stared at each other; but at last the bird blinked and the west was victorious. The raven skin was hanging on the pole, the two sides were getting angry, and a fight portended. Thunder cloud roared, but failed to uproot Sea fog's house, but when Sea fog's wind blew, the mountain houses went down. They then raced to La Jolla in the mountains. Many became exhausted, but Eagle, Chickenhawk, and Raven now won for the east from Butterfly and Grasshopper. Another race was north to San Gorgonio Mountain, through the open country, and Antelope of the plains beat Deer of the mountains. A second match led through the rugged hills, and Deer earned his revenge. So they contested in the first *Notush*. The Yokuts have faintly reminiscent tales of contests between hill and valley people.

The *Ashwut maknash* or eagle killing was an anniversary held for chiefs—the Diegueño say for their dance leaders. Probably both accounts are correct for both tribes. Eagle and condor nests were personal and hereditary property. The young were taken from them and reared. In the ceremony, made at night in the *wamkish*, the eagle was danced with, and finally " shot " to death with a magic stick. Actually his heart was pressed in, but the trick was known only to the toloache initiates. The relatives of the dead man wailed and his successor gave away property to the invited performers. This arrangement pervades all Luiseño mourning rites: the home village issues the invitation and provides food and gifts, the guests perform the ceremony and receive the presents. The eagle's body was ritually burned or buried.

The *Yunish matakish* has already been described.

COSMOGONY.

The basis of the Luiseño origin tradition is a group of ideas that are widespread in southern California. But in the ritualistic cosmogony these appear in a very specialized shape. First, the concept of prime origins by birth, instead of a process of making, is more thoroughly worked out than by perhaps any other American tribe except possibly some of the Pueblos. Secondly, there is a remarkable attempt at abstract conceptualizing, which, though it falls short of success, leaves an impression of boldness and of a rude but vast grandeur of thought. The result is that the beginning of the Luiseño genesis reads far more, in spirit at least, like the opening of a Polynesian cosmogonic chant than like an American Indian tradition of the world origin.

It is a gratification to record this fact, and perhaps worth while remembering it, since it reveals the cultural worth that lies exposed but overlooked in the achievements of many an obscure tribe. The civilization of the California Indians was so nearly equally rudimentary that the temptation is great to regard it as a unitary if not a negligible datum. But we need only approach this civilization in a spirit free from haste, and it becomes apparent as endlessly diversified instead of monotonously homogeneous, flowering in the most unexpected places, and with all its childlikeness not devoid here and there of elements of subtlety and nobility. Few California tribes may have reached the attainments of the Luiseño; but each was possessed of its cultural individuality and endowed with potentialities that have now been cut off but which must continue to summon respect.

This is the story:

The first were *Kyuvish*, " vacant," and *Atahvish*, " empty," male and female, brother and sister. Successively, these called themselves and became *Omai*, "not alive," and *Yamai*, " not in existence "; *Whaikut Piwkut*, " white pale," the Milky Way, and *Harurai Chatutai*, " boring lowering "; *Tukomit*, " night," with the implication of " sky," and *Tamayowut*, " earth." She lay with her feet to the north; he sat by her right side; and she spoke: " I am stretched, I am extended. I shake, I resound. I am diminished, I am earthquake. I revolve, I roll. I disappear." Then he answered: " I am night, I am inverted (the arch of the heavens). I cover. I rise, I ascend. I devour, I drain (as death). I seize, I send away (the souls of men). I cut, I sever (life)."

These attributes were not yet; but they would be. The four double existences were not successive generations: they were transitions, manifestations of continuing beings.

Then as the brother took hold of her and questioned, she named each part of her body, until they were united. He assisted the births with the sacred *paviut* stick, and the following came forth singly or in pairs, ceremonial objects, religious acts, and avenging animals:

Hair (symbolical of the spirit) and *Nahut* (the mystic *wanawut* figure?)
Rush basket and throwing stick.
Paint of rust from springs and paint of pond scum.
Water and mud.
Rose and blackberry, which sting for Chungichnish.
Tussock grass and sedge, with which the sacred pits for girls were lined.
Salt grass (and grass?)
Bleeding and first periods.

These were human; and so were the next born, the mountains and rocks and things of wood now on the earth; and then followed the badger; Altair the buzzard; the feared meteor *Takwish;* the subterranean water monster *Chorwut; towish,* the spirit of man that survives the corpse; the black oak; "yellow-pine-canoe cottonwood" (a receptacle for feathers); *kimal chehenish,* the pole and offerings of the *Notush* mourning; the ash tree; the plant *isla;* the large brake fern; the black rattlesnake; the red rattlesnake; spider; tarantula hawk; raven; bear; sting ray; *tukmal,* the winnowing basket used in initiation; *shomkul papaiwish,* sea fish and urine for ceremonial sprinkling; *topal tamyush,* mortar and toloache mortar.

All these were the first people, touching one another in the obscurity, far in the north. They traveled to Darkening Dusk, where something high stopped them; then to Hill Climbing, the impassably narrow canyon; then to the lake at Elsinore; then to Temecula. There *Hainit Yunenkit* made the sun and the first people raised him in a net four times to the sky. There also Wiyot, bewitched by Frog, sickened and after long illness died. Under the direction of Kingbird, he was burned, but only after Coyote had stolen his heart. Kingbird announced his return: "Wiyot rises, Wiyot the moon," and all saw him in the west, soon to appear in the east. Eagle, knowing what was now in the world, went or sent his spirit north, east, south, west to escape, but finding *pi'mukvul*, death, everywhere, returned to Temecula, and, accepting his future fate of being danced with and killed, died. Deer, too, after a long evasion, resigned himself to death when he was told of the feathers that would wing the arrows sped after him. And last, Night, here at Temecula, divided the people, gave them the languages which they have now, and sent them to their fixed abodes.

Other versions, as among almost all tribes, vary indefinitely in minor content. The long list of sacred births in particular is never given alike. But the tenor of the conceptualizing is always the same; and every old man knows at least phases of this cosmogony, and is aware of their place and significance. We face, in short, more than the philosophizing of a gifted individual endeavoring to rise above the concrete and naive crudities of his age and land. The cultural creation of a nation lies before us.

Besides the migration legends embodied in the story of the origin of things, the Luiseño tell traditions that are primarily geographical.

Nahachish, "glutton, the disease consumption, old age, or male," a great man at Temecula, had the hook broken down on which he hung his abundance of food, and, starving, began to travel. Near Aguanga he was given gruel (which is light gray), so, saying "My stomach is *picha* (whitish)" he named the place Pichanga. On Palomar he was again fed, until his belly burned, and he uttered "My stomach is nettle, *shakishla*," and the place became Shakishna. At Kayawahana he knelt and drank and left his footprints. Sovoyami he named because he was chilled, Pumai because he whistled, Yapichai for a feast witnessed, and Tomka because he was fed. Where he drank he called the place Pala, "water," and Pamai, "small water," and a muddy spot Yuhwamai. Below Pala, seeds were ground for him into meal too fine to handle, and he was poisoned. Perishing, he turned homeward, but died and became a rock just before he could arrive.

There are probably many other tales of this strange character—trivial or meaningless to us, surcharged with associations to the native.

THE SOUL.

The life or soul was called *shun*, Juaneño -*suni*, "heart." This was the part of the person believed to go to the stars.

The *towish*, Juaneño *touch*, was the ghost, and was applied both to a corpse and to the spirit detached from it. Its translation as "devil" is of course inaccurate, but yet not wholly of wrong implication, since a haunting ghost would work harm; otherwise it would not have been feared so vigorously and directed to depart. It is probable that it was the *towish* which went into the ground to what was known as *tolmar* or *tolmal*, which was also the name given to the symbolic pit in the center of the ground painting. As to the meaning of *tolmal*, compare the phrase *ha-tolmik*, translated as "infierno," but said literally to mean "he is gone."

Kwinamish, "root" or "origin," is much used to designate the spirit, apparently as such, or in the living, without the implication of death which attaches to *towish*.

Yula, "hair," has already been mentioned as a frequent symbolic designation of the spiritual.

The Juaneño *piuch* or "breath" should, on the analogy of *touch-towish*, appear in Luiseño as *piwish*. This word is actually found as a name of the Milky Way, particularly where this is coordinated, as in the ground painting, with the *towish* and *kwinamish*.

Huhlewish is said to have the signifiance of "religion" or "sacred matters."

Potish is a dream. The shamans are said to have their "dreams" tell them how to proceed with the treatment of a patient. Just what this may or may not imply as to a conception of a guardian spirit is not certain.

The word used in the sense of Algonkin *manitou*, Siouan *wakan*, Iroquois *orenda*, Yokuts *tipin*, and our "supernatural," is not known, except for one mention of *towauya*, evidently from the stem of *towish*.

Takwish, literally "eater" or "eating," denotes not so much a class of spirits as one particular monster or divinity that makes his home on San Jacinto Mountain, carries off and devours human beings, and appears usually as a low-flying meteor or ball of lightning, but also in birdlike form or as a man in feathers. Sight of him portends disaster and death. He also enters prominently into myth, but as an independently acting being, unassociated either positively or negatively with Wiyot or Chungichnish. His origin is thought to have been in Diegueño land, where he is known as *Chaup*, and Poway is mentioned as his birthplace. Part of his career was run among the Luiseño, especially in association with Temecula, so often mentioned in song and story; and his final abode is the great peak San Jacinto, where Cahuilla, Serrano, and Luiseño territory met. The Luiseño leave the first part of his history to the Diegueño, but narrate freely his later actions. There is a wideness of international outlook in these relations that is characteristic of the southern Californians, but unheard of elsewhere in the State.

Wite, *witiak*, or *witiako* was a sort of greeting spoken when one encountered a raven, the messenger of Chungichnish.

SHAMANISM.

None of the several investigators who have recorded information on the Luiseño make very clear mention of a belief in the familiar or guardian spirit. The same holds true of all other southern California tribes, whereas north of Tehachapi the guardian spirit is regularly and specifically referred to as the source of shamanistic power. Knowledge for the south is admittedly imperfect; but the tenor of the sources on the two regions is too uniformly distinct to allow of any inference but that the attitude of the cultures differed. For the Yuma and Mohave, indeed, it can be asserted positively that they did not know this class of spirits. Now it is interesting that no mention of personally owned spirits is made in any account of the several Pueblo groups. Nor is there anything definite from the Navaho. As to the Apache, there exists an extensive monograph on their medicine men; and it is significant that while this describes numerous charms, and discusses the practice of magic, it nowhere alludes in unmistakable manner to guardian spirits. For the Pima, statements as to guardian spirits are also somewhat indefinite, whereas it is specifically stated that the most important shamans are those who receive their ability from their fathers.

It may be concluded, therefore, that in the area which includes the Southwest and southern California, the idea of the guardian spirit, which is so basic in the conception of shamanism among the American Indians at large, is either lacking or very imperfectly developed.

Among the Pueblos the organized fraternities cure disease and may likely have crowded not only the guardian spirit belief but the shaman himself out of the culture. With the river Yumans, the shaman dreams indeed, but of an ancient divinity; and other men who do not practice medicine dream of him too, and quite similarly. For the Juaneño, Boscana reports that the toloache initiates had the animal or being visioned in their intoxication as protector through life. This is an undoubted approach to the guardian spirit idea. But the drug was drunk as part of a cult, initiation into which marked civic and religious maturity; it was not taken by individuals to acquire medical faculties. It seems, therefore, that the factors which have displaced the guardian spirit belief vary locally. The inference is that the concept, for some unknown reason, lacked vigor throughout the area, and that in consequence substitutes for it arose independently among several groups.

An alternative interpretation would be that the organizing of religion and intrusting of its exercise to official priests suppressed the guardian spirit type of individualistic shamanism among the Pueblos, and that this negative influence spread from this culturally most advanced group to other southwestern tribes as far as the Pacific, local groups of the tribes substituting diverse customs more or less of their own devising.

There is, it is true, one Luiseño statement to the effect that shamans dream of "a rock, a mountain, a person, or something similar" and receive songs from this object of their dream. But this reference is too vague to count for much. The mountain or person might be mythological, as among the Mohave; that is, an ancient bestowing divinity rather than a present and controllable spirit.

On the other hand, it is significant that of the three special classes of shamans known to all the Indians of central California, the bear doctors, rain doctors, and rattlesnake doctors, the latter are the only ones not known to the Luiseño and their neighbors.

The practices of the curing shamans are the conventional ones, in spite of the difference in conceptual attitude. They suck, blow tobacco smoke, spurt water or saliva over the patient, rub, or wave feathers over him. Sickness is considered to be largely the result of witchcraft—that is, of malevolent shamans—and counter-bewitchings and outright slayings were frequent. Sympathetic and perhaps imitative magic were liberally practiced in this connection; hair, nails, and blood carefully concealed. As in the remainder of California, except on the Colorado, disease was thought to be caused by the presence of a physical object in the body rather than by an affection of the soul. Thus sucking was the foremost reliance of the physician. True, there are monsters or water spirits, the *pavawut*, *koyul*, and *yuyungviwut*, that not only drown people but steal their souls and make them sick; but the immediate cause of the illness in native opinion is perhaps the diet of frogs that the *yuyungviwut* imposes upon his or her captive and enforced spouse.

The shaman, Spanish hechizero, is called *pula;* the toloache initiate, *pumal.* The probable etymological connection of these two words has already been commented on in the chapter on the Juaneño.

CALENDAR AND ASTRONOMY.

The Luiseño had more star names than most Californians. This superiority may be connected with their belief that the dead turned into stars. In all southern California constellations are named in ritual, and particularly in song, much more frequently than in the northern part of the State, and play a more important part even than in the ceremonies of the Southwest. But where the Mohave and Yuma sing over and over of Orion and the Pleiades, the Luiseño appear to have had designations for all first-magnitude stars. The known appellations are: *Hula'ch-um,* Orion's belt, and *Chehay-am,* the Pleiades, usually mentioned together; *Nukulish,* Antares; *Nukulish po-ma,* "his hand," Arcturus; *Yungavish,* "buzzard," Altair; *Yungavish po-ma,* Vega; *Yungavish po-cheya,* "his headdress," a star near Altair; *Waunish,* Spica; *Ngoiwut chawochmush,* Fomalhaut; *Tukmi iswut-um pom-shun,* "night wolves [1] their hearts," the North Star, which does not move. The Pleiades were girls once, and Aldebaran is their pursuer Coyote.

The only planet recognized was Venus, called *Eluchah,* "leavings," as of food over night.

The Milky Way, *piwish* or *ahuta,* had several esoteric designations, and was more than the mere ghosts' road of most Californians. It was symbolically associated with the spirit of dead man, *towish,* with the sacred cord *wanawut*—itself representative of life—and probably with the mystic being *Whaikut Piwkut,* "white grayish," one of the preexistences of Night and Earth.

The Luiseño calendar has been preserved, but is not well understood. Eight periods are named. None of the terms has been translated; and their season and order are not certain. They are *Tasmoyil* (grass is green), *Tawut, Tausanal* (grass sere), *Tovakal* (fallen leaves), *Novanut, Pahoyil, Nemoyil* (deer are fat), *Somoyil.* Each has two divisions, the first designated by a diminutive form with *alu'mal,* "lean," the second by the addition of *mokat,* "large." Thus, *Tasmoi-mal alu'mal* and *Tasmoyil mokat.* The "lean" and "large" evidently refer to the appearance of the moon. If we add to eight lunar months two longer unnamed or overlooked periods at the solstices, we have a calendar similar in plan to the peculiar

---

[1] There are no wolves in southern California; but *iswut* is from the stem of *isil,* coyote. Possibly the word has come to denote the jaguar.

one described from the Juaneño. But a comparison of the names of the periods fails to reveal the least verbal resemblance; and the Luiseño names may have been seasonal without exact lunar correlation.

MORALITY.

A nation's ethical practices can best be judged by the foreigner; its code, by its own statements. We are fortunate in possessing extended addresses, recorded in the native dialect, of the kind that the Luiseño were wont to deliver to their boys and girls. The occasion was ritualistic, but it marked also the entry of the young people into manhood and womanhood, and much of what is enjoined is purely ethical with reference to daily life. The avengers are supernatural and determined by the prevailing cult, the punishment is concretely physical. One must respect his elders, listen to them, give them food freely, not eat meals secretly, refrain from anger, be cordial and polite to one's relatives-in-law. Then one will be stout, warm, and long haired, will grow old in good health and have children to whom to pass on counsel, be talked of when death comes, and have one's spirit go to the sky to live. The disobedient and heedless will be bitten by the rattlesnake or spider, they will vomit blood, swell up, go lame, fall into wasting cough; their eyes will granulate, their children be sickly. Fortune or misfortune hangs over every act. Virtue is far from being its own reward— it is the only path that leads to prosperity. Back of all hovers the unnamed figure of Chungichnish, whose messengers and instruments execute many of the punishments. But the afflictions are stated as inevitable facts: there is no allusion to the deity's will or pleasure, nor any outright reference to his anger. He is very far from being as personal as Yahweh; yet there is no concept of any law, nothing that we should call a principle, only an inexorable causality manifest in innumerable specific but endlessly varying instances. One does not reason about this sequence nor stop to bow before an omnipotent personality behind it. One merely adjusts himself to events as to the stress of nature, and takes measures for a wise arrangement of life instead of a series of troubles, in the same spirit as one might provide against storm and starvation. The Luiseño made efforts, indeed, to wrestle with the mysteries of the spiritual, but he attempted them through myth and religion; in his morality and aspect of life he is without exaltation, fatalistic, and a resigned materialist like most American Indians.

On the purely ethical side, one trait stands out which is also a general American rather than a tribal characteristic. There is no provision against theft, assault, rape, witchcraft, or murder, nor any

mention of them. Such violent extremes are too obvious for condemnation, as incest was to the ancient Aryans. It is only with
written codes that such horrid violations of the bases of morality
seem to demand attention—not because they become more frequent,
but because then silence concerning them would in the nature of
things be an avowed condonation. The Indian, beyond taboos and
cult observances, centers his attention on the trivial but unremitting
factors of personal intercourse; affability, liberality, restraint of
anger and jealousy, politeness. He, whom we are wont to regard as
dark, reserved, and latent with cruelties and passions, sets up an
open, even, unruffled, slow, and pleasant existence as his ideal. He
preaches a code of manners rather than morals. He thinks of character, of its expression in the innumerable but little relations of daily
life, not of right or wrong in our sense. It is significant that these
words do not exist in his language. In California, at least, the
Indian speaks only of " good " and " bad"; elsewhere he may add
the terms " straight " and " crooked."

A part of the sermon addressed to boys over the sand painting:

See these, these are alive, this is bear-mountain lion; these are going to
catch you if you are not good and do not respect your elder relatives and
grown-up people. And if you do not believe, these are going to kill you; but
if you do believe, everybody is going to see your goodness and you then will
kill bear-mountain lion. And you will gain fame and be praised, and your
name will be heard everywhere.

See this, this is the raven, who will shoot you with bow and arrow if you
do not put out your winnowing basket. Harken, do not be a dissembler, do
not be heedless, do not eat food of overnight (i. e., do not secretly eat food
left after the last meal of the day). Also you will not get angry when you
eat, nor must you be angry with your elder relations.

The earth hears you, the sky and wood mountain see you. If you will
believe this you will grow old. And you will see your sons and daughters, and
you will counsel them in this manner, when you reach your old age. And if
when hunting you should kill a hare or rabbit or deer, and an old man should
ask you for it, you will hand it to him at once. Do not be angry when you
give it, and do not throw it to him. And when he goes home he will praise you,
and you will kill many, and you will be able to shoot straight with the
bow. . . .

When you die your spirit will rise to the sky and people will blow (three
times) and will make rise your spirit. And everywhere it will be heard that
you have died. And you will drink bitter medicine, and will vomit, and your
inside will be clean, and illness will pass you by, and you will grow old, if you
heed this speech. This is what the people of long ago used to talk, that they
used to counsel their sons and daughters. In this manner you will counsel
your sons and daughters. . . .

This is the breaker; this will kill you. Heed this speech and you will grow
old. And they will say of you: He grew old because he heeded what he was
told. And when you die you will be spoken of as those of the sky, like the stars.
Those it is said were people, who went to the sky and escaped death. And
like those will rise your soul (*towish*). . . .

The counsel to girls is similar:

See, these are alive; these will think well of you if you believe; and if you do not believe, they are going to kill you; if you are heedless, a dissembler, or stingy. You must not look sideways, must not receive a person in your house with anger; it is not proper. You will drink hot water when you menstruate, and when you are pregnant you will drink bitter medicine.

This will cause you to have your child quickly, as your inside will be clean. And you will roast yourself at the fire (after childbirth), and then your son or daughter will grow up quickly, and sickness will not approach you. But if you are heedless you will not bear your child quickly, and people will speak of your heedlessness.

Your elder relatives you must think well of; you will also welcome your daughters-in-law and your brothers-in-law when they arrive at your house. Pay heed to this speech, and at some future time you will go to their house, and they are going to welcome you politely at their house. Do not rob food of overnight; if you have a child it will make him costive; it is also going to make your stomach swell; your eyes are also going to granulate. Pay attention to this speech; do not eat venison or jack rabbit, or your eyes will granulate, and people will know by your eyes what you have done. And as your son or daughter will grow up, you will bathe in water, and your hair will grow long, and you will not feel cold, and you will be fat, if you bathe in water. And after the adolescence rite you will not scratch yourself with your hands; you will scratch yourself with a stick; your body will have pimples if you scratch yourself with your hands. Do not neglect to paint yourself, and people will see, and you will grow old, if you pay attention to this speech, and you will see your sons and daughters.

See these old men and women; these are those who paid attention to this counsel, which is of the grown-up people, and they have already reached old age. Do not forget this that I am telling you; pay heed to this speech, and when you are old like these old people, you will counsel your sons and daughters in like manner, and you will die old. And your spirit will rise northwards to the sky, like the stars, moon, and sun. Perhaps they will speak of you and will blow (three times) and (thereby) cause to rise your spirit and soul to the sky.

Sermons somewhat like those of the Luiseño were probably preached in other parts of California; but they have not been preserved. The harangues of the Wintun chiefs are somewhat similar, but vaguer in tenor, fuller of repetitions, and thoroughly tedious to us for their unceasing injunctions to do what the occasion of itself demands to be done. The Luiseño did not revel quite so untiringly in the obvious when they talked to the young people for their good.

SOCIETY.

Luiseño society presents a somewhat confused picture. Some of its subdivisions exercise religious functions; their relations to the soil have been disturbed by the invasion of Spaniard and American; and wasting of numbers has caused an irregular consolidation of groups.

The totemic moieties of the Serrano and of central California are lacking, except possibly on the northern border about Saboba. There are patrilinear family groups, and unions of these into ceremonial groups. Both bear nontotemic names, which are totally different in each locality.

The patrilinear family groups or "clans" are known as *tunglam*, "names," or *kamalum*, "sons, children," in distinction from the *kecham* ("houses"?), the larger territorial or national groups. People married into neither the father's nor the mother's "clan." This suggests that these clans consisted of actual kinsmen. Their number confirms this interpretation; some 80 are known, with part of Luiseño territory unaccounted for. On this basis the average "clan" would comprise only 25 or 30 souls, a number well within the limits of traceable blood. The total distinctness of the "clan" names in each district also argues for their being families of local origin.

The clan names are now borne by the Indians as if they were Spanish family names. They have a varied character. Many are verbal, some descriptive, some denote animals or objects, or occasionally places.

Thus, at Rincon, there are the *Omish*, "bloody," *Kalak*, "quickly," *Michah*, "rammed, stuffed," *Ngesikat*, "scrapers, grazers," *Shovenish*, "disagreeable," *Chevish*, "pulling apart," and *Kewewish*, "fox"; at Pauma the *Mahlanga*, "palm place," *Kengish*, "ground squirrel," *Shokchum*, "scratchers," *Chat*, "white owl," *Ayal*, "know(?)," and *Pauval*. It may be that some of these appellations are of nickname quality.

The religious groups or ."parties" are known to the Luiseño as *not* or *nota* (plural *nonotum*), which is also the word for "chief." They are described as consisting of a chief, his "clan," members of other clans that are chief-less or greatly reduced, and individuals who have quarreled and broken with their proper "party." Their number is therefore less, their size greater, than that of the "clans." This may also have been true in ancient times. All ceremonies are in the hands of these "parties," each of which, however, generally performs the same rites as all the others. They might therefore be described as a series of parallel religious societies, resting on a clan basis, or more exactly, on consanguinity or personal affiliation with a chief who is at once head of a group of coresident kinsmen and a responsible undertaker of rituals. There is, however, no inherent relation between the social bodies and the ceremonies—nothing in any public rite that is peculiar to a social group. The families and parties built around them have merely been utilized as a means of executing ceremonies.

The present Rincon and former Kuka organizations are:

Anoyum, "coyotes," so called on account of reputed greediness at gatherings; proper name, *Kengichum*, "ground squirrels." *Omish* clan or family; also *Tovik* and *Suvish* families, which formerly acted independently but now have no chiefs.

Ivangawish, "sitting apart," also a nickname; originally called *Nahyam,* from the ancestor of the *Kalak* family, *Nahnahkwis—nahat* means walking stick or cane.

Ehvayum or *Temekwiyum,* "Temeculas"—Ehva and Temeku' both denoting that place. *Ngesikat* family.

Sengyum, "gravels," or *Seveyum. Shovenish* family, said to have come from a gravelly place.

Navyam, "prickly pears," or *Siwakum. Siwak* family. Now extinct.

The *Michah, Chevish,* and *Kewewish* families adhere to the foregoing ceremonial groups.

At Pauma the three parties are the *Mahlangum, Sokchum,* and *Pauvalum,* all named after families. Pichanga, which is said once to have had 17 families, has two religious organizations, the *Seyingoish* and the *Kiungahoish,* the latter founded in 1915 and given the name of an extinct Temecula party.

Occasionally rites are said to be the property of particular organizations. Thus at Rincon, the *morahash* dance belongs to the Anoyum, the *tanish* to the Ivangawish. This condition seems to be a result of the dwindling of ceremonies, or their becoming identified, for a period and within a locality, with individuals of particular interest or ability. A division of function is clearly not the essential purpose of the "parties." The *morahash* is danced by the Luiseño of all districts, as well as by their neighbors, so that it can not be regarded as the specific rite characteristic of one local society. So far as such association exists, it must be due to a temporary or recent loss of this or that ceremony by other societies.

But the basic parallelism of the "parties" did not prevent certain songs, localized migration traditions, landmarks, and perhaps territorial claims, from being the property of particular families or societies. Such possessions seem eminently characteristic of "clans" or organizations centered on lines of descent. The public rituals were essentially communal or national, however completely their performances may have been entrusted to family societies.

It is clear that the chief was the fulcrum of Luiseño society. The religious group was called "a chief," the social group was "the children." A chief ordered ceremonies, his assistant, the *paha',* executed them. A chief-less family was nothing but a body of individuals, dependent for religious activity on personal affiliation with other groups: a family with a chief was *ipso facto* a religious society. It is conceivable that many of the surnames which the Luiseño now possess are the personal names of chiefs in authority when this European habit was adopted. The one thing that is wholly obscure is the relation of the chief to the territorial or political group. There can scarcely have been several family chiefs of equal standing at the head of such a group, and the families were so small that they could not have been the sole political units. Possibly there were always chief-less families, and in a large community the chief of a certain family may have been accorded primacy over his colleagues. The hereditary principle was strong. In default of male heirs, a woman sometimes succeeded, and a widow might exercise a sort of regency for her son. Nothing is on record concerning the chief's riches. This omission is in itself significant. It is not unlikely that the chief was kept in position to entertain and lead by contributions from his " children." If so, his office brought him wealth. It is clear that it was not his property that made him chief.

There was a definite installation of a new chief, a night rite called *unanisha noti*, held in the *wamkish*, with singing, dancing, eating, and no doubt long speeches.

Gifts or payments were expected by a bride's family, but a reputation for industry or ability in the hunt weighed for as much as the wealth formally tendered as basis to marriage. The usual Californian semicouvade was in force: fasting from meat and quiescence were enjoined on both parents for 20 to 40 days, on pain of the child's physical welfare. The umbilical cord was buried. Women withdrew each month from the house and slept and ate apart for a few days. Parent-in-law taboos seem unknown. Hunters ate no game of their own killing, on pain of losing their luck. A violation could be amended by public confession.

CHAPTER 48.

THE CUPEÑO AND CAHUILLA.

THE CUPEÑO.

TRIBAL RELATIONS.

The Cupeño are one of the smallest distinct groups in California. They state that they possessed only two permanent villages: Kupa—whence their Spanish name—near the famous hot springs of Warner's ranch, usually called merely Agua Caliente, a designation that has also been applied to the tribe; and Wilakal, in Luiseño Wolak, at San Ysidro. The Diegueño call the two sites Hakupin and Ephi. The entire territory controlled by the inhabitants of these two settlements is a mountainous district on the headwaters of the San Luis Rey, not over 10 miles by 5 in extent—a sort of Doris in an Indian Greece.

The Cupeño appear to have no name for themselves, other than Kupa-ngakitom, "Kupa-people," and perhaps Wilaka-ngakitom. Their language they call Panahil. The Diegueño call them Hekwach, which is a generic Yuman designation for the Cahuilla. The Cupeño name the Serrano Tamankamyam, the Cahuilla Tamikochem, the Diegueño Kichamkochem, the Luiseño Kawikochem, perhaps all of them terms based on the cardinal directions.

The hot springs seem to have drawn the residence of various Indians for two or three generations, and some years ago the Cupeño were removed, with several other settlements, to Pala. Indian censuses, being more frequently based on location than on exact tribal discrimination, have therefore either ignored the Cupeño or exaggerated their strength. In 1910 there were not far from 200. Anciently, 500 must be set as their maximum.

It is above all their speech that warrants a separate recognition of the Cupeño. This is of the Luiseño-Cahuilla branch of Shoshonean, but more than a mere dialect of either of these tongues. Luiseño and Cahuilla have many words in common which in Cupeño are quite different. When Cupeño agrees with one and differs from the other, the resemblance is more frequently with Cahuilla. In accord with this fact is the Diegueño name of the tribe, which classes it with the Cahuilla. So small a body of people as the Cupeño could not, however, have developed so distinctive an idiom while in their recent intimate juxtaposition to two larger groups of the same origin. A former period of isolation, or of special contact with aliens, is indicated. We must infer, accordingly, that the Cupeño detached themselves from the still somewhat undifferentiated Luiseño-Cahuilla group at some former time, moved to their present abode, and later were overtaken by their more numerous kinsmen; or, that they represent a southerly advance guard which was crowded back into intimacy with its congeners by an expansion of the Diegueño. In either event, relations with the Diegueño appear to have been an important factor in Cupeño tribal history.

SOCIAL ORGANIZATION.

The Cupeño scheme of society is less disintegrated than the Luiseño, but appears also to have been modified in the past century. Its present form is this:

Moieties.	Clans.	Ceremonial groups.
1. *Istam* ("Coyotes")	1. *Nauwilot* ("body louse")	"Party" 1.
	2. *Changalangalish*	
	3. *Kauval*	
	4. *Po-tama-toligish* ("his tooth black")	"Party" 2.
2. *Tuktum* ("Wild cats")	5. *Aulingawish, Auliat* ("blood ——")	"Party" 3.
	6. *Sivimoat*	
	7. *Djutnika*	

The totem of the moiety is called *wala*, "great-great-grandparent," but there is no belief in descent from the totem animal. A sort of good-natured opposition is recognized between the moieties, whose members frequently taunt each other with being unsteady and slow witted, respectively. Mourning ceremonies are made by moieties, but the complementary moiety always participates. Throughout California the contact of the moiety scheme with religion was largely on the side of mourning rites. There is an association here which is undoubtedly of historical significance.

The nature of the " clans " is less clear. As there were several, and the Cupeño had only two villages, they can scarcely have been local bodies. Their appellations also do not seem to be based on place names. They are used as outright family names by the modern Indians; but this can hardly be old practice. The functions of the clans are said to have been chiefly religious. In recent years, as some of them dwindled in numbers, their members ceased their own ceremonies and affiliated themselves with other clans, most of the Cupeño say: in this way the "parties" became established. Others regard the "clans" as only synonymous designations of the religious "party" units. At any rate, the Cupeño designate both clan and party by the latter term in speaking English, and call them both *nout* in their own language. This word also means chief, and is found, as *nota* and *net*, among the Luiseño and Cahuilla. Each clan had its chief, it is said, and there were neither village nor moiety chiefs. At present there is a chief for each "party," besides a tribal political head chosen at the instigation of the whites. Each *nout* had a *paha* or ceremonial director, as among the Luiseño and Serrano; also a *kutvovosh*, who seems to have served as his speaker, messenger, fire tender, and assistant.

RELIGION.

The Cupeño call the toloache initiation *manit paninil*, "Jimson weed drinking." The director of this holds his post through inheritance, it is said, and is also known as *nout*. The *morahash* whirling dance was called *pukavihat*. The girls' adolescence rite, *aulinil* or *ülunika*, included the usual "roasting," and a ring dance in which the people were grouped by moieties. This ceremony is described as made by the girl's clan, but the statement may refer rather to her patrilinear kinsmen, who would generally constitute at least a considerable portion of a clan. *Piniwahat* is the singing of maledictions against "clan" enemies.

The mourning ceremonies are the *pisatuil*, *süshomnil*, and *nangawil*, apparently corresponding to the Luiseño *tuvish*, *chuchamish*, and *tauchanish*. The moieties constantly function in these. Each rite is made by the moiety to which the dead person belonged, and the other is invited. In all of them the guests sing during the early part of the night, the rite makers after midnight. In both the *süshomnil* and *nangawil* property is thrown away as well as burned, and this is seized and kept by members of the opposite moiety. The materials for the figures in the *nangawil* are prepared by the mourning moiety, and then assembled—for pay—by the invited one. This ceremony is said to last three days. The eagle killing ceremony is also in the hands of one moiety at a time, with the other present as guests. This organization by moieties must give the Cupeño mourning ceremonies a different color from those of the nonmoiety Luiseño, which in other respects they appear to resemble closely.

Cupeño mythology is closest to that of the Cahuilla, it would seem, and even perhaps more closely related to that of the Serrano than to that of the adjacent Luiseño. Tumayowit ("earth") and Mukat were the first deities and the creators or progenitors of everything in it. They led mankind southward to their approximate present seats. Either identified or associated with these two gods were Coyote and Wild Cat, who emerged from the halves of a primeval bag hanging in space. Mankind was already in existence, but in mud and darkness. Tumayowit and Mukat disagreed. The former wished death to be and finally descended to a lower world. Mukat caused people to quarrel, and was finally poisoned, by the wish of men, through Frog eating his voidings. Coyote was sent away on a pretext, but returned and seized Mukat's heart from the funeral pyre. The Cupeño were exterminated by their neighbors, only one baby boy, Hübüyak, escaping with his Diegueño mother. As he grew up, he rejoined his kinsmen of Coyote moiety and Kauval clan who had remained at Saboba (in historic Luiseño territory), returned to Kupa, slaughtered the destroyers of his people, and settled there with two Luiseño wives, to become the progenitor of the Cupeño of today. The Wild Cat moiety came to Kupa later.

Mukat is obviously the equivalent of Wiyot, but Tumayowit, the earth mother, appears here, as among the Cahuilla, as a man, if there is no error. This part of the myth suggests the Diegueño and Yuman belief in two first hostile brother gods.

THE CAHUILLA.

HISTORY AND HABITAT.

The Cahuilla, with 750 souls, are to-day one of the important tribes of California. Originally they may have numbered 2,500. They are Catholic and speak Spanish; but, although generally included among the Mission Indians, they were only to a slight extent brought under mission control in the first third of the nineteenth century. The western division may have been partially affiliated with the submission at San Bernardino, and those from the vicinity of Cahuilla Valley, or some of them, appear to have been within the sphere of San Luis Rey or its station at Pala. After secularization, many of the Cahuilla entered into relations with the Spaniards on the grants in the fertile portion of southern California, either as seasonal visitors or more permanent peons. This brought them in some numbers into Serrano and Gabrielino territory and has led to the attribution of part of the habitat of the former people to the Cahuilla by some authorities. Of late years this westward movement from the desert and mountains has slackened. The Government has developed water and protected Indian rights, and the Cahuilla live regularly in their old homes—an instance of the enduring attachment of the California nations to their ancestral soil. There are fewer reservations than there once were villages; but they are rather fairly distributed through the same regions.

The name Cahuilla is in universal use, but its origin is obscure. Reid, our principal authority on the Gabrielino, says that the word means "masters"; but this has not been confirmed. Indians of all tribes regard the designation as of Spanish origin. The Yuman group about Ensenada Bay in Baja California, who are practically one people with the Diegueño, have sometimes been called Cahuillas; but whatever basis of local or official usage this appellation may have, it is unfortunate, since speech proves the Bajeños to have no connection at all with the American Cahuilla. There is also a Yokuts Kawia tribe, on Kaweah River, whose name, however, seems to be a coincidence. The Yokuts say Kä'wia or Gä'wia, while Cahuilla is of course Kawi'a. This is its universal pronunciation. The spellings Coahuilla and Coahuila, although the more frequent and established in government usage, are therefore erroneous; they would be pronounced Kwawia or Kwawila. The latter seems a mere confusion with the name of the Mexican State of Coahuila.

The Cahuilla are called Yuhikt-om or Kwimkuch-um ("easterners") by the Luiseño, Tamikoch-em by the Cupeño, Kitanemun-um by the Serrano proper, Kwitanem-um by the Chemehuevi, Hakwicha by the Mohave, and a dialectic equivalent of Hakwicha by the other Yuman groups that know them.

Cahuilla territory is somewhat irregular, but may be defined as the inland basin between the San Bernardino Range and the range extending southward from Mount San Jacinto; with a few spillings over into the headwaters of coast drainage. There are three natural topographical divisions.

The first comprises San Gorgonio Pass, lying nestled between the giant peaks of Mounts San Bernardino, San Gorgonio, and San Jacinto, all over 10,000 feet high. With this belongs Palms Springs Canyon, and the westward draining San Timoteo Canyon.[1] The elevation of the inhabited sites is between 1,500 and 2,500 feet. Serrano and Luiseño adjoin. The natives of this district, who are here

[1] This is in error. San Gorgonio Pass and San Timoteo Canyon were in Serrano possession, as set forth in the footnote appended to the section on the Serrano. Palm Springs Canyon thus remains as the focus of this Cahuilla group, and their boundary should be run northward or northeastward from Mount San Jacinto instead of forming the westward arm shown in Plates 1 and 57. The hill near White Water probably marked their limit against the Serrano and not against the Desert Cahuilla. The Serrano do not reckon the Palm Springs division as Cahuillas. They are said to call them Wanupiapayum and Tüpamukiyam; which, however, appear also as names of Serrano local groups.

designated as the Western or Pass Cahuilla, speak a somewhat different though intelligible dialect to the remainder of the group. Their range extended to Kawishmu, a hill a little east of White Water.

Southeastward is the Colorado Desert, partly below sea level, and forming an old arm of the Gulf of California. The southern end of this totally arid valley, occasionally watered by overflows from the great Colorado into New River—which looks on the map like an affluent but is really a spillway flowing in opposite direction from the main stream—was in the possession of the Kamia or other Yuman groups. The northern end, down to about Salton Sea, was Cahuilla. Most of this district is exceedingly fertile under irrigation, and has been partly reclaimed. In native times it appeared most forbiddingly desert. But its tremendous depression brought the ground waters near the surface, so that in many localities mesquite trees throve and the Cahuilla obtained water in comparatively shallow wells. The people here are the Kitanemun-um of the Serrano, our Desert Cahuilla.

The third division lived in the mountains south of San Jacinto Peak, chiefly in fairly watered canyons well up the less favored side of the range, overlooking the inland desert, as at Santa Rosa, Los Coyotes, and San Ygnacio. At one point these people were across the divide, in Pacific Ocean drainage. This is the district centering in the patch now known as " Coahuila Reservation "—though it harbors only a small minority of the entire group—on the head of the Santa Margarita. The elevation of these habitats is from 3,000 to 4,000 feet. The speech is said to be distinguishable from that of the desert; but the difference is insignificant, and the desert and mountain divisions might be grouped together.

Plate 57 shows a few important sites in part of the habitat of the Cahuilla. Other place names are: Kavinish, Indian Wells; Pal tewat, Indio; Pal seta, Cabezon; Temalwahish, La Mesa; Sokut Menyil, Martinez; Lawilvan or Sivel, Alamo; Tova, Agua Dulce; Wewutnowhu, Santa Rosa. San Ygnacio is both Pachawal and Sapela. Most of these seem to be old names of specific villages, but now refer to tracts or reservations. Other sites are mentioned in the list of clans under " Society " below.

PLANT FOODS.

The principal supplies of food drawn from plants by the Cahuilla are rather accurately known, and while somewhat more varied than usual owing to the range of the group from low desert to high and fairly watered mountains, may be considered typical of the Indians of the southern part of the State.

Oaks, of course, require reasonable precipitation and moderate elevation, so that they are available in quantities to only a part of the Cahuilla; but the acorns were utilized wherever obtainable and treated as by the other Californians. *Quercus lobata* was the species that the Cahuilla had most frequently accessible to them.

In the sunken desert, where the roots of the mesquite can in many places penetrate to ground water, the fruit of this tree was the staple food. Both the bean or honey and the screw mesquite (*Prosopis juliflora* and *pubescens*) were employed, the whole fruits being ground in wooden mortars. The former variety was the more important; the latter is sweeter.

Agaves and yuccas were less vital to the Cahuilla than to the mountain tribes of western Arizona and probably the Chemehuevi and Koso, but were made use of in the same way. The thick, short, succulent, sweet stalks were roasted in stone-lined and covered pits. The waxy flowers as well as the fruits of some species were eaten cooked.

Nearly every variety of cactus was made use of. Most generally the fruit was consumed, but the fleshy stalks or leaves of some species helped out when diet became scant, and sometimes buds or seeds are edible.

The native palm bears clusters of a small fruit which was not neglected.

Nearly every conifer, from pine to juniper, had its seeds eaten. The most important variety is the Nevada nut pine, *Pinus monophylla*, seeds of which were harvested by the Cahuilla in the same manner as by the Koso, the cones being roasted to extract the nuts.

Many plants furnished what is usually known by its Mexican name pinole—the Aztec original *pinolli* is significant of the wide distribution of the food habit—that is, seed flour. The most important kind was chia, *Salvia columbariae*, Cahuilla *pasal*. Other sages and a variety of plants were also made use of: *Atriplex lentiformus, Artemisia tridentata, Sisimbrium canescens, Lasthenia glabrata, Chenopodium fremontii*. These were all gathered with the seed beater (Fig. 57), parched or roasted with coals

Fig. 57. — Cahuilla seed beater.

shaken in a basket or pottery tray, and ground. The meal was eaten dry, boiled, or baked into heavy doughy cakes, according to species.

California is nowhere a berry country. The Cahuilla have available several varieties which are rather of the nature of small fruits. In some of these the seeds are perhaps of more food value than the flesh. Thus, in the wild plum, *Prunus*, Cahuilla *chamish*, Mexican *yslay*, the kernel of the pit is crushed, leached, and boiled like acorn flour. Manzanita, *Arctostaphylos*, is treated similarly. The berries of the elder, *Sambucus mexicana*, and of sumac, *Rhus trilobata*, are also dried. The influence of acorn-seed processes in the use of these food materials is evident. The arid to subarid climate of California produces fruits whose paucity of juicy pulp allows them to be made into meal; but a people unaccustomed to grinding would hardly have applied the process to varieties consumable otherwise.

Root parts of plants are of little service to the Cahuilla, whose dry habitat allows but a sparse growth of the lily-like bulb plants that are important farther north in the State. Flowers, on the other hand, are often thick and sappy.

Those of species of yucca, agave, sumac, and ocatilla (*Fouquiera spinosa*) are boiled, either fresh or after drying.

Altogether, more than 60 varieties of plants are known to have served the Cahuilla as food in one form or another, and the whole number may have been twice as great. It is obvious that a non-farming people living in a country of little game and limited fertility would be likely to leave no source of wild plant food idle which lay within their capacity to utilize. The value of ethnobotanical studies lies in a comprehension of the processes followed, and a determination of the manner in which these have positively and negatively affected methods of securing food. It is clear that a few well-developed processes were applied to the limits of applicability, rather than that the best possible method was independently devised for each product of nature. Thus grinding and drying stand out among the Cahuilla; the seed beater is more important than the digging stick. The true significance of the processes, of course, is clear only with the totality of the botanical environment in view. For this reason the plants and parts not utilized are as important to an interpretative understanding as those made use of; but on this side little information has been recorded.

MORTAR AND METATE.

The Cahuilla do not neatly square their metates, as the Mohave do, but use an irregularly rectangular or oval slab. Most specimens have only part of their surfaces worn, obviously by a circular motion. The rub stone sometimes is only a bowlder ground flat. Another form is dressed into an oval, and rather thin. This type could also be used for rotary grinding. In general, the implement is of the California type, as described in the chapters on the Maidu and Luiseño, and is more properly designated "grinding slab" than "metate."

But there are many "manos" that are as evenly squared as a brick, and even longer and narrower. These can be utilized only with a back and forth motion. Some metates, too, show that they have been rubbed with such a stone. Now the Cahuilla of to-day often grind wheat; and it is therefore a question whether this southwestern type of metate was frequent among them anciently, or whether its use has been stimulated by contact with Mexicans. The settlers from Mexico must have brought many metates of lava with them, or manufactured them after their arrival. Apparently the utensil was in daily service in every poorer Spanish Californian household for several generations; and from this source it penetrated, in its standard Mexican form with three legs, to the Indians. Occasional examples are still in use in Indian hands in central as well as southern California. Fragments have even been discovered in the surface layers of the San

Francisco Bay shell mounds and in graves on the Santa Barbara coast.

The southern California mortar is a block of stone hollowed out, when new, some 2 or 3 inches, but gradually wearing deeper. The hopper is by no means always employed. If present, it is always attached with asphalt or gum. Neither of the two central and northern types of mortar is known—the bedrock hole and the slab with loose, superposed hopper.

The pestle, as in central California, is frequently only a long cobble, sometimes slightly dressed at the grinding end or along one side (Fig. 58, b).

For mesquite beans and perhaps other foods, the desert Cahuilla use a deep wooden mortar sunk into the ground. This has its counterpart on the Colorado River; but the Cahuilla form appears to average a more extended section of log and deeper hole. A pestle of unusual

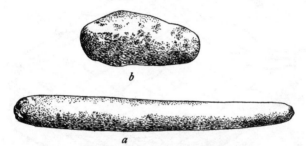

b

a

FIG. 58.—Cahuilla stone pestles for wooden (a) and for stone (b) mortar.

length, often 2 feet, is necessitated. To prevent undue weight, this must be made slender; and in turn, dressing is involved (Fig. 58, a). The pestle for the wooden mortar is therefore quite different from the much more roughly shaped form used on stone.

It is doubtful if the Cahuilla-Mohave wooden mortar is connected with that of the valley Wintun and Yokuts. One is used for mesquite, the other for acorns. The former has a deep, pointed pit: the other contains a broad bowl-shaped basin, in the center of which is a small shallow excavation in which all the actual pounding is done. The southern mortar of wood is perhaps a device to meet some particular quality of the mesquite bean; that of central California is clearly a substitute for a more general form in stone.

Somewhere in acornless southeastern California, probably from the Chemehuevi to the Eastern Mono, and in parts of Nevada, a very large and deep cone-shaped mortar of stone occurs, worked with a long and sharp but thick pestle of extraordinary weight. This seems to be connected with the wooden mortar of southern California.

The mountain Cahuilla, as well as the Luiseño and Diegueño, who have acorns but no mesquite, have not been observed to possess wooden mortars; and no pestle of wood has been reported from California except from the Mohave.

BASKETRY.

Cahuilla basketry is that of all the "Mission Indians" of southern California. Chumash ware alone was somewhat different, though clearly of the same type. It is a rather heavy but regular basketry, coiled on bundles of *Epicampes* grass stems, the wrapping being either sumac splints or *Juncus* rush. The varying shades of the latter produce a mottled effect, which is pleasing to most civilized people, though it is not certain that the natives sought it equally. But they obviously appreciated the lustrous texture of the rush,

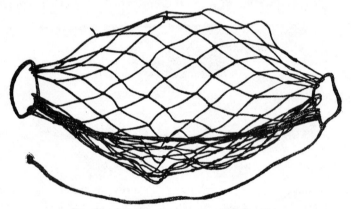

Fig. 59.—Cahuilla carrying net.   (Cf. Fig. 53.)

which, as used for the groundwork, is normally buff in color, while red or brown lengths of stem serve for designs, and even olive and distinctly yellow shades can be obtained. Only black was produced by dyeing. The prevailing pattern arrangement is one of encircling bands.

The forms are as standardized and nearly as few as the materials. They are nearly flat plates; shallow flaring bowls; a large deeper basket; a small receptacle with slightly constricted mouth, the equivalent of the Chumash-Yokuts-Chemehuevi "bottle-neck," but without trace of a shoulder; and the woman's cap.

The large basket serves for storage and carriage. It differs fundamentally from the carrying basket of all central and northern California. It is close coiled instead of open twined; is flat bottomed instead of an inverted cone; and broader than deep. It is obviously not a form that originated for transport, but a receptacle or pot put secondarily to burden use. The explanation is found in the carrying net, which renders the precise shape of the contained basket of little moment.

The net has the form of a small hammock with a mesh of from 3 to 5 inches, the ends being gathered on heavy loops, which are joined by an adjustable rope passing across the cap-protected forehead (Fig. 59). Similar nets are found in central California to as far north as the Pomo without an accompanying alteration of the carrying basket from its conical form. The inference is that the central Californians employed the net only occasionally, the southern Shoshoneans regularly. All that is actually known of the use of the implement corroborates this conclusion. The net must therefore be regarded as of southern origin. It is a localized device: the adjacent Southwest reverts to the basket or employs the carrying frame; the Shoshonean Plateau appears to use the Californian cone basket.

It may be added that the Pomo carrying net has the headband woven in, so that the capacity can not be altered—a· fact which indicates that it is designed only for certain specific usages.

The large, coiled, fairly deep storage and transport basket of the south may therefore be regarded as probably an original cooking vessel, and is certainly a form which elsewhere is used for cooking. It is not so used by the Cahuilla to-day, as indeed is not to be expected of a pottery making people. The history of the vessel can hardly be understood in full without more precise knowledge of the baskets in which the inland Gabrielino—who made no pots and were too remote from steatite to use it generally—did their cooking.

The same vessel undoubtedly served formerly, as it does to-day, for a general receptacle; but that it was not primarily a store basket is suggested by two circumstances. The first is that the ancient Chumash possessed a taller, larger, and distinctly bellied basket, similar to that of northwestern California in form, but coiled instead of twined. This was indubitably made for storing only. The second fact is that the Cahuilla (Pl. 60), the Mohave, and apparently the Luiseño also, make an outdoor granary. This is not set vertically and worked into posts, as among the Sierra tribes, but laid flat on the ground, on a rock, or on a scaffold. It is made of long stalks of wormwood, *Artemisia*, among the Cahuilla, or arrow weed, *Pluchea*, with the Mohave, and put together in bundles much on the plan of a bird's nest, without textile process. The Mohave and desert Cahuilla form is up to 6 feet in diameter, generally low, and without bottom. This type is mostly used to hold mesquite. The mountain Cahuilla make a smaller but taller form with bottom for their acorns. The entire device is obviously one that is serviceable only in an arid climate: there is no thatch or provision for cover except horizontally

laid stalks that would not turn rain. This granary, together with
the opportunities afforded by rock crevices in a dry country, make a
true storage basket unnecessary in most of southern California. The
large "mission" basket would be convenient to contain as much food
as might be wanted about the house; it was not intended to hold provisions for the winter, nor was it serviceable for the purpose.

The small and more or less globular basket of the Cahuilla and
their neighbors was no doubt sometimes useful as a deposit for awls
and other little things; it must also have served particularly as a
gift and as an offering in the mourning anniversary.

The basketry cap of southern California has the shape of a fairly
tall frustum. Except for material and texture, it is identical with
the Yokuts and Koso cap. This southern coiled form appears to
have only a remote historical connection with the overlay-twined cap
of northernmost California, which is low and more or less convex
in profile, and whose range, toward the south at least, is exactly coterminous with that of the basket art that does not know coiling.
The northern cap is worn habitually; southern women don theirs
when they carry a load. The intervening tribes, such as Maidu,
Miwok, and Pomo, use no headwear. A third type is represented in
California among the Chemehuevi, and appears to be representative
of the Shoshonean Plateau. This is diagonally twined, peaked, and
sometimes has the design painted on. It seems that this form links
the northern and southern California types geographically, rendering the distribution of the object continuous over an arc of territory. This arc and the Pacific Ocean inclose the north central Californian capless area. A distribution of this kind makes it obvious
that it is a specific reason, and not mere failure of diffusion, that has
kept the central Californians from use of the cap; and establishes
some possibility that they once wore it and subsequently abandoned
the custom.

The Great Basin type of cap is found among Cahuilla and
Diegueño beside the coiled form. Both are shown in Plate 73, d.

The mortar hopper of the Cahuilla and other southerners is started
on a hoop. Here is a truly interrupted distribution. The north
twines its hopper, the south coils, the middle area dispenses with
the article.

Uniformity of technique, material, pattern, and even fineness of
finish of all coiled ware, irrespective of the nature of the basket, is
almost absolute among the Cahuilla and their neighbors, and is one
of the most marked traits of their art.

The commonest twined basket of southern California is a small
or moderate sized openwork vessel of *Juncus* stems, used both as a
receptacle and, after lining with leaves or similar material, for

leaching. The weave is essentially simple twining, with considerable doubling and zigzagging of warp. The introduction of these variants seems random, the only apparent purpose being to keep the interstices approximately equal in area. No attention is paid to uniformity of mesh or to an even surface. The result is a basket that seems deliberately crude and unworkmanlike.

The seed beater has become a frame rather than a basket with the Cahuilla. It is nothing but a bundle of three, six, or a dozen sticks, wrapped together at one end to form a handle, and more or less spread fanwise at the other end over a hoop. A single crosspiece may bisect the circle and give stiffness, but is not always introduced. Modern pieces have the fan and hoop very roughly lashed together with cord, rag strips, or wire. As no old specimens have been preserved, this imperfect workmanship may possibly be ascribable to modern degeneracy. But the analogous crudeness of the openwork basket, as contrasted with the full maintenance of careful finish in all coiled ware to the present time, suggests that the Cahuilla beater was always made hastily and imperfectly. This is the more likely because on the one hand it is scarcely a true basket and on the other reaches its southernmost known range in southern California. The concept has become feeble, its execution half-hearted. (Fig. 57.)

The only other twined vessel known to have been made in the region of "mission" basketry is the pitched or asphalted water jug with constricted neck, and the occurrence of this is doubtful for the Cahuilla. The Chemehuevi and Kawaiisu manufacture a coated jug in diagonal twining and with pointed or round bottom, a type belonging to the Shoshonean Plateau and the western part of the Southwest. The Chumash made a bellied bottle that would stand up, and used simple twining. The Gabrielino, who also had no pottery, may have had the same type; the preserved description of their water vessel unfortunately is not clear. The Chumash and Chemehuevi forms probably met in the Serrano region, although here also exact knowledge fails. For Cahuilla, Luiseño, and Diegueño there is only a single and vague reference; and as these peoples made pottery, the occurrence of the basketry water bottle among them must be considered somewhat doubtful, and was probably at most occasional.

The southern California basket art thus reveals these traits. Twining is remarkably undeveloped. Types that are twined elsewhere in the State are either lacking in the south, replaced by coiled substitutes, or amazingly crude. The center of the art rests in coiling to a much higher degree than elsewhere. The coiled ware is connected with that of central California, especially of the San Joaquin Valley, but is reduced to a single well-maintained manner universally ap-

plied. The occurrence of pottery among the Cahuilla, Luiseño, and
Diegueño has unquestionably contributed to this condition of their
basketry. As soon as neighboring regions without pottery are entered, such as the Santa Barbara Channel or Tehachapi Mountain
district, the rigid restriction to a single style ceases, and twining
flourishes beside coiling.

POTTERY.

The pottery made by the Cahuilla, Luiseño, and Diegueño, which
did not extend to the Gabrielino but probably to the Serrano,
apparently had its immediate origin in the lower Colorado Valley,
from which it continues also in the opposite direction to the Seri.
It is a coiled and smoothed unslipped ware, made of clay that burns
red, with tempering of crushed rock; very thin walled, light, but
fragile and porous. Patterns are linear, solid areas being confined chiefly to fillings in of the favorite acute angle; and are
painted on in yellow ocher, which fires to a somewhat deeper red
than the clay. The Cahuilla and Luiseño more frequently omit designs, but when they add them, do so in typical Mohave style, which
is suggestive of tattoo and face-paint patterns; but they employ a
red substance in place of yellow ocher. Black designs occur (Pl. 62),
and though rare are of interest because unknown to the Mohave.
They are said to have been produced with black mineral; the surface is more highly polished and the lines finer. The forms of vessels seem to have been less numerous than with the Mohave; at least,
spoons, plates, and oval platters have not been found. The moderns
occasionally make specialties, like jars with three or four mouths,
which do not occur among the Mohave, where the art remained
vigorous in purely native condition until recently; but these may be
fanciful inventions under American stimulus. Something similar
has occurred among the Yuma, whose old pottery seems to have
nearly disappeared before crude and bastard forms made as
curiosities.
   The introduction of this art from the Colorado River to the desert
and the coast is not altogether recent, as the presence of sherds in
the upper layers of an ancient site at La Jolla proves. The apparent
absence of pottery from the lower deposits can not yet be stressed,
because examination has been too far from exhaustive to make negative conclusions dependable. On the other hand, it can not be
doubted that the art came to the coast from the east at no very
remote period.
   That the ultimate source of the pottery industry of the entire region
is from the Southwest proper is also certain. But again, hasty conclusions must be avoided. Nothing like the Mohave-Luiseño ware

has been found in any ancient or recent Pueblo culture; an area wholly or nearly without pottery separates the Colorado River from the westerly edge of the district of Pueblo architecture; and from the river to the coast there are no traces of any other form of the art.

The ware most nearly resembling that of southern California seems to be a red pottery with one-colored pattern found up the Gila and at least as far into Sonora as the Papago country. This similarity, together with the modern Seri one, points to Sonora rather than the Pueblos as the specific source of the southern California art.

HOUSES.

The Cahuilla house is thatched. Its original form has not been satisfactorily determined. At present it is rectangular and set on forked posts. There is a distinct ridge and considerable slope to the roof. The walls may be plastered with mud or adobe. This type of dwelling has unquestionably been influenced by the Mexican *jacal* or the American house; but to what degree is uncertain. On the desert larger and more nearly square houses with nearly flat roof and without sharp corners may be seen which somewhat suggest the Mohave house minus its covering of sand. These are probably more nearly aboriginal. The mud coating of the walls of the pitched-roof houses is certainly not native. The Mohave follow the same practice, but it is positively known to be recent with them.

In the mountains a type survived until recently which lacks walls. Two, four, or six posts are set up rather close together and connected across their crotched tops by short logs. From these, poles are then radiated to the ground, and some sort of thatch bound on. Such a dwelling suggests a reduction of the Miwok semisubterranean house or assembly chamber, but is probably more immediately connected with the Luiseño and Mohave houses; a covering of earth could be easily added or omitted. Stumps in abandoned settlements at the edge of the desert conform to this structural plan. But the question remains whether this type of house was built by all the Cahuilla or restricted to those in a certain topography; and further, whether it represents the standard house, or a form used in summer or for temporary purposes.

Uncertainty also surrounds the sweat house. The Serrano and Pass Cahuilla made this chamber. For the Mountain Cahuilla the sweat house has not been mentioned; but they may have had it. For the Desert Cahuilla the case is more doubtful. The next tribes to the east, those of the Colorado River, do not know the sweat house.[2]

---

[2] A recent study of the Cahuilla by L. Hooper (see bibliography) leaves the use of sweat houses and earth-covered houses somewhat obscure, but establishes the existence of sweat houses.

The sweat house of the Pass region is oval and small, about 12 by 8 feet, and of a man's height in the middle (Pl. 60). The only opening is the door on ground level. Inside from this is the fireplace, and beyond, two center posts, connected by a transverse beam. From this poles run down to the edge of the rather shallow excavation. The whole is then laid with brush and earth. The structure is too small for dancing or assemblies: all through southern California the sweat house is used only for sweating.

This sweat house agrees closely in plan with the old type of Cahuilla dwelling that has been discussed.

The ramada or shade is of the usual type: a roof of foliage on posts. In the desert it forms a sort of porch in front of the door, and is frequently surrounded in whole or part by a windbreak—both devices known also to the Mohave.

The brush inclosure for ceremonial purposes has not been reported from the Cahuilla, but may have been made by them.

WEAPONS.

The Cahuilla bow is that of all southern California—long, narrow, thick, and unbacked. It is made of mesquite, inferior specimens of willow, or palm-leaf stem; in the mountains probably of other materials. The arrow is of two kinds: cane with a wooden foreshaft, as among the Chemehuevi and Yokuts, or a single sharpened stem of *Artemisia*, without head, the Mohave type. The grooved straightener and polisher of steatite, which was heated, occurs throughout the south, and has already been mentioned as the regular accompaniment of the cane or reed arrow.

The thrusting war club with thick cylindrical head was used by the Cahuilla. This is a form found from the Pueblos to the Gabrielino.

The curved flat rabbit-killing stick of southwestern type was known to all the southern Californians (Fig. 55).

VARIOUS UTENSILS.

The Cahuilla cradle was a ladderlike frame like that of the Mohave and Diegueño. The relation of this generic southern California type to the other forms found in California has been discussed in the section dealing with the Yokuts. Whether the Cahuilla used a hooplike wickerwork hood of splints such as the Mohave attach to their frames is not recorded, but seems likely. (Pl. 39, *b*.)

The hammock-shaped carrying net (Fig. 59) is often suspended in the house to hold a sleeping baby. This may be an aboriginal custom, but there is no certainty on the point.

The desert habitat of most of the Cahuilla is probably responsible for their nonuse of the two commonest Californian string materials, *Apocynum* and *Asclepias*. Instead they employ the leaf fibers of the mescal, *Agave deserti*, and the bark of the reed, *Phragmites communis*. The latter plant is called *wish*, but this word in Luiseño denotes *Apocynum cannabinum*.

The mealing brush of soaproot fibers, *Chlorogalum pomeridianum*, is also replaced by one of agave among the Cahuilla.

The straight flute has four holes usually set roughly in two pairs by rule of thumb or eye, and therefore productive of arbitrary intervals rendering the instrument unsuited for accompaniment to the voice.

For strung shell money the Cahuilla are known to have used the *Olivella* type of thin, curving disks, but the more massive currency of clam must also have reached them.

SOCIETY.

The social organization of the Cahuilla has been less broken and altered in the past century than that of the Luiseño, and may therefore afford a truer picture of the society of the latter people than their own present institutions. At the same time the information about the Cahuilla is not wholly clear. As among the Serrano, the moieties stand out definitely, the "clans" are less certain.

The Cahuilla moieties are patrilinear, totemic, and exogamous. They are called *Istam*, after *isil*, the coyote, and *Tuktum*, after the wild cat, *tukut; -am, -um*, is the plural ending. Endogamy occurs now and then, as among the Miwok; it may or may not have been tolerated in native days.

The " clans " are very numerous, small, and associated with localities or named after places. All clan members insist on their direct kinship and descent in the male line from a comparatively recent ancestor. No recorded clan names and village names agree. Two or more clans might inhabit one village. The members of a single clan sometimes live in different villages, and the Cahuilla do not seem to regard this condition as a modern innovation. All this leaves it doubtful whether the clans are bodies of the kind usually implied by this term, or only families of actual blood kindred named after a spot with which they are or once were associated. Their moiety affiliations prove nothing in this matter, since under patrilinear moieties either patrilinear clans or patrilinear families must automatically form part of the moieties.

The recorded Cahuilla clans are nearly all from the desert division:

Coyote moiety.

Sawala-kiktum. Formerly with the Wild Cat *Nanha-yum* and *Ayelmukut* and Coyote *Ikoni-kiktum* in the village of Ekwawinet at La Mesa, 2 miles south of Coachella. Now at Torros Reservation.

Ikoni-kiktum. See last.

Taukat-im. Southwest of Coachella.

Wora'i-kiktum. At Indio.

Sewakil. South of Indio.

Masuvich-um. On Martinez Reservation. The name is said to refer to a sandy place.

Wiit-am, "grasshoppers." On Martinez Reservation.

Mumlait-im. On Martinez Reservation.

Wansau-wum. On Martinez Reservation. Named from *wanyish,* stream, because once flooded out.

Iviat-um. At Agua Dulce.

Sasalma-yum. At Agua Dulce.

Kaunakal-kiktum. At Agua Dulce. This group is said once to have lived at a place where *kaunakal* shrubs grew.

Kauwistamila-kiktum. At Agua Dulce.

A'atsat-um, "good ones." Formerly at Indian Wells.

Wanisiwau-yam. At Mecca.

Tevi-nga-kiktum. At Alamo.

Wiyist-am. At San Ysidro.

Havinawich-um. At Palm Springs.

Amna'avich-um, "large ones." Northwest of Palm Springs.

Hunavati-kiktum. Southeast of Banning. Perhaps Serrano.

Wild Cat moiety.

Palkausinakela, "seepage from a spring." Figtree John, west of Salton Sea.

Panatka-kiktum. Now at Thermal; came from west of there.

Tui-kiktum. Southeast of Thermal.

Isil-sivayauwich-um. South of Coachella.

Wanki-nga-kiktum. South of Coachella.

Nanha-yum, Tel-kiktum, and *Ayelmukut.* At La Mesa, south of Coachella.

Panasa-kiktum. Southeast of Coachella.

Wansinga-tamyangahuch-um. Northeast of Coachella.

Walpunidi-kiktum. At Alamo.

Palpunivikt-um. At Alamo.

Tamula-kiktum. Near Alamo.

Tamolanich-im. At Agua Dulce.

Awal-im, "dogs," a nickname. At Martinez.

Autaat-em. West or southwest of Coachella, now at Martinez.

Wavicht-em—wavish, mesquite. At Indian Wells; now at Thermal and Mecca.

Kauwis-paumiyawich-em, "living in the rocks at Kauwis," *i. e.* at Palm Springs. Now at Mecca.

Kauwis-i-kiktum, "living at Kauwis." Perhaps one group with the last. Now at Palm Springs and Coachella.

Kilyi-nga-kiktum. On Mission Creek. Perhaps Serrano.

Iswet-um, "wolves," a nickname; in Spanish, Lobos, used in the form Lugo, as a modern family name. On Cahuilla Reservation. This is the only mountain Cahuilla clan recorded, and is so prominent on its reservation as to give the impression that *Iswetum* may have been a synonym for all the people of the district. The wolf is not an inhabitant of southern California.

Wakwai-kiktum. Formerly near Warner's ranch, that is, neighbors of the Cupeño. Now at Wakwi or Maulim on Torros Reservation.

The ending *-kiktum* on many of these names is from the stem *ki,* "live" or "house."

The Cahuilla word for "clan" is *tahelo,* which is probably from the stem *tah, atah,* "person," occurring in several Shoshonean languages of southern California.

The chief, *net,* and his assistant or ceremonial director, *paha,* held office in the clan, it is said.

The totemism of the moieties extends to ritual and myth. Images for the *nukil* or mourning anniversary are made by each moiety for the other. Temayowit and Mukat, the first gods, born in the Milky Way, are thought to have been companions of Coyote and Wild Cat, respectively. The moon is a woman of Coyote moiety, made by Temayowit, the sun a Wild Cat man who went to the sky.

Their possession of names and affiliation with the moieties render it probable that the enumerated groups of the Cahuilla approached the nature of clans. But the relation of the clans to the local or political units, to the moieties, to blood families, and to chieftainship and religious groups is far from clear for any of the southern California Shoshoneans.

RELIGION.

Considering the importance of the Cahuilla, their strength in survivors, and the interest attaching both on account of their varied environment and their position midway between the Gabrielino and the Mohave ceremonial foci, regrettably little is known of their religion.

Their creation myth seems to have been of Serrano type, but with the deities named as among the Cupeño.

The mourning anniversary was called *Nukil* or *Hemnukuwin.* Images were used.

The same may be said of the adolescence rite, *Aulolil* or *Pemiwoluniwom,* in which the girl was "roasted."

Whether the Chungichnish religion reached the Cahuilla of the pass is not certain. It probably obtained some foothold among those of the mountains. It did not exist in the desert. The Cahuilla there do not know Chungischnish, drink no toloache publicly, make no sand paintings, and hold no eagle ceremony. According to the Mohave, they sing several cycles analogous to their own song series.

There may be some forced native equating in this statement, but there is probably at least some basis of fact. The desert Cahuilla knew the toloache plant and admit that they drank it, but apparently only as occasional individuals intent on wealth or some other special aspect of fortune. This is very nearly the Mohave attitude toward the drug.[3]

On the whole, therefore, it would seem that the Cahuilla possessed the basic and generalized elements of southern California religion; lacked—at least in their most characteristic habitat—its developed Chungichnish form; and had come instead under a certain degree of Mohave or Colorado River influence. This influence is likely to have been indirect, since there is practically no mention of outright communications between the Cahuilla and the Mohave.

---

[3] L. Hooper, The Cahuilla Indians (see bibliography), gives, among other new data, an account of a Jimson-weed initiation which appears to refer to the Pass division.

CHAPTER 49.

THE DIEGUEÑO AND KAMIA.

THE DIEGUEÑO.

YUMAN STOCK.

With the Diegueño, more fully San Diegueños, we return once more to the much scattered Hokan family and enter upon consideration of the last of the stocks represented in California—the Yuman.

The Yuman stock is internally classified on the basis of speech as follows, Californian tribes being starred:

Lower California division: Kiliwi; Cochimi; Akwa'ala.

Central division, centering on the lower Colorado River: * Mohave; * Halchidhoma; * Yuma; Kohuana; Halyikwamai; Cocopa; * Kamia; * Diegueño; Maricopa.

Arizona Plateau division: Havasupai; Walapai; Tulkepai ("Tonto"); Yavapai.

TERRITORY AND DIVISIONS.

Diegueño land was washed by the ocean on the west and bordered by the holdings of the Luiseño, Cupeño, and Cahuilla on the north. For the east and south no precise limits can be set. The Diegueño of the north, about Mesa Grande and San Felipe, declare that they did not live beyond the eastern foot of the mountains. But what group owned the desert tract to the east, from Salton Sea to the now fertile Imperial Valley and New River district, has never been fully established. On the map most of the district in question has been assigned tentatively to the Kamia; in the section on whom the problem is discussed further.

Southward, the Diegueño shade off into the closely allied Yuman bands of northernmost Baja California. At Ensenada, 60 miles south of San Diego, the speech is still close to that of the Diegueño. The Indians through this stretch have no group names for each other, except by directions. They distinguish between the Diegueños, those formerly connected with the mission of San Diego, and the

Bajeños, the inhabitants of Lower or Baja California. But this is merely a reflection of the political separateness of American and Mexican. The congeners across the line have not thriven, and ethnologically they are wholly unknown, except for statements of the most general character; but the scant indications point to no ethnic demarcation of moment at or even near the international border.

Within the part of California occupied by the Diegueño two not very different dialects are spoken besides some minor subdialects. The two principal dialects have usually been designated as the northern and the southern, although " northwestern " and " southeastern " would be more exact. A number of differences of custom are known, but much of the available information concerns the two groups jointly, so that it is difficult to treat them other than as a unit. Their careful distinction by future students is indispensable.

Both dialects extended across the international boundary, but their position is such as to make it appear that the northern belonged primarily to American and the southern to Mexican California. The southern dialect includes, in American California, only the modern districts of Campo, La Posta, Manzanita, Guyapipe, and La Laguna.

It is probable that the Diegueño, or at least the northern branch, called themselves merely Ipai, people. They do sometimes call themselves " southern people," Kawak-upai, or " western people," Awik-upai, with reference to their neighbors; but these are not true national designations. Thus the Diegueño of Mesa Grande are Kawak-upai with reference to the Luiseño, and those of San Felipe as regards the Cupeño; but at San Felipe the real Kawak-upai should be the Campo people. The southern Diegueño sometimes call themselves Kamiai or Kamiyahi; which once more intrudes the vexed question of who the Kamia were.

To the Luiseño and Cupeño all the Diegueño are simply " southerners ": Kichamkuchum or Kichamkochem. The Mohave know them as Kamia'-ahwe, that is, " foreign " or remote Kamia.

Diegueño names for their neighbors are: Kohwai, perhaps also Hakunyau, the Luiseño; Hekwach, the Cupeño, and no doubt originally the Cahuilla also, although the latter are now known by their usual name, which the Indians declare to be of Spanish origin; Techahet, probably a place, is also recorded for the Cupeño or Cahuilla; Yuma or Yum (probably a recent name), Inyakupai (" eastern people "), or Yakiyak, the Yuma; although some distinguish between the Kwichan or Yuma proper, said to be on the Colorado or beyond it, and the Yakiyak to the west of the Kwichan; Kwikapa, the Cocopa; Chimuwowo, the Chemehuevi; Humkahap, the Mohave; Mitlchus in the northern dialect, or Haiku in the southern, the Americans; Pinyai, the Mexicans.

The name Kamia seems to be unknown to the northern Diegueño, except, in the form Kamiai, as a designation for the inhabitants of the district of San Pascual, near the Luiseño frontier. The occurrence of this name at San Pascual may possibly be due to the settlement there of a group of southern Diegueño during or after mission times. With the Cupeño there was intimate association and considerable intermarriage, at least from the vicinity of San Felipe. The Cocopa are said not to have voyaged into northern Diegueño territory, but the Chemehuevi were occasional visitors in search of food. The Mohave seem very little known in the district of Mesa Grande and San Felipe. They probably made their journeys to Manzanita and other southern points, where references to their songs and sacred mountain occur.

The western portion of Diegueño territory is shown in detail on Plate 57. Other place names are Emitl-kwatai, Campo; Amat-kwa'-ahwat, farther up on the same stream; Amai'-tu, La Posta; Ewiapaip, from which we have made Guyapipe; Inyahkai and Aha-hakaik, La Laguna; Hawi, Vallecitos; Ahta, "cane," or Hapawu, Carrizo. Most of these are little reservations now; but it seems as if many of the reservations constituted by the government in this region, as among the Luiseño and Cahuilla, had an ancient village community as their nucleus.

Settled places that can not be located with any definiteness are Awaskal, Kohwat, Maktati, Maramoido, Matamo, Meti, Pokol, Shana, and Tapanke, mentioned in Spanish sources, Hanwi, Hasumel, Kamachal, Kokwitl, and Suapai in American. South of the boundary, some of them perhaps in what may be considered Diegueño limits, were Ahwat, Mat-ahwat-is, Hasasei, Hata'am, Hawai, Inomasi, Kwalhwut, Netlmol, and Wemura. The Hakum were inland near the border: that is, a village of this name evidently stood in or near Jacumba Pass.

Other settlements are given below in the clan lists under "Society."

Beyond their own territories the northern Diegueño knew Salton as Esily, "Salt," or Esilyeyaka; the mud volcanoes as Hakwicholol; Mount San Jacinto as Emtetei-Chaup-ny-uwa, "Chaup's house peak."

HISTORY AND NUMBERS.

San Diego was the first mission founded in upper California; but the geographical limits of its influence were the narrowest of any, and its effect on the natives comparatively light. There seem two reasons for this: first, the stubbornly resisting temper of the natives; and second, a failure of the rigorous concentration policy enforced elsewhere. Whether this second cause was itself the result of the first, or was due to an inability of the almost arid region to support a large population by agriculture without irrigation, is not wholly clear.

The spirit of the Diegueño toward the missionaries was certainly quite different from the passiveness with which the other Californians received the new religion and life. They are described as proud, rancorous, boastful, covetous, given to jests and quarrels, passionately devoted to the customs of their fathers, and hard to handle. In short, they possessed their share of resoluteness. Not especially formidable as foes, they at least did not shrink from warlike attempts. Within a month of the founding of the mission an attack was made for plunder. In its seventh year, the mission, meanwhile removed to its present site, was definitely attacked, partly burned, and three Spaniards, including one of the priests, killed. This was the only Franciscan to meet martyrdom at Indian hands in the entire history of the

California missions. Three years later it was necessary to send an expedition against the hostiles of Pamo.

Christianity also took hold of the natives very slowly. The initial year of the mission did not bring a single baptism; in the first five, less than a hundred neophytes were enrolled. After this, progress was more rapid: but the very success of the priests appears to have been the stimulus that drove the unconverted into open hostility. There can be little doubt that this un-Californian attitude can be ascribed to a participation by the Diegueño in the spirit of independence characteristic of the other Yuman tribes.

The Diegueño population, with the Kamia of American California included, may have reached 3,000. To-day there are between 700 and 800. This is a higher percentage of survival than is enjoyed by any other missionized group of California. The cause must be ascribed to the slowness of the Diegueño to submit and their retention of a greater degree of freedom of movement and residence. It was not until 55 years after its foundation that San Diego attained its maximum of converts. Other missions fell into heavy numerical decline in a much shorter period, and were only partly able to check the decrease by drawing upon importations from more and more remote districts. San Diego never harbored any Indians but Diegueños.

The total baptisms in 65 years were a few over 6,000. Three generations to a century would make this figure indicate a standing population of 3,000. But the native rate of reproduction may have been faster, and if so the numbers at a given time would have been less. Ten years before the mission reached its populational acme the annual death rate was 35 per thousand. This suggests more rapid breeding than is common to modern civilized communities; but it is probably not a high figure for a primitive community, and was certainly far below the mortality obtaining at other missions during their periods of activity.

RELIGION.

Diegueño religion is so largely compounded of the same elements as that of the Luiseño that its detailed consideration would be repetition. This is evident from the accompanying tabulation, the native names in which may serve as points of identification in future studies.

This similarity is probably in part ancient, but has undoubtedly been accentuated by the southeastward sweep of the Chungichnish toloache cult about a century ago. The southern Diegueño, in fact, did not come definitely under the influence of the movement until about the period of American occupation. It is characteristic of the effect of speech diversity in California that ceremonial names were translated or replaced by the Diegueño, not taken over. Only in the songs, the words and melody of which tend to form a close unit in the Indian mind, did outright borrowing of speech occur; and in these it took place on an extensive scale. A large proportion of Diegueño songs are in a foreign tongue; and this is generally not Luiseño or Cahuilla, as the singers believe, but Gabrielino.

TABLE 7.—ELEMENTS OF RELIGION IN SOUTHERN CALIFORNIA.

Religious elements.	Diegueño.	Luiseño.	Other groups.
Ceremonial enclosure	himak ("they dance"?), akiuch.	wamkish; hotahish, the fence.	Juaneño, wankech; Gabrielino yoba.
Ceremonial manager or dancé leader.	kwaipai	paha'	Serrano, Cupeño, Cahuilla, paha'.
Toloache initiates	(1)	pumal-um	Juaneño, pupl-em.
Shaman	kwasiyai	pula	Juaneño, pul.
"Tatahuila" dance (Pl. 55)	tapakwirp	morahash; totawish, the performer.	Juaneño, tobet (=towet?) the costume; Cupeño, pukavihat, the dance.
Eagle feather skirt	yipehai	palat	Juaneño, palet.
Headdress of owl feathers on stick.	tsekwirp, winyeyi.	cheyat	
Erect headdress on band	talo	apuma; hainit	Juaneño, eneat.
Stick headed with crystal	kotat	paviut	
Toloache mortar	kalmo	tamyush	
Net figure for initiation	minyu	wanawut	
Toloache	kusi, kus	naktomush, the plant; mani, the preparation; pa'nish mani, the drinking.	Juaneño, pivat ("tobacco"); Cupeño manit paninil, the rite.
Bull-roarer	air	momlahpish	
Sand painting	(1)	tarohaish	Juaneño,[1] Gabrielino.[1]
Clothes-burning rite	watlma	chuchamish	Cupeño, süshomnil.
Image-burning rite	keruk, wukeruk	tauchanish	Cupeño, nangawil; Cahuilla, nukil, hemnukuwin.
Mourning rite for initiates	ocham	yunish matakish	Gabrielino.[1]
Eagle mourning rite	ehpa ima ("eagle dance").	ashwut maknash ("eagle killing")	Juaneño, panes, the bird.
Girls' adolescence rite	atanuk, akil	wekenish, (yuninish?).	Cupeño, aulinil, ülunika; Cahuilla, aulolil.
Fire dance	(1)	(1)	
Initiates' dance	hortloi, (hutltui)	tanish	
Ordeal of stinging ants	(2)	antish	Juaneno.[1]
Race at dying or new moon	(1)	(1)	Juaneño.[1]
Songs of invective and contempt.	(1)	nyachish	Gabrielino,[1] Cupeño, piniwahat.
Pole in Notush mourning	(2)	kutumit	Fernandeño, kotumut.
Cannibal spirit, meteor, fireball.	Chaup, Kuyahomar.	Takwish	Cahuilla, Takwish; Juaneño, Takwich ("Tacuieh").

[1] Occurs, but name unrecorded.   [2] Lacking.

The name Chungichnish did not enter the Diegueño idiom. While it is difficult to believe that they took over the ritual without the least knowledge of the associated deity, such knowledge can not have been profound, since there is no trace of it in the available myths. The Diegueño call the Chungichnish practices simply *awik*, " western."

Being recent among them, this cult has not invaded all rites to the same extent as among the Luiseño. The girls' adolescence ceremony, for instance, is totally free from Chungichnish coloring, and must be regarded as belonging to an older stratum of religion, although not necessarily an originally Diegueño one, since the Diegueño elements of this rite recur among the Luiseño plus Chungichnish additions. The adolescence ceremony, in fact, seems to have been worked out and to have spread over the entire coastward part of southern California so long ago that it became wholly naturalized among each group with a nearly uniform character.

Apart from the stronger hold of the Chungichnish cultus among the Luiseño, the two peoples differ definitely in religious outlook. This diversity has been noted by all careful observers, and is the more marked because of the close similarity of the concrete elements making up the two religions and the practical identity of the cultures on their material and economic side. The Luiseño are mystics, crude but earnest. The Diegueño are left untouched by the abstruse. The actual—picturesque or decorative but either visible or tangible—is what interests them. The sacred order of births of the essences of things does not occur in their narrow cosmogony. The dying god Wiyot, representative of humanity, is slighted in their traditions for the sea serpent that was beheaded, the wonderworking boy Chaup, the blind brother of the creator, or other individuals remarkable only for their peculiarities of magic. The relation of the two mythologies, with reference to those of all southern California, is discussed in detail in the chapter on the Yuma. No trace of the Luiseño esoteric system of double terms for all sacred objects or concepts has been found among even the most immediately contiguous Diegueño. The sand paintings of the two peoples have already been described as perceptibly different workings out of a single idea.

In some measure these differences may be due to the Diegueño having been subject to an eastern influence from their Yuman kinsmen of the lower Colorado River, from which the Luiseño were guarded by the intervening Cahuilla. This influence undoubtedly existed. Its spring was probably in large measure the Mohave nation; but wherever it originated, it was chiefly transmitted to the Diegueño proper by the Yuma and Kamia. As between the river tribes and the Diegueño, there is no doubt that the current flowed from the former to the latter.

The effects of this stimulation or borrowing are visible at several points. The Diegueño, in the mythic basis of part of their ritual, make much of the sacred mountain of the Mohave, Avikwame, which they called Wikami, although sometimes they relocate it at a lower peak near Yuma. They sing song cycles admitted by the Mohave as equivalent to their own, in part as identical. *Orup* and *Tutomunp* songs phonographed among the southern Diegueño have been promptly recognized and correctly named by the Mohave. Whether they would have similarly known Luiseño songs of *Temenganesh*, *Pï'mukvul*, or *Nokwanish* is very doubtful. The Diegueño mourning rite with images is called *Keruk*—it is said after the name of the booth which is burned at the climax. The Yuma also consume a shade at their anniversary and call one of the two kinds of songs in the rite *Karu'uka*. That the Luiseño, whose speech is radically diverse, do not know this name, proves nothing; but it is significant that they are not mentioned as burning any structure. More intimate knowledge may bring to light hundreds of other points of contact.

It is extremely desirable, in this connection, that something intimate may yet be ascertained as to the religion of the Cahuilla. In origin, they are one with the Luiseño and Gabrielino. Their position is such that they may well have received ritual influence from the river tribes to the same degree as the Diegueño. The Mohave speak of the Cahuilla cults in terms of their own; but this may be because they themselves, situated at the center of an area of religious dispersion, know no other rites. The Diegueño refer to the Cahuilla as if in their beliefs and practices they were one with the Luiseño. Yet this may indicate nothing much more than that they recognized the Cahuilla and Luiseño as allied nations distinct from themselves. Moreover, the Mohave have in mind the Cahuilla of the desert, the Diegueño probably those of the mountains, immediate neighbors and associates of the Luiseño. We, on the other hand, are so little informed about the Cahuilla that we do not know positively how far the respective influences of Avikwame and Chungichnish prevailed among them.

A complete list of the known song series or cycles of the southern Diegueño is included in a comparative discussion in the chapter on the Yuma (Table 8).

As to the Diegueño, once more, a distinct eastern and Yuman importation can accordingly be recognized in their religion in addition to a more recent northwestern and Shoshonean one. When both are accounted for, we are face to face with a native Diegueño basis. But how much of this is original Diegueño it is impossible to say. Its outstanding elements—the girls' rite with its roasting, the use of toloache in some way, the mourning anniversary with images, the stringing of songs into cycles or classes, a type of cosmogony—are all common to an array of tribes, stretching in some cases into central California and in others into Arizona. There is nothing to suggest that the Diegueño were especially prominent or creative among this group of nations. We may rather conclude from their marginal position, with the unnavigable sea at their back and the extremely poor and hard-pressed peoples of Baja California on their right hand, that, other things equal, they received more often than they gave; and, as one people among many, conditions were far from equal. Most of the substratum even of their religion, then, is likely to have had its ultimate devising in the hands of other nations; and all that we can point to as specifically Diegueño in source are the superficial details peculiar to them. Fuller knowledge will no doubt add to the number of these, but, on the other hand, is also certain to reduce the number at other points as it uncovers the presence of this or that trait, as yet recorded only for the Diegueño, among their neighbors also.

The following are the principal of these peculiarities:

The Diegueño girls' ceremony being free of the Chungichnish atmosphere, and therefore containing more magic and less religion, refers primarily to the girls' physiological well-being during life, whereas the Luiseño, having more nearly equated the ceremony with that for boys, make of it almost an initiation into a cult, with sermons over the sand painting, an ordeal of retaining swallowed tobacco, foot racing, and painting of rocks by the candidate. In place of these features, the Diegueño use the *atulku*, a large crescentic stone, heated and placed between the girls' legs to soften the abdominal tissues and render motherhood easy and safe. These stones have been spoken of as sacred. No doubt they were. But their use was a practical one, in native opinion, not symbolical or esoteric.

Cremation among the Diegueño was followed by a gathering of the ashes, which, placed in a jar of pottery, were buried or hidden among remote rocks. The apparel of the dead person was saved for the clothes-burning ceremony, but no mention is made of the preliminary rite of washing called *Tuvish* by the Luiseño.

The image ceremony begins with a night of wailing. On the six succeeding nights the images are marched around the fire and dancing and singing continue until morning. The figures are of mats stuffed with grass, the features indicated in haliotis shell. The faces of those representing men are painted black, of women, red. On the last of the six nights, at daybreak, the images, together with a great quantity of property, are put into the *keruk*, a small semi-circular house of brush open to the east in which the images have previously been stored, and the whole is burned to a song "Goes *katomi* to your house." *Katomi* may denote essence, or spirit; the meaning is not certainly known. The purpose of the rite is said to be to keep the dead content, prevent their return, and assuage the grief of the survivors, who at once cease mourning.

The Diegueño danced and raced for the revival of the moon toward the end of its waning; the Juaneño when it was new; for the Luiseño, both periods are mentioned.

The Diegueño keep or don their ceremonial paraphernalia in a "house" or enclosure called *kwusich-ny-awa*. The meaning of this term is not known but *kwusich* recalls *kwasiyai*, shaman, and *awa* is house. It is not recorded whether the *kwusich-ny-awa* was a special religious structure or a living house temporarily set apart for sacred purposes. It may have been nothing but a small brush fence such as the Luiseño built near the main *wamkish*.

East is the primary ceremonial direction to the Diegueño, as north is to the Luiseño and usually to the Mohave. The ceremonial enclosures open in these directions, but both Diegueño and Luiseño occasionally state the entrance to have been on the side characteristic of the other tribe.

The Diegueño are the only tribe in California as yet known to possess a system of color-direction symbolism. This is: East, white; south, green-blue; west, black; north, red. It is interesting that there is little if any idea of a circuit of the directions or fixed sequence of the colors, as in the Southwest. The Diegueño thinks of two pairs of directions, each with its balance of colors, white-black or red-blue. If he falters, which is not infrequently, the confusion is within the pair.

From this directional symbolism it might be inferred that the ceremonial number of the Diegueño was four, as it is to a very marked degree among the Mohave and Yuma. This, however, is true chiefly of Diegueño mythology; and it may be remarked that the color symbolism has so far been found only in traditions. In ritual, things are done three times, or six times in a pair of threes, almost always; four is rare, five and seven do not occur. This conflict is rather remarkable and seems very un-Indian. It has an analogue in an indeterminateness of sacred number among the Luiseño, where three and four both occur, but the feeling for number seems curiously deficient. With the Juaneño, five rather looms up, but there is no certainty. With the Gabrielino, 4 and its multiple 8 secure primacy once more; but there is also a tendency toward 6 and 12, and perhaps 7, which in turn prevail among the Serrano and Yokuts.

SHAMANISM.

The shaman, *kwasiyai*, is said by the Diegueño to have been born as such. He may have owned guardian spirits, but information to this effect is very vague. There were bear doctors as well as shamans who could turn themselves into eagles. The weather maker was called *kwamyarp*.

Curing was effected by sucking blood or the disease object, either with the mouth or through a pipe; by kneading and pressing; and by blowing tobacco smoke. Suspected shamans were done away with.

CALENDAR.

The Diegueño calendar had six named divisions and no more, which have been independently recorded twice.

Season.	Weather.	First count.	Second count.
November	cold	ilya–kwetl	
December	snow	heha–nimsup	namasap (white).
January	cold	hatai	tai.
February	rain	heha–psu	pswi, kwurh.
March	rain	hatya–matinya	matanai.
April	growth	ihy–anidja	anaha.

Kwurh of the second count may possibly stand for *-kwetl* of the first and have been misplaced.

The round of six was gone through twice each year. Although the month names refer to wintry phenomena, they were repeated in summer. That the divisions were lunar is shown by the fact that the names in the second list were obtained with the prefix *hatlya*, "moon."

The Diegueño reckoning is an exact duplicate of the Zuñi calendar, except for appearing not to begin at the solstices. This default may be an error, or due to an imperfect adjustment. The Luiseño and Juaneño calendar was almost certainly based on the solstices, and the annual repetition of the Diegueño count very strongly suggests a primary recognition of two fixed points within the year; and these can hardly have been any events other than the solstices. The Zuñi-Diegueño reckoning flows more evenly for short periods than the Juaneño-Luiseño system of combining four or five months with two longer solstitial periods; but after each few years it must require a violent wrench to readjust it. The Juaneño plan seems rather more advanced in that it has departed farther from a mere seasonal year divided by lunations toward a true solar year.

SOCIETY.

The Diegueño were divided into exogamous patrilineal clans. Their system, like that of the Luiseño, is, however, a vestigial or rudimentary one, evidently because they were situated at the edge of the Californian area of clans. The totemic moieties of more northerly nations are lacking. So are the totemic names of the cognate Yuman tribes to the east. The clans are definitely associated with localities in the native mind. Their names, so far as translatable, give the impression of being place names, perhaps of narrowly limited spots. Married women went to live with their husbands' people. The following are the known clans. There were undoubtedly others:

Northern Diegueño "clans."

Matuwir ("hard"), south of Mesa Grande.
Shrichak ("an owl"), at Pamo in winter, Mesa Grande in summer.
U'u ("an owl"), at Pamo and Mesa Grande.
Kwitlp, at Pamo and Mesa Grande.
Hesitl ("manzanita"), at Tauwi, San Jose, on Warner's ranch, adjoining the Cupeño.
Paipa, at Santa Ysabel.
Esun, at Santa Ysabel.
Kwaha ("estafiate"), at Santa Ysabel.
Hipuwach, at Santa Ysabel.
Tumau ("grasshopper"), now at Capitan Grande, formerly at Mesa Grande, Santa Ysabel, and elsewhere. Reckoned as distinct from the Tumau clan of the southern Diegueño.
Kukuro ("dark, shady"), now at Mesa Grande, formerly at Mission San Diego and Tiajuana, original location uncertain.
Lachapa (short?), location uncertain.

Southern Diegueño "clans."

Kwitak, at Campo.
Nahwach, at Miskwatnuk, north of Campo.
Yachap, at Hakisap, northeast of Campo.
Hitlmawa, at Snauyaka, Manzanita.
Kwamai ("wishing to be tall"), at Pilyakai, near La Posta.
Saikul, at Matajuai.
Kwatl ("hide"), at Hakwaskwak, in Jacumba Valley.
Hetmiel, at Hakwasik, east of Tecate Divide below Jacumba Valley on American soil; now near Campo.
Kanihich or *Kwinhich*, in southwestern Imperial Valley; now at Campo.
Hayipa, at Hakwino, Cameron Lake, in southwestern Imperial Valley.
Hakisput, at Hachupai in Imperial Valley.
Tumau ("grasshopper"), near Brawley in Imperial Valley; now among the Yuma.
Miskwis, location unknown.

These locations tend to connect the southern Diegueño with the nonfarming division of the elusive Kamia. That Imperial Valley was owned by a group called Kamia is clear; whether these were more nearly allied to the agricultural totemic Kamia on the Colorado or to the hunting, nontotemic Kamiai or "southern Diegueño" of the mountains of San Diego County is less certain.

The southern Diegueño having been less disturbed by civilization, their list probably represents the aboriginal status more closely. From this it would appear that each "clan" owned a tract and that each locality was inhabited by members of one clan, plus their introduced wives. The *kwaipai* or chief of the clan had direction of ceremonies, which were largely or wholly made by clans as such. This is a gentile system reduced to a skeleton; the only unquestionable clan attribute is the exogamy. Patrilinear descent proves nothing, since the wholly ungentile tribes of California reckon and inherit in the male line. It is not unlikely that the scheme had its origin in pure village communities or small political groups among whom a prevalent exogamy hardened into a prescription, while the name of one of a number of spots in their habitat became generally accepted as their appellation. Only a slight readjustment in these directions would be required to convert the Yurok villages, the Pomo communities, or the Yokuts tribes into "clans." In short, it is doubtful whether the term clan is applicable.[1]

The northern Diegueño data suggest a more definitely social system. Pamo had a chief (*kwaipai*) for the village or community as well as for each clan living there, besides *koreau* or assistant chiefs in the clans. But the northern Diegueño were shuffled into the mission and mission stations and out again after secularization, and it would be venturesome to draw inferences from statements that may refer to conditions either 50 or 150 years old.

The Diegueño word for clan is *simus*, which may be from a Yuman stem meaning "name."

CUSTOMS.

The semicouvade was practiced by Diegueño and Luiseño alike. For a month after a birth father and mother alike did no avoidable

---

[1] Spier (see bibliography) lists the following southern Diegueño clans: Kwaha, Waipuk ("kingsnake"), Huhlwa ("twined basket"), Oswai, Hlich ("worthless"), Kalyarp ("butterfly"), Hotum ("drum"—an object learned from the Spaniards), Kwalnyitl ("black"), Paipa, Nihkai; plus several previously recorded: Tuman, Lyacharp, Neeihhawach, Hitlmiarp, Kwatl, Kwitark, Kwamai, Miskwis, Kwinehich, Hitlmawa, Saikur. A map gives their situations, which seem to be their summer haunts, hunted and gathered over from spring to autumn. Winter was spent in mixed groups in the eastern foothills, at the desert's edge. Clans sometimes fought; they owned eyries and most food products of their tract, but not acorns. Local exogamy was normal but not studied; there was no preferential marriage between clans; residence after marriage was patrilocal. Clans seem to have been without totemic associations. Each had a chief, the office being generally hereditary, but with some selection among heirs by the people. The principal functions of the chief were to admonish and to hold the mourning ceremony; his necessary qualification, generosity. Other than their names, there is little in all this to mark the "clans" as being more than local bands or miniature "tribes" of the usual Californian type.

work, shunned exposure, and refrained from meat and salt—the usual food taboos of the region.

The umbilical cord, after severing, was coiled on the infant's abdomen. After it fell off, it was carefully buried. This is also a Luiseño custom.

Suicide by jealous women is said to have been not rare.

The entire scalp, including the ears, was cut from fallen foes and preserved. The event was celebrated in a night of dancing by men and women in the ceremonial inclosure. It is said that the dancers took turns at setting the scalp on their own heads.

The standard game of the Diegueño is guessing, *homarp*, Spanish peon, played as by the Luiseño. The hoop and poles have gone out of use. Women's dice are of Mohave type: four little boards, painted or burned. These are said to be in use only among the southern division, and to be a " Mohave " importation.

DRESS.

Men went naked. A braided girdle of agave fiber evidently served for carrying and not to support a breechclout. Women's wear was the usual two-piece petticoat. The hinder garment, *teparau*, was of willow bark; the front apron, of the same material or of close strings, perhaps partly braided or netted. The footgear, which was worn only on rough or thorny ground, was a sandal of agave fiber, cushioned to the thickness of a half inch or more.

Both sexes wore their hair long. The men bunched it on their crowns. The women allowed it to hang loose, but trimmed the front at the eyebrows, and often set on their heads a coiled basketry cap.

Tattooing, *ukwich*, was somewhat random and variable. Women bore more designs than men, as a rule, and two or three vertical lines on the chin were the commonest pattern, but forehead, cheeks, arms, and breast were not exempt. Women were tattooed in connection with the adolescence ceremony. A cactus thorn pricked charcoal into the skin.

HOUSES.

The house in the mountains, and apparently on the coast also, was earth covered. Three posts, planted in a row, were connected by a short ridge log, on which poles were then leaned from the sides. A layer of *hiwat* brush kept the superimposed soil from sifting or washing in. The door was not oriented. The elliptical outline, sharp roof, and absence of walls approximate this structure to the Luiseño and Cahuilla house; but the regular roofing with earth, exacted by neither the mild climate of the coast nor the heat of the desert edge, points to an influence of the cognate tribes on the Colorado River.

The sweat house, *tawip*, is described as smaller but higher than the dwelling. Its center rested on four posts set in a square. The roof was like that of the living house. The fire was between the posts and the door. Men sweated regularly in the evening; women did not enter at any time. This is the farthest known occurrence of the typical Californian sweat house; the Mohave and Yuma did not know any device of the kind.

Wells, *setlmehwatl*, were dug with sticks. Like the Cahuilla, the Diegueño declare this to have been a practice of the pre-Spanish days. Permanent springs are not numerous on the eastern slope of the mountains.

FOOD, ARTS, AND IMPLEMENTS.

About San Diego Bay fish and mollusks formed the basis of subsistence. Inland the range of food was similar to that of the mountain Luiseño and Cahuilla. Toward the desert baked "mescal," *amatl*, looms up as a staple. In spite of their affinity to the farming Kamia, the Diegueño never attempted the practice of agriculture.

The mortar was that of the Luiseño, but usually made in a smaller bowlder, and often sunk into the ground. The bed-rock mortar was also known.

The same pottery is made by the Diegueño as by their neighbors. A reddish clay is mixed with finely crushed rock, coiled, shaped with a stone and a wooden paddle called *hiatltut*, and fired. Nowadays it is usually unornamented. Formerly patterns were customary, it is said; but this seems doubtful. Cook pots and water jars are the common forms. Bowls and plates of clay seem to be largely replaced by baskets.

Basketry is of the type general in southern California; but in addition a variety of soft textiles in basket shape, close-twined sacks or wallets, were made of string materials, especially milkweed. These are unparalleled in California except for some ancient specimens found in the southern San Joaquin Valley (Pl. 63), and for somewhat similar wares made by the Mohave and Yuma, but executed to-day in civilized materials and coarsened technique.

The war club, *hitlchahwai*, was of heavy mesquite wood, and of typical southwestern form, that is, with a cylindrical enlargement at the head.

String was either red or white, apparently as it was made of milkweed, *hotl*, or yucca, *pyatl*. Heavier cordage, and the burden net, *katari*, were usually of yucca.

Carrying nets and sacks are made in the "bowline on a bight" stitch among the northern Diegueño, with the double loop or square knot among the southern Diegueño. This is but another of several indications that the two groups were further cleft in culture than their similarity of dialect and inclusion under a common Spanish name would indicate.

On San Diego Bay tule balsas were used; perhaps canoes also. The paddles were double bladed, as among the Chumash.

What appear to be olivella or other small univalve shells were dug out of the ground in the eastern desert and made into necklaces by the interior Diegueño. They were called *ahchitl*. These may have been living shells in the banks of New River, but are more likely to have been ancient remains from former lake beds or overflowed districts in the region below sea level.

Pipes, *mukwin*, were 6 or 8 inches long, tubular, and either of stone or of pottery. The former may be presumed to have been used in religion, the latter for every-day smoking. The Mohave also make pipes of clay, but they are much shorter. A pipe of cane is also mentioned by the Diegueño.

Like all the tribes of southern California, the Diegueño had no drum. The rattle was a gourd or turtle shell, both of which were called *ahnatl*. The gourd is probably recent. A deer-hoof rattle was used in the mourning anniversary.[2]

THE KAMIA.

The Kamia, Kamya, Comeya, or Quemaya are a Yuman tribe between San Diego and the lower Colorado whose identity is not altogether clear, while their territory is even more doubtful.

These are the facts about them.

In 1775 the Quemaya were said by Garcés to live in the mountains from about the latitude of the south end of Salton Sea to San Diego, to eat mescal like a hunting group, but to visit the lower Colorado River for agricultural food. Hardy in 1826 described the Axua (ahwe, "foreign") as on the Colorado,

---

[2] Spier (see bibliography) has recently added important notes on the southern Diegueño. There are no bear or weather shamans, though both are known from northern neighbors. The Jimson-weed initiation is made by a "clan," viz, the people of a locality, mostly of one clan; members of any clan are included among the initiates. The ceremony is simple: The ground painting contains no figures of animals; the net figure (Luiseño *wanawut*) is not used; the whirling dance (*tipkwirp*) is not made; the fire ceremony is made after the Jimson-weed drinking. There is no clothes-burning ceremony separate from the image ceremony. Wild plums are pounded, leached, and cooked like acorns. The metate is often unsquared, its hollow oval. Rabbits are netted; small rodents taken in a stone deadfall baited with an acorn; snares are not used. Houses are for winter use only, gabled with a ridgepole in two forked posts, and covered with earth. The flat-roofed shade is not built. The diagonally twined cap is said to be for women, the coiled cap for men. Good blankets contain an average of 20 jack-rabbit or 40 cottontail skins. They serve mainly as bedding, but are also worn as ponchos. Trees are felled by fire, wedges not used. Cord is of mescal, milkweed, or human hair, not of yucca, nettle, or reed. The old rattle was of deer hoofs or clay, gourds being a Mohave importation, and turtle shells not used. Sinew-backing of the bow is known as a Chemehuevi trait. Soapstone arrow straighteners are preferable to clay ones. Arrowheads of stone are for large game only. Clubs were curved or spiked, not cylinder headed. The "moons" of the year have six names only, repeated, and seem to denote seasons rather than lunations. Other recent papers on the Diegueño, by G. G. Heye and E. H. Davis, are also cited in the bibliography.

above the mouth of the Gila, fishing and farming. Whipple in 1849 distinguished the Comaiyah from the Yuma or Kwichyana and put them on New River near Salton Sea. The modern Yuma know the eastern or "southern" Diegueño, as they have been called in the present work, as Kamya, and appear to include the western or "northern Diegueño" with the Shoshonean Cahuilla under the designation Hakwichya. The Mohave distinguished between the Kamia, and the Kamia ahwe or foreign, strange Kamia, whose dialects, habits, and territory were distinct. The Kamia they describe as farmers, and as living on the Colorado below the Yuma, but wholly on the west side; which may mean that they ranged considerably back from the river. The Kamia ahwe they identify with the Diegueño, state that they did not farm, but ate snakes and other strange foods, and place them in the mountains that run south of San Jacinto Peak. Alone of all the Yuman tribes, they did not travel or visit— hence their name as "foreign" people; and captive women from them made no attempts to escape.

This evidence points to a group that held the New River district, the depressed desert valley—anciently an arm of the Gulf of California extending over most of Cahuilla territory also—that slopes from the lowest course of the Colorado northwest to the sink, nearly 300 feet below sea level, called Salton Sea, which is at irregular times dry and flooded. The people in this area, particularly in its southern or Baja California part, would naturally have an outlet toward the great river; and may have had a foothold, perhaps even their main seats, on its nearer bank. These people are here identified as probably the Kamia. Their chief residence must have been across the line in Mexican California; on the map they have been given the tract between Diegueño, Yuma, Cahuilla, and the international boundary. (Pl. 1.)

The old ownership of this stretch, which forms part of the Colorado Desert and was formerly as utterly arid as portions of it are fertile under irrigation at present, is, however, by no means established. Although likely to have been only seasonally inhabited, and in any event harboring only the slenderest population, it must nevertheless have belonged to some group. Yet what this group was remains open to some doubt. It was not the northern Diegueño, who, by the common account of themselves, the Yuma, and the Mohave, did not own beyond the eastern foot of the mountains. It was not the Cahuilla, who profess to have reached south only to Salton Sea or at most a little beyond its farther end. It may have been the Yuma, who sometimes claimed eastward to the Diegueño, and who may have visited the desert for one purpose or another, though they certainly never lived in it. In favor of this supposition is the fact that the northern Diegueño, little as they know of the Yuma, place no other group between them and themselves. On the other hand, there undoubtedly was a Kamia tribe with its distinctive dialect and a range on New River as well as on the nearer side of the lowest Colorado.

It is also possible that the owners of what is given as Kamia territory on the map and the southern Diegueño of Campo, Manzanita, and Jacumba, are the same people. These "southern Diegueño" are really southeastern and might just as correctly have been called "eastern." They call themselves Kamiai or Kamiyahi. Their situation on the map of the American State is such that they give the impression of being but the spur of a group that lives mainly in Mexican territory. From what is known of their customs, they are in fairly close affiliation with the Colorado River tribes, and under their religious influence, to nearly the same degree as the northern Diegueño cults have been shaped by the Shoshoneans beyond. All this agrees splendidly with the Yuma terminology: Kamya for the eastern Diegueño, Hakwichya for the western Diegueño together with the Shoshonean Cahuilla, to whom alone it properly refers. The application of the name Diegueño to both the southern-eastern and the northern-western group proves nothing, since it is of Spanish origin and indicative of mission affiliation, with only a secondary ethnic significance. In any event it is balanced by the similar Mohave terms for the Kamia and the Diegueño.

It may be added that the modern Diegueño of the "southern" branch voice some claim to a former ownership of the Imperial Valley. There are individuals among them who were born, or whose parents were born, in this valley, and along the eastern foot of the mountains in a latitude where these mountains belong to the northern Diegueño.

All this looks as if the southern Diegueño Kamia and the Colorado River Kamia south of the Yuma might have been a single people that stretched across the greater part of the State at its southern end and in Mexican California. The difficulty, however, is to accept as a single nation a group which at one end farmed, was divided into totemic clans, and closely resembled the Yuma in all customs, and at the opposite end of its territory was nonagricultural, nontotemic, and so similar to the northern Diegueño that it has been usually considered a part of the latter.

Enough of speculation, however. Knowledge is so scant that a certain amount of conjecture is admissible. But what is really desirable is information, which can undoubtedly still be secured, especially in Baja California. And with that statement we must leave the Kamia.

CHAPTER 50.

THE MOHAVE: CONCRETE LIFE.

Habitat and outlook, 726; appearance, 728; disposition, 729; houses, 731; agricultural and other foods, 735; pottery and basketry, 737; various utensils, 739; games, 740; totemic clans, 741; land ownership, 744; chieftainship, 745; marriage and sex, 747; names, 749; death, 749; war, 751.

HABITAT AND OUTLOOK.

With the Mohave, the third Yuman tribe to be considered, we reach for the first time a people living on a large river. The Colorado is one of the great streams of the continent, voluminous, and far longer than any within the boundaries of California. From the Mohave to its mouth its shores were occupied by a line of Yuman tribes, similar in speech, in habits, in appearance, and in disposition. This enormous Nile, flowing through narrow bottom lands bordered sharply by sandy stretches, high mesa rims, and barren mountains rising on both sides from an utterly arid desert, provides a setting wholly unlike any heretofore encountered. And its civilization is equally distinct.

The country of the Mohave is the valley which bears their name, the uppermost of a number that stretch at intervals to the sea. Above is the great defile known as Eldorado Canyon, visited now and then by Chemehuevi and Walapai, who lived above it on west and east, but unfit for habitation; and beyond comes a bend and the vast gorge that culminates in the Grand Canyon. The river civilization thus comes to a sudden upstream stop with the Mohave.

Their valley lies in what is now three States: California, Nevada, and Arizona. As the channel has flowed in recent years, most of the bottom lands lie on the eastern side; and there the bulk of the settlements were. But the land is so shut in by the high desert and so dependent on the river that it is an inevitable unit. East and west, the left bank and the right, are incidental. The stream course is a furrow that separates Arizona from California, as culturally it divides the Southwest from California; and whoever lived in the trench belonged as much, and as little, to one area as to the other.

Cottonwood Island, above Fort Mohave, was but intermittently inhabited by the Mohave. The same is true, perhaps in even greater measure, of Chemehuevi Valley below them. After the Mohave drove the Halchidhoma out of the country about Parker and below, the Chemehuevi began to drift into the valley now named after them. The Mohave probably maintained some claim to the land, although they did not use it; for they tell that they came in numbers, and by persuasion or compulsion induced the Chemehuevi to remove to Cottonwood Island at their northern limit. Here Chemehuevi and Mohave lived more or less together until about 1867, when, war breaking out between them, these Mohave outposts felt it safest to rejoin their main body below, just as certain Chemehuevi who had reoccupied Chemehuevi Valley fled from it back to the desert from which they had come. The most frequent references of the Mohave to their habitations are to the vicinity of Fort Mohave; but they lived down to the lower end of Mohave Valley, where the river enters the narrow gorge above which rise the jagged peaks known as the Needles.

For every people hitherto mentioned in this book a list of towns or villages has had some significance. When such information has not been given, ignorance has been the sole cause. The settlement is the political and social basis of life in California. The tribe, at least as a larger unit, exists hardly or not at all. The reverse is the case with the Mohave. They think in terms of themselves as a national entity, the *Hamakhava*. They think also of their land as a country, and of its numberless places. They do not think of its settlements. Where a man is born or lives is like the circumstance of a street number among ourselves, not part of the fabric of his career. The man stands in relation to the group as a whole, and this group owns a certain tract rich in associations; but the village does not enter into the scheme. In fact, the Mohave were the opposite of clannish in their inclinations. Their settlements were small, scattering, and perhaps often occupied only for short times; the people all mixed freely with one another.

With such proclivities, it is small wonder that the petty Californian feuds of locality and inherited revenge have given way among the Mohave to a military spirit, under which the tribe acted as a unit in offensive and defensive enterprise. Tribes hundreds of miles away were attacked and raided. Visits carried parties of Mohave as far as the Chumash and Yokuts. Sheer curiosity was their main motive; for the Mohave were little interested in trade. They liked to see lands; timidity did not discourage them; and they were as eager to know the manners of other peoples as they were careful to hold aloof from adopting them.

These journeyings brought with them friendships and alliances as well as enmities. The Mohave were consistently leagued with the Yuma against the Halchidhoma and Maricopa and Kohuana and Cocopa; and these belligerencies led them into hostile or amicable relations with people with whom they had but few direct contacts.

Thus the Pima and Papago, the friends of the Maricopa, became normal foes, the Yavapai and western Apache nominal friends. Against tribes of the desert and mountains the Mohave carried on few wars. Perhaps the nomads were too elusive. On the other hand, reciprocal raids into a valley thickly settled by an aggressive people thirsting for adventure and glory did not appeal to the scattered mountaineers. Thus the Chemehuevi and Mohave got along well. The Mohave constantly traversed the Chemehuevi territory that began at the western border of their own valley; and the smaller and wilder people came to be profoundly influenced by the more dominant one, as has already been recounted.

APPEARANCE.

The Mohave men are tall, long footed and limbed, large boned, and spare. The common California tendency toward obesity is rare. Their carriage is loose, slouching at times and rapid at others. They lack the graceful dignity of the Pueblo and the sedate stateliness of the Plains warrior, but are imposing to look at. In walking, they are apt to stoop and drag, but break readily into an easy trot in which they travel interminably. The women have the usual Indian inclination toward stoutness after they have borne several children, and in comparison with the men seem dumpy, but carry themselves very erect and with a pleasingly free and even gait. The color of both sexes is distinctly yellowish—as often appears in the women when they wash—but ordinarily is turned a very dark brown by dirt and exposure to the sun. (Pls. 64, 65.)

Mohave men sit with their thighs on their calves and heels, or with legs bent to one side on the ground. These are women's fashions among the Indians of the western Plains. Women at rest stretch their legs straight out, and sometimes cross their feet. This is Pueblo style, but a most indecent position for a woman among the majority of American Indians. At work, a Mohave woman tucks one leg under her, with her other knee up. This is a common female attitude in California, and convenient for certain kinds of sedentary work. When she pleases, the Mohave woman also sits with her legs folded in oriental style—the normal attitude of Navaho and Plains men. Dress may have had much influence in determining the adoption of some of these styles. Thus the "Turk position" is easily taken in the loose fiber petticoat of California, but is awkward or likely to lead to exposure in the rather long gown of unyielding buckskin worn by the eastern women. But factors other than fashion of garment have certainly been operative, particularly for men. This is one of the most interesting matters in the whole range of

PLATE 63

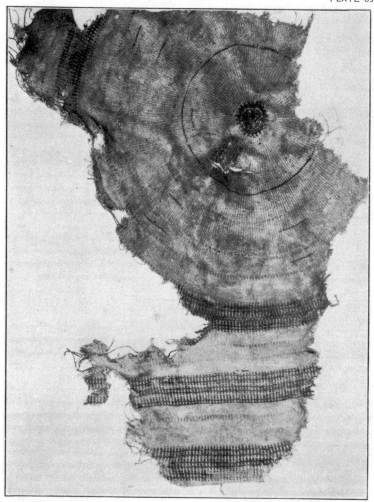

FRAGMENT OF PLAIN-TWINED, PLIABLE BAG, WITH PAT-
TERN OF HUMAN HAIR. BUENA VISTA LAKE INTER-
MENTS

PLATE 64

MOHAVE TYPES, WITH CHARACTERISTIC HAIR DRESSING.
LOWER RIGHT, A WOMAN

PLATE 65

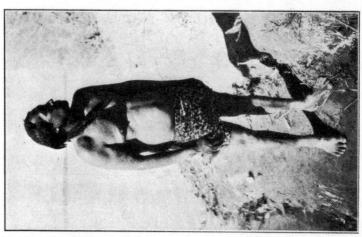

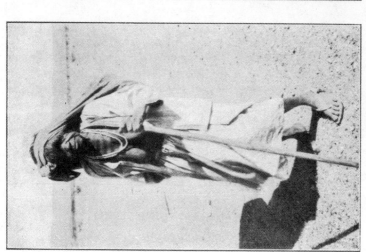

MOHAVE TYPES, SHOWING ALSO MODE OF WEARING HAIR, NOSE ROD, CANE, SANDALS, AND LOAD SLUNG
FROM HEAD

PLATE 66

Mohave

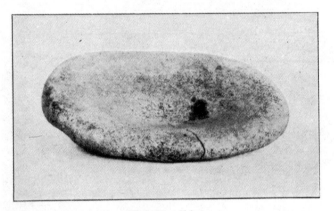

Kings River Yokuts

Cupeño

METATES AND GRINDING SLABS

customs and further knowledge for California is a great desideratum.

A very frequent Mohave gesture, apparently of embarrassment, is the quick placing of the hand over the mouth. Men especially seem addicted to this movement.

In many individuals the fingers habitually hang straight, except for a sharp bend at the farthest joint, which gives the hand a curious effect as of the legs of a crab.

Men wore, and sometimes still wear, their hair long, rolled or rather pasted into 20 or 30 ropes of about the thickness of a lead pencil. The greater the mass of these strands hanging down the back to the hip, the prouder the owner. The women trim the hair square above the eyes and let the remainder flow free, spread out over the shoulders. In mourning they cut it a little below the ears; the men clip a trifle from the ends. The hair is sometimes tied up in clay mixed with mesquite gum, to stain it black and glossy; or plain clay is allowed to dry on it in a complete casing and left for a day or two, in order to suppress parasites. As the nits survive and hatch out, the treatment requires frequent repetition.

The Mohave tattoo somewhat irregularly, although their own saying is that an untattooed person goes into a rat's hole at death instead of the proper place for spirits—as the Yahi pierce their ears with a similar purpose. Another account is that the ghosts are asked to point to the pole star, *umasakahava*, which in their new country is south; if they point northward, the rat's hole is their fate. Both sexes most commonly mark lines or rows of dots down the chin, and may add a little circle, a stripe, or a few spots on the forehead. The men are the more sparsely ornamented. Women sometimes draw a few lines across the cheeks or on the forearms. The absence of any standardized style is notable. (Fig. 46.)

The Mohave paint the face far more frequently and effectively than other California Indians. Young women in particular hardly appear at a gathering or public occasion without striking red or yellow patterns across the cheeks. Forking lines are drawn downward from the eyes, or a band passes squarely across the cheeks, and the like. The style is obviously kindred to that followed by the Seri, though not quite so inclined to fineness of execution. (Figs. 60, 61, 62.)

DISPOSITION.

The Mohave are noticeably more responsive and energetic than the other Indians of California. They are an obstinate people—amiably so, but totally unable to see anything but their own view once this has set. They are rarely sullen; although they sometimes

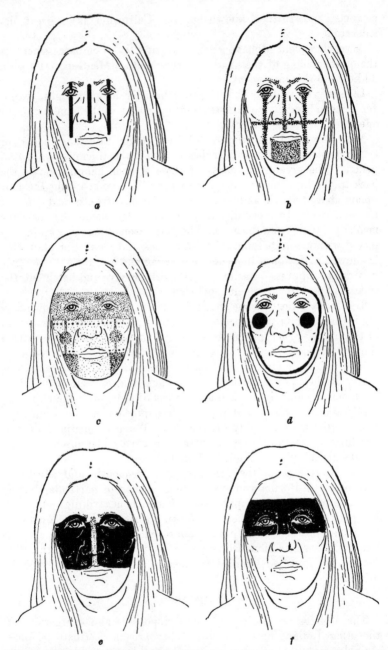

Fig. 60.—Face paints: Mohave men. *a,* Ha'avkek; *b,* "cut"; *c,* modern; *d,* for male twin; *e,* for elderly man; *f,* "lie at back of house," for old man. (Heavy and light stippling indicate red and yellow, respectively.)

sulk like children, they are more given to outbursts of temper. The women scold freely on occasion. The Californian trick of eating in a grievance is foreign to them. Ordinarily they are idle minded and therefore readily persuaded, until some prejudice is stirred. Then they become immovable, although usually without resentment. Normally they are frank, inquisitive, and inclined to be confiding. They are untidy, careless of property, and spend money freely, like eastern Indians. Only the old women evince some disposition to hoard for their funerals.

The slow, steady labor to which the Californian and the Pueblo are inclined is rarely seen among the Mohave. They either lounge in complete relaxation or plunge into sudden and strenuous activity. No physical exertion is too great for them. They make valuable laborers, except that they are rarely dependable for long periods. When they have enough, nothing can hold them to the job. In their own affairs, such as house building and farming, they often work with a veritable fury, and even when hired do not spare themselves. They eat voraciously, but endure hunger without trace of complaint. The demeanor of the men in repose has a certain reserve, as befits a people that fought for pleasure, but they unbend readily, talk volubly, and laugh freely. Jokes are greeted uproariously. All ages and sexes demonstrate their feelings openly. Young men may be seen walking with their arms around each other, fathers kiss their children irrespective of who is about, girls in love manifest their sentiment in every action. There is something very winning in the instantaneousness of the generous Mohave smile. The habitual and slow-dying distrust typical of most of the California Indians does not rest on the Mohave's mind; when he suspects, he complains or accuses. The children are remarkably free from the unconquerable shyness that most Indian youngsters, in California as elsewhere, can not shake off. They often answer even a strange white man readily. Altogether it is a nation half child, half warrior, likable in its simple spontaneity, and commanding respect with its inherent manliness—as far different from the usual California native as Frenchman and Englishman stand apart.

HOUSES.

The house has a frame of logs and poles, a thatch of the arrow weed that serves so many Mohave needs, and a covering of sand. The latter blends so gradually into the surrounding soil that it is practically impossible to give outside measurements, and the old description of the domicile as dug into a sand hill is a natural mistake. The structure has a rectangular interior, and is substantially square on a line of 20 to 25 feet. The door or front is always to the

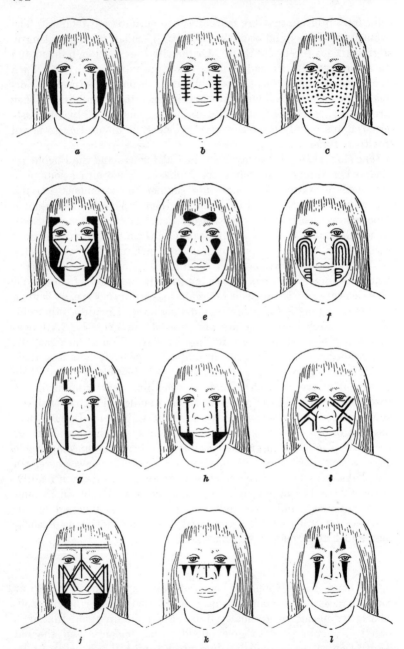

Fig. 61.—Face paints: Mohave women. *a*, "Rainbow"; *b*, "coyote teeth"; *c*, "yellow-hammer belly"; *d*, "butterfly"; *e*, "atalyka leaf"; *f*, "bent over"; *g*, *h*, hatsiratsirk; *i*, *j*, hotahpava; *k*, *l*, tatsirkatsirka. All in red or yellow.

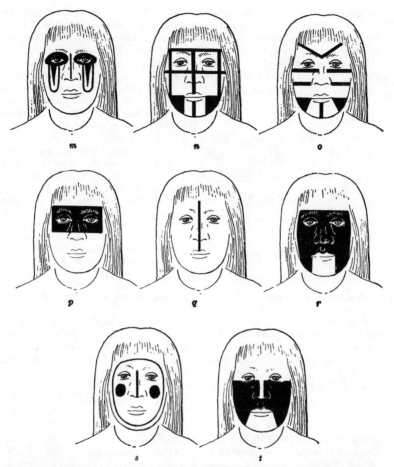

Fig. 62.—Face paints: Mohave women. *m*, "Tatsirkatsirka enclosed"; *n, o, r*, without names; *p*, "at edge of nose"; *q*, humturk; *s*, for female twin; *t*, mourning for a child. All in red or yellow except *t*, which is black.

south on account of the coldness which the frequent north wind seems to the desert dwellers to bear. (Pl. 56; Fig. 63.)

So few of the native houses of the Californians have been described accurately that the following details may not be amiss.

In the center are either four posts or two placed longitudinally, that is, in north and south line; or one; or two set transversely. The last arrangement is the commonest, but there is a name for each design. The tops of the posts are slightly hollowed, and the connecting logs laid on. The south or front wall has eight or ten posts of varying length; the back, two principal ones in the middle; the sides, about five that are still shorter. The tips of these are all connected. From the log above the center posts six or eight beams run to the back wall and an equal number forward. The latter spread into two sets of threes or fours to clear the door. From these 12 or 16 beams about 20 smaller rafters extend to each of the sides. Across these rafters sticks are laid longitudinally. The thatch in turn runs across the house. In the middle the 12 or 16 beams are directly overlaid with transverse sticks close together. In this part of the house, therefore, the sticks and the thatch run in the same direction.

The low side walls slope. About two dozen light poles are leaned against the logs that connect the five vertical posts on each side. On these leaning poles four or five long sticks are laid horizontally, and against these arrow-weed thatch is set upright, outside of which comes the banking of sand. The rear is similarly constructed. The front wall is higher, vertical, and unbanked. Sticks run across the inner as well as outer faces of its posts. In the space thus formed thatch is set and sand poured in. In the old days a mat of woven cottonwood bark closed the door at night. In front there is often a space enclosed with a windbreak of arrow weed, and almost invariably a flat shade on posts.

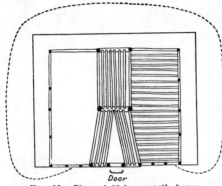

Fig. 63.—Plan of Mohave earth house.

Seen from the front, the roof is nearly level in the center, slopes about 10 degrees to the side posts, and then falls more steeply, but still at no great angle, to the ground. The profile is gently rounded, especially toward the rear, but of course terminates vertically in front. The floor is fine soft sand. (Pl. 56.)

The following are details of two houses:

Inside length to rear posts	feet	22	23
Inside length to base of rear wall	do	24	26
Inside width, side posts to side posts	do	22	24
Inside width, wall to wall base	do	24	30
Distance between 2 transversely set center posts	do		7
Width of door	do		2½
Height—center posts	do	6	6
middle of roof	do	7½	
front posts at door	do		5
at ends	do		3
back posts	do	4	4
side posts	do	3	3
door	do	6	6
Diameter—center posts	inches	10+	
door posts	do	10+	
2 middle rear posts	do	10+	
side posts	do	7–8	
log on center posts	do	12	
beams	do	5–9	
rafters	do	4–5	
Number of beams		12	16
Number of rafters		39	
Number of side posts, each side		5	5

The Mohave were without sweat houses. Prominent men put up large houses in which considerable groups of people slept. Such a house was the owner's dwelling; the others lived near by in smaller houses, but these were considered too cold for comfortable sleeping. The big houses can not be regarded as more than a sort of Mohave substitute for the sweat house, since women and children assembled there with the men—a quite un-Californian practice.

A prospective builder summoned his friends and kin to do the work, and fed them while they were busy on his behalf. His place, and that of his wife, was the corner west of the door. Other couples occupied the other corners. Girls slept along the walls, unmarried men in the center. Late in the afternoon a fire was built just inside the door. At night this was covered with sand. Smoke hung through the house, but above the heads of the reclining inmates. The myths frequently mention such houses as crowded with people.

AGRICULTURAL AND OTHER FOODS.

Mohave agriculture according to aboriginal methods began quickly to go into disuse after Americans settled among them, and it is already somewhat difficult to estimate the importance of the art to them. It may have furnished half their subsistence. The rainfall is too nominal to support any cultivated plant, and the Mohave seem to know nothing of irrigation. Annually, about May and June, the Colorado rises and floods large stretches of the bottom lands, sometimes to a distance of a mile or two. Sloughs from this overflow remain for months or through the year. The level tracts are left drenched and coated with soft mud. In this the Mohave plant; and under the fierce sun their produce shoots and ripens with marvelous rapidity. The relation of the tiller to his strip of fertile soil in the vast burning desert is therefore similar to that which obtained in primitive Egypt, and gives Mohave agriculture a character unique in native America.

Corn is planted irregularly, not in rows. The planter takes one long step more or less at random from his last hole and rams his stick into the ground for another hole. Half a dozen kernels are sunk from half a foot to a foot deep.

The wheat planter sits on the ground and makes holes at the limit of his reach a foot or two apart, and drops a number of seeds into each. This is, of course, a plant introduced by the Spaniards, but the Mohave regard it as indigenous.

Beans, pumpkins, watermelons, and cantaloupes were also planted by the Mohave. Their corn is usually white and long eared, but they distinguish blue, red, yellow, and spotted yellow and white varieties also. Beans are called white, yellow, "deer droppings" (black), and "Pleiades" (spotted). Bean-stalk fiber was a common material for cordage.

The farming implements were two: A hard, heavy staff for planting, which is nothing but the California root-digging stick somewhat enlarged and slightly flattened at the sharp end; and the cultivator, a broader piece, whose square edge is pushed flat over the ground to cut the weeds off as they sprout. The cultivator handle is usually somewhat crooked in the plane of the working edge. (Pl. 67, *a*, *b*.)

Women perhaps did most of the farm work, but the men were not averse to participating, and there may have been no formal division of labor. Even in recent years an old Mohave and his wife can frequently be seen going to their patch together—he carrying an American hoe, she preparing to pull weeds with her hands.

It is rather interesting that pottery and agriculture are definitely associated in the Mohave mind, their myths telling how the god Mastamho thought farmed food incomplete until vessels were provided to cook and eat it in. The Pueblo has little feeling of this sort. Corn is to him something so basic that it was primal; the method of causing it to flourish is his gravest concern; but he is little interested in vessels. The Mohave thinks of both as something given to him. Perhaps this sense is intensified by his situation among nations that neither farm nor bake pots.

Besides the usual native American farm products, the Mohave planted several wild herbs or grasses in their overflowed lands and gathered the seeds. These they call *akatai*, *aksamta*, *ankithi*, and *akyesa*. They are unidentified except for the last, which appears to be a species of *Rumex*.

A larger variety of seeds were collected from plants that sprang without cultivation after the recession of the river from certain tracts of the bottom lands. These include *akwava*, *kupo*, *aksama*, *hamaskwera*, *koskwaka*, and *ankika*.

The Mohave metate for corn, wheat, and beans is a rectangular block of lava on which a cylindrical muller is rubbed back and forth. It is therefore the Pueblo type of implement, except for not being boxed or set into the ground. A myth describes the metate first used by Turtle woman, in Mastamho's presence, as "rounded, not square like the metate of to-day." The narrator may have been merely thinking of a ruder implement, as would befit the time of beginnings; or it is conceivable that the native Mohave metate was of the oval Californian type, which went out of use after steel axes allowed the readier shaping of stone. (Pl. 66.)

Mesquite beans are crushed with a stone pestle in a wooden mortar, the hard seeds remaining whole. The meal is sometimes eaten raw, the seeds being shaken out of it in the hand. More commonly, water is poured on the flour to extract the sugar, and then drunk off. The dough that is left is carried to the mouth in handfuls, sucked out, and replaced, to be steeped a second time before being thrown away. Sometimes the fresh dough is patted into a huge jar-shaped cake, covered with wet sand, and baked. It comes out so hard that it has to be cracked with a stone. The seeds are spat out or swallowed whole. Mesquite screw meal is baked in the same fashion.

Fresh mesquite screw bean is " cooked " by being stored in an immense pit, perhaps 15 feet across and 4 or 5 deep, lined and covered with arrow weed. From time to time water is sprinkled on the mass. After about a month the screws turn brown and very sweet.

Mesquite of both varieties formed an important part of Mohave food. Trees are said to have been owned. In other cases a bunch of arrow weeds was hung on a tree to indicate that its yield was claimed.

Long wooden pestles were also used (Pl. 67, c)—an unknown implement in the remainder of California.

Fish were taken with seines, or driven up shallow sloughs into scoops, kwithata (Pl. 59), as large as a canoe, that were quickly lifted up. The fish of the muddy Colorado are rather soft and unpalatable to the white man, but the Mohave caught quantities and relished them. Game is very scarce in the valley, and the Mohave rarely left their country to hunt. They can have eaten meat only occasionally. They refused to touch the turtles and lizards of which the Chemehuevi and other tribes made use.

Fish are sometimes broiled on charcoal, but more often cooked into a disintegrated stew with or without corn. The tails, heads, scales, and guts are left in, only the " gall " being taken out. Such a mess is stirred and tasted with three little rods tied together in the middle, and is scooped to the mouth with the fingers. Sometimes the viscera are removed to be cooked separately.

POTTERY AND BASKETRY.

Clay is tempered with sandstone crushéd on the metate, and built up by coiling. The start of a vessel may be spiral, but its body consists of concentric rings. The paste is rolled out into a slim sausage, the length of which is roughly estimated on the vessel. It is then laid on the last coil, and any excess pinched off. It is beaten, with a light and rapid patting with a wooden paddle, against a smooth cobble held inside, and its edge finished flat by scraping between the thumb-nail and index finger. Then the next coil is added. The maker sits with the growing vessel on the thighs of her stretched legs, or with one leg flat in front of her and the other doubled under.

The paint is yellow ocher, which is put on with a little stick and burns dull red. The firing is by an open wood fire. The patterns are carelessly done and often shaky. (Pl. 68; Figs. 64, 65.)

The following are enumerated as pottery vessels:

hapurui, the water jar.

taskyena, the cook pot.

chuvava, a large cook pot, rested on three conical supports of pottery.

kam'otta, a spoon or ladle, with the handle often in the rude shape of a quail's head and hollowed to rattle. (Fig. 64.)

kayetha, a flat bowl or lipless plate. (Fig. 65.)

kakapa, an oval platter.

katela, a parcher for corn and wheat, pointed at two ends.

kayuka, an open bowl. (Fig. 64.)

The water jar is sometimes made asymmetrically and is then known as *hanemo*, "duck," from its resemblance to a swimming water bird.

kwathki seems to be the generic name for pottery.

FIG. 64.—Mohave bowl and ladle with "rain" and "fish backbone" designs.   (Cf. Pl. 68.)

Designs on vessels are named spider, rain, rainbow, fish backbone, melon markings, turtle, cottonwood leaf, coyote tooth, yellow-hammer belly, tattoo, and *hotahpam*, a style of face paint that crosses under the eye.

Mohave basketry was easily the poorest of any in California. Coiled baskets are still used in every house and their employment as drums to certain kinds of singing proves the habit to be old; but they are Chemehuevi or Maricopa trays. The Mohave made only a few flat receptacles in an irregular plain twining or open-stitch coiling (Pl. 55, *b*); fish traps or scoops in twining (Pl. 59); wicker hoods of splints for their cradles (Pl. 39, *b*); and the *kupo* carrying frame of two U-shaped sticks surrounded with thin string—a far derivation from the burden basket of California. One textile art they followed with more skill: the weaving of bags or wallets from string of bean and *akyasa* fiber, much as the Diegueño wove, it appears. At present such receptacles are made only in American yarns. Braided or woven belts with which the baby was lashed into the cradle have deteriorated similarly.

VARIOUS UTENSILS.

Now and then a stone ax made its way into the Mohave country from the Southwest, but rarely; and the implement is associated by the tribe with eastern nations. There was also no adze, and the general Californian horn wedge seems to have been unknown. Trees were not felled. If land was to be made arable, split stones were tied to handles, and with this rude tool the smaller limbs and foliage were hacked from willows. The brush was then burned about the butt to kill the tree, the stump being left standing. (Fig. 66.)

The rush raft of the Mohave was a crude affair of two bundles, with about three sticks skewered through, and some lashings of willows. The material was the flat tule, *atpilya* (probably *Typha* rush), not the round stemmed

FIG. 65.—Mohave pottery bowl. Design: "Cottonwood leaf" and "rain."

kwal'inyo (*Scirpus lacustris*). Loose tules might be laid on top. Four to six persons could be carried, those in the middle remaining dry. The balsa was pushed with a long pole. It was made for crossing the river. If the current carried it far downstream it was easier to put a new one together than to drag the old one up against the current. The men were all good swimmers. Children were some-

FIG. 66.—Mohave fire drill.

times pushed across the river in pots a yard in diameter. These vessels were made for the purpose, being too large, the Mohave say, to utilize for cooking.

Shell currency seems to have been held only in small quantity. A horse was given for half a fathom of typical Californian disk beads—a very high valuation. Most old women wore at the throat a clam shell cut into frog shape and called simply *hanye*, frog. These also were valuable. On the whole, the Mohave appear to have used shells as jewelry rather than money; in which they resembled the southwesterners. They took to imported glass beads more eagerly than most Californians. Men as well as women coiled strands of blue and white Venetian beads in thick masses around their necks; women wound them around their wrists; and donned showy shoulder capes of a network of beads. A definite style seems to have been evolved early, which made use almost wholly of the two colors mentioned; and these, it must be admitted, match pleasingly with the brown of the Mohave skin. The women's lacelike bead capes that fit snugly around the shoulders are shown in Plates 54 and 69.

GAMES.

The favored game of the Mohave was between two players, each of whom cast a long pole at a rolling hoop. The ring was thrown by the winner of the last point, and either runner was at liberty to dart his pole when he pleased. If the hoop was pierced, nothing was counted. If the ring rested on the pole with sufficient overlap that a space was visible, one point was made. Should the ring lie on the end of the pole, the score was double. If both players cast successfully, both scored. Four points won the stakes. A favorite device was to hurl one's pole between the opponent's and the hoop.

Thus the Mohave describe the game. The following record presents some discrepancies:

Two elderly men bet three dollars, as the Indians say, that is, a dollar and a half each, on a game of five points. When the score stood 2 to 1, the leader threw the tip of his pole under the ring. His opponent insisted that this was worth only 2 points, but 3 were allowed, running out the game. The players immediately bet two dollars and a half each and resumed. When the winner had scored 2 points to 3, he apparently feared to lose and quit; whereupon the new stakes of five dollars were divided in the proportion of 2 to 3.

A football race was run by two men, each with a ball of willow root.

Shinny was played with a slender curved stick and small wooden ball by "old," that is, middle aged, men, seven or eight to a side, between goal lines a third of a mile apart. Betting was public, but by individuals, the stakes being matched and deposited in pairs. The ball was put into a hole in the middle of the field, covered with soil, and trod down. Half a dozen players struck at the pit until the billet flew out. The play was fast, wild, and random, without stations or order, each contestant and many younger spectators following the ball as closely as they could. Other people stood where they pleased and stepped aside when the ball traveled toward them. Boys pointed it out in the confusion and clouds of desert dust. The striking was clean, hard, and generally successful, the aim not so good, nursing of the ball scarcely attempted. If it entered a mes-

PLATE 67

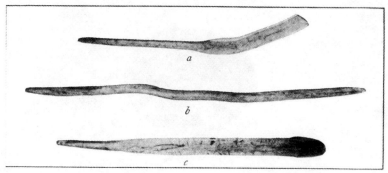

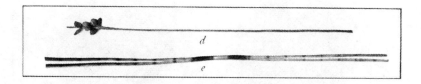

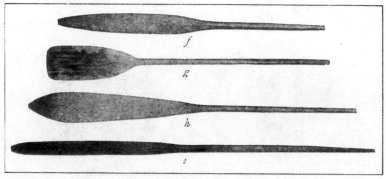

a, Mohave weedcutter; *b*, planter; *c*, wooden pestle; *d*, *e*, Pomo rattles. Paddles: *f*, *i*, Yurok;
g, Pomo; *h*, Klamath-Modoc

PLATE 68

MOHAVE POTTERY BOWLS, PATTERNED

PLATE 69

MOHAVE CREMATION

PLATE 70

YUROK WOMAN (WITH CAP) AND OLD MEN

quite thicket from which it could not be struck, it was picked out and play resumed from a pit as at the start.

The guessing game was played by four men on a side, each with one piece of cane which he hid in his hand under a mat or blanket. Pointing was at one or two of the players. An umpire stood in the middle, parceled out the twelve stick counters as they were lost, held the stakes, and threatened to burn them if the contestants quarreled too violently.

Another variety, less formal, was played between two persons, one of whom hid a bit of stick in one of four little heaps of sand. Each wrong guess lost one of the five counters from which the game was played; if the stick was found, the play was transferred.

Women played dice with four willow staves, painted in three different patterns on one side. The score has not been recorded. In the myths, boys sometimes play this game.

Women also swung the ring-and-pin. The rings were the butts of pumpkin rinds. Each ring caught counted one point, except the last one, which went for ten. When none was caught, play passed to one of the pair of opponents. A long spiral was drawn on the sand, and a mark made across this for each point, the two sides beginning at opposite ends of the line. When the tallies met, they were counted, and the victors were considered to have won the anuses of their opponents.

TOTEMIC CLANS.

The Mohave share with the other Yuman tribes of the Colorado a peculiar clan system. This comprises patrilinear, exogamous, nameless groups of totemic reference. All the women born in a clan bear an identical name, although they may in addition be known by nicknames or other epithets. These clan names are of totemic import, though they are not the word which is in common use to denote the totemic object. Thus *anya* is "sun," but the woman's clan name that "means" sun, as the Mohave say, is *Nyo'ilcha*. In a few instances there is a resemblance, as in Yuma *ave*, rattlesnake, and *Mave*, rattlesnake clan name. But in general the names appear to be archaic stems, disguised descriptions or allusions, or equivalents from other dialects. Many of the younger men and women seem to be ignorant of the totemic import of the names, and totem taboos are either lacking or slight, although the Cocopa do not kill their totem. The clans do not enter into religious activities, so far as known. In fact, the ceremonial scheme of these tribes is such that it is difficult to see how the natives could have found serious points of contact between their clan organization and cult practices if they had been so inclined. The impress which this gentile scheme makes is that it rests lightly on society and not at all on cults.

The clans are mentioned in mythology, but in a bald and formal way. At a certain point in some long myth dealing with other things a man called so and so announces or is instructed that he will take such and such a name for his daughters and his sons' female descendants. Sometimes it is added that he will settle or "take land" at a specified place. Such references can scarcely be interpreted as any strong indication of an original local basis for the clans. They seem rather to reflect the custom of the river Yumans of living in little groups of kinsmen, and therefore incidentally of clan mates, at more or less shifting sites determined by the farming fields, and scattered rather randomly through the cultivable portions of the tribal territory. At the same time it is well to remember that the "clans" of the Diegueño and southern California Shoshoneans were essentially local in native consciousness and perhaps in fact.

The known clans of the Mohave and Yuma are here listed according to their women's names and totemic implications, with the corresponding data added for several cognate tribes of Arizona and Baja California. Of these, the Kamia are the group of that name actually on the Colorado, while a series of names reported as " Maricopa from the Cocopa " have been interpreted as belonging to one of the refugee tribes formerly on the Colorado, probably the ancient " Cajuenche " or Kohuana neighbors of the Cocopa.

Nyo'ilcha, Mohave: sun, fire, deer, eagle, or beetle.

Hoalya, Mohave: moon (*haly'a*).

Mat-hachva, Mohave: wind (*mat-ha*).

Owich, Mohave: cloud.

Hipa, Mohave, Yuma, Maricopa: coyote; Maricopa also: cholla cactus.

Moha, Mohave: mountain sheep.

Siulya, Mohave: beaver.

Malyikha, Mohave: wood rat.

Kutkilya, Mohave: owl; Kohuana: yellow animal.

Motheha, Mohave: screech owl.

Masipa, Mohave: quail, possibly also coyote.

Maha, Mohave: a small bird; *Sikuma*, Yuma, Kamia: dove; Kohuana: " pigeon "; *Sakuma*, Cocopa: dove, buzzard.

Halypota, Mohave: frog; Yuma: already-done; Kohuana: a shrub.

Nyikha, Mohave: a caterpillar or worm.

Kata, Mohave: tobacco, perhaps also mescal, that is agave.

Vahadha, Mohave: tobacco.

Tilya, Mohave: mescal.

Vimaka, Mohave: bean mesquite.

Musa, Mohave: screw mesquite; *Kalsmus*, Kamia: screw mesquite; *Alymos*, Yuma: bean (?)mesquite, deer: *Kasmus*, Cocopa: beaver.

Kumadhiya, Mohave: ocatilla cactus; *Kimithi*, Maricopa: ocatilla, roadrunner.

Kwinitha, Mohave: prickly pear cactus.

Chacha, Mohave: corn or food; *Harchach*, Maricopa: white corn; Yuma: agricultural food, frog.

Waksi, Haksi, Yuma: hard earth; Kamia, undetermined; *Ksila,* Maricopa, sand.

Sinykwatl, Yuma: deer or skin; also eagle; *Sinikwus,* Kohuana: red ant; Kamia: undetermined; *Sikupas,* Yuma: red ant.

Kwaku, Maricopa: deer (Mohave: *akwaka*).

Wahas, Yuma: beaver.

Liach, Liots, Yuma: buzzard, cloud, also called "Pima" clan; Maricopa, buzzard, sun, fire; Kamia, buzzard.

Met'a, Yuma: road-runner.

Chia, Yuma: night-hawk.

Mave, Smawi', Yuma, Kohuana, Cocopa: rattlesnake (*ave*).

Estamadhun, Yuma: an insect.

Kwisku, Yuma: grasshopper, willow bark for skirt.

Sikus, Yuma, undetermined; Cocopa: salt, coyote, and two undetermined meanings.

Niu, Cocopa: deer; *Kwinis,* Kohuana: deer.

Nimi, Cocopa: wild cat.

Uru, Cocopa: night hawk (Mohave: *orro*).

Kapsas, Cocopa: frog.

Kwas, Cocopa: "Colorado river".

Kuchal, Cocopa: bark.

Wachuwal, Cocopa: undetermined.

Hutpas, Kohuana: sedge.

Salal, Kohuana: bean mesquite.

Namituch, Maricopa: bean mesquite.

Pakit, Maricopa: "buzzard."

Kunyih, Kamia: coyote, fox.

Witah, Kamia: undetermined.

Itlkamyap, Kamia: undetermined.

It is rather remarkable how divergent the lists for the several tribes are. More than two-thirds of the names are confined to a single nation. Only a sixth are found among three of the six. Not one is established among all of the tribes. The only names of any notable distribution are:

Hipa, coyote.
Sikuma, dove.
Liach, buzzard.
Mave, rattlesnake.
Sinikwus-Sikupas, red ant.
Havchacha, corn.
Kalymusa, screw mesquite.
Halypota, of variable significance.

Frequently a single name has two, three, or even five totemic implications: compare *Nyo'ilcha* at the head of the preceding list.

Analogously, the same "totem" often has entirely diverse names attached to it, sometimes perhaps within a single tribe, certainly among different tribes. For instance:

Deer: Mohave, *Nyo'ilcha;* Yuma, *Alymos;* Cocopa, *Niu;* Kohuana, *Kwinis;* Maricopa, *Kwaku.*

Coyote: Mohave, Yuma, Maricopa, *Hipa;* Cocopa, *Sikus;* Kamia, *Kunyih.*

Bean mesquite: Mohave, *Vimaka;* Yuma, *Alymos;* Kohuana, *Salal;* Maricopa, *Namituch.*

It is clear that all the agricultural Yuman tribes adhered with rather rigid uniformity to the scheme of the system, but varied its precise content freely. This is a situation of some interest, because the tendency of scholars has been to observe frequent transmission of individual elements from culture to culture, at least among primitive peoples, whereas the combinations made of these elements by individual nations have seemed much more fluctuating. In the present case the probability of diverging growths from a single source is very high.

It may be added that the indirectness of the totemic reference in this clan system finds an analogue among the Pima and Papago, whose totemic clans and moieties are also nameless, but are distinguished by their appellations for " father; " and among the Miwok, whose individual personal names connote totemic objects without expressing them.

Among the Yuma and Cocopa gray-haired women are called by their clan name with *akoi* or *wakui,* " old woman," prefixed: thus, *Akoi-hipa, Wakui-niu.* In other instances the ordinary word denoting the totem replaces the clan name: *Akoi-akwak* (deer) for *Alymos, Akoi-uru* (night-hawk) for *Chia, Wakui-panapala* (buzzard) for *Sakuma, Wakui-sih* (salt) for *Sikus.* In still other cases a third stem appears, as *Wakui-chayil* for *Kapsas* (*hanye,* frog), and *Wakui-mas* for *Kwiye* (*ihwi,* cloud). This plan is not known to be followed by the Mohave; but this people changes *Nyo'ilcha* to *Nyocha* and *Siulya* to *Kusuvilya* for a woman who has lost a child.

LAND OWNERSHIP.

Farm land was owned and could be sold for beads or other property. A brave man, the Mohave say, brought captives and spoils back from war and gave them to other men in return for tracts of land.

Quarrels of various sorts were settled by a sort of combat calculated to prevent fatalities. For instance, when the river flooded the valley, it sometimes changed the configuration of the land or washed away landmarks. A group of people might then assert the boundary of their holdings to have been at a point which their neighbors regarded as well within their own limits. A sort of pushing match, *thupirvek,* was then arranged. One man was surrounded by his friends, who tried to shove or drag him across the disputed territory, whereas their opponents struggled to carry a champion of theirs to the farthest end of the land of the aggressors. In this scuffle legs were sometimes broken and the human footballs nearly crushed and pulled to death. The stake of the contest may sometimes have been not only the stretch first in dispute but the entire arable holdings of both contestants.

If the losers were dissatisfied, they reappeared next morning at their asserted boundary, armed with willow poles a couple of inches thick and 5 or 6 feet long. Each man held a shorter stick in his left hand. The victors met them, and a stick fight, *chetmana'ak*, ensued, which might last hours. The contestants beat each other over the heads till they were weary. As they parried with their staves, no one was killed, say the Mohave, but men sometimes died afterwards, especially when they fought long on a summer's day and maggots bred in the wounds. The object of each party was to drive the other back across the disputed tract, whereupon title to it was definitely established. The dispossessed losers went to friends elsewhere and might have fields lent to them.

Such a system would have been impossible among other Californians. If these raised their hands against an opponent at all it was to kill, and the losers would scarcely have ceased to plan injury for their wrongs unless formal settlement were made.

CHIEFTAINSHIP.

The Mohave had hereditary chiefs, in the male line, whom they call *hanidhala* (from Spanish *general*); but their functions are obscure. They are much less often mentioned than the brave man or war leader, who ranked in estimation much like his counterpart among the eastern tribes of the continent, and for whom alone an anniversary mourning rite was performed; less, too, than the *kohota* or manager of entertainments, somewhat recalling the Luiseño *paha'*; and the *kwathidhe*, the "doctor" or shaman. All three of these characters acquired their prominence individually—through their dreaming, the Mohave say. Only the chief inherited—but counted for little, it would seem.

The Mohave say that when a man, instead of joining in a feast, orated while the others ate, or if he allowed his dishes, property, or house to be destroyed—presumably by those whom he had offended— he gained prestige and authority. Early travelers tell how the "chiefs" to whom they made presents promptly distributed these, keeping nothing for themselves. It is doubtful whether these accounts refer to the official hereditary chiefs or to men of influence. But it is clear that liberality and abnegation were qualities required of him who aspired to leadership.

The following narrative, which appears to relate to about 1855, illustrates the position of the *kohota* or festival chief, the nature of Mohave dances, and the attitude toward captives:

When I was a boy I saw a war party set out to help the Yuma, who had issued an invitation for a raid on the Cocopa. They killed two of the enemy and took two women captives. They returned to a place some miles south of Fort Mohave, where the entire tribe assembled. This place was among the *Mat-halya-dhoma* or northern Mohave, who already had several captives, whereas the *Kavilya-dhoma* or southern Mohave were without. The two women were brought to the *kohota* at this place, because he had asked some of his kinsmen to join the party and if captives were made to carry food and water for them and guard them so that they could be taken home to himself.

The *kohota* is a man who constantly works, builds a large house, makes dances, and provides food for all who come. When he undertakes anything, people say: " Let us help him because he works for us all." When he has nothing left, everyone contributes blankets or other property. Captives are given to him to keep. Every year he says: " Let us sing," and then the people gather and are happy.

This *kohota* sang " Pleiades." In the morning the men and the women would dance to this, facing each other. About noon they all ate. Then in the afternoon the *kohota* would call on someone who sang *Chutaha*. When the jar began to resound, the people would leave off their play or gambling and come together, the young men with feathers in their hair. Then they would dance to this, three rows of young men, one of old, and two women, until the sun had nearly set.

Then the *kohota* might say: " Let who wishes to, sing; I name no one. Let any woman sing." He would bring out his rattles. Then if women wanted to dance *Tumanpa*, they brought a rattle to a man who sang *Tumanpa*, and so for " Raven " and *Vinimulya* and *Vinimulya-hapacha*. But *Nyohaiva* is sung without rattle. The singer holds a long stick. Sometimes one other man sings with him. Many women stand about him, shoulder to shoulder, moving one foot at a time sidewise to the left, their hands hanging, the circle revolving. When the singer swings his stick, they step with their knees bent. All five of these dances may be going on at tne same time. As soon as one song is finished, another is begun; they dance fast because the sun is nearly gone, and the women sweat.

So they did this time when the captives were brought in. As it began to be dusk, they stopped, and all went to the river and washed off their paint in order that the two captives might not cause them to be sick. Having returned and dried themselves, they ate, and then began dancing again. They sang the same songs as before, and sometimes also *Chuhuecha*, or " Cane," though these are not danced to; or *Ohuera*.

And some men sang *Tudhulva*, and they gambled to that by a fire. They played that all night. I was a boy but I was there.

In the morning the *kohota* said: " Now all bathe. Then come back in two days and we will dance again."

So in two days they all assembled once more, and danced again the whole day and the whole night. In the morning they continued singing while the *kohota* took the two slaves, one in each hand, and started toward the river. Behind him came those who were singing *Tumanpa*, then the *Vinimulya-hapacha* singers. All the people followed him. When he came near the river, he ran and leaped in with the captives. Everyone plunged after him. This was to make the two Cocopa women Mohaves, so that they would not bring sickness on the people. They had waked me at daybreak to take part. Being a small boy, I did not want to jump into the water, but they compelled me.

Then the *kohota* sent the people home and took the two captives into his house. He said: " Perhaps these young women will bear children. These children will grow up half Mohave and half Cocopa, and because they belong to both tribes, there may be no more fighting."

The captives were sisters, both called *Orro*, which is a Cocopa name for women and means nighthawk in Mohave. After two or three years one of them was married and had a child. The other one did not marry. Then, after a time, the *kohota* said: "Everything is peaceable. Fighting has stopped. Let us not keep her since all tribes are friends. We will send her home." So a party of men took the unmarried girl to the Yuma, where the Cocopa met her and brought her home. Her sister remained with the Mohave and is living yet and her son is a man. She is still called Orro.

MARRIAGE AND SEX.

The Mohave are at least as loose as any California Indians, and far franker about sexual relations. Marriage is a living together at will, and divorce is separation when either is so inclined. No mention is made of any bride purchase or wedding ceremony. A woman that is notoriously unstable becomes conspicuous and is called *kama-luik*, but there seems to be no serious criticism of either men or women on the score of conduct dictated by sex feeling. The old do not exhort the young to be continent, but urge them to enjoy themselves while they may. This indiscriminateness has perhaps contributed to a higher social position, or at least greater freedom, of women among the Mohave than is usual. They sit, eat, laugh, work, and converse freely with the men, and the children display little less bashfulness. In the realm of religion, however, women are very subsidiary. They rarely join the men's singing, tell myths, or become shamans; and there is not a single song series for women.

A Mohave brought a second wife into his house, where she occupied a separate corner. The first wife was urged by her kin to be silent and put up with the unwelcome situation. After a time she left her husband for another. This one soon displayed an ugly disposition, and when angry would throw out her property or tear up her new front petticoat of bean strings. Finally she buried her food, packed up, and left, telling him to save persuasion as she would not return. They have now become old, but still do not speak. If he comes where she is, she looks away.

If two half-sisters had sons and the children of these sons married (that is, the second half-cousins) the father of the girl would say to the father of the boy: "It is not long ago that our mothers were related. You knew it. Why did you allow this?" Then he would take a horse or something from the boy's father, and the young people were permitted to remain married, not being considered relatives any longer.

Women gave birth seated. They leaned backward, but without support, and held neither rope nor stick. Another woman received the child. For a month the mother ate no salt or flesh; and, together with her husband, refrained from smoking.

Twins, *havak*, were thought to come from the sky. " We have only come to visit," they said. " Our relatives live above. Give us something and we shall stay with you for a time." They possessed clairvoyance and knowledge of supernatural things; but their " dreams " were of the sky, not of the mountain Avikwame. They must be treated alike. If one were given more of something than the other, at least in childhood, the latter became angry and went where he had come from. If one died, the other lay down and, without sickness, followed him.

The Mohave appear not to make a dance for adolescent girls: dancing is not a characteristic social form with them. The maiden is kept covered with hot sand for four nights. There is no actual pit, as among the Shoshoneans, but sand is taken from next the fire. It is likely that she is sung for, but this has not been reported. During the four days her acts are symbolical of her future. She goes about plucking leaves from arrow-weed brush—a perfectly useless labor—merely because she would forever be lazy if she remained sitting in the house. She is silent, so as not to turn gossip. If she moved her head to look about she would soon become immodest. So that she may have a clean head the remainder of her life, her mother louses her and assembles the catch in a small pot.

For 40 days the girl eats no salt, drinks only warmed liquids, and washes herself with hot water. On her next illness the period is the same; on successive occasions, 10, 8, 6, and 4 days.

The Mohave call transvestites *alyha* and hold a ceremony inducting youths into this condition. They say that a boy dreams that he is an *alyha* and then can not do otherwise. Four men who have dreamed about the ceremony are sent for, and spend the night in the house, twisting cords and gathering shredded bark for the skirt the prospective *alyha* will thereafter wear. The youth himself lies, with two women sitting by him. As they twist the cords, the men sing:

> *ihatnya vudhi* _____ roll it this way.
> *ihatnya va'ama* _____ roll it that way.

When the petticoat nears completion:

> *istum* _____ I hold it.
> *icham* _____ I place it.
> *hilyuvik* _____ it is done.
> *havirk* _____ it is finished.
> *ka'avek* _____ hear !
> *kidhauk* _____ listen !

These songs the singers dreamed when they were with the god Mastamho, and during the night they tell and sing of how they saw him ordering the first performance of this ceremony.

In the morning the two women lift the youth and take him outdoors. One of the singers puts on the skirt and dances to the river
in four stops, the youth following and imitating. Then all bathe.
Thereupon the two women give the youth the front and back pieces
of his new dress and paint his face white. After four days he is
painted again and then is an *alyha*. Such persons speak, laugh,
smile, sit, and act like women. They are lucky at gambling, say
the Mohave, but die young. It is significant that a variety of
venereal sickness which they treat is also called *alyha*.

Sometimes, but more rarely, a girl took on man's estate, among
both Yuma and Mohave, and was then known as *hwami*, and might
marry women. There was no ceremony to mark her new status.

NAMES.

The Mohave are vehement in their observance of the name taboo
of the dead, and are bashful about their names before strangers, but
readily accept and even take for themselves names of the most un-
dignified sort. A phrase that strikes as apt or novel or alludes to a
trivial incident is the basis of many names. There is not the least
shrinking from obscenity, even in such personal connection as this.
The other Californians are sufficiently shameless in their conversation on occasion, but the Mohave delight in filthy speech habitually.
Some men assume names of this character in the hope of attracting
or impressing women. These are typical men's names: Earth-
tongue, Proud-coyote, Yellow-thigh, Foreign-boy, Girl's-leg, Hawk's-
track, Doctor's-sack, Shoots-mountain-sheep, Sells-eagle, Muskmelon,
Rope, Gartersnake, Man-dies-bone-castrated-coyote.

Kweva-namaua-napaua, of which the second element means
" father's mother " and the third " father's father," is a violent insult
uttered by angry women, evidently because of its reference to ancestors normally dead. In a contrary spirit of delicacy the Mohave
referred to the father's settlement or kin as on the right, the mother's
as on the left, or designated the places from which the father's kin
sprang as *ny-amata-kothare*, and the mother's as *hanavasut*. The
indirectness of the allusion allowed these phrases to be used on certain occasions without sting.

DEATH.

The Mohave have the appalling habit of beginning their wailing
and singing some hours before an expected death. If the patient
possesses unexpected vitality, the singing may go on for two or three
days. In certain crucial cases the effect must be adverse; but the
probability is that the mourning usually commences only after the
sick person has indicated his expectation of dying, and that he is

comforted by the unrestrained solicitude and grief of the crowd of
his kinsmen and friends. General mourning after death goes on only
for a very few hours; unless a death has occurred suddenly, when
time must be allowed to assemble the relatives. A trench is scooped
out near the house, willow or cottonwood logs piled above it, the body
laid on with its head to the south, burning arrow weeds applied, and
when the fire has sunk into the pit, sand is pushed over it. There
are no cemeteries. The house and shade are immediately set on fire
with all their contents. While the pyre is blazing, the shouts and
lamentations are at their height, property is thrown into the flames,
and people even strip themselves of their garments. All relatives,
however remote, attend the cremation and weep; afterwards, only
the closest kin cry for a few days, then go about their affairs as if
nothing had happened. The loud lamentations must be extremely
exhausting. For an entire night a father may sing *Tumanpa*, or
whatever he knows, at the top of his voice for a dying son, while the
mother alternates wails with speaking aloud until her voice comes in
a whisper. An uncle shouts in jerky sentences how Mastamho made
the river, or some other myth that he has dreamed, while others seem
to " preach " in competition with him, or lament more inchoately,
and the sitting women cry *alalalai* or weep mutely. Of course grief
is not spontaneous in all, but it is expressed most unrestrainedly; the
cries that arise at the moment of death are piercing; and the quick
fierce cremation with the circle of abandoned mourners makes a scene
whose intensity is unforgettably impressive. (Pl. 69.)

For four days after a death the kin eat no salt, fish, flesh, or fat,
incense themselves with the smoke of arrow weed, and wash with
steepings of the peeled root of the same plant, in order not to fall ill.

The Mohave enact a special mourning for men with an illustrious
war record and perhaps for chiefs. This seems to be held either
immediately after cremation or some days or weeks later; but
strangely enough is called "Annual" by them in English, as if it
were an anniversary. The native name is *Nyimich*, "mourning,"
or *Hitpachk*, which seems to refer to the running in the rite, or
Nyimi-chivauk, "cry-put." The mourners, distinguished men, and
old people sit crowded close under a shade, crying and singing for
a night, or a day and a night. Almost constantly there is some old
man " preaching "—speaking on mythological subjects in loud, detached, jerky words or pressed-out phrases. This is called *nyimi-
chekwarek*, " mourning-talk." For hours 12 men run back and forth
over a cleared and dampened space south of the shade. One shouts
and directs; one holds a war club and is the leader; two carry bows
and arrows; four have sticks with loops of beads; and four others
carry sticks from which feathers dangle in pairs. Sometimes a

woman and a mounted man are stationed on each flank of the 12 runners, several of whom wear large bunches of feathers on their heads. The running back and forth is a conventionalized representation of warfare, and occasionally an imitative act may be recognized. In the morning the dead warrior's house, his property, the shade, and all the paraphernalia of the runners are burned, and the entire assemblage bathes.

The destroying of property with the dead is a subject of much concern to most Mohave, and frequently discussed. It is called *upily-m* or *ch-upily-k*. One man wants his flute laid on his breast when he is burned, another his rattle, a third his feathers. Old women with difficulty keep a horse alive on gathered mesquite in order that it may be killed and eaten at their funeral. When a man has sung for his dying or dead son. he throws away and gives him— *chupilyk*—his songs.

An old woman had saved some odds and ends of property for *chupilyk* for herself. When she sold them, she declared her intention of buying food, which would pass into her body and thus be destroyed with her. She was perhaps half humorous in her remarks, but at the same time evidently explaining to her conscience.

WAR.

War was carried on with four weapons, according to native reckoning: the unbacked bow of willow, *otisa*, a little less than a man in length; the arrow, *ipa*, of *Pluchea sericea*, the arrow-weed which serves so many uses, feathered but unforeshafted and untipped; the mallet headed club, *halyahwai*, of mesquite wood; and the *tokyeta* or straight stick club of screw mesquite wood. Shields and lances were known, but very little used. At long-range fighting, the headless arrow penetrated but a short distance, and many a warrior returned covered with wounds, the Mohave say. Their myths make some of their heroes bristle like a porcupine at the end of a battle, and speak of men dying subsequently from wounds more frequently than during a fight. The ambition of combatants was to come to close quarters, and here execution was often deadly. No man was accounted really brave who had not distinguished himself in this hand-to-hand fighting; and in surprise attacks on settlements it was the rule. A leader sometimes rushed into the opposing ranks, grasped an opponent, and threw him over his shoulders, thus at the same time shielding his own head from the foe and exposing his victim to the blows of his followers. Such struggles often ceased when one or two had been slain and their heads secured as trophies to be scalped at leisure; but at other times the mêlée became general and losses were heavy. The straight club was for breaking heads; the mallet was thrust upward endwise to crush in an opponent's face after his long hair had been seized with the free hand. This style of fighting was not confined to ambuscades and desperate resistances of those who had been trapped, but sometimes marked the termination of an open combat. The Mohave prized courage above all other virtues, and it can not be denied them.

Brave men dreamed especially of the morning star and of certain hawks.

When war parties went out, each man carried a gourd of water and a gourd of ground wheat which furnished his sole subsistence for 15 days. Travelers professed to journey four days without any food. Horses were rarely used in war or travel, in fact seem to have been kept chiefly for food and show. The Mohave move across the country in a trot that carries them over long distances rapidly. They seem not inferior to the southwestern and Sonora Indians in this ability. Bits of *ihore* willow were often chewed to keep the mouth moist. If hail or showers threatened, the bow was sometimes cased to protect the string. In battle and at other times a belt was worn; under the back of this, arrows were thrust.

Triumphal scalps consisted of the entire skin of the head except a triangle consisting of nose, mouth, chin, and throat; and with their long locks they must have made magnificent trophies. They were celebrated over in the *Yakatha'alya*. The scalp was put on a pole set up in an open field or playground, *mat'ara*. Near by was a shade, under which the old people sat, the women calling *pilelelelele*. Young men and women painted their hair white and danced for four days and nights. The songs were from any of the standard series, irrespective of their content. After each period of dancing, the youths and girls bathed and smoked themselves over a fire of human dung to escape sickness. The celebration was directed by the *kohota*, and was held near his house. He alone could touch the scalp, and might keep it for another dance a year later; but even he had to incense himself eight times each of the four days.

A constant object of Mohave war parties was the capture of girls or young women. Other prisoners were not taken. The Mohave speak of these captives as "slaves," but the word by which they were designated, *ahwe*, means only "strangers." They were not violated; in fact, a ceremony had to be made over them else they would bring sickness into the land; and even after this purification they seem more generally not to have been married. They were given work, but not often abused, except under suspicion of trying to escape. In fact, their usual treatment appears to have been rather kindly, and they were sometimes assigned seed and a patch of field for their personal subsistence. The economic life was far too simple to allow of such captives being seriously exploited, and they needed constant watching to keep; yet the Mohave were sufficiently intent to hold them to even purchase the captives of other tribes. Their curious attitude in the matter is distinctly southwestern.

The last great fight of the Mohave occurred in 1857 or 1858, a short time after their successful raid against the Cocopa, the celebration of which has been described. The same five leaders were at the head of this more disastrous expedition, which was directed against their hereditary foe, the Maricopa. The Mohave, in a party whose numbers are not exactly known but estimated by themselves at about 200, were joined at Avi-kwa-hasala by 82 Yuma and a considerable body of Yavapai and a contingent from a more remote tribe whom the Mohave call *Yavapaya-hwacha*, "traveling" or "nomadic Yavapai," and the description of whose appearance and manners exactly fits the Apache. The Maricopa summoned the Hatpa or Pima, "a large tribe of many villages," as the Mohave found to their cost. The battle took place at Avi-vava, in an open plain. The Apache fought fiercely for a time but fled when things turned against them, and escaped without a fatality. The Yavapai followed but lost seven. The majority of warriors of these tribes were probably mounted, whereas the river nations fought on foot. A part of the Mohave and all the Yuma were surrounded and exterminated after a most determined hand-to-hand fight. Sixty Mohave fell and 80 of the 82 Yuma—Humara-va'acha and Kwasanya being the only survivors of the latter. The Yuma refused to flee and stood in a dense mass. When the foe charged, they attempted to grasp and drag him into their body, where he was hacked to pieces with great knives.

It is this style of fighting, based on a readiness to clinch with the enemy in mortal issue, that was characteristic of the Yuman river tribes, as well as the Pima, and that allowed the latter people, quiet farmers as they were, to more than hold their own against the untiringly aggressive but unstable Apache. The same quality of fortitude has found notable expression among another agricultural tribe, the Yaqui of Sonora.

The Mohave reckon that a war party returning from an attack on the Maricopa sleeps one night on Maricopa soil, five in Yavapai territory, one among the Walapai, and on the eighth evening reaches the foot of Mohave Valley. The distance is 150 miles by air, considerably more over the ground, and most of the country totally desert.

CHAPTER 51.

THE MOHAVE: DREAM LIFE.

DREAMING.

The Mohave adhere to a belief in dreams as the basis of everything in life, with an insistence equaled only by the Yurok devotion to the pursuit of wealth. Not only all shamanistic power but most myths and songs, bravery and fortune in war, success with women or in gaming, every special ability, are dreamed. Knowledge is not a thing to be learned, the Mohave declare, but to be acquired by each man according to his dreams. For "luck" they say *sumach ahot*, "good dreaming," and "ill starred" is "bad dreams." Nor is this a dreaming by men so much as by unconscious infants in their mothers or even earlier, when their *matkwesa*, their shadows, stood at Avikwame or played at Aha'av'ulypo. "I was there, I saw him," a myth teller says of his hero, or of the death of the god Matavilya; and each shaman insists that he himself received his powers from Mastamho at the beginning of the world. So deep are these convictions, especially as old age comes on, that most Mohave can no longer distinguish between what they have received from other men and what is their own inward experience. They learn, indeed, as much as other people; but since learning seems an almost valueless nothing, they dream over, or believe they have first dreamed, the things which they in common with every Mohave know. It is a strange attitude, and one that can grow only out of a remarkable civilization.

There is, too, an amazing timelessness in these beliefs, which finds reflection in every myth. The precise time of day or night of each trivial supernatural event is specified, but the briefest moments suffice for the growth from boyhood to adult age, for the transformation from person to animal, for the making of a mountain or the ordering of an everlasting institution. Just so a Mohave can not tell a story or a dream without naming the exact spot at which each character journeyed or slept or stood or looked about; but four steps bring the god to the center of the earth or the source of the river, and his arms reach to the edges of the sky.

Dreams, then, are the foundation of Mohave life; and dreams throughout are cast in mythological mold. There is no people whose activities are more shaped by this psychic state, or what they believe to be such, and none whose civilization is so completely, so deliberately, reflected in their myths.

SONG SERIES.

Public ceremonies or rituals as they occur among almost all native Americans can not be said to be practiced by the Mohave. Even dances are little developed among them, being little more than an occasional addition to certain cycles of familiar songs. These cycles or series number about 30, each designated by a name. The songs in each are comparatively uniform, in fact little more than variations on a single theme; and although no two of the 100 or 200 songs of one series are identical, the Mohave need hear only a few bars of any song to recognize its kind. All the cycles have their songs strung on a thread of myth, of which the singer is conscious, although practically nothing of the story appears in the brief, stylistically chosen, and distorted words of the songs. Sometimes a night is spent by a singer entertaining a houseful of people with alternate recital and singing; but such occasions seem not to have been common. Many singers declare that they have never told their whole tale through and sung their songs from beginning to end at one sitting. It is in accord with this statement that some men appear to know the whole of a song cycle but only parts of its myth; and that to the public at large all the songs are more or less familiar, but the stories much less known.

The singers generally state that they have dreamed the myth and cycle; sometimes admit that they have learned them from listening to older relatives; and occasionally declare that they first learned them in part and then dreamed the whole. One or more of an old man's sons or brothers or brothers' sons usually sing the same cycles; others have dreamed a different one. Some men, and they are not a few, profess to know, and sing and tell, three or four series. The same cycle is often sung quite differently by men not connected in blood or by personal association, and the story appears to vary to a nearly equal degree.

At funerals, and in case of an anticipated death for many hours before, mourning consists largely of singing from these cycles. A dying man's kin know his songs and sing them; for a man not given

to singing, or a woman, or a child, the chief mourners sing from
their own cycles. The Mohave appear to be aware, and tell readily,
what songs will be sung at the funeral of any person with whom
they are well acquainted. As the same songs are substantially the
only ones which they use for pleasure, this definite association
with death seems strange; but the content, or rather implication, of
all of them is so mythological, and at the same time so vague and
so conventionalized according to familiar patterns, that any song is
intrinsically about equally suitable for any occasion. A singer evidently does not think of the reference or lack of reference of his song
to the funeral or the celebration which is going on at the moment.
Music is proper, and he sings what he knows. The mythology that
is touched upon is one of the materials of which his fabric is made,
and nothing more. When a man has sung for his dead son, he
breaks the rattle and declares that he has thrown his song away;
but after a time his association of grief vanishes, and when next
he sings, it is from the same series. He certainly would recur to
it at the next death.

About a third of the cycles are said by the Mohave to belong to
shamans and to serve the curing of particular sicknesses. These
seem to be regarded with some disfavor and to be little used on other
occasions; but all that is known of them shows them to be nearly the
same as the nonshamanistic cycles, and to be based on myths of
the identical type. The remainder are variously classified, according
to the proper instrument that accompanies the singing, whether or
not they can be danced to, whether the tale contains episodes of
war, and so on. *Hæcha* and *Chutaha*, for instance, are sung chiefly
as an occasion for dancing. But again, neither their songs nor story
appear to present any marked peculiarities.

The myths are enormously long, and almost invariably relate the
journey of either a single person, or of a pair of brothers with or
without a following, beginning with their coming into existence and
ending with their transformation into an animal or a landmark.
This journey, which is sometimes described as occupying two or
three days, but is really a timeless life history of the hero, is given
with the greatest detail of itinerary; but incidents of true narrative
interest are few, often irrelevant to the main thread of the story,
and usually can be found in very similar form in entirely distinct
cycles. But each locality reached, whether on the river, in the
desert, or among distant mountains, is named, and its features are
frequently described. All that happens, however, at most of these
stops is that the hero thinks of something that he has left behind
or that will happen, marvels at the appearance of a rock, sees a
badger, catches a wood rat, has night come on and watches the stars,

or suddenly, and in the same vein, plots the death of his brother and companion. As a story the whole is meaningless. In fact, the narrator is sometimes guilty of gross inconsistencies as he goes along, and when asked to resummarize his tale, usually outlines it altered. The plot is evidently a framework on which episodes of ornamental significance can be hung.

We are thus face to face with a style of literature which is as frankly decorative as a patterned textile. The pattern is far from random; but it is its color and intricacy, its fineness or splendor, that have meaning, not the action told by its figures; and as a simple but religious people don the same garment for festivity or worship, for dress or interment, provided only it is gorgeously pleasing enough, so the Mohave weave their many myths in one ornamental style and sing them on every occasion that calls for music. Something of this quality has already been found in the tales of the Gabrielino and chants of the Luiseño. But the Mohave are perhaps more single-minded, more extreme and less conscious, and therefore more expert, in their national manner.

The same with the songs. As a narrator comes to each spot in his story, he sings so many songs. If, after his conclusion, he is asked to repeat the songs that belong to a certain place, he may sing four instead of six, and insist that there were no more. He is truthful: comparison shows that he is now singing other variations of his fundamental theme; and the words are likely to be different. What he has in mind is clearly only the theme, certain manners of varying it, a certain stock of words to be fitted to the melody. This might be anticipated. It would be impossible for ordinary men to remember definitely the sequence and the precise minor shadings of the varying rhythms and melodic embellishments of 150 songs all cast in the same mold. The gifted individual might do this; but it does not attract him. In short, the skeleton of the plot, its geography, the basic tune and the kind and scope of its variations, are held somewhat plastically in mind; everything else is more or less improvised, with frequent recourse to remembrances of other singers and even diverse series.

Some examples of songs will illustrate:

Tumanpa-vanyume:

Words of song.	Mohave.	English.
tiyakayami	tayamk	move
kachaik	hacha	Pleiades
hayangamanui varam	(=kiyuk)	(see!)

Goose:

nahaiyamim	nyahaim-	At Nyahaim-
kuvayanghim	kuvara	kuvara
tinyamauch	tinyam	night
kwidhauvangai	kuvidhauk	have

Another:

himangauch	*iamk*	go
tawimangai	*matawemk*	travel to
inyamaut	*iny-amata*	my land
hangaii.		

Turtle:

kwinyavai	At Hakwinyava
kutinyam hakwinyk	dark imagine (make a dark place—a house—by thinking)
havasu	blue

The same:

hinyora	is marked
hiama (for *himata*)	her body (the turtle's)
akwatha	yellow

Nyohaiva:

amatuanga	at Amataya'ama
sumakwanga	dream
sumakahuwam	dream

Raven:

ahnalya	gourd-rattle
oalya	I show
viv'aum	standing

The following song is:

ahnalya	gourd-rattle
idhauk	I hold
amaim ichiak	upward raise it
viv'aum	standing

And the one after:

idhauk	I hold it
akanavek	I tell of it
viv'aum	standing
achidhumk	I look hither
achikavak	I look thither
viv'aum	standing

The next song, the first of the following group:

tinyam-kalchieska	the night bat
himan kuyamk	rising flies
akanavek	I tell it
sivarek	I sing it

Another Raven song:

ahpe	metate
hamuchye	muller
tawam	grinding
tadhi (*cha*) *tawam*	corn grinding

The first song of this cycle:

humik	Now both
pi'ipaik	being persons (*i. e.*, alive)
nakwidhauk	we sit here

And the last:

matahaik (for *mat-hak*)	the wind
ikwerevik	whirls

It is clear that very little of the plot gets into the song: insufficient to render it intelligible to those who have not learned or heard the story; although the words themselves may be readily recognizable.

THE SEVERAL SERIES: TUMANPA TYPE.

Tumanpa comes in three varieties: *Tumanpa akyulya*, long; *Tumanpa uta'uta*, *atatuana*, *taravika*, or *halyadhompa*, short, odd, or crooked; and *Tumanpa Vanyume*, of the Vanyume or Serrano of Mohave River. The first two differ in the length of their songs. The myth is the same and takes, with the songs, a night to go through. The story begins at Aha'av'ulypo at the death of Matavilya and then relates the rather eventless journey of an old man and woman, brother and sister, first north to Okalihu, then south along the river past Bill Williams Fork, then eastward, until at Chimusam-kuchoiva, near Aubrey in Arizona, the two marry and turn into rock. Another version takes them first into the Providence Mountains west of Aha'av'ulypo, omits the marriage, but ends at the same locality. There are practically no events except the journey itself. Instead, the things which the Tumanpa see, their thoughts about them and names for them, are entered into at length: a battle, scalping, the newly made river, driftwood, rats and other animals, the constellations, and so on indefinitely and no doubt differently in the mouth of each reciter.

Tumanpa Vanyume has an obscure history. Some Mohave say that it was learned by them from Tavaskan, a chief at Tejon. This would make him a Kitanemuk, but this dialect and Vanyume are both Serrano and not very different. Others declare that the songs were learned from certain Mohave-speaking relatives of Tavaskan and are therefore in Mohave, although the myth is told in the Vanyume language and is unintelligible; much as the Cocopa sing another variety of the same cycle, *Tumanpa ahwe*, "foreign Tumanpa," in words intelligible to the Mohave and believed by them to be in their own speech, whereas they can not understand the accompanying story. Cocopa is Yuman speech, and it may well be that the phrases which occur over and over in all Yuman songs are sufficiently similar to be recognizable; but Serrano is a Shoshonean language. In any event the *Tumanpa Vanyume* songs sung by the Mohave have Mohave words; and they agree that the inevitable journey narrated in the story begins at Aha'av'ulypo, progresses to Matavilya-vova near Barstow, and ends at Aviveskwikaveik, south of Boundary Cone at the rim of Mohave Valley. Barstow is Vanyume territory, and possibly that is all that this tribe has to do with the cycle.

Vinimulya and *Vinimulya-hapacha*—the first is also called *Vinimulya-tahanna*, "Vinimulya indeed "—are stories of fighting. They are often coupled with *Tumanpa*, " Raven," and *Nyohaiva* as a group of series that are sung at celebrations, even the women participating, and men and women dancing. These cycles tell of war, lend themselves to play, and are free from any suspicion of shamanistic powers in the Mohave mind.

Vinimulya-hapacha lasts from near sunset to the middle of the following afternoon. One version begins at "Gourd mountain" in Chemehuevi or other Shoshonean territory, 200 or 300 miles northwest of Avikwame; comes into Mohave Valley; and ends "at" Aviwatha (New York Mountains), Savetpilya (Charleston Peak), Harrakarraka, and Komota, four widely separated places belonging to the Chemehuevi.

Another account makes the hero Umas-kwichipacha, a Mohave, leave his home, Aha-kwa'a'i, in Mohave Valley and settle for a year with his people in the Providence Mountains, historic Chemehuevi territory. On his impending return, the people in Mohave Valley crediting him with warlike intent, he goes first past Hatalompa far downstream to Aha-kwatpava below Ehrenberg, then turns back and after a number of days' marches reaches Kwaparveta at the lower end of the valley. The residents there flee up the valley and Umas-kwichipacha with all his followers, men, women, and children, pursues, until he reaches his old home Aha-kwa'a'i. There he gathers booty and settles. His daughter Ilya-owich-maikohwera, angered at his suggestion that she take a husband, runs off to the Walapai for a year. On her return, Umas-kwichipacha starts up the valley, the residents fleeing before him under the leadership of his younger brother Savilyuvava to Sokwilya-hihu near Fort Mohave. There they make a stand, Savilyuvava is killed and scalped, his daughter made captive, and his people driven across the river. Next the hero attacks the Ipa'ahma, "quail people," who also flee across the river and join the defeated party of Savilyuvava at Avi-kutaparva, a few miles above. There they and Umas-kwichipacha defy and revile each other across the river, mentioning each other's kin. Then he returns to the Providence Mountains, where one of his people, Umas-elyithe, dies from wounds received in the battle.

This is clearly a "clan legend," though of the peculiar form favored by the Mohave. While the narrator does not regard it necessary to mention the fact in his story, he thinks of all Umaskwichipacha's people—as well as his brother's—as having daughters named Owich.

Akaka, "Raven," tells of the birth from the ground, where Matavilya's house was burned after his death at Aha'av'ulypo, of the two raven brothers, Humar-kwidhe and Humar-hanga. They move toward the door and sing of their toys, buzzers of cane; then, that there will be war; then face and reach out in the four directions and thereby obtain gourd rattles. Then they sing of the bat of night, Orion and the Pleiades, hostile tribes in the south, the dust of an approaching war party, the battle at dawn, captive women, scalped foes, the return journey northward past Bill Williams Fork, announcement of victory, gathering of the people, and the dance of celebration. They continue singing, telling of the birds to be heard before dawn, of food in the grinding, of people gathering to play at

Miakwa'orva. Now they move nearer the door, are able to stand and walk, and tell of their bodies and what those who dream of them will sing. They go outside the door, wondering what their shape will be and where they shall go, and take new names. Feathers begin to grow on them and they commence to fly. It dawns, and the older brother announces that he will follow the darkness as it passes from east to west, and go southwestward to live, as the crow, with the Kamia. The younger takes the name Tinyam-hatmowaipha, " dusky night," will be the raven, and stay in the Mohave land. The wind puffs and they soar off with it.

This is a curious tale within a tale, if it can be called a story at all. The heroes do nothing but move 30 feet, sing all night, and disappear at daybreak. What they sing of is precisely what any Mohave would be likely to sing of if he sat up. The story is thus but a pallid reflection of the conventional subjects of Mohave singing. The version outlined comprises some 186 songs in about 32 groups.

Nyohaiva differs from those that precede in being sung without gourd rattle accompaniment. The singer stands leaning on a stick. The tale is one of war.

Nyohaiva, the insect called *yanathakwa'ataya*, was a woman who grew out of the ground at Miakwa'orva, near the northern end of Mohave Valley. She moved southward, went east from opposite Needles into the mountains, gave a bow and knife to Hamatholaviya that the Walapai might live by hunting, returned to the river, leaped far down, accepted a new name, Ath'inkumedhi, from Nyahunemkwayava, but rejected several men who claimed her as sister. At Akwaka-hava, somewhere in the old Halchidhoma country, she was offered food and plotted against by Kimkusuma, Ochouta, and their two brothers, who wished to eat her. She found her relatives' bones, beat the people of Akwaka-hava in a contest for them, and defied them to war. She went downstream to Avi-haly'a and Avenyava and prepared the people for war. They assembled, and she appointed three leaders besides herself. On the way up they met her brother, on whom horns were growing, and she sent him to the east to become a mountain sheep. As the party approached Akwaka-hava, Nyohaiva put the foe to sleep with a magic ball, entered the house with her three companions, carried off the sleeping Ochouta, and decapitated him with her thumb-nail. She took the head northward to Amata-ya'ama, near Parker, still in old Halchidhoma territory, where four *alyha* men-women lived, and made the scalp dance. Ochouta's skull she threw far south, where it became the rock Avi-melyakyeta at Picacho near Yuma. Then she herself turned into a black rock near Amata-ya'ama.

One narrator sang 33 groups of from 1 to 5 songs, 107 in all, in reference to the myth outlined.

" SALT " TYPE.

" Salt," " Deer," and " Turtle " are sometimes mentioned with " Tumanpa short " as sung indoors during the long winter nights, apparently in contrast to " Tumanpa long," the two *Vinimulya*,

"Raven," and *Nyohaiva*, which lent themselves to outdoor dancing when the people gathered for amusement. All the singings of the present group except "Turtle," which uses no rattle, were also danced to, but only on the limited scale which a crowded house allowed. Thus in "Deer," women accompanied the singer, and a few men danced. In "Salt," three men stood by the singer facing four women inside the door, and the two lines danced four steps forward and back. The singer might make a knot in a string of his own length as he finished each song.

"Salt," *Ath'i*, uses the rattle. One version begins at Aha'av'ulypo and ends at Yava'avi-ath'i, near Daggett, in Vanyume country. Another, whose 25 groups of 115 songs take a night and a day to traverse, tells of four mountain-sheep brothers who journeyed from Aha'av'ulypo, after Matavilya's death, eastward and then north through the Walapai country to Ati'siara, where the two oldest sank into the ground and blew back their brothers, who wished to follow them. The younger brothers went north, then west, crossed the course of the future river at Ukaliho, passed the Providence Mountains, and reached Hayakwiranya-mat'ara, east of Mojave station in Kawaiisu or Vanyume land. On the way they saw and talked or disputed about their tears, their powers and future, several insects, rats, birds, and tobacco plants, meteors and constellations, and a lake which they took to be the sea. Then they turned southeastward across the desert, and finally at Himekuvauva, a day's journey west of Parker, their tears turned into salt and they into stone. The Chemehuevi now gather salt there, the Mohave say, and sing what they have dreamed about Salt, beginning at the point where the Mohave leave off.

Akwaka, "Deer," is sung to the gourd rattle. It seems to be of no great length, so that it can be completed within a night. Most of the songs are those of the deer, but the last of the cycle are put in the mouths of the true heroes of the myth, Numeta the older brother and Hatakulya the younger. These seem to be the mountain lion and the jaguar; wild cat is *nume*. The Mohave say that Numeta's tail stands up, Hatakulya's hangs.

When Matavilya died, the two feline brothers sank into the ground at Aha'av'ulypo, emerged to the north at Hatakulya-nika, sank in again, and reappeared far west at Avi-kwinyehore, beyond San Bernardino. There they made two deer of clay, cleansed them by rain, and thought of the bow and hunting of the eastern mountain tribes. The deer stood and looked at the earth, sun, sky, and coming of night, and then journeyed eastward across the San Bernardino Range, through the Mohave Desert, past the New York Mountains and Avikwame, across the Colorado River at Idho-kuva'ira and Karaerva near Fort Mohave, by the foot of Boundary Cone, south, then up by Aha-kuvilya wash, and east to Amata-kwe-hoalya, "pine land," the Walapai Mountains. Their experiences are of the sort conventional in Mohave song myths; they find grass, see the morning star, swim with difficulty across the river, meet antelopes and wild cats.

From the Walapai Mountains a path led eastward which Numeta and Hatakulya had made for them. The female believed the tracks to be left from the beginning of the world, but the male knew that his makers were waiting for him and that disaster portended: he had "dreamed badly." Where the trail stopped, Numeta and Hatakulya were in wait: the older unskillfully made a noise with his bow, but the younger shot and wounded the male deer, which ran eastward and died at Amata'-ahwata-kuchinakwa. The brothers followed, so that the Walapai and Yavapai of that country might know how to hunt, found the dead body, but quarreled about its division. Numeta went back to the Walapai Mountains; Hatakulya, taking only the deer's heart, to Ahta-kwatmenva, east of Kingman, also in Walapai country. The female deer went on to Avi-melyahweke, mountains also in Arizona, but far south, opposite Parker. Such is the myth: the songs begin only at the New York Mountains, Aviwatha, and end at Amata'-ahwata-kuchinakwa. The last song is:

kwora'aka'o'ewich	old man (brother)
achwodhavek	divide
himata	its body
hikwiva	its horns
chathkwilva	skin
kosmava	sinews

Kapeta, "Turtle," is sung to the beating of a basket with a rod. This person was born last in the great house of Mastamho on Avikwame. She came into existence on the west side of the house, hence the Chemehuevi, who live in that direction, eat turtle. The singing seems to be thought to begin at Aha-kwi'-ihore, near the New York Mountains. The story progresses through the various mountains west of the river belonging to the Chemehuevi. Then it tells how Turtle went east to Hakwinyava, in Pima land, and built herself a house.

CHUHUECHA TYPE.

Chuhuecha, *Ohwera*, *Ahta*, and *Satukhota* are also classed by the Mohave as good singings because those who know them do not become shamans in old age.

The heroes of *Chuhuecha* are the two brothers called *Hayunye*, an insect, perhaps the cricket, that is said to sing *Chuhuecha* now as it chirps. A record obtained includes 169 songs in 83 groups. The singer begins in the evening to beat his basket with a bundle of stems and tells of Aha'av'ulypo and the sickness and funeral of Matavilya. By the middle of the night his story is at Analya-katha, northwest of the Providence Mountains, in Chemehuevi land; in the morning at Kwiya-selya'aya, where the river flows through Chemehuevi Valley. In the evening he begins again, but sings only a short time and ends his tale at the sea—the Gulf of California, in Papago land. At first the two brothers' experience are of the usual insignificant and descriptive kind. Later in the story, the elder wins the younger at gambling and maltreats him. From their house at Avi-melyahweke in Arizona the younger goes far down river and gets a wife among the Alakwisa, then kills much game, wins his brother's body at dice, kills him, and throws his corpse south to grow as cane. Then he turns to stone. His wife goes far east to the Pima country, and bears a miraculous boy, who grows up in four days, journeys to the sea, and turns into low cane. His mother follows and becomes the shore bird *minturisturisa* (the snipe?). Where the plot is nomi-nal, the songs are numerous; as the story becomes humanly interest-ing, the songs are few and hurried. *Chuhuecha* is not danced to.

Ohwera has the eagle as its hero, and revolves at least in part about the New York Mountains and the Chemehuevi country north-west of the Mohave. The singer strikes together two bundles of stems. A sort of dance can accompany the singing. Six men and two women kneel on one leg, then stamp the forward foot slightly to each beat of the music.

Ahta, or "Cane," also called "tall cane," *Ahta'-amalya'e*, is a long story, with more plot than most cycles. The singer strikes a double beat on a Chemehuevi basket with a stick. There is no dancing.

Satukhota has much the same plot as the Diegueño story of *Kuya-homar*, but the Mohave know nothing of this, and connect their series with a Maricopa version called *Satukhota*. Its geographical setting indicates that they are right. The story is said to begin at Aha-kutot-namomampa near the Bill Williams Fork of the Colo-rado. Kwa'akuya-inyohava, "west old woman," surviving alone after a flood, gives birth to two boys, Para'aka and Pa'ahana, who grow up, take cane, make flutes, and attract the two far-away daugh-ters of Masayava-kunauva, who lives at Koakamata, near Maricopa Wells. They marry the girls, go off with them, and are killed by their wives' kin in the Papago country, but are avenged by their son Kwiya-humar. *Satukhota* and "Cane" appear to have much plot in common. The *Satukhota* singer smites his palm against his breast.

"PLEIADES" TYPE.

Hacha or "Pleiades," and *Chutaha*, which refers to the long-billed wading bird *minsakulita*, stand apart from all others in being pri-marily dance singings, although the Mohave list them indiscrimi-nately with the others. There is some justification for this attitude because there are long myths for both, beginning at Aha'av'ulypo. There are only two Pleiades songs and two *Chutaha*, these being sung over and over for hours. There seems to be no instrument of percussion used in the former. For *Chutaha*, a trench perhaps 4 feet long and a few inches wide is scooped out with the foot and sprinkled to compact its walls. At one end a tray-shaped Cheme-huevi basket is laid and beaten; at the other, a large pot is set as a resonance chamber. The dances, which are made at least primarily for the fun of them, are conducted as follows:

The Pleiades singer stands under a shade with his back to the sun. Behind him young men stand abreast, and behind these, their elders. They wear feather-hung rabbit skin ropes over their shoulders. Facing the singer are a row of girls and one of older women. All sing with him for a time. Then he ceases, but they continue to dance. They bend and raise the body, make a long stride forward with the right knee elevated, bend again, and step back. As the men step backward, the women step forward, and vice versa.

In *Chutaha*, when the basket is struck with the palm, the jar gives out a deep booming, and the people assemble. Abreast with the singer is a kneeling line of elderly men facing east; behind him, two women selected for their loud voices, their bodies painted red, their hair white; in front, looking toward the sun, sit three rows of younger men. They wear tufts of white heron or crane feathers on their heads, or strings of these feathers down their backs. A passage is left through their ranks. Down this path runs an old man, one arm raised behind him, the other pointing forward and down. He shouts: " Hu! once, once, once," the drummer smites his basket, and all clap hands. Again the runner comes, but calls: " Twice, twice, twice (*haviktem*)," and as all answer " Yes," and clap again, the drummer and singer begin. Soon the singer raises his hand and the row of old men arises. Each one holds a stick of his own length and merely nods his head to the music. Again the singer signals, and the three rows of young men, 40 or 50 in number, kneel, and the first rank stands and sings. One of them raises his arms and the second row rises and joins in the song; and then the third on signal from the second. Finally the two women sing, their shrill voices rising above the great chorus. The young men's dancing is a slight flexing of the knees, the arms hanging slack. As the leader in the middle of each row raises his hand, they drop farther, perhaps a foot each time. The dance is continued until everyone is tired. It is very clear that the Mohave are not dance specialists. Unison mass effect makes up to them for variety and meaning of movement.

It is doubtful whether either Pleiades or *Chutaha* is sung at funerals. Their four songs are known to every one, but their public execution seems to be left to the dance or play director, the *kohota*.

VARIOUS SERIES.

Nyavadhoka, *Halykwesa*, *Ohulya*, and *Kamtoska* are little known. The first has its myth begin at Aha'av'ulypo. The singer slaps his thigh. In *Halykwesa* he kneels before a basket and beats it with a stick. There is no dancing. The singing is considered short, lasting only part of the night. The story begins at Av'athamulya; the hero traveled to the sea, presumably the Gulf of California, and became a univalve shell. In *Ohulya* the basket is beaten both with the stick and with the hand, which suggests a double or syncopated rhythm. The hero of the tale is the rat, who began his career at Avihalykwa'ampa. The *Kamtoska* singer also uses a basket. This singing tells of an unidentified brownish bird with the cry " *tos, tos*."

Some of the Mohave count *Tudhulva*, the hand game, as a song series. There seems to be an associated story into which coyote enters. When besides dances, traditions, funeral rites, and shamanistic practices, even games are reckoned in one common group, it is clear that the standardized formula into which these varied activities have been fitted must have deeply impressed the civilization.

In addition to *Tumanpa Vanyume*, the Mohave follow several other foreign singings. *Chiyere*, "birds" (that is, in general), was learned by one or more individuals from the Yuma. They are said not to know the story. The rattle is used and the songs can be danced to. *Av'alyunu* is also from the Yuma. The myth begins at Aha'av'ulypo. *Alysa* is from the Kamia. The singer rattles, and men and women dance in a circle, an arrangement that is rare in native Mohave dances.

" GOOSE " SERIES.

The shamanistic song series that follow seem to comprise only a portion of the curative practices of the Mohave, and on the other hand to be only partly shamanistic, since some of them are in dispute as " doctor " singings, and the myths that accompany them are, in some cases, of the same tenor as the stories of the nonshamanistic series. Perhaps the present group, or some of its cycles, are shamanistic in association rather than practice. Thus the Mohave say that those who sing them become doctors when they grow old. At the same time these cycles are not danced to, do not use the rattle, and seem not to be sung at funerals, so that they must present a quite different aspect to the native mind from the preceding ones.

Yellaka or " Goose " is one of these " doctor's singings," but the cure which it serves is not known. It begins at the source of the river, and describes, with much detail but little incident, the journey to the sea of a company of birds with the goose and later the grebe as their leader. The musical theme is unusually simple in one of the renditions; a second is rather different in melody and rhythm. The stories of these two versions seem to be similar in scheme, but far apart in particulars. Since other cycles probably vary equally in the mouths of different individuals, a synopsis of the two Goose versions may be of interest. It may be added that the two singers who gave the information were relatives, although not close kin. The first was a young man, who also knew and sang *Nyohaiva*. His rendition, according to his own itemizing, comprised over 400 songs in 66 groups. The second was an old man, who professed to sing no other series. His Goose songs fell into 89 groups, and required two nights and a half to complete.

Version 1.

Song-group 1: at Nyahaim-kwidhik (" wet-lie ") or Nyahaim-kwiyuma (" wet-see "). Pahuchacha (Mastamho) makes the river and Goose (Yellaka) comes out followed by other birds, still unformed. (8 songs.)

2: they go to Nyahaim-kuvara, in the San Francisco Mountains in Arizona and return. (6 songs.)

3: they go to Kwathakapaya, Mount San Gorgonio near San Bernardino. (4.)

4: they return to Nyahaim-kwidhik. (10.)

5–8: south to Nyahaim-korema, Nyahaim-kumaika, Nyahaim-kuchapaiva, Nyahaim-kwattharva. (4, 4, 8, 10 songs.)

9–11: started on their long journey down the Colorado River, the birds think themselves equal to Goose; he teaches them to know right and left, and shows them foam. (8, 5, 10.)

12, 13: at Nyahaim-kwachava. They think he will die, and Raven, Roadrunner, and Gold-eye ask him for names. (4, 2.)

14: at Hatakulya-nikuya. Raven is named and flies off. (5.)

15, 16: at Hatavilya-kuchahwerva. Roadrunner and Gold-eye are named. (4, 5.)

17: at Amata-hamak. Goose is sick but bars the way to the others by stretching his wings. (15.)

18: at Thaweva. He sinks and they think him dead. (6.)

19–21: at Aha'av'ulypo. Only his heart still lives. He dies, Halykupa (Grebe) takes his place, and orders the insect Han'ava to wail for him. (10, 10, 10.)

22, 23: at Ahakekachvodhauva Grebe gives half the birds to Minse'atalyke to lead, but the channel rejoins at Wathalya. (10, 14.)

24–27: going on, Grebe hears a supernatural noise from Avikwame, makes the birds swim in a straight row, and names the places Ahaikusoerva and Avikunu'ulya. (5, 5, 4, 5.)

28–31: approaching Avikwame, Grebe tells four names of Pahuchacha, warns the birds not to heed him as his power is antagonistic to theirs, and succeeds in passing the mountain. (8, 6, 10, 10.)

32: at Akwaka'iova, near Fort Mohave, they sleep. (13.)

33: Halykupa pretends to hear a noise of Goose far ahead. (18.)

34: at Hachiokwatveva. Four birds, led by Han'avachipa (Gnat catcher?), select land to become people. (10.)

35: at Avihalykwa'ampa. Grebe resolves to take the land. (10.)

36: at Hayakwira-hidho. A white beaver dams the river with its tail, but Grebe passes. (6.)

37: at Idholya-idhauva they land. (4.)

38: at Himekoata they sleep and Grebe makes a rock for them to breed on in future. (10.)

39–41: at Hachehumeva, Omaka, Aspalya-pu'umpa, their feathers sprout, they look back where they have come from, and think of that place. (5, 6, 4.)

42: at Selya'aya-kwame. Grebe tells them they are birds, but they do not understand. (6.)

43: at Hakuchyepa, Bill Williams fork, Woodpecker flies off. (4.)

44–47: at Avi-sokwilya-hatai, where they sleep, Quail, Oriole, Nighthawk, and Mockingbird take their characteristics and the last announces day break. (6, 6, 6, 10.)

48, 49: at Avi-vataya and Avi-vera Grebe has them try walking on land and tells them they are not yet fully formed. (6, 8.)

50, 51: at Aha-kutinyam he tells them how to lay eggs and Mud-hen does so. (8, 4.)

52–54: at Aha-takwatparva and Kuvukwilya they hear a noise far in the south and Grebe tells them it comes from their brothers who have come into existence from Goose's body which floated south to the sea. They try to walk on land, but faint, and Grebe makes wind and hail for them. (3, 3, 4.)

55, 56: at Aha-kumitha the wet from their feathers makes a spring and as they go on Grebe names a place To'oska. (4, 3.)

57–59: at Yellaka-hime ("goose-foot") they try to fly but their gooselike toes fail to leave the ground. At Aha-dhauvaruva they return to the water and hear a noise ahead near Yuma. (6, 4, 4.)

60: at Avi-kunyura they speculate over their ultimate appearance. (4.)

61–64: at Hukthilya they hear Pakyetpakyet, at Kwenyokuvilyo Ahanisata, at Amata-kutkyena Kwilolo, who have grown from Goose's body. They go on and see the ocean. (4, 2, 4, 5.)

65–66: at the sea, Minturisturisa (Snipe?) dives and arises with a necklace of shells. All go on the ocean except Grebe, Wood-duck, and Sakatathera. The latter wishes to return north and become a person. (6, 4.)

Here end the songs, but as in many Mohave singings, the story continues. The three birds rise halfway to the sky, where they can see the ocean on all sides of the earth, and try to alight on Avikwame, but come down on Avi-kwahwata, farther south. They proceed upstream, sleep at Savechivuta, go on to Hachiokwatveva near Fort Mohave where the four birds led by Han'avachipa have chosen tracts of land and become people. The three are unable to eat the edible food offered them. They announce that they have come to take the land. The first settlers resist successfully and Wood-duck and Han'avachipa are wounded. The three wanderers think Mastamho may be able to do something for them, go on north, and meet him at Hokusava, where the god is turning various beings into finished birds. He gives mythic names to the three, who go off as birds. Mastamho returns in four steps to the head of the river, makes fish, sand, and rocks, deliberates, turns into the bird Sakwithei, and flies away.

Version 2.

Song-group 1: at Nyahaim-kwiyuma ("wet-see"), the mythical source of the river, where many eggs hatch.

Groups 3 to 5 and 11 to 12 are devoted to the names of Goose.

15: at Avi-kwatulya.

19: at Avak-tinyam. Tinyam-hwarehware and Han'ava, two insects, cry in their house when they see Goose, here called Masahai-tachuma, coming at the head of many birds.

24: at Selya'aya-ita.

28: at Avi-kutaparva.

29: at Kara'erva, near Fort Mohave.

32: at Avi-halykwa'ampa.

33: at Mat'ara ("playing field "), near Needles.

36: at Hokyampeva.

40: at Sankuvanya. Goose turns white and thinks himself like the gulls he sees.

43: at Hakuchyepa, the mouth of Bill Williams fork, Goose takes the main channel, other birds follow a blind slough and must return.

44: at Amata-kutudhunya. It becomes night and the birds quarrel whether it will be light again. Goose tells of the owl and night birds.

47: he tells of Orion and the Pleiades.

48: Goose awakes and tells of a dream in which they were at the sea.

51: the birds swim on downstream abreast, they being now where the river is widest.

55 to 56: at Hatusalya. Goose tells of sitting on the beach of the sea.

59: at Kuvukwilya. Mastamho is there, but Goose announces that they will pass on.

69: Goose dreams he sees the ocean, the others say that it is a mesa; they quarrel.

70: at Yiminalyek, in Yuma country.

77: at Avi-aspa or Amata-kutkyena, below Yuma territory.

81: they have gone to Amata-hakwachtharva, apparently another name for the place at which they began.

86: they grow feathers and begin to fly.

88: at Hokusava.

89: at Amata-minyoraiva, north of Mastamho's mountain Avikwame.

OTHER SEMI-SHAMANISTIC SERIES.

Halykupa, "Grebe," is the chief character of the latter part of the Goose story. There seems to be a distinct *Halypuka* or "Loon" singing, for which a basket is beaten. Those who dream this shout like the bird at the "annual" mournings and have the repute of not living long.

Ahakwa'ilya seems to be named from the dragon-fly larva. A basket is beaten. This is both specified and denied as a shamanistic cycle.

Sampulyka, "Mosquito," also uses a basket as instrument.

Wellaka cures diarrhea.

Hikupk has to do with venereal disease.

Apena, "Beaver," begins its story with Matavilya still alive at the source of the river. It is sung by shamans who cure neck swellings caused by the beaver, can smoke tobacco while diving, and prevent the river from washing away banks on which houses stand. *Ichul-yuye* may be another singing connected with the beaver, or perhaps is only the name of the sickness which the *Apena* dreamer cures.

Humahnana, a hard, black, malodorous beetle, and *Ipam-imicha*, "person cries," begin their tale at Aha'av'ulypo, use no accompaniment to their songs, and serve to cure the sickness *ichudhauva* caused by eating a bird wounded by hawks, as well as the *ichiekanyamasava*, diarrheal illness which befalls infants whose fathers eat game killed by themselves instead of giving it away. *Ipam-imicha* also has to do with the "foreign-sickness" caused by eating strange food, and is thus connected with *Yaroyara*, which serves the same purpose and also commences at Aha'av'ulypo. All four of these singings, if they are indeed distinct, are held by the Mohave to be truly shamanistic in their details of Matavilya's sickness and funeral.

Hayakwira is a cycle concerned with another kind of rattlesnake than the *Ave* songs and story described below under "Shamanism." *Chamadhulya* is allied to *Hayakwira.*

MYTHOLOGY.

Besides the tales that form the thread of their song cycles, the Mohave tell at least three other kinds of myths, which ordinarily are not sung to. There is, first, an origin myth, of a type generic in southern California. Second, there are long pseudohistorical narrations, which contain suggestions of migration legends and clan traditions, but are too thoroughly cast in the standard molds of Mohave mythology to evince these qualities very clearly. Lastly, there are coyote stories and miscellaneous tales, which, if they do nothing else, prove that the Mohave can on occasion be reasonably brief.

This is the cosmogony; for which the Mohave seem to have no name other than "dream tale" or "shaman's tale":

The first were Sky and Earth, male and female, who touched far in the west, across the sea. Then were born from them Matavilya, the oldest; Frog, his daughter, who was to cause his death; his younger brother or son Mastamho, his successor and greater than he; and all men and beings. In four strides Matavilya led them upward to Aha'-av'ulypo, "house-post water," in Eldorado Canyon on the Colorado, above Mohave land; the center of the earth, as he found by stretching his arms. There he made his "dark round," the first house. With an unwitting indecency he offended his daughter, and plotting against him, she swallowed his voidings, and he knew that he should die, and told the people. Coyote, always suspected, was sent away for fire, and then Fly, a woman, rubbed it on her thigh. Coyote raced back, leaped over Badger, the short man in the ring of people, snatched the god's heart from the pyre, and escaped with it. Mastamho directed the mourning, and Han'ava, the cicada, first taught how to wail. Korokorapa, also called Hiko or Haiko, "white man," alone had sat unmoved as Matavilya lay dying, now sank into the ground with noise, and returned westward to Pi'in, the place of universal origin.

Matavilya's ashes offended, and wind, hail, and rain failed to obliterate them. In four steps Mastamho strode far north, plunged his cane of breath and spittle into the earth, and the river flowed out. Entering a boat, Mastamho journeyed with mankind to the sea, twisting and tilting the boat or letting it run straight as he wished wide bottom lands or sharp canyons to frame the river. He returned with the people on his arms, surmounted the rising waters to the mountain Akokahumi, trod the water down, and took his followers upstream to the northern end of what was to be the Mohave country. Here he heaped up the great pointed peak Avikwame—more exactly Avikwa'ame—Newberry or Dead Mountain as the Americans call it, where he, too, built himself a house. It is of this house that shamans dream, for here their shadows were as little boys in the face of Mastamho, and received from him their ordained powers, confirmed by tests on the spot. Here, too, Mastamho made the people shout, and the fourth time day and sun and moon appeared.

Then he plotted the death of "sky-rattlesnake," Kammay-aveta, also called Umas-ereha, a great power far south in the sea. Message after message was sent him; he knew that the sickness which he was summoned to cure was pretended; but at last he came, amid rain and thunder, stretching his vast length from ocean to mountain. As his head entered the great house it was cut off. It rolled back to the sea in the hope of reconstituting its living body, but became only an ocean monster; while from his blood and sweat and juices came rattlesnakes and noxious insects whose powers some shamans combat. This was the first shaman killed in the world.

Now Mastamho's work was nearly done. To Walapai, Yavapai, Chemehuevi, Yuma, and Kamia he gave each their land and mountains, their foods, and their speech, and sent them off. The youngest, the Mohave, he taught to farm, to cook in pottery, to speak and count as was best fit for them, and to stay in the country. Then, meditating as to his own end, he stretched his arms, grew into *saksak* the fish eagle, and flew off, without power or recollection, ignorant and infested with vermin.

"GREAT TALES."

The migration or war myths are of the type of the *Vinimulya-hapacha* cycle stories. Their groups of people who travel and fight seem all to be regarded as Mohave, and each of them to stand in the narrator's mind for a body of kinsmen in the male line; but his interest is in their doings, not in their organization, and their clan affiliations are rarely mentioned, or sometimes contradictorily. The geography, as always among the Mohave, is gone into very minutely, and centers in Mohave Valley, but the marches and settlements are made to extend for long distances in all directions. These stories are called *ich-kanava*, "great tellings," and while of similar tenor, appear to vary greatly according to the narrator. They are, of course, dreamed, in native opinion, and are staggeringly prolix. One, which the narrator, a blind old man, had sometimes told from for a night, or until his hearers went to sleep, but never completely through, he recited on six days for a total of 24 hours, and then was still far from the end. He evidently was wholly unable to estimate its length.

Such stories simply can not be condensed. An outline becomes as dry a skeleton of names and places as certain passages of the priestly writer of the Pentateuch. The central events, the battles themselves, are trivial. The point, and to the native the interest of the whole, evidently lies in the episodes and a certain treatment of them; which is so peculiar, so uninteresting even, to those habituated to other literary manners, that it must be admitted as a very definite style, in the inward sense of that word. A comparison with the Iliad with the wrath of Achilles omitted, or the Mahabharata without the careers of its five brother heroes, gives some rude suggestion of the quality. If Mohave civilization had been advanced enough to allow of their finding some clear central theme to hold together the welter of detail and names, their "great tales" would no doubt seem impressive to us. A fragment of one may serve to give some hint of the epic breadth of manner.

Part of a Hipahipa Legend.

Amainyavererkwa and Ichehwekilyeme, his son, were at Amata-tasilyka. They were there four days. Then Ichehwekilyeme went fishing. He visited his friends, some to the north and some to the south, through the whole Mohave Valley, and gave them fish. The next day he went again. His people said: "Take food with you," and wanted to give him mixed corn and pumpkin seeds, but he said: "I will not carry a load. I shall travel light." So he took only his fish net and went off on a run. On his way he followed a lake (or slough), *Aha'-inya* (some miles south of Fort Mohave). When he had caught fish, the people there crowded around him. He gave them his catch and they cut up the fish and ate them. When they had thus pleased themselves, they killed Ichehwekilyeme with a club and hid his body and ran off. The men who did this were Hinyorilya-vahwilya, Hinyorilya-vanaka, Hinyorilya-vapaya, and Hinyorilya-va'ava. When the people (at large) had scattered abroad, these four had returned and settled at Avinya-kapuchora and Kwinalya-kutikiorva, near Aha'-inya. They were Hipahipa (the mythic name of a clan, whose women bore the name Kutkilya, which is still in use). Now that they had killed Ichehwekilyeme, they ran off far to the east to Chivakaha, Aha-kupone, Aha-kuvilya, and Avinyesko.

Amainyavererkwa became distressed about his son and searched for him. As he had friends everywhere, he thought perhaps the young man might be at Aha-talompa (near the southern end of the valley), or perhaps at Kuhuinye. Or he thought he might be at Avi-kw-ahoato, or Avi-kutaparva, or Kwiya-kavasu, or Kwiya-kulyike, or Hu'ulyechupaiva, or at Avi-tutara (apparently all in Mohave Valley). As he had friends at all these places, he thought of them, and in the morning put on his sandals and went southward. As he traveled, he looked over these places. By noon he had come down to the last one. Then he returned and by night reached his house in the north (of the valley) without having found his son. His people crowded thickly around him, but he said that he had not heard news nor seen tracks. He felt very bad.

Then Ampotakerama was the only one there who thought: "Perhaps the young man became as if crazy or blind. Perhaps he was drowned, or ran off." Ampotakerama thought thus all that night.

Now Umase'aka lived at Amata-tasilyka also. But he said nothing. Ahalya'-asma was chief there also, and so were Ahamakwinyuenyeye, Nyemelyekwesi'ika, and Ha'ampa-kwa'akwenya. They too thought. But Amainyavererkwa said nothing. He only lay and slept while the others were thinking.

When the sun was up, the others all told him: "Eat a little." But Amainyavererkwa said: "I feel bad. I want to go north. When I come back and have found my boy I shall eat." So he started.

When he returned, all crowded around him again. He said: "I have looked everywhere. I have no more friends among whom I can search. I think my son is lost." Then all cried and had tears in their eyes.

In the morning Amainyavererkwa went up river once more. This time he went farther and traveled until he came to Asesmava. There he slept. In the morning he went on. He visited all his friends and received to eat whatever kinds of food they ate different from his own. He thought that perhaps his son had gone up for the purpose of eating these strange foods. Late in the afternoon he came to Amata-akwata, Kukake, Ahtanye-ha, and Avinyidho. He inquired there among his friends. It was now sunset and his friends gave him to eat, but told him they had not seen his son. He ate a little and slept there that night.

In the morning he ate a little again. His friends gave him red paint and feathers which he packed and put on his shoulder and then he started (south) homeward.

At sunset he came to Akwereha. He had no one living there, but lay and slept there. He thought: "I will call this place Akwereha, and all will call it by this name when they tell stories. And I will leave my paint and feathers here, and will call it also Amata-sivilya-kwidhaua (feather-having-place)."

In the morning he went on, and while it was still early came to Kwakitupeva and Kwasekelyekete (Union Pass, north of Fort Mohave). There he drank a little. He was now feeling very bad on account of his son. Then he began to run until he came to Amata-kamota'ara. There he drank again and then ran on until he came to Ammo-heva (Hardyville). Having drunk once more, he went on until he came to Ismavakoya and Mach-ho. There he looked to see how far he still had to go. Then he began running again. He ran until he came to Akweretonyeva. Then he thought: "I am nearly at my house now." So he walked fast until he came to Selya'aya-kumicha, and then to the top of Amai-kwitasa. Then he looked toward his house at Amata-tasilyka. As he stood, he saw that it was dusty about his house as if there were wind there. The dust was from the many people.

When he returned home he again thought of the north. He wanted to go north once more to look for his son. Then in the morning he took his sandals and started. He came to Oachavampeva, Asmalya-kuvachaka, Amata-kumata'ara, and Avi-tunyora. At Avi-tunyora lived Himekuparakupchula. He was a shaman and knew everything that happened. It was he that Amainyavererkwa went to see. Himekuparakupchula had two sons, Thumeke'-ahwata, the older, and Ahwe-mestheva, the younger. He himself was too old to walk. When Amainyavererkwa came, his two sons set him up and leaned against him to support him. He was so old that he could hardly talk.

Amainyavererkwa sat down near him and said: "My son is lost." Himekuparakupchula said: "I am the man who knows everything. No one has told me of this matter, but I know it. Here are my two sons. The oldest is not very able. The younger knows something. Call him. He is playing about with a bow. Call him and ask him. He knows. He has dreamed like myself." So they called Ahwe-mestheva, and the boy came. He said: "I know. I am like the old man, my father." He was ready to go back with Amainyavererkwa. But he only sat and said that he knew and made no movement. Amainyavererkwa asked: "You will be sure to come?" Ahwe-mestheva said: "Yes; I shall surely come southward."

Then Amainyavererkwa started back to his house. When he had gone a short way he looked back but did not see the boy coming. He went on, looking back, but still Ahwe-mestheva did not come. Then he thought: "I do not think he will come. He has not seen. He is only a little boy. He is not man enough and does not know and so will not come." But when he reached Ammo-heva he looked again and saw the boy coming. Then he thought: " He is really coming." When he reached Amata-kwilyisei he stood and looked and again saw him coming. Then all at once the boy was no longer apparent. He was traveling under the ground. Therefore Amainyavererkwa did not see him. He kept looking back in vain. Then at last he saw him traveling underground. He went on and reached his house in the afternoon and said: "Ahwe-mestheva is coming. He will be here soon."

When Ahwe-mestheva arrived carrying bow and arrows everything was prepared. They had made a little hut of *idho* willows, sticking them into the ground and tying the tops together. As the boy came in front of the hut he threw his bow and arrows forward on the ground. Then he stood, kicked the ground, and jumped up on the roof of the hut so that it shook. Then he jumped up, then down on the ground again, and stood outside the hut. He said: " I said that I knew everything. Now I shall sing. I shall sing four times." Then he sang as follows (the words are distorted to fit the rhythm) :

"Akwetinyam ithapikali, at night I see clearly."

"(Matkwesa) ikakorenye ikanamave, (my shadow) speaks and tells me (all)."

"Akwetinyam ithapiwaye, at night I see brightly."

" Ikanavek kwanumadhe, I shall tell it (all) here (in time)."

When he had sung these four songs he went into the little house.

When he was inside he said : " I know the man's name. It is Ichehwekilyeme. He went fishing. Four men killed him. Their names are Hinyorilya-vahwilya, Hinyorilya-vanaka, Hinyorilya-vapaya, and Hinyorilya-va'ava. The people here wanted to give him corn and pumpkin seeds to take with him, but he would not. Then he went. These people found him fishing. He said to them : ' You are traveling and are hungry. Build a fire and I shall give you to eat.' Then these four men answered : ' It is good.' Then they killed him. In the water was a stump. There they dragged him and fastened his body down with a stick so that no one would see and know."

Thus the boy Ahwe-mestheva knew and told everything, and so the people discovered what had become of Ichehwekilyeme.

Then his father, Amainyavererkwa, went to Aha'-inya and found the body and took it out of the water. Then they burned Ichehwekilyeme with his best clothes and property, and cried at the house. Then the boy Ahwe-mestheva said : " That is all. I go now." He shot an arrow northward and started home.

When he returned, he told the old man Himekuparakupchula, his father : " I found him." His father said : " It is good. Perhaps they will do something about it (fight). I do not yet know it, but perhaps they will." Then he said to his oldest son, Thumeke'-ahwata : " Go down to them and let me know what they will do." So the older son started. He reached Amata-tasilyka at sunset. Amainyavererkwa said : " We do not yet know. I have nothing to say. There is one man here who speaks and we follow. He is Ampota-kerama, and he is thinking now. I know that people sometimes " steal " (ambush shamans who have caused deaths). I have seen them doing that. But I think that bad and we shall not do it. Perhaps Ampota-kerama will know something to do."

And Ampota-kerama said : " I am trying to know how we shall start a fight. Perhaps we shall play *kachoakwek* with them (a game of kicking at one another with the heels). Perhaps in that way we shall be able to pick a quarrel and seize and kill them. Or perhaps we shall play *hachohwesavek* (a game in which balls of mud are put on the ends of poles and slung at the opposing party). If they beat us, we can become angry and fight. Perhaps we shall play with hoop and poles. If the ring lies so that the pole shows inside, we shall say that we can not see it clear. Then he who threw the pole will say: 'I can see it.' We shall say: 'No; it is not a score.' Perhaps in that way there will be a quarrel and a fight will begin." So they were thinking of that.

Here the recorded tale breaks off. The above is evidently little more than a beginning.

SHAMANISM.

Shamanism is deeply stained by the beliefs that pervade all Mohave thought. The shaman's experiences begin in myth at the world origin and are myth in form. The god Mastamho gave their special powers to all shamans of to-day, who own no private spirit allies. Their songs have words of the same cast as the myths on which are based all songs of pleasure or funeral. One class is dreamed like the other. There is no theory of disease objects projected into human bodies. Hence the physician sucks little if at all. The patient's soul, his "shadow," is affected or taken away; the shaman brings it back because he has dreamed, while Mastamho was regulating the world, of the mythical person that became a certain thing or animal, and saw the nature of its power of operation for human good or ill; and he counteracts this power with his own, with song or breath or spittle, blowing or laying on of hands or other action, as his own shadow then saw and was instructed. There is no philosophy of disease and treatment more diverse than this from the beliefs of the north and central Californians.

A single example, even though in condensation, may make this attitude plain.

A shaman's story.

At Aha'av'ulypo, the account begins, all the people were in the dark house that Matavilya made. "I shall die," he said when the Frog, the shaman, his daughter, had made him sick. Six persons were there and listened to him and grieved and went off when he had died: Tumanpa long, Tumanpa short, Chuhuecha, Salt, Nyavadhoka, and Av'alyunu (these song cycles are here personified).

Then follows the story of Matavilya's funeral, of the making of the river by Mastamho, and the killing of the gigantic Sky-Rattlesnake. From the glue in his joints, *himata-halai*, eggs, were formed, out of which came Achyeka, Yellow ant, the oldest, who took the name Humara-kadhucha. From *himata-haka-malya*, his "body form," grew Halytota, Spider, who called himself Ampota-nyunye, "road dust." Menisa, Scorpion, was born from Sky-Rattlesnake's sweat, and from his blood Ave, Rattlesnake, the youngest. These took the names Ampota-kuhudhurre and Ampota-himaika.

While these four took shape, Mastamho taught some of the people to know three sicknesses and their cure: *hayakwira* (a kind of rattlesnake distinct from *ave*), *isuma* (dream), and *ichhulyuye* (beaver). Of these sicknesses I know, says the narrator, but I do not treat them because they were not given to me. But Ave-rattlesnake, Scorpion, Halytota-spider, and Achyeka-ant are mine. Four rows of people stood at Avikwame before Mastamho, and these four sat there also, and my shadow was there. "Now he comes," Mastamho said of me. "Listen to him. What he says is true. I gave it to him." Then the four were ashamed and feared and hung their heads and did not want to hear, because I knew them and was above them.

Then Mastamho took all the people downstream to Avi-kutaparva, to the New York Mountains, and far west to Avi-hamoka, "three mountains," which is toward Tehachapi from Mojave station. The four went there too, but on the north, by their own road. There Rattlesnake marked himself with white dust, with dark dust, with white cloud, with dark cloud, and went with Mastamho and others eastward to Koskilya near Parker. There Mastamho ordained a line between the Mohave to the north and the Pima, the Halchidhoma, and the Kohuana to the south. There they prepared for war against the southerners, traveled against them at Ahpe-hwelyeve near Ehrenberg, attacked and fought, and took a Halchidhoma and a Kohuana scalp under Rattlesnake's lead. Then they returned to "Three Mountains" and made a dance over the scalps.

Rattlesnake lives there at Three Mountains. He has a road to every tribe. Often he thinks of war and wants to bite a person. "I like him," he says of a man, "I want him as a friend to be here." Then he asks the mountain. If the mountain says yes, the man will die; but if the mountain is silent, the man will be bitten and live. One road goes straight from Three Mountains to my heart, says the narrator, and I hear the singing and talking there. Then I know whether a person will live or die. When Rattlesnake or Spider has bitten him, he takes his shadow. If he brings it all the way to Three Mountains, the man dies. But if I can stop the shadow near Three Mountains, then I sing again at each place on the road and each time we are farther, until when I arrive with it here the man is well. At every place on the way I stand and sing and prevent the shadow's going on.

Spider also thinks of biting persons. He thinks (sings):

*Oyach-kwa'-anyayi*_____	my breath is bright.
*iha-kwa'-anyayi*_____	my spittle is bright.
*iha-kwa'-akwithva*_____	my spittle is tough.
*oyach-kwa'-akwithva*_____	my breath is tough.

"In the north, in the south, my breath is not hot. In the east my breath is hot. When the sun rises, I put up my hands. When they are warm, I lay them on my face, and my breath becomes hot. Hiha-nyunye, 'saliva-road,' is my name. My roads are four. They are not on earth, but high, in the sky. As Rattlesnake has done, so I will do. I am thinking of my friend whom I wish. I want his shadow on my road. My north road is cold, my south road is cold, but when I bite in the east it is hot. I do not want my friend at night, I want him when the sun rises in the east and my breath becomes hot in him," says Spider.

Then I see Spider start out on his sky road when he wishes to bite. North of Avikwame, at Lyehuta, lives the chief of Rattlesnakes, Ampota-nyamatham-tamakwa. Him I hear Spider asking; and if he will not allow, Spider can do nothing. When he permits, Spider bites with his four teeth, and bright-spittle and hot-spittle go into the person's body and make it clear. Then I can look through the man, and he rolls about in sweat. Spider ties his heart around with spittle. I see it like that. If I am summoned from far away, the heart may be wrapped twice when I arrive. Then I walk four times around the man on the left side (sunwise) and break the roads that Spider has made to his heart, and he sits up and spits out what Spider has put into him, and is well. But if Spider has tied his heart four times around when I arrive and it is tight, the man is killed. I can do nothing then.

If Spider has bitten a person without the assent of the mountain or of the great Rattlesnake, and the man is cured, Spider is full of breath, and goes off and dies somewhere. His shadow goes up, without legs, a round thing, *ampota-yara*, that rolls in the clouds, invisible, and makes rain.

There is another one, Halyota-kunemi, "brave spider," that brings on diarrhœa, and that warriors dream of. I know that one's name, but I did not dream about him. And so with Ave-hakthara, the short rattlesnake, that is brave and always wants to war: he too went off to one side from where I was, and knowledge about him was not given me.

But Scorpion at Three Mountains took the name Matkwesam-havika, "Shadow-companion," and meditated what his form would be. He too made four roads, but they are underground. At the end of the road to the east, he made Tarantula by his word; at the north, Rock Spider; west, Firefly; south, Kwithohwa, a longish yellow spider. These four own the winds and clouds, which are their breath. But the rain from these clouds is bitter. I can make it fall, and sometimes when the crops are dry, people ask me to make it, but I refuse because it is not good. Scorpion asked these four at the ends for the power to kill. But they did not answer him, hence he only wounds, and a man who is strong needs no treatment. Sweat is harmless, and that is what Scorpion was born from. He also went down the river to ask four great rattlesnakes for power, but one after the other would not give it to him.

Achyeka-ant was the oldest of the four. He, too, made four roads of spittle and breath. Then he called himself "night body," Kutinyam-himata, and sank down to the heart of the earth, *amata-hiwa*. There he was no longer a person, but a yellow ant; and there he made four more roads in the darkness. He emerged, and now called himself "bright body," Himata'-anyayi, who would live in the roots of a tree, the heart of a tree, and make his house there. His body is here on earth, his shadow below. It is his night body, the underground shadow, that bites men. It goes through the veins, of which one leads to the heart. He eats the heart and the man begins to die. He is a long time dying; but at last Achyeka takes the man's shadow with him to his house. But he failed to make stone and earth alive as he tried. So I take a very fine earth, rub it between my hands, and put it on the sick person's body. So I stop the roads to the middle place of Achyeka, and bring the person's shadow back to him, and he becomes well.

The complete interweaving of shamanistic beliefs and curative practices with the national mythology, and the complete dependence, in native opinion, of both on individual dreaming, are fully exemplified by the foregoing personal narrative.

The following is a purely objective description of the treatment extended for snake bite by another shaman.

When the shaman is notified, he immediately begins to sing where he is, in order to produce a cooling wind and sprinkle of rain for the wounded man. When he arrives where the patient is lying with his head to the south in front of his house, he sings standing at a little distance from him, first on his north, then on his west, south, and east. Should he sing a fifth song, the sick man would die. Only the man's wife may sit by him; all others are at a distance.

The shaman forbids everyone to drink until the sun has set, and takes no water himself, because the rattlesnake does not drink. He sits awake, and at midnight and in the morning sings his four songs over again. Then he goes home and the patient is cured.

If a man eats fish caught in his own net while this is new, the ghosts, *nyavedhi*, of the fish take away his shadow, *matkwesa*. Then he becomes drowsy and feeble, and a shaman must sing the soul back. But the shaman must not stay too long in the village of the dead, or the departed among his own kin are likely to seize and try to hold him with them in affection.

STATUS OF THE SHAMAN.

The Mohave are astoundingly frank in telling of how they kill their doctors or shamans, and some of the latter reciprocate with unforced declarations of the harm they have done. This is a native summary:

Doctors are despatched for blighting the crops; for repeatedly attending a patient but killing instead of curing him; for having said about a sick person: "I wish you would die;" and for admitting responsibility for deaths. There is a doctor now who stands at funerals and says aloud: "I killed him." Doctors and brave men are alike. The latter say: "I do not wish to live long." A doctor says: "I shall not live a long time. I wish to die. That is why I kill people. Why do you not kill me?" Or he may hand a stick to a man and say: "I killed your father." Or he may come and tell a sick person: "Don't you know that it is I that am killing you? Must I grasp you and despatch you with my hands before you will try to kill me?"

The Mohave tell of such utterances as if they were frequent, and there is little doubt that certain shamans, particularly those under suspicion, now and then launched into a very delirium of provocation and hate—an intensity of emotion rare among other Californians. In general, they unquestionably believe their spirit experiences and power to be actual.

The following autobiographical anecdote well illustrates the native attitude:

When I was young, I was once with a friend at a shaman's house. My friend proposed that we kill him. I took my bow and four arrows and said to the shaman: "I am going to shoot doves." He assented. When I returned, the shaman seemed to be asleep under the shade before his house. My friend was indoors, and said: "He is sleeping." I took a (steel) ax and swung at the shaman's head. I struck him in the cheek. As he sat up, no blood came from the wound. Then suddenly a torrent gushed out. My companion became frightened, ran off, returned, struck at the shaman's head, but hit only his legs, and ran off, hardly able to drag his own. Two women had been sitting near, lousing each other, and at first had not seen what we did. Then they began to cry and wail. I crossed the river, and found some men gambling, and sat with them. In the afternoon I said: "I have killed so and so." They thought I was boasting. "Yes, do it," they said. "That will be good. Too many people are dying." "I have done it already," I answered. Soon the dead man's relatives came, and it seemed that we should fight with sticks. But on the next day the shaman's son announced that he would not fight, and nothing further happened.

TOLOACHE.

The Mohave know the Jimson weed and its qualities, but give no evidence of having been at all influenced by the toloache cult of the Shoshonean tribes. They make no ceremony connected with the plant. Individuals drink a decoction of the leaves taken from the west side of the bush—those on the east are considered poison—become unconscious for four days, dream, and thus acquire luck in gambling. This appears to be similar to the desert Cahuilla practice and indicates a semishamanistic use of the drug analogous to its status among the Pueblos.

THE GHOST DANCE.

The Mohave took up the later or eastern ghost dance, whereas most California tribes either were influenced by the less known first wave or escaped both. The movement was introduced by a Southern Paiute, and appears to have left no impress at all on the Mohave consciousness. They had their own peculiar and satisfying scheme of dreaming, and by 1890 were still so wholly absorbed in their native way of doing things that they hardly realized that they were living in a new and destructive atmosphere.

RELIGION AND KNOWLEDGE.

It is interesting that the Mohave are frequently in argument about each other's religious knowledge. Some one announces that he has dreamed one of the less common cycles: others deny that there is such a myth or cycle, or refuse to admit more than that the assertor says so. A man begins a story. Suddenly another interrupts with the reproof that what is being told is nothing, a mere mixture of things as diverse as *Chutaha* and coyote tales. The narrator insists that he has dreamed it so and it is correct. He is told that his dreams are bad; and usually he subsides. Whether a certain man is or is not a shaman, or is a legitimate one, or will become a shaman, and what his power really is for, are all matters on which whoever is minded expresses his opinion freely.

The Mohave display far more sense of the value of numbers than the average Californian Indian. They are constantly using such figures as "5 or 6"—"5, 6" they say—and "40 or 50," apparently with a reasonably correct idea of the numbers denoted, especially if persons are referred to.   They are not much given to tallies, and one rarely sees them operating with counters or marks in the sand. Simple addition or subtraction of numbers below 100 they carry on readily in their heads.

The number 4 is brought into myth and religious act at every opportunity.

There is a word for year, *kwathe*, but its etymology is unknown.

The Mohave are utterly unlike the true southwestern Indians, and essentially in the status of the central and northern California tribes, in lacking fetishes or any artistic or concretely expressed symbolism.   The Shoshoneans of southern California express the Pueblo spirit much more nearly in their sand paintings and ritualistic implements.   In fact the gap between the southwesterners proper and the Yumans of the Colorado is profound as regards religion.   There is no trace among the latter of kiva, altar, mask, offering, priest, initiation, fraternity, or color symbolism, all so characteristic of the town-dwelling tribes.   Most of these elements recur, though in abbreviation or pallid substitute, among the Luiseño and Gabrielino; but among the Mohave they are replaced by the wholly predominant factor of dreaming.

CHAPTER 52.

THE YUMA.

RELATION OF THE YUMA AND MOHAVE.

The Yuma have provided a name not only for an Arizona city and county and a fort and reservation in California—all adjoining the great stream of the Colorado—but for the entire family of tribes to which they, the Mohave, the Diegueño, and many others belong. This does not mean that they were the central or prominent tribe of the group; for such nomenclatures become established by accident or by unconscious fancies of the civilized ear for designations of picturesque or facile sound. As a matter of fact, the Mohave seem to have been at least as numerous as the Yuma ever since they were known, equally solidary, rather more venturesome and addicted to travel to far parts, and probably more active in their inward life; since not only their religious concepts but their songs, the very words thereof, and their sacred places are known farther than Yuma influence penetrated. That the general lower Colorado culture to which both tribes adhered was in its origin and elementals more largely the creation of one tribe than of the other or of some still different group of the region, it is impossible to say. The original focus of the culture is almost certain to have been where there was the greatest agglomeration of tribes, about the mouth of the Gila, rather than at the upstream limit of the valley lands where the Mohave were situate. The lower river was also nearer to influences from the south and down the Gila from the east, the direction in which higher cultures lay. Yet one receives the impression that the most concentrated, energetic, and characteristic form of the river civilization in the past century or two has been that which it took among the Mohave.

It also happens that the Mohave are better known than the Yuma, so that even if a less extended description of the latter people were

not justified by circumstances, it would be inevitable. The following account is therefore limited to comparisons of the two tribes on
matters in which they are known to differ. In their agriculture,
manufacture, clothing, hairdress, houses, warfare, and tribal sense,
the Yuma and Mohave seem to be virtually identical.

TRIBAL AND HISTORICAL FACTS.

The Yuma call themselves Kwichyana or Kuchiana, and are
known to all the other Yumans by dialectic variants of this name,
whose meaning is not known to them. The Chemehuevi call them
Hukwats, the Apache denominate them together with other tribes
of the family: Hatilshe. A Spanish designation is Garroteros,
clubbers, perhaps with reference to their mallet or pestle-shaped
war clubs. The name Yuma first appears in Kino in 1702. Its
origin is not positively known. It has been thought a misapplication of *yamayo*, the word denoting a chief's son; but this interpretation seems only a conjecture. The existence of such titles for the
hereditary successors of chieftainship is, however, of interest as
parallel to Gabrielino and Juaneño custom.

The tribe may be estimated at 2,500 or more souls before contact
with the whites. Garcés in 1776 thought there were 3,000. The
number in 1905 was put at 900, in 1910 at 834.

The territory of the Yuma was the Colorado bottom about the
mouth of the Gila. They are said to have occupied the main stream
for 15 miles above and 60 miles below the confluence; but the latter
figure is almost certainly too high. It would bring the Yuma almost
to the Gulf of California, between which and themselves a number
of other tribes of allied lineage intervened. In distinction from the
Mohave, they seem to have inhabited chiefly the western bank of
the river; but such choices are probably dictated by considerations
of local topography.

The Yuma may have been among the first tribes discovered by
Caucasians in California. In 1540, two years before Cabrillo
sighted the channel islands, Alarcon, operating in conjunction with
the Coronado expedition to Zuñi, sailed up the great Rio de los
Tizones, the "Firebrand River" or Colorado, and established contact with the natives. He hardly penetrated as far as Mohave
territory—his 85 leagues would carry him there only if the river
flowed straight. But he certainly passed what were later the seats
of the Yuma, and may have seen their ancestors; although Oñate
in 1605 tells us nothing of any people in whom we can recognize

the Yuma, and the first positively identifiable mention of them is that of Kino, a century later. Alarcon's brief notices of the Indians accord well with the disposition and customs of the historic Yuman peoples of the river. It is also in agreement with what is known as to freedom of intertribal relations in the region, that Alarcon found the natives informed as to details of the equipment and appearance of the Spaniards who had reached New Mexico but a few months before.

While it has been asserted that Oñate reached the Yuma, his Cohuanas are the Kohuana, a separate tribe nearer the gulf; and the Ozaras whom he found at the mouth of the Gila are so described as to give the impression that they were a Piman rather than Yuman people. Kino and Garcés, like most lone travelers of resoluteness and tact, encountered few difficulties from the Yuma; but when two missions were soon after established among them they were wiped out within a year, in 1781. After the acquisition of California by the United States and the setting in of the overland tide of travel there were the usual troubles, and Fort Yuma was established to hold the tribe in check; but there was no notable resistance to the Americans.

In international friendships and enmities the Yuma belonged on the side of the Mohave and were hostile to the Maricopa in the great division that extended through the tribes of southern California and western Arizona, as already outlined with reference to the Chemehuevi. They seem, however, to have been more friendly to the Kamia, and through them with the Diegueño proper, than were the Mohave. It was probably their ancient feud with the Maricopa that embroiled them with the Pima, a peaceable but sturdy nation of farmers, against whom the volatile military ambition of the river tribes repeatedly dashed itself. The last great undertaking of the Yuma was against these people, and ended disastrously in 1858.

DREAMING.

The direct basis of all religion—tradition, ritual song, and shamanistic power—is individual dreaming, in the opinion of the Yuma. They hold to this belief as thoroughly and consistently as the Mohave. An autobiographic statement by one of their medicine men and myth narrators reveals this attitude more convincingly than it can be summarized in general statements:

Before I was born I would sometimes steal out of my mother's womb while she was sleeping, but it was dark and I did not go far. Every good doctor (*kwasidhe*, almost synonymous with *sumach*, "dreamer") begins to understand before he is born. When a little boy I took a trip to Avikwame Mountain and slept at its base. I felt of my body with my two hands, but found it was not there (*sic*). It took me four days and nights to go there. Later I became able to approach even the top of the mountain. At last I reached the willow-roof (shade) in front of the dark-house there. Kumastamho was within. It was so dark that I could hardly see him. He was naked and very large. Only a few great doctors were in there with him, but a crowd of men stood under the shade before the house. I now have power to go to Kumastamho any time. I lie down and try, and soon I am up there again with the crowd. He teaches me to cure by spitting (blowing frothy saliva) and sucking. One night Kumastamho spat up blood. He told me: "Come here, little boy (this is a characteristic concept), and suck my chest." I placed my hands on his ribs and sucked his sickness out. Then he said: "You are a consumption dreamer. When anybody has consumption lay your hands on him and suck the pain out continually, and in four months he will be well." It takes four days to tell about Kwikumat and Kumastamho (the origin myth). I was present (*i. e.*, at the happenings told in this myth) from the very beginning (*sic*), and saw and heard all. I dreamed a little of it at a time. I would then tell it to my friends. The old men would say: "That is right! I was there and heard it myself." Or they would say: "You have dreamed badly. That is not right." And they would tell me right. So at last I learned the whole of it right.

Just so, the Mohave in general admit frankly that they have learned much of their knowledge of songs and stories from their older relatives, and yet insist that they possess all this knowledge through dreams; and like the Yuma, every narrator is convinced that he was present at the ancient events he tells of. If these tribes could express themselves in our abstract terminology, they would probably say that the phenomena of dreams have an absolute reality but that they exist in a dimension in which there is no time and in which there is no distinction between spiritual and material.

SONG-MYTH-RITES IN THE LOWER COLORADO REGION.

The narrative song cycles which largely take the place of dances among the Mohave, and have been mentioned for the Chemehuevi and Luiseño, are very much less known among the Yuma, the fragmentary information available being mostly from Mohave sources. The accessible data for all the Yuman tribes and some of their Shoshonean neighbors are gathered in the appended table. From this collocation it is clear that some song series have traveled widely and are so definitely international at present that their tribal origin can perhaps never be ascertained. It appears further that the Mohave have been most active in this religio-aesthetic manifestation. On the one hand they have borrowed freely, on the other they have probably been drawn upon by their neighbors to an at least equal extent.

At any rate, they possess much the largest number of cycles: 20 which they claim as their own, besides at least 10 more sung by doctors. Seven of the 20 are shared by one or more other tribes, and are likely to be of foreign devising. But the remainder are, so far as known, purely Mohave; and this is a greater number of series than has been recorded for any other people in the region. And it is not likely that the disproportion is altogether due to incompleteness of information. The Chemehuevi, for instance, themselves assert that they possess no more than four kinds of singings.

TABLE 8.—YUMAN SONG CYCLES.[1]

Mohave	Yuma	Maricopa	Cocopa	Kamia	Diegueño	Yavapai[3]	Chemehuevi	Serrano[3]	Cahuilla
Birds[4]	Birds								Birds.
Av'alyunu[4]	Av'alyunu								
Alysa[4]			Alysa	Alysa					
Tumanpa			Tumanpa		Tu-tomump[5]			Tumanpa[6]	Tumanpa[7]
Raven				Raven					
Salt		Salt			Salt		Salt		
Turtle									Turtle.
Deer		Deer					Deer		
Eagle[8]		Eagle			(9)				
Kwiya-humara[10]					Kuya-homar				
Shaman?'s[11]							Shaman's.		
	Frog								
	Mat-hamuchicha								
	Chichohoichva	Taris[13]							
	Harraupa	Buzzard			Orup[18]				
		Mockingbird							
				Pi'ipa[14]					
						Rabbit.			
							Mountain sheep.		
	Ohoma[15]				Keruk[16]				
	Karu'uka[16]				Kachahwar[17]				
					Awi-kunchi[18]				
				Hakile	Akil[19]				
					Hortloi[20]				
					Tuharl.				
					Tipai.				
					Isa[22]				
(21)									

1 Data on Maricopa, Diegueño, and Chemehuevi from themselves; for all other tribes from Mohave informants. The tribes heading the last three columns are Shoshonean groups adjacent to Yumans. The Diegueño series except the Keruk are known only from the Southern division of the group. The Mohave add that the Maricopa sing the equivalent of their own *Satukhota* or *Kutiya-humara; Kampanyka,* bat; *Sakachara,* a bird called *sakacheka* in Mohave; and *Avadho,* an underground insect or chrysalis.

2 And Walapai.

3 The "Vanyume" of the Mohave. Possibly the Kawaiisu are meant.

4 Borrowed by the Mohave from the Yuma.

5 Said to be sung with Mohave words, and a phonographed song was promptly identified by the Mohave as their "Long Tumanpa." Also mentioned as *Tomanp.*

6 The Mohave sing this "Vanyume Tumanpa" in addition to two kinds of their own.

7 Said to be called *Tangilvere* by themselves, equated by the Mohave with Tumanpa.

8 About the eagle; called *Ohuera.*

9 The Diegueño practice a mourning rite in which an eagle is killed. This ceremony is practiced also by the Juaneño and Luiseño, and some of the Diegueño believe that it reached them from the latter people. Its songs, however, are in Diegueño, and appear to outline a story.

10 Name of the hero; the story and songs are called *Satukhota.*

11 The Mohave name ten or more kinds of doctor's singings.

12 Or *Urop.* A phonographed song was recognized by the Mohave as from the Yuma *Harrawpa.*

13 Compare *min-turis-turis,* the Mohave name of a waterbird.

14 This word means "person" in Mohave.

15 Two kinds of songs used at the mourning commemoration.

16 The commemorative mourning ceremony: *Wu-keruk* in the Southern dialect. The words seem to be Diegueño. The *Keruk* is said to contain *Cheyotai* or *Chayautai* songs, which perhaps should be reckoned separately.

17 Or *Achawhal.* A basket is rubbed: *chahwar* is said to mean "rub." The words are Southern Diegueño from Jacumba. The story tells of two brothers. The younger loses a contest and is killed by the older who goes to Maricopa land.

18 Sung to make fair weather. Diegueño words. The hero of the story is *Kwilyu.*

19 *Atanuk* or *Akil* is the girls' adolescence ceremony. Perhaps *Atanuk* refers to the rite, *Akil* to the songs. The words are Diegueño: the songs are not recognized by the Mohave, who seem to perform no public ritual for their girls.

20 *Hortloi, Hultuyp,* or *Hurlturli* is the Diegueño name of the dance of the introduced toloache cult. While this does not seem to have been mythologized by them, they evidently fit it into the scheme familiar to themselves.

21 Mohave cycles peculiar to themselves are omitted from this table. They are described in the preceding chapter.

22 Spier (see bibliography) gives the following southern Diegueño song cycles: Hasa' (=Isa ? birds); Tomanp (=Tu-tomunp); Ispa (eagle); Hahwar (scraping basket; =Kachahwar); Horhloi (=Horhloi); Tohar (rattle; =Tuharl); Tipai (people; =Tipai); Djokwar (speech); Tasitl (rattle); Hehltamataie (hair); Nyimi (wild-cat) and Parhau (fox), associated; Nyikwar (crane?); also, of doubtful independence: Orup (sad, mourning) and Chahotai (big song); and Nyiman-kumar (=Kuya-homar), equated with Tomanp. Tipai and Horhloi are recognized as of Shoshonean origin.

Mohave stimulation is further shown in the fact that their sacred peak Avikwame or Dead Mountain is sung about by the Yuma and Diegueño, and, according to the Mohave themselves, by the Walapai and Maricopa; although the corresponding mythic center of the Chemehuevi, Charleston Peak, is in their own territory. Aha'av'-ulypo or Eldorado Canyon to the north of Avikwame, which is almost equally important in Mohave tradition, is also known to the Yuma. Some of the Mohave song narratives begin or end far afield, toward Tehachapi or in the Yavapai country or in Sonora; but the two places mentioned certainly dominate their mythic geography, and this point of view is reflected in Yuma story, and to a less degree among the Diegueño. It should be mentioned that some Diegueño accounts place their "Wikami" at Picacho Peak near Yuma.

A comparison of the songs—both words and tune—which appear to be the concrete elements most frequently and completely transmitted, should readily solve most of the interrelations of source and of borrowing by the several tribes. The narrative material has presumably been much more thoroughly broken up and recombined in its wanderings from nation to nation; and the social use and ritual setting of the cycles are also likely to vary considerably according to tribe.

ORIGIN TRADITIONS OF SOUTHERN CALIFORNIA.

The account of origins of the Yuma, Mohave, Diegueño, and Maricopa is more or less completely known, for some of these tribes in several versions. All the stories agree sufficiently closely to allow of the recognition of a typical creation myth characteristic of the central Yuman tribes. It may be expected that the more remote northeastern and southwestern members of the family participated in this conglomerate of beliefs to a considerable extent. Much of the myth is shared with the neighboring Shoshoneans of southern California. The give and take between the two groups can not yet be determined fully. But certain distinctive Yuman and Shoshonean ideas emerge clearly.

The Shoshonean creation has been designated as a myth of emergence, in the sense that mankind and all things in the world are born from mother Earth, with Sky or Night as father. The divinity Wiyot, or whatever he may be called, is not the maker but the first born, the leader and instructor, of men. As a matter of fact, such was the belief only of the Luiseño, Juaneño, and perhaps Gabrielino. The hinterland tribes—Cupeño, Cahuilla, and Serrano—evince only traces of cosmic interest. With them, the world begins with two quarreling brothers, of whom one causes and the other opposes death, and one retires to the sky, the other into the earth—is named Earth, even, in some accounts. One of the pair manufactures mankind.

This is also in general the Yuman idea; but these people add the fact that the two brothers, the creator and his death-instituting opponent, are born at the bottom of the sea, and that the younger emerges blinded by the salt water. In most Yuman accounts this concept of water origin is somewhat hesitatingly blended with earth-sky parentage. The Mohave alone have substituted for the ocean origin a direct birth from the great mother and father, have reduced the part of the antagonistic younger brother to a minimum, forgotten his blindness, and hold men to have been born with the gods, not made by them. Their cosmogony therefore assumes the same philosophy as that of the Luiseño-Gabrielino—a philosophy of distinctly Pueblo type; whereas the other tribes of the region, Yuman as well as Shoshonean, adhere to a more personalized and concrete conception. As the Mohave and Luiseño-Gabrielino are not in contact, in fact are separated by tribes like the Cahuilla, their cosmogonies can not be traced to a directly common source. They may be specializations, erected more or less independently, through a reweighting of particular ideas which in halting and ineffective form were once or are still the common property of all the Indians of southern California. Two mythological strata can therefore be recognized as regards cosmogony. The underlying one is represented by the Serrano, Cahuilla, Diegueño, and in the main by the Yuma and Maricopa. The upper crops out among the Gabrielino-Luiseño and, some distance away, among the Mohave, with some indications among the Yuma.

In the underlying stratum the Yuman names of the creator and his brother are Tuchaipa and Kokomat or Yokomatis. These designations are common to such distant tribes as the Diegueño and Maricopa, and must therefore be regarded as part of an old Yuman inheritance. But a curious inconsistence prevails. The Diegueño sometimes combine the names into Chaipa-Komat or Chakumat and apply this term to the creator, or call him Mayoha, which perhaps refers to the sky. At other times Chaipa-Komat is the earth from which the first man is made by the creator. The Yuma call the creator Kwikumat, whereas his companion, who is no longer his brother, is merely Blind Old Man. The Mohave introduce an entirely new name, Matavilya, for the leading divinity, and retain only faint traces of the concept of his companion who disappears under ground.

The creator makes men from clay: the younger brother attempts the same, but misshapes his creatures, who turn into web-footed birds—which, it may be added, play a considerable part in the song cycles of some Mohave shamans.

The great divinity, whether creator or leader, offends his daughter Frog, and is killed by her swallowing his voidings. This concept of the dying god, and of the mourning for him, is universal among Yumans and Shoshoneans, and is probably the dominant and most poignantly felt motive of every mythology in southern California. Its analogue in the Aztec Quetzalcoatl story has already been commented upon; but it is important that no parallel is known among the Pueblos or any true southwestern people. There may have been connections with the central and south Mexican story through Sonora. But except for dim suggestions, the development of the idea is probably local. All the Californians make much of the origin of death; and the Yuman and southern Shoshonean tale appears to think less of the impending end of the great god himself than of the fate of humanity as typified by him.

Everywhere there follows a concrete and circumstantial narration of the preparations for the divinity's cremation, of Coyote's plans to possess himself of his heart, of the measures taken to prevent this design, and of Coyote's success and consequent execration. The Juaneño are the only people known to have accompanied this story with a ritualistic practice; but the custom may have been more widely spread. This funerary cannibalism clearly rests upon generic Californian ideas of death and acts due the dead; and it is characteristic that its known occurrence is among those of the southern Californians nearest to the central part of the State, in which a similar custom is reported from the Pomo, although, of course, without a trace of the associated mythology. The custom further emphasizes what the flavor of the myth itself indicates: that the dying god motive is largely a native rather than an imported product.

Some Diegueño versions omit the death of Tuchaipa and consequently Coyote's theft also. This may be mere incompleteness of record; but as the myths in question are all from southerly Diegueño territory, it is not impossible that there existed a south Yuman area, centering in Baja California, in which these episodes were dispensed with. This would indicate that the dying god concept developed in southern California proper, where its ritualistic counterpart also has its seat, and inclines the balance toward a Shoshonean rather than a Yuman origin for the idea and its principal associations.

The Mohave rather slight Matavilya-Tuchaipa: his chief function is to die. His son, or, according to some accounts, younger brother, Mastamho, enters at far greater length into the narration, as the shaper and ordainer of things on the earth, and the instructor of men in all cultural relations. With the Yuma, the disproportion is not so marked; but Ku-mastamho is still of great importance.

Maricopa tradition, so far as it is fragmentarily known, does not mention this second great divinity; and the Diegueño do not know him. There is also no specific Shoshonean parallel: Chungichnish, who appears after Wiyot's death, is far too vague and shadowy a figure to compare with the practically active and more human Mastamho. This divinity seems therefore to be a creation of the Mohave; and this conclusion is confirmed by his definite association with the mountain Avikwame.

One other episode the Yuma and Mohave share with the Diegueño. Sky-Rattlesnake—Kammayaveta, Maihaiowit, Maiaveta, or Umas-ereha—is sent from his ocean abode to Avikwame, where, on entering the house, his head is chopped off or he is burned. The motive is punishment of the doctor of evil design or the desire to acquire his ritualistic knowledge. This is an incident not recorded among any Shoshonean tribe; but the monster recurs in the Zuñi Kolowisi and is an ancient southwestern concept with water associations.

The specific common Yuman elements in this cosmogony are the rising out of the deep of the creator Tuchaipa, the blindness, opposition, and miscreations of his brother Kokomat, and the killing of Maiaveta. The complex of ideas associated with the dying god and Coyote's theft of his heart is a general Yuman possession, more likely to have originated among the Shoshoneans. Besides the fluctuating and often vague belief in Sky and Earth as the initial parents of all else, this set of Wiyot-Matavilya concepts is the principal theme of wide scope common to the two families of tribes. The Mohave have most largely developed the non-Yuman elements of the tradition, as well as the Mastamho cycle, which appears to be a special growth that has assimilated a variety of minor elements of Yuman origin. The Yuma stand next to the Mohave in both points. It does not seem that the contacts of these tribes with Shoshoneans were as numerous as the contacts of the Diegueño, but they evidently assimilated more because they were more inclined to mythologize. The difference is one between the comparatively active and specialized culture of the river tribes and a more generic, simple, and apathetic civilization among the Diegueño.

It is rather remarkable how closely the Maricopa adhere to the common Yuman tradition, if the record is to be trusted, whereas their national fortunes in the historic period have been intimately linked with those of the Pima, and the nearest of their kinsmen—the Yuma, Yavapai, and Mohave—have been their hereditary foes. The inference is that the Maricopa, like the Halchidhoma whom they subsequently received, were resident on the Colorado at no very ancient period. This is indicated also by their speech, which is said to be almost identical with Yuma, but perceptibly different from the dialects of the Yuman nomadic mountain tribes of western Arizona.

It has indeed often been asserted that the Maricopa were an offshoot from the Colorado River tribes; but all such statements appear to be assumptions based only on the knowledge that the tribe of Piman associations spoke a Yuman language, and to have been devoid, hitherto, of substantiation by definite historical evidence. How far the general civilization of the Maricopa retains its original cast, or, on the other hand, has yielded to the influences of their alien but allied neighbors, it is impossible to say, in the almost total absence of exact information about them; but, like the Havasupai, they bid fair to present valuable material for a study in the interesting problem of native American acculturation.

MOURNING AND ADOLESCENCE CEREMONIES.

The Yuma mourning ceremony, which is called *Nyimits*, "crying," and, like that of the Mohave, is generally known in English as an "Annual," appears to be made especially for distinguished warriors, and not for hereditary chiefs, rich men, or the dead of the community at large. This flavoring is distinctly eastern, although the commemoration concept itself is preeminently characteristic of California. The eastern cast appears in several features, such as mimic warfare and the use of a shield.

The rites are held under an open shade, where two lines of men sing *Karu'uka* and *Ohoma* songs during the night. The former are at the west end, the latter at the east, but both face toward the dawn. As this approaches, they dance in turn, and then, after it is day, dance again to the east of the shade. During the last Karu'uka singing, a handled skin drawn over a willow hoop and feathered at the edge, in other words a shield, is displayed; and as a climax, the shade is set on fire and an arrow shot against the shield, whereupon it and the bow and arrow are cast upon the blazing pile. There are other features of a dramatic character whose place in the rite is not clear. Two armed men run, another pair pursues shoulder to shoulder, the first turn and discharge an arrow which the hinder twain, separating, allow to pass between them. There is also said to be a pair of riders who avoid arrows; and apparently some symbolic taunting with death in war. The dualism that obviously pervades the performance, in spite of formal adherence to the four-folding ceremonial pattern of the tribe, seems also connected with the idea of antithesis in combat.

The *Ohoma* singers carry a sort of arrow feathered at both ends; the *Karu'uka* party is led with a deer-hoof rattle. *Karu'uka* has already been mentioned as being the same word as the Diegueño *Keruk;* but the latter rite is a much more typical Californian mourning ceremony.

This, except for an allusion to its use by the Diegueño, is the most westerly known occurrence of the shield, whose distribution stretches through the Pima and Apache to the Pueblo and Plains tribes. Neither the Yuma nor the Mohave, however, appear to have used the implement very extensively in actual warfare, and there is no mention of any heraldry in connection with it. The true Californians fought naked, or, in the north, in body armor.

The Yuma hold an adolescence ceremony for girls, but its specific traits are too obscure to allow comparisons. As among the Mohave, there is no record of a tribal or societal initiation of boys. Since the coast tribes as well as the Pueblos on the other side practice initiations, even agreeing in such details as the employment of sand paintings, the absence of this set of customs among the Colorado River tribes is significant of their specialization in religion.

TOLOACHE.

The Yuma dreamers know and use Jimson weed, *smalykapita*,[1] Mohave *malykatu*, much as the Mohave do, to stimulate their dreams; in other words, as individual shamans. This differentiates the employment of the plant from its utilization by the Gabrielino and adjacent tribes, to whom it is the center of the initiation complex. The Yuma-Mohave attitude seems to be that of the Pueblos, to judge by the Zuñi, who use the drug in medical practice and to attain second sight. The Walapai and White Mountain Apache employ the plant. The association of Jimson weed with religion is probably continuous from the San Joaquin Valley to southern Mexico. Toloache is an Aztec word and the plant was worshipped. While little is known of its employment, it may be presumed to have been sacred to the tribes of northern Mexico, except where unobtainable or relegated to obscurity by the peyote cult. At bottom, therefore, the southern California toloache religion may confidently be ascribed to ideas that, like so much else in North America, originated in Mexico or Central America. On the other hand, as a specific growth this religion is unquestionably local, the Colorado Valley and Pueblo use of toloache being of much more elementary character in a more highly organized religious setting. In short, we are dealing here with an instance of connection between California and the Southwest in which historical priority must as usual be given to the more advanced region; and yet to regard the Californian manifestations as merely an imperfect loan from the Southwest would be erroneous. It is only the source that the Pueblos contributed, and a borrowed source at that. The growths upon it were independent: in fact, that of the humbler people the more luxuriant.

THE SWEAT HOUSE.

A parallel condition is presented by the sweat house, except that the discontinuity in recent times is emphasized by the lack of the institution among the spatially intermediate Yumans of the great

---

[1] Probably *Datura discolor* instead of the *D. meteloides* used in most of the remainder of California. See footnote, page 502.

river. Neither the Yuma, the Mohave, nor, it seems, the Pima and Papago of Arizona know the universal Californian sweat house. On the other hand, the sweat house correlates with the Pueblo kiva or estufa, which in spite of a possible augmentation of its sacred character under pressure from the Spaniard, retains some of its former functions of man's club and sleeping place; while even its religious associations are never wholly wanting in California. A failure to connect the kiva and the sweat house would be more than shortsighted. But an immediate derivation of the latter from the former would not only be hasty on general grounds, but directly contradicted by the Yuman gap. Here, too, then, we find entirely new associations clustering about the institution in its Pacific coast range; even possibly an enlargement of the sweat house into the dance house or assembly chamber of the Sacramento Valley tribes, and its definite affiliation with the masked society cult, every particular trait of which has obviously been devised on the spot. Again, also, we have the indication of an ultimate source in Mexico, the home of the temescal; and, to illustrate the principle one step farther, there is the Plains sweat lodge, the idea of which must be carried back to the same root, but whose concrete form, as well as its place in religion and daily custom, are markedly different from those of temescal, kiva, or California sweat house.

Incidentally, the cultural importance of the sweat house is one of the bonds that links the Yurok and Hupa to the Californian peoples, in spite of the numerous features which their civilization shares with that of the North Pacific coast in its narrower sense. The latter tract scarcely knows the sweat house.

The house is ritually significant to the Yuma and Mohave in myth, song, and symbolism, but is not itself ritually employed to any extent. It is referred to as "dark house" and "dark round." The open sided roof shade has similar though weaker associations as a concept; while actually used in cult, the structure is scarcely sacred. The ceremonial enclosure constructed by the group of peoples influenced by the Gabrielino is as foreign to the river tribes as the sweat house, but reappears among the Navaho, and may have a true homologue in the court or plaza in which most Pueblo dances are performed.

THE MOHAVE-YUMA CULTURE.

A balance may now be struck between the cultural affiliations of the lower Colorado tribes with the Indians respectively of the Southwest and of California, especially of southern California. Civilizational traits such as pottery and emergence myths, which are common to all three areas, may be left out of this consideration.

The Yuma and Mohave share with the southwestern peoples agriculture; totemic clan exogamy; a tribal sense; a considerable military spirit and desire for warlike renown; and the shield; all of which are un-Californian. They also agree with the southwesterners in lacking several generic or widespread Californian traits: a regard for wealth; basketry as a well-cultivated art; and the use of toloache in an organized cult.

On the other hand, they resemble the Californians and differ from the southwesterners in reckoning descent paternally; in holding public religious mourning commemorations; in hereditary chieftainship; and in the lack of architecture in stone, a priestly hierarchy, masks, depictive art, the loom, and body dress on a notable scale.

It is clear that there is substantially no less and no more reason for reckoning the river tribes in the Southwest than in the California culture area.

That they are more than merely transitional is revealed by a number of peculiarities. These, strangely enough for a people of intermediate location, are mostly negative: they lack the sweat house, the ceremonial enclosure, the initiating society, and the sand painting which the Gabrielino and Luiseño on their west share with the Pueblos and Navahos to the east.

The positive particularities of moment are all clearly and closely interrelated, and may be designated as the peculiar system of song-myth-rites with its reduction of dancing to a minimum and its basis of belief in an unusual form of dreams which also lend a characteristic color to shamanism. In this one association of religious traits, accordingly, rests the active distinctiveness of Yuma-Mohave culture; and to this growth must be attributed the local suppression of elements like the sweat house and the secret society.

It seems likely that when the culture of the Sonoran tribes shall be better known, it may link at least as closely as that of the Pueblos with that of the lower Colorado tribes and explain much of the genesis of the latter.

CHAPTER 53.

OTHER YUMAN TRIBES.

THE NATIONS ON THE COLORADO.

Besides the Mohave and Yuma, at least five other tribes of the same lineage once occupied the shores of the Colorado. Of these, only the Cocopa and Kamia retain their identity, and the latter are few. The others are extinct or merged. In order upstream these tribes were the Cocopa, Halyikwamai, Alakwisa, Kohuana, Kamia, Yuma, Halchidhoma, and Mohave.

THE COCOPA.

The Cocopa, called Kwikapa by the Mohave, held the lowest courses of the river, chiefly, it would seem, on the west bank. They have survived in some numbers, but have, and always had, their seats in Baja California. They are mentioned by name as early as 1605.

THE HALYIKWAMAI OR KIKIMA.

The Halyikwamai, as the Mohave call them, are the Quicama or Quicoma of Alacon in 1540, the Halliquamallas of Oñate in 1605, the Quiquima or Jalliquamay of Garcés in 1776, and therefore the first California group to have a national designation recorded and preserved. Oñate puts them next to the Cocopa, on the east bank of the Colorado, Garcés on the west bank between the Cocopa and the Kohuana. Garcés estimated them to number 2,000, but his population figures for this region are high, especially for the smaller groups. It seems impossible that three or four separate tribes should each have shrunk from 2,000 or 3,000 to a mere handful in less than a century during which they lived free and without close contact with the whites.

The discrepancies between the habitat assigned by one authority on the left bank and the other on the right, for this and other tribes, are of little moment. It is likely that every nation on the river owned both sides, and shifted from one to the other, or divided, according to the exigencies of warfare, fancy, or as the channel and farm lands changed. The variations in linear position along the river, on the contrary, were due to tribal migrations dependent on hostilities or alliances.

HALYIKWAMAI AND AKWA'ALA.

The Mohave, who do not seem to know the name Quigyuma or Quiquima, say that the Halyikwamai survive, but know them only as mountaineers west of the river. West of the Cocopa, that is, in the interior of northernmost Baja California, they say is Avi-aspa, " Eagle Mountain," visible from the vicinity of Yuma; and north of it another large peak called Avi-savet-kyela. Between the two mountains is a low hilly country. This and the region west of Avi-aspa is the home of the Akwa'ala or Ekwa'ahle, a Yuman tribe whose speech seems to the Mohave to be close to the Walapai dialect and different from Diegueño. They were still there in some numbers about 30 years ago, the Mohave say, and rode horses. They did not farm. They were neighbors of the Kamia-ahwe or Diegueño, and occasionally met the Mohave at Yuma or among the Cocopa.

The Halyikwamai, the Mohave say, adjoined the Akwa'ala on the north, near the Yuma, and, like the Akwa'ala, were hill dwellers. They also did not farm, but migrated seasonally into the higher mountains to collect mescal root, *vadhilya*. They did not, in recent times, come to the river even on visits, evidently on account of the old feuds between themselves and the Yuma and Kamia. In the last war expedition which the Yuma and Mohave made against the Cocopa, about 1855, the Akwa'ala and Halyikwamai were allied with the Cocopa.

It would seem, therefore, that the Halyikwamai or Quigyuma or Quiquima are an old river tribe that was dispossessed by its more powerful neighbors, took up an inland residence, and of necessity abandoned agriculture.

THE ALAKWISA.

The country of the Alakwisa is occasionally mentioned by the Mohave in traditions, but the tribe seems to have been extinct for some time, and fancy has gathered a nebulous halo about its end. Here is the story of an old Mohave.

When I was young an old Mohave told me how he had once come homeward from the Cocopa, and after running up along the river for half a day, saw house posts, charcoal, broken pottery, and stone mortars. He thought the tract must still be inhabited, but there was no one in sight. He ran on, and in the evening reached the Kamia, who told him that he had passed through the old Alakwisa settlements. His Kamia friends said that they had never seen the Alakwisa, the tribe having become extinct before their day, but that they had heard the story of their end. It is as follows:

There was a small pond from which the Alakwisa used to draw their drinking water, and which had never contained fish. Suddenly it swarmed with fish. Some dug wells to drink from, but these, too, were full of fish. They took them, and, although a few predicted disaster, ate the catch. Women began to fall over dead at the metate or while stirring fish mush, and men at their occupations. They were playing at hoop and darts, when eagles fought in the air, killed each other, and fell down. The Alakwisa clapped their hands, ran up, and gleefully divided the feathers, not knowing that deaths had already occurred in their homes. As they wrapped the eagle feathers, some of them fell over dead; others lived only long enough to put the feathers on.

Another settlement discovered a jar under a mesquite tree, opened it, and found four or five scalps. They carried the trophies home, mounted them on poles, but before they reached the singer, some of them dropped lifeless, and others fell dead in the dance. So one strange happening crowded on another, and each time the Alakwisa died swiftly and without warning. Whole villages perished, no one being left to burn the dead or the houses, until the posts remained standing or lay rotting on the ground, as if recently abandoned. So the Kamia told my old Mohave friend about the end of the Alakwisa.

Fabulous as is this tale, it is likely to refer to an actual tribe, although the name Alakwisa may be only a synonym of story for Halyikwamai or some other familiar term of history.

THE KOHUANA.

The Kohuana, Kuhuana, or Kahuene of the Mohave, are the Coana of Alarcón and the Cohuana of Oñate, who in 1605 found them in nine villages above the Halyikwamai. Garcés in 1776 called them Cajuenche, put them on the east side of the Colorado, also above the Halyikwamai and below the Kamia, and estimated there were 3,000 of them. Their fortunes ran parallel with those of the Halchidhoma, and the career of the two tribes is best considered together.

THE KAMIA AND YUMA.

Next above were the Kamia, also recorded as the Comeya, Quemaya, Comoyatz, or Camilya, who have already been discussed. There is much confusion concerning them, owing to the fact that besides the farming tribe on the river, who alone are the true Kamia of the Mohave, the Southern Diegueño call themselves Kamiai, and the Mohave call all the Diegueño "foreign Kamia." It is, however, well established that a group of this name was settled on the Colorado adjacent to the Yuma.

The Yuma have also been reviewed separately.

THE HALCHIDHOMA.

The Halchidhoma or Halchadhoma, as the Mohave know them, were unquestionably at one time an important nation, suffered reverses, and at last completely lost their identity among the Maricopa, although there are almost certain to be survivors to-day with that tribe. Oñate found them the first tribe on the river below the Gila. Kino, a century later, brings them above the Gila. They had no doubt taken refuge here from the Yuma or other adjacent enemies, but can have profited little by the change, since it brought them nearer the Mohave, who rejoiced in harrying them. Garcés makes them extend 15 leagues northward along the river to a point an equal distance south of Bill Williams Fork. He was among them in person and succeeded in patching up a temporary peace between them and the Mohave. He calls them Alchedum and Jalchedunes, but they can scarcely still have numbered 2,500 in 1776, as he reports.

The Mohave report that the Kohuana and Halchidhoma once lived along the river at Parker, about halfway between the Mohave and Yuma territories. This period must have been subsequent to 1776, since the location corresponds with that in which Garcés found the Halchidhoma, whereas in his day the Kohuana were still below the Yuma. Evidently they, too, found living too uncomfortable in the turmoil of tribes below the confluence of the Gila—the Mohave say that they lived at Aramsi on the east side of the stream below the Yuma and were troubled by the latter—and followed the Halchidhoma to the fertile but unoccupied bottom lands farther up. If they had been free of a quarrel with the Mohave, their union with the Halchidhoma brought them all the effects of one.

It must have been about this period of joint residence that the Halchidhoma, attempting reprisals, circuited eastward and came down on the Mohave from the Walapai Mountains. In this raid they captured a Mohave girl at Aha-kwa'-a'i, with whom they returned to their home at Parker, and then sold to the Maricopa. Subsequently, in an attack on the latter tribe, the Mohave found a woman who, instead of fleeing, stood still with her baby, and when they approached, called to them that she was the captive. They took her back, she married again, and had another son, Cherahota, who was still living in 1904. Her half-Maricopa son grew up among the Mohave, and becoming a shaman, was killed near Fort Mohave. This indicates that he reached a tolerable age.

But the preponderance of numbers and aggressions must have been on the side of the Mohave, because they finally drove both Halchidhoma and Kohuana south from Parker, back toward the

Yuma. The Halchidhoma settled at Aha-kw-atho'ilya, a long salty "lake" or slough, that stretched for a day's walk west of the river at the foot of the mountains. The Kohuana removed less far, to Avi-nya-kutapaiva and Hapuvesa, but remained only a year, and then settled farther south, although still north of the Halchidhoma.

After a time the Mohave appeared in a large party, with their women and children. They would scarcely have done this if their foes had retained any considerable strength. It was a five days' journey from Mohave Valley to the Kohuana. The northerners claimed the Kohuana as kinsmen but kept them under guard while the majority of their warriors went on by night. They reached the settlements of the Halchidhoma in the morning, the latter came out, and an open fight ensued, in which a few Halchidhoma were killed, while of the Mohave a number were wounded but none fell. In the afternoon, the Mohave returned—pitched battles rarely ended decisively among any of these tribes—and announced to the Kohuana that they had come to live with them. They also invited the Halchidhoma to drive them out; which the latter were probably too few to attempt. For four days the Mohave remained quietly at the Kohuana settlements doctoring their wounded. They had probably failed to take any Halchidhoma scalps, since they made no dance. The four days over, they marched downstream again, arrived in the morning, and fought until noon, when they paused to retire to the river to drink. The Halchidhoma used this breathing space to flee. They ran downstream, swam the river to the eastern bank, and went on to Ava-chuhaya. The Mohave took six captives and spoiled the abandoned houses.

After about two days, the Mohave account proceeds, they went against the foe once more, but when they reached Ava-chuhaya found no one. The Halchidhoma had cut east across the desert to take refuge with the Hatpa-'inya, the "East Pima," or Maricopa. Here ends their career; and it is because of this merging of their remnant with the Maricopa that when the Mohave are asked about the latter tribe they usually declare them to have lived formerly on the river between themselves and the Yuma: the Halchidhoma are meant. There can be little doubt that the Maricopa, too, were once driven from the river to seek an asylum near the alien and powerful Pima; but the Spanish historical notices place them with the latter people on the Gila for so long a time back—to at least the beginning of the eighteenth century—that their migration must far antedate the period which native tradition traverses.

The Mohave decided to stay on in the land above Aha-kw-atho'ilya, which the Halchidhoma had possessed, expecting that the latter would return. They remained all winter. There is said to have been no one left in the Mohave country.   In spring, when the mesquite was nearly ripe and the river was soon to rise and open the planting season, they returned, traveling three days.   The Kohuana went with them under compulsion, but without the Mohave having to use force.

For five years the Kohuana lived in Mohave Valley.   Then they alleged an equally close kinship with the Yuma and a wish to live among them.   The Mohave allowed them to go.   Ten days' journey brought them to their ancient foes.   After four years of residence here, one of their number was killed by the Yuma and his body hidden.   His kinsmen found it and resolved to leave as soon as their going would not be construed as due to a desire for revenge—an interpretation that might bring an immediate Yuma attack upon them. They waited a year; and then their chief, Tinyam-kwacha-kwacha, "Night traveler," a man of powerful frame, so tall that a blanket reached only to his hips, led them eastward between the mountains Kara'epe and Avi-hachora up the Gila.   They found the Maricopa at Maricopa Wells, recounted the many places at which they had lived, and asked for residence among their hosts.   Aha-kurrauva, the Maricopa chief, told them to remain forever.

So the Mohave story, the date of which may refer to the period about 1820 to 1840.   In 1851 Bartlett reported 10 "Cawina" surviving among the Maricopa.   But this was an underestimation, as a further Mohave account reveals.

About 1883 the same Mohave who is authority for the foregoing, having been told by certain Kohuana who had remained among the Mohave, or by their half-Mohave descendants, that there were kinsmen of theirs with the Maricopa, went to Tempe and there found not only Kohuana but Halchidhoma, although the Americans regarded them both as Maricopa.   The Kohuana chief was Hatpa'-ammay-ime, "Papago-foot," an old man, whom Ahwanchevari, the Maricopa chief, had appointed to be head over his own people. Hatpa'-ammay-ime had been born in the Maricopa country, but his father, and his father's sister, who was still living, were born while the Kohuana spent their five years among the Mohave.   He enumerated 6 old Kohuana men as still living and 10 young men—36 souls in all, besides a few children in school.

These statements, if accurate, would place the Kohuana abandonment of the river at least as early as 1820; and the date agrees with the remark of an old Mohave, about 1904, that the final migration of the tribe occurred in his grandfather's time.   It does not reconcile with the fact that a son of the Mohave woman taken captive by the Halchidhoma—who are said to have fled to the Maricopa 10 years earlier than the Kohuana—was yet living in 1904.   In any event, in

1776 both tribes were still on the Colorado and sufficiently numerous to be reckoned substantially on a par with the Yuma and Mohave; in 1850, when the American came, they were merged among the Maricopa, and of the seven or eight related but warring Yuman nations that once lived on the banks of the stream, there remained only three, the Cocopa, Yuma, and Mohave, and a fragment of a fourth, the Kamia. The drift has quite clearly been toward the suppression of the smaller units and the increase of the larger, a tendency probably influential on the civilization of the region, and perhaps stimulative in its effects.

TRIBES ENCOUNTERED BY OÑATE IN 1605.

The native information now accumulated allows the valuable findings of the Oñate expedition of 1605, as related by Zárate-Salmeron, to be profitably summarized, reinterpreted, and compared with those of later date.

In Mohave Valley, a 10 days' journey from the mouth of the river, as the natives then reckoned and still count, Oñate found the Amacavas or Amacabos. This tribe has therefore occupied substantially the same tract for at least three centuries. Their "Curraca," or "Lord," is only *kwora'aka*, "old man."

Five leagues downstream through a rocky defile brought Oñate to Chemehuevi Valley, where more Mohave lived.

Below the Mohave, evidently in the region about Parker or beyond, Oñate encountered an allied nation of the same speech, the Bahacechas. This name seems unidentifiable. Their head, Cohota, was so named for his office: he is the *kohota* or entertainment chief of the Mohave.

On the river of the Name of Jesus, the Gila, Oñate found a less affable people of different appearance and manners and of difficult speech, who claimed 20 villages all the way up that stream. These he calls Ozaras, a name that can also not be identified. The Relation gives the impression that this tribe stood apart from all those on the Colorado. They do not seem to be the Maricopa, whose speech even to-day is close to that of the river tribes. The most convincing explanation is that they were the Pima or Papago or at least some Piman division, who then lived farther down the Gila than subsequently. This agrees with the statement that they extended to the shores of the sea.

Along the Colorado from the Gila to the ocean all the Colorado nations were like the Bahacechas in dress and speech—that is, Yumans.

The first were the Halchidoma, in 8 pueblos, the northernmost alone said to contain 160 houses and 2,000 people.

Next came the Cohuana in 9 villages, of 5,000 inhabitants, of whom 600 accompanied the expedition.

Below were the Agolle, Haglli, or Haclli, in 5 (or 100!) settlements, and next the Halliquamalla or Agalecquamaya, 4,000 or 5,000 strong, of whom more than 2,000 assembled from 6 villages.

Finally, in 9 pueblos, reaching down to where the river became brackish 5 leagues above its mouth, were the Cocopa.

The mythical island Ziñogaba in the sea sounds as if it might be named from "woman," *thenya'aka* in Mohave, and *ava*, "house." Its chieftainess, Ciñaca cohota, is certainly "woman-*kohota*." "Acilla," the ocean, is Mohave *hatho'ilya*. Other modern dialects have " s " where Mohave speaks " th." It is clear that the languages of the Colorado have changed as little in three centuries as the speech of the Chumash that Cabrillo recorded.

CHANGES IN THREE CENTURIES.

Apart from the Ozara, on the Gila, Oñate thus encountered seven Yuman nations on the left bank of the Colorado. Five of these are familiar, two appear under unknown designations, and the Yuma and Kamia are not mentioned. Possibly they remained on the California side of the river and thus failed of enumeration. But if the foreign Ozara held the Gila to its mouth there would have been no place for the Yuma in their historic seats.

Alarcón's data, the earliest of all for the region or for any part of California, specify the Quicama (Halyikwamai), Coana (Kohuana), and Cumana (Kamia?), and allude to many elements of the culture of later centuries: maize, beans, squashes or gourds, pottery, clubs, dress, coiffure, transvestites, cremation, intertribal warfare, attitude toward strangers, relations with the mountain tribes; as well as characteristic temperamental traits—enthusiasm, resistance to fatigue, stubbornness under provocation, an ebullient emotionality.

Alarcón and Melchior Diaz in 1540, Oñate in 1605, Kino in 1702, and Garcés in 1776, accordingly found conditions on the river much as they were when the American came. The tribes battled, shifted, and now and then disappeared. The uppermost and lowest were the same for 300 years: the Mohave and Cocopa. Among the conflicts, customs remained stable. If civilization developed, it was inwardly; the basis and manner of life were conservative.

CHAPTER 54.

ARTS OF LIFE.

This and the following two chapters on society and religion abandon the nationally descriptive presentation which has so far been followed for a comparative one. They are included for the convenience of those whose interest is generally ethnographic rather than intensive or local; but they make no attempts at completeness. On topics for which information is abundant or fruitfully summarizable it is collected here and reviewed. Subjects on which knowledge is irregular, or profuse but miscellaneous, or complicated by intricate considerations, have been omitted. For all such matter, the reader is referred to the appropriate passages in the tribal accounts which make the body of this book, and which can be assembled through the subject index.

DRESS.

The standard clothing of California, irrespective of cultural provinces, was a short skirt or petticoat for women, and either nothing at all for men or a skin folded about the hips. The breechclout is frequently mentioned, but does not seem to have been aboriginal. The sense of modesty as regards men was very slightly developed. In many parts all men went wholly naked except when the weather demanded protection, and among all groups old men appear to have gone bare of clothing without feeling of impropriety. The women's skirt was everywhere in two pieces. A smaller apron was worn in front. A larger back piece extended at least to the hips and frequently reached to meet the front apron. Its variable materials are of two classes, buckskin and plant fibers. Local supply was the chief factor in determining choice. If the garment was of skin, its lower half was slit into fringes. This allowed much greater freedom of movement, but the decorative effect was also felt and made use of. Of vegetable fibers the most frequently used was the inner bark of trees shredded and gathered on a cord. Grass, tule, ordinary cordage, and wrapped thongs are also reported.

As protection against rain and wind, both sexes donned a skin blanket. This was either thrown over the shoulders like a cape, or wrapped around the body, or passed over one arm and under the other and tied or secured in front. Sea-otter furs made the most prized cloak of this type where they could be obtained. Land otter, wildcat, deer, and almost every other kind of fur was not disdained. The woven blanket of strips of rabbit fur or bird skin sometimes rendered service in this connection, although primarily an article of bedding.

There was not much sewing. It was performed with bone awls, apparently of the same types as used in basket coiling (Fig. 67, a–h). In the northwest, where no coiled baskets were made, awls were used to slit lamprey eels.

The typical California moccasin, which prevailed over central and northwestern California, was an unsoled, single-piece, soft shoe, with one seam up the front and another up the heel. This is the Yurok, Hupa, and Miwok type. The front seam is puckered, but sometimes with neat effect. The heel seam is sometimes made by a thong drawn through. The Lassik knew a variant form, in which a single seam from the little toe to the outer ankle sufficed. The draw string varied: the Miwok did without, the Lassik placed it in front of the ankle, the Yurok followed the curious device of having the thong, self-knotted inside, come out through the sole near its edge, and then lashing it over instep and heel back on itself. This is an arrangement that would have been distinctly unpractical on the side of wear had the moccasins been put on daily or for long journeys. Separate soles of rawhide are sometimes added, but old specimens are usually without, and the idea does not seem to be native. The moccasin comes rather higher than that of the Plains tribes, and appears not to have been worn with its ankle portion turned down. Journeys, war, wood gathering are the occasions mentioned for the donning of moccasins; as well as cold weather, when they were sometimes lined with grass. They were not worn about the village or on ordinary excursions.

The Modoc and Klamath moccasin stands apart through eastern modification. It appears to have been without stiff sole, but contained three pieces: the sole and moccasin proper, reaching barely to the ankle; a U-shaped inset above the toes, prolonged into a loose tongue above; and a strip around the ankles, sewed to the edge of the main piece, and coming forward as far as the tongue. The main piece has the two seams customary in California. The ankle piece can be worn turned down or up; the draw string passes across the front of the tongue. The Atsugewi moccasin is also three-piece and therefore probably similar in plan.

Southern California is a region of sandals; but the desert Cahuilla wore a high moccasin for travel in the mountains. The

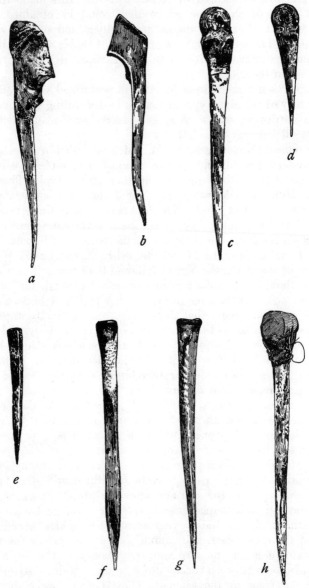

FIG. 67.—Bone awls. *a*, Pomo; *b*, Maidu; *c*, *d*, *e*, Yokuts; *f*, Yuki; *g*, *h*, Miwok.

hard sole curls over the thick but soft upper, and is sewed to it from the inside by an invisible stitch. The upper has its single seam at the back. The front is slit down to the top of the instep, and held together by a thong passed through the edges once or twice. The appearance of this moccasin is southwestern, and its structure nearly on the plan of a civilized shoe. It reaches well up on the calf.

Moccasins and leggings in an openwork twining of tule fibers were used in northeastern California and among the Clear Lake Pomo as a device for holding a layer of soft grass against the foot for warmth.

The skin legging is rarer than the moccasin. It was made for special use, such as travel through the snow.

The only snowshoe used in California is a rather small oval hoop, across which from one to three thongs or grape-vines are tied longitudinally and transversely (Fig. 68, a–d). The nearest parallels are in prehistoric pieces from the cliff-dweller area (Fig. 68, e).

In southern California the sandal of the Southwest begins to appear. In its character-istic local form it consists of mescal fiber, untwisted bundles of which are woven back and forth across a looped cord, forming a pad nearly an inch thick. (Pl. 62.) The Colo-rado River tribes have aban-

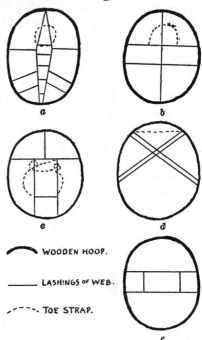

WOODEN HOOP.

LASHINGS OF WEB.

TOE STRAP.

Fig. 68.—The Californian snowshoe. a, Kla-math-Modoc, two-ply rawhide thong; b, Maidu, wrapped thong; c, Yurok, two-ply or four-ply grapevine; d, Nongatl, double thong, untwisted; e, prehistoric, Mesa Verde, Colo.

doned the use of this form of sandal, if ever they possessed it. In recent years they have worn simple rawhide sandals; but their very slender opportunities to hunt render it doubtful whether this is a type that antedates the introduction of horses and cattle among them. The Chemehuevi are said to have worn true moccasins. There is no clear report of any sandal north of Tehachapi.

The woman's basketry cap, a brimless cone or dome, is generally considered a device intended to protect against the chafe of the pack strap. That this interpretation is correct is shown by the fact that in the south the cap is worn chiefly when a load is to be carried; whereas in the north, where custom demands the wearing of the cap at all ordinary times, it is occasionally donned also by men when it becomes of service to them in the handling of a dip net which is steadied with the head. The woman's cap is not, however, a generic California institution. In the greater part of the central area it is unknown. Its northern and southern forms are quite distinct. Rather surprisingly, their distribution shows them to be direct adjuncts or dependents of certain basketry techniques. The northern cap coincides with the *Xerophyllum* technique and is therefore always made in overlaid twining. (Pls. 14, 70, 71, 73, *f*.) The range of the southern cap appears to be identical with that of baskets made on a foundation of *Epicampes* grass, and is accordingly a coiled product. (Pls. 53, 73, *d*.) There can be no question that tribes following other basketry techniques possessed the ability to make caps; but they did not do so. It is curious that an object of evident utilitarian origin, more or less influenced by fashion, should have its distribution limited according to the prevalence of basketry techniques and materials.

Two minor varieties of the cap occur. Among the Chemehuevi the somewhat peaked, diagonally twined cap of the Great Basin Shoshoneans was in use. It also occurs among the typical southern California tribes as far as the southern Diegueño by the side of the coiled cap. (Pl. 73, *d*.) This is likely to have been a comparatively recent invasion from the Great Basin, since coexistence of two types side by side among the same people is a condition contrary to prevailing ethnic precedent.

The Modoc employ but little overlay twining, and most of their caps are wholly in their regular technique of simple twining with tule materials. The Modoc cap averages considerably larger and is more distinctly flat topped than that of the other northern Californians.

The hair net worn by men (pls. 55, *a*, 72) centers in the region of the Kuksu religion, but its distribution seems most accurately described as exclusive of that of the woman's cap. Thus the Kato probably used the net and not the cap; the adjacent Wailaki reversed the situation. There are a few overlappings, as among the Yokuts, who employed both objects. The head net is also reported for the Shasta of Shasta Valley, but may have penetrated to them with the Kuksu elements carried into this region in recent years by the ghost dance.

Some tattooing (Figs. 45, 46) was practiced by most groups; facially more often than on the body, and more by women than by men. The most abundant patterns, taking in the whole cheeks, are found in the region of the Yuki and Wailaki; elsewhere the jaw is chiefly favored.

PLATE 71

HUPA WOMAN AND MEN

PLATE 72

FROM BUENA VISTA LAKE INTERMENTS

Above, head net and hair rolled in fashion of Lower Colorado tribes; below, cotton blanket, probably
of Pueblo manufacture, with rude armholes punched out

PLATE 73

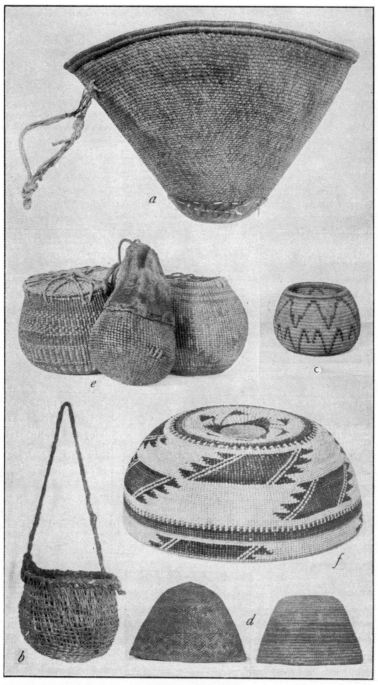

BASKETS AND CAPS

a, Chemehuevi carrying basket, diagonally twined; *b*, Luiseño, crude plain twining; *c*, Cahuilla; *d*, Cahuilla caps, diagonally twined and coiled; *e*, Yurok tobacco baskets; *f*, Yurok cap

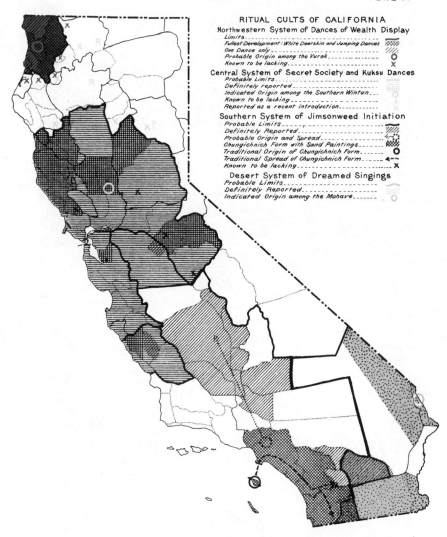

PLATE 74

RITUAL CULTS OF CALIFORNIA

Northwestern System of Dances of Wealth Display

Limits
Fullest Development: White Deerskin and Jumping Dances
One Dance only
Probable Origin among the Yurok
Known to be lacking

Central System of Secret Society and Kuksu Dances

Probable Limits
Definitely reported
Indicated Origin among the Southern Wintun
Known to be lacking
Reported as a recent introduction

Southern System of Jimsonweed Initiation

Probable Limits
Definitely Reported
Probable Origin and Spread
Chungichnich Form with Sand Paintings
Traditional Origin of Chungichnich Form
Traditional Spread of Chungichnich Form
Known to be lacking

Desert System of Dreamed Singings

Probable Limits
Definitely Reported
Indicated Origin among the Mohave

HOUSES.

The houses of native California are difficult to classify except in summary fashion. The extreme forms are well differentiated, but are all connected by transitions. The frame house of the Yurok and Hupa is a definite type whose affinity with the larger plank house of the North Pacific coast is sufficiently evident. Southward and eastward from the Yurok it becomes smaller and more rudely made. Bark begins to replace the split or hewn planks, and before long a conical form made wholly of bark slabs is attained. This in turn, if provided with a center post, need only be covered with soil to serve as the simple prototype of the large semisubterranean house of the Sacramento Valley. Again, the bark is often partly replaced by poles and sticks. If these are covered with thatch we have a simple form of the conical brush house. This in turn also attains the gabled, rectangular form of the plank house, as with the Cahuilla, or again is made oval, or round and domed, as among the Pomo and Chumash. In the latter case it differs from the semisubterranean house only in the lack of earth covering and its consequent lighter construction. A further transition is afforded by the fact that the earth house almost invariably has foliage of some kind as its topmost covering immediately below the dirt surfacing of the roof. The brush house is often dug out a short distance. The Chumash threw the earth from the excavation up against the walls for a few feet. The earth-covered house proper is only a little deeper and has the covering extending all the way over.

Neither shape, skeleton structure, nor materials, therefore, offer a satisfactory basis for the distinction of sharp types. A classification that would be of value would have to rest on minute analysis, preceded in many cases by more accurate information than is now available. Among numerous tribes the old types of houses have long since gone out of use. Among most of the remainder they have been at least partly modified, and the majority of early descriptions are too summary to be of great service.

Nor does a consideration of distributions hold much present promise of fuller understanding. The earth-covered house was made from the Modoc, Achomawi, and Yuki south to the Miwok; then again in the extreme part of southern California. The bark house is found chiefly among mountain tribes, but no very close correlation with topography appears. The well-fashioned plank house is definitely to be associated with the northwestern culture. The earth lodge of the Sacramento Valley region is evidently connected with the Kuksu religion on one side, since the southward distribution of the two appears to coincide. Northward, however, this form of house extends considerably beyond the cult. The southern earth lodge probably has the center of its distribution among the Colorado River tribes. It appears to have penetrated somewhat farther west than the religious influences emanating from this district. From the Chumash to the southern valley Yokuts communal houses were in use. But the larger specimens of the earth lodges of the Sacramento Valley district must also have sheltered more people than we reckon to a family, and the same is definitely stated for the thatched houses of some of the Pomo.

As regards outward affiliations, there is the same uncertainty. Are we to reckon the semisubterranean house of interior British Columbia as one in type with the Navaho hogan simply because the two are roofed with earth; or is the hogan essentially of the type of the Plains tepee by reason of its conical shape and tripod foundation? Until such broader problems are answered, it would probably be premature to interpret the history of dwellings in aboriginal California.[1]

Views and plans of dwellings and dance houses will be found in Plates 9, 11, 12, 13, 46, 56, and Figures 4, 19, 23, 24, 25, 35, 39, 63.

The separate hut for the woman in her periodical illness seems to be a northern Californian institution. Information is irregular, but the groups who affirm that they formerly erected such structures are the Yurok, Karok, Hupa; probably the other northwestern tribes; the Shasta and Modoc; the northern Maidu; and apparently the Pomo. The Yuki and Sinkyone deny the practice, but their position renders unconfirmed negative statements somewhat doubtful. South of the Golden Gate there is no clear reference to separate huts for women except among the Luiseño, and the Yokuts specifically state that they did not build them.

SWEAT HOUSES.

The sweat house is a typical California institution, if there is any; yet, characteristically, it was not in universal use. The Colorado River tribes lacked it or any substitute; and a want of reference to the structure among a series of Shoshonean desert tribes—the easternmost Cahuilla, the Chemehuevi, the eastern Mono—indicates that these must perhaps be joined to the agricultural Yumans. The nonuse of the sweat house among the Yuma and Mohave appears to be of considerable significance, since on their other side the edifice was made by some of the nomadic tribes of the Southwest, and—as the kiva or estufa—a related type is important among the Pueblos.

The Californian sweat house is an institution of daily, not occasional, service. It is a habit, not a medicinal treatment; it enters into

---

[1] A searching analysis of house types in California has recently been made by F. Krause (see bibliography).

ceremony indirectly rather than specifically as a means of purification. It is the assembly of the men and often their sleeping quarters. It thus comes to fulfill many of the functions of a club; but is not to be construed as such, since ownership or kinship or friendship, not membership, determines admission; and there is no act of initiation.

In line with these characteristics, the California sweat house is a structure, not a few boughs over which a blanket is thrown before entry is made. It is earth covered, except in the northwest, where an abundance of planks roof a deep pit. Consequently, a substantial construction is requisite. A center post is often, or always, set up; logs, at any rate, have to be employed.

Warmth was produced directly by fire, never by steam generated on heated stones. While the smoke was densest the inmates lay close to the floor. Women were never admitted except here and there on special ceremonial occasions, when sweating was a subsidiary feature or wholly omitted.

In general, the sweat house was somewhat smaller than the living house. This holds of the northwestern tribes, the Yokuts, and those of southern California. In the region of the Kuksu religion the dance house or ceremonial assembly chamber, built much like the sweat house elsewhere but on a much ampler scale, has come to be known as "sweat house" to both Indians and whites. It is not certain how far this large structure really replaced the true sweat house in and about the Sacramento Valley. The two seem generally to have existed side by side, as is known to have been the case among the Pomo and Patwin, but the smaller edifice has lost its proper identity in description under the unfortunate looseness of nomenclature; much as among tribes like the Yana and Achomawi the Indians now speak of "sweat houses" inhabited by families. In these latter cases, however, there is some indication that the earth-covered dwellings were on occasion used for sweating. Some careful, because belated, inquiries remain to be made.

In extreme northeastern California the Plains form of sweat house has obtained a foothold: a small dome of willows covered with mats, large enough for a few men to sit up in, heated by steam. This is established for the Modoc, while less complete descriptions suggest the same for the Shasta, Achomawi, and Washo; but among at least some of these groups the steam sweat house is of modern introduction.

It is rather notable that there is no indication of any fusion or hybridization of the Californian and the eastern types of sweat house, even in the region where they border. This condition is typical of cultural phenomena in native America, and probably throughout the world, as soon as they are viewed distributionally rather than in their developmental sequence. Civilizations shade by endless transitions. Their elements wander randomly, as it seems, with little reference to the circumstances of their origin. But analogous or logically equivalent elements rigidly exclude each other more often than they intergrade.

Sweat houses are illustrated in Plates 10, 13, 14, 56, 60, and Figures 5, 6.

BOATS.

Native California used two types of boat—the wooden canoe and the tule balsa or shaped raft of rushes. Their use tends to be exclusive without becoming fully so. Their distribution is determined by cultural far more than by physiographic factors.

The northwestern canoe was employed on Humboldt Bay and along the open, rocky coast, but its shape as well as range indicate it to have been devised for river use. It was dug out of half a redwood log, was square ended, round bottomed, of heavy proportions, but nicely finished with recurved gunwales and carved-out seat. A similar if not identical boat was used on the southern Oregon coast beyond the range of the redwood tree. The southern limit is marked by Cape Mendocino and the navigable waters of Eel River. Inland, the Karok and Hupa regularly used canoes of Yurok manufacture, and occasional examples were sold as far upstream as the Shasta. This boat is a river type, only secondarily used on the ocean, and evidently a local specialization of an old North Pacific coast form. (Pls. 3, 5, 13, 15.)

The southern California canoe was a seagoing vessel, indispensable to the Shoshonean and Chumash islanders of the Santa Barbara group, and considerably employed also by the mainlanders of the shore from Point Concepcion and probably San Luis Obispo as far south as San Diego. It was usually of lashed planks, either because solid timber for dugouts was scarce, or because dexterity in woodworking rendered such a construction less laborious. The dugout form seems also to have been known, and perhaps prevailed among the manually clumsier tribes toward San Diego. A double-bladed paddle was used. The southern California canoe was maritime. There were no navigable rivers, and on the few sheltered bays and lagoons the balsa was sufficient and generally employed. The ends of this canoe seem to have been sharp and raised and the beam narrow. It is not certain whether the Chumash canoe was built entirely of planks or was a dugout with planks added.

A third type of canoe had a limited distribution in favorable localities in northern California, ranging about as far as overlay twining, and evidently formed part of the technological culture characteristic of this region. A historical community of origin with the northwestern redwood canoe is indubitable, but it is less clear whether the northeastern canoe represents the original type from which the northwestern developed as a specialization, or whether the latter, originating under northern influences, gave rise to the northeastern form as a marginal deterioration. This northeastern canoe was of pine or fir, burned and chopped out, narrow of beam, without definite shape. It was made by the Shasta, Modoc. Atsugewi, Achomawi, and northernmost Maidu.

The balsa has a nearly universal distribution, so far as drainage conditions permit, the only groups that wholly rejected it in favor of the canoe being the group of typical northwestern tribes. It is reported from the Modoc, Achomawi, Northern Paiute, Wintun, Maidu, Pomo, Costanoans, Yokuts, Tübatulabal, Luiseño, Diegueño, and Colorado River tribes. For river crossing, a bundle or group of bundles of tules sufficed. On large lakes and bays well-shaped vessels, with pointed and elevated prow and raised sides, were often navigated with paddles. The balsa does not appear to have been in use north of California, but it was known in Mexico, and probably has a continuous distribution, except for gaps due to negative environment, into South America.

Except for Drake's reference to boats among the Coast Miwok— perhaps to be understood as balsas—there is no evidence that any form of boat was in use on the ocean from below Monterey Bay to Cape Mendocino. A few logs were occasionally lashed into a rude raft when seal or mussel rocks were to be visited.

A number of interior groups ferried goods, children, and perhaps even women across swollen streams in large baskets or—in the south—pots. Swimming men propelled and guarded the little vessels. This custom is established for the Yuki, Yokuts, and Mohave, and was no doubt participated in by other tribes.

The rush raft was most often poled; but in the deep waters of San Francisco Bay the Costanoans propelled it with the same double-bladed paddle that was used with the canoe of the coast and archipelago of southern California, whence the less skillful northerners may be assumed to have derived the implement. The double paddle is extremely rare in America; like the " Mediterranean " type of arrow release, it appears to have been recorded only from the Eskimo. The Pomo of Clear Lake used a single paddle with short, broad blade. The northwestern paddle is long, narrow, and heavy, having to serve both as " pole " and as " oar "; that of the Klamath and Modoc, whose waters were currentless, is of more normal shape. (Pl. 67, *f–h*.) Whether the southerners employed the one-bladed paddle in addition to the double-ended one does not seem to be known.

Plants appear to have furnished a larger part of the diet than animals in almost all parts of California. Fish and mollusks were probably consumed in larger quantities than flesh in regions stocked with them, especially the salmon-carrying rivers of northern California, the Santa Barbara Archipelago, Clear and Klamath Lakes, the larger bays like that of San Francisco, and in a measure the immediate coast everywhere. Of game, the rodents, from jack rabbits to gophers, together with birds, evidently furnished more food the seasons through than deer and other ruminants. Foods rejected varied locally, of course, but in general northern California looked upon dog and reptile flesh as poisonous, but did not scruple to eat earthworms, grasshoppers, hymenopterous larvæ, certain species of caterpillars, and similar invertebrates when they could be gathered in sufficient masses to make their consumption worth while. In south central California the taboos against dogs and reptiles were less universal, and south of Tehachapi and east of the Sierra snakes and lizards were eaten by a good many groups. In much the greater part of the State acorns constituted a larger part of the diet than any other food, and a lengthy though simple technique of gathering, hulling, drying, grinding, sifting, leaching, and cooking had been devised. Many other seeds and fruits were treated similarly; buckeyes (*Aesculus*), for instance, and the seeds of various grasses, sages, compositæ, and the like. These were whipped into receptacles with seed beaters, which varied only in detail from one end of the State to the other (Pls. 24, *b*, 29, 50; Fig. 57); collected in close-woven or glue-smeared conical baskets (Pl. 73, *a;* contrast the open-work basket for acorns and loads, Pls. 9, 14, 23, *b*); parched with coals in trays; winnowed by tossing in trays; ground; and then eaten either dry, or, like acorn meal, as lumps of unleavened bread baked by the open fire or as boiled gruel. Leaching was on sand which drained off the hot water. In the north, the meal was spread directly on the sand (Pl. 14); in central California fir leaves were often interposed; in the south, also an openwork basket. Pulverization was either by pounding in a mortar or rubbing on the undressed metate or oval grinding slab (Pls. 16, 44, 45, 60, 66; Figs. 27, 58). The history and interrelations of the various types of these implements is somewhat intricate and has been discussed in the chapters on the Maidu, Chumash, Luiseño, and Cahuilla. The grinding process had become a well-established cultural pattern. Besides seeds, dried salmon, vertebræ, whole small rodents, berries, and fruits were often pulverized, especially for storage. In analogous manner, other processes of the acorn and seed preparation complex were extended to various foods: leaching to wild plums, parching to grasshoppers and caterpillars (Pl. 61). This complex clearly dominates the food habits of California.

Where the acorn fails, other foods are treated similarly, though sometimes with considerable specialization of process; the mesquite bean in the southern desert, the piñon nut east of the Sierra, the water lily in the Klamath-Modoc Lakes.

Agriculture had only touched one periphery of the State, the Colorado River bottom, although the seed-using and fairly sedentary habits of virtually all the other tribes would have made possible the taking over of the art with relatively little change of mode of life. Evidently planting is a more fundamental innovation to people used to depending on nature than it seems to those who have once acquired the practice. Moreover, in most of California the food supply, largely through its variety, was reasonably adequate, in spite of a rather heavy population—probably not far from one person to the square mile on the average. In most parts of the State there is little mention of famines.

More detailed reflections on the food quest of the California Indian have been expressed in the last of the chapters on the Yokuts.

FISHING.

In fresh-water and still bays fish are more successfully taken by rude people with nets or weirs or poison than by line. Fishhooks are therefore employed only occasionally. This is the case in California. There was probably no group that was ignorant of the fishhook, but one hears little of its use. The one exception was on the southern coast, where deep water appears to have restricted the use of nets. The prevalent hook in this region was an unbarbed or sometimes barbed piece of haliotis cut almost into a circle. Elsewhere the hook was in use chiefly for fishing in the larger lakes, and in the higher mountains where trout were taken. It consisted most commonly of a wooden shank with a pointed bone lashed backward on it at an angle of 45° or less. Sometimes two such bones projected on opposite sides (Fig. 28). The gorget, a straight bone sharpened on both ends and suspended from a string in its middle, is reported from the Modoc, but is likely to have had a wider distribution.

The harpoon was probably known to every group in California whose territory contained sufficient bodies of water. The Colorado River tribes provide the only known exception. The type of harpoon is everywhere substantially identical. The shaft, being intended for thrusting and not throwing, is long and slender. The foreshaft is usually double, one prong being slightly longer than the other, presumably because the stroke was most commonly delivered at an angle to the bottom. The toggle heads are small, of bone and wood tightly wrapped with string and pitched. The socket is most frequently in or near the end. The string leaving the head at or near the middle, the socket end serves as a barb. This rather rude device is sufficient because the harpoon is rarely employed for game larger than a salmon. The lines are short and fastened to the shaft.

A heavier harpoon which was perhaps hurled was used by the northwestern coast tribes for taking sea lions. Only the heads have been preserved. These are of bone or antler and possess a true barb as well as socket. A preserved Chumash harpoon has a detachable wooden foreshaft tipped with a flint blade and lashed-on bone barb. The foreshaft itself serves as toggle.

There is one record of the spear thrower; also a specimen from the Chumash. This is of wood and is remarkable for its excessively short, broad, and unwieldy shape. It is probably authentic, but its entire uniqueness renders caution necessary in drawing inferences from this solitary example.

The seine for surrounding fish, the stretched gill net, and the dip net were known to all the Californians, although many groups had occasion to use only certain varieties. The form and size of the dip net, of course, differed according as it was used in large or small streams, in the surf, or in standing waters. The two commonest forms of frame were a semicircular hoop bisected by the handle, and two long diverging poles crossed and braced in the angle (Pls. 4, 7). A kite-shaped frame was sometimes employed for scooping (Pl. 6). Nets without poles had floats of wood or tule stems. The sinkers were grooved or nicked stones, the commonest type of all being a flat beach pebble notched on opposite edges to prevent the string slipping. Perforated stones are known to have been used as net sinkers only in northwestern California, and even there they occur by the side of the grooved variety. They are usually distinguishable without difficulty from the perforated stone of southern and central California which served as a digging stick weight, by the fact that their perforation is normally not in the middle (Fig. 7). The northwesterners also availed themselves of naturally perforated stones.

Fish weirs were used chiefly in northern California, where the streams carry salmon. In the northwest such "dams" sometimes became the occasion of important rituals. Fish traps are shown in Plates 33 and 59.

Fish poison was fed into small streams and pools by a number of tribes: the Pomo, Yana, Yokuts, and Luiseño are mentioned, and indicate that the practice was widely spread. Buckeyes, the squirting cucumber, and soaproot (*Chlorogalum*) as well as probably other plants were employed.

HUNTING.

Among hunting devices, the bow was the most important. Deer were frequently approached by the hunter covering himself with a deer hide and putting on his own head a stuffed deer head (Pl. 8; Fig. 31). This method seems not to have been reported from the south. This area also used snares little, if at all; whereas in the northwest deer were perhaps snared more often than shot. Dogs seem to have been used in hunting chiefly in northern California. Driving large game into a brush fence or over a cliff was a rather unusual practice, though specifically reported from the Mountain Maidu. The surrounding of game—rabbits, antelope, occasionally deer or elk—was most practicable in relatively open country and is therefore reported chiefly from the southern two-thirds of the State. Rabbits were frequently driven into long, low, loose nets. Through southern California a curved throwing stick of southwestern type, of boomerang shape but unwarped (Fig. 55), was used to kill rabbits, other small game, and perhaps birds. Traps, other than snares for deer, quail, and pigeons, were little developed. Deadfalls are occasionally reported for rodents. The Achomawi caught large game in concealed pits.

BOWS.

The bow was self, long, and narrow in the south, sinew-backed, somewhat shorter, thin, and flat in northern and central California. Of course, light unbacked bows were used for small game and by boys everywhere. The material varied locally. In the northwest the bow is of yew and becomes shorter and broader than anywhere else; the wood is pared down to little greater thickness than the sinew, the edge is sharp, and the grip much pinched. Good bows, of course, quickly went out of use before firearms, so that few examples have been preserved except low-grade modern pieces intended for birds and rabbits. But sinew backing is reported southward to the Yokuts and Koso. The Yokuts name of the Kitanemuk meant "large bows." This group, therefore, is likely to have used the southern self bow. On the other hand, the short Chemehuevi bow was sinew backed, and a backed Chumash specimen has been preserved.

The following are measurements of the California bows in one museum:

	Length in inches.	Width in sixteenths of inches.	Thickness in sixteenths of inches.
Sinew-backed:			
Yurok (6)	32–52	[1] 22–40	5–9
Tolowa (2)	39	[1] 24–30	9–10
Yahi (2)	44–54	[1] 28–30	10–12
Northern Wintun? (2)	44–45	22–24	11–12
Miwok? (1)	44	22	14
Self:			
Klamath–Modoc (3)	40–43	[1] 25–35	9–14
Pomo (1)	56	[1] 20	13
Yokuts (8)	40–56	19–24	8–14
Luiseño (1)	64	19	16
Cahuilla (6)	52–56	17–20	10–15
Mohave (7)	53–70	18–22	12–17

[1] Grip pinched in from this maximum.

The arrow was normally two-pieced, its head most frequently of obsidian, which works finer and smaller as well as sharper than flint. The butt end of the point was frequently notched for a sinew lashing. The foreshaft was generally set into the main shaft. For small game shot at close range one-piece arrows frequently sufficed; the stone head was also omitted or replaced by a blunted wooden point. Cane was used as main shaft wherever it was available, but nowhere exclusively. From the Yokuts south to the Yuma the typical fighting arrow was a simple shaft without head, quantity rather than effectiveness of ammunition appearing the desideratum. The same tribes, however, often tipped their deer arrows with stone.

The arrow release has been described for but three groups. None of these holds agree, and two are virtually new for America. The Maidu release is the primary one, the Yahi a modification of the Mongolian, the Luiseño the pure Mediterranean, hitherto attributed in the New World only to the Eskimo. This remarkable variety in detail is not wholly uncharacteristic of California.

The arrow, in the north, was bent straight in a hole cut through a slab of wood (Pl. 16), and polished with *Equisetum* or in two grooved pieces of sandstone. The southern straightener and polisher is determined by the cane arrow: a transversely grooved rectangle of steatite set by the fire. Among pottery-making tribes clay might replace steatite. This southwestern form extends north to the Yokuts and Mono (Pl. 49); the Maidu possessed it in somewhat aberrant form.

TEXTILES.

Basketry is unquestionably the most developed art in California. It is of interest that the principle which chiefly emerges in connection with the art is that its growth has been in the form of what ethnologists are wont to name " complexes." That is to say, materials, processes, forms, and uses which abstractly considered bear no intrinsic relation to one another, or only a slight relation, are in fact bound up in a unit. A series of tribes employs the same forms, substances, and techniques; when a group is reached which abandons one of these factors, it abandons most or all of them, and follows a characteristically different art.

This is particularly clear of the basketry of northernmost California. At first sight this art seems to be distinguished chiefly by the outstanding fact that it knows no coiling processes. Its southern line of demarcation runs between the Sinkyone and Kato, the Wailaki and Yuki, through Wintun and Yana territory at points that have not been determined with certainty, and between the Achomawi (or more strictly the Atsugewi) and the Maidu. Northward the art extends far into Oregon west of the Cascades. The Klamath and Modoc do not fully adhere to it, although their industry is a related one.

Further examination reveals a considerable number of other traits that are universally followed by the tribes in the region in question. Wicker and checker work, which have no connection with coiling, are also not made. Of the numerous varieties of twining, the plain weave is substantially the only one employed, with some use of subsidiary strengthening in narrow belts of three-strand twining. The diagonal twine is known, but practiced only sporadically. Decoration is wholly in overlay twining, each weft strand being faced with a colored one. The materials of this basketry are hazel shoots for warp, conifer roots for weft, and *Xerophyllum*, *Adiantum*, and alder-dyed *Woodwardia* for white, black, and red patterns, respectively. All of these plants appear to grow some distance south of the range of this basketry. At least in places they are undoubtedly sufficiently abundant to serve as materials. The limit of distribution of the art can therefore not be ascribed to botanical causes. Similarly, there is no reason why people should stop wearing basketry caps and pounding acorns in a basketry hopper (Pl. 24, *a*) because their materials or techniques are different. That they do evidences the strength of this particular complex. (Compare Pls. 23, 24, 73, *e*, *f*.)

In southern California a definite type of basket ware is adhered to with nearly equal rigidity. The typical technique here is coiling, normally on a foundation of straws of *Epicampes* grass. The sewing material is sumac or *Juncus*. Twined ware is subsidiary, is roughly done (Pl. 73, *b*), and is made wholly in *Juncus*, a material that, used alone, forbids any considerable degree of finish. Here again the basketry cap (Pl. 73, *d*) and the mortar hopper (Pl. 44, *a*) appear, but are limited toward the north by the range of the technique. (Compare Pls. 55, *c, e;* 73, *c.*)

From southern California proper this basketry has penetrated to the southerly Yokuts and the adjacent Shoshonean tribes. Chumash ware also belongs to the same type, although it generally substitutes *Juncus* for the *Epicampes* grass. Both the Chumash and the Yokuts and Shoshoneans in and north of the Tehachapi Mountains have developed one characteristic form not found in southern California proper—the shouldered basket with constricted neck. This is represented in the south by a simpler form—a small globular basket. The extreme development of the "bottle neck" type is found among the Yokuts, Kawaiisu, and Tübatulabal. The Chumash on the one side, and the willow-using Chemehuevi on the other, round the shoulders of these vessels so as to show a partial transition to the southern California prototype. (Compare Yokuts, Pl. 50; Mono and Kawaiisu, Pl. 55, *d, e;* Chumash, Pls. 50, 52, 53, 54; Chemehuevi, Pls. 59, 73, *a.*)

The Colorado River tribes slight basketry to a very unusual degree. (Pl. 55, *b.*) They make a few very rude trays and fish traps. The majority of their baskets they seem always to have acquired in trade from their neighbors. Their neglect of the art recalls its similar low condition among the Pueblos, but is even more pronounced. Pottery making and agriculture are perhaps the influences most specifically responsible; although it is observable that the river tribes show little skill or interest in anything mechanical or economic.

Central California from the Yuki and Maidu to the Yokuts is an area in which coiling and twining occur side by side. There were probably more twined baskets made but they were manufactured for rougher usage and were generally undecorated. Show pieces were almost invariably coiled. The characteristic technique is therefore perhaps coiling, but the two processes were nearly in balance. The materials are not as uniform as in the north or south. The most characteristic plant is perhaps the redbud, *Cercis occidentalis*, which furnished the red and often the white surface in coiling and twining. Willows are also widely used; and *Carex* root fibers provide the Pomo and Yokuts with a splendid material for weft and especially wrapping. Dogwood, maple, hazel, pine, tule, and grape are also employed, some rather consistently by a single group or two, others only occasionally, but over a wide area. The most common techniques are coiling with triple foundation and plain twining. Diagonal twining is, however, more or less followed, and lattice twining, single-rod coiling, and wickerwork all have a local distribution, including in each case the Pomo. Twining with overlay is never practiced. Forms are variable, but not to any notable extent. Oval baskets were made in the Pomo region, but there was no shape of as pronounced a character as the southern Yokuts bottle neck.

It is rather clear that a number of local basketry arts developed in central California on this generic foundation. The most complex of these is without any question that of the Pomo and their immediate neighbors. The many specialties and peculiarities of this art have been set forth in detail in the account of this group. It may only be added that the Pomo appear to be the only central Californian group that habitually makes twined baskets with patterns.

Another definite center of development includes the Washo and in some measure the Miwok. Both of these groups practiced single-rod coiling and have evolved a distinctive style of ornamentation characterized by a certain lightness of decorative touch. (Pls. 76, 55, f.) This ware, however, shades off to the south into Yokuts basketry with its southern California affiliations, and to the north into Maidu ware.

The latter in its pure form is readily distinguished from Miwok as well as Pomo basketry, but presents few positive peculiarities. Costanoan and Salinan baskets have perished so completely that no very definite idea of them can be formed. It is doubtful whether a marked local type prevailed in this region. The Yuki, wedged in between the Pomo and tribes that followed the northern California twining, make a ware which in spite of its simplicity can not be confounded with that of any other group in California (Pl. 75); this in spite of the general lack of advancement which pervades their culture.

It thus appears that we may infer that a single style and type underlies the basketry of the whole of central California; that this has undergone numerous local diversifications due only in part to the materials available, and extending on the other hand into its purely decorative aspects; and that the most active and proficient of these local superstructures was that for which the Pomo were responsible, their creation, however, differing only in degree from those which resulted from analogous but less active impulses elsewhere. In central California, therefore, a basic basketry complex is less rigidly developed, or preserved, than in either the north or the south. The flora being substantially uniform through central California, differences in the use of materials are generally in themselves significant of incipient national diversifications.

The Modoc constitute a subtype within the area of twining. They overlay chiefly when they use *Xerophyllum* or quills, it would seem; and the majority of their baskets, which are composed of tule fibers of several shades, are in plain twining. But the shapes and patterns of their ware have clearly been developed under the influences that guide the art of the surrounding tribes, and the cap and hopper occur among them.

It is difficult to decide whether the Modoc art is to be interpreted as a form of the primitive style on which the modern overlaying complex is based, or as an adaptation of the latter to a new and widely useful material. The question can scarcely be answered without full consideration of the basketry of all Oregon.

The awl with which coiled basketry was made, and with which such little sewing as existed was performed, was usually of bone, in the desert south also of spines. Figure 67 shows a series of central Californian forms. Among the northwestern tribes, who did not coil, a blunter awl survives in use for dressing lamprey eels; and buckskin was presumably sewn with sharp specimens.

Cloth is unknown in aboriginal California. Rush mats are twined like baskets or sewn. The nearest approach to a loom is a pair of sticks on which a long cord of rabbit fur is wound back and forth to be made into a blanket by the intertwining of a weft of the same material, or of two cords. The Maidu, perhaps the Chumash, and therefore probably other tribes also, made similar blankets of strips of goose or duck skin, and in other cases of feather-wrapped cords. The rabbit-skin blanket has, of course, a wide distribution outside of California; that of bird skins may have been devised locally.

POTTERY.

The distribution of pottery in California reveals this art as due to southwestern influences. It is practiced by the Yuma, Mohave, and other Colorado River tribes; sporadically by the Chemehuevi; more regularly by the Diegueño, Luiseño, Cupeño, Serrano, and Cahuilla; probably not by the Gabrielino; with the Juaneño status unknown.

A second area, in which cruder pottery is made (Pl. 51), lies to the north, apparently disconnected from the southern California one. In this district live the southern and perhaps central Yokuts, the Tübatulabal, and the western Mono. This ware seems to be pieced with the fingers; it is irregular, undecorated, and the skill to construct vessels of any size was wanting.

PLATE 75

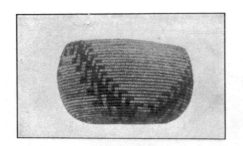

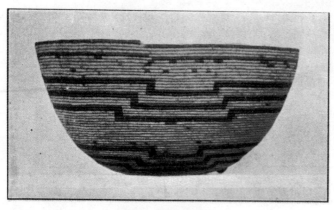

YUKI BASKETS

PLATE 76

MIWOK COILED BASKETS, TRIPLE AND
SINGLE ROD FOUNDATION

PLATE 77

KAROK USING FIRE DRILL

PATWIN HESI DANCERS

PATWIN HESI APPROACH, WITH
FLAG, INFLUENCED BY MOD-
ERN GHOST DANCE CULT

PLATE 78

YAHI SHOOTING IN HUNTER'S POSITION,
AND DRILLING FIRE

The southern Californians tempered with crushed rock, employed a clay that baked dull reddish, laid it on in thin spiral coils, and smoothed it between a wooden paddle and a pebble. They never corrugated, and no slipped ware has been found in the region; but there is some variety of forms—bowls, jars, pots, oval plates, short-handled spoons, asymmetrical and multiple-mouthed jars, pipes—executed in a considerable range of sizes. Designs were solely in yellow ocher, and frequently omitted. They consisted chiefly of patterns of angular lines, with or without the corners filled in. Curves, solidly painted areas, and semirealistic figures were not attempted. (Pls. 49, 62, 68; Figs. 64, 65.) The ware is light, brittle, and porous. The art during the last generation has been best preserved among the Mohave, and seems at all times to have attained greatest development on the Colorado River. But the coast tribes may have been substantial equals before they came under Caucasian influence; except that they decorated less. An affinity with Pima and Seri ware is unmistakable; but it is far from attaining identity. There is no direct or specific resemblance to any present or ancient Pueblo pottery; but rather close parallels in prehistoric ware from the Papago and Gila country. This argues either a local origination of Colorado River pottery under generic southwestern influence or a more direct stimulus or importation from Sonora. Potsherds indistinguishable from the modern ware occur on the surface of ancient sites on the Diegueño coast. Whether they extend to the earlier deposits remains to be ascertained; but they testify that the art is not an entirely recent one. Pottery was not established in California as a direct adjunct of agriculture, its distribution being considerably greater.

MUSICAL INSTRUMENTS.

The rattle is of three kinds in the greater part of California: the split clap stick for dancing (Pls. 67, *e*, 77), the gravel-filled cocoon bunch for shamanistic practices and ritualistic singing (Fig. 37; Pl. 67, *d*), and the bundle of deer hoofs for the adolescent girl. South of Tehachapi these are mostly replaced by a single form, whose material varies between turtle shell and gourd according to region. The northwest does not use rattles except in the adolescence ceremony; in which some tribes, such as the Hupa and Sinkyone, employ a modification of the clap stick, the Karok, Tolowa, and others the more general deer hoofs. The latter are known as far south as the Diegueño, but seem to be associated with hunting or mourning ceremonies at this end of the State. The clap stick penetrated south to the Gabrielino.

The notched scraper or musical rasp has been reported only from the Salinans.

California is a drumless region, except in the area of the Kuksu cult. There a foot drum, a segment of a large cylinder of wood, is set at the back of the dance house, and held very sacred. Various substitutes exist elsewhere: the Yurok beat a board with a paddle, the Maidu and Diegueño strike or rub baskets, the Mohave do the same before a resounding jar. But these accompaniments belong to gambling or shamans' or narrative songs; none of the substitutes replace dance drums.

Whistles of bone or cane are employed far more frequently in dances than the drum by practically all tribes, in fact, although of course in quite different connections.

The bull-roarer has been reported from several scattered tribes. (Pl. 44, d–f.) As might be expected, its function is religious, but is not well known and seems to have varied. To the Luiseño it was a summons. It was not used by the northwestern nations.

The only true musical instrument in our sense is the flute, an open reedless tube, blown across the edge of one end. Almost always it has four holes, often more or less grouped in two pairs, and is innocent of any definite scale. It is played for self-recreation and courtship. (Pl. 43.) The Mohave alone know a reeded flageolet.

The musical or resonant bow, a sort of jew's-harp, the only stringed instrument of California, has been recorded among the Pomo, Maidu, Yokuts, and Diegueño, and no doubt had a wider distribution. It was tapped as a restful amusement, and sometimes in converse with spirits.

It is remarkable, although abundantly paralleled among other Indians, that the only two instruments capable of producing a melody were not used ceremonially. The cause must be their imperfection. The dance was based on song, which an instrument of rhythm could enrich, but with which a mechanically produced melody would have clashed.

It is also a curious fact that the comparatively superior civilization of the northwestern tribes was the one that wholly lacked drum, bull-roarer, and musical bow, and made minimal employ of rattles.

MONEY.

Two forms of money prevailed in California: the dentalium shell, imported from the far north; and the clamshell disk bead. Among the strictly northwestern tribes dentalia were alone standard. In a belt stretching across the remainder of the northern end of the State, and limited very nearly, to the south, by the line that marks the end of the range of overlay twined basketry, dentalia and disks were used side by side. Beyond, to the end of the State, dentalia were so sporadic as to be no longer reckoned as money, and clam currency was the medium of valuation. It had two sources of supply. On Bodega Bay the resident Coast Miwok and neighboring Pomo gathered the shells of *Saxidomus aratus* or *gracilis*. From Morro Bay near San Luis Obispo to San Diego there occurs another large clam, *Tivela* or *Pachydesma crassatelloides*. Both of these were broken, the pieces roughly shaped, bored, strung, and then rounded and polished on a sandstone slab. The disks were from a third of an inch to an inch in diameter, and from a quarter to a third of an inch thick, and varied in value according to size, thickness, polish, and age. The Pomo supplied the north; southern and central California used *Pachydesma* beads. The southern Maidu are said to have had the latter, which fact, on account of their remoteness from supply, may account for the higher value of the currency among them than with the Yokuts. But the Pomo *Saxidomus* bead also reached them.

From the Yokuts and Salinans southward, money was measured on the circumference of the hand. The exact distance traversed by the string varied somewhat according to tribe; the value in our terms appears to have fluctuated locally to a greater degree. The available data on this system have been brought together in Table 6 in the chapter on the Chumash. The Pomo, Wintun, and Maidu seem not to have known the hand scale. They measured their strings in the rough by stretching them out, and appear to have counted the beads when they wished accuracy.

Associated with the two clam moneys were two kinds of valuables, both in cylindrical form. The northern was of magnesite, obtained in southeastern Pomo territory. This was polished and on baking took on a tawny or reddish hue, often variegated. These stone cylinders traveled as far as the Yuki and the Miwok. From the south came similar but longer and slenderer pieces of shell, white to violet in color, made sometimes of the columella of univalves, sometimes out of the hinge of a large rock oyster or rock clam, probably *Hinnites giganteus*. The bivalve cylinders took a finer grain and seem to have been preferred. Among the Chumash such pieces must have been fairly common, to judge from grave finds. To the inland Yokuts and Miwok they were excessively valuable. Both the magnesite and the shell cylinders were perforated longitudinally, and often constituted the center piece of a fine string of beads; but, however displayed, they were too precious to be properly classifiable as ornaments. At the same time their individual variability in size and quality, and consequently in value, was too great to allow them to be reckoned as ordinary money. They rank rather with the obsidian blades of northwestern California, as an equivalent of precious stones among ourselves.

The small univalve *Olivella biplicata* and probably other species of the same genus were used nearly everywhere in the State. In the north they were strung whole; in central and southern California, frequently broken up and rolled into thin, slightly concave disks, as by the southwestern Indians of to-day. Neither form had much value. The olivella disks are far more common in graves than clam disks, as if a change of custom had taken place from the prehistoric to the historic period. But a more likely explanation is that the olivellas accompanied the corpse precisely because they were less valuable, the clam currency either being saved for inheritance, or, if offered, destroyed by fire in the great mourning ceremony.

Haliotis was much used in necklaces, ear ornaments, and the like, and among tribes remote from the sea commanded a considerable price; but it was nowhere standardized into currency.

TOBACCO.

Tobacco, of two or more species of *Nicotiana*, was smoked everywhere, but by the Yokuts, Tübatulabal, Kitanemuk, and Costanoans it was also mixed with shell lime and eaten.

The plant was grown by some of the northern groups: the Yurok, Hupa, and probably Wintun and Maidu. This limited agriculture restricted to the people of a small area remote from tribes with farming customs is remarkable. The Hupa and Yurok are afraid of wild tobacco as likely to have sprung from a grave; but it is as likely that the cultivation produced this unreasonable fear by rendering the use of the natural product unnecessary, as that the superstition was the impetus to the cultivation.

Tobacco was offered religiously by the Yurok, the Yahi, the Yokuts, and presumably by most or all other tribes; but exact data are lacking, offering being a rather limited practice of the Californians.

The pipe is found everywhere, and with insignificant exceptions is tubular. In the northwest it averages about 6 inches long and is of hard wood scraped somewhat concave in profile, the bowl lined with inset soapstone. For some distance about the Pomo area the pipe is longer, the bowl end abruptly thickened to 2 inches, the stem slender. In the Sierra Nevada the pipe runs to only 3 or 4 inches and tapers somewhat to the mouth end. The Chumash pipe has been preserved only in its stone exemplars. These usually resemble the Sierra type, but are often longer, normally thicker, and more frequently contain a brief mouthpiece of bone. Ceremonial specimens are sometimes of obtuse angular shape. The pottery-making tribes of the south used clay pipes most commonly. These were short, with shouldered bowl end. In all the region from the

Yokuts south, in other words wherever the plant was available, a simple length of cane frequently replaced the worked pipe; and among all tribes shamans had all-stone pieces at times. The Modoc pipe was essentially eastern: a stone head set on a wooden stem. The head is variable, as if it were a new and not yet established form: a tube, an L, intermediate forms, or a disk. (Compare Fig. 29 with Pl. 30.)

The Californians were light smokers, rarely passionate. They consumed smaller quantities of tobacco than most eastern tribes and did not dilute it with bark. Smoking was of little formal social consequence, and indulged in chiefly at bedtime in the sweat house. The available species of *Nicotiana* were pungent and powerful in physiological effect, and quickly produced dizziness and sleep.

VARIOUS.

The ax and the stone celt are foreign to aboriginal California. The substitute is the wedge or chisel of antler—among the Chumash of whale's bone—driven by a stone. This maul is shaped only in northwestern California. (Pl. 19.) The extreme south and southeast of the State seem to have lacked even the wedge. An adz of shell lashed to a curved stone handle is restricted to the northwestern area. (Pl. 19.)

The commonest string materials are the bark or outer fibers of dogbane or Indian hemp, *Apocynum cannabinum*, and milkweed, *Asclepias*. From these fine cords and heavy ropes are spun by hand. Nettle string is reported from two groups as distant as the Modoc and the Luiseño. Other tribes are likely to have used it also as a subsidiary material. In the northwest, from the Tolowa to the Coast Yuki, and inland at least to the Shasta, Indian hemp and milkweed are superseded by a small species of iris, *I. macrosiphon*, from each leaf of which thin, tough, silky fibers are scraped out. The manufacture is very tedious, but results in an unusually fine, hard, and even string. In the southern desert *Agave* fibers yield a coarse, stiff cordage, and the reed, *Phragmites*, is also said to be used. Barks of various kinds, mostly from unidentified species, are used for wrappings and lashings by many tribes, and grapevine is a convenient tying material for large objects. Practically all Californian cordage, of whatever weight, was two-ply before Caucasian contact became influential; although three-ply bow strings have been reported.

The carrying net is essentially southern so far as California is concerned, but connects geographically as well as in type with a net used by the Shoshonean women of the Great Basin. It was in use among all the southern Californians except those of the Colorado River and possibly the Chemehuevi, and extended north to the

Yokuts and Koso. (Figs. 53, 59.) The shape of the utensil is that of a small hammock of large mesh, gathered at the ends on loops which can be brought together by a heavy cord. A varying type occurs in an isolated region to the north among the Pomo and Yuki. Here the ends of the net are carried into a continuous headband. This arrangement does not permit of a contraction or expansion to accommodate the load as in the south. The net has also been mentioned for the Costanoans, but its type there remains unknown. It is possible that these people served as transmitters of the idea from the south to the Pomo. A curious device is reported from the Maidu. The pack strap, when not of skin, is braided or more probably woven. Through its larger central portion the warp threads run free without weft. This arrangement allows them to be spread out and to enfold a small or light load somewhat in the fashion of a net.

The carrying frame of the Southwest has no analogy in California except on the Colorado River. Here two looped sticks are crossed and their four lengths connected with light cordage. Except for the disparity in weight between the frame and the shell of the covering, this type would pass as a basketry form, and at bottom it appears to be such. The ordinary openwork conical carrying basket of central and northern California is occasionally strengthened by the lashing in of four heavier rods. In the northeastern corner of the State, where exterior influences from other cultures are recognizable, the carrier is sometimes of hide fastened to a frame of four sticks.

The storage of acorns or corresponding food supplies is provided for in three ways in California. All the southern tribes construct a large receptacle of twigs irregularly interlaced like a bird's nest. This is sometimes made with a bottom, sometimes set on a bed of twigs and covered in the same way. The more arid the climate, the less does construction matter. Mountain tribes make the receptacle with bottom and lid and small mouth. In the open desert the chief function of the granary is to hold the food together, and it becomes little else than a short section of hollow cylinder. Nowhere is there a worked-out technique. The diameter is from 2 to 6 feet. The setting is always outdoors, sometimes on a platform, often on bare rocks, and occasionally on the ground. (Pl. 60.) The Chumash seem not to have used this type of receptacle.

In central California a cache or granary is used which can also not be described as a true basket. It differs from the southern form in usually being smaller in diameter but higher, in being constructed of finer and softer materials, and in depending more or less directly in its structure on a series of posts which at the same time elevate it from the ground. This is the granary of the tribes in the Sierra

Nevada, used by the Wintun, Maidu, Miwok (Pl. 38), and Yokuts, and in somewhat modified form—a mat of sticks covered with thatch—by the western or mountain Mono. It has penetrated also to those of the Pomo of Lake County who are in direct communication with the Wintun.

In the remainder of California large baskets—their type, of course, determined by the prevailing style of basketry (Pls. 9, 54)—are set indoors or perhaps occasionally in caves or rock recesses. In the desert south there was some storage in jars hidden in cliff crevices.

The flat spoon or paddle for stirring gruel is widely spread in California, but far from universal. It has been found among all the northwestern tribes, the Achomawi, Atsugewi, Shasta, Pomo, Wappo, southern Maidu, northern Miwok, Washo, and Diegueño. The Yokuts and southern Miwok, at times also the Washo, use instead a looped stick, which is also convenient for handling hot cooking stones. The Colorado River tribes, who stew more civilized messes of corn, beans, or fish in pots, tie three rods together for a stirrer. Plates 17, 44, and Figure 38 illustrate types of stirrers.

Cradles or baby carriers (Pls. 35, 39, 40) have been discussed in one of the chapters on the Yokuts.

Fire was made only by the drill, except that the Pomo are said sometimes to have scraped together two rough pieces of quartz. The materials of the fire drill (Pls. 77, 78; Fig. 66) varied considerably according to locality; borer and hearth were sometimes of the same wood. The drill, whether for fire or for perforation, was always twirled by hand rubbing. The Pomo pump-drill is taken over from the Spaniards.

CHAPTER 55.

SOCIETY.

POLITICAL ORGANIZATION.

Tribes did not exist in California in the sense in which the word is properly applicable to the greater part of the North American Continent. When the term is used in the present work, it must therefore be understood as synonymous with "ethnic group" rather than as denoting political unity.

The marginal Mohave and the Yuma are the only Californian groups comparable to what are generally understood as "tribes" in the central and eastern United States: namely a fairly coherent body of from 500 to 5,000 souls, usually averaging not far from 2,000; speaking in almost all cases a distinctive dialect or at least subdialect; with a political organization of the loosest, perhaps; but nevertheless possessed of a considerable sentiment of solidarity as against all other bodies, sufficient ordinarily to lead them to act as a unit. The uniquely enterprising military spirit displayed by the Yuma and Mohave is undoubtedly connected with this sense of cohesion.

The extreme of political anarchy is found in the northwest, where there is scarcely a tendency to group towns into higher units, and where even a town is not conceived as an essential unit. In practice a northwestern settlement was likely to act as a body, but it did so either because its inhabitants were kinsmen or because it contained a man of sufficient wealth to have established personal relations of obligation between himself and individual fellow townsmen not related to him in blood. The Yurok, Karok, and Hupa, and probably several of the adjacent groups, simply did not recognize any organization which transcended individuals and kin groups.

In north central California the rudiments of a tribal organization are discernible among the Pomo, Yuki, and Maidu, and may be assumed to have prevailed among most other groups. A tribe in this region was a small body, evidently including on the average not much

more than 100 souls. It did not possess distinctive speech, a number
of such tribes being normally included in the range of a single dialect.
Each was obviously in substance a " village community," although the
term " village " in this connection must be understood as implying a
tract of land rather than a settlement as such. In most cases the
population of the little tribe was divided between several settlements,
each presumably consisting of a few households more or less connected by blood or marriage; but there was also a site which was regarded as the principal one inhabited. Subsidiary settlements were
frequently abandoned, reoccupied, or newly founded. The principal
village was maintained more permanently. The limits of the territory of the group were well defined, comprising in most cases a natural drainage area. A chief was recognized for the tribe. There is
some indication that his elevation was normally subject to popular
approval, although hereditary privileges are likely to have limited
selection to particular lineages. The minor settlements or groups of
kinsmen had each their lesser chief or headman. There was usually
no name for the tribe as such. It was designated either by the
name of its principal settlement or by that of its chief. Among foreigners these little groups sometimes bore names which were used
much like true tribal names; but on an analysis these generally
prove to mean only " people of such and such a place or district."
This type of organization has been definitely established for the
Wailaki, Yuki, Pomo, and Patwin, and is likely to have prevailed
as far south as the Miwok in the interior and the Costanoans or
Salinans on the coast and inland to the Maidu and Yana. In the
northeast, among Shasta, Atsugewi, and Achomawi, there are reports of chiefs recognized over wider districts, which would suggest
somewhat larger political units.

The Yokuts, and apparently they alone, attained a nearer approach
to a full tribal system. Their tribes were larger, ranging from 150
to 400 or 500 members, possessed names which do not refer to localities, and spoke distinctive dialects, although these were often only
slightly divergent from the neighboring tongues. The territory of
each tribe was larger than in the region to the north, and a principal
permanent village rarely looms up with prominence.

The Shoshoneans of Nevada, and with them those of the eastern
desert fringe of California, possessed an organization which appears
to be somewhat akin to that of the Yokuts. They were divided into
groups of about the same size as the Yokuts, each without a definite
metropolis, rather shifting within its range, and headed by a chief
possessing considerable influence. The groups were almost throughout named after a characteristic diet: thus, " fish eaters " or " moun-

tain-sheep eaters." It is not known how far each of these tribes possessed a unique dialect: if they did, their speech distinctness was in most cases minimal. Owing to the open and poorly productive nature of the country, the territory of each of these Shoshonean groups of the Great Basin was considerably more extensive than in the Yokuts habitat.

Political conditions in southern California are obscure, but are likely to have been generally similar to those of north central California. Among the Chumash, towns of some size were inhabited century after century, and these undoubtedly were the centers if not the bases of political groups. Among the Serrano and Diegueño, groups that have been designated as "clans" appear to have been pretty close equivalents of the Pomo tribelets or "village communities" in owning a drainage territory, in the size of this area, and in their numbers. Cahuilla, Cupeño, and Luiseño may also prove to conform. The larger towns of the Gabrielino and Chumash may represent concentrations like those of the Patwin and Clear Lake Pomo. In at least part of southern California, however, the local groups were assigned to totemic moieties and practiced habitual if not rigorous exogamy. They may therefore be the typical tribelets of other parts of the State somewhat remodeled under the influence of a social pattern.

The Mohave and other Yuman tribes of the Colorado Valley waged war as tribal units. Their settlements were small, shifting, apparently determined in the main by the location of their fields, and enter little into their own descriptions of their life. It is clear that a Mohave's sense of attachment was primarily to his people as a body, and secondarily to his country. The California Indian, with the partial exception of the Yokuts, always gives the impression of being attached first of all to a spot, or at most a few miles of stream or valley, and to his blood kindred or a small group of lifelong associates and intimates.

It should be added that the subject of political organization and government is perhaps in as urgent need of precise investigation as any other topic in the field of California ethnology.

THE CHIEF.

Chieftainship is wrapped in the obscurity of the political organization to which it is related. There were hereditary chiefs in most parts of California. But it is difficult to determine how far inheritance was the formally instituted avenue to office, or was only actually operative in the majority of instances. In general, it seems that chieftainship was more definitely hereditary in the southern half or two-thirds of the State than in the north. Wealth was a factor of some consequence in relation to chieftainship everywhere, but its influence seems also to have varied according to locality. In the south, liberality perhaps counted for more than possession of wealth. The northwestern tribes had rich men of great influence, but no chiefs. Being without political organizations, they could not well have had the latter.

The degree of authority of the chief is difficult to estimate. This is a matter which can not be judged accurately from the relations between native groups and intruders belonging to a more highly civilized alien race. To understand the situation as between the chief and his followers in the routine of daily life, it is necessary to have at command a more intimate knowledge of this life before its disturbance by Caucasian culture than is available for most Californian groups. It seems that the authority of the chief was considerable everywhere as far north as the Miwok, and by no means negligible beyond; while in the northwest the social effect of wealth was so great as to obtain for the rich a distinctly commanding position. Among certain of the Shoshoneans of southern California the chief, the assistant or religious chief, and their wives or children, were all known by titles; which fact argues that a fairly great deference was accorded them. Their authority probably did not lag much behind. Both the Juaneño and the Chumash are said to have gone to war to avenge slights put upon their chiefs. The director of rituals as an assistant to the head chief is a southern California institution. Somewhat similar is the central Yokuts' practice of having two chiefs for each tribe, one to represent each exogamous moiety. The chief had speakers, messengers, or similar henchmen with named offices, among the Coast Miwok, the interior Miwok, the Yokuts, the Juaneño, and no doubt among other groups.

The headman of a settlement seems to have been head of a group of kinsmen and must be distinguished from the heads of political groups, although this is usually difficult in the absence of detailed information because the same word often denotes both offices.

The chief was everywhere distinctly a civil official. If he commanded also in battle, it seems to have been only through the accident of being a distinguished warrior as well. The usual war leader was merely that individual in the group who was able to inspire confidence through having displayed courage, skill, and enterprise in combat. It is only natural that his voice should have carried weight even in time of peace, but he seems not to have been regarded as holding an office. This distinction between the chief and the military leader appears to apply even to the warlike Yuma and Mohave.

There were no hereditary priests in California. A religious office often passed from father to son or brother's son, but the successor took his place because his kinship had caused him to acquire the necessary knowledge, rather than in virtue of his descent as such.

The shaman, of course, was never an official in the true sense of the word, inasmuch as his power was necessarily of individual acquisition and varied directly according to his supernatural potency, or, as we should call it, his gifts of personality.

SOCIAL STRATIFICATION.

Social classes of different level are hardly likely to develop in so primitive a society as that of California. It is therefore highly distinctive of the northwestern area that the social stratification which forms so important an element in the culture of the North Pacific coast appears among these people with undiminished vigor. The heraldic and symbolic devices of the more advanced tribes a thousand miles to the north are lacking among the Yurok: the consciousness of the different value of a rich and a poor man is as keen among them as with the Kwakiutl or the Haida.

The northwest perhaps is also the only part of California that knew slavery. This institution rested wholly upon an economic basis here. The Chumash may have held slaves; but precise information is lacking. The Colorado River tribes kept women captives from motives of sentiment, but did not exploit their labor.

Wealth was by no means a negligible factor in the remainder of California, but it clearly did not possess the same influence as in the northwest. There seems to have been an effort to regulate matters so that the chief, through the possession of several wives, or through contributions, was in a position to conduct himself with liberality, especially toward strangers and in time of need. On the whole, however, he was wealthy because he was chief rather than the reverse. Among the Colorado River tribes a thoroughly democratic spirit prevailed as regards property, and there is a good deal of the Plains sentiment that it behooves a true man to be contemptuous of material possessions.

EXOGAMY AND TOTEMISM.

California was long regarded as a region lacking clans, group totems, or other exogamous social units. The Colorado River tribes were indeed known to be divided into clans, and the Miwok into moieties, both carrying certain rather indirect totemic associations. But these seemed to be isolated exceptions. More recent information, however, shows that some form of gentile organization was prevalent among nearly all groups from the Miwok south to the

Yuma; and the principal types which this organization assumes have become clear in outline.

In brief, the situation, which is reviewed in Figure 69, is this: Almost everywhere within the area in question the units are exogamous. Nearly always they are totemic. Descent is invariably patrilinear. In the extreme south or southeast the division of society is on

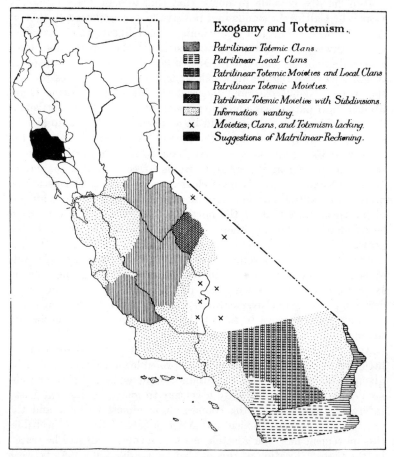

FIG. 69.—Exogamy and totemism in California.

the basis of multiple clans, in the San Joaquin Valley of moieties, in the middle—that is, roughly in the region of the northern part of southern California—there are clans and moieties. Toward the head of the San Joaquin Valley there is a tract over which clans, moieties, and totems are all lacking. This tongue of clanless area seems to represent an intrusive influence from the desert Shoshoneans on the east. It perhaps did not disrupt the continuity of totemic social organization between central and southern California, since there is no definite information available on the most southwesterly group of the Yokuts, the Chumash, the Kitanemuk, or the Gabrielino. The map suggests the possibility that at least some of these groups possessed moieties or totems and thus served to link central and southern California into one continuous chain.

It is hardly possible to doubt that this totemic clan or moiety system of California stands in a positive historic relation to that of the Southwest. The fact of its being a patrilinear system, whereas the southwestern Indians reckon descent in the female line, indicates only that the connection is ancient and indirect. Both the other North American regions in which totemic clans or moieties prevail, the North Pacific coast and the eastern side of the continent, are divided into patrilinear and matrilinear subareas. The continental distribution is such that it would be more than hazardous to assume the patrilinear institutions of the North Pacific, the East, and the Southwest-California area to have been derived from one common source, and the matrilinear institutions of the same three regions from a second origin. It is as clear as such matters can be that a system of gentile organization developed around three centers— of which at least that of the north Pacific coast is likely to have been independent of the others—and that within each area, with the growth and diversification of the institution, paternal and then maternal reckoning grew up. Such seeming to be the course of development, we need be under no hesitation in linking the totemic exogamy of California with that of the Southwest, in spite of its decisive patrilinear character; and this conclusion holds even if the exogamy should prove to be but slightly or brokenly connected on the map with that of the Southwest.

As to the age of exogamy in the two regions, there can be little doubt that as in most matters probable precedence should be given to the Southwest on the ground of the generally greater richness of its culture. It is only necessary to guard against the hasty inference that, because the connection is almost certain, and the radiation from New Mexico and Arizona into California probable, this movement has been a recent one whose course can still be traced by the present location of this or that particular tribe. As between the patrilineate of the Californians, on the other hand, and the matrilineate of the Pueblos, the former, representing a presumably older type, may well prove to be at least equally ancient in absolute time.

The clans of the Colorado River tribes are fairly numerous, a dozen or more for each group. They have no names as such, but are each characterized by the use of a single name borne by all the women of a clan. These women's names can often not be analyzed, but are understood by the Indians as denotive of an animal or object which is clearly the totem of the clan. This system is common without material modification to all the Yumans of the river, but the totemic references vary considerably, and the women's names even more. The latter must have fluctuated with considerable readiness, since only a small proportion of the total number known are common even to two tribes. The clans enter into myth, but are without ritual function. Details will be found in the first of the chapters on the Mohave.

With the Diegueño and Luiseño the system loses many of its characteristics. Totemism, direct or indirect, is wholly lacking. The groups are numerous and small. Their names when translatable are mostly those of localities, or have reference to a locality. The native theory is clearly that each clan is a local kin group. How far this was actually the case is difficult to determine positively.

With the Cupeño, Cahuilla, and Serrano, the institution is reinvigorated. The local groups persist as among the Luiseño and Diegueño and bear similar names. They are classed, however, in two great totemic moieties, named after the coyote and wild cat. With the Serrano, at least, the moieties do not determine marriage, groups of the same moiety sometimes intermarrying more or less regularly.

From here on northward follows the gap in our knowledge. It is, however, certain that the Shoshonean Kawaiisu and Tübatulabal, and the southern Yokuts such as the Yaudanchi and Yauelmani, were at least substantially free from the influence of any exogamous system.

When this negative or doubtful zone has been passed through, we find ourselves well in the San Joaquin Valley. Here, among the central Yokuts, according to some slender indications among the Salinans, probably among the northern Yokuts, and among all the Sierra Miwok, clans have wholly disappeared. The exogamous moiety, however, remains, and its totemic aspects are rather more developed than in the south. The Miwok carry the totemic scheme farthest, dividing the universe as it were into totemic halves, so that all its natural contents are potential totems of one or the other moiety. Among the other groups of this region the totemism is generally restricted to a limited number of birds or animals. Moieties are variously designated as land and water, downstream and upstream, blue jay and coyote, bullfrog and coyote, or bear and deer. The totem is spoken of as the " dog," that is, domestic animal or pet, of each individual. Among the Miwok the personal name refers to an animal or object of the individual's moiety, but the totem itself is hardly ever expressed in the name, the reference being by some implication which can hardly be intelligible to those who do not know the individual and his moiety.

The western Mono, at least in the northern part of their range, have come under the influence of the Miwok-Yokuts system, but this has assumed a somewhat aberrant shape among them. They subdivide each moiety into two groups which might be called clans except for the fact that they are not exogamous. The names of these groups have not yielded to certain translation. The Mono themselves seem to identify them with localities, which may be a correct representation of the facts, but is scarcely yet established.

Matrilinear descent has once been reported for a single Yokuts tribe, the Gashowu, but is so directly at variance with all that is known of the institutions of the region as to be almost certainly an error of observation. On the other hand, there are more positive indications of a reckoning in the female line among some of the Pomo and Wappo; and these are the more credible because the Pomo lie outside of the exogamic and totemic area of California. The facts pointing to Pomo matrilineate are, however, slight; and it is clear that the institution was at most a sort of suggestion, an undeveloped beginning or last vestige, and not a practice of much consequence.

Totemic taboos were little developed in California. Among most groups the totem seems to have been killed and eaten without further thought. Belief in descent from the totem is also weak or absent, except for some introduction of the moiety totems into the cosmogony of the Shoshoneans of the south.

The exogamic groups of California have rather fewer religious functions than is customary in North America. The Colorado River clans seem to have no connection with ritual. The clans of the Shoshoneans were perhaps, in some tribes, the bodies that conducted ceremonies, the instruments for ritual execution; although the rites were in no sense peculiar, but substantially identical for each clan. It appears also that these ritually functioning groups or " parties " sometimes included several " clans " and admitted individuals who had broken away from their hereditary bodies. It is thus likely that these religious bodies really crystallized around chiefs rather than on a clan basis. Indeed, the word for such a religiously functioning group is merely the word for chief. In the San Joaquin Valley the moieties assume ceremonial obligations, usually reciprocal, and evidently in the main in connection with the mourning anniversary; but these arrangements begin to fade out toward the north, among the Miwok.

MARRIAGE.

Marriage is by purchase almost everywhere in California, the groups east of the Sierra and those on the Colorado River providing the only exceptions. Among the latter there is scarcely a formality observed. A man and woman go to live together and the marriage is recognized as long as the union endures. While some form of bride purchase is in vogue over the remainder of the State, its import is very different according to locality. The northwestern tribes make it a definite, commercial, negotiated transaction, the absence of which prior to living together constitutes a serious injury to the family of the girl, whereas a liberal payment enhances the status of both bride and groom. In the southern half of the State, and among the mountaineers of the north, payment has little more significance than an observance. It might be described as an affair of manners rather than morals. Formal negotiations are often omitted, and in some instances the young man shows his intentions and is accepted merely on the strength of some presents of game or the rendering of an ill-defined period of service before or after the union. Even within comparatively restricted regions there is considerable difference in this respect between wealthy valley dwellers and poor highlanders: the northern Maidu furnish an interesting case in point.

So far as known the levirate or marriage of the widow by her dead husband's brother was the custom of all California tribes except those of the Colorado River. The same may be said of the widower's marriage to his dead wife's sister, or in cases of polygamy to two sisters or to a mother and daughter. These customs must therefore be looked upon as basic and ancient institutions. The uniformity of their prevalence is in contrast to the many intergrading forms assumed by the marriage act, and in contrast also to the differences as regards exogamy, render it probable that if an attempt be made to bring the levirate and marriage with the wife's sister into relation with these other institutions, the former must be regarded as antecedent—as established practices to which marriage, exogamy, and descent conformed.

VARIOUS SOCIAL HABITS.

A rigid custom prescribes that the widow crop or singe off her hair and cover the stubble as well as her face with pitch, throughout a great part of central California. This defacement is left on until the next mourning anniversary or for a year or sometimes longer. The groups that are known to follow this practice are the Achomawi, Shasta, Maidu, Wintun, Kato, Pomo, and Miwok; also the Chukchansi, that is, the northern hill Yokuts. Among the southern

Yokuts the widow merely does not wash her face during the period in which she abstains from eating meat. Beyond the Yokuts, there is no reference to the custom; nor is it known from any northwestern people.

A mourning necklace is northern. The northwestern tribes braid a necklace which is worn for a year or longer time after the death of a near relative or spouse. The Achomawi and northwestern Maidu, perhaps other groups also, have their widows put on a necklace of lumps of pitch.

A belt made of the hair cut from her head was worn by the widow among the Shastan tribes, that is the Shasta, Achomawi, and Atsugewi. With the Yokuts and in southern California belts and hair ties and other ornaments of human hair reappear, but do not have so definite a reference to mourning.

The couvade was observed by nearly all Californians, but not in its "classic" form of the father alone observing restrictions and pretending to lie in. The usual custom was for both parents to be affected equally and for the same period. They observed food restraints and worked and traveled as little as possible in order to benefit their child; they did not ward illness from the infant by shamming it themselves. The custom might well be described as a semicouvade. It has been reported among the Achomawi, Maidu, Yuki, Pomo, Yokuts, Juaneño, and Diegueño. Among the Yurok, Hupa, Shasta, and with them presumably the Karok and other northwestern tribes, there are restrictions for both parents, but those for the father are much shorter.

Fear toward twins is known to be felt by the Yurok, Achomawi, and northwestern Maidu of the hills. It is likely to have prevailed more widely, but these instances suggest a most acute development of the sentiment in northern California.

The child's umbilical cord was saved, carefully disposed of, or specially treated. The Diegueño, Luiseño, Juaneño, and Chukchansi Yokuts buried it. The Tachi Yokuts tied it on the child's abdomen. The Hupa and Yurok kept it for a year or two, then deposited it in a split tree.

KINSHIP TABOOS.

The taboo which forbids parents-in-law and children-in-law to look each other in the face or speak or communicate was a central Californian custom. It is recorded for the Kato, Pomo, Maidu, Miwok, Yokuts, and western Mono; with whom at least the southerly Wintun must probably be included. The Yuki, the eastern Mono, the Tübatulabal, and the Kawaiisu seem not to have adhered to the practice, whose distribution is therefore recognizable as holding over a continuous and rather regular area. There is no mention of the habit in regard to any northwestern or southern tribe. Actually, the mother-in-law is alone specified in some instances, but these may be cases of loose or incomplete statements. Accuracy also necessitates the statement that among the Kato and Pomo the custom had rather a feeble hold, and that these people did not hesitate to address a parent-in-law as long as they spoke in the plural or third person— a device which the Miwok and western Mono also made use of as an allowable circumvention of the taboo when there was the requisite occasion.

It may be added that among the Yana and the western Mono, two far-separated and unrelated peoples, brother and sister also used plural address. For the Yana it is stated that a certain degree of avoidance was also observed; but this was not very acute. This custom can be looked for with some likelihood among the intervening nations, but to predict it would be rash. There are many purely local developments in Californian culture: witness the sex diversity of speech among the Yana.

As in other parts of America, no reason for the custom can be obtained from the natives. It is a way they have, they answer; or they would be ashamed to do otherwise. That they feel positive humiliation and repugnance at speaking to a mother-in-law is certain; but this sentiment can no more be the cause of the origin of the custom than a sense of shame can itself have produced the manifold varieties of dress current among mankind. It can hardly be doubted that a sense of delicacy with reference to sexual relations lies at the root of the habit. But to imagine that a native or unhistorically minded civilized person might really be able to explain the source of any of his institutions or manners is to be unreasonable.

DISPOSAL OF THE DEAD.

The manner of disposing of the dead fluctuated greatly according to region in California. The areas in which cremation was practiced seem to aggregate somewhat larger than those in which burial was the custom, but the balance is nearly even, and the distribution quite irregular. Roughly, five areas can be distinguished. (Fig. 70.)

Southern California burned.[1]

Interment was the rule over a tract which seems to extend from the Great Basin across the southern Sierras to the Chumash and Santa Barbara Islands. This takes in the Chemehuevi, the eastern Mono, the Tübatulabal, the southern Yokuts, the Chumash, and perhaps a few of the adjacent minor Shoshonean groups.

A second region of cremation follows. This consists of the entire central Sierra Nevada, the San Joaquin Valley except at its

---

[1] The Vanyume should be added to the southern cremation area delineated in Figure 70.

head, the lower Sacramento Valley, and the coast region for about the same distance. Roughly, the range is from the Salinans and central Yokuts to the Pomo and southern Maidu.

The second area of burial takes in all of the tribes under the influence of the northwestern culture, and in addition to them the

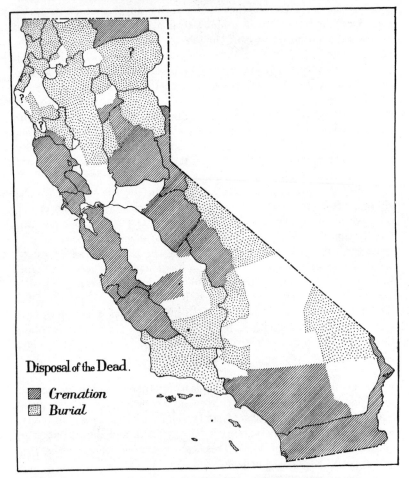

FIG. 70.—Cremation and earth burial in California.

Yuki, at least the majority of the Wintun, and most of the northern Maidu.

The Modoc in the northeastern corner of the State again cremate. For the adjoining Achomawi the evidence conflicts. It is possible that this northern region was connected with the central area of cremation through the Yahi and northwestern Maidu of the foothills.

It seems impossible to establish any correlation between custom and environment in this matter. Treeless and timbered regions both cremated and in other cases interred.

It does appear that the southern and central culture areas can be described as regions of prevailing cremation, the northwestern culture as one of burial. The practice of each of the two interring regions has to some extent penetrated the adjacent parts of the central area. Interment, however, extends farther beyond the outer limits of the northwestern culture than almost all other institutions or elements which are definitely characteristic of the northwest—basketry and dentalia for instance. Furthermore, there is the curious tongue of burying peoples from the Santa Barbara Islands to the eastern Mono. This group can scarcely correspond to any primary cultural stratum.

WAR.

Warfare throughout California was carried on only for revenge, never for plunder or from a desire for distinction. The Mohave and Yuma must, indeed, be excepted from this statement, but their attitude is entirely unique. Perhaps the cause that most commonly originated feuds was the belief that a death had been caused by witchcraft. No doubt theft and disputes of various sorts also contributed. Once ill feeling was established, it was likely to continue for long periods.

Torture has been reported as having been practiced by several tribes, such as the Maidu and the Gabrielino. It appears to have been considered merely a preliminary to the execution of captives, which was the victors' main purpose. As a rule, men who could be seized in warfare were killed and decapitated on the spot. Women and children were also slaughtered more frequently than enslaved. The Colorado River tribes made a point of capturing young women, but did not abuse them. There is no record of any attempt to hold men as prisoners.

Scalps were taken in the greater part of California, brought home in triumph, and celebrated over, usually by a dance around a pole. Women as well as men generally participated. Some tribes made the dance indoors, others outside. There was no great formality about this scalp dance of victory. It may often have been celebrated with great abandon, but its ritual was loose and simple. The Mohave and Yuma alone show some organization of the ceremony, coupled with a considerable manifestation of dread of the scalps themselves —a southwestern trait.

It is rather difficult to decide how far the scalp taken was literally such and how far it was the entire head. A fallen foe that could be operated upon in safety and leisure was almost always decapitated, and his head brought home. Sometimes it is said that this head was danced with. In other localities it was skinned at the first opportunity and the scalp alone used in the dance. The scalp, however, was always a larger object than we are accustomed to think of with the habits of eastern tribes in mind. The skin taken usually extended to the eyes and nose, and included the ears. There is no evidence of an endeavor to preserve scalps as permanent trophies to the credit of individuals; nor of a feeling that anything was lost by a failure to secure scalps, other than that an occasion for a pleasant celebration might be missed thereby.

It is significant that it remains doubtful whether the Yokuts, the Valley Maidu, and the Pomo took scalps or performed a scalp dance. If they did so, it was clearly with less zest than most of their neighbors. All of the tribes in question are peoples of lowland habitat, considerable wealth, and comparative specialization of culture.

In the northwestern area no scalps were taken, and the victory dance was replaced by one of incitement before battle. In this dance the fully armed warriors stood abreast, with one or more of their number moving before them. With the Yurok and Hupa, and perhaps some of their immediate neighbors also, this dance was also or particularly made when two hostile parties gathered for settlement of a feud; and, as might be expected, as often as not resulted in a new fight instead of the desired peace. The northwestern habit of not scalping extended at least as far south as the Sinkyone and as far east as the Shasta. The Wintun on the Trinity River are also said to have taken no scalps and may therefore be supposed to have practiced the associated form of incitement dance. Finally, there is an echo of the Yurok custom from as far away as the Maidu of the northern Sacramento Valley, who it is said had a war dance performed by armed negotiators.

The battle weapon of California was the bow. Spears have been mentioned as in use by a number of tribes, but all indications are that they were employed only sporadically in hand-to-hand fighting and not for hurling from the ranks. It is probable that they were serviceable in an ambush or early morning rush upon the unsuspecting sleepers in a settlement. In a set fight the spear could not be used against a row of bowmen by unarmored and unorganized warriors.

Southern California used the Pueblo type of war club, a rather short, stout stick expanded into a longitudinal mallet head. This seems to have been meant for thrusting into an opponent's face rather than for downright clubbing. The Mohave, at any rate, knew a second form of club, a somewhat longer, straight, and heavy stick, which served the specific purpose of breaking skulls. In central California mentions of clubs are exceedingly scarce. If they were used they were probably nothing but suitable sticks. When it came to hand-to-hand fighting the central Californian was likely to have recourse to the nearest stone. Rocks were also favored by the northwestern tribes, but in addition there are some examples of a shaped war club of stone in this region. This club was a little over a foot long and rudely edged, somewhat in the shape of a narrow and thick paddle blade. This type has affiliations with the more elaborate stone and bone clubs used farther north on the Pacific coast.

Slings seem to have been known to practically all the California tribes as toys, and in some parts were used effectively for hunting water fowl. The only definite reports of the use of slings in warfare are from the Wintun of Trinity River and the western Mono, both mountaineers.

The shield, which is so important to the Plains Indian and to the southwestern warrior, was known in California only to the Mohave, Yuma, and perhaps Diegueño—that is to say, the local representatives of the Yuman family. It was a round piece of unornamented hide. There is no reference to symbolism, and it appears to have been carried only occasionally. Not a single original specimen has been preserved. Much as tribes like the Mohave speak of war, they rarely mention the shield, and its occurrence among them and their kinsmen is of interest chiefly as an evidence that the distribution of this object reached the Pacific coast at one point at least.

Armor enters the State at the other end as an extension from another extra-Californian culture. It is either of elk hide or of rods twined with string in waistcoat shape. (Pl. 18.) The rod type is reported from the northwestern tribes, the Achomawi, and the northern mountain Maidu. Elkskin armor has been found among the same groups, as well as among the Modoc, Shasta, northern valley Maidu, and Wailaki. These closely coincident distributions indicate that the two armor types are associated, not alternative; and that, confined to the northernmost portion of the State, they are to be understood as the marginal outpost of a custom that centers in the culture of the North Pacific coast.

The greater part of central California appears to have been armorless and shieldless.

GAMING.

The endless games of the North American Indians have been reduced by Mr. Stewart Culin to a few fundamental types:

> Games of dexterity:
> > With a dart—
> > > Outdoor—Hoop and pole.
> > > Hand—Ring and pin.
> > With a ball—Shinny, lacrosse, etc.
> Games of chance:
> > Pure chance—Dice.
> > Guessing—Hand or stick.

Among amateurs, the guessing games come out entirely according to luck; among skillful players they depend on concealment and reading of facial and bodily expression, and are therefore in reality games of mental ability, or rather of will and character.

As a rule, all of these games were known to all the California Indians, and, with some exceptions, no game existed in more than one form among the same group.

The hoop-and-pole game was perhaps the chief one which was entirely unknown in some districts. The Yurok and Hupa did not possess it, and it seems to have been lacking also through the remainder of the northwestern part of the State. It is an interesting circumstance, illustrating in one of several concrete ways the fact that at the northwestern corner of California is ethnographically the last southern frontier of the North Pacific coast "culture area," that this hoop-and-pole game, favorite over a large part of the continent, also holds but a small part in the amusements of most of the coast tribes from Oregon to Alaska.

The dignity of this game is upheld at the opposite end of the State, where the Mohave deem it the means of gambling best befitting a man. They play it with a small string-wound hoop, and long poles that are slid so as to fall, if possible, on or under the rolling hoop when this finally comes to rest. The Luiseño and Diegueño, the other tribes of the south, the Salinan and Costanoan groups, the Maidu, the Pomo, the Shasta, and the Modoc, played substantially the same game. Among the Yokuts, Mono, and Miwok of the Sierra Nevada, youths and boys played a simpler and typically Californian variety. A small block was thrown or slid, and then poles darted after it. This must be a slovenly degeneration of an original hoop game.

The ring-and-pin or hand variety of the same game, in which several rings or loops are strung to the butt end of a pin on which they are to be caught, is widespread in California, but varies characteristically according to habits of life and, ultimately, environment.

The fishing tribes of the northwest, as far south as the middle course of Eel River, including the Tolowa, Yurok, Hupa, Chimariko, Shasta, and Sinkyone (Fig. 14), employed salmon vertebræ as "rings." On the headwaters of Eel River, where the streams run smaller and hunting must largely replace fishing, the Wailaki used deer bones. In the South, the Luiseño favored acorn cups; while the agricultural Mohave made their rings of pumpkin rind. The Klamath and Modoc employed a single-looped ball, made of the same tule rush that is the material of most of their industries. Maidu and Yokuts did without this game, so far as known.

Of the many possible varieties of ball games, each group usually specialized on one. The Pomo played a kind of lacrosse, with a rude small net. Still simpler rackets are found among the southern Maidu. With the Miwok and Yokuts the net has degenerated into a mere loop at the end of a stick, serving to pick up or pocket the ball rather than bat it. Among both these groups this rudimentary form of the racket is perhaps due to the shinny stick being the standard form of ball-propelling implement. The Miwok women, but not the men, also batted a soft hair-stuffed ball with baskets resembling the common utilitarian seed beater.

The Mohave knew nothing of lacrosse, but clung to simple shinny, played with a small block or ball and plain curved sticks. With these they played as our boys play shinny or hockey on the ice.

It would have been difficult to find many suitable fields for such an active free-running game in the rocky canyons of the northwestern tribes; even the bars and river benches are narrow, rough, and uneven. Here, accordingly, the game was played with a double ball of two string-tied blocks of wood, impossible to propel far by striking, and requiring to be picked up with the end of the stick and thrown. Maneuvering thus took the place of speed; the players grappled like wrestlers, and a number of men could participate within a small area. (Pl. 79.)

Elsewhere than in the northwest the double-ball game is essentially or wholly one for women, as over most of the continent. This is the case among the Shasta, Modoc, Achomawi, Washo, Maidu, and Miwok. Among the last three groups the "ball" has degenerated into merely the connecting string, though this is heavy and sometimes knotted at the ends.

Through most of the south, and along the coast as far north at least as Monterey, sticks or bats were often dispenesd with, and the game became essentially a football race. The contestants covered a long distance, each hurling, with his feet only, his little wooden ball. Speed and endurance were counted as even more valuable factors toward victory than skill in manipulation. Diegueño, Luiseño, Costanoan, and presumably the intervening groups competed in this way, which was familiar also to the Indians of Arizona. The Chumash, however, knew shinny; and in the interior the ball race had penetrated to the Maidu and Miwok. This latter people followed all the varieties of ball play: rackets for men and for women, shinny, double ball for women, and football race.

Dice were everywhere preeminently if not entirely a woman's game. A set numbered four, six, or eight, each only two-sided; the count of the various combinations of pieces falling face up or face down varied locally.

The Yurok, Tolowa, Wiyot, and Hupa used four mussel-shell disks; the Pomo, Wailaki, and northern Yokuts, six split sticks; the Mohave, Diegueño, and Luiseño, four painted boards; the southern Yokuts, Chumash, and Chemehuevi, filled walnut shells. (Fig. 54.) Among the Miwok split acorns were employed; and among the Mono, acorn cups. The Modoc used either the Californian sticks or a northern type consisting of four beaver teeth. Some tribes played on a flat basket, others on a stone.

The ball game, whatever its character, was well fitted for competition between towns or districts, and was often heavily backed with stakes; but, except with the Mohave and perhaps the Yokuts, who favored respectively the rolling hoop and the shinny stick, the gambling game above all others, and therefore the man's game par excellence, among the California tribes, was the "hand" or "grass" game, a contest of guessing. Tremendous energy and concentration were thrown into this play, which was passionately followed. Songs and sometimes drumming were regular features, without which the stimulus to play hard would be weakened, and the contestants' luck magically diminished. Actually, the singing and rhythmic swaying aided the hiding player to conceal his knowledge of the location of the "ace" by enabling him better to control his expression.

A public ritual, a dance, even a mourning ceremony, could hardly take place without the accompaniment, at least at the conclusion, of the guessing game. It is hard for us to realize to the full the large degree to which this amusement or occupation entered into the life not so much of a professional class of gamblers as of all the California Indians. Their avarice, and the importance to them of their wealth, hardly allowed them to bet as recklessly, and to strip themselves as completely of all belongings on a run of ill luck, as some of the eastern tribes, with whom liberality rather than possession carried prestige; but they made up in the frequency, the duration, and the tenacity of their play.

PLATE 79

DOUBLE-BALL SHINNY AT HUPA: PAIRS OF PLAYERS WRES-
TLING TO KEEP EACH OTHER FROM THE BALL

PLATE 80

NORTHERN MIWOK FEATHER CAPE WORN BY MOCHILO PER-
FORMER IN KUKSUYU DANCE

Two types of the game occur, and these do not differ fundamentally. In the northwest a bundle of 25 or 50 slender rods is used, one being painted in the center. These sticks are shuffled, in sight of the opponent, with a peculiar rolling twist, divided behind the back, and then shown, the middle portions concealed in the hands. After some deliberation, and frequent false or pretended starts, the opponent guesses for the hand containing the one marked stick, indicating his decision by pointing past the other hand. If he is right, he wins nothing but the privilege of playing; if wrong, one counter goes to the player, who shuffles again. An expert player always knows the place of the marked rod among its many plain fellows, even behind his back, and frequently displays it alone against the pack in his other hand, to tempt his opponent to incline to the latter; or, divining the tendency of his mind, misleads him with a single unmarked rod.

Shasta women, the northern Wintun, and the Modoc play like the northwestern tribes; but through the remainder of the State, from the Shasta men and Achomawi to the Diegueño, the implements are two small bones, or short sticks, one of them marked with a band. These are concealed in the two hands behind the back, under a mat, or often wound in two wisps of grass in view of the opponent, whence the popular American name of the game. Some tribes use only one small bone, guessing for the full hand; mostly they employ four, handled by two men on a side; the southern Indians usually attach string loops to pass over the fingers; but such differences do not seriously alter the course of the play.

The counters are everywhere sticks. Contrary to our custom, the Indians rarely begin with an equal number of markers on the two sides, but with a neutral pile from which winnings are allotted to this or that contestant. Only after this stock is exhausted do they begin to win from each other; and the game continues until one side is without sticks. This may be an affair of minutes. But if fortunes are fluctuating and ability even, one contest may be prolonged for hours. If the losers, without a word, continue to play, they are understood to bet in the ensuing game an amount the equal of that which was staked by both parties in the first game. At least such is the Hupa custom.

Among the Mohave several varieties of the guessing games are played. One of these, shared by them with some of the tribes of the Southwest, is a smaller informal affair pertaining to idle moments. A bit of stick is hidden in one of four little hillocks of sand. Dexterity of manipulation and perception seems the deciding factor instead of control of the features.

The Coast Miwok, some of the Maidu, and the Washo, played the regular "hand" game, but also guessed whether the number of a handful of manipulated sticks was odd or even. Among the Pomo the sticks were counted off by fours after the remainder had been guessed at. This procedure is suggestive of a Chinese form of gambling, but the geographical compactness of the area over which this subtype of guessing game is found indicates its distribution from a native origin.

The "four-stick game" of Mr. Culin is another local variety, which has been found only among the Lutuami, Achomawi, northern Paiute, and Washo—all at least partly Californian—and possibly the Chinook of Oregon. Among most or all of these tribes it does not replace but occurs by the side of the usual guessing game. Two of the sticks are heavy, two short and thin. The guessing is for the order in which they are grouped under a basket or mat.

When one reflects that in reality chance is no greater factor in the standard forms of the guessing game than in the American national card game, the decisive element being the match of character against character, the fascination which the game exercises on the Indian's mind is easy to understand.

The economic basis of life and the estimation of the purpose of wealth among the Indians are so different from our own, that gambling, instead of incurring odium, was not only sanctioned but approved. Nevertheless the underlying human similarity of the emotional processes connected with the practice is revealed in a most interesting way by the common belief in a connection between success at play and in relations with the opposite sex: "Luck in love," the reverse at cards, and vice versa, is our proverbial superstition. But the Indian, regarding, like the ancient Hebrew and ourselves, sexual affairs as normally destructive of supernatural or magical potency, draws in a particular case an opposite inference. Two Yokuts myths relate how the favorite hero of these tales, Limik, the prairie falcon, was uniformly successful in winning all stakes, in the one case at shinny, in the other with the hoop and poles, until the coyote was induced to disguise himself as the victor and thus take advantage of the latter's wife. As soon as this misfortune, although unknown, befell the falcon, his luck turned, until he had lost everything. The modern gambler would perhaps expect the opposite event.

RELIGION AND KNOWLEDGE.

SHAMANISM.

The shamanistic practices of most California groups are fairly uniform, and similar to those obtaining among the North American Indians generically. The primary function of the California shaman is the curing of disease. The latter is almost always considered due to the presence in the body of some foreign or hostile object, rarely to an abstraction or injury of the soul. The Mohave are the only tribe for whom there is definite record that shamans recovered souls, though the attitude of other southern Californians is such that the belief may well have prevailed among them also. Over most of California the shaman's business is the removal of the disease object, and this in the great majority of cases is carried out by sucking. Singing, dancing, and smoking tobacco, with or without the accompaniment of genuine trance conditions, are the usual diagnostic means. Manipulation of the body, brushing it, and blowing of breath, saliva, or tobacco smoke are sometimes resorted to in the extraction of the disease object.

As contrasted with the general similarity of the practices of the established shaman, there is a considerable diversity of methods employed by the prospective shaman in the acquisition of his supernatural powers. This diversity is connected with a variety of beliefs concerning guardian spirits.

In central California, from the Wailaki and Maidu to the Yokuts, the guardian spirit is of much the same character as with the Indians of the central and eastern United States, and is obtained in much the same way. A supernatural being in animal or other form is seen and conversed with during a trance or dream. Sometimes the spirits come to a man unsought, sometimes there is a conscious attempt to acquire them.

For southern California information on these matters is tantalizingly scant and vague. The few statements recorded from Indians seem mostly made under the pressure of questioning. It remains to be established that a definite belief in personal guardian spirits obtained in southern California. This doubt is strengthened by the fact that the concept of the guardian spirit, and, consequently, the institution of shamanism in its most commonly accepted form, seem to have been very weak among the tribes of the southwestern United States, especially the Pueblos.

Among the Colorado River tribes it is certain that there was no belief in a guardian spirit of the usual kind. Shamans derived their power by dreaming of the Creator or some ancient divinity, or, as they themselves sometimes describe it, from having associated before their birth—in other words, during a previous spiritual existence—with the gods or divine animals that were on earth at the beginning. The culture of the Colorado River tribes is so specialized that a positive inference from them to the remaining southern Californians would be unsound; but it must be admitted that their status increases the probability that the latter tribes did not share the central Californian and eastern ideas as to the source of shamanistic power.

In northern California, and centering as usual among the northwestern tribes, beliefs as to the source of shamanistic power take a peculiar turn. Among peoples like the Yurok the guardian in the ordinary sense scarcely occurs. The power of the shaman rests not on the aid or control of a spirit, but upon his maintenance in his own body of disease objects which to nonshamans would be fatal. These "pains" are animate and self-moving, but are always conceived as minute, physically concrete, and totally lacking human shape or resemblance. Their acquisition by the shaman is due to a dream in which a spirit gives them to him or puts them in his body. This spirit seems most frequently to be an ancestor who has had shamanistic power. The dream, however, does not constitute the shaman as such, since the introduced "pain" causes illness in him as in other persons. His condition is diagnosed by accepted shamans, and a long and rigorous course of training follows, whose object is the inuring of the novice to the presence of the "pains" in his body and the acquisition of control over them. Fasting and analogous means are employed for this purpose, but the instruction of older shamans seems to be regarded as an essential feature, culminating in what is usually known as the "doctors' dance." This dance is therefore substantially a professional initiation ceremony. There is no doubt that it provided the opportunity for the establishment of shamans' societies as organized bodies, but this step seems never to have been taken in California.

From the Yurok and Hupa this peculiar type of shamanism spreads out gradually, losing more and more of its elements, to at least as far as the Maidu. Already among the Shasta the shaman controls spirits as well as " pains," but the name for the two is identical. With the Achomawi and Maidu the " pain " and the spirit are differently designated. Here the doctor's concern in practice still is more largely with the " pains," but his control of them rests definitely upon his relation to his spirits and their continued assistance. The doctor dance persists among all these tribes. It is practiced also by the northerly Wintun and Yuki. The Yuki shamans possess and acquire spirits very much like the central Californians, and the spirits are sometimes animals. The " pain " is still of some importance among them, however, and they and the Wintun agree in calling it " arrowhead." A line running across the State south of the Yuki, and probably through Wintun and Maidu territory about its middle, marks the farthest extension of remnants of the northwestern type of shaman.

Among the Pomo there is no mention of the doctor dance, while indications of a considerable use of amulets or fetishes suggest that entirely different sets of concepts obtain.[1] The Miwok and Yokuts also knew of nothing like a " doctor dance," and with them it would seem that the Maidu of the south may have to be included.

It may be added that central and southern California are a unit in regarding shamanistic power as indifferently beneficent or malevolent. Whether a given shaman causes death or prevents it is merely a matter of his inclination. His power is equal in both directions. Much disease, if not the greater part, is caused by hostile or spiteful shamans. Witchcraft and the power of the doctor are therefore indissolubly bound up together. The unsuccessful shaman, particularly if repeatedly so, was thought to be giving prima facie evidence of evil intent, and earnest attempts to kill him almost invariably followed.

In the northwest this intertwining of the two aspects of supernatural power was slighter. Shamans were much less frequently killed, and then rather for refusal to give treatment or unwillingness to return pay tendered for treatment, than for outright witchcraft. A person who wished to destroy another had recourse to magical practice. This northwestern limitation of shamanism is perhaps connected with the fact that among the tribes where it was most marked the shaman was almost invariably a woman. In these matters, too, tribes as far as the Maidu shared in some measure in the beliefs which attained their most clear-cut form among the Yurok and Hupa.

---

[1] See footnote, p. 259.

The use of supernatural spirit power was on the whole perhaps more largely restricted to the treatment or production of disease in California than in most other parts of aboriginal North America. There is comparatively little reference to men seeking association with spirits for success in warfare, hunting, or love, although it is natural that ideas of this kind crop out now and then. There are, however, three specialties which in the greater part of the State lead to the recognition of as many particular kinds of shamans or " doctors," as they are usually known in local usage. These are rain or weather doctors, rattlesnake doctors, and bear doctors.

The rain doctor seems generally to have exercised his control over the weather in addition to possessing the abilities of an ordinary shaman. Very largely he used his particular faculty like the prophet Samuel, to make impression by demonstrations. All through the southern half of the State there were men who were famous as rain doctors, and the greatest development of the idea appears to have been in the region where central and southern California meet. Control of the weather by shamans was, however, believed in to the northern limit of the State, although it was considerably less made of. there. The groups within the intensive northwestern culture are again in negative exception.

The rattlesnake doctor is also not northwestern, although tribes as close to the focus of this culture as the Shasta knew the institution. His business, of course, was to cure snake bites; in some cases also to prevent them. Among the Yokuts a fairly elaborate ceremony in which rattlesnakes were juggled with was an outgrowth of these beliefs. Less important or conspicuous demonstrations of the same sort seem also to have been made among a number of other tribes, since we know that the northern Maidu of the valley had some kind of a public rattlesnake ceremony conducted by their shamans. There appears to have been some inclination to regard the sun as the spirit to which rattlesnake doctors particularly looked.

The bear doctor was recognized over the entire State from the Shasta to the Diegueño. The Colorado River tribes, those of the extreme northwest, and possibly those of the farthest northeastern corner of the State, are the only ones among whom this impressive institution was lacking. The bear shaman had the power to turn himself into a grizzly bear. In this form he destroyed enemies.

The most general belief, particularly in the San Joaquin Valley and southern California, was that he became actually transmuted. In the region of the Wintun, Pomo, and Yuki, however, it seems to have been believed that the bear doctor, although he possessed undoubted supernatural power, operated by means of a bear skin and other paraphernalia in which he encased himself.[2] Generally bear shamans were thought invulnerable, or at least to possess the power of returning to life. They inspired an extraordinary fear and yet seem rather to have been encouraged. It is not unlikely that they were often looked upon as benefactors to the group to which they belonged and as exercising their destructive faculties chiefly against its foes. In some tribes they gave exhibitions of their power; in others, as among the Pomo, the use of their faculties was carefully guarded from all observation. Naturally enough, their power was generally considered to be derived from bears, particularly the grizzly. It is the ferocity and tenacity of life of this species that clearly impressed the imagination of the Indians, and a more accurately descriptive name of this caste would be "grizzly bear shamans."

Throughout northern California a distinction is made between the shaman who sings, dances, and smokes in order to diagnose, in other words, is a clairvoyant, and a second class endowed with the executive power of sucking out disease objects, that is, curing sickness. This grouping of shamans has been reported from the Hupa, Wiyot, Nongatl, Yuki, Pomo, and Maidu. It has not been mentioned among more southerly peoples. It thus coincides in its distribution with the concept of the "pain" as a more or less animate and self-impelled thing, and the two ideas can scarcely be interpreted as other than connected. The sucking shaman seems to be rated higher than the one that only sings; as is only natural, since his power in some measure presupposes and includes that of his rival. It is not unlikely, however, that certain singing shamans were believed to possess an unusual diagnostic power against illness, and no doubt all such matters as finding lost objects and foretelling the future were their particular province.

CULT RELIGIONS.

The cults or definitely elaborated religions of California have been described in detail in the accounts given of the peoples among whom they are perhaps most intensively practiced, and who may be assumed to have had somewhat the largest share in their development: the Yurok, Wintun (compare especially Tables 1–4), Gabrielino and Luiseño (see also Table 7), and Mohave (Table 8). The respective ranges of the four systems are plotted on Plate 74. Certain comparative aspects of these cult types will be considered here.

It appears from Plate 74 that the specific northwestern cultus is separated from that of north central California by a belt of tribes that participate in neither.

---

[2] There may be confusion as regards this area, either in the customs themselves or in the information about them, between true bear shamans and bear impersonators in Kuksu rituals.

The religions of north central and southern California, or Kuksu and "toloache," on the other hand, seem to have overlapped in the region of the northern Yokuts and Salinans. It is unlikely that the two cults existed side by side with undiminished vigor among the same people; one was probably much abbreviated and reduced to subsidiary rank, while the other maintained itself in flourishing or substantially full status. Unfortunately the tribes that seem to have shared the two religions are the very ones whose institutions have long since melted away, so that data are exceedingly elusive. It is not improbable that fuller knowledge would show that the two religions reacted toward each other like the basketry complexes that have been discussed: namely, that they were preserved integrally, and normally to the exclusion of each other.

This seems on the whole to be what has happened in southern California, where the Jimson-weed religion emanating from the Gabrielino and the system of song-myth cycles issuing from the Colorado River tribes existed side by side to only a limited extent among the Diegueño and perhaps some of the Cahuilla and Serrano. Even in these cases of partial mixture it is possible that the condition is not ancient. A recent wave of propaganda for the Jimson-weed cult radiated southward and perhaps eastward from the Gabrielino during mission times—may in fact have succeeded in then gaining for the first time a foothold—particularly because civilization had sapped the strength of the older cults in regions where these had previously been of sufficient vitality to keep out this "toloache" religion.

In any event there are certain ceremonies of wide distribution in California which must be considered as belonging to a more generalized and presumably older stratum of native civilization than any of the four great cults referred to. Most prominent among these simpler rituals is the adolescence ceremony for girls. The dance of war or victory occupies second place. To these must be added in northwestern and north central California the shamans' dance for instruction of the novice, and in north and south central California various exhibitions by classes or bodies of shamans. Generally speaking, all these rites are dwarfed among each people in proportion as the nation adheres to one of the four organized cults; but they rarely disappear wholly. They are usually somewhat colored by ritualistic ideas developed in the greater cults. Thus the adolescence rites of the Hupa, the Maidu, and the Luiseño are by no means uniform. And yet, with the partial exception of the latter, they have not been profoundly shaped by the cults with which they are in contact, and can certainly not be described as having been incorporated in these cults. In short, these old or presumably ancient rites, which are all animated by essentially individual motives as opposed to communal or world purposes, evince a surprising vitality which has enabled them to retain certain salient traits with but little modification during periods when it may be supposed that the more highly florescent religions grew or were replaced by others.

The mourning anniversary belongs to neither class and is best considered separately.

The Kuksu and toloache systems shared the idea of initiation into a society. This organization was always communal. The organization of the society was also of very simple character, particularly in the south. In the Kuksu society two grades of initiates were recognized, besides the old men of special knowledge who acted as directors.[3]

The Kuksu cult impersonates spirits and has developed a fair wealth of distinctive paraphernalia and disguises for the several mythic characters. This is a feature which probably developed on the spot. It can not well have reached central California from either the Southwestern or the North Pacific coast areas, since the intervening nations for long distances do not organize themselves into societies; not to mention that the quite diverse northwestern and toloache religions are present as evidences of growths that would have served to block the transmission of such influences.

The dances and costumes of the toloache cult are extremely simple. Ritual actions refer unceasingly to mythology, and the ground painting is only one of several manifestations of an actively symbolizing impulse, but there are no disguises or impersonations. The vision-producing drug gives the cult an inward-looking and mystic character and discourages meaningless formalism.

The cults of the Colorado River tribes are bare of any inclination toward the formation of associations or bodies of members. They rest on dreams, or on imitations of other practitioners which are fused with inward experiences and construed as dreams. These dreams invariably have a mythological cast. Ritually the cults consist essentially of long series of songs, but most singers know a corresponding narrative. Dancing is minimal, and essentially an adjunct for pleasure. Concretely expressed symbolism is scarcely known; disguises, ground paintings, altars, religious edifices, drums, and costumes are all dispensed with.

The northwestern cults adhere minutely to certain traditional forms, but these forms per se have no meaning. There is no trace of any cult organizations. The esoteric basis of every ceremony is the recitation of a formula, which is a myth in dialogue. The formulas are jealously guarded as private property. Major rites

---

[3] It is doubtful whether the Miwok, Yokuts, Costanoans, and Salinans—in other words, the southern Kuksu dancing tribes—possessed a society.

always serve a generic communal or even world-renewing purpose and may well be described as new year rites. Dance costumes and equipments are splendid but wholly unsymbolic. All performances are very rigorously attached to precise localities and spots.

It is clear that as these four cults are followed from northwestern California southeastward to the lower Colorado, there is a successive weakening of the dance and all other external forms, of physical apparatus, of association with particular place or structure; and an increase of personal psychic participation, of symbolism and mysticism, of speculation or at least emotion about human life and death, and of intrinsic interweaving of ritualistic expression with myth. The development of these respective qualities has nothing to do with the development of principles of organization, initiation, and impersonation or enactment, since the latter principles are adhered to in the middle of our area and unknown at the extremities.

As organizations, the Kuksu and toloache cult associations are decidedly weak. They aim usually to include all adult males, and even where some attempt at discrimination is made, as perhaps among the Wintun, the proportion of those left out of membership seems to be small. There is no internal hierarchy; recognized priests can scarcely be spoken of with propriety; and there never is an elaboration of structure through the coexistence of parallel and equivalent societies within the community. On all these sides, the Californian religious bodies are much less developed than those of the Southwest and the Plains.

To compensate for the simplicity of organization in the Kuksu and toloache religions, initiation looms up largely, according to some reports almost as if it were the chief function of the bodies. Novices were often given a formal and prolonged education. Witness the *woknam*, the "lie-dance" or "school" of the Yuki, the orations of the Maidu and Patwin, the long moral lectures to Luiseño boys and girls. That these pedagogical inclinations are an inherent part of the idea of the religious society is shown by the fact that the Yurok and Mohave, who lack societies, do not manifest these inclinations, at least not in any formal way. In the Southwest, education seems less important than in California, relatively to the scheme of the whole religious institution; and for the Plains the difference is still greater. It appears, therefore, that these two aspects, initiation and organization, stand in inverse ratio of importance in North American cult societies.

Police and military functions of religious societies are very strongly marked among the Plains tribes; are definitely exercised by the bow or warrior societies of the Southwest, and perhaps stand out larger in native consciousness than in our own, since ethnologists have usually approached the religious bodies of this area from the side of cult rather than social influence; but such functions are exceedingly vague and feeble in California. There may have been some regulation of profane affairs by the body of initiates; but the chiefs and other civil functionaries are the ones almost always mentioned in such matters in California. There certainly was no connection of the cult societies with warfare. The first traces of an association of cult and war appear on the Colorado River, where societies do not exist. The negativeness of the California religious bodies in this regard is to be construed as an expression of their lack of development of the organization factor.

In spite of their performance of communal and often public rituals, American religious societies are never wholly divorced from shamanism, that is, the exercise of individual religious power; and one of their permanent foundations or roots must be sought in shamanism. On the Plains there is a complete transition from societies based on voluntary affiliation, purchase, age, war record, or other nonreligious factors, to such as are clearly nothing but more or less fluctuating groups of individuals endowed with similar shamanistic powers. Farther east the Midewiwin is little more than an attempt at formal organization of shamanism. In the Southwest, among the Pueblos, the fraternal as opposed to the communal religious bodies can be looked upon, not indeed as shamans' associations, but as societies one of whose avowed purposes—perhaps the primary one—is curative, and which have largely replaced the shaman acting as an individual. Among the Navaho the greatest ceremonies seem to be curative. In California we have the similarity of name between the Luiseño shaman and initiates, *pul-a* and *pu-pl-em*, already commented on; and the *lit* or doctoring of the Yuki societies as practically their only function besides that of perpetuating themselves by initiation. In spite of their loose structure and comparative poverty of ritual, it can not, however, be maintained that the societies of California are more inclined to be shamanistic than those of the other two regions.

Perhaps the most distinctive character of the two Californian cult societies is their freedom from any tendency to break up into, or to be accompanied by, smaller and equivalent but diverse societies as in the Plains, Southwest, and North Pacific coast regions.

Dance costumes and ornaments are illustrated in Plates 3, 42, 58, 59. 61, 77, 80, and Figures 20, 21, 44.

THE MOURNING ANNIVERSARY.

The anniversary or annual ceremony in memory of the dead bulks so large in the life of many California tribes as to produce a first impression of being one of the most typical phases of Californian culture. As a matter of fact, the institution was in force over only about half of the State: southern California and the Sierra Nevada region. There can be little doubt that its origin is southern. The distribution itself so suggests. The greatest development of mourning practices is found among the Gabrielino and Luiseño. It is not that their anniversary is much more elaborate than that of other groups—the use of images representing the dead is common to the great majority of tribes—but it is that these southerners have a greater number of mourning rites. Thus the Luiseño first wash the clothes of the dead, then burn them, and finally make the image ceremony. Of this they know two distinct forms, and in addition there are special mourning rites for religious initiates, and the eagle dance, which is also a funerary ceremony. Another circumstance that points to southern origin is the fact that the anniversary is held by nearly all tribes in the circular brush enclosure, which is not used by the Miwok and Maidu for other purposes, whereas in southern California it is the only and universal religious structure. Finally, there are no known connections between the anniversary and the Kuksu cult of the Miwok and Maidu, whereas the Jimson-weed religion of southern California presents a number of contacts with the mourning ceremony.

It is a fair inference that the anniversary received its principal development among the same people that chiefly shaped the Jimson-weed cult, namely, the Gabrielino or some of their immediate neighbors. It is even possible that the two sets of rites flowed northward in conjunction, and that the anniversary outreached its mate because the absence of the Jimson-weed plant north of the Yokuts checked the invasion of the rites based upon it.

The Mohave and Yuma follow an aberrant form of mourning which is characteristic of their general cultural position with reference to the remainder of southern California. Their ceremony is held in honor of distinguished individual warriors, not for the memory of all the dead of the year. The mourners and singers sit under a shade, in front of which young men engage in mimic battle and war exploits. There are no images and no brush enclosures. The shade is burned at the conclusion, but there is no considerable destruction of property such as is so important an element of the rite elsewhere in California.

An undoubted influence of the anniversary is to be recognized in a practice shared by a number of tribes just outside its sphere of distribution: the southern Wintun, Pomo, Yuki, Lassik, and perhaps others. These groups burn a large amount of property for the dead at the time of the funeral.   Somewhat similar are the eastern Mono practices.

Some faint traces, not of the mourning anniversary itself, indeed, but rather of the point of view which it expresses, are found even among the typical northwestern tribes. Among the Yurok and Hupa custom has established a certain time and place in every major dance as the occasion for an outburst of weeping. The old people in particular remember the presence of their departed kinsmen at former presentations of this part of the ceremony, and seem to express their grief spontaneously.

On the question of the time of the commemoration, more information is needed. It appears rather more often not to fall on the actual anniversary. Among some of the southern tribes it may be deferred several years; with the Mohave it seems to be held within a few weeks or months after death; the Sierra tribes mostly limit it to a fixed season—early autumn.

GIRLS' ADOLESCENCE CEREMONY.

Probably every people in California observed some rite for girls at the verge of womanhood: the vast majority celebrated it with a dance. The endless fluctuations in the conduct of the ceremony are indicated in Table 9. It appears that in spite of a general basic similarity of the rite, and the comparatively narrow scope imposed on its main outlines by the physiological event to which it has reference, there are very few features that are universal. These few, among which the use of a head scratcher and the abstention from flesh are prominent, are of a specifically magical nature. The wealth of particular features restricted to single nations, and therefore evidently developed by them, is rather remarkable, and argues that the Californians were not so much deficient in imagination and originality as in the ability to develop these qualities with emotional intensity to a point of impressiveness. There is every reason to believe that this inference applies with equal force to many phases of Californian civilization. It merely happens that an unusually full series of details is available for comparison on the rite for girls.

It has been noted several times that poor and rude tribes make much more of the adolescence ceremony in California than those possessed of considerable substance and specialized institutions. In this connection it is only necessary to cite the Yurok as contrasted with the Sinkyone, the Pomo as against the Yuki, valley Maidu against those of the mountains, Yokuts against Washo, Mohave against Diegueño. Precedence in general elaboration of culture must in every instance be given to the former people of each pair; and yet it is the second that makes, and the first that does not make, an adolescence ceremony. This condition warrants the inference that the puberty rite belongs to the generic or basic stratum of native culture, and that it has decayed among those nations that succeeded in definitely evolving or establishing ceremonials whose associations are less intimately personal and of a more broadly dignified import.

In the northern half of the State the idea is deep rooted that the potential influence for evil of a girl at the acme of her adolescence is very great. Even her sight blasts, and she is therefore covered or concealed as much as possible. Everything malignant in what is specifically female in physiology is thought to be thoroughly intensified at its first appearance. So far as known, all the languages of this portion of California possess one word for a woman in the periodic illness of her sex, and an entirely distinct term for a girl who is at the precise incipiency of womanhood.

A second concept is also magical: that the girl's behavior at this period of intensification is extremely critical for her nature and conduct forever after. Hence the innumerable prescriptions for gathering firewood, industry, modest deportment, and the like.

This concept pervades also the reasoning of the tribes in the southern end of the State, but is rather overshadowed by the more special conviction that direct physiological treatment is necessary to insure future health. Warmth appears to be considered the first requisite in the south. Cold water must not be drunk under any circumstances, bathing must be in heated water; and in the sphere of Gabrielino-Luiseño influence, the girl is cooked or roasted, as it were, in a pit, which seems modeled on the earth oven. The idea of her essential malignancy is comparatively weak in the south.

The southern concepts have penetrated in diluted form into the San Joaquin Valley region, along with so many other elements of culture. On the other hand, the Mohave, and with them presumably the Yuma, practice a type of ceremony that at most points differs from that of the other southern Californians, and provides an excellent exemplification of the profound aloofness of the civilization of these agricultural tribes of the Colorado River.

The deer-hoof rattle is consciously associated with the girls' ceremony over all northern California. Since there is a deep-seated antithesis of taboo between everything sexual on the one hand, and everything referring to the hunt, the deer as the distinctive game animal, and flesh on the other, the use of this particular rattle can hardly be a meaningless accident. But the basis of the inverting association has not become clear, and no native explanations seem to have been recorded.

A few Athabascan tribes replace the deer-hoof rattle by a modification of the clap-stick which provides the general dance accompaniment throughout central California, but which is not otherwise used in the northwest. In southern California the deer-hoof rattle is known, but is employed by hunters among the Luiseño, by mourners among the Yumans.

The scarcity of the ritualistic number 4 in Table 9 may be an accident of tribal representation in the available data, but gives the impression of having some foundation in actuality and a significance.

TABLE 9. THE ADOLESCENCE CEREMONY FOR GIRLS.

[Present, x; absent, o.]

Tribe	Special features.	Repetitions of ceremony.	Duration: nights.	General license.	Tattooed.	Ears pierced.	Drinks no water.	Fasts from salt.	Fasts from meat.	Head scratcher.	Girl bathes.	Girl works.	Girl carries wood.	Girl runs.	"Roasting" in pit.	Girl covered.	Eyeshade.	Deerhoof rattle.	Dance indoors.	Dance outdoors.	Dance abreast.	Dance in circle.	Girl dances.	Men dance.	Women dance.	Dancing.	Singing.
Yurok	Leaps toward morning star.		10				x			x	x						x									o	
Karok			10				x		x		o		x	o	o			x	o	x	x	x	x	x	x	x	x
Hupa	Pared stick rattle; painted boards; girl peers into haliotis shells.	3	10						x	x	x		x	x		x		o	x	o		o	o	x		x	x
Tolowa																		x								x	x
Wiyot	10 or 5 nights: concluding dance by women in water.		10						x							x		o	x		x			x	x	x	x
Sinkyone		2	5						x														x		x	x	x
Yuki	Pared stick rattle; girl keeps awake; hair over her eyes.			x				x	x	x						x			x		x		x		x	x	x
Pomo									x	x																o	
Modoc																								x		x	x
Shasta	Girl keeps awake; does not look about; east is symbolic direction.	3	5	x													x	x			x	x	x	x	x	x	x
Achomawi	Girl must not look at world.	3	10		x			x	x	x		x	x		x		x	x	x	x	x	x	x	x	x	x
Mountain Maidu		2	5		x			x	x	x	x	x	x		x		x	o	x	x	x	x	x	x	x	x
Hill Maidu	Girl in ring of fire.		10	x				x	x	x	x				x		x			o	x	x	o	x	x	x
Valley Maidu								x							x			x							o	x
Central Miwok	Girl in trench in house.							x										x			x		x	x		
Washo			5																				x		x	x
Yokuts	Girl uses no cold water.		4														o								o	
Tübatulabal	Girl in pit; roasting not sure.								x	x				x									x			

Girl forbidden all work; tobacco drunk.

Sand painting; tobacco eating ordeal, rocks painted; girl forbidden all work.

Cresentic stone applied; girl forbidden all work; tobacco drunk; period in pit indefinite.

Girl washes 40 days with warm water; drinks no cold water; loused by mother; lies in hot sand.

	2			6
	3	3?		
	×	×	×	
		×		
	×	×	×	×
	×	×	×	
	×	×	×	
		o	o	×
		o	o	×
		o	o	
		×	o	
	×	×	×	[×]
	×	×		
		o	o	o
		o		
				o
	×		×	o
	o			o
	×	×		o
	×	×	×	o
	×	×	×	o
Cahuilla	×	×	×	
Luiseño				
Diegueño				
Mohave				

BOYS' INITIATIONS.

The description which has sometimes been made of Californian religion as characterized by initiation and mourning rites does not appear to be accurate. Mourning customs, so far as they are crystallized into formal and important ceremonies, are confined to a single wave of southern origin and definitely limited distribution—the mourning anniversary. The girls' adolescence rite, on the other hand, is universal, and clearly one of the ancient constituents of the religion of all California as well as considerable tracts outside.

Boys were initiated into the two great organized religions of the State, the Kuksu and the toloache cult. Important as the initiation ceremonies were in these cults, it would, however, be misleading to regard them as primary: logically, at any rate, the cult comes first; the initiation is a part of it. When, therefore, we subtract these two religions, there is left almost nothing in the nature of initiations for boys parallel to the girls' adolescence ceremony.

The only clear instance is in the northeastern corner of the State among the Achomawi and Shasta, primarily the former. These people practice an adolescence rite for boys comparable to the more widespread one for girls. Among each of them a characteristic feature is the whipping of the boy with a bow string. The Achomawi also pierce the boy's ears and make him fast, besides which he performs practices very similar to the deliberate seeking after supernatural power indulged in by the tribes of the Plains. The entire affair is very clearly an adolescence rather than an initiation rite, an induction into a status of life, and not into an organized group. It may be looked upon as a local extension to boys of concepts that are universal in regard to girls.

In southern California there is sometimes a partial assimilation of the boys' toloache initiation and of the girls' adolescence ceremony. Thus the Luiseño construct ground paintings for both, deliver analogous orations of advice to both, and put both sexes under similar restrictions. The Kawaiisu are said to give toloache to both boys and girls.

But these local and incomplete developments are very far from equating the initiations for the two sexes; and neither balances with mourning ceremonies. The girls' adolescence, the boys' initiation into a society, and the mourning anniversary clearly have distinct origins so far as California is concerned, and represent separate cultural planes.

NEW YEAR OBSERVANCES.

A first-salmon ceremony was shared by an array of tribes in northern California. The central feature was usually the catching and eating of the first salmon of the season; after which fishing was open to all. These features constitute the ceremony one of public magic. The tribes from which some observance of this kind has been reported are the Tolowa, Yurok, Hupa, Karok, Shasta, Achomawi, and northern mountain Maidu. The list is probably not complete; but it may be significant that all the groups included in it are situated in the extreme north of the State, whereas salmon run in abundance, wherever there are streams of sufficient size to receive them, as far south as San Francisco Bay. It thus seems probable that the distribution of the rite was limited not only by the occurrence of the fish but also by purely cultural associations. Its range, for example, is substantially identical with that of the northern type of overlaid basketry.

The first-salmon ceremony is clearly of the type of new year's rituals, but is the only well-marked instance of this type yet found in California outside of the hearth of the northwestern culture. The idea of ceremonial reference to the opening of the year or season seems not to have been wholly wanting in north central California, especially where the Kuksu religion prevailed, but there is no record of its having been worked out into a definite ritual concept. In the northwest there were first-acorn and world-renewing ceremonies as well as the first-salmon rite. With the Karok these contained the superadded feature of new-fire making. All this, however, was an essentially local development among the small group of tribes who had advanced the northwestern culture to its most intense status.

In other words, an annual salmon producing or propitiating act of magical nature and of public rather than individual reference is usual in the northern part of the State, as well as in Oregon, and is therefore presumably an ancient institution. Among the specifically northwestern tribes this act later became associated with a ritualistic spectacle, either the Deerskin or the Jumping dance, which probably had no original connection with the magical performance; after which the combination of magic act and dance was applied to other occasions of a first fruits or New Year's character.

OFFERINGS.

Offerings of feathered wands are reported from the Chumash, the Costanoans, and the Maidu, and may therefore be assumed to have had a considerably wider distribution in the central parts of California, although neither Yuki nor Pomo seem to know the device. The idea is that of the prayer stick or prayer plume of the Southwest, and there is probably a connection between the practices of the two regions; although this may be psychological, that is, indirectly cultural, rather than due to outright transmission. This inference is supported by the fact that there is no reference to anything like the offering of feather wands in southern California where southwestern influences are, of course, most immediate. In fact, the practice of setting out offerings of any kind is so sparsely mentioned for southern California that it must be concluded to have been but slightly developed. The Californian feather wand was of somewhat different shape from the southwestern prayer plume. It appears usually to have been a stick of some length from which single feathers were loosely hung at one or two places. The northwestern tribes are free from the practice.

Another ultimate connection with the Southwest is found in offerings or sprinklings of meal. These have been recorded for the Pomo, the Maidu, the Costanoans, and the Serrano. In some instances it is not clear whether whole seeds or flour ground from them was used, and it is even possible that the meal was sometimes replaced by entire acorns. The southern California tribes should perhaps be included, since the use of meal or seeds in the ground painting might be construed as an offering. The custom seems, however, to have been more or less hesitating wherever it has been reported. It certainly lacks the full symbolic implications and the ritualistic rigor which mark it in the Southwest. Among the Yokuts and probably their mountain neighbors offerings of eagle down appear to have been more characteristic than of seeds or meal. The northwestern tribes can again be set down with positiveness as not participating in the custom.

THE GHOST DANCE.

The ghost dance, which swept northern California with some vehemence from about 1871 to 1873 or 1874, is of interest because of its undoubted connection with the much more extensive and better known wave of religious excitement that penetrated to the Indians of half of the United States about 1889 and 1890, and which left most of the Californians totally untouched. Both movements had their origin among the Northern Paiute of Nevada, and from individuals in the same family. The author of the early phophesies may have been the father and was, at any rate, an older kinsman of Wovoka or Jack Wilson, the later prophet or Messiah. The ideas of the two movements and their ritual were substantially identical. There is thus little doubt that even their songs were similar, although, unfortunately, these were not recorded for the earlier movement until after its fusion with other cults.

The question arises why the religious infection which originated twice in the same spot in an interval of 15 or 20 years should at the first occasion have obtained a powerful, although fleeting, foothold in northern California alone, and on its recrudescence should have spread to the Canadian boundary and the Mississippi River. That the Californians remained impassive toward the second wave is intelligible on the ground of immunity acquired by having passed through the first. But that a religion which showed its inherent potentiality by spreading to wholly foreign tribes should in 1870 have been unable to make any eastward progress and in 1890 sweep like wildfire more than a thousand miles to the east is remarkable. The only explanation seems to be that the bulk of the Indian tribes in the United States in 1870 had not been reduced to the necessary condition of cultural decay for a revivalistic influence to impress them. In other words, the native civilization of northern California appears to have suffered as great a disintegration by 1870, 20 or 25 years after its first serious contact with the whites, as the average tribe of the central United States had undergone by 1890, or from 50 to 100 years after similar contact began. As regards the Plains tribes, among whom the second ghost dance reached its culmination, there may be ascribed to the destruction of the buffalo the same influence on the breaking up of their old life as the sudden overwhelming swamping of the natives by the California gold seekers. In each case an interval of from 10 to 20 years elapsed from the dealing of the substantial death blow to the native civilization until the realization of the change was sufficiently profound to provide a fruitful soil for a doctrine of restoration.

Individual tribes had, of course, been subject to quite various fortunes at the hands of the whites when either ghost dance reached them. But it is also known that they accorded the movement many locally diverse receptions. Some threw themselves into it with an almost unlimited enthusiasm of hope; others were only slightly touched or remained aloof. This is very clear from Mooney's classical account of the greater ghost dance, and it can be conjectured that an intensive study would reveal the skeptical negative tribes to have been so situated that their old life did not yet appear to themselves as irrevocably gone, or as so thoroughly subject to the influences of Caucasian civilization that they had accepted the change as final. Then, too, it must be remembered that the wave, as it spread, developed a certain psychological momentum of its own, so that tribes which, if left to themselves or restricted to direct intercourse with the originators of the movement, might have remained passive, were infected by the frenzy of differently circumstanced tribes with whom they were in affiliation.

The same phenomena can be traced in the history of the California ghost dance, imperfect as our information concerning it is. The Karok and Tolowa seem to have projected themselves into the cult with greater abandonment than the Yurok. The Hupa, at least to all intents, refused to participate. This is perhaps to be ascribed to the fact that they were the only tribe in the region leading a stable and regulated reservation life. But it is not clear whether this circumstance had already led them to a conscious though reluctant acceptance of the new order of things, or whether some other specific cause must be sought.

On many of the northernmost tribes the effect of the ghost dance was quite transient, and it left no traces whatever. It was perhaps already decadent when the Modoc war broke out. At any rate it is no longer heard of after the termination of that conflict. How far the Modoc war may have been indirectly fanned by the doctrine remains to be ascertained. Its immediate occasion seems not to have been religious.

Somewhat farther south the ghost dance took firmer root among tribes like the Pomo and southern Wintun, which were beyond the most northerly missions but which had been more or less under mission influence and whose lands had been partly settled by Mexicans in the period between secularization and the Americanization of California. The old Kuksu ceremonies were now not only revived but made over. A new type of songs, paraphernalia, and ritual actions came into existence; and these have maintained themselves in some measure until to-day they are strongly interwoven with the aboriginal form of religion. The Wintun at least, and presumably the Pomo also, are still conscious, however, of the two elements in their present cults, and distinguish them by name. *Saltu* are the spirits that instituted the ancient rites, *boli* those with whom the modern dances are associated.

This amalgamation, strangely enough, resulted in the carrying of the Kuksu religion, at a time when it was essentially moribund, to tribes which in the days of its vitality had come under its influence only marginally or not at all. Evidently the ghost dance element acted as a penetrating solvent and carrier. The central Wintun took the mixed cult over from the southern Wintun, and the use since 1872 of typical Kuksu paraphernalia as far north as the Shasta of Shasta Valley evidences the extent of this movement.

None of the tribes within the mission area seems to have been in the least affected by the ghost dance. This is probably not due to their being Catholics or nominal Catholics, but rather to the fact that their life had long since been definitively made over. Groups like the Yokuts, of which only portions had been missionized and these rather superficially, also did not take up the ghost dance. The cause in this case presumably lies between their geographical remoteness and the fact that most of their intercourse was with missionized tribes.

The Modoc were perhaps the first Californian people to receive the early ghost dance from the Northern Paiute. It is hard to conceive that the Achomawi should have been exempt, but unfortunately there appear to be no records concerning them on this point. The

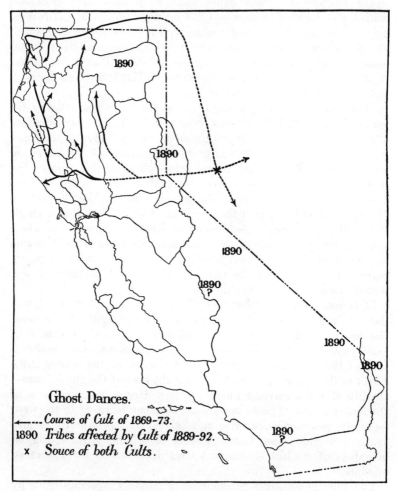

Ghost Dances.

←.... *Course of Cult of 1869-73.*
1890 *Tribes affected by Cult of 1889-92.*
x *Souce of both Cults.*

FIG. 71.—Ghost dance movements in California.

same may be said of the mountain Maidu. From the Modoc, at any rate, the cult was carried to the Shasta. These transmitted it still farther down the Klamath to the Karok. From there it leaped the Siskiyou Mountains to the Tolowa, from whom the lower Yurok of the river and of the coast took their beliefs. The upper Yurok were less affected and the Hupa scarcely at all. Here we lose track

of the spread of the dance. Probably all the Athabascan tribes between the Whilkut and the Wailaki, at least those that survived in
sufficient numbers, came under ghost dance influence, but the direction in which this influence progressed seems to have been from the
south northward. Their dance appears to have been associated
with the erection of large round dance houses of central Californian
type. The traced course of the movement is: southern Wintun of
the Sacramento Valley; Long Valley Wintun; southeastern Pomo;
eastern Pomo; southern, central, and northern Pomo; Huchnom;
Yuki, Kato, and Wailaki; and north to the Hayfork Wintun, Whilkut, and perhaps Chilula. (Fig. 71.)

It has already been mentioned how in the Sacramento Valley the
ghost dance spread from south to north. To this it may be added
that the Yana received the cult from the valley Maidu to the south
of them. The question then arises how the dance reached the southern Wintun. There is no known information on this point. The
movement may conceivably have traveled directly westward from
the Northern Paiute through Washo and southern Maidu. Yet, on
the whole, it is likely that the entry into California was at a single
point; that is, through the Modoc and Klamath tribes, from whom
the cult spread southward until, reaching its extreme limit among
the southern Wintun, it recrystallized and then flowed back northward. Inquiry among the southern Maidu and northern Miwok
would probably determine this issue.

It is not known whether any of the Miwok took up the ghost
dance. In a number of localities they have during the last generation or so erected circular or octagonal dance houses of wood without
earth covering. These look very much like a ghost dance modification of the old semisubterranean dance house of the Kuksu cults.
Forty or fifty years ago—that is, about the time of the ghost dance—
the hill Miwok received a number of new dances, including some of
the Kuksu series. These came from Costanoan territory to the west,
but quite possibly represent a cult revival of the imperfectly missionized northernmost valley Yokuts or Plains Miwok, original
neighbors of the hill Miwok, but later domiciled at the Costanoan
missions.[1]

The 1890 ghost dance is reported by Mooney, specifically or by
implication, for the Achomawi, Washo, Mono, Koso, Yokuts of
Tule River, Luiseño or other "mission" groups, Chemehuevi, and
Mohave. The Washo, eastern Mono, Chemehuevi, and perhaps
Koso could hardly have escaped participation. The Achomawi may
have been rendered susceptible by a failure to take part in 1872.
The Mohave were never seriously affected. The Yokuts and Luiseño
were no doubt interested, but seem never to have practiced the cult.

---

[1] The northern Miwok of 1923 know nothing of the ghost dance.

No tribe in California retained for more than a very short time any phase of this second ghost dance religion.

CALENDAR.

The California Indian did not record the passage of long intervals of time. No one knew his own age nor how remote an event was that had happened more than two or three years ago. Tallies seem not to have been kept for any purpose, and no sticks notched annually have been found or reported in the State. Most groups had not even a word for "year," but employed "world," "summer," or "winter" instead. Where there appear to be words meaning "year," they seem as often as not to denote "season," that is, a half year.

Probably every tribe, however, had a system of measuring time within the year. This was by the universally known method of naming and reckoning lunations in the round of the seasons. The point of interest in this method to the historian of culture rests in the means taken to adjust the eternally varying and essentially irreconcilable lunar and solar phenomena. Half a dozen such calendars are known from California. These clearly belong to three types, evidently representative of the three cultures of which so much mention has been made in this book.

The Maidu knew 12 moons, named after seasonal occurrences. The series began in spring, and appears not to have been controlled by any solar phenomenon. There can accordingly scarcely have been a consistent method, however rude, of adjusting the moon count to the year. When the discrepancy became too insistent, something was presumably stretched or the reckoning simply suspended until matters seemed to tally again. The whole scheme is essentially descriptive of terrestrial events, and has as little reference to astronomical events as a system can have and still be called a calendar. In line with this attitude of the Maidu is the fact that they made definite recognition of the seasons, as shown by a neat nomenclature. It should also be added that the upland Maidu counted only the winter moons, those of the summer being left unnamed.

The Yurok calendar has a more astronomical basis, although simple enough; and the descriptive element is almost lacking. The moons are numbered, not named, at least up to the tenth; the remaining ones have descriptive appellations. The year begins definitely at the winter solstice. The summer solstice may have been noted also, but does not enter into the system. There was a clear recognition of the essential problem of a year calendar, some individuals counting twelve moons and others thirteen. The solution must have been less clearly formulated, since it is stated that disputes often took place as to the proper designation of the current moon. Yet recognition of the solstice as a primary point, however inaccurately it may have been determined by offhand appearances without mechanically aided observations, would prevent any excessively gross errors or long-continued conflict of opinion.

The Yurok system is undoubtedly connected with that of the North Pacific coast, where the moons are also frequently numbered and fitted into the frame afforded by the solstices.

The Modoc calendar seems to be a weakening of the Yurok one. Basically, the moons are numbered, although their actual names are those of the fingers of the hand. But the beginning of the round is in summer and is determined by a seasonal harvest; there is no mention of the solstices; and none of an intercalary thirteenth month.

The Huchnom and Pomo mostly used descriptive moon names, but some "finger months" are included.[4]

In southern California the moon names are probably descriptive, but the fixed points of the calendar, and the means of its more or less automatic correction, are the two solstices. The Diegueño have only six month names; which means that the second half-year repeats and balances the first, and presumably that the two solstices are pivotal. The Juaneño and Luiseño do not repeat month designations within the year, but the former name only five and the latter but four periods in each half year. This scheme makes the nonlunar periods which include the solstices long and somewhat variable, but also accentuates them as primary.[5] All three varieties of this calendar must at times have been productive of difficulty within the haf-year, but as a perpetual system the scheme is obviously self-correcting. Whether any of the southern California tribes took actual observations of the solstices is not known.

This southern calendar is clearly allied to that of the tribes of the Southwestern States, who also deal in solstices but describe their moons. The Diegueño six-name plan is that of the Zuñi. The Pueblos definitely determined the solstices with fair accuracy by observations made on the horizon from established spots. It is possible that they were led to this procedure by their permanent residences. These would at least afford an advantage and perhaps a stimulus in this direction.

Astronomical knowledge not directly used in time reckoning was slight in northern and central California. The planets were too

---

[4] It appears (see footnote, p. 209) that both finger-count and descriptive calendars might coexist among one group in this region, and that the year sometimes began with the winter solstice. This suggests that central Californian and North Pacific coast customs have met in the Pomo area.

[5] It has been doubted whether the southern California periods tally with lunations in native consciousness, even though they are called "moons." See footnote, p. 723.

difficult to trouble with, except for Venus when it was the morning star. The Pleiades are the constellation most frequently mentioned, and seem to have had a designation among every tribe. Myths usually make them dancing girls, as in so many parts of the world. This may prove to be one of the concepts of independent or directly psychological origin which have so often been sought but are so difficult to establish positively. Orion's belt is probably recognized with the next greatest frequency, and then possibly Ursa Major. There are some references to Polaris as the immovable star. The Milky Way is known everywhere, and quite generally called the ghosts' road. In southern California stellar symbolism begins to be of some consequence, and half a dozen constellations and several isolated first magnitude stars are named in addition to those recognized farther north.

NUMERATION.

The round numbers familar to the Californians in ritual and myth are low, as among all American Indians. In the north, from the Tolowa and Sinkyone to the Achomawi and mountain Maidu, 5 or its multiple 10 is in universal use in such connections (Table 10). In the region of the well-defined Kuksu cult 4 takes its place, although the Pomo evince some inclination to supplement it by 6. To the south there is enough uncertainty to suggest that no one number stood strongly in the foreground. The Yokuts favor 6, but without much emphasis. The Gabrielino employed 5, 6, and 7 in addition to 4; among the Juaneño, 5 is most commonly mentioned; for the Luiseño, probably 3; among the Diegueño, 3 is clearly prevalent in ritual, 4 in myth. For a group of American nations with a definite ceremonial cult, and that comprising sacred paintings of the world, this is an unusually vague condition. Only the Colorado River tribes are positive: 4 is as inevitably significant to them as to all the Indians of the Southwest.

Directional reference of the ritualistic number is manifest in the Kuksu tribes, but everywhere else is wanting or at least insignificant, except with the Yuman groups. Here there is some tendency to balance opposite directions; single pairs are even mentioned alone. North or east has the precedence. In the Kuksu region there is a definite sequence of directions in sinistral circuit; but the starting point varies from tribe to tribe. Association of colors with the directions has been reported only from the Diegueño. Its general absence is an instance of the comparatively low development of ritualistic symbolism in California.

TABLE 10.—RITUAL NUMBERS AND METHODS OF NUMERATION.

Group.	Ritual number.				Units of count.		
					1–10	11–19	20+
Yurok			5, 10		10	10	10
Wiyot			5, 10		10	10	10
Karok			5, 10		5	10	10
Chimariko					5	10	10
Tolowa					10	10	10
Hupa, Chilula			5, 10		10	10	10
Sinkyone			5		5	.....	10
Wailaki					5	.....	10
Kato					5	5	10
Coast Yuki					5	5	10
Yuki		* 4		(6)	8	8	64
Wappo		*			5	10	10
Pomo		* 4		(* 6)	¹ 5	² 5	10, 20
Coast Miwok					10	10	10
Shasta			5, 10		5	10	10
Modoc			5		5	10	10
Achomawi			(5)		5	10	10
Yana			(5)		5	10	20
Wintun—							
Northern					5	10	.....
Central					5	5	.....
Southern		* 4			5	5, 10	20, 10
Maidu—							
Mountain			* 5		5	10	10
Hill		4	5		5	5, 10	20, 10
Valley		* 4	(5)		5	5	20
Southern					5	5	10
Miwok—							
Northern					10	5	20
Central		4			10	5	20
Southern					10	10	10
Yokuts—							
Central				6	10	10	10
Southerly	3			6, 12	10	10	10
Costanoan			(5)		³ 10	10	10
Esselen					5	.....	.....
Salinan					4	16	16
Chumash					4	16	16

* Referred to cardinal directions.
¹ 10 among northeastern Pomo.
² 10 among northeastern and southern Pomo.
³ 5 among southern Costanoans.

TABLE 10.—RITUAL NUMBERS AND METHODS OF NUMERATION—Continued.

Group.	Ritual number.					Units of count.		
						1-10	11-19	20+
Washo						5	10	10
Eastern Mono		4				10		
Tübatulabal						10		
Chemehuevi						10		
Serrano						5	10	10
Gabrielino		4, 8	(10)	6	(7)	5	5	5
Cahuilla						5	10	10
Luiseño	(3)	(* 4)				5	5	5
Diegueño	4 3	* 4				5		10
Yuma						5	10	10
Mohave		* 4				5	10	10

* Referred to cardinal directions.   4 4 predominates in myth, 3 in ritual action.

The same Table 10 shows also the distribution in California of methods of counting—the basis of all mathematical science. Mankind as a whole, and even the most advanced nations, count as the fingers determine. But it is obvious that the unit or basis of numeration can be one hand, or two, or the fingers plus the toes, that is, "one man." This gives a choice between quinary, decimal, and vigesimal systems. Whether from an inherent cause or because of a historical accident, practically all highly civilized nations count by tens, with hundred as the next higher unit. Peoples less advanced in culture, however, are fairly equally divided between a decimal numeration and one which operates somewhat more concretely or personally with fives and twenties. So, too, with the Californians. But to judge correctly their inclinations as between these two possibilities, it is necessary to distinguish between their use of low and high numbers.

For the first 10 numerals the majority of the Californians have stems only for 1 to 5. The words for 6 to 9 are formed from those for 1 to 4. This system is replaced chiefly in three regions by a truly decimal one, in which the word for 7, for instance, bears no relation to that for 2. The first of these three tracts holds the two Algonkin divisions of California, the Wiyot and Yurok; and a few immediately adjacent Athabascan groups, notably the Hupa and Tolowa. The second area comprises the Yokuts, Miwok, and most of the Costanoans—in short, the southern half of the Penutian family. In the third area are the Plateau Shoshoneans east of the Sierra Nevada.

These distributions reflect geographical position rather than linguistic affinities. The northern Penutians, southern Athabascans, and southern California Shoshoneans count by fives instead of tens. The map makes it look as if decimal numeration had been taken over by the Hupa and Tolowa in imitation of the method of their Algonkin neighbors; but the difficulty in this connection is that the great mass of eastern Algonkins count by fives instead of straight to ten.

For the higher numbers, the corresponding choice is between a system based on 20 and 400, or on 10 and 100. In this domain the decimal system prevails, showing that the quinary and vigesimal methods, even if inherently associated, are not inseparable. The situation may be summed up by saying that from 20 up, all California counts decimally except the people of two areas. The first comprises half or more of the Pomo, most of the southern Wintun, in general the western Maidu, and the northerly divisions of the interior Miwok. This is precisely the region of intensive development of the Kuksu cults. Here the count is by twenties. The second area is that of the Gabrielino and Luiseño, with whom the Fernandeño, Juaneño, and perhaps Cupeño must be included, but no others. (These peoples strictly do not count by twenties, but by multiplying fives.) Now, this, strangely enough, is precisely the tract over which the Chungichnish religion had penetrated in its full form. The connection between a system of religious institutions and a method of numeration in daily life is very difficult to understand, and the bonds must be indirect and subtle. That they exist, however, and that it is more than an empty coincidence that we are envisaging, is made almost indisputable by the fact that the northern tract of decimal counting for low numbers coincides very nearly with the area of the northwestern culture in its purest form as exemplified by New Year's rites and the Deerskin dance.

That the basing of the vigesimal on the quinary count, although usual, is by no means necessary, is shown by the northern and central Miwok, who count the first 10 numbers decimally, but proceed from 10 to 20 by adding units of 5, and beyond with units of 20. That a people should count first 5 and then another 5 and then proceed to operate systematically with the higher unit of 10, is not so very foreign to our way of thinking. But that our own psychic processes are by no means necessarily binding is proved by this curious Miwok practice of beginning with ten straight numeral words, then counting twice by fives, and finally settling into a system of twenties.

Two other totally divergent methods of counting are found in California. The Chumash and Salinans count by fours, with 16 as higher unit, the Yuki by eights and sixty-fours. The latter operate by laying pairs of twigs into the spaces between the fingers. Thus the anomaly is presented of an octonary system based on the hand. The Yuki operate very skillfully by this method: when they are asked to count on the fingers like their neighbors, they work slowly and with frequent errors. Both these systems run contrary to speech affinity: the Chumash and Salinans are the only Hokans that count by fours; and the Coast Yuki, Huchnom, and Wappo related to the Yuki know nothing of their system of eights.

Every count that can progress beyond one hand involves arithmetical operations of some sort, usually addition. But other processes crop out with fair frequency in California. Nine, fourteen, and nineteen are sometimes formed from the unit next above. The word for 4 is often a reduplicated or expanded 2; or 8 a similar formation from 4. Two-three for 6, three-four for 12, and three-five for 15 all occur here and there; and the Luiseño count by an indefinitely repeated system of multiplication, as "4 times 5 times 5."

The degree to which mathematical operations were conducted other than in the counts themselves has been very little examined into. The Pomo speak of beads by ten and forty thousands. Every group in the State, apparently, knew how to count into the hundreds; how often its members actually used these higher numbers, and on what occasions, is less clear. Rapid and extended enumeration argues some sense of the value of numbers, and it is likely that people like the Pomo and Patwin developed such a faculty by their counting of beads. Of direct mathematical operations there is less evidence. An untutored Yuki can express offhand in his octonary nomenclature how many fingers he has; he evidently can not multiply 10 by 2: for he finds it necessary to count his hands twice over to enable him to answer. An old Mohave knows at once that 4 times 4 is 16; but 4 times 8 presents a problem to be solved only by a sorting and adding up of counters. No Californian language is known to have any expression for fractions. There is always a word for half, but it seems to mean "part" or "division" rather than the exact mathematical ratio.

CHAPTER 57.

POPULATION.

PREVIOUS ESTIMATES AND COMPUTATIONS.

The strength of the aboriginal population is as difficult to estimate in California as in most parts of America. Early figures of general range, like Powers's 700,000, are almost invariably far too high, and those of more restricted application are either obvious impressionistic exaggerations or fail to specify accurately the areas really involved.

There has been only one attempt to approach the subject in a critical spirit, and to arrive at conclusions by computation in place of guess. This is a valuable essay by Dr. C. Hart Merriam, which takes the Franciscan mission statistics as a basis. The argument runs as follows:

In 1834 there were upward of 30,000 converted Indians. A ratio of one gentile to every three neophytes may be assumed for this period for the territory tapped by the missions. This gives 40,000. The population at the missions had, however, long suffered a heavy decrease. At least 10,000 must therefore be added to reach the true numbers before contact with the Spaniards: total, 50,000. The area in question comprises only one-fifth of the nondesert part of the State. Hence, natural conditions in the mission strip being on the average in no way superior to those elsewhere, there were 250,000 Indians in the fertile and semifertile portions of California. Add 10,000 for the deserts, and a grand total of 260,000 is reached.

Some of the factors in this computation are taken very conservatively; others must be gravely questioned. The assumption of the representativeness of the mission territory in productiveness seems fair. The proportion of four natives in 1834 where there had been five in 1769 is, if anything, too low, in view of the enormous mortality at some of the missions. The proportion of converts to gentiles may be accepted as reasonable, statistics being totally lacking. On the other hand, the vague report of over 30,000 in 1834, the year of secularization, is less entitled to credence than the exact figure of 24,634 for 1830.

That the tracts drawn upon for the missions covered only a fifth of the nondesert parts of the State is, however, an undervaluation, as can be seen by a glance at Figure 72. The outer, broken line on that map, indicating the limits of partial missionization, is the one that must be considered in this connection, since we are allowing for territory that still contained wild Indians as well as neophytes. It is evident that this line includes very nearly a third of the whole State, and certainly more than a third of the nondesert areas.

A recomputation then might start with 25,000; add a third for gentiles, making 33,000; and possibly half to that as an allowance for decrease from 1769 to 1830; total for the mission area about 1770, 50,000. Multiplying by 3 yields 150,000. An addition of 10,000 for desert areas might be insisted on; but if so, at least an equal deduction would have to be made for the fertile portions of the State being less than three times the mission area; so that the result of 150,000 would stand. This cuts Dr. Merriam's total nearly in half.

It must be pointed out that the mission data are of such a character that they can not be used with any accuracy except after a far more painstaking analysis than they have yet been subjected to. We hear constantly of a jumble of tribes at most of the establishments, and sometimes they are designated so as to be recognizable, but their relative proportions remain obscure. A study of the baptismal registers, where these give birthplaces, may provide some notion of the strength of the various groups for certain periods at a few of the missions; and from such conclusions an estimate of the size of the tribes represented at all the establishments between 1769 and 1834 might be derivable. Before this can be done, however, the location of the rancherias mentioned must be worked out with at least approximate precision. Another difficulty is that the ratios changed enormously. In 60, or even in 30 years, the unremitting mortality undoubtedly shrank the numbers of the first converts from the immediate vicinity very heavily; while neophytes from a distance began to come in only gradually, but then, until a certain point was reached, ever more rapidly. Thus, there were Yokuts at missions founded on Costanoan, Salinan, Chumash, and perhaps Shoshonean soil; but whether in 1810 and again in 1830 they constituted, at any one point, 5 or 20 or 60 per cent of the converted population, there is at present no means of deciding.

A RECONSIDERATION OF THE DATA.

For many years the present writer had set the native population of the State at 150,000. This was avowedly a guess, based on numerous scattered impressions, which, however, seemed at least as reliable as any computation can be at present. Later, he was inclined to shift the figure toward 100,000 rather than at 150,000. In the preparation of the present work the matter was once more gone into, and as exhaustively as possible. The method followed was to take up each group separately, giving consideration to all possible elements of knowledge, and checking these against each other. The variety of sources of information, unsatisfactory as most of these are separately, is considerable. There are, for instance, early estimates of travelers and settlers; the conclusions of ethnologists familiar with the people at a later time; the number of known villages or village sites; the tribal count in the Federal census of 1910, which was undertaken conscientiously and carried out very reasonably; the apparent rapidity of decrease in various areas; the availability of food supply in each habitat; and indications of the ratio of density of population in adjacent areas of differing surface and environment. The figures thus obtained more or less independently for each tribe, dialect group, or stock, were then brought together, rounded to the nearest half thousand, in Table 11, and yielded a total of 133,000.

TABLE 11.—INDIAN POPULATION OF CALIFORNIA, 1770 AND 1910.

Groups.	1770	1910	Groups.	1770	1910
Yurok	2,500	700	Northern Paiute in Cal-		
Karok	1,500	800	ifornia	500	300
Wiyot	1,000	100	Eastern and western		
Tolowa	1,000	150	Mono	4,000	1,500
Hupa	1,000	500	Tübatulabal	1,000	150
Chilula, Whilkut	1,000	(*)	Koso, Chemehuevi, Ka-		
Mattole	500	(*)	waiisu	1,500	500
Nongatl, Sinkyone,			Serrano, Vanyume,		
Lassik	2,000	100	Kitanemuk, Alliklik.	3,500	150
Wailaki	1,000	200	Gabrielino, Fernan-		
Kato	500	(*)	deño, San Nicoleño	5,000	(*)
Yuki	2,000	100	Luiseño	4,000	500
Huchnom	500	(*)	Juaneño	1,000	(*)
Coast Yuki	500	(*)	Cupeño	500	150
Wappo	1,000	(*)	Cahuilla	2,500	800
Pomo	8,000	1,200	Diegueño, Kamia	3,000	800
Lake Miwok	500	(*)	Mohave (total)	3,000	1,050
Coast Miwok	1,500	(*)	Halchidhoma (emi-		
Shasta	2,000	100	grated since 1800)	1,000	....
Chimariko, New River,			Yuma (total)	2,500	750
Konomihu, Okwanu-				136,000	15,400
chu	1,000	(*)	Total of groups marked *	....	450
Achomawi, Atsugewi	3,000	1,100			
Modoc in California	500	(*)			15,850
Yana	1,500	(*)	Less river Yumans in		
Wintun	12,000	1,000	Arizona	3,000	850
Maidu	9,000	1,100			
Miwok (Plains and					15,000
Sierra)	9,000	700	Non-Californian Indians		
Yokuts	18,000	600	now in California	....	350
Costanoan	7,000	(*)	Affiliation doubtful or		
Esselen	500	(*)	not reported	....	1,000
Salinan	3,000	(*)			
Chumash	10,000	(*)	Total	133,000	16,350
Washo in California	500	300			

It must be admitted that as each individual figure is generally nothing but an estimate, or an average of possible conjectures, the total can make no claim to precision. It represents only an opinion; but at least this opinion is the formulation of years of attention to all possible aspects of the question. A different impression may be truer, and perhaps can some day be verified.

Many of the figures for individual tribes in Table 11 may excite protest on the part of those specially familiar with a group. But it is believed that if some have been put too low, others are excessively liberal. Thus, 9,000 for the Maidu may seem a small total, but the student who has most carefully investigated these people judges 4,000 to be a conservative estimate. The numbers for the Mohave and Yuma are smaller than the prepioneer Garcés reported. Perhaps he was correct; but if so, the shortage is likely to be more than made up, in the State total, by the allowance of 9,000 for the Plains and Sierra Miwok, not to mention the high figure of 18,000 for the Yokuts. At any rate, the list represents the best that the writer conscientiously believes himself capable of proffering. And he is confident, in his own conviction, that he has not erred by more than a fourth from reality.

Of course there is no intention of offering the figure of 133,000 with the least idea of its specific correctness. It is meant only to indicate with some exactness the point near which the true value probably falls. A better expression might be to say that the population was from 120,000 to 150,000. But for broader computations, into which California might enter only as a small element, some precise formulation is necessary, and the 133,000 arrived at is the figure of all those in its vicinity that seems to have a little the greatest verisimilitude.

The plan of multiplicative calculation has been attempted on the basis of one people, the Yokuts. The computation can be followed in detail in chapter 32. The conclusion does not seem to have the same strength as that just arrived at, but it yields the interesting and perhaps significant corroboration of 130,000 maximum.

COMPARISON WITH THE POPULATION OF THE CONTINENT.

There is one other test that can be applied: Comparison with the remainder of the continent. Mr. James Mooney, who has devoted assiduous years to the problem of native population, arrives at a judgment of 846,000 souls for the United States and 202,000 in Canada, Alaska, and Greenland, or about 1,050,000 for America north of Mexico, with an estimate of error of less than 10 per cent. California covers a twentieth of the area of the country, or about a fortieth of the larger tract. On the basis of the present estimate of 133,000, this would allot to California nearly 16 per cent of the aboriginal population of the United States, as compared with 5 per cent of the area, or a relative density more than three times as great. This surely is liberal, no matter how highly we may rate the fertility of the Golden State and overlook its very considerable areas of minimal productivity.

In fact, the ratio is really higher, since Mr. Mooney's estimate of 846,000 seems to contain the figure of 260,000 for California. If for 260,000 we substitute 133,000, the total for the United States sinks to 719,000, and the California proportion rises to between 18 and 19 per cent. The density, similarly, is almost one person per square mile for California, as against one to every 4 plus miles over the remainder of the country. If we remember Death Valley, the Colorado and Mohave Deserts, the northern lava flows, and the high Sierra, this disproportion seems sufficient, if not excessive.

Comparison with outside territories therefore produces nothing to compel an enlargement of the estimate arrived at, in fact rather indicates that the reckoning of 133.000 is already thoroughly liberal. On the same basis, the result of Dr. Merriam's computation is incredible: 260,000 Indians in California, only 586,000 in all the other States and not more than 788,000 in the whole continent north of the Rio Grande, is a proportion that shatters conceivability. It is true that Mr. Mooney has evidently been thoroughly conservative in his estimates for the eastern and central United States with whose Indians he is most familiar from personal experience. But if this has been the inclination, for the larger part of the continent, of the admitted authority on the subject, a similar restraint is not only permissible but almost requisite in approaching the present more limited inquiry.

THE MISSION AREA.

A calculation made from Table 11 and Figure 72, of the number of Indians in the region affected by the missions, yields the following probabilities:

Pomo	3, 000	Esselen	500
Yukian	1, 000	Salinan	3, 000
Miwok	4, 000	Chumash	10, 000
Maidu	1, 000	Shoshonean	15, 000
Wintun	4, 000	Yuman	2, 500
Yokuts	13, 000		
Costanoan	7, 000	Total	64, 000

On the basis of the area involved being a third or not quite a third of the State, this figure of 64,000 would yield a total of very nearly 200,000, which is as near to Dr. Merriam's final conclusion as to the number advanced in the present work. Justice compels this admission; but the result thus attained seems not so much to compel an upward revision of the results already arrived at, as to indicate the unreliability of the multiplicative method.

POPULATION BY SPEECH FAMILIES.

The following compilation from Table 11 of the relative strength of the several native families in California may be of interest:

Families.	1770	1910
Penutian:		
Pen group: Maidu, Wintun, Yokuts.............. 39,000		
Uti group: Miwok, Costanoan.................... 18,000		
Total...	57,000	3,500
Hokan:		
Northern group: Shastan, Chimariko, Karok,		
Yana.. 9,000		
Pomo... 8,000		
Washo in California.............................. 500		
Southwestern group: Esselen, Salinan, Chumash.. 13,500		
Yuman (9,500, less 3,000 in Arizona)............. 6,500		
Total..	37,500	6,000
Shoshonean:		
Plateau branch.................................. 6,000		
Kern River branch............................... 1,000		
Southern California branch....................... 16,500		
Total..	23,500	4,050
Athabascan.......................................	7,000	1,000
Yukian...	4,000	200
Algonkin (Yurok, Wiyot)...........................	3,500	800
Lutuami in California.............................	500	300
Total..	133,000	15,850

DECREASE OF POPULATION.

There is one Indian in California to-day for every eight that lived in the same area before the white man came. To attain even this fractional proportion of one-eighth, half and mixed bloods, totaling nearly 30 per cent according to the census of 1910, must be included. It is true that a certain number of scattered individuals of much diluted blood, and individuals mainly of Indian blood but wholly Mexicanized in their mode of life, all of whom no longer habitually speak a native tongue, have probably succeeded in identifying themselves so completely with the Caucasian population as to have escaped the Indian census takers. But the total of such persons is not likely to exceed a few hundreds; and it seems only reasonable to omit them from any count of Indians.

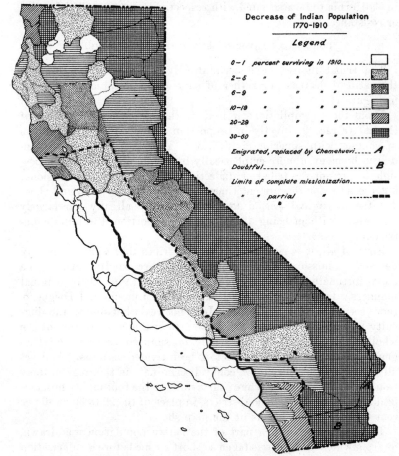

FIG. 72.—Decrease of native population from 1770 to 1910.

The causes of this decline of nearly 90 per cent within a period ranging, according to locality, from only 6 to 14 decades, are obscure. New diseases and alteration of diet, clothing, and dwellings have undoubtedly contributed largely. But civilized and semicivilized communities are often subject to similar influences, and thrive; whereas the native of low civilization, in many parts of the world, passes away. The ultimate explanation must therefore undoubtedly take into account, and perhaps in primary place, a set of cultural factors as well as the more obvious organic or physiological ones; and these cultural factors have never been determined, athough an untold quantity of conjecture and assertion has been formulated on the subject. But it may be of interest and service to set forth with some precision of detail those immediate conditions that appear in California to be associated with respectively greater tribal fatality or resistance.

CONDITIONS FAVORING SURVIVAL AND DECLINE.

The tribal figures have been already given in Table 11, and the ratio of decrease, or rather of survival, is graphically depicted in Figure 72.

From these compilations it is clear that, in general, decrease of the native race is directly in proportion to immediacy and fullness of contact with superior civilization. This fact would have been driven home even more emphatically by the map if it had been possible to present the tribal or dialectic areas in smaller subdivisions; but the data for the present time scarcely suffice for this, and those for the aboriginal period are unfortunately already too largely estimatory without being drawn fine and apportioned to minute districts.

First of all, it is established that the tribes that were completely devoted to mission life are gone. Many are wholly extinct; the most fortunate may amount to one-hundredth of their original numbers. In the extreme south, among the Luiseño and Diegueño, there seems to be an exception. It is not real; but due to the difficulty just mentioned: data are lacking to enable a separation of the wholly missionized from the partly missionized Luiseño and Diegueño. Both groups have therefore been treated as units. And yet all indications are that if we could discriminate in this region, there would be less than 5 per cent of survivors for the thoroughly missionized Luiseño and Diegueño districts, in place of the 20 to 30 or 40 per cent that the rough blocks of the map show.

The tracts from which part of the native population was drawn, or from which all of it was taken so short a time before secularization that a considerable proportion of the tribes was able to return to their old homes after 1834, tell the same story.

It must have caused many of the fathers a severe pang to realize, as they could not but do daily, that they were saving souls only at the inevitable cost of lives. And yet such was the overwhelming fact. The brute upshot of missionization, in spite of its kindly flavor and humanitarian root, was only one thing: death.

What the Franciscan commenced with his concentrations, the American finished by mere settlement, and extended to the hitherto unopened portions of the State. Where his cities sprang up, there was soon not an Indian within miles. In farming districts he lingered a little longer in scattered families. In the timbered hills, in the higher habitable Sierra, in the broken coast ranges, above all in the deserts and half deserts that skirt the eastern edge and make up a large part of the southern end of the State, the native maintained himself in some measure. The occasional homesteader, the cattle ranger, the lumberman, even the miner if he did not stay too long, were not present in force enough to blast him more than in partial measure. Outside of the mission district the preservation of the Indian population of California is in inverse ratio to the density of the white population. The tints of a map of one of these two factors need only to be reversed to serve as a substantially correct map of the other.

There are some exceptions: A number of hill tribes that have vanished completely in 60 years, or are on the very brink of extinction. Such are the Chimariko, New River Shasta, Konomihu, Okwanuchu, southern Yana, and Yahi in the north; and the Yokuts tribes of the Poso and Buena Vista foothill groups in the south; and, in only slightly less degree, all the Athabascan tribes between the Hupa and the Wailaki, the Shasta, the northern and central Yana, and the Vanyume. All these lived in remote places, where the white man never was abundant, and is still thinly sown; and yet they have perished. But they were small groups—all of them in numbers and many of them in territory as well. And they were all rude even in native culture; which is equivalent to saying that they were poor; in short, that the margin which they had established between themselves and the minimum limit of existence was narrower than that of other tribes. Thus, the maladjustment caused by even a light immigration of Americans was enough to push them over the precipice.

That this coincidence is no idle one is clear from the circumstance that neighboring tribes—in valleys or on larger streams, more populous, richer, and of more elaborated customs—have usually maintained themselves proportionally better in spite of heavier or at least equal contact with the whites. Compare the Yurok, Hupa, and Karok, the richest and most civilized tribes in the State, of whom from a quarter to a half survive, with the half dozen just-cited groups of Athabascan and Shastan mountaineers who inclose them on three sides, of none of whom even one person in twenty remains. Match, too, the wild Yana with the adjacent populous and comparatively refined Maidu and Wintun: at best a bare 5 per cent of maintenance in one case, 8 to 12 in the other. And so with the Yokuts Paleuyami, Chulamni, and Tuhohi, against their kinsmen the Yauelmani and Yaudanchi. Even as between the Yuki and the Pomo a similar relation prevails. The latter are more accessible lowlanders, they held rich farming lands, and were invaded by a much heavier stream of colonization; yet they have maintained themselves three or four times as successfully, relatively.

One further element is to be considered in this last class of cases. In the fifties and sixties the white settlers, however enterprising, were still sparse. Where a tribe numbered 2,000 or 3,000 closely concentrated people, it may sometimes have seemed venturesome to the whites to give way to passion and commence a warfare of extermination. Moreover, the natives furnished labor, services, perhaps even food, and soon acquired some means to make their trade worth while. Much, therefore, tended toward a preservation of amicable relations. A little group of hill men, however, was of small potential use; they were too scattered to be available for work, and too poor to buy much; they were likely to be so hungry as to kill cattle or horses on opportunity, and thereby to sow the seeds of a conflict; and however brave and desperate, they were not strong enough to be seriously feared.

RESERVATION INFLUENCE.

The first reservations established by Federal officers in California were little else than bull pens. They were founded on the principle, not of attempting to do something for the native, but of getting him out of the white man's way as cheaply and hurriedly as possible. The reason that the high death rate that must have prevailed among these makeshift assemblages was not reported on more emphatically is that the Indians kept running away even faster than they could die.

The few reservations that were made permanent have on the whole had a conserving influence on the population after they once settled into a semblance of reasonable order. They did little enough for the Indian directly; but they gave him a place which he could call his own, and where he could exist in security and in contact with his own kind. In this way the many scattered tracts in southern California that came under the jurisdiction of the Mission-Tule Agency have helped to preserve the numbers of Luiseño, Diegueño, and Cahuilla. The Hoopa reserve has done the same for the Hupa. Round Valley Reservation did not check a heavy decrease of the native Yuki, nor Tule River of the Yaudanchi; but, on the other hand, the number of introduced Wailaki, Wintun, and Maidu surviving on the former, and of Yauelmani on the latter, is almost certainly greater than if these people had been allowed to shift for themselves.

PROGRESSION OF THE DECLINE.

Doctor Merriam's estimate of the population at different dates in the nineteenth century tells a graphic story, even though the initial figures seem, for reasons already discussed, too high.

1800	260, 000	1860	35, 000
1834	210, 000	1870	30, 000
1849	100, 000	1880	20, 500
1852	85, 000	1890	18, 000
1856	50, 000	1900	15, 500

The decrease is saddening, however cautiously we may assume the absolute numbers. But excessive exaggerations need also be guarded against, such as the statement sometimes cited that 70,000 California Indians died of epidemic diseases in a few years following 1830.

INHABITED AND UNINHABITED AREAS.

The parts of native California which actually contained permanent settlements at one time or another formed a small fraction of the total area of the State. It is true that there were probably no regions which remained wholly unvisited, that most tracts were likely to be frequented seasonally for some food that they yielded, and that large areas came in this way to be wandered over and camped on. But there were no true nomadic tribes in California. Every group had some spot that it considered its home; here stood its most durable houses, and here the winters, or a considerable part of each year, were normally lived. It is these spots that were not distributed randomly over the whole extent of California, but clung to main water courses, valleys or their edges, and the more open canyons. The higher mountains, dense timber, rolling hills, the plains in the intervals between streams, and, of course, the vast preponderance of the deserts never held permanent settlements. In short, the Indian did not think of territory in terms of plane area as we do. Every representation of group lands as filling areas on the map is therefore misleading and must be considered a makeshift tolerable only as long as our precise knowledge of the facts remains inadequate for most regions.

CHAPTER 58.

PLACE NAMES.

TYPES OF PLACE NAMES.

It is well known to all who are sufficiently interested in the American Indian's point of view to make any inquiry into such matters, that the names which he gives to his settlements and to localities are normally descriptive, or at most based on some trivial but unusual happening. Romantic Indian names have been coined by romantic Americans through a species of prevalent self-deception. Just as we actually have Smithville or Warner or Leadville or Salmon Creek or Bald Mountain and leave Bridal Veil and Lover's Leap for occasional show places frequented by the idle and emotionally poor but hungry tourist, so the Indian will have his "clover valley" or "red rock" or "snow mountain" or "deer-watering place" or "bear fell down" and never dream of a "home of the mists" or "great Spirit's abode." His place names now and then are based on allusions to his mythology; but even in that case he is convinced that the event in question really happened, and that the formation of the ground or of a rock is evidence that it happened there.

All this applies to the California Indian as to the American Indian in general. There are, however, certain points in which native place names differ from our own. They are never based on the names of persons. They are also rarely if ever taken over from another language. The California Indian translates into his own tongue the place names of his neighbors or of the aliens whom his ancestors may long ago have gradually dispossessed; or he makes up a descriptive name of his own. Names of the type of our Washington, Philadelphia, Massachusetts, and Detroit are therefrore unrepresented among the Indians.

NORTH CENTRAL CALIFORNIA.

Some examples from tribes of the most diverse speech will illustrate.

The following are typical Yuki place names: Red rock, bent over, brush mouth, wide madroña, woodpecker sits on rock, for crossing water (a ford),

892

salmon rock, snail rock, strong rock, peak, wormwood hole, water mouth, wide rock, dust flat, large dust, ground water, alder creek, flint hole, willow stream, deer eat pepperwood mouth, bear water, large water, sand, white rock ridge, white flower barrier, live-oak peak, good earth, tangled pines, wolf hole peak, pine-nut flat, wide water hole, skunk hole, hissing water drink (a hot spring), tan-oak hole, mountain-live-oak crotch, tree sifting-basket, rock, alder mouth, fir peak, large brush ridge, buckeye peak, large rocks together, sore canyon, large canyon, brush stands, cedars stand, windy rock.

Pomo names of settlements and camp sites run along similar lines: Wind tree (i. e., wind-bent tree), pine hole, hollow trail, tobacco hole, obsidian creek, shady, madroña flat, bear throws out, hand bog, grind pepperwood-nuts, hollow mussel, under the rock, east corner, milk-snake builds, dam mouth, willow valley, water-lily valley, string valley, rock mountain, scorched sweat-house, red-ant house, owl mountain, between the ground, clover corner, crow water, hand hangs, large, cold water valley, ground-squirrel water, valley end, between the rocks, north valley, old water place, rock house, large sand, mellow ashes, red mountain, river mouth, earth sweathouse, peeled tree, west point, south coyote gulch, bark fallen across, clover place, coyote house, west mountain, burned sweat house, pestle rock, west canyon, white-willow canyon, angelica mountain.

Some of these names evidently refer to episodes and to mythical incidents, and a few must be taken metaphorically, but the majority are directly descriptive of natural or conspicuous features or of the abundance of an animal or plant.

NORTHWESTERN CALIFORNIA.

A few Karok and Yurok town names: In the basket, upper dam, lower dam, make a dam, lake, ghosts, pepperwoods, great large, trail descends, clay, watch for ducks, they dance.

Athabascan place names frequently end in suffixes meaning " place " or " in "; but the body of the word is similar in character to those in other languages. Thus the towns shown on the Chilula map (Fig. 13), excepting the first, the eleventh, and the fifteenth, are named in order: Waterfall place, in the small glade, large timber point, near the large timber, down-hill ridge runs on, lying bones place, facing the water place, door upstream place, in the flat, flying dust place, among the willows place, projecting willows place, Yurok house place, in the slide, among the wild-syringa place.

SOUTH CENTRAL CALIFORNIA.

Yokuts place names seem unusually simple, because this language is averse to compounded words, but their meanings are nevertheless of the usual character. For instance, for villages: Cane, ground-squirrels' holes, salt grass, arrow, drink, markings, gate, deer's hole, clover, Jimson weed, bone, hole, sowing, wind, brush-shades. Most of these end in the locative -u in the original, but as this is only a case ending, it has not been translated. Yokuts place names are: Water's fall, dog's hole, rattlesnake's holes, eye, hot-spring, supernatural. Being tribally organized, the Yokuts also possess a few towns named in accord with their political divisions, though it is possible that these villages once bore specific local names. Thus: Tulamniu, Tahayu, Kochoyu, Dalinau, Suksanau, Kiawitnau: Tulamni place, Tuhohi place, Kechayi place, Dalinchi place, Chukchansi place, Koyeti place. It is not certain whether the spot was named after the tribe or the tribe after the village. The lack

of exact agreement between the corresponding place and group names may
be due to prevailing employment of the latter in the mouths of aliens of
somewhat divergent dialect.

SOUTHERN CALIFORNIA.

Chumash names are also generally uncompounded: Bowstring, beach, moon,
my eye, my ear, yucca, fish. These are all village names.

A few southern California Shoshonean place names can be added: Poison-
oak, willow, doves drink, small woods, small roses, water, warm water, at the
salt, river, pine water, alkali water, deer moon, cottonwood, pines, ears, roadrunner's mortar.

With the Mohave elaborately compounded names are once more encountered.
They are often of an unwieldly length. They are also more inclined to be
colored by fancy than among the other Californians; that is, a fair proportion
of the names are not directly descriptive of a visible feature, or of a practice customary there. For instance: Mortar mountain, three mountains, blue
mountain, sharp mountain, lizard mountain, willow water, faecal sand, owls
regarding each other, duck water, pine land rattlesnake tooth, hawk nose, see
deer, yellow waterhole, fear slough, covered with sand, no water, water tears
through, thick *akyasa* plants, lie in the middle, beaver house, tule water, football surmounts, dove's breast, whispering place, mosquito cannot, retches, cut
earth, fat earth, gambling-ring place, four mortars, fight with club, yellow ocher
washed open.

Diegueño names are sometimes simple, sometimes of Mohave type: hollow
over, far above, my water, large valley, red earth, white earth, middle of the
sky, lie on rock, flows in opposite, wrap around neck, hot water, rain above,
large mountain, Chaup's house mountain, large, foam, pair of live oaks stands.

MEANINGLESS NAMES.

In all the native languages there are some place names that can
not be translated by the Indians. The number of these, however,
reduces rapidly in proportion to the degree to which the language
has been studied and resolved into its elements. There is probably
everywhere a residuum of unanalyzable names, which long usage has
crystallized into a meaningless form. But there is also every indication that this residuum is smaller than among ourselves, and that
in general the California Indian is more conscious, at least potentially, of the denotation of his place names than we are. Where we
are content with an age-old term without inquiring into what it may
signify, or when called upon for a new name, apply the name of a
settler or repeat a geographical designation familiar from another
part of the world, the Indian draws upon his imaginative faculties
and makes a word. Only, this imagination is observant, practical,
and directly descriptive, and not intended to be exercised poetically.

TABLE 12.—SOURCE OF SOME CALIFORNIA PLACE NAMES OF INDIAN ORIGIN.

Acalanes..... Costanoan (?) village (?).
Aguanga..... I uiseño place name.
Ahwahnee.... Miwok village in Yosemite valley.
Algootoon.... Perhaps Luiseño "raven."
Anacapa..... Chumash.
Anapamu.... Chumash.
Ausaymas.... Costanoan village.
Azusa......... Gabrielino place name; perhaps "skunk place."
Bally .... Wintun "peak."
Bohemotash.. Wintun "large —."
Bolbones..... Costanoan village.
Bully Choop.. Wintun "peak —."
Buriburi...... Costanoan village.
Cahto........ Pomo "lake" or "mush water."
Cahuenga.... Gabrielino place name.
Cahuilla...... Given as "master," but doubtful if Indian.
Calleguas..... Chumash "my head."
Calpella...... Pomo "mussel carrier."
Camulos...... Chumash "my mulus," a fruit.
Capay........ Wintun "stream."
Carquinez.... Wintun village.
Caslamayomi. Pomo or Coast Miwok "— place."
Castac........ Chumash "my eye."
Caymus...... Wappo village.
Chagoopa..... Probably Mono.
Chanchelulla. Probably Wintun.
Chemehuevi.. Probably the Mohave name of a Shoshonean tribe.
Choenimne... Yokuts tribe.
Cholame..... Salinan village.
Chowchilla... Yokuts tribe.
Cleone....... Pomo village.
Collayomi.... Coast Miwok "— place."
Coloma....... Maidu village.
Colusa....... Wintun village.
Concow....... Maidu "valley place."
Cosmit....... Diegueño place name.
Coso.......... Probably Shoshonean.
Cosumnes..... Miwok village.
Cotati........ Coast Miwok village.
Cucamonga... Gabrielino village.
Cuyama...... Chumash place name.
Cuyamaca.... Diegueño "rain above."

Guajome..... Luiseño place name.
Gualala....... Pomo "stream mouth."
Guatay....... Diegueño "large."
Guenoc....... Indian, but unidentified.
Guesisosi..... Probably Wintun.
Guilicos..... Coast Miwok name of a Wappo village.
Guyapipe..... Diegueño "rock lie on."
Hanaupah.... Shoshonean.
Hetch Hetchy Miwok name of a plant.
Hettenchow.. Wintun "camass valley."
Homoa....... Serrano place name.
Honcut...... Maidu village.
Hoopa....... Yurok name of Athabascan valley.
Horse Linto... Athabascan village.
Huasna...... Probably Chumash village.
Hueneme.... Chumash place name.
Huichica...... Coast Miwok village.
Hyampom... Wintun "— place."
Iaqua........ Athabascan, Yurok, Wiyot, etc., salutation.
Iñaja......... Diegueño "my water."
Inyo......... Possibly Shoshonean.
Ivanpah...... Probably Southern Paiute.
Jalama....... Chumash village.
Jamacha..... Diegueño name of a wild squash-like plant.
Jamul........ Diegueño "foam."
Jolon......... Probably Salinan.
Juristac...... Costanoan "— at."
Jurupa....... Serrano place name.
Kaweah..... Yokuts tribe.
Kaiaiauwa.... Possibly Miwok.
Kekawaka... Probably Indian, but unidentified.
Kenoktai..... Pomo "woman mountain."
Kenshaw.... Probably Wintun.
Kibesillah.... Pomo "rock flat."
Kimshew.... Maidu "— stream."
Klamath..... Probably either Lutuami "people" or Chinook name of the group.
Koip......... Probably Mono "mountain sheep."
Kuna........ Perhaps Mono "firewood."

TABLE 12.—SOURCE OF SOME CALIFORNIA PLACE NAMES OF INDIAN ORIGIN—Con.

Lasseck......	Name of an Athabascan chief.	Omjumi......	Perhaps Maidu "rock —."
Locoallomi...	Coast Miwok name of a Wappo village.	Omo..........	Miwok village.
		Omochumnes.	Miwok "people of Umucha."
Loconoma....	Wappo "goose-town."	Ono.........	Possibly Wintun "head."
Lompoc......	Chumash village.	Orestimba ...	Perhaps Costanoan "bear —."
Lospe........	Possibly Chumash.		
Malibu......	Chumash village.	Orick........	Yurok village.
Mallacomes...	Wappo village.	Osagon........	Yurok place name.
Marin........	Probably Spanish name of a Coast Miwok Indian headman.	Otay........	Diegueño "brushy."
		Pacoima......	Perhaps a Gabrielino place name.
Matajuai......	Diegueño "white earth."	Pala..........	Luiseño "water."
Matilija......	Chumash place name.	Pamo........	Probably a Diegueño place name.
Mattole......	Probably Wiyot or Athabascan.		
		Panamint.....	Name of a Shoshonean division.
Mettah......	Yurok village.		
Modoc.......	Lutuami "south."	Paskenta.....	Wintun "under the bank."
Mohave......	Mohave name of themselves.		
		Pauba........	Perhaps a Luiseño place name.
Mokelumne...	Miwok "people of Mokel," a village.		
		Pauja.........	Diegueño place name.
Monache.....	Yokuts name of a Shoshonean division.	Pauma.......	Luiseño village.
		Pecwan......	Yurok village.
Mono........	Same as Monache.	Petaluma.....	Coast Miwok "flat back."
Moorek......	Yurok village.		
Moristul......	Wappo "north valley."	Piru..........	Shoshonean name of a Chumash village: a plant.
Morongo......	Serrano local group.		
Muah........	Probably Mono.		
Mugu........	Chumash "beach."		
Musalacon....	Pomo, perhaps a chief's name.	Pismo........	Perhaps a Chumash place name.
Muscupiabe...	Serrano place name.	Piute, Pahute.	A Shoshonean division.
Najalayegua..	Chumash village.	Pohono.......	Probably Miwok.
Napa.........	Probably Pomo "harpoon point."	Pomo........	Pomo "people."
		Poonkiny....	Yuki "wormwood."
Natoma......	Maidu "north place" or "upstream people."	Poway.......	Diegueño or Luiseño.
		Requa.......	Probably a Yurok village.
Nimshew.....	Maidu "large stream."	Saboba.......	Luiseño place name.
Nipomo.......	Chumash village.	Sanel.........	Pomo village: "dance house."
Nojogui......	Probably a Chumash village.		
		Saticoy.......	Chumash village.
Nomcult......	Wintun "west people."	Sequan.......	Diegueño name of a bush.
Nopah........	Perhaps Shoshonean.	Sequit........	Chumash or Gabrielino.
Noyo.........	Pomo village.	Sespe........	Chumash village; perhaps "fish."
Ojai..........	Chumash "moon."		
Olanche......	Perhaps a form of Yaudanchi, a Yokuts tribe.	Shasta.......	Uncertain; most likely name of a Shasta headman.
Olema.......	Coast Miwok "coyote valley."		
		Simi..........	Chumash place name.
Oleta........	Perhaps Miwok.	Siskiyou.....	Uncertain; perhaps Oregon Indian.
Olompali....	Coast Miwok "south —."		

TABLE 12.—SOURCE OF SOME CALIFORNIA PLACE NAMES OF INDIAN ORIGIN—Con.

Sisquoc....... Probably a Chumash place name.
Skukum...... Chinook jargon "strong."
Somis........ Chumash village.
Sonoma...... Probably a Wappo suffix, meaning "village of."
Soquel........ Probably a Costanoan village.
Sotoyome.... Pomo "place of Soto," a chief.
Suey......... Perhaps a Chumash place name.
Suisun........ Wintun village or tribe.
Surper....... Yurok village.
Suscol........ Wintun village.
Taboose...... Perhaps a Mono Shoshonean word.
Tache........ Yokuts tribe.
Tahoe........ Washo "lake."
Tahquitz.... Luiseño divinity.
Taijiguas..... Chumash village.
Tajauta....... Probably G a b r i e l i n o place name.
Tamalpais.... Coast Miwok "bay mountain."
Tapu......... Chumash "yucca."
Tatu........ Pomo name for the Huchnom.
Tecuya....... Yokuts name of the Chumash.
Tehachapi... Yokuts, perhaps also Shoshonean, place name.
Tehama...... Wintun village.
Tehipite..... Perhaps a Mono Shoshonean word.
Tejunga..... Gabrielino place name.
Temecula..... Luiseño village; possibly "sun —."
Tenaya....... Miwok chief.
Tepusquet.... Perhaps a Chumash place name.

Tequepis.... Chumash village.
Tinaquaic.... Perhaps a Chumash place name.
Tinemaha..... Perhaps Shoshonean.
Tishtangatang Hupa village.
Tissaack...... Miwok place name of mythological origin.
Tocaloma..... Probably a Coast Miwok place name.
Tolenas....... Wintun village.
Tomales...... Coast Miwok "bay."
Toowa....... Probably a Mono word.
Topanga...... Gabrielino place name.
Topa Topa... Chumash place name.
Truckee...... Name of a Northern Paiute chief.
Tulucay..... Wintun village, "red."
Tuolumne.... Probably a Yokuts tribe.
Ukiah....... Pomo "south valley."
Ulatus........ Wintun village or division.
Ulistac...... Costanoan "at ulis."
Un Bully..... Wintun "— peak."
Usal.......... Pomo "south —."
Wahtoke..... Yokuts "pine nut."
Weeyot...... Yurok name of the Wiyot.
Weitchpec.... Yurok village: "at the forks."
Winum Bully. Wintun "— peak."
Yallo Bally... Wintun "snow peak."
Ydalpom..... Wintun "north — place."
Yokohl...... Yokuts tribe.
Yolo.......... Wintun village.
Yosemite..... Miwok: usually said to mean "grizzly bear;" perhaps "killers."
Yreka........ Probably Shasta name for Mount Shasta.
Yuba......... Maidu village.
Yucaipa..... Serrano place name.
Yuma........ Probably Indian, but unidentified.

CHAPTER 59.

CULTURE PROVINCES.

AREAS OF DISTINCTIVE CIVILIZATION IN CALIFORNIA.

Constant outright and implied reference has been made through this book to the three or four areas of culture, or ethnic provinces. distinguishable in native California. Roughly, the Tehachapi Range and the vicinity of Point Concepcion mark off the southern from the central type of civilization, while the northwestern extends south to a line running from Mount Shasta to Cape Mendocino or a little beyond. East of the crest of the Sierra Nevada the culture of central California changes into that of Nevada, or more properly of the Great Basin. In the south, the Colorado River, with some of the adjoining desert, must be set apart from the mountain and coast tracts.

Yet any map creates an erroneous impression of internal uniformity and coherence. Thus, all in all, the Yokuts are probably more similar to the Wintun in the totality of their life than to the Gabrielino. But innumerable cultural elements have reached the Yokuts from the south, and they themselves have very likely developed local peculiarities of which some have filtered across the mountains to the Gabrielino. Consequently any presentation which tended to create the impression that the Yokuts and Wintun belonged to a block of nations in which certain traits were standard and exclusive would mislead.

Just so in the northwest. The moment the Yurok and Hupa are left behind, central Californian traits begin to appear even among their most immediate neighbors. These increase in number and intensity among the peoples to the south and east. After a time we find ourselves among tribes such as the Coast Yuki, who undoubtedly appertain to the central province. Yet these still make string or bury the dead or do various other things in the most distinctive northwestern manner.

CENTERS OF CIVILIZATION.

On the other hand, certain centers or hearths of the several types of culture become apparent rather readily and the increase of information, instead of distracting and confusing the impressions first formed, strengthens them: each focus becomes narrower and more distinct.

NORTHWESTERN.

Thus there seems no possible ground to doubt that the center of gravity and principal point of influence of the northwestern culture was the limited area occupied by the Yurok, Karok, and Hupa. Its precise point of gathering has been discussed in the first chapter of this book.

CENTRAL.

The heart of the central province is not quite so definite, but unquestionably lay between the Pomo, the more southerly Wintun or Patwin, and the Valley Maidu; with the Wintun, as the middle one of the three, the most likely leaders.

SOUTHERN.

In the south, one center is recognizable on or near the coast. The most developed peoples about this were the Chumash, Gabrielino, and Luiseño. As regards religion and institutions, we happen to know by far the most about the Luiseño; but there is direct evidence that a considerable part of Luiseño customs was imported from the Gabrielino, and precedence must therefore be given to this people. As to the choice between them and the Chumash, the Gabrielino must again be favored. Our knowledge of Chumash practices is scant, but there is so complete an absence of indications of their having seriously influenced the institutions of their neighbors that their civilization, at least on this side, can hardly have had the potency of that of the Gabrielino. A complication is indeed caused by material culture, which so far as it can be reconstructed from early descriptions, and particularly through the evidence of archaeology, was most developed among the Chumash and among a special branch of the Gabrielino who through their island habitat were in closest communication with the Chumash. Again, however, Chumash example did not reach far; and it is therefore likely that it is a localized development of technology which confronts us among the Chumash, as against a much more penetrating and influential growth of social and religious institutions among the Gabrielino.

COLORADO RIVER.

The hearth of the type of culture which radiated from the Colorado River must beyond doubt be sought either among the Mohave or the Yuma. As between the two, the Mohave are probably entitled to precedence, both because they were the more populous tribe, and because it appears to be solely their influence which has reached to northern groups like the Chemehuevi, whereas southern tribes like the Diegueño give unmistakable evidence of having been affected by the Mohave as well as by the nearer Yuma.

Geographical position, on the other hand, would point to the Yuma, who are not only more centrally situated than the Mohave with reference to tribes of the same lineage, but have their seats at the mouth of the chief affluent of the Colorado, the Gila, up and down which there must have gone on considerable communication with the Pima, the non-Yuman tribe of the Southwest which on the whole seems to be culturally most nearly related to the Yumans of the Colorado Valley. The Yuma had the Cocopa and other groups below them toward the mouth of the river; but above the Mohave as well as to their west there lived only Shoshoneans. Further, the Diegueño and the various Yuman groups of the northern half of Baja California are much more nearly in contact with the Yuma. General probability would therefore lead to an expectation of the focus of the Yuman culture of the Colorado being below the Mohave, among or near the Yuma. It seems not unlikely that if we could trace the history of this area sufficiently far back such would prove to have been the case, but that in recent centuries the Mohave, owing to an increase in numbers or for some other reason, have taken the lead in cultural productivity.

These four centers are indicated by crosses on the map in Figure 74.

AN IRREGULARITY.

Several peculiar traits, some of them positive and some of them negative, are found in a region which forms a sort of tongue separating the San Joaquin Valley from southern California. This region lacks pottery, which occurs on both sides of it; practices burial instead of cremation; is without exogamic institutions, which are also known both to the north and south; and is the area in which the so-called "bottle-neck" basket is dominant. The distribution of these several cultural elements is not identical, but in general they

characterize the peoples from the southern Yokuts and Tübatulabal
to the Chumash. A radiation from the latter people can scarcely
be thought of because specifically Chumash features do not occur
among the peoples inhabiting the more northerly part of the tongue.
A possible Shoshonean influence from the Great Basin must be dis-
allowed on parallel grounds. In fact, the traits in question are so
few and diverse that it is doubtful whether they have any historical
connection. If they are intrinsically associated it is perhaps chiefly
through the fact that this middle and upland region failed to be
reached in certain respects by both central and southern influences.

NATURE OF THE CENTERS.

It would, of course, be a grave mistake to assume that the whole
of each type of culture had emanated from the group or small array
of groups situated at its focus. Every tribe must be viewed as contributing to the civilization or civilizations of which it partakes. It
is only that the most intensive development or greatest specialization
of culture has occurred at the hearth. This renders it probable that
more influences have flowed out from the center to the peripheries
than in the opposite direction. But the movement must necessarily
always have been reciprocal in considerable degree. What has probably happened in many cases is that the tribe which carried a certain
set of practices and institutions farthest came thereby to attain a
status in which it reacted more powerfully upon its neighbors in
other respects, so that the civilizational streams which gathered into
it were made over and caused to stream out again. In this sense
the central or focal groups may have been influential in coloring to
some degree the culture of their entire areas, while contributing in
each case probably only a very small proportion of the substance
thereof.

It will be seen that the cultural centers as here described are those
indicated on the religious map (Pl. 74). In part this coincidence may
be due to a rather heavy weighting of religious factors in the estimation of culture wholes—a procedure that seems necessary, since a
definitely organized set of cults is like the flower to the plant—unquestionably one of the highest products of civilization. But the
constitution of society, the use of wealth and attitude toward it, the
material arts and industries, the type of mythology, music, and what
may be called literature, correspond almost without exception, in
the degrees of their complexity or specialization, to the elaborateness of religion. This cult map, then, although not an accurate geographical representation of the distribution of native civilizations
in California, probably indicates their history about as well as would
any averaged outline, and serves to balance or even correct the neces-

sarily arbitrary delimitations which a culture province map like Figure 74 attempts.

RELATION TO POPULATION AND PHYSIOGRAPHY.

It need hardly be added that a considerable concentration of population would be expectable at the focus of each province, together with a perceptible thinning out of numbers toward the margins. This, so far as can be judged, was the case. It is, however, of interest that diverse topographies are represented by the centers. In the northwest, the distinctive physiographic feature of the focal area is streams of sufficient size to be navigable and rich in salmon; in the central province it is the heart of a great valley; in the south a group of islands and a mainland shore washed by still ocean reaches; and at the southeast the vast Colorado with its annually overflowed bottom lands in the midst of a great desert. No single type of physical environment can therefore be said to have been permanently stimulative to concentration of numbers and the furtherance of civilization in California; except that there is a clear tendency for cultural focus to be situated on important drainage.

The annual run-off of the Klamath at Keno, before it has received notable affluents, is over $1\frac{1}{2}$ million acre-feet, which may be estimated to be perhaps doubled in its lower course. The Colorado at Yuma carries 16 millions; the Sacramento at Red Bluff over 10 millions, to which the Feather, Yuba, and American add nearly 13 millions. The total flow through Carquinez Straits, after considerable diversion for irrigation, is about 26 million acre-feet, derived probably more than three-fourths from the Sacramento and less than one-fourth from the San Joaquin half of the interior valley. It is evident that the Yurok, southern Wintun, and Yuma-Mohave centers of culture are closely correlated with the points of maximal flow of the three greatest drainage systems of California; although as between these three centers the degree of cultural advancement does not correlate with the relative amount of drainage. That is, on comparison of one area with another, inference that the one situated on the larger stream will be the more advanced in type of civilization does not hold for this part of the continent; but within one drainage or series of parallel and related drainages the advancement is greatest at the point of largest flow.

That the cultural importance of an ocean frontage must not be overestimated for California is clear from the relation of the Coast Yurok to the River Yurok, of the Wiyot to the Hupa, of the Pomo of the coast to those of Russian River and Clear Lake, of the Costanoans and Esselen to Yokuts, where, as discussed in previous chapters, the interior people seem in each case to have been the more prosperous.

NORTHWESTERN CALIFORNIA AND THE NORTH PACIFIC COAST CULTURE.

All of the cultures of California are without question at least partly related in origin to more widely spread civilizations outside the State.

The northwestern culture is obviously part of that generally known as the culture of the North Pacific coast. The center of this larger civilization is clearly in Brit-ish Columbia, but this center is so remote that any specific comparison of the Yurok and Hupa with the Kwakiutl or Haida would be unprofitable. In Washington and Oregon, however, three subtypes of this culture are recognizable, after exclusion of three inland cultures: that of the Plateau east of the Cascades; the curiously simple culture of the Kalapuya in the Willamette Valley; and of the Lutuamian Klamath and Modoc in the Klamath Lake basin. The three coastal provinces, which chiefly come into question in a comparison with north California, are, in order from the north, and as sketched in Figure 73:

FIG. 73.—Subculture areas on the Pacific coast of the United States.

(1) *Puget Sound*, with all or part of the Olympic Peninsula, and probably the southeastern portion of Vancouver Island and the opposite coast of British Columbia. The groups in this area are clearly dependent for much of their culture on the Kwakiutl and other tribes to the north. Coast Salish groups are the principal ones in this province.

(2) *The Lower Columbia*, up to The Dalles, with the coast from about Shoalwater Bay on the north to lower Umpqua River on the south. The Chinook were nearly central and perhaps dominant. Other members were the Yakonan Alsea and Siuslaw, the most southerly of the coast Salish, and a few Athabascans.

(3) *Southwestern Oregon*, probably from the Umpqua and the Calapooya Mountains and inland to the Cascade Range. The principal stream is Rogue River, but the Coquille and upper Umpqua seem to have formed part. The abutment is on four ethnic subprovinces: the Lower Columbian just outlined, the Kalapuyan of the Willamette, the Lutuamian of the Klamath Lake drainage, and the northwest Californian of the Klamath River. The majority of the inhabitants were Athabascans; the other groups were the Kus and Takelma and a branch of the Shasta. The Takelma, except for being wholly off the coast, may be taken as typical.

Table 13 summarizes the principal comparable ethnic traits of these three regions and of northwestern California. It appears at once that northwestern California and southwestern Oregon are very closely related, so much so, in fact, as to constitute but a single area. They agree about three times out of four in the cases in which either of them differs from the Lower Columbia. The latter in turn seems rather more closely connected with Puget Sound than with southwestern Oregon, whether chiefly as a marginal dependent or, as seems more likely, as a separate center of some distinctness, can scarcely yet be decided, and need not be in the present connection. The important fact is that the general culture of the coast is decisively altered somewhere in the region of the Umpqua Mountains, and that thence south, as far as it prevails at all, that is, to Cape Mendocino, it is substantially uniform. In other words, we need not recognize three provinces of the coast culture in Oregon and Washington and a fourth in California: there were only three south of the forty-ninth parallel. The first lay in Washington with some extension into British Columbia; the second was mainly Oregonian with some overlap into Washington; the third centered in northern California but ran well into Oregon.

TABLE 13.—COAST CULTURES OF NORTHERN CALIFORNIA, OREGON, AND WASHINGTON.

	Northwestern California.	Southwestern Oregon.	Lower Columbia.	Puget Sound.
BODY AND DRESS.				
Head deformation	None.	None.	Universal; sign of free birth.	General.
Tattooing:				
Women	Chin almost solidly covered.	Three stripes on chin.	Little; none on face.	Little; none on face.
Men	Measuring lines on arm.	Measuring lines on arm.		
Women's hair	2 clubs in front.	2 clubs[1]	Parted, but flowing.	
Nose ornament	Dentalium[2]	Dentalium.	Dentalium.	Probably none.
Woman's hat	Brimless cap.	Brimless cap[3]	Brim, peak, and knob.	Same; or flattened cone.
Man's hat	None[4]	Fur cap.	}	
Man's deerskin shirt	None[4]	Worn.	None.	None.
Man's leggings	In snow only[4]	Reported.	Only inland.	
Man's robe	Of deer fur.	Of deer fur.	Twined fur strips or mountain goat wool.	Woven cedar bark or dog hair.
Woman's petticoat	Fringed deerskin; shaman's of fiber.	Fiber.	Fiber.	Fiber.
Woman's deerskin gown	None[4]	Mentioned as if customary[5].	Only inland.	
HOUSES.				
Material	Redwood where available.	Sugar pine, cedar; poor people: bark.	Cedar; inland: bark.	Cedar.
Position of planks	Vertical.	Vertical.	Vertical.	Horizontal.
Breadth (feet)	20.	12.	Up to 30 or 40.	Up to 60.

[1] Takelma: men shamans.
[2] Karok, Tolowa; Yurok and Hupa bore the nose of the dead.
[3] Takelma imported caps from California.
[4] The Shasta agree with the Oregonians.
[5] The Takelma speak of a gown with fringes of *Xerophyllum*: perhaps a hybrid of gown and Yurok petticoat, or a confused description of the latter.

TABLE 13.—COAST CULTURES OF NORTHERN CALIFORNIA, OREGON, AND WASHINGTON—Continued.

	Northwestern California.	Southwestern Oregon.	Lower Columbia.	Puget Sound.
HOUSES—continued.				
Length (feet)	23	15–20	Up to 100	Up to 500.
Subdivisions	None[6]	None	Present	Present.
Mat beds	On floor	On floor; girls on platform	On raised platform	On raised platform.
Excavation	Center of house only, 2–5 feet	Whole area, 1–5 feet	Whole area, 3–5 feet	Whole area, 3–5 feet.
Entrance	Round	Rectangular	Round or oval	Round or oval.
Door	Sliding	Sliding	Hung	
Ridges	Two	One	One	None; shed roof.
Carving or painting	None	None	Found	Found.
Summer house	No	Brush hut	Rush lodge	
Inmates	7–8	10+?	Several families	Several families.
SWEAT HOUSE.				
Permanent, sunk	Oblong, of planks, no earth covering	Rectangular, of planks, earth covered	Referred to in myths	Doubtful.
Movable[7]	None	For women only	None on coast; inland, doubtful	Doubtful.
Occupance	6–7 men sleep in	6 men sleep in		
Heat	Fire	Steam from hot stones	Doubtful	
CANOE.				
Material	Redwood		Cedar	Cedar.
Length (feet)	18		Up to 40 or 50	40–50.
Shape	Blunt prow	"Like butcher's tray"	Sharp prow; blunt inland	Sharp prow.

Painted or carved	No	Yes	Yes
Coasting voyages	No	Yes	Yes
BASKETRY.			
Twining:			
Warp	Hazel	Hazel or willow	
Weft	Split conifer roots	Split roots	Split roots
White patterns	Xerophyllum tenax	probably Xerophyllum	Xerophyllum tenax
Black patterns	Maidenhair fern	mud dyed	
Red patterns	Alder dyed	Alder dyed	
Decorating technique	Overlaid (faced) weft	Probably overlaid weft	Wrapped twining; false embroidery
Checker and twill work	None	Not mentioned	Made
Coiling	None	None	Inland; North of Columbia: imbricated
Wallets and bags	None	Not mentioned	Made
Conical burden basket	Yes	Yes	Not mentioned
Mortar hopper	Yes	Yes	
Cradle	Twined	Twined	Wooden
FOOD.			
Salmon	Staple	Important	Staple
Acorns	Staple	Staple among Takelma	No
Camass and bulbs	Some bulbs	Some bulbs	Important
Wasp larvæ	Eaten	Eaten	
Tobacco	Cultivated	Cultivated	Little used

[6] Except a little anteroom for the storage of wood.

[7] The Plains type: low and small, of mats thrown over willows.

TABLE 13.—COAST CULTURES OF NORTHERN CALIFORNIA, OREGON, AND WASHINGTON—Continued.

	Northern California.	Southwestern Oregon.	Lower Columbia.	Puget Sound.
UTENSILS.				
Salmon harpoon	Two-pronged	Apparently two-pronged		
Seed beater	Of basketry	A stick		
Slab mortar	Used	Used		
Mush paddle	Used	Used		
Spoons	Elk antler; geometric carving	Elk antler	Mountain sheep or goat; geometric carving	Mountain sheep or goat; animal carving
Wooden troughs or bowls	Rude, unornamented		Well made, ornamented	
Joined boxes	None		Probably only imported	Made.
Drum	None	None (among Takelma)		
SOCIETY.				
Cause of social rank	Possession of wealth	Possession of wealth	Possession of wealth	Birth plus wealth.
Foundation of slavery	Debt	Debt	War	War.
Slave sacrifice	No	No	Occasional	Occasional.
Village exogamy	No	No	No	
Clans	No	No trace	No trace	
Descent	Paternal	Paternal	Paternal	Paternal.
Potlatch	No	No record	Unimportant	Important.
Measurement of dentalia	By fives or number to arm length.	By tens	By number to fathom	
Burial	In ground, recumbent	In ground, sitting	In canoes; inland, in houses.	In canoes or boxes, often elevated.

WAR.			
Armor	Of rods or elk hide	"Elk hide over rods," hide helmets.	Of rods or elk hide
Shield	None.	Not reported.	Few: probably inland only.
War dance	Of incitement or settlement, not scalp dance.	Of incitement, apparently.	
RELIGION.			
Masks or societies	None.	None.	None. **Some.**
Formulas	Long, narrative or dramatic.	Brief, type of prayers.	
Girls' adolescence ceremony	Yes [8]	Yes [9]	Yes. **Yes.**
Ritual number	5, 10.	5.	5. **5.**
Cause of disease	Pain object in body.	Pain object in body.	Pain object or theft of soul.
Source of shaman's power	Pain objects received from spirits.	Spirits.	Spirits. **Spirits.**
Sex of shamans	Chiefly women.	Men or women.	Chiefly men.
Non-shamans own spirits	Rarely.	Sometimes.	Generally.

[8] Weakest among the Yurok.

[9] The Takelma ceremony is very similar to that of Karok and Shasta. The girl may not look about, wears a visor of bluejay feathers, sleeps with her head in a mortar hopper. For five days men and women dance in a circle.

NORTHWESTERN CALIFORNIA AND OREGON.

The cultural predominance of the California over the Oregon tract within this last area can scarcely be proved outright, because the life of the tribes of southwestern Oregon broke and decayed very quickly on contact with the Americans and has been but sadly portrayed. Yet this very yielding perhaps indicates a looseness of civilizational fiber. There may have been highly developed rituals held in southwestern Oregon comparable to the Yurok Deerskin dance, which have not only perished but been forgotten; but it is far more likely that the reason the ceremonies of this region vanished without a trace is that they never amounted to much nor had a deep hold on native life. The Gabrielino have been longer subject to Caucasian demoralization and are as substantially extinct as any Oregon group; but there is no doubt as to their religious and general cultural preeminence over their neighbors. The southern Wintun have been cuffed about for a century and are nearly gone, but it is reasonably clear that the Kuksu cult and culture centered among them. If the Rogue River tribes had cultivated a religion surpassing or even rivaling that of the groups on the Klamath, it is scarcely conceivable that its very memory should have dissolved in two generations.

Where direct evidence is available, it uniformly points the same way. The Yurok house is larger as well as more elaborate than that of the Takelma; the sweat house more specialized; the shamanism appreciably more peculiar; the formulas and myths show a much more distinct characterization. The Takelma give the impression of being not only on a level similar to that of the Shasta, but specifically like them in many features; and the Shasta have been seen to be culturally subsidiary to the Yurok and Karok. What holds for the Takelma there is no reason to doubt held for the Athabascans who nearly surrounded them. The lower Klamath thus is the civilizational focus of the drainage of the Rogue and probably of most of the Umpqua.

CAUSE OF THE PREDOMINANCE OF NORTHWESTERN CALIFORNIA.

This predominance could be laid theoretically to two causes: Exposure to external ethnic influences, or physiographic environment. Extraneous cultural influence can be dismissed in this case. The center of the coast civilization as a whole lay north; the Oregonians were the nearer to it. Central California has given too little to the Klamath region to be of moment—or at least gave only underlying elements, not those specializations that mark the cultural preeminence which is being considered. The latter quality it did not possess, as against northwestern California. Natural environment, therefore, must be the cause; and sufficient explanation is found in the fact that the Klamath is the largest stream entering the Pacific between the Sacramento-San Joaquin on the south and the Columbia on the north—the third largest, in fact, that debouches from this face of the United States. The large stream held the largest number of inhabitants; and, particularly on its lower reaches, allowed them to accumulate densely. This concentration provided the opportunity, or was the cause, however we may wish to put it, of a more active prosecution of social life.

CAUSE OF SOUTHWARD ABRIDGMENT.

It may seem strange that the peak or focus of this culture should be eccentric, that Yurok influence, to call it such, should have extended several times as far to the north as to the south, particularly that it should penetrate to remote parallel streams and not to the headwaters of its own drainage system. Such an objection may seem theoretically valid, but there is precedent to the contrary. The culmination of the North Pacific coast culture as a whole is probably found among the Haida, near the northern end of its long belt. In the Southwest the Pueblos of the Rio Grande have for centuries been culturally predominant, and yet they lie on the eastern edge of the province.

There is accordingly no reason for hesitating to accept as a fact the much more rapid southward than northward fading out of the northwestern culture.

There does not seem to be a satisfactory physiographic explanation for this unequal distribution. That the Trinity and the Eel soon become small streams in a rugged country as their course is followed should not have been sufficient to prevent unchecked spread up them of northwestern influences, since the northwestern culture is well established in a similar environment on the upper Rogue and Umpqua. It would seem, accordingly, that the cause has been a social one. Such a cause can only be sought in the presence of another civilization, in this case that of central California, as represented by the Kuksu dancing nations, and particularly the Pomo. The Pomo subtype of the central culture may therefore be considered as having been established about as long as that of the Yurok. This inference is corroborated by the fact that about the head of the Sacramento Valley, to which the Kuksu cult and basketry of Pomo type have not made their way and where most specific central Californian influences are weak, numerous elements of northwestern civilization have penetrated almost across the breadth of the State.

Physiography can, however, be called in to explain why the culture of the Yurok did not flow more freely east and northeast up its main stream, the Klamath, to the Lutuami. The elevated lake habitat of these people is very different from the region of coastal streams. Moreover, it is nearly shut off from them by the southern end of the great Cascade Range, but is rather open toward the Great Basin and the more northerly Plateau.

THE LUTUAMI SUBCULTURE.

The Lutuamian or Klamath Lakes culture or subculture, as represented in this work by the Modoc, corresponds well with this setting. It reveals some specializations, such as its *wokas* and tule industries, that are obviously founded on peculiar environment. There are some northwestern influences, but rather vague ones. The basis of the culture is perhaps central California, with some Great Basin or Plateau admixture. Since the introduction of the horse, the Lutuami mode of life has evidently been modified analogously to that of the Plateau peoples of the Columbia, although less profoundly; and with the horse came a number of cultural elements from the Plateau, if not from the Plains; of which some went on to the Shasta and Achomawi. This recent modification appears to have given Lutuami culture a more un-Californian aspect than it originally possessed. Neither the Kalapuya nor the Klamath-Modoc were a numerous enough people nor a sufficiently advanced one to have possessed a truly distinctive civilization. The Kalapuya are gone, but nearly a thousand Lutuami remain, and as soon as their society and religion are seriously inquired into, their cultural affiliations will no doubt become clearer.

DRAINAGE, CULTURE, AND SPEECH.

As regards the part of environment in general, it is clear that the culture provinces of the Pacific frontage of the United States are essentially based on natural areas, particularly of drainage. Thus the central Californian province consists of the great interior valley of that State with the adjacent coast. The Plateau is the drainage of the Columbia above the Cascade Range; the Great Basin, the area which finds no outlet to the sea. The one exception is northwestern California, whose ethnic boundary on the north cuts across the Umpqua, and on the south across the Klamath, the Trinity, and the Eel. The streams in this district have a northward trend, and it appears that both the Lower Columbia and the northwestern culture retained enough of the seaboard character of the British Columbia civilization to enable them better to cling along the coast than to push up the long narrow valleys that nearly parallel it.

At the same time there is not a single distinctly maritime culture in the entire stretch from Cape Flattery to Baja California, except in a measure that of Puget Sound. Lower Columbia and northwestern California clearly are river civilizations; that of central California evinces an almost complete negation of understanding or use of the sea. In southern California the acme of culture is indeed attained in and opposite the little Santa Barbara Archipelago; but the great bulk of the province is a canoeless, arid tract.

In nearly every case, too, the province is either composed mainly of people of one stock or family, or one such group dominates civilizationally.

Puget Sound: Salish preponderant, Wakash perhaps most characteristic.

Lower Columbia: Chinook most numerous and distinctive.

Willamette (distinctness doubtful): wholly Kalapuyan.

Klamath Lakes (distinctness doubtful): wholly Lutuami.

Northwestern California: Athabascans in the majority, Algonkins culturally dominant.

Central California: distinctly a Penutian province with Hokan fringes.

Southern California: Shoshonean, although the Chumash are not without consequence.

Lower Colorado: Yuman, with perhaps some Shoshonean margin.

Great Basin: Almost solidly Shoshonean.

Plateau: about balanced between Sahaptin and Salish.

It is also notable that in spite of this massing no province is populated wholly by people of one origin. The two apparent exceptions are areas so weak culturally that their proper independence is doubtful.

SOUTHERN CALIFORNIA AND THE SOUTHWESTERN PROVINCE.

Both the Southern California and Lower Colorado cultures present numerous relations to the great Southwestern province, and it is not open to doubt that many of their constituent elements can be traced back to an origin among the Pueblos or the ancestors or cultural kinsmen of the Pueblos. At the same time it would be a very summary and misleading procedure to consider these provinces an outright part of the Southwest. New foci have formed on the spot. If these are to be canceled out merely because they are secondary to an older, more active hearth of influences among the Pueblos, it would be equally justifiable to dismiss the culture of the latter as superficial and unimportant on the ground that its basic constituents have largely radiated out of Mexico. Understanding of the ultimate sources is, of course, indispensable to interpretation, but ramifications and new starts are of no less consequence to an understanding of the history of cultural growths. A direct merging of all the collateral branches into a single type merely on the ground of their relationship would lead to a prevention of the recognition of cultural individuality, as it might be termed, and thereby defeat the very end of truly historical inquiry. In the preceding pages it has been the constant endeavor to point out those elements in the native life of the southern end of California that can be considered as derived from the culture of the Southwest, and at the same time to determine how far the groupings of these elements and the social attitudes thereby established have remained specifically Southwestern or have become regionally peculiar.

The considerable distinctiveness that obtains in the south is perhaps most pregnantly illustrated by the fact that of the two subtypes there, the one geographically nearer to the Southwest proper, that of the Lower Colorado River, is on the whole not appreciably more similar to that of the Pueblos than is the one which has its center on the coast among the Gabrielino and their neighbors. Many things link the Mohave with the Pueblos and with the so-called nomadic tribes of Arizona. Other elements, such as the sand painting, have, however, been pointed out which are common to the Gabrielino and the Southwesterners proper and in which the Mohave and the Yuma do not participate. These elements may be somewhat the less numerous; but. so far as can be judged in the present state of knowledge, as reviewed in the chapter on the Yuma, the balance between the two classes is nearly even. From this condition the only conclusion possible is that southwesern influences have infiltrated southern California slowly, irregularly, and disjointedly, with the result that these influences have been worked over into new combinations and even into new products faster than they arrived.

A searching examination of the relation of the southern California and Lower Colorado subcultures to the Southwest will prove of great interest because it will presumably unravel much of the history of civilization in all of these regions. Such an examination can not yet be conducted with satisfaction because the mother culture of Arizona and New Mexico, probably at once the greatest and the most compact native civilization of the continent north of Mexico, and the one which documents and archeology combine to illuminate most fully, has not yet been adequately conceptualized. Agriculture, pottery, stone architecture, clans, masked fraternities, dramatizing rituals are the ethnic activities that rise before the mind; but not one is universal in the Southwest. If the Apache and Havasupai are not southwestern, they are nothing at all; and yet one or both of them fail on every one of these supposed touchstones.

In fact, while ethnologists speak constantly of the Southwest as if it were a well-defined ethnic unit, what they generally have in mind is the Pueblos with perhaps the addition of their town-dwelling ancestors or of the interspersed and Pueblo-influenced Navaho. No satisfying picture that gives proper weight to the unsettled as well as the agricultural tribes has yet been drawn; at least not so as to serve for detailed comparative analysis. The Pima are closely linked with the Pueblos, and in other respects with the Lower Colorado tribes, but to unite them nonchalantly with either would be inadmissible. But so far as they are southwestern, the Papago are; and if the Papago, then, in some measure at least, the Yaqui and Seri also.

The truth is that the Southwest is too insistently complex to be condensed into a formula or surrounded with a line on the map. Essentially this is true of every culture. The Haida no more represent the Chinook and the Yurok than the Hopi can be made to stand for the Pima, nor will an average struck in either case do justice to the essence of the Haida and Hopi ethnos. Such condensing efforts can be condoned only as preliminary steps to historical inquiry, as narrowly ethnological classifications which clear the way to an understanding of civilizational events. Elsewhere in America cultures are often relatively simple and the time element not present to disturb a purely geographical view; hence the inadequacy of such reductions is less impressed on the student. But in the Southwest the factor of temporal order obtrudes instead of eluding us blankly. Two diverse strains, the life of the town dwellers and of the country dwellers, remain distinct yet are interminably interwoven. Regional differences are striking in short distances and without notable environmental basis. And it is clear that the foundation of everything southwestern is Mexican, and yet that everything in the Southwest has taken its peculiar shape and color on the spot. In short, a history of southwestern civilization lies within measurable sight, but the antecedent analysis, which must include southern California, has not yet been made.

CENTRAL CALIFORNIA AND THE GREAT BASIN.

While the north and south of aboriginal California are to be construed as marginal regions of greater extraneous cultures, central California remains isolated. It can not be viewed as a subsidiary because the potent civilization on which it might depend does not exist. Its north and the south being accounted for, and the ocean lying on the west, the only direction remaining open for any set of influences is the east, and this is the area of the barren Great Basin, populated by tribes of no greater advancement than the central Cali-

fornians—perhaps even less developed. These tribes could not, therefore, well serve as carriers of culture into central California, if we
may judge by analogy with the spread of civilization in other parts
of the world. As a matter of fact, they did not. Specific culture
elements characteristic of the Plains have not penetrated into California. A few such traits that are discernible in northeastern Cali-

FIG. 74.—Major culture areas and centers of development within California.

fornia have evidently come in not across the Great Basin but down
the Columbia River and through the interior peoples of Oregon.
Moreover, it is questionable whether these elements have chiefly
entered California anciently or rather as an adjunct of the white
man and the horse. Nor have Southwestern influences penetrated
central California to any appreciable extent by way of the Great
Basin. Where Southwestern elements are traceable in central California, as in the San Joaquin Valley, it is usually probable that
they represent an immediate outflow from southern California.

Yet it is certain that central California and the Great Basin are regions of close cultural kinship. It is true that the food supply and material resources of the interior semidesert have enforced a mode of life which makes a quite different impression. Analogies have therefore been little dwelt upon. Absence of definite records concerning the Shoshoneans of the Great Basin render exact comparisons somewhat difficult even now. Both regions, however, lack in common most of the characteristic traits of the culture adjacent to them; and it is only necessary to set side by side their basketry, their houses, their technical processes or the schemes of their societies, to be convinced that the bonds between the two areas are numerous and significant. This kinship may be expected to be revealed convincingly as soon as a single intensive study of any Great Basin tribe is made from other than a Plains point of view.[1]

It has been the custom among ethnologists to recognize a " Plateau area " as possessing a common although largely negative culture. Our exact information to date regarding the peoples of this " Plateau " is almost wholly from the northern part of the area inhabited by the Salish. It is manifestly hasty to assume for the Shoshoneans of the Great Basin, which constitutes the southern half of this greater " Plateau," substantial cultural identity with the Sahaptin and interior Salish of the north. The latter have been subjected to powerful although incomplete influences from the North Pacific coast proper as well as from the Plains. Plains influences have penetrated also to the Shoshoneans, but the North Pacific coast could hardly have had much effect, and certainly not a direct one, in the Great Basin. The coastward tract here is central California; and we could therefore anticipate, on theoretical grounds, that it had affected the Great Basin Shoshoneans much as the North Pacific coast has influenced the Salish of the Plateau proper, that is, of the upper Columbia and Fraser.

This is exactly the condition to which the available facts point. The civilization of central California is less sharply characterized and less vigorous than that of the coast of British Columbia. Its influences could therefore hardly have been as penetrating. There must have been more give and take between Nevada and central California than between the interior and the coastal districts of British Columbia. But the kinship is clearly of the same kind, and the preponderance of cultural energy is as positively (though less strikingly) on the coast in one tract as in the other. The Kuksu cult and the institutions associated with it have not flowed directly into Utah and Idaho, nor even in any measure into Nevada, but they indicate a dominance of cultural effectiveness, which, merely in a somewhat lower degree, relates central California to the Great Basin substantially as the North Pacific coast is related to the northern Plateau.

---

[1] See Lowie in bibliography.

THE IDEA OF A CALIFORNIAN CULTURE AREA.

The "California culture area" of the older American ethnology therefore fades away. The north of the State, on broader view, is part of a great non-Californian culture; the south likewise. The middle region, on the other hand, is dominant, not dominated, within the larger area of which it forms part; but its distinctiveness is only a superstructure on a basic type of civilization that extends inland far beyond the limits of the California of to-day. Analogously, local cultural patterns have been woven on the fabric, respectively, of the far-stretched civilization of the north; and, twice, on that of the south. Thus, in a close aspect, not one but four centers of diffusion, or, in the customary phraseology, four types and provinces of culture, must be recognized in California. Figure 74 summarizes these conclusions.

PREHISTORY.

DATA.

California is a fairly rich field for prehistoric antiquities. There have probably been discovered since the American occupation at least a million specimens, about one in a hundred of which has found a resting place in a public museum or become available as a permanent record for science to draw on. But the ancient objects are widely scattered in the ground, and the absence of ruins and earthworks has made the discovery of inhabited sites largely a matter of accident. Systematic exploration is therefore comparatively unremunerative, unless undertaken on an intensive scale. Only in two regions are artifacts and burials found in some concentration.

The more profitable and best exploited of these areas consists of the Santa Barbara Islands and the coast of the Santa Barbara Channel. The other takes in the winding shores of San Francisco Bay. In both instances the former inhabited sites are readily revealed by the presence of shell and sometimes of ashes. The channel district was the more heavily populated and the art of the natives distinctly more advanced. This region has therefore been extensively dug over by enthusiasts, and a number of really valuable collections have been amassed and deposited in public institutions. The San Francisco Bay shell mounds yield a smaller quantity of less interesting material. Now and then a nest of burials proves a fairly rich pocket, but in general not more than two or three implements can be secured for each cubic yard of soil turned over,[1] and the majority of these are simple bone awls, broken pestle ends, arrow points, and the like. On the other hand, some of the diggings in these northern mounds have been conducted in a scientific manner; with

---

[1] Artifacts secured per cubic yard of excavation: Emeryville shell mound, 2; Ellis Landing, 0.5; Castro, 0.2; Gunther Island (Humboldt Bay), 3.

the result that some attempt can be made to interpret the period, manner of life, and development of culture of the ancient inhabitants. It is likely that the southern area will allow of much more ample conclusions once it is investigated with definite problems in view.

ANCIENT SITES.

The number of prehistoric sites is known to have been very considerable wherever topography and climate and food supply encouraged settlement. Figures 75 to 77 suggest the density and continuity of occupation on San Diego Bay, as well as on two of the islands of the Santa Barbara group. For San Francisco and Humboldt Bays in the north, larger maps have been published. These districts comprise the principal shore lines in California that face on sheltered waters. The surf-beaten cliffs which constitute the remainder of the coast undoubtedly held a smaller population. Their numerous short transverse streams, most of them with half-filled mouths, offered the natives many sheltered sites, but the remains indicate that these were frequently occupied only as temporary or intermittent camps.

FIG. 75.—Prehistoric sites about San Diego Bay. (Data by Nelson and Welty.)

Away from the coast, the ancient sites are much more difficult to detect, and data are so scattering that any present endeavor to map the sites, even for restricted districts, is out of the question, although painstaking investigation usually reveals abundant evidences of occupation.

On San Francisco Bay something over half of the bulk of the deposits left by the prehistoric occupants is shell. This, with the soil and rock and ash that have become mixed in, has usually accumulated to some height, forming a distinct and sometimes a conspicuous rounded elevation. The sites in this region are therefore well described by their common designation of "shell mounds."

Elsewhere, even on the coast, shell usually forms a smaller proportion of the soil or refuse left by ancient villages, except perhaps for certain localities in the Santa Barbara district.   In consequence the mound formation is generally also less visible.   Table 14 combines the available data on this point.

ANTIQUITY.

The shores of San Francisco Bay have been subsiding in recent periods, as the geologist reckons time.   These shores are mostly low and frequently bordered by an extensive tidal marsh.   Some of the mounds appear to have been established at the water's edge and have been affected by this subsidence.   They grew up faster than the land sank, and thus remained convenient for occupation, but their bases have become submerged or covered with inorganic deposits.   The exact depth to which this subsidence has taken place

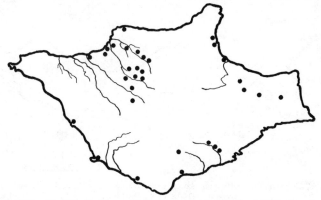

FIG. 76.—Prehistoric sites on Santa Rosa Island.   (Data of P. M. Jones.)

is somewhat laborious to ascertain, and has been determined for only a few of the ten or more mounds known to be partly drowned. The bases of these range from 3 to 18 feet below the ocean level of to-day.   This fact makes a respectable antiquity for the beginning of their occupation certain.

Some of the mounds on San Francisco Bay remained inhabited until the historic period.   Early Spanish travelers, it is true, do not refer definitely to shell mounds, but it is only natural that as between a site and a group of houses filled with people, the latter would be the first to attract attention.   A number of objects of European source have been found in the upper layers of these mounds, sometimes in association with burials: adobe bricks, a crucifix, medals, three-legged metates of Mexican type, and the like.

The Emeryville and Ellis Landing mounds, two of the largest and best explored on San Francisco Bay, have been estimated by their excavators to possess an age, respectively, of from one to several thousand and from three to four thousand years. The latter figure is arrived at by an ingenious computation. The Ellis Landing mound contains a million and a quarter cubic feet of material. About 15 house pits were recently still visible on it. If contemporaneously occupied, these would indicate a population of about a hundred. The Indians ate fish, game, acorns, seeds, and roots. A per capita allowance of fifty mussels a day, or an equivalent in other molluskan species, for adults and children, therefore seems liberal. Five thousand mussel shells crush down, per experiment, to a quarter as many cubic inches. Ash, rock, and other débris would bring the daily accumulation to about a cubic foot for the entire settlement. At a rate of deposition amounting to 300 to 400 cubic feet annually, 3,500 years would be required to build up 1,260,000 feet. There are too many indeterminate factors in such a calculation to allow its results

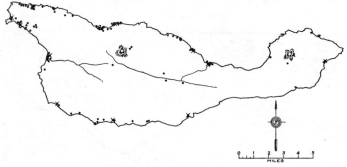

Fig. 77.—Prehistoric sites on Santa Cruz Island. The largest middens are crossed. (Data of L. Outhwaite.)

to be pressed rigidly; but it seems reasonable. The bottom of the mound now being 18 feet below sea level, a subsidence of half a foot per century is indicated. The population may have averaged more than 100; but this would be rather a high figure for a native Californian village. It may have been augmented seasonally by visitors from the interior, but to compensate, its own inhabitants are likely to have spent five or six months of each year in the hills away from their mussels. However the question is approached, 3,500 years seems a conservative deduction.

A check has been attempted by another investigator. Fourteen per cent of Ellis Landing mound, according to a number of analyzed samples, is ash—a weight of over 7,000 tons. Assuming 3,500 years, we have a production of 11 pounds daily. The woods available in the vicinity yield less than 1 per cent of ash. Hence more than 1,200 pounds of wood were burned daily, or, on the previous estimate of population, about 80 pounds per family of 7 persons.

As a woman can carry this bulk in one load, the figure appears conservative. In other words, a test of the factors assumed in the first calculation yields a credible result.

Of course, many mounds are smaller, less or not at all depressed below sea level, and evidently more recent and shorter lived. But again, Ellis Landing may be by no means the most ancient. It seems extremely probable, therefore, that a minimum duration of 3,000 years must be allowed for the shell mound period on San Francisco Bay.

COMPOSITION OF SHELL MOUNDS.

The constituents that go to make up the coast mounds are classified in Table 14. Charcoal never amounts to more than a fraction of 1 per cent of the weight of the total bulk and has been counted as ash. Fish, bird, and mammal bones compose from 1 part in 400 down to mere traces. Soil includes rock, sand and gravel. The proportion of this varies noticeably, but is usually explained by topographical considerations. Gunther Island is sand and peat, Sausalito a rocky site, Castro several miles from the shore, Half Moon Bay on a slide from a hillside, Point Loma on a narrow shelf along the side of the headland. In the other mounds the inorganic material is less abundant, and does not fall below a sixth or rise above a third in weight of the whole mass.

TABLE 14.—PERCENTAGE COMPOSITION OF CALIFORNIA SHELL MOUNDS.

	Shell.	Ash.	Soil.
Humboldt Bay—Gunther Island	16	2	82
San Francisco Bay:			
Emeryville	60	14	26
West Berkeley	53	24	23
Ellis Landing	70	14	16
Carquinez	55	27	18
San Rafael	54	25	21
Greenbrae	65	13	22
Sausalito	55	4	41
San Francisco (Presidio)	57	16	27
San Mateo Point	59	6	35
San Mateo	59	11	30
Castro	26	10	64
Coast south of San Francisco—Half Moon Bay	57	4	39
San Diego Bay—Point Loma	29	5	66

The ratio of shell to ash varies more, but its fluctuations are also partly intelligible. It is highest, about 14:1, at Half Moon Bay, an exposed spot more suited for occasional camping than continuous residence, and at Sausalito, where shelter, wood, and water are available but where abundance of clams may seasonally have drawn people from some distance about. The average proportion, 4 or 5:1, is found at Emeryville, Ellis Landing, Greenbrae, and San Mateo (on three sides of San Francisco Bay), and is only slightly exceeded on San Diego and Humboldt Bays. The ratio is low, between 2:1 and 3:1, at Carquinez, which is well up on brackish water; at San Rafael, an essentially inland site; Castro, also away from tidewater; and West Berkeley, where wealth of net sinkers indicates a fishing village rather than a mollusk-gathering station.

On San Francisco Bay the commonest shell in the mounds is the mussel, *Mytilus edulis*. This is regularly the prevailing mollusk. Next common, but far more irregularly distributed, is the common soft-shell clam, *Macoma nasuta*. The small local oyster, *Ostrea lurida*, is abundant at San Mateo, where the modern cultivated beds of introduced oysters are located, at West Berkeley, and at Emeryville, but scarce elsewhere. All three of these species are still regularly on the American market. The large ocean mussel, *Mytilus californianus*, is of importance, in examined mounds, only in those on the outlet to the bay, namely San Francisco and Sausalito. Barnacles constitute from 1 to 6 per cent of the total weight of shell. Their occurrence is such as to indicate that they were collected with the other mollusks or with driftwood to which they adhered. Haliotis is everywhere sparsely represented.

TABLE 15.—MOLLUSKAN PROPORTIONS (BY WEIGHT) IN SHELL MOUNDS.

	Mussel.	Clam.	Oyster.	Ocean mussel.	Barnacles.	Dust and unidentifiable fragments.
Emeryville	35	18	8	(1)	2	34
West Berkeley	41	4	19	(1)	2	32
Ellis Landing	35	36	(1)	....	1	25
Carquinez	68	(1)	(1)	....	1	29
San Rafael	44	(1)	(1)	(1)	5	48
Greenbrae	47	1	1	(1)	3	46
Sausalito	24	23	(1)	2	3	41
San Francisco	19	12	(1)	18	6	39
San Mateo Point	34	....	22	....	5	37
San Mateo	33	(1)	31	(1)	3	31

¹ Less than 1 per cent.

Castro, whose location makes it abnormal in other ways, contains only traces of mussel and clam, and a small proportion of oyster. The dominant species is the horn shell, *Cerithidea californica*, a variety available at other mound sites, but usually neglected there in favor of more palatable foods. Next in abundance at Castro is *Pholas pacificus*, which is rare elsewhere. Crab carapaces are also far more conspicuous at Castro than at any other explored site of the region.

It is quite apparent that the molluskan fauna of San Francisco Bay has not changed appreciably. even in its local distribution since the shell mounds were inhabited; and the topography and hydrography of the district are also likely to have remained substantially constant during the elapsed period of occupation.

On the open ocean at Half Moon Bay the native sea foods possessed a quite different range. *Tegula funebralis* was secured in greatest quantity, the *californianus* mussel came next, and *Paphia staminea* was obtained occasionally. The bay species are scarcely represented.

In the north, along the steep coast beyond Trinidad, the large ocean mussel seems to be the chief shell constituent of the refuse left by villages. The only quantitative determinations are from the sandy and marshy shores of Humboldt Bay, where the Gunther Island mound yielded *Schizothaerus nuttallii*, 23 per cent; *Macoma nasuta* (clam), 17; *Cardium corbis* (scallop), 14; *Paphia staminea*, 12; *Paphia tenerrima*, 1; *Saxidomus gigantea*, 1; *Mytilus edulis* and barnacles, trace; unidentifiable, 28. These are probably fairly representative proportions for the district. Yet a camp site on Freshwater slough, near Eureka, had about 58 per cent of its shell *edulis* mussel, with 34 per cent unidentifiable. On the other hand a coast site near Cape Mendocino showed the large mussel, *californianus*, predominant; " clam " and " cockle " next; and a sea snail, a conical shell, and haliotis frequent. The species recovered at the spot are *Mytilus californianus; Purpura crispata* and *saxicola; Acmaea pelta, spectrum,* and *mitra; Tapes staminea; Pholas californica; Fissurella aspera; Chrysodomus dirus; Haliotis rufescens; Chlorostoma funebrale* and *brunneum;* and *Helix Townsendiana.*

ANCIENT CULTURE PROVINCES.

Exploration of prehistoric sites anywhere in the State rarely reveals anything of moment that is not apparent in the life of the recent natives of the same locality. This rule applies even to limited districts. The consequence is that until now the archaeology of

California has but rarely added anything to the determinations of ethnology beyond a dim vista of time, and some vague hints toward a recognition of the development of culture. But as regards endeavor in this direction, practically nothing has yet been achieved.

Nor do the local varieties of culture seem to have advanced or receded or replaced one another to any extent. Objects of Santa Barbara type are found only in the Santa Barbara district and practically never about San Francisco Bay. Humboldt Bay yields some variant types, but these are again peculiar to the locality. How ancient these may be, can not yet be stated, but they are certainly not mere recent types. Moreover, there is no indication whatever that the San Francisco Bay culture ever prevailed at Humboldt Bay, and it is certain that the characteristics of the culture of the latter district never penetrated far enough south to be even partly represented in the former region.

In other words, the upshot of the correlation of the findings of archaeology and ethnology is that not only the general Californian culture area, but even its subdivisions or provinces, were determined a long time ago and have ever since maintained themselves with relatively little change.

PURELY PREHISTORIC IMPLEMENTS.

In regard to a few utensils, we do know that customs have changed. Prominent among these are the mortar and metate. The mortar is found practically everywhere in California, and in most localities is rather frequent underground. But over a considerable part of the State, comprising roughly its northern half, it was not used by the historic tribes, at least not in portable form or for the purpose of grinding acorns. In this area it either consists of an excavation in bedrock, or is a small instrument used for crushing tobacco or meat, or is made of a basketry hopper set on a slab. It is therefore probable that at some time in the past, more or less remote, a change came over northern California which led to the abandonment of the large movable acorn mortar of stone in favor of these other devices. Even in the southern half of the State this mortar was not so extensively used in recent times as the frequency of the type among prehistoric remains has led to being generally believed.

The metate or grinding slab seems to have come in about as the mortar went out of use. The evidence is less complete, but it is significant that there are no metates in the San Francisco shell mounds, although a slab mortar is now and then to be found. It is possible that the historic but little known Costanoans and Coast Miwok of San Francisco Bay followed their ancestors or predecessors on the spot in going without the metate; but it would be rather surprising if they had done so, in view of the fact that modern interior tribes in the same latitude, such as the Miwok and Maidu, and even those farther north, grind on the metate, and that all the coast tribes from San Francisco Bay north uniformly employ the pounding slab. The latter may be a modification of the mortar under the influence of the metate in regions influenced by the metate culture but into which the metate proper did not penetrate. This rather intricate point has been discussed more fully in the chapters on the Maidu, Chumash, Luiseño, and Cahuilla.

In prehistoric deposits on Humboldt Bay, and at several interior points in extreme northern California, have been found examples of an ornamental stone object which can hardly have been anything but a club. It is of animal shape, the head fairly defined, the tail serving as handle, and the legs projecting somewhat as if they were spikes. This is a type with affiliations in Oregon and on the Columbia River, and was not used by any historic tribe in California. These animal-shaped clubs are almost certainly to be connected with the simpler edged fighting club of stone used by the recent Indians of northwestern California.

DEVELOPMENT OF CIVILIZATION ON SAN FRANCISCO BAY.

Enough mounds have been systematically excavated in the San Francisco Bay region to make possible a fairly accurate comparison of the culture represented by the deep, early strata with that partially preserved in the upper, late layers.

A number of difficulties must be mentioned. The mounds are highest at the center and slope toward the edges. The periphery is generally later than the middle of the base. A reckoning from the ground level upward would therefore be misleading. On the other hand, measurements of depth from the surface are not quite accurate because the mounds usually built up fastest in their central portions. A foot of mound material near the periphery may therefore stand for a period considerably longer—or sometimes less—than that required for a like thickness to accumulate in the middle. Theoretically, the correct procedure would accordingly be to follow lines of deposition in instituting comparisons; but this is not practical, stratification being confined to limited areas and often wholly imperceptible. In spite of some variation of age for the several parts

of each mound, depths have therefore had to be calculated by absolute measurement from the modern surfaces.

In most cases, much more material was removed from the upper
than from the lower levels of mounds. But the proportion varies
according to the circumstances of excavation at each site. Absolute
frequency of the various classes of implements, therefore, proves
nothing. The number of objects of the several types has accordingly
been expressed in percentage of the total number of artifacts discovered in each level.

Still other factors disturb. The mounds are very unequal in bulk
and in height, and the excavations have removed quite different
volumes. Collectors also preserve and classify their finds in somewhat divergent manners.

All these circumstances render any exactly reliable comparisons impossible at present. It is, however, fortunate that enough data are
on record to allow of any inferences at all; and, with due heed to
the considerations mentioned, the evidence may therefore be proceeded with.

Table 16 shows the relative frequency, as compared with all recovered articles of manufacture, of tools of obsidian, a material found
only at some distance—some 25 to 50 miles—from the bay shores,
and therefore a valuable index of tribal intercommunication; of
mortars, pestles, and awls, three implements that are basic in the industrial life of all aboriginal Californians; and of a special class of
well-finished objects of plummet-like shape, the so-called "charm
stones," which presumably bore associations of magic and religion.
In the mounds of medium height, which go down to a depth of 8
to 12 feet, all three of these classes of objects, except charm stones,
are found quite generally down to the lowest levels. They occur
in the same ratio in the higher and in general presumably more
ancient mounds whose thickness extends to 20 and 30 feet. In fact
in both of those from which data are available, at Emeryville and
Ellis Landing, even charm stones are still relatively abundant at a
greater depth than is attained by the six other mounds. This fact
renders it likely that the absence of charm stones in the lowest 2 to
4 feet of the moderate deposits is due either to accident or to the
low probability that objects of such comparative rarity as charm
stones would normally occur in the small total number of artifacts
that is characteristic of the bottom-most levels of all the bay shell
heaps.

TABLE 16.—PERCENTAGES OF TOTAL ARTIFACTS CONSTITUTED BY CERTAIN IMPLEMENTS ACCORDING TO DEPTH IN SHELL MOUNDS.

CHIPPED IMPLEMENTS OF OBSIDIAN.

Mounds.	Depth in 2-foot and 4-foot intervals.									
	2	4	6	8	10	12	14	18	22	26
San Rafael.................	0	0	23	100	.....	.....	.....	.....	.....	.....
Greenbrae..................	37	5	27	0	17	33	.....	.....	.....	.....
Sausalito..................	14	5	0	0	17	0	.....	.....	.....	.....
Ellis Landing [1]............	0	0	1	0	42	0	0	0	29	8
Emeryville [2]..............	0	0	0	50	0	0	0	0	0	0
Visitacion (Bay Shore)....	0	0	3	0	0	.....	.....	.....	.....	.....
San Mateo.................	0	12	0	0	.....	.....	.....	.....	.....	.....
Castro....................	6	0	0	6	.....	.....	.....	.....	.....	.....

MORTARS AND PESTLES.

San Rafael.................	25	0	18	0	.....	.....	.....	.....	.....	.....
Greenbrae..................	37	26	7	33	33	17	.....	.....	.....	.....
Sausalito..................	43	10	14	7	17	25	.....	.....	.....	.....
Ellis Landing	25	17	32	18	0	56	50	22	7	25
Emeryville.................	56		0	10	33	0	0	45	18	40
Visitacion.................	14	27	6	0	0	.....	.....	.....	.....	.....
San Mateo.................	22	19	33	29	.....	.....	.....	.....	.....	.....
Castro....................	37	22	23	33	.....	.....	.....	.....	.....	.....

BONE AWLS.

San Rafael.................	8	22	0	0	.....	.....	.....	.....	.....	.....
Greenbrae..................	12	37	27	0	17	17	.....	.....	.....	.....
Sausalito..................	0	30	14	0	8	12	.....	.....	.....	.....
Ellis Landing..............	9	30	6	13	0	0	0	0	7	0
Emeryville.................	0	0	0	30	33	50	25	18	0	0
Visitacion.................	14	36	14	0	0	.....	.....	.....	.....	.....
San Mateo.................	11	0	0	29	.....	.....	.....	.....	.....	.....
Castro....................	0	0	23	17	.....	.....	.....	.....	.....	.....

CHARM STONES.

San Rafael.................	8	0	6	0	.....	.....	.....	.....	.....	.....
Greenbrae..................	0	0	7	0	0	0	.....	.....	.....	.....
Sausalito..................	0	0	0	20	0	0	.....	.....	.....	.....
Ellis Landing..............	14	17	14	18	8	9	17	0	0	0
Emeryville.................	0	0	25	0	0	0	25	6	0	0
Visitacion.................	0	9	9	0	0	.....	.....	.....	.....	.....
San Mateo.................	22	0	22	0	.....	.....	.....	.....	.....	.....
Castro....................	0	3	6	0	.....	.....	.....	.....	.....	.....

[1] Excavation of 1907-1908.   [2] Excavation of 1906.

In short, then, all the classes of objects in question occur at the bottom, middle, and top of the mounds, and the table shows that they occur with substantially the same frequency. In other words, the natives of the San Francisco Bay region traded the same materials from the same localities one or two or three thousand years ago as when they were discovered at the end of the eighteenth century. They ate the same food, in nearly the same proportions (only mammalian bones became more abundant in higher levels), prepared it in substantially the same manner, and sewed skins, rush mats, and coiled baskets similarly to their recent descendants. Even their religion was conservative, since the identical charms seem to have been regarded potent. In a word, the basis of culture remained identical during the whole of the shell-mound period.

When it is remembered that the best authority—estimating, indeed, but using as exact data as possible and proceeding with scientific care—puts the beginning of this period at more than 3,000 years ago, it is clear that we are here confronted by a historical fact of extraordinary importance. It means that at the time when Troy was besieged and Solomon was building the temple, at a period when even Greek civilization had not yet taken on the traits that we regard as characteristic, when only a few scattering foundations of specific modern culture were being laid and our own northern ancestors dwelled in unmitigated barbarism, the native Californian already lived in all essentials like his descendant of to-day. In Europe and Asia, change succeeded change of the profoundest type. On this far shore of the Pacific, civilization, such as it was, remained immutable in all fundamentals. Even as some measure of progress shall be determined by continued investigation, it is probable that this will prove to have been unusually slow and slight. There are few parts of the world, even those inhabited by dark-skinned savages, where such a condition can be regarded as established. The permanence of Californian culture, therefore, is of far more than local interest. It is a fact of significance in the history of civilization.

If it be objected that the period dealt with is after all conjectural rather than established, the import of our inference may be diminished; but it is not destroyed. Cut the estimate of 3,500 years in half, or even to one-third: we are still carried back to the time of Charlemagne. The elapsed millennium has witnessed momentous alterations in Europe, in India, in Japan; even the Mohammedan countries, China, Central Asia, and Malaysia, have changed deeply in civilization, while our part of America has stood still.

PARALLEL CONDITIONS ELSEWHERE.

No similar computations can yet be made for ancient remains in other parts of California, because the débris deposits elsewhere have indeed been ransacked for finds, but no accurate record of the precise depth of each specimen has been preserved. Yet the fact that no site shows objects appearing to belong to two types of culture, except for some potsherds close to the surface about San Diego; that the finds at various sites over whole districts are uniform, and even the districts usually merge into each other—all these circumstances indicate that relatively little transformation and but slight succession of civilizations occurred in prehistoric California.

It may be added that in a review of the archaeology of the continent Doctor Dixon has found the Californian conditions to be typical of the entire Pacific coast, whereas in the Atlantic region and Mississippi Valley exact inquiry has often brought to light decisive evidence of two or several types of culture in each region. Types must, of course, be interpreted as periods; and Doctor Dixon connects the comparatively rapid succession of these in the East with a much greater tendency toward movements of population, as known in the historic period and supported by tradition for earlier times. Instability of population may not have been the only, perhaps not even the principal, cause of eastern instability of culture; but it is a fact that there is scarcely any record or even legend of migrations in California.

In the Southwest changes in the types of prehistoric remains are striking, and a definite sequence of ceramic wares, and behind these of civilizations, is being determined. Southwestern influences are so numerous in southern California that something of the tendency toward change may be expected to be discovered there as soon as sufficiently painstaking search is undertaken at ancient sites. This is the more likely because southern California differs from the remainder of the State in revealing some evidence of shifts of population.

LOCAL UNIFORMITY OF THE SAN FRANCISCO BAY DISTRICT.

The averaging constancy of the figures in Table 16 rests upon a very conspicuous irregularity in detail. But this wavering is indicative only of the limitation of data. Not over a couple of dozen charm stones or obsidian pieces of provenience of known depth are available from any one mound, and the total number of artifacts recovered from the largest excavations at single sites is only a few hundred. By the time these are distributed among several layers the numbers are so small that chance must vary their distribution considerably. With successive levels, particularly at the lower and comparatively barren depths, yielding, say, one, two, and no objects of a given class, the corresponding percentages can easily be 5, 33, and zero. Burials, which occur scatteringly, contain pockets of specimens and add further to the irregularity of distribution over small sections of mounds. The variation in frequencies from layer to layer, therefore, allows of no inferences; it is the absence of drift in cultural direction, from bottom to top of any mound as a whole, that is significant.

The tendency toward uniformity is almost as great for locality as for time. Table 17 gathers the data on this point. It is notable that the variations in frequency of many classes of objects is about as great between successive excavations in the same mound as between distinct sites. Thus Emeryville in 1902 yielded 9 per cent of mortars and pestles and about 30 per cent of awls; in 1906 the respective results were 26 and 12. In short, variations must again be ascribed largely to chance.

TABLE 17.—PERCENTAGES OF CLASSES OF ARTIFACTS ACCORDING TO LOCALITY OF SHELL MOUNDS.

Mound.	Total specimen depth.	Total specimens obtained.	Percentages.							
			Obsidian.	Mortars and pestles.	Sinkers.	Charm stones.	Ornaments of beads or bone or shell.	Awls.	Wedges	All others.
	Feet.									
San Rafael	7	42	19	14	0	5	2	7	2	51
Greenbrae	12	60	17	22	0	1	8	22	2	28
Sausalito	12	84	5	15	12	5	19	13	0	31
Ellis Landing, 1906	13	92	9	11	1	11	5	10	0	53
Ellis Landing, 1907–8	25	260	4	24	10	13	11	12	1	25
West Berkeley, 1902	....	314	4	5	44	3	2	4	0	38
Emeryville, 1902	[1] 25	[2] 340	[1] 7	9	1	3	[1] 7	[1] 30	4	39
Emeryville, 1906	24	65	8	26	0	5	3	12	0	46
Visitacion (Bay Shore)	9	75	1	12	1	7	19	19	0	41
San Mateo	8	41	4	24	0	10	10	7	5	40
Castro	8	87	2	27	0	5	21	8	1	36

[1] Approximate.

[2] The total number is about 600, but this includes waste chips, broken bones, and similar pieces which have not been counted from the other mounds. That the correction to 340 makes the total comparable to the other totals is indicated by the figure 39 in the last column, which is also the average of the 10 other figures in that column.

There are a few exceptions. The two highest frequencies for charm stones are both furnished by Ellis Landing. The probable inference is that the settlement here was a center of some particular shamanistic or ceremonial activity. Such a development would be most likely in a large town, and this the size of the mound indicates the place to have been. It is illustrative of the lack of flow pervading Californian culture that the flowering of this religious manifestation was not a transient phase, but something that endured for many centuries, as evidenced by the comparative regularity of the high proportion of charm stones at this site.

West Berkeley, on the other hand, was mainly a fishing settlement. Nearly half of its discovered artifacts are sinkers—flattish pebbles nicked on two sides for the string that bound them to the lower edge of the seine net. That it was more than a camp is clear from the extent and depth of the deposits, as well as the burials and ceremonial and ornamental pieces which they contain. The spot may have been unusually favorable for taking fish. Yet Ellis Landing and West Berkeley, but a few miles on either side, contain only the usual low percentage of sinkers; and however much the aboriginal West Berkeleyans fished, the little mountain of shells they left behind proves them not to have neglected mollusks as a food supply.

Obsidian comes from Clear Lake and the head of Napa Valley, occasionally also in small lumps from upper Sonoma Valley. One should expect it to follow two routes in its distribution around San Francisco Bay—along the north and west border of San Pablo Bay to the Golden Gate, or across Carquinez Straits and southward along the eastern shore of San Francisco Bay proper. By either route the peninsular district of San Mateo and San Francisco would be the last to be reached. Analysis of the finds exactly tallies with these inferences from geography. San Rafael and Greenbrae, most northerly and nearest the source of supply, actually show much the heaviest proportion of obsidian implements; Visitacion, San Mateo, and Castro, the most southerly mounds and on the peninsula, the smallest frequency.

THE LOWER SAN JOAQUIN VALLEY.

In the delta region of the great interior valley, particularly in the vicinity of Stockton, several special objects have been found in sufficient numbers to insure their being characteristic of the region. These include narrow cylindrical jars or vases of steatite; clay balls, either plain or incised, perhaps slung shots for water fowl or substitutes for cooking stones in the alluvial region; neatly worked obsidian blades of about a finger's length and crescentically shaped; and thin ornaments of either haliotis or mussel shell cut into forms ranging from that of a human outline to more conventionalized figures, which, if they were of civilized origin, would suggest the form of a stringed musical instrument. The distribution of these types is so well localized as to give a first impression of a specific ancient subculture. But the area is one from which the historic tribes were early drained into the missions, so that historic data which would enable a comparison on the basis of ethnology are practically nil.

It is therefore quite possible that we are confronted by the usual phenomenon of a culture proceeding undisturbed from prehistoric times until its elimination by the Caucasian; with merely the peculiarity that its modern phase disappeared before being observed. This solution is indicated by the fact that investigations among the Miwok have developed that the so-called " Stockton curves " of obsidian were known to these Indians, the blades being attached to the fingers in imitation of bear claws by dancers who impersonated the animal. It seems rather likely that if the northern valley ·Yokuts survived in condition to depict the culture of their great-grandfathers, they would be able to explain most of the other types, which now appear isolated or peculiar, as something familiar in the region when the Spaniards came.

THE UPPER SAN JOAQUIN VALLEY.

A rather remarkable discovery of burials near the shores of Buena Vista Lake at the head of the San Joaquin Valley, in a territory that was historically Yokuts, seems at first sight to reveal a stronger influence of southern California, and even of the Southwest, than is discernible among the modern Indians of this region. (Pls. 41, 63, 72, 81.) A carefully preserved eagle skull with eyes of haliotis, for instance, suggested a definite connection with the Luiseño and Diegueño eagle-killing ceremony, until it became known that the modern Yokuts also practiced a mourning rite over eagles. But a specimen of a wooden club of the " potato-masher " type standard in southern California and the Southwest—unfortunately not preserved, but of definite description—does point to the conclusion indicated.

The same may be said of a number of bags twined in basketry technique but of soft string materials. (Pl. 63.) These are similar to the bags or wallets made by the Diegueño and Mohave, and bear an especial likeness, at any rate superficially, to utensils of the so-called " basket makers " who once lived at Grand Gulch, in southern Utah.

Another point is of interest. The hair preserved with some of the Buena Vista Lake skulls is wound or contained in typical central Californian head nets, but the hair itself is plastered in the long pencil-shaped masses which in the historic period the Colorado River tribes, and so far as known no others, followed as their fashion. (Pl. 72.) Yet the remains are those of natives of the region. So many of the objects preserved with them are articles of household use, and the interment of the dead is so precise, that there can be no suspicion of a party of raiding warriors having been slain and buried far from home.

PLATE 81

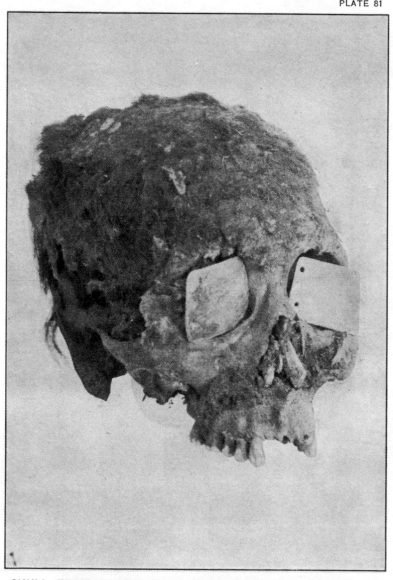

SKULL FROM NEAR BUENA VISTA LAKE, EDGE OF TULARE
VALLEY

PLATE 82

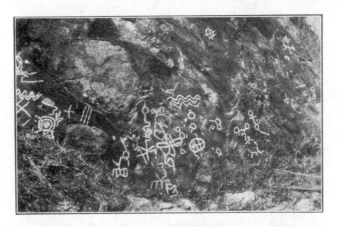

PETROGLYPHS FROM THE SIERRA NEVADA

From above, down: Rock Creek near Bishop; Upper Stanislaus River;
Tehipite, Middle Fork of Kings River

Perhaps of greatest interest in this collection is an unornamented cotton blanket unquestionably made among one of the settled tribes of New Mexico or Arizona. This is one of the few authentic instances of long distance trade of any manufactured article either into or out of California. It is, however, suggestive that the last wearer of this blanket was certainly not following the style customary among the people who wove it. He had roughly cut into it two ragged holes for his arms, so that he could put it about himself somewhat as a coat. (Pl. 72.) Had the maker intended the blanket to be worn in this fashion, he might have woven it in one piece, but would have trimmed and seamed the holes.

Unfortunately there is no indication whatever of the age of this very unusual find. It represents a series of burials uncovered by natural causes and detached from the village to which they belonged. At any rate, if the latter stood in the vicinity, it left no evidences of refuse or other accumulation. The state of preservation of many of the articles is such as to suggest comparative recency. But as against this is to be set the high aridity of the district. The interments may not be more than a few centuries old; but they are certainly pre-Spanish.

THE SANTA BARBARA REGION.

The Santa Barbara Islands and mainland contain in their ancient graves the greatest number of unique forms and specialized types to be found in California. Unfortunately the historical culture of the Chumash and island Shoshoneans has been so completely wiped out that in the majority of instances it is quite impossible to say whether the peculiar objects dug out of graves were or were not in use by the Indians of 150 years ago. So far as seems safe, they have been tentatively connected with the technological and religious practices of these Indians, in the chapter on the Chumash. It does not seem possible to interpret them more decisively, or worth while to speculate upon them at greater length, until either additional historical information becomes accessible upon this group, or systematic excavations enable the characterization of the several periods and types of culture that may be represented in the prehistoric deposits of the region.

A word may be added about two types of implements in regard to which there has been some controversy: a stone ring or perforated disk, and a pear or plummet shaped object. It has been affirmed that the former was a club head, or again a net sinker. But the holed disk is most common in the Chumash region, and the surviving Chumash unanimously declare that it was slipped as a weight over the root-digging sticks of their women. The size and shape and all evidences of wear on the pieces confirm this interpretation. That now and then such a stone may have been used for a hammer or for cracking acorns is entirely natural, but marks indicative of such occasional secondary utilization can not be stretched into a basis for theories. The net sinker of California was a beach pebble, nicked or notched on opposite edges, or sometimes grooved. Anything more finished or ornate would have been a sheer waste of labor, which would not have appealed to so practical minded a people as the Californians; at any rate not in an occupation in which religion did not directly enter. The only exception that must be made to the interpretation of the round perforated stone as a digging stone weight is provided by a few specimens found slenderly hafted and feathered in a cave that contained several hundred other clearly ceremonial objects.

The plummet-shaped stone, which is often very symmetrically ground and well polished, and sometimes made of attractively colored or banded rock, is without doubt a ceremonial object. At least, every interpretation obtained from recent Indians is to the effect that stones of this type were amulets or fetishes for luck in hunting and fishing. They may possibly also have been used by rain-making shamans. The fact that traces of asphalt show some of these pieces to have been suspended is, of course, no proof of their having been used as sinkers, true plummets, or weaving weights. In fact, one such charm stone was actually found, only a few years ago, suspended from a string over a fishing place near an Indian settlement in the San Joaquin Valley. Whether these stones, which are most common in central California but are also known from Chumash territory, were originally made as charms, or whether they served some other purpose and were only put to magical use when they were discovered by later generations of natives, it is impossible to decide with certainty; but the positive knowledge as to their recent employment should weigh more heavily in the student's mind than any conjecture, no matter how appealing, as to what their still earlier use may have been.

PICTURED ROCKS.

About 50 sites with carved or painted rocks have become known in California. These range from bowlders bearing a few scratches to walls of caves or overhanging cliffs covered with a long assemblage of figures in red, yellow, black, and white. Their distribution (Fig. 78) is by no means uniform. About half occur in territory occupied in the historic period by Shoshoneans. Nearly all the remainder are in areas immediately adjacent to Shoshonean tracts. Other parts of California are practically devoid of such monuments of the past.

This distribution can not be accounted for by environment. It is true that the open plains of the great valley and the heavy redwood belt would furnish few exposed stones suitable for inscribing. But the half-forested broken country north and south of San Francisco and the foothills of the Sierra offer abundant opportunities which the inhabitants of these regions availed themselves of most sparsely.

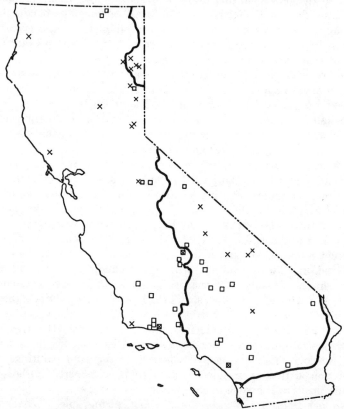

Fig. 78.—Distribution of petrographs. Squares, carved; crosses, painted; crossed squares, carved and painted. The lines are the limits of recent Shoshonean territory.

On the other hand, petrographs are common throughout the Great Basin, which was solidly tenanted by Shoshoneans. The inference is therefore strong that these people are mainly responsible for the painted and carved rocks of California, in part through the work of their ancestors' hands and partly by their influence on their neighbors. (Pl. 82.)

The most remarkable pictographs are those in the Chumash country, beginning with the famous Corral Rock in the Carrizo

Plains, the largest and most notable group in the State (Pl. 83);
stretching to the vicinity of Santa Barbara; and extending thence
easterly into Gabrielino land in the Sierra Madre and northeasterly
among the Yokuts in the southern Sierra Nevada. These pictographs
are almost all painted in several colors, protected from the weather
and well preserved except for defacings by civilized vandals, and inclined to the representation of recognizable figures—men, animals,
suns, and the like. Outside of this area carvings preponderate.
Although sometimes extensive, these are simpler, circles, spirals,
zigzags, rows of triangles, and other geometric designs prevailing,
usually in quite irregular arrangement.

It is true that the distinction between paintings and incised stones
must be made with caution. Stone is so much slower to work than
pigment that an equal effort would lead to much less elaborate results; and many of the carvings may originally have been over-
painted, the color quickly washing out in exposed locations, such as
granite outcrops. Yet caves and smooth overhangs occur in many
regions outside the district of the Chumash, Gabrielino, and southern Yokuts, and there can be little doubt that had the inhabitants
of the remoter regions felt impelled to produce complicated or life-
like pictures, they would have found the opportunity to make them,
and that their handiwork would have been more frequently preserved than is the case. The cave paintings of the south, therefore,
represent a particular art, a localized style or cult. This can be
connected, in all probability, with the technological art of the
Chumash and island Shoshoneans, as manifest in the occasional
carvings of whales, quadrupeds, and the like in steatite. Since these
paintings farther fall well within the region of the toalache religion,
in fact their distribution coincides fairly closely with the area in
which this religion was strongest, and since its cult was in certain
tracts worked out in visible symbols such as the sand painting, an
association with this religion is also to be considered, although
nothing positive is known in the matter.

Two questions are always asked about pictographs: What do
they mean? and How old are they? Neither can be answered.
The modern Indians are always familiar with them as landmarks,
but can give as little information as the visitor, except to say that
they have always been there. No connected story can be deciphered
from any of the groups of symbols, and many are so obviously
nonrepresentative as to leave even a speculative imagination baffled
for a clew. Many of the pictures may have been made by shamans;
but again there is no specific evidence pointing in this direction,
and it is quite possible that medicine men were not connected with
the making of any. Luiseño girls paint granite bowlders at the

PLATE 83

FIGURES FROM THE PAINTED ROCK OF CARRIZO PLAINS

conclusion of their adolescence rites. But this seems a local custom. and the paintings made in accordance with it are of different character from those found in caves farther north. They would in any case wash off in a generation or two. It has sometimes been conjectured that the symbols served as boundary marks, direction signs, or for some analogous practical purpose. Yet this interpretation fits neither their character, their location, nor the habits of native life. The Indian knew the limits of his territory and his way around in it; and as for strangers, his impulse would have been to obscure their path rather than blazon it.

The uncertainty is equal as regards age. Many of the pictures need not be more than two or three hundred years old, since all evidence goes to show that nothing survived in California tradition for even half a dozen lifetimes, except possibly in a garb wholly altered into myth. On the other hand, the sheltered paintings, and some of the deeper cut rocks, may well be several times as ancient. The only hope of a partial solution of this question seems to lie in an examination by mineralogists and geologists entitled to an opinion as to the resistance of stones, severity of exposure, and the rate of surface disintegration under given climatic conditions.

PRONUNCIATION OF NATIVE WORDS.

Many an Indian language contains more different sounds than the Roman alphabet has letters. If, according to a basic rule of philology, a distinct character were to be employed for each distinct sound, an alphabet of several hundred characters would have had to be devised for this book, since there are nearly a hundred native dialects in California of which some record has been made, and the vast majority of these contain sounds that are not identical. Such a scheme of orthography is both impracticable and unnecessary for anything but purely linguistic studies. On the other hand, the writing of Indian words with the current English values of the letters—sometimes falsely called "phonetic"—was out of the question, because words written in this way can often be read in two or three ways. If anyone can correctly pronounce a foreign word written by the English method, it is not because he can read it, but because his tongue remembers the pronunciation. It is impossible to convey to others a fixed pronunciation of alien terms rendered in English orthography.

The system of spelling followed in this work employs only letters of the Roman alphabet and three or four diacritical marks. In general, the vowel signs have the sound of the letters in the languages of the continent of Europe, the consonant signs the sound of the English letters. This system does not permit of any one of the Indian languages referred to being pronounced with absolute correctness. On the other hand, if the description of the sound or sounds denoted by each letter is carefully observed, this spelling will permit of the pronunciation of the native terms in this book with sufficient accuracy for an Indian to recognize all the words quoted from his dialect.

a   as in *father*, sometimes as in *what;* in Yurok only, sometimes as in *bad.*

b   usually a little more difficult to distinguish from p than in English.

c   not employed; s or k has been written instead.

ch.   as in English, or nearly so.

d   somewhat as in English; but its quality is like that of b, its tongue position like t.

dh   in Mohave and Luiseño only, like th in English *the.*

dj   as in English, but with some approach to ch quality (compare b, d, g).

e   as in *met, there;* sometimes like a in *mate.*

f   rare; the upper lip touches the lower lip, not the teeth.

g   as in *go*, but harder to distinguish from k than in English; in Yurok, always a "fricative," that is, like g in Spanish *gente* or colloquial German *wagen*; in Pomo, and occasionally in other languages, both values of g occur, but are designated by the one letter.

h   sometimes as in English; occasionally fainter; sometimes more harshly made with constriction at the back of the mouth, producing a sound equal, or nearly so, to Spanish j or German ch. H must always be sounded, even at the end of words.

hl   a "surd" l, made without vibration of the vocal cords.

hw   a "surd" w, much like wh in English *which.*

i   as in *pin*, long or short, or as in *machine*, long or short.

j   not used, except in dj.

k in languages which possess g, is as in English; in those which do not, it is usually somewhat nearer g than is English k, at least at the beginning and in the middle of words. Indian k is often pronounced much farther back in the mouth than English k.

l never quite the same as in English, but near enough in sound to be unmistakable.

m substantially as in English.

n substantially as in English.

ng as in English *singing*, not as in *finger*.

o as in *come, ore;* when long, sometimes like o in *note*, more frequently like aw in *law*.

p as in English, but with a tendency of approach toward b like that of k toward g.

q not used; kw has been written instead.

r much as in German, French, Spanish, or Irish brogue; only in Yurok it is "soft" as in American English. Yurok er is a vowel.

s is a sound of the same type as English s, though rarely quite identical. In languages like Yana and Mohave, in which sh has not been written, s is usually as similar in effect to English sh as to English s.

sh much as in English, but probably never quite the same.

t tends to approach d as k does g. Pomo, Yuki, Costanoan, Yokuts, Luiseño, Diegueño, Mohave, and perhaps other languages, possess one t made with the tip of the tongue against the teeth, and another against the front palate, the latter sounding almost like English tr; but the two sounds have been represented by one letter.

th in Mohave only, like English th in *thin*.

tl an "affricative surd" l, much like tl in English *little*.

u as in *rule*, long or short; or as in *full*, long or short; never as in *unit*.

ü in Shoshonean, Chumash, Yokuts, Miwok, Maidu, is spoken with the tongue in position for u, the lips formed as if for i or e. It is almost the "opposite" in articulation from German ü or French u.

v in Shoshonean, Mohave, and Karok; the lower lip touches the upper, not the teeth.

w as in English, or nearly so.

x not used. The sound of English x is represented by ks; the "fricative palatal" sound usually denoted by x in works on American Indian languages is here represented by h.

y as in English.

z as in English zebra.

zh rare; like s in *pleasure* or z in *azure*.

’ the so-called glottal stop; a contraction of the larynx or Adam's apple, closing the breath passage; a cessation of sound, or pause, and therefore inaudible except sometimes as a faint click or catch. When written after p, t, k, ch, ts, tl, the closing of the larynx is usually simultaneous with the first part of the consonant, while the last portion of the sound is reenforced and has to the ear something of the quality of a smack or crack.

denotes the accented or most loudly spoken vowel of the word. Accent is generally less marked in the Californian Indian languages than in English, and its designation has been omitted in all but a few instances.

when used, denotes a long vowel; but as a rule, length and shortness of vowels have not been distinguished. Lengthened consonants are represented by being written twice. This device does not indicate shortness of the preceding vowel as in English.

BIBLIOGRAPHY.

A classification by numbers according to subject will be found at the end of the alphabetic bibliography.

1. ABBOTT, C. C. Chipped stone implements. Mortars and pestles. Steatite cooking pots. Articles made of wood. Smoking pipes of stone. Miscellaneous objects made of stone. Musical instruments. In [Putnam, F. W.] Rept. U. S. Geog. Surv. west of the 100th Meridian [Wheeler Surv. Rept.], vol. VII, Archaeology, pp. 49–69, 70–92, 93–116, 122–124, 125–134, 190–217, 234–238, Washington, 1879.

2. ALARCON, FERNANDO. Relation, 1540. Hakluyt, Voyages, vol. III, London, 1600; repr. 1810: Ternaux-Compans, Voyages, vol. IX, Paris, 1838.

3. ANDERSON, R. A. Fighting the Mill Creeks. Chico, 1909.
   [The title indicates the nature of this booklet. The Mill Creeks are the Yahi.]

4. ANGEL, MYRON. La piedra pintada. The painted rock of California. A Legend. Los Angeles, 1910.

5. ARROYO DE LA CUESTA, FELIPE. Grammar of the Mutsun language. Shea's Library of American Linguistics, vol. IV, New York, 1861.

6. ———. Vocabulary of the Mutsun language. Ibid., vol. VIII, 1862.
   [A valuable collection by a competent Franciscan missionary. See Mason, J. Alden.]

7. BAEGERT, JACOB. Nachrichten von der Amerikanischen Halbinsel Californien. Mannheim, 1772. Partly translated by Charles Rau, Smithsonian Reports for 1863 and 1864, Washington, 1864, 1865.
   [Very valuable for Baja California, especially the extinct tribes of the southern half of the peninsula. The little book is probably the most spiritedly abusive description of a primitive people ever written by a priest, and certainly one of the most picturesque.]

8. BAER, K. E. VON, and HELMERSEN, G. VON. Beiträge zur Kentniss des Russischen Reiches. St. Petersburg, 1839.

9. BANCROFT, H. H. The native races of the Pacific states. The works of H. H. Bancroft, vols. I–V, San Francisco, 1883.
   [These five volumes on the aborigines are a fair sample of the thirty-nine that comprise the entire remarkable collection. They contain much that is based on manuscript material, or, if in print, is otherwise accessible with difficulty. Nothing that bears on the subject is omitted. Most of the volumes are excellently written. All the material is externally organized. Yet the series remains an immense drifting miscellany, without real plan, inner unity, or definite point of view but extremely valuable for the numerous important items that it embodies.]

10. BARRETT, S. A. Basket designs of the Pomo Indians. Amer. Anthrop., n. s. vol. VII, pp. 648–653, 1905.

11. ———. Ceremonies of the Pomo Indians. Univ. Cal. Publs. Amer. Archaeol. and Ethnol., vol. XII, pp. 397–441, 1917.

12. ———. A composite myth of the Pomo Indians. Jour. Amer. Folk-lore, vol. XIX, pp. 37–51, 1906.

13. BARRETT, S. A. The ethno-geography of the Pomo and neighboring Indians. Univ. Cal. Publs. Amer. Archaeol. and Ethnol., vol. VI, pp. 1–332, 1908.
   [A mine of data. Pages 28–36 reprint the account of Drake's landing in California.]

14. ———. The geography and dialects of the Miwok Indians. Ibid., vol. VI, pp. 333–368, 1908.

15. ———. Indian opinions of the earthquake of 1906. Jour. Amer. Folk-lore, vol. XIX, p. 324, 1906.

16. ———. The material culture of the Klamath Lake and Modoc Indians. Univ. Cal. Publs. Amer. Archaeol. and Ethnol., vol. V, pp. 239–292, 1910.

17. ———. Myths of the Southern Sierra Miwok. Ibid., vol. XVI, pp. 1–28, 1919.

18. ———. A new Moquelumnan territory in California. Amer. Anthrop., n. s. vol. V, p. 730, 1903.

19. ———. Pomo Bear doctors. Univ. Cal. Publs. Amer. Archaeol. and Ethnol., vol. XII, pp. 443–465, 1917.

20. ———. Pomo buildings. Holmes Anniversary Volume, pp. 1–17, Washington, 1916.

21. ———. Pomo Indian basketry. Univ. Cal. Publs. Amer. Archaeol. and Ethnol., vol. VII, pp. 133–306, 1908.
   [Perhaps the fullest description ever written of the basket art of any one native people.]

22. ———. The Pomo in the Sacramento valley of California. Amer. Anthrop., n. s. vol. VI, 189–190, 1904.

23. ———. Totemism among the Miwok Indians. Journ. Amer. Folk-lore, vol. XXI, p. 237, 1908.

24. ———. The Washo Indians. Bull. Public Mus. of Milwaukee, vol. II, no. 1, pp. 1–52, 1917.
   [Mainly a description of implements, but about all there is on the Washo.]

25. ———. The Wintun Hesi ceremony. Univ. Cal. Publs. Amer. Archaeol. and Ethnol., vol. XIV, pp. 437–488, 1919.
   [A Kuksu ritual influenced by the ghost-dance.]

26. BARRINGTON, DAINES. Journal of a Spanish voyage in 1775 by Don Antonio Maurelle. Miscellanies, pp. 471–534, London, 1781.

27. BARROWS, DAVID PRESCOTT. The ethno-botany of the Coahuilla Indians of southern California. Univ. of Chicago, 1900.
   [A spirited little book. Perhaps the best introduction to a study of the southern California Indians. The ethno-botany is excellent, and the author manages to present much of the culture along with it. One of the most human doctor's dissertations ever written.]

28. BARTLETT, J. R. Personal Narrative of explorations and incidents . . . connected with the United States and Mexican Boundary Commission, 1850–53. Vols. I–II. New York, 1854.
   [An excellent book, with some valuable data on the tribes of southern California.]

29. BEACH, WM. W. The Indian miscellany. Albany, 1877.

30. BEECHEY, FREDERIC W. Narrative of a voyage to the Pacific and Berings strait, to cooperate with the Polar expeditions. Vols. I–II, London, 1831.

31. BLEDSOE, A. J. Indian wars of the Northwest. San Francisco, 1885.
   [Written from the settler's point of view and without interest in the Indian as such, but contains some glimpses of ethnology.]

32. BOAS, FRANZ. Anthropometrical observations on the Mission Indians of Southern California. Proc. Amer. Asso. Adv. Sci., vol. XLIV, pp. 261–269, 1895.
   [All that there is on the racial type of this group.]

33. ———. Anthropometry of Central California. Bull. Amer. Mus. Nat. Hist., vol. XVII, pt. 4, pp. 347–380, 1905.
   [Maidu, Wintun, Achomawi, Pomo, Yuki, Wailaki.]

34. ———. Notes on the Tillamook. Univ. Cal. Publs. Amer. Archaeol. and Ethnol., vol. XX, no. 1 (in press, 1923).
   [Of comparative value for northwestern California.]

35. ———. Traditions of the Tillamook Indians. Journ. Amer. Folk-lore, vol. XI, pp. 23–38, 133–150, 1898.
   [Some California allusions.]

36. ———. Zur Anthropologie der Nordamerikanischen Indianer. Verhandlungen der Berliner Anthropologischen Gesellschaft, pp. 367–411, May, 1895.
   [Among the mass of summarized data are bodily measurements of several Californian groups.]

37. BODEGA Y QUADRA. Primero viage, 1775. Anuario de la Direccion de Hidrografia, Año III, 1864, Madrid, 1865.

38. BOLTON, H. E., ed. Expedition to San Francisco Bay in 1770. Diary of Pedro Fagés. Univ. Cal., Acad. Pac. Coast Hist., Publs., vol. II, no. 3, pp. [141]–[159], 1911.

39. ———. Father Escobar's relation of the Oñate expedition to California. Catholic Historical Review, vol. V, pp. 19–41, 1919.

40. ———. Kino's Historical Memoir of Pimería Alta. Cleveland, 1919.

41. ———. Spanish exploration in the Southwest, 1542–1706. New York, 1916.
   [Contains authoritative translations of the Relation of Cabrillo, the Diary of Vizcaino, and the Journey of Oñate.]

42. BOSCANA, GERONIMO. Chinigchinich. English translation in Robinson, Alfred, Life in California, New York, 1846. (The Spanish original is probably lost. Alexander Taylor reprinted the English version in the California Farmer, vol. XIII. The Robinson book has also been reprinted, but without the Chinigchinich.)
   [This account of the religion and social customs of the Juaneño is by far the most valuable document on the California Indians preserved from the pen of any of the Franciscan missionaries. It is written in a spirited style, is based on unusually full knowledge, and is done with understanding. The ethnologist with local interest is at times puzzled how much of it to assign to Juaneño and how much to Gabrielino sources.]

43. BOURKE, J. G. Notes on the cosmogony and theogony of the Mojave Indians. Journ. Amer. Folk-lore, vol. II, pp. 169–189, 1889.
   [Excellent material somewhat confused.]

44. BOWERS, STEPHEN. Santa Rosa Island. Rept. Smithson. Inst. for 1877, pp. 316–320, Washington, 1878.

45. BRINTON, DANIEL G. The American Race. New York, 1891.

46. BROWNE, J. ROSS. The Indian reservations of California. Harper's Magazine, August, 1861. Reprinted in Beach, Indian Miscellany, pp. 303–322, Albany, 1877.
   [Vigorous and to the point, but overdrawn.]

47. Buchanan, R. C.   Number, characteristics, etc., of the Indians of California, Oregon, and Washington. H. R. Ex. Doc. No. 76 (Serial no. 906), 34th Cong., 3d sess., Washington, 1857.

48. Burns, L. M.   Digger Indian legends.   Land of Sunshine, vol. xiv, pp. 130–134, 223–226, 310–314, 397–402, 1901.
    [Shasta coyote tales.]

49. Buschmann, J.   Die Sprachen Kizh und Netela von Neu Californien. Abhandlungen der Königlichen Akademie der Wissenschaften zu Berlin, 1855, pp. 499–531, 1856.
    [Gabrielino and Juaneño.]

50. ———.   Die Spuren der Aztekischen Sprache im nördlichen Mexico und höheren amerikanischen Norden. Ibid., 1854, 2d suppl. vol., pp. 1–819, 1859.
    [A monumentally painstaking analysis of the linguistic materials available at the time from northern Mexico, the Southwest, and California.]

51. Caballeria [y Collell, Juan].   History of the city of Santa Barbara. Santa Barbara, 1892.
    [Contains a chapter on a Chumash dialect.]

52. Caballeria, Juan.   History of San Bernardino valley. San Bernardino, 1902.

    Cabrillo, Juan Rodriguez.   See Ferrel, B.

53. Carr, Lucien.   Measurements of crania from California. Twelfth Ann. Rept. Peabody Museum, pp. 497–505, 1880.
    [Skulls from the Santa Barbara region.]

54. ———.   Observations on the crania from the Santa Barbara Islands. Rept. U. S. Geog. Surv. west of the 100th Meridian [Wheeler Surv. Rept.], vol. vii, Archaeology, pp. 277–292, Washington, 1879.

55. Chamisso, Adelbert von.   Reise um die Welt, 1815–1818. Hildburghausen, 1869.

56. Chapman, C. E., ed.   Expedition on the Sacramento and San Joaquin rivers in 1817. Diary of Fray Narciso Duran. Univ. Cal., Acad. Pacific Coast History, Publs., vol. ii, no. 5, pp. [329]–[349], 1911.

57. Chesnut, V. K.   Plants used by the Indians of Mendocino county, California. Cont. U. S. National Herbarium, vol. vii, no. 3, Washington, 1902.

58. Chever, E. E.   The Indians of California. Amer. Naturalist, vol. iv, pp. 129–148, 1870.
    [A pioneer's notes on the Maidu.]

59. Choris, L.   Voyage pittoresque autour du Monde. Paris, 1822. (Includes sections by Cuvier, Chamisso, Gall.)

60. Clark, Galen.   Indians of the Yosemite Valley and vicinity, their history, customs, and traditions. Yosemite, 1904.

61. Clavigero, F. X.   Storia della California. Vols. i–ii. Venice, 1789. Spanish translation, Historia de la Antigua ó Baja California. Mexico, 1852.

    Costansó Miguél.   See Hemert-Engert, Adolph van, and Teggart, Frederick J.

62. Coues, Elliott, ed.   On the trail of a Spanish pioneer. The diary and itinerary of Francisco Garcés, 1775–76. Vols. i–ii. New York, 1900.
    [A well translated and splendidly annotated version of the diary of an intrepid explorer and priest, rich in data of the greatest value. The ethnological comments are by F. W. Hodge.]

63. COVILLE, FREDERICK V.   Notes on the plants used by the Klamath Indians of Oregon. Cont. U. S. Nat. Herbarium, vol. v, no. 2, Washington, 1897.

64. ———. The Panamint Indians of California. Amer. Anthrop., vol. v, pp. 351–361, 1892.
[Brief but good, and there is little else on these people.]

65. ———. Wokas, a primitive food of the Klamath Indians. Rept. U. S. Nat. Mus. for 1902, pp. 727–739, Washington, 1904.
[Model scientific report—clear, concise, exhaustive, and interesting. It shows the possibilities that lie in intelligent ethno-botanical studies.]

66. CULIN, STEWART.   Games of the North American Indians.   Twenty-fourth Rept. Bur. Amer. Ethn., Washington, 1907.
[California is well represented in this exhaustive monograph.]

67. CURTIN, JEREMIAH.   Achomawi myths.   Edited by Roland B. Dixon. Journ. Amer. Folk-lore, vol. XXII, pp. 283–287, 1909.

68. ———.   Creation myths of primitive America.   Boston, 1898.
[9 Wintun and 13 Yana myths, told at length with the stylistic peculiarities and comments characteristic of the author.]

69. ———.   Myths of the Modocs.   Boston, 1912.

70. DALTON, O. M.   Notes on an ethnographical collection.   Intern. Achiv für Ethnog., B. x, pp. 225–245, 1897.

71. DAVIS, EDWARD H.   The Diegueño ceremony of the death images.   Contr. Mus. Am. Indian Heye Found., vol. v, no. 2, pp. 7–33, 1919.

72. ———.   Early cremation ceremonies of the Luiseño and Diegueño Indians of Southern California.   Indian Notes and Monographs, vol. VII, no. 3, pp. 87–110, 1921.

73. DIXON, ROLAND B.   Achomawi and Atsugewi tales.   Journ. Amer. Folk-lore, vol. XXI, pp. 159–177, 1908.

74. ———.   Basketry designs of the Maidu Indians of California.   Amer. Anthrop., n. s. vol. II, pp. 266–276, 1900.

75. ———.   Basketry designs of the Indians of Northern California.   Bull. Amer. Mus. Nat. Hist., vol. XVII, pp. 1–32, 1902.

76. ———.   The Chimariko Indians and language.   Univ. Cal. Publs. Amer. Archaeol. and Ethnol., vol. v, pp. 293–380, 1910.
[The results of a study undertaken just prior to the extinction of this tribe.]

77. ———.   Linguistic relationships within the Shasta-Achomawi stock. International Congress of Americanists, XVth sess., vol. II, pp. 255–263, Quebec, 1907.

78. ———.   Maidu: an illustrative sketch.   Bull. 40, Bur. Amer. Ethn. (Handbook of American Indian Languages), pt. 1, pp. 683–734, Washington, 1911.
[A rather complete account of Maidu grammar.]

79. ———.   Maidu myths.   Bull. Amer. Mus. Nat. Hist., vol. XVII, pp. 33–118, 1902.
[Perhaps the most generally interesting collection of native traditions ever made in California.]

80. ———.   Maidu texts.   Publs. Amer. Ethnol. Soc., vol. IV, 1912.
[The only considerable body of texts published in any Californian language except Athabascan, Yana, and Klamath-Modoc.]

81. ———.   The mythology of the Shasta-Achomawi.   Amer. Anthrop., n. s. vol. VII, pp. 607–612, 1905.

82. DIXON, ROLAND B.   The Northern Maidu.   Bull. Amer. Mus. Nat. Hist., vol. XVII, pp. 119–346, 1905.
[Easily the most comprehensive and valuable ethnological study of any one group of California Indians.]

83. ———.   Notes on the Achomawi and Atsugewi of northern California. Amer. Anthrop., n. s. vol. X, pp. 208–220, 1908.
[Brief, but the best there is on these people.]

84. ———.   Outlines of Wintun grammar.   Putnam Anniversary Volume, pp. 461–476, New York, 1909.
[All that is known of the structure of this important tongue.]

85. ———.   The pronominal dual in the languages of California.   Boas Anniversary Volume, pp. 80–84, New York, 1906.

86. ———.   The Shasta.   Bull. Amer. Mus. Nat. Hist., vol. XVII, pp. 381–498, 1907.
[Second only to the author's " Northern Maidu " in value.]

87. ———.   The Shasta-Achomawi: a new linguistic stock with four new dialects.   Amer. Anthrop., n. s. vol. VII, pp. 213–217, 1905.

88. ———.   Shasta myths.   Journ. Amer. Folk-lore, vol. XXIII, pp. 8–37, 364–370, 1910.

89. ———.   Some coyote stories from the Maidu Indians of California.   Ibid., vol. XIII, pp. 267–270, 1900.

90. ———.   Some shamans of northern California.   Ibid., vol. XVII, pp. 23–27, 1904.

91. ———.   System and sequence in Maidu mythology.   Ibid., vol. XVI, pp. 32–36, 1903.

92. DIXON, ROLAND B., *and* KROEBER, A. L.   Linguistic families in California. Univ. Cal. Publs. Amer. Archaeol. and Ethnol., vol XVI, pp. 47–118, 1919.

93. ———.   The native languages of California.   Amer. Anthrop., n. s. vol. V, pp. 1–26, 1903.
[A classification of stocks according to types.]

94. ———.   New linguistic families in California.   Ibid., n. s. vol. XV, pp. 647–655, 1913.

95. ———.   Numerical systems of the languages of California.   Ibid., n. s. vol. IX, 663–690, 1907.

96. ———.   Relationship of the Indian languages of California.   Science, n. s. vol. XXXVII, p. 225, 1913.

97. DORSEY, GEORGE A.   Certain gambling games of the Klamath Indians. Amer. Anthrop., n. s. vol. III, pp. 14–27, 1901.

98. ———.   Indians of the Southwest.   1903.
[This exceedingly useful handbook, issued by the Atchison, Topeka, and Santa Fe Railway System, contains notes on Mohave, Chemehuevi, Yuma, Yokuts, Mono, and Miwok on pp. 193–216.]

99. DORSEY, J. OWEN.   The Gentile system of the Siletz tribes.   Journ. Amer. Folk-lore, vol. III, pp. 227–237, 1890.
[The " gentes " are villages.   The Californian Tolowa are included.]

DRAKE, SIR FRANCIS.   *See* Early English Voyages; *and* Barrett, S. A., the ethno-geography of the Pomo and neighboring Indians.

100. DuBois, CONSTANCE GODDARD.   Diegueño mortuary ollas.   Amer. Anthrop., n. s. vol. IX, pp. 484–486, 1907.

101. DuBois, Constance Goddard. Diegueño myths and their connections with the Mohave. International Congress of Americanists, XVth sess., 1906, vol. II, pp. 129–134, Quebec, 1907.

102. ——. The mythology of the Diegueños. Jour. Amer. Folk-lore, vol. XIV, pp. 181–185, 1901.

103. ——. The mythology of the Diegueños. International Congress of Americanists, XIIIth sess., New York, 1902, pp. 101–106, 1905.

104. ——. Mythology of the Mission Indians. Journ. Amer. Folk-lore, vol. XVII, pp. 185–188, 1904.

105. ——. The religion of the Luiseño and Diegueño Indians of Southern California. Univ. Cal. Publs. Amer. Archaeol. and Ethnol., vol. VIII, pp. 69–186, 1908.
[An unusually sympathetic portrayal of a remarkable native religion.]

106. ——. Religious ceremonies and myths of the Mission Indians. Amer. Anthrop., n. s. vol. VII, pp. 620–629, 1905.

107. ——. The story of the Chaup: a myth of the Diegueños. Journ. Amer. Folk-lore, vol. XVII, pp. 217–242, 1904.
[Valuable.]

108. ——. Two types or styles of Diegueño religious dancing. International Congress of Americanists, XVth sess., 1906, vol. II, pp. 135–138, Quebec, 1907.

109. Duflot de Mofras, Eugène. Exploration du Territoire de l'Oregon, des Californies, et de la Mer Vermeille. Vols. I–II. Paris, 1844.

Duran, Narciso. See Chapman, C. E.

110. Dutcher, B. H. Piñon gathering among the Panamint Indians. Amer. Anthrop., vol. VI, pp. 377–380, 1893.

111. Early English voyages to the Pacific coast of America. (From their own, and contemporary English, accounts.) Sir Francis Drake.—III. Out West, vol. XVIII, no. 1, pp. 73–80, Jan. 1903. See also Barrett, S. A.
[Perhaps the most readily accessible republication of the passages descriptive of native life in the principal account of Drake's landing in Nova Albion.]

112. Early Western history. From documents never before published in English. Diary of Junipero Serra; Loreto to San Diego, March 28–June 30, 1769. Out West, vol. XVI, pp. 293–296, 399–406, 513–518, 635–642, 1902; vol. XVII, pp. 69–76, 1902.
[Mostly Baja California, but there is some mention of the people later called Diegueño.]

113. Eisen, Gustav. An Account of the Indians of the Santa Barbara Islands in California. Sitzungsberichte der Königlichen Boehmischen Gesellschaft der Wissenschaften, II Klasse, Prag, 1904.
[A compilation done with intelligence.]

114. Elliott, W. W., and Company, publishers, History of Humboldt County, California. San Francisco, 1881.

115. Emory, W. H. Notes of a military reconnaissance from Fort Leavenworth in Missouri to San Diego in California, made in 1846–47. Washington, 1848.

116. ——. United States and Mexican Boundary Survey. Report. Vol. I. Washington, 1857. (H. R. Ex. Doc. 135, 34th Cong., 1st sess.)

117. ENGELHARDT, ZEPHRYIN. Franciscans in California. Harbor Springs, Michigan, 1897.
    [A considerable number of facts about the Indians, mostly from sources otherwise accessible with difficulty, are included in this story of the missions and missionaries.]

118. ———. The missions and missionaries of California. Vols. I–IV. San Francisco, 1908–1914.
    [An important history, containing many passages of ethnological moment.]

EWBANK, THOMAS. See Whipple, A. W., Ewbank and Turner.

FAGÉS, PEDRO. See Bolton, H. E.; Priestley, H. I.; Ternaux-Compans, Henri.

119. FARRAND, LIVINGSTON. Notes on the Alsea Indians of Oregon. Amer. Anthrop., n. s. vol. III, pp. 239–247, 1901.
    [Of service for comparisons with the tribes of northwestern California.]

120. ———. Shasta and Athapascan myths from Oregon. Edited by L. J. Frachtenberg. Journ. Amer. Folk-lore, vol. XXVIII, pp. 207–242, 1915.

FASSIN, A. G. See Tassin.

121. FAYE, PAUL-LOUIS. Notes on the Southern Maidu. Univ. Cal. Publs. Amer. Archaeol. and Ethnol., vol. XX, no. 3 (in press, 1923).

122. FERREL, B. Relation or diary of the voyage which Rodriguez Cabrillo made. Translation with notes by H. W. Henshaw. Rept. U. S. Geog. Surv. west of the 100th Meridian [Wheeler Surv. Rept.], vol. VII, Archaeology, pp. 293–314, Washington, 1879. Transl. in Bolton, Spanish exploration in the Southwest, pp. 13–39, New York, 1916.

FONT, PEDRO. See Teggert, Frederick J., ed.

123. FORBES, ALEXANDER. A history of lower and upper California. London, 1839.

124. FREDERICK, M. C. Some Indian paintings. Land of Sunshine, vol. XV, no. 4, pp. 223–227, 1901.
    [Pictographs near Santa Barbara.]

125. FREELAND, L. S. Pomo doctors and poisoners. Univ. Cal. Publs. Amer. Archaeol. and Ethnol., vol. XX, no 4 (in press, 1923).

126. FRÉMONT, J. C. The exploring expedition to the Rocky Mountains, Oregon and California. Auburn and Buffalo, 1854.

127. ———. Geographical memoir upon Upper California. Washington, 1848.

128. ———. Report of an exploring expedition to Oregon and northern California. Washington, 1845.

129. FRIEDERICI, GEORG. Die Schiffahrt der Indianer. Stuttgart, 1907.

130. FRY, WINIFRED S. Humboldt Indians. Out West, vol. XXI, pp. 503–514, 1904.

131. GALIANO, D. A. Relacion del viage hecho por las goletas Sutil y Mexicana. Madrid, 1802.

132. GALLATIN, ALBERT. Hale's Indians of Northwest America. Trans. Amer. Ethn. Soc., vol. II, pp. xxiii–clxxxviii, 1–130, New York, 1848.
    [Includes Californian groups.]

133. ———. A synopsis of the Indian tribes in North America. Trans. Amer. Antiq. Soc. (Archaeologia Americana), vol. II, 1836.

GARCÉS, FRANCISCO. See Coues, Elliott, ed.

134. GATSCHET, ALBERT S. Analytical report upon Indian dialects spoken in southern California. U. S. Geog. Surv. west of the 100th Meridian, Ann. Rept. [of the Chief of Engineers] for 1876, Appendix JJ, pp. 550–563, Washington, 1876.

135. ———. Classification into seven linguistic stocks of western Indian dialects contained in forty vocabularies. Rept. U. S. Geog. Surv. west of the 100th Meridian [Wheeler Surv. Rept.], vol. VII, Archaeology, pp. 403–485, 1879.

136. ———. Indian languages of the Pacific states and territories. Magazine of Amer. Hist., March, 1877.

137. ———. The Klamath Indians of southwestern Oregon. Cont. N. Amer. Ethnol., vol. II, pts. 1 and 2, Washington, 1890.
   [An enormous and carefully done monograph, mainly texts, grammar, and dictionary, also an ethnographic sketch. The Modoc are included with the Klamath.]

138. ———. Songs of the Modoc Indians. Amer. Anthrop., vol. VII, pp. 26–31, 1894.

139. ———. Specimen of the Chûmĕto language. American Antiquarian, vol. V, pp. 71–73, 173–180, 1883.
   [Sketch of the Southern Miwok dialect.]

140. ———. Der Yuma-Sprachstamm. Zeitschrift für Ethnologie, B. IX, pp. 341–350, 366–418, 1877; B. XV, pp. 123–147, 1883; B. XVIII, pp. 97–122, 1886.
   [Scholarly work on crude materials. The contribution should by now be long out of date, but investigations of this stock have been neglected, and the work remains of value.]

141. ———. Zwölf Sprachen aus dem Südwesten Nord-Amerikas. Weimar, 1876.

142. GIBBS, GEORGE. Journal of the Expedition of Colonel Redick M'Kee . . . through Northwestern California . . . in 1851. In Schoolcraft, Indian Tribes, vol. III, pp. 99–177, Phila., 1853.
   [A valuable report.]

143. ———. Observations on some of the Indian dialects of Northern California. Ibid., pp. 420–423. Continued under the title " Vocabularies of Indian languages in Northwest California." Ibid., pp. 428–445.

144. ———. Tribes of western Washington and northwestern Oregon. Cont. N. Amer. Ethnol., vol. I, pp. 157–241, Washington, 1877.
   [Contains some allusions to California and is important for comparisons of the Indians of California with those farther north.]

145. GIFFORD, EDWARD WINSLOW. California kinship terminologies. Univ. Cal. Publs. Amer. Archaeol. and Ethnol., vol. XVIII, pp. 1–285, 1922.
   [The fullest study of the kind attempted for any area.]

146. ———. Clans and moieties in Southern California. Ibid., vol. XIV, pp. 155–219, 1918.

147. ———. Composition of California shellmounds. Ibid., vol. XII, pp. 1–29, 1916.
   [Bears on questions of fauna, topographic change, age, etc.]

148. ———. Dichotomous social organization in south central California. Ibid., vol. XI, pp. 291–296, 1916.

149. ———. Miwok moieties. Ibid., vol. XII, pp. 139–194, 1916.
   [A thorough account of the organization of society.]

150. ———. Miwok myths. Ibid., vol. XII, pp. 283–338, 1917.

151. GIFFORD, EDWARD WINSLOW. Pomo lands on Clear Lake. Ibid., vol. xx, no. 5 (in press, 1923).

152. ———. Tübatulabal and Kawaiisu kinship terms. Ibid., vol. xii, pp. 219–248, 1917.

153. GODDARD, PLINY EARLE. Athapascan (Hupa). Bull. 40, Bur. Amer. Ethn. (Hankbook of American Indian Languages), pt. 1, pp. 85–158, Washington, 1911.

154. - ———. Chilula texts. Univ. Cal. Publs. Amer. Archaeol. and Ethnol., vol. x, pp. 289–379, 1914.

155. ———. Elements of the Kato language. Ibid., vol. xi, pp. 1–176, 1912.

156. ———. Habitat of the Wailaki. Ibid., vol. xx, no. 6 (in press, 1923).

157. ———. Hupa texts. Ibid., vol. i, pp. 89–368, 1904.
    [The first of a valuable series of collections of texts from the Athabascan languages of California by this author.]

158. ———. The Kato Pomo not Pomo. Amer. Anthrop., n. s. vol. v, pp. 375–376, 1903.

159. ———. Kato texts. Univ. Cal. Publs. Amer. Archaeol. and Ethnol., vol. v, pp. 65–238, 1909.

160. ———. Lassik tales. Journ. Amer. Folk-lore, vol. xix, pp. 133–140, 1906.

161. ———. Life and culture of the Hupa. Univ. Cal. Publs. Amer. Archaeol. and Ethnol., vol. i, pp. 1–88, 1903.
    [The best written general monograph on a California tribe, and the first coherent picture of the culture of northwestern California. The only defect of the work is its brevity.]

162. ———. The morphology of the Hupa language. Ibid., vol iii, 1905.
    [An exhaustive grammar.]

163. ———. Notes on the Chilula Indians of northwestern California. Ibid., vol. x, pp. 265–288, 1914.
    [Sums up what is known.]

164. ———. The phonology of the Hupa language. Ibid., vol. v, pp. 1–20, 1907.

165. ———. Wayside shrines in northwestern California. Amer. Anthrop., n. s., vol., xv, pp. 702–703, 1913.

166. HALDEMAN, S. S. Beads. Rept. U. S. Geog. Surv. west of the 100th meridian [Wheeler Surv. Rept.], vol. vii, Archaeology, pp. 263–271, 1879.

167. HALE, HORATIO. Ethnology and philology. U. S. Exploring Expedition during the years 1838–1842, under the command of Charles Wilkes, U. S. N. Vol. vi. Phila., 1846.

168. HALL, SHARLOT M. The burning of a Mojave chief. Out West, vol. xviii, pp. 60–65, 1903.

169. HARDACRE, EMMA C. Eighteen years alone. Scribner's Monthly, pp. 657–664, September, 1880.
    [The story of the lone woman of San Nicolas Island, the last of her people.]

170. HARRINGTON, JOHN PEABODY. A Yuma account of origins. Journ. Amer. Folk-lore, vol. xxi, pp. 324–348, 1908.
    [An important scholarly presentation.]

HELMERSEN, G. VON. See Baer, K. E. von, and Helmersen.

171. HEMERT–ENGERT, ADOLPH VAN, and TEGGART, FREDERICK J., eds. The narrative of the Portolá expedition of 1769–1770, by Miguel Costanso. Univ. Cal. Acad. Pac. Coast Hist., Publs. vol. i, no. 4, pp. [91]–[159], 1910.

172. HENLY, THOMAS J. California Indians. In Schoolcraft, Indian Tribes, vol. VI, Table XXXV, pp. 715–718, Phila., 1857.

173. HENSHAW, H. W. The aboriginal relics called "Sinkers" or "Plummets." Amer. Journ. Archaeol., vol. I, pp. 105–114, 1885.

174. ———. A new linguistic family in California. Amer. Anthrop., vol. III, pp. 45–49, 1890.
    [Esselen.]

175. ———. Perforated stones from California. Bull. 2, Bur. Amer. Ethn., Washington, 1887.
    [Concise, definite, and convincing.]

176. HEYE, GEORGE G. Certain aboriginal pottery from Southern California. Indian Notes and Monographs, vol. VII, no. 1, pp. [1]–[46]. 1919.

177. ———. Certain artifacts from San Miguel Island, California. Ibid., no. 4, pp. [1]–[211]. 1921.

178. HISTORY OF MENDOCINO COUNTY, CALIFORNIA. [Lyman L. Palmer, historian. Sometimes cited as by Alley Bowen and Company, the publishers.] San Francisco, 1880.

179. HISTORY OF NAPA AND LAKE COUNTIES, CALIFORNIA. [Lyman L. Palmer, historian. Sometimes cited under Slocum, Bowen and Company, the publishers.] San Francisco, 1880.

180. HITTELL, THEODORE H. History of California. Vols. I–IV. San Francisco, 1885–1897.

181. HODGE, F. W., ed. Handbook of American Indians North of Mexico. Bull. 30, Bur. Amer. Ethn., pts. 1–2, Washington, 1907–1910.
    HODGE, F. W. See Coues, Elliott, ed.

182. HOFFMAN, W. T. Hugo Reid's account of the Indians of Los Angeles county, California. Bull. Essex Institute, vol. XVII, 1885. [See Reid, Hugo.]

183. ———. Miscellaneous ethnographic observations on Indians inhabiting Nevada, California, and Arizona. Tenth Ann. Rept. U. S. Geol. and Geog. Surv. [Hayden Survey], Washington, 1878.

184. ———. Remarks on aboriginal art in California and Queen Charlotte's Island. Proc. Davenport Acad. Nat. Sci., vol. IV, pp. 105–122, 1884.
    [Petroglyphs.]

185. HOLDER, C. F. The ancient islanders of California. Pop. Sci. Mo., pp. 658–662, March, 1896.

186. HOLMES, WILLIAM H. Anthropological studies in California. Rept. U. S. Nat. Mus. for 1900, pp. 155–188, Washington, 1902.
    [A traveler's observations on various groups of Indians from the Maidu to the Diegueño, incidental to studies of the antiquity of man, done with a master hand. The paper is as exact as it is readable.]

187. ———. Preliminary revision of the evidence relating to auriferous gravel man in California. Amer. Anthrop., n. s. vol. I, pp. 107–121, 614–645, 1899. Reprinted in Smithsonian Report for 1899, pp. 419–472, Washington, 1901.
    [The findings are negative, but in the best manner of this lucid and brilliant master.]

188. HOOPER, LUCILE. The Cahuilla Indians. Univ. Cal. Publs. Amer. Archaeol. and Ethnol., vol. XVI, pp. 315–380, 1920.

189. HOUGH, WALTER. Primitive American armor. Rept. U. S. Nat. Mus. for 1893, pp. 625–651, Washington, 1895.

190. HRDLIČKA, ALEŠ. Contribution to the physical anthropology of California. Univ. Cal. Publs. Amer. Archaeol. and Ethnol., vol. IV, pp. 49–64, 1906.
       [A careful study of skulls from central California.]

191. ——. Skeletal remains suggesting or attributed to early man in North America. Bull. 33, Bur. Amer. Ethn., Washington, 1907.

192. ——. Stature of Indians of the Southwest and of northern Mexico. Putnam Anniversary Volume, pp. 405–426, New York, 1909.
       [Includes the lower Colorado tribes.]

193. HUDSON, J. W. An Indian myth of the San Joaquin Basin. Journ. Amer. Folk-lore, vol. XV, pp. 104–106, 1902.

194. ——. Pomo basket makers. Overland Monthly, 2d ser., vol. XXI, pp. 561–578, 1893.

195. ——. Pomo wampum makers. Ibid., vol. XXX, pp. 101–108, 1897.

196. HUMBOLDT, F. H. ALEXANDER DE. Essai politique sur le Royaume de la Nouvelle-Espagne. Vols. I–V, Paris, 1811. Translated by John Black, vols. I–IV, London, 1811.

197. INDIAN AFFAIRS (U. S.). Office of Indian Affairs (War Department). Reports, 1825–1848. Report of the Commissioner (Department of the Interior), 1849–1917.

198. JACKSON, HELEN M. H., and KINNEY, ABBOT. Report on the condition and needs of the Mission Indians of California. Washington, 1883.

199. JAMES, GEORGE WHARTON. Indian basketry. New York, 1904.

200. ——. The legend of Tauquitch and Algoot. Journ. Amer. Folk-lore, vol. XVI, pp. 153–159, 1903.

201. ——. A Saboba origin-myth. Journ. Amer. Folk-lore, vol. XV, pp. 36–39, 1902.

202. JOHNSTON, ADAM. The California Indians—their manners, customs, and history. In Schoolcraft, Indian Tribes, vol. IV, pp. 221–226, Phila., 1854.

203. JOHNS[T]ON, ADAM. Indian tribes, or bands, of the Sacramento Valley, California. In Schoolcraft, Indian Tribes, vol. VI, Table XXIX, p. 710, Phila., 1857.

204. ——. Languages of California. Ibid., vol. IV, pp. 406–415, Phila., 1854.

205. JOHNSTON, ADAM. [Report on the Indians of the Sacramento river and the Sierra Nevada.] Report of the Commissioner of Indian Affairs for 1850, pp. 122–125. (Sen. Ex. Docs. vol. I, 31st Cong., 2d sess.)

206. JONES, PHILIP MILLS. Mound Excavations near Stockton. Univ. Cal. Pub. Amer. Archaeol. and Ethnol., vol. XX, no. 7 (in press, 1923).

207. KELSEY, C. E. Report of the Special Agent for California Indians. Carlisle, Pa., 1906.

208. KERN, E. M. Indian customs of California. In Schoolcraft, Indian Tribes, vol. V, pp. 649–650, Phila., 1855.

KINNEY, ABBOT. See Jackson, Helen M. H., and Kinney.

KINO, FATHER. See Bolton, H. E.

KOSTROMITONOW. See Baer, K. E. von.

209. KOTZEBUE, OTTO VON. Voyage of discovery into the South Sea and Behring's Strait, 1815–1818. Translated by H. F. Lloyd. Vols. I–III. London, 1821.

210. KRAUSE, FRITZ. Die kultur der kalifornischen Indianer in ihrer bedeutung für die ethnologie und die nordamerikanische völkerkunde. Institut für Völkerkunde, erste Reihe, Bd. 4, pp. 1–98, Leipzig, 1921.
[A scholarly interpretation.]

211. KROEBER, A. L. The anthropology of California. Science, n. s. vol. XXVII, pp. 281–290, 1908.

212. ———. The archaeology of California. Putnam Anniversary Volume, pp. 1–42, New York, 1909.

213. ———. Basket designs of the Indians of northwestern California. Univ. Cal. Publs. Amer. Archaeol. and Ethnol., vol. II, pp. 104–164, 1905.

214. ———. Basket designs of the Mission Indians of California. Anthrop. Pap. Amer. Mus. Nat. Hist., vol. XX, pp. 147–183, 1922.

215. ———. At the bedrock of history. Sunset [Magazine], vol. XXV, pp. 255–260, 1910.
[An archeological discovery in the San Joaquin valley.]

216. ———. California basketry and the Pomo. Amer. Anthrop., n. s., vol. XI, pp. 233–249, 1909.

217. ———. California culture provinces. Univ. Cal. Publs. Amer. Archaeol. and Ethnol., vol. XVII, pp. 151–169, 1920.

218. ———. California kinship systems. Ibid., vol. XII, pp. 339–396, 1917.

219. ———. California place names of Indian origin. Ibid., vol. XII, pp. 31–69, 1916.

220. ———. The Chumash and Costanoan languages. Ibid., vol. IX, pp. 237–271, 1910.

221. ———. The coast Yuki of California. Amer. Anthrop., n. s. vol. V, pp. 729–730, 1903.

222. ———. The dialectic divisions of the Moquelumnan family. Ibid., n. s. vol. VIII, pp. 652–663, 1906.

223. ———. Elements of culture in native California. Univ. Cal. Publs. Amer. Archaeol. and Ethnol., vol. XIII, pp. 259–328, 1922.

224. ———. Ethnography of the Cahuilla Indians. Ibid., vol. VIII, pp. 29–68, 1908.

225. ———. On the evidences of the occupation of certain regions by the Miwok Indians. Ibid., vol. VI, pp. 369–380, 1908.

226. ———. A Ghost dance in California. Journ. Amer. Folk-lore, vol. XVII, pp. 32–35, 1904.

227. ———. The history of native culture in California. Univ. Cal. Publs. Amer. Archaeol. and Ethnol., vol. XX, no. 8 (in press, 1923).

228. ———. Indian myths from south central California. Ibid., vol. IV, pp. 167–250, 1907.
[Mainly Yokuts, but also Miwok and Costanoan tales, and comparisons.]

229. ———. Ishi, the last aborigine. World's Work, pp. 304–308, July, 1912.

230. ———. The languages of the coast of California north of San Francisco. Univ. Cal. Publs. Amer. Archaeol. and Ethnol., vol. IX, pp. 273–435, 1911.
[Miwok, Pomo, Yuki, Wiyot, Yurok, Karok.]

231. ———. The languages of the coast of California south of San Francisco. Ibid., vol. II, pp. 29–80, 1904.
[Chumash, Salinan, Esselen, Costanoan.]

232. KROEBER, A. L.* A Mission record of the California Indians. Ibid., vol. VIII, pp. 1–27, 1908.

233. ———. Notes on Shoshonean dialects of southern California. Ibid., vol. VIII, pp. 235–269, 1909.

234. ———. Origin tradition of the Chemehuevi Indians. Journ. Amer. Folk-lore, vol. XXI, pp. 240–242, 1908.

235. ———. Phonetic constituents of the native languages of California. Univ. Cal. Publs. Amer. Archaeol. and Ethnol., vol. X, pp. 1–12, 1911.

236. ———. Phonetic elements of the Mohave language. Ibid., pp. 45–96.

237. ———. Preliminary sketch of the Mohave Indians. Amer. Anthrop., n. s. vol. IV, pp. 276–285, 1902.

238. ———. The religion of the Indians of California. Univ. Cal. Publs. Amer. Archaeol. and Ethnol., vol. IV, pp. 319–356, 1907.

239. ———. Serian, Tequistlatecan, and Hokan. Ibid., vol. XI, pp. 279–290, 1915.

240. ———. Shoshonean dialects of California. Ibid., vol. IV, pp. 65–166, 1907.
[Contains considerable ethno-geography and a tribal classification.]

241. ———. Two myths of the Mission Indians of California. Journ. Amer. Folk-lore, vol. XIX, pp. 309–321, 1906.

242. ———. Types of Indian culture in California. Univ. Cal. Publs. Amer. Archaeol. and Ethnol., vol. II, pp. 81–103, 1904.

243. ———. The Washo language of east central California and Nevada. Ibid., vol. IV, pp. 251–317, 1907.

244. ———. Wishosk myths. Journ. Amer. Folk-lore, vol. XVIII, pp. 85–107, 1905.
[Wiyot.]

245. ———. Wiyot folk-lore. Ibid., vol. XXI, pp. 37–39, 1908.

246. ———. The Yokuts and Yuki languages. Boas Anniversary Volume, pp. 64–79, New York, 1906.

247. ———. The Yokuts language of south central California. Univ. Cal. Publs. Amer. Archaeol. and Ethnol., vol. II, pp. 165–377, 1907.
[Contains a classification of tribes.]

248. ———. Yokuts names. Journ. Amer. Folk-lore, vol. XIX, pp. 142–143, 1906.

249 ———. Yuman tribes of the Lower Colorado. Univ. Cal. Publs. Amer. Archaeol. and Ethnol., vol. XVI, pp. 475–485, 1920.

———. See Dixon, Roland B., and Kroeber.

250. KROEBER, HENRIETTE ROTHSCHILD. Wappo myths. Journ. Amer. Folk-lore, vol. XXI, pp. 321–323, 1908.

251. LANGSDORFF, G. H. VON. Voyages and travels, 1803–1807. Vols. I–II. London, 1813–14. Translation of: Bemerkungen auf einer Reise um die Welt. Frankfurt, 1812.

252. LATHAM, R. G. On the languages of New California. Proc. Philol. Soc. London, 1852–53, vol. VI, pp. 72–86, London, 1854.

253. ———. On the languages of northern, western, and central America. Trans. Philol. Soc. London, 1856, pp. 57–118, London, 1857.

254. ———. Opuscula. Essays chiefly philological and ethnographical. London, 1860.

255. LEWIS, ALBERT BUELL. Tribes of the Columbia valley and the coast of Washington and Oregon. Memoirs of the Amer. Anthrop. Asso., vol. I, pt. 2, pp. 147–209, 1906.
[Important for the study of the relations of the cultures of California to those of the north.]

256. LOEFFELHOLZ, K. VON. Die Zoreisch-Indianer der Trinidad-Bai (Californien). Mitth. Anthrop. Ges. Wien, vol. XXIII, pp. 101–123, 1893.
[Yurok of Tsurau in 1857.]

257. LOEW, OSCAR. Notes upon the ethnology of southern California and adjacent regions. U. S. Geog. Surv. of Terr. west of the 100th Meridian, Ann. Rept. [Chief of Engineers] for 1876, Appendix JJ, Washington, 1876.

258. LOUD, LLEWELLYN L. Ethnogeography and archaeology of the Wiyot territory. Univ. Cal. Publs. Amer. Archaeol. and Ethnol., vol. XIV, pp. 221–436, 1918.
[The first detailed report of archaeological exploration in the north of California.]

259. LOWIE, ROBERT H. Culture connection of California and Plateau Shoshonean tribes. Ibid., vol. XX, no. 9 (in press, 1923).

260. LUMMIS, CHAS. F. The exiles of Cupa. Out West, vol. XVI, pp. 465–479; [continued under the title of] Two days at Mesa Grande, pp. 602–612, 1902.

261. LYON, C. How the Indians made stone arrow-heads. Historical Magazine, vol. III, p. 214, 1859.

262. MALLERY, GARRICK. Pictographs of the North American Indians. Fourth Rept. Bur. Ethn., pp. 3–256, Washington, 1886.
[Pp. 30–33 relate to California.]

263. ———. Picture writing of the American Indians. Tenth Rept. Bur. Ethn., Washington, 1893.
[There are some California data.]

264. McKEE, REDICK. California Coast Tribes north of San Francisco, 1851. In Schoolcraft, Indian Tribes, vol. VI, Table XXX, p. 711, Phila., 1857.

265. ———. Report of expedition leaving Sonoma August 9, 1851 . . . to the Klamath. Sen. Ex. Doc. No. 4 (Serial no. 688), 33d Cong., Special sess., Washington, 1853.

———. See M'Kee, Redick.

266. McKERN, W. C. Functional families of the Patwin. Univ. Cal. Publs. Amer. Archaeol. and Ethnol., vol. XIII, pp. 235–258, 1922.

267. ———. Patwin houses. Ibid., vol. XX, no. 10 (in press, 1923).

McLEAN, JOHN J. See Rau, Charles.

268. MASON, J. ALDEN. The ethnology of the Salinan Indians. Univ. Cal. Publs. Amer. Archaeol. and Ethnol., vol. X, pp. 97–240, 1912.
[A careful comparative study of the broken data available on this group.]

269. ———. The language of the Salinan Indians. Ibid., vol. XIV, pp. 1–154, 1918.

270. ———. The Mutsun dialect of Costanoan, based on the vocabulary of [Arroyo] De la Cuesta. Ibid., vol. XI, pp. 399–472, 1916.
[The author has drawn a grammar and classified list of stems from a disordered phrase-book.]

271. MASON, OTIS T. Aboriginal American basketry. Rept. U. S. Nat. Mus. for 1902, pp. 171–548, Washington, 1904.
[The classic work on the subject, beautifully illustrated. California receives its due share of treatment.]

272. ———. Cradles of the American aborigines. Rept. U. S. Nat. Mus. for 1897, pp. 161–212, Washington, 1889.
[Pp. 178–184 refer to California.]

273. ———. The Ray collection from Hupa Reservation. Ann. Rept. Smithsonian Institution for 1886, pt. 1, pp. 205–239, Washington, 1889.
[The first accurate description of utensils typical of the culture of northwestern California. A few implements from Round Valley and northeastern California have got mixed in: Figures 20–25, 30–31, 35, 38–40, 56, 61–65, 68–69, 111–114.]

274. ———. The throwing-stick in California. Amer. Anthrop., vol. v, p. 66, 1892.

275. MATIEGKA, H. Ueber Schädel und Skelette von Santa Rosa [Island]. Sitzungsberichte der Königlichen Gesellschaft der Wissenschaften, Jahrgang 1904, pp. 1–121, Prag, 1905.
[An exhaustive anthropometric report on new material.]

MAURELLE, ANTONIO. See Barrington, Daines.

276. MENEFEE, C. A. Historical and descriptive sketch book of Napa, Sonoma, Lake, and Mendocino. Napa City, 1873.

277. MEREDITH, H. C. Archaeology of California: Central and Northern California. In Moorehead, W. K., Prehistoric implements, Section ix, pp. 258–294, Cincinnati, [1900].

278. MERRIAM, C. HART. The dawn of the world: myths and weird tales told by the Mewan Indians of California. Cleveland, 1910.
[Prepared for the general public, but contains some priceless fragments of the traditions of perished groups.]

279. ———. Distribution and classification of the Mewan stock of California. Amer. Anthrop., n. s. vol. ix, pp. 338–357, 1907.
[Full of important data on the ethno-geography of the Miwok and their valley neighbors.]

280. ———. Distribution of Indian tribes in the southern Sierra and adjacent parts of the San Joaquin valley, California. Science, n. s. vol. xix, pp. 912–917, 1914.
[An attempt to conform the distribution of Indians to biological life zones. The ethnic data are valuable.]

281. ———. The Indian population of California. Amer. Anthrop., n. s. vol. vii, pp. 594–606, 1905.
[The only serious attempt to approach this subject critically.]

282 ———. Indian village and camp sites in Yosemite Valley. Sierra Club Bulletin, vol. x, pp. 202–209, San Francisco, 1917.

283. ———. Some little-known basket materials. Science, n. s. vol. xvii, p. 826, 1903.

284. ———. Totemism in California. Amer. Anthrop., n. s. vol. x, pp. 558–562, 1908.

285. MERRIAM, JOHN C. Recent cave exploration in California. Amer. Anthrop., n. s. vol. viii, pp. 221–228, 1906.

286. ———. Recent cave exploration in California. International Congress of Americanists, XVth sess., 1906, vol. ii, pp. 139–146, Quebec, 1907.

287. MERRILL, RUTH EARL. Plants used in basketry by the California Indians. Univ. Cal. Publs. Amer. Archaeol. and Ethnol., vol. xx, no. 13 (in press, 1923).

288. MICHELSON, TRUMAN H. Two alleged Algonquian languages of California. Amer. Anthrop., n. s. vol. xvi, pp. 361–367, 1914.
[Wiyot and Yurok.]

289. MILLER, JOAQUIN. Life amongst the Modocs. London, 1873.

290. MILLER, M. L. The so-called California Diggers. Popular Science Monthly, vol. L, pp. 201–214, 1897.

291. ———. Der Untergang der Maidu oder Diggerindianer in Kalifornien. Globus, B. LXXII, pp. 111–113, Braunschweig, 1897.

292. M'KEE, REDICK. Indian population of Northwestern California. In Schoolcraft, Indian Tribes, vol. III, p. 634, Phila., 1853.
———. See McKee, Redick.

293. MÖLLHAUSEN, B. Diary of a journey from the Mississippi to the coasts of the Pacific with a U. S. exploring expedition. Vols. I–II. London, 1860.

294. ———. Wanderungen durch die Prairien und Wüsten des westlichen Nord-amerika. Leipzig, 1860.

295. MOONEY, JAMES. The Ghost-dance religion. Fourteenth Rept. Bur. Ethn., pt. 2, Washington, 1896.
[This monumental and unique work contains brief notices of the Northern Paiute and Washo.]

296. ———. Notes on the Cosumnes tribes of California. Amer. Anthrop., vol. III, pp. 259–262, 1890.
[Data from Col. Z. A. Rice, who "recollects" stone axes, scaffold burial, boiling in clay-lined pits, and terrapin rattles worn on the knee!]

MOOREHEAD, W. K. See Yates, L. G.; Meredith, H. C.

MOURELLE, F. A. See Maurelle.

297. NELSON, E. W. The Panamint and Saline Valley Indians. Amer. Anthrop., vol. IV, pp. 371–372, 1891.

298. NELSON, N. C. The Ellis Landing shellmound. Univ. Cal. Publs. Amer. Archaeol. and Ethnol., vol. VII, pp. 357–426, 1910.
[This and the monograph by Uhle are the only scientific accounts dealing at any length with particular California shellmounds.]

299. ———. Flint working by Ishi. Holmes Anniversary Volume, pp. 397–402, Washington, 1916.

300. ———. Shellmounds of the San Francisco bay region. Univ. Cal. Publs. Amer. Archaeol. and Ethnol., vol. VII, pp. 309–356, 1909.
[The classic paper on the subject. Its only fault is that it leaves off before discussing culture in detail.]

301. O'KEEFE, J. J. The buildings and churches of the Mission of Santa Barbara. Santa Barbara, 1886.

302. OETTEKING, BRUNO. Morphological and metrical variation in skulls from San Miguel Island, California. I, The sutura nasofrontalis. Indian Notes and Monographs, vol. VII, no. 2, pp. [47]–[85], 1920.

OÑATE. See Zárate-Salmerón.

303. PALMER, EDWARD. Plants used by the Indians of the United States. Amer. Nat., vol. XII, pp. 593–606, 646–655, 1878.
[The flora of southern California figures largely in this paper.]

304. PALMER, FRANK M. Nucleus of Southwestern Museum. Out West, vol. XXII, pp. 23–34, 1905.
[Partial description of the Palmer-Campbell collection of southern California archæology.]

305. PALOU, F. Noticias de la Nueva California. Vols. I–IV. San Francisco, 1874.

306. ——. Noticias de las Californias. Documentos para la Historia de Mexico, ser. IV, vols. VI–VII, 1857.

307. ——. Relacion Historica de la vida . . . de . . . Fray Junípero Serra. Mexico, 1787. (*Same*, English trans. by Rev. J. Adam, San Francisco, 1884.)

308. PÉROUSE, J. F. G. DE LA. Voyage autour du monde. Vols. I–IV. Paris, 1797.

309. POPE, SAXTON T. The medical history of Ishi. Univ. Cal. Publs. Amer. Archaeol. and Ethnol., vol. XIII, pp. 175–213, 1920.

310. ——. Yahi archery. Ibid., pp. 103–152, 1918.

PORTOLÁ, G. DE. *See* Teggart, F. J., *ed.*; Smith, Donald E., and Teggart.

311. POWELL, J. W. Indian linguistic families of America north of Mexico. Seventh Rept. Bur. Amer. Ethn., pp. 1–142, Washington, 1891.

312. POWERS, STEPHEN. Aborigines of California: an Indo-Chinese study. Atlantic Monthly, pp. 313–323, March, 1874.
[A wild little speculation.]

313. ——. Tribes of California [and variant titles]. Overland Monthly, 1st ser., vols. VIII–XIV, *passim*, 1872–75.
[The basis of the following.]

314. ——. Tribes of California. Cont. N. Am. Ethn., vol. III, Washington, 1877. (Includes Appendix: Linguistics, by J. W. Powell.)
[The value of this remarkable work has been discussed in the preface. It is fundamental.]

315. PRIESTLEY, HERBERT I., *ed.* The Colorado River campaign, 1781–1782. Diary of Pedro Fagés. Univ. Cal., Acad. Pac. Coast Hist. Publs., vol. III, no. 2, pp. [133]–[233], 1913.

316. PURDY, CARL. Pomo Indian baskets and their makers. Out West, vol. XV, no. 6, pp. 438–449, December, 1901; vol. XVI, no. 1, pp. 8–19; no. 2, pp. 151–158; no. 3, pp. 262–273, 1902.
[Useful.]

317. PUTNAM, F. W. Evidence of the work of man on objects from Quaternary caves in California. Amer. Anthrop., n. s. vol. VIII, pp. 229–235, 1906.

318. ——, *and others.* Reports upon archaeological and ethnological collections from vicinity of Santa Barbara. Rept. U. S. Geog. Surv. west of the 100th Meridian [Wheeler Surv. Rept.], vol. VII, Archaeology, Washington, 1879.
[This comprehensive volume on the region of the archipelago is still the fundamental work on the archaeology of California. It contains sections by C. C. Abbott, Lucien Carr, A. S. Gatschet, S. S. Haldeman, H. W. Henshaw, Paul Schumacher, H. C. Yarrow, which are separately cited.]

319. PUTNAM, G. R. A Yuma cremation. Amer. Anthrop., vol. VIII, pp. 264–267, 1895.

320. RADIN, PAUL. Wappo Texts. First Series. Univ. Cal. Publs. Amer. Archaeol. and Ethnol. (in press, 1923).
[One of the few large collections of native texts from California.]

321. RAU, CHARLES. Prehistoric fishing in Europe and North America. Smithson. Cont. Knowledge, vol. xxv, Washington, 1884.

[Pages 254–256 refer to California shell mounds, especially a site near Cape Mendocino examined by John J. McLean.]

322. READ, CHARLES H. An account of a collection of ethnographical specimens formed during Vancouver's voyage. Journ. Anthrop. Inst. Great Britain and Ireland, vol. xxi, pp. 99–108, 1892.

[Chumash spear thrower, harpoon, etc.]

323. REID, [or RIED] HUGO. The Indians of Los Angeles County. Los Angeles Star, 1852. Republished by Alexander S. Taylor in the California Farmer, vol. xiv, Jan 11–Feb. 8, 1861. [See W. J. Hoffman.]

[The fullest data on the Gabrielino.]

324. RILEY, J. H. Vocabulary of the Kah-we'yah and Kah-so'-wah Indians. Historical Magazine, 2d ser., vol. iii, pp. 238–240, 1868.

[The tribes are Yokuts, the vocabulary is Miwok.]

325. RIVET, PAUL. Recherches anthropologiques sur la Basse Californie. Jour. Soc. Americ., n. s., vol. vi, pp. 147–253, 1909.

326. ROYCE, CHARLES C. Indian land cessions in the United States. Eighteenth Rept. Bur. Amer. Ethn., pt. 2, pp. 521–694, Washington, 1899.

[A useful work. California is of course represented.]

327. RUSSELL, FRANK. The Pima Indians. Twenty-sixth Rept. Bur. Amer. Ethn., pp. 3–389, Washington, 1908.

[An extremely valuable work, describing a tribe usually reckoned as Southwestern but presenting innumerable resemblances to those of the lower Colorado river.]

328. RUST, HORATIO N. A cache of stone bowls in California. Amer. Anthrop., n. s. vol. viii, pp. 686–687, 1906.

329. ——. The obsidian blades of California. Amer. Anthrop., n. s. vol. vii, pp. 688–695, 1905.

330. ——. A puberty ceremony of the Mission Indians. Amer. Anthrop., n. s. vol. viii, pp. 28–32, 1906.

331. SANCHEZ, NELLIE VAN DE GRIFT. Spanish and Indian place names of California. San Francisco, 1914.

[The best general work on the subject.]

332. SAPIR, EDWARD. The fundamental elements of Northern Yana. Univ. Calif. Publs. Amer. Archaeol. and Ethnol., vol. xiii, pp. 215–234, 1922.

333. ——. Luck-stones among the Yana. Journ. Amer. Folk-lore, vol. xxi, p. 42, 1908.

334. ——. Notes on the Takelma Indians of southwestern Oregon. Amer. Anthrop., n. s. vol. ix, pp. 251–275, 1907.

[An invaluable little paper dealing with a region on which practically nothing else is available. The data are only fragments of memories, but the author presents them with such discriminating precision that they picture the culture accurately.]

335. ——. The position of Yana in the Hokan stock. Univ. Cal. Publs. Amer. Archaeol. and Ethnol., vol. xiii, pp. 1–34, 1917.

336. ——. Religious ideas of the Takelma Indians of southwestern Oregon. Journ. Amer. Folk-lore, vol. xx, pp. 33–49, 1907.

337. ——. Song recitative in Paiute mythology. Ibid., vol. xxiii, pp. 455–472, 1910.

338. ——. Terms of relationship and the levirate. Amer. Anthrop., n. s. vol. xviii, pp. 327–337, 1916.

[Largely Yahi.]

339. SAPIR, EDWARD.   Text analyses of three Yana dialects.   Univ. Cal. Publs. Amer. Archaeol. and Ethnol., vol. xx, no. 15 (in press, 1923).

340. ———.   Wiyot and Yurok, Algonkin languages of California.   Amer. Anthrop., n. s. vol. xv, pp. 617–646, 1913.

341. ———.   Yana terms of relationship.   Univ. Cal. Publs. Amer. Archaeol. and Ethnol., vol. xiii, pp. 153–173, 1918.

342. ———.   Yana texts.   Ibid., vol. ix, pp. 1–235, 1910.
[A scholarly work, as important ethnologically as philologically.]

343. SCHMIDT, W.   Die Altstämme Nordamerikas.   Festschrift Eduard Seler, pp. 471–502, Stuttgart, 1922.
[Mostly on the tribes of California. A reconstructive historical interpretation of their culture.]

344. SCHOOLCRAFT, HENRY R.   Historical and statistical information, respecting the history, condition and prospects of the Indian tribes of the United States.   Vols. i–vi.   Philadelphia, 1851–57.   Same, printed under the title "Archives of Aboriginal Knowledge," vols. i–vi, Philadelphia, 1860.
[See Gibbs, Henly, Johnson, Kern, M'Kee. There is a California passage by Schoolcraft himself in vol. v, pp. 214–217.]

345. SCHUMACHER, PAUL.   Ancient graves and shell-heaps of California.   Ann. Rept. Smithson. Inst. for 1874, pp. 335–350, Washington, 1875.
[Careful work in the little explored coast region of San Luis Obispo.]

346. ———.   Die anfertigung der angelhaken aus muschelschalen bei den früheren bewohnern der inseln im Santa Barbara Canal.   Arch. für Anthrop., vol. viii, pp. 223–224, 1875.

347. ———.   The method of manufacture of several articles by the former Indians of southern California.   [Eleventh] Ann. Rept. Peabody Mus., vol. ii, pp. 258–268, 1878.
[Stone pots, mortars, digging stick weights, pipes.]

348. ———.   The method of manufacture of soapstone pots.   Rept. U. S. Geog. Surv. west of the 100th meridian [Wheeler Surv. Rept.], vol. vii, Archaeology, pp. 117–121, 1879.

349. ———.   The methods of manufacturing pottery and baskets among the Indians of Southern California.   [Twelfth] Ann. Rept. Peabody Mus., vol. ii, pp. 521–525, 1880.

350. ———.   Remarks on the kjökken-möddings on the northwest coast of America.   Ann. Rept. Smithson. Inst. for 1873, pp. 354–362, Washington, 1874.
[Southern Oregon coast.]

351. ———.   Researches in the kjökkenmöddings and graves of a former population of the Santa Barbara Islands and the adjacent mainland.   Bull. U. S. Geol. Surv., vol. iii, pp. 37–56, Washington, 1877.
[Useful.]

352. SCOULER, JOHN.   Observations on the indigenous tribes of the N. W. coast of America.   Journ. Royal Geog. Soc., vol. xi, pp. 215–249, London, 1841.
[Includes the Coulter vocabularies.]

SERRA, JUNÍPERO.   See Early Western history.

353. SINCLAIR, W. J.   Recent investigations bearing upon the question of the occurrence of Neocene man in the auriferous gravels of California.   Univ. Cal. Publs. Amer. Archaeol. and Ethnol., vol. vii, pp. 107–130, 1908.

354. SITJAR, BONAVENTURE.   Vocabulary of the language of San Antonio Mission, California.   Shea's library of Amer. Linguistics, vol. vii, New York, 1861.

SLOCUM, BOWEN AND COMPANY. *See* History of Napa and Lake Counties, California.

355. SMITH, DONALD E., *and* TEGGART, FREDERICK J., *eds.* Diary of Gaspar de Portolá during the California expedition of 1769–1770. Univ. Cal., Acad. Pacific Coast History, Pubs., vol. I, no. 3, pp. [31]–[89], 1909.

356. SMITH, WAYLAND H. The relief of Campo. Out West, vol. XXII, pp. 13–22, 1905.

357. SPARKMAN, PHILIP STEDMAN. The culture of the Luiseño Indians. Univ. Cal. Publs. Amer. Archaeol. and Ethnol., vol. VIII, pp. 187–234, 1908.
[Compact. Fullest on the material side of the civilization.]

358. ———. A Luiseño tale. Journ. Amer. Folk-lore, vol. XXI, pp. 35–36, 1908.

359. ———. Sketch of the grammar of the Luiseño language. Amer. Anthrop., n. s. vol. VII, pp. 656–662, 1905.

360. SPENCER, D. L. Notes on the Maidu Indians of Butte County. Journ. Amer. Folk-lore, vol. XXI, pp. 242–245, 1908.

361. SPIER, LESLIE. Southern Diegueño customs. Univ. Cal. Publs. Amer. Archaeol. and Ethnol., vol. XX, no. 16 (in press, 1923).

362. SPINDEN, H. J. The Nez Percé Indians. Mem. Amer. Anthrop. Asso., vol. II, pp. 171–274, 1908.
[The best account of a group having many affinities with the Klamath and Modoc.]

363. STEARNS, ROBERT E. C. On certain aboriginal implements from Napa County, California. Amer. Nat., vol. XVI, pp. 203–209, 1882.

364. ———. Ethno-conchology. Rept. U. S. Nat. Mus. for 1887, pp. 297–334, 1889.
[Useful.]

365. ———. On the Nishinam game of " Ha " and the Boston game of " Props." Amer. Anthrop., vol. III, pp. 353–358, 1890.

366. ———. Shell-money. Amer. Nat., vol. III, pp. 1–5, 1869.

367. STEWART, GEORGE W. Two Yokuts traditions. Journ. Amer. Folk-lore, vol. XXI, pp. 237–239, 1908.

368. ———. A Yokuts creation myth. Ibid., vol. XIX, p. 322, 1906.

369. STRATTON, R. B. Captivity of the Oatman girls. New York, 1857.
[Tries hard to be lurid, but a few facts on the Mohave have crept in.]

370. TASSIN [or " FASSIN "], A. G. The Concow Indians. Overland Monthly, 2d ser., vol. IV, pp. 7–14, 1884.

371. ———. Un-koi-to; the Savior. A legend of the Concow Indians. Ibid., pp. 141–150, 1884.

372. TAYLOR, ALEXANDER S. Bibliografa Californica, 1510–1865. Sacramento Union, June 25, 1863–March 13, 1866.

373. ———. Indianology of California. California Farmer and Journal of Useful Sciences, vols. XIII–XX, San Francisco, Feb. 22, 1860, to Oct. 30, 1863.
[A very miscellaneous but famous and valuable collection of data on every aspect of the Indian history of the state. The author was untrained as a scholar, indefatigable in his inquiries, and a most industrious compiler. He obtained access to many rare publications and to a number of manuscript sources no longer available, and omitted nothing that he could publish or republish. Very few files of the California Farmer are extant and a republication of the Indianology, with annotations and corrections of typographical errors, is greatly to be desired.]

374. TEGGART, FREDERICK J., *ed.* The Anza expedition of 1775–1776. Diary of Pedro Font. Univ. Cal., Acad. Pac. Coast Hist., Pubs., vol. III, no. 1, pp. [1]–[131], 1913.

375. ———. The official account of the Portolá expedition of 1769–1770. Ibid., vol. I, no. 2, pp. [15]–[29], 1909.
[The first of a series of important editions and translations of documents bearing on the Spanish exploration of California.]

376. ———. The Portolá expedition of 1769–1770. Diary of Miguel Costansó. Ibid., vol. II, no. 4, pp. [161]–[327], 1911.

TEGGART, FREDERICK J. *See* Smith, Donald E., and Teggart.

377. TEN KATE, H. Materiaux pour servir à l'anthropologie de la presqu'île californienne. Bull. Soc. d'Anthrop., pp. 551–569, 1884.

378. TERNAUX-COMPANS, HENRI, *tr.* Voyage en Californie, par D. Pedro Fagés. Nouvelles Annales des Voyages, vol. CI, pp. 145–182, 311–347, Paris, 1844.
[The Spanish text, with English translation by H. I. Priestley, is in press in Univ. Cal., Acad. Pac. Coast Hist. Publ., under the title, Pedro Fagés, Noticias de Monterey.]

379. THOMPSON, LUCY. To the American Indian. Eureka, California, 1916.
[Written by a Yurok on the Yurok. Valuable.]

TURNER, W. W. *See* Whipple, A. W., Ewbank, and Turner.

380. UHLE, MAX. The Emeryville shellmound. Univ. Cal. Publs. Amer. Archaeol. and Ethnol., vol. VII, pp. 1–106, 1907.
[An exhaustive description and interpretation by an investigator of wide comparative experience.]

381. UNITED STATES DEPARTMENT OF COMMERCE. Bureau of the Census. Indian population in the United States and Alaska, 1910. Washington, 1915.
[The results of the first effort of the Bureau to obtain particular statistics on the Indian, and the only census worth anything as regards the Indians of California. Sections on Number, Tribes, Sex, Age, Fecundity, and Vitality by R. B. Dixon.]

382. U. S. GEOGRAPHICAL SURVEYS OF THE TERRITORY OF THE U. S. WEST OF THE 100TH MERIDIAN, in charge of First Lieut. Geo. M. Wheeler. Reports. Vol. VII, Archaeology, Washington, 1879. (*See* Putnam, F. W.)

383. VANCOUVER, GEORGE. Voyage of discovery to the North Pacific Ocean, and round the world, 1790–95. Vols. I–III. London, 1798.

VAN HEMERT ENGERT, ADOLPH. *See* Hemert-Engert, Adolph van.

384. VENEGAS, MIGUEL. Noticia de la California, y de su conquista temporal y espiritual hasta el tiempo presente. Vols. I–III. Madrid, 1757. *Same,* English trans., vols. I–II, London, 1759; *Same,* French trans., vols. I–III, Paris, 1767.

385. VIZCAINO, SEBASTIAN. Diary of Sebastian Vizcaino, 1602–1603. Transl. in Bolton, Spanish exploration in the Southwest, pp. 52–103, New York, 1916.

VON BAER, K. E. *See* Baer, K. E. von.

VON HELMERSEN, G. *See* Baer, K. E. von, and Helmersen.

386. WARDLE, H. NEWELL. Stone implements of surgery (?) from San Miguel Island, California. Amer. Anthrop., n. s. vol. XV, pp. 656–660, 1913.

387. WASHINGTON, F. B. Customs of the Indians of western Tehama county. Journ. Amer. Folk-lore, vol. XIX, p. 144, 1906.

388. WATERMAN, T. T. Analysis of the Mission Indian creation story. Amer. Anthrop., n. s. vol. XI, 41–55, 1909.

389. WATERMAN, T. T. Diegueño identification of color with the cardinal points. Journ. Amer. Folk-lore, vol. XXI, pp. 40–42, 1908.

390. ———. The last wild tribe of California. Pop. Sci. Mo., pp. 233–244, March, 1915.
[Story of the extinction of the Yahi.]

391. ———. Native musical instruments of California, and some others. Out West, vol. XXVIII, pp. 276–286, 1908.

392. ———. The phonetic elements of the Northern Paiute language. Univ. Cal. Publs. Amer. Archaeol. and Ethnol., vol. X, pp. 13–44, 1911.

393. ———. The religious practices of the Diegueño Indians. Ibid., vol. VIII, pp. 271–358, 1910.
[A vivid and accurate portrayal.]

394. ———. The Yana Indians. Ibid., vol. XIII, pp. 35–102, 1918.

395. ———. Yurok affixes. Ibid., vol. XX, no. 18 (in press, 1923).

396. ———. Yurok geography. Ibid., vol. XVI, pp. 177–314, 1920.
[An exhaustive study of the ethnogeographical basis of a culture, with many references to the culture.]

WHEELER, GEORGE M. See U. S. Geographical Survey West of the 100th Meridian.

397. WHIPPLE, A. W., EWBANK, THOMAS, and TURNER, WM. W. Report upon the Indian tribes. U. S. War Dept. Repts. of Explorations and Surveys . . . for a Railroad from the Mississippi River to the Pacific Ocean, 1853–4, vol. III, Washington, 1855.
[Some useful data on the Mohave and Chemehuevi.]

398. WILKES, CHARLES. Western America, including California and Oregon. Philadelphia, 1849.

———. See Hale, Horatio.

399. WILLOUGHBY, CHARLES C. Feather mantles of California. Amer. Anthrop., n. s. vol. XXIV, pp. 432–437, 1922.

400. WOOD, L. K. The discovery of Humboldt bay. Humboldt Times (Eureka, California), 1856.
[Probably most accessible in W. W. Elliott and Co.'s History of Humboldt County, 1881, one of the innumerable anonymous compilations, avowed only by their publishers, of which H. H. Bancroft's " Works " is the most ambitious and glorified example. Many of the county histories contain data that are not available elsewhere.]

401. WOODRUFF, CHARLES E. Dances of the Hupa Indians. Amer. Anthrop., vol. V, pp. 53–61, 1892.

402. WOODS, ETHEL B. La Piedra Pintada de la Carrisa.
[Privately printed, San Luis Obispo, California.]

403. WOOSLEY, DAVID J. Cahuilla tales. Journ. Amer. Folk-lore, vol. XXI, pp. 239–240, 1908.

404. WOZENCRAFT, O. M. [Report on the Indians of California.] Rept. Com. Ind. Aff. for 1851, pp. 224–231, 242–249, Washington, 1851. (Sen. Ex. Docs. vol. III, 32d Cong., 1st sess.)

405. WRANGELL, FERDINAND VON. Observations recueillies par l'Amiral Wrangell sur les habitants des côtes nord-ouest de l'Amérique; extraites du Russe par M. le prince Emanuel Galitzin. Nouvelles Annales des Voyages, tome I, Paris, 1853.

406. YARROW, H. C. Report of the operations of a special party for making ethnological researches in the vicinity of Santa Barbara. Rept. U. S. Geog. Surv. west of the 100th Meridian [Wheeler Surv. Rept.], vol. VII, Archaeology, pp. 32–46, Washington, 1879.

407. YATES, L. G. Aboriginal weapons of California. Overland Monthly, 2d ser., vol. XXVII, pp. 337–342, 1896.

408. ———. Archaeology of California: Southern California. In Moorehead, W. K., Prehistoric Implements, Section VII, pp. 230–252, Cincinnati, [1900].

409. ———. Charmstones or " plummets " from California. Ann. Rept. Smithson. Inst. for 1886, pp. 296–305, Washington, 1889.

410. ———. The deserted homes of a lost people. Overland Monthly, 2d ser., vol. XXVII, pp. 538–544, 1896.
    [The Chumash islanders.]

411. ———. Fragments of the history of a lost tribe. Amer. Anthrop., vol. IV, pp. 373–376, 1891.

412. ———. Indian medicine men. Overland Monthly, 2d ser., vol. XXVIII, pp. 171–182, 1896.
    [A little on California is included.]

413. ———. Indian petroglyphs in California. Overland Monthly, 2d ser., vol. XXVIII, pp. 657–661, 1896.

414. ———. Prehistoric man in California. Santa Barbara, 1887.

415. ZÁRATE-SALMERÓN. Relacion. Translated in Land of Sunshine, vol. XI, no. 6; vol. XII, nos. 1 and 2, Nov., 1899, to Jan., 1900. Transl. in Bolton, Spanish exploration in the Southwest, pp. 268–280, New York, 1916.
    [Oñate's trip from New Mexico to California in 1604–05. The last section is of the greatest importance for the Yuman tribes of the Colorado.]

CLASSIFICATION OF TITLES BY SUBJECT.

LANGUAGES.

PHYSICAL TYPES.

CLASSIFIED SUBJECT INDEX

A. TANGIBLE CULTURE

BODY AND DRESS:

Body garments, 76, 173, 240, 276, 283, 292, 310, 317, 326, 405, 467, 519, 572, 597, 634, 651, 654, 721, 804.

Robes, capes, 76, 173, 276, 327, 406, 416, 467, 519, 546, 615, 634, 654, 805, 935.

Hats and caps, 76, 92, 155, 173, 311, 327, 332, 467, 532, 548, 561, 591, 597, 654, 698, 700, 807, 808; pl. 2, 53, 55, 71, 73.

Hair nets, 156, 173, 276, 293, 405, 416, 808, 934; pl. 55, 72.

Footgear, 76, 144, 240, 283, 292, 311, 317, 323, 327, 405, 519, 597, 654, 721, 805, 807; pl. 62.

Snowshoe, 76, 295, 327, 405, 410, 807.

Coiffure, 77, 293, 299, 406, 519, 598, 633, 721, 729, 803, 934; pl. 57, 64, 72.

Comb, 327, 406, 519.

Ornaments, 240, 406, 739.

Paint, 56, 186, 729, 730, 732, 733, 765; pl. 61.

Tattoo, 77, 146, 173, 215, 293, 311, 357, 406, 467, 519, 520, 521, 641, 651, 675, 721, 729, 808.

Deformation, mutilations, 77, 240, 311, 326, 406, 519; pl. 65.

Postures, 520, 728.

SUBSISTENCE:

Foods, 40, 84, 144, 174, 238, 309, 323, 358, 409, 467, 523–527, 547, 591, 615, 631, 694, 814.

Food preferences, 88, 293, 411, 649.

Foods, rejected, 84, 111, 216, 310, 409, 526, 547, 631, 652, 737, 814.

Insects, worms, etc., 84, 111, 409, 525, 527, 592, 652; pl. 61.

Fish, mollusks, 84, 409, 467, 525, 722, 737, 920, 922–925, 933.

Nets, weirs, fish traps, 58, 85, 93, 132, 148, 174, 213, 214, 246, 294, 309, 325, 359, 410, 415, 529, 652, 737, 815, 816, 933; pl. 4, 6, 7, 33, 59, 67.

Fishhooks, 326, 564, 652, 815.

Fish poison, 529, 652, 817.

Snaring, trapping, 86, 213, 294, 309, 326, 528, 530, 615, 652, 817; pl. 46.

Surrounding, 144, 409, 528, 817.

Decoys, 86, 342, 359, 410, 528, 652, 817; pl. 8.

Other hunting methods, 144, 174, 294, 295, 326, 395, 410, 530, 652, 652, 817.

Ethnobotany, 649, 694–696.

Digging stick, 563, 736, 935.

Seed beater, 91, 172, 291, 332, 415, 701, 814; pl. 24, 29.

Mortar, pestle, hopper, metate, grinding slab, 87, 91, 148, 153, 172, 214, 284, 291, 323, 358, 411, 448, 527–528, 548, 562, 572, 592, 631, 653, 695–698, 700, 722, 736, 737, 814, 926–930, 932; pl. 16, 24, 44, 45, 60, 66.

Pulverized food, 293, 294, 323, 409, 528, 572, 592, 649, 652, 695, 736, 814.

SUBSISTENCE—Continued.

Storage, 85, 91, 242, 294, 309, 410, 447, 548, 561, 592, 598, 618, 699, 828; pl. 38, 54, 60.

Leaching, 88, 293, 467, 524, 527, 649, 814; pl. 14.

Cooking, 87, 156, 527, 592, 652, 654, 695, 722, 737, 814; pl. 23.

Stirrers, 87, 172, 291, 310, 411, 446, 447, 527, 572, 737, 829; pl. 17, 44.

Spoons, 93, 147, 174, 205, 284, 290, 310, 411; pl. 20.

Salt, 84, 174, 256, 294, 310, 340, 363, 467, 530, 546, 747, 762.

Agriculture, 597, 722, 735, 797, 803, 815; pl. 67.

HOUSES:

Earth house, 175, 276, 290, 312, 317, 327, 340, 358, 365, 407, 447, 572, 654, 704, 721, 731, 809, 811; pl. 56.

Plank house, 12, 18, 39, 78, 140, 289, 809; pl. 9, 10, 12.

Bark house, 111, 140, 141, 144, 146, 175, 213, 240, 284, 311, 317, 358, 407, 447, 468, 522, 572, 809.

Thatch or mat house, 241, 328, 340, 407, 468, 521, 522, 557, 572, 598, 608, 612, 618, 628, 634, 650, 703, 809; pl. 46.

Sweat house and dance house, 12, 41, 80, 140, 141, 144, 147, 156, 175, 189, 205, 213, 241, 284, 290, 312, 317, 328, 358, 365, 375, 387, 446, 447, 468, 522, 557, 572, 591, 608, 618, 628, 655, 703, 704, 722, 735, 793, 810; pl. 10, 13, 14, 56, 60.

Menstrual house, 80, 150, 254, 290, 299, 329, 358, 402, 409, 810.

Camps, shades, 140, 176, 241, 290, 311, 327, 358, 482, 506, 522, 655, 704, 765.

Partitions, beds, 79, 81, 290, 358, 409, 521, 557, 612.

Furniture, 79, 80, 93, 558; pl. 9, 10, 19.

TRANSPORTATION:

Boats, 83, 111, 126, 147, 155, 214, 243, 277, 291, 310, 329, 416, 558, 630, 634, 652, 654, 723, 812–813; pl. 3, 5, 13, 15.

Balsa and raft, 243, 277, 329, 359, 416, 468, 531, 608, 630, 652, 654, 723, 739, 813.

Paddles, 83, 330, 468, 559, 723, 813; pl. 67.

Ferrying, 35, 83, 174, 739, 813.

Carrying basket or frame, 91, 153, 172, 247, 291, 532, 571, 591, 597, 698, 699, 738, 814, 828; pl. 23, 24, 54, 73.

Carrying net, 173, 240, 247, 416, 467, 533, 592, 698, 699, 704, 722, 828.

Water basket (bottle), 533, 561, 571, 591, 597, 605, 628, 634, 701; pl. 53, 55.

Cradle, baby carrier, 92, 248, 291, 323, 327, 358, 534–537, 571, 704, 738, 829; pl. 35, 39, 40.

WEAPONS:

Bow and arrow, 89, 214, 277, 310, 332, 417, 530, 545, 559, 572, 591, 597, 632, 650, 652, 704, 751, 817–818; pl. 18, 78.

Quiver, 90, 323, 417, 752.

Arrow release, 417, 652, 818; pl. 18, 78.

GENERAL INDEX

A CATALOGUE OF SELECTED DOVER BOOKS
IN ALL FIELDS OF INTEREST

A CATALOGUE OF SELECTED DOVER BOOKS
IN ALL FIELDS OF INTEREST

THE NOTEBOOKS OF LEONARDO DA VINCI, edited by J.P. Richter. Extracts from manuscripts reveal great genius; on painting, sculpture, anatomy, sciences, geography, etc. Both Italian and English. 186 ms. pages reproduced, plus 500 additional drawings, including studies for Last Supper, Sforza monument, etc. 860pp. 7⅞ x 10¾. USO 22572-0, 22573-9 Pa., Two vol. set $12.00

ART NOUVEAU DESIGNS IN COLOR, Alphonse Mucha, Maurice Verneuil, Georges Auriol. Full-color reproduction of Combinaisons ornementales (c. 1900) by Art Nouveau masters. Floral, animal, geometric, interlacings, swashes — borders, frames, spots — all incredibly beautiful. 60 plates, hundreds of designs. 9⅜ x 8¹/₁₆. 22885-1 Pa. $4.00

GRAPHIC WORKS OF ODILON REDON. All great fantastic lithographs, etchings, engravings, drawings, 209 in all. Monsters, Huysmans, still life work, etc. Introduction by Alfred Werner. 209pp. 9⅛ x 12¼. 21996-8 Pa. $6.00

EXOTIC FLORAL PATTERNS IN COLOR, E.-A. Seguy. Incredibly beautiful full-color pochoir work by great French designer of 20's. Complete Bouquets et frondaisons, Suggestions pour étoffes. Richness must be seen to be believed. 40 plates containing 120 patterns. 80pp. 9⅜ x 12¼. 23041-4 Pa. $6.00

SELECTED ETCHINGS OF JAMES A. McN. WHISTLER, James A. McN. Whistler. 149 outstanding etchings by the great American artist, including selections from the Thames set and two Venice sets, the complete French set, and many individual prints. Introduction and explanatory note on each print by Maria Naylor. 157pp. 9⅜ x 12¼. 23194-1 Pa. $5.00

VISUAL ILLUSIONS: THEIR CAUSES, CHARACTERISTICS, AND APPLICATIONS, Matthew Luckiesh. Thorough description, discussion; shape and size, color, motion; natural illusion. Uses in art and industry. 100 illustrations. 252pp.
21530-X Pa. $2.50

TEN BOOKS ON ARCHITECTURE, Vitruvius. The most important book ever written on architecture. Early Roman aesthetics, technology, classical orders, site selection, all other aspects. Stands behind everything since. Morgan translation. 331pp.
20645-9 Pa. $3.50

THE CODEX NUTTALL, A PICTURE MANUSCRIPT FROM ANCIENT MEXICO, as first edited by Zelia Nuttall. Only inexpensive edition, in full color, of a pre-Columbian Mexican (Mixtec) book. 88 color plates show kings, gods, heroes, temples, sacrifices. New explanatory, historical introduction by Arthur G. Miller. 96pp. 11⅜ x 8½. 23168-2 Pa. $7.50

AGAINST THE GRAIN (A REBOURS), Joris K. Huysmans. Filled with weird images, evidences of a bizarre imagination, exotic experiments with hallucinatory drugs, rich tastes and smells and the diversions of its sybarite hero Duc Jean des Esseintes, this classic novel pushed 19th-century literary decadence to its limits. Full unabridged edition. Do not confuse this with abridged editions generally sold. Introduction by Havelock Ellis. xlix + 206pp. 22190-3 Paperbound **$2.50**

VARIORUM SHAKESPEARE: HAMLET. Edited by Horace H. Furness; a landmark of American scholarship. Exhaustive footnotes and appendices treat all doubtful words and phrases, as well as suggested critical emendations throughout the play's history. First volume contains editor's own text, collated with all Quartos and Folios. Second volume contains full first Quarto, translations of Shakespeare's sources (Belleforest, and Saxo Grammaticus), Der Bestrafte Brudermord, and many essays on critical and historical points of interest by major authorities of past and present. Includes details of staging and costuming over the years. By far the best edition available for serious students of Shakespeare. Total of xx + 905pp. 21004-9, 21005-7, 2 volumes, Paperbound **$11.00**

A LIFE OF WILLIAM SHAKESPEARE, Sir Sidney Lee. This is the standard life of Shakespeare, summarizing everything known about Shakespeare and his plays. Incredibly rich in material, broad in coverage, clear and judicious, it has served thousands as the best introduction to Shakespeare. 1931 edition. 9 plates. xxix + 792pp. 21967-4 Paperbound $4.50

MASTERS OF THE DRAMA, John Gassner. Most comprehensive history of the drama in print, covering every tradition from Greeks to modern Europe and America, including India, Far East, etc. Covers more than 800 dramatists, 2000 plays, with biographical material, plot summaries, theatre history, criticism, etc. "Best of its kind in English," *New Republic*. 77 illustrations. xxii + 890pp. 20100-7 Clothbound **$10.00**

THE EVOLUTION OF THE ENGLISH LANGUAGE, George McKnight. The growth of English, from the 14th century to the present. Unusual, non-technical account presents basic information in very interesting form: sound shifts, change in grammar and syntax, vocabulary growth, similar topics. Abundantly illustrated with quotations. Formerly *Modern English in the Making*. xii + 590pp. 21932-1 Paperbound **$4.00**

AN ETYMOLOGICAL DICTIONARY OF MODERN ENGLISH, Ernest Weekley. Fullest, richest work of its sort, by foremost British lexicographer. Detailed word histories, including many colloquial and archaic words; extensive quotations. Do not confuse this with the Concise Etymological Dictionary, which is much abridged. Total of xxvii + 830pp. 6½ x 9¼. 21873-2, 21874-0 Two volumes, Paperbound **$10.00**

FLATLAND: A ROMANCE OF MANY DIMENSIONS, E. A. Abbott. Classic of science-fiction explores ramifications of life in a two-dimensional world, and what happens when a three-dimensional being intrudes. Amusing reading, but also useful as introduction to thought about hyperspace. Introduction by Banesh Hoffmann. 16 illustrations. xx + 103pp. 20001-9 Paperbound **$1.50**

THE JOURNAL OF HENRY D. THOREAU, edited by Bradford Torrey, F.H. Allen. Complete reprinting of 14 volumes, 1837-1861, over two million words; the sourcebooks for Walden, etc. Definitive. All original sketches, plus 75 photographs. Introduction by Walter Harding. Total of 1804pp. 8½ x 12¼.
20312-3, 20313-1 Clothbd., Two vol. set $50.00

MASTERS OF THE DRAMA, John Gassner. Most comprehensive history of the drama, every tradition from Greeks to modern Europe and America, including Orient. Covers 800 dramatists, 2000 plays; biography, plot summaries, criticism, theatre history, etc. 77 illustrations. 890pp. 20100-7 Clothbd. $10.00

GHOST AND HORROR STORIES OF AMBROSE BIERCE, Ambrose Bierce. 23 modern horror stories: The Eyes of the Panther, The Damned Thing, etc., plus the dreamessay Visions of the Night. Edited by E.F. Bleiler. 199pp. 20767-6 Pa. $2.00

BEST GHOST STORIES, Algernon Blackwood. 13 great stories by foremost British 20th century supernaturalist. The Willows, The Wendigo, Ancient Sorceries, others. Edited by E.F. Bleiler. 366pp. USO 22977-7 Pa. $3.00

THE BEST TALES OF HOFFMANN, E.T.A. Hoffmann. 10 of Hoffmann's most important stories, in modern re-editings of standard translations: Nutcracker and the King of Mice, The Golden Flowerpot, etc. 7 illustrations by Hoffmann. Edited by E.F. Bleiler. 458pp. 21793-0 Pa. $3.95

BEST GHOST STORIES OF J.S. LEFANU, J. Sheridan LeFanu. 16 stories by greatest Victorian master: Green Tea, Carmilla, Haunted Baronet, The Familiar, etc. Mostly unavailable elsewhere. Edited by E.F. Bleiler. 8 illustrations. 467pp.
20415-4 Pa. $4.00

SUPERNATURAL HORROR IN LITERATURE, H.P. Lovecraft. Great modern American supernaturalist brilliantly surveys history of genre to 1930's, summarizing, evaluating scores of books. Necessary for every student, lover of form. Introduction by E.F. Bleiler. 111pp. 20105-8 Pa. $1.50

THREE GOTHIC NOVELS, ed. by E.F. Bleiler. Full texts Castle of Otranto, Walpole; Vathek, Beckford; The Vampyre, Polidori; Fragment of a Novel, Lord Byron. 331pp. 21232-7 Pa. $3.00

SEVEN SCIENCE FICTION NOVELS, H.G. Wells. Full novels. First Men in the Moon, Island of Dr. Moreau, War of the Worlds, Food of the Gods, Invisible Man, Time Machine, In the Days of the Comet. A basic science-fiction library. 1015pp.
USO 20264-X Clothbd. $6.00

LADY AUDLEY'S SECRET, Mary E. Braddon. Great Victorian mystery classic, beautifully plotted, suspenseful; praised by Thackeray, Boucher, Starrett, others. What happened to beautiful, vicious Lady Audley's husband? Introduction by Norman Donaldson. 286pp. 23011-2 Pa. $3.00

EGYPTIAN MAGIC, E.A. Wallis Budge. Foremost Egyptologist, curator at British Museum, on charms, curses, amulets, doll magic, transformations, control of demons, deific appearances, feats of great magicians. Many texts cited. 19 illustrations. 234pp. USO 22681-6 Pa. $2.50

THE LEYDEN PAPYRUS: AN EGYPTIAN MAGICAL BOOK, edited by F. Ll. Griffith, Herbert Thompson. Egyptian sorcerer's manual contains scores of spells: sex magic of various sorts, occult information, evoking visions, removing evil magic, etc. Transliteration faces translation. 207pp. 22994-7 Pa. $2.50

THE MALLEUS MALEFICARUM OF KRAMER AND SPRENGER, translated, edited by Montague Summers. Full text of most important witchhunter's "Bible," used by both Catholics and Protestants. Theory of witches, manifestations, remedies, etc. Indispensable to serious student. 278pp. 6⅝ x 10. USO 22802-9 Pa. $3.95

LOST CONTINENTS, L. Sprague de Camp. Great science-fiction author, finest, fullest study: Atlantis, Lemuria, Mu, Hyperborea, etc. Lost Tribes, Irish in pre-Columbian America, root races; in history, literature, art, occultism. Necessary to everyone concerned with theme. 17 illustrations. 348pp. 22668-9 Pa. $3.50

THE COMPLETE BOOKS OF CHARLES FORT, Charles Fort. Book of the Damned, Lo!, Wild Talents, New Lands. Greatest compilation of data: celestial appearances, flying saucers, falls of frogs, strange disappearances, inexplicable data not recognized by science. Inexhaustible, painstakingly documented. Do not confuse with modern charlatanry. Introduction by Damon Knight. Total of 1126pp.
23094-5 Clothbd. $15.00

FADS AND FALLACIES IN THE NAME OF SCIENCE, Martin Gardner. Fair, witty appraisal of cranks and quacks of science: Atlantis, Lemuria, flat earth, Velikovsky, orgone energy, Bridey Murphy, medical fads, etc. 373pp. 20394-8 Pa. $3.50

HOAXES, Curtis D. MacDougall. Unbelievably rich account of great hoaxes: Locke's moon hoax, Shakespearean forgeries, Loch Ness monster, Disumbrationist school of art, dozens more; also psychology of hoaxing. 54 illustrations. 338pp. 20465-0 Pa. $3.50

THE GENTLE ART OF MAKING ENEMIES, James A.M. Whistler. Greatest wit of his day deflates Wilde, Ruskin, Swinburne; strikes back at inane critics, exhibitions. Highly readable classic of impressionist revolution by great painter. Introduction by Alfred Werner. 334pp. 21875-9 Pa. $4.00

THE BOOK OF TEA, Kakuzo Okakura. Minor classic of the Orient: entertaining, charming explanation, interpretation of traditional Japanese culture in terms of tea ceremony. Edited by E.F. Bleiler. Total of 94pp. 20070-1 Pa. $1.25